BUSINESS STATISTICS

The McGraw Hill Series in Operations and Decision Sciences

SUPPLY CHAIN MANAGEMENT

Bowersox, Closs, Cooper, and Bowersox
Supply Chain Logistics Management
Fifth Edition

Johnson
Purchasing and Supply Management
Sixteenth Edition

Simchi-Levi, Kaminsky, and Simchi-Levi
Designing and Managing the Supply Chain: Concepts, Strategies, Case Studies
Fourth Edition

Stock and Manrodt
Fundamentals of Supply Chain Management

PROJECT MANAGEMENT

Larson and Gray
Project Management: The Managerial Process
Eighth Edition

SERVICE OPERATIONS MANAGEMENT

Bordoloi, Fitzsimmons, and Fitzsimmons
Service Management: Operations, Strategy, Information Technology
Ninth Edition

MANAGEMENT SCIENCE

Hillier and Hillier
Introduction to Management Science: A Modeling and Case Studies Approach with Spreadsheets
Sixth Edition

BUSINESS RESEARCH METHODS

Schindler
Business Research Methods
Fourteenth Edition

BUSINESS FORECASTING

Keating and Wilson
Forecasting and Predictive Analytics
Seventh Edition

BUSINESS SYSTEMS DYNAMICS

Sterman
Business Dynamics: Systems Thinking and Modeling for a Complex World

OPERATIONS MANAGEMENT

Cachon and Terwiesch
Operations Management
Second Edition

Cachon and Terwiesch
Matching Supply with Demand: An Introduction to Operations Management
Fourth Edition

Jacobs and Chase
Operations and Supply Chain Management
Sixteenth Edition

Jacobs and Chase
Operations and Supply Chain Management: The Core
Fifth Edition

Schroeder and Goldstein
Operations Management in the Supply Chain: Decisions and Cases
Eighth Edition

Stevenson
Operations Management
Fourteenth Edition

Swink, Melnyk, and Hartley
Managing Operations Across the Supply Chain
Fourth Edition

BUSINESS STATISTICS

Bowerman, Drougas, Duckworth, Froelich, Hummel, Moninger, and Schur
Business Statistics and Analytics in Practice
Ninth Edition

Doane and Seward
Applied Statistics in Business and Economics
Seventh Edition

Doane and Seward
Essential Statistics in Business and Economics
Third Edition

Lind, Marchal, and Wathen
Basic Statistics for Business and Economics
Tenth Edition

Lind, Marchal, and Wathen
Statistical Techniques in Business and Economics
Eighteenth Edition

Jaggia and Kelly
Business Statistics: Communicating with Numbers
Fourth Edition

Jaggia and Kelly
Essentials of Business Statistics: Communicating with Numbers
Second Edition

BUSINESS ANALYTICS

Jaggia, Kelly, Lertwachara, and Chen
Business Analytics: Communicating with Numbers

BUSINESS MATH

Slater and Wittry
Practical Business Math Procedures
Thirteenth Edition

Slater and Wittry
Math for Business and Finance: An Algebraic Approach
Second Edition

Fourth Edition

BUSINESS STATISTICS

Communicating with Numbers

Sanjiv Jaggia
California Polytechnic State University

Alison Kelly
Suffolk University

BUSINESS STATISTICS, FOURTH EDITION

Published by McGraw Hill LLC, 1325 Avenue of the Americas, New York, NY 10121.

This book is printed on acid-free paper.

1 2 3 4 5 6 7 8 9 LWI 24 23 22 21

ISBN 978-1-260-71630-6 (bound edition)
MHID 1-260-71630-9 (bound edition)
ISBN 978-1-264-21887-5 (loose-leaf edition)
MHID 1-264-21887-7 (loose-leaf edition)

Portfolio Manager: *Noelle Bathurst*
Product Developer: *Ryan McAndrews*
Marketing Manager: *Harper Christopher*
Content Project Managers: *Pat Frederickson and Jamie Koch*
Buyer: *Laura Fuller*
Designer: *Matt Diamond*
Content Licensing Specialist: *Traci Vaske*
Cover Image: *McGraw Hill*
Compositor: *SPi Global*

Library of Congress Cataloging-in-Publication Data

Names: Jaggia, Sanjiv, 1960- author. | Kelly, Alison, author.
Title: Business statistics : communicating with numbers / Sanjiv Jaggia, California Polytechnic State University, Alison Kelly, Suffolk University.
Description: Fourth edition. | New York, NY : McGraw-Hill Education, [2022] | Includes bibliographical references and index.
Identifiers: LCCN 2020036782 | ISBN 9781260716306 (hardcover ; alk. paper) | ISBN 9781264218882 (ebook)
Subjects: LCSH: Commercial statistics.
Classification: LCC HF1017 .J34 2022 | DDC 519.5—dc23
LC record available at https://lccn.loc.gov/2020036782

mheducation.com/highered

Dedicated to Chandrika, Minori, John, Megan, and Matthew

ABOUT THE AUTHORS

Sanjiv Jaggia

Courtesy Sanjiv Jaggia

Sanjiv Jaggia is a professor of economics and finance at California Polytechnic State University in San Luis Obispo. Dr. Jaggia holds a Ph.D. from Indiana University and is a Chartered Financial Analyst (CFA®). He enjoys research in statistics and data analytics applied to a wide range of business disciplines. Dr. Jaggia has published numerous papers in leading academic journals and has co-authored three successful textbooks, two in business statistics and one in business analytics. His ability to communicate in the classroom has been acknowledged by several teaching awards. Dr. Jaggia resides in San Luis Obispo with his wife and daughter. In his spare time, he enjoys cooking, hiking, and listening to a wide range of music.

Alison Kelly

Alison Kelly is a professor of economics at Suffolk University in Boston. Dr. Kelly holds a Ph.D. from Boston College and is a Chartered Financial Analyst (CFA®). Dr. Kelly has published in a wide variety of academic journals and has co-authored three successful textbooks, two in business statistics and one in business analytics. Her courses in applied statistics and econometrics are popular with students as well as working professionals. She has also served as a consultant for a number of companies; her most recent work focused on how large financial institutions satisfy requirements mandated by the Dodd-Frank Act. Dr. Kelly resides in Hamilton, Massachusetts, with her husband, daughter, and son. In her spare time, she enjoys exercising and gardening.

Courtesy Alison Kelly

Business Statistics: Communicating with Numbers

Reviewer Quotes

"[Jaggia and Kelly's text is] an introductory statistics textbook which is rigorous in statistics with modern technology embedded."

-Qiang Zhen, University of North Florida

"This introductory statistics book is relevant and approachable. The book and its materials support teaching in various modalities. It offers an applied orientation with a reasonable and appropriate theoretical foundation."

-Kathryn Ernstberger, Indiana University Southeast

"The authors . . . do an excellent job of introducing the concepts. Illustrations, modern and relevant examples and applications, and exercises. . . This is a well-rounded and excellent textbook in introductory statistics and data analysis."

-Mohammad A. Kazemi, University of North Carolina, Charlotte

"This book and its accompanying online resources is ideal for an introductory in statistics with an emphasis in business. There is a thoughtful balance between concepts and applications."

-Ted Galanthay, Ithaca College

"Excellent coverage. . . It is a great book."

-Ricardo S. Tovar-Silos, Lamar University

A Unique Emphasis on Communicating with Numbers Makes Business Statistics Relevant to Students

We wrote *Business Statistics: Communicating with Numbers* because we saw a need for a contemporary, core statistics text that sparked student interest and bridged the gap between how statistics is taught and how practitioners think about and apply statistical methods. Throughout the text, the emphasis is on communicating with numbers rather than on number crunching. In every chapter, students are exposed to statistical information conveyed in written form. By incorporating the perspective of practitioners, it has been our goal to make the subject matter more relevant and the presentation of material more straightforward for students. Although the text is application-oriented and practical, it is also mathematically sound and uses notation that is generally accepted for the topic being covered.

From our years of experience in the classroom, we have found that an effective way to make statistics interesting is to use timely applications. For these reasons, examples in *Business Statistics* come from all walks of life, including business, economics, sports, health, housing, the environment, polling, and psychology. By carefully matching examples with statistical methods, students learn to appreciate the relevance of statistics in our world today, and perhaps, end up learning statistics without realizing they are doing so.

Continuing Key Features

The fourth edition of *Business Statistics* reinforces and expands six core features that were well-received in earlier editions.

Integrated Introductory Cases. Each chapter begins with an interesting and relevant introductory case. The case is threaded throughout the chapter, and once the relevant statistical tools have been covered, a synopsis—a short summary of findings—is provided. The introductory case often serves as the basis of several examples in other chapters.

Writing with Data. Interpreting results and conveying information effectively is critical to effective decision making in a business environment. Students are taught how to take the data, apply it, and convey the information in a meaningful way.

Unique Coverage of Regression Analysis. Relevant coverage of regression without repetition is an important hallmark of this text.

Written as Taught. Topics are presented the way they are taught in class, beginning with the intuition and explanation and concluding with the application.

Integration of Microsoft Excel® and R. Students are taught to develop an understanding of the concepts and how to derive the calculation; then Excel and R are used as a tool to perform the cumbersome calculations.

Connect. Connect is an online system that gives students the tools they need to be successful in the course. Through guided examples and LearnSmart adaptive study tools, students receive guidance and practice to help them master the topics.

Features New to the Fourth Edition

In the fourth edition of *Business Statistics,* we have made substantial revisions that address the current needs of the market. These revisions are based on the feedback of countless reviewers and users of our earlier editions.

The emphasis in this edition has been to strengthen the connection between business statistics and data analytics. More than ever, colleges and universities across the United States and abroad are incorporating business analytics into their curricula, and businesses are scrambling to find qualified professionals who can translate statistical analysis into decisions that improve performance. We believe that the fourth edition will not only introduce students to data analytics, but will also excite them to further explore the field. There are four major innovations in this edition.

Descriptive: More emphasis on data preparation and visualization

- New sections devoted to data preparation in Chapter 1
- New sections devoted to data visualization methods in Chapter 2
- Discussion of subsetted means in Chapter 3
- Discussion of pivot tables used to analyze empirical probabilities in Chapter 4

Predictive: Significant rewrite of regression and forecasting

- Streamlined discussion of goodness-of-fit measures in Chapter 14
- Revised section on model assumptions and common violations in Chapter 15
- Improved visualizations to explore nonlinear models in Chapters 16, 17, and 18
- New subsection on accuracy rates for binary choice models in Chapter 17
- Separate sections devoted to linear and nonlinear forecasting models in Chapter 18

Technology: More reliance on statistical software and Connect

- Greater use of Excel and R in solving problems
- Expanded R instructions in all regression and forecasting chapters
- Excel and/or R instructions included in most exercises in Connect
- Improved Connect product to facilitate teaching in an online environment

Storytelling: More relevant discussion

- Numerous new examples, exercises, and case studies
- Updated data to make the applications more current
- Big data used in the writing sections for Chapters 1, 2, 3, 15, 16, and 17
- Big data used for suggested case studies in several chapters

Students Learn Through Real-World Cases and Business Examples . . .

Integrated Introductory Cases

Each chapter opens with a real-life case study that forms the basis for several examples within the chapter. The questions included in the examples create a roadmap for mastering the most important learning outcomes within the chapter. A synopsis of each chapter's introductory case is presented when the last of these examples has been discussed. Instructors of distance learners may find these introductory cases particularly useful.

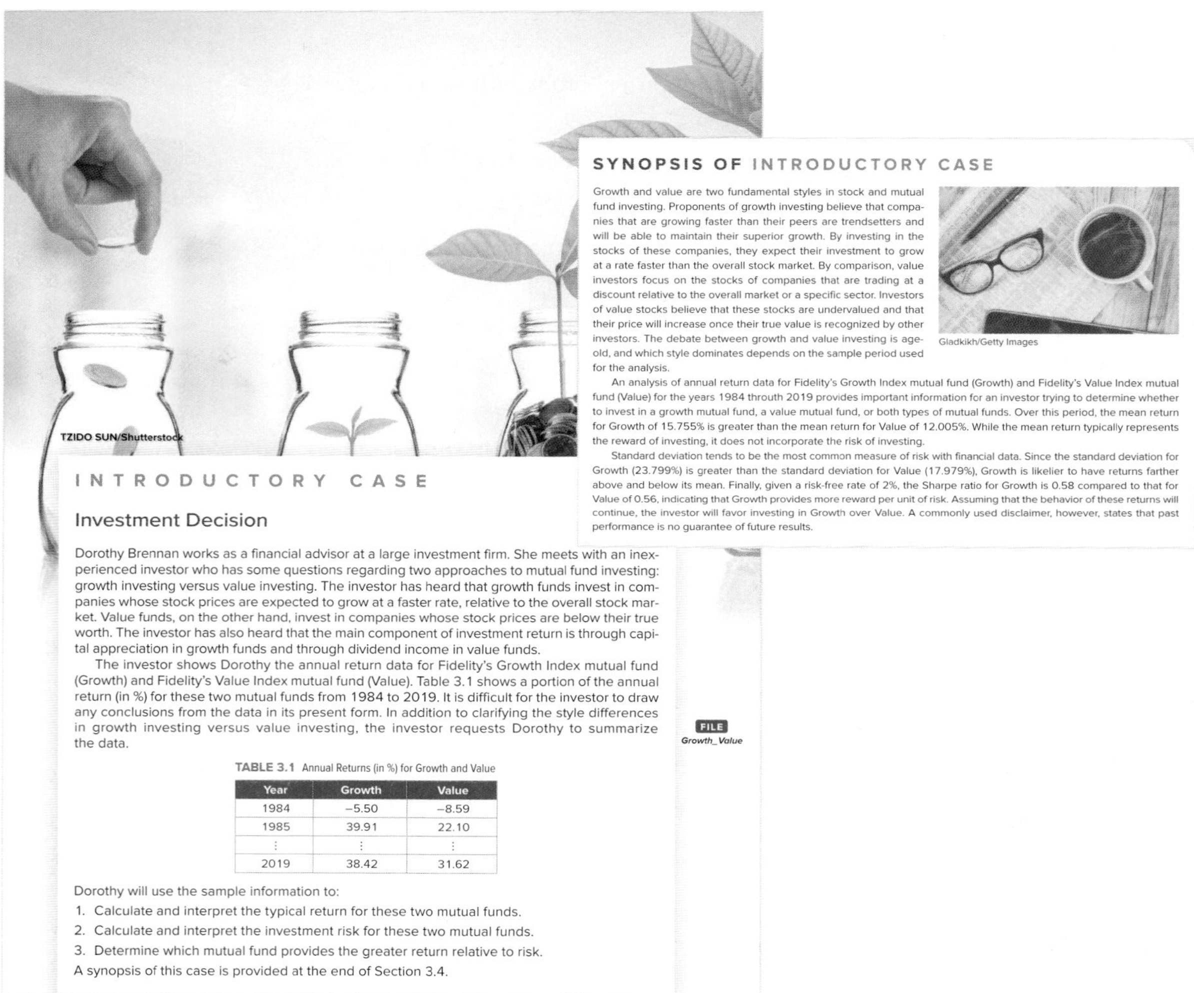

TZIDO SUN/Shutterstock

INTRODUCTORY CASE

Investment Decision

Dorothy Brennan works as a financial advisor at a large investment firm. She meets with an inexperienced investor who has some questions regarding two approaches to mutual fund investing: growth investing versus value investing. The investor has heard that growth funds invest in companies whose stock prices are expected to grow at a faster rate, relative to the overall stock market. Value funds, on the other hand, invest in companies whose stock prices are below their true worth. The investor has also heard that the main component of investment return is through capital appreciation in growth funds and through dividend income in value funds.

The investor shows Dorothy the annual return data for Fidelity's Growth Index mutual fund (Growth) and Fidelity's Value Index mutual fund (Value). Table 3.1 shows a portion of the annual return (in %) for these two mutual funds from 1984 to 2019. It is difficult for the investor to draw any conclusions from the data in its present form. In addition to clarifying the style differences in growth investing versus value investing, the investor requests Dorothy to summarize the data.

FILE *Growth_Value*

TABLE 3.1 Annual Returns (in %) for Growth and Value

Year	Growth	Value
1984	−5.50	−8.59
1985	39.91	22.10
⋮	⋮	⋮
2019	38.42	31.62

Dorothy will use the sample information to:

1. Calculate and interpret the typical return for these two mutual funds.
2. Calculate and interpret the investment risk for these two mutual funds.
3. Determine which mutual fund provides the greater return relative to risk.

A synopsis of this case is provided at the end of Section 3.4.

SYNOPSIS OF INTRODUCTORY CASE

Growth and value are two fundamental styles in stock and mutual fund investing. Proponents of growth investing believe that companies that are growing faster than their peers are trendsetters and will be able to maintain their superior growth. By investing in the stocks of these companies, they expect their investment to grow at a rate faster than the overall stock market. By comparison, value investors focus on the stocks of companies that are trading at a discount relative to the overall market or a specific sector. Investors of value stocks believe that these stocks are undervalued and that their price will increase once their true value is recognized by other investors. The debate between growth and value investing is age-old, and which style dominates depends on the sample period used for the analysis.

Gladkikh/Getty Images

An analysis of annual return data for Fidelity's Growth Index mutual fund (Growth) and Fidelity's Value Index mutual fund (Value) for the years 1984 throuth 2019 provides important information for an investor trying to determine whether to invest in a growth mutual fund, a value mutual fund, or both types of mutual funds. Over this period, the mean return for Growth of 15.755% is greater than the mean return for Value of 12.005%. While the mean return typically represents the reward of investing, it does not incorporate the risk of investing.

Standard deviation tends to be the most common measure of risk with financial data. Since the standard deviation for Growth (23.799%) is greater than the standard deviation for Value (17.979%), Growth is likelier to have returns farther above and below its mean. Finally, given a risk-free rate of 2%, the Sharpe ratio for Growth is 0.58 compared to that for Value of 0.56, indicating that Growth provides more reward per unit of risk. Assuming that the behavior of these returns will continue, the investor will favor investing in Growth over Value. A commonly used disclaimer, however, states that past performance is no guarantee of future results.

and Build Skills to Communicate Results

Writing with Data

One of our most important innovations is the inclusion of a sample report within every chapter. Our intent is to show students how to convey statistical information in written form to those who may not know detailed statistical methods. For example, such a report may be needed as input for managerial decision making in sales, marketing, or company planning. Several similar writing exercises are provided at the end of every Writing with Data section. Each chapter also includes a synopsis that addresses questions raised from the introductory case. This serves as a shorter writing sample for students. Instructors of large sections may find these reports useful for incorporating writing into their statistics courses.

6.4 WRITING WITH DATA

Case Study

Professor Lang is a professor of economics at Salem State University. She has been teaching a course in Principles of Economics for over 25 years. Professor Lang has never graded on a curve since she believes that relative grading may unduly penalize (benefit) a good (poor) student in an unusually strong (weak) class. She always uses an absolute scale for making grades, as shown in the two left columns of Table 6.4.

TABLE 6.4 Grading Scales with Absolute Grading versus Relative Grading

Absolute Grading		Relative Grading	
Grade	Score	Grade	Probability
A	92 and above	A	0.10
B	78 up to 92	B	0.35
C	64 up to 78	C	0.40
D	58 up to 64	D	0.10
F	Below 58	F	0.05

A colleague of Professor Lang's has convinced her to move to relative grading, because it corrects for unanticipated problems. Professor Lang decides to experiment with grading based on the relative scale as shown in the two right columns of Table 6.4. Using this relative grading scheme, the top 10% of students will get A's, the next 35% B's, and so on. Based on her years of teaching experience, Professor Lang believes that the scores in her course follow a normal distribution with a mean of 78.6 and a standard deviation of 12.4.

Professor Lang wants to use this information to calculate probabilities based on the absolute scale and compare them to the probabilities based on the relative scale. Then, she wants to calculate the range of scores for grades based on the relative scale and compare them to the absolute scale. Finally, she want to determine which grading scale makes it harder to get higher grades.

Sample Report— Absolute Grading versus Relative Grading

Many teachers would confess that grading is one of the most difficult tasks of their profession. Two common grading systems used in higher education are relative and absolute. Relative grading systems are norm-referenced or curve-based, in which a grade is based on the student's relative position in class. Absolute grading systems, on the other hand, are criterion-referenced, in which a grade is related to the student's absolute performance in class. In short, with absolute grading, the student's score is compared to a predetermined scale, whereas with relative grading, the score is compared to the scores of other students in the class.

Let X represent a grade in Professor Lang's class, which is normally distributed with a mean of 78.6 and a standard deviation of 12.4. This information is used to derive the grade probabilities based on the absolute scale. For instance, the probability of receiving an A is derived as $P(X \geq 92) = P(Z \geq 1.08) = 0.14$. Other probabilities, derived similarly, are presented in Table 6.5.

TABLE 6.5 Probabilities Based on Absolute Scale and Relative Scale

Grade	Probability Based on Absolute Scale	Probability Based on Relative Scale
A	0.14	0.10
B	0.38	0.35
C	0.36	0.40
D	0.07	0.10
F	0.05	0.05

Unique Coverage and Presentation . . .

Unique Coverage of Regression Analysis

Our coverage of regression analysis is more extensive than that of the vast majority of texts. This focus reflects the topic's importance in the emerging field of data analytics. We combine simple and multiple regression in one chapter, which we believe is a seamless grouping and eliminates needless repetition. The detailed Excel and R instructions eliminate the need for tedious manual calculations. Three more in-depth chapters cover statistical inference, nonlinear relationships, dummy variables, and the linear probability and the logistic regression models. The emphasis in all chapters is on conceptualization, model selection, and interpretation of the results with reference to professionally created figures and tables.

Chapter 14: Regression Analysis
Chapter 15: Inference with Regression Models
Chapter 16: Regression Models for Nonlinear Relationships
Chapter 17: Regression Models with Dummy Variables

The authors have put forth a novel and innovative way to present regression which in and of itself should make instructors take a long and hard look at this book. ***Students should find this book very readable and a good companion for their course.***

Harvey A. Singer, *George Mason University*

Inclusion of Important Topics

We have incorporated several important topics, often ignored in traditional textbooks, including data preparation, pivot tables, geometric mean return, Sharpe ratio, accuracy rates, etc. From our experience from working outside the classroom, we have found that professionals use these topics on a regular basis.

THE SHARPE RATIO

The Sharpe ratio measures the extra reward per unit of risk. The Sharpe ratio for an investment I is computed as

$$\frac{\bar{x}_I - \bar{R}_f}{s_I},$$

where $\bar{x}_I$ is the mean return for the investment, $\bar{R}_f$ is the mean return for a risk-free asset such as a Treasury bill (T-bill), and s_I is the standard deviation for the investment.

Written as Taught

We introduce topics just the way we teach them; that is, the relevant tools follow the opening application. Our roadmap for solving problems is

1. Start with intuition
2. Use Excel or R to estimate the appropriate model,
3. Communicate the results.

We use worked examples throughout the text to illustrate how to apply concepts to solve real-world problems.

that Make the Content More Effective

Integration of Microsoft Excel and R

We prefer that students first focus on and absorb the statistical material before replicating their results with a computer. Solving each application manually provides students with a deeper understanding of the relevant concept. However, we recognize that embedding computer output is often necessary in order to avoid cumbersome calculations or the need for statistical tables. Microsoft Excel and R are the primary software packages used in this text. We chose Excel and R over other statistical packages based on their widespread use and reviewer feedback. For instructors who prefer to focus only on Excel, the R instructions sections are easily skipped. We provide brief guidelines for using Minitab, SPSS, and JMP in chapter appendices.

Using Excel

We use Excel's **BINOM.DIST** function to calculate binomial probabilities. We enter =BINOM.DIST(x, n, p, TRUE or FALSE) where x is the number of successes, n is the number of trials, and p is the probability of success. For the last argument, we enter TRUE if we want to find the cumulative probability function $P(X \leq x)$ or FALSE if we want to find the probability mass function $P(X = x)$.

a. In order to find the probability that exactly 70 American adults are Facebook users, $P(X = 70)$, we enter =BINOM.DIST(70, 100, 0.68, FALSE) and Excel returns 0.0791.

b. In order to find the probability that no more than 70 American adults are Facebook users, $P(X \leq 70)$, we enter =BINOM.DIST(70, 100, 0.68, TRUE) and Excel returns 0.7007.

c. In order to find the probability that at least 70 American adults are Facebook users, $P(X \geq 70) = 1 - P(X \leq 69)$, we enter =1–BINOM.DIST(69, 100, 0.68, TRUE) and Excel returns 0.3784.

Using R

We use R's **dbinom** and **pbinom** functions to calculate binomial probabilities. In order to calculate the probability mass function $P(X = x)$, we enter dbinom(x, n, p) where x is the number of successes, n is the number of trials, and p is the probability of success. In order to calculate the cumulative probability function $P(X \leq x)$, we enter pbinom(x, n, p).

a. In order to find $P(X = 70)$, we enter:

```
> dbinom(70, 100, 0.68)
```

And R returns: 0.07907911.

b. In order to find $P(X \leq 70)$, we enter:

```
> pbinom(70, 100, 0.68)
```

And R returns: 0.7006736.

c. In order to find $P(X \geq 70) = 1 - P(X \leq 69)$, we enter:

```
> 1 - pbinom(69, 100, 0.68)
```

And R returns: 0.3784055.

Real-World Exercises and Case Studies that Reinforce the Material

Mechanical and Applied Exercises

Chapter exercises are a well-balanced blend of mechanical, computational-type problems followed by more ambitious, interpretive-type problems. We have found that simpler drill problems tend to build students' confidence prior to tackling more difficult applied problems. Moreover, we repeatedly use many data sets—including house prices, sales, personality types, health measures, expenditures, stock returns, salaries, and debt—in various chapters of the text. For instance, students first use these real data to calculate summary measures, make statistical inferences with confidence intervals and hypothesis tests, and finally, perform regression analysis.

Mechanics

39. Consider the following population data:

34	42	12	10	22

a. Calculate the range.
b. Calculate MAD.
c. Calculate the population variance.
d. Calculate the population standard deviation.

40. Consider the following population data:

0	−4	2	−8	10

a. Calculate the range.
b. Calculate MAD.
c. Calculate the population variance.
d. Calculate the population standard deviation.

41. Consider the following sample data:

40	48	32	52	38	42

a. Calculate the range.
b. Calculate MAD.
c. Calculate the sample variance.
d. Calculate the sample standard deviation.

42. Consider the following sample data:

− 10	12	−8	−2	−6	8

a. Calculate the range.
b. Calculate MAD.
c. Calculate the sample variance and the sample standard deviation.

Applications

43. FILE ***Prime.*** The accompanying table shows a portion of the annual expenditures (in $) for 100 Prime customers.

Customer	Expenditures
1	1272
2	1089
⋮	⋮
100	1389

a. What were minimum expenditures? What were maximum expenditures?
b. Calculate the mean and the median expenditures.
c. Calculte the variance and the standard devation.

44. FILE ***StockPrices.*** Monthly closing stock prices for Firm A and Firm B are collected for the past five years. A portion of the data is shown in the accompanying table.

Observation	Firm A	Firm B
1	39.91	42.04
2	42.63	41.64
⋮	⋮	⋮
60	87.51	75.09

a. Calculate the sample variance and the sample standard deviation for each firm's stock price.
b. Which firm's stock price had greater variability as measured by the standard deviation?
c. Which firm's stock price had the greater relative dispersion?

45. FILE ***Rental.*** A real estate analyst examines the rental market in a college town. She gathers data on monthly rent and the square footage for 40 apartments. A portion of the data is shown in the accompanying table.

Monthly Rent	Square Footage
645	500
675	648
⋮	⋮
2,400	2,700

a. Calculate the mean and the standard deviation for monthly rent.
b. Calculate the mean and the standard deviation for square footage.
c. Which sample data exhibit greater relative dispersion?

46. FILE ***Revenues.*** The accompanying data file shows the annual revenues (in $ millions) for Corporation A and Corporation B for the past 13 years.
a. Calculate the coefficient of variation for Corporation A.
b. Calculate the coefficient of variation for Corporation B.
c. Which variable exhibits greater relative dispersion?

47. FILE ***Census.*** The accompanying data file shows, among other variables, median household income and median house value for the 50 states.
a. Calculate and discuss the range of household income and house value.
b. Calculate the sample MAD and the sample standard deviation of household income and house value.
c. Discuss why we cannot directly compare the sample MAD and the standard deviations of the two variables.

Features that Go Beyond the Typical

Conceptual Review

At the end of each chapter, we present a conceptual review that provides a more holistic approach to reviewing the material. This section revisits the learning outcomes and provides the most important definitions, interpretations, and formulas.

CONCEPTUAL REVIEW

LO 14.3 Estimate and interpret the multiple linear regression model.

The multiple linear regression model allows more than one explanatory variable to be linearly related with the response variable y. It is defined as $y = \beta_0 + \beta_1 x_1 + \beta_2 x_2 + \cdots + \beta_k x_k + \varepsilon$, where y is the response variable, $x_1, x_2, \ldots, x_k$ are the k explanatory variables, and ε is the random error term. The coefficients $\beta_0, \beta_1, \ldots, \beta_k$ are the unknown parameters to be estimated. We again use the OLS method to arrive at the following sample regression equation: $\hat{y} = b_0 + b_1 x_1 + b_2 x_2 + \cdots + b_k x_k$, where $b_0, b_1, \ldots, b_k$ are the estimates of $\beta_0, \beta_1, \ldots, \beta_k$, respectively.

For each explanatory variable x_j ($j = 1, \ldots, k$), the corresponding slope coefficient b_j is the estimated regression coefficient. It measures the change in the predicted value of the response variable $\hat{y}$, given a unit increase in the associated explanatory variable x_j, *holding all other explanatory variables constant.* In other words, it represents the partial influence of x_j on $\hat{y}$.

LO 14.4 Interpret goodness-of-fit measures.

The standard error of the estimate s_e is the standard deviation of the residual and is calculated as $s_e = \sqrt{\frac{SSE}{n-k-1}}$, where SSE is the error sum of squares. The standard error of the estimate is a useful goodness-of-fit measure when comparing models; the model with the smaller s_e provides the better fit.

The coefficient of determination R^2 is the proportion of the sample variation in the response variable that is explained by the sample regression equation. It falls between 0 and 1; the closer the value is to 1, the better the model fits the sample data.

Adjusted R^2 adjusts R^2 by accounting for the number of explanatory variables k used in the regression. In comparing competing models with different numbers of explanatory variables, the preferred model will have the highest adjusted R^2.

Instructors: Student Success Starts with You

Tools to enhance your unique voice

Want to build your own course? No problem. Prefer to use our turnkey, prebuilt course? Easy. Want to make changes throughout the semester? Sure. And you'll save time with Connect's auto-grading too.

65%
Less Time Grading

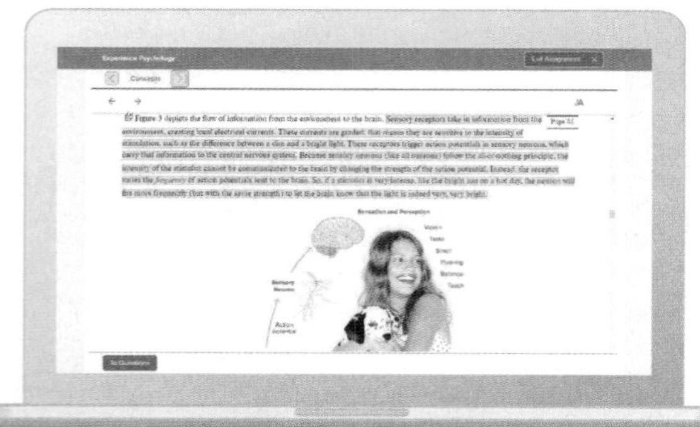

Laptop: McGraw Hill; Woman/dog: George Doyle/Getty Images

Study made personal

Incorporate adaptive study resources like SmartBook® 2.0 into your course and help your students be better prepared in less time. Learn more about the powerful personalized learning experience available in SmartBook 2.0 at **www.mheducation.com/highered/connect/smartbook**

Affordable solutions, added value

Make technology work for you with LMS integration for single sign-on access, mobile access to the digital textbook, and reports to quickly show you how each of your students is doing. And with our Inclusive Access program you can provide all these tools at a discount to your students. Ask your McGraw Hill representative for more information.

Padlock: Jobalou/Getty Images

Solutions for your challenges

A product isn't a solution. Real solutions are affordable, reliable, and come with training and ongoing support when you need it and how you want it. Visit **www.supportateverystep.com** for videos and resources both you and your students can use throughout the semester.

Checkmark: Jobalou/Getty Images

Students: Get Learning that Fits You

Effective tools for efficient studying

Connect is designed to make you more productive with simple, flexible, intuitive tools that maximize your study time and meet your individual learning needs. Get learning that works for you with Connect.

Study anytime, anywhere

Download the free ReadAnywhere app and access your online eBook or SmartBook 2.0 assignments when it's convenient, even if you're offline. And since the app automatically syncs with your eBook and SmartBook 2.0 assignments in Connect, all of your work is available every time you open it. Find out more at **www.mheducation.com/readanywhere**

"I really liked this app—it made it easy to study when you don't have your text-book in front of you."

- Jordan Cunningham, Eastern Washington University

Calendar: owattaphotos/Getty Images

Everything you need in one place

Your Connect course has everything you need—whether reading on your digital eBook or completing assignments for class, Connect makes it easy to get your work done.

Learning for everyone

McGraw Hill works directly with Accessibility Services Departments and faculty to meet the learning needs of all students. Please contact your Accessibility Services Office and ask them to email accessibility@mheducation.com, or visit **www.mheducation.com/about/accessibility** for more information.

Top: Jenner Images/Getty Images, Left: Hero Images/Getty Images, Right: Hero Images/Getty Images

Remote Proctoring & Browser-Locking Capabilities

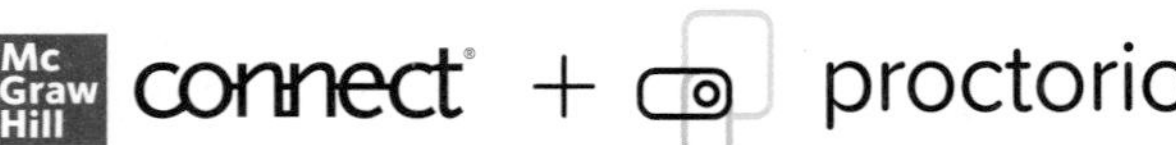

New remote proctoring and browser-locking capabilities, hosted by Proctorio within Connect, provide control of the assessment environment by enabling security options and verifying the identity of the student.

Seamlessly integrated within Connect, these services allow instructors to control students' assessment experience by restricting browser activity, recording students' activity, and verifying students are doing their own work.

Instant and detailed reporting gives instructors an at-a-glance view of potential academic integrity concerns, thereby avoiding personal bias and supporting evidence-based claims.

What Resources are Available for Instructors?

Instructor Library

The Connect Instructor Library is your repository for additional resources to improve student engagement in and out of class. You can select and use any asset that enhances your lecture. The *Connect* Instructor Library includes:

- PowerPoint presentations
- Excel Data Files
- Test Bank
- Instructor's Solutions Manual
- Digital Image Library

Tegrity Campus: Lectures 24/7

Tegrity Campus is integrated in Connect to help make your class time available 24/7. With Tegrity, you can capture each one of your lectures in a searchable format for students to review when they study and complete assignments using Connect. With a simple one-click start-and-stop process, you can capture everything that is presented to students during your lecture from your computer, including audio. Students can replay any part of any class with easy-to-use browser-based viewing on a PC or Mac.

Educators know that the more students can see, hear, and experience class resources, the better they learn. In fact, studies prove it. With Tegrity Campus, students quickly recall key moments by using Tegrity Campus's unique search feature. This search helps students efficiently find what they need, when they need it, across an entire semester of class recordings. Help turn all your students' study time into learning moments immediately supported by your lecture. To learn more about Tegrity, visit http://tegritycampus.mhhe.com.

ALEKS

ALEKS is an assessment and learning program that provides individualized instruction in Business Statistics, Business Math, and Accounting. Available online in partnership with McGraw Hill, ALEKS interacts with students much like a skilled human tutor, with the ability to assess precisely a student's knowledge and provide instruction on the exact topics the student is most ready to learn. By providing topics to meet individual students' needs, allowing students to move between explanation and practice, correcting and analyzing errors, and defining terms, ALEKS helps students to master course content quickly and easily.

ALEKS also includes an instructor module with powerful, assignment-driven features and extensive content flexibility. ALEKS simplifies course management and allows instructors to spend less time with administrative tasks and more time directing student learning. To learn more about ALEKS, visit www.aleks.com.

MegaStat for Microsoft Excel

MegaStat by J. B. Orris of Butler University is a full-featured Excel add-in that is available online through the MegaStat website at **www.mhhe.com/megastat** or through an access card packaged with the text. It works with Excel 2016, 2013, and 2010 (and Excel: Mac 2016). On the website, students have 10 days to successfully download and install MegaStat on their local computer. Once installed, MegaStat will remain active in Excel with no expiration date or time limitations. The software performs statistical analyses within an Excel workbook. It does basic functions, such as descriptive statistics, frequency distributions, and probability calculations, as well as hypothesis testing, ANOVA, and regression. MegaStat output is carefully formatted, and its ease-of-use features include Auto Expand for quick data selection and Auto Label detect. Since MegaStat is easy to use, students can focus on learning statistics without being distracted by the software. MegaStat is always available from Excel's main menu. Selecting a menu item pops up a dialog box. Screencam tutorials are included that provide a walkthrough of major business statistics topics. Help files are built in, and an introductory user's manual is also included.

What Resources are Available for Students?

Integration of Excel Data Sets. A convenient feature is the inclusion of an Excel data file link in many problems using data files in their calculation. The link allows students to easily launch into Excel, work the problem, and return to Connect to key in the answer and receive feedback on their results.

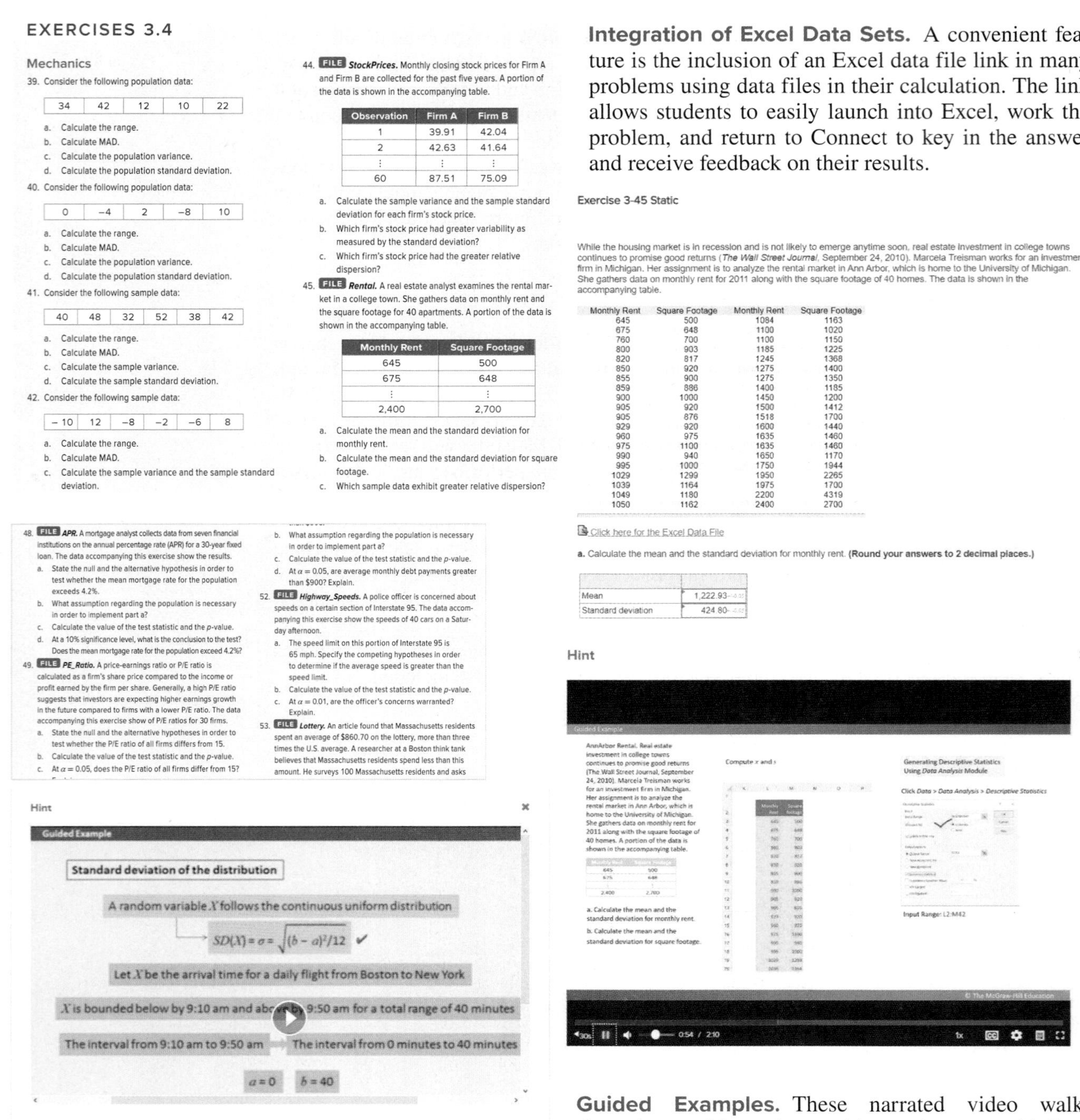

Guided Examples. These narrated video walkthroughs provide students with step-by-step guidelines for solving selected exercises similar to those contained in the text. The student is given personalized instruction on how to solve a problem by applying the concepts presented in the chapter. The video shows the steps to take to work through an exercise. Students can go through each example multiple times if needed.

The Connect Student Resource page is the place for students to access additional resources. The Student Resource page offers students quick access to the recommended study tools, data files, and helpful tutorials on statistical programs.

McGraw Hill Customer Care Contact Information

At McGraw Hill, we understand that getting the most from new technology can be challenging. That's why our services don't stop after you purchase our products. You can e-mail our product specialists 24 hours a day to get product training online. Or you can search our knowledge bank of frequently asked questions on our support website.

For customer support, call **800-331-5094** or visit **www.mhhe.com/support**. One of our technical support analysts will be able to assist you in a timely fashion.

ACKNOWLEDGMENTS

We would like to acknowledge the following people for providing useful comments and suggestions for past and present editions of all aspects of *Business Statistics.*

John Affisco *Hofstra University*
Mehdi Afiat *College of Southern Nevada*
Mohammad Ahmadi *University of Tennessee–Chattanooga*
Sung Ahn *Washington State University*
Mohammad Ahsanullah *Rider University*
Imam Alam *University of Northern Iowa*
Mostafa Aminzadeh *Towson University*
Ardavan Asef-Vaziri *California State University*
Antenah Ayanso *Brock University*
Scott Bailey *Troy University*
Jayanta Bandyopadhyay *Central Michigan University*
Samir Barman *University of Oklahoma*
Douglas Barrett *University of North Alabama*
John Beyers *University of Maryland*
Arnab Bisi *Purdue University–West Lafayette*
Gary Black *University of Southern Indiana*
Randy Boan *Aims Community College*
Matthew Bognar *University of Iowa*
Juan Cabrera *Ramapo College of New Jersey*
Scott Callan *Bentley University*
Gregory Cameron *Brigham Young University*
Kathleen Campbell *St. Joseph's University*
Alan Cannon *University of Texas–Arlington*
Michael Cervetti *University of Memphis*
Samathy Chandrashekar *Salisbury University*
Gary Huaite Chao *University of Pennsylvania–Kutztown*
Sangit Chatterjee *Northeastern University*
Leida Chen *California Polytechnic State University*
Anna Chernobai *Syracuse University*
Alan Chesen *Wright State University*
Juyan Cho *Colorado State University–Pueblo*
Alan Chow *University of South Alabama*
Bruce Christensen *Weber State University*
Howard Clayton *Auburn University*
Robert Collins *Marquette University*
M. Halim Dalgin *Kutztown University*
Tom Davis *University of Dayton*
Matthew Dean *University of Maine*
Jason Delaney *University of Arkansas–Little Rock*
Ferdinand DiFurio *Tennessee Tech University*
Matt Dobra *UMUC*
Luca Donno *University of Miami*
Joan Donohue *University of South Carolina*
David Doorn *University of Minnesota*
James Dunne *University of Dayton*
Mike Easley *University of New Orleans*
Erick Elder *University of Arkansas–Little Rock*
Ashraf ElHoubi *Lamar University*
Roman Erenshteyn *Goldey-Beacom College*
Kathryn Ernstberger *Indiana University*
Grace Esimai *University of Texas–Arlington*
Soheila Fardanesh *Towson University*
Carol Flannery *University of Texas–Dallas*
Sydney Fletcher *Mississippi Gulf Coast Community College*
Andrew Flight *Portland State University*
Samuel Frame *Cal Poly San Luis Obispo*
Priya Francisco *Purdue University*
Vickie Fry *Westmoreland County Community College*
Ed Gallo *Sinclair Community College*
Glenn Gilbreath *Virginia Commonwealth University*
Robert Gillette *University of Kentucky*
Xiaoning Gilliam *Texas Tech University*
Mark Gius *Quinnipiac University*
Malcolm Gold *Saint Mary's University of Minnesota*
Michael Gordinier *Washington University*
Deborah Gougeon *University of Scranton*
Don Gren *Salt Lake Community College*
Thomas G. Groleau *Carthage College*
Babita Gupta *CSU Monterey Bay*
Robert Hammond *North Carolina State University*
Sheila Diann Hammon *Athens State University*
Jim Han *Florida Atlantic University*
Elizabeth Haran *Salem State University*
Jack Harshbarger *Montreat College*
Edward Hartono *University of Alabama–Huntsville*

Clifford Hawley *West Virginia University*
Santhi Heejebu *Cornell College*
Paul Hong *University of Toledo*
Ping-Hung Hsieh *Oregon State University*
Marc Isaacson *Augsburg College*
Mohammad Jamal *Northern Virginia Community College*
Robin James *Harper College*
Molly Jensen *University of Arkansas*
Craig Johnson *Brigham Young University–Idaho*
Janine Sanders Jones *University of St. Thomas*
Vivian Jones *Bethune–Cookman University*
Yogesh Joshi *Kingsborough Community College*
Jerzy Kamburowski *University of Toledo*
Howard Kaplon *Towson University*
Krishna Kasibhatla *North Carolina A&T State University*
Mohammad Kazemi *University of North Carolina–Charlotte*
Ken Kelley *University of Notre Dame*
Lara Khansa *Virginia Tech*
Esther C. Klein *St. Francis College*
Ronald Klimberg *St. Joseph's University*
Andrew Koch *James Madison University*
Subhash Kochar *Portland State University*
Brandon Koford *Weber University*
Randy Kolb *St. Cloud State University*
Vadim Kutsyy *San Jose State University*
Francis Laatsch *University of Southern Mississippi*
David Larson *University of South Alabama*
John Lawrence *California State University–Fullerton*
Shari Lawrence *Nicholls State University*
Radu Lazar *University of Maryland*
David Leupp *University of Colorado–Colorado Springs*
Carel Ligeon *Auburn University–Montgomery*
Carin Lightner *North Carolina A&T State University*
Constance Lightner *Fayetteville State University*
Scott Lindsey *Dixie State College of Utah*
Ken Linna *Auburn University–Montgomery*
Andy Litteral *University of Richmond*
Jun Liu *Georgia Southern University*
Chung-Ping Loh *University of North Florida*
Salvador Lopez *University of West Georgia*
John Loucks *St. Edward's University*
Cecilia Maldonado *Georgia Southwestern State University*
Farooq Malik *University of Southern Mississippi*
Brent Marinan *University of Arizona*
Ken Mayer *University of Nebraska–Omaha*
Bradley McDonald *Northern Illinois University*
Elaine McGivern *Duquesne University*
John McKenzie *Babson University*
Norbert Michel *Nicholls State University*
John Miller *Sam Houston State University*
Virginia Miori *St. Joseph's University*
Prakash Mirchandani *University of Pittsburgh*
Jason Molitierno *Sacred Heart University*
Elizabeth Moliski *University of Texas–Austin*
Joseph Mollick *Texas A&M University–Corpus Christi*
James Moran *Oregon State University*
Khosrow Moshirvaziri *California State University–Long Beach*
Tariq Mughal *University of Utah*
Patricia Mullins *University of Wisconsin–Madison*
Kusum Mundra *Rutgers University–Newark*
Anthony Narsing *Macon State College*
Robert Nauss *University of Missouri–St. Louis*
Satish Nayak *University of Missouri–St. Louis*
Thang Nguyen *California State University–Long Beach*
Mohammad Oskoorouchi *California State University–San Marcos*
Barb Osyk *University of Akron*
Bhavik Pathak *Indiana University South Bend*
Melissa Patterson *Chabot College*
Scott Paulsen *Illinois Central College*
James Payne *Calhoun Community College*
Norman Pence *Metropolitan State College of Denver*
Dane Peterson *Missouri State University*
Joseph Petry *University of Illinois–Urbana/Champaign*
Courtney Pham *Missouri State University*
Martha Pilcher *University of Washington*
Cathy Poliak *University of Wisconsin–Milwaukee*
Simcha Pollack *St. John's University*
Hamid Pourmohammadi *California State University–Dominguez Hills*
Tammy Prater *Alabama State University*
Zbigniew H. Przasnyski *Loyola Marymount University*
Manying Qiu *Virginia State University*
Troy Quast *Sam Houston State University*
Michael Racer *University of Memphis*
Srikant Raghavan *Lawrence Technological University*
Bharatendra Rai *University of Massachusetts–Dartmouth*
Michael Aaron Ratajczyk *Saint Mary's University of Minnesota*
Tony Ratcliffe *James Madison University*
David Ravetch *University of California*
Bruce Reinig *San Diego State University*
Darlene Riedemann *Eastern Illinois University*

David Roach *Arkansas Tech University*
Carolyn Rochelle *East Tennessee State University*
Alfredo Romero *North Carolina A&T State University*
Ann Rothermel *University of Akron*
Jeff Rummel *Emory University*
Deborah Rumsey *The Ohio State University*
Stephen Russell *Weber State University*
William Rybolt *Babson College*
Fati Salimian *Salisbury University*
Fatollah Salimian *Perdue School of Business*
Samuel Sarri *College of Southern Nevada*
Jim Schmidt *University of Nebraska–Lincoln*
Patrick Scholten *Bentley University*
Bonnie Schroeder *Ohio State University*
Sue Schou *Boise State University*
Pali Sen *University of North Florida*
Donald Sexton *Columbia University*
Vijay Shah *West Virginia University–Parkersburg*
Dmitriy Shaltayev *Christopher Newport University*
Soheil Sibdari *University of Massachusetts–Dartmouth*
Prodosh Simlai *University of North Dakota*
Harvey Singer *George Mason University*
Harry Sink *North Carolina A&T State University*
Don Skousen *Salt Lake Community College*
Robert Smidt *California Polytechnic State University*
Gary Smith *Florida State University*
Antoinette Somers *Wayne State University*
Ryan Songstad *Augustana College*
Erland Sorensen *Bentley University*
Arun Kumar Srinivasan *Indiana University–Southeast*
Anne-Louise Statt *University of Michigan–Dearborn*
Scott Stevens *James Madison University*
Alicia Strandberg *Temple University*
Linda Sturges *Suny Maritime College*
Wendi Sun *Rockland Trust*
Bedassa Tadesse *University of Minnesota*
Pandu Tadikamalta *University of Pittsburgh*
Roberto Duncan Tarabay *University of Wisconsin–Madison*
Faye Teer *James Madison University*
Deborah Tesch *Xavier University*
Patrick Thompson *University of Florida*
Satish Thosar *University of Redlands*
Ricardo Tovar-Silos *Lamar University*
Quoc Hung Tran *Bridgewater State University*
Elzbieta Trybus *California State University–Northridge*
Fan Tseng *University of Alabama–Huntsville*
Silvanus Udoka *North Carolina A&T State University*
Shawn Ulrick *Georgetown University*
Bulent Uyar *University of Northern Iowa*
Ahmad Vakil *Tobin College of Business*
Tim Vaughan *University of Wisconsin–Eau Claire*
Raja Velu *Syracuse University*
Holly Verhasselt *University of Houston–Victoria*
Zhaowei Wang *Citizens Bank*
Rachel Webb *Portland State University*
Kyle Wells *Dixie State College*
Alan Wheeler *University of Missouri–St. Louis*
Mary Whiteside *University of Texas–Arlington*
Blake Whitten *University of Iowa*
Rick Wing *San Francisco State University*
Jan Wolcott *Wichita State University*
Rongning Wu *Baruch College*
John Yarber *Northeast Mississippi Community College*
John C. Yi *St. Joseph's University*
Kanghyun Yoon *University of Central Oklahoma*
Mark Zaporowski *Canisius College*
Ali Zargar *San Jose State University*
Dewit Zerom *California State University*
Eugene Zhang *Midwestern State University*
Ye Zhang *Indiana University–Purdue University–Indianapolis*
Yi Zhang *California State University–Fullerton*
Yulin Zhang *San Jose State University*
Qiang Zhen *University of North Florida*
Wencang Zhou *Baruch College*
Zhen Zhu *University of Central Oklahoma*

The editorial staff of McGraw Hill are deserving of our gratitude for their guidance throughout this project, especially Noelle Bathurst, Pat Frederickson, Ryan McAndrews, Harper Christopher, Jamie Koch, and Matt Diamond.

We would also like to thank Jenna Eisenman, Matthew Hawke, and Megan Hawke for their outstanding research assistance.

BRIEF CONTENTS

CONTENTS

CHAPTER 5

DISCRETE PROBABILITY DISTRIBUTIONS 160

CHAPTER 6

CONTINUOUS PROBABILITY DISTRIBUTIONS 200

PART FOUR

Basic Inference

CHAPTER 7

SAMPLING AND SAMPLING DISTRIBUTIONS 238

CHAPTER 8

INTERVAL ESTIMATION 278

CHAPTER 9

CHAPTER 10

CHAPTER 11

CHAPTER 12

PART FIVE
Advanced Inference

CHAPTER 13
ANALYSIS OF VARIANCE 438

CHAPTER 14
REGRESSION ANALYSIS 482

CHAPTER 15
INFERENCE WITH REGRESSION MODELS 514

CHAPTER 16
REGRESSION MODELS FOR NONLINEAR RELATIONSHIPS 556

CHAPTER 17

REGRESSION MODELS WITH DUMMY VARIABLES 588

PART SIX

Supplementary Topics

CHAPTER 18

FORECASTING WITH TIME SERIES DATA 622

CHAPTER19

RETURNS, INDEX NUMBERS, AND INFLATION 658

CHAPTER 20

NONPARAMETRIC TESTS 682

APPENDIXES

BUSINESS STATISTICS

1 Data and Data Preparation

LEARNING OBJECTIVES

After reading this chapter, you should be able to:

LO **1.1** **Explain the various data types.**

LO **1.2** **Describe variables and types of measurement scales.**

LO **1.3** **Inspect and explore data.**

LO **1.4** **Apply data subsetting.**

In just about any contemporary human activity, we use statistics to analyze large amounts of data for making better decisions. Managers, consumers, sports enthusiasts, politicians, and medical professionals are increasingly turning to data to boost a company's revenue, deepen customer engagement, find better options on consumer products, prevent threats and fraud, succeed in sports and elections, provide better diagnoses and cures for diseases, and so on. In this chapter, we will describe various types of data and measurement scales of variables that are used in statistics.

It is important to note that after obtaining relevant data, we often spend a considerable amount of time on inspecting and preparing the data for subsequent analysis. In this chapter, we will discuss a few important data preparation tasks. We will use counting and sorting of relevant variables to inspect and explore data. Finally, we will discuss a commonly used technique called subsetting, where only a portion (subset) of the data is used for the analysis.

Yuliia Mazurkevych/Shutterstoick

INTRODUCTORY CASE

Gaining Insights into Retail Customer Data

Organic Food Superstore is an online grocery store that specializes in providing organic food products to health-conscious consumers. The company offers a membership-based service that ships fresh ingredients for a wide range of chef-designed meals to its members' homes. Catherine Hill is a marketing manager at Organic Food Superstore. She has been assigned to market the company's new line of Asian-inspired meals. Research has shown that the most likely customers for healthy ethnic cuisines are college-educated millennials (born between 1982 and 2000).

In order to spend the company's marketing dollars efficiently, Catherine wants to focus on this target demographic when designing the marketing campaign. With the help of the information technology (IT) group, Catherine has acquired a representative sample that includes each customer's identification number (CustID), sex (Sex), race (Race), birthdate (BirthDate), whether the customer has a college degree (College), household size (HHSize), annual income (Income), total spending (Spending), total number of orders during the past 24 months (Orders), and the channel through which the customer was originally acquired (Channel). Table 1.1 shows a portion of the data set.

TABLE 1.1 A Sample of Organic Food Superstore Customers

CustID	Sex	Race	BirthDate	...	Channel
1530016	Female	Black	12/16/1986	...	SM
1531136	Male	White	5/9/1993	...	TV
⋮	⋮	⋮	⋮	⋮	⋮
1579979	Male	White	7/5/1999	...	SM

Customers

Catherine wants to use the Customers data set to:

1. Identify Organic Food Superstore's college-educated millennial customers.
2. Compare the profiles of female and male college-educated millennial customers.

A synopsis of this case is provided at the end of Section 1.3.

LO 1.1

1.1 TYPES OF DATA

Explain the various types of data.

In general, data are compilations of facts, figures, or other contents, both numerical and nonnumerical. Data of all types and formats are generated from multiple sources. Insights from all of these data improves a company's bottom-line and enhances consumer experience. At the core, business statistics benefits companies by developing better marketing strategies, deepening customer engagement, enhancing efficiency in procurement, uncovering ways to reduce expenses, identifying emerging market trends, mitigating risk and fraud, etc. We often find a large amount of data at our disposal. However, we also derive insights from relatively small data sets, such as from consumer focus groups, marketing surveys, or reports from government agencies.

Every day, consumers and businesses use data from various sources to help make decisions. In order to make intelligent decisions in a world full of uncertainty, we have to understand statistics—the language of data. In the broadest sense, statistics is the science of extracting useful information from data. Three steps are essential for doing good statistics. An important first step for making decisions is to find the right data, which are both complete and lacking any misrepresentation, and prepare it for the analysis. Second, we must use the appropriate statistical tools, depending on the data at hand. Finally, an important ingredient of a well-executed statistical analysis is to clearly communicate information into verbal and written language. It is important to note that numerical results are not very useful unless they are accompanied with clearly stated actionable business insights.

DATA AND STATISTICS

Data are compilations of facts, figures, or other contents, both numerical and nonnumerical. Statistics is the science that deals with the collection, preparation, analysis, interpretation, and presentation of data.

In the introductory case, Catherine wants to target college-educated millennials when designing the marketing campaign so that she spends the company's marketing dollars efficiently. Before we analyze the information that Catherine has gathered, it is important to understand different types of data and measurement scales of variables. In this section, we focus on data types.

LO 1.1

Sample and Population Data

Explain the various types of data.

We generally divide the study of statistics into two branches: descriptive statistics and inferential statistics. **Descriptive statistics** refers to the summary of important aspects of a data set. This includes collecting data, organizing the data, and then presenting the data in the form of charts and tables. In addition, we often calculate numerical measures that summarize the data by providing, for example, the typical value and the variability of the variable of interest. Today, the techniques encountered in descriptive statistics account for the most visible application of statistics—the abundance of quantitative information that is collected and published in our society every day. The unemployment rate, the president's approval rating, the Dow Jones Industrial Average, batting averages, the crime rate, and the divorce rate are but a few of the many "statistics" that can be found in a reputable newspaper on a frequent, if not daily, basis. Yet, despite the familiarity of descriptive statistics, these methods represent only a minor portion of the body of statistical applications.

The phenomenal growth in statistics is mainly in the field called inferential statistics. Generally, **inferential statistics** refers to drawing conclusions about a large set of data—called a **population**—based on a smaller set of **sample** data. A population is defined as all members of a specified group (not necessarily people), whereas a sample is a subset of that particular population. In most statistical applications, we must rely on sample data in order to make inferences about various characteristics of the population.

Figure 1.1 depicts the flow of information between a population and a sample. Consider, for example, a 2016 Gallop survey that found that only 50% of millennials plan to stay at their current job for more than a year. Researchers use this sample result, called a **sample statistic,** in an attempt to estimate the corresponding unknown **population parameter.** In this case, the parameter of interest is the percentage of *all* millennials who plan to be with their current job for more than a year.

FIGURE 1.1 Population versus Sample

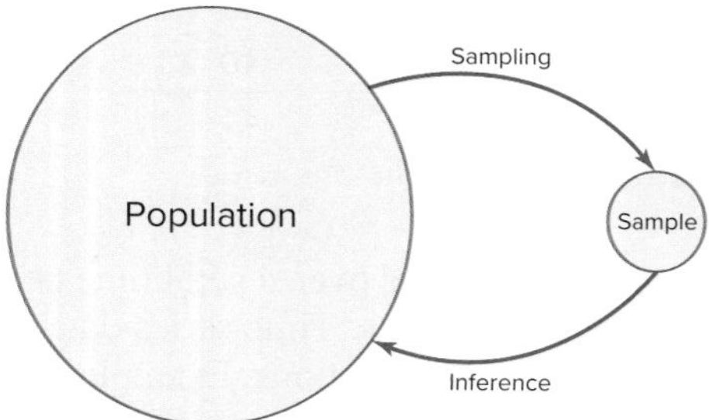

> POPULATION VERSUS SAMPLE
>
> A population consists of all items of interest in a statistical problem. A sample is a subset of the population. We analyze sample data and calculate a sample statistic to make inferences about the unknown population parameter.

It is generally not feasible to obtain population data due to prohibitive costs and/or practicality. We rely on sampling because we are unable to use population data for two main reasons.

- **Obtaining information on the entire population is expensive.** Consider how the monthly unemployment rate in the United States is calculated by the Bureau of Labor Statistics (BLS). Is it reasonable to assume that the BLS counts every unemployed person each month? The answer is a resounding NO! In order to do this, every home in the country would have to be contacted. Given that there are approximately 160 million individuals in the labor force, not only would this process cost too much, it would take an inordinate amount of time. Instead, the BLS conducts a monthly sample survey of about 60,000 households to measure the extent of unemployment in the United States.
- **It is impossible to examine every member of the population.** Suppose we are interested in the average length of life of a Duracell AAA battery. If we tested the duration of each Duracell AAA battery, then in the end, all batteries would be dead and the answer to the original question would be useless.

Cross-Sectional and Time Series Data

Sample data are generally collected in one of two ways. **Cross-sectional data** refer to data collected by recording a characteristic of many subjects at the same point in time, or without regard to differences in time. Subjects might include individuals, households, firms, industries, regions, and countries.

Table 1.2 is an example of a cross-sectional data set. It lists the team standings for the National Basketball Association's Eastern Conference at the end of the 2018–2019 season. The eight teams may not have ended the season precisely on the same day and time, but the differences in time are of no relevance in this example. Other examples of cross-sectional data include the recorded grades of students in a class, the sale prices of single-family homes sold last month, the current price of gasoline in different cities in the United States, and the starting salaries of recent business graduates from the University of Connecticut.

TABLE 1.2 2018–2019 NBA Eastern Conference

Team name	Wins	Losses	Winning percentage
Milwaukee Bucks	60	22	0.732
Toronto Raptors*	58	24	0.707
Philadephia 76ers	51	31	0.622
Boston Celtics	49	33	0.598
Indiana Pacers	48	34	0.585
Brooklyn Nets	42	40	0.512
Orlando Magic	42	40	0.512
Detroit Pistons	41	41	0.500

*The Toronto Raptors won their first NBA title during the 2018–2019 season.

Time series data refer to data collected over several time periods focusing on certain groups of people, specific events, or objects. Time series data can include hourly, daily, weekly, monthly, quarterly, or annual observations. Examples of time series data include the hourly body temperature of a patient in a hospital's intensive care unit, the daily price of General Electric stock in the first quarter of 2020, the weekly exchange rate between the U.S. dollar and the euro over the past six months, the monthly sales of cars at a dealership in 2020, and the annual population growth rate of India in the last decade. In these examples, temporal ordering is relevant and meaningful.

Figure 1.2 shows a plot of the national homeownership rate in the U.S. from 2000 to 2018. According to the U.S. Census Bureau, the national homeownership rate in the first quarter of 2016 plummeted to 63.6% from a high of 69.4% in 2004. An explanation for the decline in the homeownership rate is the stricter lending practices caused by the housing market crash in 2007 that precipitated a banking crisis and deep recession. This decline can also be attributed to home prices outpacing wages in the sample period.

FIGURE 1.2 Homeownership Rate (in %) in the U.S. from 2000 through 2018

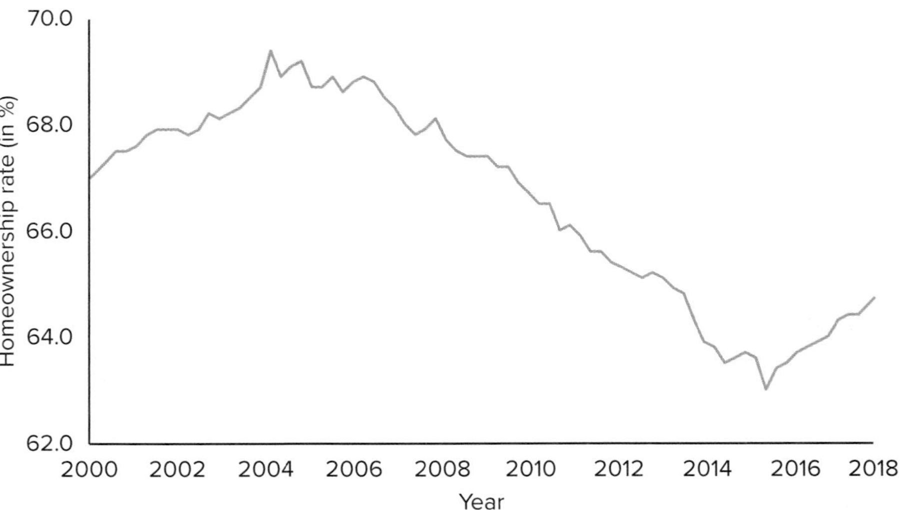

Structured and Unstructured Data

When you think of data, the first image that probably pops in your head is lots of numbers and perhaps some charts and graphs. In reality, data can come in multiple forms. For example, information exchange in social networking websites such as Facebook, LinkedIn, and Twitter also constitute data. In order to better understand the various forms of data, we make a distinction between structured and unstructured data.

Generally, **structured data** reside in a predefined, row-column format. We use spreadsheet or database applications to enter, store, query, and analyze structured data.

Examples of structured data include numbers, dates, and groups of words and numbers, typically stored in a tabular format. Structured data often consist of numerical information that is objective and is not open to interpretation.

Point-of-sale and financial data are examples of structured data and are usually designed to capture a business process or transaction. Examples include the sale of retail products, money transfer between bank accounts, and the student enrollment in a university course. When individual consumers buy products from a retail store, each transaction is captured into a record of structured data.

Consider the sales invoice shown in Figure 1.3. Whenever a customer places an order like this, there is a predefined set of data to be collected, such as the transaction date, shipping address, and the units of product being purchased. Even though a receipt or an invoice may not always be presented in rows and columns, the predefined structure allows businesses and organizations to translate the data on the document into a row-column format.

Tranquility Home and Garden

8 Harmony Drive

San Francisco, CA 94126

Phone: (415) SOL-SAVE

Date: July, 20, 2017

Invoice number: A9239145-W

Customer Name: Kevin Lau

Street Address: 123 Solstice Circle

State/Province: California

Telephone: (415) 234-4550

Account Number: KL0927

City: San Francisco

Postal Code: 94126

Product code	Product description	Units ordered	Price per unit	Extended Price
421-L	8W LED light bulbs	27	$7.59	$204.93
389-P	Chlorine removing shower filter	6	$19.99	$119.94
682-K	Compostable cutlery (box sets)	5	$14.99	$74.95
			Total amount:	$399.82
			Sales Tax:	$31.99
			Shipping fee:	$6.99
			Grand total:	$438.80

FIGURE 1.3 A sample invoice from a retail transaction

For decades, companies and organizations relied mostly on structured data to run their businesses and operations. Today, with the advent of the digital age, most experts agree that only about 20% of all data used in business decisions are structured data. The remaining 80% are unstructured.

Unlike structured data, **unstructured data** (or unmodeled data) do not conform to a predefined, row-column format. They tend to be textual (e.g., written reports, e-mail messages, doctor's notes, or open-ended survey responses) or have multimedia contents (e.g., photographs, videos, and audio data). Even though these data may have some implied structure (e.g., a report title, e-mail's subject line, or a time stamp on a photograph), they are still considered unstructured as they do not conform to a row-column model required in most database systems. Social media data such as Twitter, YouTube, Facebook, and blogs are examples of unstructured data.

Big Data

Nowadays, businesses and organizations generate and gather more and more data at an increasing pace. The term **big data** is a catch-phrase, meaning a massive amount of both structured and unstructured data that are extremely difficult to manage, process, and analyze using traditional data-processing tools. Despite the challenges, big data present great opportunities to gain knowledge and business intelligence with potential game-changing impacts on company revenues, competitive advantage, and organizational efficiency.

More formally, a widely accepted definition of big data is "high-volume, high-velocity and/or high-variety information assets that demand cost-effective, innovative forms of information processing that enable enhanced insight, decision making, and process automation" (www.gartner.com). The three characteristics (the three Vs) of big data are:

- **Volume:** An immense amount of data is compiled from a single source or a wide range of sources, including business transactions, household and personal devices, manufacturing equipment, social media, and other online portals.
- **Velocity:** In addition to volume, data from a variety of sources get generated at a rapid speed. Managing these data streams can become a critical issue for many organizations.
- **Variety:** Data also come in all types, forms, and granularity, both structured and unstructured. These data may include numbers, text, and figures as well as audio, video, e-mails, and other multimedia elements.

In addition to the three defining characteristics of big data, we also need to pay close attention to the veracity of the data and the business value that they can generate. **Veracity** refers to the credibility and quality of data. One must verify the reliability and accuracy of the data content prior to relying on the data to make decisions. This becomes increasingly challenging with the rapid growth of data volume fueled by social media and automatic data collection. **Value** derived from big data is perhaps the most important aspect of any statistical project. Having a plethora of data does not guarantee that useful insights or measurable improvements will be generated. Organizations must develop a methodical plan for formulating business questions, curating the right data, and unlocking the hidden potential in big data.

Big data, however, do not necessarily imply complete (population) data. Take, for example, the analysis of all Facebook users. It certainly involves big data, but if we consider all Internet users in the world, Facebook users are only a very large sample. There are many Internet users who do not use Facebook, so the data on Facebook do not represent the population. Even if we define the population as pertaining to those who use online social media, Facebook is still one of many social media portals that consumers use. And because different social media are used for different purposes, data collected from these sites may very well reflect different populations of Internet users; this distinction is especially important from a strategic business standpoint. Therefore, Facebook data are simply a very large sample.

In addition, we may choose not to use big data in its entirety even when they are available. Sometimes it is just inconvenient to analyze a very large data set as it is computationally burdensome, even with a modern, high-capacity computer system. Other times, the additional benefits of working with big data may not justify the associated costs. In sum, we often choose to work with relatively smaller data sets drawn from big data.

STRUCTURED, UNSTRUCTURED, AND BIG DATA

Structured data are data that reside in a predefined, row-column format, while unstructured data do not conform to a predefined, row-column format. Big data is a term used to describe a massive amount of both structured and unstructured data that are extremely difficult to manage, process, and analyze using traditional data-processing tools. Big data, however, do not necessary imply complete (population) data.

In this textbook, we will focus on traditional statistical methods applied to structured data. Sophisticated tools to analyze unstructured data are beyond the scope of this textbook.

Data on the Web

Comstock Images/Jupiterimages

The explosion in the field of statistics and data analytics is partly due to the growing availability of vast amounts of data and improved computational power. Many experts believe that 90% of the data in the world today were created in the last two years alone. These days, it has become easy to access data by simply using a search engine like Google. These search engines direct us to data-providing websites. For instance, searching for economic data may lead you to the Bureau of Economic Analysis (www.bea.gov), the Bureau of Labor Statistics (www.bls.gov/data), the Federal Reserve Economic Data (research.stlouisfed.org), and the U.S. Census Bureau (www.census.gov/data.html). These websites provide data on inflation, unemployment, GDP, and much more, including useful international data.

The National Climatic Data Center (www.ncdc.noaa.gov/data-access) provides a large collection of environmental, meteorological, and climate data. Similarly, transportation data can be found at www.its-rde.net. The University of Michigan has compiled sentiment data found at www.sca.isr.umich.edu. Several cities in the United States have publicly available data in categories such as finance, community and economic development, education, and crime. For example, the Chicago data portal data.cityofchicago.org provides a large volume of city-specific data. Excellent world development indicator data are available at data.worldbank.org. The happiness index data for most countries are available at www.happyplanetindex.org/data.

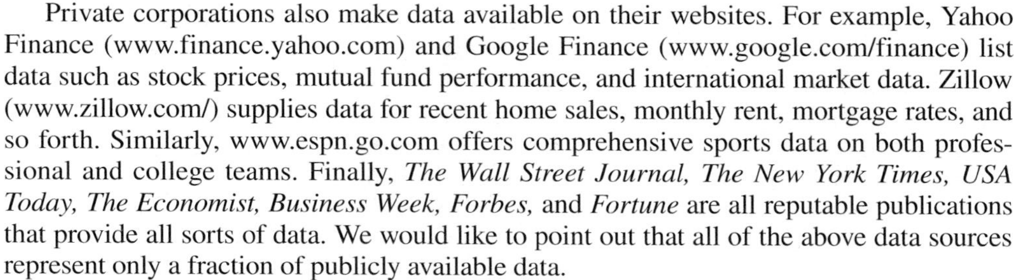

Private corporations also make data available on their websites. For example, Yahoo Finance (www.finance.yahoo.com) and Google Finance (www.google.com/finance) list data such as stock prices, mutual fund performance, and international market data. Zillow (www.zillow.com/) supplies data for recent home sales, monthly rent, mortgage rates, and so forth. Similarly, www.espn.go.com offers comprehensive sports data on both professional and college teams. Finally, *The Wall Street Journal, The New York Times, USA Today, The Economist, Business Week, Forbes,* and *Fortune* are all reputable publications that provide all sorts of data. We would like to point out that all of the above data sources represent only a fraction of publicly available data.

EXERCISES 1.1

Applications

1. A few years ago, it came as a surprise when Apple's iPhone 4 was found to have a problem. Users complained of weak reception, and sometimes even dropped calls, when they cradled the phone in their hands in a particular way. A survey at a local store found that 2% of iPhone 4 users experienced this reception problem.
   a. Describe the relevant population.
   b. Is 2% associated with the population or the sample?
2. Many people regard video games as an obsession for youngsters, but, in fact, the average age of a video game player is 35 years old. Is the value 35 likely the actual or the estimated average age of the population? Explain.
3. An accounting professor wants to know the average GPA of the students enrolled in her class. She looks up information on Blackboard about the students enrolled in her class and computes the average GPA as 3.29. Describe the relevant population.
4. Recent college graduates with an engineering degree continue to earn high salaries. An online search revealed that the average annual salary for an entry-level position in engineering is $65,000.
   a. What is the relevant population?
   b. Do you think the average salary of $65,000 is computed from the population? Explain.
5. Research suggests that depression significantly increases the risk of developing dementia later in life. Suppose that in a study involving 949 elderly persons, it was found that 22% of those who had depression went on to develop dementia, compared to only 17% of those who did not have depression.
   a. Describe the relevant population and the sample.
   b. Are the numbers 22% and 17% associated with the population or a sample?

6. Go to www.zillow.com and find the sale price of 20 single-family homes sold in Las Vegas, Nevada, in the last 30 days. Structure the data in a tabular format and include the sale price, the number of bedrooms, the square footage, and the age of the house. Do these data represent cross-sectional or time series data?
7. Go to www.finance.yahoo.com to get the current stock quote for Home Depot (ticker symbol = HD). Use the ticker symbol to search for historical prices and create a table that includes the monthly adjusted close price of Home Depot stock for the last 12 months. Do these data represent cross-sectional or time series data?
8. Go to *The New York Times* website at www.nytimes.com and review the front page. Would you consider the data on the page to be structured or unstructured? Explain.
9. Conduct an online search to compare small hybrid vehicles (e.g., Toyota Prius, Ford Fusion, Chevrolet Volt) on price, fuel economy, and other specifications. Do you consider the search results structured or unstructured data? Explain.
10. Find Under Armour's annual revenue from the past 10 years. Are the data considered structured or unstructured? Explain. Are they cross-sectional or time series data?
11. Ask 20 of your friends about their online social media usage, specifically whether or not they use Facebook, Instagram, and Snapchat; how often they use each social media portal; and their overall satisfaction of each of these portals. Create a table that presents this information. Are the data considered structured or unstructured? Are they cross-sectional or time series data?

LO 1.2

1.2 VARIABLES AND SCALES OF MEASUREMENT

Describe variables and types of measurement scales.

For any statistical analysis, we invariably focus on people, firms, or events with particular characteristics. When a characteristic of interest differs in kind or degree among various observations (records), then the characteristic can be termed a **variable.** Marital status and income are examples of variables because a person's marital status and income vary from person to person. Variables are further classified as either **categorical** (qualitative) or **numerical** (quantitative). The observations of a categorical variable represent categories, whereas the observations of a numerical variable represent meaningful numbers. For example, marital status is a categorical variable, whereas income is a numerical variable.

For a categorical variable, we use labels or names to identify the distinguishing characteristic of each observation. For instance, a university may identify each student's status as either at the undergraduate or the graduate level, where the education level is a categorical variable representing two categories. Categorical variables can also be defined by more than two categories. Examples include marital status (single, married, widowed, divorced, separated), IT firm (hardware, software, cloud), and course grade (A, B, C, D, F). It is important to note that categories are often converted into numerical codes for purposes of data processing, which we will discuss in later chapters.

For a numerical variable, we use numbers to identify the distinguishing characteristic of each observation. Numerical variables, in turn, are either discrete or continuous. A **discrete variable** assumes a countable number of values. Consider the number of children in a family or the number of points scored in a basketball game. We may observe values such as 3 children in a family or 90 points being scored in a basketball game, but we will not observe fractions such as 1.3127 children or 92.4724 scored points. The values that a discrete variable assumes need not be whole numbers. For example, the price of a stock for a particular firm is a discrete variable. The stock price may take on a value of $20.37 or $20.38, but it cannot take on a value between these two points.

A continuous variable is characterized by uncountable values within an interval. Weight, height, time, and investment return are all examples of continuous variables. For example, an unlimited number of values occur between the weights of 100 and 101 pounds, such as 100.3, 100.625, 100.8342, and so on. In practice, however, continuous variables are often measured in discrete values. We may report a newborn's weight (a continuous variable) in discrete terms as 6 pounds 10 ounces and another newborn's weight in similar discrete terms as 6 pounds 11 ounces.

CATEGORICAL AND NUMERICAL VARIABLES

A variable is a general characteristic being observed on a set of people, objects, or events, where each observation varies in kind or degree.

- The observations of a categorical variable assume names or labels.
- The observations of a numerical variable assume meaningful numerical values. A numerical variable can be further categorized as either discrete or continuous. A discrete variable assumes a countable number of values, whereas a continuous variable is characterized by uncountable values within an interval.

EXAMPLE 1.1

In the introductory case, Catherine Hill has been assigned to help market Organic Food Superstore's new line of Asian-inspired meals. With the help of the IT group, she has acquired a representative sample of customers at her store. Determine which of the variables in the sample are categorical or numerical and, if numerical, determine if they are discrete or continuous.

SOLUTION:

The variables Sex, Race, College, and Channel are categorical, merely representing labels. We also treat Birthdate as a categorical variable, with numerous categories, even though it contains numbers. Note that we can easily convert date of birth to a numerical variable age by simply subtracting it from the current date. On the other hand, HHSize, Income, Spending, and Orders are numerical variables because the observations are all meaningful numbers. Note that all of the numerical variables in this example are discrete because they can only assume a countable number of values; in other words, they are not characterized by uncountable values within an interval.

The Measurement Scales

In order to choose the appropriate techniques for summarizing and analyzing variables, we need to distinguish between the different measurement scales. The observations for any variable can be classified into one of four major measurement scales: nominal, ordinal, interval, or ratio. Nominal and ordinal scales are used for categorical variables, whereas interval and ratio scales are used for numerical variables. We discuss these scales in ascending order of sophistication.

The **nominal scale** represents the least sophisticated level of measurement. If we are presented with nominal observations, all we can do is categorize or group them. The observations differ merely by name or label. Table 1.3 lists the 30 publicly-owned companies, as of February 2019, that comprise the Dow Jones Industrial Average (DJIA). The DJIA is a stock market index that shows how these large U.S.-based companies have traded during a standard trading session in the stock market. Table 1.3 also indicates where stocks of these companies are traded: on either the National Association of Securities Dealers Automated Quotations (Nasdaq) or the New York Stock Exchange (NYSE). These observations are classified as nominal scale because we are simply able to group or categorize them. Specifically, only five stocks are traded on the Nasdaq, whereas the remaining 25 are traded on the NYSE.

Often, we substitute numbers for the particular categorical characteristic or trait that we are grouping. For instance, we might use the number 0 to show that a company's stock is traded on the Nasdaq and the number 1 to show that a company's stock is traded on the NYSE. One reason why we do this is for ease of exposition; always referring to the National Association of Securities Dealers Automated Quotations, or even the Nasdaq, can be awkward and unwieldy.

TABLE 1.3 Companies of the DJIA and Exchange Where Stock is Traded

Company	Exchange	Company	Exchange
3M (MMM)	NYSE	Johnson & Johnson (JNJ)	NYSE
American Express (AXP)	NYSE	JPMorgan Chase (JPM)	NYSE
Apple (AAPL)	Nasdaq	McDonald's (MCD)	NYSE
Boeing (BA)	NYSE	Merck (MRK)	NYSE
Caterpillar (CAT)	NYSE	Microsoft (MFST)	Nasdaq
Chevron (CVX)	NYSE	Nike (NKE)	NYSE
Cisco (CSCO)	Nasdaq	Pfizer (PFE)	NYSE
Coca-Cola (KO)	NYSE	Procter & Gamble (PG)	NYSE
Disney (DIS)	NYSE	Travelers (TRV)	NYSE
DowDupont (DWDP)	NYSE	United Health (UNH)	NYSE
ExxonMobil (XOM)	NYSE	United Technologies (UTX)	NYSE
Goldman Sachs (GS)	NYSE	Verizon (VZ)	NYSE
Home Depot (HD)	NYSE	Visa (V)	NYSE
IBM (IBM)	NYSE	Wal-Mart (WMT)	NYSE
Intel (INTC)	Nasdaq	Walgreen (WBA)	Nasdaq

Compared to the nominal scale, the **ordinal scale** reflects a stronger level of measurement. With ordinal observations, we are able to both categorize and rank them with respect to some characteristic or trait. The weakness with ordinal observations is that we cannot interpret the difference between the ranked observations because the actual numbers used are arbitrary. Consider, for example, hotel reviews where consumers are asked to classify the service at a particular hotel as excellent (5 stars), very good (4 stars), good (3 stars), fair (2 stars), or poor (1 star). We summarize the categories and their respective ratings in Table 1.4.

TABLE 1.4 Hotel Survey Categories with Ratings

Category	Rating
Excellent	5
Very good	4
Good	3
Fair	2
Poor	1

In Table 1.4, the number attached to excellent (5 stars) is higher than the number attached to good (3 stars), indicating that the response of excellent is preferred to good. However, we can easily redefine the ratings, as we show in Table 1.5.

TABLE 1.5 Hotel Survey Categories with Redefined Ratings

Category	Rating
Excellent	100
Very good	80
Good	70
Fair	50
Poor	40

In Table 1.5, excellent still receives a higher number than good, but now the difference between the two categories is 30 points (100 – 70), as compared to a difference of 2 points (5 – 3) when we use the first classification. In other words, differences between categories are meaningless with ordinal observations. (We also should note that we could reverse the ordering so that, for instance, excellent equals 40 and poor equals 100; this renumbering would not change the nature of the observations.)

As mentioned earlier, observations of a categorical variable are typically expressed in words but are coded into numbers for purposes of data processing. When summarizing the results of a categorical variable, we typically count the number of observations that fall into each category or calculate the percentage of observations that fall into each category. However, with a categorical variable, we are unable to perform meaningful arithmetic operations, such as addition and subtraction.

With observations that are measured on the **interval scale,** we are able to categorize and rank them as well as find meaningful differences between them. The Fahrenheit scale for temperatures is an example of interval-scaled variable. Not only is 60 degrees Fahrenheit hotter than 50 degrees Fahrenheit, the same difference of 10 degrees also exists between 90 and 80 degrees Fahrenheit.

The main drawback of an interval-scaled variable is that the value of zero is arbitrarily chosen; the zero point of an interval-scaled variable does not reflect a complete absence of what is being measured. No specific meaning is attached to 0 degrees Fahrenheit other than to say it is 10 degrees colder than 10 degrees Fahrenheit. With an arbitrary zero point, meaningful ratios cannot be constructed. For instance, it is senseless to say that 80 degrees is twice as hot as 40 degrees; in other words, the ratio 80/40 has no meaning.

The **ratio scale** represents the strongest level of measurement. The ratio scale has all the characteristics of the interval scale as well as a true zero point, which allows us to interpret the ratios between observations. The ratio scale is used in many business applications. Variables such as sales, profits, and inventory levels are expressed on the ratio scale. A meaningful zero point allows us to state, for example, that profits for firm A are double those of firm B. Variables such as weight, time, and distance are also measured on a ratio scale because zero is meaningful.

Unlike nominal- and ordinal-scaled variables (categorical variables), arithmetic operations are valid on interval- and ratio-scaled variables (numerical variables). In later chapters, we will calculate summary measures, such as the mean, the median, and the variance, for numerical variables; we cannot calculate these measures for categorical variables.

MEASUREMENT SCALES

The observations for any variable can be classified into one of four major measurement scales: nominal, ordinal, interval, or ratio.

- Nominal: Observations differ merely by name or label.
- Ordinal: Observations can be categorized and ranked; however, differences between the ranked observations are meaningless.
- Interval: Observations can be categorized and ranked, and differences between observations are meaningful. The main drawback of the interval scale is that the value of zero is arbitrarily chosen.
- Ratio: Observations have all the characteristics of an interval-scaled variable as well as a true zero point; thus, meaningful ratios can be calculated.

Nominal and ordinal scales are used for categorical variables, whereas interval and ratio scales are used for numerical variables.

Tween_Survey

EXAMPLE 1.2

The owner of a ski resort two hours outside Boston, Massachusetts, is interested in serving the needs of the "tween" population (children aged 8 to 12 years old). He believes that tween spending power has grown over the past few years, and he wants their skiing experience to be memorable so that they want to return. At the end of last year's ski season, he asked 20 tweens the following four questions.

- Q1. On your car drive to the resort, which music streaming service was playing?
- Q2. On a scale of 1 to 4, rate the quality of the food at the resort (where 1 is poor, 2 is fair, 3 is good, and 4 is excellent).
- Q3. Presently, the main dining area closes at 3:00 pm. What time do you think it should close?
- Q4. How much of your own money did you spend at the lodge today?

A portion of their responses is shown in Table 1.6. Identify the scale of measurement for each variable used in the survey. Given the tween responses, provide suggestions to the owner for improvement.

TABLE 1.6 Tween Responses to Resort Survey

Tween	Music Streaming	Food Quality	Closing Time	Own Money Spent ($)
1	Apple Music	4	5:00 pm	20
2	Pandora	2	5:00 pm	10
⋮	⋮	⋮	⋮	⋮
20	Spotify	2	4:30 pm	10

SOLUTION:

- Q1. Responses for music streaming service are nominal because the observations differ merely in label. Twelve of the 20 tweens, or 60%, listened to Spotify. If the resort wishes to contact tweens using this means, then it may want to direct its advertising dollars to this streaming service.
- Q2. Food quality responses are on an ordinal scale because we can both categorize and rank the observations. Eleven of the 20 tweens, or 55%, felt that the food quality was, at best, fair. Perhaps a more extensive survey that focuses solely on food quality would reveal the reason for their apparent dissatisfaction.
- Q3. Closing time responses are on an interval scale. We can say that 3:30 pm is 30 minutes later than 3:00 pm, and 6:00 pm is 30 minutes later than 5:30 pm; that is, differences between observations are meaningful. The closing time responses, however, have no apparent zero point. We could arbitrarily define the zero point at 12:00 am, but ratios are still meaningless. In other words, it makes no sense to form the ratio 6:00 pm/3:00 pm and conclude that 6:00 pm is twice as long a time period as 3:00 pm. A review of the closing time responses shows that the vast majority (19 out of 20) would like the dining area to remain open later.
- Q4. The tweens' responses with respect to their own money spent at the resort are on a ratio scale. We can categorize and rank observations as well as calculate meaningful differences. Moreover, because there is a natural zero point, valid ratios can also be calculated. Seventeen of the 20 tweens spent their own money at the lodge. It does appear that the discretionary spending of this age group is significant. The owner would be wise to cater to some of their preferences.

EXERCISES 1.2

Applications

12. Which of the following variables are categorical and which are numerical? If the variable is numerical, then specify whether the variable is discrete or continuous.
   a. Points scored in a football game.
   b. Racial composition of a high school classroom.
   c. Heights of 15-year-olds.
13. Which of the following variables are categorical and which are numerical? If the variable is numerical, then specify whether the variable is discrete or continuous.
   a. Colors of cars in a mall parking lot.
   b. Time it takes each student to complete a final exam.
   c. The number of patrons who frequent a restaurant.
14. In each of the following scenarios, define the type of measurement scale.
   a. A kindergarten teacher marks whether each student is a boy or a girl.
   b. A ski resort records the daily temperature during the month of January.
   c. A restaurant surveys its customers about the quality of its waiting staff on a scale of 1 to 4, where 1 is poor and 4 is excellent.
15. In each of the following scenarios, define the type of measurement scale.
   a. An investor collects data on the weekly closing price of gold throughout the year.
   b. An analyst assigns a sample of bond issues to one of the following credit ratings, given in descending order of credit quality (increasing probability of default): AAA, AA, BBB, BB, CC, D.
   c. The dean of the business school at a local university categorizes students by major (i.e., accounting, finance, marketing, etc.) to help in determining class offerings in the future.
16. In each of the following scenarios, define the type of measurement scale.
   a. A meteorologist records the amount of monthly rainfall over the past year.
   b. A sociologist notes the birth year of 50 individuals.
   c. An investor monitors the daily stock price of BP following the 2010 oil disaster in the Gulf of Mexico.
17. **FILE** ***Major.*** A professor records the majors of her 30 students. A portion of the data is shown in the accompanying table.

Student	Major
1	Accounting
2	Management
⋮	⋮
30	Economics

   a. What is the measurement scale of the Major variable?
   b. Summarize the results in tabular form.
   c. What information can be extracted from the data?
18. **FILE** ***DOW.*** The accompanying table shows a portion of the 30 companies that comprise the Dow Jones Industrial Average (DJIA). For each company, the data set lists the year that it joined the DJIA, its industry, and its stock price (in $) as of February 15, 2019.

Company	Year	Industry	Price
3M (MMM)	1976	Health Care	208.9
American Express (AXP)	1982	Finance	107.4
⋮	⋮	⋮	⋮
Walgreen (WBA)	2018	Health Care	73.43

   a. What is the measurement scale of the Industry variable?
   b. What is the measurement scale of the Year variable? What are the strengths of this type of measurement scale? What are its weaknesses?
   c. What is the measurement scale of the Price variable? What are the strengths of this type of measurement scale?

1.3 DATA PREPARATION

As noted earlier, after obtaining relevant data, we often spend a considerable amount of time on inspecting and preparing the data for subsequent analysis. In this section, we will discuss a few important data preparation tasks. We first count and sort the observations of relevant variables in order to inspect and explore the data. We also discuss a commonly used technique called subsetting where only on a portion (subset) of the data are used for the statistical analysis.

Counting and Sorting

LO 1.3

Inspect and explore data.

In addition to visually reviewing data, counting and sorting are among the very first tasks most data analysts perform to gain a better understanding and insights into the data.

Counting and sorting data help us verify that the data set is complete or that it may have missing values, especially for important variables. Sorting data also allows us to review the range of values for each variable. We can sort data based on a single variable or multiple variables.

In Example 1.3, we demonstrate how to use counting and sorting features in Excel and R to inspect and gain insights into the data.

EXAMPLE 1.3

FILE *Gig*

BalanceGig is a company that matches independent workers for short-term engagements with businesses in the construction, automotive, and high-tech industries. The 'gig' employees work only for a short period of time, often on a particular project or a specific task. A manager at BalanceGig extracts the employee data from their most recent work engagement, including the hourly wage (Wage), the client's industry (Industry), and the employee's job classification (Job). A portion of the ***Gig*** data set is shown in Table 1.7.

TABLE 1.7 Gig Employee Data

EmployeeID	Wage	Industry	Job
1	32.81	Construction	Analyst
2	46	Automotive	Engineer
⋮	⋮	⋮	⋮
604	26.09	Construction	Other

The manager suspects that data about the gig employees are sometimes incomplete, perhaps due to the short engagement and the transient nature of the employees. She would like to find the number of missing observations for the Wage, Industry, and Job variables. In addition, she would like information on the number of employees who (1) worked in the automotive industry, (2) earned more than $30 per hour, and (3) worked in the automotive industry and earned more than $30 per hour. Finally, the manager would like to know the hourly wage of the lowest- and the highest-paid employees at the company as a whole and the hourly wage of the lowest- and the highest-paid accountants who worked in the automotive and the tech industries.

Use counting and sorting functions in Excel and R to find the relevant information requested by the manager, and then summarize the results.

Important: Due to different fonts and type settings, copying and pasting Excel or R functions from this text directly into Excel or R may cause errors. When such errors occur, you may need to replace special characters such as quotation marks and parentheses or delete extra spaces in the functions.

SOLUTION:

Using Excel

a. Open the ***Gig*** data file. Note that the employee data are currently sorted by their employee ID in column A. Scroll to the end of the data set and note that the last record is in row 605. With the column heading in row 1, the data set has a total of 604 records.

b. We use two Excel functions, **COUNT** and **COUNTA,** to inspect the number of observations in each column. The **COUNT** function counts the number of cells that contain numeric observations and, therefore, can only apply to the EmployeeID and Wage variables. The **COUNTA** function counts the number of cells that are not empty and is applicable to all four variables. Because Wage is a numerical variable, we can enter either =COUNT(B2:B605) or

=COUNTA(B2:B605) in an empty cell to count the number of observations for Wage. We get 604, implying that there are no missing observations. We enter =COUNTA(C2:C605) and =COUNTA(D2:D605) in empty cells to count the number of observations for the Industry (column C) and Job (column D) variables. Because these two variables are non-numerical, we use **COUNTA** instead of **COUNT.** Verify that the number of observations for Industry and Job are 594 and 588, respectively, indicating that there are 10 and 16 blank or missing observations, respectively, for these two variables.

c. To count the number of employees in each industry, we use the **COUNTIF** function. Entering =COUNTIF(C2:C605,"=Automotive") in an empty cell will show that 190 of the 604 employees worked in the automotive industry. Similarly, entering =COUNTIF(B2:B605,">30") in an empty cell will show that 536 employees earned more than $30 per hour. Note that the first parameter in the **COUNTIF** function is the range of cells to be counted, and the second parameter specifies the selection criterion. Other logical operators such as >=, <, <=, and <> (not equal to) can also be used in the **COUNTIF** function.

d. To count the number of employees with multiple selection criteria, we use the **COUNTIFS** function. For example, entering =COUNTIFS(C2:C605, "=Automotive", B2:B605,">30") in an empty cell will show that 181 employees worked in the automotive industry and earned more than $30 per hour. Additional data ranges and selection criteria can be added in corresponding pairs. The >=, <, <=, and <> operators can also be used in the **COUNTIFS** function.

e. To sort all employees by their hourly wage, highlight cells A1 through D605. From the menu, click **Data > Sort** (in the Sort & Filter group). Make sure that the *My data has headers* checkbox is checked. Select Wage for the *Sort by* option and choose the *Smallest to Largest* (or ascending) order. Click **OK.**

At the top of the sorted list, verify that there are three employees with the lowest hourly wage of $24.28. To sort data in descending order, repeat step e but choose the *Largest to Smallest* (or descending) order. Verify that the highest hourly wage is $51.00.

f. To sort the data based on multiple variables, again highlight cells A1:D605 and go to **Data > Sort.** Choose Industry in the *Sort by* option and the *A to Z* (or ascending) order. Click the *Add Level* button and choose Job in the *Then by* option and the *A to Z* order. Click the *Add Level* button again and choose Wage in the second *Then by* option and the *Smallest to Largest* order. Click **OK.** We see that the lowest- and the highest-paid accountants who worked in the automotive industry made $28.74 and $49.32 per hour, respectively.

Similarly, sorting the data by industry in descending order (*Z to A*) and then by job classification and hourly wage in ascending order reveals that the lowest- and the highest-paid accountants in the Tech industry made $36.13 and $49.49 per hour, respectively.

g. To resort the data set to its original order, highlight cells A1:D605 and go to **Data > Sort.** Select each of the *Then by* rows and click the *Delete Level* button. Choose EmployeeID in the *Sort by* option and the *Smallest to Largest* order.

Using R

Before following all R instructions, make sure that you have read Appendix A ("Getting Started with R"). We assume that you have downloaded R and RStudio and that you know how to import an Excel file. Throughout the text, our goal is to provide the simplest way to obtain the relevant output. We denote all function names in **boldface** and all options within a function in *italics*.

a. Import the ***Gig*** data file into a data frame (table) and label it myData. Keep in mind that the R language is case sensitive.

b. We use the **dim** function in R to count the number of observations and variables. Verify that the R output shows 604 observations and four variables. Enter:

```
> dim(myData)
```

c. Two common functions to display a portion of data are **head** and **View**. The **head** function displays the first few observations in the data set, and the **View** function (case sensitive) displays a spreadsheet-style data viewer where the user can scroll through rows and columns. Verify that the first employee in the data set is an analyst who worked in the construction industry and made $32.81 per hour. Enter:

```
> head(myData)
> View(myData)
```

d. R stores missing values as *NA*, and we use the **is.na** function to identify the observations with missing values. R labels observations with missing values as "True" and observations without missing values as "False." In order to inspect the Industry variable for missing values, enter:

```
> is.na(myData$Industry)
```

e. For a large data set, having to look through all observations is inconvenient. Alternately, we can use the **which** function together with the **is.na** function to identify "which" observations contain missing values. The following command identifies 10 observations by row number as having a missing value in the Industry variable. Verify that the first observation with a missing Industry value is in row 24. Enter:

```
> which(is.na(myData$Industry))
```

f. To inspect the 24th observation, we specify row 24 in the myData data frame. Enter:

```
> myData[24,]
```

Note that there are two elements within the square bracket, separated by a comma. The first element identifies a row number (also called row index), and the second element after the comma identifies a column number (also called column index). Leaving the second element blank will display all columns. To inspect an observation in row 24 and column 3, we enter myData[24, 3]. In a small data set, we can also review the missing values by scrolling to the specific rows and columns in the data viewer produced by the **View** function.

g. To identify and count the number of employees with multiple selection criteria, we use the **which** and **length** functions. In the following command, we identify which employees worked in the automotive industry with the **which** function and count the number of these employees using the **length** function. The double equal sign (==), also called equality operator, is used to check whether the industry is automotive. In R, text characters such as 'Automotive' are enclosed in quotation marks. Enter:

```
> length(which(myData$Industry=='Automotive'))
```

We can also use the >, >=, <, <=, and != (not equal to) operators in the selection criteria. For example, using the following command, we can determine the number of employees who earn more than $30 per hour. Enter:

```
> length(which(myData$Wage > 30))
```

Note that there are 190 employees in the automotive industry and there are 536 employees who earn more than $30 per hour.

h. To count how many employees worked in a particular industry and earned more than a particular wage, we use the & operator. The following command shows that 181 employees worked in the automotive industry and earned more than $30 per hour. Enter:

```
> length(which(myData$Industry=='Automotive' & myData$Wage > 30))
```

i. We use the **order** function to sort the observations of a variable. In order to sort the Wage variable and store the ordered data frame in a new data frame called sortedData1, enter:

```
> sortedData1 <- myData[order(myData$Wage),]
> View(sortedData1)
```

The **View** function shows that the lowest and highest hourly wages are $24.28 and $51.00, respectively. By default, the sorting is performed in ascending order. To sort in descending order, enter:

```
> sortedData1 <- myData[order(myData$Wage, decreasing = TRUE),]
```

j. To sort data by multiple variables, we specify the variables in the **order** function. The following command sorts the data by industry, job classification, and hourly wage, all in ascending order, and stores the ordered data in a data frame called sortedData2. Enter:

```
> sortedData2 <- myData[order(myData$Industry, myData$Job,
myData$Wage),]
> View(sortedData2)
```

The **View** function shows that the lowest-paid accountant who worked in the automotive industry made $28.74 per hour.

k. To sort the data by industry and job classification in ascending order and then by hourly wage in descending order, we insert a minus sign in front of the wage variable. We store the resulting ordered data in a data frame called sortedData3. Verify that the highest-paid accountant in the automotive industry made $49.32 per hour. Enter:

```
> sortedData3 <- myData[order(myData$Industry, myData$Job,
-myData$Wage),]
> View(sortedData3)
```

l. The industry and job classification variables are non-numerical. As a result, to sort the data by industry in descending order and then by job classification and hourly wage in ascending order, we use the **xtfrm** function with the minus sign in front of the Industry variable. Enter:

```
> sortedData4 <- myData[order(-xtfrm(myData$Industry), myData$Job,
myData$Wage),]
> View(sortedData4)
```

The **View** function reveals that the lowest- and the highest-paid accountants in the technology industry made $36.13 and $49.49 per hour, respectively.

m. To sort the data by industry, job, and hourly wage, all in descending order, we use the *decreasing* option in the **order** function. Verify that the highest-paid sales representative in the technology industry made $48.87. Enter:

```
> sortedData5 <- myData[order(myData$Industry, myData$Job,
myData$Wage, decreasing = TRUE),]
> View(sortedData5)
```

n. To export the sorted data from step m as a comma-separated value file, we use the **write.csv** function. Verify that the exported file is in the default folder (e.g., My Document on Microsoft Windows). Other data frames in **R** can be exported using a similar statement. Enter:

```
> write.csv(sortedData5,"sortedData5.csv")
```

Summary

- There are a total of 604 records in the data set. There are no missing values in the Wage variable. The Industry and Job variables have 10 and 16 missing values, respectively.
- 190 employees worked in the automotive industry, 536 employees earned more than $30 per hour, and 181 employees worked in the automotive industry and earned more than $30 per hour.
- The lowest and the highest hourly wages in the data set are $24.28 and $51.00, respectively. The three employees who had the lowest hourly wage of $24.28 all worked in the construction industry and were hired as Engineer, Sales Rep, and Accountant, respectively. Interestingly, the employee with the highest hourly wage of $51.00 also worked in the construction industry in a job type classified as Other.
- The lowest- and the highest-paid accountants who worked in the automotive industry made $28.74 and $49.32 per hour, respectively. In the technology industry, the lowest- and the highest-paid accountants made $36.13 and $49.49 per hour, respectively. Note that the lowest hourly wage for an accountant is considerably higher in the technology industry compared to the automotive industry ($36.13 > $28.74).

A Note on Handling Missing Values

There are two common strategies for dealing with missing values. The **omission** strategy recommends that observations with missing values be excluded from subsequent analysis. The **imputation** strategy recommends that the missing values be replaced with some reasonable imputed values. For numerical variables, it is common to replace the missing values with the average (typical) values across relevant observations. For categorical variables, it is common to impute the most predominant category. Further details regarding the imputation strategy are beyond the scope of this text.

LO 1.4

Apply data subsetting

Subsetting

The process of extracting portions of a data set that are relevant to the analysis is called **subsetting.** For example, a multinational company has sales data for its global operations, and it creates a subset of sales data by country and performs analysis accordingly. For time series data, which are data indexed in time order, we may choose to create subsets of recent observations and observations from the distant past in order to analyze them separately. Subsetting can also be used to eliminate observations that contain missing values, low-quality data, or outliers. Sometimes, subsetting involves excluding variables that contain redundant information, or variables with excessive amounts of missing values.

SUBSETTING

Subsetting is the process of extracting a portion of a data set that is relevant for subsequent statistical analysis or when the objective of the analysis is to compare two subsets of the data.

In Example 1.4, we demonstrate how to use subsetting functions in Excel and R to select or exclude variables and/or observations from the original data set.

EXAMPLE 1.4

In the introductory case, Catherine Hill wants to gain a better understanding of Organic Food Superstore's customers who are college-educated millennials, born between 1982 and 2000. She feels that sex, household size, annual income, total spending, total number of orders, and channel through which the customer was acquired are useful for her to create a profile of these customers. Use Excel and R to first identify college-educated millenial customers in the ***Customers*** data file. Then, create subsets of female and male college-educated millenial customers and provide a summary of the results.

SOLUTION:

Using Excel

a. Open the ***Customers*** data file.

b. We first filter the data set to include only college-educated millennials. Select the data range A1:J201. From the menu choose **Home > Sort & Filter > Filter.** The column headings (A1 through J1) will turn into drop-down boxes.

c. Click on the drop-down box in E1 (College). Uncheck *(Select all),* then check the box next to *Yes.* Click **OK.** This step shows only those customers who have a college degree (Yes) by hiding those who don't (No) in the data set.

d. Click on the drop-down box in D1 (BirthDate). Select **Date filters > Between.** See Figure 1.4. In the *Custom AutoFilter* dialog box, enter 1/1/1982 next to the *is after or equal to* box or select the date from the calendar object. Select *And* and enter 12/31/1999 next to the is *before or equal to* box or select the date from the calendar object. Click **OK.** The data set now only displays college-educated millennials who were born between 1982 and 2000.

FIGURE 1.4 Excel's AutoFilter dialog box

e. Select the entire filtered data that are left in the worksheet. Copy and paste the filtered data to a new worksheet. Verify that the new worksheet contains 59 observations of college-educated millennials. Rename the new worksheet as *College-Educated Millennials.*

f. We now exclude the variables that are not relevant to the current analysis. In the *College-Educated Millennials* worksheet, select cell A1 (CustID). From the menu choose **Home > Delete > Delete Sheet Columns** to remove the CustID column. Repeat this step for the Race, BirthDate, and College columns from the data set.

g. To subset the college-educated millennials data by sex, select column A. From the menu choose **Home > Sort & Filter > Sort A to Z.** If prompted, select *Expand the selection* in the *Sort Warning* dialog box and click *Sort.* The observations are now sorted by sex in alphabetic order. The female customer observations are followed by male customer observations.

h. Create two new worksheets and assign the worksheet names *Female* and *Male.* Copy and paste the female and male customer observations, including the column headings, to the new *Female* and *Male* worksheets, respectively. Table 1.8 shows a portion of the results.

TABLE 1.8 College-Educated Millennial Customers

a) Female College-Educated Millennials

Sex	HHSize	Income	Spending	Orders	Channel
Female	5	53000	241	3	SM
Female	3	84000	153	2	Web
⋮	⋮	⋮	⋮	⋮	⋮
Female	1	52000	586	13	Referral

b) Male College-Educated Millennials

Sex	HHSize	Income	Spending	Orders	Channel
Male	5	94000	843	12	TV
Male	1	97000	1028	17	Web
⋮	⋮	⋮	⋮	⋮	⋮
Male	5	102000	926	10	SM

Using R

a. Import the ***Customers*** data file into a data frame (table) and label it myData.

b. To select college-educated millennials, we first select all customers with a college degree. Recall that the double equal sign (==) is used to check whether the College observation is Yes. Enter:

```
> college <- myData[myData$College=='Yes', ]
```

c. We now use the Birthdate variable to select the millennials who were born between 1982 and 2000. R usually imports the date values as text characters, and, therefore, we first need to convert the BirthDate variable into the date data type using the **as.Date** function. The option format = "%m/%d/%Y" indicates that the BirthDate variable is in the mm/dd/yyyy format. For example, in order for R to read dates such as 01/13/1990, enter:

```
> college$BirthDate <- as.Date(college$BirthDate, format =
"%m/%d/%Y")
```

Other common date formats include "%Y-%m-%d", "%b %d, %Y", and "%B %d, %Y" that will read dates specified as 1990-01-13, Jan 13, 1990, and January 13, 1990, respectively.

d. We also use the **as.Date** function to specify the cutoff dates, January 1, 1982, and December 31, 1999, before using them as selection criteria for selecting the millennials in our data. Enter:

```
> cutoffdate1 <- as.Date("01/01/1982", format = "%m/%d/%Y")
> cutoffdate2 <- as.Date("12/31/1999", format = "%m/%d/%Y")
> millenials <- college[college$BirthDate >= cutoffdate1 &
college$BirthDate <= cutoffdate2, ]
```

Use the **View** function to verify that the millennials data frame contains 59 college-educated millennials.

e. To include only the Sex, HHSize, Income, Spending, Orders, and Channel variables in the millenials data frame, we specify the column indices of these variables using the **c** function. Enter:

```
> subset1 <- millenials[ , c(2, 6, 7, 8, 9, 10)]
```

Alternately, we can create a new data frame by specifying the names of the variables to include. Enter:

```
> subset2 <- millenials[ , c("Sex", "HHSize", "Income",
"Spending", "Orders", "Channel")]
```

Use the **View** function to verify that subset1 and subset2 data are identical.

f. R imports non-numerical variables such as Sex and Channel as text characters. Before further subsetting and examining the data, we convert Sex and Channel into categorical variables (called factors in R) by using the **as.factor** function. Enter:

```
> subset1$Sex <- as.factor(subset1$Sex)
> subset1$Channel <- as.factor(subset1$Channel)
```

To verify that the Channel variable has been converted into a factor or a categorical variable, enter:

```
> is.factor(subset1$Channel)
```

This command returns TRUE if the variable is a factor, and FALSE otherwise.

g. To create two subsets of data based on Sex, we use the **split** function. Enter:

```
> sex <- split(subset1, subset1$Sex)
```

The sex data frame contains two subsets: Female and Male. We can now view the Female and Male subsets. Enter:

```
> View(sex$Female)
> View(sex$Male)
```

Verify that there are 21 female college-educated millennials and 38 male college-educated millennials. Your results should be similar to Table 1.8.

A Note on Subsetting Based on Data Ranges

In some situations, we might simply want to subset data based on data ranges. For example, we use the following statement to subset customers data to include observations 1 to 50 and observations 101 to 200. Enter:

```
> dataRanges <- myData[c(1:50, 101:200),]
```

SYNOPSIS OF INTRODUCTORY CASE

hbpictures/Shutterstock

Catherine Hill has been assigned to help market Organic Food Superstore's new line of Asian-inspired meals. In order to understand the potential target market for this product, Catherine subsetted the data that contain a representative sample of the company's customers to include only college-educated millennials. She also partitioned the data set into two subsets based on sex to compare the profiles of female and male college-educated millennials.

The data show that an overwhelming portion of the male customers were acquired through social media ads, while female customers tend to be enticed by web ads or referrals. Catherine plans to use these results to design and run a series of social media ads about the new product line with content that targets male customers. For female customers, she plans to focus her marketing efforts on web banner ads and the company's referral program.

Furthermore, as the male customers seem to place more frequent but smaller orders than female customers do, Catherine plans to work with her marketing team to develop some cross-sell and upsell strategies that target male customers. Given the fact that the company's male college-educated millennial customers tend to be high-income earners, Catherine is confident that with the right message and product offerings, her marketing team will be able to develop strategies for increasing the total spending of these customers.

EXERCISES 1.3

Mechanics

19. **FILE** ***Exercise_1.19.*** The accompanying data set contains two numerical variables, x_1 and x_2.
    a. For x_2, how many of the observations are equal to 2?
    b. Sort x_1 and then x_2, both in ascending order. After the variables have been sorted, what is the first observation for x_1 and x_2?
    c. Sort x_1 and then x_2, both in descending order. After the variables have been sorted, what is the first observation for x_1 and x_2?
    d. Sort x_1 in ascending order and x_2 in descending order. After the variables have been sorted, what is the first observation for x_1 and x_2?
    e. How many missing values are there in x_1 and x_2?

20. **FILE** ***Exercise_1.20.*** The accompanying data set contains three numerical variables, x_1, x_2, and x_3.
    a. For x_1, how many of the observations are greater than 30?
    b. Sort x_1, x_2, and then x_3 all in ascending order. After the variables have been sorted, what is the first observation for x_1, x_2, and x_3?
    c. Sort x_1 and x_2 in descending order and then x_3 in ascending order. After the variables have been sorted, what is the first observation for x_1, x_2, and x_3?
    d. How many missing values are there in x_1, x_2, and x_3?

21. **FILE** ***Exercise_1.21.*** The accompanying data set contains three numerical variables, x_1, x_2, and x_3, and one categorical variable, x_4.
    a. For x_4, how many of the observations are less than three?
    b. Sort x_1, x_2, x_3, and then x_4 all in ascending order. After the variables have been sorted, what is the first observation for x_1, x_2, x_3, and x_4?
    c. Sort x_1, x_2, x_3, and then x_4 all in descending order. After the variables have been sorted, what is the first observation for x_1, x_2, x_3, and x_4?
    d. How many missing values are there in x_1, x_2, x_3, and x_4?
    e. How many observations are there in each category in x_4?

22. **FILE** ***Exercise_1.22.*** The accompanying data set contains four variables, x_1, x_2, x_3, and x_4.
    a. Subset the data set to include only observations that have a date on or after May 1, 1975 for x_3. How many observations are in the subset data?
    b. Subset the original data set based on the binary 1/0 values for x_4. How many observations are in each of the two subsets?

23. **FILE** ***Exercise_1.23.*** The accompanying data set contains five variables, x_1, x_2, x_3, x_4, and x_5.
    a. Subset the data set to include only x_2, x_3, and x_4. How many missing values are there in these three variables?
    b. Remove all observations that have "Own" as the value for x_2. Then remove all observations that have values lower than 150 for x_3. How many observations remain in the data set?

24. **FILE** ***Exercise_1.24.*** The accompanying data set contains five variables, x_1, x_2, x_3, x_4, and x_5. There are missing values in the data set.
    a. Which variables have missing values?
    b. Which observations have missing values?
    c. Omit all observations (rows) that have missing values. How many observations remain in the data set?

Applications

25. **FILE** ***SAT.*** The following table lists a portion of the average writing and math SAT scores for the 50 states as well as the District of Columbia, Puerto Rico, and the U.S. Virgin Islands for the year 2017 as reported by the College Board.

State	Writing	Math
Alabama	595	571
Alaska	562	544
⋮	⋮	⋮
Wyoming	633	635

    a. Sort the data by writing scores in descending order. Which state has the highest average writing score? What is the average math score of that state?
    b. Sort the data by math scores in ascending order. Which state has the lowest average math score? What is the average writing score of that state?
    c. How many states reported an average math score higher than 600?
    d. How many states reported an average writing score lower than 550?

26. **FILE** ***Fitness.*** A social science study conducts a survey of 418 individuals about how often they exercise, marital status, and annual income. A portion of the data is shown in the accompanying table.

ID	Exercise	Married	Income
1	Always	Yes	106299
2	Sometimes	Yes	86570
⋮	⋮	⋮	⋮
418	Often	No	92690

a. Sort the data by annual income. Of the 10 highest income earners, how many of them are married and always exercise?
b. Sort the data by marital status and exercise both in descending order. How many of the individuals who are married and exercise sometimes earn more than $110,000 per year?
c. How many missing values are there in each variable?
d. How many individuals are married and unmarried?
e. How many married individuals always exercise? How many unmarried individuals never exercise?

27. **FILE** ***Demographics.*** The accompanying table shows a portion of the data for an individual's income (Income in $1,000s), age, sex (F = female, M = male), and marital status (Married; Y = yes, N = no).

Individual	Income	Age	Sex	Married
1	87	46	F	Y
2	97	52	M	Y
⋮	⋮	⋮	⋮	⋮
890	69	44	F	N

a. Count the number of males and females in the data.
b. What percentages of males and females are married?
c. Of the 10 individuals with the highest income, how many are married males.
d. What are the highest and the lowest incomes of males and females?
e. What are the highest and lowest incomes of married and unmarried males?

28. **FILE** ***Travel_Plan.*** Jerry Stevenson is the manager of a travel agency. He wants to build a model that can predict whether or not a customer will travel within the next year. He has compiled a data set that contains the following variables: whether the individual has a college degree (College), annual household spending on food (FoodSpend in $), annual income (Income in $), and whether the customer has plans to travel within the next year (TravelPlan, 1 = have travel plans; 0 = do not have travel plans). A portion of the data is shown in the accompanying table.

College	FoodSpend	Income	TravelPlan
Yes	1706.89	49412	1
No	2892.9	55416	0
⋮	⋮	⋮	⋮
No	2617	50900	0

a. Which variables have missing values?
b. Omit all observations (rows) that have missing values. How many observations are removed due to missing values?
c. In order to better understand his customers with high incomes, Jerry wants to create a subset of the data that only includes customers with annual incomes higher than $75,000 and who plan to travel within the next year. Subset the data to build the list of customers who meet these criteria. How many observations are in this subset?

29. **FILE** ***Population.*** The US Census Bureau records the population for the 50 states each year. The accompanying table shows a portion of these data for the years 2010 to 2018.

State	2010	2011	. . .	2018
Alabama	4,785,448	4,798,834	. . .	4,887,871
Alaska	713,906	722,038	. . .	737,438
⋮	⋮	⋮	⋮	⋮
Wyoming	564,483	567,224	. . .	577,737

a. Create two subsets of the state population data: one with 2018 population greater than or equal to 5 million and one with 2018 population less than 5 million. How many observations are in each subset?
b. In the subset of states with 5 million or more people, remove the states with over 10 million people. How many states were removed?

30. **FILE** ***Football_Players.*** Denise Lau is an avid football fan and religiously follows every game of the National Football League. During the 2017 season, she meticulously keeps a record of how each quarterback has played throughout the season. Denise is making a presentation at the local NFL fan club about these quarterbacks. The accompanying table shows a portion of the data that Denise has recorded, with the following variables: the player's name (Player), team's name (Team), completed passes (Comp), attempted passes (Att), completion percentage (Pct), total yards thrown (Yds), average yards per attempt (Avg), yards thrown per game (Yds/G), number of touch downs (TD), and number of interceptions (Int).

Player	Team	Comp	. . .	Int
Aaron Rodgers	GB	154	. . .	6
Alex Smith	KC	341	. . .	5
⋮	⋮	⋮	⋮	⋮
Tyrod Taylor	BUF	263	. . .	4

a. Are there any missing values in the data set? If there are, which variables have missing values? Which observations have missing values?

b. Omit all observations (rows) that have missing values. How many observations are removed due to missing values?

c. Denise also wants to remove outlier cases where the players have less than five touchdowns or more than 20 interceptions. Remove these observations from the data set. How many observations were removed from the data?

31. **FILE** ***Salaries.*** Ian Stevens is a human resource analyst working for the city of Seattle. He is performing a compensation analysis of city employees. The accompanying data set contains three variables: Department, Job Title, and Hourly Rate (in $). A few hourly rates are missing in the data.

Department	Job Title	Hourly Rate
Public Utilities	Res&Eval Asst	32.81
Sustainability & Environ Dept	StratAdvsr3,Exempt	62.27
⋮	⋮	⋮
Public Utilities	Capital Prjts Coord, Asst	42.71

a. Split the data set into a number of subsets based on Department. How many subsets are created?

b. Which subset contains missing values? How many missing values are in that data set?

1.4 WRITING WITH DATA

TechSales_Reps

Case Study

Cassius Weatherby is a human resources manager at a major technology firm that produces software and hardware products. He would like to analyze the net promoter score (NPS) of sales professionals at the company. The NPS measures customer satisfaction and loyalty by asking customers how likely they are to recommend the company to others on a scale of 0 (unlikely) to 10 (very likely). This measure is an especially important indicator for the company's software business as a large percentage of the sales leads come from customer referrals. Cassius wants to identify relevant factors that are linked with the NPS that a sales professional receives. These insights can help the company make better hiring decisions and develop a more effective training program.

With the help of the company's IT group, a data set with over 20,000 observations of sales professionals is extracted from the enterprise data warehouse. The relevant variables include the product line to which the sales professional is assigned, age, sex, the number of years with the company, whether the sales professional has a college degree, personality type based on the Myers-Briggs personality assessment, the number of professional certificates acquired, the average score from the 360-degree annual evaluation, base salary, and the average NPS received. Cassius is tasked with inspecting and reviewing the data and preparing a report for the company's top management team.

Sample Report–Evaluation of Net Promoter Scores

The net promoter score (NPS) is a key indicator of customer satisfaction and loyalty. It measures how likely a customer would recommend a product or company to others. Because our software line for business relies heavily on customer referrals to generate sales leads, the NPS that our sales professionals receive is a key indicator of our company's future success.

dizain/Shutterstock

From a total of about 20,000 records of sales professionals, we select only the sales professionals in the software product group and divide them into two categories: those with an average NPS below nine and those with an average NPS of nine or ten. When a customer gives a sales professional an NPS of nine or ten, the customer is considered "enthusiastically loyal," meaning that they are very likely to continue purchasing from us and refer their colleagues to our company. Based on the NPS categorization, we then divide the sales professionals into two categories: those with zero to three professional certificates and those with four or more professional certificates. Table 1.9 shows the results. Of the 12,130 sales professionals in the software product group, we find that 65.57% have earned less than 4 professional certificates, whereas 34.43% have earned four or more. However, there appears to be a link between those with 4 or more professional certificates and NPS values. For those who received an NPS of nine or ten, we find that 62.60% have earned at least four professional certificates. Similarly, for those who received an NPS of below nine, we find that 73.00% earned less than four professional certificates.

Although this might simply suggest that high-achieving employees tend to be self-motivated to earn professional certificates, we also believe that sales professionals with sufficient technical knowledge can effectively communicate and assist their customers in finding technology solutions, which will lead to increased customer satisfaction and loyalty. Our training and development program must place a greater emphasis on helping the employees earn relevant certifications and acquire necessary technical knowledge.

TABLE 1.9 Sales Professionals by the Number of Certificates and NPS Value

Number of certificates	Full Sample (n = 12,130)	NPS $<$ 9 (n = 9,598)	NPS $\geq$ 9 (n = 2,532)
0 to 3	65.57%	73.00%	37.40%
4 or more	34.43%	27.00%	62.60%

Based on NPS categorization, we then divide the sales professionals into categories based on personality type. Table 1.10 shows the results. In addition to professional certification, we find that personality types are linked with NPS values. Among the four personality types, Diplomats and Explorers account for 72.69% of all the sales professionals in the software group. However, when we divide the employees based on the NPS values, these two personality types account for 91.63% of the group with an average NPS of nine or ten, whereas they account for only 67.69% for the below nine NPS group.

TABLE 1.10 Sales Professionals by Personality Type and NPS Value

Myers-Briggs Personality Type	Full Sample (n = 12,130)	NPS $<$ 9 (n = 9,598)	NPS $\geq$ 9 (n = 2,532)
Analyst	12.13%	14.47%	3.24%
Diplomat	35.62%	33.07%	45.30%
Explorer	37.07%	34.62%	46.33%
Sentinel	15.19%	17.84%	5.13%

We also examined NPS variations by other variables such as age, sex, education attainment, sales, and commission but did not find considerable differences in NPS categorization. Other variables such as salary and the tenure of the employee with the company are not included in our initial analysis.

Based on the insights from this analysis, we request that the company appoint an analytics task force to conduct a more comprehensive analysis of sales professionals. We strongly suggest that the analysis focus on professional certification and personality, among relevant factors for determining the NPS value. At a minimum, two goals of the task force should include making recommendations on (1) a redesign of our training and development program to focus on helping employees acquire relevant professional certificates and (2) the efficacy of using personality types as part of the hiring decision.

Suggested Case Studies

As discussed in the chapter, data from an endless number of online sources are available for us to explore and investigate. Here are some suggested case studies using online as well as the data that accompany the text.

Report 1.1 Finland is the happiest country in the world, according to the 2018 Happiness Index Report by the United Nations (http://www.worldhappiness.report). In fact, several Scandinavian countries have consistently held the top spots among the 156 countries included in the annual Happiness Index Report in the past several years. Visit the Happiness Index website, download and explore online data, and write a report on your choice of countries, focusing on variables such as social support, healthy life expectancy at birth, freedom to make life choices, and generosity.

Report 1.2 FILE ***House_Price.*** Choose any two campus towns and focus on variables representing the sale price, beds, baths, square footage, lot size, and the house type. Describe the variable type and scales of measurement for each variable. Further, make a comparison between the two campus towns.

Report 1.3 FILE ***College_Admissions.*** Choose any college and focus on variables representing parents' education, gender (male or female), race (white, Asian, or other), high school GPA, and SAT/Act scores, and admission decision. Describe the variable type and scales of measurement for each variable. Further, subset the data by race to report any patterns that you observe for these selected variables.

Report 1.4 FILE ***TechSales_Reps.*** Use data on employees in the software product group with a college degree for variables representing sex (female or male), personality type, salary, and net promoter score. Describe the variable type and scales of measurement for each variable. Further, subset the data by personality type to report any patterns that you observe for these selected variables.

CONCEPTUAL REVIEW

LO 1.1 Explain the various data types.

Data are compilations of facts, figures, or other contents.

A population consists of all items of interest in a statistical problem; a sample is a subset of that population.

Cross-sectional data contain values of a characteristic of many subjects at the same point in time or without regard to differences in time. Time series data contain values of a characteristic of a subject over time.

Structured data conform, but unstructured data do not conform, to a predefined row-column format.

Big data is a term used to describe a massive amount of both structured and unstructured data that are extremely difficult to manage, process, and analyze using traditional data processing tools. Big data, however, does not necessary imply complete (population) data.

LO 1.2 **Describe variables and types of measurement scales.**

Variables are classified as categorical or numerical. The observations of a categorical variable represent categories, whereas the observations of a numerical variable represent meaningful numbers.

Numerical variables are further classified as discrete or continuous. A discrete variable assumes a countable number of values, whereas a continuous variable is characterized by uncountable values within an interval.

All data measurements can be classified into one of four major categories.

- The nominal scale represents the least sophisticated level of measurement. The observations on a nominal scale differ merely by name or label. These observations are then simply categorized or grouped by name.
- The observations on an ordinal scale can be categorized *and* ranked; however, differences between the ranked observations are meaningless.
- The interval scale is a stronger measurement scale as compared to nominal and ordinal scales. Observations on the interval scale can be categorized and ranked, and differences between observations are meaningful. The main drawback of the interval scale is that the value of zero is arbitrarily chosen; this implies that ratios constructed for an interval-scaled variable bear no significance.
- The ratio scale represents the strongest level of measurement. A ratio-scaled variable has all the characteristics of an interval-scaled variable as well as a true zero point; thus, meaningful ratios can be calculated.

Nominal and ordinal scales are used for categorical variables, whereas interval and ratio scales are used for numerical variables.

LO 1.3 **Inspect and explore data.**

After obtaining relevant data, we often spend a considerable amount of time on inspecting and preparing the data for subsequent analysis.

Counting and sorting data help us verify that the data set is complete or that it may have missing values, especially for important variables. Sorting data also allows us to review the range of values for each variable to gain a better understanding and insights into the data. We can sort data based on a single variable or multiple variables.

LO 1.4 **Apply data subsetting.**

Subsetting is the process of extracting a portion of a data set that is relevant for subsequent statistical analysis or when the objective of the analysis is to compare two subsets of the data. It is also used to eliminate observations that contain missing values, low quality data, or outliers. Sometimes, subsetting involves excluding variables that contain redundant information.

ADDITIONAL EXERCISES

32. According to *Statistica.com,* the average life expectancies in the United States for those born in 2019 is 76 years for men and 81 years for women.
    a. Describe the relevant population for the average life expectancy estimates.
    b. Are the average life expectancies computed from sample or population data?

33. Ask 20 of your friends whether they live in a dormitory, a rental unit, or other form of accommodation. Also find out their approximate monthly lodging expenses. Create a table that uses this information. Are the data considered structured or unstructured? Are they cross-sectional or time series data?

34. Go to the U.S. Census Bureau website at www.census.gov and search for the most recent median household income for Alabama, Arizona, California, Florida, Georgia, Indiana, Iowa, Maine, Massachusetts, Minnesota, Mississippi, New Mexico, North Dakota, and Washington. Do these data represent cross-sectional or time series data? Comment on the regional differences in income.

35. FILE ***Retailer.*** An online retail company is trying to predict customer spending in the first three months of the year. Brian Duffy, the marketing analyst of the company, has compiled a data set on 200 existing customers that includes sex (Sex: Female/Male), annual income in 1,000s (Income), age (Age, in years), and total spending in the first three months of the year (Spending). A portion of the data is shown in the accompanying table.

Sex	Income	Age	Spending
Male	87.50	52	156.88
Female	66.50	43	275.16
⋮	⋮	⋮	⋮
Male	51.90	61	159.51

a. Which of the above variables are categorical and which are numerical?
b. What is the measurement scale of each of the above variable?

36. FILE ***Vacation*** Vacation destinations often run on a seasonal basis, depending on the primary activities in that location. Amanda Wang is the owner of a travel agency in Cincinnati, Ohio. She has built a database of the number of vacation packages (Vacation) that she has sold over the last 12 years. A portion of the data is shown in the accompanying table.

Year	Quarter	Vacation
2008	1	500
2008	2	147
⋮	⋮	⋮
2019	4	923

a. What is the measurement scale of the Year variable? What are the strengths of this type of measurement scale? What are its weaknesses?
b. What is the measurement scale of the Quarter variable? What is a weakness of this type of measurement scale?
c. What is the measurement scale of the Vacation variable? What are the strengths of this type of measurement scale?

37. FILE ***Spend.*** A company conducts a consumer survey with questions about home ownership (OwnHome: Yes/No), car ownership (OwnCar: Yes/No), annual household spending on food (Food), and annual household spending on travel (Travel). A portion of the data is shown in the accompanying table.

ID	OwnHome	OwnCar	Food	Travel
1	Yes	Yes	5472.43	827.4
2	No	Yes	9130.73	863.55
⋮	⋮	⋮	⋮	⋮
500	No	No	6205.97	3667.5

a. Sort the data by home ownership, car ownership, and the travel spending all in descending order. How much did the first customer on the ordered list spend on food?
b. Sort the data only by the travel spending amount in descending order. Of the 10 customers who spend the most on traveling, how many of them are homeowners? How many of them are both homeowners and car owners?
c. How many missing values are there in each variable?
d. How many customers are homeowners?
e. How many customers are homeowners but do not own a car?

38. FILE ***Admission.*** College admission is a competitive process where, among other things, the SAT and high school GPA scores of students are evaluated to make an admission decision. The accompanying data set contains the admission decision (Decision; Admit/Deny), SAT score, Female (Yes/No), and high school GPA (HSGPA) for 1,230 students. A portion of the data is shown in the accompanying table.

Student	Decision	SAT	Female	HSGPA
1	Deny	873	No	2.57
2	Deny	861	Yes	2.65
⋮	⋮	⋮	⋮	⋮
1230	Admit	1410	No	4.28

a. Count the number of male and female students.
b. What percentages of male and female students are admitted?
c. Of the 10 students with the highest HSGPA, how many are males?
d. Of the 10 students with the lowest SAT, how many are females?
e. What are the highest and the lowest SAT scores of admitted male and female students?

39. FILE ***Longitudinal.*** The accompanying table contains a portion of data from the National

Longitudinal Survey (NLS), which follows over 12,000 individuals in the United States over time. Variables in this analysis include the following information on individuals: Urban (1 if lives in urban area, 0 otherwise), Siblings (number of siblings), White (1 if white, 0 otherwise), Christian (1 if Christian, 0 otherwise), FamilySize, Height, Weight (in pounds), and Income (in $).

Urban	Siblings	White	. . .	Income
1	8	1	. . .	0
1	1	1	. . .	40000
⋮	⋮	⋮	⋮	⋮
1	2	1	. . .	43000

a. Are there any missing values in the data set? If there are, which variables have missing values? Which observations have missing values?
b. Omit all observations (rows) that have missing values. How many observations are removed due to missing values?

40. **FILE** ***Stocks.*** Investors usually consider a variety of information to make investment decisions. The accompanying table displays a sample of large publicly traded corporations and their financial information. Relevant information includes stock price (Price), dividend as a percentage of share price (Dividend), price to earnings ratio (PE), earnings per share (EPS), and lowest and highest share prices within the past 52 weeks (Lowest and Highest).

Name	Price	Dividend	. . .	High
3M	189.09	2.48	. . .	190.54
Abbott Lab	45.00	2.34	. . .	45.83
⋮	⋮	⋮	⋮	⋮
Zoetis	53.07	0.79	. . .	56.50

a. Are there any missing values in the data set? If there are, which variables have missing values?
b. Omit all observations (rows) that have missing values. How many complete observations are in the subset?
c. The financial analyst is most interested in companies with a price to earnings ratio less than 15. Remove all observations from the subset in part b for which PE equals 15 or more. How many observations are left in the data set?

2 Tabular and Graphical Methods

LEARNING OBJECTIVES

After reading this chapter you should be able to:

LO **2.1** **Construct and interpret a frequency distribution for a categorical variable.**

LO **2.2** **Construct and interpret a bar chart and a pie chart.**

LO **2.3** **Construct and interpret a contingency table and a stacked bar chart for two categorical variables.**

LO **2.4** **Construct and interpret a frequency distribution for a numerical variable.**

LO **2.5** **Construct and interpret a histogram, a polygon, and an ogive.**

LO **2.6** **Construct and interpret a scatterplot, a scatterplot with a categorical variable, and a line chart.**

LO **2.7** **Construct and interpet a stem-and-leaf diagram.**

People often have difficulty processing information provided by data in its raw form. A useful way of interpreting data effectively is through data visualization. In this chapter, we present several tabular and graphical tools that help us organize and present data.

We first construct a frequency distribution for a categorical variable. A frequency distribution is a tabular method for condensing and summarizing data. For visual representations of a categorical variable, we construct a bar chart and a pie chart. We then examine the relationship between two categorical variables by constructing a contingency table and a stacked column chart.

For a numerical variable, we again construct a frequency distribution. In addition to giving us an overall picture of where the data tend to cluster, a frequency distribution for a numerical variable also shows us how the data are spread out from the lowest observation to the highest observation. For visual representations of a numerical variable, we construct a histogram, a polygon, and an ogive.

Finally, we show how to construct a scatterplot, which graphically depicts the relationship between two numerical variables. We will find that a scatterplot is a very useful tool when conducting correlation and regression analysis, topics discussed in depth later in the text. We also discuss additional data visualizations including a scatterplot with a categorical variable, a line chart, and a stem-and-leaf diagram.

Ilene MacDonald/Alamy Stock Photo

INTRODUCTORY CASE

House Prices in Punta Gorda, Florida

The year-round warm weather and the lack of state income tax are two of the many reasons why people love to call Florida home. It is especially attractive to baby boomers wanting a warmer climate for their golden years.

Matthew Edwards is a relocation specialist for a real estate firm in Punta Gorda, a small city on the west coast of Florida. Recently, Matthew has seen an increase in the number of people from the Northeast who want to live in Punta Gorda. He would like to prepare a summary of house prices for future clients. For 40 recent real estate transactions, he collects data on the house price (Price in $1,000s), the square footage of the house (Sqft), the number of bedrooms (Beds), the number of Bathrooms (Baths), the year the house was built (Built), and the type of house (either Single or Condo). Table 2.1 shows a portion of the data.

TABLE 2.1 Recent Real Estate Transactions in Punta Gorda, Florida

FILE *PG_Sales*

Transaction	Price	Sqft	Beds	Baths	Built	Type
1	200	1684	3	2	2005	Single
2	435	2358	3	2.5	2017	Single
⋮	⋮	⋮	⋮	⋮	⋮	⋮
40	192	1154	2	2	2019	Condo

In his preliminary analysis, Matthew wants to use the sample information to

1. Make summary statements concerning the range of house prices.
2. Comment on where house prices tend to cluster.
3. Examine the relationship between a house price and its size.

A synopsis of this case is provided in Section 2.4.

2.1 METHODS TO VISUALIZE A CATEGORICAL VARIABLE

LO 2.1

Construct and interpret a frequency distribution for a categorical variable.

In this section, we present several tabular and graphical tools that help us organize and present data concerning a single variable. We first examine common ways to summarize a categorical variable.

Recall from Chapter 1 that a categorical variable consists of observations that represent labels or names. For example, participants in a survey are often asked to indicate their sex or race, or provide ratings of a product. When presented with a categorical variable, it is often useful to summarize the data with a **frequency distribution**.

> A FREQUENCY DISTRIBUTION FOR A CATEGORICAL VARIABLE
>
> A frequency distribution for a categorical variable groups the data into categories and records the number of observations that fall into each category. The relative frequency for each category equals the proportion of observations in each category.

A Frequency Distribution for a Categorical Variable

Suppose the Human Resources department of a large technology company maintains relevant personnel information regarding each employee's personality type based on the Myers-Briggs assessment. The Myers-Briggs assessment breaks down personality types into four categories:

- Analyst: An analyst tends to be open-minded and strong-willed. He/she likes to work independently and usually approaches things from a very practical perspective.
- Diplomat: A diplomat cares about people and tends to have a lot of empathy toward others.
- Explorer: An explorer tends to be very good at making quick, rational decisions in difficult situations.
- Sentinel: A sentinel likes stability, order, and security, and tends to be hard working and meticulous.

Table 2.2 shows a portion of the Myers-Briggs assessment results for 1,000 employees. The Personality variable is a categorical variable that is of nominal scale, because the observations merely represent labels. Data presented in this format—that is, in raw form—are very difficult to interpret. Converting the raw data into a frequency distribution is often a first step in making the data more manageable and easier to assess.

FILE
Myers_Briggs

TABLE 2.2 Personality Types

Employee	Personality
1	Diplomat
2	Diplomat
⋮	⋮
1000	Explorer

As shown in Table 2.3, the four categories of the Personality variable form the first column of a frequency distribution. We then record the number of employees that fall into each category. We can readily see from Table 2.3 that Explorer occurs with the most frequency, while Analyst occurs with the least frequency.

In some applications, especially when comparing data sets of differing sizes, our needs may be better served by focusing on the relative frequency for each category rather than its frequency. The relative frequency for each category is calculated by dividing the frequency by the sample size. For example, the relative frequency for Explorer is 404/1,000 = 0.404. We can easily convert a relative frequency into a percent frequency by multiplying the relevant relative frequency by 100. So, given Explorer's relative frequency of 0.404, we can say that 40.4% of the employees are Explorers. In addition to showing each category's frequency, Table 2.3 also shows each category's relative frequency and percent frequency.

TABLE 2.3 Frequency Distribution for the Personality Variable

Personality	Frequency	Relative Frequency	Percent Frequency
Analyst	116	0.116	11.6
Diplomat	324	0.324	32.4
Explorer	404	0.404	40.4
Sentinel	156	0.156	15.6

We can visualize the information found in the frequency distribution by constructing various graphs. A graphical representation often portrays the variable more dramatically, as well as simplifies interpretation. A **bar chart** and a **pie chart** are two widely used graphical representations for a categorical variable

A Bar Chart

LO 2.2

Construct and interpret a bar chart and a pie chart.

We first construct a vertical **bar chart**, sometimes referred to as a column chart. In a vertical bar chart, the height of each bar is equal to the frequency or the relative frequency of the corresponding category. Figure 2.1 shows the bar chart for the Personality variable.

FIGURE 2.1 Bar chart for the Personality variable

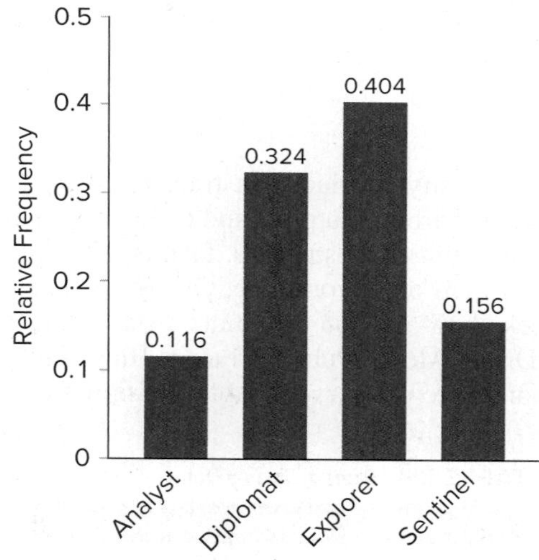

> **A BAR CHART**
>
> A bar chart depicts the frequency or the relative frequency for each category of the categorical variable as a series of horizontal or vertical bars, the lengths of which are proportional to the values that are depicted.

A Pie Chart

A pie chart is a circle that is cut into slices, or sectors, such that each sector is proportional to the size of the category we wish to display. For instance, in the Myers-Briggs example, we found that the relative frequency for Explorer is 0.404. Since a circle contains 360 degrees, the portion of the circle representing Explorers encompasses $0.404 \times 360 = 145.44$ degrees. Calculations for the other three categories can be obtained in a similar manner.

Figure 2.2 shows the pie chart for the Myers-Briggs example. We see that Figure 2.1 and Figure 2.2 reveal the same information in different ways; that is, the most common personality types at this firm are Explorer and Diplomat. The least common personality types are Sentinel and Analyst.

FIGURE 2.2 A pie chart for the Myers-Briggs example

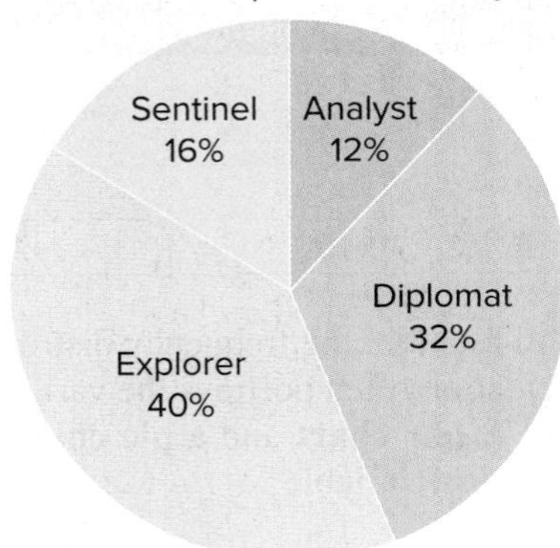

A PIE CHART

A pie chart is a segmented circle whose segments portray the relative frequency of each category for a categorical variable.

EXAMPLE 2.1

FILE *Transit_Survey*

Recently, an urban university conducted a transportation survey as part of its commitment to reduce its carbon footprint and comply with the federal Clean Air Act. The survey was distributed to students, faculty, and staff members in order to learn the patterns of their daily commute. One of the questions asked: During a typical school week, how do you commute from home to school? Possible responses included Drive_Alone, Public_Transit, Bicycle, Walk, and Other. Six hundred people responded to the survey. Table 2.4 shows a portion of the survey results.

TABLE 2.4 ***Transit_Survey*** Data

Respondent	Mode of Transportation
1	Bicycle
2	Public_Transit
⋮	⋮
600	Walk

Construct a frequency distribution, a bar chart, and a pie chart using Excel and R. Then, summarize the results.

Important: Due to different fonts and type settings, copying and pasting Excel or R functions from this text directly into Excel or R may cause errors. When such errors occur, you may need to replace special characters such as quotation marks and parentheses or delete extra spaces in the functions.

SOLUTION:

Using Excel

a. Open the ***Transit_Survey*** data file.

b. Enter the column headings Mode of Transportation and Number of Respondents in cells D1 and E1, respectively. Enter the column heading Drive_Alone in cell D2. Enter the formula =COUNTIF(A2:A601, "Drive_Alone") in cell E2. Enter the column heading Public_Transit in cell D3. Enter the formula =COUNTIF(A2:A601, "Public_Transit") in cell E3. Enter the column heading Bicycle in cell D4. Enter the formula =COUNTIF(A2:A601, "Bicycle") in cell E4. Enter the column heading Walk in cell D5. Enter the formula =COUNTIF(A2:A601, "Walk") in cell E5. Enter the column heading Other in cell D6. Enter the formula =COUNTIF(A2:A601, "Other") in cell E6. Table 2.5 shows the frequency distribution.

TABLE 2.5 Frequency Distribution for Transit Survey Example

Mode of Transportation	Number of Respondents
Drive_Alone	57
Public_Transit	273
Bicycle	111
Walk	141
Other	18

c. For a bar chart, select cells D2:E6. From the menu, choose **Insert > Insert Bar Chart** and select the option on the top left side. (If you are having trouble finding this option after selecting **Insert**, look for the horizontal bars above **Charts**.) Figure 2.3 shows the bar chart. Note that in this instance we have constructed a horizontal bar chart. If you wish to construct a vertical bar chart, then you would choose **Insert > Column Chart**.

Formatting (regarding axis titles, gridlines, etc.) can be done by selecting the '+' sign at the top right of the chart or by selecting **Add Chart Elements** from the menu. Check the box next to *Data Labels* in the *Chart Elements* popup box to display frequencies in the bar chart (or the column chart).

FIGURE 2.3 Bar chart for Transit Survey example

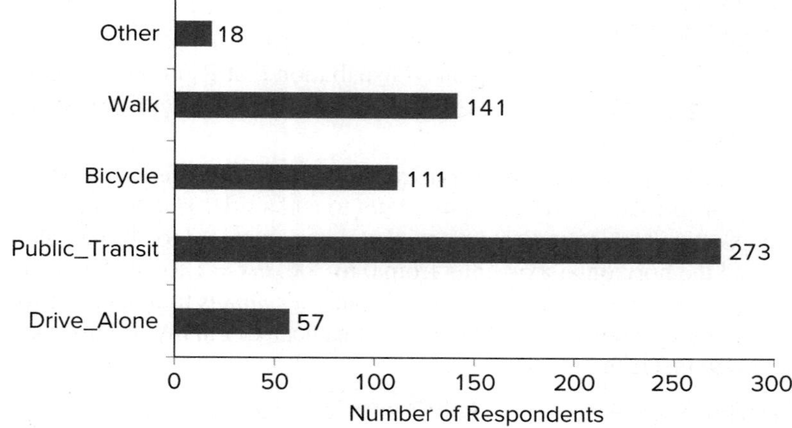

d. For a pie chart, select cells D2:E6. From the menu, choose **Insert > Pie > 2-D Pie** and select the graph on the top left. (If you are having trouble finding this option after selecting **Insert**, look for the circle above Charts.) Figure 2.4 shows the pie chart. See Step c for formatting.

FIGURE 2.4 Pie chart for the Transit Survey example

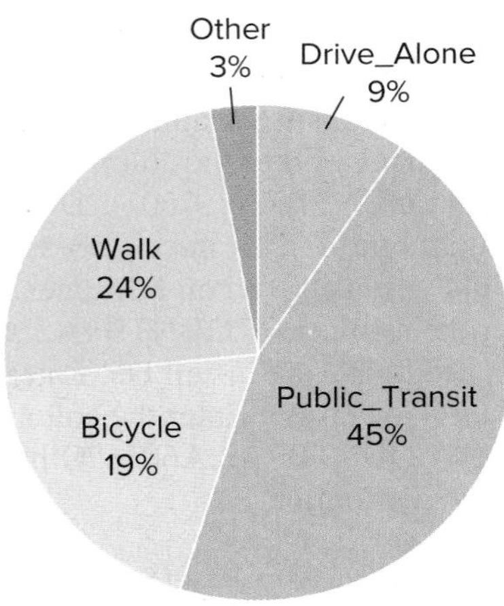

Using R

As mentioned in Chapter 1, before following all R instructions, make sure that you have read Appendix A ("Getting Started with R"). We assume that you have downloaded R and RStudio, and that you know how to import an Excel file. Throughout the text, our goal is to provide the simplest way to obtain the relevant output. We denote all function names in **boldface** and all options within a function in *italics*. It is important to keep in mind that R is case sensitive.

a. Import the ***Transit_Survey*** data file into a data frame (table) and label it myData.

b. We use the **table** function to create a frequency distribution labeled Frequency. As outlined in Appendix A, we typically identify a variable within a data frame using the expression $var, where var denotes the variable name. Here, we need to enclose the variable name with single quotations because the variable name, Mode of Transportation, consists of more than one word. If you retype Frequency, you will see that the resulting frequency distribution is not very attractive. For this reason, we use the **View** function to create a more appealing frequency distribution. The **View** function creates a spreadsheet-style data viewer. Enter:

```
> Frequency <- table(myData$'Mode of Transportation')
> Frequency
> View(Frequency)
```

The only difference in the frequency distribution that R produces compared to the one that appears in Table 2.5 is that the category names are arranged in alphabetical order.

c. We use the **barplot** function to construct a bar chart. R offers a number of options for formatting. Here, we use *main* to add a title, *xlab* to provide a label for the x-axis, *horiz* to indicate a horizontal bar chart, *col* to define color, *xlim* to extend the horizontal axis units from 0 to 300, *las* = 1 to display the category names perpendicular to the y-axis, and *cex.names* to reduce the font size of the category names so that they are not truncated. Finally, we use the **abline** function to insert the y-axis.

```
> barplot(Frequency,main="Bar Chart for Transit Survey",
xlab="Number of Respondents", horiz=TRUE, col="blue",
xlim=c(0,300), las=1, cex.names=0.5)
> abline(v=0)
```

There are a few differences in the bar chart that R produces compared to the one that appears in Figure 2.3, but these differences are cosmetic.

d. We use the **pie** function to construct a pie chart. For options within the function, we use *main* to designate a title.

```
> pie(Frequency, main="Pie Chart for Transit Survey")
```

There are differences in the pie chart that R produces compared to Figure 2.4, but again, these differences are cosmetic.

Summary

Table 2.5, Figure 2.3, and Figure 2.4 reveal that the most common commuting mode at this urban university is public transportation. Walking and riding a bicycle are the next most common commuting modes. These results are not surprising for a university that is located in a city.

Cautionary Comments When Constructing or Interpreting Charts or Graphs

As with many of the analytical methods that we examine throughout this text, the possibility exists for unintentional, as well as purposeful, distortions of graphical information. As a careful researcher, you should follow these basic guidelines:

- The simplest graph should be used for a given set of data. Strive for clarity and avoid unnecessary adornments.
- Axes should be clearly marked with the numbers of their respective scales; each axis should be labeled.
- When creating a bar chart or a histogram (discussed in Section 2.3), each bar/rectangle should be of the same width. Differing widths create distortions.
- The vertical axis should not be given a very high value as an upper limit. In these instances, the data may appear compressed so that an increase (or decrease) of the data is not as apparent as it perhaps should be. For example, Figure 2.5(a) plots the daily price for a barrel of crude oil for the first quarter of the year. Due to Middle East unrest at this time, the price of crude oil rose from a low of \$83.13 per barrel to a high of \$106.19 per barrel, or approximately 28% $\left(= \frac{106.19 - 83.13}{83.13}\right)$. However, because Figure 2.5(a) uses an unreasonably high value as an upper limit on the vertical axis (\$325), the rise in price appears dampened. Figure 2.5(b) shows a vertical axis with an upper limit of \$110; this value better reflects the upper limit observed during this time period.

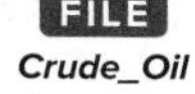

Crude_Oil

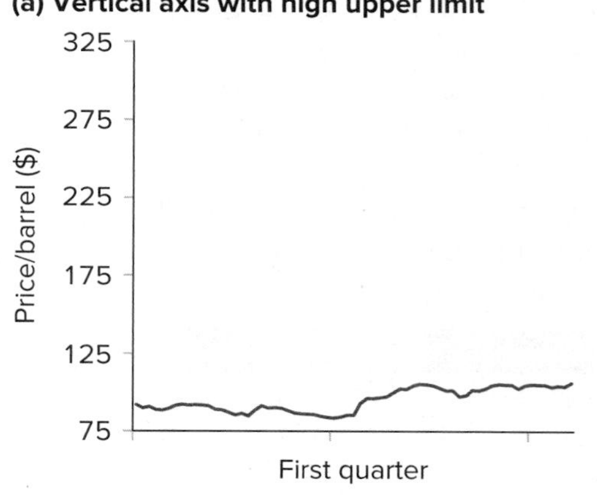

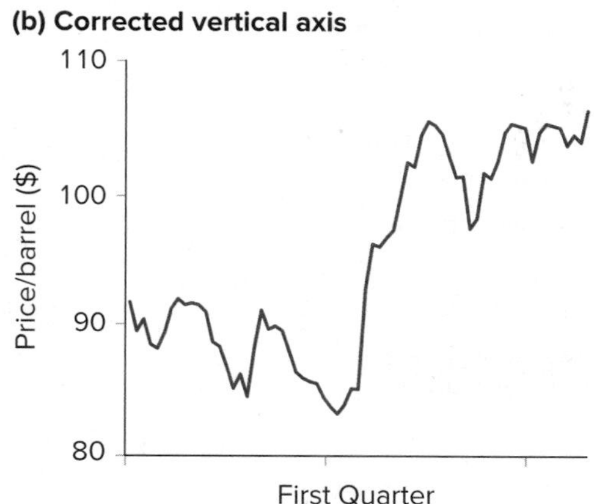

FIGURE 2.5 Misleading vertical axis: unreasonably high upper limit

FILE
Retail

- The vertical axis should not be stretched so that an increase (or decrease) of the data appears more pronounced than warranted. For example, Figure 2.6(a) charts the daily closing stock price of a large retailer for the week of April 4. It is true that the stock price declined over the week from a high of $60.15 to a low of $59.46; this amounts to a $0.69 decrease, or an approximate 1% decline. However, because the vertical axis is stretched, the drop in stock price appears more dramatic. Figure 2.6(b) shows a vertical axis that has not been stretched.

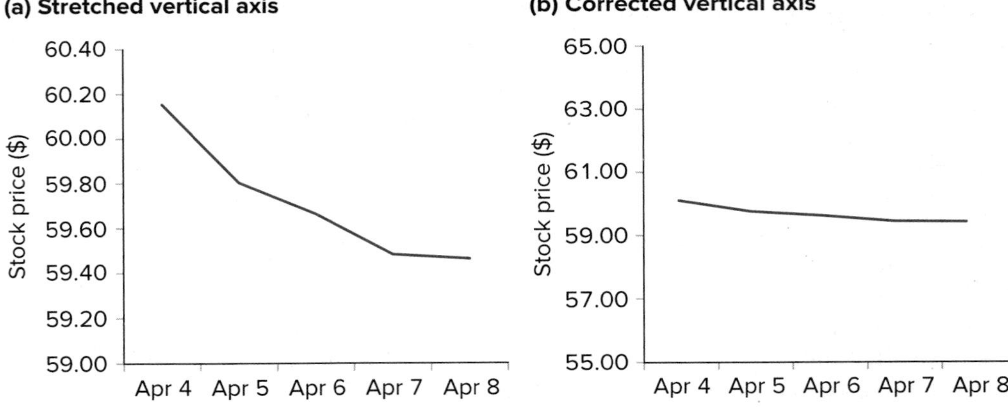

FIGURE 2.6 Misleading scale on vertical axis: stretched scale

EXERCISES 2.1

Applications

1. Fifty pro-football rookies were rated on a scale of 1 to 5, based on performance at a training camp as well as on past performance. A ranking of 1 indicated a poor prospect, whereas a ranking of 5 indicated an excellent prospect. The following frequency distribution was constructed.

Rating	Frequency
1	4
2	10
3	14
4	18
5	4

   a. How many of the rookies received a rating of 4 or better? How many of the rookies received a rating of 2 or worse?
   b. Construct the relative frequency distribution. What proportion received a rating of 5?
   c. Construct a bar chart. Comment on the findings.

2. The following frequency distribution shows the counts of sales of men's shirts at an online retailer over the weekend.

Size	Frequency
Small	80
Medium	175
Large	210
X-Large	115

   a. Construct the relative frequency distribution. What proportion of sales were for a medium-sized shirt?
   b. Construct a bar chart. Comment on the findings.

3. The following frequency distribution summarizes the counts of purchases by day of the week for a major domestic retailer.

Day	Frequency
Mon	2,504
Tue	2,880
Wed	3,402
Thur	3,566
Fri	4,576
Sat	5,550
Sun	5,022

   a. Construct the relative frequency distribution. What proportion of the purchases occurred on Wednesday?
   b. Construct a bar chart using relative frequencies. Comment on the findings.

4. In 2018, the U.S. Census Bureau provided the following frequency distribution for the number of people (in 1,000s) who live below the poverty level by region.

Region	Number of People
Northeast	6,373
Midwest	7,647
South	16,609
West	9,069

a. Construct the relative frequency distribution. What proportion of people who live below the poverty level live in the Midwest?

b. Construct a bar chart. Comment on the findings.

5. A recent poll of 3,057 individuals asked: "What's the longest vacation you plan to take this summer?" The following relative frequency distribution summarizes the results.

Response	Relative Frequency
A few days	0.21
A few long weekends	0.18
One week	0.36
Two weeks	0.25

a. Construct the frequency distribution. How many people are going to take a one-week vacation this summer?

b. Construct a bar chart. Comment on the findings.

6. FILE ***Dining.*** A local restaurant is committed to providing its patrons with the best dining experience possible. On a recent survey, the restaurant asked patrons to rate the quality of their entrées. The responses ranged from 1 to 5, where 1 indicated a disappointing entrée and 5 indicated an exceptional entrée. A portion of the 200 responses is as follows:

Response	Rating
1	3
2	5
⋮	⋮
200	4

a. Construct the frequency distribution that summarizes the results from the survey. Which rating appeared with the most frequency?

b. Construct a bar chart. Are the patrons generally satisfied with the quality of their entrées? Explain.

7. FILE ***Health.*** Patients at North Shore Family Practice are required to fill out a questionnaire that gives the doctor an overall idea of each patient's health. The first question is: "In general, what is the quality of your health?" The patient chooses Excellent, Good, Fair, or Poor. A portion of the 150 responses is as follows:

Response	Quality
1	Fair
2	Good
⋮	⋮
150	Good

a. Construct the frequency distribution that summarizes the results from the questionnaire. What is the most common response to the questionnaire?

b. Construct a bar chart. How would you characterize the health of patients at this medical practice? Explain.

8. FILE ***Millennials.*** A few years ago, a study found that 35% of millennials (Americans born between 1981 and 1996) identified themselves as not religious. A researcher wonders if this finding is consistent today. She surveys 600 millennials and asks them to rate their faith. Possible responses were Very Religious, Somewhat Religious, Slightly Religious, and Not Religious. A portion of the 600 responses is as follows:

Response	Faith
1	Slightly Religious
2	Slightly Religious
⋮	⋮
600	Somewhat Religious

a. Construct the frequency distribution that summarizes the results from the survey. What is the most common response to the survey?

b. Construct a pie chart. Do the researcher's results appear consistent with those found by the earlier study? Explain.

9. FILE ***Status.*** A statistics instructor is interested in the class status of her students, which is defined as freshman, sophomore, junior, or senior. She downloads her roster, a portion of which is shown in the following table.

Student	Status
1	Sophomore
2	Freshman
⋮	⋮
60	Senior

a. Construct the frequency and relative frequency distributions. How many freshmen are in her class? What percentage of the class are sophomores?

b. Construct the pie chart. Summarize the findings.

10. The accompanying figure plots the monthly stock price of a large construction company from July 2017 through March 2019. The stock has experienced tremendous growth over this time period, almost tripling in price. Does the figure reflect this growth? If not, why not?

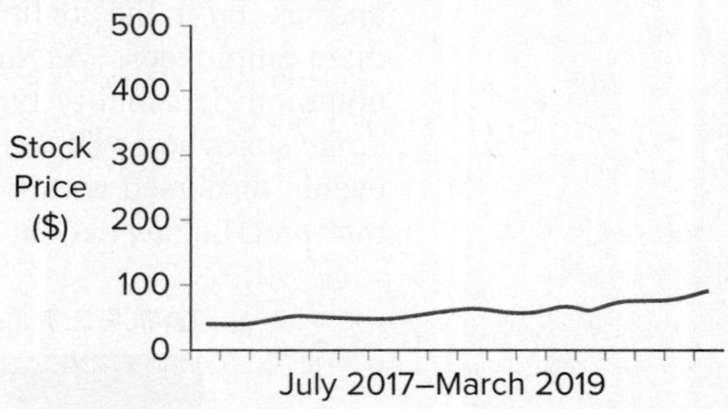

11. Annual sales at a small pharmaceutical firm have been rather stagnant over the most recent five-year period, exhibiting only 1.2% growth over this time frame. A research analyst prepares the accompanying graph for inclusion in a sales report.

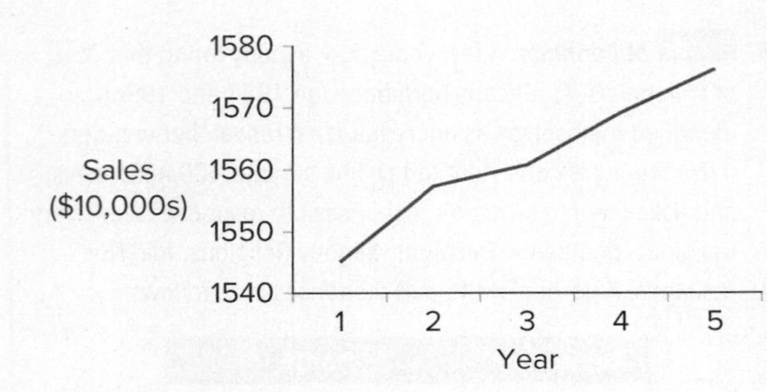

Does this graph accurately reflect what has happened to sales over the last five years? If not, why not?

LO 2.3

2.2 METHODS TO VISUALIZE THE RELATIONSHIP BETWEEN TWO CATEGORICAL VARIABLES

Construct and interpret a contingency table and a stacked bar chart.

In the last section we presented tabular and graphical methods that described one categorical variable. However, we may be interested in the relationship between two categorical variables; that is, we may want to examine whether one categorical variable systematically influences the other.

Here, we introduce a contingency table and a stacked column chart, two common tabular and graphical methods that help us summarize the relationship between two categorical variables. These summary methods are widely used in marketing as well as other business applications. Consider the following example.

A Contingency Table

Suppose we expand the ***Myers_Briggs*** data set discussed in Section 2.1 so that it now includes information on an employee's personality type and sex—two categorical variables. Table 2.6 shows a portion of the expanded data set, ***Myers_Briggs2***.

FILE *Myers_Briggs2*

TABLE 2.6 Expanded Myers-Briggs Assessment Results

Employee	Personality	Sex
1	Diplomat	Female
2	Diplomat	Female
⋮	⋮	⋮
1000	Explorer	Male

Perhaps we are interested in whether certain personality types are more prevalent among males versus females. We can use a contingency table to us summarize the data. A **contingency table** shows the frequencies for two categorical variables. Table 2.7 shows the contingency table for the 1,000 employees cross-classified by personality type and sex. From the contingency table, we see that there are 492 female employees and 508 male employees. As we found in Section 2.1, Diplomats and Explorers are the most common personality types. We also see, for example, that 55 females are considered Analysts, wheras 61 males fall into this category. Female and male employees appear evenly dispersed within each category. The contingency table allows us to present and interpret the raw data in a much more manageable format.

TABLE 2.7 Contingency Table for Expanded Myers-Briggs Example

	Personality				
Sex	**Analyst**	**Diplomat**	**Explorer**	**Sentinel**	**Total**
Female	55	164	194	79	**492**
Male	61	160	210	77	**508**
Total	**116**	**324**	**404**	**156**	**1000**

> **A CONTINGENCY TABLE**
>
> A contingency table shows the frequencies for two categorical variables, x and y, where each cell represents a mutually exclusive combination of the pair of x and y values.

A Stacked Column Chart

The information in a contingency table can be shown graphically using a **stacked column chart**. A stacked column chart is an advanced version of the bar chart that we discussed in Section 2.1. It is designed to visualize more than one categorical variable, plus it allows for the comparison of composition within each category.

Figure 2.7 shows the stacked column chart for personality type and sex. Each column in the chart represents all the employees of a particular personality type, and the two segments in each column represent female employees and male employees. Again, the stacked column chart shows that Diplomats and Explorers are the most common personality types; plus, it appears that female and male employees are equally distributed among each category.

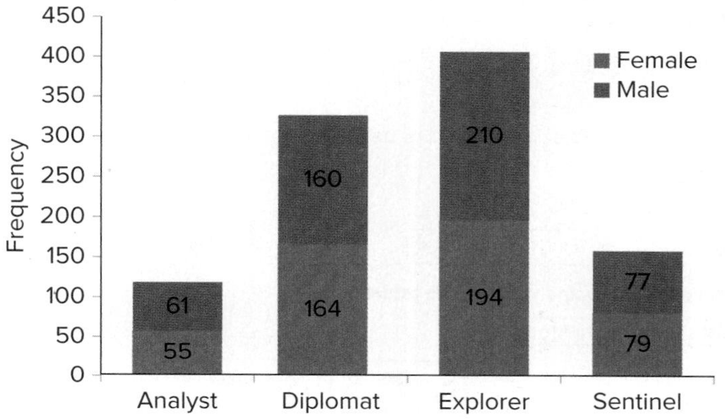

FIGURE 2.7 A stacked column chart for personality type and sex

> **A STACKED COLUMN CHART**
>
> A stacked column chart graphically depicts a contingency table. It is designed to visualize more than one categorical variable, plus it allows for the comparison of composition within each category.

In order to illustrate the construction of a contingency table and a stacked column chart, consider the following example.

EXAMPLE 2.2

An online retailer recently sent e-mails to customers that included a promotional discount. The retailer wonders whether there is any relationship between a customer's location in the U.S. (Midwest, Northeast, South, or West) and whether the customer made a purchase with the discount (yes or no). Table 2.8 shows a portion of the results from 600 e-mail accounts.

Promotion

TABLE 2.8 Promotion Responses

Email	Location	Purchase
1	West	yes
2	Northeast	yes
⋮	⋮	⋮
600	South	no

Construct a contingency table and a stacked column chart using Excel and R, and then summarize the results.

SOLUTION:

Using Excel

a. Open the ***Promotion*** data file.

b. Click anywhere on the data (we choose cell A5). From the menu, select **Insert > Pivot Table**. Figure 2.8 shows the *Create PivotTable* dialog box. Because we clicked on the data before creating a pivot table, the default option in *Select a table or range* should already be populated. We choose to place the pivot table in the existing worksheet beginning in cell E1. Check the box next to the *Add this data to the Data Model* option. Then click **OK**.

FIGURE 2.8 Excel's Create PivotTable Dialog Box

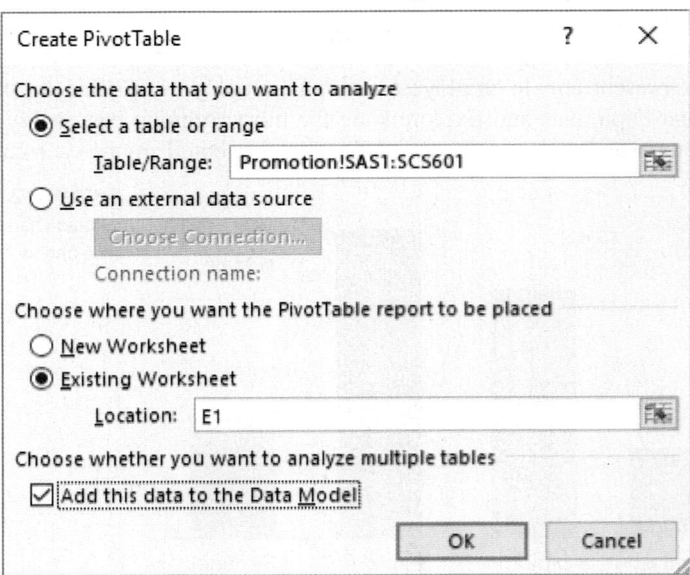

c. A menu will appear on the right side of the screen called *PivotTable Fields*. In the top of this menu you will see all of the variables in our data set. In the bottom part of the menu, there is a grid with four fields: Filters, Rows, Columns, and Values; see Figure 2.9. Drag the Location variable to the Rows field. Drag the Purchase variable to the Columns field. Drag the Email variable to the Values field. If the Email variable in the Values field is not presented as a count (for example, it may be presented as a sum), you will need to change it. Click the arrow below the Values field and select *Value Field Settings*. In the dialog box, select the *Summarize value field by* tab, and then, in the drop-down menu, select *Count*. Click **OK**.

FIGURE 2.9 Excel's Pivot Table Fields

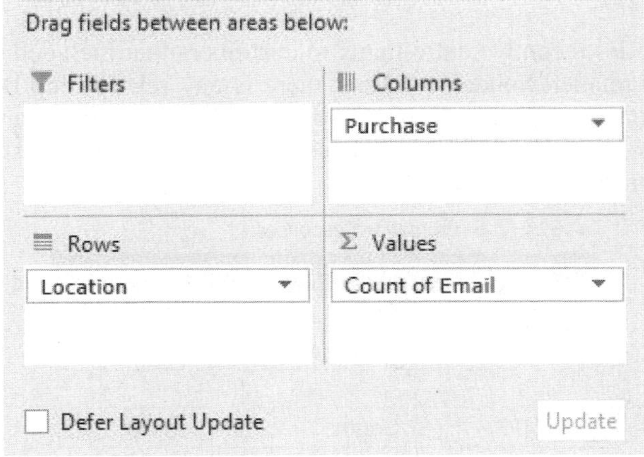

The resulting contingency table should be similar to Table 2.9.

TABLE 2.9 Contingency Table for the Promotion Example

	Purchase		
Location	No	Yes	Total
Midwest	107	77	**184**
Northeast	41	102	**143**
South	24	130	**154**
West	18	101	**119**
Total	**190**	**410**	**600**

Sometimes it is preferable to convert counts to percentages, as shown in Table 2.10. In order to make this change, go back to the *Value Field Settings* dialog box, select the *Show values as* tab, and in the drop-down menu select *% of Grand Total.*

TABLE 2.10 Percent Table for the Promotion Example

	Purchase		
Location	No	Yes	Total
Midwest	17.83%	12.83%	**30.67%**
Northeast	6.83%	17.00%	**23.83%**
South	4.00%	21.67%	**25.67%**
West	3.00%	16.83%	**19.83%**
Total	**31.67%**	**68.33%**	**100.00%**

d. We now illustrate how to create a stacked column chart using the contingency table. Make sure that the contingency table shows counts as in Table 2.9. Select the cells E2:G6. Choose **Insert > Insert Column or Bar Chart > Stacked Column**.

Formatting (regarding axis titles, gridlines, etc.) can be done by selecting the '+' sign at the top right of the chart or by selecting **Add Chart Elements** from the menu. Check the box next to *Data Labels* in the *Chart Elements* pop-up box to display frequencies in the column chart. The resulting stacked column chart is shown in Figure 2.10.

FIGURE 2.10 A stacked column chart for the Promotion example

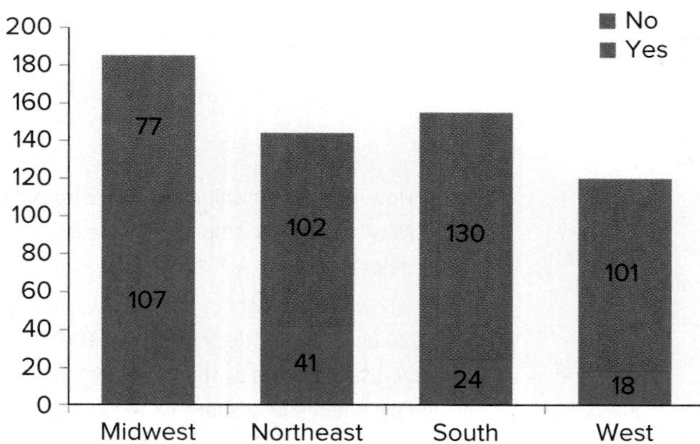

Using R

a. Import the ***Promotion*** data file into a data frame (table) and label it myData.

b. In order to create a contingency table, labeled as myTable, we use the **table**(*row, column*) function and specify the *row* and *column* variables.

If you retype myTable, you will see a contingency table that resembles Table 2.9. If we use the **prop.table** function, then R returns cell proportions that, when converted to percentages, are the same as those that appear in Table 2.10. Enter:

```
> myTable <- table(myData$Location, myData$Purchase)
> myTable
> prop.table(myTable)
```

c. To create a stacked column chart similar to Figure 2.10, we need to first create a contingency table with the Purchase variable in rows and the Location variable in columns. Enter:

```
> myNewTable <- table(myData$Purchase, myData$Location)
```

d. We use the **barplot** function to construct a column chart. As we saw when constructing a bar chart, R offers a number of options for formatting. Here we use *main* to add a title; *col* to define colors for the segments of the columns; *legend* to create a legend; *xlab* and *ylab* to provide labels for the x-axis and y-axis, respectively; and *ylim* to extend the vertical axis units from 0 to 200. Enter:

```
> barplot(myNewTable, main=“Location and Purchase”,
col=c('blue','red'), legend=rownames(myNewTable), xlab='Location',
ylab='Count', ylim = c(0,200))
```

The resulting stacked column chart should look similar to Figure 2.10.

Summary

Compared to Table 2.8 with just raw data, Table 2.9, Table 2.10, and Figure 2.10 present the results of the Promotion example in a much more informative format. We can readily see that of the 600 e-mail recipients, 410 of them made a purchase using the promotional discount. With a 68.33% positive response rate, this marketing strategy seemed successful. However, there do appear to be some differences depending on location. Recipients residing in the South and West were a lot more likely to make a purchase (130 out of 154 and 101 out of 119, respectively) compared to those residing in the Midwest (77 out of 184). It would be wise for the retailer to examine if there are other traits that the customers in the South and West share (age, sex, etc.). That way, in the next marketing campaign, the e-mails can be even more targeted.

EXERCISES 2.2

Applications

12. The following contingency table shows shipments received by a large firm. The shipments have been cross-classified by Vendor (I, II, and III) and Quality (Defective and Acceptable).

	Quality	
Vendor	**Defective**	**Acceptable**
I	14	112
II	10	70
III	22	150

a. How many shipments did the firm receive?

b. How many of the shipments were defective?

c. How many of the shipments were from Vendor II?

d. How many of the shipments were from Vendor I and were defective?

13. The following contingency table shows inspection records for 630 units of a particular product. The records have been cross-classified by the inspector's decision (Pass and Fail) and the inspector's experience (Low, Medium, and High).

	Experience		
Decision	**Low**	**Medium**	**High**
Pass	152	287	103
Fail	16	46	26

a. How many of the units passed inspection? How many of the units failed inspection?
b. How many of the units were inspected by inspectors with high experience?
c. What proportion of the units were inspected by inspectors with low experience?
d. What proportion of the units were inspected by inspectors with medium experience and failed inspection?

14. FILE ***Bar.*** At a local bar in a small Midwestern town, beer and wine are the only two alcoholic options. The manager conducts a survey on the bar's customers over the past weekend. Customers are asked to identify their sex (male or female) and their drink choice (beer, wine, or soft drink). A portion of the responses is shown in the accompanying table.

Customer	Sex	Drink Choice
1	male	beer
2	male	beer
⋮	⋮	⋮
270	female	soft drink

a. Construct a contingency table that cross-classifies the data by Sex and Drink Choice. How many of the customers were male? How many of the customers drank wine?
b. Given that a customer is male, what is the likelihood that he drank beer? Given that a customer is female, what is the likelihood that she drank beer?
c. Construct a stacked column chart. Comment on the findings.

15. FILE ***Friends.*** Many believe that it is not feasible for men and women to be just friends, while others argue that this belief may not be true anymore because gone are the days when men worked and women stayed at home and the only way they could get together was for romance. A researcher conducts a survey on 186 students. The students are asked their sex (male or female) and if it is feasible for men and women to be just friends (yes or no). A portion of the responses is shown in the accompanying table.

Student	Sex	Feasible
1	female	yes
2	female	yes
⋮	⋮	⋮
186	male	no

a. Construct a contingency table that cross-classifies the data by Sex and Feasible. How many of the students were female? How many of the students felt that it was feasible for men and women to be just friends?
b. What is the likelihood that a male student feels that men and women can be just friends? What is the likelihood that a female student feels that men and women can be just friends?
c. Construct a stacked column chart. Do male and female students feel the same or differently about this topic? Explain.

16. FILE ***Shift.*** Metalworks, a supplier of fabricated industrial parts, wonders if there is any connection between when a component is constructed (Shift is equal to 1, 2, or 3) and whether or not it is defective (Defective is equal to Yes or No). The supplier collects data on the construction of 300 components. A portion of the data is shown in the accompanying table.

Component	Shift	Defective
1	1	No
2	1	Yes
⋮	⋮	⋮
300	3	No

a. Construct a contingency table that cross-classifies the data by Shift and Defective. How many components constructed during Shift 1 were defective? How many components constructed during Shift 2 were not defective?
b. Given that the component was defective, what is the likelihood that it was constructed during Shift 2? Given that the component was defective, what is the likelihood that it was constructed during Shift 3? Does there seem to be any connection between when a component is constructed and whether or not it is defective? Explain.
c. Construct a stacked column chart. Are the defect rates consistent across all shifts? Explain.

17. FILE ***Athletic.*** A researcher at a marketing firm examines whether the age of a consumer matters when buying athletic clothing. Her initial feeling is that Brand A attracts a younger customer, whereas the more established companies (Brands B and C) draw an older clientele. For 600 recent purchases of athletic clothing, she collects data on a customer's age (Age equals 1 if the customer is under 35, 0 otherwise) and the brand name of the athletic clothing (A, B, or C). A portion of the data is shown in the accompanying table.

Purchase	Age	Brand
1	1	A
2	1	A
⋮	⋮	⋮
600	0	C

a. Construct a contingency table that cross-classifies the data by Age and Brand. How many of the purchases were for Brand A? How many of the purchases were from customers under 35 years old?
b. Given that the purchase was made by a customer under 35 years old, what is the likelihood that the customer purchased Brand A? Brand B? Brand C? Do the data seem to support the researcher's belief? Explain.
c. Construct a stacked column chart. Does there appear to be a relationship between the age of the customer and the brand purchased?

18. FILE ***Study.*** A report suggests that business majors spend the least amount of time on course work compared to all other college students. A provost of a university conducts a similar survey on 270 students. Students are asked their major (business or nonbusiness) and if they study hard (yes or no), where study hard is defined as spending at least 20 hours per week on course work. A portion of the responses is shown in the accompanying table.

Student	Major	Study Hard
1	business	yes
2	business	yes
⋮	⋮	⋮
270	nonbusiness	no

a. Construct a contingency table that cross-classifies the data by Major and Study Hard. How many of the students are business majors? How many of the students study hard?

b. Given that the student is a business major, what is the likelihood that the student studies hard? Given that the student is a nonbusiness major, what is the likelihood that the student studies hard? Do the data seem to support the findings in the report? Explain.

c. Construct a stacked column chart. Comment on the findings.

2.3 METHODS TO VISUALIZE A NUMERICAL VARIABLE

LO 2.4

Construct and interpret a frequency distribution for a numerical variable.

In Section 2.1 we summarized a categorical variable using a frequency distribution, a bar chart, and a pie chart. Here, we turn our attention to a numerical variable.

Recall that with a numerical variable, each observation represents a meaningful amount or count. Examples of numerical variables include the number of patents held by pharmaceutical firms (count) and household incomes (amount). Although different in nature from a categorical variable, we still use a frequency distribution to summarize a numerical variable.

A Frequency Distribution for a Numerical Variable

When we constructed a frequency distribution for a categorical variable, the raw data could be categorized in a well-defined way; we simply counted the number of observations in each category. For a numerical variable, instead of categories, we construct a series of intervals (sometimes called classes). We must make certain decisions about the number of intervals, as well as the width of each interval. When making these decisions, we consider the following guidelines.

- *Intervals are mutually exclusive.* For example, suppose the first two intervals of a frequency distribution are defined as $300 < x \leq 400$ and $400 < x \leq 500$, where x is the value of an observation. If $x = 400$, then it would fall into the first interval. In other words, intervals do not overlap, and each observation falls into one, and only one, interval.
- *The total number of intervals in a frequency distribution usually ranges from 5 to 20.* Smaller data sets tend to have fewer intervals than larger data sets. Recall that the goal of constructing a frequency distribution is to summarize the data in a form that accurately depicts the group as a whole. If we have too many intervals, then this advantage of the frequency distribution is lost. Similarly, if the frequency distribution has too few classes, then considerable accuracy and detail are lost.
- *Intervals are exhaustive.* The total number of intervals covers the entire sample (or population).

- *Interval limits are easy to recognize and interpret.* For example, the intervals $-10 < x \leq 0$, $0 < x \leq 10$, etc. are preferred to the intervals $-8 < x \leq 2$, $2 < x \leq 12$, etc. Also, as a starting point for approximating the width of each interval, we often use the formula:

$$\frac{\text{Maximum} - \text{Minimum}}{\text{Number of Intervals}},$$

where Maximum and Minimum refer to the largest and smallest observations, respectively, for the variable of interest. Generally, the width of each interval is the same for each interval. If the width varied between intervals, then comparisons between different intervals could be misleading.

A FREQUENCY DISTRIBUTION FOR A NUMERICAL VARIABLE

For a numerical variable, a frequency distribution divides the data into nonoverlapping intervals and records the number of observations that falls into each interval.

The Price variable from the introductory case is a numerical variable. Recall that each observation for this variable reflects the price of a house (in \$1,000s) for a sample of 40 houses in Punta Gorda, Florida. Here we will create a frequency distribution with six intervals. The minimum and maximum observations for the Price variable are 125 and 649, respectively. (Obtaining summary measures will be discussed in Chapter 3.) Using the approximation formula to find the width of each interval, we calculate:

$$\frac{\text{Maximum} - \text{Minimum}}{\text{Number of Intervals}} = \frac{649 - 125}{6} = 87.33.$$

However, intervals with a width of 87.33 would not have limits that are easily recognizable. For this reason, we will define the lower limit of the first interval as 100 (rather than 125) and have each interval be of width 100 (rather than 87.33); that is, the intervals are: $100 < x \leq 200$, $200 < x \leq 300$, etc., where x is the price of a house (in \$1,000s). The first column of Table 2.11 shows the six intervals.

TABLE 2.11 Frequency Distribution for Price

Interval (in \$1,000s)	Frequency
$100 < x \leq 200$	9
$200 < x \leq 300$	16
$300 < x \leq 400$	8
$400 < x \leq 500$	4
$500 < x \leq 600$	2
$600 < x \leq 700$	1

Once we have clearly defined the intervals for the Price variable, the next step is to count and record the number of observations that fall into each interval. The second column of Table 2.11 shows the resulting frequencies. Soon, we will construct a frequency distribution in Excel and R. We note that the sum of the frequencies is 40 ($= n$), which confirms that we have included each observation in the frequency distribution. While it is true that some detail is lost because we no longer see the raw data, we are able to extract more useful information. Consider Example 2.3.

EXAMPLE 2.3

Use Table 2.11 to answer the following questions.

a. What is the range of house prices over this time period?

b. Which interval has the highest frequency?

c. How many houses sold for more than \$600,000?

SOLUTION:

a. House prices ranged from \$100,000 up to \$700,000 over this time period.

b. The \$200,000 up to \$300,000 interval has the highest frequency with 16 observations.

c. Only one house sold for more than \$600,000.

We can extend the frequency distribution in Table 2.11 by constructing a relative frequency distribution, a cumulative frequency distribution, and a cumulative relative frequency distribution. We discuss each one next.

Analogous to the relative frequency distribution that we calculated for a categorical variable, we find the relative frequency for a numerical variable by dividing the frequency for each interval by the sample size. For example, we observe that nine houses sold in the interval $100 < x \leq 200$. We calculate $9/40 = 0.225$, and conclude that 22.5% of the houses sold in this price range. We make similar calculations for each interval. The third column of Table 2.12 shows the relative frequency distribution for the Price variable. We note that when we sum the relative frequencies, we should get one, or, due to rounding, a number very close to one.

TABLE 2.12 Extended Frequency Distributions for Price

Interval (in \$1,000s)	Frequency	Relative Frequency	Cumulative Frequency	Cumulative Relative Frequency
$100 < x \leq 200$	9	0.225	9	0.225
$200 < x \leq 300$	16	0.400	$9 + 16 = 25$	$0.225 + 0.400 = 0.625$
$300 < x \leq 400$	8	0.200	$9 + 16 + 8 = 33$	$0.225 + 0.400 + 0.200 = 0.825$
$400 < x \leq 500$	4	0.100	$9 + 16 + \cdots + 4 = 37$	$0.225 + 0.400 + \cdots + 0.100 = 0.925$
$500 < x \leq 600$	2	0.050	$9 + 16 + \cdots + 2 = 39$	$0.225 + 0.400 + \cdots + 0.050 = 0.975$
$600 < x \leq 700$	1	0.025	$9 + 16 + \cdots + 1 = 40$	$0.225 + 0.400 + \cdots + 0.025 = 1.000$

For a numerical variable, we can also construct a cumulative frequency distribution. A cumulative frequency distribution shows the number of observations that fall below the upper limit of a particular interval. The fourth column of Table 2.12 shows values for cumulative frequency. The cumulative frequency of the first interval is the same as the frequency of the first interval—here, that value is 9. However, the interpretation is different. With respect to the frequency column, 9 houses sold in the \$100,000 up to \$200,000 range. With respect to the cumulative frequency column, 9 houses sold for \$200,000 or less. To obtain the cumulative frequency for the second interval, we add its frequency, 16, with the preceding frequency, 9, and obtain 25. So, 25 houses sold for \$300,000 or less. We find the cumulative frequencies of the remaining intervals in a like manner. Note that the cumulative frequency of the last interval is equal to the sample size of 40. This indicates that all 40 houses sold for \$700,000 or less.

The cumulative relative frequency for a particular interval indicates the proportion (fraction) of the observations that falls below the upper limit of that particular interval. We can calculate the cumulative relative frequency of each interval in one of two ways: (1) We can sum successive relative frequencies, or (2) we can divide each interval's cumulative frequency by the sample size. In the last column of Table 2.12, we show the first way. The value for the first interval is the same as the value for its relative frequency—here, that value is 0.225. For the second interval, we add 0.225 to 0.400 and obtain 0.625; this value indicates that 62.5% of the houses sold for \$300,000 or less. We continue calculating cumulative relative frequencies in this manner until we reach the last class. Here, we get the value one, which means that 100% of the houses sold for \$700,000 or less.

RELATIVE FREQUENCY, CUMULATIVE FREQUENCY, AND CUMULATIVE RELATIVE FREQUENCY DISTRIBUTIONS

For a numerical variable:

- A relative frequency distribution records the proportion (or the fraction) of observations that falls into each interval;
- A cumulative frequency distribution records the number of observations that falls below the upper limit of a particular interval; and
- A cumulative relative frequency distribution records the proportion (or fraction) of observations that falls below the upper limit of a particular interval.

EXAMPLE 2.4

Use Table 2.12 to answer the following questions.

a. What proportion of the houses sold in the $300,000 to $400,000 range?

b. How many of the houses sold for $500,000 or less?

c. What proportion of the houses sold for $400,000 or less? More than $400,000?

SOLUTION:

a. The relative frequency distribution shows that 0.20 of the houses sold in the $300,000 to $400,000 range.

b. The cumulative frequency distribution shows that 37 of the houses sold for $500,000 or less.

c. The cumulative relative frequency distribution shows that 0.825 of the houses sold for $400,000 or less, implying that 0.175 sold for more than $400,000.

A Histogram

LO 2.5

Construct and interpret a histogram, a polygon, and an ogive.

Next we show a number of ways to graphically depict a frequency distribution for a numerical variable. We start with a **histogram**, which is essentially the counterpart to the vertical bar chart that we use for a categorical variable.

When constructing a histogram, we typically mark off the interval limits along the horizontal axis. The height of each bar represents either the frequency or the relative frequency for each interval. No gaps appear between the interval limits.

A HISTOGRAM

A histogram is a series of rectangles where the width and height of each rectangle represent the interval width and frequency (or relative frequency) of the respective interval.

The advantage of a histogram is that we can quickly see where most of the observations tend to cluster, as well as the spread and shape of the variable. In general, the shape of most distributions can be categorized as either symmetric or skewed. A symmetric distribution is one that is a mirror image of itself on both sides of its center. That is, the location of values below the center corresponds to those above the center. As we will see in Chapter 3, the smoothed histogram for many variables approximates a bell-shaped curve, which is indicative of the well-known normal distribution. Figure 2.11(a) shows a histogram with a symmetric distribution. If the edges were smoothed, this histogram would look somewhat bell-shaped.

If the distribution is not symmetric, then it is either positively skewed or negatively skewed. Figure 2.11(b) shows a histogram with a positively skewed distribution or one that is skewed to the right. The long tail that extends to the right reflects the presence of a small number of relatively large observations. Figure 2.11(c) shows a histogram with a negatively skewed distribution or one that is skewed to the left because it has a long tail extending off to the left. A negatively skewed distribution has a small number of relatively small observations.

FIGURE 2.11 Histograms with differing shapes

(c) Negatively skewed distribution

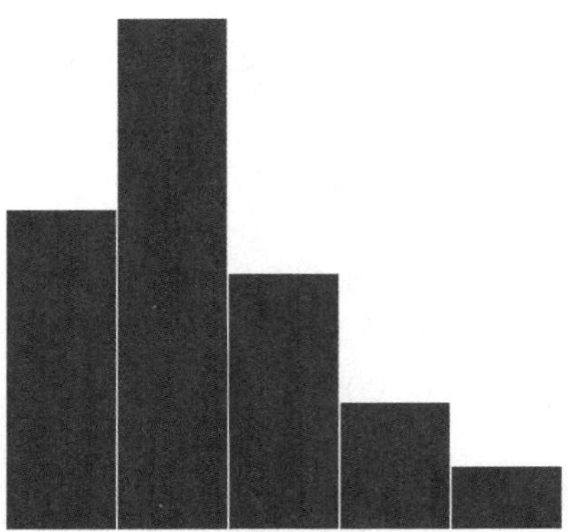

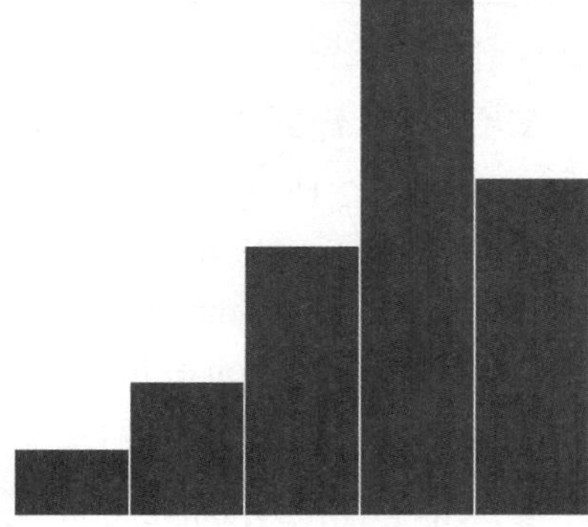

EXAMPLE 2.5

FILE *PG_Sales*

Use Excel and R to replicate the frequency distribution for the Price variable in Table 2.11. Construct the variable's histogram. Is the distribution symmetric? If not, is it positively or negatively skewed?

SOLUTION:

As mentioned earlier, when we construct a frequency distribution for a numerical variable, we need to make some decisions about the number of intervals, as well as the width of each interval. There are no steadfast rules, but we outlined a number of guidelines that one should follow. Using these guidelines for the Price variable, we decide to have six intervals, each of width 100, where the lower limit of the first interval is 100.

Using Excel

a. Open the ***PG_Sales*** data file.

b. Enter the column heading Interval Limits in cell H1, and in cells H2 through H7 enter the upper limit of each interval, so 200, 300, 400, 500, 600, and 700. The reason for these entries will be explained shortly.

c. From the menu choose **Data** > **Data Analysis** > **Histogram** > **OK**. (Note: If you do not see the **Data Analysis** option under **Data**, you must add in Excel's **Analysis Toolpak** option.)

d. See Figure 2.12. In the *Histogram* dialog box, next to *Input Range,* select the Price observations. Excel uses the term "bins" for the interval limits. If we leave the *Bin Range* box empty, Excel creates evenly distributed intervals using the minimum and maximum values as end points. This approach is rarely satisfactory. In order to construct a histogram that is more informative, we use the upper limits of each interval as the bin values. Next to *Bin Range,* we select cells H1:H7 (the Interval Limits observations). We check the *Labels* box because we have included the headings Price and Interval Limits as part of the selection. Under *Output Options,* select *Output Range* and enter cell J1, and then select **Chart Output**. Click **OK**.

FIGURE 2.12 Excel's dialog box for a histogram

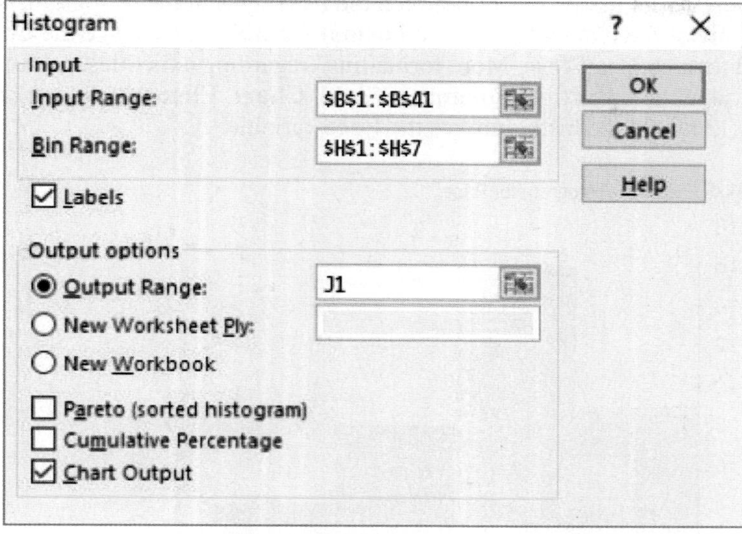

Excel returns both the frequency distribution and the histogram for the Price variable; however, for presentation purposes, it needs some cleaning up. Let's start with the frequency distribution. The first column of the frequency distribution shows only the upper limits for each interval. Generally, the lower limit and the upper limit for each interval should be explicit. (We should note that Excel defines its intervals by including the value of the upper limit for each interval. For example, if the value 200 appeared as an observation for the Price variable, then Excel would account for this observation in the first interval.) In the first column of Table 2.13, we show well-defined interval limits as well as a new heading.

Also, in the event that the given interval limits do not include all the observations, Excel automatically adds another interval labeled "More" to the resulting frequency distribution and histogram. Because we observe zero observations in this interval, we delete this interval for expositional purposes.

Once we have the frequency distribution, we can easily find relative frequency, cumulative frequency, and cumulative relative frequency. For example, in order to calculate the relative frequency for each interval, we label cell K1 as Relative Frequency. We then go to cell K2 and enter =J2/40. We then select cell J2, drag down to cell J7, and from the menu we choose **Home > Fill > Down**. The third column of Table 2.13 shows the relative frequencies for each interval.

TABLE 2.13 Formatting the Frequency Distribution in Excel

Interval (in $1,000s)	Frequency	Relative Frequency
$100 < x \leq 200$	9	0.225
$200 < x \leq 300$	16	0.400
$300 < x \leq 400$	8	0.200
$400 < x \leq 500$	4	0.100
$500 < x \leq 600$	2	0.050
$600 < x \leq 700$	1	0.025

Now let's turn to the histogram. Excel graphs a frequency histogram rather than a relative frequency histogram. Both histograms look the same; the only difference is the unit of measurement on the vertical axis. For the frequency histogram, the frequency of each interval is used to represent the height, whereas for the relative frequency histogram, the proportion (or the fraction) of each interval is used to represent the height.

Because Excel leaves spaces between the rectangles in the histogram, we right-click on any of the rectangles, choose **Format Data Series**, change the *Gap Width* to 0, and then choose **Close**. More formatting (regarding axis titles, gridlines, etc.) can be done by selecting **Format > Add Chart Element** from the menu. Figure 2.13 shows the histogram for the Price variable.

FIGURE 2.13 Histogram for Price

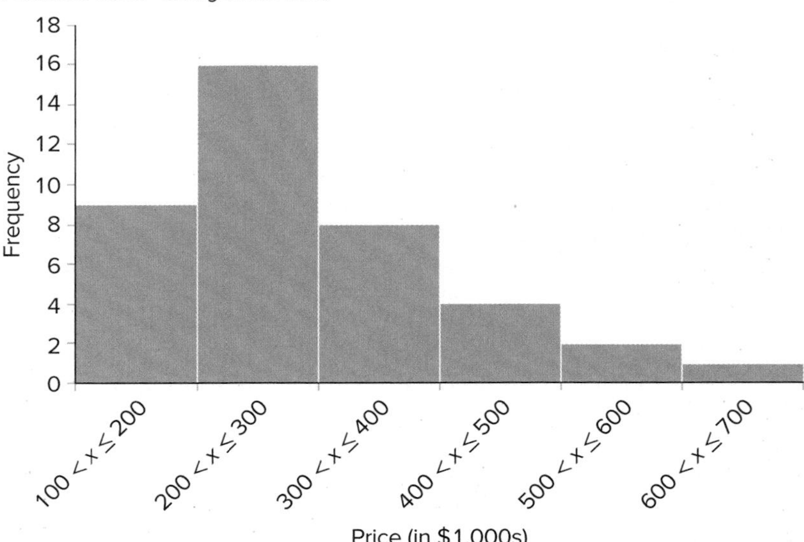

Note that you can construct a frequency distribution by using Excel's COUNTIF function that we used in Section 2.1. You can then use the resulting frequency distribution to plot a histogram. The Histogram option in Excel's Analysis Toolpak allows us to construct both the frequency distribution and the histogram with one command. Plus, Excel's Analysis Toolpak comes in handy in later chapters in the text.

Using R

a. Import the ***PG_Sales*** data file into a data frame (table) and label it myData.

b. We first define the intervals using the **seq** function. The first argument in the function is the lower limit of the first interval, the next argument is the upper limit of the last interval, and the last argument defines the width of each interval. Enter:

```
> intervals <- seq(100, 700, by=100)
```

c. We then use the **cut** function with *left* and *right* options to ensure that the intervals are open on the left and closed on the right; that is, $100 < x \leq 200$, $200 < x \leq 300$, etc. Enter:

```
> price.cut <- cut(myData$Price, intervals, left=FALSE, right=TRUE)
```

d. We use the **table** function to create a frequency distribution labeled price.freq. If you retype price.freq, you will see that the resulting frequency distribution is not very attractive. For these reasons, we use the **View** function to create a more appealing frequency distribution. Enter:

```
> price.freq <- table(price.cut)
> price.freq
> View(price.freq)
```

The frequency distribution that R produces should be comparable to Table 2.13.

e. We use the **hist** function to construct a histogram. We define the *breaks* option using the intervals that we defined in step b. Again, we set the *right* option equal to TRUE so that the intervals are right-closed (implying left-opened). As in previous examples, we also use the options *main*, *xlab*, *ylab*, and *col*. Enter:

```
> hist(myData$Price, breaks=intervals, right=TRUE, main="Histogram
for Price (in $1,000s)", xlab="Price (in $1,000s)", col="blue")
```

The histogram that R produces should be comparable to Figure 2.13.

Summary

From Table 2.13, we see that the range of observations for Price is between \$100,000 and \$700,000. The \$200,000 to \$300,000 interval has the highest frequency with 16 observations. Figure 2.3 shows that the distribution for Price is not symmetric; rather, it is positively skewed with a tail running off to the right. There are a few houses that sold in the upper price intervals, but the majority of sales were in the lower intervals. This is not an uncommon finding for house price distributions.

A Polygon

A **polygon** provides another convenient way of depicting a frequency distribution. It too gives a general idea of the shape of a distribution. Like the histogram, we place either the frequency or the relative frequency of the distribution on the y-axis, and the upper and lower limits of each interval on the x-axis. We plot the midpoint of each interval with its corresponding frequency or relative frequency. We then connect neighboring points with a straight line.

A POLYGON

A polygon connects a series of neighboring points where each point represents the midpoint of a particular class and its associated frequency or relative frequency.

If we choose to construct a polygon for the Price variable, we first calculate the midpoint of each interval; thus, the midpoint for the first interval is $\frac{100+200}{2} = 150$, and similarly, the midpoints for the remaining intervals are 250, 350, 450, 550, and 650. We treat each midpoint as the x-coordinate and the respective frequency or relative frequency as the y-coordinate. After plotting the points, we connect neighboring points. In order to close off the graph at each end, we add one interval below the lowest interval (so, $0 < x \leq 100$ with midpoint 50) and one interval above the highest interval (so, $700 < x \leq 800$ with midpoint 750) and assign each of these intervals zero frequencies. Table 2.14 shows the relevant coordinates for plotting a polygon for the Price variable. We use relative frequency to represent the y-coordinate.

TABLE 2.14 Coordinates for Plotting Relative Frequency Polygon

Interval	x-coordinate (midpoint)	y-coordinate (relative frequency)
$0 < x \leq 100$	50	0
$100 < x \leq 200$	150	0.225
$200 < x \leq 300$	250	0.400
$300 < x \leq 400$	350	0.200
$400 < x \leq 500$	450	0.100
$500 < x \leq 600$	550	0.050
$600 < x \leq 700$	650	0.25
$700 < x \leq 800$	750	0

Figure 2.14 plots a relative frequency polygon for the Price variable. As expected, the polygon, like the histogram in Figure 2.13, is not symmetric. It is positively skewed.

FIGURE 2.14 A polygon for the Price variable

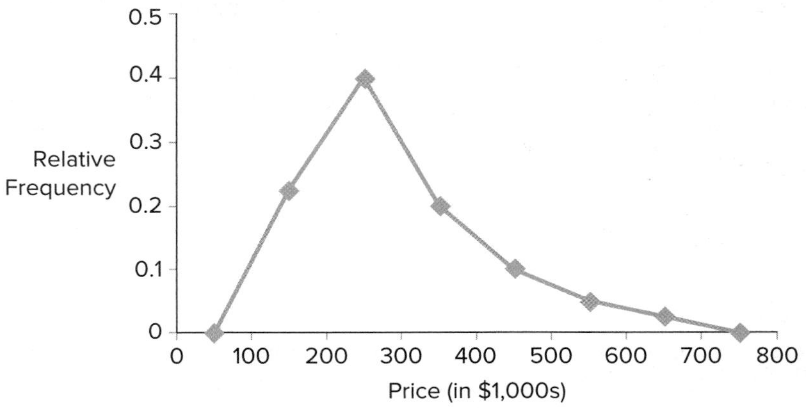

An Ogive

In many instances, we might want to convey information by plotting an **ogive** (pronounced "ojive").

> **AN OGIVE**
>
> An ogive connects a series of neighboring points where each point represents the upper limit of a particular interval and its associated cumulative frequency or cumulative relative frequency.

An ogive differs from a polygon in that we use the upper limit of each interval as the x-coordinate and the cumulative frequency or cumulative relative frequency of the corresponding interval as the y-coordinate. After plotting the points, we connect neighboring points. Lastly, we close the ogive only at the lower end by intersecting the x-axis at the lower limit of the first interval. Table 2.15 shows the relevant coordinates for plotting an ogive for the Price variable. We choose to use cumulative relative frequency as the y-coordinate since the resulting graph tends to have more interpretive appeal. The use of cumulative frequency would not change the shape of the ogive, just the unit of measurement on the y-axis. Recall that we calculated both cumulative frequency and cumulative relative frequency for the Price variable in Table 2.12.

TABLE 2.15 Coordinates for the Ogive for the Price variable

Interval	x-coordinate (upper limit)	y-coordinate (cumulative relative frequency)
Lower limit of first class	100	0
$100 < x \leq 200$	200	0.225
$200 < x \leq 300$	300	0.625
$300 < x \leq 400$	400	0.825
$400 < x \leq 500$	500	0.925
$500 < x \leq 600$	600	0.975
$600 < x \leq 700$	700	1

Figure 2.15 plots the ogive for the Price variable. In general, we can use an ogive to approximate the proportion of observations that are less than a specified value on the horizontal axis. Consider an application to the Price variable in Example 2.6.

FIGURE 2.15 An ogive for the Price variable

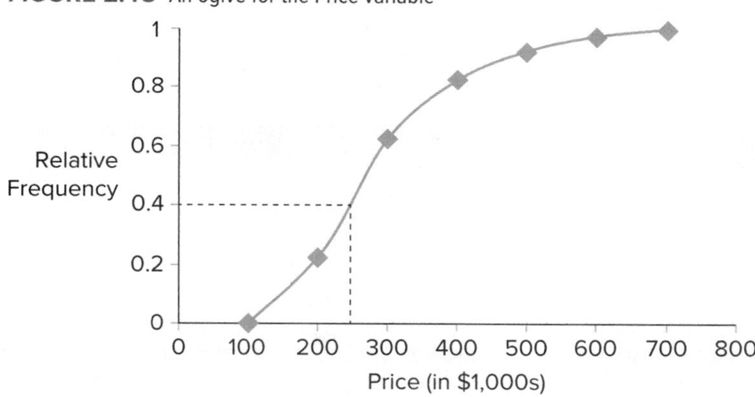

EXAMPLE 2.6

Using Figure 2.15, approximate the percentage of houses that sold for less than $250,000.

SOLUTION:

We draw a vertical line that starts at 250 and intersects the ogive. We then follow the line to the vertical axis and read the relative frequency. We conclude that approximately 40% of the houses sold for less than $250,000.

Using Excel and R Construct a Polygon and an Ogive

We replicate the polygon in Figure 2.14 using Excel and R. For both software, the directions for an ogive are the same, but we would use the ***Ogive*** data file.

Using Excel

A. Open the ***Polygon*** data file (this is a simplified version of the data in Table 2.14).

B. Select the values in the x and y columns and choose **Insert > Scatter**. Select the box at the middle right. (If you are having trouble finding this option after selecting **Insert**, look for the graph with data points above **Charts**.)

C. Formatting (regarding axis titles, gridlines, etc.) can be done by selecting **Format > Add Chart Element** from the menu.

Using R

A. Import the ***Polygon*** data file into a data frame (table) and label it myData. (This is a simplified version of the data in Table 2.14.)

B. We make a scatterplot using the **plot**(*y*~*x*, . . .) function. As in previous examples, we also use the options *xlab* and *ylab*. We add lines to the scatterplot using the **lines** function. Enter:

```
> plot(myData$y ~ myData$x, ylab="Relative Frequency", xlab="Prices
  (in $1,000s)")
> lines(myData$y ~ myData$x)
```

EXERCISES 2.3

Mechanics

19. Consider the following frequency distribution:

Interval	Frequency
$10 < x \leq 20$	12
$20 < x \leq 30$	15
$30 < x \leq 40$	25
$40 < x \leq 50$	4

a. Construct the relative frequency distribution. What proportion of the observations are in the interval $20 < x \leq 30$?

b. Construct the cumulative frequency distribution. How many of the observations are less than 40?

c. Construct the cumulative relative frequency distribution. What proportion of the observations are less than 30?

20. Consider the following frequency distribution:

Interval	Frequency
$1{,}000 < x \leq 1{,}100$	22
$1{,}100 < x \leq 1{,}200$	38
$1{,}200 < x \leq 1{,}300$	44
$1{,}300 < x \leq 1{,}400$	16

a. Construct the relative frequency distribution. What proportion of the observations are more than 1,100 but no more than 1,200?

b. Construct the cumulative frequency distribution. How many of the observations are 1,300 or less?

c. Construct the cumulative relative frequency distribution. What proportion of the observations are 1,300 or less? More than 1,300?

21. Consider the following cumulative frequency distribution:

Interval	Cumulative Frequency
$15 < x \leq 25$	30
$25 < x \leq 35$	50
$35 < x \leq 45$	120
$45 < x \leq 55$	130

a. Construct the frequency distribution. How many observations are more than 35 but no more than 45?

b. Construct the cumulative relative frequency distribution. What proportion of the observations are 45 or less?

c. Graph the histogram. Is the distribution symmetric?

22. Consider the following relative frequency distribution:

Interval	Relative Frequency
$-20 < x \leq -10$	0.04
$-10 < x \leq 0$	0.28
$0 < x \leq 10$	0.26
$10 < x \leq 20$	0.22
$20 < x \leq 30$	0.20

a. Suppose this relative frequency distribution is based on a sample of 50 observations. Construct the frequency distribution. How many of the observations are more than −10 but no more than 0?

b. Construct the cumulative frequency distribution. How many of the observations are 20 or less?

c. Graph the polygon. Is the distribution symmetric?

23. Consider the following cumulative relative frequency distribution.

Interval	Cumulative Relative Frequency
$150 < x \leq 200$	0.10
$200 < x \leq 250$	0.35
$250 < x \leq 300$	0.70
$300 < x \leq 350$	1

a. Construct the relative frequency distribution. What proportion of the observations are more than 250 but no more than 300?

b. Graph the ogive. Use the ogive to find the proportion of observations that are less than 300.

24. Using 5,000 observations, the following histogram summarizes Variable *X*.

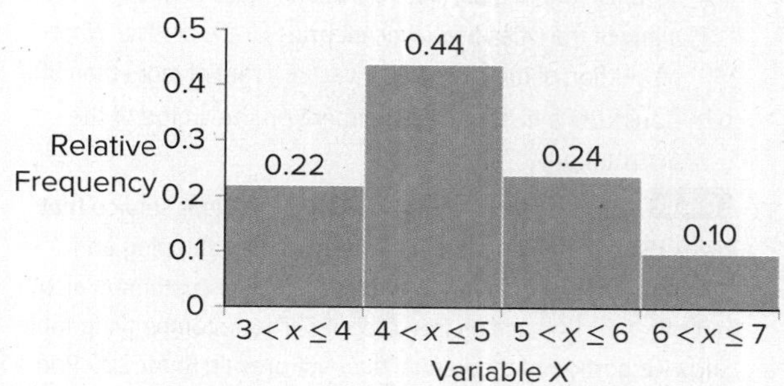

a. Is the distribution symmetric? If not, is it positively or negatively skewed?

b. What proportion of the observations are greater than 5?

c. How many of the observations are less than or equal to 5?

25. Using 3,000 observations, the following histogram summarizes Variable *X*.

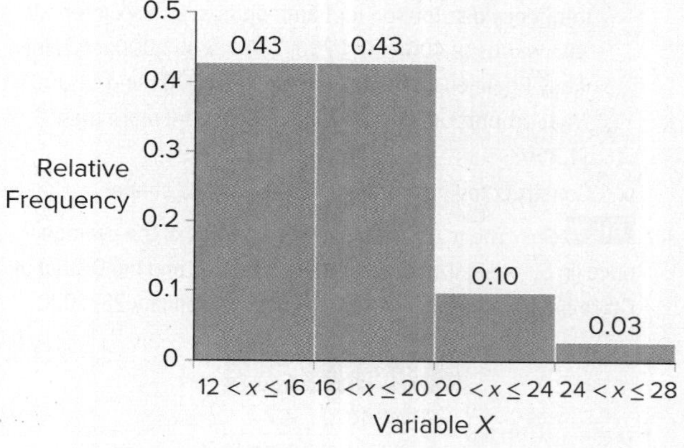

a. Is the distribution symmetric? If not, is it positively or negatively skewed?

b. What proportion of the observations are less than or equal to 20?

c. How many of the observations are greater than 20?

26. Using 1,000 observations, the following ogive summarizes Variable *X*.

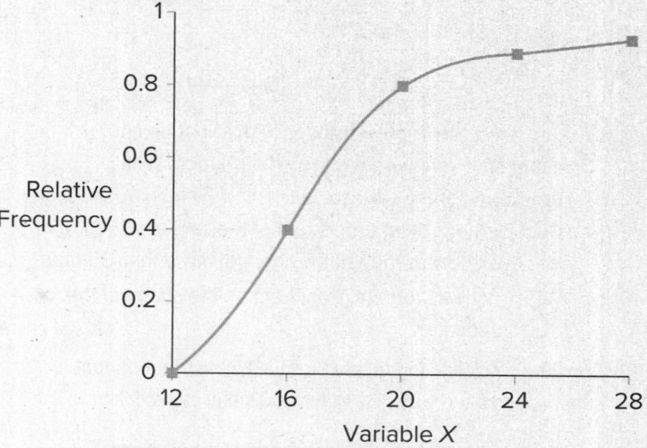

a. Approximate the proportion of observations that are less than 16.

b. Approximate the number of observations that are greater than 20.

27. **FILE** ***Exercise_2.27.*** The accompanying data file shows 100 observations for Variable *X*.

a. Construct the frequency distribution using 6 intervals with widths of $3 < x \leq 5$, $5 < x \leq 7$, etc. How many of the observations are greater than 7 but less than or equal to 9?

b. Construct the relative frequency distribution. What proportion of the observations are greater than 5 but less than or equal to 7?

c. Construct the histogram. Is the distribution symmetric?

28. **FILE** ***Exercise_2.28.*** The accompanying data file shows 100 observations for Variable *X*.

a. Construct the frequency distribution using 5 intervals with widths of $-10 < x \leq 0$, $0 < x \leq 10$, etc. How many of the observations are greater than 0 but less than or equal to 10?

b. Construct the relative frequency and the cumulative relative frequency distribution. What proportion of the observations are greater than 10 but less than or equal to 20? What proportion of the observations are greater than 20?

c. Construct the ogive. Use the ogive to approximate the proportion of the observations that are less than 15.

Applications

29. A researcher conducts a mileage economy test involving 80 cars. The frequency distribution describing average miles per gallon (mpg) appears in the following table.

Average mpg	Frequency
$15 < x \leq 20$	15
$20 < x \leq 25$	30
$25 < x \leq 30$	15
$30 < x \leq 35$	10
$35 < x \leq 40$	7
$40 < x \leq 45$	3

a. Construct the relative frequency distribution and cumulative relative frequency distribution. What proportion of the cars got more than 20 mpg but no more than 25 mpg? What proportion of the cars got 35 mpg or less? What proportion of the cars got more than 35 mpg?

b. Construct a histogram. Comment on the shape of the distribution.

30. Consider the following relative frequency distribution that summarizes the returns (in %) for 500 small cap stocks.

Return (%)	Relative Frequency
$-20 < x \leq -10$	0.04
$-10 < x \leq 0$	0.25
$0 < x \leq 10$	0.42
$10 < x \leq 20$	0.25
$20 < x \leq 30$	0.04

a. Construct the frequency distribution and the cumulative relative frequency distribution. How many of the stocks had a return of more than 10% but no more than 20%? What proportion of the stocks had a return of 10% or less?

b. Construct a polygon. Comment on the shape of the distribution.

c. Construct an ogive. Approximate the proportion of small cap stocks that had a return of 15% or less.

31. The manager at a water park constructed the following frequency distribution to summarize attendance in July and August.

Attendance	Frequency
$1,000 < x \leq 1,250$	5
$1,250 < x \leq 1,500$	6
$1,500 < x \leq 1,750$	10
$1,750 < x \leq 2,000$	20
$2,000 < x \leq 2,250$	15
$2,250 < x \leq 2,500$	4

a. Construct the relative frequency distribution and the cumulative relative frequency distribution. What proportion of the time was attendance more than 1,750 but no more than 2,000? What proportion of the time was attendance 1,750 or less? What proportion of the time was attendance more than 1,750?

b. Construct a histogram. Comment on the shape of the distribution.

32. Fifty cities provided information on vacancy rates (in %) in local apartments in the following frequency distribution.

Vacancy Rate (%)	Relative Frequency
$0 < x \leq 3$	0.10
$3 < x \leq 6$	0.20
$6 < x \leq 9$	0.40
$9 < x \leq 12$	0.20
$12 < x \leq 15$	0.10

a. Construct the frequency distribution, the cumulative frequency distribution, and the cumulative relative frequency distribution. How many of the cities had a vacancy rate of more than 6% but no more than 9%? How many of the cities had a vacancy rate of 9% or less? What proportion of the cities had a vacancy rate of more than 9%?

b. Construct a histogram. Comment on the shape of the distribution.

33. **FILE** ***Prime.*** Amazon Prime is a $119-per-year service that gives the company's customers free two-day shipping and discounted rates on overnight delivery. Prime customers also get other perks, such as free e-books. The accompanying table shows a portion of the annual expenditures (in $) for 200 Prime customers.

Customer	Expenditure
1	1272
2	1089
⋮	⋮
200	1390

a. Construct the frequency distribution and the relative frequency distribution for Expenditures. Use six intervals with widths of $400 < x \leq 700$; $700 < x \leq 1,000$; etc. How many Prime customers spent between $701 and $1,000? What proportion of Prime customers spent more than $1,300?

b. Construct the histogram. Comment on its shape.

34. **FILE** ***Gas.*** The following table lists a portion of the average price (in $) for a gallon of gas for the 50 states and the District of Columbia as reported by AAA Gas Prices on January 28, 2020.

State	Price
Alabama	2.27
Alaska	2.98
⋮	⋮
Wyoming	2.57

a. Construct the frequency distribution for the average price of gas. Use six intervals with widths of $2.00 < x \leq 2.30$; $2.30 < x \leq 2.60$; etc. Which interval had the highest frequency? How many of the states had average gas prices greater than $2.90?

b. Construct the histogram. Is the distribution symmetric? If not, is it positively or negatively skewed?

35. **FILE** ***Texts.*** The following table lists a portion of the number of weekly text messages sent by 150 teenagers.

Teen	Texts
1	630
2	516
⋮	⋮
150	535

a. Construct the frequency distribution and the relative frequency distribution for the number of text messages. Use five intervals with widths of $500 < x \leq 600$; $600 < x \leq 700$; etc. How many teens sent more than 700 text messages but no more than 800 text messages? What proportion of the teens sent more than 800 text messages?

b. Construct a polygon. Is the distribution symmetric? If not, is it positively or negatively skewed.

c. Construct an ogive. Use the ogive to approximate the proportion of teens who sent more than 850 text messages.

36. **FILE** ***Admission.*** The accompanying data file contains the SAT scores for 1,230 students who applied to a selective university.

a. Construct the frequency distribution and the relative frequency distribution for SAT scores. Use eight intervals with widths of $800 < x \leq 900$; $900 < x \leq 1000$; etc. Which interval had the highest frequency? How many students scored in the top interval? What proportion of students scored in the interval $900 < x \leq 1000$?

b. Construct a polygon. Is the distribution symmetric?

c. Construct an ogive. Use the ogive to approximate the proportion of students who scored 1200 or less.

2.4 MORE DATA VISUALIZATION METHODS

LO 2.6

Construct and interpret a scatterplot, a scatterplot with a categorical variable, and a line chart.

In this section, we present three additional visualization methods: a scatterplot, a scatterplot with a categorical variable, and a line chart. Each graph is relatively easy to construct and often conveys very useful information.

A Scatterplot

In many instances we are interested in the relationship between two numerical variables. People in virtually every discipline examine how one numerical variable systematically influences another numerical variable. Consider, for instance, how

- Incomes vary with education.
- Sales vary with advertising expenditures.
- Stock prices vary with corporate profits.
- Crop yields vary with the use of fertilizer.
- Cholesterol levels vary with dietary intake.
- House prices vary with square footage.

When examining the relationship between two numerical variables, a **scatterplot** often proves to be a powerful first step in any analysis.

> A SCATTERPLOT
>
> A scatterplot is a graphical tool that helps in determining whether or not two numerical variables are related in some systematic way. Each point in the diagram represents a pair of observations of the two variables.

When constructing a scatterplot, we generally refer to one of the variables as x and the other variable as y. We then plot each pairing: (x_1, y_1), (x_2, y_2), and so on. Once the data are plotted, the graph may reveal that

- A linear relationship exists between the two variables;
- A nonlinear relationship exists between the two variables; or
- No relationship exists between the two variables.

For example, Figure 2.16(a) shows points on a scatterplot clustered together along a line with a negative slope; we infer that the two variables have a negative linear relationship. Figure 2.16(b) depicts a positive nonlinear relationship; as x increases, y tends to increase at an increasing rate. The points in Figure 2.16(c) are scattered with no apparent pattern; thus, there is no relationship between the two variables.

FIGURE 2.16 Scatterplots depicting relationships between two variables

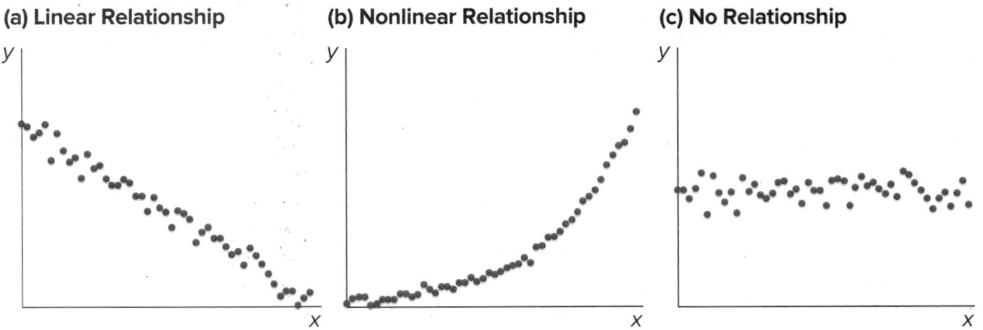

In order to illustrate a scatterplot, consider the following example.

EXAMPLE 2.7

FILE
PG_Sales

Recall that the ***PG_Sales*** data file from the introductory case lists the selling price (Price in $1,000s) and the square footage (Sqft) for a sample of 40 houses. Construct a scatterplot of Price against Sqft using Excel and R. Then summarize the results.

SOLUTION:

Using Excel

a. Open the ***PG_Sales*** data file.

b. When constructing a scatterplot in Excel, we place the variables of interest in columns next to one another. Moreover, our steps are simplified if we place the variable that we want denoted on the x-axis in the first column (here, Sqft) and the variable that we want denoted on the y-axis in the second column (here, Price). We simultaneously select the observations for Sqft and Price and choose **Insert > Insert Scatter or Bubble Chart > Scatter**. (If you are having trouble finding this option, look for the graph with data points above **Charts**.) The resulting scatterplot should be similar to Figure 2.17.

FIGURE 2.17 A scatterplot of Price against Sqft

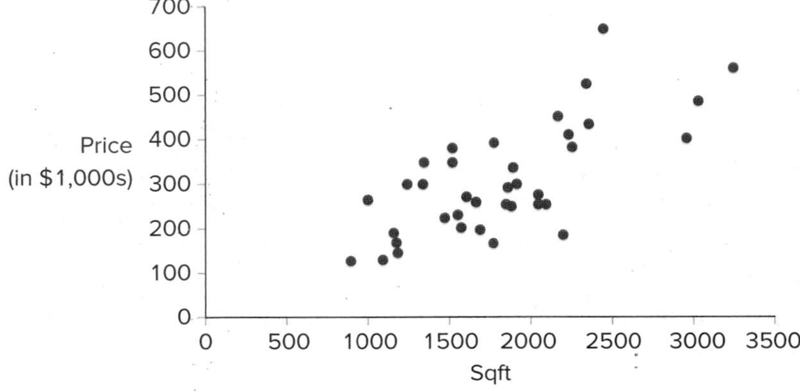

c. Formatting (regarding axis titles, gridlines, etc.) can be done by selecting **Format > Add Chart Element** from the menu.

Using R

a. Import the ***PG_Sales*** data file into a data frame (table) and label it myData.

b. In order to construct a scatterplot, we use the **plot**(*y~x*, . . .) function. We use the *pch* option to choose the marker for the data points—in particular, *pch* = 16 displays filled circles as data markers. As in previous examples, we also use the options *main*, *xlab*, *ylab*, and *col*. Enter:

```
> plot(myData$Price~myData$Sqft, main="A scatterplot of Price
against Sqft", xlab="Sqft", ylab="Price (in $1,000s)",
col="chocolate", pch=16)
```

The resulting scatterplot should be similar to Figure 2.17.

Summary

From Figure 2.17, we can infer that there is a positive relationship between the selling price of a house and its square footage; that is, the bigger the house, the more it is worth.

A Scatterplot with a Categorical Variable

In the last example we showed the relationship between two numerical variables using a scatterplot. We plotted price against square footage, and found a positive relationship between these two variables. If we have a third variable in the data set, say the property type (a single-family home, a multi-family home, etc.), we can incorporate this categorical variable within the scatterplot by using different colors or symbols. This allows us to see if the relationship between price and square footage differs across different property types. This plot is referred to as a **scatterplot with a categorical variable**.

A SCATTERPLOT WITH A CATEGORICAL VARIABLE

A scatterplot with a categorical variable modifies a basic scatterplot by incorporating a categorical variable. It is common to encode the categorical variable through point color. Giving each point a distinct hue makes it easy to show its membership to a respective category.

We illustrate the use of a scatterplot with a categorical variable in the following example.

EXAMPLE 2.8

The ***PG_Sales*** data file from the introductory case lists the selling price (Price), the square footage (Sqft), and a categorical variable labeled Type for a sample of 40 houses. The Type variable has two categories: Single for a single-family house and Condo for a condominium. Use Excel and R to construct a scatterplot of selling price against square footage that also incorporates the Type variable. Summarize the results.

PG_Sales

SOLUTION:

Using Excel

a. Open the ***PG_Sales*** data file.

b. In order to create a scatterplot that incorporates a categorical variable, the categorical variable should be sorted by category. Here, the Type variable is already sorted; that is, the first 30 houses are Single and the remaining 10 houses are Condo. Select **Insert > Insert Scatter or Bubble Chart > Scatter**. This creates a placeholder for the scatterplot in the worksheet.

c. Select **Design > Select Data.** In the *Select Data Source* dialog box, click the *Add* button. This opens the *Edit Series* dialog box so that you can select the data for the x-axis and the y-axis of the scatterplot. Enter "Single" as the *Series name,* select cells C2 through C31 as the *Series X values,* and select cells B2 through B31 as the *Series Y values.* Click **OK** in the *Edit Series* dialog box. This plots selling price against square footage for the 30 single-family houses.

d. Click *Add* to open the *Edit Series* dialog box. Enter "Condo" as the *Series name,* select cells C31 through C41 as the *Series X values,* and select cells B31 through B41 as the *Series Y values.* Click **OK** in the *Edit Series* dialog box. This plots selling price against square footage for the 10 condominiums. Click **OK** in the *Select Data Source* dialog box.

e. Formatting (regarding axis titles, gridlines, etc.) can be done by selecting **Format > Add Chart Element** from the menu. The resulting scatterplot should be similar to Figure 2.18.

FIGURE 2.18 A scatterplot of Price against Sqft incorporating type of house

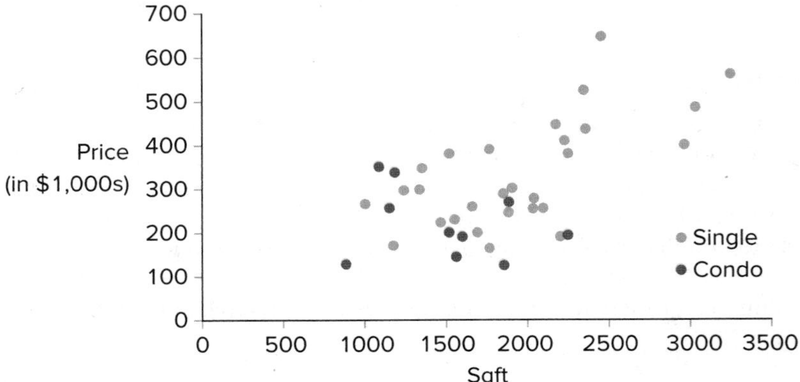

Using R

a. Import the ***PG_Sales*** data file into a data frame (table) and label it myData.

b. To create a scatterplot that incorporates the Type variable, we use the **plot** function. As in previous examples, we use the options *main*, *xlab*, *ylab*, *pch*, and *col*. The shapes and colors of the markers are based on the categories of the Type variable. Enter:

```
> plot(myData$Price~myData$Sqft, main="A scatterplot of
Price against Sqft incorporating type of house", xlab = "Sqft",
ylab = "Price (in $1,000s)", pch=16,
col=ifelse(myData$Type == "Condo", 20, 26))
```

c. We add a legend on the bottom right of the scatterplot using the **legend** function. Enter:

```
> legend("bottomright", legend=c("Condo", "Single"), pch=16,
col=c(20, 26))
```

The resulting scatterplot should be similar to Figure 2.18.

Summary

From Figure 2.18, we see a positive linear relationship between square footage and sale price. That is, larger houses tend to sell for a higher price. This relationship holds true for both single-family houses and condominiums. We also see that, in general, condominiums are smaller and sell for lower prices as compared to single-family houses.

SYNOPSIS OF INTRODUCTORY CASE

Florida has always been an attractive destination for retirees. In addition to very mild winters and generally warm summers, Florida is also considered one of the most tax-friendly states in the country. Matthew Edwards, a relocation specialist, has recently been approached by a number of clients for help with a house purchase. He reviews the selling prices of 40 recent house sales in Punta Gorda to prepare a summary report.

After constructing various frequency distributions, Matthew finds that prices ranged from $100,000 up to $700,000 over this time period. The most houses (16) sold in the $200,000 to $300,000 price range. The vast majority of houses sold for $400,000 or less; only 17.5% sold for more than $400,000.

Not surprisingly, Matthew also finds a strong relationship between square footage and price; that is, bigger houses are more expensive. This information is important for clients to form realistic expectations for the kind of house they can afford.

Brand X Pictures/Getty Images

A Line Chart

A **line chart** displays a numerical variable as a series of consecutive observations connected by a line. A line chart is especially useful for tracking changes or trends over time. For example, if we use a line chart to plot a firm's sales over time, then we can easily tell whether sales follow an upward, a downward, or a steady trend. It is also easy for us to identify any major changes that happened in the past on a line chart.

When multiple lines are plotted in the same chart, we can compare these observations on one or more dimensions. For example, if we simultaneously plot the historical sales of Firm A alongside its competitor Firm B, we would be able to compare the trends and the rates of change of the two firms. We may even detect interesting patterns such as whether a drop in the sales of Firm A coincides with a surge in the sales of Firm B.

> **A LINE CHART**
>
> A line chart connects the consecutive observations of a numerical variable with a line. It tends to be used to track changes of the variable over time.

In order to illustrate the use of a line chart, consider the following example.

EXAMPLE 2.9

The ***Apple_Merck*** data file contains monthly stock prices for Apple, Inc. and Merck & Co. for the years 2016 through 2019. A portion of the data is shown in Table 2.16. Use Excel and R to construct line charts for the stock prices for Apple and Merck. Then, summarize the results.

Apple_Merck

TABLE 2.16 Monthly Stock Prices for Apple and Merck, 2016–2019

Date	Apple	Merck
1/1/2016	90.96	44.98
2/1/2016	90.35	44.57
⋮	⋮	⋮
12/1/2019	293.65	90.33

SOLUTION:

Using Excel

a. Open the ***Apple_Merck*** data file.

b. Highlight cells B1 through C49 and then, from the menu, select **Insert > Insert Line or Area Chart > Line**. Select the option on the top left.

c. Select **Design > Select Data** and click the *Edit* button under *Horizontal (Category) Axis Labels.* In the *Axis Labels* dialog box, highlight cells A2 through A49 in the *Axis label range* box. Click **OK**. The dates appear along the horizontal axis. Due to space limitations, Excel does not display every date.

d. Formatting (regarding axis titles, gridlines, etc.) can be done by selecting **Format > Add Chart Element** from the menu. The resulting line chart should be similar to Figure 2.19.

FIGURE 2.19 Monthly stock prices for Apple and Merck

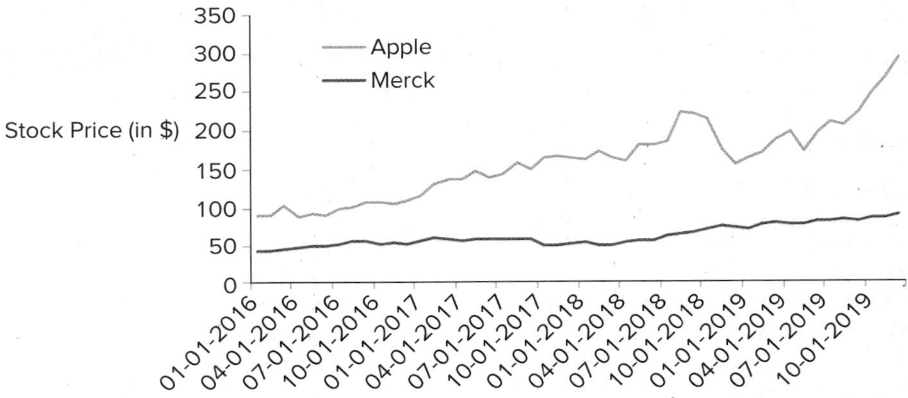

Using R

a. Import the ***Apple_Merck*** data file into a data frame (table) and label it myData.

b. We first use the **plot** function to create a line chart for Apple. Here we use the options *type* to define the type of plot where "l" means line; and *ylim* to provide limits on the y-axis. As in previous examples, we also use the options *main, xlab, ylab,* and *col.* Enter:

```
> plot(myData$Apple~myData$Date, main="Monthly stock prices for
Apple and Merck", xlab="Date", ylab="Monthly Stock Price (in $)",
col = "blue", type = "l", ylim=c(0,300))
```

c. We then incorporate a red line for Merck's stock prices using the **lines** function. Enter:

```
> lines(myData$Merck~myData$Date, col="red", type = "l")
```

d. We add a legend on the top left of the chart using the **legend** function. The *lty* =1 option specifies that the legend is based on the two solid lines. Enter:

```
> legend("topleft", legend=c("Apple", "Merck"), col=c("blue",
"red"), lty=1)
```

The resulting line chart should be similar to Figure 2.19.

Summary

The line charts in Figure 2.19 show the monthly stock prices for Apple and Merck over the years 2016 through 2019. Both stocks rose over this period which is not surprising given the growth in the U.S. economy over this time period. However, the rise in Apple's stock price is far more dramatic as compared to Merck's stock price. There is also a lot more volatility in Apple's stock price. Specifically, we see a dramatic decline in Apple's stock at the end of 2018. This dip corresponded to news that the company would no longer offer unit sales data for its products. At the time, some wondered if this lack of transparency presaged weaker iPhone sales in the future. Fortunately for Apple, this prediction did not materialize.

EXERCISES 2.4

Applications

37. FILE ***Test_Scores.*** The accompanying table shows a portion of midterm and final grades for 32 students. Construct a scatterplot of Final against Midterm. Describe the relationship.

Student	Final	Midterm
1	86	78
2	94	97
⋮	⋮	⋮
32	91	47

38. FILE ***Life_Obesity.*** The accompanying table shows a portion of life expectancies (in years) and obesity rates (in %) for the 50 states and the District of Columbia. Construct a scatterplot of Life Expectancy against Obesity. Describe the relationship.

State	Life Expectancy	Obesity
Alabama	75.4	36.3
Alaska	78.3	34.2
⋮	⋮	⋮
Wyoming	78.3	28.8

39. FILE ***Consumption.*** The accompanying table shows a portion of quarterly data for real personal consumption (Consumption in $) and real personal disposable income (Income in $) for the years 2000–2019. Construct a scatterplot of Consumption against Income. Describe the relationship.

Date	Consumption	Income
Q1, 2000	8520.71	9338.68
Q2, 2000	8603.01	9441.95
⋮	⋮	⋮
Q4, 2019	13411.94	15100.13

40. FILE ***Return.*** In order to diversify risk, investors are often encouraged to invest in assets whose returns have either a negative relationship or no relationship. The accompanying table shows a portion of the annual returns (in %) for two assets over the past 20 years. Construct a scatterplot of Return B against Return A. In order to diversify risk, would the investor be wise to include both of these assets in her portfolio? Explain.

Year	Return A	Return B
1	−20	2
2	−5	0
⋮	⋮	⋮
20	10	2

41. FILE ***HighSchool_SAT.*** The accompanying table shows a portion of the average SAT math score (Math), the average SAT writing score (Writing), the number of test takers (Test Taker), and whether the school is a private or public school (Type) for 25 high schools in a major metropolitan area.

School	Math	Writing	Test Taker	Type
1	456	423	228	Public
2	437	393	475	Public
⋮	⋮	⋮	⋮	⋮
25	592	592	127	Private

Construct a scatterplot that shows the math score on the x-axis and the writing score on the y-axis. Use different colors or symbols to show whether the high school is a private or public school. Describe the relationships between math score, writing score, and school type. Does the relationship between math score and writing score hold true for both private and public schools?

42. FILE ***Car_Price.*** The accompanying table shows a portion of data consisting of the selling price, the age, and the mileage for 20 used sedans.

Price	Age	Mileage
13590	6	61485
13775	6	54344
⋮	⋮	⋮
11988	8	42408

a. Construct a scatterplot of Price against Age. Describe the relationship.

b. Construct a scatterplot of Price against Mileage. Describe the relationship.

c. Convert Mileage into a categorical variable, Mileage_Category, by assigning all cars with less than 50,000 miles to the " Low_Mileage" category and the rest to the "High_Mileage" category. How many cars are in the "High_Mileage" category?
d. Construct a scatterplot using Price, Age, and Mileage_Category. Use different colors or symbols to show cars that belong to the different mileage categories. Describe the relationships between price, age, and mileage of these used sedans. Does the relationship between price and age hold true for both mileage categories?

43. FILE ***InternetStocks.*** A financial analyst wants to compare the performance of the stocks of two internet companies, Amazon (AMZN) and Alphabet (GOOG). She records the monthly closing prices of the two stocks for the years 2016 through 2019. A portion of the data is shown in the accompanying table. Construct a line chart that shows the movements of the two stocks over time using two lines each with a unique color. Describe the overall trend of price movement for the two stocks. Which stock shows the greater trajectory of price appreciation?

Date	AMZN	GOOG
1/1/2016	587.00	742.95
2/1/2016	552.52	697.77
⋮	⋮	⋮
12/1/2019	1847.84	1337.02

44. FILE ***India_China.*** It is believed that India will overtake China to become the world's most populous nation much sooner than previously thought (*CNN,* June 19, 2019). The accompanying data file contains the population data, in millions, for India and China from 1960 to 2017. Construct a line chart that shows the changes in the two countries' populations over time using two lines each with a unique color. Describe the overall trend of population growth in the two countries. Which country shows the faster population growth during the past 40 years?

Year	India	China
1960	449.48	667.07
1961	458.49	660.33
⋮	⋮	⋮
2017	1339.18	1386.40

LO 2.7

2.5 A STEM-AND-LEAF DIAGRAM

Construct and interpret a stem-and-leaf diagram.

John Tukey (1915–2000), a well-known statistician, provided another visual method for displaying a numerical variable. A **stem-and-leaf diagram** gives an overall picture of where the observations are centered and how they are dispersed from the center.

A STEM-AND-LEAF DIAGRAM

A stem-and-leaf diagram is constructed by separating each observation of a numerical variable into two parts: a *stem,* which consists of the leftmost digits, and a *leaf,* which consists of the last digit.

In order to illustrate the construction of a stem-and-leaf diagram, consider the following example.

EXAMPLE 2.10

FILE
Wealth_World

Table 2.17 shows the ages of the 25 wealthiest people in the world in 2019. Construct and interpret the stem-and-leaf diagram for the Age variable.

TABLE 2.17 Wealthiest People in the World, 2019

Rank	Name	Age	Rank	Name	Age
1	Jeff Bezos	56	14	Francoise Bettencourt Meyers	66
2	Bill Gates	64			
3	Warren Buffet	89	15	Jim Walton	71
4	Bernard Arnault	70	16	Alice Walton	70
5	Carlos Slim Hellu	80	17	Rob Walton	75
6	Amancio Ortega	83	18	Steve Ballmer	63
7	Larry Ellison	75	19	Ma Huateng	48
8	Mark Zuckerberg	35	20	Jack Ma	55
9	Michael Bloomberg	77	21	Hui Ka Yan	61
10	Larry Page	46	22	Sheldon Adelson	86
11	Charles Koch	84	23	Michael Dell	54
12	Mukesh Ambani	62	24	Phil Knight	81
13	Sergey Brin	46	25	David Thomson	62

SOLUTION:

For each observation for Age, the number in the tens spot denotes the stem, and the number in the ones spot denotes the leaf. We then identify the lowest and highest observations for Age. Mark Zuckerberg is the youngest person of this group at 35 (stem: 3, leaf: 5) and Warren Buffet is the oldest at 89 (stem: 8 and leaf: 9). As shown in Panel A of Table 2.18, we can then infer that the values of the stem range from 3 to 8.

TABLE 2.18 Constructing a Stem-and-Leaf Diagram for Age

Panel A		Panel B		Panel C	
Stem	Leaf	Stem	Leaf	Stem	Leaf
3		3	5	3	5
4		4	6 6 8	4	6 6 8
5	6	5	6 5 4	5	4 5 6
6		6	4 2 6 3 1 2	6	1 2 2 3 4 6
7		7	0 5 7 1 0 5	7	0 0 1 5 5 7
8		8	9 0 3 4 6 1	8	0 1 3 4 6 9

We then begin with the wealthiest man in the world, Jeff Bezos, whose age of 56 gives us a stem of 5 and a leaf of 6. We place a 6 in the row corresponding to a stem of 5, as shown in Panel A of Table 2.18. We continue this process with all the other ages and obtain the values in Panel B. Finally, in Panel C we arrange each individual leaf row in ascending order; this is the stem-and-leaf diagram in its final form.

The stem-and-leaf diagram (Panel C) presents the original 25 observations in a more organized form. From the diagram we can readily observe that the ages range from 35 to 89. The majority of people in this group are over 60. In fact, there are six people in their 60s, six people in their 70s, and six people in their 80s.

A stem-and-leaf diagram is similar to a histogram turned on its side with the added benefit of retaining the original observations. From this stem-and-leaf diagram, we finally note the distribution is not symmetric; it is negatively skewed.

EXERCISES 2.5

Mechanics

45. **FILE** ***Exercise_2.45.*** The accompanying data file contains 20 observations for Variable *X*.
    a. Construct a stem-and-leaf diagram. What are the lowest and highest observations?
    b. Is the distribution symmetric? Explain.

46. **FILE** ***Exercise_2.46.*** The accompanying data file contains 20 observations for Variable *X*.
    a. Construct a stem-and-leaf diagram. What are the lowest and highest observations?
    b. Is the distribution symmetric? Explain.

Applications

47. **FILE** ***Body_Temp.*** The accompanying data file contains body temperature readings for 20 patients who arrived at Overbrook Hospital emergency room over the weekend.
    a. Construct a stem-and-leaf diagram. What are the lowest and highest readings?
    b. Is the distribution symmetric? Explain.

48. **FILE** ***City_Temp.*** The accompanying data file contains the high temperatures for 40 cities in the United States for a day in July.
    a. Construct a stem-and-leaf diagram. What are the lowest and highest temperatures?
    b. Is the distribution symmetric? Explain.

49. **FILE** ***Speed.*** A police officer is concerned with excessive speeds on a portion of Interstate 90 with a posted speed limit of 65 miles per hour. The accompanying data file contains the speeds that he recorded for 25 cars and trucks. Construct a stem-and-leaf diagram. Are the officer's concerns warranted?

50. **FILE** ***Age.*** France was the winner of the FIFA 2018 World Cup, beating Croatia by a score of 4-2. The accompanying data file shows the ages of the players from both teams. Construct a stem-and-leaf diagram for the ages for each country. Comment on similarities and differences.

2.6 WRITING WITH DATA

Case Study

FILE *College_Admissions*

Camilla Jones works as data analyst in the Admissions office at a selective four-year university in North America. Every year, before making any important admissions decisions, the university reviews information on the applicant pool. Today, Camilla focuses on the School of Business and Economics. Camilla will use tabular and graphical methods to summarize the various demographic and academic variables.

Sample Report—Summary of Applicant Pool for College Admission

As in previous years, the Admissions office strives to support and serve a diverse and talented array of prospective students while fulfilling institutional expectations and strategic priorities. Just as prospective students are anxious about receiving an acceptance letter, our office is concerned about meeting our enrollment target. One of the first steps in the acceptance process is to summarize the applicant pool. The following report focuses on applicants to the School of Business and Economics.

Photographs in the Carol M. Highsmith Archive, Library of Congress, Prints & Photographs Division

This year, the School of Business and Economics received 4,103 applications, the most in the School's history. First, we provide some demographic summaries. Figure 2.20(a) shows that 59% of the applicants are male and 41% are female. Figure 2.20(b) shows that the majority of the applicants are white (54%). Asians make up 20% of the applicant pool, whereas Other (blacks, Latinxs, etc.) are the remaining 26%.

FIGURE 2.20 Demographics of Applicant Pool

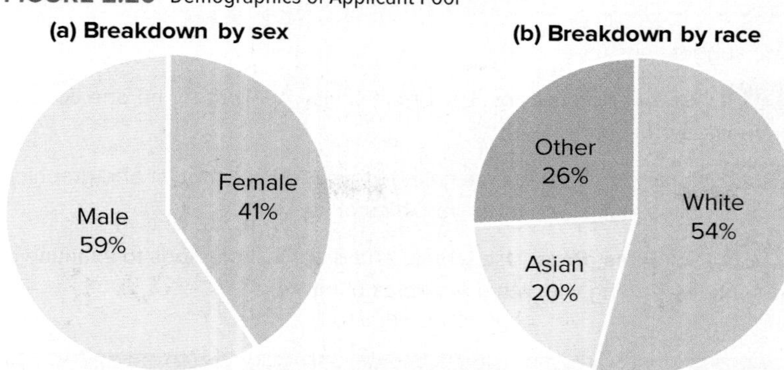

Two important factors that are considered for admission are a student's high school record and performance on standardized tests. Here we summarize the grade point averages (GPAs) and the SAT scores of the applicant pool. The left three columns of Table 2.19 show the frequency and relative frequency distributions for GPA. Notably, 55% of the GPAs are higher than 3.5 and only 14% are below a 3.0. The high school record of the applicant pool appears very strong.

The right three columns of Table 2.19 show the frequency distribution for SAT scores. The national average SAT score is about 1060. In the applicant pool, 85% have SAT scores higher than 1000; moreover, 44% have SAT scores higher than 1200. These findings are similar to those found for GPA. However, as compared to GPA, the proportion of high SAT scores is lower and the proportion of low scores is a bit higher. This is not entirely surprising given the rise in grade inflation in both secondary and higher education.

TABLE 2.19 Frequency Distributions for GPA and SAT scores

GPA	Frequency	Relative Frequency	SAT	Frequency	Relative Frequency
$x \leq 2.5$	83	0.02	$x \leq 800$	74	0.02
$2.5 < x \leq 3.0$	490	0.12	$800 < x \leq 1000$	569	0.14
$3.0 < x \leq 3.5$	1258	0.31	$1000 < x \leq 1200$	1650	0.40
$3.5 < x \leq 4.0$	1693	0.41	$1200 < x \leq 1400$	1457	0.36
$4.0 < x \leq 4.5$	579	0.14	$1400 < x \leq 1600$	353	0.09

Figure 2.21 shows the histograms for GPA and SAT scores. Both distributions are negatively skewed, reinforcing the findings from the frequency distributions; that is, the majority of GPA and SAT scores are clustered in the upper end of both distributions.

FIGURE 2.21 Histograms for GPA and SAT scores.

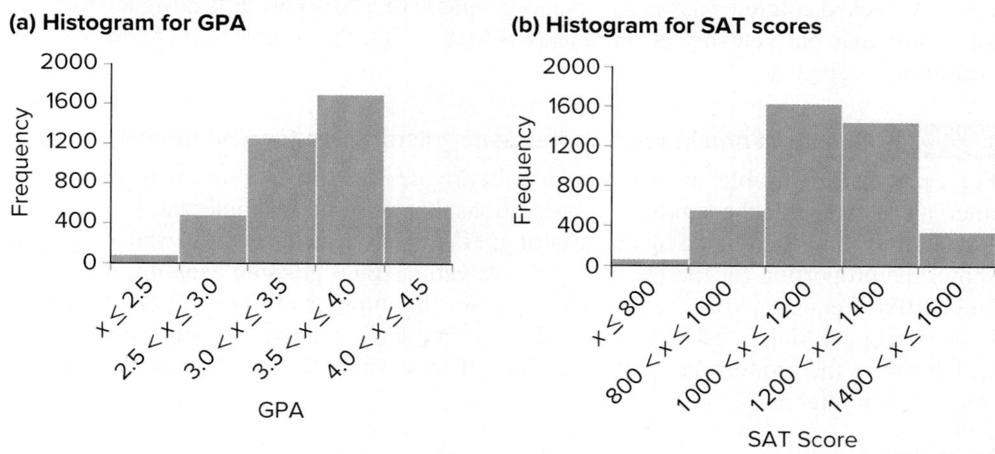

Not only is the applicant pool for the School of Business and Economics the largest ever, it also appears relatively diverse and very competitive. The School will face difficult decisions in the near future.

Suggested Case Studies

Here are some suggestions for analysis.

Report 2.1 FILE ***College_Admissions.*** Perform a similar analysis to the one conducted in this section, but choose another school.

Report 2.2 FILE ***House_Price.*** Choose a college town and use tabular and graphical methods to examine house prices along with other variables of interest.

Report 2.3 FILE ***TechSales_Reps.*** Use tabular and graphical methods to examine the salaries of sales representatives along with other variables of interest.

CONCEPTUAL REVIEW

LO 2.1 Construct and interpret a frequency distribution for a categorical variable.

For a categorical variable, a frequency distribution groups observations into categories and records the number of observations that fall into each category. A relative frequency distribution shows the proportion (or the fraction) of observations in each category.

LO 2.2 Construct and interpret a bar chart and a pie chart.

A bar chart and a pie chart are graphical representations of a frequency distribution for a categorical variable. A bar chart depicts the frequency or the relative frequency for each category of the categorical variable as a series of horizontal or vertical bars. A pie chart is a segmented circle that clearly portrays the categories of the categorical variable.

LO 2.3 Construct and interpret a contingency table and a stacked bar chart for two categorical variables.

A contingency table shows the frequencies for two categorical variables, x and y, where each cell in the table represents a mutually exclusive combination of the pair of x and y observations. A contingency table can be shown graphically using a stacked column chart. A stacked column chart is an advanced version of a bar chart. It is designed to visualize more than one categorical variable, plus it allows for the comparison of composition within each category.

LO 2.4 Construct and interpret a frequency distribution for a numerical variable.

For a numerical variable, a frequency distribution divides the data into nonoverlapping intervals, and records the number of observations that falls into each interval. A frequency distribution can be extended by constructing: (1) a relative frequency distribution which shows the proportion (or the fraction) of observations that falls into each interval; (2) a cumulative frequency distribution which shows the number of observations that falls below the upper limit of each interval; and (3) a cumulative relative frequency distribution which shows the proportion (or the fraction) of observations that falls below the upper limit of each interval.

LO 2.5 Construct and interpret a histogram, a polygon, and an ogive.

A histogram and a polygon are graphical representations of a frequency distribution or a relative frequency distribution for a numerical variable. A casual inspection of these graphs reveals where most of the observations tend to cluster, as well as the general shape and spread of the variable. An ogive is a graphical representation of a cumulative frequency distribution or cumulative relative frequency distribution.

LO 2.6 **Construct and interpret a scatterplot, a scatterplot with a categorical variable, and a line chart.**

A scatterplot is a graphical tool that helps in determining whether or not two numerical variables are related in some systematic way. Each point in the diagram represents a pair of observations of the two variables. A scatterplot with a categorical variable modifies a basic scatterplot by incorporating a categorical variable. It is common to encode the categorical variable through point color. Giving each point a distinct hue makes it easy to show its membership to a respective category. Finally, a line chart connects the consecutive observations of a numerical variable with a line. It tends to be used to track changes of the variable over time.

LO 2.7 **Construct and interpret a stem-and-leaf diagram.**

A stem-and-leaf diagram is another visual method for displaying a numerical variable. It is constructed by separating each observation of the variable into a *stem,* which consists of the leftmost digits, and a *leaf,* which consists of the last digit. Like a histogram and a polygon, a stem-and-leaf diagram gives an overall picture of where the observations are centered and how the observations are dispersed from the center.

ADDITIONAL EXERCISES

51. FILE ***CEO.*** The accompanying table shows a portion of the highest degrees earned by a sample of 200 chief executive officers (CEOs) in the United States.

CEO	Degree
1	Bachelor's
2	Master's
⋮	⋮
200	Master's

a. Construct the frequency and the relative frequency distributions. Do most CEOs in the United States have advanced degrees, such as a Master's degree or a PhD? What percentage of CEOs do not have at least a Bachelor's degree?
b. Construct the bar chart. Summarize the findings.

52. FILE ***AdultChild.*** A recent survey of 400 Americans asked whether or not parents do too much for their young adult children. A portion of the results is shown in the accompanying table.

Respondent	Response
1	Too much
2	Too much
⋮	⋮
400	Just right

a. Construct the frequency and the relative frequency distributions. How many respondents felt that parents do too much for their adult children? What proportion of respondents felt that parents do too little for their adult children?
b. Construct the pie chart. Summarize the findings.

53. FILE ***Bookstores.*** A national bookstore chain is trying to understand customer preferences at various store locations. The marketing department has acquired a list of 500 of the most recent transactions from four of its stores. The data set includes the record number (Record), which one of its four stores sold the book (BookStore), and the type of book sold (BookType). A portion of the data is shown in the accompanying table.

Record	BookStore	BookType
1	Store2	Biography
2	Store2	Children book
⋮	⋮	⋮
500	Store4	Romance

a. Construct a contingency table. Which store had the most transactions? Which type of book had the most transactions?

b. Construct a stacked column chart. Which store has the most transactions for Romance books? Which store has the most transactions for Sci-fi books?

54. FILE ***TShirts.*** A company that sells unisex t-shirts is interested in finding out the color and size of its best-selling t-shirt. The accompanying data file contains the size, color, and quantity of t-shirts that were ordered during the last 1,000 transactions. A portion of the data is shown in the accompanying table.

Transaction	Quantity	Size	Color
1	1	XL	White
2	3	M	Gray
⋮	⋮	⋮	⋮
1000	1	S	Red

a. Construct a contingency table that shows the total quantity sold for each color and size combination. How many size M red t-shirts were sold? How many size XL white t-shirts were sold?

b. Construct a stacked column chart. Which two color and size combinations are the most popular ones? Which two are the least popular ones?

55. FILE ***StockPrice.*** The following table lists a portion of the monthly stock price (in $) for Firm A over the past five years (60 months).

Observation	Price
1	51.78
2	50.29
⋮	⋮
60	89.33

a. Construct the frequency distribution for the monthly stock price. Use five intervals with widths of $40 < x \leq 50$; $50 < x \leq 60$; etc. Which interval had the highest frequency? How many times was the stock price between $40 and $50?

b. Construct the relative frequency, the cumulative frequency, and the cumulative relative frequency distributions. What proportion of the time was the stock price between $50 and $60? How many times was the stock price $70 or less? What proportion of the time was the stock price more than $70?

c. Construct the histogram. Is the distribution symmetric? If not, is it positively or negatively skewed?

56. FILE ***Wages.*** The manager of a human resources department of a large manufacturing firm gathers data on the hourly wage (in $), years of education, and age for 80 employees. The accompanying table shows a portion of the data.

Observation	Wage	Education	Age
1	17.54	12	76
2	20.93	10	61
⋮	⋮	⋮	⋮
80	23.66	12	49

a. Construct the frequency distribution, the relative frequency distribution, and the cumulative relative frequency distribution for the hourly wage. Use seven intervals with widths of $10 < x \leq 15$; $15 < x \leq 20$; etc. What proportion of the time were hourly wages between $15 and $35? What proportion of the time were hourly wages more than $35?

b. Construct the polygon. Is the distribution approximately symmetric?

c. Construct the ogive. Use the ogive to approximate the proportion of hourly wages that are less than $25.

57. FILE ***Wages.*** Refer to the previous exercise for a description of the data.

a. Construct a scatterplot of Wage against Education. Describe the relationship.

b. Construct a scatterplot of Wage against Age. Describe the relationship.

58. FILE ***Healthy_Living.*** Healthy living has always been an important goal for any society. Most would agree that a diet that is rich in fruits and vegetables (FV) and regular exercise have a positive effect on health, while smoking has a negative effect on health. The accompanying table shows a portion of the percentage of these variables observed in various states in the United States.

State	Health	FV	Exercise	Smoking
AK	88.7	23.3	60.6	14.6
AL	78.3	20.3	41.0	16.4
⋮	⋮	⋮	⋮	⋮
WY	87.5	23.3	57.2	15.2

a. Construct a scatterplot of Health against Exercise. Describe the relationship.

b. Construct a scatterplot of Health against Smoking. Describe the relationship.

59. FILE ***Pick_Errors.*** The distribution center for an online retailer has been experiencing quite a few "pick errors" (i.e., retrieving the wrong item). Although the warehouse manager thinks most errors are due to inexperienced workers, she believes that a training program also may help

to reduce them. Before sending all employees to training, she examines data from a pilot study of 30 employees. Information is collected on the employee's annual pick errors (Errors), experience (Exper in years), and whether or not the employee attended training (Train equals 1 if the employee attended training, 0 otherwise). A portion of the data is shown in the accompanying table.

Employee	Errors	Exper	Train
1	13	9	0
2	3	27	0
⋮	⋮	⋮	⋮
30	4	24	1

a. Construct a scatterplot of pick errors against experience. Interpret the results.
b. Construct a scatterplot of pick errors against experience that also incorporates the Train variable (categorical). Interpret the results.

60. FILE ***Birth_Life.*** The accompanying data file contains information on the life expectancy (Life_Exp in years), the birth rate (Birth_Rate in percent), and the level of development (Development) for 10 countries. A portion of the data is shown in the accompanying table.

Country Name	Life_Exp	Birth_Rate	Development
Congo, Dem. Rep.	50.00	45.96	Developing
India	62.59	26.46	Developing
⋮	⋮	⋮	⋮
Japan	81.08	9.40	Developed

a. Construct a scatterplot of birth rate against life expectancy. Interpret the results.
b. Construct a scatterplot of birth rate against life expectancy that also incorporates the Development variable (categorical). Interpret the results.

61. FILE ***Exchange_Rate.*** Consider the exchange rate of the $ (USD) with € (Euro) and $ (USD) with £ (Pound). The accompanying table shows a portion of the exchange rates from January 2018 to January 2020.

Date	Euro	Pound
2018-01-01	1.2197	1.3824
2018-02-01	1.2340	1.3961
⋮	⋮	⋮
2020-01-01	1.1098	1.3076

Construct a line chart that shows the movements of the exchange rates over time using two lines each with a unique color. Describe and interpret the overall trend of each currency against the USD.

62. FILE ***Growth.*** The accompanying table shows a portion of the growth rate in revenues (in %) for Starbucks and McDonald's for the years 2010 through 2019.

Year	Starbucks	McDonald's
2010	9.53	5.85
2011	9.27	12.17
⋮	⋮	⋮
2019	7.24	0.25

Construct a line chart that shows the movements of the growth rates over time using two lines each with a unique color. Describe and interpret the overall trend for each firm.

63. FILE ***Wealth_USA.*** The accompanying table lists a portion of the ages and net worth of the 25 wealthiest people in the United States in 2019.

Rank	Name	Age	Net_Worth
1	Jeff Bezos	56	131.0
2	Bill Gates	64	96.5
⋮	⋮	⋮	⋮
25	Thomas Peterffy	75	17.1

a. Construct a stem-and-leaf diagram. What are the ages of the youngest and oldest people in this group?
b. Is the distribution symmetric? Explain.

64. FILE ***PEG.*** The price-to-earnings growth ratio, or PEG ratio, is the market's valuation of a company relative to its earnings prospects. A PEG ratio of 1 indicates that the stock's price is in line with growth expectations. A PEG ratio less than 1 suggests that the stock of the company is undervalued (typical of value stocks), whereas a PEG ratio greater than 1 suggests the stock is overvalued (typical of growth stocks). The accompanying table shows a portion of PEG ratios for 30 large companies.

Company	PEG
1	1.4
2	0.9
⋮	⋮
30	1.2

a. Construct a stem-and-leaf diagram. What are the lowest and highest PEG ratios? Which range of PEG ratios had the highest frequency?
b. Is the distribution symmetric? Explain.

APPENDIX 2.1 Guidelines for Other Software Packages

The following section provides brief commands for Minitab, SPSS, and JMP. Import the specified data file into the relevant software spreadsheet prior to following the commands.

Minitab

Bar Chart

FILE *Myers_Briggs*

(Replicating Figure 2.1) From the menu, choose **Graph > Bar Chart**. Under **Bars Represent** select **Counts of unique values**, and choose **Simple** for bar chart type. In the next dialog box, under **Categorical variables**, select Personality.

Pie Chart

FILE *Myers_Briggs*

(Replicating Figure 2.2) From the menu, choose **Graph > Pie Chart**. Select **Chart counts of unique values**, and under **Categorical variables**, select Personality.

Contingency Table

FILE *Myers_Briggs2*

(Replicating Table 2.7) From the menu, choose **Stat > Tables > Cross Tabulation and Chi Square**. Select **Raw data (categorical variables)**. For **Rows**, select Sex, and for **Columns**, select Personality.

Stacked Column Chart

(Replicating Figure 2.7) From the menu, choose **Graph > Bar Chart.** Under **Bars Represent**, select **Counts of unique values** and choose **Stacked** for bar chart type. In the next dialog box, under **Categorical variables**, select Personality and Sex.

Histogram

A. (Replicating Figure 2.13) From the menu, choose **Graph > Histogram > Simple**. In the next dialog box, under **Graph variables**, select Price.

B. Double-click *x*-axis and select **Edit Scale**. Under **Major Tick Positions**, choose **Position of Ticks** and enter 100 200 300 400 500 600 700. Under **Scale Range**, deselect **Auto** for *Minimum* and enter 100. Then deselect **Auto** for *Maximum* and enter 700. Select the **Binning** tab. Under **Interval Type**, select **Cutpoint**. Under **Interval Definition**, select **Midpoint/Cutpoint Definitions** and enter 100 200 300 400 500 600 700.

Polygon/Ogive

(Replicating Figure 2.14 and Figure 2.15) From the menu, choose **Graph > Scatterplot > With Connect Line**. Under **Y variables** select y, and under **X variables** select x.

Scatterplot

(Replicating Figure 2.17) From the menu, choose **Graph > Scatterplot > Simple**. Under **Y variables**, select Price, and under **X variables**, select Sqft.

Scatterplot with Categorical Variable

(Replicating Figure 2.18) From the menu, choose **Graph > Scatterplot > With Groups**. Under **Y variables**, select Price, and under **X variables**, select Sqft. **Under Categorical variables for grouping (0-3)**, select Type.

Line Chart

(Replicating Figure 2.19) From the menu, choose **Graph > Time Series Plot > Multiple**. Under **Series**, select Apple and Merck. Select **Time/Scale**, and under **Time Scale**, select **Calendar** and then **Month Year**. Under **Start Values**, select **One set for all variables**, and then under **Month** enter 1 and under **Year** enter 2016.

SPSS

Bar Chart

(Replicating Figure 2.1) From the menu, choose **Graphs > Chart Builder**. Under the **Gallery** tab, then under **Choose from**, select **Bar**. Drag the **Simple Bar** icon (top left) to the Gallery. Drag Personality to the **X-axis**.

Pie Chart

(Replicating Figure 2.2) From the menu, choose **Graphs > Chart Builder**. Under the **Gallery** tab, then under **Choose from**, select **Pie**. Drag the **Pie Chart** icon to the Gallery. Drag Personality to **Slice by**.

Contingency Table

(Replicating Table 2.7) From the menu, choose **Analyze > Descriptive Statistics > Crosstabs**. Under **Row(s)**, select Sex, and under **Column(s)**, select Personality.

Stacked Column Chart

(Replicating Figure 2.7) From the menu, choose **Graphs > Chart Builder**. Under the **Gallery** tab, then under **Choose from**, select **Bar**. Drag the **Stacked Bar** icon (third from the left) to the Gallery. Drag Personality to the **X-axis**, and drag Sex to **Stack: set color**.

Histogram

A. (Replicating Figure 2.13) From the menu, choose **Graphs > Chart Builder**. Under the **Gallery** tab, then under **Choose from**, select **Histogram**. Drag the **Simple Histogram** icon (top left) to the Gallery. Drag Price to **X-axis**, then double-click on Price. Under the **Element Properties** tab, next to **Minimum**, deselect **Automatic** and enter 100 under **Custom**; next to **Maximum**, deselect **Automatic** and enter 700 under **Custom**, next to **Major Increment**, deselect **Automatic** and enter 100; and next to **Origin**, deselect **Automatic** and enter 100.

B. In the output window, double-click on one of the bars. Choose the **Binning** tab, and under **X Axis**, deselect **Automatic**, and select **Interval width**, and enter 100. Click **Apply**.

Polygon/Ogive

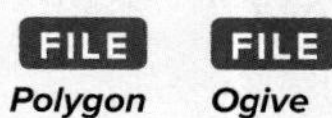

(Replicating Figure 2.14 and Figure 2.15) From the menu, choose **Graphs > Chart Builder**. Under the **Gallery** tab, then under **Choose from**, select **Scatter/Dot**. Drag the **Simple Scatter** icon (top left) to the Gallery. Drag x to the **X-axis** and drag y to **Y-axis**. In the output window, double-click on the graph to open the **Chart Editor**. From the menu, select **Element > Interpolation Line**.

Scatterplot

(Replicating Figure 2.17) From the menu, choose **Graphs > Chart Builder**. Under the **Gallery** tab, then under **Choose from**, select **Scatter/Dot**. Drag the **Simple Scatter** icon (top left) to the Gallery. Drag Sqft to the **X-axis** and drag Price to **Y-axis**.

Scatterplot with Categorical Variable

FILE
PG_Sales

(Replicating Figure 2.18) From the menu, choose **Graphs > Chart Builder**. Under the **Gallery** tab, then under **Choose from**, select **Scatter/Dot**. Drag the **Grouped Scatter** icon (third from top left) to the Gallery. Drag Sqft to the **X-axis**, drag Price to **Y-axis**, and drag Type to **Set Color**.

Line Chart

FILE
Apple_Merck

(Replicating Figure 2.19) From the menu choose **Graphs > Legacy Dialogs > Line**. Select **Multiple** and under **Data in Chart Are**, select **Summaries of separate variables**. Click **Define**. Under **Lines Represent**, select Apple and Merck. Under **Category Axis**, select Date.

JMP

Bar Chart

FILE
Myers_Briggs

(Replicating Figure 2.1) From the menu, choose **Graph > Graph Builder**. From the menu of chart types, select the **Bar** icon. Drag Personality to the **X** axis.

Pie Chart

FILE
Myers_Briggs

(Replicating Figure 2.2) From the menu, choose **Graph > Graph Builder**. From the menu of chart types, select the **Pie Chart** icon. Drag Personality to the **X** axis.

Contingency Table

FILE
Myers_Briggs2

(Replicating Table 2.7) From the menu, choose **Analyze > Fit Y by X**. Drag Personality to **Y, Response box,** and drag Sex to **X, Factor** box.

Stacked Column Chart

FILE
Myers_Briggs2

(Replicating Figure 2.7) From the menu, choose **Graph > Graph Builder**. From the menu of chart types, select the **Bar** icon. Under **Bar** and next to **Bar Style**, select **Stacked**. Drag Personality to the **X** axis, and drag Sex to **Overlay**.

Histogram

FILE
PG_Sales

A. (Replicating Figure 2.13) From the menu, choose **Analyze > Distributions**. Select Price and click **Y, Columns**. By default, JMP constructs a horizontal layout. For a vertical layout, select the red arrow next to Price and then choose **Display Options**. Deselect the **Horizontal Layout** option.

B. Double-click on the values on the x-axis in order to open the dialog box for the **X Axis Settings**. Under the **Scale**, enter 100 for **Minimum** and enter 700 for **Maximum**. Under **Tick/Bin Increment**, verify that **Increment** is set to 100.

Polygon/Ogive

FILE *Polygon* FILE *Ogive*

(Replicating Figure 2.14 and Figure 2.15) From the menu, choose **Graph > Graph Builder**. From the menu of chart types, select the **Line** icon. Drag x to the **X** axis and drag y to the **Y** axis.

Scatterplot

FILE
PG_Sales

(Replicating Figure 2.17) From the menu, choose **Graph > Graph Builder**. From the menu of chart types, select the **Scatter** icon. Drag Sqft to the **X** axis and drag Price to the **Y** axis.

Scatterplot with Categorical Variable

(Replicating Figure 2.18) From the menu, choose **Graph > Graph Builder**. From the menu of chart types, select the **Scatter** icon. Drag Sqft to the **X** axis, drag Price to the **Y** axis, and drag Type to **Overlay**.

Line Chart

(Replicating Figure 2.19) From the menu choose **Graph > Legacy > Overlay Plot**. Select Apple and click **Y**, select Merck and click **Y**, and select Date and click **X**.

3 Numerical Descriptive Measures

LEARNING OBJECTIVES

After reading this chapter you should be able to:

LO **3.1** **Calculate and interpret measures of central location.**

LO **3.2** **Interpret a percentile and a boxplot.**

LO **3.3** **Calculate and interpret a geometric mean return and an average growth rate.**

LO **3.4** **Calculate and interpret measures of dispersion.**

LO **3.5** **Explain mean-variance analysis and the Sharpe ratio.**

LO **3.6** **Apply Chebyshev's theorem, the empirical rule, and *z*-scores.**

LO **3.7** **Calculate and interpret measures of association.**

In Chapter 2, we used tables and graphs in order to extract meaningful information from data. In this chapter, we focus on numerical descriptive measures. These measures provide precise, objectively determined values that are easy to calculate, interpret, and compare with one another.

We first calculate several measures of central location, which attempt to find a typical or central value for the data. In addition to analyzing the center, we then examine how the data vary around the center. Measures of dispersion gauge the underlying variability of the data.

We use measures of central location and dispersion to introduce some popular applications, including the Sharpe ratio, Chebyshev's theorem, the empirical rule, and the *z*-score.

Finally, we discuss measures of association that examine the linear relationship between two variables. These measures assess whether two variables have a positive linear relationship, a negative linear relationship, or no linear relationship.

TZIDO SUN/Shutterstock

INTRODUCTORY CASE

Investment Decision

Dorothy Brennan works as a financial advisor at a large investment firm. She meets with an inexperienced investor who has some questions regarding two approaches to mutual fund investing: growth investing versus value investing. The investor has heard that growth funds invest in companies whose stock prices are expected to grow at a faster rate, relative to the overall stock market. Value funds, on the other hand, invest in companies whose stock prices are below their true worth. The investor has also heard that the main component of investment return is through capital appreciation in growth funds and through dividend income in value funds.

The investor shows Dorothy the annual return data for Fidelity's Growth Index mutual fund (Growth) and Fidelity's Value Index mutual fund (Value). Table 3.1 shows a portion of the annual return (in %) for these two mutual funds from 1984 to 2019. It is difficult for the investor to draw any conclusions from the data in its present form. In addition to clarifying the style differences in growth investing versus value investing, the investor requests Dorothy to summarize the data.

FILE *Growth_Value*

TABLE 3.1 Annual Returns (in %) for Growth and Value

Year	Growth	Value
1984	−5.50	−8.59
1985	39.91	22.10
⋮	⋮	⋮
2019	38.42	31.62

Dorothy will use the sample information to:

1. Calculate and interpret the typical return for these two mutual funds.
2. Calculate and interpret the investment risk for these two mutual funds.
3. Determine which mutual fund provides the greater return relative to risk.

A synopsis of this case is provided at the end of Section 3.4.

LO 3.1

3.1 MEASURES OF CENTRAL LOCATION

Calculate and interpret measures of central location.

The term *central location* relates to the way data tend to cluster around some middle or central value. Measures of central location attempt to find a typical or central value that describes the data. Examples include finding a typical value that describes the return on an investment, the number of defects in a production process, the salary of a business graduate, the rental price in a neighborhood, the number of orders for a subscription-based service, and so on.

The Mean

The **arithmetic mean** is the primary measure of central location. Generally, we refer to the arithmetic mean as simply the **mean** or the **average.** In order to calculate the mean of a variable, we simply add up all the observations and divide by the number of observations in the population or sample. Consider the following example.

FILE
Growth_Value

EXAMPLE 3.1

Use the ***Growth_Value*** data file from the introductory case to calculate and interpret the mean return for Growth and the mean return for Value.

SOLUTION: Let's start with the mean return for Growth. We first add all the returns and then divide by the number of returns as follows:

$$\text{Growth: } \frac{(-5.50) + 39.91 + \cdots + 38.42}{36} = 15.755$$

Similarly, we calculate the mean return for Value as:

$$\text{Value: } \frac{(-8.59) + 22.10 + \cdots + 31.62}{36} = 12.005$$

Thus, over the 36-year period 1984–2019, the mean return for Growth was greater than the mean return for Value, or equivalently, 15.755% > 12.005%. These means represent typical annual returns resulting from one-year investments. We will see throughout this chapter, however, that we would be ill-advised to invest in a mutual fund solely on the basis of its average return.

All of us have calculated a mean before. What might be new for some of us is the notation used to express the mean as a formula. For instance, when calculating the mean return for Growth, we let $x_1 = -5.50$, $x_2 = 39.91$, and so on, and let n represent the number of observations in the sample. So our calculation for the mean can be written as

$$\text{Mean} = \frac{x_1 + x_2 + \cdots + x_n}{n}.$$

The mean of the sample is referred to as $\bar{x}$ (pronounced x-bar). Also, we can denote the numerator of this formula using summation notation, which yields the following compact formula for the **sample mean**: $\bar{x} = \frac{\Sigma x_i}{n}$. We should also point out that if we had all the observations for Growth, instead of just the observations for the past 36 years, then we would have been able to calculate the **population mean** μ as $\mu = \frac{\Sigma x_i}{N}$ where μ is the Greek letter mu (pronounced as "mew") and N is the number of observations in the population.

MEASURE OF CENTRAL LOCATION: THE MEAN

For sample observations $x_1, x_2, \ldots, x_n$, the sample mean $\bar{x}$ is computed as

$$\bar{x} = \frac{\Sigma x_i}{n}.$$

For population observations $x_1, x_2, \ldots, x_N$, the population mean μ is computed as

$$\mu = \frac{\Sigma x_i}{N}.$$

The calculation method is identical for the sample mean and the population mean except that the sample mean uses n observations and the population mean uses N observations, where $n < N$. We refer to the population mean as a parameter and the sample mean as a statistic. As mentioned in Chapter 1, a parameter describes a population, whereas a statistic describes a sample. Since the population mean is generally unknown, we use the sample mean to make inferences about the population mean, which is discussed Chapters 8 and 9.

The mean is used extensively in statistics. However, it can give a misleading description of the center of the distribution in the presence of extremely small or large values, also referred to as **outliers**.

The mean is the most commonly used measure of central location. One weakness of this measure is that it is unduly influenced by outliers.

Example 3.2 highlights the main weakness of the mean.

EXAMPLE 3.2

Eight people work at Acetech, a small technology firm in Seattle. Their salaries (in $) over the past year are listed in Table 3.2. Compute the mean salary for this firm and discuss whether it accurately indicates a typical value.

TABLE 3.2 Salaries of Employees at Acetech

Title	Salary
Administrative Assistant	40,000
Research Assistant	40,000
Data Analyst	65,000
Senior Research Associate	90,000
Senior Data Analyst	100,000
Senior Sales Associate	145,000
Chief Financial Officer	150,000
President (and owner)	550,000

SOLUTION: Since the salaries of all employees of Acetech are included in Table 3.2, we calculate the population mean salary as:

$$\mu = \frac{\Sigma x_i}{N} = \frac{40{,}000 + 40{,}000 + \cdots + 550{,}000}{8} = 147{,}500$$

It is true that the mean salary for this firm is $147,500, but this value does not reflect the typical salary at this firm. In fact, six of the eight employees earn less than $147,500. This example highlights the main weakness of the mean—that is, it is very sensitive to extremely large or extremely small observations, or outliers.

The Median

Since the mean can be affected by outliers, we often also calculate the **median** as a measure of central location. The median is the middle value of a variable. It divides the data in half; an equal number of observations lie above and below the median. Many government publications and other data sources publish both the mean and the median in order to accurately portray a variable's typical value. For instance, in 2017 the U.S. Census Bureau found that the median income for American households was $61,372; however, the mean income was $86,220. It is well documented that a small number of households in the United States have income that is considerably higher than the typical American household income. As a result, these top-earning households influence the mean by pushing its value significantly above the value of the median.

MEASURE OF CENTRAL LOCATION: THE MEDIAN

The median is the middle observation in a sample or a population. The observations are arranged in ascending order (smallest to largest) and the median is calculated as

- The middle observation if n (or N) is odd, or
- The average of the two middle observations if n (or N) is even.

The median is especially useful when outliers are present.

EXAMPLE 3.3

Use the data in Table 3.2 to calculate the median salary of employees at Acetech.

SOLUTION: In Table 3.2, the data are already arranged in ascending order. We reproduce the salaries along with their relative positions.

Position:	1	2	3	4	5	6	7	8
Value:	40,000	40,000	65,000	90,000	100,000	145,000	150,000	550,000

Given eight salaries ($N = 8$), the median is the average of the observations occupying the 4th and 5th positions. Thus, the median is 95,000. Four salaries are less than $95,000 and four salaries are greater than $95,000. As compared to the mean income of $147,500 the median in this case better reflects the typical salary.

The Mode

The **mode** of a variable is the observation that occurs most frequently. A variable can have more than one mode, or even no mode. If a variable has one mode, then we say it is unimodal. If two or more modes exist, then the variable is multimodal; it is common to call it bimodal in the case of two modes. Generally, the mode's usefulness as a measure of central location tends to diminish with variables that have more than three modes.

MEASURE OF CENTRAL LOCATION: THE MODE

The mode is the most frequently occurring observation in a sample or a population. A variable may have no mode or more than one mode.

EXAMPLE 3.4

Use the data in Table 3.2 to calculate the modal salary for employees at Acetech.

SOLUTION: The salary $40,000 is earned by two employees. Every other salary occurs just once. So $40,000 is the modal salary. Just because an observation occurs with the most frequency does not guarantee that it best reflects the center of the variable. It is true that the modal salary at Acetech is $40,000, but most employees earn considerably more than this amount.

In the preceding examples, we used measures of central location to describe a numerical variable. However, in many instances we want to summarize a categorical variable, where the mode is the only meaningful measure of central location.

EXAMPLE 3.5

Kenneth Forbes is a manager at the University of Wisconsin campus bookstore. There has been a recent surge in the sale of women's sweatshirts, which are available in three sizes: Small (S), Medium (M), and Large (L). Kenneth notes that the campus bookstore sold 10 sweatshirts over the weekend in the following sizes:

Sebastian Pfeutze/Getty Images

S	L	L	M	S	L	M	L	L	M

Use the most appropriate measure of central location to find the typical size of a sweatshirt.

SOLUTION: The size of a sweatshirt is a categorical variable: S, M, or L. Here, the mode is the only relevant measure of central location. The modal size is L since it appears 5 times, as compared to S and M, which appear 2 and 3 times, respectively. Often, when examining issues relating to the demand for a product, such as replenishing stock, the mode tends to be the most relevant measure of central location.

Using Excel and R to Calculate Measures of Central Location

In general, Excel and R offer a couple of ways to calculate descriptive measures. Table 3.3 summarizes the function names for descriptive measures in these software. We will refer to these functions throughout this chapter and text. In the next example, we show how to use Excel and R to calculate measures of central location.

TABLE 3.3 Descriptive Measures and Corresponding Function Names in Excel and R

Descriptive Measure	Excel	R
Location		
Mean	=AVERAGE(array)	mean(DF$var)[a]
Median	=MEDIAN(array)	median(DF$var)
Mode	=MODE(array)	NA[b]
Minimum	=MIN(array)	min(DF$var)
Maximum	=MAX(array)	max(DF$var)
Percentile	=PERCENTILE.INC(array, p)[c]	quantile(DF$var, p)[c]
Multiple measures	*NA*	summary(DF)
Dispersion		
Range	=MAX(array)-MIN(array)	range(DF$var)[d]
Mean Absolute Deviation	=AVEDEV(array)	mad(DF$var)[e]
Sample Variance	=VAR.S(array)	var(DF$var)
Sample Standard Deviation	=STDEV.S(array)	sd(DF$var)
Shape		
Skewness	=SKEW(array)	NA
Kurtosis	=KURT(array)	NA
Association		
Sample Covariance	=COVARIANCE.S(array1,array2)	cov(DF)
Correlation	=CORREL(array1,array2)	cor(DF)

[a]The notation *DF* refers to the data frame (table) and the notation *var* refers to the variable name. The variable name should be specified in single quotations if it consists of more than one word or if it is a number.

[b]*NA* denotes that a simple function is not readily available.

[c]The parameter p takes on a value between 0 and 1.

[d]The **range** function in R returns the minimum and maximum values, so the range can be calculated by taking the difference between the two values.

[e]The **mad** function calculates the median absolute deviation, rather than the mean absolute deviation. Alternatively, we can install the 'lsr' package in R and use the **aad** function, which computes the mean absolute deviation.

EXAMPLE 3.6

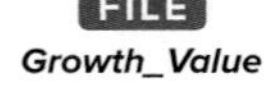

Growth_Value

Using Excel and R, calculate measures of central location for the Growth and Value variables from the introductory case. Summarize the results.

SOLUTION:

Using Excel

I. Excel's Formula Option To illustrate, we follow these steps to find measures of central location for Growth.

a. Open the ***Growth_Value*** data file.

b. In order to find the mean, find an empty cell and enter =AVERAGE(B2:B37). Verify that the output is 15.755.

c. In order to find the median, find an empty cell and enter =MEDIAN(B2:B37). Verify that the output is 15.245.

d. In order to find the mode, find an empty cell and enter =MODE(B2:B37). Verify that the output is #N/A meaning that no observation appears more than once.

If we want to calculate these measures of central location for Value, we simply replace B2:B37 with C2:C37 because the observations for Value occupy cells C2 through C37.

II. Excel's Data Analysis Toolpak Option Another way to obtain summary measures is to use Excel's Data Analysis Toolpak option. One advantage of this option is that it provides numerous summary measures using a single command.

a. Open the ***Growth_Value*** data file.

b. From the menu, choose **Data > Data Analysis > Descriptive Statistics > OK.** (Note: As mentioned in Section 2.3, if you do not see **Data Analysis** under **Data,** you must add in the **Analysis Toolpak** option.)

c. See Figure 3.1. In the *Descriptive Statistics* dialog box, click on the box next to *Input Range,* then select the headings and the observations for the Growth and Value variables. Select the options *Labels in First Row* and *Summary Statistics.* Select *Output Range* and enter cell E1. Then click **OK.**

FIGURE 3.1 Excel's Descriptive Statistics dialog box

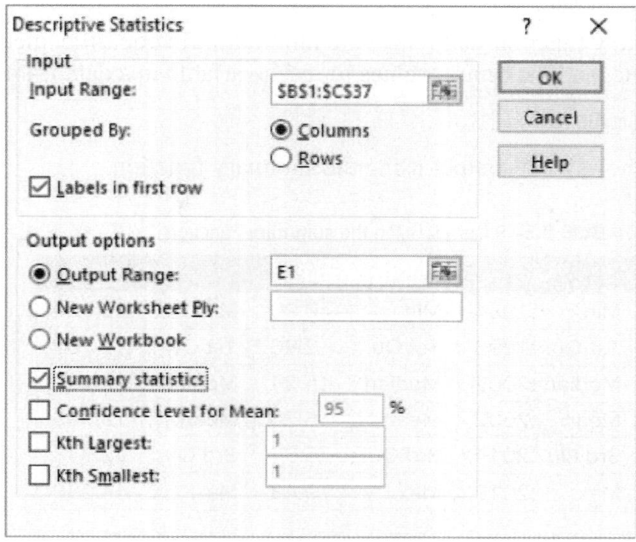

d. Table 3.4 presents the Excel output. If the output is difficult to read, highlight the output and choose **Home > Format > Column > Autofit Selection.** As noted earlier, Excel provides numerous summary measures; we have put the measures of central location in boldface.

TABLE 3.4 Excel's Output Using the Data Analysis Toolpak

Growth		Value	
Mean	**15.755**	**Mean**	**12.005**
Standard Error	3.966547567	Standard Error	2.996531209
Median	**15.245**	**Median**	**15.38**
Mode	**#N/A**	**Mode**	**#N/A**
Standard Deviation	23.7992854	Standard Deviation	17.97918725
Sample Variance	566.4059857	Sample Variance	323.2511743
Kurtosis	0.973702537	Kurtosis	1.853350762
Skewness	−0.028949752	Skewness	−1.023591081
Range	120.38	Range	90.6
Minimum	−40.9	Minimum	−46.52
Maximum	79.48	Maximum	44.08
Sum	567.18	Sum	432.18
Count	36	Count	36

Using R

As noted in Chapters 1 and 2, we denote all function names in **boldface** and all options within a function in *italics*. Also, remember that R is case sensitive.

a. Import the ***Growth_Value*** data file into a data frame (table) and label it myData.

b. The **mean** and **median** functions will return the mean and the median, respectively, for a specified variable in a data frame. In order to find the mean for Growth, enter:

```
> mean(myData$Growth)
> median(myData$Growth)
```

R returns 15.755 for the mean and 15.245 for the median. In order to find these measures of central location for Value, simply substitute Value for Growth in the code.

c. The **summary** function will return the minimum, first quartile, median, mean, third quartile, and maximum values for each variable in a data frame. Enter:

```
> summary(myData)
```

Table 3.5 shows the R output using the summary function.

TABLE 3.5 R Output Using the **summary** Function

Year*	Growth	Value
Min. :1984	Min. :−40.90	Min. :−46.520
1st Qu. :1993	1st Qu. : 2.86	1st Qu. : 1.702
Median :2002	Median : 15.24	Median : 15.380
Mean :2002	Mean : 15.76	Mean : 12.005
3rd Qu. :2011	3rd Qu. : 36.97	3rd Qu. : 22.348
Max. :2019	Max. : 79.48	Max. : 44.080

*Note that in this example, the summary statistics for the variable Year are not useful.

Summary

From Tables 3.4 and 3.5 we see that the average return for Growth is greater than the average return for the Value, 15.76% > 12.01%. Interestingly, however, the median return for Value is greater than the median return for Growth, 15.38% > 15.25%. This example illustrates why it is useful to examine both the mean and the median when summarizing central location, especially when outliers may be present. Neither variable has a mode.

Note on Symmetry

In Chapter 2, we used histograms to discuss **symmetry** and **skewness.** Recall that the distribution is symmetric if one side of the histogram is a mirror image of the other side. For a symmetric and unimodal distribution, the mean, the median, and the mode are equal. In business applications, it is common to encounter data that are skewed. The mean is usually greater than the median when the data are positively skewed and less than the median when the data are negatively skewed.

We would also like to comment on the numerical measure of skewness that Excel reports in Table 3.4, even though we will not discuss its calculation. A skewness coefficient of zero indicates the observations are evenly distributed on both sides of the mean. A positive skewness coefficient implies that extreme observations are concentrated in the right tail of the distribution, pulling the mean up, relative to the median, and the bulk of the observations lie to the left of the mean. Similarly, a negative skewness coefficient implies that extreme observations are concentrated in the left tail of the distribution, pulling the mean down, relative to the median, and the bulk of the observations lie to the right of the mean. For both Growth and Value, the skewness coefficient is negative; for Growth, however, the coefficient value of −0.0289 implies a very slight negative skew.

Subsetted Means

As discussed in Chapter 1, sometimes it is useful to subset the observations in a sample or a population. This process often reveals important information that would not be uncovered if the variable is analyzed for the entire data set. For example, in addition to reporting its total sales over the past year, a multinational company also reports sales by region. This way the company easily identifies which region has the highest or lowest sales. Consider the following example.

EXAMPLE 3.7

Online

The marketing analyst of an online retail company is trying to understand spending behavior of customers during the holiday season. She has compiled information on 130 existing customers that includes the customer's sex and spending (in $) in the following categories: clothing (Clothing), health and beauty (Health), technology (Tech), and miscellaneous items (Misc). A portion of the data is shown in Table 3.6.

TABLE 3.6 Online Spending by Females versus Males

Customer	Sex	Clothing	Health	Tech	Misc
1	Female	246	185	64	75
2	Male	171	78	345	10
⋮	⋮	⋮	⋮	⋮	⋮
130	Male	52	73	542	58

Use Excel and R to subset the data by sex and compute the corresponding average spending for each of the product categories by female and male customers. Then, help the manager determine whether it seems appropriate to target females or males for the different product categories.

SOLUTION:

Using Excel:

a. Open the ***Online*** data file.

b. We use the AVERAGEIF function. The input for the function is 1) the range of cells that are to meet a certain criteria, 2) the criteria, and 3) the cells that are to be averaged. For instance, to find the average amount that females spend on clothing, we enter =AVERAGEIF(B2:B131, "Female", C2:C131), and Excel returns 225.67. To find the average amount that males spend on clothing, we enter =AVERAGEIF(B2:B131, "Male", C2:C131), and Excel returns 97.93. The averages for the other categories can be found in a similar manner. Table 3.7 summarizes the results.

TABLE 3.7 Average Amount Spent (in $) by Females versus Males

Sex	Clothing	Health	Tech	Misc
Female	225.67	100.25	47.10	159.88
Male	97.93	100.64	310.97	85.84

Using R:

a. Import the ***Online*** data file into a data frame (table) and label it myData.

b. The **tapply** function is useful for finding means (or standard deviations—discussed in Section 3.4) of subgroups. The input for the function is 1) the outcome variable, 2) the categorical variable, and 3) the function to be performed (mean or sd). In order to find the average amount that females and males spend on clothing, enter:

```
> tapply(myData$Clothing, myData$Sex, mean)
```

And R returns:

```
Female      Male
225.66667   97.93103
```

The averages for the other categories can be found in a similar manner.

Summary:

Given the means for the two groups, the manager should target females for clothing and miscellaneous products and males for technology products. Because females and males spend approximately the same on health products, the manager need not differentiate this market.

The Weighted Mean

So far we have focused on applications where each observation of a variable contributed equally to the mean. The **weighted mean** is relevant when some observations contribute more than others. For example, a student is often evaluated on the basis of the weighted mean since the score on the final exam is typically worth more than the score on the midterm.

We might also want to calculate the mean from a frequency distribution. Recall from Chapter 2 that a frequency distribution groups the observations into non-overlapping intervals and records the number of observations in each interval. Because frequencies will likely differ for each interval, this difference will need to be incorporated into the mean.

MEASURE OF CENTRAL LOCATION: THE WEIGHTED MEAN

Let $w_1, w_2, \ldots, w_n$ denote the weights of the sample observations $x_1, x_2, \ldots, x_n$ such that $w_1 + w_2 + \cdots + w_n = 1$. The weighted mean for the sample is computed as

$$\bar{x} = \Sigma\, w_i x_i, \text{ for } i = 1, \ldots, n.$$

For a frequency distribution, we substitute the relative frequency of the ith interval for w_i, and the midpoint of the ith interval for x_i. The weighted mean for the population is computed similarly.

EXAMPLE 3.8

A student scores 60 on Exam 1, 70 on Exam 2, and 80 on Exam 3. What is the student's average score for the course if Exams 1, 2, and 3 are worth 25%, 25%, and 50% of the grade, respectively?

SOLUTION: We define the weights as $w_1 = 0.25$, $w_2 = 0.25$, and $w_3 = 0.50$. We compute the average score as $\bar{x} = \Sigma\, w_i x_i = 0.25(60) + 0.25(70) + 0.50(80) = 72.50$. Note that the unweighted mean is only 70 because it does not incorporate the higher weight given to the score on Exam 3.

EXAMPLE 3.9

In Chapter 2, we constructed a frequency distribution to summarize house prices (in \$1,000s) in Punta Gorda, Florida. Table 3.8 shows this frequency distribution. Calculate the mean house price.

TABLE 3.8 Frequency Distribution for Price

Interval (in \$1,000s)	Frequency	Relative Frequency
$100 < x \leq 200$	9	0.225
$200 < x \leq 300$	16	0.400
$300 < x \leq 400$	8	0.200
$400 < x \leq 500$	4	0.100
$500 < x \leq 600$	2	0.050
$600 < x \leq 700$	1	0.025

SOLUTION: In order to calculate the mean from a frequency distribution, we first calculate the midpoint, m_i, for each interval. The first interval is $100 < x \leq 200$, so its midpoint, m_1, equals $\frac{100 + 200}{2} = 150$. The midpoints for the other intervals are found in a similar manner.

We then use the relative frequency for each interval as its respective weight. So, the weight for the first interval is defined as $w_1 = 0.225$. The weights for the other intervals are defined in a similar manner. We compute the mean price as

$$\bar{x} = \Sigma w_i m_i = 0.225(150) + 0.400(250) + \cdots + 0.025(650) = 292.5.$$

Based on the frequency distribution of 40 houses, the mean price of houses in Punta Gorda, Florida is \$292,500.

EXERCISES 3.1

Mechanics

1. Given the following observations from a sample, calculate the mean, the median, and the mode.

8	10	9	12	12

2. Given the following observations from a sample, calculate the mean, the median, and the mode.

−4	0	−6	1	−3	−4

3. Given the following observations from a population, calculate the mean, the median, and the mode.

150	257	55	110	110	43	201	125	55

4. Given the following observations from a population, calculate the mean, the median, and the mode.

20	15	25	20	10	15	25	20	15

Applications

5. **FILE** ***Houses.*** The following table shows a portion of the sale price (in \$1,000s) for 36 homes sold in a suburb outside Chicago, Illinois. Find the mean and median sale price.

Number	Price
1	430
2	520
⋮	⋮
36	430

6. **FILE** ***Gas_Prices.*** The following table shows a portion of the average price of gas (in \$ per gallon) for the 50 states in the United States. Find the mean and the median price.

State	Price
Alaska	3.09
Alabama	1.94
⋮	⋮
Wyoming	2.59

7. **FILE** ***Life_Expectancy.*** The following table shows a portion of U.S. life expectancy (in years) for the 50 states. Find the mean and median life expectancy.

Rank	State	Life Expectancy
1	Hawaii	81.5
2	Alaska	80.9
⋮	⋮	⋮
50	Mississippi	74.8

8. **FILE** ***Prime.*** Amazon Prime is a service that gives the company's customers free two-day shipping and discounted rates on overnight delivery. Prime customers also get other perks, such as free e-books. The accompanying table shows a portion of the annual expenditures (in $) for 100 Prime customers. Find the mean and the median for annual expenditures.

Customer	Expenditures
1	1272
2	1089
⋮	⋮
100	1389

9. **FILE** ***Fitness.*** A survey of 417 individuals asks questions about how often they exercise, marital status, and annual income. The accompanying table shows a portion their responses.

ID	Exercise	Married	Income
1	Always	Yes	106299
2	Sometimes	Yes	86570
⋮	⋮	⋮	⋮
417	Often	No	92690

a. Find the mean and the median for Income.
b. Find the mean income for married individuals and the mean income for non-married individuals. Which subgroup earns more?
c. Find the mean income for individuals who always exercise and the mean income for individuals who never exercise. Which subgroup earns more?

10. **FILE** ***Spend.*** A survey of 500 individuals asks questions about home ownership (OwnHome: Yes/No), car ownership (OwnCar: Yes/No), annual household spending on food (Food), and annual household spending on travel (Travel). A portion of their responses is shown in the accompanying table.

ID	Own Home	OwnCar	Food	Travel
1	Yes	Yes	5472.43	827.40
2	No	Yes	9130.73	863.55
⋮	⋮	⋮	⋮	⋮
500	No	No	6205.97	3667.50

a. Find the mean for Food and Travel.
b. Find the mean amount spent on food for homeowners versus non-homeowners. Which subgroup spends more?
c. Find the mean amount spent on travel for homeowners versus non-homeowners. Which subgroup spends more?

11. You score 90 on the midterm, 60 on the final, and 80 on the class project. What is your average score if the midterm is worth 30%, the final is worth 50%, and the class project is worth 20%?

12. Over the past year, an investor bought common stock of Corporation A on three occasions at the following prices.

Date	Price Per Share	Number of Shares
January	19.58	70
July	24.06	80
December	29.54	50

Calculate the average price per share at which the investor bought these shares.

13. Over the past year, an investor bought common stock of Firm A on three occasions at the following prices.

Date	Price Per Share
January	94.81
July	102.67
December	115.32

a. What is the average price per share if the investor had bought 100 shares in January, 60 in July, and 40 in December?
b. What is the average price per share if the investor had bought 40 shares in January, 60 in July, and 100 in December?

14. A local hospital provided the following relative frequency distribution summarizing the weights of babies (in pounds) delivered over the month of January. Calculate the average weight.

Weight (in pounds)	Relative Frequency
$2 < x \leq 4$	0.04
$4 < x \leq 6$	0.11
$6 < x \leq 8$	0.36
$8 < x \leq 10$	0.43
$10 < x \leq 12$	0.06

15. Fifty cities provided information on vacancy rates (in %) for local apartments in the following relative frequency distribution. Calculate the average vacancy rate.

Vacancy Rate (in %)	Relative Frequency
$0 < x \leq 3$	0.10
$3 < x \leq 6$	0.10
$6 < x \leq 9$	0.20
$9 < x \leq 12$	0.40
$12 < x \leq 15$	0.20

3.2 PERCENTILES AND BOXPLOTS

LO 3.2

Interpret a percentile and a boxplot.

As discussed in Section 3.1, the median is a measure of central location that divides the observations for a variable in half; that is, half of the observations fall below the median and half fall above the median. The median is also called the 50th percentile. In many instances, we are interested in a percentile other than the 50th percentile. Here we discuss calculating and interpreting percentiles. In addition, we construct a boxplot, which is a visual representation of particular percentiles. It also helps us identify outliers and skewness in the distribution of a variable.

A Percentile

In general, the pth **percentile** divides a variable into two parts: 1) approximately p percent of the observations are less than the pth percentile, and 2) approximately $(100 - p)$ percent of the observations are greater than the pth percentile. Technically, a percentile is a measure of location, however, it is also used as a measure of relative position because it is so easy to interpret.

For example, suppose you obtained a raw score of 650 on the math portion of the SAT. It may not be readily apparent how you did relative to other students that took the same test. However, if you know that the raw score corresponds to the 75th percentile, then you know that approximately 75% of students had scores lower than your score and approximately 25% of students had scores higher than your score.

> A PERCENTILE
>
> In general, the pth percentile divides a data set into two parts:
>
> - Approximately p percent of the observations have values less than the pth percentile.
> - Approximately $(100 - p)$ percent of the observations have values greater than the pth percentile.

When we calculate the 25th, the 50th, and the 75th percentiles for a variable, we have effectively divided it into four equal parts, or quarters. Thus, the 25th percentile is also referred to as the first quartile or Q1, the 50th percentile is referred to as the second quartile or Q2, and the 75th percentile is referred to as the third quartile or Q3. These quartiles are the most commonly used percentiles.

It really only makes sense to calculate percentiles for larger data sets. For this reason, we tend to rely on software packages, like Excel or R, to make the calculations for us. Software packages often use different algorithms to calculate percentiles; however, with larger sample sizes, the differences, if any, tend to be negligible.

A common way to report descriptive measures for a variable is to use a five-number summary. A five-number summary shows the minimum value, the quartiles, and the maximum value for a variable. Consider the following example.

EXAMPLE 3.10

Use Excel and R to find the five-number summary for the Growth and Value variables from the introductory case.

FILE *Growth_Value*

SOLUTION:

Using Excel:

a. Open the ***Growth_Value*** data file.

b. We use the MIN and MAX functions to find the minimum and maximum values for a variable. For Growth we enter =MIN(B2:B37) for the minimum value and =MAX(B2:B37) for the maximum value. Similar entries are made for Value except we substitute C2:C37 for B2:B37. Table 3.9 reports the results.

c. We use the PERCENTILE.INC function to find the pth percentile in Excel. The first entry is the range of observations and the second entry is the percentile entered as a proportion. For the 25th percentile for Growth we enter =PERCENTILE.INC(B2:B37, 0.25). The 50th and the 75th percentiles are found by entering 0.50 and 0.75, respectively, for the second entry. Similar entries are made for Value except we substitute C2:C37 for B2:B37. Table 3.9 reports the results.

TABLE 3.9 Five-number Summary for Growth and Value

	Min	Q1	Q2	Q3	Max
Growth	−40.90	2.86	15.25	36.97	79.48
Value	−46.52	1.70	15.38	22.44	44.08

USING R:

a. Import the ***Growth_Value*** data file into a data frame (table) and label it myData.

b. The easiest way to find a five-number summary for a variable is to use R's **summary** function that we discussed in Section 3.1. Enter:

```
> summary(myData)
```

And R returns the values found in Table 3.9.

c. If we want to find a percentile other than a quartile, we can use R's **quantile** function. For example, in order to find the 30th percentile for Growth, enter

```
> quantile(myData$Growth,0.30)
```

And R returns: `6.92`

`30%`

A Boxplot

A boxplot, also referred to as a box-and-whisker plot, is a convenient way to graphically display the five-number summary of a variable. In general, a boxplot is constructed as follows.

a. Plot the five-number summary values in ascending order on the horizontal axis.

b. Draw a box encompassing the first and third quartiles.

c. Draw a dashed vertical line in the box at the median.

d. To determine if a given observation is an outlier, first calculate the difference between Q3 and Q1. This difference is called the **interquartile range** or IQR. Therefore, the length of the box is equal to the IQR and the span of the box contains the middle half of the observations. Draw a line ("whisker") that extends from Q1 to the minimum value that is not farther than 1.5 × IQR from Q1. Similarly, draw a line that extends from Q3 to the maximum value that is not farther than 1.5 × IQR from Q3.

e. Use an asterisk (or other symbol) to indicate points that are farther than 1.5 × IQR from the box. These observations are considered outliers.

Unfortunately, Excel does not provide a simple and straightforward way to construct a boxplot; however, R and most other statistical software packages do offer this option. We will show how to construct a boxplot in R shortly.

Consider the boxplot in Figure 3.2. The left whisker extends from Q1 to the minimum value (Min) because Min is not farther than 1.5 × IQR from Q1. The right whisker, on the other hand, does not extend from Q3 to the maximum value (Max) because there is an observation that is farther than 1.5 × IQR from Q3. The asterisk indicates that this observation is considered an outlier.

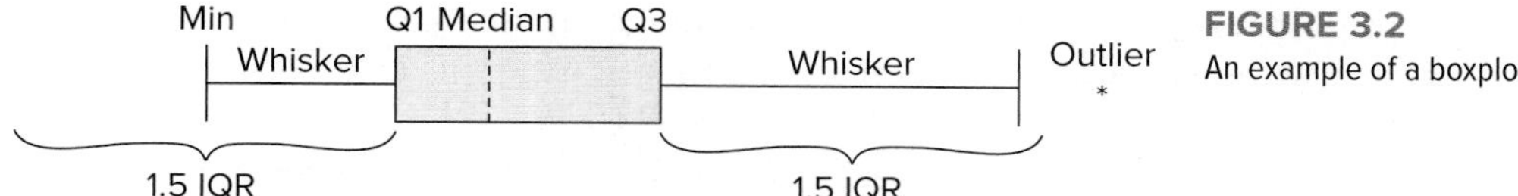

FIGURE 3.2 An example of a boxplot

A boxplot is also used to informally gauge the shape of the distribution. Symmetry is implied if the median is in the center of the box and the left and right whiskers are equidistant from their respective quartiles. If the median is left of center and the right whisker is longer than the left whisker, then the distribution is positively skewed.

Similarly, if the median is right of center and the left whisker is longer than the right whisker, then the distribution is negatively skewed. If outliers exist, we need to include them when comparing the lengths of the left and right whiskers.

From Figure 3.2, we note that the median is located to the left of center and that an outlier exists on the right side. Here the right whisker is longer than the left whisker, and if the outlier is included, then the right whisker becomes even longer. This indicates that the underlying distribution is positively skewed.

EXAMPLE 3.11

FILE *Growth_Value*

Use the five-point summaries for Growth and Value reported in Table 3.9 to answer parts a and b.

a. Find the interquartile range (IQR) for Growth. Determine whether any outliers exist. Repeat for Value.

b. Is the distribution for Growth symmetric? If not, comment on its skewness. Repeat for Value.

c. Use R to construct boxplots for Growth and Value. Are the results consistent with the findings in parts a and b? Explain.

SOLUTION:

a. For Growth:

We first calculate IQR = Q3 − Q1 = 36.97 − 2.86 = 34.11, and then we calculate the limit as 1.5 × IQR = 1.5 × 34.11 = 51.17. We find distances from Q1 − Min = 2.86 − (−40.90) = 43.76 (left whisker) and Max − Q3 = 79.48 − 36.97 = 42.51 (right whisker). Because both distances are less than 51.17, there are no outliers in the distribution.

For Value:

We first calculate IQR = Q3 − Q1 = 22.44 − 1.70 = 20.74, and then we calculate the limit as 1.5 × IQR = 1.5 × 20.74 = 31.11. We find distances from Q1 − Min = 1.70 − (−46.52) = 48.22 (left whisker) and Max − Q3 = 44.08 − 22.44 = 21.64 (right whisker). There is an outlier(s) on the left side of the distribution because the distance between Q1 and Min exceeds the limit (48.22 > 31.11).

b. For Growth:

For symmetry, we first find if the median is in the center of IQR. We calculate Median − Q1 = 15.25 − 2.86 = 12.39 and then we calculate Q3 − Median = 36.97 − 15.25 = 21.72. Because 12.39 < 21.72, the median is left of center. Next we compare the lengths of the left and right whiskers. The left whisker is slightly longer than the right whisker (43.76 > 42.51). Because the median is left of center and the left whisker is slightly longer than the right whisker, the skewness of the distribution is not clear using this method.

From the skewness coefficient (shown in Table 3.4), we find that the distribution is very slightly negatively skewed.

For Value:

It is negatively skewed because: (1) the median falls right of center in the interquartile range (Median – Q1 = 13.68 > 7.06 = Q3 – Median) and (2) the left whisker is longer than the right whisker (48.22 > 21.64).

c. We follow these steps to construct a boxplot in R.

  i. Import the ***Growth_Value*** data file into a data frame (table) and label it myData.

  ii. We use the **boxplot** function. For options within the function, we use *main* to provide a title, *xlab* to label the x-axis, *names* to label each variable, *horizontal* to construct a horizontal boxplot (as opposed to a vertical boxplot), and *col* to give color to the IQR portion. Enter:

```
> boxplot(myData$Growth, myData$Value, main= "Boxplots for Growth
and Value", xlab="Annual Returns, 1984-2019 (in percent)", names
=c("Growth","Value"), horizontal = TRUE, col="gold")
```

Figure 3.3 shows the output that R returns.

FIGURE 3.3 Boxplots for Growth and Value

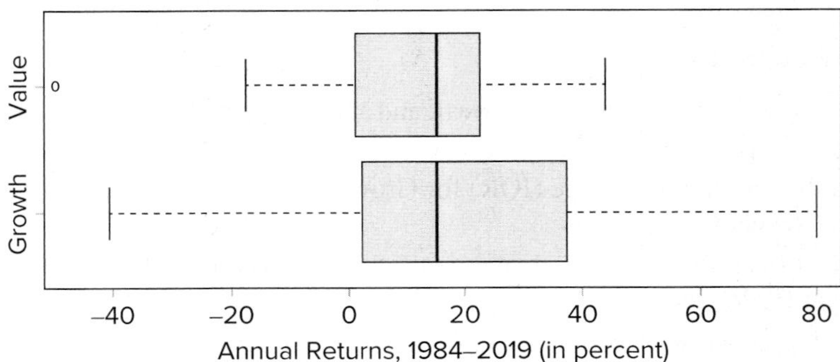

The boxplots for Growth and Value are consistent with the findings in parts a and b. For Growth, there are no outliers. The median for Growth, indicated by the bold and wider vertical line, is left of center. The left and right whiskers appear to be of similar length, so we cannot determine skewness from the boxplot. For Value, the outlier on the left-hand side of the distribution coupled with a median that falls to the right of center in the IQR box suggests that this distribution is negatively skewed.

EXERCISES 3.2

Mechanics

16. **FILE** ***Exercise_3.16.*** The accompanying data file has three variables, x_1, x_2, x_3. Calculate the 25th, 50th, and 75th percentiles for x_1. [Note: If you are using Excel to calculate percentiles, use the PERCENTILE.INC function.]

17. **FILE** ***Exercise_3.17.*** The accompanying data file has three variables, x_1, x_2, x_3.
    a. Calculate the 25th, 50th, and 75th percentiles for x_2. [Note: If you are using Excel to calculate percentiles, use the PERCENTILE.INC function.]
    b. Calculate the 20th and 80th percentiles for x_3. [Note: If you are using Excel to calculate percentiles, use the PERCENTILE.INC function.]

18. Consider the following boxplot.

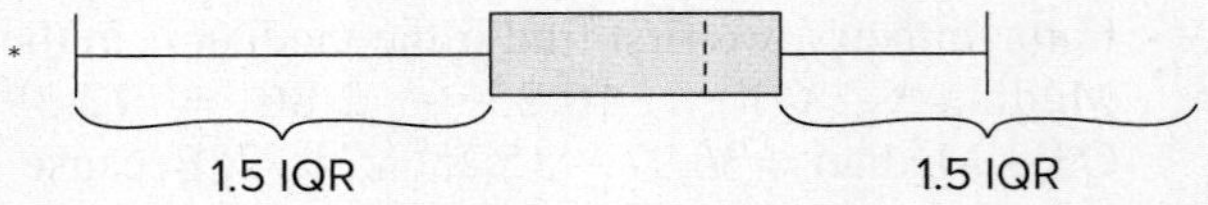

    a. Does the boxplot indicate possible outliers in the data?
    b. Comment on the skewness of the underlying distribution.

19. Consider the following boxplot.

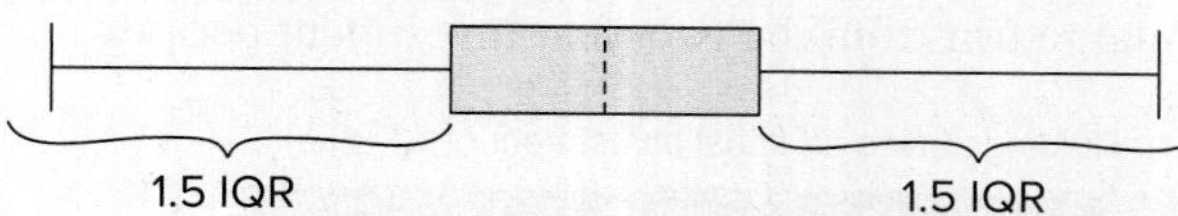

a. Does the boxplot indicate possible outliers in the data?
b. Comment on the skewness of the underlying distribution.

20. Using 500 observations, the following five-point summary was obtained for a variable.

Min	Q1	Median	Q3	Max
125	200	300	550	1300

a. Interpret Q1 and Q3.
b. Calculate the interquartile range. Determine whether any outliers exist.
c. Is the distribution symmetric? If not, comment on its skewness.

21. Using 200 observations, the following five-point summary was obtained for a variable.

Min	Q1	Median	Q3	Max
34	54	66	78	98

a. Interpret Q1 and Q3.
b. Calculate the interquartile range. Determine whether any outliers exist.
c. Is the distribution symmetric? If not, comment on its skewness.

Applications

22. FILE ***MPG.*** The data accompanying this exercise show miles per gallon (MPG) for a sample of 50 cars.
a. Calculate and interpret the 25th, 50th, and 75th percentiles. [Note: If you are using Excel to calculate percentiles, use the PERCENTILE.INC function.]
b. Calculate the interquartile range. Are there any outliers?

23. FILE ***Scores.*** The data accompanying this exercise show scores on the final in a statistics class of 40 students.
a. Calculate and interpret the 25th, 50th, and 75th percentiles. [Note: If you are using Excel to calculate percentiles, use the PERCENTILE.INC function.]
b. Calculate the interquartile range. Are there any outliers?
c. Is the distribution symmetric? If not, comment on its skewness.

24. FILE ***Census.*** The accompanying table shows a portion of median household income (Income in $) and median house value (House Value in $) for the 50 states.

State	Income	House Value
Alabama	42081	117600
Alaska	66521	229100
⋮	⋮	⋮
Wyoming	53802	174000

a. Construct a boxplot for household income and use it to identify outliers, if any, and comment on skewness.
b. Construct a boxplot for median house value and use it to identify outliers, if any, and comment on skewness.

25. FILE ***PE_Ratio.*** A price-earnings ratio or P/E ratio is calculated as a firm's share price compared to the income or profit earned by the firm per share. Generally, a high P/E ratio suggests that investors are expecting higher earnings growth in the future compared to firms with a lower P/E ratio. The accompanying table shows a portion of P/E ratios for 30 firms.

Firm	P/E Ratio
1	14
2	24
⋮	⋮
30	16

a. Calculate and interpret the 25th, 50th, and 75th percentiles. [Note: If you are using Excel to calculate percentiles, use the PERCENTILE.INC function.]
b. Construct a boxplot. Are there any outliers? Is the distribution symmetric? If not, comment on its skewness.

3.3 THE GEOMETRIC MEAN

LO 3.3

Calculate and interpret a geometric mean return and an average growth rate.

The **geometric mean** is a multiplicative average, as opposed to the arithmetic mean which is an additive average. In general, the geometric mean is smaller than the arithmetic mean and is less sensitive to outliers. It is also the relevant measure when evaluating investment returns over several years, as well as when calculating average growth rates.

The Geometric Mean Return

Suppose you invested $1,000 in a stock that had a 10% return in Year 1 and a −10% return in Year 2. The arithmetic mean suggests that by the end of Year 2, you would be right back where you started with $1,000 worth of stock. It is true that the arithmetic mean return over the two-year period is 0% ($\bar{x} = \frac{0.10 + (-0.10)}{2} = 0$); however, the arithmetic mean ignores the effects of compounding. As shown in Table 3.10 the value of your investment at the end of two years is \$990, a loss of \$10. The geometric mean return accurately captures a negative annual return from the two-year investment period.

TABLE 3.10 End of Year Holdings Given an Initial Investment of \$1,000

Year	Return %	Value at the End of Year
1	10	1,000 + 1,000×0.10 = 1,100
2	−10	1,100 + 1,100×(−0.10) = 990

THE GEOMETRIC MEAN RETURN

For multiperiod returns $R_1, R_2, \ldots, R_n$, the geometric mean return G_R is computed as

$$G_R = \sqrt[n]{(1 + R_1)\times(1 + R_2)\times \cdots \times(1 + R_n)} - 1,$$

where n is the number of multiperiod returns.

Let us revisit the above case where you invested \$1,000 in a stock that had a 10% return in Year 1 and a −10% return in Year 2. The geometric mean is computed as

$$G_R = \sqrt[2]{(1 + 0.10)\times(1 + (-0.10))} - 1 = (1.10\times 0.90)^{1/2} - 1 = -0.005, \text{ or } -0.5\%.$$

We interpret the geometric mean return as the annualized return that you will earn from a two-year investment period. Table 3.11 shows that with the computed annualized return of −0.5%, the end investment value is the same as shown in Table 3.10.

TABLE 3.11 End-of-Year Holdings Given an Initial Investment of \$1,000

Year	Annualized Return	Value at the End of Year
1	−0.5	1,000 + 1,000×(−0.005) = 995
2	−0.5	995 + 995×(−0.005) = 990

EXAMPLE 3.12

Growth_Value

Calculate the geometric mean returns for Growth and Value from the introductory case.

SOLUTION:

$$\text{Growth: } G_R = \sqrt[36]{(1 - 0.0550)\times(1 + 0.3991)\times \cdots \times(1 + 0.3842)} - 1$$
$$= (86.5350)^{1/36} - 1 = 0.1319, \text{ or } 13.19\%.$$
$$\text{Value: } G_R = \sqrt[36]{(1 - 0.0859)\times(1 + 0.2210)\times \cdots \times(1 + 0.3162)} - 1$$
$$= (34.6264)^{1/36} - 1 = 0.1035, \text{ or } 10.35\%.$$

Therefore, for the 36-year period, the annualized return for Growth is higher than that of Value, 13.19% > 10.35%.

Arithmetic Mean versus Geometric Mean

An issue that begs for explanation is the relevance of the arithmetic mean and the geometric mean as summary measures for financial returns. Both means are relevant descriptive measures for annual return; however, each has a different interpretation. The arithmetic mean is appropriate for analyzing a one-year investment, whereas the geometric mean is appropriate for analyzing a multiyear investment. For Growth, the arithmetic mean return of 15.755% is the average annual return for summarizing returns with an investment horizon of one year. Its geometric mean return of 13.19% is the average annual return when the investment horizon is 36 years. For illustration, we can think of the arithmetic mean return as the relevant metric for an investor who is saving/investing to buy a house in about a year's time. The geometric mean return is the relevant metric for an investor who is saving for retirement.

The Average Growth Rate

We also use the geometric mean when we calculate an **average growth rate.**

THE AVERAGE GROWTH RATE

For growth rates $g_1, g_2, \ldots, g_n$, the average growth rate G_g is computed as:

$$G_g = \sqrt[n]{(1+g_1)\times(1+g_2)\times\cdots\times(1+g_n)} - 1$$

where n is the number of multiperiod growth rates.

EXAMPLE 3.13

Table 3.12 shows sales for a multinational corporation (in millions of €) over the past five years.

TABLE 3.12 Sales for a multinational corporation (in millions of €)

Year	1	2	3	4	5
Sales	13,322	14,883	14,203	14,534	16,915

Calculate the growth rates for Year 1–Year 2, Year 2–Year 3, Year 3–Year 4, and Year 4–Year 5 and use them to compute the average growth rate.

SOLUTION: The growth rates for four years are computed as:

- Year 1–Year 2: $\frac{14{,}883 - 13{,}322}{13{,}322} = 0.1172$
- Year 2–Year 3: $\frac{14{,}203 - 14{,}883}{14{,}883} = -0.0457$
- Year 3–Year 4: $\frac{14{,}534 - 14{,}203}{14{,}203} = 0.0233$
- Year 4–Year 5: $\frac{16{,}915 - 14{,}534}{14{,}534} = 0.1638$

Therefore,

$$G_g = \sqrt[n]{(1+0.1172)\times(1-0.0457)\times(1+0.0233)\times(1+0.1638)} - 1$$
$$= 1.2697^{1/4} - 1 = 0.0615, \text{ or } 6.15\%.$$

Sales over the past five years had an average growth rate of 6.15% per year.

There is a simpler way to compute the average growth rate when the underlying values of the series are given. In the above example, it is cumbersome to first calculate the relevant growth rates and then use them to compute the average growth rate.

AN ALTERNATIVE FORMULA FOR THE AVERAGE GROWTH RATE

For observations $x_1, x_2, \ldots, x_n$, the average growth rate G_g is computed as

$$G_g = \sqrt[n-1]{\frac{x_n}{x_{n-1}} \times \frac{x_{n-1}}{x_{n-2}} \times \frac{x_{n-2}}{x_{n-3}} \times \cdots \times \frac{x_2}{x_1}} - 1 = \sqrt[n-1]{\frac{x_n}{x_1}} - 1,$$

where $n - 1$ is the number of distinct growth rates. Note that only the first and last observations are needed in the time series due to cancellations in the formula.

EXAMPLE 3.14

Calculate the average growth rate for the multinational corporation directly from the sales data in Table 3.12.

SOLUTION: Using the first and last observations from the time series consisting of five observations, we calculate

$$G_g = \sqrt[n-1]{\frac{x_n}{x_1}} - 1 = \sqrt[5-1]{\frac{16{,}915}{13{,}322}} - 1 = 1.2697^{1/4} - 1 = 0.0615, \text{ or } 6.15\%,$$

which is the same as in Example 3.13.

EXERCISES 3.3

Applications

26. Given the following investment returns, calculate the geometric mean return.

4%	8%	−5%	6%

27. Given the following investment returns, calculate the geometric mean return.

−3%	2%	−5%	2.7%	3.1%

28. The returns for a pharmaceutical firm are 10% in Year 1, 5% in Year 2, and −15% in Year 3. What is the annualized return for the period?

29. The returns from an investment are 2% in Year 1, 5% in Year 2, and 1.8% in the first half of Year 3. Calculate the annualized return for the entire period.

30. The returns for an auto firm are 5% in Year 1 and 3% in the first quarter of Year 2. Calculate the annualized return for the period.

31. Consider the following observations for a time series:

Year 1	Year 2	Year 3	Year 4
90	110	150	160

   a. Calculate the growth rates for Year 1–Year 2, Year 2–Year 3, and Year 3–Year 4.
   b. Calculate the average growth rate.

32. Consider the following observations for a time series:

Year 1	Year 2	Year 3	Year 4
1,200	1,280	1,380	1,520

   a. Calculate the growth rates for Year 1–Year 2, Year 2–Year 3, and Year 3–Year 4.
   b. Calculate the average growth rate.

33. Calculate the average growth rate from the following growth rates.

2.5%	3.6%	1.8%	2.2%	5.2%

34. Suppose at the beginning of Year 1 you decide to invest \$1,000 in a mutual fund. The following table shows the returns (in %) for the past four years.

Year	Annual Return
1	17.3
2	19.6
3	6.8
4	8.2

   a. Calculate and interpret the arithmetic mean return.
   b. Calculate and interpret the geometric mean return.
   c. How much money would you have accumulated by the end of Year 4?

35. The following table shows the total revenue (in $ billions) for two retailers over the past three years.

Year	Retailer 1	Retailer 2
1	77.35	48.28
2	71.29	48.23
3	66.18	47.22

a. Calculate the growth rate for Year 1–Year 2 and Year 2–Year 3 for each retailer.
b. Calculate the average growth rate for each retailer.

36. Suppose at the beginning of Year 1 you decide to invest $20,000 in a mutual fund. The following table shows the returns (in %) for the past five years.

Year	Annual Return
1	19.5
2	8.9
3	−6.0
4	−10.5
5	5.9

a. Calculate and interpret the arithmetic mean return.
b. Calculate and interpret the geometric mean return.
c. How much money would you have accumulated by the end of Year 5?

37. The following table shows the total revenue (in $ billions) for two retailers over the past three years.

Year	1	2	3
Retailer 1	379.8	404.3	408.2
Retailer 2	63.4	65.0	65.3

a. Calculate the average growth rate for each firm.
b. Which firm had the higher growth rate over the three-year period?

38. The following table shows sales for a multinational corporation (in $ millions) for the past five years.

Year	1	2	3	4	5
Sales	20,117	23,331	25,313	27,799	30,601

a. Use the growth rates for Year 1–Year 2, Year 2–Year 3, Year 3–Year 4, and Year 4–Year 5 to calculate the average growth rate.
b. Calculate the average growth rate directly from sales.

3.4 MEASURES OF DISPERSION

LO 3.4

Calculate and interpret measures of dispersion.

In Section 3.1, we focused on measures of central location in an attempt to find a typical or central value that describes a variable. It is also important to analyze how the observations vary around the center. Recall from the introductory case that the average returns for the Growth and Value mutual funds were 15.755% and 12.005%, respectively. As an investor, you might ask why anyone would put money in Value when, on average, this fund has a lower return. It turns out that the average is not sufficient when summarizing a variable. The average fails to describe the underlying variability of the variable.

We now discuss several measures of dispersion that gauge the variability of a variable. Each measure is a numerical value that equals zero if all observations are identical, and increases as the observations become more diverse. In addition to outlining how these measures of dispersion are calculated manually, we also provide instructions for obtaining these results in Excel and R. Recall that Table 3.3 in Section 3.1 provides function names for all summary measures discussed in this chapter.

The Range

The **range** is the simplest measure of dispersion; it is the difference between the maximum value and the minimum value in a sample or a population.

MEASURE OF DISPERSION: THE RANGE

The range is calculated by taking the difference between the maximum value (Max) and minimum value (Min) in a sample or a population.

$$\text{Range} = \text{Max} - \text{Min}$$

EXAMPLE 3.15

Using Excel and R, find the range for Growth and Value. What do your answers suggest?

FILE
Growth_Value

SOLUTION:

Using Excel:

a. Open the ***Growth_Value*** data file.

b. We use the MIN and MAX functions to find the range for a variable. For Growth we enter `=MAX(B2:B37)-MIN(B2:B37)` and Excel returns 120.38. For Value we enter `=MAX(C2:C37)-MIN(C2:C37)` and Excel returns 90.6.

Note too that the Descriptive Statistics option in Excel's Analysis Toolpak also reports the range for a variable.

Using R:

a. Import the ***Growth_Value*** data file into a data frame (table) and label it myData.

b. We use the **range** function. Enter:

```
> range(myData$Growth)
> range(myData$Value)
```

Verify that the range for Growth is 120.38 and the range for value is 90.6.

Summary:

Growth's range is greater than Value's range (120.38 > 90.6), which implies a greater distance between the minimum and maximum values for Growth.

The range is not considered a good measure of dispersion because it focuses solely on the extreme values and ignores every other observation in the sample or the population. While the interquartile range, IQR = Q3 − Q1, discussed in Section 3.2, does not depend on extreme values, this measure still does not incorporate all the observations.

The Mean Absolute Deviation

A good measure of dispersion should consider differences of all observations from the mean. If we simply average all differences from the mean, the positives and the negatives will cancel out, even though they both contribute to dispersion, and the resulting average will equal zero. The **mean absolute deviation** (MAD) is an average of the absolute differences between the observations and the mean.

MEASURE OF DISPERSION: THE MEAN ABSOLUTE DEVIATION (MAD)

For sample observations, $x_1, x_2, \ldots, x_n$, the sample MAD is computed as

$$\text{Sample MAD} = \frac{\Sigma|x_i - \bar{x}|}{n}.$$

For population observations, $x_1, x_2, \ldots, x_N$, the population MAD is computed as

$$\text{Population MAD} = \frac{\Sigma|x_i - \mu|}{N}.$$

EXAMPLE 3.16

Using Excel and R, find the mean absolute deviation (MAD) for Growth and Value. What do your answers suggest?

FILE *Growth_Value*

SOLUTION: We first outline how to calculate MAD manually. Recall from Example 3.1 that the sample mean for Growth is $\bar{x} = 15.755$ and the sample mean for Value is $\bar{x} = 12.005$. We calculate MAD for each variable as follows:

Growth:

$$\text{MAD} = \frac{\Sigma|x_i - \bar{x}|}{n} = \frac{|-5.50 - 15.755| + |39.91 - 15.755| + \cdots + |38.42 - 15.755|}{36}$$
$$= \frac{629.66}{36} = 17.491$$

Value:

$$\text{MAD} = \frac{\Sigma|x_i - \bar{x}|}{n} = \frac{|-8.59 - 12.005| + |22.10 - 12.005| + \cdots + |31.62 - 12.005|}{36}$$
$$= \frac{492}{36} = 13.667$$

Using Excel:

a. Open the ***Growth_Value*** data file.

b. We use the AVEDEV function to find MAD for a variable. For Growth we enter `=AVEDEV(B2:B37)`, and for Value we enter `=AVEDEV(C2:C37)`. Verify that you obtain the same values that were obtained manually.

Using R:

a. Import the ***Growth_Value*** data file into a data frame (table) and label it myData.

b. The **mad** function in R finds median absolute deviation rather than mean absolute deviation. In order to obtain the results that use the mean instead of the median in the formula for MAD, enter

```
> mean(abs(myData$Growth-mean(myData$Growth)))
> mean(abs(myData$Value-mean(myData$Value)))
```

Verify that you obtain the same values that were obtained manually.

Summary:
Growth's MAD is greater than Value's MAD (17.491 > 13.667), which implies that the observations are more dispersed for Growth.

The Variance and the Standard Deviation

The **variance** and the **standard deviation** are the two most widely used measures of dispersion. Instead of calculating the average of the absolute differences from the mean, as in MAD, we calculate the average of the squared differences from the mean. The squaring of differences from the mean emphasizes larger differences more than smaller ones; MAD weighs large and small differences equally.

The variance is defined as the average of the squared differences between the observations and the mean. The formula for the variance differs depending on whether we have a sample or a population. Also, whatever the units of the original variable, the variance has squared units. In order to return to the original units of measurement, we take the positive square root of variance, which gives us the standard deviation.

MEASURES OF DISPERSION: THE VARIANCE AND THE STANDARD DEVIATION

For sample observations $x_1, x_2, \ldots, x_n$, the sample variance s^2 and the sample standard deviation s are computed as

$$s^2 = \frac{\Sigma(x_i - \bar{x})^2}{n-1} \quad \text{and} \quad s = \sqrt{s^2}.$$

For population observations $x_1, x_2, \ldots, x_N$, the population variance σ^2 (the Greek letter sigma, squared) and the population standard deviation σ are computed as

$$\sigma^2 = \frac{\Sigma(x_i - \mu)^2}{N} \quad \text{and} \quad \sigma = \sqrt{\sigma^2}.$$

Note: The sample variance uses $n - 1$ rather than n in the denominator to ensure that the sample variance is an unbiased estimator for the population variance. The concept of an unbiased estimator is discussed in Appendix 7.2.

EXAMPLE 3.17

Using Excel and R, find the variance and the standard deviation for Growth and Value. Express the answers in the correct units of measurement. What do your answers suggest?

FILE
Growth_Value

SOLUTION: We first outline how to calculate the variance and the standard deviation manually. Recall from Example 3.1 that the sample mean for Growth is $\bar{x} = 15.755$ and the sample mean for Value is $\bar{x} = 12.005$. We calculate the variance and the standard deviation for each variable as follows:

Growth:

$$s^2 = \frac{\Sigma(x_i - \bar{x})^2}{n-1} = \frac{(-5.50 - 15.755)^2 + (39.91 - 15.755)^2 + \cdots + (38.42 - 15.755)^2}{36-1}$$

$$= \frac{19{,}824.21}{35} = 566.406(\%^2)$$

$$s = \sqrt{s^2} = \sqrt{566.406} = 23.799(\%)$$

Value:

$$s^2 = \frac{\Sigma(x_i - \bar{x})^2}{n-1} = \frac{(-8.59 - 12.005)^2 + (22.10 - 12.005)^2 + \cdots + (31.62 - 12.005)^2}{36-1}$$

$$= \frac{11{,}313.79}{35} = 323.251(\%^2)$$

$$s = \sqrt{s^2} = \sqrt{323.251} = 17.979(\%)$$

Using Excel:

a. Open the ***Growth_Value*** data file.

b. We use the VAR.S function and the STDEV.S function to find a variable's sample variance and sample standard deviation, respectively. (We use the VAR.P function and the STDEV.P function to find a variable's population variance and population standard deviation, respectively.) For Growth we enter =VAR.S(B2:B37) and =STDEV.S(B2:B37), and for Value we enter =VAR.S(C2:C37) and =STDEV.S(C2:C37). Verify that you obtain the same values that were obtained manually.

Using R:

a. Import the ***Growth_Value*** data file into a data frame (table) and label it myData.

b. We use the **var** function and the **sd** function to find a variable's sample variance and sample standard deviation, respectively. Enter:

```
> var(myData$Growth)
> sd(myData$Growth)
> var(myData$Value)
> sd(myData$Value)
```

Verify that you obtain the same values that were obtained manually.

Summary:
Growth's variance and standard deviation are greater than Value's variance and standard deviation, which implies that the observations are more dispersed for Growth. With financial data, standard deviation tends to be the most common measure of risk. Therefore, the investment risk of Growth is higher than that of Value over this time period.

The Coefficient of Variation

In some instances, analysis entails comparing the variability of two or more variables that have different means or units of measurement. The **coefficient of variation (CV)** serves as a relative measure of dispersion and adjusts for differences in the magnitudes of the means. Calculated by dividing a variable's standard deviation by its mean, CV is a unitless measure that allows for direct comparisons of mean-adjusted dispersion across different data sets.

MEASURE OF DISPERSION: THE COEFFICIENT OF VARIATION (CV)

The coefficient of variation (CV) for a variable is calculated by dividing its standard deviation by its mean.
For a sample, CV $= s/\bar{x}$.
For a population, CV $= \sigma/\mu$.

EXAMPLE 3.18

Use the information from Example 3.17 to calculate and interpret the coefficient of variation for Growth and Value.

SOLUTION: We use the sample means and the sample standard deviations to calculate CV for the two variables as

Growth: CV $= s/\bar{x} = 23.799/15.755 = 1.511$

Value: CV $= s/\bar{x} = 17.979/12.005 = 1.498$

The coefficient of variation indicates that the relative dispersion of the two variables is about the same.

EXERCISES 3.4

Mechanics

39. Consider the following population data:

34	42	12	10	22

a. Calculate the range.
b. Calculate MAD.
c. Calculate the population variance.
d. Calculate the population standard deviation.

40. Consider the following population data:

0	−4	2	−8	10

a. Calculate the range.
b. Calculate MAD.
c. Calculate the population variance.
d. Calculate the population standard deviation.

41. Consider the following sample data:

40	48	32	52	38	42

a. Calculate the range.
b. Calculate MAD.
c. Calculate the sample variance.
d. Calculate the sample standard deviation.

42. Consider the following sample data:

− 10	12	−8	−2	−6	8

a. Calculate the range.
b. Calculate MAD.
c. Calculate the sample variance and the sample standard deviation.

Applications

43. **FILE** ***Prime.*** The accompanying table shows a portion of the annual expenditures (in $) for 100 Prime customers.

Customer	Expenditures
1	1272
2	1089
⋮	⋮
100	1389

a. What were minimum expenditures? What were maximum expenditures?
b. Calculate the mean and the median expenditures.
c. Calculte the variance and the standard devation.

44. **FILE** ***StockPrices.*** Monthly closing stock prices for Firm A and Firm B are collected for the past five years. A portion of the data is shown in the accompanying table.

Observation	Firm A	Firm B
1	39.91	42.04
2	42.63	41.64
⋮	⋮	⋮
60	87.51	75.09

a. Calculate the sample variance and the sample standard deviation for each firm's stock price.
b. Which firm's stock price had greater variability as measured by the standard deviation?
c. Which firm's stock price had the greater relative dispersion?

45. **FILE** ***Rental.*** A real estate analyst examines the rental market in a college town. She gathers data on monthly rent and the square footage for 40 apartments. A portion of the data is shown in the accompanying table.

Monthly Rent	Square Footage
645	500
675	648
⋮	⋮
2,400	2,700

a. Calculate the mean and the standard deviation for monthly rent.
b. Calculate the mean and the standard deviation for square footage.
c. Which sample data exhibit greater relative dispersion?

46. **FILE** ***Revenues.*** The accompanying data file shows the annual revenues (in $ millions) for Corporation A and Corporation B for the past 13 years.
a. Calculate the coefficient of variation for Corporation A.
b. Calculate the coefficient of variation for Corporation B.
c. Which variable exhibits greater relative dispersion?

47. **FILE** ***Census.*** The accompanying data file shows, among other variables, median household income and median house value for the 50 states.
a. Calculate and discuss the range of household income and house value.
b. Calculate the sample MAD and the sample standard deviation of household income and house value.
c. Discuss why we cannot directly compare the sample MAD and the standard deviations of the two variables.

3.5 MEAN-VARIANCE ANALYSIS AND THE SHARPE RATIO

LO 3.5

Explain mean-variance analysis and the Sharpe ratio.

In the introduction to Section 3.4, we asked why any rational investor would invest in Value over Growth since the average return for Value over the time period was 12.005%, whereas the average return for Growth was 15.755%. It turns out that, in general, investments with higher returns also carry higher risk. The average return represents an investor's reward, whereas variance, or equivalently standard deviation, corresponds to risk.

According to mean-variance analysis, we can measure performance of any risky asset solely on the basis of the average and the variance of its returns.

MEAN-VARIANCE ANALYSIS

Mean-variance analysis postulates that the performance of an asset is measured by its rate of return, and this rate of return is evaluated in terms of its reward (mean) and risk (variance). In general, investments with higher average returns are also associated with higher risk.

Consider Table 3.13, which summarizes the returns for Growth and Value. It is true that an investment in Growth rather than Value provided an investor with a higher reward over this time period, as measured by the mean return. However, this same investor encountered more risk, as measured by the variance or the standard deviation.

TABLE 3.13 Mean-Variance Analysis for Growth and Value

Mutual Fund	Mean Return %	Variance %^{2}	Standard Deviation %
Growth	15.755	566.406	23.799
Value	12.005	323.251	17.979

A discussion of mean-variance analysis seems almost incomplete without mention of the **Sharpe ratio.** Nobel Laureate William Sharpe developed what he originally referred to as the "reward-to-variability" ratio. However, academics and finance professionals prefer to call it the "Sharpe ratio." The Sharpe ratio is used to characterize how well the return of an asset compensates for the risk that the investor takes. Investors are often advised to pick investments that have high Sharpe ratios.

The Sharpe ratio is defined with the reward specified in terms of the population mean and the variability specified in terms of the population standard deviation. However, we often compute the Sharpe ratio in terms of the sample mean and the sample standard deviation, where the return is usually expressed as a percent and not a decimal.

THE SHARPE RATIO

The Sharpe ratio measures the extra reward per unit of risk. The Sharpe ratio for an investment I is computed as

$$\frac{\bar{x}_I - \bar{R}_f}{s_I},$$

where $\bar{x}_I$ is the mean return for the investment, $\bar{R}_f$ is the mean return for a risk-free asset such as a Treasury bill (T-bill), and s_I is the standard deviation for the investment.

The numerator of the Sharpe ratio measures the extra reward that investors receive for the added risk taken—this difference is often called excess return. The higher the Sharpe ratio, the better the investment compensates its investors for risk.

EXAMPLE 3.19

Use the information in Table 3.13 to calculate and interpret the Sharpe ratios for Growth and Value given that the return on a 1-year T-bill is 2%.

SOLUTION Since the return on a 1-year T-bill is 2%, $\bar{R}_f = 2$. Plugging in the values of the relevant means and standard deviations into the Sharpe ratio yields

$$\text{Sharpe ratio for Growth: } \frac{\bar{x}_I - \bar{R}_f}{s_I} = \frac{15.755 - 2}{23.799} = 0.58.$$

$$\text{Sharpe ratio for Value: } \frac{\bar{x}_I - \bar{R}_f}{s_I} = \frac{12.005 - 2}{17.979} = 0.56.$$

We had earlier shown that Growth had a higher return, which is good, along with a higher variance, which is bad. We can use the Sharpe ratio to make a valid comparison between the mutual funds. Growth provides a higher Sharpe ratio than Value (0.58 > 0.56); therefore, the Growth offered more reward per unit of risk compared to Value.

SYNOPSIS OF INTRODUCTORY CASE

Growth and value are two fundamental styles in stock and mutual fund investing. Proponents of growth investing believe that companies that are growing faster than their peers are trendsetters and will be able to maintain their superior growth. By investing in the stocks of these companies, they expect their investment to grow at a rate faster than the overall stock market. By comparison, value investors focus on the stocks of companies that are trading at a discount relative to the overall market or a specific sector. Investors of value stocks believe that these stocks are undervalued and that their price will increase once their true value is recognized by other investors. The debate between growth and value investing is age-old, and which style dominates depends on the sample period used for the analysis.

Gladkikh/Getty Images

An analysis of annual return data for Fidelity's Growth Index mutual fund (Growth) and Fidelity's Value Index mutual fund (Value) for the years 1984 throuth 2019 provides important information for an investor trying to determine whether to invest in a growth mutual fund, a value mutual fund, or both types of mutual funds. Over this period, the mean return for Growth of 15.755% is greater than the mean return for Value of 12.005%. While the mean return typically represents the reward of investing, it does not incorporate the risk of investing.

Standard deviation tends to be the most common measure of risk with financial data. Since the standard deviation for Growth (23.799%) is greater than the standard deviation for Value (17.979%), Growth is likelier to have returns farther above and below its mean. Finally, given a risk-free rate of 2%, the Sharpe ratio for Growth is 0.58 compared to that for Value of 0.56, indicating that Growth provides more reward per unit of risk. Assuming that the behavior of these returns will continue, the investor will favor investing in Growth over Value. A commonly used disclaimer, however, states that past performance is no guarantee of future results.

EXERCISES 3.5

Mechanics

48. Consider the following data for two investments, A and B:

Investment A:	$x = 10\%$ and $s = 5\%$
Investment B:	$x = 15\%$ and $s = 10\%$

a. Which investment provides the higher return? Which investment provides less risk? Explain.

b. Given a risk-free rate of 1.4%, calculate the Sharpe ratio for each investment. Which investment provides the higher reward per unit of risk? Explain.

49. Consider the following data for two investments, A and B:

Investment A:	$x = 8\%$ and $s = 5\%$
Investment B:	$x = 10\%$ and $s = 7\%$

a. Which investment provides the higher return? Which investment provides less risk? Explain.

b. Given a risk-free rate of 2%, calculate the Sharpe ratio for each investment. Which investment provides the higher reward per unit of risk? Explain.

50. Consider the following returns for two investments, A and B, over the past four years:

Investment 1:	2%	8%	−4%	6%
Investment 2:	6%	12%	−8%	10%

a. Which investment provides the higher return?

b. Which investment provides less risk?

c. Given a risk-free rate of 1.2%, calculate the Sharpe ratio for each investment. Which investment has performed better? Explain.

Applications

51. Consider the following summary measures for the annual returns for Stock 1 and Stock 2 over the past 13 years.

Stock 1: $\bar{x} = 9.62\%$ and $s = 23.58\%$

Stock 2: $\bar{x} = 12.38\%$ and $s = 15.45\%$

a. Which stock had the higher average return?

b. Which stock was riskier over this time period? Given your answer in part (a), is this result surprising? Explain.

c. Given a risk-free rate of 3%, which stock has the higher Sharpe ratio? What does this ratio imply?

52. **FILE** ***Mutual Funds 1.*** The accompanying table shows a portion of the annual returns (in %) for Mutual Fund 1 and Mutual Fund 2 over the past 18 years.

Year	Mutual Fund 1	Mutual Fund 2
1	−17.46	12.28
2	−6.04	−9.61
⋮	⋮	⋮
18	30.48	14.43

a. Which fund had the higher average return?

b. Which fund was riskier over this time period?

c. Given a risk-free rate of 3%, which fund has the higher Sharpe ratio? What does this ratio imply?

53. **FILE** ***Mutual Funds 2.*** The accompanying table shows a portion of the annual returns (in %) for Mutual Fund 1 and Mutual Fund 2 over the past 17 years.

Year	Mutual Fund 1	Mutual Fund 2
1	−32.30	31.77
2	−31.70	−11.97
⋮	⋮	⋮
17	11.94	33.84

a. Compare the sample means and the sample standard deviations of the two funds.

b. Use a risk-free rate of 2% to compare the Sharpe ratios of the two funds.

3.6 ANALYSIS OF RELATIVE LOCATION

LO 3.6

Apply Chebyshev's theorem, the empirical rule, and z-scores.

The mean and the standard deviation are the most extensively used measures of central location and dispersion, respectively. Unlike the mean, it is not easy to interpret the standard deviation intuitively. All we can say is that a low value for the standard deviation indicates that the observations are close to the mean, while a high value for the standard deviation indicates that the observations are spread out. In this section, we will use Chebyshev's theorem and the empirical rule to make precise statements regarding the percentage of observations that fall within a specified number of standard deviations from the mean. We will also use the mean and the standard deviation to compute z-scores that measure the relative location of a particular observation; z-scores are also used to detect outliers.

Chebyshev's Theorem

As we will see in more detail in later chapters, it is important to be able to use the standard deviation to make statements about the proportion of observations that fall within certain intervals. Fortunately, a Russian mathematician named Pavroty Chebyshev (1821–1894) found bounds for the proportion of the observations that lie within a specified number of standard deviations from the mean.

CHEBYSHEV'S THEOREM

For any variable, the proportion of observations that lie within k standard deviations from the mean is at least $1 - 1/k^2$, where k is any number greater than 1.

EXAMPLE 3.20

A large lecture class has 280 students. The professor has announced that the mean score on an exam is 74 with a standard deviation of 8. At least how many students scored within 58 and 90?

SOLUTION: A score of 58 is two standard deviations below the mean ($\bar{x} - 2s = 74 - (2 \times 8) = 58$), while a score of 90 is two standard deviations above the mean ($\bar{x} + 2s = 74 + (2 \times 8) = 90$). Using Chebyshev's theorem and $k = 2$, we have $1 - 1/2^2 = 0.75$. In other words, Chebyshev's theorem asserts that at least 75% of the scores will fall within 58 and 90. Therefore, at least 75% of 280 students, or $0.75(280) = 210$ students, scored within 58 and 90.

This theorem holds both for a sample and for a population. For example, it implies that at least 0.75, or 75%, of the observations fall within $k = 2$ standard deviations from the mean. Similarly, at least 0.89, or 89%, of the observations fall within $k = 3$ standard deviations from the mean. The main advantage of Chebyshev's theorem is that it applies to all variables, regardless of the shape of the distribution. However, it results in conservative bounds for the percentage of observations falling in a particular interval. The actual percentage of observations lying in the interval may in fact be much larger.

The Empirical Rule

If we know that the observations are drawn from a relatively symmetric and bell-shaped distribution—perhaps by a visual inspection of the variable's histogram—then we can make more precise statements about the percentage of observations that fall within certain intervals. Symmetry and bell-shape are characteristics of the normal distribution, a topic that we discuss in Chapter 6. The normal distribution is often used as an approximation for many real-world applications. The **empirical rule** is illustrated in Figure 3.4. It provides the approximate percentage of observations that fall within 1, 2, or 3 standard deviations from the mean.

FIGURE 3.4 Graphical description of the empirical rule

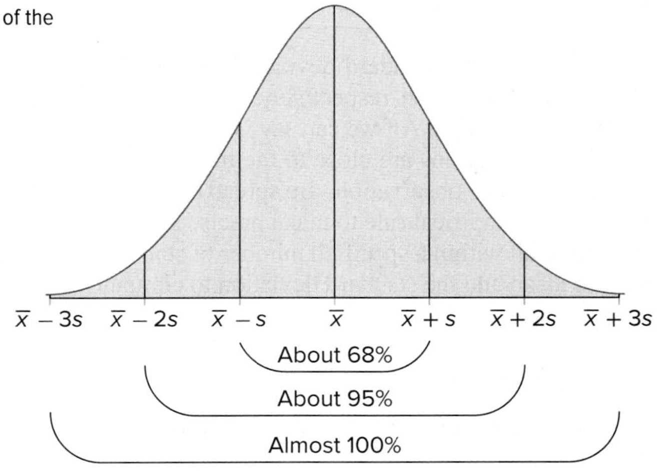

THE EMPIRICAL RULE

Given a sample mean $\bar{x}$, a sample standard deviation s, and a relatively symmetric and bell-shaped distribution:

- Approximately 68% of all observations fall in the interval $\bar{x} \pm s$,
- Approximately 95% of all observations fall in the interval $\bar{x} \pm 2s$, and
- Almost all observations fall in the interval $\bar{x} \pm 3s$.

EXAMPLE 3.21

Let's revisit Example 3.20 regarding a large lecture class with 280 students with a mean score of 74 and a standard deviation of 8. Assume that the distribution is symmetric and bell-shaped.

a. Approximately how many students scored within 58 and 90?

b. Approximately how many students scored more than 90?

SOLUTION:

a. As shown in Example 3.20, a score of 58 is two standard deviations below the mean, while a score of 90 is two standard deviations above the mean. The empirical rule states that approximately 95% of the observations fall within two standard deviations of the mean. Therefore, about 95% of 280 students, or $0.95 \times 280 = 266$ students, scored within 58 and 90.

b. We know that 90 is two standard deviations above the mean. Since approximately 95% of the observations fall within two standard deviations of the mean, we can infer that 5% of the observations fall outside the interval. Therefore, given the symmetry of the distribution, about half of 5%, or 2.5%, of 280 students scored above 90. Equivalently, about 7 students (0.025×280) scored above 90 on the exam. If the professor uses a cutoff score above 90 for an A, then only seven students in the class are expected to get an A.

The main difference between Chebyshev's theorem and the empirical rule is that Chebyshev's theorem applies to all variables, whereas the empirical rule is appropriate when the distribution of a variable is symmetric and bell-shaped. In the preceding two examples, while Chebyshev's theorem asserts that at least 75% of the students scored between 58 and 90, we are able to make a more precise statement with the empirical rule that suggests that about 95% of the students scored between 58 and 90. It is preferable to use the empirical rule if the histogram or other visual and numerical measures suggest a symmetric and bell-shaped distribution.

z-Scores

It is often instructive to use the mean and the standard deviation to find the relative location of observations within a distribution. Suppose a student gets a score of 90 on her accounting exam and 90 on her marketing exam. While the student's scores are identical in both classes, her relative position in these classes may be quite different. What if the mean score was different in the classes? Even with the same mean scores, what if the standard deviation was different in the classes? Both the mean and the standard deviation are needed to find the relative position of this student in both classes.

We use the ***z*-score** to find the relative position of an observation within a distribution by dividing the deviation of the observation from the mean by the standard deviation.

z-SCORE

A z-score is computed as

$$z = \frac{x - \bar{x}}{s},$$

where x is an observation of a variable and $\bar{x}$ and s are the variable's sample mean and the sample standard deviation, respectively.

A z-score is a unitless measure since its numerator and the denominator have the same units, which cancel out with each other. It measures the distance of a given observation from the mean in terms of standard deviations. For example, a z-score of 2 implies that the given observation is 2 standard deviations above the mean. Similarly, a z-score of -1.5 implies that the given observation is 1.5 standard deviations below the mean. Converting observations into z-scores is also called **standardizing** the observations.

EXAMPLE 3.22

The mean and the standard deviation of scores on an accounting exam are 74 and 8, respectively. The mean and standard deviation of scores on a marketing exam are 78 and 10, respectively. Find the z-scores for a student who scores 90 in both classes.

SOLUTION: The z-score in the accounting class is $z = \frac{90 - 74}{8} = 2$. Similarly, the z-score in the marketing class is $z = \frac{90 - 78}{10} = 1.2$. Therefore, the student has fared relatively better in accounting since she is two standard deviations above the mean, as compared to marketing where she is only 1.2 standard deviations above the mean.

In Section 3.2, we used boxplots as an effective tool to identify outliers. If the distribution is relatively symmetric and bell-shaped, we can also use z-scores to detect outliers. Since almost all observations fall within three standard deviations of the mean, it is common to treat an observation as an outlier if its z-score is more than 3 or less than -3. Such observations must be reviewed to determine if they should remain in the data set.

EXAMPLE 3.23

Growth_Value

Consider the information presented in the introductory case of this chapter. Use z-scores to determine if there are outliers for Growth. Is this result consistent with the boxplot constructed in Figure 3.3?

SOLUTION: The smallest and the largest observations for Growth are -40.90 and 79.48, respectively. The z-score for the smallest observation is $z = \frac{-40.90 - 15.775}{23.799} = -2.38$ and the z-score for the largest observation is $z = \frac{79.48 - 15.775}{23.799} = 2.68$. Since the absolute value of both z-scores is less than 3, it would suggest that there are no outliers for Growth. This finding is consistent with Growth's boxplot in Figure 3.3.

EXERCISES 3.6

Mechanics

54. A variable has a mean of 80 and a standard deviation of 5.
    a. Using Chebyshev's theorem, what percentage of the observations fall between 70 and 90?
    b. Using Chebyshev's theorem, what percentage of the observations fall between 65 and 95?
55. A variable has a mean of 1,500 and a standard deviation of 100.
    a. Using Chebyshev's theorem, what percentage of the observations fall between 1,300 and 1,700?
    b. Using Chebyshev's theorem, what percentage of the observations fall between 1,100 and 1,900?
56. A variable has a mean of 500 and a standard deviation of 25.
    a. Using Chebyshev's theorem, find the interval that encompasses at least 75% of the data.
    b. Using Chebyshev's theorem, find the interval that encompasses at least 89% of the data.
57. Observations are drawn from a bell-shaped distribution with a mean of 20 and a standard deviation of 2.
    a. Approximately what percentage of the observations fall between 18 and 22?
    b. Approximately what percentage of the observations fall between 16 and 24?
    c. Approximately what percentage of the observations are less than 16?
58. Consider a bell-shaped distribution with a mean of 750 and a standard deviation of 50. There are 500 observations in the data set.
    a. Approximately what percentage of the observations are less than 700?
    b. Approximately how many observations are less than 700?
59. Observations are drawn from a bell-shaped distribution with a mean of 25 and a standard deviation of 4. There are 1,000 observations in the data set.
    a. Approximately what percentage of the observations are less than 33?
    b. Approximately how many observations are less than 33?
60. Observations are drawn from a bell-shaped distribution with a mean of 5 and a standard deviation of 2.5.
    a. Approximately what percentage of the observations are positive?
    b. Approximately what percentage of the observations are not positive?
61. Data are drawn from a bell-shaped distribution with a mean of 50 and a standard deviation of 12. There are 250 observations in the data set. Approximately how many observations are more than 74?
62. Consider a sample with six observations of 6, 9, 12, 10, 9, and 8. Compute the *z*-score for each observation.
63. Consider a sample with 10 observations of −3, 8, 4, 2, −4, 15, 6, 0, −4, and 5. Use *z*-scores to determine if there are any outliers in the data; assume a bell-shaped distribution.

Applications

64. A sample of the salaries of assistant professors on the business faculty at a local university revealed a mean income of $72,000 with a standard deviation of $3,000.
    a. Using Chebyshev's theorem, what percentage of the faculty earns at least $66,000 but no more than $78,000?
    b. Using Chebyshev's theorem, what percentage of the faculty earns at least $63,000 but no more than $81,000?
65. The historical returns on a portfolio had an average return of 8% and a standard deviation of 12%. Assume that returns on this portfolio follow a bell-shaped distribution.
    a. Approximately what percentage of returns were greater than 20%?
    b. Approximately what percentage of returns were below −16%?
66. It is often assumed that IQ scores follow a bell-shaped distribution with a mean of 100 and a standard deviation of 16.
    a. Approximately what percentage of scores are between 84 and 116?
    b. Approximately what percentage of scores are less than 68?
    c. Approximately what percentage of scores are more than 116?
67. An investment strategy has an expected return of 8% and a standard deviation of 6%. Assume investment returns are bell-shaped.
    a. How likely is it to earn a return between 2% and 14%?
    b. How likely is it to earn a return greater than 14%?
    c. How likely is it to earn a return below −4%?
68. On average, an American professional football game lasts about three hours, even though the ball is actually in play only 11 minutes. Let the standard deviation be 0.4 hour.
    a. Use Chebyshev's theorem to approximate the proportion of games that last between 2.2 hours and 3.8 hours.
    b. Assume a bell-shaped distribution to approximate the proportion of games that last between 2.2 hours and 3.8 hours.
69. **FILE** ***Census.*** The accompanying data file shows, among other variables, median household income and median house value for the 50 states. Assume that the distributions for income and house value data are bell-shaped.
    a. Use *z*-scores to determine if there are any outliers for household income.
    b. Use *z*-scores to determine if there are any outliers in house value.
70. **FILE** ***Mutual Funds 2.*** The accompanying data file shows the annual returns (in percent) for Mutual Fund 1 and Mutual Fund 2 over the past 17 years. Assume that returns for both variables are bell-shaped.
    a. Use *z*-scores to determine if there are any outliers in the distribution for Mutual Fund 1.
    b. Use *z*-scores to determine if there are any outliers in the distribution for Mutual Fund 2.

LO 3.7

3.7 MEASURES OF ASSOCIATION

Calculate and interpret measures of association.

In Chapter 2, we introduced a scatterplot to visually assess whether two variables had some type of linear relationship. In this section, we present two numerical measures of association that quantify the direction and strength of the linear relationship between two variables, x and y. It is important to point out that these measures may not be appropriate when the underlying relationship between the variables is nonlinear.

A numerical measure that reveals the direction of the linear relationship between two variables is called the **covariance.** We use s_{xy} to refer to the sample covariance, and σ_{xy} to refer to the population covariance.

> MEASURE OF ASSOCIATION: THE COVARIANCE
>
> The covariance shows the direction of the linear relationship between two variables. For observations $(x_1, y_1), (x_2, y_2), \ldots, (x_n, y_n)$, the sample covariance is computed as
>
> $$s_{xy} = \frac{\Sigma(x_i - \bar{x})(y_i - \bar{y})}{n - 1}.$$
>
> For observations $(x_1, y_1), (x_2, y_2), \ldots, (x_N, y_N)$, the population covariance is computed as
>
> $$\sigma_{xy} = \frac{\Sigma(x_i - \mu_x)(y_i - \mu_y)}{N}.$$
>
> Note: As in the case of the sample variance, the sample covariance uses $n - 1$ rather than n in the denominator.

The covariance can assume a negative value, a positive value, or a value of zero.

- A negative value for covariance indicates a negative linear relationship between the two variables; on average, if x is above its mean, then y tends to be below its mean, and vice versa.
- A positive value for covariance indicates a positive linear relationship between the two variables; on average, if x is above its mean, then y tends to be above its mean, and vice versa.
- The covariance is zero if y and x have no linear relationship.

The covariance is difficult to interpret because it is sensitive to the units of measurement. That is, the covariance between two variables might be 100 and the covariance between another two variables might be 100,000, yet all we can conclude is that both sets of variables are positively related. We cannot comment on the strength of the relationships. An easier measure to interpret is the **correlation coefficient;** it describes both the direction and the strength of the linear relationship between x and y. We use r_{xy} to refer to the sample correlation coefficient and ρ_{xy} (the Greek letter rho) to refer to the population correlation coefficient.

> MEASURE OF ASSOCIATION: THE CORRELATION COEFFICIENT
>
> The correlation coefficient shows the direction and the strength of the linear relationship between two variables.
>
> The sample correlation coefficient is computed as $r_{xy} = \frac{s_{xy}}{s_x s_y}$. The population correlation coefficient is computed as $\rho_{xy} = \frac{\sigma_{xy}}{\sigma_x \sigma_y}$.

The correlation coefficient is unit-free since the units in the numerator cancel with those in the denominator. The value of the correlation coefficient falls between −1 and 1. If the correlation coefficient equals 1, then a perfect positive linear relationship exists between x and y; if it equals −1, then a perfect negative linear relationship exists between x and y. Other values for the correlation coefficient must be interpreted with reference to −1, 0, or 1. For instance, a correlation coefficient equal to −0.80 indicates a strong negative relationship, whereas a correlation coefficient equal to 0.12 indicates a weak positive relationship.

EXAMPLE 3.24

Using Excel and R, find the covariance and the correlation coefficient for Growth and Value.

SOLUTION: As a first step, it is useful to construct a scatterplot for the two variables. Figure 3.5 shows a scatterplot of Value (y) against Growth (x), and it appears that there is a positive linear relationship between the two variables.

FIGURE 3.5 Scatterplot of Value against Growth

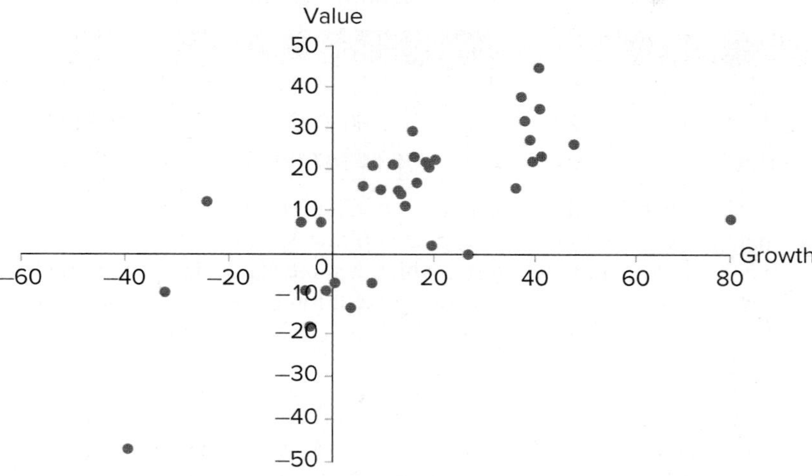

We first outline how to manually calculate the sample covariance and the sample correlation coefficient. Recall from Example 3.1 that the sample mean for Growth is $\bar{x} = 15.755$ and the sample mean for Value is $\bar{y} = 12.005$. We calculate the sample covariance as

$$s_{xy} = \frac{\Sigma(x_i - \bar{x})(y_i - \bar{y})}{n-1}$$

$$= \frac{(-5.50 - 15.755)(-8.59 - 12.055) + \cdots + (38.42 - 15.755)(31.62 - 12.005)}{36 - 1}$$

$$= \frac{9{,}996.19}{35} = 285.605$$

Recall from Example 3.17 that the sample standard deviation for Growth is $s_x =$ 23.799 and the sample standard deviation for Value is $s_y = 17.979$. We calculate the sample correlation coefficient as

$$r_{xy} = \frac{s_{xy}}{s_x s_y} = \frac{285.605}{(23.799)\,(17.979)} = 0.667$$

Using Excel:

a. Open the ***Growth_Value*** data file.

b. We use the COVARIANCE.S and CORREL functions to find the sample covariance and the sample correlation coefficient, respectively. (We use the COVARIANCE.P and CORREL functions to find the population covariance and the population correlation coefficient, respectively.) For the sample covariance, we enter `=COVARIANCE.S(B2:B37, C2:C37)`, and for the sample correlation coefficient, we enter `=CORREL(B2:B37, C2:C37)`. Verify that you obtain the same values that were obtained manually.

Using R:

a. Import the ***Growth_Value*** data file into a data frame (table) and label it myData.

b. We use the **cov** and **cor** functions to find the sample covariance and the sample correlation coefficient, respectively. Enter

```
> cov(myData)
> cor(myData)
```

For both functions, R returns a matrix that lists either the covariance or the correlation coefficient for each pairing of variables in the data frame. For example, R returns the following output after inputting the **cor** function:

	Year	Growth	Value
Year	1.00000000	−0.02985209	−0.02122542
Growth	−0.02985209	1.00000000	**0.66747118**
Value	−0.02122542	**0.66747118**	1.00000000

We are interested in the correlation coefficient between Growth and Value, which appears twice in this matrix (see boldface values). We also see the value 1 down the diagonal of the matrix, which just measures the correlation between each variable and itself. Finally, the correlation coefficient between Year and Growth and Year and Value is meaningless in this application.

Summary:

The covariance of 285.605 indicates that the variables have a positive linear relationship. In other words, on average, when one variable's return is above its mean, the other variable's return is above its mean, and vice versa. The correlation coefficient of 0.667 indicates a moderate to strong, positive linear relationship between the two variables. In order to diversify the risk in an investor's portfolio, an investor is often advised to invest in assets (such as stocks, bonds, and mutual funds) whose returns are not strongly correlated. If asset returns do not have a strong positive correlation, then if one investment does poorly, the other may still do well.

EXERCISES 3.7

Mechanics

71. Consider the following sample data:

x	12	18	20	22	25
y	15	20	25	22	27

a. Calculate the covariance.

b. Calculate and interpret the correlation coefficient.

72. Consider the following sample data:

x	−2	0	3	4	7
y	−2	−3	−8	−9	−10

a. Calculate the covariance.

b. Calculate and interpret the correlation coefficient.

APPLICATIONS

73. FILE ***MutualFunds1.*** The accompanying data file shows the annual returns (in percent) for Mutual Fund 1 and Mutual Fund 2 over the past 17 years.

a. Calculate and interpret the sample covariance between the returns.

b. Calculate and interpret the correlation coefficient.

74. FILE ***PriceDays.*** The accompanying data file shows the price of a house (Price in $1,000s) and the number of days it takes to sell the house (Days) for a sample of eight recent transactions.

a. Calculate the sample covariance. What kind of linear relationship exists?

b. Calculate and interpret the correlation coefficient.

75. FILE ***GPA.*** The director of graduate admissions at a local university is analyzing the relationship between scores on the math portion of the Graduate Record Examination (GRE) and subsequent performance in graduate school, as measured by a student's grade point average (GPA). She uses a sample of 24 students who graduated within the past five years. A portion of the data is shown in the accompanying table.

GPA	GRE
3.0	700
3.5	720
⋮	⋮
3.5	760

a. Calculate and interpret the sample covariance.
b. Calculate and interpret the correlation coefficient. Does an applicant's GRE score seem to be a good indicator of subsequent performance in graduate school?

76. FILE ***Education.*** A social scientist would like to analyze the relationship between educational attainment (in years of higher education) and salary (in $1,000s). He collects data on 20 individuals. A portion of the data is shown in the accompanying table.

Salary	Education
40	3
53	4
⋮	⋮
38	0

a. Calculate and interpret the sample covariance.
b. Calculate and interpret the correlation coefficient.

77. FILE ***Happiness_Age.*** Many attempts have been made to relate happiness with various factors. One such study relates happiness with age and finds that holding everything else constant, people are least happy when they are in their mid-40s. Data are collected on a respondent's age and his/her perception of well-being on a scale from 0 to 100; a portion of the data is presented in the accompanying table.

Age	Happiness
49	62
51	66
⋮	⋮
69	72

a. Calculate and interpret the correlation coefficient between age and happiness.
b. Construct a scatterplot to point out a flaw with the above correlation analysis.

75. FILE ***Census.*** The accompanying data file shows demographic information for the 50 states.

a. Calculate and interpret the correlation coefficient for household income and house value.
b. Calculate and interpret the correlation coefficient for household income and the percentage of the residents who are foreign born.
c. Calculate and interpret the correlation coefficient for household income and the percentage of the residents who are without a high school diploma.

3.8 WRITING WITH DATA

When confronted with a very large data set, a necessary first step for any analysis is to convert the raw data into a more meaningful form. Summary measures prove very useful. Consider the following big data case.

Case Study

An investor currently owns real estate in the college town of Blacksburg, Virginia—home to the Virginia Tech Hokies. He would like to expand his holdings by purchasing similar rental property in either Athens, Georgia, or Chapel Hill, North Carolina. As a preliminary step, he would like information on house prices in these two areas. He is interested in properties that have at least two bedrooms and that are listed for less than $1,000,000. The following report will summarize previous sales that have satisfied these criteria.

FILE
House_Price

Sample Report—Investing in College Town Real Estate

There are a number of reasons why you might consider investing in a rental property near a university. First, there's a large pool of renters, including students, faculty, and staff. Second, because many universities are unable to house their students beyond freshman year, students offer a steady stream of rental demand. Finally, university towns tend to be filled with restaurants, shopping, and nightlife. All of these factors can make it easier for you to market your property.

The following report examines house prices in Athens, Georgia—home to the University of Georgia Bulldogs—and Chapel Hill, North Carolina—home to the University of North Carolina Tar Heels. The sample consists of 293 house sales in Athens and 351 house sales in Chapel Hill. In addition, all houses in the sample had at least two bedrooms and sold for less than $1,000,000. Table 3.14 provides the most relevant summary measures for the analysis.

kali9/Getty Images

TABLE 3.14 Summary Measures for House Prices (in $) in Athens and Chapel Hill

Summary Measure	Athens, GA	Chapel Hill, NC
Mean	219,671	429,152
Median	177,500	395,000
Minimum	41,125	105,000
Maximum	910,000	950,000
Standard deviation	147,648	186,762
Coefficient of variation	0.67	0.44
Number of houses	293	351

The average house price in Athens is $219,671, as opposed to $429,152 in Chapel Hill, a difference of almost $210,000. In Athens, the median house price is $177,500, suggesting that half of the house prices are below this value and half are above this value. The corresponding value in Chapel Hill is $395,000. The difference in medians between these two cities is close to $218,000. In both cities, the median is quite a bit less than the mean, which implies that outliers, some extremely high house prices in this case, are likely present.

While the mean and the median represent where house prices tend to cluster, they do not relay information about the variability in house prices. Generally, standard deviation is used as a measure of variability. The standard deviation for house prices in Chapel Hill is greater than the standard deviation for house prices in Athens ($186,762 > $147,648), suggesting that, compared to Athens, house prices in Chapel Hill are more dispersed from the mean.

Finally, Figure 3.6 shows the boxplots of house prices for each city. The boxplots reveal two more major points with respect to house prices in these two cities:

- In each boxplot, the median is off-center within the box, being located to the left of center.
- In each boxplot, there are outliers on the right side. However, there are far fewer outliers in the Chapel Hill distribution as compared to the Athens distribution.

FIGURE 3.6 Boxplots of house prices in Athens, Georgia, and Chapel Hill, North Carolina

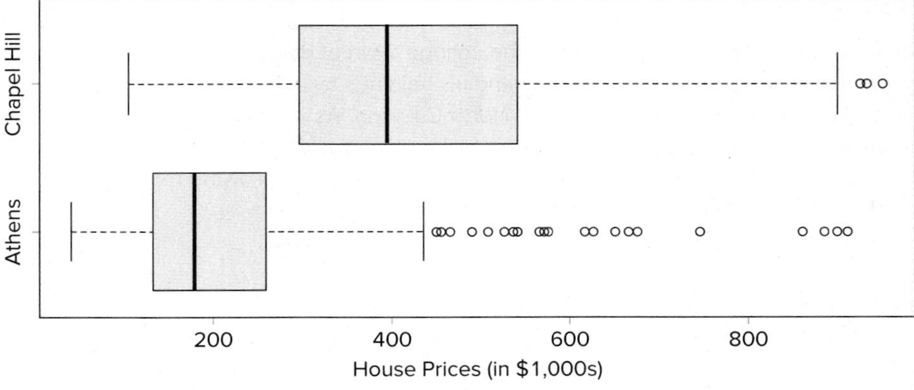

These two observations suggest that both distributions are positively skewed. This implies that the bulk of the house prices falls in the lower end of the distribution, and there are relatively few high-priced houses.

This report summarizes house prices in Athens, Georgia, and Chapel Hill, North Carolina. On average, houses in Chapel Hill are almost twice as expensive as those in Athens. Moreover, if outliers are removed from the analysis, house prices in Athens are less variable than house prices in Chapel Hill. However, before any investor purchases property in either city, many other factors should be considered, such as the size of the houses and their distance from campus.

Suggested Case Studies

Summary measures prove very useful when analyzing the big data that accompanies this text. Here are some suggestions.

Report 3.1 FILE ***House_Price.*** Perform a similar analysis to the one conducted in this section, but choose two other college towns.

Report 3.2 FILE ***College_Admissions.*** Use summary measures to examine the high school GPA and the SAT scores of those students who were admitted to the School of Business & Economics versus those students who were admitted to the School of Arts & Letters.

Report 3.3 FILE ***TechSales_Reps.*** Use summary measures to examine the salaries and the net promoter score (NPS) of sales representatives depending on their personality types and sex in the software group.

CONCEPTUAL REVIEW

LO 3.1 Calculate and interpret measures of central location.

The mean (average) is the most widely used measure of central location. The sample mean and the population mean are computed as $\bar{x} = \frac{\Sigma x_i}{n}$ and $\mu = \frac{\Sigma x_i}{N}$, respectively. One weakness of the mean is that it is unduly influenced by outliers—extremely small or large values.

The median is the middle observation of a distribution. We arrange the observations in ascending order (smallest to largest), and the median is the middle observation if n (or N) is odd. It is the average of the two middle observations if n (or N) is even. The median is an especially useful measure of central location when outliers are present.

The mode is the observation of a distribution that occurs with the most frequency. A variable may have no mode or more than one mode. If the variable is categorical, then the mode is the only meaningful measure of central location.

The weighted mean is relevant when some observations contribute more than others. In these instances, the sample mean is calculated as $\bar{x} = \Sigma w_i x_i$ where w_i is the weight associated with observation x_i. We also use the weighted mean to calculate the mean from a frequency distribution. The population mean is calculated similarly.

LO 3.2 Interpret a percentile and a boxplot.

Percentiles provide detailed information about how the observations are spread over the interval from the smallest observation to the largest observation. In general, the pth percentile divides the observations set into two parts, where approximately p percent of the observations are less than the pth percentile and the rest are greater than the pth percentile. The 25th percentile is also referred to as the first quartile (Q1), the 50th percentile is referred to as the second quartile (Q2), and the 75th percentile is referred to as the third quartile (Q3).

A boxplot displays the five-number summary (minimum, Q1, Q2, Q3, and maximum) for a variable. Boxplots are particularly useful when comparing similar information gathered at another place or time. They are also used as an effective tool for identifying outliers and skewness.

LO 3.3 Calculate and interpret a geometric mean return and an average growth rate.

The geometric mean is the multiplicative average of a variable. In general, the geometric mean is smaller than the arithmetic mean and is less sensitive to outliers.

The geometric mean is relevant when summarizing financial returns over several years. For multiperiod returns $R_1, R_2, \ldots, R_n$, the geometric mean return is computed as $G_R = \sqrt[n]{(1+R_1)\times(1+R_2)\times\cdots\times(1+R_n)} - 1$, where n is the number of multiperiod returns.

The geometric mean is also used when summarizing average growth rates. For growth rates $g_1, g_2, \ldots, g_n$, the average growth rate is computed as $G_g = \sqrt[n]{(1+g_1)\times(1+g_2)\times\cdots\times(1+g_n)} - 1$, where n is the number of multiperiod growth rates. When the underlying observations of the series are given, there is a simpler way to compute the average growth rate. For observations $x_1, x_2, \ldots, x_n$, the average growth rate is computed as $G_g = \sqrt[n-1]{\frac{x_n}{x_1}} - 1$, where $n - 1$ is the number of distinct growth rates.

LO 3.4 Calculate and interpret measures of dispersion.

The range is the difference between the maximum and the minimum observations of a variable.

The mean absolute deviation (MAD) is an average of the absolute differences between the observations and the mean of a data set. The sample MAD and the population MAD are computed as $\text{MAD} = \frac{\Sigma|x_i - \bar{x}|}{n}$ and $\text{MAD} = \frac{\Sigma|x_i - \mu|}{N}$, respectively.

The variance and the standard deviation, which are based on squared differences from the mean, are the two most widely used measures of dispersion. The sample variance s^2 and the sample standard deviation s are computed as $s^2 = \frac{(x_i - \bar{x})^2}{n-1}$ and $s = \sqrt{s^2}$, respectively. The population variance σ^2 and the population standard deviation σ are computed as $\sigma^2 = \frac{\Sigma(x_i - \mu)^2}{N}$ and $\sigma = \sqrt{\sigma^2}$, respectively. Whatever the units of the original variable, the variance has squared units. By calculating the standard deviation, we return to the original units of measurement.

The coefficient of variation CV is a relative measure of dispersion. The CV allows comparisons of variability between variables with different means or different units of measurement. The sample CV and the population CV are computed as $\text{CV} = \frac{s}{\bar{x}}$ and $\text{CV} = \frac{\sigma}{\mu}$, respectively.

LO 3.5 Explain mean-variance analysis and the Sharpe ratio.

Mean-variance analysis postulates that we measure the performance of an asset by its rate of return and evaluate this rate of return in terms of its reward (mean) and risk (variance). In general, investments with higher average returns are also associated with higher risk.

The Sharpe ratio measures extra reward per unit of risk. The Sharpe ratio for an investment I is computed as $\frac{\bar{x}_I - \bar{R}_f}{s_I}$, where $\bar{R}_f$ denotes the mean return on a risk-free asset. The higher the Sharpe ratio, the better the investment compensates its investors for risk.

LO 3.6 Apply Chebyshev's theorem, the empirical rule, and *z*-scores.

Chebyshev's theorem dictates that for any variable, the proportion of observations that lie within k standard deviations from the mean will be at least $1 - 1/k^2$, where k is any number greater than 1.

Given a sample mean $\bar{x}$, a sample standard deviation s, and a relatively symmetric and bell-shaped distribution, the empirical rule dictates that

- Approximately 68% of all observations fall in the interval $\bar{x} \pm s$,
- Approximately 95% of all observations fall in the interval $\bar{x} \pm 2s$, and
- Almost all observations fall in the interval $\bar{x} \pm 3s$.

A *z*-score, calculated as $(x - \bar{x})/s$, measures the relative location of the sample observation x. For a relatively symmetric and bell-shaped distribution, it is also used to detect outliers.

LO 3.7 Calculate and interpret measures of association.

The covariance and the correlation coefficient are measures of association that assess the direction and strength of a linear relationship between two variables, x and y.

The sample covariance s_{xy} and the population covariance σ_{xy} are computed as $s_{xy} = \frac{\Sigma(x_i - \bar{x})(y_i - \bar{y})}{n-1}$ and $\sigma_{xy} = \frac{\Sigma(x_i - \mu_x)(y_i - \mu_y)}{N}$, respectively.

The sample correlation coefficient r_{xy} and the population correlation coefficient ρ_{xy} are computed as $r_{xy} = \frac{s_{xy}}{s_x s_y}$ and $\rho_{xy} = \frac{\sigma_{xy}}{\sigma_x \sigma_y}$, respectively.

ADDITIONAL EXERCISES

79. **FILE** ***Highway.*** Many environmental groups and politicians are suggesting a return to the federal 55-mile-per-hour (mph) speed limit on America's highways. They argue that not only will a lower national speed limit reduce greenhouse emissions, it will also increase traffic safety. A researcher believes that a lower speed limit will not increase traffic safety because he feels that traffic safety is based on the variability of the speeds with which people are driving, rather than the average speed. The researcher gathers the speeds of 40 cars from a highway with a speed limit of 55 mph (Highway 1) and the speeds of 40 cars from a highway with a speed limit of 65 mph (Highway 2). A portion of the data is shown in the accompanying table.

Car	Highway 1	Highway 2
1	60	70
2	55	65
⋮	⋮	⋮
40	52	65

a. Calculate the mean and the median for each highway.

b. Calculate the standard deviation for each highway.

c. Do the data support the researcher's belief? Explain.

80. **FILE** ***Firms.*** Monthly stock prices (in $) for Firm A and Firm B are collected for five years. A portion of the data is shown in the accompanying table.

Month	Firm A	Firm B
1	63.85	75.56
2	66.04	78.68
⋮	⋮	⋮
60	89.98	126.38

a. Calculate the mean, the variance, and the standard deviation for each firm's stock price.

b. Which firm had the higher average stock price over the time period?

c. Which firm's stock price had greater dispersion as measured by the standard deviation?

81. **FILE** ***MutualFunds3.*** The accompanying table shows a portion of the annual returns (in %) for Mutual Fund 1 and Mutual Fund 2 over the past 25 years.

Year	Mutual Fund 1	Mutual Fund 2
1	−23.17	−11.98
2	−16.46	19.39
⋮	⋮	⋮
25	−10.37	−14.29

a. Which fund had the higher reward over this time period? Explain.

b. Which fund was riskier over this time period? Explain.

c. Given a risk-free rate of 2%, which fund has the higher Sharpe ratio? What does this ratio imply?

82. The manager at a water park constructed the following relative frequency distribution to summarize attendance for 60 days in July and August. Calculate the average attendance.

Attendance	Relative Frequency
$1{,}000 < x \leq 1{,}250$	0.08
$1{,}250 < x \leq 1{,}500$	0.10
$1{,}500 < x \leq 1{,}750$	0.17
$1{,}750 < x \leq 2{,}000$	0.33
$2{,}000 < x \leq 2{,}250$	0.25
$2{,}250 < x \leq 2{,}500$	0.07

83. Annual growth rates for individual firms in the toy industry tend to fluctuate dramatically, depending on consumers' tastes and current fads. Consider the following growth rates (in %) for two firms in this industry over the past five years.

Year	Firm 1	Firm 2
1	3.0	1.5
2	2.1	9.1
3	21.8	5.7
4	4.8	−0.1
5	1.2	−8.2

a. Calculate the geometric mean growth rate for each firm.

b. Use the standard deviation to evaluate the variability for each firm.

c. Which firm had the higher geometric mean growth rate? Which firm's growth rate had greater variability?

84. The following table shows the revenues (in $ millions) for Firm 1 and Firm 2 over the past three years.

Year	Firm 1	Firm 2
1	15.73	3.06
2	14.53	2.99
3	14.20	2.99

a. Calculate the average growth rate for each firm.
b. Which firm had the higher growth rate over this period?

85. FILE ***Life_Obesity.*** The accompanying data file shows life expectancies (in years) and obesity rates (in %) for the 50 states and the District of Columbia. Calculate and interpret the correlation coefficient.

86. FILE ***Test_Scores.*** The accompanying data file shows midterm and final grades for 32 students. Calculate and interpret the correlation coefficient.

87. FILE ***MutualFunds4.*** The accompanying table shows a portion of the annual returns (in %) for Mutual Fund 1 and Mutual Fund 2 over the past 37 years.

Year	Mutual Fund 1	Mutual Fund 2
1	56.32	−12.16
2	52.47	20.27
⋮	⋮	⋮
37	−8.79	−24.92

a. Which fund had the higher reward over this time period? Explain.
b. Which fund was riskier over this time period? Explain.
c. Given a risk-free rate of 2%, which fund has the higher Sharpe ratio? What does this ratio imply?

88. Refer to the previous exercise for a description of the data.
a. Construct a boxplot for Mutual Fund 1. Does the boxplot suggest that outliers exist?
b. Use z-scores to determine if there are any outliers for Mutual Fund 1. Are your results consistent with part a? Explain why or why not.
c. Construct a boxplot for Mutual Fund 2. Does the boxplot suggest that outliers exist?
d. Use z-scores to determine if there are any outliers for Mutual Fund 2. Are your results consistent with part c? Explain why or why not.

89. FILE ***Prime.*** The accompanying data file shows the annual expenditures (Expenditures in $) for 100 Amazon Prime customers.
a. Construct a boxplot for Expenditures. Does the boxplot suggest that outliers exist?
b. Use z-scores to determine if there are any outliers for Expenditures. Are your results consistent with part a? Explain why or why not.

90. FILE ***Gas_Prices.*** The accompanying data file shows the average price of gas (Price in $ per gallon) for the 50 states and the District of Columbia.
a. Find the mean and the median for gas price.
b. Calculate and interpret the first quartile and the third quartile for gas price. [Note: If you are using Excel, use the PERCENTILE.INC function to calculate a percentile.]
c. Calculate the sample variance and the sample standard deviation.
d. Construct a boxplot for Price. Does the boxplot suggest that outliers exist?
e. Use z-scores to determine if there are any outliers for Price. Are your results consistent with part d? Explain why or why not.

91. FILE ***Car_Prices.*** The accompanying data file shows the price, the age, and the mileage for 20 used sedans.
a. Calculate the mean price, the mean age, and the mean mileage.
b. Calculate the standard deviation for price, the standard deviation for age, and the standard deviation for mileage.
c. Calculate and interpret the correlation coefficient between price and age.
d. Calculate and interpret the correlation coefficient between price and mileage.

92. FILE ***GPA_College.*** The accompanying data file shows a student's first-year GPA in college (College GPA), SAT score (SAT), unweighted high school GPA (HS GPA), and race (White equals 1 if white, 0 otherwise) for 180 students.
a. Calculate the mean College GPA and the mean SAT.
b. Find the mean College GPA for white students and the mean College GPA for nonwhite students. Which subgroup has a higher College GPA?
c. Find the mean SAT for white students and the mean SAT for nonwhite students. Which subgroup has a higher SAT?

93. FILE ***IceCream.*** The accompanying data file shows 35 observations for an ice cream truck driver's daily income (Income in $), number of hours on the road (Hours), whether it was a hot day (Hot = 1 if the high temperature was above 85° F, 0 otherwise), and whether it was a Holiday (Holiday = 1, 0 otherwise).
a. Calculate the mean Income and the mean Hours.
b. Find the mean Income for a Hot day and the mean Income for a non-Hot day. Which subgroup has a higher Income?
c. Find the mean Income for a Holiday and the mean Income for a non-Holiday. Which subgroup has a higher Income?

APPENDIX 3.1 Guidelines for Other Software Packages

The following section provides brief commands for Minitab, SPSS, and JMP. Import the specified data file into the relevant software spreadsheet prior to following the commands.

Minitab

Calculating Summary Measures

FILE Growth_Value

(Replicating Table 3.4) From the menu, choose **Stat > Basic Statistics > Display Descriptive Statistics**. Under **Variables**, select Growth and Value. Choose **Statistics**, and then select the summary measures that you wish to calculate, such as Mean, Standard deviation, etc.

Constructing a Boxplot

FILE Growth_Value

A. (Replicating Figure 3.3) From the menu, choose **Graph > Boxplot > Multiple Y's > Simple**.

B. Under **Graph variables,** select Growth and Value. Choose **Data View.** Choose **Interquartile range box, Outlier symbols, Individual symbols,** and **Median connect line**.

C. Choose **Scale** and select the box in front of **Transpose value and category scales.**

Calculating the Covariance and the Correlation Coefficient

(Replicating Example 3.24) From the menu, choose **Stat > Basic Statistics > Covariance** (choose **Covariance** to calculate the correlation coefficient). Under **Variables**, select Growth and Value.

SPSS

Calculating Summary Measures

(Replicating Table 3.4) From the menu, choose **Analyze > Descriptive Statistics > Descriptives**. Under **Variable(s)**, select Growth and Value. Choose **Options**. Select the summary measures that you wish to calculate, such as Mean, Std. deviation, etc.

Constructing a Boxplot

(Replicating Figure 3.3) From the menu choose **Graphs > Legacy Dialogs > Boxplot.** Select **Simple** and under **Data in Chart Are**, select **Summaries of separate variables.** Click **Define**. Under **Boxes Represent**, select Growth and Value.

Calculating the Covariance and the Correlation Coefficient

(Replicating Example 3.24) From the menu, choose **Analyze > Correlate > Bivariate.** Under **Variables**, select Growth and Value. Under **Correlation Coefficients**, select **Pearson.** Choose **Options**. Under **Statistics,** select **Cross-product deviations and covariances.**

JMP

Calculating Summary Measures and Constructing a Boxplot

(Replicating Table 3.4 and Figure 3.3) From the menu, choose **Analyze > Distribution.** Drag Growth and Value to the **Y, Columns** box.

Calculating the Covariance and the Correlation Coefficient

FILE Growth_Value

A. (Replicating Example 3.24) From the menu, choose **Analyze > Multivariate Methods > Multivariate**. Drag Growth and Value to the **Y, Columns** box.

B. Click the red triangle beside **Multivariate**. Select **Covariance Matrix.**

4 Introduction to Probability

LEARNING OBJECTIVES

After reading this chapter you should be able to:

LO **4.1** **Describe fundamental probability concepts.**

LO **4.2** **Apply the rules of probability.**

LO **4.3** **Calculate and interpret probabilities from a contingency table.**

LO **4.4** **Apply the total probability rule and Bayes' theorem.**

LO **4.5** **Use a counting rule to calculate the probability of an event.**

Every day we make choices about issues in the presence of uncertainty. By figuring out the chances of various events, we are better prepared to make the more desirable choices. For example, given the weather forecast, we determine whether we should wear a jacket or carry an umbrella. Similarly, retailers tweak their sales force in anticipation of an increase or decrease in shoppers, and the Federal Reserve adjusts interest rates based on its anticipation of growth and inflation. Probability is simply the likelihood that something will happen under uncertainty.

This chapter presents the essential probability tools needed to frame and address many real-world issues involving uncertainty. Probability theory turns out to be the very foundation for statistical inference, and numerous concepts introduced in this chapter are essential for understanding later chapters.

Halfpoint/Shutterstock

INTRODUCTORY CASE

24/7 Fitness Center Annual Membership

24/7 Fitness Center is a high-end, full-service gym and recruits its members through advertisements and monthly open house events. Each open house attendee is given a tour and a one-day pass. Potential members register for the open house event by answering a few questions about themselves and their exercise routine. The fitness center staff places a follow-up phone call with the potential member and sends information to open house attendees by mail in the hopes of signing the potential member up for an annual membership.

Janet Williams, a manager at 24/7 Fitness Center, wants to develop a data-driven strategy for selecting which new open house attendees to contact. From 400 past open house attendees, she knows the outcome (Enroll or Not Enroll) of a follow-up phone call regarding a club membership. In addition, she has information on age in years of attendees, where age is binned into groups Under 30, Between 30 and 50, and Over 50. Table 4.1 shows a portion of the data.

TABLE 4.1 24/7 Fitness Center Enrollment and Age Data ($n = 400$)

FILE
Gym

Attendee	Age Group	Outcome
1	Between 30 and 50	Not Enroll
2	Over 50	Enroll
⋮	⋮	⋮
400	Between 30 and 50	Enroll

Janet wants to use the sample information to

a. Construct a contingency table and use it to calculate and interpret relevant empirical probabilities concerning age and enrollment.

b. Use the empirical probabilities to develop a data-driven strategy for selecting open house attendees.

A synopsis of this case is provided at the end of Section 4.3.

LO 4.1

4.1 FUNDAMENTAL PROBABILITY CONCEPTS

Describe fundamental probability concepts.

We are better prepared to deal with uncertainty if we know the probabilities that describe which events are likely and which are unlikely. A **probability** is defined as follows.

> A probability is a numerical value that measures the likelihood that an event occurs. This value is between zero and one, where a value of zero indicates an *impossible* event and a value of one indicates a *definite* event.

In order to define an event and assign the appropriate probability to it, it is useful to first establish some terminology and impose some structure on the situation.

An **experiment** is a process that leads to one of several possible outcomes. The diversity of the outcomes of an experiment is due to the uncertainty of the real world. When you purchase a new computer, there is no guarantee as to how long it will last before any repair work is needed. It may need repair in the first year, in the second year, or after two years. You can think of this as an experiment because the actual outcome will be determined only over time. Other examples of an experiment include whether a roll of a fair die will result in a value of 1, 2, 3, 4, 5, or 6; whether the toss of a coin results in heads or tails; whether a project is finished early, on time, or late; whether the economy will improve, stay the same, or deteriorate; and whether a ball game will end in a win, loss, or tie.

A **sample space**, denoted by S, of an experiment contains all possible outcomes of the experiment. For example, suppose the sample space representing the letter grade in a course is given by $S = \{A, B, C, D, F\}$. The sample space for an experiment need not be unique. For example, in the above experiment, we can also define the sample space with just P (pass) and F (fail) outcomes; that is, $S = \{P, F\}$. Note that if the teacher also gives out an I (incomplete) grade, then neither of these sample spaces are valid because they do not contain all possible outcomes of the experiment.

EXAMPLE 4.1

A snowboarder competing in the Winter Olympic Games is trying to assess her probability of earning a medal in her event, the ladies' halfpipe. Construct the appropriate sample space.

SOLUTION: The athlete's attempt to predict her chances of earning a medal is an experiment because, until the Winter Games occur, the outcome is unknown. We formalize an experiment by constructing its sample space. The athlete's competition has four possible outcomes: gold medal, silver medal, bronze medal, and no medal. We formally write the sample space as $S = \{\text{gold, silver, bronze, no medal}\}$.

Events

An **event** is a subset of the sample space. A simple event consists of just one of the possible outcomes of an experiment. Getting an A in a course is an example of a simple event. An event may also contain several outcomes of an experiment. For example, we can define an event as getting a passing grade in a course; this event is formed by the subset of outcomes A, B, C, and D.

Let us define two events from Example 4.1, where one event represents "earning a medal" and the other denotes "failing to earn a medal." These events are **exhaustive** because they include all outcomes in the sample space. In the earlier grade-distribution example, the events of getting grades A and B are not exhaustive events because they do not include many feasible grades in the sample space. However, the events P and F, defined as "pass" and "fail," respectively, are exhaustive.

Another important probability concept concerns **mutually exclusive** events. For two mutually exclusive events, the occurrence of one event precludes the occurrence of the other. Suppose we define the two events "at least earning a silver medal" (outcomes of gold and silver) and "at most earning a silver medal" (outcomes of silver, bronze, no medal). These two events are exhaustive because no outcome of the experiment is omitted. However, in this case, the events are not mutually exclusive because the outcome "silver" appears in both events. Going back to the grade-distribution example, while the events of getting grades A and B are not exhaustive, they are mutually exclusive, because you cannot possibly get an A as well as a B in the same course. However, getting grades P and F are mutually exclusive and exhaustive. Similarly, the events defined as "at least earning a silver medal" and "at most earning a bronze medal" are mutually exclusive and exhaustive.

EXPERIMENTS AND EVENTS

- An experiment is a process that leads to one of several possible outcomes. A sample space, denoted *S*, of an experiment contains all possible outcomes of the experiment.
- An event is any subset of outcomes of the experiment. It is called a simple event if it contains a single outcome.
- Events are exhaustive if all possible outcomes of an experiment belong to the events.
- Events are mutually exclusive if they do not share any common outcome of an experiment.

For any experiment, we can define events based on one or more outcomes of the experiment and also combine events to form new events. The **union** of two events, denoted $A \cup B$, is the event consisting of all outcomes in A or B. A useful way to illustrate these concepts is through the use of a Venn diagram, named after the British mathematician John Venn (1834–1923). Figure 4.1 shows a Venn diagram where the rectangle represents the sample space S and the two circles represent events A and B. The union $A \cup B$ is the portion in the Venn diagram that is included in either A or B.

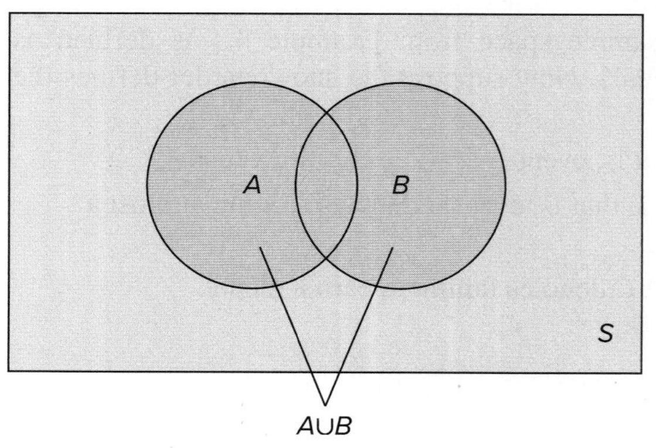

FIGURE 4.1
The union of two events, $A \cup B$

The **intersection** of two events, denoted $A \cap B$, is the event consisting of all outcomes in A and B. Figure 4.2 depicts the intersection of two events A and B. The intersection $A \cap B$ is the portion in the Venn diagram that is included in both A and B.

FIGURE 4.2
The intersection of two events, $A \cap B$

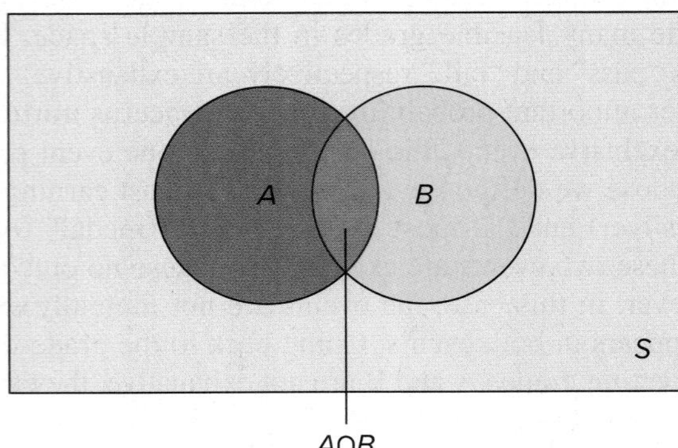

The **complement** of event A, denoted A^c, is the event consisting of all outcomes in the sample space S that are not in A. In Figure 4.3, A^c is everything in S that is not included in A.

FIGURE 4.3
The complement of an event, A^c

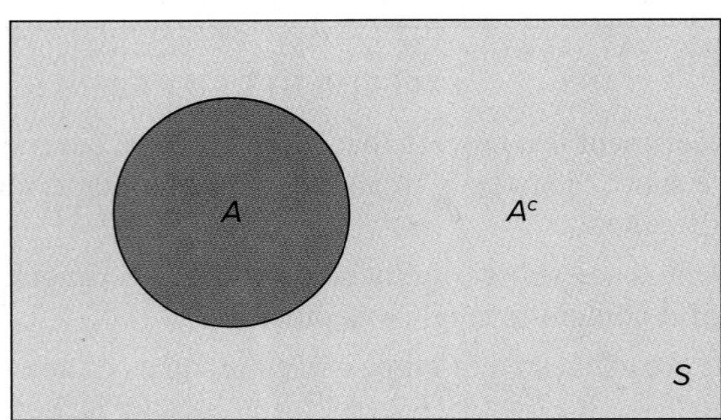

COMBINING EVENTS

- The union of two events, denoted $A \cup B$, is the event consisting of all outcomes in A or B.
- The intersection of two events, denoted $A \cap B$, is the event consisting of all outcomes in A and B.
- The complement of event A, denoted A^c, is the event consisting of all outcomes in the sample space S that are not in A.

EXAMPLE 4.2

Recall that the snowboarder's sample space from Example 4.1 is defined as $S = \{\text{gold, silver, bronze, no medal}\}$. Now suppose the snowboarder defines the following three events:

- $A = \{\text{gold, silver, bronze}\}$; that is, event A denotes earning a medal;
- $B = \{\text{silver, bronze, no medal}\}$; that is, event B denotes earning at most a silver medal; and
- $C = \{\text{no medal}\}$; that is, event C denotes failing to earn a medal.

a. Find $A \cup B$ and $B \cup C$.

b. Find $A \cap B$ and $A \cap C$.

c. Find B^c.

SOLUTION:

a. The union of A and B denotes all outcomes common to A or B; here, the event $A \cup B = \{\text{gold, silver, bronze, no medal}\}$. Note that there is no double counting of the outcomes "silver" or "bronze" in $A \cup B$. Similarly, we have the event $B \cup C = \{\text{silver, bronze, no medal}\}$.

b. The intersection of A and B denotes all outcomes common to A and B; here, the event $A \cap B = \{\text{silver, bronze}\}$. The event $A \cap C = \emptyset$, where $\emptyset$ denotes the null (empty) set; no common outcomes appear in both A and C.

c. The complement of B denotes all outcomes in S that are not in B; here, the event $B^c = \{\text{gold}\}$.

Assigning Probabilities

Now that we have described a valid sample space and the various ways in which we can define events from that sample space, we are ready to assign probabilities. When we arrive at a probability, we generally are able to categorize the probability as a subjective probability, an empirical probability, or a classical probability. Regardless of the method used, there are two defining properties of probability.

THE TWO DEFINING PROPERTIES OF PROBABILITY

1. The probability of any event A is a value between 0 and 1; that is, $0 \leq P(A) \leq 1$.
2. The sum of the probabilities of any list of mutually exclusive and exhaustive events equals 1.

Suppose the snowboarder from Example 4.1 believes that there is a 10% chance that she will earn a gold medal, a 15% chance that she will earn a silver medal, a 20% chance that she will earn a bronze medal, and a 55% chance that she will fail to earn a medal. She has assigned a **subjective probability** to each of the simple events. She made a personal assessment of these probabilities without referencing any data. Subjective probabilities differ from person to person and may contain a high degree of personal bias.

The snowboarder believes that the most likely outcome is failing to earn a medal since she gives that outcome the greatest chance of occurring at 55%. When formally writing out the probability that an event occurs, we generally construct a probability statement. Here, the probability statement might take the form: $P(\{\text{no medal}\}) = 0.55$, where P("event") represents the probability that a given event occurs. Table 4.2 summarizes these events and their respective subjective probabilities. Note that here the events are mutually exclusive and exhaustive.

TABLE 4.2 Snowboarder's Subjective Probabilities

Event	Probability
Gold	0.10
Silver	0.15
Bronze	0.20
No medal	0.55

Reading from the table we can readily see, for instance, that she assesses that there is a 15% chance that she will earn a silver medal, or $P(\{\text{silver}\}) = 0.15$. We should note that all the probabilities are between the values of zero and one, and they add up to one, thus meeting the defining properties of probability.

Suppose the snowboarder wants to calculate the probability of earning a medal. In Example 4.2, we defined "earning a medal" as event A, so the probability statement takes the form $P(A)$. We calculate this probability by summing the probabilities of the outcomes in A, or equivalently,

$$P(A) = P(\{\text{gold}\}) + P(\{\text{silver}\}) + P(\{\text{bronze}\}) = 0.10 + 0.15 + 0.20 = 0.45.$$

EXAMPLE 4.3

Given the events in Example 4.2 and the probabilities in Table 4.2, calculate the following probabilities.

a. $P(B \cup C)$

b. $P(A \cap C)$

c. $P(B^c)$

SOLUTION:

a. The probability that event B or event C occurs is

$$P(B \cup C) = P(\{\text{silver}\}) + P(\{\text{bronze}\}) + P(\{\text{no medal}\})$$
$$= 0.15 + 0.20 + 0.55 = 0.90.$$

b. The probability that event A and event C occur is

$P(A \cap C) = 0$; recall that there are no common outcomes in A and C.

c. The probability that the complement of B occurs is

$$P(B^c) = P(\{\text{gold}\}) = 0.10.$$

In many instances, we calculate probabilities by referencing data based on the observed outcomes of an experiment. The **empirical probability** of an event is the observed relative frequency with which an event occurs. The experiment must be repeated a large number of times for empirical probabilities to be accurate. For example, it may be misleading to report a default rate of 0.40 if payments are delinquent in 2 out of 5 new loans. The probability would be reliable if the default is based on a much larger number of new loans.

EXAMPLE 4.4

The frequency distribution in Table 4.3 summarizes the ages of the richest 400 Americans. Suppose we randomly select one of these individuals.

a. What is the probability that the individual is at least 50 but less than 60 years old?

b. What is the probability that the individual is younger than 60 years old?

c. What is the probability that the individual is at least 80 years old?

TABLE 4.3 Frequency Distribution of Ages of 400 Richest Americans

Ages	Frequency
< 40	13
40 up to 50	24
50 up to 60	67
60 up to 70	113
70 up to 80	117
80 up to 90	55
≥ 90	11

SOLUTION: In Table 4.3a, we first label each outcome with letter notation; for instance, the outcome "< 40" is denoted as event *A*. Next we calculate the relative frequency of each event and use the relative frequency to denote the probability of the event.

TABLE 4.3a Relative Frequency Distribution of Ages of 400 Richest Americans

Ages	Event	Frequency	Relative Frequency
< 40	*A*	13	13/400 = 0.0325
40 up to 50	*B*	24	0.0600
50 up to 60	*C*	67	0.1675
60 up to 70	*D*	113	0.2825
70 up to 80	*E*	117	0.2925
80 up to 90	*F*	55	0.1375
≥ 90	*G*	11	0.0275

a. The probability that an individual is at least 50 but less than 60 years old is

$$P(C) = \frac{67}{400} = 0.1675.$$

b. The probability that an individual is younger than 60 years old is

$$P(A \cup B \cup C) = \frac{13 + 24 + 67}{400} = 0.260.$$

c. The probability that an individual is at least 80 years old is

$$P(F \cup G) = \frac{55 + 11}{400} = 0.165.$$

In a more narrow range of well-defined problems, we can sometimes deduce probabilities by reasoning about the problem. The resulting probability is a **classical probability**. Classical probabilities are often used in games of chance. They are based on the assumption that all outcomes of an experiment are equally likely. Therefore, the classical probability of an event is computed as the number of outcomes belonging to the event divided by the total number of outcomes.

EXAMPLE 4.5

Suppose our experiment consists of rolling a six-sided die. Then we can define the appropriate sample space as $S = \{1, 2, 3, 4, 5, 6\}$.

a. What is the probability that we roll a 2?

b. What is the probability that we roll a 2 or 5?

c. What is the probability that we roll an even number?

SOLUTION: Here we recognize that each outcome is equally likely. So with 6 possible outcomes, each outcome has a 1/6 chance of occurring.

a. The probability that we roll a 2, $P(\{2\})$, is thus 1/6 or 0.1667.

b. The probability that we roll a 2 or 5, $P(\{2\}) + P(\{5\})$, is $1/6 + 1/6 = 1/3$ or 0.3333.

c. The probability that we roll an even number, $P(\{2\}) + P(\{4\}) + P(\{6\})$, is $1/6 + 1/6 + 1/6 = 1/2$ or 0.50.

CATEGORIZING PROBABILITIES

- A subjective probability is calculated by drawing on personal and subjective judgment.
- An empirical probability is calculated as a relative frequency of occurrence.
- A classical probability is based on logical analysis rather than on observation or personal judgment.

Since empirical and classical probabilities generally do not vary from person to person, they are often grouped as objective probabilities.

According to the famous **law of large numbers,** the empirical probability approaches the classical probability if the experiment is run a very large number of times. Consider, for example, flipping a fair coin 10 times. It is possible that heads may not show up exactly 5 times and, therefore, the relative frequency may not be 0.50. However, if we flip the fair coin a very large number of times, heads will show up approximately half of the time. This would make the empirical probability equal to the classical probability of 0.50.

EXERCISES 4.1

Mechanics

1. Determine whether the following probabilities are best categorized as subjective, empirical, or classical probabilities.
   a. Before flipping a fair coin, Sunil assesses that he has a 50% chance of obtaining tails.
   b. At the beginning of the semester, John believes he has a 90% chance of receiving straight A's.
   c. A political reporter announces that there is a 40% chance that the next person to come out of the conference room will be a Republican, since there are 60 Republicans and 90 Democrats in the room.
2. A sample space S yields five equally likely events, A, B, C, D, and E.
   a. Find $P(D)$.
   b. Find $P(B^c)$.
   c. Find $P(A \cup C \cup E)$.
3. You roll a die with the sample space $S = \{1, 2, 3, 4, 5, 6\}$. You define A as $\{1, 2, 3\}$, B as $\{1, 2, 3, 5, 6\}$, C as $\{4, 6\}$, and D as $\{4, 5, 6\}$. Determine which of the following events are exhaustive and/or mutually exclusive.
   a. A and B
   b. A and C
   c. A and D
   d. B and C
4. A sample space, S, yields four simple events, A, B, C, and D, such that $P(A) = 0.35$, $P(B) = 0.10$, and $P(C) = 0.25$.
   a. Find $P(D)$.
   b. Find $P(C^c)$.
   c. Find $P(A \cup B)$.

Applications

5. Jane Peterson has taken Amtrak to travel from New York to Washington, DC, on six occasions, of which three times the train was late. Therefore, Jane tells her friends that the probability that this train will arrive on time is 0.50. Would you label this probability as empirical or classical? Why would this probability not be accurate?
6. Consider the following scenarios to determine if the mentioned combination of attributes represents a union or an intersection.
   a. There are two courses that seem interesting to you, and you would be happy if you can take at least one of them.
   b. There are two courses that seem interesting to you, and you would be happy if you can take both of them.
7. Consider the following scenarios to determine if the mentioned combination of attributes represents a union or an intersection.
   a. A marketing firm is looking for a candidate with a business degree and at least five years of work experience.
   b. A family has decided to purchase a Toyota minivan or a Honda minivan.
8. You apply for a position at two firms. Let event A represent the outcome of getting an offer from the first firm and event B represent the outcome of getting an offer from the second firm.
   a. Explain why events A and B are not exhaustive.
   b. Explain why events A and B are not mutually exclusive.
9. An alarming number of U.S. adults are either overweight or obese. The distinction between overweight and obese is made on the basis of body mass index (BMI), expressed as

weight/height^2. An adult is considered overweight if the BMI is 25 or more but less than 30. An obese adult will have a BMI of 30 or greater. A recent study suggests that 33.1% of the adult population in the United States is overweight and 35.7% is obese. Use this information to answer the following questions.

a. What is the probability that a randomly selected adult is either overweight or obese?
b. What is the probability that a randomly selected adult is neither overweight nor obese?
c. Are the events "overweight" and "obese" exhaustive?
d. Are the events "overweight" and "obese" mutually exclusive?

10. At four community health centers on Cape Cod, Massachusetts, 15,164 patients were asked to respond to questions designed to detect depression. The survey produced the following results.

Diagnosis	Number
Mild	3,257
Moderate	1,546
Moderately Severe	975
Severe	773
No Depression	8,613

a. What is the probability that a randomly selected patient suffered from mild depression?
b. What is the probability that a randomly selected patient did not suffer from depression?
c. What is the probability that a randomly selected patient suffered from moderately severe to severe depression?
d. Given that the national figure for moderately severe to severe depression is approximately 6.7%, does it appear that there is a higher rate of depression in this summer resort community? Explain.

4.2 RULES OF PROBABILITY

LO 4.2

Apply the rules of probability.

In the previous section, we discussed how the probability of an event is assigned. Here we present various rules that are used to combine the probabilities of events.

The **complement rule** follows from one of the defining properties of probability: The sum of probabilities assigned to simple events in a sample space must equal one. Therefore, for an event A and its complement A^c, we get $P(A) + P(A^c) = 1$. Rearranging this equation, we obtain the complement rule.

THE COMPLEMENT RULE

The probability of the complement of event A is derived as

$$P(A^c) = 1 - P(A).$$

The complement rule is quite straightforward, but it is widely used and powerful.

EXAMPLE 4.6

A manager at Moksha Yoga Center believes that 37% of female and 30% of male open house attendees will purchase a membership.

a. What is the probability that a randomly selected female open house attendee will not purchase a membership?

b. What is the probability that a randomly selected male open house attendee will not purchase a membership?

SOLUTION:

a. Let's define A as the event that a randomly selected female open house attendee will purchase a membership; thus, $P(A) = 0.37$. In this problem, we are interested in the complement of A. So $P(A^c) = 1 - P(A) = 1 - 0.37 = 0.63$.

b. Similarly, we define B as the event that a randomly selected male open house attendee will purchase a membership, so $P(B) = 0.30$. Thus, $P(B^c) = 1 - P(B) = 1 - 0.30 = 0.70$.

The **addition rule** allows us to find the probability of the union of two events. Suppose we want to find the probability that either event A occurs or event B occurs, so in probability terms, $P(A \cup B)$. Recall from Figures 4.1 and 4.2 that the union, $A \cup B$, is the portion in the Venn diagram that is included in A or B, whereas the intersection, $A \cap B$, is the portion in the Venn diagram that is included in both A and B.

If we try to obtain $P(A \cup B)$ by simply summing $P(A)$ with $P(B)$, then we overstate the probability because we double-count the probability of the intersection of A and B, $P(A \cap B)$. It is common to refer to $P(A \cap B)$ as the **joint probability** of events A and B. When implementing the addition rule, we sum $P(A)$ and $P(B)$ and then subtract $P(A \cap B)$ from this sum.

THE ADDITION RULE

The probability that event A or event B occurs is derived as

$$P(A \cup B) = P(A) + P(B) - P(A \cap B).$$

EXAMPLE 4.7

Anthony feels that he has a 75% chance of getting an A in Statistics and a 55% chance of getting an A in Managerial Economics. He also believes he has a 40% chance of getting an A in both classes.

a. What is the probability that he gets an A in at least one of these courses?

b. What is the probability that he does not get an A in either of these courses?

SOLUTION:

a. Let $P(A_S)$ correspond to the probability of getting an A in Statistics and $P(A_M)$ correspond to the probability of getting an A in Managerial Economics. Thus, $P(A_S) = 0.75$ and $P(A_M) = 0.55$. In addition, the joint probability that Anthony gets an A in both classes, $P(A_S \cap A_M) = 0.40$. In order to find the probability that he receives an A in at least one of these courses, we use the addition rule and calculate:

$$P(A_S \cup A_M) = P(A_S) + P(A_M) - P(A_S \cap A_M) = 0.75 + 0.55 - 0.40 = 0.90.$$

b. The probability that he does not receive an A in either of these two courses is actually the complement of the union of the two events; that is, $P((A_S \cup A_M)^c)$. We use the complement rule as well as the information from part a and calculate:

$$P((A_S \cup A_M)^c) = 1 - P(A_S \cup A_M) = 1 - 0.90 = 0.10$$

An alternative expression that correctly captures the required probability is $P(A_S^c \cap A_M^c)$, which is the probability that he does not get an A Statistics and he does not get an A in Managerial Economics. A common mistake is to calculate the probability as $1 - P(A_S \cap A_M) = 1 - 0.40 = 0.60$, which simply indicates that there is a 60% chance that Anthony will not get an A in both courses. This is clearly not the required probability that Anthony does not get an A in either course.

Note that for mutually exclusive events A and B, the joint probability is zero; that is, $P(A \cap B) = 0$. We need not concern ourselves with double-counting, and, therefore, the probability of the union is simply the sum of the two probabilities.

In business applications, the probability of interest is often a **conditional probability.** Examples include the probability that a customer will make an online purchase conditional on receiving an e-mail with a discount offer; the probability of making a six-figure salary conditional on getting an MBA; and the probability that sales will improve conditional on the firm launching a new marketing campaign.

Let's use an example to illustrate the concept of conditional probability. Suppose the probability that a recent business college graduate finds a suitable job is 0.80. The probability of finding a suitable job is 0.90 if the recent business college graduate has prior work experience. Here, the probability of an event is conditional on the occurrence of another event. If A represents "finding a job" and B represents "prior work experience," then $P(A) = 0.80$ and the conditional probability is denoted as $P(A|B) = 0.90$. In this example, the probability of finding a suitable job increases from 0.80 to 0.90 when conditioned on prior work experience. In general, the conditional probability, $P(A|B)$, is greater than the **unconditional probability,** $P(A)$, if B exerts a positive influence on A. Similarly, $P(A|B)$ is less than $P(A)$ when B exerts a negative influence on A. Finally, if B exerts no influence on A, then $P(A|B)$ equals $P(A)$. It is common to refer to "unconditional probability" simply as "probability."

We rely on the Venn diagram in Figure 4.2 to explain the conditional probability. Because $P(A|B)$ represents the probability of A conditional on B (B has occurred), the original sample space S reduces to B. The conditional probability $P(A|B)$ is based on the portion of A that is included in B. It is derived as the ratio of the probability of the intersection of A and B to the probability of B.

CONDITIONAL PROBABILITY

The probability that event A occurs given that event B has occurred is derived as

$$P(A|B) = \frac{P(A \cap B)}{P(B)}.$$

EXAMPLE 4.8

Economic globalization is defined as the integration of national economies into the international economy through trade, foreign direct investment, capital flows, migration, and the spread of technology. Although globalization is generally viewed favorably, it also increases the vulnerability of a country to economic conditions of other countries. An economist predicts a 60% chance that country A will perform poorly and a 25% chance that country B will perform poorly. There is also a 16% chance that both countries will perform poorly.

a. What is the probability that country A performs poorly given that country B performs poorly?

b. What is the probability that country B performs poorly given that country A performs poorly?

c. Interpret your findings.

SOLUTION: We first write down the available information in probability terms. Defining event A as "country A performing poorly" and event B as "country B performing poorly," we have the following information: $P(A) = 0.60$, $P(B) = 0.25$, and $P(A \cap B) = 0.16$.

a. $P(A|B) = \frac{P(A \cap B)}{P(B)} = \frac{0.16}{0.25} = 0.64$

b. $P(B|A) = \frac{P(A \cap B)}{P(A)} = \frac{0.16}{0.60} = 0.27$

c. It appears that globalization has definitely made these countries vulnerable to the economic woes of the other country. The probability that country A performs poorly increases from 60% to 64% when country B has performed poorly. Similarly, the probability that country B performs poorly increases from 25% to 27% when conditioned on country A performing poorly.

In some situations, we are interested in finding the joint probability $P(A \cap B)$. Using the conditional probability formula $P(A|B) = \frac{P(A \cap B)}{P(B)}$, we can easily derive $P(A \cap B) = P(A|B)P(B)$. Because we calculate the product of two probabilities to find $P(A \cap B)$, we refer to it as the **multiplication rule** for probabilities.

THE MULTIPLICATION RULE

The joint probability of events A and B is derived as

$$P(A \cap B) = P(A|B)P(B).$$

EXAMPLE 4.9

A manager believes that 14% of consumers will respond positively to the firm's social media campaign. Also, 24% of those who respond positively will become loyal customers. Find the probability that the next recipient of their social media campaign will react positively and will become a loyal customer.

SOLUTION: Let the event R represent a consumer who responds positively to a social media campaign and the event L represent a loyal customer. Therefore, $P(R) = 0.14$ and $P(L|R) = 0.24$. We calculate the probability that the next recipient of a social media campaign will react positively and become a loyal customer as $P(R \cap L) = P(L|R)P(R) = 0.24 \times 0.14 = 0.0336$.

Of particular interest to researchers is whether or not two events influence one another. Two events are **independent** if the occurrence of one event does not affect the probability of the occurrence of the other event. Similarly, events are considered **dependent** if the occurrence of one is related to the probability of the occurrence of the other. We generally determine the independence of two events by comparing the conditional probability of one event, for instance $P(A|B)$, to the probability, $P(A)$. If these two probabilities are the same, we say that the two events, A and B, are independent; if the probabilities differ, the two events are dependent.

INDEPENDENT VERSUS DEPENDENT EVENTS

Two events, A and B, are independent if $P(A|B) = P(A)$ or, equivalently, $P(A \cap B) = P(A|B)P(B) = P(A)P(B)$. Otherwise, the events are dependent.

EXAMPLE 4.10

Suppose that for a given year there is a 2% chance that your desktop computer will crash and a 6% chance that your laptop computer will crash. Moreover, there is a 0.12% chance that both computers will crash. Is the reliability of the two computers independent of each other?

SOLUTION: Let event D represent the outcome that your desktop crashes and event L represent the outcome that your laptop crashes. Therefore, $P(D) = 0.02$, $P(L) = 0.06$, and $P(D \cap L) = 0.0012$. The reliability of the two computers is independent because

$$P(D|L) = \frac{P(D \cap L)}{P(L)} = \frac{0.0012}{0.06} = 0.02 = P(D).$$

In other words, if your laptop crashes, it does not alter the probability that your desktop also crashes. Equivalently, we show that the events are independent because $P(D \cap L) = P(D)P(L) = 0.0012$.

EXERCISES 4.2

Mechanics

11. Let $P(A) = 0.65$, $P(B) = 0.30$, and $P(A|B) = 0.45$.
    a. Calculate $P(A \cap B)$.
    b. Calculate $P(A \cup B)$.
    c. Calculate $P(B|A)$.
12. Let $P(A) = 0.55$, $P(B) = 0.30$, and $P(A \cap B) = 0.10$.
    a. Calculate $P(A|B)$.
    b. Calculate $P(A \cup B)$.
    c. Calculate $P((A \cup B)^c)$.
13. Let A and B be mutually exclusive events with $P(A) = 0.25$ and $P(B) = 0.30$.
    a. Calculate $P(A \cap B)$.
    b. Calculate $P(A \cup B)$.
    c. Calculate $P(A|B)$.
14. Let A and B be independent events with $P(A) = 0.40$ and $P(B) = 0.50$.
    a. Calculate $P(A \cap B)$.
    b. Calculate $P((A \cup B)^c)$.
    c. Calculate $P(A|B)$.
15. Let $P(A) = 0.15$, $P(B) = 0.10$, and $P(A \cap B) = 0.05$.
    a. Are A and B independent events? Explain.
    b. Are A and B mutually exclusive events? Explain.
    c. What is the probability that neither A nor B takes place?
16. Consider the following probabilities: $P(A) = 0.40$, $P(B) = 0.50$, and $P(A^c \cap B^c) = 0.24$. Find:
    a. $P(A^c|B^c)$
    b. $P(A^c \cup B^c)$
    c. $P(A \cup B)$
17. Consider the following probabilities: $P(A^c) = 0.30$, $P(B) = 0.60$, and $P(A \cap B^c) = 0.24$. Find:
    a. $P(A|B^c)$
    b. $P(B^c|A)$
    c. Are A and B independent events? Explain.

Applications

18. Only 20% of students in a college ever go to their professor during office hours. Of those who go, 30% seek minor clarification and 70% seek major clarification.
    a. What is the probability that a student goes to the professor during her office hours for a minor clarification?
    b. What is the probability that a student goes to the professor during her office hours for a major clarification?
19. The probabilities that stock A will rise in price is 0.40 and that stock B will rise in price is 0.60. Further, if stock B rises in price, the probability that stock A will also rise in price is 0.50.
    a. What is the probability that at least one of the stocks will rise in price?
    b. Are events A and B mutually exclusive? Explain.
    c. Are events A and B independent? Explain.
20. Fraud detection has become an indispensable tool for banks and credit card companies to combat fraudulent credit card transactions. A fraud detection firm raises an alarm on 5% of all transactions and on 80% of fraudulent transactions. What is the probability that the transaction is fraudulent if the firm does not raise an alarm? Assume that 1% of all transactions are fraudulent.
21. Dr. Miriam Johnson has been teaching accounting for over 20 years. From her experience, she knows that 60% of her students do homework regularly. Moreover, 95% of the

students who do their homework regularly pass the course. She also knows that 85% of her students pass the course.

a. What is the probability that a student will do homework regularly and also pass the course?
b. What is the probability that a student will neither do homework regularly nor will pass the course?
c. Are the events "pass the course" and "do homework regularly" mutually exclusive? Explain.
d. Are the events "pass the course" and "do homework regularly" independent? Explain.

22. Records show that 5% of all college students are foreign students who also smoke. It is also known that 50% of all foreign college students smoke. What percent of the students at this university are foreign?

23. An analyst estimates that the probability of default on a seven-year AA-rated bond is 0.06, while that on a seven-year A-rated bond is 0.13. The probability that they will both default is 0.04.
    a. What is the probability that at least one of the bonds defaults?
    b. What is the probability that neither the seven-year AA-rated bond nor the seven-year A-rated bond defaults?
    c. Given that the seven-year AA-rated bond defaults, what is the probability that the seven-year A-rated bond also defaults?

24. Mike Danes has been delayed in going to the annual sales event at one of his favorite apparel stores. His friend has just texted him that there are only 20 shirts left, of which 8 are in size M, 10 in size L, and 2 in size XL. Also 9 of the shirts are white, 5 are blue, and the remaining are of mixed colors. Mike is interested in getting a white or a blue shirt in size L. Define the events A = Getting a white or a blue shirt and B = Getting a shirt in size L.
    a. Find $P(A)$, $P(A^c)$, and $P(B)$.
    b. Are the events A and B mutually exclusive? Explain.
    c. Would you describe Mike's preference by the events $A \cup B$ or $A \cap B$?

25. In general, shopping online is supposed to be more convenient than going to stores. However, according to a poll, 87% of people have experienced problems with an online transaction. Forty-two percent of people who experienced a problem abandoned the transaction or switched to a competitor's website. Fifty-three percent of people who experienced problems contacted customer-service representatives.
    a. What proportion of people did not experience problems with an online transaction?
    b. What proportion of people experienced problems with an online transaction and abandoned the transaction or switched to a competitor's website?
    c. What proportion of people experienced problems with an online transaction and contacted customer-service representatives?

26. A manufacturing firm just received a shipment of 20 assembly parts, of slightly varied sizes, from a vendor. The manager knows that there are only 15 parts in the shipment that would be suitable. He examines these parts one at a time.
    a. Find the probability that the first part is suitable.
    b. If the first part is suitable, find the probability that the second part is also suitable.
    c. If the first part is suitable, find the probability that the second part is not suitable.

27. Apple products have become a household name in America. Suppose that the likelihood of owning an Apple product is 61% for households with kids and 48% for households without kids. Suppose there are 1,200 households in a representative community, of which 820 are with kids and the rest are without kids.
    a. Are the events "household with kids" and "household without kids" mutually exclusive and exhaustive? Explain.
    b. What is the probability that a household is without kids?
    c. What is the probability that a household is with kids and owns an Apple product?
    d. What is the probability that a household is without kids and does not own an Apple product?

28. Bank regulators are renewing efforts to require Wall Street executives to cut back on bonuses. Despite that, it is believed that 10 out of 15 members of the board of directors of a company are in favor of the bonus. Suppose two members are randomly selected by the media.
    a. What is the probability that both of them are in favor of the bonus?
    b. What is the probability that neither of them is in favor of the bonus?

29. Christine has asked Dave and Mike to help her move into a new apartment on Sunday morning. She has asked them both, in case one of them does not show up. From past experience, Christine knows that there is a 40% chance that Dave will not show up and a 30% chance that Mike will not show up. Dave and Mike do not know each other and their decisions can be assumed to be independent.
    a. What is the probability that both Dave and Mike will show up?
    b. What is the probability that at least one of them will show up?
    c. What is the probability that neither Dave nor Mike will show up?

30. According to the Census's Population Survey, the percentage of children with two parents at home is the highest for Asian people and lowest for black people. It is reported that 85% of Asian, 78% of white, 70% of Hispanic, and 38% of black children have two parents at home. Suppose there are 500 students in a representative school, of which 280 are white, 50 are Asian, 100 are Hispanic, and 70 are black.

a. Are the events "Asian" and "black" mutually exclusive and exhaustive? Explain.
b. What is the probability that a child is not white?
c. What is the probability that a child is white and has both parents at home?
d. What is the probability that a child is Asian and does not have both parents at home?

31. According to results from the Spine Patient Outcomes Research Trial, or SPORT, surgery for a painful, common back condition resulted in significantly reduced back pain and better physical function than treatment with drugs and physical therapy. SPORT followed 803 patients, of whom 398 ended up getting surgery. After two years, of those who had surgery, 63% said they had a major improvement in their condition, compared with 29% among those who received nonsurgical treatment.
   a. What is the probability that a patient had surgery? What is the probability that a patient did not have surgery?
   b. What is the probability that a patient had surgery and experienced a major improvement in his or her condition?
   c. What is the probability that a patient received nonsurgical treatment and experienced a major improvement in his or her condition?

32. According to a survey by two United Nations agencies and a nongovernmental organization, two in every three women in the Indian capital of New Delhi are likely to face some form of sexual harassment in a year. The study also reports that women who use public transportation are especially vulnerable. Suppose the corresponding probability of harassment for women who use public transportation is 0.82. It is also known that 28% of women use public transportation.
   a. What is the probability that a woman takes public transportation and also faces sexual harassment?
   b. If a woman is sexually harassed, what is the probability that she had taken public transportation?

4.3 CONTINGENCY TABLES AND PROBABILITIES

LO 4.3

Calculate and interpret probabilities from a contingency table.

As discussed in Chapter 2, a **contingency table** proves very useful when examining the relationship between two categorical variables. It shows the frequencies for two categorical variables, x and y, where each cell represents a mutually exclusive combination of the pair of x and y observations. Contingency tables are widely used in marketing as well as other business applications. In this section, we will use them to calculate empirical probabilities of relevant events.

In the introductory case, Janet would like to use the information on age groups and enrollment outcome to develop a data-driven strategy for selecting which new open house attendees to contact. Table 4.4 displays the contingency table that shows the frequencies for age groups and enrollment outcome of 24/7 Fitness Center past attendees.

TABLE 4.4 Enrollment and Age Frequencies of Attendees

	Age Group			
Outcome	Under 30 (*U*)	Between 30 and 50 (*B*)	Over 50 (*O*)	Total
Enroll (*E*)	24	72	44	140
Not Enroll (*N*)	84	88	88	260
Total	108	160	132	400

As you can see, there are two outcomes regarding club membership (Enroll and Not enroll) and three age groups of open house attendees (Under 30, Between 30 and 50, and Over 50). There are 400 open house attendees of which 108 are under 30 years old, 160 are between 30 and 50 years old, and 132 are over 50 years old. Furthermore, 140 open house attendees enrolled and 260 did not enroll in the fitness center.

Recall that we can estimate an empirical probability by calculating the relative frequency of the occurrence of the event. To make calculating these probabilities less cumbersome, it is often useful to denote each event with letter notation. In Table 4.4, we let the letters E and N denote the events "Enroll" and "Not Enroll", respectively. Similarly, we use the letters U, B, and O to denote the events "Under 30", "Between 30 and 50", and "Over 50", respectively.

The following example illustrates how to calculate empirical probabilities when the data are presented in the form of a contingency table.

EXAMPLE 4.11

Use the contingency table in Table 4.4 to answer the following questions.

a. What is the probability that a randomly selected attendee enrolls in the fitness center?

b. What is the probability that a randomly selected attendee is over 50 years old?

c. What is the probability that a randomly selected attendee enrolls in the fitness center and is over 50 years old?

d. What is the probability that a randomly selected attendee enrolls in the fitness center or is over 50 years old?

e. What is the probability that an attendee enrolls in the fitness center, given that he/she is over 50 years old?

SOLUTION:

a. $P(E) = \frac{140}{400} = 0.35$; there is a 35% chance that a randomly selected attendee enrolls in the fitness center.

b. $P(O) = \frac{132}{400} = 0.33$; there is a 33% chance that a randomly selected attendee is over 50 years old.

c. $P(E \cap O) = \frac{44}{400} = 0.11$; there is a 11% chance that a randomly selected attendee enrolls in the fitness center and is over 50 years old.

d. $P(E \cup O) = \frac{24 + 72 + 44 + 88}{400} = 0.57$; there is a 57% chance that a randomly selected attendee enrolls in the fitness center or is over 50 years old. Alternatively, we can use the addition rule to compute this probability as $P(E \cup O) = P(E) + P(O) - P(E \cap O) = 0.35 + 0.33 - 0.11 = 0.57$.

e. We wish to calculate the conditional probability, $P(E|O)$. When the information is in the form of a contingency table, calculating a conditional probability is rather straightforward. We are given the information that the attendee is over 50 years old, so the relevant sample size shrinks from 400 attendees to 132 attendees. We can ignore all attendees who are under 30 years old or between 30 and 50 years old. Thus, of the 132 attendees who are over 50 years old, 44 of them enroll in the fitness center. Therefore, the probability that an attendee enrolls in the fitness center, given that he/she is over 50 years old is calculated as $P(E|O) = \frac{44}{132} = 0.33$. Alternatively, we can use the conditional probability formula to compute this probability as $P(E|O) = \frac{P(E \cap O)}{P(O)} = \frac{0.11}{0.33} = 0.33$.

Arguably, a more convenient way of expressing relevant probabilities is to convert the contingency table to a joint probability table. The frequency in each cell is divided by the number of outcomes in the sample space, which in this example is 400. Table 4.5 shows the results.

TABLE 4.5 Converting a Contingency Table to a Joint Probability Table

	Age Group			
Outcome	Under 30 (*U*)	Between 30 and 50 (*B*)	Over 50 (*O*)	Total
Enroll (*E*)	0.06	0.18	0.11	0.35
Not Enroll (*N*)	0.21	0.22	0.22	0.65
Total	0.27	0.40	0.33	1.00

The values in the interior of the table represent the probabilities of the intersection of two events, which as noted earlier are also referred to as **joint probabilities**. For instance, the probability that an attendee enrolls in the fitness center and is over 50 years old, denoted $P(E \cap O)$, is 0.11. Similarly, we can readily read from this table that there is a 22% chance that an attendee does not enroll in the fitness center and is between 30 and 50 years old, or $P(N \cap B) = 0.22$.

The values in the margins of Table 4.5 represent unconditional probabilities, also referred to as **marginal probabilities.** For example, the probability that a randomly selected attendee is over 50 years old is $P(O) = 0.33$. Similarly, the probability that an attendee enrolls in the fitness center is $P(E) = 0.35$.

Note that the conditional probability is basically the ratio of a joint probability to a marginal probability. Take for example the conditional probability $P(E|O) = \frac{(P(E \cap O))}{P(O)}$ where the numerator is the joint probability, $P(E \cap O)$, and the denominator is the marginal probability, $P(O)$. Using joint and marginal probabilities, we can calculate, for example, $P(E|O) = \frac{0.11}{0.33} = 0.33$.

EXAMPLE 4.12

Use the joint probability table in Table 4.5 to answer the following questions.

a. Calculate the conditional probabilities of enrolling in the fitness center for the different age groups.

b. Is age related to enrollment? Explain using probabilities.

SOLUTION:

a. For the event "Under 30", the conditional probability of enrolling is calculated as $P(E|U) = \frac{P(E \cap U)}{P(U)} = \frac{0.06}{0.27} = 0.22$. Similarly, for the other age groups, we compute $P(E|B) = \frac{P(E \cap B)}{P(B)} = \frac{0.18}{0.40} = 0.45$ and $P(E|O) = \frac{P(E \cap O)}{P(O)} = \frac{0.11}{0.33} = 0.33$.

b. If age and enrollment were independent, then $P(E|U) = P(E|B) = P(E|O) = P(E)$. In other words, the probability of enrollment will not be impacted by the age of attendees. Earlier, we found the unconditional probability of enrolling as $P(E) = 0.35$. Because the conditional probabilities of enrolling found in part a differ from $P(E)$, we can conclude that age and enrollment are not independent. The manager should focus on the attendees in the age group "Between 30 and 50" because they have the highest probability of buying a gym membership.

A Note on Independence with Empirical Probabilities

It is important to note that the conclusions about independence, such as the one made in Example 4.12, are informal because they are based on empirical probabilities computed from given sample information. In Example 4.12, these empirical probabilities are likely to change if a different sample of 400 attendees is used. Formal tests of independence are discussed in Chapter 12.

SYNOPSIS OF INTRODUCTORY CASE

Erik Isakson/Getty Images

Gyms and exercise facilities usually have a high turnover rate among their members. Like other gyms, 24/7 Fitness Center relies on recruiting new members on a regular basis in order to sustain its business and financial well-being. Janet Williams, a manager at 24/7 Fitness Center, analyzes data from the gym's past open houses. She wants to gain a better insight into which attendees are likely to purchase a gym membership after attending an open house.

After careful analysis of the contingency table representing frequencies for age groups and enrollment outcome of attendees, several interesting observations are made. From a sample of 400 past attendees, 27% are younger than 30 years old, 40% are between 30 and 50 years old, and 33% are over 50 years old. It is also determined that 35% of all attendees enroll in 24/7 fitness center. Further inspection of the contingency table reveals that the probability of enrollment depends on the age of the attendees. In particular, the attendees who are between 30 and 50 years old have a 45% likelihood of enrolling in the fitness center, which is the highest of all age groups. The corresponding likelihood of enrollment is 22% for under 30 years old and 33% for over 50 years old.

Overall, with a simple analysis of the contingency table, Janet is able to identify individual open house attendees who are likely to purchase a gym membership. With this insight, she can train her staff to regularly analyze the monthly open house data in order to help 24/7 Fitness Center grow its membership base.

EXERCISES 4.3

Mechanics

33. Consider the following contingency table.

	B	B^c
A	26	34
A^c	14	26

a. Convert the contingency table into a joint probability table.
b. What is the probability that A occurs?
c. What is the probability that A and B occur?
d. Given that B has occurred, what is the probability that A occurs?
e. Given that A^c has occurred, what is the probability that B occurs?
f. Are A and B mutually exclusive events? Explain.
g. Are A and B independent events? Explain.

34. Consider the following joint probability table.

	B_1	B_2	B_3	B_4
A	0.09	0.22	0.15	0.20
A^c	0.03	0.10	0.09	0.12

a. What is the probability that A occurs?
b. What is the probability that B_2 occurs?
c. What is the probability that A^c and B_4 occur?
d. What is the probability that A or B_3 occurs?
e. Given that B_2 has occurred, what is the probability that A occurs?
f. Given that A has occurred, what is the probability that B_4 occurs?

Applications

35. A poll asked 3,228 16- to 21-year-olds whether or not they are likely to serve in the U.S. military. The following joint probability table, cross-classified by sex and race, reports the proportion of those polled who responded that they are likely or very likely to serve in the active-duty military.

	Race		
Sex	Hispanic	Black	White
Male	0.335	0.205	0.165
Female	0.145	0.105	0.045

a. What is the probability that a randomly selected respondent is female?
b. What is the probability that a randomly selected respondent is Hispanic?
c. Given that a respondent is female, what is the probability that she is Hispanic?
d. Given that a respondent is white, what is the probability that the respondent is male?
e. Are the events "Male" and "White" independent? Explain using probabilities.

36. A report suggests that business majors spend the least amount of time on course work than all other college students. A provost of a university decides to conduct a survey where students are asked if they study hard, defined by spending at least 20 hours per week on course work. Of 120 business majors included in the survey, 20 said that they studied hard, as compared to 48 out of 150 nonbusiness majors who said that they studied hard.
a. Construct a contingency table that shows the frequencies for the variables Major (business or nonbusiness) and Study Hard (yes or no).
b. Find the probability that a business major spends less than 20 hours per week on course work.
c. What is the probability that a student studies hard?
d. If a student spends at least 20 hours on course work, what is the probability that he/she is a business major? What is the corresponding probability that he/she is a nonbusiness major?

37. Research suggests that Americans are becoming increasingly polarized on issues pertaining to the environment. It is reported that 70% of Democrats see signs of global warming as compared to only 30% of Republicans who feel the same. Suppose the survey was based on 400 Democrats and 400 Republicans.
a. Construct a contingency table that shows frequencies for the variables Political Affiliation (Democrat or Republican) and Global Warming (yes or no).
b. Find the probability that a Republican sees signs of global warming.
c. Find the probability that a person does not see signs of global warming.
d. If a person sees signs of global warming, what is the probability that this person is a Democrat?

38. **FILE** ***Happiness.*** There have been numerous attempts that relate happiness with income. In a recent survey, 290 individuals were asked to evaluate happiness (Yes or No) and income (Low, Medium, or High). The accompanying table shows a portion of the data.

Individual	Income	Happy?
1	Low	No
2	Low	Yes
⋮	⋮	⋮
290	High	Yes

a. Use the data to construct a contingency table.
b. Find the probability that a randomly selected individual feels happy.
c. Find the probability that a low-income individual feels happy. Find the corresponding probabilities for medium-income and high-income individuals.
d. Is income related to happiness? Explain using probabilities.

39. **FILE** ***Crash.*** The California Highway Patrol (CHP) routinely compiles car crash data in California. The accompanying table shows a portion of the data for Santa Clara county. It shows information on the type of car crash (Head-On or Not Head-On) and light (Daylight or Not Daylight).

ID	Crash	Light
1	Not Head-On	Not Daylight
2	Not Head-On	Daylight
⋮	⋮	⋮
4858	Not Head-On	Not Daylight

a. Use the data to construct a contingency table.
b. Find the probability that a randomly selected car crash is a head-on.
c. Find the probability that a randomly selected car crash is at daylight.
d. Find the probability that the car crash is a head-on, given daylight. Find the corresponding probability given not daylight.
e. Is crash related to light? Explain using probabilities.

40. The research team at a leading perfume company is trying to test the market for its newly introduced perfume. In particular the team wishes to look for sex and international differences in the preference for this perfume. They sample 2,500 people internationally and each person in the sample is asked to try the new perfume and list his/her preference. The following table reports the results.

Preference	Sex	America	Europe	Asia
Like it	Men	210	150	120
	Women	370	310	180
Don't like it	Men	290	150	80
	Women	330	190	120

a. What is the probability that a randomly selected man likes the perfume?
b. What is the probability that a randomly selected Asian likes the perfume?
c. What is the probability that a randomly selected European woman does not like the perfume?
d. What is the probability that a randomly selected American man does not like the perfume?
e. Are the events "Men" and "Like Perfume" independent in (i) America, (ii) Europe, and (iii) Asia? Explain using probabilities.
f. Internationally, are the events "Men" and "Like Perfume" independent? Explain using probabilities.

41. More and more households are struggling to pay utility bills given high heating costs. Particularly hard hit are households with homes heated with propane or heating oil. Many of these households are spending twice as much to stay warm this winter compared to those who heat with natural gas or electricity. A representative sample of 500 households was taken to investigate if the type of heating influences whether or not a household is delinquent in paying its utility bill. The following table reports the results.

	Type of Heating			
Delinquent in Payment?	Natural Gas	Electricity	Heating Oil	Propane
Yes	50	20	15	10
No	240	130	20	15

a. What is the probability that a randomly selected household uses heating oil?
b. What is the probability that a randomly selected household is delinquent in paying its utility bill?
c. What is the probability that a randomly selected household uses heating oil and is delinquent in paying its utility bill?
d. Given that a household uses heating oil, what is the probability that it is delinquent in paying its utility bill?
e. Given that a household is delinquent in paying its utility bill, what is the probability that the household uses electricity?
f. Are the events "Heating Oil" and "Delinquent in Payment" independent? Explain using probabilities.

4.4 THE TOTAL PROBABILITY RULE AND BAYES' THEOREM

LO 4.4

Apply the total probability rule and Bayes' theorem.

In this section, we present two important rules in probability theory: the total probability rule and Bayes' theorem. The **total probability rule** is a useful tool for breaking the computation of a probability into distinct cases. **Bayes' theorem** uses this rule to update the probability of an event that has been affected by a new piece of evidence.

The Total Probability Rule and Bayes' Theorem

Often in business the probability of an event is not readily available from the given information. The total probability rule expresses the probability of an event in terms of joint or conditional probabilities. Let $P(A)$ denote the probability of an event of interest. We can express $P(A)$ as the sum of probabilities of the intersections of A with some mutually exclusive and exhaustive events corresponding to an experiment. For instance, consider event B and its complement B^c. Figure 4.4 shows the sample space partitioned into these two mutually exclusive and exhaustive events. The circle, representing event A, consists entirely of its intersections with B and B^c. According to the total probability rule, $P(A)$ equals the sum of $P(A \cap B)$ and $P(A \cap B^c)$.

FIGURE 4.4

The total probability rule:
$P(A) = P(A \cap B) + P(A \cap B^c)$

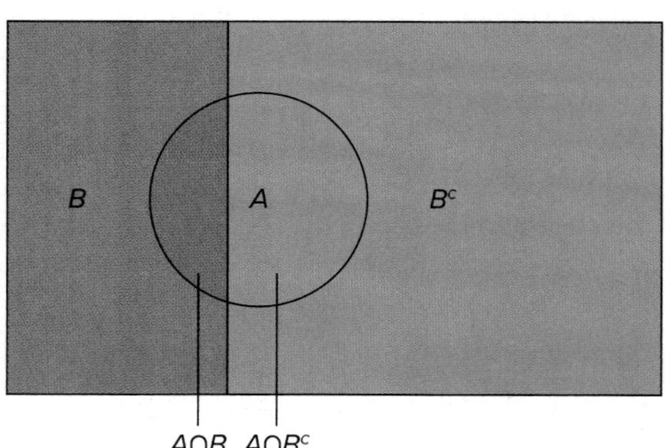

Oftentimes the joint probabilities needed to compute the total probability are not explicitly specified. Therefore, we use the multiplication rule to derive these probabilities from the conditional probabilities as $P(A \cap B) = P(A|B)P(B)$ and $P(A \cap B^c) = P(A|B^c)P(B^c)$.

The total probability rule is also needed to derive Bayes' theorem. Bayes' theorem is a procedure for updating probabilities based on new information. The original probability is an unconditional probability called a **prior probability,** in the sense that it reflects only what we know now before the arrival of any new information. On the basis of new information, we update the prior probability to arrive at a conditional probability called a **posterior probability.**

Suppose we know that 99% of the individuals who take a lie detector test tell the truth. Therefore, the prior probability of telling the truth is 0.99. Suppose an individual takes the lie detector test and the results indicate that the individual lied. Bayes' theorem updates a prior probability to compute a posterior probability, which in this example is essentially a conditional probability based on the information that the lie detector has detected a lie.

Let $P(B)$ denote the prior probability and $P(B \mid A)$ the posterior probability. Note that the posterior probability is conditional on event A, representing new information. Recall the conditional probability formula from Section 4.2:

$$P(B \mid A) = \frac{P(A \cap B)}{P(A)}.$$

In some instances, we may have to evaluate $P(B \mid A)$, but we do not have explicit information on $P(A \cap B)$ or $P(A)$. However, given information on $P(B)$, $P(A \mid B)$, and $P(A \mid B^c)$, we can use the total probability rule to find $P(B \mid A)$, as shown in the following definition box.

THE TOTAL PROBABILITY RULE AND BAYES' THEOREM

The total probability rule expresses the probability of event A in terms of joint or conditional probabilities. Given events B and B^c, the probability of event A can be found as

$$P(A) = P(A \cap B) + P(A \cap B^C) = P(A \mid B)P(B) + P(A \mid B^C)P(B^C).$$

Bayes' Theorem is a method for updating a prior probability, $P(B)$, to a posterior probability, $P(B \mid A)$. The posterior probability can be found as

$$P(B \mid A) = \frac{P(A \cap B)}{P(A \cap B) + P(A \cap B^c)} = \frac{P(A \mid B)P(B)}{P(A \mid B)P(B) + P(A \mid B^c)P(B^c)}.$$

In the above formula, we have used Bayes' theorem to update the prior probability $P(B)$ to the posterior probability $P(B \mid A)$. Equivalently, we can use Bayes' theorem to update the prior probability $P(A)$ to derive the posterior probability $P(A \mid B)$ by interchanging the events A and B in the above formula.

EXAMPLE 4.13

In a lie-detector test, an individual is asked to answer a series of questions while connected to a polygraph (lie detector). This instrument measures and records several physiological responses of the individual on the basis that false answers will produce distinctive measurements. Assume that 99% of the individuals who go in for a polygraph test tell the truth. These tests are considered to be 95% reliable. In other words, there is a 95% chance that the test will detect a lie if an individual actually lies. Let there also be a 0.5% chance that the test erroneously detects a lie even when the individual is telling the truth. An individual has just taken a polygraph test and the test has detected a lie. What is the probability that the individual was actually telling the truth?

SOLUTION:

First we define some events and their associated probabilities. Let D and T correspond to the events that the polygraph detects a lie and that an individual is telling the truth, respectively. We are given that $P(T) = 0.99$, implying that $P(T^c) = 1 - 0.99 = 0.01$. In addition, we formulate $P(D \mid T^c) = 0.95$ and $P(D \mid T) = 0.005$. We need to find $P(T \mid D)$ when we are not explicitly given $P(D \cap T)$ and $P(D)$. We can use Bayes' theorem to find

$$P(T|D) = \frac{P(D \cap T)}{P(D)} = \frac{P(D \cap T)}{P(D \cap T) + P(D \cap T^c)} = \frac{P(D|T)P(T)}{P(D|T)P(T) + P(D|T^c)P(T^c)}.$$

Although we can use this formula to solve the problem directly, we use Table 4.6 to help solve the problem systematically.

TABLE 4.6 Computing Posterior Probabilities for Example 4.13

Prior Probability	Conditional Probability	Joint Probability	Posterior Probability
$P(T) = 0.99$	$P(D \mid T) = 0.005$	$P(D \cap T) = 0.00495$	$P(T \mid D) = 0.3426$
$P(T^c) = 0.01$	$P(D \mid T^c) = 0.95$	$P(D \cap T^c) = 0.00950$	$P(T^c \mid D) = 0.6574$
$P(T) + P(T^c) = 1$		$P(D) = 0.01445$	$P(T \mid D) + P(T^c \mid D) = 1$

The first column presents prior probabilities and the second column shows related conditional probabilities. We first compute the denominator of Bayes' theorem by using the total probability rule, $P(D) = P(D \cap T) + P(D \cap T^c)$. Joint probabilities are calculated as products of conditional probabilities with their corresponding prior probabilities. For instance, in Table 4.6, in order to obtain $P(D \cap T)$, we multiply $P(D \mid T)$ with $P(T)$, which yields $P(D \cap T) = 0.005 \times 0.99 = 0.00495$. Similarly, we find $P(D \cap T^c) = 0.95 \times 0.01 = 0.00950$. Thus, according to the total probability rule, $P(D) = 0.00495 + 0.00950 = 0.01445$. Finally, $P(T|D) = \frac{P(D \cap T)}{P(D \cap T) + P(D \cap T^c)} = \frac{0.00495}{0.01445} = 0.3426$.

The prior probability of an individual telling the truth is 0.99. However, given the new information that the polygraph detected the individual telling a lie, the posterior probability of this individual telling the truth is now revised downward to 0.3426.

Extensions of the Total Probability Rule and Bayes' Theorem

So far we have used the total probability rule as well as Bayes' theorem based on two mutually exclusive and exhaustive events, namely, B and B^c. We can easily extend the analysis to include n mutually exclusive and exhaustive events, $B_1, B_2, \ldots, B_n$.

EXTENSIONS OF THE TOTAL PROBABILITY RULE AND BAYES' THEOREM

Let $B_1, B_2, \ldots, Bn$ represent n mutually exclusive and exhaustive events for $i = 1, 2, \ldots, n$. The total probability rule extends to

$$P(A) = P(A \cap B_1) + P(A \cap B_2) + \cdots + P(A \cap B_n) = P(A \mid B_1)P(B_1) + P(A \mid B_2)P(B_2) + \cdots + P(A \mid B_n)P(B_n).$$

We can use Bayes' Theorem to find the posterior probability as

$$P(B_i|A) = \frac{P(A \cap B_i)}{P(A \cap B_1) + P(A \cap B_2) + \cdots + P(A \cap B_n)} = \frac{P(A|B_i)P(B_i)}{P(A \mid B_1)P(B_1) + P(A \mid B_2)P(B_2) + \cdots + P(A \mid B_n)P(B_n)}.$$

EXAMPLE 4.14

Scott Myers is a security analyst for a telecommunications firm called Webtalk. Although he is optimistic about the firm's future, he is concerned that its stock price will be considerably affected by the condition of credit flow in the economy. He believes that the probability is 0.20 that credit flow will improve significantly, 0.50 that it will improve only marginally, and 0.30 that it will not improve at all. He also estimates that the probability that the stock price of Webtalk will go up is 0.90 with significant improvement in credit flow in the economy, 0.40 with marginal improvement in credit flow in the economy, and 0.10 with no improvement in credit flow in the economy.

a. Based on Scott's estimates, what is the probability that the stock price of Webtalk goes up?

b. If we know that the stock price of Webtalk has gone up, what is the probability that credit flow in the economy has improved significantly?

SOLUTION: As always, we first define the relevant events and their associated probabilities. Let S, M, and N denote significant, marginal, and no improvement in credit flow, respectively. Then $P(S) = 0.20$, $P(M) = 0.50$, and $P(N) = 0.30$. In addition, if we allow G to denote an increase in stock price, we formulate $P(G \mid S) = 0.90$, $P(G \mid M) = 0.40$, and $P(G \mid N) = 0.10$. We need to calculate $P(G)$ in part a and $P(S \mid G)$ in part b. Table 4.7 aids in assigning probabilities.

TABLE 4.7 Computing Posterior Probabilities for Example 4.14

Prior Probability	Conditional Probability	Joint Probability	Posterior Probability
$P(S) = 0.20$	$P(G \mid S) = 0.90$	$P(G \cap S) = 0.18$	$P(S \mid G) = 0.4390$
$P(M) = 0.50$	$P(G \mid M) = 0.40$	$P(G \cap M) = 0.20$	$P(M \mid G) = 0.4878$
$P(N) = 0.30$	$P(G \mid N) = 0.10$	$P(G \cap N) = 0.03$	$P(N \mid G) = 0.0732$
$P(S) + P(M) + P(N) = 1$		$P(G) = 0.41$	$P(S \mid G) + P(M \mid G) + P(N \mid G) = 1$

a. In order to calculate $P(G)$, we use the total probability rule, $P(G) = P(G \cap S) + P(G \cap M) + P(G \cap N)$. The joint probabilities are calculated as products of conditional probabilities with their corresponding prior probabilities. For instance, in Table 4.7, $P(G \cap S) = P(G \mid S)P(S) = 0.90 \times 0.20 = 0.18$. Therefore, the probability that the stock price of Webtalk goes up equals $P(G) = 0.18 + 0.20 + 0.03 = 0.41$.

b. According to Bayes' theorem, $P(S|G) = \frac{P(G \cap S)}{P(G)} = \frac{P(G \cap S)}{P(G \cap S) + P(G \cap M) + P(G \cap N)}$. We use the total probability rule in the denominator to find $P(G) = 0.18 + 0.20 + 0.03 = 0.41$. Therefore, $P(S|G) = \frac{P(G \cap S)}{P(G)} = \frac{0.18}{0.41} = 0.4390$. Note that the prior probability of a significant improvement in credit flow is revised upward from 0.20 to a posterior probability of 0.4390.

EXERCISES 4.4

Mechanics

42. Let $P(A) = 0.70$, $P(B \mid A) = 0.55$, and $P(B \mid A^c) = 0.10$. Find the following probabilities:
    a. $P(A^c)$
    b. $P(A \cap B)$ and $P(A^c \cap B)$
    c. $P(B)$
    d. $P(A \mid B)$

43. Complete the following probability table.

Prior Probability	Conditional Probability	Joint Probability	Posterior Probability
$P(B) = 0.85$	$P(A \mid B) = 0.05$	$P(A \cap B) =$	$P(B \mid A) =$
$P(B^c) =$	$P(A \mid B^c) = 0.80$	$P(A \cap B^c) =$	$P(B^c \mid A) =$
Total =		$P(A) =$	Total =

44. Let a sample space be partitioned into three mutually exclusive and exhaustive events, B_1, B_2, and B_3. Complete the following probability table.

Prior Probabilities	Conditional Probabilities	Joint Probabilities	Posterior Probabilities
$P(B_1) = 0.10$	$P(A \mid B_1) = 0.40$	$P(A \cap B_1) =$	$P(B_1 \mid A) =$
$P(B_2) =$	$P(A \mid B_2) = 0.60$	$P(A \cap B_2) =$	$P(B_2 \mid A) =$
$P(B_3) = 0.30$	$P(A \mid B_3) = 0.80$	$P(A \cap B_3) =$	$P(B_3 \mid A) =$
Total =		$P(A) =$	Total =

Applications

45. Christine has always been weak in mathematics. Based on her performance prior to the final exam in Calculus, there is a 40% chance that she will fail the course if she does not have a tutor. With a tutor, her probability of failing decreases to 10%. There is only a 50% chance that she will find a tutor at such short notice.
    a. What is the probability that Christine fails the course?
    b. Christine ends up failing the course. What is the probability that she had found a tutor?

46. An analyst expects that 20% of all publicly traded companies will experience a decline in earnings next year. The analyst has developed a ratio to help forecast this decline. If the company is headed for a decline, there is a 70% chance that this ratio will be negative. If the company is not headed for a decline, there is a 15% chance that the ratio will be negative. The analyst randomly selects a company and its ratio is negative. What is the posterior probability that the company will experience a decline?

47. The State Police are trying to crack down on speeding on a particular portion of the Massachusetts Turnpike. To aid in this pursuit, they have purchased a new radar gun that promises greater consistency and reliability. Specifically, the gun advertises ± one-mile-per-hour accuracy 98% of the time; that is, there is a 0.98 probability that the gun will detect a speeder, if the driver is actually speeding. Assume there is a 1% chance that the gun erroneously detects a speeder even when the driver is below the speed limit. Suppose that 95% of the drivers drive below the speed limit on this stretch of the Massachusetts Turnpike.
    a. What is the probability that the gun detects speeding and the driver was speeding?
    b. What is the probability that the gun detects speeding and the driver was not speeding?
    c. Suppose the police stop a driver because the gun detects speeding. What is the probability that the driver was actually driving below the speed limit?

48. According to data from the *National Health and Nutrition Examination Survey,* 33% of white, 49.6% of black, 43% of Hispanic, and 8.9% of Asian women are obese. In a representative town, 48% of women are white, 19% are black, 26% are Hispanic, and the remaining 7% are Asian.
    a. Find the probability that a randomly selected woman in this town is obese.
    b. Given that a woman is obese, what is the probability that she is white?
    c. Given that a woman is obese, what is the probability that she is black?
    d. Given that a woman is obese, what is the probability that she is Asian?

49. An analyst thinks that next year there is a 20% chance that the world economy will be good, a 50% chance that it will be neutral, and a 30% chance that it will be poor. She also predicts probabilities that the performance of a start-up firm, Creative Ideas, will be good, neutral, or poor for each of the economic states of the world economy. The following table presents probabilities for three states of the world economy and the corresponding conditional probabilities for Creative Ideas.

State of the World Economy	Probability of Economic State	Performance of Creative Ideas	Conditional Probability of Creative Ideas
Good	0.20	Good	0.60
		Neutral	0.30
		Poor	0.10
Neutral	0.50	Good	0.40
		Neutral	0.30
		Poor	0.30
Poor	0.30	Good	0.20
		Neutral	0.30
		Poor	0.50

    a. What is the probability that the performance of the world economy will be neutral and that of Creative Ideas will be poor?
    b. What is the probability that the performance of Creative Ideas will be poor?
    c. The performance of Creative Ideas was poor. What is the probability that the performance of the world economy had also been poor?

50. A crucial game of the Los Angeles Lakers basketball team depends on the health of their key player. According to his doctor's report, there is a 40% chance that he will be fully fit to play, a 30% chance that he will be somewhat fit to play, and a 30% chance that he will not be able to play at all. The coach has estimated the chances of winning at 80% if the player is fully fit, 60% if he is somewhat fit, and 40% if he is unable to play.
    a. What is the probability that the Lakers will win the game?
    b. You have just heard that the Lakers won the game. What is the probability that the key player had been fully fit to play in the game?

4.5 COUNTING RULES

LO 4.5

Use a counting rule to calculate the probability of an event.

In several areas of statistics, including the binomial distribution discussed in the next chapter, the calculation of probabilities involves defining and counting outcomes. Here we discuss principles and shortcuts for counting. Specifically, we explore the factorial, combination, and permutation notations. In certain circumstances, we find that counting rules can aid in calculating the probability of an event.

When we are interested in counting the arrangements of a given set of n items, we use the **factorial formula,** denoted $n!$. In other words, given n items, there are $n!$ ways of arranging them. We apply the factorial when there are no groups—we are only arranging a given set of n items.

THE FACTORIAL FORMULA

The number of ways to assign every member of a group of size n to n slots is calculated using the factorial formula:

$$n! = n \times (n-1) \times (n-2) \times (n-3) \times \cdots \times 1$$

By definition, $0! = 1$.

EXAMPLE 4.15

A little-league coach has nine players on his team and he has to assign each of the players to one of nine positions (pitcher, catcher, first base, etc.). In how many ways can the assignments be made?

SOLUTION: The first player may be assigned to nine different positions. Then eight positions remain. The second player can be assigned to eight different positions. The third player can be assigned to seven different positions, and so on, until the ninth and last player can be assigned in only one way. The total number of different assignments is equal to $9! = 9 \times 8 \times \cdots \times 1 = 362{,}880$.

We apply the combination formula and the permutation formula to two groups of predetermined size. When the order of the arrangement does not matter, we use the **combination formula**.

THE COMBINATION FORMULA

The number of ways to choose x objects from a total of n objects, where the order in which the x objects are listed *does not matter,* is calculated using the combination formula:

$${}_nC_x = \binom{n}{x} = \frac{n!}{(n-x)!x!}$$

EXAMPLE 4.16

The little-league coach from Example 4.15 recruits three more players so that his team has backups in case of injury. Now his team totals 12.

a. How many ways can the coach select nine players from the 12-player roster?

b. If each of the lineups from part a is equally likely, what is the probability that the coach selects a particular lineup?

SOLUTION:

a. This is a combination problem because we are simply interested in placing 9 players on the field. We have no concern, for instance, as to whether a player pitches, catches, or plays first base. In other words, the order in which the players are selected is not important. We make use of the combination formula as follows:

$$_{12}C_9 = \binom{12}{9} = \frac{12!}{(12-9)! \times 9!} = \frac{12 \times 11 \times \cdots \times 1}{(3 \times 2 \times 1) \times (9 \times 8 \times \cdots \times 1)} = 220.$$

b. Given that each lineup in part a is equally likely, the probability that any one lineup occurs is 1/220 = 0.0045.

When the order of the arrangement matters, we use the **permutation formula**. Generally, we look for a specific reference to "order" being important when applying the permutation formula.

THE PERMUTATION FORMULA

The number of ways to choose x objects from a total of n objects, where the order in which the x objects is listed *does matter,* is calculated using the permutation formula:

$$_nP_x = \frac{n!}{(n-x)!}$$

EXAMPLE 4.17

Now suppose the little league coach from Example 4.16 recognizes that the nine positions of baseball are quite different. It matters whether one player is pitching or whether that same player is in the outfield.

a. In how many ways can the coach assign his 12-player roster to the nine different positions?

b. If each of the lineups from part a are equally likely, what is the probability that the coach selects a particular lineup?

SOLUTION:

a. This is a permutation problem because the order in which the coach assigns the positions matters. For example, a lineup that has one player playing in the outfield is different from a lineup that has that same player pitching. We calculate the answer as follows:

$$_{12}P_9 = \frac{12!}{(12-9)!} = \frac{12 \times 11 \times \cdots \times 1}{3 \times 2 \times 1} = 79{,}833{,}600.$$

Comparing the answers we obtained from Examples 4.16 and 4.17, we see there is a big difference between the number of arrangements when the position of the player does not matter versus the number of arrangements when the position is important.

b. Given that each lineup in part a is equally likely, the probability that any one lineup occurs is 1/79,833,600 ≈ 0.0000; that is, the probability approaches zero.

EXERCISES 4.5

Mechanics

51. Calculate the following values.
    a. 8! and 6!
    b. ${}_8C_6$
    c. ${}_8P_6$
52. Calculate the following values.
    a. 7! and 3!
    b. ${}_7C_3$
    c. ${}_7P_3$

Applications

53. Twenty cancer patients volunteer for a clinical trial. Ten of the patients will receive a placebo and 10 will receive the trial drug. In how many different ways can the researchers select 10 patients to receive the trial drug from the total of 20?
54. At a local elementary school, a principal is making random class assignments for her eight teachers. Each teacher must be assigned to exactly one job. In how many ways can the assignments be made?
55. There are 10 players on the local basketball team. The coach decides to randomly pick five players to start the game.
    a. In how many different ways can the coach select five players to start the game if order does not matter?
    b. In how many different ways can the coach select five players to start the game if order (the type of position, i.e., point guard, center, etc.) matters?
56. A horse-racing fan is contemplating the many different outcomes in an eight-horse race.
    a. How many different outcomes are possible if only the first three places are considered and ranking (first, second, and third) is important?
    b. If each of the outcomes in part a is equally likely, what is the probability of selecting the winning outcome?
    c. How many different outcomes are possible if only the first three places are considered and ranking (first, second, and third) is not important?
    d. If each of the outcomes in part c is equally likely, what is the probability of selecting the winning outcome?
57. David Barnes and his fiancée Valerie Shah are visiting Hawaii. At the Hawaiian Cultural Center in Honolulu, they are told that 2 out of a group of 8 people will be randomly picked for a free lesson of a Tahitian dance.
    a. What is the probability that both David and Valerie get picked for the Tahitian dance lesson?
    b. What is the probability that Valerie gets picked before David for the Tahitian dance lesson?
58. Jacqueline Fibbe manages 10 employees at a small ice cream store in Beverly Farms, MA. She assigns three employees for each eight-hour shift.
    a. If order is not important, in how many different ways can she select three employees from the total of 10 for each eight-hour shift?
    b. Megan H. is one of the 10 employees. If the assignment of employees is random, how many of the shifts in part a will include Megan H.?

4.5 WRITING WITH DATA

Case Study

SEASTOCK/Shutterstock

Support for marijuana legalization in the United States has grown remarkably over the past few decades. In 1969, when the question was first presented, only 12% of Americans were in favor of its legalization. This support had increased to over 25% by the late 1970s. While support was stagnant from 1981 to 1997, the turn of the century brought a renewed interest in its legalization, with the percentage of Americans in favor exceeding 30% by 2000 and 40% by 2009.

Alexis Lewis works for a drug policy institute that focuses on science, health, and human rights. She is analyzing the demographic breakdown of marijuana supporters. Using results from a 2016 survey, she has found that support for marijuana legalization varies considerably depending on a person's age group. Alexis compiles information on support based on age group as shown in Table 4.8.

TABLE 4.8 Percentage Support for Legalizing Marijuana by Age Group

Age Group	Support
Millennial (18–35)	71%
Generation X (36–51)	57%
Baby Boomer (52–70)	56%
Silent (71 and older)	33%

Alexis finds that another important factor determining the fate of marijuana legalization concerns each age group's ability to sway the vote. For adults eligible to vote as of 2016, she breaks down each age group's voting power. The Millennial, Generation X, Baby Boomer, and Silent generations account for 31%, 25%, 31%, and 13% of the voting population, respectively.

Alexis wants to use this information to calculate and interpret relevant probabilities to better understand the support for the legalization of marijuana in the United States.

Sample Report—Linking Support for Legalizing Marijuana with Age Group

Driven by growing public support, the legalization of marijuana in America has been moving at a breakneck speed in recent years. As of 2016, marijuana is now legal in some form in 28 states and in Washington, DC. Even recreational marijuana is gaining support, becoming legal in Alaska, California, Colorado, Maine, Massachusetts, Nevada, Oregon, Washington, and Washington, DC. Changing demographics can help explain how the tide has turned in marijuana's favor, especially since Millennials (those between the ages of 18 and 35) are on the verge of becoming the nation's largest living generation.

A 2016 survey provides interesting data regarding support for marijuana legalization. Two factors seem to drive support for the issue: generation (or age group) and the relative size of a generation's voting bloc. For ease of interpretation, let *M, G, B,* and *S* denote "Millennial," "Generation X," "Baby Boomer," and "Silent" generations, respectively. Based on data from the survey, the following probability statements can be formulated with respect to the relative size of each generation's voting bloc: $P(M) = 0.31$, $P(G) = 0.25$, $P(B) = 0.31$, $P(S) = 0.13$. In other words, Millennials and Baby Boomers have the most voting power, each comprising 31% of the voting population; the Generation X and Silent generations represent 25% and 13% of the voting population, respectively.

Now let L denote "support for legalizing marijuana." Again, based on data from the survey, conditional probabilities can be specified as $P(L \mid M) = 0.71$, $P(L \mid G) = 0.57$, $P(L \mid B) = 0.56$, and $P(L \mid S) = 0.33$. Therefore, the probability that a randomly selected adult supports legal marijuana and is in the Millennial generation is determined as $P(L \cap M) = 0.71 \times 0.31 = 0.2201$. Similarly, $P(L \cap G) = 0.1425$, $P(L \cap B) = 0.1736$, and $P(L \cap S) = 0.0429$. By combining all generations, we deduce the total probability of support for legalizing marijuana as $P(L) = 0.2201 + 0.1425 + 0.1736 + 0.0429 = 0.5791$; in 2016, a staggering 58% of Americans support the legalization of marijuana. Table 4.9 is the joint probability table that summarizes unconditional and joint probabilities.

TABLE 4.9 Joint Probability Table for the Support for Legalizing Marijuana by Age Group

	Legalizing Marijuana		
Age Group	Support	Do not Support	Total
Millennial (18–35)	0.2201	0.0899	0.31
Generation X (36–51)	0.1425	0.1075	0.25
Baby Boomer (52–70)	0.1736	0.1364	0.31
Silent (71 and older)	0.0429	0.0871	0.13
Total	0.5791	0.4209	1.00

To put it in perspective, suppose that there are 1,000 randomly selected adult attendees at a conference. The results imply that there would be about 310 Millennial, 250 Generation X, 310 Baby Boomer, and 130 Silent attendees. Further, the supporters of marijuana legalization would include about 220 Millennial, 143 Generation X, 174 Baby Boomer, and 43 Silent attendees.

Millennials, with roughly 31% of the overall electorate, are now as large a political force as Baby Boomers. In general, Millennials tend to be liberal on social issues such as gay rights, immigration, and marijuana. This shift in population has not gone unnoticed by political parties, which all hope to court the more than 75 million of these eligible young voters.

Suggested Case Studies

Report 4.1 It is not uncommon to ignore the thyroid gland of women during pregnancy. This gland makes hormones that govern metabolism, helping to regulate body weight, heart rate, and a host of other factors. If the thyroid malfunctions, it can produce too little or too much of these hormones. Hypothyroidism, caused by an untreated underactive thyroid in pregnant women, carries the risk of impaired intelligence in the child. According to one research study, 62 out of 25,216 pregnant women were identified with hypothyroidism. Nineteen percent of the children born to women with an untreated underactive thyroid had an I.Q. of 85 or lower, compared with only 5% of those whose mothers had a healthy thyroid. It was also reported that if mothers have their hypothyroidism treated, their children's intelligence would not be impaired. In a report calculate and discuss (a) the likelihood that a woman suffers from hypothyroidism during pregnancy and later has a child with an I.Q. of 85 or lower, (b) the number of children in a sample of 100,000 who are likely to have an I.Q. of 85 or lower if the thyroid gland of pregnant women is ignored. Compare and comment on your answer to part b with the corresponding number if all pregnant women are tested and treated for hypothyroidism.

Report 4.2 It has generally been believed that it is not feasible for men and women to be just friends. Others argue that this belief may not be true anymore since gone are the days when men worked, and women stayed at home and the two got together only for romance. In a survey, 600 heterosexual college students were asked if it was feasible for men and women to be just friends of which 282 reported that it was not. In the survey, there were 240 male students of which 57.5% reported that it was not feasible for men and women to be just friends. Use these results to compute relevant probabilities to examine if men and women can be just friends and how the belief differs across the sexes.

Report 4.3 It is reported that rising gas prices have made California residents less resistant to offshore drilling. A Field Poll survey shows that a higher proportion of Californians supported the idea of drilling for oil or natural gas along the state's coast than a decade ago. Assume that random drilling for oil only succeeds 5% of the time. An oil company has just announced that it has discovered new technology for detecting oil. The technology is 80% reliable. That is, if there is oil, the technology will signal "oil" 80% of the time. Let there also be a 1% chance that the technology erroneously detects oil, when in fact no oil exists. In a report, use this information to compute and interpret the probability that, on a recent expedition, oil existed but the technology detected "no oil" in the area.

Report 4.4 FILE ***College_Admissions.*** Explore the data on two categorical variables denoting admission decision (Admitted) and the college that a student applies to (College). Construct a contingency table and calculate and interpret relevant probabilities to examine the relative independence of the three colleges.

CONCEPTUAL REVIEW

LO 4.1 Describe fundamental probability concepts.

- An experiment is a process that leads to one of several possible outcomes.
- A sample space, denoted S, of an experiment contains all possible outcomes of the experiment.
- An event is any subset of outcomes of an experiment, and is called a simple event if it contains a single outcome.
- Events are exhaustive if all possible outcomes of an experiment belong to the events.
- Events are mutually exclusive if they do not share any common outcome of an experiment.
- A probability is a numerical value that measures the likelihood that an event occurs. It assumes a value between zero and one, where a value zero indicates an impossible event and a value one indicates a definite event.
- The two defining properties of a probability are (1) the probability of any event A is a value between 0 and 1, $0 \leq P(A) \leq 1$, and (2) the sum of the probabilities of any list of mutually exclusive and exhaustive events equals 1.
- A subjective probability is calculated by drawing on personal and subjective judgment. An empirical probability is calculated as a relative frequency of occurrence. A classical probability is based on logical analysis rather than on observation or personal judgment.

LO 4.2 Apply the rules of probability.

- The complement rule is used to find the probability of the complement of event A: $P(A^c) = 1 - P(A)$.
- The addition rule is used to find the probability that event A or event B occurs: $P(A \cup B) = P(A) + P(B) - P(A \cap B)$.
- The conditional probability that event A occurs given that event B has occurred is found as: $P(A \mid B) = \frac{P(A \cap B)}{P(B)}$.
- The multiplication rule is used to find the probability that event A and event B occur: $P(A \cap B) = P(A \mid B)P(B)$.
- Events A and B are independent if $P(A \mid B) = P(A)$, or equivalently, $P(A \cap B) = P(A)P(B)$. Otherwise, the events are dependent.

LO 4.3 Calculate and interpret probabilities from a contingency table.

A contingency table generally shows frequencies for two categorical variables, x and y, where each cell represents a mutually exclusive combination of x-y observations. Empirical probabilities are easily calculated as the relative frequency of the occurrence of the event.

LO 4.4 Apply the total probability rule and Bayes' theorem.

The total probability rule expresses the probability of event A in terms of joint or conditional probabilities. Given events B and B^C, the probability of event A can be found as $P(A) = P(A \cap B) + P(A \cap B^C) = P(A \mid B)P(B) + P(A \mid B^C)P(B^C)$.

Bayes' Theorem is a method for updating a prior probability, $P(B)$, to a posterior probability, $P(B \mid A)$. The posterior probability of event B can be found as $P(B \mid A) = \frac{P(A \cap B)}{P(A)} = \frac{P(A \cap B)}{P(A \cap B) + P(A \cap B^c)} = \frac{P(A \mid B)P(B)}{P(A \mid B)P(B) + P(A \mid B^c)P(B^c)}$.

The total probability rule and Bayes' Theorem can easily be extended to include n mutually exclusive and exhaustive events, $B_1, B_2, \ldots, B_n$.

LO 4.5 Use a counting rule to calculate the probability of an event.

- The number of ways to assign every member of a group of size n to n slots is calculated using the factorial formula as $n! = n \times (n-1) \times (n-2) \times \cdots \times 1$.
- The number of ways to choose x objects from a total of n objects, where the order in which the x objects are listed *does not matter,* is calculated using the combination formula as ${}_nC_x = \binom{n}{x} = \frac{n!}{(n-x)!x!}$.
- The number of ways to choose x objects from a total of n objects, where the order in which the x objects is listed *does matter,* is calculated using the permutation formula as ${}_nP_x = \frac{n!}{(n-x)!}$
- In certain circumstances, these counting rules can aid in calculating relevant probabilities.

ADDITIONAL EXERCISES

59. According to a global survey of 4,400 parents of children between the ages of 14 to 17, 44% of parents spy on their teen's Facebook account. Assume that American parents account for 10% of all parents of teens with Facebook accounts, of which 60% spy on their teen's Facebook account. Suppose a parent is randomly selected, and the following events are defined: A = selecting an American parent and B = selecting a spying parent.
    a. Based on the above information, what are the probabilities that can be established?
    b. Are the events A and B mutually exclusive and/or exhaustive? Explain.
    c. Are the events A and B independent? Explain.
    d. What is the probability of selecting an American parent given that she/he is a spying parent?
60. The subscription e-commerce market has grown substantially including subscription boxes that provide a recurring delivery of niche products. E-commerce firms pay attention to the churn rate defined as the percentage of subscribers who discontinue their subscriptions. It is estimated that the monthly churn rate for subscription boxes is 12% for female customers and 9% for male customers. It is also found that 62% of all subscription box customers are females. Find the probability that a randomly selected customer will be a male who churns within a month.
61. Henry Chow is a stockbroker working for Merrill Lynch. He knows from past experience that there is a 70% chance that his new client will want to include U.S. equity in her portfolio and a 50% chance that she will want to include foreign equity. There is also a 40% chance that she will want to include both U.S. equity and foreign equity in her portfolio.
    a. What is the probability that the client will want to include U.S. equity if she already has foreign equity in her portfolio?
    b. What is the probability that the client decides to include neither U.S. equity nor foreign equity in her portfolio?
62. The Easy Credit Company reports the following table representing a breakdown of customers according to the amount they owe and whether a cash advance has been made. An auditor randomly selects one of the accounts.

Amounts owed by customers	Cash Advance?	
	Yes	No
\$0 – 199.99	245	2,890
\$200 – 399.99	380	1,700
\$400 – 599.99	500	1,425
\$600 – 799.99	415	940
\$800 – 999.99	260	480
\$1,000 or more	290	475
Total Customers	2,090	7,910

a. What is the probability that a customer received a cash advance?
b. What is the probability that a customer owed less than $200 and received a cash advance?
c. What is the probability that a customer owed less than $200 or received a cash advance?
d. Given that a customer received a cash advance, what is the probability that the customer owed $1,000 or more?
e. Given that a customer owed $1,000 or more, what is the probability that the customer received a cash advance?
f. Are the events "receiving a cash advance" and "owing $1,000 or more" mutually exclusive? Explain using probabilities.
g. Are the events "receiving a cash advance" and "owing $1,000 or more" independent? Explain using probabilities.

63. The following frequency distribution shows the ages of India's 40 richest individuals. One of these individuals is selected at random.

Ages	Frequency
30 up to 40	3
40 up to 50	8
50 up to 60	15
60 up to 70	9
70 up to 80	5

a. What is the probability that the individual is between 50 and 60 years of age?
b. What is the probability that the individual is younger than 50 years of age?
c. What is the probability that the individual is at least 60 years of age?

64. How much you smile in your younger days can predict your later success in marriage. The analysis is based on the success rate in marriage of people over age 65 and their smiles when they were only 10 years old. Researchers found that only 11% of the biggest smilers had been divorced, while 31% of the biggest frowners had experienced a broken marriage.
a. Suppose it is known that 2% of the people are the biggest smilers at age 10 and divorced in later years. What percent of people are the biggest smilers?
b. If 25% of people are considered to be the biggest frowners, calculate the probability that a person is a biggest frowner at age 10 and divorced later in life.

65. Anthony Papantonis, owner of Nauset Construction, is bidding on two projects, A and B. The probability that he wins project A is 0.40 and the probability that he wins project B is 0.25. Winning Project A and winning Project B are independent events.
a. What is the probability that he wins project A or project B?
b. What is the probability that he does not win either project?

66. Wooden boxes are commonly used for the packaging and transportation of mangoes. A convenience store in Morganville, New Jersey, regularly buys mangoes from a wholesale dealer. For every shipment, the manager randomly inspects two mangoes from a box containing 20 mangoes for damages due to transportation. Suppose the chosen box contains exactly three damaged mangoes.
a. Find the probability that the first mango is not damaged.
b. Find the probability that neither of the mangoes is damaged.
c. Find the probability that both mangoes are damaged.

67. A study shows that unemployment does not impact males and females in the same way. According to a Bureau of Labor Statistics report, 8.5% of those who are eligible to work are unemployed. The unemployment rate is 8.8% for eligible men and only 7.0% for eligible women. Suppose 52% of the eligible workforce in the United States consists of men.
a. You have just heard that another worker in a large firm has been laid off. What is the probability that this worker is a man?
b. You have just heard that another worker in a large firm has been laid off. What is the probability that this worker is a woman?

68. According to the CGMA Economic Index, which measures executive sentiment across the world, 18% of all respondents expressed optimism about the global economy. Moreover, 22% of the respondents from the United States and 9% from Asia felt optimistic about the global economy.
a. What is the probability that an Asian respondent is not optimistic about the global economy?
b. If 28% of all respondents are from the United States, what is the probability that a respondent is from the United States and is optimistic about the global economy?
c. Suppose 22% of all respondents are from Asia. If a respondent feels optimistic about the global economy, what is the probability that the respondent is from Asia?

69. A professor of management has heard that eight students in his class of 40 have landed an internship for the summer. Suppose he runs into two of his students in the corridor.
   a. Find the probability that neither of these students has landed an internship.
   b. Find the probability that both of these students have landed an internship.

70. FILE ***Machine.*** Being able to predict machine failures before they happen can save millions of dollars for manufacturing companies. Manufacturers want to be able to perform preventive maintenance or repairs in advance to minimize machine downtime and often install electronic sensors to monitor the machines and their surrounding environment. A manager of a firm wants to explore the effect of percentage humidity (Low, Medium, or High) on machine failure (Yes or No). The accompanying table shows a portion of the data.

Machine	Humidity	Failure
1	Medium	No
2	Medium	No
⋮	⋮	⋮
480	High	Yes

   a. Use the data to construct a contingency table.
   b. Find the probability that a randomly selected machine fails.
   c. Find the probability that a randomly selected machine operates in high humidity.
   d. Find the probability that a machine fails, given high humidity. Find the corresponding probabilities given low and medium humidity.
   e. Is machine failure related to humidity? Explain using probabilities.

71. At a local bar in a small Midwestern town, beer and wine are the only two alcoholic options. The manager noted that of all male customers who visited over the weekend, 150 ordered beer, 40 ordered wine, and 20 asked for soft drinks. Of female customers, 38 ordered beer, 20 ordered wine, and 12 asked for soft drinks.
   a. Construct a contingency table that shows frequencies for the categorical variables Sex (male or female) and Drink Choice (beer, wine, or soft drink).
   b. Find the probability that a customer orders wine.
   c. What is the probability that a male customer orders wine?
   d. Are the events "Wine" and "Male" independent? Explain using probabilities.

72. A study in the *Journal of the American Medical Association* found that patients who go into cardiac arrest while in the hospital are more likely to die if it happens after 11 pm. The study investigated 58,593 cardiac arrests that occurred during the day or evening. Of those, 11,604 survived to leave the hospital. There were 28,155 cardiac arrests during the shift that began at 11 pm, commonly referred to as the graveyard shift. Of those, 4,139 survived for discharge. The following contingency table summarizes the results of the study.

	Survived for Discharge	Did not Survive for Discharge	Total
Day or Evening Shift	11,604	46,989	58,593
Graveyard Shift	4,139	24,016	28,155
Total	15,743	71,005	86,748

   a. What is the probability that a randomly selected patient experienced cardiac arrest during the graveyard shift?
   b. What is the probability that a randomly selected patient survived for discharge?
   c. Given that a randomly selected patient experienced cardiac arrest during the graveyard shift, what is the probability the patient survived for discharge?
   d. Given that a randomly selected patient survived for discharge, what is the probability the patient experienced cardiac arrest during the graveyard shift?
   e. Are the events "Survived for Discharge" and "Graveyard Shift" independent? Explain using probabilities. Given your answer, what type of recommendations might you give to hospitals?

73. It has been reported that women end up unhappier than men later in life, even though they start out happier. Early in life, women are more likely to fulfill their family life and financial aspirations, leading to greater overall happiness. However, men report a higher satisfaction with their financial situation and family life, and are thus happier than women, in later life. Suppose the results of the survey of 300 men and 300 women are presented in the following table.

Response to the question "Are you satisfied with your financial and family life?"

	Age		
Response by Women	20 to 35	35 to 50	Over 50
Yes	73	36	32
No	67	54	38

	Age		
Response by Men	**20 to 35**	**35 to 50**	**Over 50**
Yes	58	34	38
No	92	46	32

a. What is the probability that a randomly selected woman is satisfied with her financial and family life?
b. What is the probability that a randomly selected man is satisfied with his financial and family life?
c. For women, are the events "Yes" and "20 to 35" independent? Explain using probabilities.
d. For men, are the events "Yes" and "20 to 35" independent? Explain using probabilities.

74. An analyst predicts that there is a 40% chance that the U.S. economy will perform well. If the U.S. economy performs well, then there is an 80% chance that Asian countries will also perform well. On the other hand, if the U.S. economy performs poorly, the probability of Asian countries performing well goes down to 0.30.
a. What is the probability that both the U.S. economy and the Asian countries will perform well?
b. What is the probability that the Asian countries will perform well?
c. What is the probability that the U.S. economy will perform well, given that the Asian countries perform well?

75. Apparently, depression significantly increases the risk of developing dementia later in life. In a study, it was reported that 22% of those who had depression went on to develop dementia, compared to only 17% of those who did not have depression. Suppose 10% of all people suffer from depression.
a. What is the probability of a person developing dementia?
b. If a person has developed dementia, what is the probability that the person suffered from depression earlier in life?

76. According to data from the *National Health and Nutrition Examination Survey,* 36.5% of adult women and 26.6% of adult men are at a healthy weight. Suppose 50.52% of the adult population consists of women.
a. What proportion of adults is at a healthy weight?
b. If an adult is at a healthy weight, what is the probability that the adult is a woman?
c. If an adult is at a healthy weight, what is the probability that the adult is a man?

77. Suppose that 60% of students do homework regularly. It is also known that 80% of students who had been doing homework regularly end up doing well in the course (get a grade of A or B). Only 20% of students who had not been doing homework regularly end up doing well in the course.
a. What is the probability that a student does well in the course?
b. Given that a student did well in the course, what is the probability that the student had been doing homework regularly?

78. There is a growing public support for marijuana law reform, with polls showing more than half the country is in favor of some form of marijuana legalization. However, opinions on marijuana are divided starkly along political party lines. The results of a survey are shown in the following table. In addition, assume that 27% of Americans identify as Republicans, 30% as Democrats, and 43% as independents.

Political Party	Support
Republican	41%
Democrat	66%
Independent	63%

a. Calculate the probability that a randomly selected American adult supports marijuana legalization and is a Republican.
b. Calculate the probability that a randomly selected American adult supports marijuana legalization and is a Democrat.
c. Calculate the probability that a randomly selected American adult supports marijuana legalization and is an independent.
d. What percentage of American adults support marijuana legalization?
e. If a randomly selected American adult supports marijuana legalization, what is the probability that this adult is a Republican?

79. A national survey finds that there is a big gender divide between Americans when identifying as feminist or strong feminist. The results of the survey are shown in the following table. In addition, assume that 50.8% of the American population is female and 49.2% is male.

Gender	Feminist or Strong Feminist
Female	66%
Male	41%

a. Calculate the probability that a randomly selected American adult is a female who also identifies as feminist or strong feminist.
b. Calculate the probability that a randomly selected American adult is a male who also identifies as feminist or strong feminist.

c. What percentage of American adults identify as feminist or strong feminist?

d. If a randomly selected American adult identifies as feminist or strong feminist, what is the probability that this adult is a female?

80. According to the Census's Population Survey, the percentage of children with two parents at home is the highest for Asian people and lowest for black people. It is reported that 85% of Asian children have two parents at home versus 78% of white, 70% of Hispanic, and 38% of black. Suppose there are 500 students in a representative school of which 280 are white, 50 are Asian, 100 are Hispanic, and 70 are black.

a. What is the probability that a child has both parents at home?

b. If both parents are at home, what is the probability the child is Asian?

c. If both parents are at home, what is the probability the child is black?

81. Prior to the start of the season, a sports analyst is attempting to predict the end-of-season rankings of the 10 teams in a conference.

a. How many different ways can the teams be ranked if ties are not considered?

b. How many different outcomes are possible if only the first three places are considered and ranking (first, second, and third) is important?

c. If each of the outcomes in part b is equally likely, what is the probability that the sports analyst selects the correct end-of-season outcome?

d. How many different outcomes are possible if only the first three places are considered and ranking (first, second, and third) is not important?

e. If each of the outcomes in part d is equally likely, what is the probability that the sports analyst selects the correct end-of-season outcome?

82. Assume high school coach Emily Williams has seven possible swimmers for a four-person relay team.

a. If the order for the freestyle relay is unimportant, how many different relay teams are possible?

b. Assume for the medley relay team that order is important; how many different teams are possible?

c. Swimmer Michael P. is one of the seven swimmers. If the assignment of swimmers is random, how many of the teams in part a will include Michael P.?

5 Discrete Probability Distributions

LEARNING OBJECTIVES

After reading this chapter you should be able to:

LO **5.1** **Describe a discrete random variable and its probability distribution.**

LO **5.2** **Calculate and interpret summary measures for a discrete random variable.**

LO **5.3** **Calculate and interpret summary measures to evaluate portfolio returns.**

LO **5.4** **Calculate and interpret probabilities for a binomial random variable.**

LO **5.5** **Calculate and interpret probabilities for a Poisson random variable.**

LO **5.6** **Calculate and interpret probabilities for a hypergeometric random variable.**

In this chapter, we extend our discussion about probability by introducing the concept of a random variable. A random variable summarizes the results of an experiment in terms of numerical values. It can be classified as discrete or continuous depending on the range of values that it assumes. A discrete random variable assumes a countable number of distinct values, whereas a continuous random variable is characterized by uncountable values within an interval.

In this chapter, we focus on a discrete random variable and its associated probability distribution. Examples of discrete random variables include the number of sales people who hit their target for the quarter, the number of refinancing applications in a sample of 100 homeowners, and the number of cars lined up at a toll booth. We calculate summary measures for a discrete random variable, including its mean, variance, and standard deviation. Using properties of random variables, we are able to apply these summary measures to describe portfolio returns. Finally, we discuss three widely used discrete probability distributions: the binomial, the Poisson, and the hypergeometric distributions.

Jewel Samad/AFP/Getty Images

INTRODUCTORY CASE

Available Staff for Probable Customers

Starbucks is facing stiff competition and it is not coming from other coffee chains. Trendy coffee shops, emerging all over the country, are now competing with Starbucks clientele. The growth of daily consumption of gourmet coffee coupled with low capital investment has prompted entrepreneurs to start their own specialty coffee shops aimed at a younger, more affluent demographic.

Anne Jones, a manager at a local Starbucks, is concerned about how the stiff competition from trendy coffee shops might affect business at her store. Anne knows that a typical Starbucks customer visits the chain between 15 and 18 times a month, making it among the nation's most frequented retailers. She believes that her loyal Starbucks customers will average 18 visits to the store over a 30-day month. To decide staffing needs, Anne knows that she needs a solid understanding about the probability distribution of customer arrivals. If too many employees are ready to serve customers, some employees will be idle, which is costly to the store. However, if not enough employees are available to meet demand, this could result in losing angry customers who choose not to wait for service.

Anne wants to use the above information to

1. Calculate the expected number of visits from a typical Starbucks customer in a specified time period.
2. Calculate the probability that a typical Starbucks customer visits the chain a certain number of times in a specified time period.

A synopsis of this case is provided in Section 5.5.

LO 5.1

5.1 RANDOM VARIABLES AND DISCRETE PROBABILITY DISTRIBUTIONS

Describe a discrete random variable and its probability distribution.

We often have to make important decisions in the face of uncertainty. For example, a car dealership has to determine the number of cars to hold on its lot when the actual demand for cars is unknown. Similarly, an investor has to select a portfolio when the actual outcomes of investment returns are not known. This uncertainty is captured by what we call a **random variable.** A random variable summarizes outcomes of an experiment with numerical values.

We generally use the uppercase letter X to denote a random variable and a lowercase letter x to denote the value that X may assume. A **discrete random variable** assumes a countable number of distinct values such as x_1, x_2, x_3, and so on. A **continuous random variable,** on the other hand, is characterized by uncountable values within an interval. Unlike the case of a discrete random variable, we cannot describe the possible values of a continuous random variable X with a list $x_1, x_2, \ldots$ because the value $(x_1 + x_2)/2$, not in the list, might also be possible.

> DISCRETE VERSUS CONTINUOUS RANDOM VARIABLES
>
> - A random variable is a function that assigns numerical values to the outcomes of an experiment.
> - A discrete random variable assumes a countable number of distinct values.
> - A continuous random variable is characterized by uncountable values in an interval.

Examples of discrete random variables include the number of sales people who hit their target for the quarter, the number of employees leaving a firm in a given year, or the number of firms filing for bankruptcy in a given month. Similarly, the return on a mutual fund, the completion time of a task, or the volume of beer sold as 16 ounces are examples of continuous random variables. In this chapter, we focus on discrete random variables. Details of continuous random variables will be presented in Chapter 6.

The Discrete Probability Distribution

Every discrete random variable is associated with a **probability distribution,** also called the **probability mass function,** that provides the probability that the random variable X assumes a particular value x, or equivalently, $P(X = x)$. We can also define the random variable in terms of its **cumulative distribution function,** or, equivalently, $P(X \leq x)$. There are two defining properties of all discrete probability distributions.

> TWO KEY PROPERTIES OF DISCRETE PROBABILITY DISTRIBUTIONS
>
> - The probability of each value x is a value between 0 and 1, or equivalently, $0 \leq P(X = x) \leq 1$.
> - The sum of the probabilities equals 1. In other words, $\Sigma P(X = x_i) = 1$, where the sum extends over all values x of X.

We can view a discrete probability distribution in several ways, including tabular, algebraic, and graphical forms.

EXAMPLE 5.1

Suppose we roll a a six-sided die and define the number rolled as the random variable. Present the probability distribution in a tabular form.

SOLUTION: When we roll a six-sided die, the possible values that X assumes are x = 1, 2, 3, 4, 5, or 6. Because each of the outcomes is equally likely, the probability that X assumes any of the six possible values is $1/6 = 0.1667$. Table 5.1 shows the probability distribution for rolling a six-sided die. When a probability distribution is presented as a probability mass function, we can easily deduce, for instance, that $P(X=5)=0.1667$.

TABLE 5.1 Probability Distribution for Rolling a Die

x	1	2	3	4	5	6
$P(X = x)$	0.1667	0.1667	0.1667	0.1667	0.1667	0.1667

There are two tabular ways to represent a discrete probability distribution. We can specify the probability that the random variable assumes a specific value, as shown in Table 5.1. Alternatively, we can represent by its cumulative probability distribution. The cumulative probability distribution is convenient when we are interested in finding the probability that the random variable assumes a range of values rather than a specific value. For the random variable defined in Example 5.1, the cumulative probability distribution is shown in Table 5.2.

TABLE 5.2 Cumulative Probability Distribution for Rolling a Die

x	1	2	3	4	5	6
$P(X \leq x)$	0.1667	0.3333	0.5000	0.6667	0.8333	1

If we are interested in finding the probability of rolling a four or less, $P(X \leq 4)$, we see from the cumulative probability distribution that this probability is 4/6. At the same time, we can use the cumulative probability distribution to find the probability that the random variable assumes a specific value. For example, $P(X = 3)$ can be found as $P(X \leq 3) - P(X \leq 2) = 0.5000 - 0.3333 = 0.1667$.

In many instances, we can express a probability distribution by applying an algebraic formula. A formula representation of the probability distribution for rolling a six-sided die

$$P(X=x) = \begin{cases} 0.1667 & \text{if } x = 1, 2, 3, 4, 5, 6 \\ 0 & \text{otherwise} \end{cases}$$

Thus, from the formula we can ascertain that $P(X = 5) = 0.1667$ and $P(X = 7) = 0$.

In order to graphically depict a probability distribution, we place all values x of X on the horizontal axis and the associated probabilities $P(X = x)$ on the vertical axis. We then draw a line segment that emerges from each x and ends where its height equals $P(X = x)$. Figure 5.1 graphically illustrates the probability distribution for rolling a six-sided die.

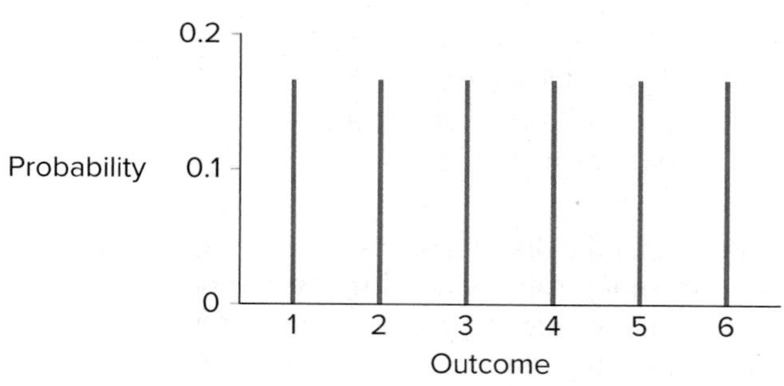

FIGURE 5.1 Probability distribution for rolling a six-sided die

We would like to point out that the probability distribution for rolling a die in Example 5.1 represents a **discrete uniform distribution,** which has the following characteristics:

- The distribution has a finite number of specified values.
- Each value is equally likely.
- The distribution is symmetric.

EXAMPLE 5.2

The number of homes that a realtor sells over a one-month period has the probability distribution shown in Table 5.3.

TABLE 5.3 Probability Distribution for the Number of Houses Sold

Number of Houses Sold	Probability
0	0.30
1	0.50
2	0.15
3	0.05

a. Is this a valid probability distribution?

b. What is the probability that the realtor does not sell any houses in a one-month period?

c. What is the probability that the realtor sells at most one house in a one-month period?

d. What is the probability that the realtor sells at least two houses in a one-month period?

e. Graphically depict the probability distribution and comment on its symmetry/skewness.

SOLUTION:

a. We first note that the random variable X denotes the number of houses that the realtor sells over a one-month period, and the possible values of X are 0, 1, 2, or 3. The probability distribution is valid because it satisfies the following two conditions: (1) all probabilities fall between 0 and 1, and (2) the probabilities sum to 1 $(0.30 + 0.50 + 0.15 + 0.05 = 1)$.

b. In order to find the probability that the realtor does not sell any houses in a one-month period, we find $P(X = 0) = 0.30$.

c. We find the probability that a realtor sells at most one house as $P(X \leq 1) = P(X = 0) + P(X = 1) = 0.30 + 0.50 = 0.80$.

d. We find the probability that the realtor sells at least two houses as $P(X \geq 2) = P(X = 2) + P(X = 3) = 0.15 + 0.05 = 0.20$.
Note that since the sum of the probabilities over all values of X equals 1, we can also find the above probability as $P(X \geq 2) = 1 - P(X \leq 1) = 1 - 0.80 = 0.20$.

e. The graph in Figure 5.2 shows that the distribution is not symmetric; rather, it is positively skewed. There are small chances of selling two or three houses in a one-month period. The most likely outcome by far is selling one house over a one-month period, with a probability of 0.50.

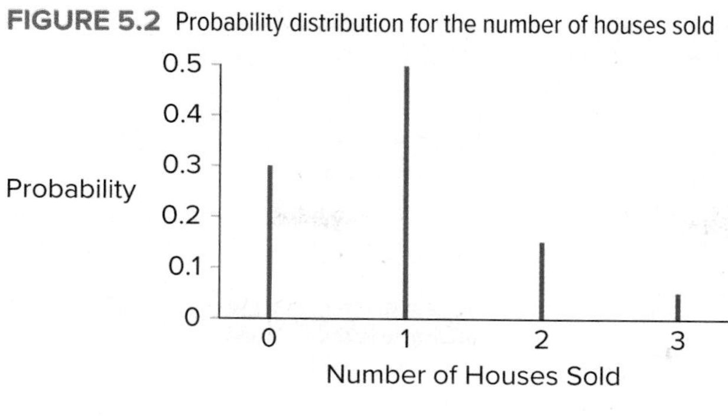

FIGURE 5.2 Probability distribution for the number of houses sold

EXERCISES 5.1

Mechanics

1. Consider the following discrete probability distribution.

x	15	22	34	40
$P(X = x)$	0.14	0.40	0.26	0.20

   a. Is this a valid probability distribution? Explain.
   b. Graphically depict this probability distribution.
   c. What is the probability that the random variable X is less than 40?
   d. What is the probability that the random variable X is between 10 and 30?
   e. What is the probability that the random variable X is greater than 20?

2. Consider the following discrete probability distribution.

x	−25	−15	10	20
$P(X = x)$	0.35	0.10		0.10

   a. Complete the probability distribution.
   b. Graphically depict the probability distribution and comment on the symmetry of the distribution.
   c. What is the probability that the random variable X is negative?
   d. What is the probability that the random variable X is greater than −20?
   e. What is the probability that the random variable X is less than 20?

3. Consider the following cumulative probability distribution.

x	0	1	2	3	4	5
$P(X \leq x)$	0.15	0.35	0.52	0.78	0.84	1

   a. Calculate $P(X \leq 3)$.
   b. Calculate $P(X = 3)$.
   c. Calculate $P(2 \leq X \leq 4)$.

4. Consider the following cumulative probability distribution.

x	−25	0	25	50
$P(X \leq x)$	0.25	0.50	0.75	1

   a. Calculate $P(X \leq 0)$.
   b. Calculate $P(X = 50)$.
   c. Is this a discrete uniform distribution? Explain.

Applications

5. Identify the possible values of the following random variables. Which of the random variables are discrete?
   a. The numerical grade a student receives in a course.
   b. The grade point average of a student.
   c. The salary of an employee, defined in figures (four-figure, five-figure, etc.).
   d. The salary of an employee defined in dollars.

6. Identify the possible values of the following random variables. Which of the random variables are discrete?
   a. The advertised size of a round Domino's pizza.
   b. The actual size of a round Domino's pizza.
   c. The number of daily visitors to Yosemite National Park.
   d. The age of a visitor to Yosemite National Park.

7. India is the second most populous country in the world, with a population of over 1 billion people. Although the government has offered various incentives for population control, some argue that the birth rate, especially in rural India, is still too high to be sustainable. A demographer assumes the following probability distribution for the household size in India.

Household Size	Probability
1	0.05
2	0.09
3	0.12
4	0.24
5	0.25
6	0.12
7	0.07
8	0.06

a. What is the probability that there are fewer than 5 members in a household in India?
b. What is the probability that there are 5 or more members in a household in India?
c. What is the probability that the number of members in a household in India is strictly between 3 and 6?
d. Graphically depict this probability distribution and comment on its symmetry.

8. A financial analyst creates the following probability distribution for the performance of an equity income mutual fund.

Performance	Numerical Score	Probability
Very poor	1	0.14
Poor	2	0.43
Neutral	3	0.22
Good	4	0.16
Very good	5	0.05

a. Comment on the optimism or pessimism depicted in the analyst's estimates.
b. Convert the above probability distribution to a cumulative probability distribution.
c. What is the probability that this mutual fund will do at least Good?

9. A basketball player is fouled while attempting to make a basket and receives two free throws. The opposing coach believes there is a 55% chance that the player will miss both shots, a 25% chance that he will make one of the shots, and a 20% chance that he will make both shots.
a. Construct the appropriate probability distribution.
b. What is the probability that he makes no more than one of the shots?
c. What is the probability that he makes at least one of the shots?

10. Using new economic data, an analyst believes that there is a 75% chance that the consumer confidence index will fall by more than 10% and only a 5% chance that it will rise by more than 5%. She scores the confidence index as 1 if it falls by more than 10%, 2 if the change is between –10% and 5%, and 3 if it rises by more than 5%.
a. According to the analyst, what is the probability that the confidence score is 2?
b. According to the analyst, what is the probability that the confidence score is not 1?

11. Professor Sanchez has been teaching Principles of Economics for over 25 years. He uses the following scale for grading.

Grade	Numerical Score	Probability
A	4	0.10
B	3	0.30
C	2	0.40
D	1	0.10
F	0	0.10

a. Depict the probability distribution graphically. Comment on whether or not the probability distribution is symmetric.
b. Convert the probability distribution to a cumulative probability distribution.
c. What is the probability of earning at least a B in Professor Sanchez's course?
d. What is the probability of passing Professor Sanchez's course?

12. Jane Wormley is a professor of management at a university. She expects to be able to use her grant money to fund up to two students for research assistance. While she realizes that there is a 5% chance that she may not be able to fund any student, there is an 80% chance that she will be able to fund two students.
a. What is the probability that Jane will fund one student?
b. Construct a cumulative probability distribution for the number of students that Jane will be able to fund.

13. Fifty percent of the customers who go to Auto Center for tires buy four tires and 30% buy two tires. Moreover, 18% buy fewer than two tires, with 5% buying none.
a. What is the probability that a customer buys three tires?
b. Construct a cumulative probability distribution for the number of tires bought.

LO 5.2

5.2 EXPECTED VALUE, VARIANCE, AND STANDARD DEVIATION

Calculate and interpret summary measures for a discrete random variable.

The analysis of probability distributions is useful because it allows us to calculate probabilities associated with the different values that the random variable assumes. In addition, it helps us calculate summary measures for a random variable. These summary measures include the mean, the variance, and the standard deviation.

Summary Measures

One of the most important probabilistic concepts in statistics is that of the **expected value,** also referred to as the population mean. The expected value of the discrete random variable X, denoted by $E(X)$ or simply, μ, is a weighted average of all possible values of X. The mean μ of the random variable X provides us with a measure of the central location of the distribution of X, but it does not give us information on how the various values are dispersed from μ. We again use the measures of variance and standard deviation to indicate whether the values of X are clustered about μ or widely scattered from μ.

SUMMARY MEASURES FOR A DISCRETE RANDOM VARIABLE

Consider a discrete random variable X with values $x_1, x_2, x_3, \ldots$, which occur with probabilities $P(X = x_i)$. The expected value of X is calculated as

$$E(X) = \mu = \Sigma x_i P(X = x_i).$$

The variance of X, denoted as $Var(X)$ or σ^2, is calculated as

$$Var(X) = \sigma^2 = \Sigma(x_i - \mu)^2 \; P(X = x_i).$$

The standard deviation of X, denoted as $SD(X)$ or σ, is calculated as

$$SD(X) = \sigma = \sqrt{\sigma^2}.$$

EXAMPLE 5.3

Brad Williams is the owner of a large car dealership in Chicago. Brad decides to construct an incentive compensation program that equitably and consistently compensates employees on the basis of their performance. He offers an annual bonus of \$10,000 for superior performance, \$6,000 for good performance, \$3,000 for fair performance, and \$0 for poor performance. Based on prior records, he expects an employee to perform at superior, good, fair, and poor performance levels with probabilities 0.15, 0.25, 0.40, and 0.20, respectively. Table 5.4 lists the bonus amount, performance type, and the corresponding probabilities.

TABLE 5.4 Probability Distribution for Compensation Program

Bonus (in \$1,000s)	Performance Type	Probability
10	Superior	0.15
6	Good	0.25
3	Fair	0.40
0	Poor	0.20

a. Calculate the expected value of the annual bonus amount.

b. Calculate the variance and the standard deviation of the annual bonus amount.

c. What is the total annual amount that Brad can expect to pay in bonuses if he has 25 employees?

SOLUTION:

a. Let the random variable X denote the bonus amount (in \$1,000s) for an employee. The first and second columns of Table 5.5 represent the probability distribution of X. The calculations for the mean are provided in the third column. We weigh each outcome by its respective probability, $x_i P(X = x_i)$, and then sum these weighted values. Thus, as shown at the bottom of the third column, $E(X) = \mu = \Sigma x_i P(X = x_i) = 4.2$, or \$4,200. Note that the expected value is not one of the possible values of X; that is, none of the employees will earn a bonus of \$4,200. We generally interpret expected value as a long-run average.

TABLE 5.5 Calculations for Example 5.3

x_i	$P(X = x_i)$	$x_i P(X = x_i)$	$(x_i - \mu)^2 P(X = x_i)$
10	0.15	$10 \times 0.15 = 1.5$	$(10 - 4.2)^2 \times 0.15 = 5.05$
6	0.25	$6 \times 0.25 = 1.5$	$(6 - 4.2)^2 \times 0.25 = 0.81$
3	0.40	$3 \times 0.40 = 1.2$	$(3 - 4.2)^2 \times 0.40 = 0.58$
0	0.20	$0 \times 0.20 = 0$	$(0 - 4.2)^2 \times 0.20 = 3.53$
		Total = 4.2	Total = 9.97

b. The last column of Table 5.5 shows the calculation for the variance. We first calculate each x_i's squared difference from the mean $(x_i - \mu)^2$, weigh each value by the appropriate probability, $(x_i - \mu)^2 P(X = x_i)$, and then sum these weighted squared differences. Thus, as shown at the bottom of the last column, $Var(X) = \sigma^2 = \Sigma(x_i - \mu)^2 P(X = x_i) = 9.97$, or 9.97 (in (\$1,000s)^2). The standard deviation is the positive square root of the variance, $SD(X) = \sigma = \sqrt{9.97} = 3.158$, or \$3,158.

c. In part a we found that the expected bonus of an employee is \$4,200. Since Brad has 25 employees, he can expect to pay \$4,200 × 25 = \$105,000 in bonuses.

Risk Neutrality and Risk Aversion

An important concept in economics, finance, and psychology relates to the behavior of consumers under uncertainty. Consumers are said to be **risk neutral** if they are indifferent to risk and care only about their expected gains. They are said to be **risk-averse** if they care about risk and, if confronted with two choices with the same expected gains, they prefer the one with lower risk. In other words, a risk-averse consumer will take a risk only if it entails a suitable compensation. A **risk-loving** consumer may be willing to take a risk even if the expected gain is negative.

Consider a seemingly fair gamble where you flip a coin and get \$10 if it is heads and lose \$10 if it is tails, resulting in an expected gain of zero ($10 \times 0.5 - 10 \times 0.5 = 0$). A risk-neutral consumer is indifferent about participating in this gamble. For a risk-averse consumer, the pain associated with losing \$10 is more than the pleasure of winning \$10. Therefore, the consumer will not want to participate in this seemingly fair gamble because there is no reward to compensate for the risk. Example 5.4 expands on this type of consumer behavior.

A CONSUMER'S RISK PREFERENCE

- A risk-neutral consumer completely ignores risk and makes his/her decisions solely on the basis of expected gains.
- A risk-averse consumer demands a positive expected gain as compensation for taking risk.
- A risk-loving consumer may be willing to take a risk even if the expected gain is negative.

EXAMPLE 5.4

You have a choice of receiving $1,000 in cash or receiving a beautiful painting from your grandmother. The actual value of the painting is uncertain. You are told that the painting has a 20% chance of being worth $2,000, a 50% chance of being worth $1,000, and a 30% chance of being worth $500. What should you do?

SOLUTION: Let the random variable X represent the painting's value. Table 5.6 shows the probability distribution for X.

TABLE 5.6 Probability Distribution for the Value of the Painting

x	$P(X = x)$
2,000	0.20
1,000	0.50
500	0.30

We calculate the expected value as

$$E(X) = \Sigma x_i P(X = x_i) = 2{,}000 \times 0.20 + 1{,}000 \times 0.50 + 500 \times 0.30$$
$$= \$1{,}050.$$

Since the expected value of the painting is more than $1,000, it may appear that the right choice is to pick the painting over $1,000 in cash. This choice, however, is based entirely on the expected value of the painting, paying no attention to risk. While the expected value of $1,050 is more than $1,000, the painting entails some risk. For instance, there is a 30% chance that it may be worth only $500. Therefore, a risk-neutral consumer will take the painting because its expected value exceeds the risk-free cash value of $1,000. This consumer is not concerned with risk. A risk lover will be thrilled to take the painting. For a risk-averse consumer, however, the decision is not clear-cut. It depends on the risk involved in picking the painting and how much he/she wants to be compensated for this risk. One way to resolve this issue is to define the utility function of the consumer, which in essence conveys the degree of risk aversion. A risk-averse consumer will pick the risky prospect if the expected utility (not the expected money) of the risky prospect exceeds the utility of a risk-free alternative. Further details are beyond the scope of this text.

EXERCISES 5.2

Mechanics

14. Calculate the mean, the variance, and the standard deviation of the following discrete probability distribution.

x	5	10	15	20
$P(X = x)$	0.35	0.30	0.20	0.15

15. Calculate the mean, the variance, and the standard deviation of the following discrete probability distribution.

x	−23	−17	−9	−3
$P(X = x)$	0.50	0.25	0.15	0.10

Applications

16. The number of homes that a realtor sells over a one-month period has the following probability distribution.

Number of Houses Sold	Probability
0	0.30
1	0.50
2	0.15
3	0.05

a. On average, how many houses is the realtor expected to sell over a one-month period?

b. What is the standard deviation of this probability distribution?

17. A marketing firm is considering making up to three new hires. Given its specific needs, the management feels that there is a 60% chance of hiring at least two candidates. There is only a 5% chance that it will not make any hires and a 10% chance that it will make all three hires.
   a. What is the probability that the firm will make at least one hire?
   b. Find the expected value and the standard deviation of the number of hires.
18. An analyst has developed the following probability distribution for the rate of return for a common stock.

Scenario	Probability	Rate of Return (in %)
1	0.30	−5
2	0.45	0
3	0.25	10

   a. Calculate the expected rate of return.
   b. Calculate the variance and the standard deviation of this probability distribution.
19. Organizers of an outdoor summer concert in Toronto are concerned about the weather conditions on the day of the concert. They will make a profit of $25,000 on a clear day and $10,000 on a cloudy day. They will take a loss of $5,000 if it rains. The weather channel has predicted a 60% chance of rain on the day of the concert. Calculate the expected profit from the concert if the likelihood is 10% that it will be sunny and 30% that it will be cloudy.
20. Mark Underwood is a professor of economics at Indiana University. He has been teaching Principles of Economics for over 25 years. Professor Underwood uses the following scale for grading.

Grade	Probability
A	0.10
B	0.30
C	0.40
D	0.10
F	0.10

Calculate the expected numerical grade in Professor Underwood's class using 4.0 for A, 3.0 for B, etc.
21. The manager of a publishing company plans to give a $20,000 bonus to the top 15%, $10,000 to the next 30%, and $5,000 to the next 10% of sales representatives. If the publishing company has a total of 200 sales representatives, what is the expected bonus that the company will pay?
22. An appliance store sells additional warranties on its refrigerators. Twenty percent of the buyers buy the limited warranty for $100 and 5% buy the extended warranty for $200. What is the expected revenue for the store from the warranty if it sells 120 refrigerators?
23. You are considering buying insurance for your new laptop computer, which you have recently bought for $1,500. The insurance premium for three years is $80. Over the three-year period there is an 8% chance that your laptop computer will require work worth $400, a 3% chance that it will require work worth $800, and a 2% chance that it will completely break down with a scrap value of $100. Should you buy the insurance? (Assume risk neutrality.)
24. Four years ago, Victor purchased a very reliable automobile. His warranty has just expired, but the manufacturer has just offered him a 5-year, bumper-to-bumper warranty extension. The warranty costs $3,400. Victor constructs the following probability distribution with respect to anticipated costs if he chooses not to purchase the extended warranty.

Cost (in $)	Probability
1,000	0.25
2,000	0.45
5,000	0.20
10,000	0.10

   a. Calculate Victor's expected cost.
   b. Given your answer in part a, should Victor purchase the extended warranty? (Assume risk neutrality.) Explain.
25. An investor considers investing $10,000 in the stock market. He believes that the probability is 0.30 that the economy will improve, 0.40 that it will stay the same, and 0.30 that it will deteriorate. Further, if the economy improves, he expects his investment to grow to $15,000, but it can also go down to $8,000 if the economy deteriorates. If the economy stays the same, his investment will stay at $10,000.
   a. What is the expected value of his investment?
   b. Should he invest the $10,000 in the stock market if he is risk neutral?
   c. Is the decision clear-cut if he is risk averse? Explain.
26. You are considering two mutual funds as an investment. The possible returns for the funds are dependent on the state of the economy and are given in the accompanying table.

State of the Economy	Fund 1 (in %)	Fund 2 (in %)
Good	20	40
Fair	10	20
Poor	−10	−40

You believe that the likelihood is 20% that the economy will be good, 50% that it will be fair, and 30% that it will be poor.
   a. Find the expected value and the standard deviation of returns for Fund 1.
   b. Find the expected value and the standard deviation of returns for Fund 2.
   c. Which fund will you pick if you are risk averse? Explain.

27. Investment advisors recommend risk reduction through international diversification. International investing allows you to take advantage of the potential for growth in foreign economies, particularly in emerging markets. Janice Wong is considering investment in either Europe or Asia. She has studied these markets and believes that both markets will be influenced by the U.S. economy, which has a 20% chance for being good, a 50% chance for being fair, and a 30% chance for being poor. Probability distributions of the returns for these markets are given in the accompanying table.

State of the U.S. Economy	Returns in Europe (in %)	Returns in Asia (in %)
Good	10	18
Fair	6	10
Poor	−6	−12

a. Find the expected value and the standard deviation of returns in Europe and Asia.
b. What will Janice pick as an investment if she is risk neutral?
c. Discuss Janice's decision if she is risk averse.

5.3 PORTFOLIO RETURNS

LO 5.3

Calculate and interpret summary measures to evaluate portfolio returns.

As discussed in Chapter 3, we often evaluate investment opportunities using expected return as a measure of reward and variance or standard deviation as a measure of risk. Consider two assets where Asset A is expected to have a return of 12% and Asset B is expected to have a return of 8% for the year. While Asset A is attractive in terms of its reward, an investor may still choose Asset B over Asset A if the risk associated with Asset A is too high. In other words, both reward as well as risk are relevant for evaluating the investment.

So far we have considered assets separately. However, most investors hold a **portfolio** of assets, where a portfolio is defined as a collection of assets such as stocks and bonds. As in the case of an individual asset, an investor is concerned about the reward as well as the risk of a portfolio. The derivations of the expected return and the variance of a portfolio depend on some important results regarding the joint distribution of random variables.

Let X and Y represent two random variables of interest, denoting, say, the returns of two assets. Since an investor may have invested in both assets, we would like to evaluate the portfolio return formed by a linear combination of X and Y. The following properties for random variables are useful in evaluating portfolio returns.

Properties of Random Variables

Given two random variables X and Y, the expected value of their sum, $E(X + Y)$, is equal to the sum of their individual expected values, $E(X)$ and $E(Y)$, or

$$E(X + Y) = E(X) + E(Y).$$

Using algebra, it can be shown that the variance of the sum for two random variables, $Var(X + Y)$, yields

$$Var(X + Y) = Var(X) + Var(Y) + 2Cov(X, Y).$$

where Cov is the covariance between the random variables X and Y.
For given constants a and b, the expected value and the variance results are extended as

$$E(aX + bY) = aE(X) + bE(Y), \text{ and}$$
$$Var(aX + bY) = a^2 Var(X) + b^2 Var(Y) + 2abCov(X, Y).$$

Summary Measures for a Portfolio

We are now in a position to derive the expected return and the variance for a portfolio based on these properties. For the sake of simplicity, consider a portfolio consisting of only two assets, Asset A and Asset B. These assets, for instance, may represent stocks and bonds. Following popular notation in finance, let R_A and R_B be the random variables of interest, representing the returns for assets A and B, respectively. It is important to note that a portfolio is described not only by its assets but also by its portfolio weights. Consider a portfolio with a total value of \$5,000, with \$1,000 invested in Asset A and \$4,000 in Asset B. The portfolio weights are derived as

$$w_A = \frac{1{,}000}{5{,}000} = 0.20 \quad \text{and} \quad w_B = \frac{4{,}000}{5{,}000} = 0.80.$$

Note that the portfolio weights add up to one; that is, $w_A + w_B = 0.20 + 0.80 = 1$. We then define the portfolio return R_p as a linear combination of the individual returns,

$$R_p = w_A R_A + w_B R_B.$$

PORTFOLIO EXPECTED RETURN

Given a portfolio with two assets, Asset A and Asset B, the expected return for the portfolio $E(R_p)$ is computed as

$$E(R_p) = w_A E(R_A) + w_B E(R_B),$$

where w_A and w_B are the portfolio weights ($w_A + w_B = 1$) and $E(R_A)$ and $E(R_B)$ are the expected returns on assets A and B, respectively.

EXAMPLE 5.5

Consider an investment portfolio of \$40,000 in Stock A and \$60,000 in Stock B. Calculate the expected return for this portfolio based on the information in Table 5.7.

TABLE 5.7 Summary Measures for Stock A and Stock B

Stock A	Stock B
$E(R_A) = \mu_A = 9.5$	$E(R_B) = \mu_B = 7.6$
$SD(R_A) = \sigma_A = 12.93$	$SD(R_B) = \sigma_B = 8.20$
$Cov(R_A, R_B) = \sigma_{AB} = 18.60$	

SOLUTION: First we compute the portfolio weights. Since \$40,000 is invested in Stock A and \$60,000 in Stock B, we compute

$$w_A = \frac{40{,}000}{100{,}000} = 0.40 \quad \text{and} \quad w_B = \frac{60{,}000}{100{,}000} = 0.60.$$

Thus, using the formula for portfolio expected return, we compute

$$E(R_p) = (0.40 \times 9.5) + (0.60 \times 7.6) = 3.80 + 4.56 = 8.36.$$

Note that the portfolio expected return of 8.36% is lower than the expected return of investing entirely in Stock A with an expected return of 9.5%, yet higher than the expected return of investing entirely in Stock B with an expected return of 7.6%.

The risk of the portfolio depends not only on the individual risks of the assets but also on the interplay between the asset returns. For example, if one asset does poorly, the second asset may serve as an offsetting factor to stabilize the risk of the overall portfolio. This result will work as long as the return of the second asset is not perfectly correlated with the return of the first asset. Similar to the covariance $Cov(x, y) = \sigma_{xy}$ introduced in Chapter 3, the covariance $Cov(R_A, R_B) = \sigma_{AB}$ helps determine whether the linear relationship between the asset returns is positive, negative, or zero. Recall that an easier measure to interpret is the correlation coefficient ρ, which describes both the direction and the strength of the linear relationship between two random variables. The value of the correlation coefficient falls between −1 and 1. The closer the value is to 1, the stronger is the positive linear relationship between the variables. Similarly, the closer the value is to −1, the stronger is the negative linear relationship between the variables. Let $\rho_{AB} = \frac{\sigma_{AB}}{\sigma_A \sigma_B}$ denote the correlation coefficient between the returns R_A and R_B.

With information on either the covariance or the correlation coefficient for the two returns, we can now determine the portfolio variance.

PORTFOLIO VARIANCE

The portfolio variance, $Var(R_p) = Var(w_A R_A + w_B R_B)$, is computed as

$$Var(R_p) = w_A^2 \sigma_A^2 + w_B^2 \sigma_B^2 + 2 w_A w_B \sigma_{AB}$$

or, equivalently,

$$Var(R_p) = w_A^2 \sigma_A^2 + w_B^2 \sigma_B^2 + 2 w_A w_B \rho_{AB} \sigma_A \sigma_B$$

where σ_A^2 and σ_B^2 are the variances for Asset A and Asset B, respectively, σ_{AB} is the covariance between Asset A and Asset B, and ρ_{AB} is the correlation coefficient between Asset A and Asset B.

The portfolio standard deviation $SD(R_p)$ is then calculated as the positive square root of the portfolio variance.

EXAMPLE 5.6

Using the information in Example 5.5, solve the following:

a. Calculate and interpret the correlation coefficient between the returns for Stock A and Stock B.

b. Calculate the portfolio variance using both formulas.

c. Calculate the portfolio standard deviation.

d. Comment on the findings.

SOLUTION:

a. We calculate the correlation coefficient as $\rho_{AB} = \frac{\sigma_{AB}}{\sigma_A \sigma_B} = \frac{18.60}{12.93 \times 8.20} = 0.1754$. This value implies that the returns have a positive linear relationship, though the magnitude of the relationship is weak (ρ_{AB} is well below 1).

b. Using the first formula for portfolio variance, we calculate

$$\begin{aligned} Var(R_p) &= w_A^2 \sigma_A^2 + w_B^2 \sigma^2{}_B + 2 w_A w_B \sigma_{AB} \\ &= (0.40)^2(12.93)^2 + (0.60)^2(8.20)^2 + 2(0.40)(0.60)(18.60) \\ &= 26.75 + 24.21 + 8.93 \\ &= 59.89. \end{aligned}$$

Using the alternative formula for portfolio variance, we calculate

$$\begin{aligned} Var(R_p) &= w_A^2\sigma_A^2 + w_B^2\sigma_B^2 + 2w_A w_B \rho_{AB}\sigma_A\sigma_B \\ &= (0.40)^2(12.93)^2 + (0.60)^2(8.20)^2 \\ &\quad + 2(0.40)(0.60)(0.1754)(12.93)(8.20) \\ &= 26.75 + 24.21 + 8.93 \\ &= 59.89. \end{aligned}$$

Using either formula, the portfolio variance is 59.89 $(\%)^2$.

c. The portfolio standard deviation is $SD(R_p) = \sqrt{59.89} = 7.74$, or 7.74%.

d. We note how the portfolio standard deviation (risk) of 7.74% is lower than the risk of 12.93% of investing entirely in Stock A, as well as the risk of 8.20% of investing entirely in Stock B. This occurs because the returns of Stock A and Stock B have a correlation of only 0.1754. This example highlights the benefits of properly diversifying your portfolio in order to reduce risk. In general, the benefits of diversification depend on the correlation between the assets: the lower the correlation, the larger the benefit.

EXERCISES 5.3

28. What are the portfolio weights for a portfolio that has 100 shares of Stock X that sell for $20 per share and 200 shares of Stock Y that sell for $12 per share?

29. You own a portfolio that has $4,400 invested in stocks and $5,600 invested in bonds. What is the expected return of the portfolio if stocks and bonds are expected to yield a return of 9% and 5%, respectively?

30. A portfolio has $200,000 invested in Asset X and $300,000 in Asset Y. Consider the summary measures in the following table.

Measures	Asset X	Asset Y
Expected return (%)	8	12
Standard deviation (%)	12	20
Correlation coefficient	0.40	

a. Calculate the portfolio weights for Asset X and Asset Y.
b. Calculate the expected return for the portfolio.
c. Calculate the standard deviation for the portfolio.

31. An analyst has predicted the following returns for Stock A and Stock B in three possible states of the economy.

State	Probability	A	B
Boom	0.3	0.15	0.25
Normal	0.5	0.10	0.20
Recession	?	0.02	0.01

a. What is the probability of a recession?
b. Calculate the expected return for Stock A and Stock B.
c. Calculate the expected return for a portfolio that is invested 55% in A and 45% in B.

32. A pension fund manager is considering three mutual funds for investment. The first one is a stock fund, the second is a bond fund, and the third is a money market fund. The money market fund yields a risk-free return of 4%. The inputs for the risky funds are given in the following table.

Fund	Expected Return (in %)	Standard Deviation (in %)
Stock fund	14	26
Bond fund	8	14

The correlation coefficient between the stock and the bond funds is 0.20.

a. What is the expected return and the variance for a portfolio that invests 60% in the stock fund and 40% in the bond fund?
b. What is the expected return and the variance for a portfolio that invests 60% in the stock fund and 40% in the money market fund? *[Hint: Note that the correlation coefficient between the portfolio and the money market fund is zero.]*
c. Compare the portfolios in parts a and b with a portfolio that is invested entirely in the bond fund.

33. You have $400,000 invested in a well-diversified portfolio. You inherit a house that is presently worth $200,000. Consider the summary measures in the following table:

Investment	Expected Return (in %)	Standard Deviation (in %)
Old portfolio	6	16
House	8	20

The correlation coefficient between your portfolio and the house is 0.38.

a. What is the expected return and the standard deviation for your portfolio comprising your old portfolio and the house?
b. Suppose you decide to sell the house and use the proceeds of $200,000 to buy risk-free T-bills that promise a 3% rate of return. Calculate the expected return and the standard deviation for the resulting portfolio. [*Hint: Note that the correlation coefficient between any asset and the risk-free T-bills is zero.*]

5.4 THE BINOMIAL DISTRIBUTION

LO 5.4

Calculate and interpret probabilities for a binomial random variable.

Different types of experiments generate different probability distributions. In the next three sections, we discuss three special cases: the binomial, the Poisson, and the hypergeometric probability distributions. Here we focus on the binomial distribution. Before we can discuss the binomial distribution, we first must ensure that the experiment satisfies the conditions of a **Bernoulli process,** which is a particular type of experiment named after the person who first described it, the Swiss mathematician James Bernoulli (1654–1705).

A BERNOULLI PROCESS

A Bernoulli process consists of a series of n independent and identical trials of an experiment such that on each trial:

- There are only two possible outcomes, conventionally labeled success and failure; and
- The probabilities of success and failure remain the same from trial to trial.

We use p to denote the probability of success, and therefore, $1 - p$ is the probability of failure.

A **binomial random variable** is defined as the number of successes achieved in the n trials of a Bernoulli process. The possible values of a binomial random variable include $0, 1, \ldots, n$. Many experiments fit the conditions of a Bernoulli process. For instance:

- A customer defaults or does not default on a loan.
- A consumer reacts positively or negatively to a social media campaign.
- A drug is either effective or ineffective.
- A college graduate applies or does not apply to graduate school.

Our goal is to attach probabilities to various outcomes of a Bernoulli process. The result is a **binomial probability distribution,** or simply, a **binomial distribution.**

A binomial random variable X is defined as the number of successes achieved in the n trials of a Bernoulli process. The binomial distribution for X shows the probabilities associated with the possible values of X.

We will eventually arrive at a general formula that helps us derive a binomial distribution. First, however, we will use a specific example and construct a **probability tree** in order to illustrate the possible outcomes and their associated probabilities.

EXAMPLE 5.7

From past experience, a manager of an upscale shoe store knows that 85% of her customers will use a credit card when making purchases. Suppose three customers are in line to make a purchase.

a. Does this example satisfy the conditions of a Bernoulli process?

b. Construct a probability tree.

c. Using the probability tree, derive the probabilities associated with a binomial random variable.

SOLUTION:

a. This example satisfies the conditions of a Bernoulli process because a customer either uses a credit card (labeled success), with an 85% likelihood, or does not use a credit card (labeled failure), with a 15% likelihood. Moreover, given a large number of customers, these probabilities of success and failure do not change from customer to customer.

b. We can use a probability tree whenever an experiment can be broken down into stages. Here we can view each stage as a trial. We let S denote the outcome that a customer uses a credit card and F denote the outcome that a customer does not use a credit card. Figure 5.3 shows the probability tree for this example. Starting from the unlabeled node on the left, customer 1 has an 85% chance of using a credit card and a 15% chance of not using one. The branches emanating from customer 1 denote conditional probabilities of customer 2 using a credit card, given whether or not customer 1 used a credit card. However, since we assume that the trials of a Bernoulli process are independent, customer 2 has the same 85% chance of using a credit card and a 15% chance of not using one regardless of what customer 1 uses. The same holds for the probabilities for customer 3. The fourth column shows that there are eight possible events at the end of the probability tree. We are able to obtain relevant probabilities by using the multiplication rule for independent events. For instance, following the top branches throughout the probability tree, we calculate the probability that all three customers use a credit card as $(0.85)(0.85)(0.85) = 0.6141$. The probabilities for the remaining events are found in a similar manner.

c. Since we are not interested in identifying the particular customer who uses a credit card, but rather the number of customers who use a credit card, we can combine events with the same number of successes, using the addition rule

FIGURE 5.3 Probability tree for Example 5.7

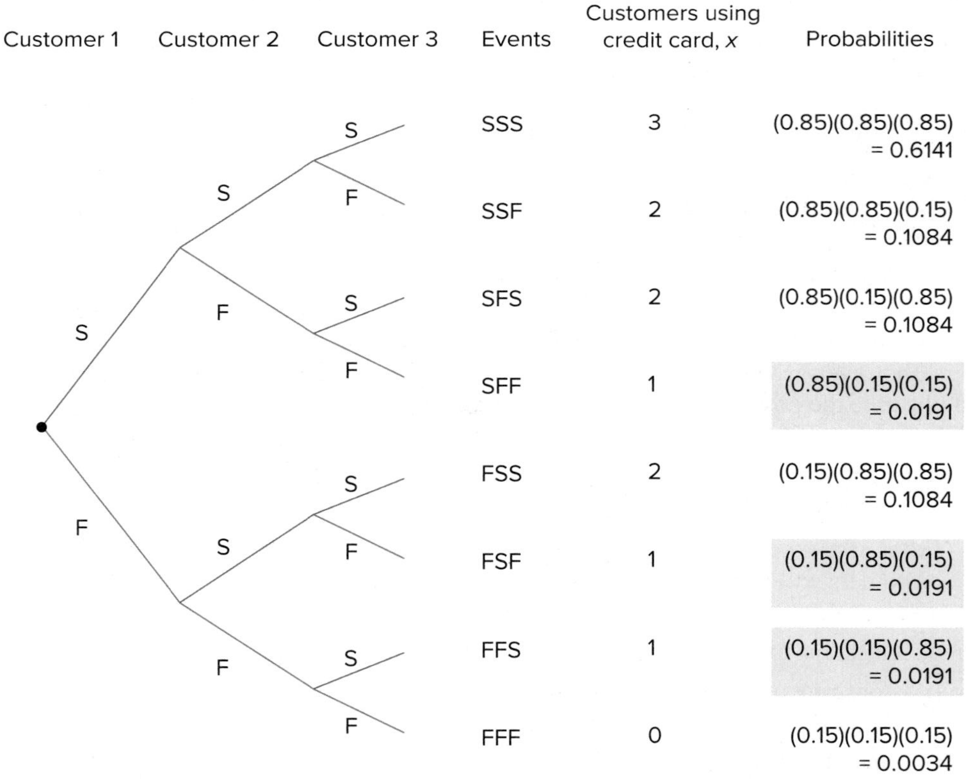

Customer 1	Customer 2	Customer 3	Events	Customers using credit card, x	Probabilities
S	S	S	SSS	3	(0.85)(0.85)(0.85) = 0.6141
S	S	F	SSF	2	(0.85)(0.85)(0.15) = 0.1084
S	F	S	SFS	2	(0.85)(0.15)(0.85) = 0.1084
S	F	F	SFF	1	(0.85)(0.15)(0.15) = 0.0191
F	S	S	FSS	2	(0.15)(0.85)(0.85) = 0.1084
F	S	F	FSF	1	(0.15)(0.85)(0.15) = 0.0191
F	F	S	FFS	1	(0.15)(0.15)(0.85) = 0.0191
F	F	F	FFF	0	(0.15)(0.15)(0.15) = 0.0034

for mutually exclusive events. For instance, in order to find the probability that one customer uses a credit card, we add the probabilities that correspond to the outcome $x = 1$ (see shaded areas in Figure 5.3): $0.0191 + 0.0191 + 0.0191 = 0.0573$. Similarly, we calculate the remaining probabilities corresponding to the other values of X and construct the probability distribution shown in Table 5.8.

TABLE 5.8 Binomial Probabilities for Example 5.7

x	$P(X = x)$
0	0.0034
1	0.0573
2	0.3252
3	0.6141

Note that the probabilities add up to 1.0.

Fortunately, we do not have to construct a probability tree each time we want to construct a binomial distribution. We can use the following formula for calculating probabilities associated with a binomial random variable.

THE BINOMIAL DISTRIBUTION

For a binomial random variable X, the probability of x successes in n Bernoulli trials is

$$P(X = x) = \binom{n}{x} p^x (1 - p)^{n-x} = \frac{n!}{x!(n - x)!} p^x (1 - p)^{n-x}$$

for $x = 0, 1, 2, \ldots, n$. By definition, $0! = 1$.

The formula consists of two parts:

- The first term, $\binom{n}{x} = \frac{n!}{x!(n-x)!}$, tells us how many sequences with x successes and $n - x$ failures are possible in n trials. We refer to the first term as the binomial coefficient, which is really the familiar combination formula used to find the number of ways to choose x objects from a total of n objects, where the order in which the x objects are listed *does not matter.* For instance, in order to calculate the number of sequences that contain exactly 1 credit card user in 3 trials, we substitute $x = 1$ and $n = 3$ into the formula and calculate $\binom{n}{x} = \frac{n!}{x!(n-x)!} = \frac{3!}{1!(3-1)!} = \frac{3 \times 2 \times 1}{(1) \times (2 \times 1)} = 3$. So there are three sequences having exactly 1 success—we can verify this result with Figure 5.3.
- The second part of the equation, $p^x(1 - p)^{n-x}$, represents the probability of any particular sequence with x successes and $n - x$ failures. For example, we can obtain the probability of 1 success in 3 trials from row 4, row 6, or row 7 in the last column of Figure 5.3 (see shaded areas) as

$$\left.\begin{array}{l} \text{row 4: } 0.85 \times 0.15 \times 0.15 \\ \text{row 6: } 0.15 \times 0.85 \times 0.15 \\ \text{row 7: } 0.15 \times 0.15 \times 0.85 \end{array}\right\} \quad \text{or} \quad (0.85)^1 \times (0.15)^2 = 0.019.$$

In other words, each sequence consisting of 1 success in 3 trials has a 1.91% chance of occurring.

In order to obtain the overall probability of getting 1 success in 3 trials, we then multiply the binomial coefficient by the probability of obtaining the particular sequence, or here, $3 \times 0.0191 = 0.0573$. This is precisely the probability that we found for $P(X = 1)$ using the probability tree.

Moreover, we could use the formulas shown in Section 5.2 to calculate the expected value, the variance, and the standard deviation for any binomial random variable. Fortunately, for the binomial distribution, these formulas simplify to $E(X) = np$, $Var(X) = np(1 - p)$, and $SD(X) = \sqrt{np(1-p)}$. The simplified formula for the expected value is rather intuitive in that if we know the probability of success p of an experiment and we repeat the experiment n times, then on average, we expect np successes.

SUMMARY MEASURES FOR A BINOMIAL RANDOM VARIABLE

If X is a binomial random variable, then

$$E(X) = \mu = np,$$
$$Var(X) = \sigma^2 = np(1 - p), \text{ and}$$
$$SD(X) = \sigma = \sqrt{np(1-p)}.$$

For instance, for the binomial probability distribution assumed in Example 5.7, we can derive the expected value with the earlier general formula as

$$E(X) = \Sigma x_i P(X = x_i) = (0 \times 0.0034) + (1 \times 0.0573) + (2 \times 0.3252) + (3 \times 0.6141) = 2.55.$$

However, an easier way is to use $E(X) = np$ and thus calculate the expected value as $3 \times 0.85 = 2.55$. Similarly, the variance and the standard deviation can be easily calculated as

$$Var(X) = \sigma^2 = np(1 - p) = 3 \times 0.85 \times 0.15 = 0.38 \text{ and}$$
$$SD(X) = \sigma = \sqrt{np(1-p)} = \sqrt{0.38} = 0.62.$$

EXAMPLE 5.8

In the United States, about 30% of adults have four-year college degrees (*U.S. Census Bureau,* July 31, 2018). Suppose five adults are randomly selected.

a. What is the probability that none of the adults has a college degree?

b. What is the probability that no more than two of the adults have a college degree?

c. What is the probability that at least two of the adults have a college degree?

d. Calculate the expected value, the variance, and the standard deviation of this binomial distribution.

e. Graphically depict the probability distribution and comment on its symmetry/skewness.

SOLUTION: First, this problem satisfies the conditions for a Bernoulli process with a random selection of five adults, $n = 5$. Here, an adult either has a college degree, with probability $p = 0.30$, or does not have a college degree, with probability $1 - p = 1 - 0.30 = 0.70$. Given a large number of adults, in the United States, it is reasonable to assume that the probability that an adult has a college degree stays the same from adult to adult.

a. In order to find the probability that none of the adults has a college degree, we let $x = 0$ and find

$$P(X=0) = \frac{5!}{0!(5-0)!} \times (0.30)^0 \times (0.70)^{5-0}$$
$$= 1 \times 1 \times 0.1681 = 0.1681.$$

In other words, from a random sample of five adults, there is a 16.81% chance that none of the adults has a college degree.

b. We find the probability that no more than two adults have a college degree as

$$P(X \leq 2) = P(X=0) + P(X=1) + P(X=2).$$

We have already found $P(X = 0)$ from part a. So we now compute $P(X = 1)$ and $P(X = 2)$:

$$P(X=1) = \frac{5!}{1!(5-1)!} \times (0.30)^1 \times (0.70)^{5-1} = 0.3602$$

$$P(X=2) = \frac{5!}{2!(5-2)!} \times (0.30)^2 \times (0.70)^{5-2} = 0.3087$$

Next we sum the three relevant probabilities and obtain $P(X \leq 2) = 0.1681 + 0.3602 + 0.3087 = 0.8370$. From a random sample of five adults, there is an 83.70% likelihood that no more than two of them will have a college degree.

c. We find the probability that at least two adults have a college degree as

$$P(X \geq 2) = P(X=2) + P(X=3) + P(X=4) + P(X=5).$$

We can solve this problem by calculating and then summing each of the four probabilities, from $P(X = 2)$ to $P(X = 5)$. A simpler method uses one of the key properties of a probability distribution, which states that the sum of the probabilities over all values of X equals 1. Therefore, $P(X \geq 2)$ can be written as $1 - [P(X = 0) + P(X = 1)]$. We have already calculated $P(X = 0)$ and $P(X = 1)$ from parts a and b, so

$$P(X \geq 2) = 1 - [P(X=0) + P(X=1)] = 1 - (0.1681 + 0.3602) = 0.4717.$$

From a random sample of five adults, there is a 47.17% likelihood that at least two adults will have a college degree.

d. We use the simplified formulas to calculate the mean, the variance, and the standard deviation as

$$E(X) = \mu = np = 5 \times 0.30 = 1.5 \text{ adults},$$
$$Var(X) = \sigma^2 = np(1-p) = 5 \times 0.30 \times 0.70 = 1.05\,(\text{adults})^2, \text{ and}$$
$$SD(X) = \sigma = \sqrt{np(1-p)} = \sqrt{1.05} = 1.02 = 1.02 \text{ adults}.$$

e. Before we graph this distribution, we first show the complete binomial distribution for Example 5.8 in Table 5.9.

TABLE 5.9 Binomial Distribution with $n = 5$ and $p = 0.30$

x	$P(X = x)$
0	0.1681
1	0.3602
2	0.3087
3	0.1323
4	0.0284
5	0.0024

This binomial distribution is graphically depicted in Figure 5.4. When randomly selecting five adults, the most likely outcome is that exactly one adult will have a college degree. The distribution is not symmetric; rather, it is positively skewed. In later chapters, we will learn that the binomial distribution is approximately symmetric when the sample size n is large.

FIGURE 5.4 Binomial distribution with $n = 5$ and $p = 0.30$

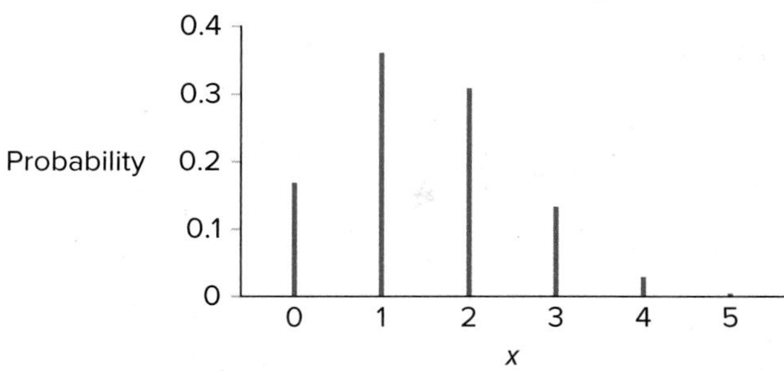

Using Excel and R to Obtain Binomial Probabilities

As you may have noticed, at times it is somewhat tedious and cumbersome to solve binomial distribution problems using the formulas. This issue becomes even more pronounced when we encounter large values for n and we wish to determine probabilities where X assumes a wide range of values. Table 5.10 shows Excel and R functions that we can use to solve problems associated with discrete probability distributions. Example 5.9 illustrates the use of these functions with respect to the binomial distribution. We will refer back to Table 5.10 in later sections of this chapter when we discuss the Poisson and hypergeometric distributions.

TABLE 5.10 Discrete Probability Distributions and Function Names in Excel and R

Distribution	Excel	R
Binomial		
$P(X = x)$:	=BINOM.DIST (x, n, p, FALSE)	dbinom(x, n, p)
$P(X \leq x)$:	=BINOM.DIST(x, n, p, TRUE)	pbinom(x, n, p)
Poisson		
$P(X = x)$:	=POISSON.DIST(x, μ, FALSE)	dpois (x, μ)
$P(X \leq x)$:	=POISSON.DIST(x, μ, TRUE)	ppois (x, μ)
Hypergeometric		
$P(X = x)$:	=HYPGEOM.DIST(x, n, S, N, FALSE)	dhyper(x, S, $N - S$, n)
$P(X \leq x)$:	=HYPGEOM.DIST(x, n, S, N, TRUE)	phyper(x, S, $N - S$, n)

EXAMPLE 5.9

People turn to social media to stay in touch with friends and family members, catch the news, look for employment, and be entertained. According to a recent survey, 68% of all U.S. adults are Facebook users. Consider a sample of 100 randomly selected American adults.

a. What is the probability that exactly 70 American adults are Facebook users?

b. What is the probability that no more than 70 American adults are Facebook users?

c. What is the probability that at least 70 American adults are Facebook users?

SOLUTION: We let X denote the number of American adults who are Facebook users. We also know that $p = 0.68$ and $n = 100$.

Using Excel

We use Excel's **BINOM.DIST** function to calculate binomial probabilities. We enter =BINOM.DIST(x, n, p, TRUE or FALSE) where x is the number of successes, n is the number of trials, and p is the probability of success. For the last argument, we enter TRUE if we want to find the cumulative probability function $P(X \leq x)$ or FALSE if we want to find the probability mass function $P(X = x)$.

a. In order to find the probability that exactly 70 American adults are Facebook users, $P(X = 70)$, we enter =BINOM.DIST(70, 100, 0.68, FALSE) and Excel returns 0.0791.

b. In order to find the probability that no more than 70 American adults are Facebook users, $P(X \leq 70)$, we enter =BINOM.DIST(70, 100, 0.68, TRUE) and Excel returns 0.7007.

c. In order to find the probability that at least 70 American adults are Facebook users, $P(X \geq 70) = 1 - P(X \leq 69)$, we enter =1–BINOM.DIST(69, 100, 0.68, TRUE) and Excel returns 0.3784.

Using R

We use R's **dbinom** and **pbinom** functions to calculate binomial probabilities. In order to calculate the probability mass function $P(X = x)$, we enter dbinom(x, n, p) where x is the number of successes, n is the number of trials, and p is the probability of success. In order to calculate the cumulative probability function $P(X \leq x)$, we enter pbinom(x, n, p).

a. In order to find $P(X = 70)$, we enter:

```
> dbinom(70, 100, 0.68)
```

And R returns: 0.07907911.

b. In order to find $P(X \leq 70)$, we enter:

```
> pbinom(70, 100, 0.68)
```

And R returns: 0.7006736.

c. In order to find $P(X \geq 70) = 1 - P(X \leq 69)$, we enter:

```
> 1 - pbinom(69, 100, 0.68)
```

And R returns: 0.3784055.

EXERCISES 5.4

Mechanics

34. Assume that X is a binomial random variable with $n = 5$ and $p = 0.35$. Calculate the following probabilities.
    a. $P(X = 0)$
    b. $P(X = 1)$
    c. $P(X \leq 1)$

35. Assume that X is a binomial random variable with $n = 6$ and $p = 0.68$. Calculate the following probabilities.
    a. $P(X = 5)$
    b. $P(X = 4)$
    c. $P(X \geq 4)$

36. Assume that X is a binomial random variable with $n = 8$ and $p = 0.32$. Calculate the following probabilities.
    a. $P(3 < X < 5)$
    b. $P(3 < X \leq 5)$
    c. $P(3 \leq X \leq 5)$

37. Let the probability of success on a Bernoulli trial be 0.30. In five Bernoulli trials, what is the probability that there will be (a) four failures, and (b) more than the expected number of failures?

38. Let X represent a binomial random variable with $n = 150$ and $p = 0.36$. Find the following probabilities.
    a. $P(X \leq 50)$
    b. $P(X = 40)$
    c. $P(X > 60)$
    d. $P(X \geq 55)$

39. Let X represent a binomial random variable with $n = 200$ and $p = 0.77$. Find the following probabilities.
    a. $P(X \leq 150)$
    b. $P(X > 160)$
    c. $P(155 \leq X \leq 165)$
    d. $P(X = 160)$

Applications

40. According to a survey by Transamerica Center for Health Studies, 15% of Americans still have no health insurance. Suppose five individuals are randomly selected.
    a. What is the probability that all five have health insurance?
    b. What is the probability that no more than two have health insurance?
    c. What is the probability that at least four have health insurance?
    d. What is the expected number of individuals who have health insurance?
    e. Calculate the variance and the standard deviation for this probability distribution.

41. At a local community college, 40% of students who enter the college as freshmen go on to graduate. Ten freshmen are randomly selected.
    a. What is the probability that none of them graduates from the local community college?
    b. What is the probability that at most nine will graduate from the local community college?
    c. What is the expected number that will graduate?

42. It is reported that only 26% of Americans have confidence in U.S. banks, which is still far below the pre-recession level of 41% reported in June 2007.
    a. What is the probability that fewer than half of four Americans have confidence in U.S. banks?
    b. What would have been the corresponding probability in 2007?

43. It is estimated that approximately 45% of baby boomers—are still in the workforce. Six baby boomers are selected at random.
    a. What is the probability that exactly one of the baby boomers is still in the workforce?
    b. What is the probability that at least five of the baby boomers are still in the workforce?
    c. What is the probability that fewer than two of the baby boomers are still in the workforce?
    d. What is the probability that more than the expected number of the baby boomers are still in the workforce?

44. A study finds that approximately 43% of millennials are not investing in stocks, bonds, real estate and more. This is a problem because people who start investing when they are first starting their careers have more time to generate returns that will help them accomplish their financial goals. Six millennials are randomly selected.
    a. What is the expected number of millennials who are not investing? What is the corresponding standard deviation?
    b. What is the probability that less than two millennials are not investing?
    c. What is the probability that all millennials are investing?

45. Sikhism, a religion founded in the 15th century in India, is going through turmoil due to a rapid decline in the number of Sikh youths who wear turbans. The tedious task of combing and tying up long hair and a desire to assimilate has led to approximately 25% of Sikh youths giving up the turban.
    a. What is the probability that exactly two in a random sample of five Sikh youths wear a turban?
    b. What is the probability that two or more in a random sample of five Sikh youths wear a turban?
    c. What is the probability that more than the expected number of Sikh youths wear a turban in a random sample of five Sikh youths?
    d. What is the probability that more than the expected number of Sikh youths wear a turban in a random sample of 10 Sikh youths?

46. According to the U.S. Census, roughly half of all marriages in the United States end in divorce. Researchers from leading universities have shown that the emotions aroused by one person's divorce can transfer like a virus, making divorce contagious. A split-up between immediate friends increases a person's own chances of getting divorced from 36% to 63%, an increase of 75%.
    a. Compute the probability that more than half of four randomly selected marriages will end in divorce.
    b. Redo part a if it is known that the couple's immediate friends have split up.
    c. Redo part a if it is known that none of the couple's immediate friends has split up.
47. Sixty percent of a firm's employees are men. Suppose four of the firm's employees are randomly selected.
    a. What is more likely, finding three men and one woman or two men and two women?
    b. Do you obtain the same answer as in part a if 70% of the firm's employees had been men?
48. The principal of an architecture firm tells her client that there is at least a 50% chance of having an acceptable design by the end of the week. She knows that there is only a 25% chance that any one designer would be able to do so by the end of the week.
    a. Would she be correct in her statement to the client if she asks two of her designers to work on the design, independently?
    b. If not, what if she asks three of her designers to work on the design, independently?
49. Suppose 40% of recent college graduates plan on pursuing a graduate degree. Fifteen recent college graduates are randomly selected.
    a. What is the probability that no more than four of the college graduates plan to pursue a graduate degree?
    b. What is the probability that exactly seven of the college graduates plan to pursue a graduate degree?
    c. What is the probability that at least six but no more than nine of the college graduates plan to pursue a graduate degree?
50. A manager at 24/7 Fitness Center is strategic about contacting open house attendees. With her strategy, she believes that 40% of the attendees she contacts will purchase a club membership. Suppose she contacts 20 open house attendees.
    a. What is the probability that exactly 10 of the attendees will purchase a club membership?
    b. What is the probability that no more than 10 of the attendees will purchase a club membership?
    c. What is the probability that at least 15 of the attendees will purchase a club membership?
51. Fraud detection has become an indispensable tool for banks and credit card companies to combat fraudulent credit card transactions. A fraud detection firm has detected minor fraudulent activities in 1.31% of transactions, and serious fraudulent activities in 0.87% of transactions. Assume that fraudulent transactions remain stable.
    a. What is the probability that there are minor fraudulent activities in fewer than 2 out of 100 transactions?
    b. What is the probability that there are serious fraudulent activities in fewer than 2 out of 100 transactions?

5.5 THE POISSON DISTRIBUTION

LO 5.5

Calculate and interpret probabilities for a Poisson random variable.

Another important discrete probability distribution is the **Poisson distribution,** named after the French mathematician Simeon Poisson (1781–1849). It is particularly useful in problems that deal with finding the number of occurrences of a certain event over time or space, where space refers to area or region. For simplicity, we call these occurrences "successes." Before we can discuss the Poisson distribution, we first must ensure that our experiment satisfies the conditions of a **Poisson process.**

A POISSON PROCESS

An experiment satisfies a Poisson process if

- The number of successes within a specified time or space interval equals any integer between zero and infinity.
- The number of successes counted in nonoverlapping intervals are independent.
- The probability of success in any interval is the same for all intervals of equal size and is proportional to the size of the interval.

For a Poisson process, we define the number of successes achieved in a specified time or space interval as a **Poisson random variable.**

Like the Bernoulli process, many experiments fit the conditions of a Poisson process. For instance:

- The number of customers who use a new banking app in a day.
- The number of spam e-mails received in a month.
- The number of defects in a 50-yard roll of fabric.
- The number of bacteria in a specified culture.

We use the following formula for calculating probabilities associated with a Poisson random variable.

THE POISSON DISTRIBUTION

For a Poisson random variable X, the probability of x successes over a given interval of time or space is

$$P(X = x) = \frac{e^{-\mu}\mu^x}{x!},$$

for $x = 0, 1, 2, \ldots$, where μ is the mean number of successes and $e \approx 2.718$ is the base of the natural logarithm.

As with the binomial random variable, we have simplified formulas to calculate the variance and the standard deviation of a Poisson random variable. An interesting fact is that the mean of the Poisson random variable is equal to the variance.

SUMMARY MEASURES FOR A POISSON RANDOM VARIABLE

If X is a Poisson random variable, then

$$E(X) = \mu$$
$$Var(X) = \sigma^2 = \mu, \quad \text{and}$$
$$SD(X) = \sigma = \sqrt{\mu}.$$

EXAMPLE 5.10

We can now address questions first posed by Anne Jones in the introductory case of this chapter. Recall that Anne is concerned about staffing needs at the Starbucks that she manages. She has specific questions about the probability distribution of customer arrivals at her store. Anne believes that the typical Starbucks customer averages 18 visits to the store over a 30-day month. She has the following questions:

a. How many visits should Anne expect in a 5-day period from a typical Starbucks customer?

b. What is the probability that a customer visits the chain five times in a 5-day period?

c. What is the probability that a customer visits the chain no more than two times in a 5-day period?

d. What is the probability that a customer visits the chain at least three times in a 5-day period?

SOLUTION: In applications of the Poisson distribution, we first determine the mean number of successes in the relevant time or space interval. We use the Poisson process condition that the probability that success occurs in any interval is the same for all intervals of equal size and is proportional to the size of the interval. Here, the relevant mean will be based on the rate of 18 visits over a 30-day month.

a. Given the rate of 18 visits over a 30-day month, we can write the mean for the 30-day period as $\mu_{30} = 18$. For this problem, we compute the proportional mean for a 5-day period as $\mu_5 = 3$ because $\frac{18 \text{ visits}}{30 \text{ days}} = \frac{3 \text{ visits}}{5 \text{ days}}$. In other words, on average, a typical Starbucks customer visits the store three times over a 5-day period.

b. In order to find the probability that a customer visits the chain five times in a 5-day period, we calculate

$$P(X = 5) = \frac{e^{-3}3^5}{5!} = \frac{(0.0498)(243)}{120} = 0.1008.$$

c. For the probability that a customer visits the chain no more than two times in a 5-day period, we find $P(X \leq 2) = P(X = 0) + P(X = 1) + P(X = 2)$. We calculate the individual probabilities, and then find the sum:

$$P(X = 0) = \frac{e^{-3}3^0}{0!} = \frac{(0.0498)(1)}{1} = 0.0498,$$

$$P(X = 1) = \frac{e^{-3}3^1}{1!} = \frac{(0.0498)(3)}{1} = 0.1494, \quad \text{and}$$

$$P(X = 2) = \frac{e^{-3}3^2}{2!} = \frac{(0.0498)(9)}{2} = 0.2240.$$

Thus, $P(X \leq 2) = 0.0498 + 0.1494 + 0.2240 = 0.4232$. There is approximately a 42% chance that a customer visits the chain no more than two times in a 5-day period.

d. We write the probability that a customer visits the chain at least three times in a 5-day period as $P(X \geq 3)$. Initially, we might attempt to solve this problem by evaluating $P(X \geq 3) = P(X = 3) + P(X = 4) + P(X = 5) + \cdots$. However, given the infinite number of possible successes over any interval, we cannot solve a Poisson problem this way. Here, we find $P(X \geq 3)$ as $1 - [P(X = 0) + P(X = 1) + P(X = 2)]$. Based on the probabilities in part c, we have $P(X \geq 3) = 1 - [0.0498 + 0.1494 + 0.2240] = 1 - 0.4232 = 0.5768$. Thus, there is about a 58% chance that a customer will frequent the chain at least three times in a 5-day period.

Figure 5.5 graphs the Poisson distribution $P(X = x)$ with $\mu = 3$, for x ranging from 0 to 8. The most likely outcomes are when x equals 2 and x equals 3, and the distribution is positively skewed. Remember that, theoretically, the values that the Poisson random variable assumes are infinitely countable, but the probabilities approach zero beyond those shown here.

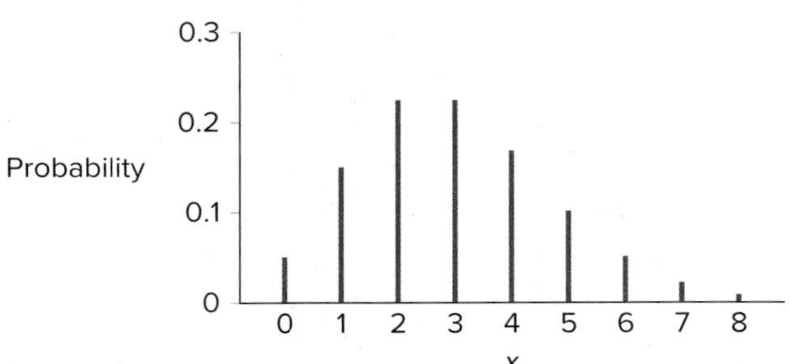

FIGURE 5.5 Poisson distribution with $\mu = 3$

SYNOPSIS OF INTRODUCTORY CASE

Anne Jones, the manager of a Starbucks store, is concerned about how the emergence of trendy coffee shops might affect foot traffic at her store. A solid understanding of the likelihood of customer arrivals is necessary before she can make further statistical inference. Historical data allow her to assume that a typical Starbucks customer averages 18 visits to a Starbucks store over a 30-day month. With this information and the knowledge that she can model customer arrivals using the Poisson distribution, she deduces that a typical customer averages three visits in a 5-day period. The likelihood that a typical customer frequents her store five times in a 5-day period is approximately 10%. Moreover, there is approximately a 42% chance that a typical customer goes to Starbucks no more than two times in a 5-day period, while the chances that this customer visits the chain at least three times is approximately 58%. These preliminary probabilities will prove vital as Anne plans her future staffing needs.

Shutterstock

Using Excel and R to Obtain Poisson Probabilities

Like the binomial formula, the manual use of the Poisson formula can become quite cumbersome, especially when the values of x and μ become large. Excel and R again prove useful when calculating Poisson probabilities. Table 5.10 shows Excel and R functions that we can use to find Poisson probabilities. Example 5.11 illustrates the use of these functions.

EXAMPLE 5.11

The sales volume of craft beer continues to grow, amounting to 24% of the total beer market in the U.S. (*USA Today,* April 2, 2019). It has been estimated that 1.5 craft breweries open every day. Assume this number represents an average that remains constant over time.

a. What is the probability that no more than 10 craft breweries open every week?

b. What is the probability that exactly 10 craft breweries open every week?

SOLUTION: We let X denote the number of craft breweries that open every week and compute the weekly mean, $\mu = 1.5 \times 7 = 10.5$.

Using Excel

We use Excel's **POISSON.DIST** function to calculate Poisson probabilities. We enter =POISSON.DIST(x, μ, TRUE or FALSE) where x is the number of successes over some interval and μ is the mean over this interval. For the last argument, we enter TRUE if we want to find the cumulative probability function $P(X \leq x)$ or FALSE if we want to find the probability mass function $P(X = x)$.

a. In order to find the probability that no more than 10 craft breweries open every week, $P(X \leq 10)$, we enter =POISSON.DIST(10, 10.5, TRUE) and Excel returns 0.5207. There is a 52.07% chance that no more than 10 craft breweries open every week.

b. In order to find the probability that exactly 10 craft breweries open every week, $P(X = 10)$, we enter =POISSON.DIST(10, 10.5, FALSE) and Excel returns 0.1236. There is a 12.36% chance that 10 craft breweries open every week.

Using R

We use R's **dpois** and **ppois** functions to calculate Poisson probabilities. In order to calculate the probability mass function $P(X = x)$, we enter dpois(x, μ) where x is the number of successes over some interval and μ is the mean over this interval. In order to calculate the cumulative probability function $P(X \leq x)$, we enter ppois(x, μ).

a. In order to find $P(X \leq 10)$, we enter:

```
> ppois(10, 10.5)
```

And R returns: 0.5207381.

b. In order to find $P(X = 10)$, we enter:

```
> dpois(10, 10.5)
```

And R returns: 0.1236055.

EXERCISES 5.5

Mechanics

52. Assume that X is a Poisson random variable with $\mu = 1.5$. Calculate the following probabilities.
    a. $P(X = 1)$
    b. $P(X = 2)$
    c. $P(X \geq 2)$

53. Assume that X is a Poisson random variable with $\mu = 4$. Calculate the following probabilities.
    a. $P(X = 4)$
    b. $P(X = 2)$
    c. $P(X \leq 1)$

54. Let the mean success rate of a Poisson process be 8 successes per hour.
    a. Find the expected number of successes in a half-hour period.
    b. Find the probability of at least two successes in a given half-hour period.
    c. Find the expected number of successes in a two-hour period.
    d. Find the probability of 10 successes in a given two-hour period.

55. Assume that X is a Poisson random variable with $\mu = 15$. Calculate the following probabilities.
    a. $P(X \leq 10)$
    b. $P(X = 13)$
    c. $P(X > 15)$
    d. $P(12 \leq X \leq 18)$

56. Assume that X is a Poisson random variable with $\mu = 20$. Calculate the following probabilities.
    a. $P(X < 14)$
    b. $P(X \geq 20)$
    c. $P(X = 25)$
    d. $P(18 \leq X \leq 23)$

Applications

57. Which of the following probabilities are likely to be found using a Poisson distribution?
    a. The probability that there will be six leaks in a specified stretch of a pipeline.
    b. The probability that at least 10 students in a class of 40 will land a job right after graduation.

c. The probability that at least 50 families will visit Acadia National Park over the weekend.
d. The probability that no customer will show up in the next five minutes.

58. Which of the following scenarios are likely to represent Poisson random variables?
    a. The number of violent crimes in New York over a six-week period.
    b. The number of defaults out of 100 bank loans.
    c. The number of scratches on a 2-by-1-foot portion of a large wooden table.
    d. The number of patients in a 50-person drug trial for whom the drug will be effective.
59. On average, there are 12 potholes per mile on a particular stretch of the state highway. Suppose the potholes are distributed evenly on the highway.
    a. Find the probability of finding fewer than two potholes in a quarter-mile stretch of the highway.
    b. Find the probability of finding more than one pothole in a quarter-mile stretch of the highway.
60. A tollbooth operator has observed that cars arrive randomly at an average rate of 360 cars per hour.
    a. Find the probability that two cars arrive during a specified one-minute period.
    b. Find the probability that at least two cars arrive during a specified one-minute period.
    c. Find the probability that 40 cars arrive between 10:00 am and 10:10 am.
61. A textile manufacturing process finds that on average, two flaws occur per every 50 yards of material produced.
    a. What is the probability of exactly two flaws in a 50-yard piece of material?
    b. What is the probability of no more than two flaws in a 50-yard piece of material?
    c. What is the probability of no flaws in a 25-yard piece of material?
62. Motorists arrive at a Gulf gas station at the rate of two per minute during morning hours.
    a. What is the probability that more than two motorists will arrive at the Gulf gas station during a one-minute interval in the morning?
    b. What is the probability that exactly six motorists will arrive at the Gulf gas station during a five-minute interval in the morning?
    c. How many motorists can an employee expect in her three-hour morning shift?
63. Airline travelers should be ready to be more flexible as airlines once again cancel thousands of flights this summer. The Coalition for Airline Passengers Rights, Health, and Safety averages 400 calls a day to help stranded travelers deal with airlines. Suppose the hotline is staffed for 16 hours a day.
    a. Calculate the average number of calls in a one-hour interval, 30-minute interval, and 15-minute interval.
    b. What is the probability of exactly six calls in a 15-minute interval?
    c. What is the probability of no calls in a 15-minute interval?
    d. What is the probability of at least two calls in a 15-minute interval?
64. New Age Solar installs solar panels for residential homes. Because of the company's personalized approach, it averages three home installations daily.
    a. What is the probability that New Age Solar installs solar panels in at most four homes in a day?
    b. What is the probability that New Age Solar installs solar panels in at least three homes in a day?
65. According to a government report, the aging of the U.S. population is translating into many more visits to doctors' offices and hospitals. It is estimated that an average person makes four visits a year to doctors' offices and hospitals.
    a. What are the mean and the standard deviation of an average person's number of monthly visits to doctors' offices and hospitals?
    b. What is the probability that an average person does not make any monthly visits to doctors' offices and hospitals?
    c. What is the probability that an average person makes at least one monthly visit to doctors' offices and hospitals?
66. A study finds that American adults are watching an average of five hours and four minutes, or 304 minutes, of television per day.
    a. Find the probability that an average American adult watches more than 320 minutes of television per day.
    b. Find the probability that an average American adult watches more than 2,200 minutes of television per week.
67. Last year there were 24,584 age-discrimination claims filed with the Equal Employment Opportunity Commission. Assume there were 260 working days in the fiscal year for which a worker could file a claim.
    a. Calculate the average number of claims filed on a working day.
    b. What is the probability that exactly 100 claims were filed on a working day?
    c. What is the probability that no more than 100 claims were filed on a working day?

5.6 THE HYPERGEOMETRIC DISTRIBUTION

LO 5.6

Calculate and interpret probabilities for a hypergeometric random variable.

In Section 5.4, we defined a binomial random variable X as the number of successes in the n trials of a Bernoulli process. The trials, according to a Bernoulli process, are independent and the probability of success does not change from trial to trial. The **hypergeometric distribution** is appropriate in applications where we cannot assume that the trials are independent.

Consider a box full of production items, of which 10% are known to be defective. Let success be labeled as the draw of a defective item. The probability of success may not be the same from trial to trial; it will depend on the size of the population and whether the sampling was done with or without replacement. Suppose the box consists of 20 items of which 10%, or 2, are defective. The probability of success in the first draw is 0.10 (= 2/20). However, the probability of success in subsequent draws will depend on the outcome of the first draw. For example, if the first item was defective, the probability of success in the second draw will be 0.0526 (= 1/19), while if the first item was not defective, the probability of success in the second draw will be 0.1053 (= 2/19).

In the preceding example, we assumed sampling without replacement; in other words, after an item is drawn, it is not put back in the box for subsequent draws. Therefore, the binomial distribution is not appropriate because the trials are not independent and the probability of success changes from trial to trial. The binomial distribution would be appropriate if we sample with replacement since, in that case, for each draw there will be 20 items, of which 2 are defective, resulting in an unchanging probability of success. Moreover, the dependence of the trials can be ignored if the population size is very large relative to the sample size. For instance, if the box consists of 10,000, items, of which 10%, or 1,000, are defective, then the probability of success in the second draw will be either 999/9,999 or 1,000/9,999, which are both approximately equal to 0.10.

We use the hypergeometric distribution in place of the binomial distribution when we are sampling without replacement from a population whose size N is not significantly larger than the sample size n. The **hypergeometric random variable** is the number of successes achieved in the n trials of a two-outcome experiment, where the trials are not assumed to be independent.

THE HYPERGEOMETRIC DISTRIBUTION

For a hypergeometric random variable X, the probability of x successes in a random selection of n items is

$$P(X = x) = \frac{\binom{S}{x}\binom{N-S}{n-x}}{\binom{N}{n}},$$

for $x = 0, 1, 2, \ldots, n$ if $n \leq S$ or $x = 0, 1, 2, \ldots, S$ if $n > S$, where N denotes the number of items in the population of which S are successes.

The formula consists of three parts:

- The first term in the numerator, $\binom{S}{x} = \frac{S!}{x!(S-x)!}$, represents the number of ways x successes can be selected from S successes in the population.
- The second term in the numerator, $\binom{N-S}{n-x} = \frac{(N-S)!}{(n-x)!(N-S-n+x)!}$, represents the number of ways $(n - x)$ failures can be selected from $(N - S)$ failures in the population.
- The denominator, $\binom{N}{n} = \frac{N!}{n!(N-n)!}$, represents the number of ways a sample of size n can be selected from the population of size N.

As with the binomial and Poisson distributions, simplified formulas can be used to calculate the mean, the variance, and the standard deviation for a hypergeometric random variable.

SUMMARY MEASURES FOR A HYPERGEOMETRIC RANDOM VARIABLE

If X is a hypergeometric random variable, then

$$E(X) = \mu = n\left(\frac{S}{N}\right),$$

$$Var(X) = \sigma^2 = n\left(\frac{S}{N}\right)\left(1 - \frac{S}{N}\right)\left(\frac{N-n}{N-1}\right), \text{ and}$$

$$SD(X) = \sigma = \sqrt{n\left(\frac{S}{N}\right)\left(1 - \frac{S}{N}\right)\left(\frac{N-n}{N-1}\right)}.$$

EXAMPLE 5.12

Wooden boxes are commonly used for the packaging and transportation of mangoes. A convenience store in Morganville, New Jersey, regularly buys mangoes from a wholesale dealer. For every shipment, the manager randomly inspects five mangoes from a box containing 20 mangoes for damages due to transportation. Suppose the chosen box contains exactly two damaged mangoes.

a. What is the probability that one out of five mangoes used in the inspection is damaged?

b. If the manager decides to reject the shipment if one or more mangoes are damaged, what is the probability that the shipment will be rejected?

c. Calculate the expected value, the variance, and the standard deviation of the number of damaged mangoes used in the inspection.

SOLUTION: The hypergeometric distribution is appropriate because the probability of finding a damaged mango changes from draw to draw (sampling is without replacement and the population size N is not significantly more than the sample size n). We use the following values to solve the problems: $N = 20$, $n = 5$, $S = 2$.

a. The probability that one out of five mangoes is damaged is $P(X = 1)$. We calculate

$$P(X = 1) = \frac{\binom{2}{1}\binom{20-2}{5-1}}{\binom{20}{5}} = \frac{\left(\frac{2!}{1!1!}\right)\left(\frac{18!}{4!14!}\right)}{\left(\frac{20!}{5!15!}\right)} = \frac{(2)(3{,}060)}{15{,}504} = 0.3947.$$

Therefore, the likelihood that exactly one out of five mangoes is damaged is 39.47%.

b. In order to find the probability that one or more mangoes are damaged, we need to calculate $P(X \geq 1)$. We note that $P(X \geq 1) = 1 - P(X = 0)$ where

$$P(X = 0) = \frac{\binom{2}{0}\binom{20-2}{5-0}}{\binom{20}{5}} = \frac{\left(\frac{2!}{0!2!}\right)\left(\frac{18!}{5!13!}\right)}{\left(\frac{20!}{5!15!}\right)} = \frac{(1)(8{,}568)}{15{,}504} = 0.5526.$$

Therefore, the probability that the shipment will be rejected equals $P(X \geq 1) = 1 - P(X = 0) = 1 - 0.5526 = 0.4474$.

c. We use the simplified formulas to obtain the mean, the variance, and the standard deviation as

$$E(X) = n\left(\frac{S}{N}\right) = 5\left(\frac{2}{20}\right) = 0.50,$$

$$Var(X) = n\left(\frac{S}{N}\right)\left(1 - \frac{S}{N}\right)\left(\frac{N-n}{N-1}\right) = 5\left(\frac{2}{20}\right)\left(1 - \frac{2}{20}\right)\left(\frac{20-5}{20-1}\right) = 0.3553,$$

$$SD(X) = \sqrt{0.3553} = 0.5960.$$

Using Excel and R to Obtain Hypergeometric Probabilities

Since it is tedious to solve for hypergeometric probabilities by hand, we typically use the computer to aid in the calculations. Table 5.10 shows Excel and R functions that we can use to find hypergeometric probabilities. Example 5.13 illustrates the use of these functions.

EXAMPLE 5.13

Employment for management analysts is projected to grow 14% from 2018 to 2028, much faster than the average for all occupations (*Bureau of Labor Statistics*, May 2020). Among 25 applicants for a management analyst position, 15 have college degrees in business. Suppose four applicants are randomly chosen for interviews.

a. What is the probability that none of the applicants has a college degree in business?

b. What is the probability that no more than two of the applicants have college degrees in business?

SOLUTION: We let X denote the number of applicants with a college degree in business. We know that $n = 4$, $S = 15$, and $N = 25$.

Using Excel

We use Excel's **HYPGEOM.DIST** function to calculate hypergeometric probabilities. We enter =HYPGEOM.DIST(x, n, S, N, TRUE or FALSE) where x is the number of successes in the sample, n is the sample size, S is the number of successes in the population, and N is the population. For the last argument, we enter TRUE if we want to find the cumulative probability function $P(X \leq x)$ or FALSE if we want to find the probability mass function $P(X = x)$.

a. In order to find the probability that none of the applicants has a college degree in business, $P(X = 0)$, we enter =HYPGEOM.DIST(0, 4, 15, 25, FALSE) and Excel returns 0.0166.

b. In order to find the probability that no more than two of the applicants have a college degree in business, $P(X \leq 2)$, we enter =HYPGEOM.DIST(2, 4, 15, 25, TRUE) and Excel returns 0.5324.

Using R

We use R's **dhyper** and **phyper** functions to calculate hypergeometric probabilities. In order to calculate the probability mass function $P(X = x)$, we enter dhyper(x, S, $N - S$, n) where x is the number of successes in the sample, S is the number of successes in the population, $N - S$ is the number of failures in the population, and n is the sample size. In order to calculate the cumulative probability function $P(X \leq x)$, we enter phyper(x, S, $N - S$, n).

a. In order to find $P(X = 0)$, we enter:

```
> dhyper(0, 15, 10, 4)
```

And R returns: 0.01660079.

b. In order to find $P(X \leq 2)$, we enter:

```
> phyper(2, 15, 10, 4)
```

And R returns: 0.5324111.

EXERCISES 5.6

Mechanics

68. Assume that X is a hypergeometric random variable with $N = 25$, $S = 3$, and $n = 4$. Calculate the following probabilities.
    a. $P(X = 0)$
    b. $P(X = 1)$
    c. $P(X \leq 1)$

69. Assume that X is a hypergeometric random variable with $N = 15$, $S = 4$, and $n = 3$. Calculate the following probabilities.
    a. $P(X = 1)$
    b. $P(X = 2)$
    c. $P(X \geq 2)$

70. Compute the probability of no successes in a random sample of three items obtained from a population of 12 items that contains two successes. What are the expected number and the standard deviation of the number of successes from the sample?

71. Assume that X is a hypergeometric random variable with $N = 50$, $S = 20$, and $n = 5$. Calculate the following probabilities.
    a. $P(X = 2)$
    b. $P(X \geq 2)$
    c. $P(X \leq 3)$

72. Compute the probability of at least eight successes in a random sample of 20 items obtained from a population of 100 items that contains 25 successes. What are the expected number and the standard deviation of the number of successes?

Applications

73. Suppose you have an urn of ten marbles, of which five are red and five are green. If you draw two marbles from this urn, what is the probability that both marbles are red? What is the probability that at least one of the marbles is red?

74. A professor of management has heard that eight students in his class of 40 have landed an internship for the summer. Suppose he runs into three of his students in the corridor.
    a. Find the probability that none of these students has landed an internship.
    b. Find the probability that at least one of these students has landed an internship.

75. It is known that 10 out of 15 members of the board of directors of a company are in favor of paying a bonus to its executives. Suppose three members are randomly selected by the media.
    a. What is the probability that all of them are in favor of a bonus?
    b. What is the probability that at least two members are in favor of a bonus?

76. Many programming teams work independently at a large software company. The management has been putting pressure on these teams to finish a project on time. The company currently has 18 large programming projects, of which only 12 are likely to finish on time. Suppose the manager decides to randomly supervise three such projects.
    a. What is the probability that all three projects finish on time?
    b. What is the probability that at least two projects finish on time?

77. David Barnes and his fiancée Valerie Shah are visiting Hawaii. There are 20 guests registered for orientation. It is announced that 12 randomly selected registered guests will receive a free lesson of Tahitian dance.
    a. What is the probability that both David and Valerie get picked for the Tahitian dance lesson?
    b. What is the probability that neither of them gets picked for the Tahitian dance lesson?

78. The National Science Foundation is fielding applications for grants to study climate change. Twenty universities apply for a grant, and only four of them will be awarded. If Syracuse University and Auburn University are among the 20 applicants, what is the probability that these two universities will receive a grant? Assume that the selection is made randomly.

79. A committee of 40 members consists of 24 men and 16 women. A subcommittee consisting of 10 randomly selected members will be formed.
    a. What are the expected number of men and women on the subcommittee?
    b. What is the probability that at least half of the members on the subcommittee will be women?

80. Powerball is a jackpot game with a grand prize starting at $20 million and often rolling over into the hundreds of millions. The winner may choose to receive the jackpot prize paid over 29 years or as a lump-sum payment. For $1 the player selects six numbers for the base game of Powerball. There are two independent stages of the game. Five balls are randomly drawn from 59 consecutively numbered white balls. Moreover, one ball, called the Powerball, is randomly drawn from 39 consecutively numbered red balls. To be a winner, the numbers selected by the player must match the numbers on the randomly drawn white balls as well as the Powerball.

   a. What is the probability that the player is able to match the numbers of two out of five randomly drawn white balls?
   b. What is the probability that the player is able to match the numbers of all five randomly drawn white balls?
   c. What is the probability that the player is able to match the Powerball for a randomly drawn red ball?
   d. What is the probability of winning the jackpot? [*Hint: Remember that the two stages of drawing white and red balls are independent.*]

5.7 WRITING WITH DATA

Case Study

Image Source/Getty Images

Senior executives at Skyhigh Construction, Inc., participate in a pick-your-salary plan. They choose salaries in a range between $125,000 and $150,000. By choosing a lower salary, an executive has an opportunity to make a larger bonus. If Skyhigh does not generate an operating profit during the year, then no bonuses are paid. Skyhigh has just hired two new senior executives, Allen Grossman and Felicia Arroyo. Each must decide whether to choose *Option* 1: a base pay of $125,000 with a possibility of a large bonus or *Option* 2: a base pay of $150,000 with a possibility of a bonus, but the bonus would be one-half of the bonus under Option 1.

Grossman, 44 years old, is married with two young children. He bought his home at the height of the market and has a rather large monthly mortgage payment. Arroyo, 32 years old, just completed her MBA at a prestigious Ivy League university. She is single and has no student loans due to a timely inheritance upon entering graduate school. Arroyo just moved to the area so she has decided to rent an apartment for at least one year. Given their personal profiles, inherent perceptions of risk, and subjective views of the economy, Grossman and Arroyo construct their individual probability distributions with respect to bonus outcomes shown in Table 5.11.

TABLE 5.11 Grossman's and Arroyo's Probability Distributions

	Probability	
Bonus (in $)	**Grossman**	**Arroyo**
0	0.35	0.20
50,000	0.45	0.25
100,000	0.10	0.35
150,000	0.10	0.20

Jordan Lake, an independent human resources specialist, is asked to use the above probability distributions to help Grossman and Arroyo decide whether to choose Option 1 or Option 2 for his/her compensation package.

Sample Report—Comparison of Salary Plans

Skyhigh Construction, Inc., has just hired two new senior executives, Allen Grossman and Felicia Arroyo, to oversee planned expansion of operations. As senior executives, they participate in a pick-your-salary plan. Each executive is given two options for compensation:

Option 1: A base pay of $125,000 with a possibility of a large bonus.
Option 2: A base pay of $150,000 with a possibility of a bonus, but the bonus would be one-half of the bonus under *Option 1*.

Grossman and Arroyo understand that if the firm does not generate an operating profit in the fiscal year, then no bonuses are paid. Each executive has constructed a probability distribution given his/her personal background, underlying risk preferences, and subjective view of the economy.

Given the probability distributions and with the aid of expected values, the following analysis will attempt to choose the best option for each executive. Grossman, a married father with two young children, believes that Table 5.12 best reflects his bonus payment expectations.

TABLE 5.12 Calculating Grossman's Expected Bonus

Bonus (in $), x_i	Probability, $P(x_i)$	Weighted Value, $x_iP(x_i)$
0	0.35	$0 \times 0.35 = 0$
50,000	0.45	$50{,}000 \times 0.45 = 22{,}500$
100,000	0.10	$100{,}000 \times 0.10 = 10{,}000$
150,000	0.10	$150{,}000 \times 0.10 = 15{,}000$
		Total = 47,500

Expected bonus, $E(X)$, is calculated as a weighted average of all possible bonus values and is shown at the bottom of the third column of Table 5.12. Grossman's expected bonus is $47,500. Using this value for his bonus, his salary options are

Option 1: $125,000 + $47,500 = $172,500
Option 2: $150,000 + (1/2 × $47,500) = $173,750

Grossman should choose *Option 2* as his salary plan.

Arroyo is single with few financial constraints. Table 5.13 shows the expected value of her bonus given her probability distribution.

TABLE 5.13 Calculating Arroyo's Expected Bonus

Bonus (in $), x_i	Probability, $P(x_i)$	Weighted Value, $x_iP(x_i)$
0	0.20	$0 \times 0.20 = 0$
50,000	0.25	$50{,}000 \times 0.25 = 12{,}500$
100,000	0.35	$100{,}000 \times 0.35 = 35{,}000$
150,000	0.20	$150{,}000 \times 0.20 = 30{,}000$
		Total = 77,500

Arroyo's expected bonus amounts to $77,500. Thus, her salary options are

Option 1: $125,000 + $77,500 = $202,500
Option 2: $150,000 + (1/2 × $77,500) = $188,750

Arroyo should choose *Option 1* as her salary plan.

Suggested Case Studies

Report 5.1. An extended warranty is a prolonged warranty offered to consumers by the warranty administrator, the retailer, or the manufacturer. An extended warranty for a laptop is being offered for $80. It will cover any repair job that a newly purchased laptop may need over the next three years. Research shows that the likelihood of a repair job over the next three years is 13% for a minor repair, 8% for a major repair, and 3% for a catastrophic repair. The extended warranty will save the consumer $70 for a minor repair, $340 for a major repair, and $800 for a catastrophic repair. In a report, use this information to evaluate the expected gain or loss to a consumer who buys the extended warranty. Determine what kind of a consumer (risk neutral, risk averse, or both) will buy this extended warranty.

Report 5.2. Call centers are used for receiving or transmitting a large volume of inquiries by telephone. At a call center in India, employees are expected to make an average of 60 calls per day, where they market a product for an American company. It is estimated that the probability of a conversion (purchase) for each call is 4%. The average revenue for the company is $20 for each conversion. In a report, use this to compute the daily expected revenue for the company for an employee. Also, analyze the probabilities and the resulting revenue for 0, 1, 2, 3, 4, 5, and 6 conversions by an employee.

Report 5.3. Ina Wang is a manager at Sunnyville Bank in California. The bank has recently developed a new mobile banking app. In addition to features like mobile check deposit, seamless money transfers, and bill pay, the new app also lets customers track accounts from different financial institutions and turns their mobile device into a digital wallet. Ina is exploring staffing needs for customer service employees whose role is to provide customers with information regarding the new app and address their problems and concerns. To decide on staffing needs, she understands the importance of understanding the probability distribution of customer calls. Having too many customer service employees adds to the cost and having too few results in losing angry customers who choose not to wait for service. On a typical weekday, there is an average of 68 customer calls in the morning and 84 customer calls in the afternoon. In a report, use this information to compute the probability of morning and afternoon calls between 0 and 10, 10 and 20, . . . , and 90 and 100. Graph these distributions and summarize the findings.

CONCEPTUAL REVIEW

LO 5.1 Describe a discrete random variable and its probability distribution.

A random variable summarizes outcomes of an experiment with numerical values. A discrete random variable assumes a countable number of distinct values, whereas a continuous random variable is characterized by uncountable values in an interval.

The probability distribution or the probability mass function provides the probability that a discrete random variable X assumes a particular value x, or equivalently, $P(X = x)$. The cumulative probability distribution function is defined as $P(X \leq x)$.

LO 5.2 Calculate and interpret summary measures for a discrete random variable.

For a discrete random variable X with values $x_1, x_2, x_3, \ldots$, which occur with probabilities $P(X = x_i)$, the expected value of X is calculated as $E(X) = \mu = \Sigma x_i P(X = x_i)$. The variance of X is calculated as $Var(X) = \sigma^2 = \Sigma(x_i - \mu)^2 P(X = x_i)$. The standard deviation of X is calculated as $SD(X) = \sigma = \sqrt{\sigma^2}$.

LO 5.3 Calculate and interpret summary measures to evaluate portfolio returns.

A portfolio return R_p is represented as a linear combination of the individual returns.

The expected return for a portfolio with two assets is $E(R_p) = w_A E(R_A) + w_B E(R_B)$, where R_A and R_B represent asset returns and w_A and w_B are the corresponding portfolio weights.

The variance for the portfolio is $Var(R_p) = w_A^2 \sigma_A^2 + w_B^2 \sigma_B^2 + 2 w_A w_B \sigma_{AB}$, or equivalently, $Var(R_p) = w_A^2 \sigma_A^2 + w_B^2 \sigma_B^2 + 2 w_A w_B \rho_{AB} \sigma_A \sigma_B$. Here, σ_A^2 and σ_B^2 are the variances for Asset A and Asset B, respectively; σ_{AB} is the covariance and ρ_{AB} is the correlation coefficient between the assets.

LO 5.4 Calculate and interpret probabilities for a binomial random variable.

A Bernoulli process is a series of n independent and identical trials of an experiment such that on each trial there are only two possible outcomes, conventionally labeled "success" and "failure." The probabilities of success and failure, denoted p and $1 - p$, remain the same from trial to trial.

For a binomial random variable X, the probability of x successes in n Bernoulli trials is $P(X = x) = \binom{n}{x} p^x (1 - p)^{n-x} = \frac{n!}{x!(n-x)!} p^x (1 - p)^{n-x}$ for $x = 0, 1, 2, \ldots, n$.

The expected value, the variance, and the standard deviation of a binomial random variable are $E(X) = \mu = np$, $Var(X) = \sigma^2 = np(1 - p)$, and $SD(X) = \sigma = \sqrt{np(1-p)}$, respectively.

LO 5.5 Calculate and interpret probabilities for a Poisson random variable.

A Poisson random variable counts the number of occurrences of a certain event over a given interval of time or space. For simplicity, we refer to these occurrences as "successes." It is appropriate when the probability of success in any interval is the same for all intervals of equal size and is proportional to the size of the interval.

For a Poisson random variable X, the probability of x successes over a given interval of time or space is $P(X = x) = \frac{e^{-\mu}\mu^x}{x!}$ for $x = 0, 1, 2, \ldots$, where μ is the mean number of successes and $e \approx 2.718$ is the base of the natural logarithm.

The expected value, the variance, and the standard deviation of a Poisson distribution are $E(X) = \mu$, $Var(X) = \sigma^2 = \mu$, and $SD(X) = \sigma = \sqrt{\mu}$, respectively.

LO 5.6 Calculate and interpret probabilities for a hypergeometric random variable.

The hypergeometric distribution is appropriate in applications where the trials are not independent and the probability of success changes from trial to trial. It is used in place of the binomial distribution when sampling occurs without replacement from a population whose size N is not significantly larger than the sample size n.

For a hypergeometric random variable X, the probability of x successes in a random selection of n items is $P(X = x) = \frac{\binom{S}{x}\binom{N-S}{n-x}}{\binom{N}{n}}$ for $x = 0, 1, 2, \ldots, n$ if $n \leq S$ or $x = 0, 1, 2, \ldots, S$ if $n > S$, where N denotes the number of items in the population of which S are successes.

The expected value, the variance, and the standard deviation of a hypergeometric distribution are $E(X) = \mu = n\left(\frac{S}{N}\right)$, $Var(X) = \sigma^2 = n\left(\frac{S}{N}\right)\left(1 - \frac{S}{N}\right)\left(\frac{N-n}{N-1}\right)$, and $SD(X) = \sigma = \sqrt{n\left(\frac{S}{N}\right)\left(1 - \frac{S}{N}\right)\left(\frac{N-n}{N-1}\right)}$, respectively.

ADDITIONAL EXERCISES

81. An analyst developed the following probability distribution for the rate of return for a common stock.

Scenario	Probability	Rate of Return (in %)
1	0.25	− 15
2	0.35	5
3	0.40	10

a. Calculate the expected rate of return.
b. Calculate the variance and the standard deviation of this probability distribution.

82. The investment team at a high tech company is considering an innovative start-up project. According to its estimates, the company can make a profit of $5 million if the project is very successful and $2 million if it is somewhat successful. It also stands to lose $4 million if the project fails. Calculate the expected profit or loss for the company if the probabilities that the project is very successful and somewhat successful are 0.10 and 0.40, respectively.

83. Consider the following information on the expected return for companies X and Y.

Economy	Probability	X (in %)	Y (in %)
Boom	0.20	30	10
Neutral	0.50	10	20
Poor	0.30	− 30	5

a. Calculate the expected value and the standard deviation of returns for companies X and Y.
b. Calculate the correlation coefficient if the covariance between X and Y is 88.

84. A professor uses a relative scale for grading. She announces that 60% of the students will get at least a B, with 15% getting A's. Also, 5% will get a D and another 5% will get an F. Assume that no incompletes are given in the course. Let Score be defined by 4 for A, 3 for B, 2 for C, 1 for D, and 0 for F.
   a. Find the probability that a student gets a B.
   b. Find the probability that a student gets at least a C.
   c. Compute the expected value and the standard deviation of Score.

85. An investor owns a portfolio consisting of two mutual funds, A and B, with 35% invested in A. The following table lists the inputs for these funds.

Measures	Fund A	Fund B
Expected Value	10	5
Variance	98	26
Covariance	22	

   a. Calculate the expected value for the portfolio return.
   b. Calculate the standard deviation for the portfolio return.

86. Fifty percent of the customers who go to Auto Center for tires buy four tires and 30% buy two tires. Moreover, 18% buy fewer than two tires, with 5% buying none.
   a. Find the expected value and the standard deviation of the number of tires a customer buys.
   b. If Auto Center makes a $15 profit on every tire it sells, what is its expected profit if it services 120 customers?

87. Forty-four percent of consumers with credit cards carry balances from month to month. Four consumers with credit cards are randomly selected.
   a. What is the probability that all four consumers carry a credit card balance?
   b. What is the probability that fewer than two consumers carry a credit card balance?
   c. Calculate the expected value, the variance, and the standard deviation for this distribution.

88. Rent-to-own (RTO) stores allow consumers immediate access to merchandise in exchange for a series of weekly or monthly payments. The agreement is for a fixed time period. At the same time, the customer has the flexibility to terminate the contract by returning the merchandise. Suppose an RTO store makes a $200 profit on appliances when the customer ends up owning the merchandise by making all payments. It makes a $20 profit when the customer returns the product and a loss of $600 when the customer defaults. Let the return and default probabilities be 0.60 and 0.05, respectively.
   a. Construct a probability distribution for the profit per appliance.
   b. What is the expected profit for a store that sells 200 rent-to-own contracts?

89. According to the Department of Transportation, 27% of domestic flights are delayed. Suppose five flights are randomly selected at an airport.
   a. What is the probability that all five flights are delayed?
   b. What is the probability that all five are on time?

90. Apple products have become a household name in America, with 51% of all households owning at least one Apple product.
   a. What is the probability that two in a random sample of four households own an Apple product?
   b. What is the probability that all four in a random sample of four households own an Apple product?
   c. In a random sample of 100 households, find the expected value and the standard deviation for the number of households that own an Apple product.

91. Email spam refers to unsolicited email messages sent in bulk. Recent estimates suggest that spam messages account for 55% of all email traffic. Suppose a service department receives 100 emails daily.
   a. What is the probability that exactly 50 are spam messages?
   b. What is the probability that more than 50 are spam messages?
   c. What is the probability that at least 50 are spam messages?

92. According to a survey, approximately 19% of employers have eliminated perks or plan to do so in the next year. Suppose 30 employers are randomly selected.
   a. What is the probability that exactly ten of the employers have eliminated or plan to eliminate perks?
   b. What is the probability that at least ten employers, but no more than 20 employers, have eliminated or plan to eliminate perks?
   c. What is the probability that at most eight employers have eliminated or plan to eliminate perks?

93. Studies have shown that bats can consume an average of ten mosquitoes per minute.
   a. Calculate the average number of mosquitoes that a bat consumes in a 30-second interval.
   b. What is the probability that a bat consumes four mosquitoes in a 30-second interval?

c. What is the probability that a bat does not consume any mosquitoes in a 30-second interval?
d. What is the probability that a bat consumes at least one mosquito in a 30-second interval?

94. The police have estimated that there are 12 major accidents per day on a particular 10-mile stretch of a national highway. Suppose the incidence of accidents is evenly distributed on this 10-mile stretch of the highway.
    a. Find the probability that there will be fewer than eight major accidents per day on this 10-mile stretch of the highway.
    b. Find the probability that there will be more than two accidents per day on a one-mile stretch of this highway.

95. A professor has learned that three students in her class of 20 will cheat on the exam. She decides to focus her attention on four randomly chosen students during the exam.
    a. What is the probability that she finds at least one of the students cheating?
    b. What is the probability that she finds at least one of the students cheating if she focuses on six randomly chosen students?

96. Suppose you draw three cards, without replacement, from a deck of well-shuffled cards. Remember that each deck consists of 52 cards, with 13 each of spades, hearts, clubs, and diamonds.
    a. What is the probability that you draw all spades?
    b. What is the probability that you draw two or fewer spades?
    c. What is the probability that you draw all spades or all hearts?

97. Find the probability that an Internal Revenue Service (IRS) auditor will catch four income tax returns with illegitimate deductions if he randomly selects five returns from among 20 returns, of which 10 contain illegitimate deductions.

98. A committee of 10 is to be chosen from 50 people, 25 of whom are Republicans and 25 Democrats. The committee is chosen at random.
    a. What is the probability that there will be five Republicans and five Democrats?
    b. What is the probability that a majority of the committee will be Republicans?

APPENDIX 5.1 Guidelines for Other Software Packages

The following section provides brief commands for Minitab, SPSS, and JMP.

Minitab

The Binomial Distribution

(Replicating Example 5.9a) From the menu, choose **Calc > Probability Distributions > Binomial.** Select **Probability**. (For a cumulative probability function, select **Cumulative probability.**) Enter 100 as the **Number of trials** and 0.68 as the **Event probability.** Select **Input constant** and enter the value 70.

The Poisson Distribution

(Replicating Example 5.11a) From the menu, choose **Calc > Probability Distributions > Poisson.** Select **Cumulative probability**. (For a probability mass function, select **Probability.**) Enter 10.5 for the **Mean.** Select **Input constant** and enter the value 10.

The Hypergeometric Distribution

(Replicating Example 5.13a) From the menu, choose **Calc > Probability Distributions > Hypergeometric.** Select **Probability**. (For a cumulative probability function, select **Cumulative probability.**) Enter 25 for the **Population size (N),** 15 for **Event count in population (M),** and 4 for the **Sample size (n).** Select **Input constant** and enter 0.

SPSS

Note: In order for the calculated probability to be seen on the spreadsheet, SPSS must first "view" data on the spreadsheet. For this purpose, enter a value of zero in the first cell of the first column.

The Binomial Distribution

(Replicating Example 5.9a) From the menu, choose **Transform > Compute Variable.** Under **Target Variable,** type pdfbinomial. In the **Numeric Expression** box, enter PDF. BINOM(70, 100, 0.68). (For a cumulative probability function, enter CDF.BINOM(x, n, p).)

The Poisson Distribution

(Replicating Example 5.11a) From the menu, choose **Transform > Compute Variable.** Under **Target Variable,** type cdfpoisson. In the **Numeric Expression** box, enter CDF. POISSON(10, 10.5). (For a probability mass function, enter PDF.POISSON(x, μ).)

The Hypergeometric Distribution

(Replicating Example 5.13a) From the menu, choose **Transform > Compute Variable.** Under **Target Variable,** type pdfhyper. In the **Numeric Expression** box, enter PDF. HYPER(0, 25, 4, 15). (For a cumulative probability function, enter CDF.HYPER(x, N, n, S).)

JMP

Note: In order for the calculated probability to be seen on the spreadsheet, JMP must first "view" data on the spreadsheet. For this purpose, enter a value of zero in the first cell of the first column.

The Binomial Distribution

(Replicating Example 5.9a) Right-click at the top of the column in the spreadsheet view and select **Formula.** Choose **Discrete Probability > Binomial Probability.** (For a cumulative probability function, select **Binomial Distribution.**) Enter 0.68 for **p,** 100 for **n,** and 70 for **k.**

The Poisson Distribution

(Replicating Example 5.11a) Right-click at the top of the column in the spreadsheet view and select **Formula.** Choose **Discrete Probability > Poisson Distribution.** (For a probability mass function, select **Poisson Probability.**) Enter 10.5 for **lambda** and 10 for **k.**

The Hypergeometric Distribution

(Replicating Example 5.13a) Right-click at the top of the column in the spreadsheet view and select **Formula.** Choose **Discrete Probability > Hypergeometric Probability.** (For a cumulative probability function, select **Hypergeometric Distribution.**) Enter 25 for **N,** 15 for **K,** 4 for **n,** and 0 for **x.** (Use the menu at the top to delete the insertions for an optional odds ratio.)

6 Continuous Probability Distributions

LEARNING OBJECTIVES

After reading this chapter you should be able to:

LO **6.1** **Describe a continuous random variable.**

LO **6.2** **Calculate and interpret probabilities for a random variable that follows the continuous uniform distribution.**

LO **6.3** **Explain the characteristics of the normal distribution.**

LO **6.4** **Calculate and interpret probabilities for a random variable that follows the normal distribution.**

LO **6.5** **Calculate and interpret probabilities for a random variable that follows the exponential distribution.**

LO **6.6** **Calculate and interpret probabilities for a random variable that follows the lognormal distribution.**

In Chapter 5, we classified a random variable as either discrete or continuous. A discrete random variable assumes a countable number of distinct values, such as the number of houses that a realtor sells in a month, the number of defective pieces in a sample of 20 machine parts, and the number of cars lined up at a toll booth. A continuous random variable, on the other hand, is characterized by uncountable values within an interval. Examples of a continuous random variable include the investment return on a mutual fund, the waiting time at a toll booth, and the amount of soda in a cup. In all of these examples, it is impossible to list all possible values of the random variable.

In this chapter, we focus on continuous random variables. Most of this chapter is devoted to the normal distribution, which is the most extensively used continuous probability distribution and is the cornerstone of statistical inference. Other important continuous distributions discussed are the continuous uniform, the exponential, and the lognormal distributions.

Vision SRL/Getty Images

INTRODUCTORY CASE

Demand for Salmon

Akiko Hamaguchi is the manager of a small sushi restaurant called Little Ginza in Phoenix, Arizona. As part of her job, Akiko has to purchase salmon every day for the restaurant. For the sake of freshness, it is important that she buys the right amount of salmon daily. Buying too much may result in wastage, and buying too little may disappoint some customers on high-demand days.

Akiko has estimated that the daily consumption of salmon is normally distributed with a mean of 12 pounds and a standard deviation of 3.2 pounds. She has always bought 20 pounds of salmon every day. Often, this amount of salmon has resulted in wastage. As part of cost cutting, Akiko is considering a new strategy. She will buy salmon that is sufficient to meet the daily demand of customers on 90% of the days.

Akiko wants to use this information to

1. Calculate the probability that the demand for salmon at Little Ginza is above 20 pounds.
2. Calculate the probability that the demand for salmon at Little Ginza is below 15 pounds.
3. Determine the amount of salmon that should be bought daily so that the restaurant meets demand on 90% of the days.

A synopsis of this case is provided in Section 6.2.

LO 6.1

6.1 CONTINUOUS RANDOM VARIABLES AND THE UNIFORM DISTRIBUTION

Describe a continuous random variable.

As discussed in Chapter 5, a discrete random variable X assumes a countable number of distinct values such as x_1, x_2, x_3, and so on. A continuous random variable, on the other hand, is characterized by uncountable values within an interval. Unlike the case of a discrete random variable, we cannot describe the possible values of a continuous random variable X with a list $x_1, x_2, \ldots$ because the value $(x_1 + x_2)/2$, not in the list, might also be possible. Examples of continuous random variables include the return on a mutual fund, the completion time of a task, or the volume of beer sold as 16 ounces.

For a discrete random variable, we can compute the probability that it assumes a particular value x, or written as a probability statement, $P(X = x)$. For instance, for a binomial random variable with a given probability of success p, we can calculate the probability of exactly one success in n trials; that is, $P(X = 1)$.

The probability that a continuous random variable assumes a particular value x is zero; that is, $P(X = x) = 0$. This occurs because we cannot assign a nonzero probability to each of the uncountable values and still have the probabilities sum to one. For a continuous random variable, it is meaningful to calculate the probability within some specified interval. Therefore, for a continuous random variable, $P(a \leq X \leq b) = P(a < X < b) = P(a \leq X < b) = P(a < X \leq b)$, because $P(X = a)$ and $P(X = b)$ are both zero.

As discussed in Chapter 5, every discrete random variable is associated with a probability distribution, also called the probability mass function, that provides the probability that the random variable X assumes a particular value x, or equivalently, $P(X = x)$. For a continuous random variable, the counterpart to the probability mass function is called the probability density function, denoted by $f(x)$. The graph of $f(x)$ approximates the relative frequency polygon for the population. The probability that the continuous random variable assumes a value within an interval, say $P(a \leq X \leq b)$, is defined as the area under $f(x)$ between points a and b. Moreover, the entire area under $f(x)$ over all values of x must equal one; this is equivalent to the fact that, for discrete random variables, the probabilities add up to one.

THE PROBABILITY DENSITY FUNCTION

The probability density function $f(x)$ for a continuous random variable X has the following properties:

- $f(x) \geq 0$ for all possible values x of X, and
- the area under $f(x)$ over all values x of X equals one.

As in the case for a discrete random variable, we can use the cumulative distribution function, denoted by $F(x)$, to compute probabilities for a continuous random variable. For a value x of the random variable X, $F(x) = P(X \leq x)$ is simply the area under the probability density function up to the value x.

If you are familiar with calculus, then you will recognize that this cumulative distribution function $F(x)$ is the integral of $f(u)$ for values less than or equal to x. Similarly, $P(a \leq X \leq b) = F(b) - F(a)$ is the integral of $f(u)$ between points a and b. Fortunately, we do not necessarily need the knowledge of integral calculus to compute probabilities for the continuous random variables discussed in this text.

LO 6.2

Calculate and interpret probabilities for a random variable that follows the continuous uniform distribution.

The Continuous Uniform Distribution

One of the simplest continuous probability distributions is called the **continuous uniform distribution.** This distribution is appropriate when the underlying random variable has an equally likely chance of assuming a value within a specified range. Uniformly distributed random variables are often used to approximate the delivery time of an appliance, the scheduled flight time between cities, and the waiting time for a campus bus. Any specified range for each of the above random variables can be assumed to be equally probable.

Suppose you are informed that your new refrigerator will be delivered between 2:00 pm and 3:00 pm. Let the random variable X denote the delivery time of your refrigerator. This variable is bounded below by 2:00 pm and above by 3:00 pm for a total range of 60 minutes. It is reasonable to infer that the probability of delivery between 2:00 pm and 2:30 pm equals 0.50 (=30/60), as does the probability of delivery between 2:30 pm and 3:00 pm. Similarly, the probability of delivery in any 15-minute interval equals 0.25 (=15/60), and so on.

Figure 6.1 depicts the probability density function for a continuous uniform random variable. The values a and b on the horizontal axis represent its lower and upper limits, respectively. The continuous uniform distribution is symmetric around its mean μ, computed as $\frac{a+b}{2}$. In the refrigerator delivery example, the mean is $\mu = \frac{2+3}{2} = 2.5$, implying that you expect the delivery at 2:30 pm. The standard deviation σ of a continuous uniform variable equals $\sqrt{(b-a)^2/12}$.

FIGURE 6.1 Continuous uniform probability density function

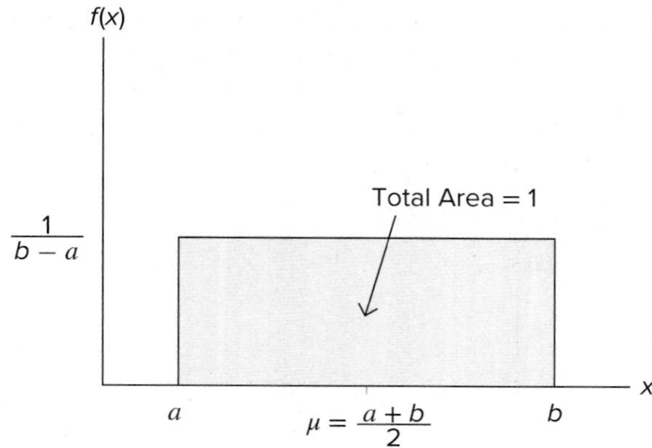

It is important to emphasize that the height of the probability density function does not directly represent a probability. As mentioned earlier, for all continuous random variables, it is the area under $f(x)$ that corresponds to probability. For the continuous uniform distribution, the probability is essentially the area of a rectangle, which is the base times the height. Therefore, the probability is easily computed by multiplying the length of a specified interval (base) with $f(x) = \frac{1}{b-a}$ (height).

THE CONTINUOUS UNIFORM DISTRIBUTION

A random variable X follows the continuous uniform distribution if its probability density function is

$$f(x) = \begin{cases} \dfrac{1}{b-a} & \text{for } a \leq x \leq b \\ 0 & \text{for } x < a \text{ or } x > b \end{cases}$$

where a and b represent the lower limit and the upper limit, respectively, that the random variable assumes.

The expected value and the standard deviation of X are computed as

$$E(X) = \mu = \frac{a+b}{2} \quad \text{and} \quad SD(X) = \sigma = \sqrt{(b-a)^2/12}.$$

EXAMPLE 6.1

A manager of a local drugstore is projecting next month's sales for a particular cosmetic line. She knows from historical data that sales follow a continuous uniform distribution with a lower limit of \$2,500 and an upper limit of \$5,000.

a. What are the mean and the standard deviation for the distribution?

b. What is the probability that sales exceed \$4,000?

c. What is the probability that sales are between \$3,200 and \$3,800?

SOLUTION:

a. With a lower limit of $a = 2{,}500$ and an upper limit of $b = 5{,}000$, we calculate the mean and the standard deviation for this continuous uniform distribution as

$$\mu = \frac{a+b}{2} = \frac{2{,}500 + 5{,}000}{2} = 3{,}750, \text{ or } \$3{,}750, \text{ and}$$

$$\sigma = \sqrt{(b-a)^2/12} = \sqrt{(5{,}000 - 2{,}500)^2/12} = 721.69, \text{ or } \$721.69.$$

b. When solving for the probability that sales exceed \$4,000, we find $P(X > 4{,}000)$, which is the area between 4,000 and 5,000, as shown in Figure 6.2. The base of the rectangle equals $5{,}000 - 4{,}000 = 1{,}000$ and the height equals $\frac{1}{5{,}000 - 2{,}500} = 0.0004$. Thus, $P(X > 4{,}000) = 1{,}000 \times 0.0004 = 0.40$.

FIGURE 6.2 Area to the right of 4,000

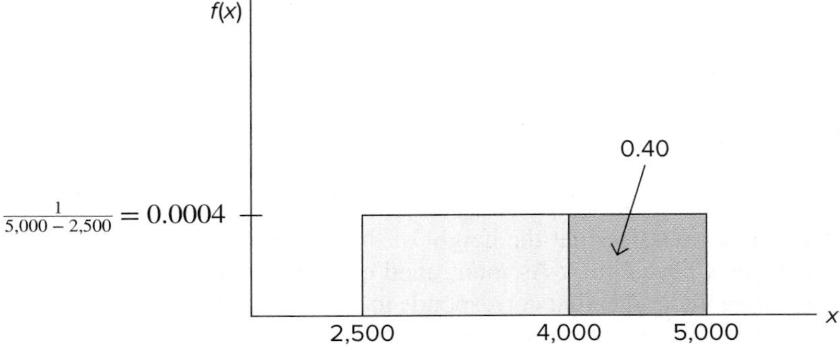

c. When solving for the probability that sales are between \$3,200 and \$3,800, we find $P(3{,}200 \leq X \leq 3{,}800)$. Using the same methodology as in part b, we multiply the base times the height of the rectangle, as shown in Figure 6.3. Therefore, we obtain the probability as $(3{,}800 - 3{,}200) \times 0.0004 = 0.24$.

FIGURE 6.3 Area between 3,200 and 3,800

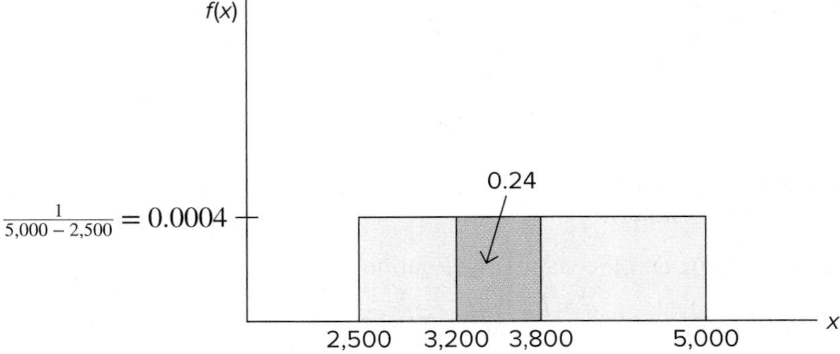

EXERCISES 6.1

Mechanics

1. The cumulative probabilities for a continuous random variable X are $P(X \leq 10) = 0.42$ and $P(X \leq 20) = 0.66$. Calculate the following probabilities.
   a. $P(X > 10)$
   b. $P(X > 20)$
   c. $P(10 < X < 20)$
2. For a continuous random variable X with an upper bound of 4, $P(0 \leq X \leq 2.5) = 0.54$ and $P(2.5 \leq X \leq 4) = 0.16$. Calculate the following probabilities.
   a. $P(X < 0)$
   b. $P(X > 2.5)$
   c. $P(0 \leq X \leq 4)$
3. For a continuous random variable X, $P(20 \leq X \leq 40) = 0.15$ and $P(X > 40) = 0.16$. Calculate the following probabilities.
   a. $P(X < 40)$
   b. $P(X < 20)$
   c. $P(X = 40)$
4. A random variable X follows the continuous uniform distribution with a lower bound of 5 and an upper bound of 35.
   a. What is the height of the density function $f(x)$?
   b. What are the mean and the standard deviation for the distribution?
   c. Calculate $P(X > 10)$.
5. A random variable X follows the continuous uniform distribution with a lower bound of −2 and an upper bound of 4.
   a. What is the height of the density function $f(x)$?
   b. What are the mean and the standard deviation for the distribution?
   c. Calculate $P(X \leq -1)$.
6. A random variable X follows the continuous uniform distribution with a lower limit of 10 and an upper limit of 30.
   a. Calculate the mean and the standard deviation for the distribution.
   b. What is the probability that X is greater than 22?
   c. What is the probability that X is between 15 and 23?
7. A random variable X follows the continuous uniform distribution with a lower limit of 750 and an upper limit of 800.
   a. Calculate the mean and the standard deviation for the distribution.
   b. What is the probability that X is less than 770?

Applications

8. Suppose the price of electricity follows the continuous uniform distribution with a lower bound of 12 cents per kilowatt-hour and an upper bound of 20 cents per kilowatt-hour.
   a. Calculate the average price of electricity.
   b. What is the probability that the price of electricity is less than 15.5 cents per kilowatt-hour?
   c. A local carnival is not able to operate its rides if the price of electricity is more than 14 cents per kilowatt-hour. What is the probability that the carnival will need to close?
9. The arrival time of an elevator in a 12-story dormitory is equally likely at any time during the next 4 minutes.
   a. Calculate the expected arrival time.
   b. What is the probability that an elevator arrives in less than 1½ minutes?
   c. What is the probability that the wait for an elevator is more than 1½ minutes?
10. The Netherlands is one of the world leaders in the production and sale of tulips. Suppose the heights of the tulips in the greenhouse of Rotterdam's Fantastic Flora follow a continuous uniform distribution with a lower bound of 7 inches and an upper bound of 16 inches. You have come to the greenhouse to select a bouquet of tulips, but only tulips with a height greater than 10 inches may be selected. What is the probability that a randomly selected tulip is tall enough to pick?
11. The scheduled arrival time for a daily flight from Boston to New York is 9:25 am. Historical data show that the arrival time follows the continuous uniform distribution with an early arrival time of 9:15 am and a late arrival time of 9:55 am.
    a. Calculate the mean and the standard deviation of the distribution.
    b. What is the probability that a flight arrives late (later than 9:25 am)?
12. You were informed at the nursery that your peach tree will definitely bloom sometime between March 18 and March 30. Assume that the bloom times follow a continuous uniform distribution between these specified dates.
    a. What is the probability that the tree does not bloom until March 25?
    b. What is the probability that the tree will bloom by March 20?
13. You have been informed that the assessor will visit your home sometime between 10:00 am and 12:00 pm. It is reasonable to assume that his visitation time is uniformly distributed over the specified two-hour interval. Suppose you have to run a quick errand at 10:00 am.
    a. If it takes 15 minutes to run the errand, what is the probability that you will be back before the assessor visits?
    b. If it takes 30 minutes to run the errand, what is the probability that you will be back before the assessor visits?

6.2 THE NORMAL DISTRIBUTION

The **normal probability distribution**, or simply the **normal distribution**, is the familiar bell-shaped distribution. It is also referred to as the Gaussian distribution.[1] The normal distribution is the most extensively used probability distribution in statistical work. One reason for this common use is that the normal distribution closely approximates the probability distribution for a wide range of random variables of interest. Examples of random variables that closely follow a normal distribution include:

- Salary of employees in a tech firm
- Scores on the SAT exam
- Cumulative debt of college graduates
- Advertising expenditure of firms
- Rate of return on an investment

Whenever possible, it is instructive to analyze the underlying data to determine if the normal distribution is appropriate for a given application. There are various ways to do this, including inspecting histograms (Chapter 2) and boxplots (Chapter 3) for symmetry and bell shape. In this chapter, we simply assume that the random variable in question is normally distributed and focus on finding probabilities associated with this type of random variable. The computation of these probabilities is easy and direct.

Another important function of the normal distribution is that it serves as the cornerstone of statistical inference. Recall from Chapter 1 that the study of statistics is divided into two branches: descriptive statistics and inferential statistics. Statistical inference is generally based on the assumption of the normal distribution and serves as the major topic in the remainder of this text.

LO 6.3

Explain the characteristics of the normal distribution.

Characteristics of the Normal Distribution

- The normal distribution is **bell-shaped** and **symmetric** around its mean; that is, one side of the mean is just the mirror image of the other side. The mean, the median, and the mode are all equal for a normally distributed random variable.
- The normal distribution is **described by two parameters**—the population mean μ and the population variance σ^2. The population mean describes the central location and the population variance describes the dispersion of the distribution.
- The normal distribution is **asymptotic** in the sense that the tails get closer and closer to the horizontal axis but never touch it. Thus, theoretically, a normal random variable can assume any value between minus infinity and plus infinity.

A graph depicting the normal probability density function is often referred to as the normal curve or the bell curve. The following example relates the normal curve to the location and the dispersion of the normally distributed random variable.

EXAMPLE 6.2

Suppose we know that the ages of employees in Industries A, B, and C are normally distributed. We are given the following information on the relevant parameters:

Industry A	Industry B	Industry C
μ = 42 years	μ = 36 years	μ = 42 years
σ = 5 years	σ = 5 years	σ = 8 years

[1]The discovery of the normal (Gaussian) distribution is often credited to Carl Friedrich Gauss (1777–1855), even though some attribute the credit to De Moivre (1667–1754), who had earlier discovered it in the context of simplifying the binomial distribution calculations.

Graphically compare the ages of employees in Industry A with Industry B. Repeat the comparison in Industry A with Industry C.

SOLUTION: Since the mean age of employees in Industry A is greater than that in Industry B, the normal curve for Industry A is located to the right of Industry B as shown in Figure 6.4. Both curves show equal dispersion from the mean, given that the standard deviations are the same.

FIGURE 6.4 Normal probability density function for two values of μ along with $\sigma = 5$

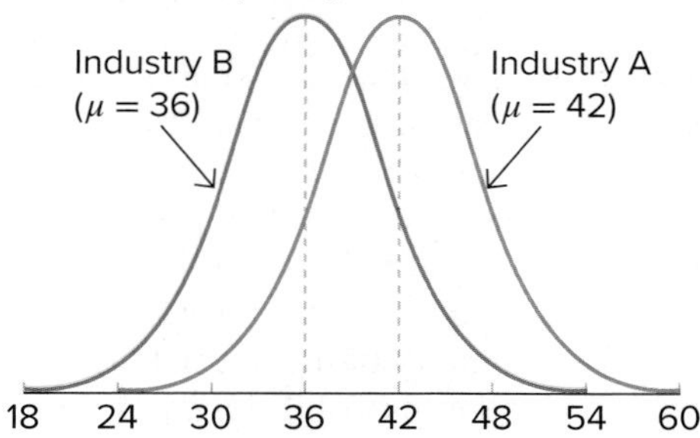

Since the mean age of employees in Industry A and Industry C is the same, the normal curves for each industry have the same center as shown in Figure 6.5. However, since the standard deviation for Industry A is less than that of Industry C, the normal curve for Industry A is less dispersed. Its peak is higher than that of Industry C, reflecting the fact that an employee's age is likelier to be closer to the mean age in Industry A. Figures 6.4 and 6.5 show that we can capture the entire distribution of any normally distributed random variable based on its mean and variance (or standard deviation).

FIGURE 6.5 Normal probability density function for two values of σ along with $\mu = 42$

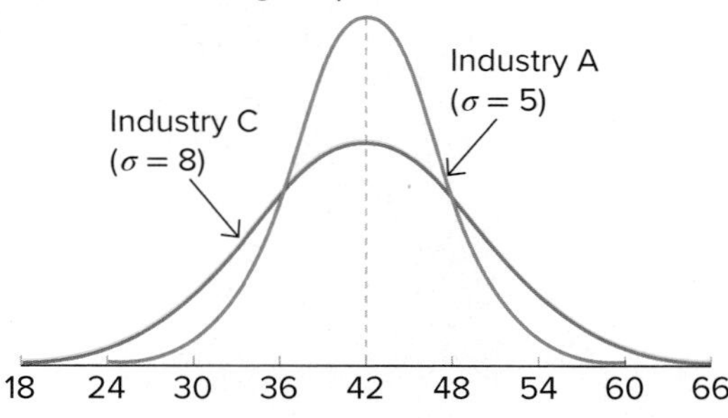

We generally use the cumulative distribution function $F(x)$ to compute probabilities for a normally distributed random variable, where $F(x) = P(X \leq x)$ is simply the area under $f(x)$ up to the value x. As mentioned earlier, we do not necessarily need the knowledge of integral calculus to compute probabilities for the normal distribution. Instead, we rely on a table to find probabilities. We can also compute probabilities with certain calculators, Excel, R, and other statistical packages. The specifics of how to use the table are delineated next.

The Standard Normal Distribution

The **standard normal distribution** is a special case of the normal distribution with a mean equal to zero and a standard deviation (or variance) equal to one. Using the letter Z to denote a random variable with the standard normal distribution, we have $\mu = E(Z) = 0$

and $\sigma = SD(Z) = 1$. As usual, we use the lowercase letter z to denote the value that the standard normal variable Z may assume.

The value z is the z-score that we discussed in Chapter 3. It measures the number of standard deviations a given value is away from the mean. For example, a z-score of 2 implies that the given value is 2 standard deviations above the mean. Similarly, a z-score of -1.5 implies that the given value is 1.5 standard deviations below the mean. As mentioned in Chapter 3, converting values into z-scores is called standardizing the data.

We will first show how to compute probabilities related to the standard normal distribution. Later, we will show that any normal distribution is equivalent to the standard normal distribution when the unit of measurement is changed to measure standard deviations from the mean.

Virtually all introductory statistics texts include a **standard normal table**, also referred to as the z table, that provides areas (probabilities) under the z curve. However, the format of these tables is sometimes different. In this text, the z table provides cumulative probabilities $P(Z \leq z)$; this table appears on two pages in Appendix B and is labeled Table 1. The left-hand page provides cumulative probabilities for z values less than or equal to zero. The right-hand page shows cumulative probabilities for z values greater than or equal to zero. Given the symmetry of the normal distribution and the fact that the area under the entire curve is one, other probabilities can be easily computed.

> THE STANDARD NORMAL DISTRIBUTION
>
> The standard normal random variable Z is a normal random variable with $E(Z) = 0$ and $SD(Z) = 1$. The z table provides cumulative probabilities $P(Z \leq z)$ for positive and negative z values.

Figure 6.6 represents the standard normal probability density function (z distribution). Because the random variable Z is symmetric around its mean of zero, $P(Z < 0) = P(Z > 0) = 0.5$. As is the case with all continuous random variables, we can also write the probabilities as $P(Z \leq 0) = P(Z \geq 0) = 0.5$.

FIGURE 6.6 Standard normal probability density function

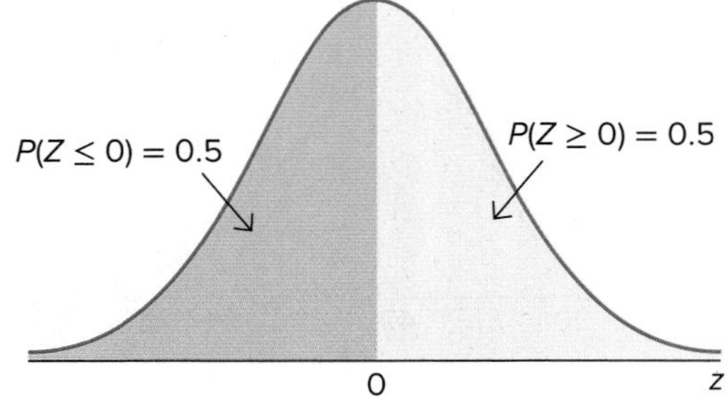

Finding a Probability for a Given z Value

As mentioned earlier, the z table provides cumulative probabilities $P(Z \leq z)$ for a given z. Consider, for example, a cumulative probability $P(Z \leq 1.52)$. Since $z = 1.52$ is positive, we can look up this probability from the right-hand page of the z table in Appendix B; Table 6.1 shows a portion of the table.

TABLE 6.1 Portion of the Right-Hand Page of the z Table

z	0.00	0.01	0.02
0.0	0.5000	0.5040	↓
0.1	0.5398	0.5438	↓
⋮	⋮	⋮	⋮
1.5	→	→	0.9357

The first column of the table, denoted as the z column, shows values of z up to the tenth decimal point, while the first row of the table, denoted as the z row, shows hundredths values. Thus, for $z = 1.52$, we match 1.5 on the z column with 0.02 on the z row to find a corresponding probability of 0.9357. The arrows in Table 6.1 indicate that $P(Z \leq 1.52) = 0.9357$.

Figure 6.7 shows the cumulative probability corresponding to $z = 1.52$. Note that $P(Z \leq 1.52) = 0.9357$ represents the area under the z curve to the left of 1.52. Therefore, the area to the right of 1.52 can be computed as $P(Z > 1.52) = 1 - P(Z \leq 1.52) = 1 - 0.9357 = 0.0643$.

FIGURE 6.7 Cumulative probability with respect to $z = 1.52$

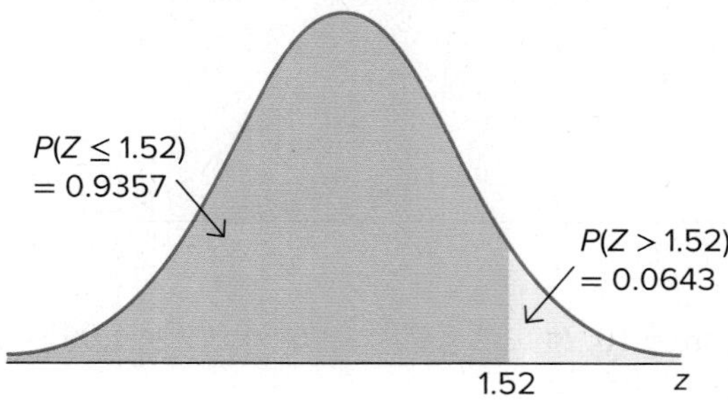

Suppose we want to find $P(Z \leq -1.96)$. Since z is a negative value, we can look up this probability from the left-hand page of the z table; Table 6.2 shows a portion of the table with arrows indicating that $P(Z \leq -1.96) = 0.0250$. Figure 6.8 shows the corresponding probability. As before, the area to the right of -1.96 can be computed as $P(Z > -1.96) = 1 - P(Z \leq -1.96) = 1 - 0.0250 = 0.9750$.

TABLE 6.2 Portion of the Left-Hand Page of the z Table

z	0.00	0.01	0.02	0.03	0.04	0.05	0.06
−3.9	0.0000	0.0000	0.0000	0.0000	0.0000	0.0000	↓
−3.8	0.0001	0.0001	0.0001	0.0001	0.0001	0.0001	↓
⋮	⋮	⋮	⋮	⋮	⋮	⋮	⋮
−1.9	→	→	→	→	→	→	0.0250

FIGURE 6.8 Cumulative probability with respect to $z = -1.96$

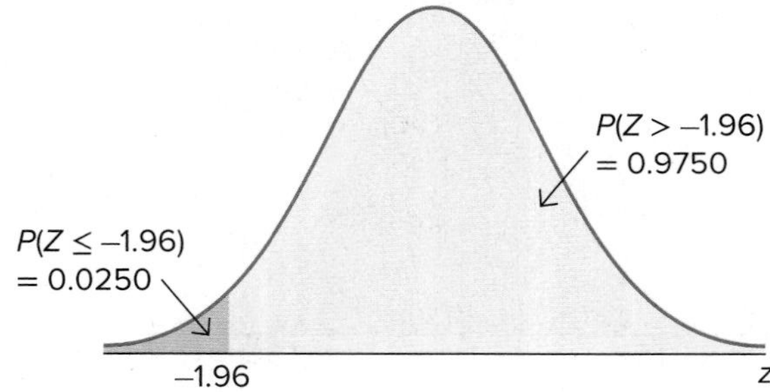

EXAMPLE 6.3

Find the following probabilities for the standard normal random variable Z.

a. $P(0 \leq Z \leq 1.96)$

b. $P(1.52 \leq Z \leq 1.96)$

c. $P(-1.52 \leq Z \leq 1.96)$

d. $P(Z > 4)$

SOLUTION: It always helps to start by highlighting the relevant probability in the z graph.

a. As shown in Figure 6.9, the area between 0 and 1.96 is equivalent to the area to the left of 1.96 minus the area to the left of 0. Therefore, $P(0 \leq Z \leq 1.96) = P(Z \leq 1.96) - P(Z < 0) = 0.9750 - 0.50 = 0.4750$.

FIGURE 6.9 Finding the probability between 0 and 1.96

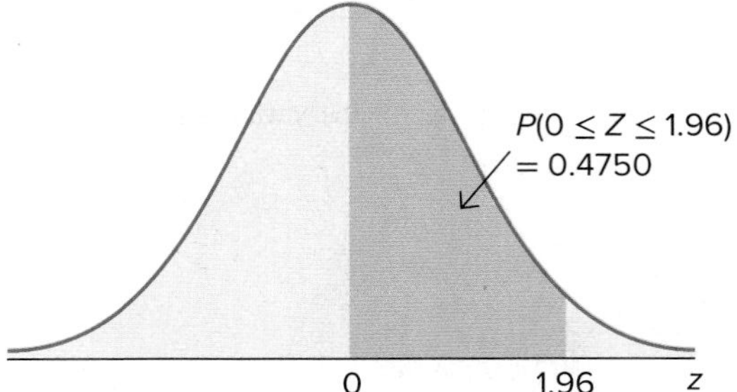

b. As shown in Figure 6.10, $P(1.52 \leq Z \leq 1.96) = P(Z \leq 1.96) - P(Z < 1.52) = 0.9750 - 0.9357 = 0.0393$.

FIGURE 6.10 Finding the probability between 1.52 and 1.96

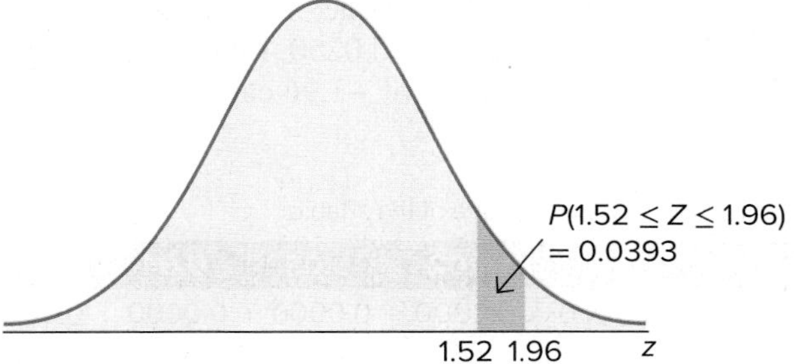

c. From Figure 6.11, $P(-1.52 \leq Z \leq 1.96) = P(Z \leq 1.96) - P(Z < -1.52) = 0.9750 - 0.0643 = 0.9107$.

FIGURE 6.11 Finding the probability between −1.52 and 1.96

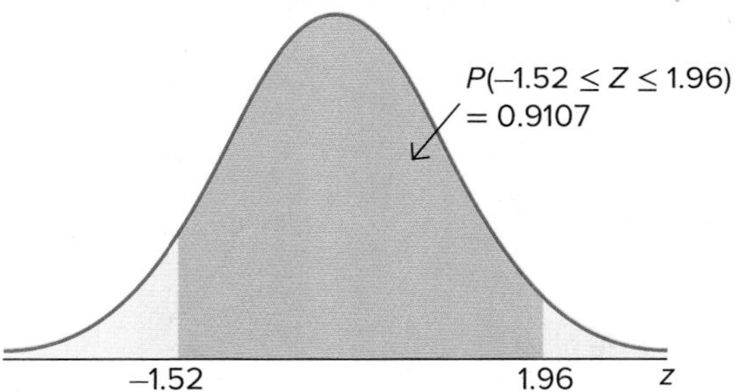

d. $P(Z > 4) = 1 - P(Z \leq 4)$. However, the z table only goes up to 3.99 with $P(Z \leq 3.99) = 1.0$ (approximately). In fact, for any z value greater than 3.99, it is acceptable to treat $P(Z \leq z) = 1.0$. Therefore, $P(Z > 4) = 1 - P(Z \leq 4) = 0$.

Finding a *z* Value for a Given Probability

So far we have computed probabilities for given z values. Now we will evaluate z values for given probabilities.

EXAMPLE 6.4

For the standard normal variable Z, find the z values that satisfy the following probability statements.

a. $P(Z \leq z) = 0.6808$

b. $P(Z \leq z) = 0.90$

c. $P(Z \leq z) = 0.0643$

d. $P(Z > z) = 0.0212$

e. $P(-z \leq Z \leq z) = 0.95$

SOLUTION: As mentioned earlier, it helps to first highlight the relevant probability in the z graph. Recall, too, that the z table lists z values along with the corresponding cumulative probabilities. Noncumulative probabilities can be evaluated using symmetry.

a. Since the probability is already in a cumulative format—that is, $P(Z \leq z) = 0.6808$—we simply look up 0.6808 from the body of the table (right-hand side) to find the corresponding z value from the row/column of z. Table 6.3 shows the relevant portion of the z table, and Figure 6.12 depicts the corresponding area. Therefore, $z = 0.47$.

TABLE 6.3 Portion of the z Table for Example 6.4a

z	0.00	0.01	0.02	0.03	0.04	0.05	0.06	0.07
0.0	0.5000	0.5040	0.5080	0.5120	0.5160	0.5199	0.5239	↑
0.1	0.5398	0.5438	0.5478	0.5517	0.5557	0.5596	0.5636	↑
⋮	⋮	⋮	⋮	⋮	⋮	⋮	⋮	⋮
0.4	←	←	←	←	←	←	←	0.6808

FIGURE 6.12 Finding z given $P(Z \leq z) = 0.6808$

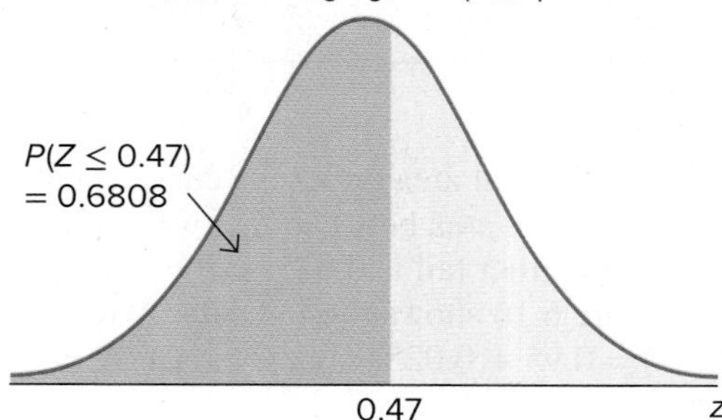

b. When deriving z for $P(Z \leq z) = 0.90$, we find that the z table (right-hand side) does not contain the cumulative probability 0.90. In such cases, we use the closest cumulative probability to solve the problem. Therefore, z is approximately equal to 1.28, which corresponds to a cumulative probability of 0.8997. Figure 6.13 shows this result graphically.

FIGURE 6.13 Finding z given $P(Z \leq z) = 0.90$

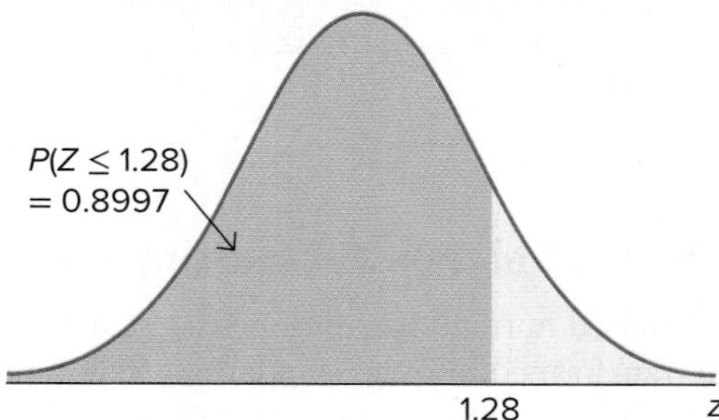

c. As shown in Figure 6.14, the z value that solves $P(Z \leq z) = 0.0643$ must be negative because the probability to its left is less than 0.50. We look up the cumulative probability 0.0643 in the table (left-hand side) to get $z = -1.52$.

FIGURE 6.14 Finding z given $P(Z \leq z) = 0.0643$

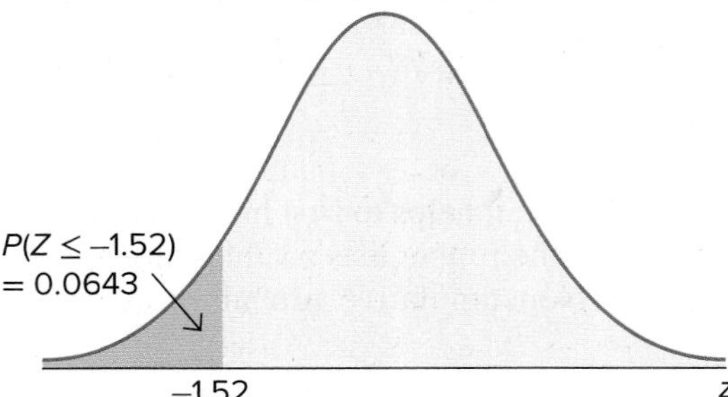

d. When deriving z for $P(Z > z) = 0.0212$, we have to find a z value such that the probability to the right of this value is 0.0212. Since the table states cumulative probabilities, we look up $P(Z \leq z) = 1 - 0.0212 = 0.9788$ in the table (right-hand side) to get $z = 2.03$. Figure 6.15 shows the results.

FIGURE 6.15 Finding z given $P(Z > z) = 0.0212$

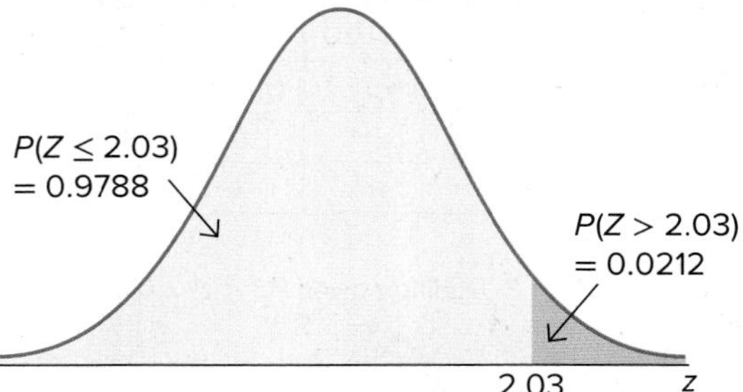

e. Because we know that the total area under the curve equals one, and we want to find $-z$ and z such that the area between the two values equals 0.95, we can conclude that the area in either tail is 0.025; that is, $P(Z < -z) = 0.025$ and $P(Z > z) = 0.025$. Figure 6.16 shows these results. We then use the cumulative probability, $P(Z \leq z) = 0.95 + 0.025 = 0.975$, to find $z = 1.96$.

FIGURE 6.16 Finding z given $P(-z \leq Z \leq z) = 0.95$

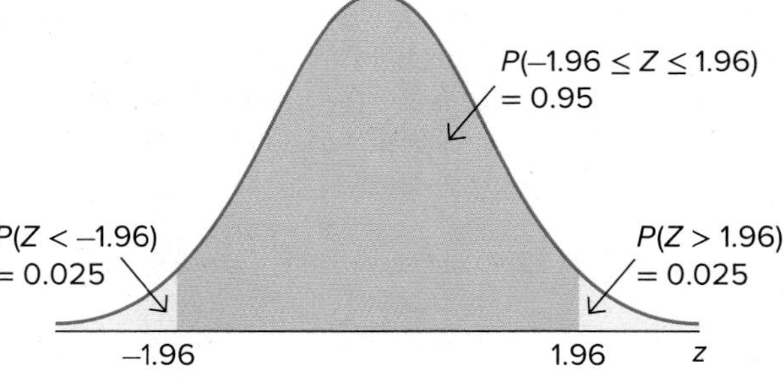

LO 6.4

Calculate and interpret probabilities for a random variable that follows the normal distribution.

The Transformation of Normal Random Variables

The importance of the standard normal distribution arises from the fact that any normal random variable can be transformed into the standard normal random variable to derive the relevant probabilities. In other words, any normally distributed random variable X

with mean μ and standard deviation σ can be transformed (standardized) into the standard normal variable Z with mean zero and standard deviation one. We transform X into Z by subtracting from X its mean and dividing by its standard deviation; this is referred to as the **standard transformation**.

THE STANDARD TRANSFORMATION: CONVERTING X INTO Z

Any normally distributed random variable X with mean μ and standard deviation σ can be transformed into the standard normal random variable Z as

$$Z = \frac{X - \mu}{\sigma}.$$

Therefore, any value x has a corresponding value z given by

$$z = \frac{x - \mu}{\sigma}.$$

As illustrated in Figure 6.17, if the x value is at the mean—that is, $x = \mu$—then the corresponding z value is $z = \frac{\mu - \mu}{\sigma} = 0$. Similarly, if the x value is at one standard deviation above the mean—that is, $x = \mu + \sigma$—then the corresponding z value is $z = \frac{\mu + \sigma - \mu}{\sigma} = 1$. Therefore, by construction, $E(Z) = 0$ and $SD(Z) = 1$.

FIGURE 6.17 Transforming X with mean μ and standard deviation σ to Z

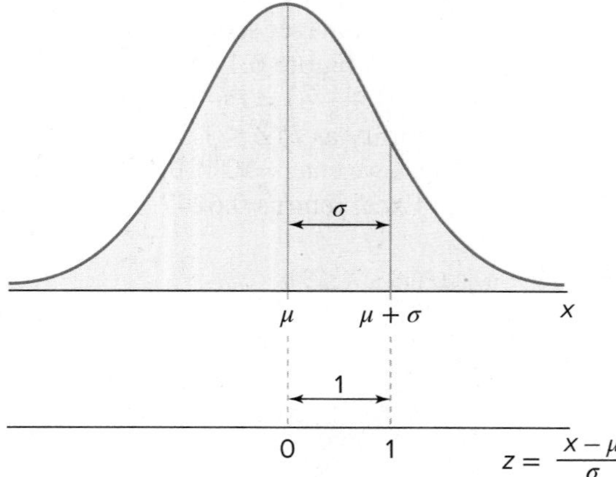

In the next two examples, we show how to solve any normal distribution problem using the z table. We then replicate the results using Excel. R instructions will be introduced later in this section.

EXAMPLE 6.5

Scores on a management aptitude exam are normally distributed with a mean of 72 and a standard deviation of 8.

a. What is the probability that a randomly selected manager will score above 60?

b. What is the probability that a randomly selected manager will score between 68 and 84?

SOLUTION: Let X represent scores with $\mu = 72$ and $\sigma = 8$.

a. The probability that a manager scores above 60 is $P(X > 60)$. Figure 6.18 shows the probability as the shaded area to the right of 60. We derive $P(X > 60) = P\left(Z > \frac{60 - 72}{8}\right) = P(Z > -1.5)$. Using the z table, we find $P(Z > -1.5) = 0.9332$.

FIGURE 6.18 Finding $P(X > 60)$

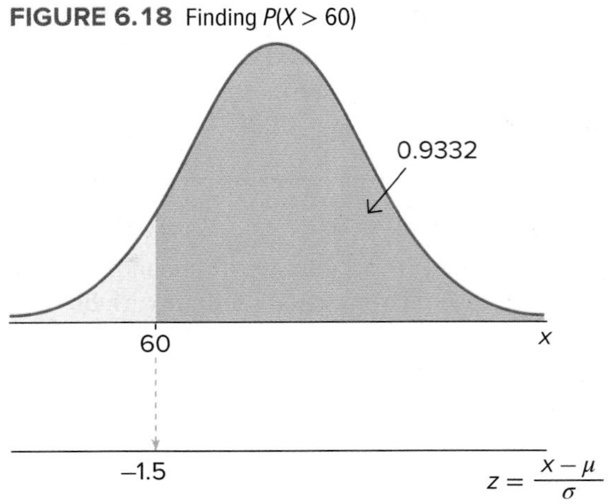

We will now use Excel's **NORM.DIST** to solve for probabilities. We enter =NORM.DIST(*x*, μ, σ, TRUE or FALSE) where x is the value to be evaluated, μ is the mean of the distribution, and σ is the standard deviation of the distribution. If we enter TRUE for the last argument, then Excel returns the cumulative probability function $P(X \leq x)$. If we enter FALSE for the last argument, then Excel returns the height of the normal distribution at the point x. In order to find $P(X > 60)$, we enter =1-NORM.DIST(60, 72, 8, TRUE), and Excel returns 0.9332.

b. When solving for the probability that a manager scores between 68 and 84, we find $P(68 \leq X \leq 84)$. The shaded area in Figure 6.19 shows this probability. We derive $P(68 \leq X \leq 84) = P\left(\frac{68-72}{8} \leq Z \leq \frac{84-72}{8}\right) = P(-0.5 \leq Z \leq 1.5)$. Using the z table we find this probability as $P(Z \leq 1.5) - P(Z < -0.5) = 0.9332 - 0.3085 = 0.6247$. Using Excel, we enter =NORM.DIST(84, 72, 8, TRUE) - NORM.DIST(68, 72, 8, TRUE), and Excel returns 0.6247.

FIGURE 6.19 Finding $P(68 \leq X \leq 84)$

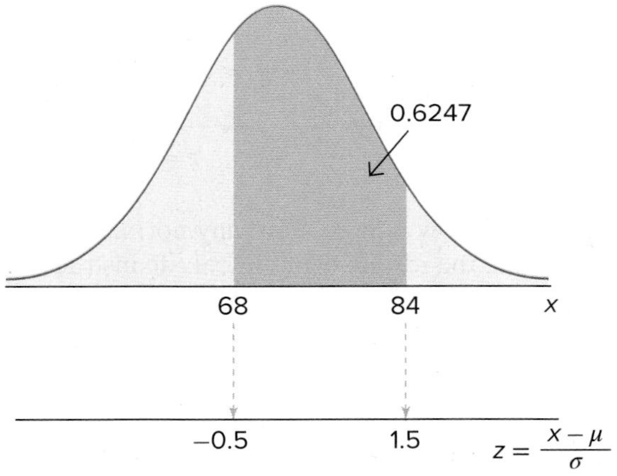

0.6247
68 84 X
−0.5 1.5 $z = \frac{x - \mu}{\sigma}$

Note: The probabilities computed with the z table may differ slightly from the probabilities computed with Excel's NORM.DIST function because of rounding to 2-decimal places with the z table.

So far we have used the standard transformation to compute probabilities for given x values. We can use the **inverse transformation**, $x = \mu + z\sigma$, to compute x values for given probabilities.

THE INVERSE TRANSFORMATION: CONVERTING Z INTO X

The standard normal variable Z can be transformed to the normally distributed random variable X with mean μ and standard deviation σ as $X = \mu + Z\sigma$.

Therefore, any value z has a corresponding value x given by $x = \mu + z\sigma$.

EXAMPLE 6.6

Scores on a management aptitude examination are normally distributed with a mean of 72 and a standard deviation of 8.

a. What is the lowest score that will place a manager in the top 10% (90th percentile) of the distribution?

b. What is the highest score that will place a manager in the bottom 25% (25th percentile) of the distribution?

SOLUTION: Let X represent scores on a management aptitude examination with $\mu = 72$ and $\sigma = 8$.

a. The 90th percentile is a numerical value x such that $P(X < x) = 0.90$. Using the z table (right-hand side), we find the corresponding z value that satisfies $P(Z < z) = 0.90$ as $z = 1.28$. We then solve $x = \mu + z\sigma = 72 + 1.28 \times 8 = 82.24$. Therefore, a score of 82.24 or higher will place a manager in the top 10% of the distribution (see Figure 6.20).

FIGURE 6.20 Finding x given $P(X < x) = 0.90$

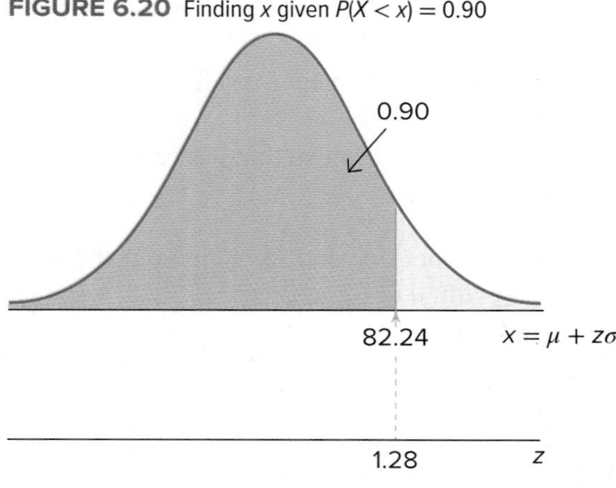

We can also use Excel's NORM.INV to find a particular x value. We enter =`NORM.INV(cumulprob, μ, σ)`, where cumulprob is the cumulative probability associated with the value x, μ is the mean of the distribution, and σ is the standard deviation of the distribution. In order to find the value of x that satisfies P(X < x) = 0.90, we enter =`NORM.INV(0.90, 72, 8)`, and Excel returns 82.25. Note that this value is slightly different from the manual calculations because of rounding with the z table.

b. The 25th percentile is a numerical value x such that $P(X < x) = 0.25$. Using the z table (left-hand side), we find the corresponding z value that satisfies $P(Z < z) = 0.25$ as $z = -0.67$. We then solve $x = 72 - 0.67(8) = 66.64$. Therefore, a score of 66.64 or lower will place a manager in the bottom 25% of the distribution (see Figure 6.21). Using Excel, we enter =`NORM.INV(0.25, 72, 8)`, and Excel returns 66.60, which is again slightly different because of rounding.

FIGURE 6.21 Finding x given $P(X < x) = 0.25$

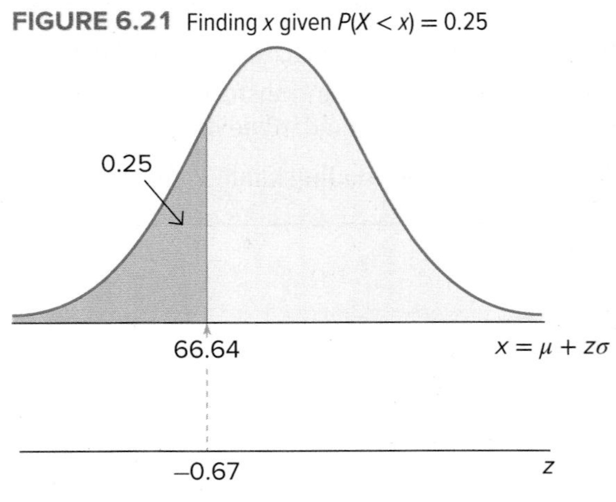

EXAMPLE 6.7

We can now answer the questions first posed by Akiko Hamaguchi in the introductory case of this chapter. Recall that Akiko would like to buy the right amount of salmon for daily consumption at Little Ginza. Akiko has estimated that the daily consumption of salmon is normally distributed with a mean of 12 pounds and a standard deviation of 3.2 pounds. She wants to answer the following questions:

a. What is the probability that the demand for salmon at Little Ginza is above 20 pounds?

b. What is the probability that the demand for salmon at Little Ginza is below 15 pounds?

c. How much salmon should be bought so that it meets customer demand on 90% of the days?

SOLUTION: Let X denote customer demand for salmon at the restaurant. We solve this problem using Excel, with $\mu = 12$ and $\sigma = 3.2$.

a. In order to find the probability that the demand for salmon is more than 20 pounds, or $P(X > 20)$, we enter `=1 - NORM.DIST(20, 12, 3.2, TRUE)`. Excel returns 0.0062.

b. In order to find the probability that the demand for salmon is less than 15 pounds, or $P(X < 15)$, we enter `=NORM.DIST(15, 12, 3.2, TRUE)`. Excel returns 0.8257.

c. In order to compute the required amount of salmon that should be purchased to meet demand on 90% of the days, we solve for x in $P(X \leq x) = 0.90$. We enter `=NORM.INV(0.9,12,3.2)`, and Excel returns 16.10. Therefore, Akiko should buy 16.10 pounds of salmon daily to ensure that customer demand is met on 90% of the days.

Using R for the Normal Distribution

We use R's **pnorm** function to find probabilities associated with the normal distribution. In order to find $P(X \leq x)$, we enter pnorm(x, μ, σ, lower.tail = TRUE), where x is the value to be evaluated, μ is the mean of the distribution, and σ is the standard deviation of the distribution. If we enter lower.tail=FALSE, then R returns $P(X > x)$. Referring back to part a of Example 6.7, if we want to find $P(X > 20)$ with $\mu = 12$ and $\sigma = 3.2$, we enter:

```
> pnorm(20,12,3.2, lower.tail=FALSE)
```

R returns: 0.006209665

Referring back to part b of Example 6.7, if we want to find $P(X < 15)$ with $\mu = 12$ and $\sigma = 3.2$, we enter:

```
> pnorm(15,12,3.2, lower.tail=TRUE)
```

R returns: 0.8257493

We use R's **qnorm** function to find a particular x value. We enter qnorm(*cumulprob*, μ, σ), where cumulprob is the cumulative probability associated with the value x, μ is the mean of the distribution, and σ is the standard deviation of the distribution. Referring back to part c of Example 6.7, if we want to to find the value of x that satisfies $P(X < x) = 0.90$ with $\mu = 12$ and $\sigma = 3.2$, we enter:

```
> qnorm(0.90,12,3.2)
```

R returns: 16.10097

A Note on the Normal Approximation of the Binomial Distribution

Recall from Chapter 5 that it is tedious to compute binomial probabilities with the formula when we encounter large values for n. As it turns out, with large values for n, the binomial distribution can be approximated by the normal distribution. Based on this normal distribution approximation, with mean $\mu = np$ and standard deviation $\sigma = \sqrt{np(1 - p)}$, we can use the z table to compute relevant binomial probabilities. Some researchers believe that the discovery of the normal distribution in the 18th century was due to the need to simplify the binomial probability calculations. The popularity of this method, however, has been greatly reduced by the advent of computers. As we learned in Chapter 5, it is easy to compute exact binomial probabilities with Excel and R; thus, there is less need to approximate. The normal distribution approximation, however, is extremely important when making an inference for the population proportion p, which is a key parameter of the binomial distribution. In later chapters, we will study the details of this approximation and how it is used for making inferences.

SYNOPSIS OF INTRODUCTORY CASE

Akiko Hamaguchi is a manager at a small sushi restaurant called Little Ginza in Phoenix, Arizona. She is aware of the importance of purchasing the right amount of salmon daily. While purchasing too much salmon results in wastage, purchasing too little can disappoint customers who may choose not to frequent the restaurant in the future. In the past, she has always bought 20 pounds of salmon daily. A careful analysis of her purchasing habits and customer demand reveals that Akiko is buying too much salmon. The probability that the demand for salmon would exceed 20 pounds is very small at 0.0062. Even a purchase of 15 pounds satisfies customer demand on 82.57% of the days. In order to execute her new strategy of meeting daily demand of customers on 90% of the days, Akiko should purchase approximately 16 pounds of salmon daily.

gkrphoto/Getty Images

EXERCISES 6.2

Mechanics

14. Find the following probabilities based on the standard normal variable Z.
    a. $P(Z > 1.32)$
    b. $P(Z \leq -1.32)$
    c. $P(1.32 \leq Z \leq 2.37)$
    d. $P(-1.32 \leq Z \leq 2.37)$

15. Find the following probabilities based on the standard normal variable Z.
    a. $P(Z > 0.74)$
    b. $P(Z \leq -1.92)$
    c. $P(0 \leq Z \leq 1.62)$
    d. $P(-0.90 \leq Z \leq 2.94)$

16. Find the following probabilities based on the standard normal variable Z.
    a. $P(-0.67 \leq Z \leq -0.23)$
    b. $P(0 \leq Z \leq 1.96)$
    c. $P(-1.28 \leq Z \leq 0)$
    d. $P(Z > 4.2)$

17. Find the following z values for the standard normal variable Z.
    a. $P(Z \leq z) = 0.9744$
    b. $P(Z > z) = 0.8389$
    c. $P(-z \leq Z \leq z) = 0.95$
    d. $P(0 \leq Z \leq z) = 0.3315$

18. Find the following z values for the standard normal variable Z.
    a. $P(Z \leq z) = 0.1020$
    b. $P(z \leq Z \leq 0) = 0.1772$
    c. $P(Z > z) = 0.9929$
    d. $P(0.40 \leq Z \leq z) = 0.3368$

19. Let X be normally distributed with mean $\mu = 10$ and standard deviation $\sigma = 6$.
    a. Find $P(X \leq 0)$.
    b. Find $P(X > 2)$.
    c. Find $P(4 \leq X \leq 10)$.
    d. Find $P(6 \leq X \leq 14)$.

20. Let X be normally distributed with mean $\mu = 10$ and standard deviation $\sigma = 4$.
    a. Find $P(X \leq 0)$.
    b. Find $P(X > 2)$.
    c. Find $P(4 \leq X \leq 10)$.
    d. Find $P(6 \leq X \leq 14)$.

21. Let X be normally distributed with mean $\mu = 120$ and standard deviation $\sigma = 20$.
    a. Find $P(X \leq 86)$.
    b. Find $P(80 \leq X \leq 100)$.
    c. Find x such that $P(X \leq x) = 0.40$.
    d. Find x such that $P(X > x) = 0.90$.

22. Let X be normally distributed with mean $\mu = 2.5$ and standard deviation $\sigma = 2$.
    a. Find $P(X > 7.6)$.
    b. Find $P(7.4 \leq X \leq 10.6)$.
    c. Find x such that $P(X > x) = 0.025$.
    d. Find x such that $P(x \leq X \leq 2.5) = 0.4943$.

23. Let X be normally distributed with mean $\mu = 2{,}500$ and standard deviation $\sigma = 800$.
    a. Find x such that $P(X \leq x) = 0.9382$.
    b. Find x such that $P(X > x) = 0.025$.
    c. Find x such that $P(2500 \leq X \leq x) = 0.1217$.
    d. Find x such that $P(X \leq x) = 0.4840$.

24. The random variable X is normally distributed. Also, it is known that $P(X > 150) = 0.10$.
    a. Find the population mean μ if the population standard deviation $\sigma = 15$.
    b. Find the population mean μ if the population standard deviation $\sigma = 25$.
    c. Find the population standard deviation σ if the population mean $\mu = 136$.
    d. Find the population standard deviation σ if the population mean $\mu = 128$.

25. Let X be normally distributed with $\mu = 254$ and $\sigma = 11$.
    a. Find $P(X \leq 266)$.
    b. Find $P(250 < X < 270)$.
    c. Find x such that $P(X \leq x) = 0.33$.
    d. Find x such that $P(X > x) = 0.33$.

26. Let X be normally distributed with $\mu = -15$ and $\sigma = 9$.
    a. Find $P(X > -12)$.
    b. Find $P(0 \leq X \leq 5)$.
    c. Find x such that $P(X \leq x) = 0.25$.
    d. Find x such that $P(X > x) = 0.25$.

Applications

27. The historical returns on a balanced portfolio have had an average return of 8% and a standard deviation of 12%. Assume that returns on this portfolio follow a normal distribution.
    a. What percentage of returns were greater than 20%?
    b. What percentage of returns were below −16%?

28. Assume that IQ scores follow a normal distribution with a mean of 100 and a standard deviation of 16.
    a. What is the probability that an individual scores between 84 and 116?
    b. What is the probability that an individual scores less than 68?
    c. What is the lowest score that will place an individual in the top 1% of IQ scores?

29. The average rent in a city is $1,500 per month with a standard deviation of $250. Assume rent follows the normal distribution.
   a. What percentage of rents are between $1,250 and $1,750?
   b. What percentage of rents are less than $1,250?
   c. What percentage of rents are greater than $2,000?
30. A professional basketball team averages 80 points per game with a standard deviation of 10 points. Assume points per game follow the normal distribution.
   a. What is the probability that a game's score is between 60 and 100 points?
   b. What is the probability that a game's score is more than 100 points? If there are 82 games in a regular season, in how many games will the team score more than 100 points?
31. In a rural town, the average high school teacher annual salary is $43,000. Let salary be normally distributed with a standard deviation of $18,000.
   a. What percentage of high school teachers make between $40,000 and $50,000?
   b. What percentage of high school teachers make more than $80,000?
32. Americans are increasingly skimping on their sleep. A health expert believes that American adults sleep an average of 6.2 hours on weekdays, with a standard deviation of 1.2 hours. Assume that sleep time on weekdays is normally distributed.
   a. What percentage of American adults sleep more than 8 hours on weekdays?
   b. What percentage of American adults sleep less than 6 hours on weekdays?
   c. What percentage of American adults sleep between 6 and 8 hours on weekdays?
33. The weight of turkeys is normally distributed with a mean of 22 pounds and a standard deviation of 5 pounds.
   a. Find the probability that a randomly selected turkey weighs between 20 and 26 pounds.
   b. Find the probability that a randomly selected turkey weighs less than 12 pounds.
34. Suppose that the miles-per-gallon (mpg) rating of passenger cars is a normally distributed random variable with a mean and a standard deviation of 33.8 mpg and 3.5 mpg, respectively.
   a. What is the probability that a randomly selected passenger car gets at least 40 mpg?
   b. What is the probability that a randomly selected passenger car gets between 30 and 35 mpg?
   c. An automobile manufacturer wants to build a new passenger car with an mpg rating that improves upon 99% of existing cars. What is the minimum mpg that would achieve this goal?
35. According to a company's website, the top 25% of the candidates who take the entrance test will be called for an interview. The reported mean and standard deviation of the test scores are 68 and 8, respectively. If test scores are normally distributed, what is the minimum score required for an interview?
36. A financial advisor informs a client that the expected return on a portfolio is 8% with a standard deviation of 12%. There is a 15% chance that the return would be above 16%. If the advisor is right about her assessment, is it reasonable to assume that the underlying return distribution is normal?
37. A packaging system fills boxes to an average weight of 18 ounces with a standard deviation of 0.2 ounce. It is reasonable to assume that the weights are normally distributed. Calculate the 1st, 2nd, and 3rd quartiles of the box weight.
38. According to the Bureau of Labor Statistics, it takes an average of 22 weeks for someone over 55 to find a new job, compared with 16 weeks for younger workers. Assume that the probability distributions are normal and that the standard deviation is 2 weeks for both distributions.
   a. What is the probability that it takes a worker over the age of 55 more than 19 weeks to find a job?
   b. What is the probability that it takes a younger worker more than 19 weeks to find a job?
   c. What is the probability that it takes a worker over the age of 55 between 23 and 25 weeks to find a job?
   d. What is the probability that it takes a younger worker between 23 and 25 weeks to find a job?
39. Loans that are 60 days or more past due are considered seriously delinquent. It is reported that the rate of seriously delinquent loans has an average of 9.1%. Let the rate of seriously delinquent loans follow a normal distribution with a standard deviation of 0.80%.
   a. What is the probability that the rate of seriously delinquent loans is above 8%?
   b. What is the probability that the rate of seriously delinquent loans is between 9.5% and 10.5%?
40. The time required to assemble an electronic component is normally distributed with a mean and a standard deviation of 16 minutes and 4 minutes, respectively.
   a. Find the probability that a randomly picked assembly takes between 10 and 20 minutes.
   b. It is unusual for the assembly time to be above 24 minutes or below 6 minutes. What proportion of assembly times fall in these unusual categories?
41. Research suggests that Americans make an average of 10 phone calls per day. Let the number of calls be normally distributed with a standard deviation of 3 calls.
   a. What is the probability that an American makes between 4 and 12 calls per day?
   b. What is the probability that an American makes more than 6 calls per day?
   c. What is the probability that an American makes more than 16 calls per day?

42. The manager of a night club in Boston stated that 95% of the customers are between the ages of 22 and 28 years. If the age of customers is normally distributed with a mean of 25 years, calculate its standard deviation.

43. It is reported that the average cumulative debt of recent college graduates is about $22,500. Let the cumulative debt among recent college graduates be normally distributed with a standard deviation of $7,000. If an estimated 1.8 million recent college graduates have debt, approximately how many of them have accumulated debt of more than $30,000?

44. Scores on a marketing exam are known to be normally distributed with a mean and a standard deviation of 60 and 20, respectively.
    a. Find the probability that a randomly selected student scores between 50 and 80.
    b. Find the probability that a randomly selected student scores between 20 and 40.
    c. The syllabus suggests that the top 15% of the students will get an A in the course. What is the minimum score required to get an A?
    d. What is the passing score if 10% of the students will fail the course?

45. On average, an American professional football game lasts about three hours, even though the ball is actually in play only 11 minutes. Assume that game times are normally distributed with a standard deviation of 0.4 hour.
    a. Find the probability that a game lasts less than 2.5 hours.
    b. Find the probability that a game lasts either less than 2.5 hours or more than 3.5 hours.
    c. Find the maximum value for the game time that will place it in the bottom 1% of the distribution.

46. A young investment manager tells his client that the probability of making a positive return with his suggested portfolio is 90%. If it is known that returns are normally distributed with a mean of 5.6%, what is the risk, measured by standard deviation, that this investment manager assumes in his calculation?

47. A construction company in Florida is struggling to sell condominiums. The company believes that it will be able to get an average sale price of $210,000. Let the price of these condominiums in the next quarter be normally distributed with a standard deviation of $15,000.
    a. What is the probability that the condominium will sell at a price (i) below $200,000? (ii) Above $240,000?
    b. The company is also trying to sell an artist's condo. Potential buyers will find the unusual features of this condo either pleasing or objectionable. The manager expects the average sale price of this condo to be the same as others at $210,000, but with a higher standard deviation of $20,000. What is the probability that this condo will sell at a price (i) below $200,000? (ii) Above $240,000?

48. You are considering the risk-return profile of two mutual funds for investment. The relatively risky fund promises an expected return of 8% with a standard deviation of 14%. The relatively less risky fund promises an expected return and standard deviation of 4% and 5%, respectively. Assume that the returns are approximately normally distributed.
    a. Which mutual fund will you pick if your objective is to minimize the probability of earning a negative return?
    b. Which mutual fund will you pick if your objective is to maximize the probability of earning a return above 8%?

49. First introduced in Los Angeles, the concept of Korean-style tacos sold from a catering truck has been gaining popularity nationally. This taco is an interesting mix of corn tortillas with Korean-style beef, garnished with onion, cilantro, and a hash of chili-soy-dressed lettuce. Suppose one such taco truck operates in the Detroit area. The owners have estimated that the daily consumption of beef is normally distributed with a mean of 24 pounds and a standard deviation of 6 pounds. While purchasing too much beef results in wastage, purchasing too little can disappoint customers.
    a. Determine the amount of beef the owners should buy so that it meets demand on 80% of the days.
    b. How much should the owners buy if they want to meet demand on 95% of the days?

50. While Massachusetts is no California when it comes to sun, the solar energy industry is flourishing in this state. The state's capital, Boston, averages 211.7 sunny days per year. Assume that the number of sunny days follows a normal distribution with a standard deviation of 20 days.
    a. What is the probability that Boston has less than 200 sunny days in a given year?
    b. Los Angeles averages 266.5 sunny days per year. What is the probability that Boston has at least as many sunny days as Los Angeles?
    c. Suppose a dismal year in Boston is one where the number of sunny days is in the bottom 10% for that year. At most, how many sunny days must occur annually for it to be a dismal year in Boston?
    d. Last year, Boston experienced unusually warm, dry, and sunny weather. Suppose this occurs only 1% of the time. What is the minimum number of sunny days that would satisfy the criteria for being an unusually warm, dry, and sunny year in Boston?

51. A new car battery is sold with a two-year warranty whereby the owner gets the battery replaced free of cost if it breaks down during the warranty period. Suppose an auto store makes a net profit of $20 on batteries that stay trouble-free during the warranty period; it makes a net loss of $10 on batteries that

break down. The life of batteries is known to be normally distributed with a mean and a standard deviation of 40 months and 16 months, respectively.

a. What is the probability that a battery will break down during the warranty period?

b. What is the expected profit of the auto store on a battery?

c. What is the expected monthly profit on batteries if the auto store sells an average of 500 batteries a month?

52. A certain brand of refrigerators has a length of life that is normally distributed with a mean and a standard deviation of 15 years and 2 years, respectively.

a. What is the probability a refrigerator will last less than 6.5 years?

b. What is the probability that a refrigerator will last more than 23 years?

c. What length of life should the retailer advertise for these refrigerators so that only 3% of the refrigerators fail before the advertised length of life?

6.3 OTHER CONTINUOUS PROBABILITY DISTRIBUTIONS

As discussed earlier, the normal distribution is the most extensively used probability distribution in statistical work. One reason that this occurs is because the normal distribution accurately describes numerous random variables of interest. However, there are applications where other continuous distributions are more appropriate.

The Exponential Distribution

LO 6.5

Calculate and interpret probabilities for a random variable that follows the exponential distribution.

A useful nonsymmetric continuous probability distribution is the **exponential distribution**. The exponential distribution is related to the Poisson distribution, even though the Poisson distribution deals with discrete random variables. Recall from Chapter 5 that the Poisson random variable counts the number of occurrences of an event over a given interval of time or space. For instance, the Poisson distribution is used to calculate the likelihood of a specified number of cars arriving at a McDonald's drive-thru over a particular time period or the likelihood of a specified number of defects in a 50-yard roll of fabric. Sometimes we are less interested in the *number* of occurrences over a given interval of time or space, but rather in the time that has elapsed or space encountered *between* such occurrences. For instance, we might be interested in the length of time that elapses between car arrivals at the McDonald's drive-thru or the distance between defects in a 50-yard roll of fabric. We use the exponential distribution for describing these times or distances. The exponential random variable is nonnegative; that is, the underlying variable X is defined for $x \geq 0$.

In order to better understand the connection between the Poisson and the exponential distributions, consider the introductory case of Chapter 5 where Anne was concerned about staffing needs at the Starbucks that she managed. Recall that Anne believed that the typical Starbucks customer averaged 18 visits to the store over a 30-day period. The Poisson random variable appropriately captures the number of visits, with the expected value (mean), over a 30-day period, as

$$\mu_{\text{Poisson}} = 18.$$

Since the number of visits follows the Poisson distribution, the time between visits has an exponential distribution. In addition, given the expected number of 18 visits over a 30-day month, the expected time between visits is derived as

$$\mu_{\text{Exponential}} = \frac{30}{18} = 1.67.$$

It is common to define the exponential probability distribution in terms of its *rate parameter* λ (the Greek letter lambda), which is the inverse of its mean. In the above example,

$$\lambda = \frac{1}{\mu} = \frac{1}{1.67} = 0.60.$$

We can think of the mean of the exponential distribution as the average time between arrivals, whereas the rate parameter measures the average number of arrivals per unit of time. Note that the rate parameter is the same as the mean of the Poisson distribution, when defined per unit of time. For a Poisson process, the mean of 18 visits over a 30-day period is equivalent to a mean of $18/30 = 0.60$ per day, which is the same as the rate parameter λ.

The probability density function for the exponential distribution is defined as follows.

THE EXPONENTIAL DISTRIBUTION

A random variable X follows the exponential distribution if its probability density function is

$$f(x) = \lambda e^{-\lambda x} \quad \text{for } x \geq 0,$$

where λ is a rate parameter and $e \approx 2.718$ is the base of the natural logarithm. The mean and the standard deviation of X are equal: $E(X) = SD(X) = \frac{1}{\lambda}$.

For $x \geq 0$, the cumulative distribution function of X is

$$P(X \leq x) = 1 - e^{-\lambda x}.$$

Therefore, $P(X > x) = 1 - P(X \leq x) = e^{-\lambda x}$.

The graphs in Figure 6.22 show the shapes of the exponential probability density function based on various values of the rate parameter λ.

FIGURE 6.22 Exponential probability density function for various values of λ

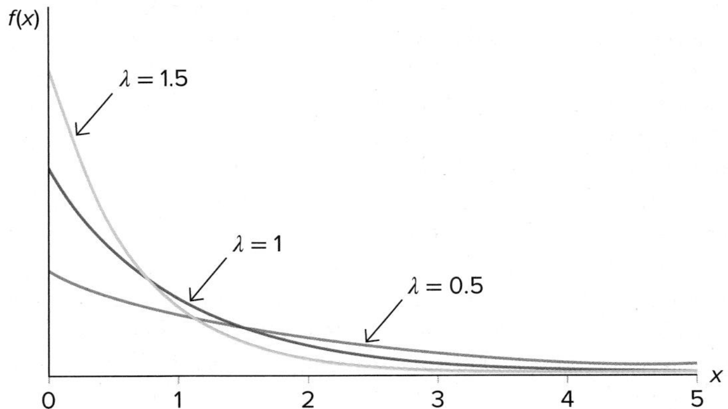

EXAMPLE 6.8

Let the time between e-mail messages during work hours be exponentially distributed with a mean of 25 minutes.

a. Calculate the rate parameter λ.

b. What is the probability that you do not get an e-mail for more than one hour?

c. What is the probability that you get an e-mail within 10 minutes?

SOLUTION:

a. Since the mean $E(X)$ equals $\frac{1}{\lambda}$, we compute $\lambda = \frac{1}{E(X)} = \frac{1}{25} = 0.04$.

b. The probability that you do not get an e-mail for more than an hour is $P(X > 60)$. We use $P(X > x) = e^{-\lambda x}$ to compute $P(X > 60) = e^{-0.04(60)} = 0.0907$. Figure 6.23 highlights this probability.

FIGURE 6.23 Finding $P(X > 60)$

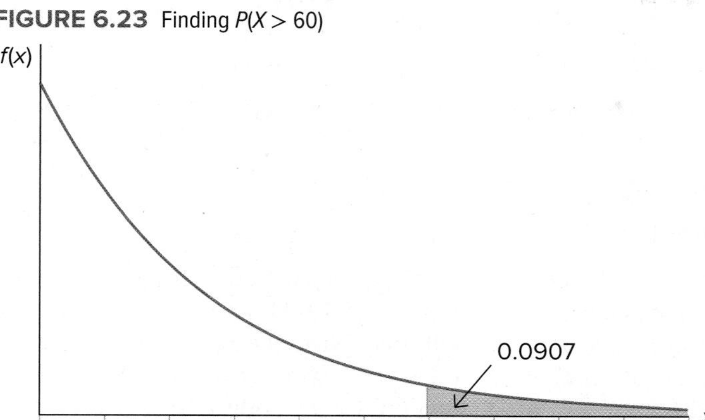

We can also use Excel's **EXPON.DIST** to solve for probabilities associated with the exponential distribution. We enter `=EXPON.DIST(x, λ, TRUE or FALSE)`, where x is the value to be evaluated and λ is the rate parameter. If we enter TRUE for the last argument, then Excel returns the cumulative probability function $P(X \leq x)$. If we enter FALSE for the last argument, then Excel returns the height of the exponential distribution at the point x. In order to find $P(X > 60)$ with $\lambda = 1/25$, we enter `=1-EXPON.DIST(60, 1/25, TRUE)`, and Excel returns 0.0907.

c. The probability that you get an e-mail within 10 minutes is $P(X \leq 10) = 1 - e^{-0.04(10)} = 1 - 0.6703 = 0.3297$. Figure 6.24 highlights this probability. Using Excel, we enter `=EXPON.DIST(10, 1/25, TRUE)`, and Excel returns 0.3297.

FIGURE 6.24 Finding $P(X \leq 10)$

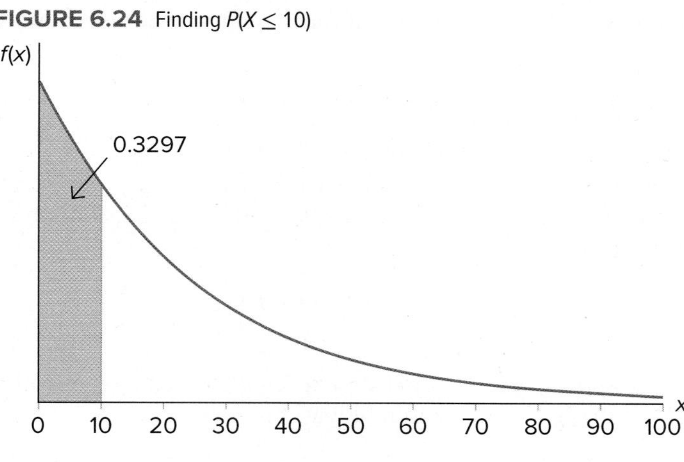

Using R for the Exponential Distribution

We use R's **pexp** function to find probabilities associated with the exponential distribution. In order to find $P(X \leq x)$, we enter pexp(x, λ, lower.tail = TRUE), where x is the value to be evaluated and λ is the rate parameter. If we enter lower.tail = FALSE, then R returns $P(X > x)$. Referring back to part b of Example 6.8, if we want to find $P(X > 60)$ with $\lambda = 1/25$, we enter:

```
> pexp(60, 1/25, lower.tail=FALSE)
```

And R returns 0.09071795.

Referring back to part c of Example 6.8, if we want to find $P(X \leq 10)$ with $\lambda = 0.04$, we enter:

```
> pexp(10, 1/25, lower.tail=TRUE)
```

And R returns 0.32968.

The exponential distribution is also used in modeling lifetimes or failure times. For example, an electric bulb with a rated life of 1,000 hours is expected to fail after about 1,000 of use. However, the bulb may burn out either before or after 1,000 hours. Thus, the lifetime of an electric bulb is a random variable with an expected value of 1,000. A noted feature of the exponential distribution is that it is "memoryless," thus implying a constant failure rate. In the electric bulb example, it implies that the probability that the bulb will burn out on a given day is independent of whether the bulb has already been used for 10, 100, or 1,000 hours.

LO 6.6

Calculate and interpret probabilities for a random variable that follows the lognormal distribution.

The Lognormal Distribution

The **lognormal distribution** is defined with reference to the normal distribution. It is positively skewed, and it is relevant for a positive random variable. Thus, it is useful for describing variables such as income, real estate values, and asset prices. Unlike the exponential distribution whose failure rate is constant, the failure rate of the lognormal distribution may increase or decrease over time. This flexibility has led to broad applications of the lognormal distribution, ranging from modeling the failure time of new equipment to the lifetime of cancer patients. For instance, in the break-in period of new equipment, the failure rate is high. However, if it survives this initial period, the subsequent failure rate is greatly reduced. The same is true for cancer survivors.

A random variable Y is lognormal if its natural logarithm $X = \ln(Y)$ is normally distributed. Alternatively, if X is a normal random variable, the lognormal variable is defined as $Y = e^X$. The probability density function for the lognormal distribution is defined as follows.

THE LOGNORMAL DISTRIBUTION

Let X be a normally distributed random variable with mean μ and standard deviation σ. The random variable $Y = e^X$ follows the lognormal distribution with a probability density function defined as

$$f(y) = \frac{1}{y\sigma\sqrt{2\pi}}\exp\left(-\frac{(\ln(y) - \mu)^2}{2\sigma^2}\right) \quad \text{for } y > 0,$$

where π equals approximately 3.14159, $\exp(x) = e^x$ is the exponential function, and $e \approx 2.718$ is the base of the natural logarithm.

The graphs in Figure 6.25 show the shapes of the lognormal density function based on various values of σ. As σ becomes smaller, the lognormal distribution starts to resemble the normal distribution.

FIGURE 6.25 Lognormal probability density function for various values of σ along with $\mu = 0$

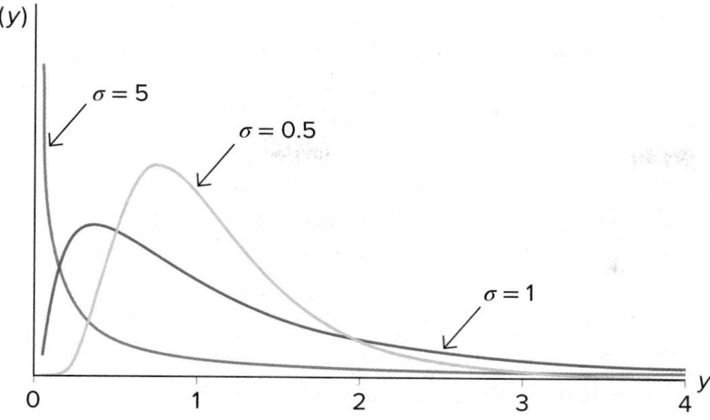

The mean and the variance of the lognormal random variable Y are related to the mean and the standard deviation of the corresponding normal random variable X.

SUMMARY MEASURES FOR THE LOGNORMAL AND NORMAL DISTRIBUTIONS

Let X be a normal random variable with mean μ and standard deviation σ, and let $Y = e^X$ be the corresponding lognormal random variable. The mean μ_Y and the standard deviation σ_Y of Y are derived as

$$\mu_Y = \exp\left(\frac{2\mu + \sigma^2}{2}\right) \quad \text{and} \quad \sigma_Y = \sqrt{(\exp(\sigma^2) - 1)\exp(2\mu + \sigma^2)}.$$

Equivalently, the mean and the standard deviation of the normal random variable $X = \ln(Y)$ are derived as

$$\mu = \ln\left(\frac{\mu_Y^2}{\sqrt{\mu_Y^2 + \sigma_Y^2}}\right) \quad \text{and} \quad \sigma = \sqrt{\ln\left(1 + \frac{\sigma_Y^2}{\mu_Y^2}\right)}.$$

EXAMPLE 6.9

Compute the mean and the standard deviation of a lognormal random variable if the mean and the standard deviation of the underlying normal random variable are as follows:

a. $\mu = 0, \sigma = 1$

b. $\mu = 2, \sigma = 1$

c. $\mu = 2, \sigma = 1.5$

SOLUTION: Because X is a normal random variable, $Y = e^X$ is the corresponding lognormal random variable with mean $\mu_Y = \exp\left(\frac{2\mu + \sigma^2}{2}\right)$ and standard deviation $\sigma_Y = \sqrt{(\exp(\sigma^2) - 1)\exp(2\mu + \sigma^2)}$.

a. Given $\mu = 0$ and $\sigma = 1$, we compute $\mu_Y = \exp\left(\frac{0 + 1^2}{2}\right) = 1.65$ and $\sigma_Y = \sqrt{(\exp(1^2) - 1)\exp(0 + 1^2)} = 2.16$.

b. Given $\mu = 2$ and $\sigma = 1$, we compute $\mu_Y = \exp\left(\frac{4+1^2}{2}\right) = 12.18$ and $\sigma_Y = \sqrt{(\exp(1^2) - 1)\exp(4 + 1^2)} = 15.97$.

c. Given $\mu = 2$ and $\sigma = 1.5$, we compute $\mu_Y = \exp\left(\frac{4+1.5^2}{2}\right) = 22.76$ and $\sigma_Y = \sqrt{(\exp(1.5^2) - 1)\exp(4 + 1.5^2)} = 66.31$.

The popularity of the lognormal distribution is also due to the fact that the probabilities of a lognormal random variable are easily evaluated by reference to the normal distribution. This is illustrated in the following example.

EXAMPLE 6.10

Let $Y = e^X$ where X is normally distributed with mean $\mu = 5$ and standard deviation $\sigma = 1.2$.

a. Find $P(Y \leq 200)$.

b. Find the 90th percentile of Y.

SOLUTION: We solve these problems by first converting them into the corresponding normal distribution problems.

a. Note that $P(Y \leq 200) = P(\ln(Y) \leq \ln(200)) = P(X \leq 5.30)$. We transform $x = 5.30$ in the usual way to get $z = \frac{5.30 - 5}{1.2} = 0.25$. From the z table, we get $P(Z \leq 0.25) = 0.5987$. Thus, $P(Y \leq 200) = P(X \leq 5.30) = P(Z \leq 0.25) = 0.5987$.

   It is easy to solve problems, related to the lognormal distribution, with Excel and R. We use Excel's LOGNORM.DIST function to find lognormal probabilities. We enter =LOGNORM.DIST(y, μ, σ, TRUE or FALSE), where y is the nonnegative value to be evaluated and μ and σ are the mean and the standard deviation of the underlying normal distribution. If we enter TRUE for the last argument, then Excel returns the cumulative probability function $P(Y \leq y)$. If we enter FALSE for the last argument, then Excel returns the height of the lognormal distribution at the point y. In order to find $P(Y \leq 200)$, we enter `=LOGNORM.DIST(200, 5, 1.2, TRUE)`, and Excel returns 0.5982. Note that this is slightly different from the manual calculations because of rounding with the z table.

b. The 90th percentile is a value y such that $P(Y < y) = 0.90$. We first note that $P(Y < y) = 0.90$ is equivalent to $P(\ln(Y) < \ln(y)) = P(X < x) = 0.90$, where $x = \ln(y)$. We look up the cumulative probability of 0.90 in the z table to get $z = 1.28$. We use the inverse transformation to derive $x = \mu + z\sigma = 5 + 1.28(1.2) = 6.536$. Finally, we compute $y = e^x = e^{6.536} = 689.52$. Therefore, the 90th percentile of the distribution is 689.52.

   We can also use Excel's **LOGNORM.INV** to find a particular y value. We enter =LOGNORM. INV(*cumulprob*, μ, σ), where cumulprob is the cumulative probability associated with the value y, μ is the mean of the underlying normal distribution, and σ is the standard deviation of the underlying normal distribution. In order to find the value of y that satisfies $P(Y < y) = 0.90$, we enter =LOGNORM.INV(0.90, 5, 1.2), and Excel returns 690.808, which is again slightly different because of rounding.

Using R for the Lognormal Distribution

We use R's **plnorm** function to find lognormal probabilities. In order to find $P(Y \leq y)$, we enter plnorm(y, μ, σ, lower.tail = TRUE), where y is the nonnegative value to be evaluated and μ and σ are the mean and the standard deviation, respectively, of the underlying normal distribution. If we enter lower.tail=FALSE for the last argument in the function, then R returns $P(Y > y)$. Referring back to part a of Example 6.10, if we want to find $P(Y \leq 200)$ with $\mu = 5$ and $\sigma = 1.2$, we enter:

```
> plnorm(200, 5, 1.2, lower.tail=TRUE) And R returns 0.598164.
```

We use R's **qlnorm** function to find a particular y value for a given cumulative probability (*cumulprob*). We enter qlnorm(*cumulprob*, μ, σ), where cumulprob is the cumulative probability associated with the value y and μ and σ are the mean and the standard deviation, respectively, of the underlying normal distribution. Referring back to part b of Example 6.10, if we want to to find the value of y that satisfies $P(Y < y) = 0.90$ with $\mu = 5$ and $\sigma = 1.2$, we enter:

```
> qlnorm(0.90, 5, 1.2)
```

And R returns 690.808.

EXERCISES 6.3

Mechanics

53. Assume a Poisson random variable has a mean of 6 successes over a 120-minute period.
    a. Find the mean of the random variable, defined by the time between successes.
    b. What is the rate parameter of the appropriate exponential distribution?
    c. Find the probability that the time to success will be more than 60 minutes.

54. Assume a Poisson random variable has a mean of four arrivals over a 10-minute interval.
    a. What is the mean of the random variable, defined by the time between arrivals?
    b. Find the probability that the next arrival would be within the mean time.
    c. Find the probability that the next arrival would be between one and two minutes.

55. A random variable X is exponentially distributed with a mean of 0.1.
    a. What is the rate parameter λ? What is the standard deviation of X?
    b. Compute $P(X > 0.20)$.
    c. Compute $P(0.10 \leq X \leq 0.20)$.

56. A random variable X is exponentially distributed with a probability density function of $f(x) = 5e^{-5x}$. Calculate the mean and the standard deviation of X.

57. A random variable X is exponentially distributed with an expected value of 25.
    a. What is the rate parameter λ? What is the standard deviation of X?
    b. Compute $P(20 \leq X \leq 30)$.
    c. Compute $P(15 \leq X \leq 35)$.

58. Let X be exponentially distributed with $\lambda = 0.5$. Compute the following values.
    a. $P(X \leq 1)$
    b. $P(2 < X < 4)$
    c. $P(X > 10)$

59. Let X be exponentially distributed with $\mu = 1.25$. Compute the following values.
    a. $P(X < 2.3)$
    b. $P(1.5 \leq X \leq 5.5)$
    c. $P(X > 7)$

60. Compute the mean and the variance of a lognormal variable $Y = e^X$ where X is normally distributed with the following mean and variance:
    a. $\mu = 3, \sigma^2 = 2$
    b. $\mu = 5, \sigma^2 = 2$
    c. $\mu = 5, \sigma^2 = 3$

61. Let $Y = e^X$ where X is normally distributed with $\mu = 1.8$ and $\sigma = 0.80$. Compute the following values.
    a. $P(Y \leq 7.5)$
    b. $P(8 < Y < 9)$
    c. The 90th percentile of Y

62. Let $Y = e^X$, where X is normally distributed. Compute the mean and the variance of X given the following information.
    a. $\mu_Y = 14, \sigma_Y^2 = 22$
    b. $\mu_Y = 20, \sigma_Y^2 = 22$
    c. $\mu_Y = 20, \sigma_Y^2 = 120$

63. Let Y have the lognormal distribution with mean 82.8 and variance 156.25. Compute the following probabilities.
    a. $P(Y > 100)$
    b. $P(80 < Y < 100)$

Applications

64. Studies have shown that bats can consume an average of 10 mosquitoes per minute. Assume that the number of mosquitoes consumed per minute follows a Poisson distribution.
    a. What is the mean time between eating mosquitoes?
    b. Find the probability that the time between eating mosquitoes is more than 15 seconds.
    c. Find the probability that the time between eating mosquitoes is between 15 and 20 seconds.

65. Last year, a study found that there was an average of one complaint every 12 seconds against large corporations. It is reasonable to assume that the time between complaints is exponentially distributed.
   a. What is the mean time between complaints?
   b. What is the probability that the next complaint will take less than the mean time?
   c. What is the probability that the next complaint will take between 5 and 10 seconds?
66. A tollbooth operator has observed that cars arrive randomly at an average rate of 360 cars per hour.
   a. What is the mean time between car arrivals at this tollbooth?
   b. What is the probability that the next car will arrive within ten seconds?
67. Customers make purchases at a convenience store, on average, every six minutes. It is fair to assume that the time between customer purchases is exponentially distributed. Jack operates the cash register at this store.
   a. What is the rate parameter λ? What is the standard deviation of this distribution?
   b. Jack wants to take a five-minute break. He believes that if he goes right after he has serviced a customer, he will lower the probability of someone showing up during his five-minute break. Is he right in this belief?
   c. What is the probability that a customer will show up in less than five minutes?
   d. What is the probability that nobody shows up for over half an hour?
68. A hospital administrator worries about the possible loss of electric power as a result of a power blackout. The hospital, of course, has a standby generator, but it, too, is subject to failure, having a mean time between failures of 500 hours. It is reasonable to assume that the time between failures is exponentially distributed.
   a. What is the probability that the standby generator fails during the next 24-hour blackout?
   b. Suppose the hospital owns two standby generators that work independently of one another. What is the probability that both generators fail during the next 24-hour blackout?
69. Prior to placing an order, the amount of time (in minutes) that a driver waits in line at a Starbucks drive-thru follows an exponential distribution with a probability density function of $f(x) = 0.2e^{-0.2x}$.
   a. What is the mean waiting time that a driver faces prior to placing an order?
   b. What is the probability that a driver spends more than the average time before placing an order.
   c. What is the probability that a driver spends more than 10 minutes before placing an order.
   d. What is the probability that a driver spends between 4 and 6 minutes before placing an order.
70. On average, the state police catch eight speeders per hour at a certain location on Interstate 90. Assume that the number of speeders per hour follows the Poisson distribution.
   a. What is the probability that the state police wait less than 10 minutes for the next speeder?
   b. What is the probability that the state police wait between 15 and 20 minutes for the next speeder?
   c. What is the probability that the state police wait more than 25 minutes for the next speeder?
71. The Bahamas is a tropical paradise made up of 700 islands sprinkled over 100,000 square miles of the Atlantic Ocean. According to the figures released by the government of the Bahamas, the mean household income in the Bahamas is $39,626 and the median income is $33,600. A demographer decides to use the lognormal random variable to model this nonsymmetric income distribution. Let Y represent household income, where for a normally distributed X, $Y = e^X$. In addition, suppose the standard deviation of household income is $10,000.
   a. Compute the mean and the standard deviation of X.
   b. What proportion of the people in the Bahamas have household income above the mean?
   c. What proportion of the people in the Bahamas have household income below $20,000?
   d. Compute the 75th percentile of the income distribution in the Bahamas.
72. Motorists arrive at a Gulf station at the rate of two per minute during morning hours. Assume that the arrival of motorists at the station follows a Poisson distribution.
   a. What is the probability that the next car's arrival is in less than one minute?
   b. What is the probability that the next car's arrival is in more than five minutes?
73. It is well documented that a typical washing machine can last anywhere between 5 to 12 years. Let the life of a washing machine be represented by a lognormal variable, $Y = e^X$, where X is normally distributed. In addition, let the mean and standard deviation of the life of a washing machine be 8 years and 4 years, respectively.
   a. Compute the mean and the standard deviation of X.
   b. What proportion of the washing machines will last for more than 10 years?
   c. What proportion of the washing machines will last for less than 6 years?
   d. Compute the 90th percentile of the life of the washing machines.

6.4 WRITING WITH DATA

Case Study

Jasper White/Image Source

Professor Lang is a professor of economics at Salem State University. She has been teaching a course in Principles of Economics for over 25 years. Professor Lang has never graded on a curve since she believes that relative grading may unduly penalize (benefit) a good (poor) student in an unusually strong (weak) class. She always uses an absolute scale for making grades, as shown in the two left columns of Table 6.4.

TABLE 6.4 Grading Scales with Absolute Grading versus Relative Grading

Absolute Grading		Relative Grading	
Grade	Score	Grade	Probability
A	92 and above	A	0.10
B	78 up to 92	B	0.35
C	64 up to 78	C	0.40
D	58 up to 64	D	0.10
F	Below 58	F	0.05

A colleague of Professor Lang's has convinced her to move to relative grading, because it corrects for unanticipated problems. Professor Lang decides to experiment with grading based on the relative scale as shown in the two right columns of Table 6.4. Using this relative grading scheme, the top 10% of students will get A's, the next 35% B's, and so on. Based on her years of teaching experience, Professor Lang believes that the scores in her course follow a normal distribution with a mean of 78.6 and a standard deviation of 12.4.

Professor Lang wants to use this information to calculate probabilities based on the absolute scale and compare them to the probabilities based on the relative scale. Then, she wants to calculate the range of scores for grades based on the relative scale and compare them to the absolute scale. Finally, she want to determine which grading scale makes it harder to get higher grades.

Sample Report—Absolute Grading versus Relative Grading

Many teachers would confess that grading is one of the most difficult tasks of their profession. Two common grading systems used in higher education are relative and absolute. Relative grading systems are norm-referenced or curve-based, in which a grade is based on the student's relative position in class. Absolute grading systems, on the other hand, are criterion-referenced, in which a grade is related to the student's absolute performance in class. In short, with absolute grading, the student's score is compared to a predetermined scale, whereas with relative grading, the score is compared to the scores of other students in the class.

Let X represent a grade in Professor Lang's class, which is normally distributed with a mean of 78.6 and a standard deviation of 12.4. This information is used to derive the grade probabilities based on the absolute scale. For instance, the probability of receiving an A is derived as $P(X \geq 92) = P(Z \geq 1.08) = 0.14$. Other probabilities, derived similarly, are presented in Table 6.5.

TABLE 6.5 Probabilities Based on Absolute Scale and Relative Scale

Grade	Probability Based on Absolute Scale	Probability Based on Relative Scale
A	0.14	0.10
B	0.38	0.35
C	0.36	0.40
D	0.07	0.10
F	0.05	0.05

The second column of Table 6.5 shows that 14% of students are expected to receive A's, 38% B's, and so on. Although these numbers are generally consistent with the relative scale restated in the third column of Table 6.5, it appears that the relative scale makes it harder for students to get higher grades. For instance, 14% get A's with the absolute scale compared to only 10% with the relative scale.

Alternatively, we can compare the two grading methods on the basis of the range of scores for various grades. The second column of Table 6.6 restates the range of scores based on absolute grading. In order to obtain the range of scores based on relative grading, it is once again necessary to apply concepts from the normal distribution. For instance, the minimum score required to earn an A with relative grading is derived by solving for x in $P(X \geq x) = 0.10$. Since $P(X \geq x) = 0.10$ is equivalent to $P(Z \geq z) = 0.10$, it follows that $z = 1.28$. Inserting the proper values of the mean, the standard deviation, and z into $x = \mu + z\sigma$ yields a value of x equal to 94.47. Ranges for other grades, derived similarly, are presented in the third column of Table 6.6.

TABLE 6.6 Range of Scores with Absolute Grading versus Relative Grading

Grade	Range of Scores Based on Absolute Grading	Range of Scores Based on Relative Grading
A	92 and above	94.47 and above
B	78 up to 92	80.21 up to 94.47
C	64 up to 78	65.70 up to 80.21
D	58 up to 64	58.20 up to 65.70
F	Below 58	Below 58.20

Once again comparing the results in Table 6.6, the use of the relative scale makes it harder for students to get higher grades in Professor Lang's courses. For instance, in order to receive an A with relative grading, a student must have a score of at least 94.47 versus a score of at least 92 with absolute grading. Both absolute and relative grading methods have their merits and teachers often make the decision on the basis of their teaching philosophy. However, if Professor Lang wants to keep the grades consistent with her earlier absolute scale, she should base her relative scale on the probabilities computed in the second column of Table 6.5.

Suggested Case Studies

Report 6.1. Body mass index (BMI) is a reliable indicator of body fat for most children and teens. The Centers for Disease Control and Prevention (CDC) reports BMI-for-age growth charts for girls as well as boys to obtain a percentile ranking. Percentiles are the most commonly used indicator to assess the size and growth patterns of children in the United States. The following table provides weight status categories and the corresponding percentiles and BMI ranges for 10-year-old boys in the United States.

Weight Status Category	Percentile Range	BMI Range
Underweight	Less than 5th	Less than 14.2
Healthy Weight	Between 5th and 85th	Between 14.2 and 19.4
Overweight	Between 85th and 95th	Between 19.4 and 22.2
Obese	More than 95th	More than 22.2

Health officials of a Midwestern town are concerned about the weight of children in their town. They believe that the BMI of their 10-year-old boys is normally distributed with mean 19.2 and standard deviation 2.6. In a report, use this information to compute the proportion of 10-year-old boys in this town that are in the various weight status categories given the BMI ranges. Discuss whether the concern of health officials is justified.

Report 6.2. Two common approaches to mutual fund investing are growth investing and value investing. Growth funds invest in companies whose stock prices are expected to grow at a faster rate, relative to the overall stock market. Value funds, on the other hand, invest in companies whose stock prices are below their true worth.

Dorothy Brennan works as a financial advisor at a large investment firm and has access to the annual return data for Fidelity's Growth Index mutual fund (Growth) and Fidelity's Value Index mutual fund (Value) for years 1984–2019. She calculates the mean and standard deviation for the Growth fund as 15.75% and 23.80%, respectively. The corresponding mean and standard deviation for the Value fund is 12.00% and 17.98%, respectively. She believes that the fund returns are stable and are normally distributed.

In a report, use the sample information to compare and contrast the Growth and Value funds for client objectives such as (a) minimizing the probability of earning a negative return and (b) maximizing the probability of earning a return greater than 10%.

Report 6.3. A variety of packaging solutions exist for products that must be kept within a specific temperature range. A cold chain distribution is a temperature-controlled supply chain. An unbroken cold chain is an uninterrupted series of storage and distribution activities that maintain a given temperature range. Cold chains are particularly useful in the food and pharmaceutical industries. A commonly suggested temperature range for a cold chain distribution in pharmaceutical industries is between 2 and 8 degrees Celsius.

Gopal Vasudeva works in the packaging branch of Merck & Co. He is in charge of analyzing a new package that the company has developed. With repeated trials, Gopal has determined that the mean temperature that this package is able to maintain during its use is 5.6°C with a standard deviation of 1.2°C. He is not sure if the distribution of temperature is symmetric or skewed to the right.

In a report, use the sample information to calculate and interpret the probability that temperature goes (a) below 2°C and (b) above 8°C, using the normal and the lognormal distribution approximations. Compare the results from the two distributions used in the analysis.

CONCEPTUAL REVIEW

LO 6.1 Describe a continuous random variable.

A continuous random variable is characterized by uncountable values within an interval. The probability that a continuous random variable X assumes a particular value x is zero; that is, $P(X = x) = 0$. Thus, for a continuous random variable, we calculate the probability within a specified interval. Moreover, the following equalities hold: $P(a \leq X \leq b) = P(a < X < b) = P(a \leq X < b) = P(a < X \leq b)$.

The probability density function $f(x)$ of a continuous random variable X is nonnegative and the entire area under this function equals one. The probability $P(a \leq X \leq b)$ is the area under $f(x)$ between points a and b.

For any value x of the random variable X, the cumulative distribution function $F(x)$ is defined as $F(x) = P(X \leq x)$.

LO 6.2 Calculate and interpret probabilities for a random variable that follows the continuous uniform distribution.

The continuous uniform distribution describes a random variable that has an equally likely chance of assuming a value within a specified range. The probability is essentially the area of a rectangle, which is the base times the height; that is, the length of a specified interval times the probability density function $f(x) = \frac{1}{b-a}$, where a and b are the lower and upper bounds of the interval, respectively.

LO 6.3 **Explain the characteristics of the normal distribution.**

The normal distribution is the most extensively used continuous probability distribution and is the cornerstone of statistical inference. It is the familiar bell-shaped distribution, which is symmetric around the mean. The normal distribution is described by two parameters: the population mean μ and the population variance σ^2.

The standard normal distribution, also referred to as the z distribution, is a special case of the normal distribution, with mean equal to zero and standard deviation (or variance) equal to one.

LO 6.4 **Calculate and interpret probabilities for a random variable that follows the normal distribution.**

Any normally distributed random variable X with mean μ and standard deviation σ can be transformed into the standard normal random variable Z as $Z = \frac{X - \mu}{\sigma}$. This standard transformation implies that any value x has a corresponding value z given by $z = \frac{x - \mu}{\sigma}$.

The standard normal variable Z can be transformed to the normally distributed random variable X with mean μ and standard deviation σ as $X = \mu + Z\sigma$. This inverse transformation implies that any value z has a corresponding value x given by $x = \mu + z\sigma$.

LO 6.5 **Calculate and interpret probabilities for a random variable that follows the exponential distribution.**

A useful nonsymmetric continuous probability distribution is the exponential distribution. A random variable X follows the exponential distribution if its probability density function is $f(x) = \lambda e^{-\lambda x}$ for $x \geq 0$, where λ is a rate parameter and $e \approx 2.718$ is the base of the natural logarithm. The mean and the standard deviation of the distribution are both equal to $1/\lambda$. For $x \geq 0$, the cumulative probability is computed as $P(X \leq x) = 1 - e^{-\lambda x}$.

LO 6.6 **Calculate and interpret probabilities for a random variable that follows the lognormal distribution.**

The lognormal distribution is another useful positively skewed distribution. Let X be a normal random variable with mean μ and variance σ^2 and let $Y = e^X$ be the corresponding lognormal variable. The mean μ_Y and standard deviation σ_Y of Y are derived as $\mu_Y = \exp\left(\frac{2\mu + \sigma^2}{2}\right)$ and $\sigma_Y = \sqrt{(\exp(\sigma^2) - 1)\exp(2\mu + \sigma^2)}$, respectively. Equivalently, the mean and standard deviation of the normal variable $X = \ln(Y)$ are derived as $\mu = \ln\left(\frac{\mu_Y^2}{\sqrt{\mu_Y^2 + \sigma_Y^2}}\right)$ and $\sigma = \sqrt{\ln\left(1 + \frac{\sigma_Y^2}{\mu_Y^2}\right)}$, respectively. Probabilities for a lognormal random variable are easily evaluated by reference to the normal distribution.

ADDITIONAL EXERCISES

74. A florist makes deliveries between 1:00 pm and 5:00 pm daily. Assume delivery times follow the continuous uniform distribution.
    a. Calculate the mean and the variance of this distribution.
    b. Determine the percentage of deliveries that are made after 4:00 pm.
    c. Determine the percentage of deliveries that are made prior to 2:30 pm.

75. A worker at a landscape design center uses a machine to fill bags with potting soil. Assume that the quantity put in each bag follows the continuous uniform distribution with low and high filling weights of 10 pounds and 12 pounds, respectively.
    a. Calculate the expected value and the standard deviation of this distribution.
    b. Find the probability that the weight of a randomly selected bag is no more than 11 pounds.
    c. Find the probability that the weight of a randomly selected bag is at least 10.5 pounds.

76. In general, normal blood pressure readings are those below 120/80 millimeters of mercury (www.mayoclinic.org, January 9, 2019). Prehypertension is suspected when the top number (systolic) is between 120 and 139 or when the bottom number (diastolic) is between 80 and 90. A recent survey reported that the mean systolic reading of Canadians is 125 with a standard deviation of 17 and the mean diastolic reading is 79 with a standard deviation of 10. Assume that diastolic as well as systolic readings are normally distributed.
    a. What proportion of Canadians are suffering from prehypertension caused by high diastolic readings?
    b. What proportion of Canadians are suffering from prehypertension caused by high systolic readings?
77. U.S. consumers are increasingly viewing debit cards as a convenient substitute for cash and checks. The average amount spent annually on a debit card is $7,790. Assume that the average amount spent on a debit card is normally distributed with a standard deviation of $500.
    a. A consumer advocate comments that the majority of consumers spend over $8,000 on a debit card. Find a flaw in this statement.
    b. Compute the 25th percentile of the amount spent on a debit card.
    c. Compute the 75th percentile of the amount spent on a debit card.
    d. What is the interquartile range of this distribution?
78. A study finds that men spend an average of $43.87 on St. Patrick's Day, while women spend an average of $29.54. Assume the standard deviations of spending for men and women are $3 and $11, respectively, and that both distributions are normally distributed.
    a. What is the probability that men spend over $50 on St. Patrick's Day?
    b. What is the probability that women spend over $50 on St. Patrick's Day?
    c. Are men or women more likely to spend over $50 on St. Patrick's Day?
79. Lisa Mendes and Brad Lee work in the sales department of an AT&T Wireless store. Lisa has been signing up an average of 48 new cell phone customers every month with a standard deviation of 22, while Brad signs up an average of 56 new customers with a standard deviation of 17. The store manager offers both Lisa and Brad a $100 incentive bonus if they can sign up more than 100 new customers in a month. Assume a normal distribution to answer the following questions.
    a. What is the probability that Lisa will earn the $100 incentive bonus?
    b. What is the probability that Brad will earn the $100 incentive bonus?
    c. Are you surprised by the results? Explain.
80. The car speeds on a certain stretch of the interstate highway I-95 are known to be normally distributed with a mean of 72 and a standard deviation of 15. You have just heard a policeman comment that about 3% of the drivers drive at extremely dangerous speeds. What is the minimum speed that the policeman considers extremely dangerous?
81. The average household income in a community is known to be $80,000. Also, 20% of the households have an income below $60,000 and another 20% have an income above $90,000. Is it reasonable to use the normal distribution to model the household income in this community?
82. The length of components produced by a company is normally distributed with a mean of 6 cm and a standard deviation of 0.02 cm. Calculate the first, second, and third quartiles of the component length.
83. Entrance to a prestigious MBA program in India is determined by a national test where only the top 10% of the examinees are admitted to the program. Suppose it is known that the scores on this test are normally distributed with a mean of 420 and a standard deviation of 80. Parul Monga is trying desperately to get into this program. What is the minimum score that she must earn to get admitted?
84. A new water filtration system is sold with a 10-year warranty that includes all parts and repairs. Suppose the life of this water filtration system is normally distributed with mean and standard deviation of 16 and 5 years, respectively.
    a. What is the probability that the water filtration system will require a repair during the warranty period?
    b. Suppose the water filtration firm makes a $300 profit for every new system it installs. This profit, however, is reduced to $50 if the system requires repair during the warranty period. Find the expected profit of the firm if it installs 1,000 new water filtration systems.
85. Suppose that the average IQ score is normally distributed with a mean of 100 and a standard deviation of 16.
    a. What is the probability a randomly selected person will have an IQ score of less than 80?
    b. What is the probability that a randomly selected person will have an IQ score greater than 125?
    c. What minimum IQ score does a person have to achieve to be in the top 2.5% of IQ scores?

86. Suppose that the annual household income in a small Midwestern community is normally distributed with a mean of $55,000 and a standard deviation of $4,500.
   a. What is the probability that a randomly selected household will have an income between $50,000 and $65,000?
   b. What is the probability that a randomly selected household will have an income of more than $70,000?
   c. What minimum income does a household need to earn to be in the top 5% of incomes?
   d. What maximum income does a household need to earn to be in the bottom 40% of incomes?
87. On a particularly busy section of the Garden State Parkway in New Jersey, police use radar guns to detect speeders. Assume the time that elapses between successive speeders is exponentially distributed with a mean of 15 minutes.
   a. Calculate the rate parameter λ.
   b. What is the probability of a waiting time less than 10 minutes between successive speeders?
   c. What is the probability of a waiting time in excess of 25 minutes between successive speeders?
88. In a local law office, jobs to a printer are sent at a rate of 8 jobs per hour. Suppose that the number of jobs sent to a printer follows the Poisson distribution.
   a. What is the expected time between successive jobs?
   b. What is the probability that the next job will be sent within five minutes?
89. According to the Federal Bureau of Investigation, there is a violent crime in the United States every 22 seconds. Assume that the time between successive violent crimes is exponentially distributed.
   a. What is the probability that there is a violent crime in the United States in the next one minute?
   b. If there has not been a violent crime in the previous minute, what is the probability that there will be a violent crime in the subsequent minute?
90. Disturbing news regarding Scottish police concerns the number of crashes involving vehicles on operational duties. Statistics showed that Scottish forces' vehicles had been involved in traffic accidents at the rate of 1,000 per year. Suppose the number of crashes involving vehicles on operational duties follows a Poisson distribution.
   a. What is the average number of days between successive crashes?
   b. What is the rate parameter of the appropriate exponential distribution?
   c. What is the probability that the next vehicle will crash within a day?
91. The mileage (in 1,000s of miles) that car owners get with a certain kind of radial tire is a random variable having an exponential distribution with a mean of 50.
   a. What is the probability that a tire will last at most 40,000 miles?
   b. What is the probability that a tire will last at least 65,000 miles?
   c. What is the probability that a tire will last between 70,000 and 80,000 miles?
92. A large technology firm receives an average of 12 new job applications every 10 days for positions that are not even advertised. Suppose the number of job applications received follows a Poisson distribution.
   a. What is the average number of days between successive job applications?
   b. What is the probability that the next job application is received within a day?
   c. What is the probability that the next job application is received between the next 1 and 2 days?
93. The relief time provided by a standard dose of a popular children's allergy medicine averages six hours with a standard deviation of two hours.
   a. Determine the percentage of children who experience relief for less than four hours if the relief time follows a normal distribution.
   b. Determine the percentage of children who experience relief for less than four hours if the relief time follows a lognormal distribution.
   c. Compare the results based on these two distributions.
94. On average, a certain kind of kitchen appliance requires repairs once every four years. Assume that the times between repairs are exponentially distributed.
   a. What is the probability that the appliance will work no more than three years without requiring repairs?
   b. What is the probability that the appliance will work at least six years without requiring repairs?
95. The mileage (in 1,000s of miles) that car owners get with a certain kind of radial tire is a random variable Y having a lognormal distribution such that $Y = e^X$, where X is normally distributed. Let the mean and the standard deviation of the life of a radial tire be 40,000 miles and 5,000 miles, respectively.

a. Compute the mean and standard deviation of *X*.
b. What proportion of the tires will last for more than 50,000 miles?
c. What proportion of the tires will last for no more than 35,000 miles?
d. Compute the 95th percentile of the life expectancy of the tire.

96. The U.S. Census Bureau reported that the median income for American households was $52,353, whereas the mean income was $71,932. Suppose income can be represented by a lognormal variable, $Y = e^X$, where *X* is normally distributed. The mean and the standard deviation of *X* are 11.1 and 0.4, respectively.
    a. What is the probability that a household's income is less than $50,000?
    b. What is the probability that a household's income is greater than $60,000?
    c. What is the lowest income that places a household in the 99th percentile?
    d. What is the highest income that places a household in the 10th percentile?

APPENDIX 6.1 Guidelines for Other Software Packages

The following section provides brief commands for Minitab, SPSS, and JMP.

Minitab

The Uniform Distribution

(Replicating Example 6.1b) From the menu, choose **Calc > Probability Distributions > Uniform.** Select **Cumulative probability.** Enter 2,500 as the **Lower endpoint** and 5,000 as the **Upper endpoint.** Select **Input constant** and enter 4,000.

The Normal Distribution

The Standard Transformation

(Replicating Example 6.8a) From the menu, choose **Calc > Probability Distributions > Normal.** Select **Cumulative probability.** Enter 7.49 for the **Mean** and 6.41 for the **Standard deviation.** Select **Input constant** and enter 10. Minitab returns $P(X \leq 10)$. Perform similar steps to find $P(X \leq 5)$, and then find the difference between the probabilities.

The Inverse Transformation

(Replicating Example 6.8b) From the menu, choose **Calc > Probability Distributions > Normal.** Select **Inverse cumulative probability.** Enter 7.49 for the **Mean** and 6.41 for the **Standard deviation.** Select **Input constant** and enter 0.90.

The Exponential Distribution

(Replicating Example 6.12) Choose **Calc > Probability Distributions > Exponential.** Select **Cumulative probability.** Enter 5 for **Scale** (since Scale = $E(X) = 5$) and 0.0 for **Threshold.** Select **Input constant** and enter 6. Minitab returns $P(X \leq 6)$. Perform similar steps to find $P(X \leq 3)$, and then find the difference between the probabilities.

The Lognormal Distribution

The Lognormal Transformation

(Replicating Example 6.13a) From the menu, choose **Calc > Probability Distributions > Lognormal.** Select **Cumulative probability.** Enter 2.6054 for the **Location** and 0.4487 for the **Scale.** Select **Input constant** and enter 20. Minitab returns $P(Y \leq 20)$.

The Inverse Transformation

(Replicating Example 6.13b) From the menu, choose **Calc > Probability Distributions > Lognormal.** Select **Inverse cumulative probability.** Enter 2.6054 for the **Location** and 0.4487 for the **Scale**. Select **Input constant** and enter 0.25.

SPSS

Note: In order for the calculated probability to be seen on the spreadsheet, SPSS must first "view" data on the spreadsheet. For this purpose, enter a value of zero in the first cell of the first column.

The Uniform Distribution

(Replicating Example 6.1b) From the menu, choose **Transform > Compute Variable.** Under **Target Variable**, enter cdfuniform. In the **Numeric Expression** box, enter `1-CDF.UNIFORM(4000,2500,5000)`.

The Normal Distribution

The Standard Transformation

(Replicating Example 6.8a) From the menu, choose **Transform > Compute Variable.** Under **Target Variable,** enter cdfnorm. In the **Numeric Expression** box, enter `CDF.NORMAL(10, 7.49, 6.41)- CDF.NORMAL(5, 7.49, 6.41)`.

The Inverse Transformation

(Replicating Example 6.8b) From the menu, choose **Transform > Compute Variable.** Under **Target Variable,** enter invnorm. In the Numeric Expression box, enter `IDF.NORMAL(0.9, 7.49, 6.41)`

The Exponential Distribution

(Replicating Example 6.12) From the menu, choose **Transform > Compute Variable.** Under **Target Variable,** enter cdfexp. In the **Numeric Expression** box, enter `CDF.EXP(6, 0.2)- CDF.EXP(3, 0.2)`.

The Lognormal Distribution

The Lognormal Transformation

(Replicating Example 6.13a) The easiest way to solve lognormal distribution problems in SPSS is to modify the normal distribution instructions. So, from the menu, choose **Transform > Compute Variable.** Under **Target Variable,** enter cdflognorm. In the **Numeric Expression box,** enter `1 - CDF.NORMAL(ln(20), 2.6054, 0.4487)`

The Inverse Transformation

(Replicating Example 6.13b) From the menu, choose **Transform > Compute Variable.** Under **Target Variable,** enter invlognorm. In the **Numeric Expression** box, enter `exp(IDF.NORMAL(0.25, 2.6054, 0.4487))`.

JMP

Note: In order for the calculated probability to be seen on the spreadsheet, JMP must first "view" data on the spreadsheet. For this purpose, enter a value of zero in the first cell of the first column.

The Normal Distribution

The Standard Transformation

(Replicating Example 6.8a) Right-click on the header at the top of the column in the spreadsheet view and select **Formula > Probability > Normal Distribution.** Enter 10 for **x**, 7.49 for **mean,** and 6.41 for **std dev.** JMP returns $P(X \leq 10)$. Perform similar steps to find $P(X \leq 5)$, and then find the difference between the probabilities.

The Inverse Transformation

(Replicating Example 6.8b) Right-click on the header at the top of the column in the spreadsheet view and select **Formula > Probability > Normal Quantile.** Enter 0.90 for **p,** 7.49 for **mean,** and 6.41 for **std dev.**

The Exponential Distribution

(Replicating Example 6.12) Right-click on the header at the top of the column in the spreadsheet view and select **Formula > Probability > Weibull Distribution.** (The exponential distribution is a special case of the Weibull distribution, when the shape parameter, equals 1.) Enter 6 for **x,** 1 for **shape,** and 5 for **scale.** JMP returns $P(X \leq 6)$. Perform similar steps to find $P(X \leq 3)$, and then find the difference between the probabilities.

The Lognormal Distribution

The Lognormal Transformation

(Replicating Example 6.13a) Right-click on the header at the top of the column in the spreadsheet view and select **Formula > Probability > GLog Distribution.** Enter 20 for **x**, 2.6054 for **mu,** 0.4487 for **sigma,** and 0 for **lambda.**
JMP returns $P(Y \leq 20)$.

The Inverse Transformation

(Replicating Example 6.13b) Right-click on the header at the top of the column in the spreadsheet view and select **Formula > Probability > GLog Quantile.** Enter 0.25 for **p,** 2.6054 for **mu,** 0.4487 for **sigma,** and 0 for **lambda.**

7 Sampling and Sampling Distributions

LEARNING OBJECTIVES

After reading this chapter you should be able to

LO 7.1 Explain common sample biases.

LO 7.2 Describe various sampling methods.

LO 7.3 Describe the sampling distribution of the sample mean.

LO 7.4 Explain the importance of the central limit theorem.

LO 7.5 Describe the sampling distribution of the sample proportion.

LO 7.6 Use a finite population correction factor.

LO 7.7 Construct and interpret control charts for numerical and categorical variables.

In the last few chapters, we had information on the population parameters, such as the population proportion and the population mean, for the analysis of discrete and continuous random variables. In many instances, we do not have information on the parameters, so we make statistical inferences on the basis of sample statistics. The credibility of any statistical inference depends on the quality of the sample on which it is based.

In this chapter, we first discuss various ways to draw a good sample and also highlight cases in which the sample misrepresents the population. It is important to note that any given statistical problem involves only one population, but many possible samples from which a statistic can be derived. Therefore, while the population parameter is a constant, the sample statistic is a random variable whose value depends on the choice of the random sample.

We then discuss how to evaluate the properties of sample statistics. In particular, we study the probability distributions of the sample mean and the sample proportion based on simple random sampling. Finally, we use these distributions to construct control charts, which are popular statistical tools for monitoring and improving quality.

KPG_Payless/Shutterstock

INTRODUCTORY CASE

Marketing Iced Coffee

Camila Fuentes is the owner of a gourmet coffee shop. She would like to increase her customer base during slow times, which primarily are Mondays through Thursdays between 1:00 pm and 4:00 pm. For one month during this time period, she decides to implement a Happy Hour when customers can enjoy a half-price iced coffee drink. Prior to the promotion Camila reviews her records and finds that customers spent, on average, \$4.18 on iced coffee with a standard deviation of \$0.84. In addition, 43% of iced-coffee customers were women and 21% were teenage girls.

After the promotion ends, Camila surveys 50 of her iced-coffee customers and finds that they had spent an average of \$4.26. In addition, 23 (46%) of the customers were women and 17 (34%) were teenage girls. Camila wants to determine if the promotion has been effective; that is, would she have gotten such business if she had chosen not to have a Happy Hour?

Camila wants to use the survey information to

1. Calculate the probability that customers spend an average of \$4.26 or more on iced coffee.
2. Calculate the probability that 46% or more of iced-coffee customers are women.
3. Calculate the probability that 34% or more of iced-coffee customers are teenage girls.

A synopsis of this case is provided at the end of Section 7.3.

LO 7.1

7.1 SAMPLING

Explain common sample biases.

A major portion of statistics is concerned with statistical inference, where we examine the problem of estimating population parameters or testing hypotheses about such parameters. Recall that a population consists of all items of interest in the statistical problem. If we had access to data that encompass the entire population, then the values of the parameters would be known and no statistical inference would be needed. Since it is generally not feasible to gather data on an entire population, we use a subset of the population, or a sample, and use this information to make statistical inference. We can think of a census and survey data as representative of population and sample data, respectively. While a census captures almost everyone in the country, a survey captures a small number of people who fit a particular category. We regularly use survey data to analyze government and business activities.

POPULATION VERSUS SAMPLE

A population consists of all items of interest in a statistical problem, whereas a sample is a subset of the population. We use a sample statistic, or simply statistic, to make inferences about the unknown population parameter.

In later chapters, we explore estimation and hypothesis testing, which are based on sample information. It is important to note that no matter how sophisticated the statistical methods are, the credibility of statistical inference depends on the quality of the sample on which it is based. A primary requisite for a "good" sample is that it be representative of the population we are trying to describe. When the information from a sample is not typical of information in the population in a systematic way, we say that **bias** has occurred.

Bias refers to the tendency of a sample statistic to systematically overestimate or underestimate a population parameter. It is often caused by samples that are not representative of the population.

Classic Case of a "Bad" Sample: The *Literary Digest* Debacle of 1936

In theory, drawing conclusions about a population based on a good sample sounds logical; however, in practice, what constitutes a "good" sample? Unfortunately, there are many ways to collect a "bad" sample. One way is to inadvertently pick a sample that represents only a portion of the population. The *Literary Digest*'s attempt to predict the 1936 presidential election is a classic example of an embarrassingly inaccurate poll.

In 1932 and amid the Great Depression, Herbert Hoover was voted out of the White House and Franklin Delano Roosevelt (FDR) was elected the 32nd president of the United States. Although FDR's attempts to end the Great Depression within four years were largely unsuccessful, he retained the general public's faith. In 1936, FDR ran for reelection against Alf Landon, the governor of Kansas and the Republican nominee. The *Literary Digest,* an influential, general-interest weekly magazine, wanted to predict the next U.S. president, as it had done successfully five times before.

After conducting the largest poll in history, the *Literary Digest* predicted a landslide victory for Alf Landon: 57% of the vote to FDR's 43%. Moreover, the *Literary Digest* claimed that its prediction would be within a fraction of 1% of the actual vote. Instead, FDR won in a landslide: 62% of the vote to Landon's 38%. So what went wrong?

The *Literary Digest* sent postcards to 10 million people (one-quarter of the voting population at the time) and received responses from 2.4 million people. The response rate of 24% (=2.4/10) might seem low to some, but in reality it is a reasonable response rate given this type of polling. What was atypical of the poll is the manner in which the *Literary Digest* obtained the respondents' names. The *Literary Digest* randomly sampled its own subscriber list, club membership rosters, telephone directories, and automobile registration rolls. This sample reflected predominantly middle- and upper-class people; that is, the vast majority of those polled were wealthier people, who were more inclined to vote for the Republican candidate. Back in the 1930s, owning a phone, for instance, was far from universal. Only 11 million residential phones were in service in 1936, and these homes were disproportionately well-to-do and in favor of Landon. The sampling methodology employed by the *Literary Digest* suffered from **selection bias**. Selection bias occurs when portions of the population are underrepresented in the sample. FDR's support came from lower-income classes whose opinion was not reflected in the poll. The sample, unfortunately, misrepresented the general electorate.

> Selection bias refers to a systematic underrepresentation of certain groups from consideration for the sample.

What should the *Literary Digest* have done differently? At a minimum, most would agree that names should have been obtained from voter registration lists rather than telephone directory lists and car registrations.

In addition to selection bias, the *Literary Digest* survey also had a great deal of **nonresponse bias**. This occurs when those responding to a survey or poll differ systematically from the nonrespondents. In the survey, a larger percentage of educated people mailed back the questionnaires. During that time period, the more educated tended to come from affluent families that again favored the Republican candidate.

> Nonresponse bias refers to a systematic difference in preferences between respondents and nonrespondents to a survey or a poll.

The most effective way to deal with nonresponse bias is to reduce nonresponse rates. Paying attention to survey design, wording, and ordering of the questions can increase the response rate. Sometimes, rather than sending out a very large number of surveys, it may be preferable to use a smaller representative sample for which the response rate is likely to be high.

It turns out that someone did accurately predict the 1936 presidential election. From a sample of 50,000 with a response rate of 10% (5,000 respondents), a young pollster named George Gallup predicted that FDR would win 56% of the vote to Landon's 44%. Despite using a far smaller sample with a lower response rate, it was far more representative of the true voting population. Gallup later founded the Gallup Organization, one of the leading polling companies of all time.

Trump's Stunning Victory in 2016

The results of the U.S. presidential election in 2016 came as a surprise to nearly everyone who had been following the national and state election polling, which consistently projected Hillary Clinton as defeating Donald Trump (www.pewresearch.org, November 9, 2016). It appears that problems with selection bias and nonresponse bias persist today. Many pollsters and strategists believe that rural white voters, who were a key demographic for Trump on Election Day, eluded polling altogether. It is also believed that the frustration and anti-institutional feelings that drove the campaign may also have aligned these same voters with an unwillingness to respond to surveys (www.politico.com, March 27, 2017).

Another theory that has gained some traction in explaining the polling missteps in the 2016 election was the presence of **social-desirability bias.** This bias occurs when voters provide incorrect answers to a survey or poll because they think that others will look unfavorably on their ultimate choices.

> Social-desirability bias refers to a systematic difference between a group's "socially acceptable" responses to a survey or poll and this group's ultimate choice.

Due to Trump's inflammatory comments, many voters did not want to be associated with him by their peers. This was perfectly exemplified by the fact that Trump consistently performed better in online polling. For example, in one aggregation of telephone polls, Clinton led Trump by nine percentage points; however, in a similar aggregation of online polls, Clinton's lead was only four percentage points (*The New York Times,* May 11, 2016). This seems to suggest that one way to battle social-desirability bias is to use online surveys. Despite their flaws, online surveys resemble an anonymous voting booth and remove the human factor of the pollsters.

LO 7.2

Describe various sampling methods.

Sampling Methods

As mentioned earlier, a primary requisite for a "good" sample is that it be representative of the population you are trying to describe. The basic type of sample that can be used to draw statistically sound conclusions about a population is a **simple random sample.**

> SIMPLE RANDOM SAMPLE
>
> A simple random sample is a sample of n observations that has the same probability of being selected from the population as any other sample of n observations. Most statistical methods presume simple random samples.

While a simple random sample is the most commonly used sampling method, in some situations, other sampling methods have an advantage over simple random samples. Two alternative methods for forming a sample are stratified random sampling and cluster sampling.

Political pollsters often employ **stratified random sampling** in an attempt to ensure that each area of the country, each ethnic group, each religious group, and so forth, is appropriately represented in the sample. With stratified random sampling, the population is divided into groups (strata) based on one or more classification criteria. Simple random samples are then drawn from each stratum in sizes proportional to the relative size of each stratum in the population. These samples are then pooled.

> STRATIFIED RANDOM SAMPLING
>
> In stratified random sampling, the population is first divided up into mutually exclusive and collectively exhaustive groups, called *strata.* A stratified sample includes randomly selected observations from each stratum. The number of observations per stratum is proportional to the stratum's size in the population. The data for each stratum are eventually pooled.

Stratified random sampling has two advantages. First, it guarantees that the population subdivisions of interest are represented in the sample. Second, the estimates of parameters produced from stratified random sampling have greater precision than estimates obtained from simple random sampling.

Suppose a public opinion survey is to be conducted to determine whether a majority of households favor the opening of a marijuana dispensary in a particular city. Assume that it is known, from previous surveys, that households with school-age children tend to oppose the opening. Seventy percent of the households in this city have school-age children. If the city pursues a proportional stratified sampling plan, then 70% of the sample will consist of households with school-age children and the remaining 30% will consist of households with no school-age children.

Cluster sampling is another method for forming a representative sample. A cluster sample is formed by dividing the population into groups (clusters), such as geographic areas, and then selecting a sample of the groups for the analysis. The technique works best when most of the variation in the population is within the groups and not between the groups. In such instances, a cluster is a miniversion of the population.

CLUSTER SAMPLING

In cluster sampling, the population is first divided up into mutually exclusive and collectively exhaustive groups, called *clusters*. A cluster sample includes observations from randomly selected clusters.

In general, cluster sampling is cheaper as compared to other sampling methods. However, for a given sample size, it provides less precision than either simple random sampling or stratified sampling. Cluster sampling is useful in applications where the population is concentrated in natural clusters such as city blocks, schools, and other geographic areas. It is especially attractive when constructing a complete list of the population members is difficult and/or costly. For example, since it may not be possible to create a full list of customers who go to Walmart, we can form a sample that includes customers only from selected stores.

STRATIFIED VERSUS CLUSTER SAMPLING

In stratified sampling, the sample consists of observations from each group, whereas in cluster sampling, the sample consists of observations from the selected groups. Stratified sampling is preferred when the objective is to increase precision, and cluster sampling is preferred when the objective is to reduce costs.

In practice, it is extremely difficult to obtain a truly random sample that is representative of the underlying population. As researchers, we need to be aware of the population from which the sample was selected and then limit our conclusions to that population. For the remainder of the text, we assume that the sample data are void of "human error." That is, we have sampled from the correct population (no selection bias); we have no nonresponse or social-desirability biases; and we have collected, analyzed, and reported the data properly.

Using Excel and R to Generate a Simple Random Sample

Excel and R provide functions that we can use to draw simple random samples. Example 7.1 illustrates the use of some of these functions.

EXAMPLE 7.1

There has been an increase in students working their way through college to offset rising tuition costs. A dean at the Orfalea College of Business (OCOB) wants to analyze the performance of her students who work while they are enrolled. For the analysis, use Excel or R to generate a random sample of 100 students drawn from 2,750 OCOB students.

SOLUTION: Since each student has a unique student identification number, we start by creating an ordered list using 1 and 2,750 as the smallest and largest student identification numbers, respectively. We then generate 100 random integers (numbers) between these values and use them to identify students based on their order on the list.

Using Excel

We use Excel's **RANDBETWEEN** function to generate random integers within some interval. We enter =RANDBETWEEN(lower, upper) where lower and upper refer to the smallest and largest integers in the interval, respectively. In this example, we enter `=RANDBETWEEN(1, 2750)`. Suppose Excel returns 983. The student whose order on the list is 983 is then selected for the sample. To generate the remaining 99 numbers, we select the cell with the value 983, drag it down 99 additional cells, and from the menu, choose **Home > Fill > Down.**

Using R

We use R's **sample** function to generate random integers within some interval. We enter sample(lower:upper, n) where lower and upper refer to the smallest and largest integers in the interval, respectively, and n denotes the sample size. We label the random sample as Sample_draw. We enter:

```
> Sample_draw <- sample(1:2750, 100)
> Sample_draw
```

EXERCISES 7.1

1. AirPods are Apple's most popular accessory product, with 35 million units sold in 2018 alone (*AppleInsider,* March 15, 2019). Suppose you are put in charge of determining the age profile of people who purchased AirPods in the United States. Explain in detail the following sampling strategies that you could use to select a representative sample.
   a. Simple random sampling
   b. Stratified random sampling
   c. Cluster sampling
2. A marketing firm opens a small booth at a local mall over the weekend, where shoppers are asked how much money they spent at the food court. The objective is to determine the average monthly expenditure of shoppers at the food court. Has the marketing firm committed any sampling bias? Discuss.
3. Natalie Min is an undergraduate in the Haas School of Business at Berkeley. She wishes to pursue an MBA from Berkeley and wants to know the profile of other students who are likely to apply to the Berkeley MBA program. In particular, she wants to know the GPA of students with whom she might be competing. She randomly surveys 40 students from her accounting class for the analysis. Discuss in detail whether or not Natalie's analysis is based on a representative sample.
4. Vons, a large supermarket in Grover Beach, California, is considering extending its store hours from 7:00 am to midnight,

seven days a week, to 6:00 am to midnight. Discuss the sampling bias in the following sampling strategies:

a. Mail a prepaid envelope to randomly selected residents in the Grover Beach area, asking for their preference for the store hours.
b. Ask the customers who frequent the store in the morning if they would prefer an earlier opening time.
c. Place an ad in the local newspaper, requesting people to submit their preference for store hours on the store's website.

5. In the previous question regarding Vons' store hours, explain how you can obtain a representative sample based on the following sampling strategies:
   a. Simple random sampling.
   b. Stratified random sampling.
   c. Cluster sampling.

7.2 THE SAMPLING DISTRIBUTION OF THE SAMPLE MEAN

As mentioned earlier, we are generally interested in the characteristics of a population. For instance, a ride sharing company is interested in the average income (population mean) in a large city. Similarly, a banker is interested in the default probability (population proportion) of mortgage holders. Recall that the population mean describes a numerical variable, and the population proportion describes a categorical variable. Since it is cumbersome, if not impossible, to analyze the entire population, we generally make inferences about the characteristics of the population on the basis of a random sample drawn from the population.

It is important to note that there is only one population, but many possible samples of a given size can be drawn from the population. Therefore, a population parameter is a constant, even though its value may be unknown. On the other hand, a statistic, such as the sample mean or the sample proportion, is a random variable whose value depends on the particular sample that is randomly drawn from the population.

PARAMETER VERSUS STATISTIC

A parameter is a constant, although its value may be unknown. A statistic is a random variable whose value depends on the chosen random sample.

Suppose that the variable of interest is the mean income in a large city. If you decide to make inferences about the population mean income on the basis of a random draw of 38 residents, then the sample mean $\overline{X}$ is the relevant statistic. Note that the value of $\overline{X}$ will change if you choose a different random sample of 38 residents. In other words, $\overline{X}$ is a random variable whose value depends on the chosen random sample. The sample mean is commonly referred to as the **estimator,** or the **point estimator,** of the population mean.

In the income example, the sample mean $\overline{X}$ is the estimator of the mean income in the large city. If the average derived from a specific sample is \$54,000, then $\overline{x} = 54{,}000$ is the **estimate** of the population mean. Similarly, if the variable of interest is the default probability of mortgage holders, then the sample proportion of defaults, denoted by $\overline{P}$, from a random sample of 80 mortgage holders is the estimator of the population proportion. If 10 out of 80 mortgage holders in a given sample default, then $\overline{p} = 10/80 = 0.125$ is the estimate of the population proportion.

ESTIMATOR AND ESTIMATE

When a statistic is used to estimate a parameter, it is referred to as an estimator. A particular value of the estimator is called an estimate.

In this section, we will focus on the probability distribution of the sample mean $\bar{X}$, which is also referred to as the sampling distribution of $\bar{X}$. Since $\bar{X}$ is a random variable, its sampling distribution is simply the probability distribution derived from all possible samples of a given size from the population. Consider, for example, a mean derived from a sample of n observations. Another mean can similarly be derived from a different sample of n observations. If we repeat this process a very large number of times, then the frequency distribution of the sample means can be thought of as its sampling distribution. In particular, we will discuss the expected value and the standard deviation of the sample mean. We will also study the conditions under which the sampling distribution of the sample mean is normally distributed.

LO 7.3

Describe the sampling distribution of the sample mean.

The Expected Value and the Standard Error of the Sample Mean

Let the random variable X represent a certain characteristic of a population under study, with an expected value, $E(X) = \mu$, and a variance, $Var(X) = \sigma^2$. For example, X could represent the income of a resident in a large city or the return on an investment. We can think of μ and σ^2 as the mean and the variance of an individual observation drawn randomly from the population of interest, or simply as the population mean and the population variance. Let the sample mean $\bar{X}$ be based on a random sample of n observations from this population. It is easy to derive the expected value and the variance of $\bar{X}$; see Appendix 7.1 for the derivations.

The expected value of $\bar{X}$ is the same as the expected value of the individual observation—that is, $E(\bar{X}) = E(X) = \mu$. In other words, if we were to sample repeatedly from a given population, the average value of the sample means will equal the average value of all individual observations in the population, or simply, the population mean. This is an important property of an estimator, called unbiasedness, that holds irrespective of whether the sample mean is based on a small or a large sample. An estimator is **unbiased** if its expected value equals the population parameter. Other desirable properties of an estimator are described in Appendix 7.2.

The variance of $\bar{X}$ is equal to $Var(\bar{X}) = \frac{\sigma^2}{n}$. In other words, if we were to sample repeatedly from a given population, the variance of the sample mean will equal the variance of all individual observations in the population, divided by the sample size, n. Note that $Var(\bar{X})$ is smaller than the variance of X, which is equal to $Var(X) = \sigma^2$. This is an intuitive result, suggesting that the variability between sample means is less than the variability between observations. Since each sample is likely to contain both high and low observations, the highs and lows cancel one another, making the variance of $\bar{X}$ smaller than the variance of X. As usual, the standard deviation of $\bar{X}$ is calculated as the positive square root of the variance. However, in order to distinguish the variability between samples from the variability between individual observations, we refer to the standard deviation of $\bar{X}$ as the **standard error** of the sample mean, computed as $se(\bar{X}) = \frac{\sigma}{\sqrt{n}}$.

THE EXPECTED VALUE AND THE STANDARD ERROR OF THE SAMPLE MEAN

The expected value of the sample mean $\bar{X}$ equals the population mean, or $E(\bar{X}) = \mu$. In other words, the sample mean is an unbiased estimator of the population mean.

The standard deviation of the sample mean $\bar{X}$ is referred to as the standard error of the sample mean. It equals the population standard deviation divided by the square root of the sample size; that is, $se(\bar{X}) = \frac{\sigma}{\sqrt{n}}$.

In Chapter 8, we will discuss that the exact standard error of an estimator is often not known and, therefore, must be estimated from the given sample data. For convenience, we use "*se*" to denote both the exact and the estimated standard errors of an estimator.

EXAMPLE 7.2

The chefs at a local pizza chain in Cambria, California, strive to maintain the suggested size of their 16-inch pizzas. Despite their best efforts, they are unable to make every pizza exactly 16 inches in diameter. The manager has determined that the size of the pizzas is normally distributed with a mean of 16 inches and a standard deviation of 0.8 inch.

a. What are the expected value and the standard error of the sample mean derived from a random sample of 2 pizzas?

b. What are the expected value and the standard error of the sample mean derived from a random sample of 4 pizzas?

c. Compare the expected value and the standard error of the sample mean with those of an individual pizza.

SOLUTION: We know that the population mean $\mu = 16$ and the population standard deviation $\sigma = 0.8$. We use $E(\overline{X}) = \mu$ and $se(\overline{X}) = \frac{\sigma}{\sqrt{n}}$ to calculate the following results.

a. With the sample size $n = 2$, $E(\overline{X}) = 16$ and $se(\overline{X}) = \frac{0.8}{\sqrt{2}} = 0.57$.

b. With the sample size $n = 4$, $E(\overline{X}) = 16$ and $se(\overline{X}) = \frac{0.8}{\sqrt{4}} = 0.40$.

c. The expected value of the sample mean for both sample sizes is identical to the expected value of the individual pizza. However, the standard error of the sample mean with $n = 4$ is lower than the one with $n = 2$. For both sample sizes, the standard error of the sample mean is lower than the standard deviation of the individual pizza. This result confirms that averaging reduces variability.

Sampling from a Normal Population

An important feature of the sampling distribution of the sample mean $\overline{X}$ is that, irrespective of the sample size n, $\overline{X}$ is normally distributed if the population X from which the sample is drawn is normally distributed. In other words, if X is normally distributed with expected value μ and standard deviation σ, then $\overline{X}$ is also normally distributed with expected value μ and standard error $\sigma / \sqrt{n}$.

SAMPLING FROM A NORMAL POPULATION

For any sample size n, the sampling distribution of $\overline{X}$ is normally distributed if the population X from which the sample is drawn is normally distributed.

If $\overline{X}$ is normally distributed, then any value $\bar{x}$ can be transformed into its corresponding value z given by $z = \frac{\bar{x} - \mu}{\sigma / \sqrt{n}}$.

EXAMPLE 7.3

Use the information in Example 7.2 to answer the following questions:

a. What is the probability that a randomly selected pizza is less than 15.5 inches?

b. What is the probability that 2 randomly selected pizzas average less than 15.5 inches?

c. What is the probability that 4 randomly selected pizzas average less than 15.5 inches?

d. Comment on the computed probabilities.

SOLUTION: Since the population is normally distributed, the sampling distribution of the sample mean is also normally distributed. Figure 7.1 depicts the shapes of the three distributions based on the population mean $\mu = 16$ and the population standard deviation $\sigma = 0.8$.

FIGURE 7.1
Normal distribution of the sample mean

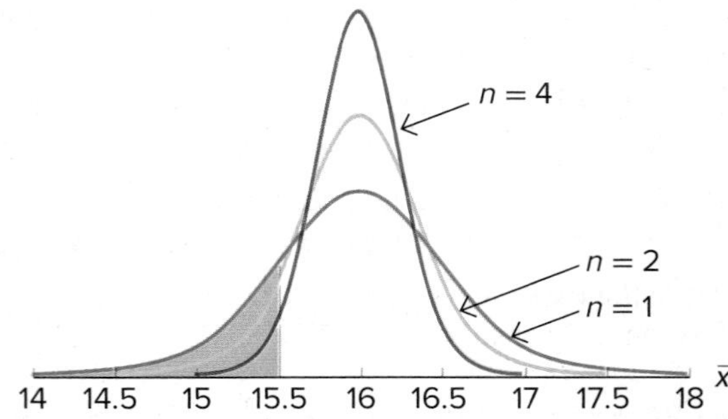

Note that when the sample size $n = 1$, the sample mean $\bar{x}$ is the same as the individual observation x.

a. We use the standard transformation to derive $P(X < 15.5) = P\left(Z < \frac{15.5 - 16}{0.8}\right) = P(Z < -0.625) = 0.2660$. There is a 26.60% chance that an individual pizza is less than 15.5 inches.

Recall that in order to find this probability in Excel, we enter `=NORM.DIST(15.5, 16, 0.8, TRUE)`; in R, we enter `pnorm(15.5, 16, 0.8, lower.tail=TRUE)`.

b. Here we use the standard transformation to derive $P(\overline{X} < 15.5) = P\left(Z < \frac{15.5 - 16}{0.8/\sqrt{2}}\right) = P(Z < -0.8839) = 0.1884$. In a random sample of 2 pizzas, there is an 18.84% chance that the average size is less than 15.5 inches.

We make a simple adjustment in the standard error to find this probability in Excel and R. In Excel, we enter `=NORM.DIST(15.5, 16, 0.8/SQRT(2), TRUE)`; in R, we enter `pnorm(15.5, 16, 0.8/sqrt(2), lower.tail=TRUE)`.

c. Again we find $P(\overline{X} < 15.5)$, but now $n = 4$. Therefore, $P(\overline{X} < 15.5) = P\left(Z < \frac{15.5 - 16}{0.8/\sqrt{4}}\right) = P(Z < -1.25) = 0.1056$. In a random sample of 4 pizzas, there is a 10.56% chance that the average size is less than 15.5 inches.

In Excel, we enter `=NORM.DIST(15.5, 16, 0.8/SQRT(4), TRUE)`; in R we enter `pnorm(15.5, 16, 0.8/sqrt(4), lower.tail=TRUE)`.

d. The probability that the average size is under 15.5 inches, for 4 randomly selected pizzas, is less than half of that for an individual pizza. This is due to the fact that while X and $\overline{X}$ have the same expected value of 16, the variance of $\overline{X}$ is less than that of X.

LO 7.4

Explain the importance of the central limit theorem.

The Central Limit Theorem

For making statistical inferences, it is essential that the sampling distribution of $\overline{X}$ is normally distributed. So far we have only considered the case where $\overline{X}$ is normally distributed because the population X from which the sample is drawn is normally distributed. What if the underlying population is not normally distributed? Here we present the **central limit theorem (CLT)**, which perhaps is the most remarkable result of probability theory. The CLT states that the sum or the average of a large number of independent observations from the same underlying distribution has an approximate normal distribution. The approximation steadily improves as the number of observations increases. In other words, irrespective of whether or not the population X is normally distributed, the sample mean $\overline{X}$ computed from a random sample of size n will be approximately normally distributed as long as n is sufficiently large.

THE CENTRAL LIMIT THEOREM FOR THE SAMPLE MEAN

For any population X with expected value μ and standard deviation σ, the sampling distribution of $\overline{X}$ will be approximately normally distributed if the sample size n is sufficiently large. As a general guideline, the normal distribution approximation is justified when $n \geq 30$.

As before, if $\overline{X}$ is approximately normally distributed, then any value $\bar{x}$ can be transformed to its corresponding value z given by $z = \frac{\bar{x} - \mu}{\sigma / \sqrt{n}}$.

Figure 7.1, discussed in Example 7.3, is not representative of the CLT principle because, for a normal population, the sampling distribution of $\overline{X}$ is normally distributed irrespective of the sample size. Figures 7.2 and 7.3, however, illustrate the CLT by using random samples of various sizes drawn from nonnormal populations. The relative frequency polygon of $\overline{X}$, which essentially represents its distribution, is generated from repeated draws (computer simulations) from the continuous uniform distribution (Figure 7.2) and the exponential distribution (Figure 7.3). Both of these nonnormal distributions were discussed in Chapter 6.

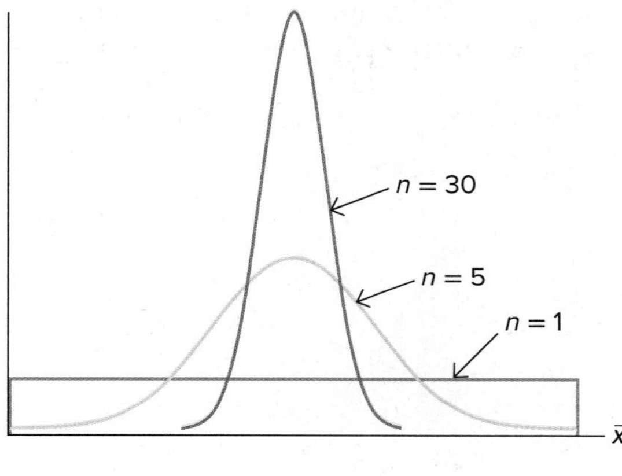

FIGURE 7.2 Sampling distribution of $\overline{X}$ when the population has a uniform distribution

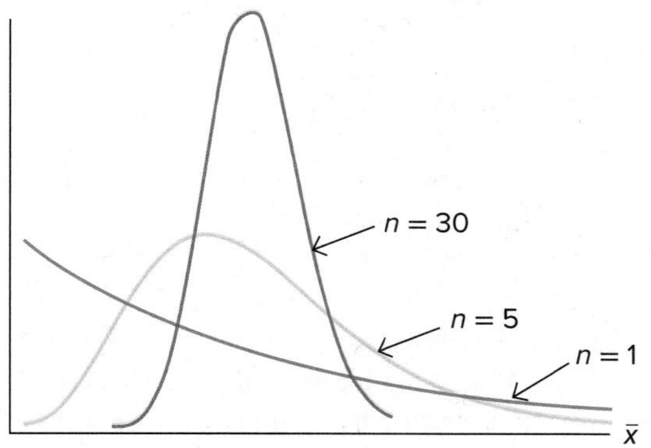

FIGURE 7.3 Sampling distribution of $\overline{X}$ when the population has an exponential distribution

Note that when the sample size $n = 1$, the sample mean is the same as the individual observation (population) with the familiar uniform and exponential shapes. With $n = 5$, the sampling distribution of $\overline{X}$ is already approximately normal when the population has the uniform distribution. With $n = 30$, the shape of the sampling distribution of $\overline{X}$ is approximately normal when the population has the exponential distribution. The CLT can similarly be illustrated with other distributions of the population. How large a sample is necessary for normal convergence depends on the magnitude of the departure of the population from normality. As mentioned earlier, practitioners often use the normal distribution approximation when $n \geq 30$.

EXAMPLE 7.4

Consider the information presented in the introductory case of this chapter. Recall that Camila wants to determine if the Happy Hour promotion has had a lingering effect on the amount of money customers spend on iced coffee. Before the promotion, customers spent an average of \$4.18 on iced coffee with a standard deviation of \$0.84. Camila reports that the average amount, based on 50 customers sampled after the campaign, is \$4.26. If Camila chose not to pursue the marketing campaign, how likely is it that customers will spend an average of \$4.26 or more on iced coffee?

SOLUTION: If Camila did not implement the Happy Hour, then spending on iced coffee would still have mean $\mu = 4.18$ and standard deviation $\sigma = 0.84$. Camila needs to calculate the probability that the sample mean is at least 4.26, or, $P(\overline{X} \geq 4.26)$. The population from which the sample is drawn is not known to be normally distributed. However, from the central limit theorem we know that $\overline{X}$ is approximately normally distributed because $n \geq 30$. Therefore, as shown in Figure 7.4, $P(\overline{X} \geq 4.26) = P\left(Z \geq \frac{4.26 - 4.18}{0.84/\sqrt{50}}\right) = P(Z \geq 0.6734) = 0.2503$. In Excel, we enter `=1-NORM.DIST(4.26, 4.18, 0.84/SQRT(50), TRUE);` in R, we enter `pnorm(4.26, 4.18, 0.84/sqrt(50), lower.tail=FALSE)`. It is quite plausible (probability = 0.2503) that in a sample of 50 customers, the sample mean is \$4.26 or more even if Camila did not implement the Happy Hour.

FIGURE 7.4 Finding $P(\overline{X} \geq 4.26)$

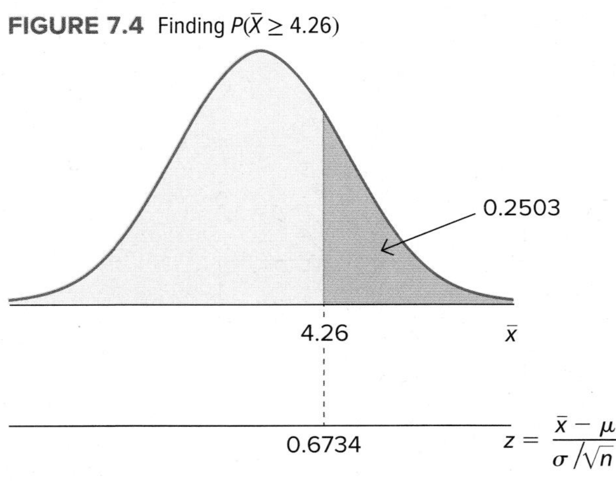

EXERCISES 7.2

Mechanics

6. A random sample is drawn from a normally distributed population with mean $\mu = 12$ and standard deviation $\sigma = 1.5$.
   a. What is the expected value and the standard error of the sampling distribution of the sample mean with $n = 20$ and $n = 40$.
   b. Can you conclude that the sampling distribution of the sample mean is normally distributed for both sample sizes? Explain.
   c. If the sampling distribution of the sample mean is normally distributed with $n = 20$, then calculate the probability that the sample mean is less than 12.5.
   d. If the sampling distribution of the sample mean is normally distributed with $n = 40$, then calculate the probability that the sample mean is less than 12.5.

7. A random sample is drawn from a population with mean $\mu = 66$ and standard deviation $\sigma = 5.5$.
   a. What is the expected value and the standard error of the sampling distribution of the sample mean with $n = 16$ and $n = 36$.
   b. Can you conclude that the sampling distribution of the sample mean is normally distributed for both sample sizes? Explain.

c. If the sampling distribution of the sample mean is normally distributed with $n = 16$, then calculate the probability that the sample mean falls between 66 and 68.

d. If the sampling distribution of the sample mean is normally distributed with $n = 36$, then calculate the probability that the sample mean falls between 66 and 68.

8. A random sample of size $n = 100$ is taken from a population with mean $\mu = 80$ and standard deviation $\sigma = 14$.

   a. Calculate the expected value and the standard error for the sampling distribution of the sample mean.

   b. What is the probability that the sample mean falls between 77 and 85?

   c. What is the probability that the sample mean is greater than 84?

9. A random sample of size $n = 50$ is taken from a population with mean $\mu = -9.5$ and standard deviation $\sigma = 2$.

   a. Calculate the expected value and the standard error for the sampling distribution of the sample mean.

   b. What is the probability that the sample mean is less than −10?

   c. What is the probability that the sample mean falls between −10 and −9?

Applications

10. According to a survey, high school girls average 100 text messages daily. Assume that the population standard deviation is 20 text messages. Suppose a random sample of 50 high school girls is taken.

    a. What is the probability that the sample mean is more than 105?

    b. What is the probability that the sample mean is less than 95?

    c. What is the probability that the sample mean is between 95 and 105?

11. Beer bottles are filled so that they contain an average of 330 ml of beer in each bottle. Suppose that the amount of beer in a bottle is normally distributed with a standard deviation of 4 ml.

    a. What is the probability that a randomly selected bottle will have less than 325 ml of beer?

    b. What is the probability that a randomly selected 6-pack of beer will have a mean amount less than 325 ml?

    c. What is the probability that a randomly selected 12-pack of beer will have a mean amount less than 325 ml?

    d. Comment on the sample size and the corresponding probabilities.

12. Despite its nutritional value, seafood is only a tiny part of the American diet, with the average American eating just 16 pounds of seafood per year. Janice and Nina both work in the seafood industry and they decide to create their own random samples and document the average seafood diet in their sample. Let the standard deviation of the American seafood diet be 5 pounds.

    a. Janice samples 30 Americans and finds an average seafood consumption of 18 pounds. How likely is it to get an average of 18 pounds or more if she had a representative sample?

    b. Nina samples 90 Americans and finds an average seafood consumption of 17.5 pounds. How likely is it to get an average of 17.5 pounds or more if she had a representative sample?

    c. Which of the two women is likely to have used a more representative sample? Explain.

13. The weight of people in a small town in Missouri is known to be normally distributed with a mean of 180 pounds and a standard deviation of 28 pounds. On a raft that takes people across the river, a sign states, "Maximum capacity 3,200 pounds or 16 persons." What is the probability that a random sample of 16 persons will exceed the weight limit of 3,200 pounds?

14. The weight of turkeys is known to be normally distributed with a mean of 22 pounds and a standard deviation of 5 pounds.

    a. What is the expected value and the standard error of the sampling distribution of the sample mean based on a random draw of 16 turkeys. Is the sampling distribution of the sample mean normally distributed? Explain.

    b. Find the probability that the mean weight of 16 randomly selected turkeys is more than 25 pounds.

    c. Find the probability that the mean weight of 16 randomly selected turkeys is between 18 and 24 pounds.

15. A small hair salon in Denver, Colorado, averages about 30 customers on weekdays with a standard deviation of 6. It is safe to assume that the underlying distribution is normal. In an attempt to increase the number of weekday customers, the manager offers a $2 discount on 5 consecutive weekdays. She reports that her strategy has worked since the sample mean of customers during this 5 weekday period jumps to 35.

    a. How unusual would it be to get a sample average of 35 or more customers if the manager had not offered the discount?

    b. Do you feel confident that the manager's discount strategy has worked? Explain.

16. A health expert evaluates the sleeping patterns of adults. Each week she randomly selects 40 adults and calculates their average sleep time. Over many weeks, she finds that 5% of average sleep time is less than 6 hours and 5% of average sleep time is more than 6.4 hours. What are the mean and standard deviation (in hours) of sleep time for the population?

17. Forty families gathered for a fund-raising event. Suppose the individual contribution for each family is normally distributed with a mean and a standard deviation of \$115 and \$35, respectively. The organizers would call this event a success if the total contributions exceed \$5,000. What is the probability that this fund-raising event is a success?

18. A doctor is getting sued for malpractice by four of her former patients. It is believed that the amount that each patient will sue her for is normally distributed with a mean of \$800,000 and a standard deviation of \$250,000.
    a. What is the probability that a given patient sues the doctor for more than \$1,000,000?
    b. If the four patients sue the doctor independently, what is the probability that the total amount that they sue her for is over \$4,000,000?

19. Suppose that the miles-per-gallon (mpg) rating of passenger cars is normally distributed with a mean and a standard deviation of 33.8 mpg and 3.5 mpg, respectively.
    a. What is the probability that a randomly selected passenger car gets more than 35 mpg?
    b. What is the probability that the average mpg of four randomly selected passenger cars is more than 35 mpg?
    c. If four passenger cars are randomly selected, what is the probability that all of the passenger cars get more than 35 mpg?

20. Suppose that IQ scores are normally distributed with a mean of 100 and a standard deviation of 16.
    a. What is the probability that a randomly selected person will have an IQ score of less than 90?
    b. What is the probability that the average IQ score of four randomly selected people is less than 90?
    c. If four people are randomly selected, what is the probability that all of them have an IQ score of less than 90?

LO 7.5

Describe the sampling distribution of the sample proportion.

7.3 THE SAMPLING DISTRIBUTION OF THE SAMPLE PROPORTION

Our discussion thus far has focused on the population mean, but many business, socio-economic, and political matters are concerned with the population proportion. For instance, a banker is interested in the default probability of mortgage holders; a superintendent may note the proportion of students suffering from the flu when determining whether to keep school open; an incumbent seeking reelection cares about the proportion of constituents that will ultimately cast a vote for him/her. In all of these examples, the parameter of interest is the population proportion p. As in the case of the population mean, we almost always make inferences about the population proportion on the basis of sample data. Here, the relevant statistic (estimator) is the sample proportion, $\overline{P}$; a particular value (estimate) is denoted by $\overline{p}$. Since $\overline{P}$ is a random variable, we need to discuss its sampling distribution.

The Expected Value and the Standard Error of the Sample Proportion

We first introduced the population proportion p in Chapter 5, when we discussed the binomial distribution. It turns out that the sampling distribution of $\overline{P}$ is closely related to the binomial distribution. Recall that the binomial distribution describes the number of successes X in n trials of a Bernoulli process where p is the probability of success; thus, $\overline{P} = \frac{X}{n}$ is the number of successes X divided by the sample size n. We can derive the expected value and the variance of the sampling distribution of $\overline{P}$ as $E(\overline{P}) = p$ and $Var(\overline{P}) = \frac{p(1-p)}{n}$, respectively. (See Appendix 7.1 for the derivations.) Note that since $E(\overline{P}) = p$, it implies that $\overline{P}$ is an unbiased estimator of p.

Analogous to our discussion in the last section, we refer to the standard deviation of the sample proportion as the standard error of the sample proportion; that is, $se(\overline{P}) = \sqrt{\frac{p(1-p)}{n}}$.

THE EXPECTED VALUE AND THE STANDARD ERROR OF THE SAMPLE PROPORTION

The expected value of the sample proportion $\overline{P}$ is equal to the population proportion, or, $E(\overline{P}) = p$. In other words, the sample proportion is an unbiased estimator of the population proportion.

The standard deviation of the sample proportion $\overline{P}$ is referred to as the standard error of the sample proportion. It equals $se(\overline{P}) = \sqrt{\frac{p(1-p)}{n}}$.

EXAMPLE 7.5

A study found that 55% of British firms experienced a cyber-attack in the past year (*BBC*, April 23, 2019).

a. What are the expected value and the standard error of the sample proportion derived from a random sample of 100 firms?

b. What are the expected value and the standard error of the sample proportion derived from a random sample of 200 firms?

c. Comment on the value of the standard error as the sample size gets larger.

SOLUTION: Given that $p = 0.55$, we can derive the expected value and the standard error of $\overline{P}$ as follows.

a. With $n = 100$, $E(\overline{P}) = 0.55$ and $se(\overline{P}) = \sqrt{\frac{0.55(1-0.55)}{100}} = 0.0497$.

b. With $n = 200$, $E(\overline{P}) = 0.55$ and $se(\overline{P}) = \sqrt{\frac{0.55(1-0.55)}{200}} = 0.0352$.

c. As in the case of the sample mean, while the expected value of the sample proportion is unaffected by the sample size, the standard error of the sample proportion is reduced as the sample size increases.

In this text, we make statistical inferences about the population proportion only when the sampling distribution of $\overline{P}$ is approximately normal. From the discussion of the central limit theorem (CLT) in Section 7.2, we can conclude that $\overline{P}$ is approximately normally distributed when the sample size is sufficiently large.

THE CENTRAL LIMIT THEOREM FOR THE SAMPLE PROPORTION

For any population proportion p, the sampling distribution of $\overline{P}$ is approximately normal if the sample size n is sufficiently large. As a general guideline, the normal distribution approximation is justified when $np \geq 5$ and $n(1-p) \geq 5$.

If $\overline{P}$ is normally distributed, then any value $\overline{p}$ can be transformed into its corresponding value z given by $z = \frac{\overline{p}-p}{\sqrt{\frac{p(1-p)}{n}}}$.

According to the CLT, the sampling distribution of $\overline{P}$ approaches the normal distribution as the sample size increases. However, as the population proportion deviates from $p = 0.50$, we need a larger sample size for the approximation. We illustrate these results by generating the sampling distribution of $\overline{P}$ from repeated draws from a population with various values of the population proportion and sample sizes. As in the case of $\overline{X}$, we use the relative frequency polygon to represent the distribution of $\overline{P}$. The simulated sampling distribution of $\overline{P}$ is based on the population proportion $p = 0.10$ (Figure 7.5) and $p = 0.30$ (Figure 7.6).

FIGURE 7.5 Sampling distribution of $\overline{P}$ when the population proportion is $p = 0.10$

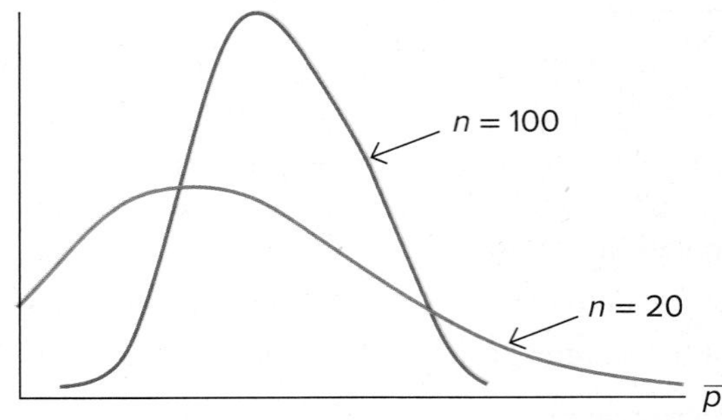

FIGURE 7.6 Sampling distribution of $\overline{P}$ when the population proportion is $p = 0.30$

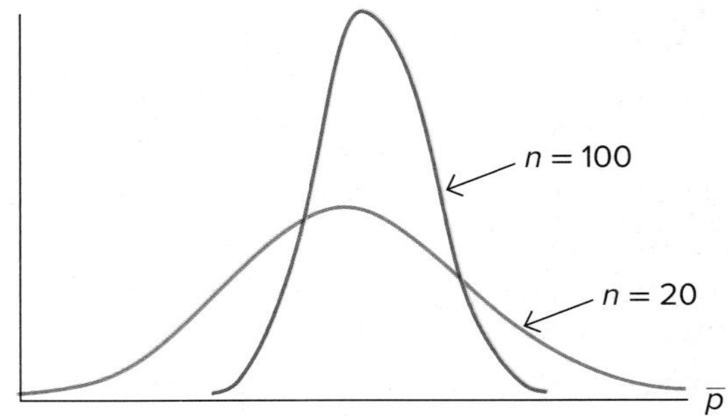

When $p = 0.10$, the sampling distribution of $\overline{P}$ does not resemble the bell shape of the normal distribution with $n = 20$ since the approximation condition $np \geq 5$ and $n(1 - p) \geq 5$ is not satisfied. However, the distribution becomes somewhat bell-shaped with $n = 100$. When $p = 0.30$, the shape of the sampling distribution of $\overline{P}$ is approximately normal because the approximation condition is satisfied with both sample sizes. In empirical work, it is common to work with large survey data, and, as a result, the normal distribution approximation is justified.

EXAMPLE 7.6

Consider the information presented in the introductory case of this chapter. Recall that Camila wants to determine if the Happy Hour promotion has had a lingering effect on the proportion of customers who are women and teenage girls. Prior to the Happy Hour promotion, 43% of the customers were women and 21% were teenage girls. Based on a random sample of 50 customers after the Happy Hour promotion, these proportions increase to 46% for women and 34% for teenage girls. Camila has the following questions.

a. If Camila chose not to pursue the Happy Hour promotion, how likely is it that 46% or more of iced-coffee customers are women?

b. If Camila chose not to pursue the Happy Hour promotion, how likely is it that 34% or more of iced-coffee customers are teenage girls?

SOLUTION: If Camila had not pursued the Happy Hour promotion, then the proportion of customers would still be $p = 0.43$ for women and $p = 0.21$ for teenage girls. With $n = 50$, the normal approximation for the sample proportion is justified for both population proportions.

a. As shown in Figure 7.7, we find that $P(\overline{P} \geq 0.46) = P\left(Z \geq \frac{0.46 - 0.43}{\sqrt{\frac{0.43(1 - 0.43)}{50}}}\right) =$ $P(Z \geq 0.4285) = 0.3341$.

FIGURE 7.7 Finding $P(\overline{P} \geq 0.46)$

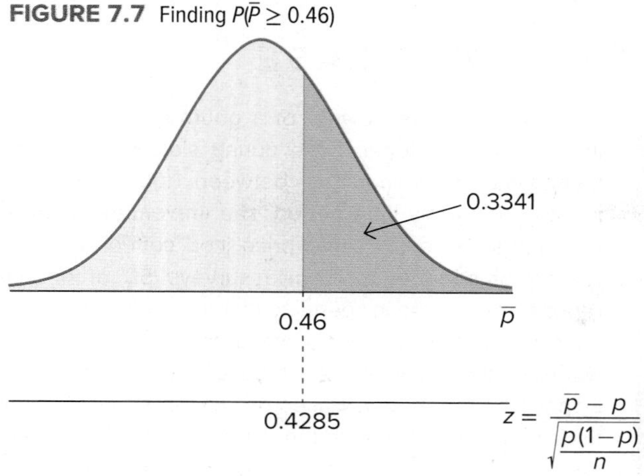

With a chance of 33.41%, it is quite plausible that the proportion of women who purchase iced coffee is at least 0.46 even if Camila did not pursue the Happy Hour promotion.

In order to find this probability in Excel, we enter `=1-NORM.DIST(0.46, 0.43, SQRT(0.43*(1-0.43)/50), TRUE)`; in R, we enter `pnorm(0.46, 0.43, sqrt(0.43*(1-0.43)/50), lower.tail=FALSE)`.

b. As shown in Figure 7.8, we find $P(\overline{P} \geq 0.34) = P\left(Z \geq \dfrac{0.34 - 0.21}{\sqrt{\frac{0.21(1-0.21)}{50}}}\right) = P(Z \geq 2.2569) = 0.0120.$

FIGURE 7.8 Finding $P(\overline{P} \geq 0.34)$

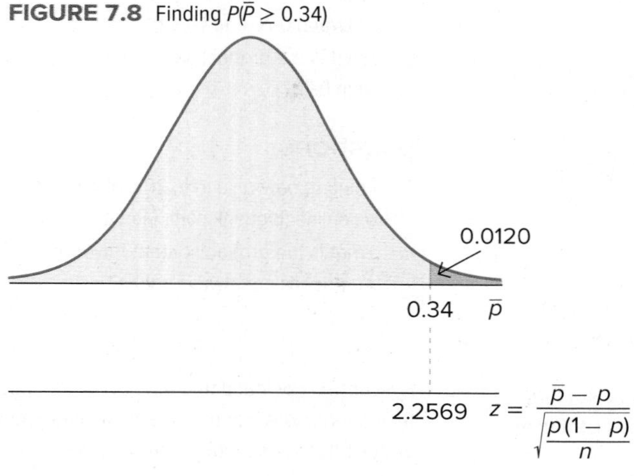

With only a 1.20% chance, it is unlikely that the proportion of teenage girls who purchase iced coffee is at least 0.34 if Camila did not pursue the Happy Hour promotion.

In order to find this probability in Excel, we enter `=1-NORM.DIST(0.34, 0.21, SQRT(0.21*(1-0.21)/50), TRUE)`; in R, we enter `pnorm(0.34, 0.21, sqrt(0.21*(1-0.21)/50), lower.tail=FALSE)`.

SYNOPSIS OF INTRODUCTORY CASE

M. Unal Ozmen/Shutterstock

Camila Fuentes, the owner of a gourmet coffee shop, would like to increase her customer base during slow times, which primarily are Mondays through Thursdays between 1:00 pm and 4:00 pm. For one month during this time period, she implements a Happy Hour when customers can enjoy a half-price iced coffee drink. After the Happy Hour promotion ends, Camila surveys 50 of her customers. She reports an increase in spending in the sample, as well as an increase in the proportion of customers who are women and teenage girls. Camila wants to determine if the increase is due to chance or due to the Happy Hour promotion. Based on an analysis with probabilities, Camila finds that higher spending in a sample of 50 customers is plausible even if she had not pursued the Happy Hour promotion. Using a similar analysis with proportions, she infers that while the Happy Hour promotion may not have necessarily increased the proportion of women customers, it seems to have attracted more teenage girls. The findings are consistent with current market research, which has shown that teenage girls have substantial income of their own to spend and often purchase items that are perceived as indulgences.

EXERCISES 7.3

Mechanics

21. Consider a population proportion $p = 0.68$.
    a. Calculate the expected value and the standard error of $\bar{P}$ with $n = 20$. Is it appropriate to use the normal distribution approximation for $\bar{P}$? Explain.
    b. Calculate the expected value and the standard error of $\bar{P}$ with $n = 50$. Is it appropriate to use the normal distribution approximation for $\bar{P}$? Explain.
22. Consider a population proportion $p = 0.12$.
    a. What is the expected value and the standard error for the sampling distribution of the sample proportion with $n = 20$ and $n = 50$?
    b. Can you conclude that the sampling distribution of the sample proportion is approximately normally distributed for both sample sizes? Explain.
    c. If the sampling distribution of the sample proportion is approximately normally distributed with $n = 20$, then calculate the probability that the sample proportion is between 0.10 and 0.12.
    d. If the sampling distribution of the sample proportion is approximately normally distributed with $n = 50$, then calculate the probability that the sample proportion is between 0.10 and 0.12.
23. A random sample of size $n = 200$ is taken from a population with a population proportion $p = 0.75$.
    a. Calculate the expected value and the standard error for the sampling distribution of the sample proportion.
    b. What is the probability that the sample proportion is between 0.70 and 0.80?
    c. What is the probability that the sample proportion is less than 0.70?

Applications

24. According to new research, 26% of Americans are (almost) always online (bigthink.com, March 20, 2018).
    a. What is the probability that fewer than 60 of 200 Americans are always online?
    b. What is the probability that more than 150 of 200 Americans are *not* always online?
25. A recent survey found that 82% of college graduates believe their degree was a good investment (cnbc.com, February 27, 2020). Suppose a random sample of 100 college graduates is taken.
    a. What is the expected value and the standard error for the sampling distribution of the sample proportion?
    b. What is the probability that the sample proportion is less than 0.80?
    c. What is the probability that the sample proportion is within $\pm$ 0.02 of the population proportion?
26. One-fifth of Britains are not using the internet (bbc.com, September 9, 2019).
    a. What is the expected value and the standard error for the sampling distribution of the sample proportion based on a sample of 200 Britains. Is it appropriate to use

the normal distribution approximation for the sample proportion? Explain.

b. What is the probability that more than 25% of Britains in the sample are not using the internet?

27. A car manufacturer is concerned about poor customer satisfaction at one of its dealerships. The management decides to evaluate the satisfaction surveys of its next 40 customers. The dealership will be fined if the number of customers who report favorably is between 22 and 26. The dealership will be dissolved if fewer than 22 customers report favorably. It is known that 70% of the dealership's customers report favorably on satisfaction surveys.
   a. What is the probability that the dealership will be fined?
   b. What is the probability that the dealership will be dissolved?

28. At an exhibit in the Museum of Science, people are asked to choose between 50 or 100 random draws from a machine. The machine is known to have 60 green balls and 40 red balls. After each draw, the color of the ball is noted and the ball is put back for the next draw. You win a prize if more than 70% of the draws result in a green ball. Would you choose 50 or 100 draws for the game? Explain.

29. Email takes up 23 percent of the average employee's workday (hbr.org, June 8, 2016).
   a. In a sample of 50 employees, what is the probability that email takes up more than 20% of their day?
   b. In a sample of 200 employees, what is the probability that email takes up more than 20% of their day?
   c. Comment on the reason for the difference between the computed probabilities in parts a and b.

7.4 THE FINITE POPULATION CORRECTION FACTOR

LO 7.6

Use a finite population correction factor.

One of the implicit assumptions we have made thus far is that the sample size n is much smaller than the population size N. In many applications, the size of the population is not even known. For instance, we do not have information on the total number of pizzas made at a local pizza chain in Cambria (Examples 7.2 and 7.3) or the total number of customers who frequent the local gourmet coffee shop (Examples 7.4 and 7.6). If the sample size is large relative to the population size, then the standard errors of the estimators must be multiplied by a correction factor. This correction factor, called the **finite population correction factor,** accounts for the added precision gained by sampling a larger percentage of the population. As a general guideline, we use the finite population correction factor $\sqrt{\frac{N-n}{N-1}}$ when the sample constitutes at least 5% of the population—that is, $n \geq 0.05N$.

THE FINITE POPULATION CORRECTION FACTOR FOR THE SAMPLE MEAN

When the sample size is large relative to the population size ($n \geq 0.05N$), the finite population correction factor is used to reduce the sampling variation of the sample mean $\overline{X}$. The resulting standard error of $\overline{X}$ is $se(\overline{X}) = \frac{\sigma}{\sqrt{n}}\sqrt{\frac{N-n}{N-1}}$. The transformation for any value $\bar{x}$ to its corresponding z value is made accordingly.

Note that the correction factor is always less than one; when N is large relative to n, the correction factor is close to one and the difference between the formulas with and without the correction is negligible.

EXAMPLE 7.7

A large introductory marketing class has 340 students. The class is divided up into groups for the final course project. Connie is in a group of 34 students. These students had averaged 72 on the midterm, when the class as a whole had an average score of 73 with a standard deviation of 10.

a. Calculate the expected value and the standard error of the sample mean based on a random sample of 34 students.

b. How likely is it that a random sample of 34 students will average 72 or lower?

SOLUTION: The population mean is $\mu = 73$ and the population standard deviation is $\sigma = 10$.

a. The expected value of the sample mean is $E(\overline{X}) = \mu = 73$. We use the finite population correction factor because the sample size $n = 34$ is more than 5% of the population size $N = 340$. Therefore, the standard error of the sample mean is $se(\overline{X}) = \frac{\sigma}{\sqrt{n}}\sqrt{\frac{N-n}{N-1}} = \frac{10}{\sqrt{34}}\sqrt{\frac{340-34}{340-1}} = 1.6294$. Note that without the correction factor, the standard error would be higher at $se(\overline{X}) = \frac{\sigma}{\sqrt{n}} = \frac{10}{\sqrt{34}} = 1.7150$.

b. We find $P(\overline{X} \le 72) = P\left(Z \le \frac{72-73}{1.6294}\right) = P(Z \le -0.6137) = 0.2697$. That is, the likelihood of 34 students averaging 72 or lower is 26.97%.

As discussed earlier, we can use Excel's NORM.DIST function or R's pnorm function to find this probability.

We use a similar finite population correction factor for the sample proportion when the sample size is at least 5% of the population size.

THE FINITE POPULATION CORRECTION FACTOR FOR THE SAMPLE PROPORTION

When the sample size is large relative to the population size ($n \ge 0.05\,N$), the finite population correction factor is used to reduce the sampling variation of the sample proportion $\overline{P}$. The resulting standard error of $\overline{P}$ is $se(\overline{P}) = \sqrt{\frac{p(1-p)}{n}}\sqrt{\frac{N-n}{N-1}}$. The transformation for any value $\overline{p}$ to its corresponding z value is made accordingly.

EXAMPLE 7.8

The home ownership rate in the United States is approximately 65% (fred.stlouisfed.org, March 28, 2020). A random sample of 80 households is taken from a small island community with 1,000 households. The home ownership rate on the island is equivalent to the national home ownership rate of 65%.

a. Calculate the expected value and the standard error for the sampling distribution of the sample proportion. Is it necessary to apply the finite population correction factor? Explain.

b. What is the probability that the sample proportion is within 0.02 of the population proportion?

SOLUTION:

a. We must apply the finite population correction factor because the sample size $n = 80$ is at least 5% of the population size $N = 1{,}000$. Therefore, $E(\overline{P}) = p = 0.65$ and

$$se(\overline{P}) = \sqrt{\frac{p(1-p)}{n}}\sqrt{\frac{N-n}{N-1}} = \sqrt{\frac{0.65(1-0.65)}{80}}\sqrt{\frac{1{,}000-80}{1{,}000-1}} = 0.0512$$

b. The probability that the sample proportion is within 0.02 of the population proportion is $P(0.63 \le \overline{P} \le 0.67)$. We find that $P(0.63 \le \overline{P} \le 0.67) = P\left(\frac{0.63-0.65}{0.0512} \le Z \le \frac{0.67-0.65}{0.0512}\right) = P(-0.3908 \le Z \le 0.3908) = 0.3041$. The likelihood that the home ownership rate is within 0.02 of the population proportion is 30.41%.

Again, we can use Excel's NORM.DIST function or R's pnorm function to find this probability.

EXERCISES 7.4

Mechanics

30. A random sample of size $n = 100$ is taken from a population of size $N = 2{,}500$ with mean $\mu = -45$ and variance $\sigma^2 = 81$.
    a. Is it necessary to apply the finite population correction factor? Explain. Calculate the expected value and the standard error of the sample mean.
    b. What is the probability that the sample mean is between -47 and -43?
    c. What is the probability that the sample mean is greater than -44?
31. A random sample of size $n = 70$ is taken from a finite population of size $N = 500$ with mean $\mu = 220$ and variance $\sigma^2 = 324$.
    a. Is it necessary to apply the finite population correction factor? Explain. Calculate the expected value and the standard error of the sample mean.
    b. What is the probability that the sample mean is less than 210?
    c. What is the probability that the sample mean lies between 215 and 230?
32. A random sample of size $n = 100$ is taken from a population of size $N = 3{,}000$ with a population proportion of $p = 0.34$.
    a. Is it necessary to apply the finite population correction factor? Explain. Calculate the expected value and the standard error of the sample proportion.
    b. What is the probability that the sample proportion is greater than 0.37?
33. A random sample of size $n = 80$ is taken from a population of size $N = 600$ with a population proportion $p = 0.46$.
    a. Is it necessary to apply the finite population correction factor? Explain. Calculate the expected value and the standard error of the sample proportion.
    b. What is the probability that the sample mean is less than 0.40?

Applications

34. Companies and institutions across industries understand that it is less expensive to prevent cyber attacks than it is to repair the damage if they happen. A researcher finds that two out of three large corporations earmark at least 5% of their IT budgets for cybersecurity. His survey was based on 1,000 large companies. What is the probability that more than 75 of 120 large companies will earmark at least 5% of their IT budgets for cybersecurity?
35. An analyst finds that the mean and the standard deviation of executive compensation for the 500 highest paid CEOs in publicly traded U.S. companies are $10.32 million and $9.78 million, respectively. A random sample of 32 CEO compensations is selected.
    a. Is it necessary to apply the finite population correction factor? Explain.
    b. Is the sampling distribution of the sample mean approximately normally distributed? Explain.
    c. Calculate the expected value and the standard error of the sample mean.
    d. What is the probability that the sample mean is more than $12 million?
36. Suppose in the previous question that a random sample of 12 CEO compensations is selected.
    a. Is it necessary to apply the finite population correction factor? Explain.
    b. Calculate the expected value and the standard error of the sample mean.
    c. Can you use the normal approximation to calculate the probability that the sample mean is more than $12 million? Explain.
37. It is expected that only 60% in a graduating class of 250 will find employment in the first round of a job search. You have 20 friends who have recently graduated.
    a. Discuss the sampling distribution of the sample proportion of your friends who will find employment in the first round of a job search.
    b. What is the probability that less than 50% of your friends will find employment in the first round of a job search?

7.5 STATISTICAL QUALITY CONTROL

LO 7.7

Construct and interpret control charts for numerical and categorical variables.

Now more than ever, a successful firm must focus on the quality of the products and services it offers. Global competition, technological advances, and consumer expectations are all factors contributing to the quest for quality. In order to ensure the production of high-quality goods and services, a successful firm implements some form of quality control. In this section, we give a brief overview of the field of **statistical quality control**.

Statistical quality control involves statistical techniques used to develop and maintain a firm's ability to produce high-quality goods and services.

In general, two approaches are used for statistical quality control. A firm uses **acceptance sampling** if it produces a product (or offers a service) and at the completion of the production process, the firm then inspects a portion of the products. If a particular product does not conform to certain specifications, then it is either discarded or repaired. There are several problems with this approach to quality control. First, it is costly to discard or repair a product. Second, the detection of all defective products is not guaranteed. Defective products may be delivered to customers, thus damaging the firm's reputation.

A preferred approach to quality control is the **detection approach**. A firm using the detection approach inspects the production process and determines at which point the production process does not conform to specifications. The goal is to determine whether the production process should be continued or adjusted before a large number of defects are produced. In this section, we focus on the detection approach to quality control.

In general, no two products or services are identical. In any production process, variation in the quality of the end product is inevitable. Two types of variation occur. **Chance variation** is caused by a number of randomly occurring events that are part of the production process. This type of variation is not generally considered to be under the control of the individual worker or machine. For example, suppose a machine fills one-gallon jugs of milk. It is unlikely that the filling weight of each jug is exactly 128 ounces. Very slight differences in the production process lead to minor differences in the weights of one jug to the next. Chance variation is expected and is not a source of alarm in the production process so long as its magnitude is tolerable and the end product meets acceptable specifications.

The other source of variation is referred to as **assignable variation**. This type of variation in the production process is caused by specific events or factors that can usually be identified and eliminated. Suppose in the milk example that the machine is "drifting" out of alignment. This causes the machine to overfill each jug—a costly expense for the firm. Similarly, it is bad for the firm in terms of its reputation if the machine begins to underfill each jug. The firm wants to identify and correct these types of variations in the production process.

Control Charts

Walter A. Shewhart, a researcher at Bell Telephone Laboratories during the 1920s, is often credited as being the first to apply statistics to improve the quality of output. He developed the **control chart**—a tool used to monitor the behavior of a production process.

THE CONTROL CHART

The most commonly used statistical tool in quality control is the control chart, which is a plot of the sample estimates of the production process over time. If the sample estimates fall in an expected range, then the production process is in control. If the sample estimates reveal an undesirable trend, then adjustment of the production process is likely necessary.

We can construct a number of different control charts where each differs by either the variable of interest and/or the type of data that are available. For a numerical variable, examples of control charts include

- The $\bar{x}$ **chart**, which monitors the *central tendency* of a production process, and
- The ***R*** **chart** and the ***s*** **chart**, which monitor the *variability* of a production process.

For a categorical variable, examples of control charts include

- The ***p*** **chart**, which monitors the *proportion* of defectives (or some other characteristic) in a production process, and
- The ***c*** **chart**, which monitors the *count* of defects per item, such as the number of blemishes on a sampled piece of furniture.

In general, all of these control charts (and others that we have not mentioned) have the following characteristics:

1. A control chart plots the sample estimates, such as $\bar{x}$ or $\bar{p}$. So as more and more samples are taken, the resulting control chart provides one type of safeguard when assessing if the production process is operating within predetermined guidelines.
2. All sample estimates are plotted with reference to a **centerline**. The centerline represents the variable's expected value when the production process is in control.
3. In addition to the centerline, all control charts include an **upper control limit (UCL)** and a **lower control limit (LCL)**. These limits indicate excessive deviation above or below the expected value of the variable of interest. A control chart is valid only if the sampling distribution of the relevant estimator is (approximately) normally distributed. Under this assumption, the control limits are generally set at three standard deviations from the centerline. The area under the normal curve that corresponds to ±3 standard deviations from the expected value is 0.9973. Thus, there is only a $1 - 0.9973 = 0.0027$ chance that the sample estimates will fall outside the limit boundaries. In general, we define the upper and lower control limits as follows:

$$\text{UCL: Expected Value} + (3 \times \text{Standard Error})$$

$$\text{LCL: Expected Value} - (3 \times \text{Standard Error})$$

If the sample estimates fall randomly within the upper and lower control limits, then the production process is deemed in control. Any sample estimate that falls above the upper control limit or below the lower control limit is considered evidence that the production process is out of control and should be adjusted. In addition, any type of patterns within the control limits may suggest possible problems with the process. One indication of a process that is potentially heading out of control is unusually long runs above or below the centerline. Another possible problem is any evidence of a trend within the control limits.

In the next example, we focus on a numerical variable and illustrate the $\bar{x}$ chart. We then turn to a categorical variable and construct the p chart.

EXAMPLE 7.9

A firm that produces one-gallon jugs of milk wants to ensure that the machine is operating properly. Every two hours, the company samples 25 jugs and calculates the following sample mean filling weights (in ounces):

$\bar{x}_1 = 128.7$	$\bar{x}_2 = 128.4$	$\bar{x}_3 = 128.0$	$\bar{x}_4 = 127.8$	$\bar{x}_5 = 127.5$	$\bar{x}_6 = 126.9$

Assume that when the machine is operating properly, $\mu = 128$ and $\sigma = 2$, and that filling weights follow the normal distribution. Can the firm conclude that the machine is operating properly? Should the firm have any concerns with respect to this machine?

SOLUTION: Here the firm is interested in monitoring the population mean. To answer these questions, we construct an $\bar{x}$ chart. As mentioned earlier, this chart relies on the normal distribution for the sampling distribution of the estimator $\bar{X}$. Recall that if we are sampling from a normal population, then $\bar{X}$ is normally distributed even for small sample sizes. In this example, we are told that filling weights follow the normal distribution, a common assumption in the literature on quality control.

For the $\bar{x}$ chart, the centerline is the mean when the process is in control. Here, we are given that $\mu = 128$. We then calculate the UCL as three standard deviations above the mean and the LCL as three standard deviations below the mean:

$$\text{UCL: } \mu + 3\frac{\sigma}{\sqrt{n}} = 128 + 3\frac{2}{\sqrt{25}} = 129.2$$

$$\text{LCL: } \mu - 3\frac{\sigma}{\sqrt{n}} = 128 - 3\frac{2}{\sqrt{25}} = 126.8$$

Figure 7.9 shows the centerline and the control limits as well as the sample means.

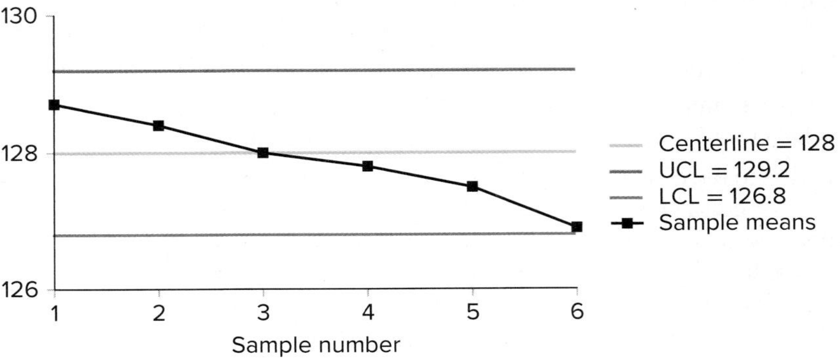

FIGURE 7.9 Mean chart for milk production process

All of the sample means fall within the UCL and the LCL, which indicates, at least initially, that the production process is in control. However, the sample means should be randomly spread between these limits; there should be no pattern. In this example, there is clearly a downward trend in the sample means. It appears as though the machine is beginning to underfill the one-gallon jugs. So even though none of the sample means lies beyond the control limits, the production process is likely veering out of control and the firm would be wise to inspect the machine sooner rather than later.

A firm may be interested in the stability of the proportion of its goods or services possessing a certain attribute or characteristic. For example, most firms strive to produce high-quality goods (or services) and thus hope to keep the proportion of defects at a minimum. When a production process is to be assessed based on sample proportions—here, the proportion of defects—then a p chart proves quite useful. Since the primary purpose of the p chart is to track the proportion of defects in a production process, it is also referred to as a fraction defective chart or a percent defective chart. Consider the next example.

EXAMPLE 7.10

A production process has a 5% defective rate. A quality inspector takes 6 samples of $n = 500$. The following sample proportions are obtained:

$\bar{p}_1 = 0.065$	$\bar{p}_2 = 0.075$	$\bar{p}_3 = 0.082$	$\bar{p}_4 = 0.086$	$\bar{p}_5 = 0.090$	$\bar{p}_6 = 0.092$

a. Construct a p chart. Plot the sample proportions on the p chart.

b. Is the production process in control? Explain.

SOLUTION:

a. The p chart relies on the central limit theorem for the normal approximation for the sampling distribution of the estimator $\bar{P}$. Recall that so long as np and $n(1 - p)$ are greater than or equal to five, then the sampling distribution of $\bar{P}$ is approximately normal. This condition is satisfied in this example. Given that the expected proportion of defects is equal to 0.05, we set the centerline at $p = 0.05$. We then calculate the UCL and the LCL as follows.

$$\text{UCL: } p + 3\sqrt{\frac{p(1-p)}{n}} = 0.05 + 3\sqrt{\frac{0.05(1-0.05)}{500}} = 0.079$$

$$\text{LCL: } p - 3\sqrt{\frac{p(1-p)}{n}} = 0.05 - 3\sqrt{\frac{0.05(1-0.05)}{500}} = 0.021$$

We note that if the UCL is a value greater than one, then we reset the UCL to one in the control chart. Similarly, if the LCL is a negative value, we reset the LCL to zero in the control chart.

Plotting the values for the centerline, the UCL, the LCL, as well as the sample proportions, yields Figure 7.10.

FIGURE 7.10 Proportion of defects

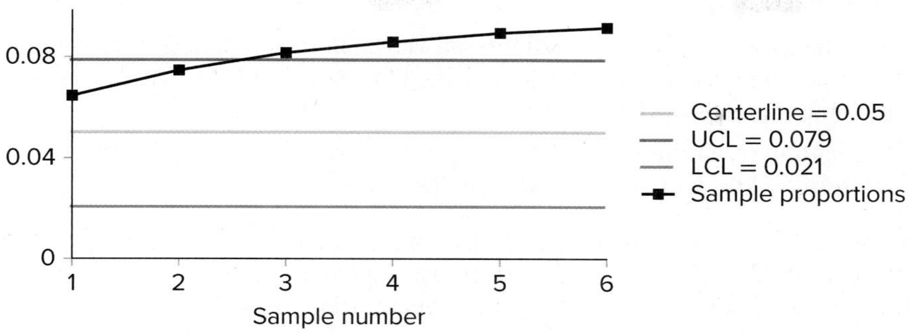

b. Four of the most recent sample proportions fall above the UCL. This provides evidence that the process is out of control and needs adjustment.

Using Excel and R to Create a Control Chart

Even though Excel does not have a built-in function to create a control chart, it is still relatively easy to construct one. If we are not given values for the centerline, the UCL, the LCL, and the sample means, then we first must provide these values in an Excel spreadsheet. Other software packages, including R, do these calculations for us. We will illustrate the construction of an $\bar{x}$ chart using Example 7.11.

EXAMPLE 7.11

JK Paints manufactures various kinds of paints in 4-liter cans. The cans are filled on an assembly line with an automatic valve regulating the amount of paint. To ensure that the correct amount of paint goes into each can, the quality control manager draws a random sample of four cans each hour and measures their amounts of paint. Since past experience has produced a standard deviation of $\sigma = 0.25$, the quality control manager has been able to calculate the LCL and the UCL as 3.625 $(= 4 - 3 \times 0.25/\sqrt{4})$ and 4.375 $(= 4 + 3 \times 0.25/\sqrt{4})$, respectively. Table 7.1 shows a portion of the results from the last 25 hours. The table also includes the sample mean of the four randomly selected cans, the LCL, the centerline, and the UCL. Create an $\bar{x}$ chart to determine whether the cans are being filled properly.

TABLE 7.1 Data for Example 7.11

FILE *Paint*

Sample	Obs. 1	Obs. 2	Obs. 3	Obs. 4	$\bar{x}$	LCL	Centerline	UCL
1	4.175	3.574	3.795	4.211	3.939	3.625	4	4.375
2	4.254	4.012	4.119	3.866	4.063	3.625	4	4.375
⋮	⋮	⋮	⋮	⋮	⋮	⋮	⋮	⋮
25	4.104	4.107	4.236	3.505	3.988	3.625	4	4.375

SOLUTION: As mentioned earlier, if only the first five columns of Table 7.1 were provided, we would have had to first populate the rest of the table by finding values for $\bar{x}$, LCL, Centerline, and UCL to make the $\bar{x}$ chart in Excel; R creates the $\bar{x}$ chart directly from the information given in columns 2 through 5.

Using Excel

a. Open the data file ***Paint***.

b. Simultaneously select the headings and values in the $\bar{x}$, LCL, Centerline, and UCL columns and choose **Insert > Line Chart > 2-D Line**. Then, choose the option on the top left.

c. Formatting (regarding axis titles, colors, etc.) can be done by selecting **Format > Add Chart Element** from the menu.

Figure 7.11 shows the control chart that Excel produces. All sample means fall within the UCL and the LCL, and they also fall randomly above and below the centerline. This indicates that the cans are being filled properly.

FIGURE 7.11 Using Excel to create a control chart

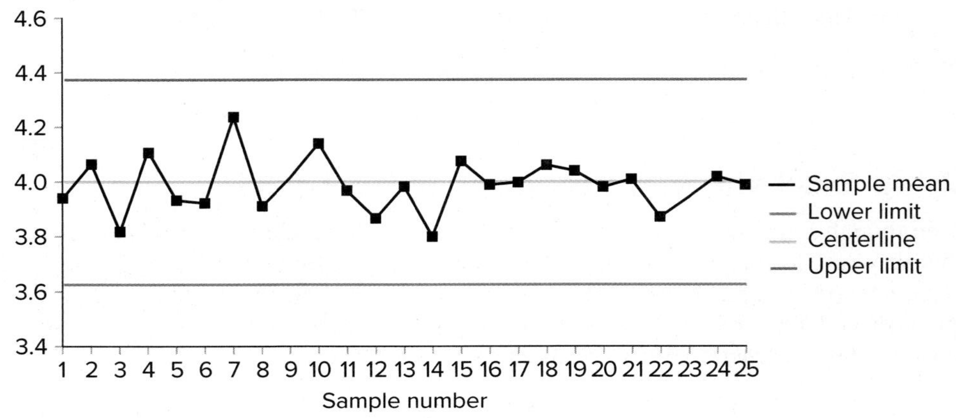

Using R

a. Import the ***Paint*** data file into a data frame (table) and label it myData.

b. Install and load the *qcc* package (where *qcc* stands for Quality Control Charts). Enter:

```
> install.packages("qcc")
> library(qcc)
```

c. We then create an $\bar{x}$ chart using the **qcc** function from the *qcc* package. Within the function, we first need to extract the data in columns 2 through 5 from the myData data frame. This is easily done with the use of square brackets. Then, for options, we use *type* to designate the type of control chart, *center* to denote the centerline, *std.dev.* to denote the standard deviation, *nsigmas* to denote the number of standard deviations from the centerline, and *title* to specify a main title for the chart. We enter:

```
> qcc(myData[, 2:5], type="xbar", center=4,
  std.dev.=0.25, nsigmas=3, title="Control Chart
  for Paint")
```

Figure 7.12 shows the control chart that R produces. We arrive at the same conclusion; that is, the cans are being filled properly.

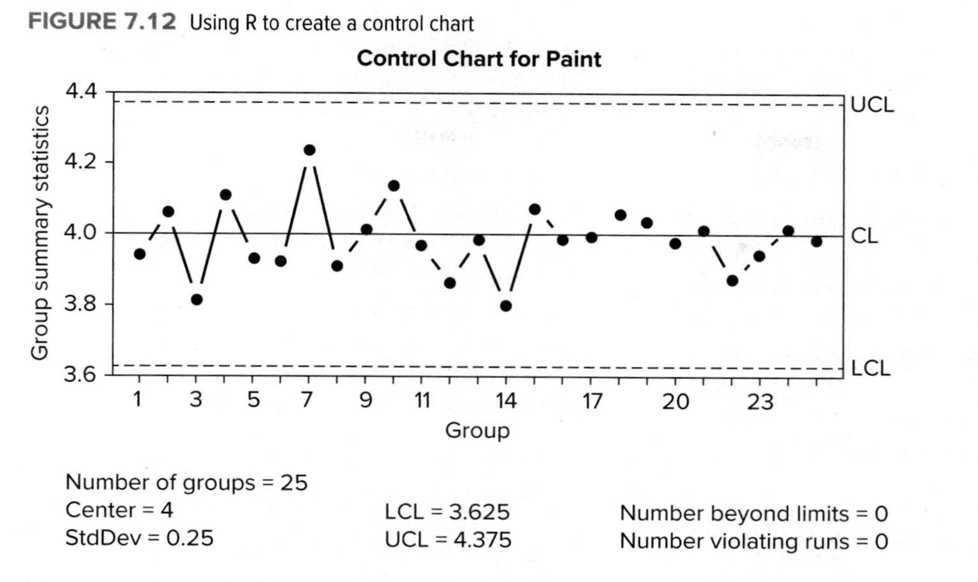

FIGURE 7.12 Using R to create a control chart

EXERCISES 7.5

Mechanics

38. Consider a normally distributed population with mean $\mu = 80$ and standard deviation $\sigma = 14$.
    a. Construct the centerline and the upper and lower control limits for the $\bar{x}$ chart if samples of size 5 are used.
    b. Repeat the analysis with samples of size 10.
    c. Discuss the effect of the sample size on the control limits.
39. Random samples of size $n = 250$ are taken from a population with $p = 0.04$.
    a. Construct the centerline and the upper and lower control limits for the p chart.
    b. Repeat the analysis with $n = 150$.
    c. Discuss the effect of the sample size on the control limits.
40. Random samples of size $n = 25$ are taken from a normally distributed population with mean $\mu = 20$ and standard deviation $\sigma = 10$.
    a. Construct the centerline and the upper and lower control limits for the $\bar{x}$ chart.
    b. Suppose six samples of size 25 produced the following sample means: 18, 16, 19, 24, 28, and 30. Plot these values on the $\bar{x}$ chart.
    c. Are any points outside the control limits? Does it appear that the process is under control? Explain.
41. Random samples of size $n = 36$ are taken from a population with mean $\mu = 150$ and standard deviation $\sigma = 42$.
    a. Construct the centerline and the upper and lower control limits for the $\bar{x}$ chart.
    b. Suppose five samples of size 36 produced the following sample means: 133, 142, 150, 165, and 169. Plot these values on the $\bar{x}$ chart.
    c. Are any points outside the control limits? Does it appear that the process is under control? Explain.
42. Random samples of size $n = 500$ are taken from a population with $p = 0.34$.
    a. Construct the centerline and the upper and lower control limits for the p chart.
    b. Suppose six samples of size 500 produced the following sample proportions: 0.28, 0.30, 0.33, 0.34, 0.37, and 0.39. Plot these values on the p chart.
    c. Are any points outside the control limits? Does it appear that the process is under control? Explain.
43. Random samples of size $n = 400$ are taken from a population with $p = 0.10$.
    a. Construct the centerline and the upper and lower control limits for the p chart.
    b. Suppose six samples of size 400 produced the following sample proportions: 0.06, 0.11, 0.09, 0.08, 0.14, and 0.16. Plot these values on the p chart.
    c. Is the production process under control? Explain.

Applications

44. Major League Baseball Rule 1.09 states that "the baseball shall weigh not less than 5 or more than 5¼ ounces" (www.mlb.com). Use these values as the lower and the upper

control limits, respectively. Assume the centerline equals 5.125 ounces. Periodic samples of 50 baseballs produce the following sample means:

$\bar{x}_1 = 5.05$	$\bar{x}_2 = 5.10$	$\bar{x}_3 = 5.15$	$\bar{x}_4 = 5.20$	$\bar{x}_5 = 5.22$	$\bar{x}_6 = 5.24$

a. Construct an $\bar{x}$ chart. Plot the sample means on the $\bar{x}$ chart.
b. Are any points outside the control limits? Does it appear that the process is under control? Explain.

45. A production process is designed to fill boxes with an average of 14 ounces of cereal. The population of filling weights is normally distributed with a standard deviation of 2 ounces. Inspectors take periodic samples of 10 boxes. The following sample means are obtained.

$\bar{x}_1 = 13.7$	$\bar{x}_2 = 14.2$	$\bar{x}_3 = 13.9$	$\bar{x}_4 = 14.1$	$\bar{x}_5 = 14.3$	$\bar{x}_6 = 13.9$

a. Construct an $\bar{x}$ chart. Plot the sample means on the $\bar{x}$ chart.
b. Can the firm conclude that the production process is operating properly? Explain.

46. FILE ***Cricket.*** Fast bowling, also known as pace bowling, is an important component of the bowling attack in the sport of cricket. The objective is to bowl at a high speed and make the ball turn in the air and off the ground so that it becomes difficult for the batsman to hit it cleanly. Kalwant Singh is a budding Indian cricketer in a special bowling camp. While his coach is happy with Kalwant's average bowling speed, he feels that Kalwant lacks consistency. He records his bowling speed on the next four overs, where each over consists of six balls. The accompanying table shows a portion of the results.

Sample	Obs. 1	Obs. 2	⋯	Obs. 6
Over 1	96.8	99.5	⋯	96.8
Over 2	99.2	100.2	⋯	98.8
Over 3	88.4	97.8	⋯	89.8
Over 4	98.4	91.4	⋯	85.9

It is fair to assume that Kalwant's bowling speed is normally distributed with a mean and a standard deviation of 94 miles per hour and 2.8 miles per hour, respectively.

a. Construct the centerline and the upper and lower control limits for the $\bar{x}$ chart. Plot the average speed of Kalwant's four overs on the $\bar{x}$ chart.
b. Is there any pattern in Kalwant's bowling that justifies his coach's concerns that he is not consistent in bowling? Explain.

47. A manufacturing process produces steel rods in batches of 1,000. The firm believes that the percent of defective items generated by this process is 5%.
a. Construct the centerline and the upper and lower control limits for the p chart.
b. An engineer inspects the next batch of 1,000 steel rods and finds that 6.2% are defective. Is the manufacturing process under control? Explain.

48. A firm produces computer chips. From past experience, the firm knows that 4% of the chips are defective. The firm collects a sample of the first 500 chips manufactured at 1:00 pm for the past two weeks. The following sample proportions are obtained:

$\bar{p}_1 = 0.044$	$\bar{p}_2 = 0.052$	$\bar{p}_3 = 0.060$	$\bar{p}_4 = 0.036$	$\bar{p}_5 = 0.028$
$\bar{p}_6 = 0.042$	$\bar{p}_7 = 0.034$	$\bar{p}_8 = 0.054$	$\bar{p}_9 = 0.048$	$\bar{p}_{10} = 0.025$

a. Construct a p chart. Plot the sample proportions on the p chart.
b. Can the firm conclude that the process is operating properly?

49. The admissions office at a local university usually admits 750 students and knows from previous experience that 25% of these students choose not to enroll at the university.
a. Construct the centerline and the upper and lower control limits for the p chart.
b. Assume that this year the university admits 750 students and 240 choose not to enroll at the university. Should the university be concerned? Explain.

50. Following customer complaints about the quality of service, a large U.S. corporation stopped routing customers to a technical support call center in Country X. Suppose the corporation's decision to direct customers to call centers outside of Country X was based on customer complaints in the last six months. The number of complaints per month for 80 randomly selected customers is shown in the accompanying table.

Month	Number of Complaints
1	20
2	12
3	24
4	14
5	25
6	22

a. Construct the centerline and the upper and lower control limits for the p chart if the corporation allows a 15% complaint rate.
b. Can you justify the corporation's decision to direct customers to call centers outside of Country X?

7.6 WRITING WITH DATA

In the Writing with Data sections in the next few chapters, we focus on case studies where the sample size is relatively small. Why is this the case? It turns out that if the sample size is sufficiently large, there is little difference in the estimates of $\overline{X}$ or the estimates of $\overline{P}$ generated by different random samples.

Recall that we use $se(\overline{X}) = \frac{\sigma}{\sqrt{n}}$ to gauge the variability in $\overline{X}$ and $se(\overline{P}) = \sqrt{\frac{p(1-p)}{n}}$ to gauge the variability in $\overline{P}$. In both cases, the variability depends on the size of the sample on which the value of the estimator is based. If the sample size is sufficiently large, then the variability virtually disappears, or, equivalently, $se(\overline{X})$ and $se(\overline{P})$ approach zero. Thus, with big data, it is not very meaningful to examine the sampling distribution of the sample mean or the sample proportion or construct quality control charts.

Case Study

Barbara Dwyer, the manager at Lux Hotel, makes every effort to ensure that customers attempting to make phone reservations wait an average of only 60 seconds to speak with a reservations specialist. She knows that this is likely to be the customer's first impression of the hotel and she wants the initial interaction to be a positive one. Since the hotel accepts phone reservations 24 hours a day, Barbara wonders if the quality of service is consistently maintained throughout the day. She takes six samples of $n = 4$ calls during each of four shifts over one 24-hour period and records the wait time of each call. A portion of the data, in seconds, is presented in Table 7.2.

Ryan McVay/Getty Images

Barbara assumes that wait times are normally distributed with a mean and standard deviation of 60 seconds and 30 seconds, respectively. She wants to use the sample information to construct a control chart for wait times. Using the control chart, she then wants to determine if the quality of service is consistently maintained throughout the day.

TABLE 7.2 Wait times for phone reservations

FILE
Lux_Hotel

Shift	Sample	Wait Time (in seconds)				Sample Mean, $\bar{x}$
Shift 1: 12:00 am–6:00 am	1	67	48	52	71	60
	2	57	68	60	66	63
	3	37	41	60	41	45
	4	83	59	49	66	64
	5	82	63	64	83	73
	6	87	53	66	69	69
⋮	⋮	⋮	⋮	⋮	⋮	⋮
Shift 4: 6:00 pm–12:00 am	19	6	11	8	9	9
	20	10	8	10	9	9
	21	11	7	14	7	10
	22	8	9	9	12	10
	23	9	12	9	14	11
	24	5	8	15	11	10

Sample Report—Customer Wait Time

When a potential customer phones Lux Hotel, it is imperative for the reservations specialist to set a tone that relays the high standard of service that the customer will receive if he/she chooses to stay at the Lux. For this reason, management at the Lux strives to minimize the time that elapses before a potential customer speaks with a reservations specialist; however, management also recognizes the need to use its resources wisely. If too many reservations specialists are on duty, then resources are wasted due to idle time. Yet, if too few reservations specialists are on duty, then the result might be unhappy customers, or worse.

In order to ensure customer satisfaction as well as an efficient use of resources, a study is conducted to determine whether a typical customer waits an average of 60 seconds to speak with a reservations specialist. Before data are collected, a control chart is constructed. The upper control limit (UCL) and the lower control limit (LCL) are set three standard deviations from the desired average of 60 seconds. Figure 7.13 shows the control chart where the centerline is at 60 seconds and the UCL and the LCL are at 105 seconds and 15 seconds, respectively. The reservation process is deemed under control if the sample means fall randomly within the control limits; otherwise, the process is out of control and adjustments should be made.

FIGURE 7.13 Sample mean wait times

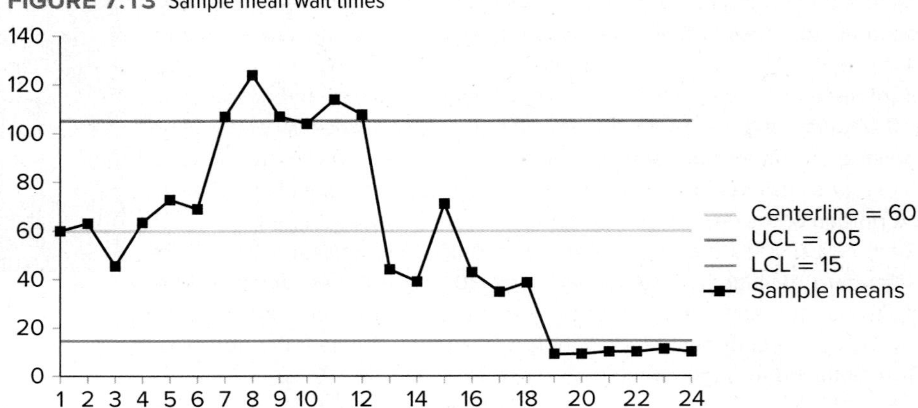

During each of four shifts, six samples of $n = 4$ calls are randomly selected over one 24-hour period and the average wait time of each sample is recorded. All six sample means from the first shift (12:00 am–6:00 am, sample numbers 1 through 6) fall within the control limits, indicating that the reservation process is in control. However, five sample means from the second shift (6:00 am–12:00 pm, sample numbers 7 through 12) lie above the UCL. Customers calling during the second shift are waiting too long before they speak with a specialist. In terms of quality standards, this is unacceptable from the hotel's perspective. All six sample means from the third shift (12:00 pm -6:00 pm, sample numbers 13 through 18) fall within the control limits, yet all sample means for the fourth shift (6:00 pm -12:00 am, sample numbers 19 through 24). fall below the LCL. Customers are waiting for very short periods of time to speak with a reservations specialist, but reservations specialists may have too much idle time. Perhaps one solution is to shift some reservations specialists from shift four to shift two.

Suggested Case Studies

Report 7.1 According to the Bureau of Economic Analysis, the savings rate of American households, defined as a percentage of the disposable personal income, was 7.90% in 2019. The reported savings rate is not uniform across the country. A public policy institute conducts two of its own surveys to compute the savings rate in the Midwest. In the first survey, a sample of 160 households is taken and the average savings rate is found to be 8.18%. Another sample of 40 households finds an average savings rate of 8.30%. Assume that the population standard deviation is 1.4%.

In a report, use this information to compute the probability of obtaining a sample mean that is at least as high as the one computed in each of the two surveys. Then use these probabilities to decide which of the two samples is likely to be more representative of the United States as a whole.

Report 7.2 In 2019, the Bureau of Labor Statistics reported that the jobless rate for college graduates under age 25 was four percent. For high school graduates under age 25 who did not enroll in college, the jobless rate was 9.1%. Cindy Chan works in the sales department of a trendy apparel company and has recently been relocated to a small town in Iowa. She finds that there are a total of 220 college graduates and 140 high school graduates under age 25 who live in this town. Cindy wants to gauge the demand for her products by the number of youths in this town who are employed.

In a report, use this information to compute the expected number of college and high school graduates who are employed. Then, report the probabilities that at least 200 college graduates and at least 100 high school graduates under age 25 are employed.

Report 7.3 FILE ***Hockey_Puck*** Hockey pucks used by the National Hockey League (NHL) and other professional leagues weigh an average of 163 grams (5.75 ounces). A quality inspector monitors the manufacturing process for hockey pucks. She takes eight samples of $n = 10$. It is believed that puck weights are normally distributed, and when the production process is in control, $\mu = 163$ and $\sigma = 7.5$.

In a report, use this information to construct a control chart for the weight of hockey pucks. Then, using the control chart, determine whether the manufacturing process is in control.

CONCEPTUAL REVIEW

LO 7.1 Explain common sample biases.

A sampling bias occurs when the information from a sample is not typical of that in the population in a systematic way. It is often caused by samples that are not representative of the population. Selection bias refers to a systematic underrepresentation of certain groups from consideration for the sample. Nonresponse bias refers to a systematic difference in preferences between respondents and nonrespondents to a survey or a poll. Social-desirability bias refers to a systematic difference between a group's "socially acceptable" responses to a survey or poll and this group's ultimate choice.

LO 7.2 Describe various sampling methods.

A simple random sample is a sample of n observations that has the same probability of being selected from the population as any other sample of n observations. Most statistical methods presume simple random samples.

A stratified random sample is formed when the population is divided into groups (strata) based on one or more classification criteria. A stratified random sample includes randomly selected observations from each stratum. The number of observations per stratum is proportional to the stratum's size in the population. The data for each stratum are eventually pooled.

A cluster sample is formed when the population is divided into groups (clusters) based on geographic areas. Whereas a stratified random sample consists of elements from each group, a cluster sample includes observations from randomly selected clusters. Stratified random sampling is preferred when the objective is to increase precision and cluster sampling is preferred when the objective is to reduce costs.

LO 7.3 Describe the sampling distribution of the sample mean.

The expected value of the sample mean $\overline{X}$ equals $E(\overline{X}) = \mu$ and the standard deviation, commonly referred to as the standard error of the sample mean, equals $se(\overline{X}) = \frac{\sigma}{\sqrt{n}}$. For any sample size, the sampling distribution of $\overline{X}$ is normal if the population is normally distributed. If $\overline{X}$ is normally distributed, then any value $\bar{x}$ can be transformed to its corresponding z value as $z = \frac{\bar{x} - \mu}{\sigma/\sqrt{n}}$.

LO 7.4 Explain the importance of the central limit theorem.

The central limit theorem (CLT) is used when the random sample is drawn from an unknown or a nonnormal population. It states that for any population X with expected value μ and standard deviation σ, the sampling distribution of $\overline{X}$ is approximately normally distributed if the sample size n is sufficiently large. As a general guideline, the normal distribution approximation is justified when $n \geq 30$.

LO 7.5 Describe the sampling distribution of the sample proportion.

The expected value of the sample proportion $\overline{P}$ equals $E(\overline{P}) = p$ and its standard error equals $se(\overline{P}) = \sqrt{\frac{p(1-p)}{n}}$. From the CLT, we can conclude that for any population proportion p, the sampling distribution of $\overline{P}$ is approximately normally distributed if the sample size n is sufficiently large. As a general guideline, the normal distribution approximation is justified when $np \geq 5$ and $n(1 - p) \geq 5$. If $\overline{P}$ is normally distributed, then any value $\bar{p}$ can be transformed to its corresponding z value as $z = \frac{\bar{p} - p}{\sqrt{\frac{p(1-p)}{n}}}$.

LO 7.6 Use a finite population correction factor.

If the sample size n is large relative to the population size N, then the standard error of the estimator must be multiplied by a correction factor. This correction factor, called the finite population correction factor, is used when the sample constitutes at least 5% of the population—that is, $n \geq 0.05N$. With the correction factor, $se(\overline{X}) = \frac{\sigma}{\sqrt{n}} \frac{N-n}{N-1}$ and $se(\overline{P}) = \sqrt{\frac{p(1-p)}{n}} \sqrt{\frac{N-n}{N-1}}$. The transformation to the corresponding z value is made accordingly.

LO 7.7 Construct and interpret control charts for numerical and categorical variables.

A control chart specifies a centerline as well as an upper control limit (UCL) and a lower control limit (LCL). In general, the UCL and the LCL are set within three standard deviations of the centerline. The UCL and the LCL for the $\bar{x}$ chart are defined as $\mu + 3\frac{\sigma}{\sqrt{n}}$ and $\mu - 3\frac{\sigma}{\sqrt{n}}$, respectively. For the p chart, these limits are defined as $p + 3\sqrt{\frac{p(1-p)}{n}}$ and $p - 3\sqrt{\frac{p(1-p)}{n}}$, respectively.

In general, if the sample estimates fall within the control limits, then the process is under control; otherwise it is out of control and adjustment is necessary. However, even if the sample estimates fall within the control limits, they must be randomly spread between the limits. If there is a trend or unusually long runs above or below the centerline, then the process may be veering out of control.

ADDITIONAL EXERCISES

51. Research has shown that physical exercise is effective at delaying the onset of deficiencies associated with an increase in brain age (magneticmemorymethod.com, November 12, 2019). For physical exercise, adults are often advised to follow a walking regimen, such as three vigorous 40-minute walks a week. As an assistant manager working for a public health institute based in Florida, you would like to estimate the proportion of adults in Miami who follow such a walking regimen. Discuss the sampling bias in the following strategies where people are asked if they walk regularly:
    a. Randomly selected adult beachgoers in Miami.
    b. Randomly selected Miami residents who are requested to disclose the information in prepaid envelopes.
    c. Randomly selected Miami residents who are requested to disclose the information on the firm's website.
    d. Randomly selected adult patients at all hospitals in Miami.
52. In the previous question regarding walking regimens of the residents of Miami, explain how you can obtain a representative sample based on the following sampling strategies:
    a. Simple random sampling.
    b. Stratified random sampling.
    c. Cluster sampling.
53. A quality control inspector periodically checks a production process. For each inspection, he selects a sample of 40 finished products and calculates the average weight. Over a long time period, he finds that five percent of the average weights are less than 9.7 pounds and five percent of the average weights are more than 10.3 pounds. What are the mean and the standard deviation (in pounds) for the population of products produced by this process?
54. The average speed of cars along Interstate 90 is 68 mph, with a standard deviation of 5 mph.
    a. What is the expected value and the standard error of the sampling distribution of the sample mean for a sample of 36 cars?
    b. Can you conclude that the sampling distribution of the sample mean is normally distributed? Explain.
    c. What is the probability that the average speed of this sample is less than 66 mph?
55. A pharmaceutical company knows that five percent of all users of a certain drug experience a serious side effect. A researcher examines a sample of 200 users of the drug.
    a. What is the probability of finding between 8 and 12 cases with side effects?
    b. What is the probability of finding more than 16 cases with side effects?
56. An automatic machine in a manufacturing process is operating properly if the length of an important subcomponent is normally distributed with a mean $\mu = 80$ cm and a standard deviation $\sigma = 2$ cm.
    a. Find the probability that the length of one randomly selected unit is less than 79 cm.
    b. Find the probability that the average length of 10 randomly selected units is less than 79 cm.
    c. Find the probability that the average length of 30 randomly selected units is less than 79 cm.
57. Trader Joe's is a privately held chain of specialty grocery stores in the United States. It has developed a reputation as a unique grocery store selling products such as gourmet foods, beer and wine, bread, nuts, cereal, and coffee. One of their best-selling nuts is a 16-ounce package of Raw California Almonds. Since it is impossible to pack exactly 16 ounces in each packet, a researcher has determined that the weight of almonds in each packet is normally distributed with a mean and a standard deviation equal to 16.01 ounces and 0.08 ounces, respectively.
    a. Discuss the sampling distribution of the sample mean based on any given sample size.
    b. Find the probability that a random sample of 20 bags of almonds will average less than 16 ounces.
    c. Suppose your cereal recipe calls for no less than 48 ounces of almonds. What is the probability that three packets of almonds will meet your requirement?
58. Georgia residents spend an average of $470.73 on the lottery, or one percent of their personal income (investopedia.com, June 25, 2019). Suppose the amount spent on the lottery follows a normal distribution with a standard deviation of $50.
    a. What is the probability that a randomly selected Georgian spent more than $500 on the lottery?
    b. If four Georgians are randomly selected, what is the probability that the average amount spent on the lottery was more than $500?

c. If four Georgians are randomly selected, what is the probability that all of them spent more than $500 on the lottery?

59. A small biotechnology firm has 250 employees. The average age of employees is 42 years with a standard deviation of 8.5 years. The human resources manager randomly selects 40 employees.
  a. What is the expected value and the standard error of the mean age from the sample? Is it necessary to use the finite correction factor? Explain.
  b. Is the sampling distribution of the sample mean approximately normally distributed? Explain.
  c. What is the probability that the sample mean is less than 40 years?

60. According to a report, scientists have identified a set of genetic variants that predicts extreme longevity with 77% accuracy (medicalnewstoday.com, Oct 22, 2018). Assume 150 patients decide to get their genomes sequenced.
  a. If the claim by scientists is accurate, what is the probability that more than 120 patients will get a correct diagnosis for extreme longevity?
  b. If the claim by scientists is accurate, what is the probability that fewer than 70% of the patients will get a correct diagnosis for extreme longevity?

61. American workers are increasingly planning to delay retirement (cnbc.com, Aug 25, 2019). A researcher finds that 35% of employed adults of age 62 and older say they have pushed back their retirement date.
  a. What is the probability that in a sample of 100 employed adults of age 62 and older, more than 40% have pushed back their retirement date?
  b. What is the probability that in a sample of 200 employed adults of age 62 and older, more than 40% have pushed back their retirement date?
  c. Comment on the difference between the two estimated probabilities.

62. **FILE** ***Packaging.*** A variety of packaging solutions exist for products that must be kept within a specific temperature range. Cold chain distribution is particularly useful in the food and pharmaceutical industries. A packaging company strives to maintain a constant temperature for its packages. It is believed that the temperature of its packages follows a normal distribution with a mean of 5 degrees Celsius and a standard deviation of 0.3 degree Celsius. Inspectors take weekly samples for 5 weeks of eight randomly selected boxes and report the temperatures in degrees Celsius. A portion of the data is given below.

Sample	Obs. 1	Obs. 2	⋯	Obs. 8
Week 1	3.98	4.99	⋯	4.95
Week 2	5.52	5.52	⋯	4.95
⋮	⋮	⋮	⋮	⋮
Week 5	5.14	6.25	⋯	4.28

  a. Construct an $\bar{x}$ chart for temperature. Plot the five weekly sample means on the $\bar{x}$ chart.
  b. Are any points outside the control limits? Does it appear that the process is in control? Explain.

63. The producer of a particular brand of soup claims that its sodium content is 50% less than that of its competitor. The food label states that the sodium content measures 410 milligrams per serving. Assume the population of sodium content is normally distributed with a standard deviation of 25 milligrams. Inspectors take periodic samples of 25 cans and measure the sodium content. The following sample means are obtained.

$\bar{x}_1 = 405$	$\bar{x}_2 = 412$	$\bar{x}_3 = 399$
$\bar{x}_4 = 420$	$\bar{x}_5 = 430$	$\bar{x}_6 = 428$

  a. Construct an $\bar{x}$ chart for sodium content. Plot the sample means on the $\bar{x}$ chart.
  b. Can the inspectors conclude that the producer is advertising the sodium content accurately? Explain.

64. Acceptance sampling is an important quality control technique, where a batch of data is tested to determine if the proportion of units having a particular attribute exceeds a given percentage. Suppose that 10% of produced items are known to be nonconforming. Every week a batch of items is evaluated and the production machines are adjusted if the proportion of nonconforming items exceeds 15%.
  a. What is the probability that the production machines will be adjusted if the batch consists of 50 items?
  b. What is the probability that the production machines will be adjusted if the batch consists of 100 items?

65. In the previous question, suppose that the management decides to use a p chart for the analysis. As noted earlier, 10% of produced items are known to be nonconforming. The firm analyzes a batch of production items for 6 weeks and computes the following percentages of nonconforming items.

Week	Nonconforming Percentage
1	5.5
2	13.1
3	16.8
4	13.6
5	19.8
6	2.0

a. Suppose weekly batches consisted of 50 items. Construct a p chart for the proportion of nonconforming items, and determine if the machine needs adjustment in any of the weeks.

b. Suppose weekly batches consisted of 100 items. Construct a p chart for the proportion of nonconforming items, and determine if the machine needs adjustment in any of the weeks.

APPENDIX 7.1 Derivation of the Mean and the Variance for $\overline{X}$ and $\overline{P}$

Sample Mean, $\overline{X}$

Let the expected value and the variance of the population X be denoted by $E(X) = \mu$ and $Var(X) = \sigma^2$, respectively. The sample mean $\overline{X}$ based on a random draw of n observations, $X_1, X_2, \ldots, X_n$, from the population is computed as $\overline{X} = \frac{X_1 + X_2 + \ldots + X_n}{n}$.

We use the properties of the sum of random variables to derive

$$E(\overline{X}) = E\left(\frac{X_1 + X_2 + \cdots + X_n}{n}\right) = \frac{E(X_1) + E(X_2) + \cdots + E(X_n)}{n}$$

$$= \frac{\mu + \mu + \cdots + \mu}{n} = \frac{n\mu}{n} = \mu.$$

Since the sample mean is based on n independent draws from the population, the covariance terms drop out and the variance of the sample mean is thus derived as

$$Var(\overline{X}) = Var\left(\frac{X_1 + X_2 + \cdots + X_n}{n}\right) = \frac{1}{n^2} Var(X_1 + X_2 + \cdots + X_n)$$

$$= \frac{1}{n^2}(Var(X_1) + Var(X_2) + \cdots + Var(X_n))$$

$$= \frac{\sigma^2 + \sigma^2 + \cdots + \sigma^2}{n^2} = \frac{n\sigma^2}{n^2} = \frac{\sigma^2}{n}.$$

Sample Proportion, $\overline{P}$

Let X be a binomial random variable representing the number of successes in n trials. Recall from Chapter 5 that $E(X) = np$ and $Var(X) = np(1 - p)$ where p is the probability of success. For the sample proportion $\overline{P} = \frac{X}{n}$,

$$E(\overline{P}) = E\left(\frac{X}{n}\right) = \frac{E(X)}{n} = \frac{np}{n} = p, \text{ and}$$

$$Var(\overline{P}) = Var\left(\frac{X}{n}\right) = \frac{Var(X)}{n^2} = \frac{np(1-p)}{n^2} = \frac{p(1-p)}{n}.$$

APPENDIX 7.2 Properties of Point Estimators

We generally discuss the performance of an estimator in terms of its statistical properties. Some of the desirable properties of a point estimator include unbiasedness, consistency, and efficiency. An estimator is **unbiased** if, based on repeated sampling from the population, the average value of the estimator equals the population parameter. In other words, for an unbiased estimator, the expected value of the point estimator equals the population parameter.

Figure A7.1 shows the sampling distributions for two estimators U_1 and U_2, which are assumed to be normally distributed. Let θ (the Greek letter read as theta) be the true parameter value of the population. Estimator U_1 is unbiased because its expected value $E(U_1)$ equals θ. Estimator U_2 is biased because $E(U_2) \neq \theta$; the degree of bias is given by the difference between $E(U_2)$ and θ.

FIGURE A7.1 The distributions of unbiased (U_1) and biased (U_2) estimators

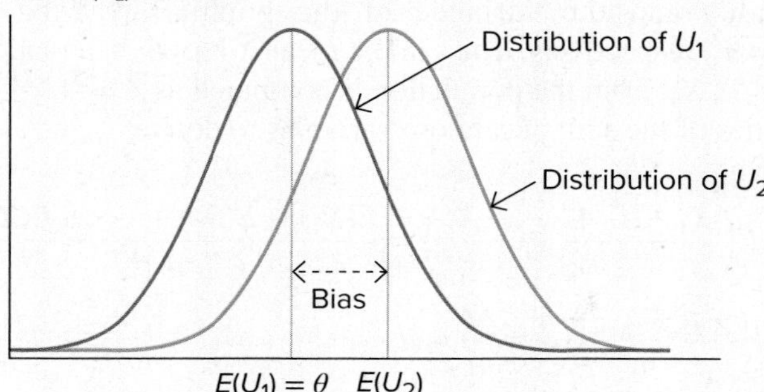

Since $E(\bar{X}) = \mu$ and $E(\bar{P}) = p$, $\bar{X}$ and $\bar{P}$ are the unbiased estimators of μ and p, respectively. This property is independent of the sample size.

We often compare the performance of the unbiased estimators in terms of their relative **efficiency**. An estimator is deemed efficient if its variability between samples is smaller than that of other unbiased estimators. Recall that the variability is often measured by the standard error of the estimator. For an unbiased estimator to be efficient, its standard error must be lower than that of other unbiased estimators. It is well documented that the estimators $\bar{X}$ and $\bar{P}$ are not only unbiased, but also efficient.

Figure A7.2 shows the sampling distributions for two unbiased estimators, V_1 and V_2, for the true population parameter θ. Again, for illustration, V_1 and V_2 follow the normal distribution. While both V_1 and V_2 are unbiased ($E(V_1) = E(V_2) = \theta$), V_1 is more efficient because it has less variability.

FIGURE A7.2 The distributions of efficient (V_1) and less efficient (V_2) estimators

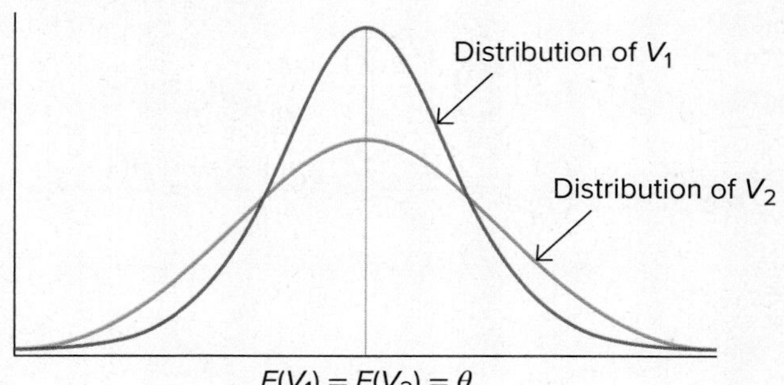

Another desirable property, which is often considered a minimum requirement for an estimator, is **consistency**. An estimator is consistent if it approaches the population parameter of interest as the sample size increases. Consistency implies that we will get the inference right if we take a large enough sample. The estimators $\bar{X}$ and $\bar{P}$ are not only unbiased, but also consistent. For instance, the sample mean collapses to the population mean ($\bar{X} \to \mu$) as the sample size approaches infinity ($n \to \infty$). An unbiased estimator is consistent if its standard error collapses to zero as the sample size increases.

The consistency of $\bar{X}$ is illustrated in Figure A7.3.

FIGURE A7.3 The distribution of a consistent estimator $\bar{X}$ for various sample sizes

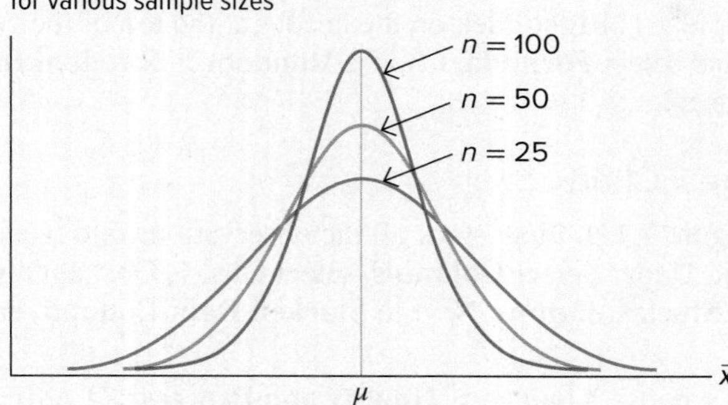

As the sample size n increases, the variability of $\bar{X}$ decreases. In particular as $n \to \infty$, $se(\bar{X}) = \sigma/\sqrt{n} \to 0$, thus implying that $\bar{X}$ is a consistent estimator of μ.

APPENDIX 7.3 Guidelines for Other Software Packages

The following section provides brief commands for Minitab, SPSS, and JMP. Where appropriate, import the specified data file into the relevant software spreadsheet prior to following the commands.

Minitab

Generating a Random Sample

(Replicating Example 7.1) From the menu, choose **Calc > Random Data > Integer.** Enter 100 as the **Number of rows of data to generate;** enter C1 for **Store in column;** enter 1 for **Minimum value** and 2,750 as **Maximum value.**

Constructing an $\bar{x}$ Chart

Paint

A. (Replicating Figure 7.11). First, stack all the observations into one column. Choose **Data > Stack > Rows.** Select Obs. 1, Obs. 2, Obs. 3, and Obs. 4. Next to **Store stacked data in,** enter Observations.

B. From the menu, choose **Stat > Control Charts > Variables Charts for Subgroups > Xbar.** Choose **All observations for a chart are in one column,** and in the box directly under this one, select Observations. For **Subgroup sizes,** enter 4. Choose **Xbar Options** and enter 4 for **Mean** and 0.25 for **Standard deviation.**

SPSS

Constructing an $\bar{x}$ Chart

A. (Replicating Figure 7.11). Reconfigure data so that all observations are in one column. From the menu, choose, **Data > Restructure > Restructure selected variables into cases**, and then follow the prompts.

B. From the menu, select **Analyze > Quality Control > Control Charts > X-bar, R, s.** Under **Process Measurement,** select trans 1, and under **Subgroups Defined by** select id. Under **Charts,** select **X-bar using standard deviation.** Choose **Options.** After **Number of Sigmas,** enter 3, and after **Minimum subgroup size,** enter 4. Choose **Statistics.** Under **Specification Limits,** enter 4.375 for **Upper,** 3.625 for **Lower,** and 4 for **Target.**

JMP

Generating a Random Sample

(Replicating Example 7.1) Right-click on the header at the top of the column in the spreadsheet view and select **Formula.** Choose **Random > Random Integer.** Enter 1 for **n1** and 2,750 for **n2.**

Constructing the $\bar{x}$ Chart

Paint

A. (Replicating Figure 7.11). First, stack all the observations into one column. Choose **Tables > Stack.** Under **Select Columns,** select Obs. 1, Obs. 2, Obs. 3, and Obs. 4, and then select **Stack Columns.** Next to **Stacked Data Column,** enter Observations. Select **OK.**

B. From the menu, choose **Analyze > Quality and Process > Control Chart > X-bar**. Drag Sample to **Subgroup** (horizontal axis) and drag Observations to **Y.**

8 Interval Estimation

LEARNING OBJECTIVES

After reading this chapter you should be able to:

LO **8.1** **Explain a confidence interval.**

LO **8.2** **Calculate a confidence interval for the population mean when the population standard deviation is known.**

LO **8.3** **Describe the factors that influence the width of a confidence interval.**

LO **8.4** **Discuss features of the *t* distribution.**

LO **8.5** **Calculate a confidence interval for the population mean when the population standard deviation is not known.**

LO **8.6** **Calculate a confidence interval for the population proportion.**

LO **8.7** **Select a sample size to estimate the population mean and the population proportion.**

In earlier chapters, we made a distinction between a population parameter, such as the population mean, and its corresponding sample statistic which is the sample mean. A sample statistic is used to make statistical inferences regarding the unknown value of the population parameter. In general, two basic methodologies emerge from the inferential branch of statistics: estimation and hypothesis testing. In this chapter, we focus on estimation which is approximating the value of an unknown population parameter. In the next chapter we will discuss hypothesis testing.

We learned in Chapter 7 that one way to estimate an unknown population parameter is to use a point estimator. A point estimator produces a single value as an estimate for the parameter. A confidence interval, on the other hand, produces a range of values as an estimate for the parameter. In this chapter, we develop and interpret confidence intervals for the population mean and the population proportion. Since obtaining a sample is one of the first steps in making statistical inferences, we also learn how an appropriate sample size is determined in order to achieve a certain level of precision in the estimates.

1000 Words/Shutterstock

INTRODUCTORY CASE

Efficiency of "Ultra-Green" Cars

A car manufacturer advertises that its new "ultra-green" car obtains an average of 100 miles per gallon (mpg) and, based on its fuel emissions, is one of the few cars that earns an A+ rating from the Environmental Protection Agency. Jared Beane, an analyst at Pinnacle Research, records the mpg for a sample of 25 "ultra-green" cars after the cars were driven equal distances under identical conditions. Table 8.1 shows a portion of the data.

TABLE 8.1 MPG for a Sample of 25 "Ultra-Green" Cars

FILE *MPG*

MPG
97
117
⋮
98

Jared would like to make statistical inferences regarding key population parameters. In particular, he wants to use the sample information to

1. Estimate the mean mpg of all ultra-green cars with 90% confidence.
2. Estimate the proportion of all ultra-green cars that obtain over 100 mpg with 90% confidence.
3. Determine the sample size that will enable him to achieve a specified level of precision in his mean and proportion estimates.

A synopsis of this case is provided at the end of Section 8.4.

LO 8.1

8.1 CONFIDENCE INTERVAL FOR THE POPULATION MEAN WHEN σ IS KNOWN

Explain a confidence interval.

Recall that a population consists of all items of interest in a statistical problem, whereas a sample is a subset of the population. Given sample data, we use the sample statistics to make inferences about the unknown population parameters, such as the population mean and the population proportion. Two basic methodologies emerge from the inferential branch of statistics: estimation and hypothesis testing. Although the sample statistics are based on a portion of the population, they contain useful information to estimate the population parameters and to conduct tests regarding the population parameters. In this chapter, we focus on estimation.

As discussed in Chapter 7, when a statistic is used to estimate a parameter, it is referred to as a point estimator, or simply an estimator. A particular value of the estimator is called a point estimate or an estimate. Recall that the sample mean $\overline{X}$ is the estimator of the population mean μ, and the sample proportion $\overline{P}$ is the estimator of the population proportion p.

Let us consider the introductory case where Jared Beane records the mpg for a sample of 25 ultra-green cars. We use the sample information in the ***MPG*** data file to compute the mean mpg of the cars as $\bar{x} = 96.52$ mpg. Similarly, since Jared is also interested in the proportion of these cars that get an mpg greater than 100, and seven of the cars in the sample satisfied this criterion, we compute the relevant sample proportion as $\bar{p} = 7/25 = 0.28$. Therefore, our estimate for the mean mpg of all ultra-green cars is 96.52 mpg, and our estimate for the proportion of all ultra-green cars with mpg greater than 100 is 0.28.

It is important to note that the above estimates are based on a sample of 25 cars and, therefore, are likely to vary between samples. For instance, the values will change if another sample of 25 cars is used. What Jared really wishes to estimate are the mean and the proportion (parameters) of all ultra-green cars (population), not just those comprising the sample. We now examine how we can extract useful information from a single sample to make inferences about these population parameters.

So far we have only discussed point estimators. Often it is more informative to provide a range of values—an interval—rather than a single point estimate for the unknown population parameter. This range of values is called a **confidence interval**, also referred to as an **interval estimate**, for the population parameter.

> CONFIDENCE INTERVAL
>
> A confidence interval, or interval estimate, provides a range of values that, with a certain level of confidence, contains the population parameter of interest.

In order to construct a confidence interval for the population mean μ or the population proportion p, it is essential that the sampling distributions of $\overline{X}$ and $\overline{P}$ follow, or approximately follow, a normal distribution. Other methods that do not require the normality condition are not discussed in this text. Recall from Chapter 7 that $\overline{X}$ follows a normal distribution when the underlying population is normally distributed; this result holds irrespective of the sample size n. If the underlying population is not normally distributed, then by the central limit theorem, the sampling distribution of $\overline{X}$ will be approximately normally distributed if the sample size is sufficiently large—that is, when $n \geq 30$. Similarly, the sampling distribution of $\overline{P}$ is approximately normally distributed if the sample size is sufficiently large—that is, when $np \geq 5$ and $n(1 - p) \geq 5$.

The main ingredient for developing a confidence interval is the sampling distribution of the underlying statistic. The sampling distribution of $\overline{X}$, for example, describes how the sample mean varies between samples. Recall that the variability between samples is measured by the standard error of $\overline{X}$. If the standard error is small, it implies that the sample means are not only close to one another, they are also close to the unknown population mean μ.

A confidence interval is generally associated with a **margin of error** that accounts for the standard error of the estimator and the desired confidence level of the interval. As we have just stressed, the sampling distributions of the estimators for the population mean and the population proportion must be approximately normally distributed. The symmetry implied by the normal distribution allows us to construct a confidence interval by adding and subtracting the same margin of error to the point estimate.

GENERAL FORMAT OF THE CONFIDENCE INTERVAL FOR μ AND p

The confidence interval for the population mean and the population proportion is constructed as

Point Estimate ± Margin of Error.

An analogy to a simple weather example is instructive. If you feel that the outside temperature is about 50 degrees, then perhaps you can, with a certain level of confidence, suggest that the actual temperature is between 40 and 60 degrees. In this example, 50 degrees is analogous to the point estimate of the actual temperature, and 10 degrees is the margin of error that is added to and subtracted from this point estimate.

We know from the introductory case study that the point estimate for the population mean mpg of all ultra-green cars is 96.52 mpg; that is, $\bar{x} = 96.52$. We can construct a confidence interval by using the point estimate as a base to which we add and subtract the margin of error.

Constructing a Confidence Interval for μ When σ Is Known

LO 8.2

Calculate a confidence interval for the population mean when the population standard deviation is known.

Let us construct the 95% confidence interval for μ when the sampling distribution of $\bar{X}$ is normally distributed. Consider the standard normal random variable Z. Using the symmetry of Z, we can compute $P(Z > 1.96) = P(Z < -1.96) = 0.025$; see Figure 8.1. Remember that $z = 1.96$ is easily determined from the z table given the probability of 0.025 in the upper tail of the distribution. Therefore, we formulate the probability statement $P(-1.96 \leq Z \leq 1.96) = 0.95$.

FIGURE 8.1 Graphical depiction of $P(Z < -1.96) = 0.025$ and $P(Z > 1.96) = 0.025$

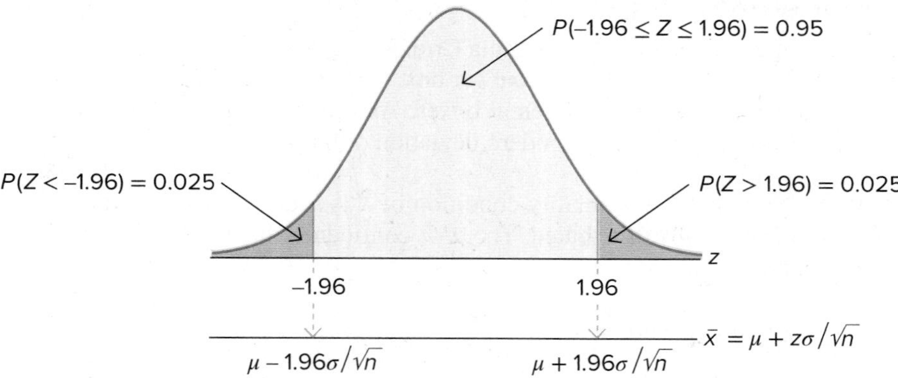

Because $Z = \frac{\bar{X} - \mu}{\sigma/\sqrt{n}}$, for a normally distributed $\bar{X}$ with mean μ and standard error $\sigma/\sqrt{n}$, we get

$$P\left(-1.96 \leq \frac{\bar{X} - \mu}{\sigma/\sqrt{n}} \leq 1.96\right) = 0.95.$$

We isolate $\bar{X}$ within the probability statement to obtain

$$P(\mu - 1.96\sigma/\sqrt{n} \leq \bar{X} \leq \mu + 1.96\sigma/\sqrt{n}) = 0.95.$$

This equation (see also the lower portion of Figure 8.1) implies that there is a 0.95 probability that the sample mean $\bar{X}$ will fall between $\mu - 1.96\sigma/\sqrt{n}$ and $\mu + 1.96\sigma/\sqrt{n}$, that is, within the interval $\mu \pm 1.96\sigma/\sqrt{n}$. If samples of size n are drawn repeatedly from a given population, 95% of the computed sample means, $\bar{x}$'s, will fall within the interval and the remaining 5% will fall outside the interval.

We do not know the population mean μ and, therefore, cannot determine if a particular $\bar{x}$ falls within the interval or not. However, we do know that $\bar{x}$ will fall within the interval $\mu \pm 1.96\sigma/\sqrt{n}$ if, and only if, μ falls within the interval $\bar{x} \pm 1.96\sigma/\sqrt{n}$. This will happen 95% of the time given how the interval is constructed. Therefore, we call the interval $\bar{x} \pm 1.96\sigma/\sqrt{n}$ the 95% confidence interval for the population mean, where $1.96\sigma/\sqrt{n}$ is its margin of error.

Confidence intervals are often misinterpreted; we need to exercise care in characterizing them. For instance, the above 95% confidence interval does *not* imply that the probability that μ falls in the confidence interval is 0.95. Remember that μ is a constant, although its value is not known. It either falls in the interval (probability equals one) or does not fall in the interval (probability equals zero). The randomness comes from $\bar{X}$, not μ, since many possible sample means can be derived from a population. Therefore, it is incorrect to say that the probability that μ falls in the $\bar{x} \pm 1.96\sigma/\sqrt{n}$ interval is 0.95. The 95% confidence interval simply implies that if numerous samples of size n are drawn from a given population, then 95% of the intervals formed by the preceding procedure (formula) will contain μ. Keep in mind that we only use a single sample to derive the estimates. Since there are many possible samples, we will be right 95% of the time, thus giving us 95% confidence.

INTERPRETING THE 95% CONFIDENCE INTERVAL

Technically, the 95% confidence interval for the population mean μ implies that for 95% of the samples, the procedure (formula) produces an interval that contains μ. Informally, we can report with 95% confidence that μ lies in the given interval. It is not correct to say that there is a 95% chance that μ lies in the given interval.

EXAMPLE 8.1

A sample of 25 cereal boxes of Granola Crunch, a generic brand of cereal, yields a mean weight of 1.02 pounds of cereal per box. Construct the 95% confidence interval for the mean weight of all cereal boxes. Assume that the weight is normally distributed with a population standard deviation of 0.03 pound.

SOLUTION: Note that the normality condition of $\bar{X}$ is satisfied since the underlying population is normally distributed. The 95% confidence interval for the population mean is computed as

$$\bar{x} \pm 1.96\frac{\sigma}{\sqrt{n}} = 1.02 \pm 1.96\frac{0.03}{\sqrt{25}} = 1.02 \pm 0.012.$$

With 95% confidence, we can report that the mean weight of all cereal boxes falls between 1.008 and 1.032 pounds.

While it is common to report the 95% confidence interval, in theory we can construct an interval of any level of confidence ranging from 0 to 100%. Let's now extend the analysis to include intervals for any confidence level. Let the Greek letter α (alpha) denote the allowed probability of error; in Chapter 9 this is referred to as the significance level. This is the probability that the estimation procedure will generate an interval that does not contain μ. The **confidence coefficient** $(1 - \alpha)$ is interpreted as the probability that the estimation procedure will generate an interval that contains μ. Thus, the probability of error α is related to the confidence coefficient and the confidence level as follows:

- Confidence coefficient = $1 - \alpha$, and
- Confidence level = $100(1 - \alpha)\%$.

For example, the confidence coefficient of 0.95 implies that the probability of error α equals $1 - 0.95 = 0.05$ and the confidence level equals $100(1 - 0.05)\% = 95\%$. Similarly, for the 90% confidence interval, the confidence coefficient equals 0.90 and $\alpha = 1 - 0.90 = 0.10$. The following statement generalizes the construction of a confidence interval for μ when σ is known.

CONFIDENCE INTERVAL FOR μ WHEN σ IS KNOWN

A $100(1 - \alpha)\%$ confidence interval for the population mean μ when the population standard deviation σ is known is computed as

$$\bar{x} \pm z_{\alpha/2}\frac{\sigma}{\sqrt{n}} \quad \text{or} \quad \left[\bar{x} - z_{\alpha/2}\frac{\sigma}{\sqrt{n}}, \bar{x} + z_{\alpha/2}\frac{\sigma}{\sqrt{n}}\right].$$

This formula is valid only if $\bar{X}$ (approximately) follows a normal distribution.

The notation $z_{\alpha/2}$ is the z value associated with the probability of $\alpha/2$ in the upper tail of the standard normal probability distribution. In other words, if Z is a standard normal random variable and α is any probability, then $z_{\alpha/2}$ represents the z value such that the area under the z curve to the right of $z_{\alpha/2}$ is $\alpha/2$, that is, $P(Z \geq z_{\alpha/2}) = \alpha/2$. Figure 8.2 depicts the notation $z_{\alpha/2}$.

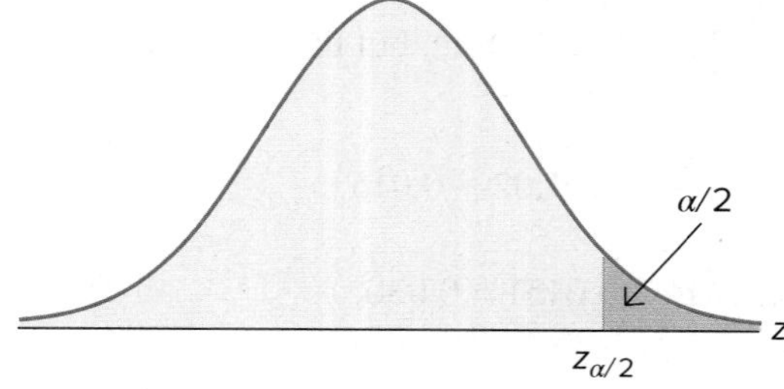

FIGURE 8.2 Graphical depiction of the notation $z_{\alpha/2}$

As discussed earlier, for the 95% confidence interval, $\alpha = 0.05$ and $\alpha/2 = 0.025$. Therefore, $z_{\alpha/2} = z_{0.025} = 1.96$. Similarly, using the z table, we can derive the following:

- For the 90% confidence interval, $\alpha = 0.10$, $\alpha/2 = 0.05$, and $z_{\alpha/2} = z_{0.05} = 1.645$.
- For the 99% confidence interval, $\alpha = 0.01$, $\alpha/2 = 0.005$, and $z_{\alpha/2} = z_{0.005} = 2.576$.

These values can also be obtained using Excel's **norm.inv** function or R's **qnorm** function with $\mu = 0$ and $\sigma = 1$. Both of these functions were discussed in Chapter 6.

The Width of a Confidence Interval

LO 8.3

Describe the factors that influence the width of a confidence interval.

The margin of error used in the computation of the confidence interval for the population mean, when the population standard deviation is known, is $z_{\alpha/2}\frac{\sigma}{\sqrt{n}}$. Since we are basically adding and subtracting this quantity from $\bar{x}$, the width of the confidence interval is two times the margin of error. In Example 8.1, the margin of error for the 95% confidence interval is 0.012 and the width of the interval is $1.032 - 1.008 = 0.024$; or equivalently, the width of the interval is $2(0.012) = 0.024$. Now let's examine how the width of a confidence interval is influenced by various factors.

I. For a given confidence level $100(1 - \alpha)\%$ and sample size n, the larger the population standard deviation σ, the wider the confidence interval.

EXAMPLE 8.1b

Let the population standard deviation in Example 8.1 be 0.05 pound instead of 0.03 pound. Compute the 95% confidence interval using the same sample mean of 1.02 pounds and the same sample size of 25.

SOLUTION: We use the same formula as before, but we use 0.05 for σ instead of 0.03:

$$1.02 \pm 1.96\frac{0.05}{\sqrt{25}} = 1.02 \pm 0.020.$$

The width has increased from 0.024 to 2(0.020) = 0.040.

II. For a given confidence level $100(1 - \alpha)\%$ and population standard deviation σ, the smaller the sample size n, the wider the confidence interval.

EXAMPLE 8.1c

Instead of 25 observations, let the sample in Example 8.1 be based on 16 observations. Compute the 95% confidence interval using the same sample mean of 1.02 pounds and the same population standard deviation of 0.03 pound.

SOLUTION: Again, we use the same formula as before, but this time we use 16 for n instead of 25:

$$1.02 \pm 1.96\frac{0.03}{\sqrt{16}} = 1.02 \pm 0.015.$$

The width has increased from 0.024 to 2(0.015) = 0.030.

III. For a given sample size n and population standard deviation σ, the greater the confidence level $100(1 - \alpha)\%$, the wider the confidence interval.

EXAMPLE 8.1d

Instead of a 95% confidence interval, compute the 99% confidence interval for Example 8.1, using the same sample mean of 1.02 pounds, the same population standard deviation of 0.03 pound, and the same sample size of 25.

SOLUTION: Again, we use the same formula as before, but this time we use the value 2.576 for $z_{\alpha/2}$ instead of 1.96:

$$1.02 \pm 2.576\frac{0.03}{\sqrt{25}} = 1.02 \pm 0.015.$$

The width has increased from 0.024 to 2(0.015) = 0.030.

The precision is directly linked with the width of the confidence interval—the wider the interval, the lower its precision. Continuing with the weather analogy, a temperature estimate of 40 to 80 degrees is imprecise because the interval is too wide to be of value. We lose precision when the sample does not reveal a great deal about the population, resulting in a wide confidence interval. Examples 8.1b and 8.1c suggest that the estimate will be less precise if the variability of the underlying population is high (σ is high) or a small segment of the population is sampled (n is small). Example 8.1d relates the width with the confidence level. For given sample information, the only way we can gain confidence is by making the interval wider. If you are 95% confident that the outside temperature is between 40 and 60 degrees, then you can increase your confidence level to 99% only by using a wider range, say between 35 and 65 degrees. This result also helps us understand the difference between precision (width of the interval) and the confidence level. There is a trade-off between the amount of confidence we have in an interval and its width.

EXAMPLE 8.2

IQ tests are designed to yield scores that are approximately normally distributed. A reporter is interested in estimating the average IQ of employees in a large high-tech firm in California. She gathers the IQ scores from 22 employees of this firm and records the sample mean IQ as 106. She assumes that the population standard deviation is 15.

a. Compute 90% and 99% confidence intervals for the average IQ in this firm.
b. Use these results to infer if the mean IQ in this firm is significantly different from the national average of 100.

SOLUTION:

a. For the 90% confidence interval, $z_{\alpha/2} = z_{0.05} = 1.645$. Similarly, for the 99% confidence interval, $z_{\alpha/2} = z_{0.005} = 2.576$.

   The 90% confidence interval is $106 \pm 1.645\frac{15}{\sqrt{22}} = 106 \pm 5.26$ or [100.74, 111.26].

   The 99% confidence interval is $106 \pm 2.576\frac{15}{\sqrt{22}} = 106 \pm 8.24$ or [97.76, 114.24].

   Note that the 99% interval is wider than the 90% interval.

b. With 90% confidence, the reporter can infer that the average IQ of this firm's employees differs from the national average, since the value 100 falls outside the 90% confidence interval, [100.74, 111.26]. However, she cannot infer the same result with 99% confidence, since the wider range of the interval, [97.76, 114.24], includes the value 100. We will study the link between estimation and testing in more detail in the next chapter.

Using Excel and R to Construct a Confidence Interval for μ When σ Is Known

We can use functions in Excel and R to construct confidence intervals. These functions are particularly useful with large data sets. Consider the following example.

EXAMPLE 8.3

Table 8.2 lists a portion of the weights (in grams) for a sample of 80 hockey pucks. Construct the 90% confidence interval for the population mean weight assuming that the population standard deviation is 7.5 grams.

TABLE 8.2 Hockey Puck Weights, $n = 80$

FILE
Hockey_Pucks

Weight
162.2
159.8
⋮
171.3

SOLUTION: We compute $\bar{x} \pm z_{\alpha/2}\frac{\sigma}{\sqrt{n}}$, or, equivalently, we find the lower and upper limits of the confidence interval: $\left[\bar{x} - z_{\alpha/2}\frac{\sigma}{\sqrt{n}}, \bar{x} + z_{\alpha/2}\frac{\sigma}{\sqrt{n}}\right]$. We are given $\sigma = 7.5$ and $n = 80$.

Using Excel

a. Open the ***Hockey_Pucks*** data file. Note that the values for weights are in cells A2 through A81.

b. Recall from Chapter 6 that Excel's **NORM.INV** function finds a particular z value for a given cumulative probability. For the 90% confidence interval, $\alpha = 0.10$ and $z_{\alpha/2} = z_{0.05}$. To find the z value such that the area under the z curve to the right of $z_{0.05}$ is 0.05 (and area to the left of $z_{0.05}$ is 0.95), we use `=NORM.INV(0.95, 0, 1)`. In order to find the lower limit of the confidence interval, we enter

`=AVERAGE(A2:A81)–NORM.INV(0.95, 0, 1) * 7.5/SQRT(80)`, and Excel returns 165.33. For the upper limit of the confidence interval, we enter `=AVERAGE(A2:A81) + NORM.INV(0.95, 0, 1) * 7.5/SQRT(80)`, and Excel returns 168.09. With 90% confidence, we conclude that the mean weight of all hockey pucks falls between 165.33 and 168.09 grams.

Using R

a. Import the ***Hockey_Pucks*** data file into a data frame and label it myData.

b. Recall from Chapter 6 that R's **qnorm** function finds a particular z value for a given cumulative probability. For the 90% confidence interval, $\alpha = 0.10$ and $z_{\alpha/2} = z_{0.05}$. To find the z value such that the area under the z curve to the right of $z_{0.05}$ is 0.05 (and area to the left of $z_{0.05}$ is 0.95), we use qnorm(0.95, 0, 1). In order to find the lower limit of the confidence interval, we enter:

```
> Lower <- mean(myData$Weight) – qnorm(0.95, 0, 1)*7.5/sqrt(80)
> Lower
```

And R returns: 165.332.

For the upper limit of the confidence interval, we enter

```
> Upper <- mean(myData$Weight) + qnorm(0.95, 0, 1)*7.5/sqrt(80)
> Upper
```

And R returns: 168.0905.

EXERCISES 8.1

Mechanics

1. Find $z_{\alpha/2}$ for each of the following confidence levels used in estimating the population mean.
   a. 90%
   b. 98%
   c. 88%
2. Find $z_{\alpha/2}$ for each of the following confidence levels used in estimating the population mean.
   a. 89%
   b. 92%
   c. 96%
3. A simple random sample of 25 observations is derived from a normally distributed population with a population standard deviation of 8.2.
   a. Is the condition that $\bar{X}$ is normally distributed satisfied? Explain.
   b. Compute the margin of error with 80% confidence.
   c. Compute the margin of error with 90% confidence.
   d. Which of the two margins of error will lead to a wider interval?
4. Consider a population with a population standard deviation of 26.8. In order to compute an interval estimate for the population mean, a sample of 64 observations is drawn.
   a. Is the condition that $\bar{X}$ is normally distributed satisfied? Explain.
   b. Compute the margin of error at the 95% confidence level.
   c. Compute the margin of error at the 95% confidence level based on a larger sample of 225 observations.
   d. Which of the two margins of error will lead to a wider confidence interval?
5. Discuss the factors that influence the margin of error for the confidence interval for the population mean. What can a practitioner do to reduce the margin of error?

Applications

6. A researcher finds that the average life expectancy for Bostonians is 78.1 years. He uses a sample of 50 Bostonians and assumes that the population standard deviation is 4.5 years.
   a. What is the point estimate for the population mean?
   b. At 90% confidence, what is the margin of error?
   c. Construct the 90% confidence interval for the population average life expectancy of Bostonians.
7. In order to estimate the mean 30-year fixed mortgage rate for a home loan in the United States, a random sample of 28 recent loans is taken. The average calculated from this sample is 5.25%. It can be assumed that 30-year fixed mortgage rates are normally distributed with a population standard deviation of 0.50%. Compute 90% and 99% confidence intervals for the population mean 30-year fixed mortgage rate.
8. A researcher in a small Midwestern town wants to estimate the mean weekday sleep time of its adult residents. He takes a random sample of 80 adult residents and records their weekday mean sleep time as 6.4 hours. Assume that the population standard deviation is fairly stable at 1.8 hours.
   a. Calculate the 95% confidence interval for the population mean weekday sleep time of all adult residents of this Midwestern town.
   b. Can we conclude with 95% confidence that the mean sleep time of all adult residents in this Midwestern town is not 7 hours?
9. A family is relocating from St. Louis, Missouri, to California. Due to an increasing inventory of houses in St. Louis, it is taking longer than before to sell a house. The wife is concerned and wants to know when it is optimal to put their house on the market. Her realtor friend informs them that the last 26 houses that sold in their neighborhood took an average time of 218 days to sell. The realtor also tells them that based on her prior experience, the population standard deviation is 72 days.
   a. What assumption regarding the population is necessary for making an interval estimate for the population mean?
   b. Construct the 90% confidence interval for the mean sale time for all homes in the neighborhood.
10. Many U.S. consumers are using debit cards to avoid accruing debt (creditkarma.com, July 27, 2019). Based on a sample of 100 U.S. consumers, a researcher finds that the average amount spent annually on a debit card is $7,790. Assume that the population standard deviation is $500.
    a. At 99% confidence, what is the margin of error?
    b. Construct the 99% confidence interval for the population mean amount spent annually on a debit card.
11. Suppose the 95% confidence interval for the mean salary of college graduates in a town in Mississippi is given by [$36,080, $43,920]. The population standard deviation used for the analysis is known to be $12,000.
    a. What is the point estimate of the mean salary for all college graduates in this town?
    b. Determine the sample size used for the analysis.
12. A manager is interested in estimating the mean time (in minutes) required to complete a job. His assistant uses a sample of 100 observations to report the confidence interval as [14.355, 17.645]. The population standard deviation is known to be equal to 10 minutes.
    a. Find the sample mean time used to compute the confidence interval.
    b. Determine the confidence level used for the analysis.
13. FILE ***PA_Debt***. A study reports that recent college graduates from Connecticut face the highest average debt of $38,510 (forbes.com, September 18, 2019). A researcher from Pennsylvania wants to determine how recent undergraduates

from that state fare. The accompanying file contains data on debt from 40 recent undergraduates. Assume that the population standard deviation is $5,000.

a. Construct the 95% confidence interval for the mean debt of all undergraduates from Pennsylvania.
b. Use the 95% confidence interval to determine if the debt of Pennsylvania undergraduates differs from that of Connecticut undergraduates.

14. **FILE** ***Hourly_Wage.*** An economist wants to estimate the mean hourly wage (in $) of all workers. The accompanying file contains data on 50 hourly wage earners. Assume that the population standard deviation is $6. Construct and interpret 90% and 99% confidence intervals for the mean hourly wage of all workers.

15. **FILE** ***Highway_Speeds.*** A safety officer is concerned about speeds on a certain section of the New Jersey Turnpike. The accompanying file contains the speeds of 40 cars on a Saturday afternoon. Assume that the population standard deviation is 5 mph. Construct the 95% confidence interval for the mean speed of all cars on that section of the turnpike. Are the safety officer's concerns valid if the speed limit is 55 mph? Explain.

8.2 CONFIDENCE INTERVAL FOR THE POPULATION MEAN WHEN σ IS UNKNOWN

So far we have considered confidence intervals for the population mean when the population standard deviation σ is known. In reality, σ is rarely known. Recall from Chapter 3 that the population variance and the population standard deviation are calculated as $\sigma^2 = \frac{\Sigma(x_i - \mu)^2}{N}$ and $\sigma = \sqrt{\sigma^2}$, respectively. It is highly unlikely that σ is known when μ is not. However, there are instances when the population standard deviation is considered fairly stable and, therefore, can be determined from prior experience. In these cases, the population standard deviation is treated as known.

Recall that the margin of error in a confidence interval depends on the standard error of the estimator and the desired confidence level. With σ unknown, the standard error of $\overline{X}$, given by $\sigma/\sqrt{n}$, can be conveniently estimated by $s/\sqrt{n}$, where s denotes the sample standard deviation. For convenience, we denote this estimate of the standard error of $\overline{X}$ also by $se(\overline{X}) = s/\sqrt{n}$.

LO 8.4

Discuss features of the *t* distribution.

The *t* Distribution

As discussed earlier, in order to derive a confidence interval for μ, it is essential that $\overline{X}$ be normally distributed. A normally distributed $\overline{X}$ is standardized as $Z = \frac{\overline{X} - \mu}{\sigma/\sqrt{n}}$ where Z follows the z distribution. Another standardized statistic, which uses the estimator S in place of σ, is computed as $T = \frac{\overline{X} - \mu}{s/\sqrt{n}}$. The random variable T follows the **Student's *t* distribution**, more commonly known as the ***t* distribution**.[1]

THE *t* DISTRIBUTION

If a random sample of size n is taken from a normal population with a finite variance, then the statistic $T = \frac{\overline{X} - \mu}{s/\sqrt{n}}$ follows the t distribution with $(n - 1)$ degrees of freedom, *df*.

[1]William S. Gossett (1876–1937) published his research concerning the *t* distribution under the pen name "Student" because his employer, the Guinness Brewery, did not allow employees to publish their research results.

The t distribution is actually a family of distributions, which are similar to the z distribution in that they are all bell-shaped and symmetric around zero. However, all t distributions have slightly broader tails than the z distribution. Each t distribution is identified by the **degrees of freedom**, or simply, df. The degrees of freedom determine the extent of the broadness of the tails of the distribution; the fewer the degrees of freedom, the broader the tails. Since the t distribution is defined by the degrees of freedom, it is common to refer to it as the t_{df} distribution.

Specifically, the degrees of freedom refer to the number of independent pieces of information that go into the calculation of a given statistic and, in this sense, can be "freely chosen." Consider the number of independent observations that enter into the calculation of the sample mean. If it is known that $\bar{x} = 20$, $n = 4$, and three of the observations have values of $x_1 = 16$, $x_2 = 24$, and $x_3 = 18$, then there is no choice but for the fourth observation to have a value of 22. In other words, three degrees of freedom are involved in computing $\bar{x} = 20$ if $n = 4$; in effect, one degree of freedom is lost.

Summary of the t_{df} Distribution

- Like the z distribution, the t_{df} distribution is bell-shaped and symmetric around 0 with asymptotic tails (the tails get closer and closer to the horizontal axis but never touch it).
- The t_{df} distribution has slightly broader tails than the z distribution.
- The t_{df} distribution consists of a family of distributions where the actual shape of each one depends on the degrees of freedom df. As df increases, the t_{df} distribution becomes similar to the z distribution; it is identical to the z distribution when df approaches infinity.

From Figure 8.3 we note that the tails of the t_2 and t_5 distributions are broader than the tails of the t_{50} distribution. For instance, for t_2 and t_5, the area exceeding a value of 3, or $P(T_{df} > 3)$, is greater than that for t_{50}. In addition, the t_{50} resembles the z distribution.

FIGURE 8.3 The t_{df} distribution with various degrees of freedom

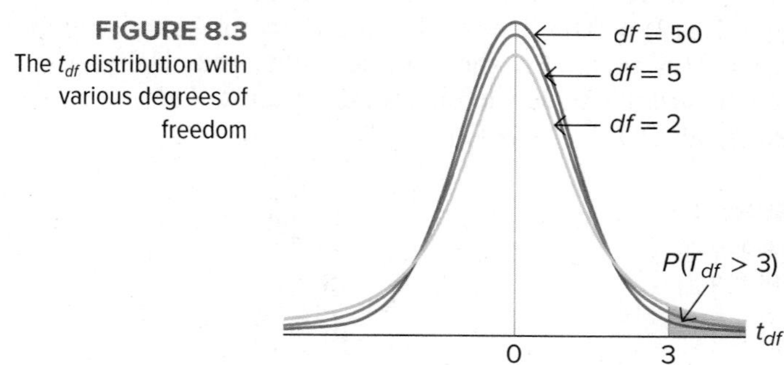

Locating t_{df} Values and Probabilities

Table 8.3 lists t_{df} values for selected upper-tail probabilities and degrees of freedom df. Table 2 of Appendix B provides a more complete table. Since the t_{df} distribution is a family of distributions identified by the df parameter, the t table is not as comprehensive as the z table. It only lists probabilities corresponding to a limited number of values. Also, unlike the cumulative probabilities in the z table, the t table provides the probabilities in the upper tail of the distribution.

TABLE 8.3 Portion of the t Table

	Area in Upper Tail, α					
df	0.20	0.10	0.05	0.025	0.01	0.005
1	1.376	3.078	6.314	12.706	31.821	63.657
⋮	⋮	⋮	⋮	⋮	⋮	⋮
10	0.879	1.372	**1.812**	2.228	2.764	3.169
⋮	⋮	⋮	⋮	⋮	⋮	⋮
∞	0.842	1.282	1.645	1.960	2.326	2.576

We use the notation $t_{\alpha,df}$ to denote a value such that the area in the upper tail equals α for a given df. In other words, for a random variable T_{df}, the notation $t_{\alpha,df}$ represents a value such that $P(T_{df} \geq t_{\alpha,df}) = \alpha$. Similarly, $t_{\alpha/2,df}$ represents a value such that $P(T_{df} \geq t_{\alpha/2,df}) = \alpha/2$. Figure 8.4 illustrates the notation.

FIGURE 8.4
Graphical depiction of $P(T_{df} \geq t_{\alpha,df}) = \alpha$

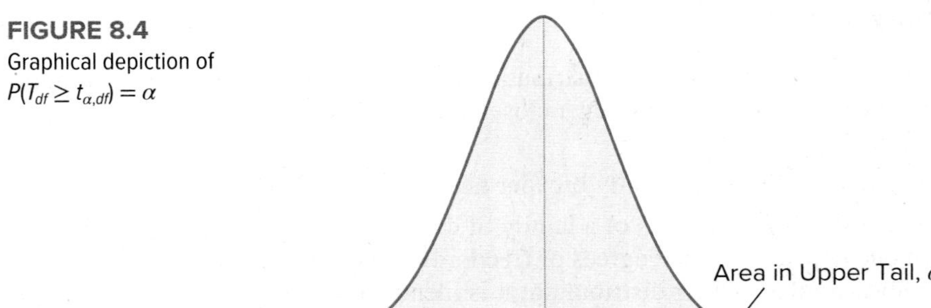

When determining the value $t_{\alpha,df}$, we need two pieces of information: α and df. For instance, suppose we want to find the value $t_{\alpha,df}$ with $\alpha = 0.05$ and $df = 10$; that is, $t_{0.05,10}$. Using Table 8.3, we look at the first column labeled df and find the row 10. We then continue along this row until we reach the column $\alpha = 0.05$. The value 1.812 indicates that $P(T_{10} \geq 1.812) = 0.05$. Due to the symmetry of the t distribution, we also get $P(T_{10} \leq -1.812) = 0.05$. Figure 8.5 shows these results graphically. Also, since the area under the entire t_{df} distribution sums to one, we deduce that $P(T_{10} < 1.812) = 1 - 0.05 = 0.95$, which also equals $P(T_{10} > -1.812)$.

FIGURE 8.5
Graph of the probability $\alpha = 0.05$ on both sides of T_{10}

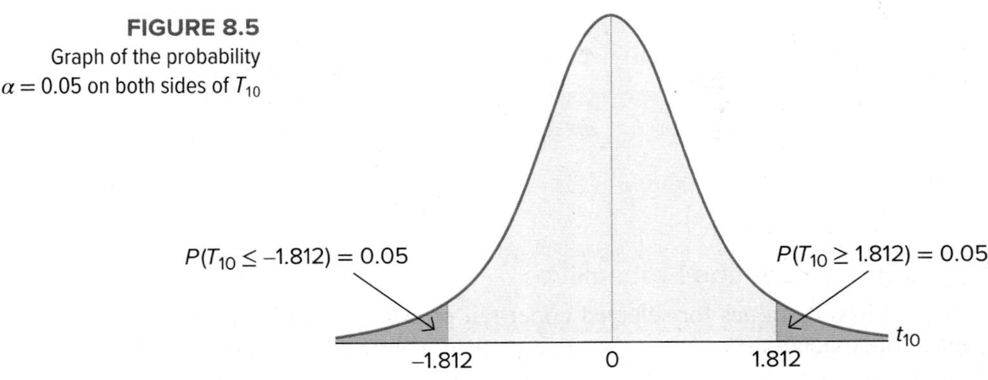

Sometimes the exact probability cannot be determined from the t table. For example, given $df = 10$, the exact probability $P(T_{10} \geq 1.562)$ is not included in the table. However, this probability is between 0.05 and 0.10 because the value 1.562 falls between 1.372 and 1.812. Similarly, $P(T_{10} < 1.562)$ is between 0.90 and 0.95. We can use Excel, R, and other statistical packages to find exact probabilities.

EXAMPLE 8.4

Compute $t_{\alpha,df}$ for $\alpha = 0.025$ using 2, 5, and 50 degrees of freedom.

SOLUTION:

- For $df = 2$, $t_{0.025,2} = 4.303$.
- For $df = 5$, $t_{0.025,5} = 2.571$.
- For $df = 50$, $t_{0.025,50} = 2.009$.

Note that the t_{df} values change with the degrees of freedom. Moreover, as df increases, the t_{df} distribution begins to resemble the z distribution. In fact, with $df = \infty$, $t_{0.025,\infty} = 1.96$, which is identical to the corresponding z value; recall that $P(Z \geq 1.96) = 0.025$.

Constructing a Confidence Interval for μ When σ Is Unknown

LO 8.5

Calculate a confidence interval for the population mean when the population standard deviation is not known.

We can never stress enough the importance of the requirement that $\overline{X}$ follows the normal distribution in estimating the population mean. Recall that $\overline{X}$ follows the normal distribution when the underlying population is normally distributed or when the sample size is sufficiently large ($n \geq 30$). We still construct the confidence interval for μ as point estimate $\pm$ margin of error. However, when the population standard deviation is unknown, we now use the t_{df} distribution to calculate the margin of error.

CONFIDENCE INTERVAL FOR μ WHEN σ IS NOT KNOWN

A $100(1 - \alpha)\%$ confidence interval for the population mean μ when the population standard deviation σ is not known is computed as

$$\bar{x} \pm t_{\alpha/2,df}\frac{s}{\sqrt{n}} \quad \text{or} \quad \left[\bar{x} - t_{\alpha/2,df}\frac{s}{\sqrt{n}}, \bar{x} + t_{\alpha/2,df}\frac{s}{\sqrt{n}}\right],$$

where $df = n - 1$ and s is the sample standard deviation. This formula is valid only if $\overline{X}$ (approximately) follows a normal distribution.

As before, $100(1 - \alpha)\%$ is the confidence level and $t_{\alpha/2,df}$ is the t_{df} value associated with the probability $\alpha/2$ in the upper tail of the distribution with $df = n - 1$. In other words, $P(T_{df} > t_{\alpha/2,df}) = \alpha/2$. It is important to note that uncertainty is increased when we estimate the population standard deviation with the sample standard deviation, making the confidence interval wider, especially for smaller samples. This is appropriately captured by the wider tail of the t_{df} distribution.

EXAMPLE 8.5

FILE *MPG*

In the introductory case of this chapter, Jared Beane wants to estimate the mean mpg for all ultra-green cars. The accompanying data file lists the mpg for a sample of 25 cars. Use this information to construct the 90% confidence interval for the population mean. Assume that mpg follows a normal distribution.

SOLUTION: The condition that $\overline{X}$ follows a normal distribution is satisfied since we assumed that mpg is normally distributed. Thus, we construct the confidence interval as $\bar{x} \pm t_{\alpha/2,df}\frac{s}{\sqrt{n}}$. This is a classic example where a statistician has access only to sample data. Since the population standard deviation is not known, the sample standard deviation has to be computed from the sample. From the sample data, we find that $\bar{x} = 96.52$ and $s = 10.697$. For the 90% confidence interval, $\alpha = 0.10$, $\alpha/2 = 0.05$, and, given $n = 25$, $df = 25 - 1 = 24$. Thus, $t_{0.05,24} = 1.711$.

The 90% confidence interval for μ is computed as

$$\bar{x} \pm t_{\alpha/2,df}\frac{s}{\sqrt{n}} = 96.52 \pm 1.711\frac{10.697}{\sqrt{25}} = 96.52 \pm 3.66 \text{ or } [92.86, 100.18].$$

Thus, Jared concludes with 90% confidence that the average mpg of all ultra-green cars is between 92.86 mpg and 100.18 mpg. Note that the manufacturer's claim that the ultra-green car will average 100 mpg cannot be rejected by the sample data since the value 100 falls within the 90% confidence interval.

Using Excel and R to Construct a Confidence Interval for μ When σ Is Unknown

Again we find that functions in Excel and R are quite useful when constructing confidence intervals. Consider the following example.

EXAMPLE 8.6

Amazon Prime is a $119-per-year service that gives the company's customers free two-day shipping and discounted rates on overnight delivery. Prime customers also get other perks, such as free e-books. Table 8.4 shows a portion of the annual expenditures (in $) for 100 Prime customers. Use Excel and R to construct the 95% confidence interval for the average annual expenditures of all Prime customers. Summarize the results.

Prime

TABLE 8.4 Annual Prime Expenditures (in $)

Customer	Expenditures
1	1272
2	1089
⋮	⋮
100	1389

SOLUTION: We compute $\bar{x} \pm t_{\alpha/2,df}\frac{s}{\sqrt{n}}$, or, equivalently, we find the lower and upper limits of the confidence interval: $\left[\bar{x} - t_{\alpha/2,df}\frac{s}{\sqrt{n}}, \bar{x} + t_{\alpha/2,df}\frac{s}{\sqrt{n}}\right]$.

Using Excel

a. Open the ***Prime*** data file. Note that the observations for the Expenditures variable are in cells B2 through B101.

b. We use Excel's **T.INV** to find a particular $t_{\alpha,df}$ value. We enter `=T.INV(cumulprob, df)`, where *cumulprob* is the cumulative probability associated with $t_{\alpha,df}$ and *df* is the degrees of freedom. For the 95% confidence interval with $n = 100$, we find $t_{0.025,99}$ using `=T.INV(0.975,99)`. Thus, in order to obtain the lower limit, we enter `=AVERAGE(B2:B101) - T.INV(0.975,99)*STDEV.S(B2:101)/SQRT(100)`. For the upper limit, we enter `=AVERAGE(B2:B101) + T.INV(0.975,99)*STDEV.S(B2:101)/SQRT(100)`.
Note: For a one-step approach to constructing a confidence interval in Excel, we can use the *Descriptive Statistics* option in its Analysis Toolpak which we discussed in Chapter 3. In the *Descriptive Statistics* dialog box, we select *Summary statistics* and *Confidence Interval for Mean.* (By default, the confidence level is set at 95%, but you easily enter another level.) In the table that Excel returns, we find the mean and the margin of error which is labeled Confidence Level(95.0%).

Using R

a. Import the ***Prime*** data file into a data frame (table) and label it myData.

b. We use R's qt function to find a particular $t_{\alpha,df}$ value. We enter `qt(cumulprob, df, lower.tail=TRUE)`, where *cumulprob* is the cumulative probability associated with $t_{\alpha,df}$ and *df* is the degrees of freedom. For the 95% confidence interval with $n = 100$, we find $t_{0.025,99}$ using `qt(0.975, 99, lower.tail=TRUE)`. Thus, in order to obtain the lower and upper limits, we enter:

```
>lower <- mean(myData$Expenditures) - qt(0.975, 99, lower.tail
=TRUE)*sd(myData$Expenditures)/sqrt(100)
>lower
>upper <- mean(myData$Expenditures) + qt(0.975, 99, lower.tail
=TRUE)*sd(myData$Expenditures)/sqrt(100)
>upper
```

Note: For a one-step approach to constructing a confidence interval in R, we can use the **t.test** function by entering: `t.test(myData$Expenditures)`. By default, R returns the 95% confidence interval for Expenditures. For a different confidence interval, you can use the option *conf.level=* and after the equal sign put the desired proportion. We will address this function in more detail in Chapter 9.

Summary

With 95% confidence, we conclude that the average annual expenditures of all Prime customers fall between $1,240.24 and $1,373.64

EXERCISES 8.2

Mechanics

16. Find $t_{\alpha,df}$ given from the following information.
    a. $\alpha = 0.025$ and $df = 12$
    b. $\alpha = 0.10$ and $df = 12$
    c. $\alpha = 0.025$ and $df = 25$
    d. $\alpha = 0.10$ and $df = 25$

17. We use the *t* distribution to construct a confidence interval for the population mean when the underlying population standard deviation is not known. Under the assumption that the population is normally distributed, find $t_{\alpha/2,df}$ for the following scenarios.
    a. A 90% confidence level and a sample of 28 observations.
    b. A 95% confidence level and a sample of 28 observations.
    c. A 90% confidence level and a sample of 15 observations.
    d. A 95% confidence level and a sample of 15 observations.

18. A random sample of 24 observations is used to estimate the population mean. The sample mean and the sample standard deviation are calculated as 104.6 and 28.8, respectively. Assume that the population is normally distributed.
    a. Construct the 90% confidence interval for the population mean.
    b. Construct the 99% confidence interval for the population mean.
    c. Use your answers to discuss the impact of the confidence level on the width of the interval.

19. Consider a normal population with an unknown population standard deviation. A random sample results in $\bar{x} = 48.68$ and $s^2 = 33.64$.
    a. Compute the 95% confidence interval for μ if $\bar{x}$ and s^2 were obtained from a sample of 16 observations.
    b. Compute the 95% confidence interval for μ if $\bar{x}$ and s^2 were obtained from a sample of 25 observations.
    c. Use your answers to discuss the impact of the sample size on the width of the interval.

20. Let the following sample of 8 observations be drawn from a normal population with unknown mean and standard deviation: 22, 18, 14, 25, 17, 28, 15, 21.
    a. Calculate the sample mean and the sample standard deviation.
    b. Construct the 80% confidence interval for the population mean.
    c. Construct the 90% confidence interval for the population mean.
    d. What happens to the margin of error as the confidence level increases from 80% to 90%?

Applications

21. FILE ***Drugstore.*** A random sample of eight drug stores shows the following prices (in $) of a popular pain reliever:

3.50	4.00	2.00	3.00	2.50	3.50	2.50	3.00

Assume the normal distribution for the underlying population to construct the 90% confidence interval for the population mean.

22. A popular weight loss program claims that with its recommended healthy diet regimen, customers lose significant weight within a month. In order to estimate the mean weight loss of all customers, a nutritionist takes a sample of 18 customers and records their weight loss

one month after joining the program. He computes the sample mean and the standard deviation of weight loss as 12.5 pounds and 9.2 pounds, respectively. He believes that weight loss is likely to be normally distributed.

a. Calculate the margin of error with 95% confidence.
b. Calculate the 95% confidence interval for the population mean.

23. **FILE** ***Customers.*** The manager of The Cheesecake Factory in Boston reports that on six randomly selected weekdays, the number of customers served was 120, 130, 100, 205, 185, and 220. She believes that the number of customers served on weekdays follows a normal distribution. Construct the 90% confidence interval for the average number of customers served on weekdays.

24. According to a survey, high school girls average 100 text messages daily. Assume that the survey was based on a random sample of 36 high school girls. The sample standard deviation is computed as 10 text messages daily.

a. Calculate the margin of error with 99% confidence.
b. What is the 99% confidence interval for the population mean texts that all high school girls send daily?

25. The Chartered Financial Analyst (CFA) designation is fast becoming a requirement for serious investment professionals. Although it requires a successful completion of three levels of grueling exams, it also entails promising careers with lucrative salaries. A student of finance is curious about the average salary of a CFA charterholder. He takes a random sample of 36 recent charterholders and computes a mean salary of $158,000 with a standard deviation of $36,000. Use this sample information to determine the 95% confidence interval for the average salary of a CFA charterholder.

26. **FILE** ***Sudoku.*** The sudoku puzzle has become very popular all over the world. It is based on a 9×9 grid and the challenge is to fill in the grid so that every row, every column, and every 3×3 box contains the digits 1 through 9. A researcher is interested in estimating the average time taken by a college student to solve the puzzle. He takes a random sample of 8 college students and records their solving times (in minutes) as 14, 7, 17, 20, 18, 15, 19, 28.

a. Construct the 99% confidence interval for the average time taken by a college student to solve a sudoku puzzle.
b. What assumption is necessary to make this inference?

27. **FILE** ***Compensation.*** Executive compensation has risen dramatically compared to the rising levels of an average worker's wage over the years. Sarah is an MBA student who decides to use her statistical skills to estimate the mean CEO compensation for all large companies in the United States. She takes a random sample of six CEO compensations (in $ millions) and obtains the following values: 8.20, 2.76, 6.57, 3.88, 6.56, and 4.10.

a. Help Sarah use the information to construct the 90% confidence interval for the mean CEO compensation for all large companies in the United States.
b. What assumption is necessary for deriving the interval estimate?
c. How can the margin of error reported in part a be reduced?

28. **FILE** ***Unemployment.*** The unemployment rates (in %) in seven major economies around the world were as follows: 5.2, 4.1, 10.0, 6.8, 3.8, 8.0, and 8.3.

a. Calculate the margin of error used in the 95% confidence level for the population mean unemployment rate. Explain the assumption made for the analysis.
b. How can we reduce the margin of error for the 95% confidence interval?
c. What is the 95% confidence interval for the mean unemployment rate?

29. **FILE** ***Footwear.*** A price-earnings ratio, or P/E ratio, is calculated as a firm's share price compared to the income or profit earned by the firm per share. Generally, a high P/E ratio suggests that investors are expecting higher earnings growth in the future compared to companies with a lower P/E ratio. An analyst takes a sample of five firms in the footwear industry and records their P/E ratios as: 26, 13, 21, 16, and 21. Let these ratios represent a random sample drawn from a normally distributed population. Construct the 90% confidence interval for the mean P/E ratio for the entire footwear industry.

30. The following table shows the annual returns (in percent) for Firm A and Firm B over the last five years.

Year	Firm A	Firm B
1	17	11
2	−8	13
3	4	7
4	39	21
5	38	22

a. Derive the 99% confidence interval for the mean return for Firm A and the 99% confidence interval for the mean return for Firm B.
b. What did you have to assume to make the above inferences?
c. Which confidence interval is wider? Explain.

31. **FILE** ***Stock_Price.*** For the first six months of the year, an analyst records the monthly closing stock price (in $) for a firm as: 71, 73, 76, 78, 81, 75.

a. Calculate the sample mean and the sample standard deviation.
b. Calculate the 90% confidence interval for the mean stock price of the firm assuming that the stock price is normally distributed.
c. What happens to the margin of error if a higher confidence level is used for the interval estimate?

32. Suppose the 90% confidence interval for the mean SAT scores of applicants at a business college is given by [1690, 1810]. This confidence interval uses the sample mean and the sample standard deviation based on 25 observations. What are the

sample mean and the sample standard deviation used when computing the interval?

33. A teacher wants to estimate the mean time (in minutes) that students take to go from one classroom to the next. His research assistant uses the sample time of 36 students to report the confidence interval as [8.20, 9.80].
    a. Find the sample mean time used to compute the confidence interval.
    b. Determine the confidence level if the sample standard deviation used for the interval is 2.365.

34. In order to attract more Millenials, a new clothing store offers free gourmet coffee and pastry to its customers. The average daily revenue over the past five-week period has been $1,080 with a standard deviation of $260. Use this sample information to construct the 95% confidence interval for the average daily revenue. The store manager believes that the coffee and pastry strategy would lead to an average daily revenue of $1,200. Use the 95% interval to determine if the manager is wrong.

35. **FILE** ***Debt_Payments.*** The accompanying data file lists average monthly debt payments (Debt in $) for 26 metropolitan areas. Construct the 90% and the 95% confidence intervals for the population mean. Compare the widths of the intervals.

36. **FILE** ***Economics.*** An associate dean of a university wishes to compare the means on the standardized final exams in microeconomics and macroeconomics. He has access to a random sample of 40 scores from each of these two courses. A portion of the data is shown in the accompanying table.

Micro	Macro
85	48
78	79
⋮	⋮
75	74

    a. Construct the 95% confidence intervals for the mean score in microeconomics and the mean score in macroeconomics.
    b. Explain why the widths of the two intervals are different.

37. **FILE** ***Math_Scores.*** Recent research shows that while the average math scores for boys and girls may be the same, there is more variability in math ability for boys than girls, resulting in some boys with soaring math skills. A portion of the data on math scores of boys and girls is shown in the accompanying table.

Boys	Girls
74	83
89	76
⋮	⋮
66	74

    a. Construct the 95% confidence intervals for the mean score of boys and the mean score of girls. Explain your assumptions.
    b. Explain why the widths of the two intervals are different.

38. **FILE** ***Startups.*** Many of today's leading companies, including Google, Microsoft, and Facebook, are based on technologies developed within universities. Lisa Fisher is a business school professor who believes that a university's research expenditure (Research in $ millions) and the age of its technology transfer office (Duration in years) are major factors that enhance innovation. She wants to know what the average values are for the Research and the Duration variables. She collects data from 143 universities on these variables. A portion of the data is shown in the accompanying table.

Research	Duration
145.52	23
237.52	23
⋮	⋮
154.38	9

    a. Construct and interpret the 95% confidence interval for the mean research expenditure of all universities.
    b. Construct and interpret the 95% confidence interval for the mean duration of all universities.

8.3 CONFIDENCE INTERVAL FOR THE POPULATION PROPORTION

LO 8.6

Calculate a confidence interval for the population proportion.

Recall that while the population mean μ describes a numerical variable, the population proportion p is the essential descriptive measure for a categorical variable. The parameter p represents the proportion of successes in the population, where success is defined by a particular outcome. Examples of population proportions include the proportion of women students at a university, the proportion of defective items in a manufacturing process, and the default probability on a mortgage loan.

As in the case of the population mean, we estimate the population proportion on the basis of its sample counterpart. In particular, we use the sample proportion $\overline{P}$ as the point estimator of the population proportion p. Also, although the sampling distribution of $\overline{P}$ is based on the binomial distribution, we can approximate it by a normal distribution for large samples, according to the central limit theorem. This approximation is valid when the sample size n is such that $np \geq 5$ and $n(1 - p) \geq 5$.

Using the normal approximation for $\overline{P}$ with $E(\overline{P}) = p$ and $se(\overline{P}) = \sqrt{p(1 - p)/n}$, and analogous to the derivation of the confidence interval for the population mean, a $100(1 - \alpha)\%$ confidence interval for the population proportion is

$$\overline{p} \pm z_{\alpha/2}\sqrt{\frac{p(1-p)}{n}} \quad \text{or} \quad \left[\overline{p} - z_{\alpha/2}\sqrt{\frac{p(1-p)}{n}}, \overline{p} + z_{\alpha/2}\sqrt{\frac{p(1-p)}{n}}\right].$$

This confidence interval is theoretically sound; however, it cannot be implemented because it uses p in the derivation, which is unknown. Since we always use large samples for the normal distribution approximation, we can also conveniently replace p with its estimate $\overline{p}$ in the construction of the interval. Therefore, for $\sqrt{\frac{p(1-p)}{n}}$, we substitute $\sqrt{\frac{\overline{p}(1-\overline{p})}{n}}$. This substitution yields a feasible confidence interval for the population proportion.

CONFIDENCE INTERVAL FOR p

A $100(1 - \alpha)\%$ confidence interval for the population proportion p is computed as

$$\overline{p} \pm z_{\alpha/2}\sqrt{\frac{\overline{p}(1-\overline{p})}{n}} \quad \text{or} \quad \left[\overline{p} - z_{\alpha/2}\sqrt{\frac{\overline{p}(1-\overline{p})}{n}}, \overline{p} + z_{\alpha/2}\sqrt{\frac{\overline{p}(1-\overline{p})}{n}}\right].$$

This formula is valid only if $\overline{P}$ (approximately) follows a normal distribution.

The normality condition is evaluated at the sample proportion $\overline{p}$. In other words, for constructing a confidence interval for the population proportion p, we require that $n\overline{p} \geq 5$ and $n(1 - \overline{p}) \geq 5$.

EXAMPLE 8.7

MPG

In the introductory case of this chapter, Jared Beane wants to estimate the proportion of all ultra-green cars that obtain over 100 mpg. The ***MPG*** data file lists the mpg for a sample of 25 cars. Use the information to construct the 90% and the 99% confidence intervals for the population proportion.

SOLUTION: In the ***MPG*** data file, we find that 25 cars obtain over 100 mpg; thus, the point estimate of the population proportion is $\overline{p} = 7/25 = 0.28$. Note that the normality condition is satisfied, because $np \geq 5$ and $n(1 - p) \geq 5$, where p is evaluated at $\overline{p} = 0.28$. With the 90% confidence level, $\alpha/2 = 0.10/2 = 0.05$; thus, we find $z_{\alpha/2} = z_{0.05} = 1.645$. Substituting the appropriate values into $\overline{p} \pm z_{\alpha/2}\sqrt{\frac{\overline{p}(1-\overline{p})}{n}}$ yields

$$0.28 \pm 1.645\sqrt{\frac{0.28(1 - 0.28)}{25}} = 0.28 \pm 0.148.$$

With 90% confidence, Jared reports that the percentage of cars that obtain over 100 mpg is between 13.2% and 42.8%.

For the 99% confidence level, we use $\alpha/2 = 0.01/2 = 0.005$ and $z_{\alpha/2} = z_{0.005} = 2.576$ to obtain

$$0.28 \pm 2.576\sqrt{\frac{0.28(1-0.28)}{25}} = 0.28 \pm 0.231.$$

At a higher confidence level of 99%, the interval for the percentage of cars that obtain over 100 MPG becomes 4.9% to 51.1%. Given the current sample size of 25 cars, Jared can gain confidence (from 90% to 99%) at the expense of precision, as the corresponding margin of error increases from 0.148 to 0.231.

EXERCISES 8.3

Mechanics

39. A random sample of 80 observations results in 50 successes.
    a. Construct the 95% confidence interval for the population proportion of successes.
    b. Construct the 95% confidence interval for the population proportion of failures.

40. Assume $\bar{p} = 0.6$ in a sample of size $n = 50$.
    a. Construct the 95% confidence interval for the population proportion.
    b. What happens to the margin of error if the sample proportion is based on $n = 200$ instead of $n = 50$?

41. A sample of 80 results in 30 successes.
    a. Calculate the point estimate for the population proportion of successes.
    b. Construct the 90% and the 99% confidence intervals for the population proportion.
    c. Can we conclude at 90% confidence that the population proportion differs from 0.5?
    d. Can we conclude at 99% confidence that the population proportion differs from 0.5?

42. A random sample of 100 observations results in 40 successes.
    a. What is the point estimate for the population proportion of successes?
    b. Construct the 90% and the 99% confidence intervals for the population proportion.
    c. Can we conclude at 90% confidence that the population proportion differs from 0.5?
    d. Can we conclude at 99% confidence that the population proportion differs from 0.5?

43. In a sample of 30 observations, the number of successes equals 18.
    a. Construct the 88% confidence interval for the population proportion of successes.
    b. Construct the 98% confidence interval for the population proportion of successes.
    c. What happens to the margin of error as you move from the 88% confidence interval to the 98% confidence interval?

Applications

44. In a sample of 400 patients, a pharmaceutical company finds that 20 of the patients experienced a serious side effect from a particular drug. Use the sample information to construct the 95% confidence interval for the population proportion of all patients who experience a serious side effect from the drug.

45. A survey of 1,026 people asked: "What would you do with an unexpected tax refund?" Forty-seven percent responded that they would pay off debts.
    a. At 95% confidence, what is the margin of error?
    b. Construct the 95% confidence interval for the population proportion of people who would pay off debts with an unexpected tax refund.

46. A sample of 5,324 Americans were asked about what matters most to them in a place to live. Thirty-seven percent of the respondents felt that good job opportunities matter most.
    a. Construct the 90% confidence interval for the proportion of Americans who feel that good job opportunities matter most in a place to live.
    b. Construct the 99% confidence interval for the proportion of Americans who feel that good job opportunities matter most in a place to live.
    c. Which of the above two intervals has a higher margin of error? Explain why.

47. An economist reports that 560 out of a sample of 1,200 middle-income American households actively participate in the stock market.
    a. Construct the 90% confidence interval for the proportion of middle-income Americans who actively participate in the stock market.
    b. Can we conclude that the percentage of middle-income Americans who actively participate in the stock market is not 50%?

48. According to a survey, 44% of adults admit to keeping money secrets from a partner (cnbc.com, February 20, 2020). Suppose this survey was based on 1,000 respondents.
    a. Compute the 90% confidence interval for the proportion of all adults who keep money secrets from a partner.

b. What is the resulting margin of error?

c. Compute the margin of error associated with the 99% confidence level.

49. In a recent poll of 760 homeowners in the United States, one in five homeowners reports having a home equity loan that he or she is currently paying off. Using a confidence coefficient of 0.90, derive the interval estimate for the proportion of all homeowners in the United States that hold a home equity loan.

50. Obesity is generally defined as 30 or more pounds over a healthy weight. A recent study of obesity reports 27.5% of a random sample of 400 adults in the United States to be obese.

a. Use this sample information to compute the 90% confidence interval for the adult obesity rate in the United States.

b. Is it reasonable to conclude with 90% confidence that the adult obesity rate in the United States differs from 30%?

51. An accounting professor is notorious for being stingy in giving out good letter grades. In a large section of 140 students in the fall semester, she gave out only 5% A's, 23% B's, 42% C's, and 30% D's and F's. Assuming that this was a representative class, compute the 95% confidence interval of the probability of getting at least a B from this professor.

52. A study found that 55% of British firms experienced a cyber-attack in the past year (bbc.com, April 23, 2019). Suppose that the study was based on 600 British firms.

a. At 95% confidence, what is the margin of error?

b. Construct the 95% confidence interval for the population proportion of British firms that experienced a cyber-attack in the past year.

c. At 95% confidence, what can be done to reduce the margin of error?

53. A survey asked 5,324 individuals: What's most important to you when choosing where to live? The responses are shown by the following frequency distribution.

Response	Frequency
Good jobs	1,969
Affordable homes	799
Top schools	586
Low crime	1,225
Things to do	745

a. Calculate the margin of error used in the 95% confidence level for the population proportion of those who believe that low crime is most important.

b. Calculate the margin of error used in the 95% confidence level for the population proportion of those who believe that good jobs or affordable homes are most important.

c. Explain why the margins of error in parts a and b are different.

54. One in five 18-year-old Americans has not graduated from high school. A mayor of a Northeastern city comments that its residents do not have the same graduation rate as the rest of the country. An analyst from the Department of Education decides to test the mayor's claim. In particular, she draws a random sample of 80 18-year-olds in the city and finds that 20 of them have not graduated from high school.

a. Compute the point estimate for the proportion of 18-year-olds who have not graduated from high school in this city.

b. Use this point estimate to derive the 95% confidence interval for the population proportion.

c. Can the mayor's comment be justified at 95% confidence?

LO 8.7

Select a sample size to estimate the population mean and the population proportion.

8.4 SELECTING THE REQUIRED SAMPLE SIZE

So far we have discussed how a confidence interval provides useful information on an unknown population parameter. We compute the confidence interval by adding and subtracting the margin of error to/from the point estimate. If the margin of error is very large, the confidence interval becomes too wide to be of much value. For instance, little useful information can be gained from a confidence interval that suggests that the average annual starting salary of a business graduate is between \$16,000 and \$64,000. Similarly, an interval estimate that 10% to 60% of business students pursue an MBA is not very informative.

Statisticians like precision in their interval estimates, which is implied by a low margin of error. If we are able to increase the size of the sample, the larger n reduces the margin of error for the interval estimates. Although a larger sample size improves precision, it also entails the added cost in terms of time and money. Before getting into data collection, it is important that we first decide on the sample size that is adequate for what we wish to accomplish. In this section, we examine the required sample size, for a desired margin of error, in the confidence intervals for the population mean μ and the population proportion p. In order to be conservative, we always round up noninteger values for the required sample size.

Selecting *n* to Estimate μ

Consider a confidence interval for μ with a known population standard deviation σ. In addition, let E denote the desired margin of error. In other words, you do not want the sample mean to deviate from the population mean by more than E for a given level of confidence. Since $E = z_{\alpha/2}\frac{\sigma}{\sqrt{n}}$, we rearrange this equation to derive the formula for the required sample size as $n = \left(\frac{z_{\alpha/2}\sigma}{E}\right)^2$. The sample size can be computed if we specify the population standard deviation σ, the value of $z_{\alpha/2}$ based on the confidence level $100(1 - \alpha)\%$, and the desired margin of error E.

This formula is based on a knowledge of σ. However, in most cases σ is not known and, therefore, has to be estimated. Note that the sample standard deviation s cannot be used as an estimate for σ because s can be computed only after a sample of size n has been selected. In such cases, we replace σ with its reasonable estimate $\hat{\sigma}$.

THE REQUIRED SAMPLE SIZE WHEN ESTIMATING THE POPULATION MEAN

For a desired margin of error E, the minimum sample size n required to estimate a $100(1 - \alpha)\%$ confidence interval for the population mean μ is

$$n = \left(\frac{z_{\alpha/2}\hat{\sigma}}{E}\right)^2,$$

where $\hat{\sigma}$ is a reasonable estimate of σ in the planning stage.

If σ is known, we replace $\hat{\sigma}$ with σ. Sometimes we use the sample standard deviation from a preselected sample as $\hat{\sigma}$ in the planning stage. Another choice for $\hat{\sigma}$ is to use an estimate of the population standard deviation from prior studies. Finally, if the minimum and maximum values of the population are available, a rough approximation for the population standard deviation is given by $\hat{\sigma} = \text{range}/4$.

EXAMPLE 8.8

Let us revisit Example 8.5, where Jared Beane wants to construct the 90% confidence interval for the mean mpg of all ultra-green cars. Suppose Jared would like to constrain the margin of error to within 2 mpg. Jared knows that the minimum and maximum values in the population are 76 mpg and 118 mpg, respectively. How large a sample does Jared need to compute the 90% confidence interval for the population mean?

SOLUTION: For the 90% confidence level, Jared finds $z_{\alpha/2} = z_{0.05} = 1.645$. He estimates the population standard deviation as $\hat{\sigma} = \text{range}/4 = (118 - 76)/4 = 10.50$. Given $E = 2$, the required sample size is

$$n = \left(\frac{z_{\alpha/2}\hat{\sigma}}{E}\right)^2 = \left(\frac{1.645 \times 10.50}{2}\right)^2 = 74.58,$$

which is rounded up to 75. Therefore, Jared needs a random sample of at least 75 ultra-green cars to constrain the margin of error to within 2 mpg.

Selecting *n* to Estimate *p*

The margin of error E for the confidence interval for the population proportion p is $E = z_{\alpha/2}\sqrt{\frac{\bar{p}(1-\bar{p})}{n}}$, where $\bar{p}$ represents the sample proportion. By rearranging, we derive the formula for the required sample size as $n = \left(\frac{z_{\alpha/2}}{E}\right)^2 \bar{p}(1 - \bar{p})$. Analogous to the case of the population mean, this formula is not feasible because it uses $\bar{p}$, which cannot be computed unless a sample of size n has already been selected. We replace $\bar{p}$ with a reasonable estimate $\hat{p}$ of the population proportion p.

THE REQUIRED SAMPLE SIZE WHEN ESTIMATING THE POPULATION PROPORTION

For a desired margin of error E, the minimum sample size n required to estimate a $100(1 - \alpha)\%$ confidence interval for the population proportion p is

$$n = \left(\frac{z_{\alpha/2}}{E}\right)^2 \hat{p}(1 - \hat{p}),$$

where $\hat{p}$ is a reasonable estimate of p in the planning stage.

Sometimes we use the sample proportion from a preselected sample as $\hat{p}$ in the planning stage. Another choice for $\hat{p}$ is to use an estimate of the population proportion from prior studies. If no other reasonable estimate of the population proportion is available, we can use $\hat{p} = 0.5$ as a conservative estimate to derive the optimal sample size; note that the required sample is the largest when $\hat{p} = 0.5$.

EXAMPLE 8.9

Let us revisit Example 8.7, where Jared Beane wants to construct the 90% confidence interval for the proportion of all ultra-green cars that obtain over 100 mpg. Jared does not want the margin of error to be more than 0.10. How large a sample does Jared need for his analysis of the population proportion?

SOLUTION: For the 90% confidence level, Jared finds $z_{\alpha/2} = z_{0.05} = 1.645$. Since no estimate for the population proportion is readily available, Jared uses a conservative estimate of $\hat{p} = 0.50$. Given $E = 0.10$, the required sample size is

$$n = \left(\frac{z_{\alpha/2}}{E}\right)^2 \hat{p}(1 - \hat{p}) = \left(\frac{1.645}{0.10}\right)^2 0.50(1 - 0.50) = 67.65,$$

which is rounded up to 68. Therefore, Jared needs to find another random sample of at least 68 ultra-green cars to constrain the margin of error to within 0.10.

SYNOPSIS OF INTRODUCTORY CASE

Mark Dierker/McGrawHill

Jared Beane, an analyst at a research firm, prepares to write a report on the new ultra-green car that boasts an average of 100 mpg. Based on a sample of 25 cars, Jared reports, with 90% confidence, that the average mpg of all ultra-green cars is between 92.86 mpg and 100.18 mpg. Jared also constructs the 90% confidence interval for the proportion of cars that obtain more than 100 mpg and reports the interval between 0.132 and 0.428. Jared wishes to increase the precision of his confidence intervals by reducing the margin of error. If his desired margin of error is 2 mpg for the population mean, he must use a sample of at least 75 cars for the analysis. Jared also wants to reduce the margin of error to 0.10 for the proportion of cars that obtain more than 100 mpg. Using a conservative estimate, he calculates that a sample of at least 68 cars is needed to achieve this goal. Thus, in order to gain precision in the interval estimate for both the mean and the proportion with 90% confidence, Jared's sample must contain at least 75 cars.

EXERCISES 8.4

Mechanics

55. The minimum and maximum observations in a population are 20 and 80, respectively. What is the minimum sample size n required to estimate μ with 80% confidence if the desired margin of error is $E = 2.6$? What happens to n if you decide to estimate μ with 95% confidence?

56. Find the required sample size for estimating the population mean in order to be 95% confident that the sample mean is within 10 units of the population mean. Assume that the population standard deviation is 40.

57. You need to compute the 99% confidence interval for the population mean. How large a sample should you draw to ensure that the sample mean does not deviate from the population mean by more than 1.2? (Use 6.0 as an estimate of the population standard deviation from prior studies).

58. What is the minimum sample size n required to estimate μ with 90% confidence if the desired margin of error is $E = 1.2$? The population standard deviation is estimated as $\hat{\sigma} = 3.5$. What happens to n if the desired margin of error decreases to $E = 0.7$?

59. In the planning stage, a sample proportion is estimated as $\hat{p} = 40/50 = 0.80$. Use this information to compute the minimum sample size n required to estimate p with 99% confidence if the desired margin of error $E = 0.12$. What happens to n if you decide to estimate p with 90% confidence?

60. What is the minimum sample size n required to estimate p with 95% confidence if the desired margin of error $E = 0.08$? The population proportion is estimated as $\hat{p} = 0.36$ from prior studies. What happens to n if the desired margin of error increases to $E = 0.12$?

61. You wish to compute the 95% confidence interval for the population proportion. How large a sample should you draw to ensure that the sample proportion does not deviate from the population proportion by more than 0.06? No prior estimate for the population proportion is available.

Applications

62. Mortgage lenders often use FICO scores to check the credit worthiness of consumers applying for real estate loans. In general, FICO scores range from 300 to 850 with higher scores representing a better credit profile. A lender in a Midwestern town would like to estimate the mean credit score of its residents. What is the required number of sample FICO scores needed if the lender does not want the margin of error to exceed 20, with 95% confidence?

63. An analyst from an energy research institute in California wishes to estimate the 99% confidence interval for the average price of unleaded gasoline in the state. In particular, she does not want the sample mean to deviate from the population mean by more than \$0.06. What is the minimum number of gas stations that she should include in her sample if she uses the standard deviation estimate of \$0.32, as reported in the popular press?

64. An analyst would like to construct 95% confidence intervals for the mean stock returns in two industries. Industry A is a high-risk industry with a known population standard deviation of 20.6%, whereas Industry B is a low-risk industry with a known population standard deviation of 12.8%.
    a. What is the minimum sample size required by the analyst if she wants to restrict the margin of error to 4% for Industry A?
    b. What is the minimum sample size required by the analyst if she wants to restrict the margin of error to 4% for Industry B?
    c. Why do the results differ if they use the same margin of error?

65. The manager of a pizza chain in Albuquerque, New Mexico, wants to determine the average size of their advertised 16-inch pizzas. She takes a random sample of 25 pizzas and records their mean and standard deviation as 16.10 inches and 1.8 inches, respectively. She subsequently computes the 95% confidence interval of the mean size of all pizzas as [15.36, 16.84]. However, she finds this interval to be too broad to implement quality control and decides to reestimate the mean based on a bigger sample. Using the standard deviation estimate of 1.8 from her earlier analysis, how large a sample must she take if she wants the margin of error to be under 0.5 inch?

66. The manager of a newly opened Target store wants to estimate the average expenditure of his customers. From a preselected sample, the standard deviation was determined to be \$18. The manager would like to construct the 95% confidence interval for the mean customer expenditure.
    a. Find the appropriate sample size necessary to achieve a margin of error of \$5.
    b. Find the appropriate sample size necessary to achieve a margin of error of \$3.

67. A budget airline wants to estimate what proportion of customers would consider paying \$12 for in-flight wireless access. Given that the airline has no prior knowledge of the proportion, how many customers would it have to sample to ensure a margin of error of no more than 0.05 for the 90% confidence interval?

68. A newscaster wishes to estimate the proportion of registered voters who support the incumbent candidate in the mayoral election. In an earlier poll of 240 registered voters, 110 had supported the incumbent candidate. Find the sample size required to construct the 90% confidence interval if the newscaster does not want the margin of error to exceed 0.02.

69. A survey reported that approximately 70% of people in the 50 to 64 age bracket have tried some type of alternative therapy (for instance, acupuncture or the use of nutrition supplements). Assume this survey was based on a sample of 400 people.
    a. Identify the relevant parameter of interest for this categorical variable and compute its point estimate as well as the margin of error with 90% confidence.
    b. You decide to redo the analysis with the margin of error reduced to 2%. How large a sample do you need to

draw? State your assumptions in computing the required sample size.

70. A report finds that two in five subprime mortgages are likely to default in the United States. A research economist is interested in estimating default rates in the state of Illinois with 95% confidence. How large a sample is needed to restrict the margin of error to within 0.06, using the reported national default rate?

71. A business student is interested in estimating the 99% confidence interval for the proportion of students who bring laptops to campus. He wants a precise estimate and is willing to draw a large sample that will keep the sample proportion within five percentage points of the population proportion. What is the minimum sample size required by this student, given that no prior estimate of the population proportion is available?

8.5 WRITING WITH DATA

Andrew Resek/McGraw-Hill Education

Todd A. Merport/Shutterstock

Callie Fitzpatrick, a research analyst with an investment firm, has been asked to write a report summarizing the weekly stock performance of Home Depot and Lowe's. Her manager is trying to decide whether or not to include one of these stocks in a client's portfolio and the average stock performance is one of the factors influencing this decision. Callie decides to use descriptive measures to summarize stock returns in her report, as well as provide confidence intervals for the average return for Home Depot and Lowe's. She collects weekly returns for each firm from January through December of 2019. A portion of the return data is shown in Table 8.5.

FILE
Weekly_Returns

TABLE 8.5 Weekly Returns (in percent) for Home Depot and Lowe's

Date	Home Depot	Lowe's
1/7/2019	3.33	3.65
1/14/2019	0.09	−2.38
⋮	⋮	⋮
12/30/2019	−1.21	−0.15

Sample Report— Weekly Stock Performance: Home Depot vs. Lowe's

Home Depot and Lowe's are the two largest home-improvement retailers in the United States. An analysis of their recent stock performance proves useful in understanding each firm's financial stability, especially when determining whether to hold either stock in a client's portfolio.

Weekly stock return data for each firm were gathered from January through December of 2019. Table 8.6 summarizes some important descriptive statistics.

TABLE 8.6 Descriptive Statistics for Weekly Returns of Home Depot and Lowe's ($n = 52$)

	Home Depot (in %)	Lowe's (in %)
Mean	0.52	0.58
Median	0.55	0.88
Minimum	−8.12	−12.52
Maximum	6.79	13.28
Standard deviation	2.78	3.77
Margin of error with 95% confidence	0.77	1.05

As compared to Home Depot, Lowe's posted both a higher average return (0.58% > 0.52%) and a higher median return (0.88% > 0.55%) over this time period. However, the standard deviation for Lowe's weekly return was higher than Home Depot's (3.77% > 2.78%), implying that an investment in Lowe's stock was riskier than an investment in Home Depot's stock.

Table 8.6 also shows the margins of error for 95% confidence intervals for the mean returns. With 95% confidence, the mean return for Home Depot fell in the range [−0.25%, 1.29%], while that for Lowe's fell in the range [−0.47%, 1.63%]. Given that these two intervals overlap, one cannot conclude that Lowe's delivered the higher reward over this period—a conclusion one may have arrived at had only the point estimates been evaluated. It is not possible to recommend one stock over the other for inclusion in a client's portfolio based solely on the mean return performance. Other factors, such as the correlation between the stock and the existing portfolio, must be analyzed before this decision can be made.

Suggested Case Studies

REPORT 8.1 FILE ***Wages.*** The accompanying data file shows the hourly wages (in $) of 30 workers with a bachelor's degree or higher, 30 workers with only a high school diploma, and 30 workers who did not finish high school. In a report, use summary measures to compare the hourly wages for the three education levels. In addition, construct and interpret confidence intervals for the mean hourly wage at each education level.

REPORT 8.2 FILE ***Fidelity Returns.*** The accompanying data file shows the annual returns for two mutual funds offered by the investment giant Fidelity. The *Fidelity Select Automotive Fund* invests primarily in companies engaged in the manufacturing, marketing, or sales of automobiles, trucks, specialty vehicles, parts, tires, and related services. The *Fidelity Select Gold Fund* invests primarily in companies engaged in exploration, mining, processing, or dealing in gold and, to a lesser degree, in other precious metals and minerals. In a report, use summary measures to compare the returns of the mutual funds. In addition, assess reward by constructing and interpreting confidence intervals for the mean return. State any assumptions that you make for the interval estimates.

REPORT 8.3 Go to https://www.realclearpolitics.com/ and find the most current approval rating for the U.S. President using the RCP average. Construct a confidence interval for the approval rating assuming that the sample size is 600. Next find the approval rating when the President first assumed office. Construct another confidence interval for the approval rating using a sample size of 600. Comment on the similarities and differences between the intervals. Repeat this process with another elected official.

CONCEPTUAL REVIEW

LO 8.1 Explain a confidence interval.

The sample mean $\overline{X}$ is the point estimator for the population mean μ, and the sample proportion $\overline{P}$ is the point estimator for the population proportion p. Sample values of the point estimators represent the point estimates for the population parameter of interest; $\overline{x}$ and $\overline{p}$ are the point estimates for μ and p, respectively. While a point estimator provides a single value that approximates the unknown parameter, a confidence interval, or an interval estimate, provides a range of values that, with a certain level of confidence, will contain the population parameter of interest.

Often, we construct a confidence interval as point estimate $\pm$ margin of error. The margin of error accounts for the variability of the estimator and the desired confidence level of the interval.

LO 8.2 Calculate a confidence interval for the population mean when the population standard deviation is known.

A $100(1 - \alpha)\%$ confidence interval for the population mean μ when the population standard deviation σ is known is computed as $\bar{x} \pm z_{\alpha/2}\frac{\sigma}{\sqrt{n}}$, where $z_{\alpha/2}\frac{\sigma}{\sqrt{n}}$ is the margin of error. This formula is valid only if $\overline{X}$ (approximately) follows a normal distribution.

LO 8.3 Describe the factors that influence the width of a confidence interval.

The precision of a confidence interval is directly linked with the width of the interval: the wider the interval, the lower its precision. A confidence interval is wider the greater the population standard deviation σ, the smaller the sample size n, and/or the greater the confidence level.

LO 8.4 Discuss features of the *t* distribution.

The t distribution is a family of distributions that are similar to the z distribution, in that they are all symmetric and bell-shaped around zero with asymptotic tails. However, the t distribution has broader tails than does the z distribution. Each t distribution is identified by a parameter known as the degrees of freedom df. The df determine the extent of broadness—the smaller the df, the broader the tails. Since the t distribution is defined by the degrees of freedom, it is common to refer to it as the t_{df} distribution.

LO 8.5 Calculate a confidence interval for the population mean when the population standard deviation is not known.

A $100(1 - \alpha)\%$ confidence interval for the population mean μ when the population standard deviation σ is not known is computed as $\bar{x} \pm t_{\alpha/2,df}\frac{s}{\sqrt{n}}$, where $df = n - 1$ and s is the sample standard deviation. This formula is valid only if $\overline{X}$ (approximately) follows a normal distribution.

LO 8.6 Calculate a confidence interval for the population proportion.

A $100(1 - \alpha)\%$ confidence interval for the population proportion p is computed as $\bar{p} \pm z_{\alpha/2}\sqrt{\frac{\bar{p}(1-\bar{p})}{n}}$, where $\bar{p}$ is the sample proportion. This formula is valid only if $\overline{P}$ (approximately) follows a normal distribution.

LO 8.7 Select a sample size to estimate the population mean and the population proportion.

For a desired margin of error E, the minimum n required to estimate μ with $100(1 - \alpha)\%$ confidence is $n = \left(\frac{z_{\alpha/2}\hat{\sigma}}{E}\right)^2$, where $\hat{\sigma}$ is a reasonable estimate of σ in the planning stage. If σ is known, we replace $\hat{\sigma}$ with σ. Other choices for $\hat{\sigma}$ include an estimate from a preselected sample, prior studies, or $\hat{\sigma} = \text{range}/4$.

For a desired margin of error E, the minimum n required to estimate p with $100(1 - \alpha)\%$ confidence is $n = \left(\frac{z_{\alpha/2}}{E}\right)^2 \hat{p}(1 - \hat{p})$, where $\hat{p}$ is a reasonable estimate of p in the planning stage. Choices for $\hat{p}$ include an estimate from a preselected sample or prior studies; a conservative estimate of $\hat{p} = 0.5$ is used when no other reasonable estimate is available.

ADDITIONAL EXERCISES

72. Over a 10-year sample period, the mean and the standard deviation of annual returns on a portfolio you are analyzing were 10% and 15%, respectively. You assume that returns are normally distributed. Construct the 95% confidence interval for the population mean.

73. **FILE** ***Salon.*** A hair salon in Cambridge, Massachusetts, reports that on seven randomly selected weekdays, the number of customers who visited the salon were 40, 30, 28, 22, 36, 16, and 50. It can be assumed that weekday customer visits follow a normal distribution.
   a. Construct the 90% confidence interval for the average number of customers who visit the salon on weekdays.
   b. Construct the 99% confidence interval for the average number of customers who visit the salon on weekdays.
   c. What happens to the width of the interval as the confidence level increases?

74. A study finds that the average U.S. worker takes 16 days of vacation each year. Assume that these data were based on a sample of 225 workers and that the sample standard deviation is 12 days.
   a. Construct the 95% confidence interval for the population mean.
   b. At the 95% confidence level, can we conclude that the average U.S. worker does not take 14 days of vacation each year?

75. **FILE** ***SLO.*** Recently, six single-family homes in San Luis Obispo County in California sold at the following prices (in $1,000s): 549, 449, 705, 529, 639, and 609.
   a. Construct the 95% confidence interval for the mean sale price in San Luis Obispo County.
   b. What assumption have you made when constructing this confidence interval?

76. A study finds that students who graduated from college in 2015 owed an average of $25,250 in student loans. An economist wants to determine if average debt has changed. She takes a sample of 40 recent graduates and finds that their average debt was $27,500 with a standard deviation of $9,120. Use the 90% confidence interval to determine if average debt has changed.

77. A machine that is programmed to package 1.20 pounds of cereal is being tested for its accuracy. In a sample of 36 cereal boxes, the sample mean filling weight is calculated as 1.22 pounds. The population standard deviation is known to be 0.06 pound.
   a. Identify the relevant parameter of interest for this numerical variable and compute its point estimate as well as the margin of error with 95% confidence.
   b. Can we conclude that the packaging machine is operating improperly?
   c. How large a sample must we take if we want the margin of error to be at most 0.01 pound with 95% confidence?

78. Scores on the math portion of the SAT are believed to be normally distributed and range from 200 to 800. A researcher from the admissions department at the University of New Hampshire is interested in estimating the mean math SAT scores of the incoming class with 90% confidence. How large a sample should she take to ensure that the margin of error is below 15?

79. A study finds that 82% of employees will likely quit because of lack of progression at the job (msn.com, January 14, 2020). Suppose this study was based on a random sample of 50 employees.
   a. Construct the 99% confidence interval for the proportion of all employees who will likely quit because of lack of progression at the job.
   b. What is the margin of error with 99% confidence?

80. **FILE** ***FundReturn.*** Over the past five years, an analyst records the annual returns (in percent) for a mutual fund as: 13, −2, 3, 18, and −14.
   a. Calculate the point estimate for μ.
   b. Construct the 95% confidence interval for μ.
   c. What assumption did you make when constructing the interval?

81. **FILE** ***MV_Houses.*** A realtor wants to estimate the mean price of houses in Mission Viejo, California. She collects a sample of 36 recent house sales (in $1,000s), a portion of which is shown in the accompanying table. Assume that the population standard deviation is 100 (in $1,000s). Construct and interpret 95% and 98% confidence intervals for the mean price of all houses in Mission Viejo, CA.

Prices
430
520
⋮
430

82. **FILE** ***MI_Life_Expectancy.*** Residents of Hawaii have the longest life expectancies, averaging 81.3 years (travelandleisure.com, July 16, 2018). A sociologist collects data on the age at death for 50 recently deceased Michigan residents. A portion of the data is shown in the accompanying table. Assume that the population standard deviation is 5 years.

Age at Death
76.4
76.0
⋮
73.6

a. Construct the 95% confidence interval for the mean life expectancy of all residents of Michigan.
b. Use the 95% confidence interval to determine if the mean life expectancy of Michigan residents differs from that of Hawaiian residents.

83. FILE ***Fastballs.*** The manager of a minor league baseball team wants to estimate the average fastball speed of two pitchers. He clocks 50 fastballs, in miles per hour, for each pitcher. A portion of the data is shown in the accompanying table.

Pitcher 1	Pitcher 2
87	82
86	92
⋮	⋮
86	93

a. Construct 95% confidence intervals for the mean speed for each pitcher.
b. Explain why the widths of the two intervals are different.

84. FILE ***Theater.*** The new manager of a theater would like to offer discounts to increase the number of tickets sold for shows on Monday and Tuesday evenings. She uses a sample of 30 weeks to record the number of tickets sold on these two days. A portion of the data is shown in the accompanying table.

Monday	Tuesday
221	208
187	199
⋮	⋮
194	180

a. Compare the margin of error for the 95% confidence intervals for the mean number of tickets sold for shows on Monday and Tuesday evenings.
b. Construct the 95% confidence intervals for the mean number of tickets sold for shows on Monday and Tuesday evenings.
c. Determine if the population mean differs from 200 for shows on Monday and Tuesday evenings.

85. FILE ***Rental.*** A real estate analyst examines the rental market in a college town. She gathers data on monthly rent and the square footage for 40 homes. A portion of the data is shown in the accompanying table.

Monthly Rent	Square Footage
645	500
675	648
⋮	⋮
2400	2700

a. Construct 90% and 95% confidence intervals for the mean rent for all rental homes in this college town.
b. Construct 90% and 95% confidence intervals for the mean square footage for all rental homes in this college town.

86. A study finds that one out of five Britains is not using the internet (bbc.com, September 9, 2019). Suppose that this study was based on 600 Britains.
a. With 95% confidence, what is the margin of error when estimating the proportion of all Britains who are not using the internet.
b. Construct the 95% confidence interval for the population proportion.

87. A recent survey of 3,057 individuals asked: "What's the longest vacation you plan to take this summer?" The following relative frequency distribution summarizes the results.

Response	Relative Frequency
A few days	0.21
A few long weekends	0.18
One week	0.36
Two weeks	0.22

a. Construct the 95% confidence interval for the proportion of people who plan to take a one-week vacation this summer.
b. Construct the 99% confidence interval for the proportion of people who plan to take a one-week vacation this summer.
c. Which of the two confidence intervals is wider?

88. Linda Barnes has learned from prior studies that one out of five applicants gets admitted to top MBA programs in the country. She wishes to construct her own 90% confidence interval for the acceptance rate in top MBA programs. How large a sample should she take if she does not want the acceptance rate of the sample to deviate from that of the population by more than five percentage points? State your assumptions in computing the required sample size.

89. FILE ***Field_Choice.*** Thirty college-bound students in Portland, Oregon, are asked about the field they would like to pursue in college. The choices offered in the questionnaire are Science, Business, and Other. Whether a student is male or female is also included in the questionnaire.

Field Choice	Sex
Business	Male
Other	Female
⋮	⋮
Science	Female

a. Compare the 95% confidence intervals for the proportion of students who would like to pursue science with the proportion who would like to pursue business.
b. Construct and interpret the 90% confidence interval for the proportion of female students who are college bound.

90. FILE ***Pedestrians.*** A study examined "sidewalk rage" in an attempt to find insight into anger's origins and offer suggestions for anger-management treatments (menshealth.com, March 1, 2019). "Sidewalk ragers" tend to believe that pedestrians should behave in a certain way. One possible strategy for sidewalk ragers is to avoid walkers who are distracted by other activities such as smoking and tourism. Sample data were obtained from 50 pedestrians in Lower Manhattan. It was noted if the pedestrian was smoking (equaled 1 if smoking, 0 otherwise) or was a tourist (equaled 1 if tourist, 0 otherwise). The accompanying table shows a portion of the data.

Smoking	Tourist
0	1
0	1
⋮	⋮
0	0

a. Construct and interpret the 95% confidence interval for the proportion of pedestrians in Lower Manhattan who smoke while walking.
b. Construct and interpret the 95% confidence interval for the proportion of pedestrians in Lower Manhattan who are tourists.

91. An economist would like to estimate the 95% confidence interval for the average real estate taxes collected by a small town in California. In a prior analysis, the standard deviation of real estate taxes was reported as $1,580. What is the minimum sample size required by the economist if he wants to restrict the margin of error to $500?

92. An employee of the Bureau of Transportation Statistics has been given the task of estimating the proportion of on-time arrivals of a budget airline. A prior study had estimated this on-time arrival rate as 78.5%. What is the minimum number of arrivals this employee must include in the sample to ensure that the margin of error for the 95% confidence interval is no more than 0.05?

93. A study finds that 85% of adults under 30 feel optimistic about the economy, but the optimism is shared by only 45% of those who are over 50. A research analyst would like to construct 95% confidence intervals for the proportion patterns in various regions of the country. She uses the reported rates to determine the sample size that would restrict the margin of error to within 0.05.
a. How large a sample is required to estimate the proportion of adults under 30 who feel optimistic about the economy?
b. How large a sample is required to estimate the proportion of adults over 50 who feel optimistic about the economy?

APPENDIX 8.1 Guidelines for Other Software Packages

The following section provides brief commands for Minitab, SPSS, and JMP. Where appropriate, import the specified data file into the relevant software spreadsheet prior to following the commands.

Minitab

Estimating μ, σ Known

Hockey_Pucks

(Replicating Example 8.3) From the menu, choose **Stat > Basic Statistics > 1-Sample Z.** Select **One or more samples, each in a column,** and then select Weight. After **Known standard deviation,** enter 7.5. Choose **Options.** Enter 90.0 for **Confidence Level.**

Estimating μ, σ Unknown

(Replicating Example 8.6) From the menu, choose **Stat > Basic Statistics > 1-Sample t.** Select **One or more samples, each in a column,** and then select Expenditures. Choose **Options.** Enter 95.0 for **Confidence Level.**

Estimating p

(Replicating Example 8.7) From the menu, choose **Stat > Basic Statistics > 1 Proportion.** Select **Summarized data.** Enter 7 for **Number of events** and 25 for **Number of trials.** Choose **Options.** Enter 90.0 for **Confidence Level** and after **Method** select **Normal approximation.**

SPSS

Estimating μ, σ Unknown

(Replicating Example 8.6) From the menu, choose **Analyze > Compare Means > One-Sample T Test.** Under **Test Variable(s),** select Expenditures. Choose **Options.** After **Confidence Interval Percentage** enter 95.

JMP

Estimating μ, σ Known

A. (Replicating Example 8.3) From the menu, choose **Analyze > Distribution.** Drag Weight to the **Y, Columns** box.

B. Click on the red triangle in the output window beside Weight. Choose **Confidence Interval > Other,** and after **Enter (1-alpha for Confidence level),** enter 0.90. Select **Use known sigma** and enter 7.5.

Estimating μ, σ Unknown

A. (Replicating Example 8.6) From the menu, choose **Analyze > Distribution.** Drag Expenditures to the **Y, Columns** box.

B. Click on the red triangle in the output window beside Expenditures. Choose **Confidence Interval > 0.95.**

9 Hypothesis Testing

LEARNING OBJECTIVES

After reading this chapter you should be able to:

LO **9.1** **Define the null hypothesis and the alternative hypothesis.**

LO **9.2** **Distinguish between Type I and Type II errors.**

LO **9.3** **Conduct a hypothesis test for the population mean when σ is known.**

LO **9.4** **Conduct a hypothesis test for the population mean when σ is unknown.**

LO **9.5** **Conduct a hypothesis test for the population proportion.**

In Chapter 8, we used confidence intervals to estimate an unknown population parameter of interest. We now focus on the second major area of statistical inference: hypothesis testing. We use a hypothesis test to challenge the status quo, or some belief about an underlying population parameter, based on sample data.

In this chapter, we develop hypothesis tests for the population mean and the population proportion. For instance, we may wish to test whether the average age of MBA students in the United States is less than 30 years or whether the percentage of defective items in a production process differs from 5%. In either case, since we do not have access to the entire population, we have to perform statistical inference on the basis of limited sample information. If the sample information is not consistent with the status quo, we use the hypothesis testing framework to determine if the inconsistency is real (that is, we contradict the status quo) or due to chance (that is, we do not contradict the status quo).

Ken Seet/Corbis Images/SuperStock

INTRODUCTORY CASE

Undergraduate Study Habits

Are today's college students studying hard or hardly studying? A study asserts that, over the past six decades, the number of hours that the average college student studies each week has been steadily dropping (*The Wall Street Journal*, April 10, 2019). In 1961, students invested 24 hours per week in their academic pursuits, whereas today's students study an average of 14 hours per week.

Susan Knight is an assistant dean of students at a large university in California. She wonders if the study trend is reflective of the students at her university. She randomly selects 35 students and asks their average study time per week (in hours). A portion of the responses is

TABLE 9.1 Number of Hours Spent Studying

FILE
Study_Hours

Hours
25
19
⋮
16

Susan wants to use the sample information to

1. Determine if the mean study time of students at her university is below the 1961 national average of 24 hours per week.
2. Determine if the mean study time of students at her university differs from today's national average of 14 hours per week.

A synopsis of this case is provided at the end of Section 9.3.

LO 9.1

9.1 INTRODUCTION TO HYPOTHESIS TESTING

Define the null hypothesis and the alternative hypothesis.

Every day people make decisions based on their beliefs about the true state of the world. They hold certain things to be true and others to be false, and then act accordingly. For example, an engineer believes that a certain steel cable has a breaking strength of 5,000 pounds or more, and then permits its use at a construction site; a manufacturer believes that a certain process yields capsules that contain precisely 100 milligrams of a drug, and then ships the capsules to a pharmacy; a manager believes that an incoming shipment contains 2%, or fewer, of defects, and then accepts the shipment. In these cases, and many more, the formation of these beliefs may have started as a mere conjecture, an informed guess, or a proposition tentatively advanced as true. When people formulate a belief in this way, we refer to it as a hypothesis. Sooner or later, however, every hypothesis eventually confronts evidence that either substantiates or refutes it. Determining the validity of an assumption of this nature is called hypothesis testing.

We use the hypothesis testing framework to resolve conflicts between two competing hypotheses on a particular population parameter of interest. We refer to one hypothesis as the **null hypothesis,** denoted H_0, and the other as the **alternative hypothesis,** denoted H_A. We think of the null hypothesis as corresponding to a presumed default state of nature or status quo. The alternative hypothesis, on the other hand, contradicts the default state or status quo.

> NULL HYPOTHESIS VERSUS ALTERNATIVE HYPOTHESIS
>
> When constructing a hypothesis test, we define a null hypothesis, denoted H_0, and an alternative hypothesis, denoted H_A. We conduct a hypothesis test to determine whether or not sample evidence contradicts H_0.

In statistics, we use sample information to make inferences regarding the unknown population parameters of interest. Here, our goal is to determine if the null hypothesis can be rejected in favor of the alternative hypothesis. An analogy can be drawn with applications in the medical and legal fields, where we can define the null hypothesis as "an individual is free of a particular disease" or "an accused is innocent." In both cases, the verdict is based on limited evidence, which in statistics translates into making a decision based on limited sample information.

The Decision to "Reject" or "Not Reject" the Null Hypothesis

The hypothesis testing procedure enables us to make one of two decisions. If sample evidence is inconsistent with the null hypothesis, we reject the null hypothesis. Conversely, if sample evidence is not inconsistent with the null hypothesis, then we do not reject the null hypothesis. It is not correct to conclude that "we accept the null hypothesis" because while the sample information may not be inconsistent with the null hypothesis, it does not necessarily prove that the null hypothesis is true.

> On the basis of sample information, we either "reject the null hypothesis" or "do not reject the null hypothesis."

Consider the example just referenced where the null is defined as "an individual is free of a particular disease." Suppose a medical procedure does not detect this disease. On the basis of this limited information, we can only conclude that we are unable to detect the disease (do not reject the null hypothesis). It does not necessarily prove that the person does not have the disease (accept the null hypothesis). Similarly, in the court example where the null hypothesis is defined as "an accused is innocent," we can conclude that the person is guilty (reject the null hypothesis) or that there is not enough evidence to convict (do not reject the null hypothesis).

Defining the Null and the Alternative Hypotheses

As mentioned earlier, we use a hypothesis test to contest the status quo, or some belief about an underlying population parameter, based on sample data. A very crucial step concerns the formulation of the two competing hypotheses, since the conclusion of the test depends on how the hypotheses are stated. As a general guideline, whatever we wish to establish is placed in the alternative hypothesis, whereas the null hypothesis includes the status quo. If we are unable to reject the null hypothesis, then we maintain the status quo or "business as usual." However, if we reject the null hypothesis, this establishes that the evidence supports the alternative hypothesis, which may require that we take some kind of action. For instance, if we reject the null hypothesis that an individual is free of a particular disease, then we conclude that the person is sick and, therefore, treatment should be prescribed. Similarly, if we reject the null hypothesis that an accused is innocent, we conclude that the person is guilty and, therefore, should be suitably punished.

In most applications, we require some form of the equality sign in the null hypothesis. (The justification for the equality sign will be provided later.) In general, the null hypothesis typically includes one of the following three signs: $=$, $\leq$, or $\geq$. Given that the alternative hypothesis states the opposite of the null hypothesis, the alternative hypothesis is then specified with the corresponding opposite sign: $\neq$, $>$, or $<$.

> As a general guideline, we use the alternative hypothesis as a vehicle to establish something new—that is, contest the status quo. In most applications, the null hypothesis regarding a particular population parameter of interest is specified with one of the following signs: $=$, $\leq$, or $\geq$; the alternative hypothesis is then specified with the corresponding opposite sign: $\neq$, $>$, or $<$.

A hypothesis test can be **one-tailed** or **two-tailed.** A two-tailed test is defined when the alternative hypothesis includes the $\neq$ sign. For example, H_0: $\mu = \mu_0$ versus H_A: $\mu \neq \mu_0$ and H_0: $p = p_0$ versus H_A: $p \neq p_0$ are examples of two-tailed tests, where μ_0 and p_0 represent hypothesized values of the population mean and the population proportion, respectively. If the null hypothesis is rejected, it suggests that the true parameter does not equal the hypothesized value.

A one-tailed test, on the other hand, involves a null hypothesis that can only be rejected on one side of the hypothesized value. For example, consider H_0: $\mu \leq \mu_0$ versus H_A: $\mu > \mu_0$. Here we reject the null hypothesis when there is substantial evidence that the population mean is greater than μ_0. It is also referred to as a right-tailed test since rejection of the null hypothesis occurs on the right side of the hypothesized mean. Another example is a left-tailed test, H_0: $\mu \geq \mu_0$ versus H_A: $\mu < \mu_0$, where the rejection of the null hypothesis occurs on the left side of the hypothesized mean. One-tailed tests for the population proportion are defined similarly.

> ONE-TAILED VERSUS TWO-TAILED HYPOTHESIS TESTS
>
> Hypothesis tests can be one-tailed or two-tailed. In a one-tailed test, we can reject the null hypothesis only on one side of the hypothesized value of the population parameter. In a two-tailed test, we can reject the null hypothesis on either side of the hypothesized value of the population parameter.

In general, we follow three steps when formulating the competing hypotheses:

1. Identify the relevant population parameter of interest.
2. Determine whether it is a one- or two-tailed test.
3. Include some form of the equality sign in the null hypothesis and use the alternative hypothesis to establish a claim.

The following examples highlight one- and two-tailed tests for the population mean and the population proportion. In each example, we want to state the appropriate competing hypotheses.

EXAMPLE 9.1

A trade group predicts that back-to-school spending will average $606.40 per family this year. A different economic model is needed if the prediction is wrong. Specify the null and the alternative hypotheses to determine if a different economic model is needed.

SOLUTION: Given that we are examining average back-to-school spending, the parameter of interest is the population mean μ. Since we want to be able to determine if the population mean differs from $606.40 ($\mu \neq 606.40$), we formulate the null and the alternative hypotheses for a two-tailed test as

$$H_0: \mu = 606.40$$
$$H_A: \mu \neq 606.40$$

The trade group is advised to use a different economic model if the null hypothesis is rejected.

EXAMPLE 9.2

An advertisement for a popular weight-loss clinic suggests that participants in its new diet program experience an average weight loss of more than 10 pounds. A consumer activist wants to determine if the advertisement's claim is valid. Specify the null and the alternative hypotheses to validate the advertisement's claim.

SOLUTION: The advertisement's claim concerns average weight loss; thus, the parameter of interest is again the population mean μ. This is an example of a one-tailed test because we want to determine if the mean weight loss is more than 10 pounds ($\mu > 10$). We specify the competing hypotheses as

$$H_0: \mu \leq 10 \text{ pounds}$$
$$H_A: \mu > 10 \text{ pounds}$$

The underlying claim that the mean weight loss is more than 10 pounds is valid if our decision is to reject the null hypothesis. Conversely, if we do not reject the null hypothesis, we cannot support the claim.

EXAMPLE 9.3

A television research analyst wishes to test a claim that more than 50% of the households will tune in for a TV episode. Specify the null and the alternative hypotheses to test the claim.

SOLUTION: This is an example of a one-tailed test regarding the population proportion p. Given that the analyst wants to determine whether $p > 0.50$, this claim is placed in the alternative hypothesis, whereas the null hypothesis is just its opposite.

$$H_0: p \leq 0.50$$
$$H_A: p > 0.50$$

The claim that more than 50% of the households will tune in for a TV episode is valid only if the null hypothesis is rejected.

EXAMPLE 9.4

It is generally believed that at least 60% of the residents in a small town in Texas are happy with their lives. A sociologist wonders whether recent economic woes have adversely affected the happiness level in this town. Specify the null and the alternative hypotheses to determine if the sociologist's concern is valid.

SOLUTION: This is also a one-tailed test regarding the population proportion p. While the population proportion has been at least 0.60 ($p \geq 0.60$), the sociologist wants to establish that the current population proportion is below 0.60 ($p < 0.60$). Therefore, the hypotheses are formulated as

$$H_0: p \geq 0.60$$
$$H_A: p < 0.60$$

In this case, the sociologist's concern is valid if the null hypothesis is rejected. Nothing new is established if the null hypothesis is not rejected.

Type I and Type II Errors

LO 9.2

Distinguish between Type I and Type II errors.

Since the decision of a hypothesis test is based on limited sample information, we are bound to make errors. Ideally, we would like to be able to reject the null hypothesis when the null hypothesis is false and not reject the null hypothesis when the null hypothesis is true. However, we may end up rejecting or not rejecting the null hypothesis erroneously. In other words, sometimes we reject the null hypothesis when we should not, or not reject the null hypothesis when we should.

We consider two types of errors in the context of hypothesis testing: a **Type I error** and a **Type II error.** A Type I error is committed when we reject the null hypothesis when the null hypothesis is true. On the other hand, a Type II error is made when we do not reject the null hypothesis when the null hypothesis is false.

Table 9.2 summarizes the circumstances surrounding Type I and Type II errors. Two correct decisions are possible: not rejecting the null hypothesis when the null hypothesis is true and rejecting the null hypothesis when the null hypothesis is false. Conversely, two incorrect decisions (errors) are also possible: rejecting the null hypothesis when the null hypothesis is true (Type I error) and not rejecting the null hypothesis when the null hypothesis is false (Type II error).

TABLE 9.2 Type I and Type II Errors

Decision	Null hypothesis is true	Null hypothesis is false
Reject the null hypothesis	Type I error	Correct decision
Do not reject the null hypothesis	Correct decision	Type II error

EXAMPLE 9.5

Consider the following hypotheses that relate to the medical example mentioned earlier.

H_0: A person is free of a particular disease
H_A: A person has a particular disease

Suppose the person takes a medical test that attempts to detect this disease. Discuss the consequences of a Type I error and a Type II error.

SOLUTION: A Type I error occurs when the medical test indicates that the person has the disease (reject H_0), but, in reality, the person is free of the disease. We often refer to this type of result as a false positive. If the medical test shows that the person is free of the disease (do not reject H_0), when the person has the disease, then a Type II error occurs. We often call this type of result a false negative. Arguably, the consequences of a Type II error in this example are more serious than those of a Type I error.

EXAMPLE 9.6

Consider the following competing hypotheses that relate to the court of law.

H_0: An accused person is innocent
H_A: An accused person is guilty

Suppose the accused person is judged by a jury of her peers. Discuss the consequences of a Type I error and a Type II error.

SOLUTION: A Type I error is a verdict that finds that the accused is guilty (reject H_0) when she is innocent. A Type II error is a verdict that finds that the accused is innocent (do not reject H_0) when she is guilty. In this example, it is not clear which of the two errors is more costly to society.

As noted in Example 9.6, it is not always easy to determine which of the two errors has more serious consequences. For given evidence, there is a trade-off between these errors; by reducing the likelihood of a Type I error, we implicitly increase the likelihood of a Type II error, and vice versa. The only way we can reduce both errors is by collecting more evidence. Let us denote the probability of a Type I error by α, the probability of a Type II error by β, and the strength of the evidence by the sample size n. Therefore, we can conclude that the only way we can lower both α and β is by increasing n. For a given n, however, we can reduce α only at the expense of a higher β and reduce β only at the expense of a higher α.

The optimal choice of α and β depends on the relative cost of these two types of errors, and determining these costs is not always easy. Typically, the decision regarding the optimal level of Type I and Type II errors is made by the management of a firm where the job of a statistician is to conduct the hypothesis test for a chosen value of α.

EXERCISES 9.1

1. Explain why the following hypotheses are not constructed correctly.
   a. H_0: $\mu \leq 10$; H_A: $\mu \geq 10$
   b. H_0: $\mu \neq 500$; H_A: $\mu = 500$
   c. H_0: $p \leq 0.40$; H_A: $p > 0.42$
   d. H_0: $\overline{X} \leq 128$; H_A: $\overline{X} > 128$
2. Which of the following statements are valid null and alternative hypotheses? If they are invalid hypotheses, explain why.
   a. H_0: $\overline{X} \leq 210$; H_A: $\overline{X} > 210$
   b. H_0: $\mu = 120$; H_A: $\mu \neq 120$
   c. H_0: $p \leq 0.24$; H_A: $p > 0.24$
   d. H_0: $\mu < 252$; H_A: $\mu > 252$
3. Explain why the following statements are not correct.
   a. "With my methodological approach, I can reduce the Type I error with the given sample information without changing the Type II error."
   b. "I have already decided how much of the Type I error I am going to allow. A bigger sample will not change either the Type I or Type II error."
   c. "I can reduce the Type II error by making it difficult to reject the null hypothesis."
   d. "By making it easy to reject the null hypothesis, I am reducing the Type I error."
4. Which of the following statements are correct? Explain if incorrect.
   a. "I accept the null hypothesis since sample evidence is not inconsistent with the null hypothesis."
   b. "Since sample evidence cannot be supported by the null hypothesis, I reject the null hypothesis."
   c. "I can establish a given claim if sample evidence is consistent with the null hypothesis."
   d. "I cannot establish a given claim if the null hypothesis is not rejected."
5. Construct the null and the alternative hypotheses for the following tests:
   a. Test if the mean weight of cereal in a cereal box differs from 18 ounces.
   b. Test if the stock price increases on more than 60% of the trading days.
   c. Test if Americans get an average of less than seven hours of sleep.
6. Define the consequences of Type I and Type II errors for each of the tests considered in the preceding question.
7. Construct the null and the alternative hypotheses for the following claims:
   a. "I am going to get the majority of the votes to win this election."
   b. "I suspect that your 10-inch pizzas are, on average, less than 10 inches in size."
   c. "I will have to fine the company since its tablets do not contain an average of 250 mg of ibuprofen as advertised."
8. Discuss the consequences of Type I and Type II errors for each of the claims considered in the preceding question.
9. A polygraph (lie detector) is an instrument used to determine if an individual is telling the truth. These tests are considered to be 95% reliable. In other words, if an individual lies, there is a 0.95 probability that the test will detect a lie. Let there also be a 0.005 probability that the test erroneously detects a lie even when the individual is actually telling the truth. Consider the null hypothesis, "the individual is telling the truth," to answer the following questions.
   a. What is the probability of a Type I error?
   b. What is the probability of a Type II error?
   c. What are the consequences of Type I and Type II errors?
   d. What is wrong with the statement, "I can prove that the individual is telling the truth on the basis of the polygraph result"?
10. The manager of a large manufacturing firm is considering switching to new and expensive software that promises to reduce its assembly costs. Before purchasing the software, the manager wants to conduct a hypothesis test to determine if the new software does reduce its assembly costs.
    a. Would the manager of the manufacturing firm be more concerned about a Type I error or a Type II error? Explain.
    b. Would the software company be more concerned about a Type I error or a Type II error? Explain.
11. The screening process for detecting a rare disease is not perfect. Researchers have developed a blood test that is considered fairly reliable. It gives a positive reaction in 98% of the people who have that disease. However, it erroneously gives a positive reaction in 3% of the people who do not have the disease. Consider the null hypothesis "the individual does not have the disease" to answer the following questions.
    a. What is the probability of a Type I error?
    b. What is the probability of a Type II error?
    c. What are the consequences of Type I and Type II errors?
    d. What is wrong with the nurse's analysis, "The blood test result has proved that the individual is free of disease"?
12. A consumer group has accused a restaurant of using higher fat content than what is reported on its menu. The group has been asked to conduct a hypothesis test to substantiate its claims.
    a. Is the manager of the restaurant more concerned about a Type I error or a Type II error? Explain.
    b. Is the consumer group more concerned about a Type I error or a Type II error? Explain.

9.2 HYPOTHESIS TEST FOR THE POPULATION MEAN WHEN σ IS KNOWN

In order to introduce the basic methodology for hypothesis testing, we first conduct a hypothesis test regarding the population mean μ under the assumption that the population standard deviation σ is known. While it is true that σ is rarely known, there are instances when σ is considered fairly stable and, therefore, can be determined from prior experience. In such cases, σ is treated as known. Fortunately, this assumption has no bearing on the overall procedure of conducting a hypothesis test, a procedure we use throughout the remainder of the text.

A hypothesis test regarding the population mean μ is based on the sampling distribution of the sample mean $\overline{X}$. In particular, it uses the fact that $E(\overline{X}) = \mu$ and $se(\overline{X}) = \sigma / \sqrt{n}$. Also, in order to implement the test, it is essential that $\overline{X}$ is normally distributed. Recall that $\overline{X}$ is normally distributed when the underlying population is normally distributed. If the underlying population is not normally distributed, then, by the central limit theorem, $\overline{X}$ is approximately normally distributed if the sample size is sufficiently large—that is, $n \geq 30$.

The basic principle of hypothesis testing is to first assume that the null hypothesis is true and then determine if sample evidence contradicts this assumption. This principle is analogous to the scenario in the court of law where the null hypothesis is defined as "the individual is innocent" and the decision rule is best described by "innocent until proven guilty."

There are two approaches to implementing a hypothesis test—the p-value approach and the critical value approach. The critical value approach is attractive when a computer is unavailable and all calculations must be done by hand. We discuss this approach in the appendix to this chapter. Most researchers and practitioners, however, favor the p-value approach since virtually every statistical software package reports p-values. In this text, we too focus on the p-value approach. We implement a four-step procedure that is valid for one- and two-tailed tests regarding the population mean, the population proportion, or any other population parameter of interest.

LO 9.3

Conduct a hypothesis test for the population mean when σ is known.

The *p*-Value Approach

Suppose a sociologist wants to establish that the mean retirement age is greater than 67 ($\mu > 67$). It is assumed that retirement age is normally distributed with a known population standard deviation of 9 years ($\sigma = 9$). We can investigate the sociologist's belief by specifying the competing hypotheses as

$$H_0: \mu \leq 67$$
$$H_A: \mu > 67$$

Let a random sample of 25 retirees produce an average retirement age of 71—that is, $\bar{x} = 71$. This sample evidence casts doubt on the validity of the null hypothesis, since the sample mean is greater than the hypothesized value, $\mu_0 = 67$. However, the discrepancy between $\bar{x}$ and μ_0 does not necessarily imply that the null hypothesis is false. Perhaps the discrepancy can be explained by pure chance. It is common to evaluate this discrepancy in terms of the appropriate test statistic.

TEST STATISTIC FOR μ WHEN σ IS KNOWN

The value of the test statistic for the hypothesis test of the population mean μ when the population standard deviation σ is known is computed as

$$z = \frac{\bar{x} - \mu_0}{\sigma / \sqrt{n}},$$

where μ_0 is the hypothesized value of the population mean. This formula is valid only if $\overline{X}$ (approximately) follows a normal distribution.

Note that the value of the test statistic z is evaluated at $\mu = \mu_0$, which explains why we need some form of the equality sign in the null hypothesis. Given that the population is normally distributed with a known standard deviation, $\sigma = 9$, we compute the value of the test statistic as $z = \frac{\bar{x} - \mu_0}{\sigma/\sqrt{n}} = \frac{71 - 67}{9/\sqrt{25}} = 2.2222$. Therefore, comparing $\bar{x} = 71$ with 67 is identical to comparing $z = 2.2222$ with 0, where 67 and 0 are the means of $\bar{X}$ and Z, respectively.

We now find the ***p*-value,** which is the likelihood of obtaining a sample mean that is at least as extreme as the one derived from the given sample, under the assumption that the null hypothesis is true as an equality—that is, $\mu_0 = 67$. Since in this example $\bar{x} = 71$, we define the extreme value as a sample mean of 71 or higher and find the p-value as $P(\bar{X} \geq 71) = P(Z \geq 2.2222) = 0.0131$. In order to find the p-value in Excel, we enter `=1-NORM.DIST(2.2222,0,1,TRUE)`; in R, we enter `pnorm(2.2222,0,1,lower.tail=FALSE)`. The Excel and R functions were detailed in earlier chapters. Figure 9.1 shows the computed p-value.

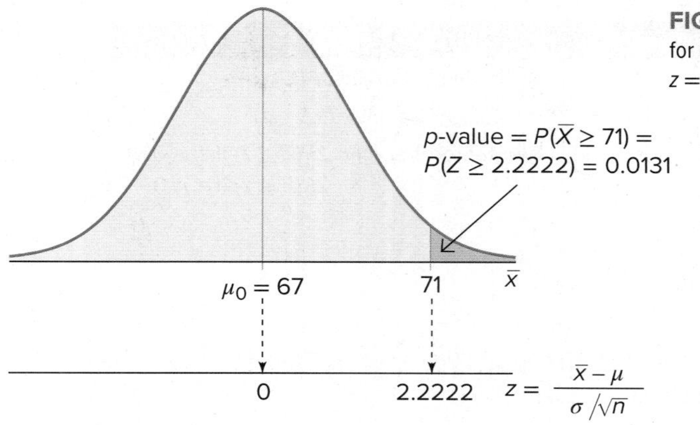

FIGURE 9.1 The p-value for a right-tailed test with $z = 2.2222$

Note that when the null hypothesis is true, there is only a 1.31% chance that the sample mean will be 71 or more. This seems like a very small chance, but is it small enough to allow us to reject the null hypothesis in favor of the alternative hypothesis? Let's see how we define "small enough."

Remember that a Type I error occurs when we reject the null hypothesis when it is true. We define the *allowed* probability of making a Type I error as α and refer to $100\alpha\%$ as the **significance level.** We generally choose a value for α *before* implementing a hypothesis test; that is, we set the rules of the game before playing. Care must be exercised in choosing α because important decisions are often based on the results of a hypothesis test, which in turn depend on α. Most hypothesis tests are conducted using a significance level of 1%, 5%, or 10%, using $\alpha = 0.01$, 0.05, or 0.10, respectively. For example, $\alpha = 0.05$ means that we allow a 5% chance of rejecting a true null hypothesis.

The p-value is referred to as the *observed* probability of making a Type I error. In the retirement example, given the p-value of 0.0131, if we decide to reject the null hypothesis, then there is a 1.31% chance that our decision will be erroneous. So, how do we decide whether or not to reject the null hypothesis, or equivalently, is this p-value "small enough"? We decide to reject the null hypothesis when the observed probability of a Type I error (the p-value) is less than the allowed probability of a Type I error (α). Or more formally, the decision rule in a hypothesis test is:

- Reject the null hypothesis if the p-value $< \alpha$, or
- Do not reject the null hypothesis if the p-value $\geq \alpha$.

Suppose we had chosen $\alpha = 0.05$ to conduct the hypothesis test in the retirement example. At this significance level, we reject the null hypothesis because $0.0131 < 0.05$. This means that the sample data support the sociologist's claim that the average retirement age is greater than 67 years old. Individuals may be working past the normal retirement age of 67 because of poor savings and/or because this generation is expected to outlive any previous generation and needs jobs to pay the bills. We should note that if α had been set at 0.01, then the findings would have been different. At this smaller significance level, the evidence does not allow us to reject the null hypothesis (0.0131 > 0.01). At the 1% significance level, we cannot conclude that the mean retirement age is greater than 67.

In the retirement age example of a right-tailed test, we calculated the p-value as $P(Z \geq z)$. Analogously, for a left-tailed test, the p-value is given by $P(Z \leq z)$. For a two-tailed test, the extreme values exist on both sides of the distribution of the test statistic. Given the symmetry of the z distribution, the p-value for a two-tailed test is twice that of the p-value for a one-tailed test. It is calculated as $2P(Z \geq z)$ if $z > 0$ or as $2P(Z \leq z)$ if $z < 0$.

THE p-VALUE APPROACH

Under the assumption that $\mu = \mu_0$, the p-value is the likelihood of observing a sample mean that is at least as extreme as the one derived from the given sample. The p-value is also referred to as the observed probability of a Type I error. Its calculation depends on the specification of the alternative hypothesis.

Alternative Hypothesis	p-value
H_A: $\mu > \mu_0$	Right-tail probability: $P(Z \geq z)$
H_A: $\mu < \mu_0$	Left-tail probability: $P(Z \leq z)$
H_A: $\mu \neq \mu_0$	Two-tail probability: $2P(Z \geq z)$ if $z > 0$ or $2P(Z \leq z)$ if $z < 0$

The decision rule is:

- Reject H_0 if the p-value $< \alpha$, or
- Do not reject H_0 if p-value $\geq \alpha$,

where α is the allowed probability of a Type I error. The significance level of a hypothesis test is defined as $100\alpha\%$.

Figure 9.2 shows the three different scenarios of determining the p-value depending on the specification of the competing hypotheses.

FIGURE 9.2 The p-values for one- and two-tailed tests

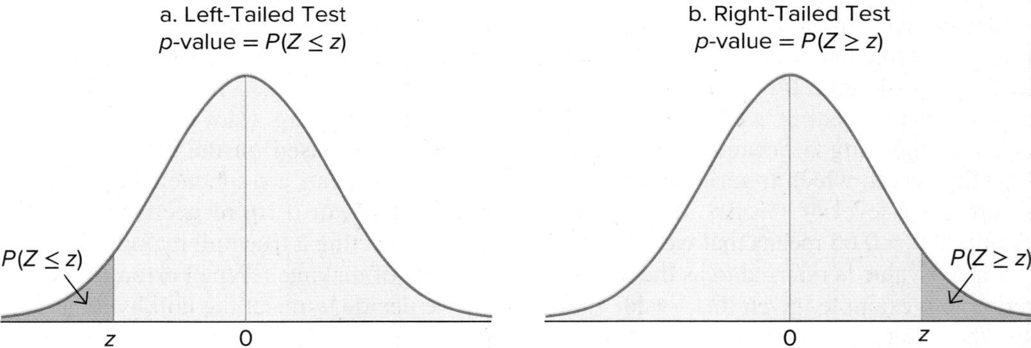

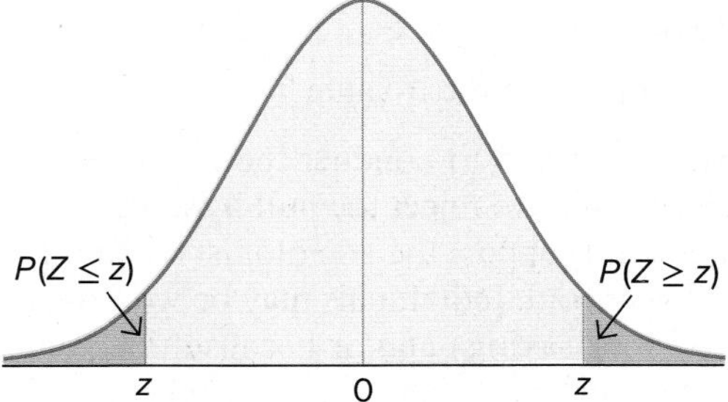

Figure 9.2a shows the p-value for a left-tailed test. Since the appropriate test statistic follows the standard normal distribution, we compute the p-value as $P(Z \leq z)$. When calculating the p-value for a right-tailed test (see Figure 9.2b), we find the area to the right of the value of the test statistic z or, equivalently, $P(Z \geq z)$. Figure 9.2c shows the p-value for a two-tailed test, calculated as $2P(Z \leq z)$ when $z < 0$ or as $2P(Z \geq z)$ when $z > 0$.

It is important to note that we *cannot* reject H_0 for a right-tailed test if $\bar{x} \leq \mu_0$ or, equivalently, $z \leq 0$. Consider, for example, a right-tailed test with the hypotheses specified as H_0: $\mu \leq 67$ versus H_A: $\mu > 67$. Here, if $\bar{x} = 65$, there is no need for formal testing since we have no discrepancy between the sample mean and the hypothesized value of the population mean. Similarly, we *cannot* reject H_0 for a left-tailed test if $\bar{x} \geq \mu_0$ or, equivalently, $z \geq 0$. We will now summarize the four-step procedure using the p-value approach.

THE FOUR-STEP PROCEDURE USING THE p-VALUE APPROACH

Step 1. Specify the null and the alternative hypotheses. We identify the relevant population parameter of interest, determine whether it is a one- or a two-tailed test and, most importantly, include some form of the equality sign in the null hypothesis and place whatever we wish to establish in the alternative hypothesis.

Step 2. Specify the significance level. Before implementing a hypothesis test, we first specify α, which is the *allowed* probability of making a Type I error.

Step 3. Calculate the value of the test statistic and the p-value. When the population standard deviation σ is known, the value of the test statistic is $z = \frac{\bar{x} - \mu}{\sigma/\sqrt{n}}$, where μ_0 is the hypothesized value of the population mean. For a right-tailed test, the p-value is $P(Z \geq z)$, and for a left-tailed test, the p-value is $P(Z \leq z)$. For a two-tailed test, the p-value is $2P(Z \geq z)$ if $z > 0$, or $2P(Z \leq z)$ if $z < 0$.

Step 4. State the conclusion and interpret results. The decision rule is to reject the null hypothesis when the p-value $< \alpha$ and not reject the null hypothesis when the p-value $\geq \alpha$. Clearly interpret the results in the context of the application.

EXAMPLE 9.7

A research analyst disputes a trade group's prediction that back-to-school spending will average \$606.40 per family this year. She believes that average back-to-school spending will differ from this amount. She decides to conduct a test on the basis of a random sample of 30 households with school-age children. She calculates the sample mean as \$622.85. She also believes that back-to-school spending is normally distributed with a population standard deviation of \$65. She wants to conduct the test at the 5% significance level.

a. Specify the competing hypotheses in order to test the research analyst's claim.

b. What is the allowed probability of a Type I error?

c. Calculate the value of the test statistic and the p-value.

d. At the 5% significance level, does average back-to-school spending differ from \$606.40?

SOLUTION:

a. Since we want to determine if the average is different from the predicted value of \$606.40, we specify the hypotheses as

$$H_0: \mu = 606.40$$
$$H_A: \mu \neq 606.40$$

b. The allowed probability of a Type I error is equivalent to the significance level of the test, which in this example is given as $\alpha = 0.05$.

c. Note that $\overline{X}$ is normally distributed since it is computed from a random sample drawn from a normal population. Since σ is known, the test statistic follows the standard normal distribution, and its value is

$$z = \frac{\bar{x} - \mu_0}{\sigma / \sqrt{n}} = \frac{622.85 - 606.40}{65 / \sqrt{30}} = 1.3862.$$

For a two-tailed test with a positive value for the test statistic, we find the p-value as $2P(Z \geq 1.3862) = 0.1657$. In order to find the p-value in Excel, we enter `=2*(1-NORM.DIST(1.3862,0,1,TRUE))`; in R we enter `2*pnorm(1.3862,0,1,lower.tail=FALSE)`.

d. The decision rule is to reject the null hypothesis if the p-value is less than α. Since $0.1657 > 0.05$, we do not reject H_0. Therefore, at the 5% significance level, we cannot conclude that average back-to-school spending differs from $606.40 per family this year. The sample data do not support the research analyst's claim.

Confidence Intervals and Two-Tailed Hypothesis Tests

A confidence interval for the population parameter is sometimes used as an alternative method for conducting a two-tailed hypothesis test. Informally, we had used this procedure when discussing confidence intervals in Chapter 8. Given that we conduct the hypothesis test at the α significance level, we can use the sample data to determine a corresponding $100(1 - \alpha)\%$ confidence interval for the population mean μ. If the confidence interval does not contain the hypothesized value of the population mean μ_0, then we reject the null hypothesis. If the confidence interval contains μ_0, then we do not reject the null hypothesis.

IMPLEMENTING A TWO-TAILED TEST USING A CONFIDENCE INTERVAL

The general specification for a $100(1 - \alpha)\%$ confidence interval for the population mean μ when the population standard deviation σ is known is computed as

$$\bar{x} \pm z_{\alpha/2}\frac{\sigma}{\sqrt{n}} \quad \text{or} \quad \left[\bar{x} - z_{\alpha/2}\frac{\sigma}{\sqrt{n}}, \bar{x} + z_{\alpha/2}\frac{\sigma}{\sqrt{n}}\right].$$

Given a hypothesized value of the population mean μ_0, the decision rule is:

- Reject H_0 if μ_0 does not fall within the confidence interval, or
- Do not reject H_0 if μ_0 falls within the confidence interval.

EXAMPLE 9.8

Use the confidence interval approach to conduct the hypothesis test described in Example 9.7.

SOLUTION: We are testing H_0: $\mu = 606.40$ versus H_A: $\mu \neq 606.40$ at the 5% significance level. We use $n = 30$, $\bar{x} = 622.85$, and $\sigma = 65$, along with $\alpha = 0.05$, to determine the 95% confidence interval for μ. We find $z_{\alpha/2} = z_{0.025} = 1.96$ and compute

$$\bar{x} \pm z_{\alpha/2}\frac{\sigma}{\sqrt{n}} = 622.85 \pm 1.96\frac{65}{\sqrt{30}} = 622.85 \pm 23.26,$$

resulting in the interval [599.59, 646.11]. Since the hypothesized value of the population mean $\mu_0 = 606.40$ falls within the 95% confidence interval, we do not reject H_0. Thus, we arrive at the same conclusion as with the p-value approach; that is, the sample data do not support the research analyst's claim that average back-to-school spending differs from $606.40 per family this year.

As shown in Example 9.8, we use the confidence interval as an alternative method for conducting a two-tailed test. It is possible to adjust the confidence interval to accommodate a one-tailed test, but we do not discuss this adjustment in this text.

One Last Remark

An important component of any well-executed statistical analysis is to clearly communicate the results. Thus, it is not sufficient to end the analysis with a conclusion that you reject the null hypothesis or you do not reject the null hypothesis. You must interpret the results, clearly reporting whether or not the claim regarding the population parameter of interest can be justified on the basis of the sample information.

EXERCISES 9.2

Mechanics

13. Consider the following hypotheses:

$$H_0: \mu \leq 12.6$$
$$H_A: \mu > 12.6$$

A sample of 25 observations yields a sample mean of 13.4. Assume that the sample is drawn from a normal population with a population standard deviation of 3.2.

a. Calculate the p-value. What is the conclusion if $\alpha = 0.10$?

b. Calculate the p-value if the above sample mean was based on a sample of 100 observations. What is the conclusion if $\alpha = 0.10$?

14. Consider the following hypotheses:

$$H_0: \mu = 100$$
$$H_A: \mu \neq 100$$

A sample of 16 observations yields a sample mean of 95. Assume that the sample is drawn from a normal population with a population standard deviation of 10.

a. Calculate the value of the test statistic.

b. Find the p-value.

c. At the 10% significance level, what is the conclusion?

15. Consider the following hypotheses:

$$H_0: \mu \geq 150$$
$$H_A: \mu < 150$$

A sample of 80 observations results in a sample mean of 144. The population standard deviation is known to be 28.

a. Calculate the value of the test statistic and the p-value.

b. Does the above sample evidence enable us to reject the null hypothesis at $\alpha = 0.01$?

c. Does the above sample evidence enable us to reject the null hypothesis at $\alpha = 0.05$?

16. A researcher wants to determine if the population mean is greater than 45. A random sample of 36 observations yields a sample mean of 47. Assume that the population standard deviation is 8.

a. Specify the competing hypotheses to test the researcher's claim.

b. Calculate the value of the test statistic.

c. Find the p-value.

d. At the 5% significance level, what is the conclusion?

17. Consider the following hypotheses:

$$H_0: \mu = 1{,}800$$
$$H_A: \mu \neq 1{,}800$$

The population is normally distributed with a population standard deviation of 440. Compute the value of the test statistic and the resulting p-value for each of the following sample results. For each sample, determine if you can reject the null hypothesis at the 10% significance level.

a. $\bar{x} = 1{,}850$; $n = 110$

b. $\bar{x} = 1{,}850$; $n = 280$

c. $\bar{x} = 1{,}650$; $n = 32$

d. $\bar{x} = 1{,}700$; $n = 32$

18. Consider the following hypothesis test:

$$H_0: \mu \leq -5$$
$$H_A: \mu > -5$$

A random sample of 50 observations yields a sample mean of −3. The population standard deviation is 10. Calculate the p-value. What is the conclusion to the test if $\alpha = 0.05$?

19. Consider the following hypothesis test:

$$H_0: \mu \leq 75$$
$$H_A: \mu > 75$$

A random sample of 100 observations yields a sample mean of 80. The population standard deviation is 30. Calculate the p-value. What is the conclusion to the test if $\alpha = 0.10$?

20. Consider the following hypothesis test:

$$H_0: \mu = -100$$
$$H_A: \mu \neq -100$$

A random sample of 36 observations yields a sample mean of −125. The population standard deviation is 42. Conduct the test at $\alpha = 0.01$.

21. Consider the following hypotheses:

$$H_0: \mu = 120$$
$$H_A: \mu \neq 120$$

The population is normally distributed with a population standard deviation of 46.

a. If $\bar{x} = 132$ and $n = 50$, what is the conclusion at the 5% significance level?

b. If $\bar{x} = 108$ and $n = 50$, what is the conclusion at the 10% significance level?

Applications

22. It is advertised that the average braking distance for a small car traveling at 65 miles per hour equals 120 feet. A transportation researcher wants to determine if the statement made in the advertisement is false. She randomly test drives 36 small cars at 65 miles per hour and records the braking distance. The sample average braking distance is computed as 114 feet. Assume that the population standard deviation is 22 feet.

a. State the null and the alternative hypotheses for the test.

b. Calculate the value of the test statistic and the p-value.

c. Use $\alpha = 0.01$ to determine if the average breaking distance differs from 120 feet.

23. Customers at Costco spend an average of $130 per trip. One of Costco's rivals would like to determine whether its customers spend more per trip. A survey of the receipts of 25 customers found that the sample mean was $135.25. Assume that the population standard deviation is $10.50 and that spending follows a normal distribution.

a. Specify the null and alternative hypotheses to test whether average spending at the rival's store is more than $130.

b. Calculate the value of the test statistic and the p-value.

c. At the 5% significance level, what is the conclusion to the test?

24. A sales manager of a used car dealership for sports utility vehicle (SUVs) believes that it takes more than 90 days, on average, to sell an SUV. In order to test his claim, he samples 40 recently sold SUVs and finds that it took an average of 95 days to sell an SUV. He believes that the population standard deviation is fairly stable at 20 days.

a. State the null and the alternative hypotheses for the test.

b. What is the p-value?

c. Is the sales manager's claim justified at $\alpha = 0.01$?

25. A researcher wants to determine if Americans are sleeping less than the recommended 7 hours of sleep on weekdays. He takes a random sample of 150 Americans and computes the average sleep time of 6.7 hours on weekdays. Assume that the population is normally distributed with a known standard deviation of 2.1 hours. Test the researcher's claim at $\alpha = 0.01$.

26. A local bottler in Hawaii wishes to ensure that an average of 16 ounces of passion fruit juice is used to fill each bottle. In order to analyze the accuracy of the bottling process, he takes a random sample of 48 bottles. The mean weight of the passion fruit juice in the sample is 15.80 ounces. Assume that the population standard deviation is 0.8 ounce.

a. State the null and the alternative hypotheses to test if the bottling process is inaccurate.

b. What is the value of the test statistic and the p-value?

c. At $\alpha = 0.05$, what is the conclusion to the hypothesis test? Make a recommendation to the bottler.

27. **FILE** ***MV_Houses.*** The data accompanying this exercise show the selling price (in $1,000s) for 36 recent house sales in Mission Viejo, California. A Realtor believes that the average price of a house is more than $500,000. Assume the population standard deviation is $100 (in $1,000s).

a. State the null and the alternative hypotheses for the test.

b. What is the value of the test statistic and the p-value?

c. At $\alpha = 0.05$, what is the conclusion to the test? Is the Realtor's claim supported by the data?

28. **FILE** ***Home.*** The data accompanying this exercise show the weekly stock price (Price in $) for a home improvement store. Assume that stock prices are normally distributed with a population standard deviation of $3.

a. State the null and the alternative hypotheses in order to test whether or not the average weekly stock price differs from $30.

b. Find the value of the test statistic and the p-value.

c. At $\alpha = 0.05$, can you conclude that the average weekly stock price does not equal $30?

29. **FILE** ***Hourly_Wage.*** The data accompanying this exercise show hourly wages (Wage in $) for 50 employees. An economist wants to test if the average hourly wage is less than $22. Assume that the population standard deviation is $6.
   a. State the null and the alternative hypotheses for the test.
   b. Find the value of the test statistic and the p-value.
   c. At $\alpha = 0.05$, what is the conclusion to the test? Is the average hourly wage less than $22?

30. **FILE** ***Undergrad_Debt.*** The accompanying data file lists the student debt for 40 recent undergraduates. A researcher believes that average student debt is more than $25,000. Assume that the population standard deviation is $5,000.
   a. Specify the competing hypotheses to test the researcher's belief.
   b. Find the value of the test statistic and the p-value.
   c. Do the data support the researcher's claim, at $\alpha = 0.10$?

9.3 HYPOTHESIS TEST FOR THE POPULATION MEAN WHEN σ IS UNKNOWN

LO 9.4

Conduct a hypothesis test for the population mean when σ is unknown.

So far we have considered hypothesis tests for the population mean μ under the assumption that the population standard deviation σ is known. In most business applications, σ is not known and we replace σ with the sample standard deviation s to estimate the standard error of $\overline{X}$ and the resulting t_{df} test statistic.

TEST STATISTIC FOR μ WHEN σ IS UNKNOWN

The value of the test statistic for the hypothesis test of the population mean μ when the population standard deviation σ is unknown is computed as

$$t_{df} = \frac{\bar{x} - \mu_0}{s/\sqrt{n}},$$

where μ_0 is the hypothesized value of the population mean, s is the sample standard deviation, n is the sample size, and the degrees of freedom $df = n - 1$. This formula is valid only if $\overline{X}$ (approximately) follows a normal distribution.

In the next two examples we use the four-step procedure for hypothesis testing for the population mean μ when the population standard deviation σ is unknown.

EXAMPLE 9.9

FILE ***Study_Hours***

In the introductory case to this chapter, the assistant dean of students at a large university in California wonders if students at her university study less than the 1961 national average of 24 hours per week. She randomly selects 35 students and asks their average study time per week (in hours). From their responses (see the ***Study_Hours*** data file), she calculates a sample mean of 16.3714 hours and a sample standard deviation of 7.2155 hours.

a. Specify the competing hypotheses to test the assistant dean's concern.

b. Calculate the value of the test statistic.

c. Find the p-value.

d. At the 5% significance level, what is the conclusion to the hypothesis test?

SOLUTION:

a. This is an example of a one-tailed test where we would like to determine if the mean hours studied is less than 24; that is, $\mu < 24$. We formulate the competing hypotheses as

$$H_0: \mu \geq 24 \text{ hours}$$
$$H_A: \mu < 24 \text{ hours}$$

b. Recall that for any statistical inference regarding the population mean, it is essential that the sample mean $\overline{X}$ is normally distributed. This condition is satisfied because the sample size is greater than 30, specifically $n = 35$. The degrees of freedom, $df = n - 1 = 34$. Given $\bar{x} = 16.3714$ and $s = 7.2155$, we compute the value of the test statistic as

$$t_{34} = \frac{\bar{x} - \mu_0}{s/\sqrt{n}} = \frac{16.3714 - 24}{7.2155/\sqrt{35}} = -6.255.$$

c. Since this is a left-tailed test, we compute the p-value as $P(T_{34} \leq t_{34})$. Table 9.3 shows a portion of the t table. Referencing Table 9.3 for $df = 34$, we find that the exact probability $P(T_{34} \leq -6.255)$, which is equivalent to $P(T_{34} \geq 6.255)$, cannot be determined. Since 6.255 is larger than any value in this row, it implies that the p-value is less than 0.005. In other words, we approximate the p-value as $P(T_{34} \leq -6.255) < 0.005$. In the next example, we will show how to use Excel and R to obtain exact p-values.

TABLE 9.3 Portion of the *t* Table

	Area in Upper Tail					
df	**0.20**	**0.10**	**0.05**	**0.025**	**0.01**	**0.005**
1	1.376	3.078	6.341	12.706	31.821	63.657
	⋮	⋮	⋮	⋮	⋮	⋮
34	0.852	1.307	1.691	2.032	2.441	2.728

d. We reject the null hypothesis since the p-value is less than $\alpha = 0.05$. At the 5% significance level, we conclude that the average study time at the university is less than the 1961 average of 24 hours per week.

Using Excel and R to Test μ When σ is Unknown

Again we find that functions in Excel and R are quite useful when calculating the value of the test statistic and the exact p-value. Consider the following example.

EXAMPLE 9.10

FILE
Study_Hours

As mentioned in the introductory case to this chapter, research finds that today's undergraduates study an average of 14 hours per week. Using the ***Study_Hours*** data file, the assistant dean would also like to test if the mean study time of students at her university differs from today's national average of 14 hours per week. At the 5% significance level, what is the conclusion to this test?

SOLUTION: Since the assistant dean would like to test if the mean study time of students at her university differs from 14 hours per week, we formulate the competing hypotheses for the test as

$$H_0: \mu = 14 \text{ hours}$$
$$H_A: \mu \neq 14 \text{ hours}$$

Using Excel

a. Open the ***Study_Hours*** data file. Note that the values for hours studied are in cells A2 through A36.

b. We use Excel's **AVERAGE** and **STDEV.S** functions to help in the calculation of the value of the test statistic $t_{df} = \frac{\bar{x} - \mu}{s/\sqrt{n}}$. We enter `=(AVERAGE(A2: A36) - 14)/(STDEV.S(A2:A36)/SQRT(35))`. Excel returns 1.9444, so $t_{34} = 1.9444$.

c. Even though Excel offers a number of functions that generate p-values, we use the **T.DIST.RT** function. If we enter `=T.DIST.RT(tdf, df)`, where t_{df} is the value of the test statistic and df is the relevant degrees of freedom, then Excel returns $P(T_{df} \geq t_{df})$; this probability is the p-value for a right-tailed test. If we enter `=1 - T.DIST.RT(tdf, df)`, then Excel returns $P(T_{df} \leq t_{df})$; this probability is the p-value for a left-tailed test. As with the z-test, the p-value for a two-tailed test is $2P(T_{df} \geq t_{df})$ if $t_{df} > 0$ or $2P(T_{df} \leq t_{df})$ if $t_{df} < 0$. Therefore, in order to find the p-value for the given two-tailed test where $t_{34} = 1.9444$, we enter `=2*T.DIST.RT(1.9444, 34)`. Excel returns 0.0602.

d. Since the p-value of 0.0602 is not less than $\alpha = 0.05$, we do not reject the null hypothesis. At the 5% significance level, we cannot conclude that the mean study time of students at the university is different from today's national average of 14 hours per week.

Using R

a. Import the ***Study_Hours*** data file into a data frame (table) and label it myData.

b. We use R's **t.test** function to obtain both the test statistic and the p-value. For options within this function, we use *alternative* to denote the specification of the alternative hypothesis (denoted as "two.sided" for a two-tailed test, "less" for a left-tailed test, and "greater" for a right-tailed test) and *mu* to denote the hypothesized value of the mean. Another feature of this function is that it automatically provides the 95% confidence interval for the mean by default; other levels can be found using the option *conf.level.* We enter

```
> t.test(myData$Hours, alternative="two.sided", mu=14)
```

Figure 9.3 shows the output that R produces. We have put the value of the test statistic and the p-value in boldface. Because the p-value of 0.0602 is not less than $\alpha = 0.05$, we do not reject the null hypothesis. At the 5% significance level, we cannot conclude that the mean study time of students at this large university in California differs from 14 hours per week.

FIGURE 9.3 R's output using t.test function

```
One sample t-test
data:  myData$Hours
t = 1.9444, df = 34, p-value = 0.06016
alternative hypothesis: true mean is not equal to 14
95 percent confidence interval:
 13.89281 18.85005
sample estimates:
mean of x
 16.37143
```

Note: If we do not have access to the raw data and only have summary statistics, then we could use R's ***pt*** function to find the p-value. In order to find the p-value for the two-tailed test in this example, we enter `2*pt(1.9444, 34, lower.tail=FALSE)`.

SYNOPSIS OF INTRODUCTORY CASE

Asia Images Group/Getty Images

A report claims that undergraduates are studying far less today as compared to six decades ago (The *Wall Street Journal*, April 10, 2019). The report finds that in 1961, students invested 24 hours per week in their academic pursuits, whereas today's students study an average of 14 hours per week. In an attempt to determine whether or not this national trend is present at a large university in California, 35 students are randomly selected and asked their average study time per week (in hours). The sample produces a mean of 16.37 hours with a standard deviation of 7.22 hours. Two hypothesis tests are conducted. The first test examines whether the mean study time of students at this university is below the 1961 national average of 24 hours per week. At the 5% significance level, the sample data suggest that the mean is less than 24 hours per week. The second test investigates whether the mean study time of students at this university differs from today's national average of 14 hours per week. At the 5% significance level, the results do not suggest that the mean study time differs from 14 hours per week. Thus, the sample results support the overall findings of the report: undergraduates study, on average, 14 hours per week, far below the 1961 average of 24 hours per week. The present analysis, however, does not explain why that might be the case. For instance, it cannot be determined whether students have just become lazier, or if with the advent of the computer, they can access information in less time.

EXERCISES 9.3

Mechanics

31. Consider the following hypotheses:

$$H_0: \mu \leq 210$$
$$H_A: \mu > 210$$

Find the *p*-value for this test based on the following sample information.

a. $\bar{x} = 216; s = 26; n = 40$
b. $\bar{x} = 216; s = 26; n = 80$
c. $\bar{x} = 216; s = 16; n = 40$
d. $\bar{x} = 214; s = 16; n = 40$

32. Which of the sample information in the preceding question enables us to reject the null hypothesis at $\alpha = 0.01$ and at $\alpha = 0.10$?

33. Consider the following hypotheses:

$$H_0: \mu = 12$$
$$H_A: \mu \neq 12$$

Find the *p*-value for this test based on the following sample information.

a. $\bar{x} = 11; s = 3.2; n = 36$
b. $\bar{x} = 13; s = 3.2; n = 36$
c. $\bar{x} = 11; s = 2.8; n = 36$
d. $\bar{x} = 11; s = 2.8; n = 49$

34. Which of the sample information in the preceding question enables us to reject the null hypothesis at $\alpha = 0.01$ and at $\alpha = 0.10$?

35. Consider the following hypotheses:

$$H_0: \mu = 50$$
$$H_A: \mu \neq 50$$

A sample of 16 observations yields a sample mean of 46. Assume that the sample is drawn from a normal population with a sample standard deviation of 10.

a. Calculate the value of the test statistic.
b. At the 5% significance level, does the population mean differ from 50? Explain.

36. In order to test if the population mean differs from 16, you draw a random sample of 32 observations and compute the sample mean and the sample standard deviation as 15.2 and 0.6, respectively. Conduct the test at the 1% level of significance.

37. In order to conduct a hypothesis test for the population mean, a random sample of 24 observations is drawn from a normally distributed population. The resulting sample mean and sample standard deviation are calculated as 4.8 and 0.8, respectively. Conduct the following tests at $\alpha = 0.05$.

a. $H_0: \mu \leq 4.5$ against $H_A: \mu > 4.5$
b. $H_0: \mu = 4.5$ against $H_A: \mu \neq 4.5$

38. Consider the following hypotheses:

$$H_0: \mu \geq -10$$
$$H_A: \mu < -10$$

A sample of 25 observations yields a sample mean of −12. Assume that the sample is drawn from a normal population with a sample standard deviation of 4.

a. Calculate the value of the test statistic.

b. At the 5% significance level, is the population mean less than −10? Explain.

39. Consider the following hypotheses:

$$H_0: \mu = 8$$
$$H_A: \mu \neq 8$$

The population is normally distributed. A sample produces the following observations:

6	9	8	7	7	11	10

Conduct the test at the 5% level of significance.

40. Consider the following hypotheses:

$$H_0: \mu \geq 100$$
$$H_A: \mu < 100$$

The population is normally distributed. A sample produces the following observations:

95	99	85	80	98	97

Conduct the test at the 1% level of significance.

Applications

41. A machine that is programmed to package 1.20 pounds of cereal in each cereal box is being tested for its accuracy. In a sample of 36 cereal boxes, the mean and the standard deviation are calculated as 1.22 pounds and 0.06 pound, respectively.

a. Set up the null and the alternative hypotheses to determine if the machine is working improperly—that is, it is either underfilling or overfilling the cereal boxes.

b. Calculate the value of the test statistic and the *p*-value.

c. At the 5% level of significance, can you conclude that the machine is working improperly? Explain.

42. The manager of a small convenience store does not want her customers standing in line for too long prior to a purchase. In particular, she is willing to hire an employee for another cash register if the average wait time of the customers is more than five minutes. She randomly observes the wait time (in minutes) for 20 customers and calculates a mean and standard deviation of 6.5 and 2.2, respectively.

a. Set up the null and the alternative hypotheses to determine if the manager needs to hire another employee.

b. Calculate the value of the test statistic and the *p*-value. What assumption regarding the population is necessary to implement this step?

c. Decide whether the manager needs to hire another employee at $\alpha = 0.10$.

43. **FILE** ***Prime.*** Amazon Prime is a $119-per-year service that gives the company's customers free two-day shipping and discounted rates on overnight delivery. Prime customers also get other perks, such as free e-books. An analyst believes that Prime customers spend more than $1,200 per year on this service. The data accompanying this exercise show the annual expenditures (in $) of 100 Prime customers.

a. Specify the null and alternative hypotheses to test the analyst's claim.

b. Calculate the value of the test statistic and the *p*-value.

c. At the 5% significance level, what is the conclusion to the test? Is the analyst's claim supported by the sample data?

44. A local brewery wishes to ensure that an average of 12 ounces of beer is used to fill each bottle. In order to analyze the accuracy of the bottling process, the bottler takes a random sample of 48 bottles. The sample mean weight and the sample standard deviation of the bottles are 11.80 ounces and 0.8 ounce, respectively.

a. State the null and the alternative hypotheses to test if the accuracy of the bottling process is compromised.

b. Do you need to make any assumption regarding the population before implementing the hypothesis test?

c. Calculate the value of the test statistic and the *p*-value.

d. At $\alpha = 0.05$, what is the conclusion to the test? Make a recommendation to the bottler.

45. Based on the average predictions of 45 economists, the U.S. gross domestic product (GDP) will expand by 2.8% this year. Suppose the sample standard deviation of their predictions was 1%. At the 5% significance level, test if the mean forecast GDP of all economists is less than 3%.

46. This past year, home prices in the Midwest increased by an average of 6.6%. A Realtor collects data on 36 recent home sales in the West. He finds an average increase in home prices of 7.5% with a standard deviation of 2%. Can he conclude that the average increase in home prices in the West is greater than the increase in the Midwest? Use a 5% significance level for the analysis.

47. A car manufacturer is trying to develop a new sports car. Engineers are hoping that the average amount of time that the car takes to go from 0 to 60 miles per hour is below 6 seconds.

The manufacturer tested 12 of the cars and clocked their performance times. Three of the cars clocked in at 5.8 seconds, 5 cars at 5.9 seconds, 3 cars at 6.0 seconds, and 1 car at 6.1 seconds. At the 5% level of significance, test if the new sports car is meeting its goal to go from 0 to 60 miles per hour in less than 6 seconds. Assume a normal distribution for the analysis.

48. **FILE** ***APR.*** A mortgage analyst collects data from seven financial institutions on the annual percentage rate (APR) for a 30-year fixed loan. The data accompanying this exercise show the results.
   a. State the null and the alternative hypothesis in order to test whether the mean mortgage rate for the population exceeds 4.2%.
   b. What assumption regarding the population is necessary in order to implement part a?
   c. Calculate the value of the test statistic and the p-value.
   d. At a 10% significance level, what is the conclusion to the test? Does the mean mortgage rate for the population exceed 4.2%?

49. **FILE** ***PE_Ratio.*** A price-earnings ratio or P/E ratio is calculated as a firm's share price compared to the income or profit earned by the firm per share. Generally, a high P/E ratio suggests that investors are expecting higher earnings growth in the future compared to firms with a lower P/E ratio. The data accompanying this exercise show P/E ratios for 30 firms.
   a. State the null and the alternative hypotheses in order to test whether the P/E ratio of all firms differs from 15.
   b. Calculate the value of the test statistic and the p-value.
   c. At $\alpha = 0.05$, does the P/E ratio of all firms differ from 15? Explain.

50. **FILE** ***MPG.*** The data accompanying this exercise show miles per gallon (MPG) for 25 'super-green' cars.
   a. State the null and the alternative hypotheses in order to test whether the average MPG differs from 95.
   b. Calculate the value of the test statistic and the p-value.
   c. At $\alpha = 0.05$, can you conclude that the average MPG differs from 95?

51. **FILE** ***Debt_Payments.*** The data accompanying this exercise show the average debt payments (Debt, in $) for 26 metropolitan areas.
   a. State the null and the alternative hypotheses in order to test whether average monthly debt payments are greater than $900.
   b. What assumption regarding the population is necessary in order to implement part a?
   c. Calculate the value of the test statistic and the p-value.
   d. At $\alpha = 0.05$, are average monthly debt payments greater than $900? Explain.

52. **FILE** ***Highway_Speeds.*** A police officer is concerned about speeds on a certain section of Interstate 95. The data accompanying this exercise show the speeds of 40 cars on a Saturday afternoon.
   a. The speed limit on this portion of Interstate 95 is 65 mph. Specify the competing hypotheses in order to determine if the average speed is greater than the speed limit.
   b. Calculate the value of the test statistic and the p-value.
   c. At $\alpha = 0.01$, are the officer's concerns warranted? Explain.

53. **FILE** ***Lottery.*** An article found that Massachusetts residents spent an average of $860.70 on the lottery, more than three times the U.S. average. A researcher at a Boston think tank believes that Massachusetts residents spend less than this amount. He surveys 100 Massachusetts residents and asks them about their annual expenditures on the lottery. The data accompanying this exercise show their responses.
   a. Specify the competing hypotheses to test the researcher's claim.
   b. Calculate the value of the test statistic and the p-value.
   c. At the 10% significance level, do the data support the researcher's claim? Explain.

LO 9.5

Conduct a hypothesis test for the population proportion.

9.4 HYPOTHESIS TEST FOR THE POPULATION PROPORTION

Recall that the population mean μ describes a numerical variable whereas the population proportion p is the essential descriptive measure for a categorical variable. The parameter p represents the proportion of observations with a particular attribute.

As in the case for the population mean, we estimate the population proportion on the basis of its sample counterpart. In particular, we use the sample proportion $\overline{P}$ to estimate the population proportion p. Recall that although $\overline{P}$ is based on the binomial distribution, it can be approximated by a normal distribution in large samples. This approximation is considered valid when $np \geq 5$ and $n(1 - p) \geq 5$. Since p is not known, we typically test the sample size requirement under the hypothesized value of the population proportion p_0. In most applications, the sample size is large and the normal distribution approximation is justified. However, when the sample size is not deemed large enough, the statistical methods suggested here for inference regarding the population proportion are no longer valid.

Recall from Chapter 7 that the mean and the standard error of the sample proportion $\overline{P}$ are given by $E(\overline{P}) = p$ and $se(\overline{P}) = \sqrt{p(1-p)/n}$, respectively. The test statistic for p is defined as follows.

TEST STATISTIC FOR p

The value of the test statistic for the hypothesis test of the population proportion p is computed as

$$z = \frac{\overline{p} - p_0}{\sqrt{p_0(1-p_0)/n}},$$

where p_0 is the hypothesized value of the population proportion. This formula is valid only if $\overline{P}$ (approximately) follows a normal distribution.

The following examples elaborate on the four-step procedure for a hypothesis test for the population proportion.

EXAMPLE 9.11

A popular weekly magazine asserts that fewer than 40% of households in the United States have changed their lifestyles because of environmental concerns. A recent survey of 180 households finds that 67 households have made lifestyle changes due to environmental concerns.

a. Specify the competing hypotheses to test the magazine's claim.

b. Calculate the value of the test statistic and the p-value.

c. At the 5% level of significance, what is the conclusion to the test?

SOLUTION:

a. We wish to establish that the population proportion is less than 0.40—that is, $p < 0.40$. Thus, we construct the competing hypotheses as

$$H_0: p \geq 0.40$$
$$H_A: p < 0.40$$

b. When evaluated at $p_0 = 0.40$ with $n = 180$, the normality requirement that $np \geq 5$ and $n(1-p) \geq 5$ is satisfied. We use the sample proportion, $\overline{p} = 67/180 = 0.3722$, to compute the value of the test statistic as

$$z = \frac{\overline{p} - p_0}{\sqrt{P_0(1-p_0)/n}} = \frac{0.3722 - 0.40}{\sqrt{0.40(1-0.40)/180}} = -0.7613.$$

Since this is a left-tailed test for the population proportion, we find the p-value as $P(Z \leq z) = P(Z \leq -0.7613) = 0.2232$. In order to find the p-value in Excel, we enter `=NORM.DIST(-0.7613,0,1,TRUE)`; in R we enter `pnorm(-0.7613,0,1,lower.tail=TRUE)`. The Excel and R functions were detailed in earlier chapters.

c. The p-value of 0.2232 is greater than the chosen $\alpha = 0.05$. Therefore, we do not reject the null hypothesis. This means that the magazine's claim that fewer than 40% of households in the United States have changed their lifestyles because of environmental concerns is not justified by the sample data at the 5% significance level. Such a conclusion may be welcomed by firms that have invested in alternative energy.

EXAMPLE 9.12

Driven by growing public support, the legalization of marijuana in America has been moving at a breakneck speed. Approximately 67% of adults say the use of marijuana should be made legal (www.pewresearch.org, November 14, 2019). A health practitioner in Ohio collects data from 200 adults and finds that 122 of them favor marijuana legalization.

a. The health practitioner believes that the proportion of adults who favor marijuana legalization in Ohio is not representative of the national proportion. Specify the competing hypotheses to test her claim.

b. Calculate the value of the test statistic and the p-value.

c. At the 10% significance level, do the sample data support the health practitioner's belief?

SOLUTION:

a. The parameter of interest is again the population proportion p. The health practitioner wants to test if the population proportion of those who favor marijuana legalization in Ohio differs from the national proportion of 0.67. We construct the competing hypotheses as

$$H_0: p = 0.67$$
$$H_A: p \neq 0.67$$

b. When evaluated at $p_0 = 0.67$ with $n = 200$, the normality requirement that $np \geq 5$ and $n(1 - p) \geq 5$ is easily satisfied. We use the sample proportion $\bar{p} = 122/200 = 0.61$ to compute the value of the test statistic as

$$z = \frac{\bar{p} - p_0}{\sqrt{p_0(1 - p_0)/n}} = \frac{0.61 - 0.67}{\sqrt{0.67(1 - 0.67)/200}} = -1.8046$$

Given a two-tailed test and $z < 0$, we compute the p-value as $2P(Z \leq z) = 2P(Z \leq -1.8046) = 0.0711$. In order to find the p-value in Excel, we enter `=2*NORM.DIST(-1.8046,0,1,TRUE)`; in R we enter `2*pnorm(-1.8046,0,1, lower.tail=TRUE)`.

c. Since the p-value of 0.0711 is less than $\alpha = 0.10$, we reject the null hypothesis. Therefore, at the 10% significance level, the proportion of adults who favor marijuana legalization in Ohio differs from the national proportion of 0.67.

EXERCISES 9.4

Mechanics

54. Consider the following hypotheses:

$$H_0: p \geq 0.38$$
$$H_A: p < 0.38$$

Calculate the p-value based on the following sample information.

a. $x = 22; n = 74$
b. $x = 110; n = 300$
c. $\bar{p} = 0.34; n = 50$
d. $\bar{p} = 0.34; n = 400$

55. Which sample information in the preceding question enables us to reject the null hypothesis at $\alpha = 0.01$ and at $\alpha = 0.10$?

56. Consider the following hypotheses

$$H_0: p = 0.32$$
$$H_A: p \neq 0.32$$

Calculate the p-value based on the following sample information

a. $x = 20; n = 66$
b. $x = 100; n = 264$
c. $\bar{p} = 0.40; n = 40$
d. $\bar{p} = 0.38; n = 180$

57. Which sample information in the preceding question enables us to reject the null hypothesis at $\alpha = 0.05$ and at $\alpha = 0.10$?

58. In order to test if the population proportion differs from 0.40, you draw a random sample of 100 observations and obtain a sample proportion of 0.48.
   a. Specify the competing hypotheses.
   b. Is the normality condition satisfied? Explain.
   c. Calculate the value of the test statistic and the p-value.
   d. At the 5% significance level, does the population proportion differ from 0.40? Explain.

59. In order to conduct a hypothesis test for the population proportion, you sample 320 observations that result in 128 successes. Conduct the following tests at $\alpha = 0.05$.
   a. $H_0: p \geq 0.45$; $H_A: p < 0.45$
   b. $H_0: p = 0.45$; $H_A: p \neq 0.45$

60. In order to test if the population proportion is greater than 0.65, you draw a random sample of 200 observations and obtain a sample proportion of 0.72.
   a. Specify the competing hypotheses.
   b. Is the normality condition satisfied? Explain.
   c. Calculate the value of the test statistic and the p-value.
   d. At the 5% significance level, is the population proportion greater than 0.65? Explain.

61. You would like to determine if the population probability of success differs from 0.70. You find 62 successes in 80 binomial trials. Implement the test at the 1% level of significance.

62. You would like to determine if more than 50% of the observations in a population are below 10. At $\alpha = 0.05$, conduct the test on the basis of the following 20 sample observations:

8	12	5	9	14	11	9	3	7	8
12	6	8	9	2	6	11	4	13	10

Applications

63. A study finds that 82% of employees will likely quit because of lack of progression at the job (msn.com, January 14, 2020). A human resources manager would like to determine whether the percentage has decreased due to uncertainty in the job market. The manager conducts an anonymous survey and finds that 150 out of 200 employees will likely quit because of lack of progression at the job.
   a. State the null and the alternative hypotheses to test the manager's claim.
   b. What is the value of the test statistic? What is the p-value?
   c. At $\alpha = 0.05$, is the manager's claim supported by the data? Explain.

64. An economist is concerned that more than 20% of American households have raided their retirement accounts to endure financial hardships such as unemployment and medical emergencies. He randomly surveys 190 households with retirement accounts and finds that 50 are borrowing against them.
   a. Set up the null and the alternative hypotheses to test the economist's concern.
   b. Calculate the value of the test statistic and the p-value.
   c. Determine if the economist's concern is justifiable at $\alpha = 0.05$.

65. The margarita is one of the most common tequila-based cocktails, made with tequila mixed with triple sec and lime or lemon juice, often served with salt on the glass rim. A common ratio for a margarita is 2:1:1, which includes 50% tequila, 25% triple sec, and 25% fresh lime or lemon juice. A manager at a local bar is concerned that the bartender uses incorrect proportions in more than 50% of margaritas. He secretly observes the bartender and finds that he used the correct proportions in only 10 out of 30 margaritas. Test if the manager's suspicion is justified at $\alpha = 0.05$.

66. Many financial institutions are unwittingly training their online customers to take risks with their passwords and other sensitive account information, leaving them more vulnerable to fraud. Researchers at the University of Michigan found design flaws in 78% of the 214 financial institution websites they studied. Is the sample evidence sufficient to conclude that more than three out of four of these websites are prone to fraud? Use a 5% significance level for the test.

67. A report suggests that older workers are the happiest employees. It documents that 70% of older workers in England feel fulfilled, compared with just 50% of younger workers. A demographer believes that an identical pattern does not exist in Asia. A survey of 120 older workers in Asia finds that 75 feel fulfilled. A similar survey finds that 58% of 210 younger workers feel fulfilled.
   a. At the 5% level of significance, test if older workers in Asia feel less fulfilled than their British counterparts.
   b. At the 5% level of significance, test if younger workers in Asia feel more fulfilled than their British counterparts.

68. A politician claims that he is supported by a clear majority of voters. In a recent survey, 24 out of 40 randomly selected voters indicated that they would vote for the politician. Is the politician's claim justified at the 5% level of significance?

69. A movie production company is releasing a movie with the hopes of many viewers returning to see the movie in the theater for a second time. Their target is to have 30 million viewers, and they want more than 30% of the viewers to want to see the movie again. They show the movie to a test audience of 200 people, and after the movie they asked them if they would see the movie in theaters again. Of the test audience, 68 people said they would see the movie again.
   a. At the 5% level of significance, test if more than 30% of the viewers will return to see the movie again.
   b. Repeat the analysis at the 10% level of significance.
   c. Interpret your results.

70. With increasing out-of-pocket healthcare costs, it is claimed that more than 60% of senior citizens are likely to make serious adjustments to their lifestyle. Test this claim at the 1% level of significance if in a survey of 140 senior citizens, 90 reported that they have made serious adjustments to their lifestyle.

71. **FILE** ***Silicon_Valley.*** According to a 2018 report by CNBC on workforce diversity, about 60% of the employees in high-tech firms in Silicon Valley are white and about 20% are Asian. Women, along with African Americans and Latinxs, are highly underrepresented. Just about 30% of all employees are women, with African Americans and Latinxs accounting for only about 15% of the workforce. Tara Jones is a recent college graduate, working for a large high-tech firm in Silicon Valley. She wants to determine if her firm faces the same diversity as in the report. She collects sex and ethnicity information on 50 employees in her firm. A portion of the data is shown in the accompanying table.

Sex	Ethnicity
Woman	White
Man	White
⋮	⋮
Man	Nonwhite

a. At the 5% level of significance, determine if the proportion of women in Tara's firm is different from 0.30.

b. At the 5% level of significance, determine if the proportion of whites in Tara's firm is more than 0.50.

Ariel Skelley/Blend Images LLC

9.5 WRITING WITH DATA

Case Study

According to a 2018 paper released by the Economic Policy Institute, a nonprofit, nonpartisan think tank in Washington, D.C., income inequality continues to grow in the United States. Over the years, the rich have become richer while working-class wages have stagnated. A local politician has been vocal regarding his concern about the welfare of Latinxs. In various speeches, he has stated that the mean salary of Latinx households in his country has fallen below the 2017 mean of approximately $50,000. He has also stated that the population of Latinx households making less than $30,000 has risen above the 2017 level of 20%. Both of his statements are based on income data for 36 Latinx households in the country. A portion of the data is shown in Table 9.4.

Latinx_Income

TABLE 9.4 Latinx Household Income (in $1,000s)

Income
23
63
⋮
47

Trevor Jones is a newspaper reporter who is interested in verifying the concerns of the local politician. He uses the sample information to determine if the mean income of Latinx households has fallen below the 2017 level of $50,000, and if the percentage of Latinx households making less than $30,000 has risen above 20%.

Sample Report—Income Inequality in the United States

One of the hotly debated topics in the United States is that of growing income inequality. This trend, which has picked up post Great Recession, is a reversal of what was seen during and after the Great Depression, where the gap between rich and poor narrowed. Market forces such as increased trade and technological advances have made highly skilled and well-educated workers more productive, thus increasing their pay. Institutional forces, such as deregulation, the decline of unions, and the stagnation of the minimum wage, have contributed to income inequality. Arguably, this income inequality has been felt by minorities, especially African Americans and Latinxs, because a very high proportion of both groups is working class.

A sample of 36 Latinx households resulted in a mean household income of $47,278 with a standard deviation of $19,524. The sample mean is below the 2017 level of $50,000. In addition, eight Latinx households, or approximately 22%, make less than $30,000. Based on these results, a politician concludes that current market conditions continue to negatively impact the welfare of Latinxs. However, it is essential to provide statistically significant evidence to substantiate these claims. Toward this end, formal tests of hypotheses regarding the population mean and the population proportion are conducted. The results of the tests are summarized in Table 9.5.

TABLE 9.5 Test Statistic Values and *p*-Values for Hypothesis Tests

Hypotheses	Test Statistic Value	*p*-value
$H_0: \mu \geq 50$ $H_A: \mu < 50$	$t_{35} = \dfrac{47.278 - 50}{19.524/\sqrt{36}} = -0.837$	0.204
$H_0: p \leq 0.20$ $H_A: p > 0.20$	$z = \dfrac{0.222 - 0.20}{\sqrt{\dfrac{(0.20)(0.80)}{36}}} = 0.333$	0.369

Given the *p*-value of 0.204, the null hypothesis regarding the population mean, specified in Table 9.5, cannot be rejected at any reasonable level of significance. Similarly, given the *p*-value of 0.369, the null hypothesis regarding the population proportion cannot be rejected. Therefore, sample evidence does not support the claims that the mean income of Latinx households has fallen below $50,000 or that the proportion of Latinx households making less than $30,000 has risen above 20%. Perhaps the politician's remarks were based on a cursory look at the sample statistics and not on a thorough statistical analysis.

Suggested Case Studies

Report 9.1 FILE ***Wellbeing.*** The Gallup-Healthways Well-Being Index provides an assessment measure of health and well-being of U.S. residents. The overall composite score is calculated on a scale from 0 to 100, where 100 represents fully realized well-being. In 2017, the overall well-being of American residents was reported as 61.5–a decline from 62.1 in 2016. The accompanying data file shows the overall well-being score for a random sample of 35 residents from South Dakota–the state with the highest level of well-being. In a report, conduct hypothesis tests to (i) determine whether the well-being score of South Dakotans is more than the national average of 61.5, and (ii) determine if fewer than 40% of South Dakotans report a score below 50. Use a reasonable significance level for the tests. Given your findings, comment on the well-being of South Dakotans at the chosen significance level.

Report 9.2 FILE ***SPAM.*** Peter Derby works as a cyber security analyst at a private equity firm. He has been asked to implement a spam detection system on the company's email server. He has access to a sample of 100 spam and legitimate e-mails with two variables: spam (1 if spam, 0 otherwise) and the number of hyperlinks in the message. Before implementing a spam detection system, we wants to better understand the company's emails. In a report, conduct hypothesis tests at a reasonable significance level to (i) determine whether more than 50% of the company's email are spam, and (ii) determine whether the average number of hyperlinks is more than 5.

Report 9.3 FILE ***Salary_MIS.*** At the bachelor's degree level, recent graduates with a concentration in management information systems (MIS) continue to land high-paying, entry level positions. This is due, in large part, to the concentration's linkage to the exploding field of data analytics. At a University of California campus, data were collected on the starting salary of business graduates (Salary in $1,000s) along with whether they have an MIS concentration (MIS=1 if yes, 0 otherwise), and whether they have a statistics minor (Statistics = 1 if yes, 0 otherwise). In a report, use the sample information to compare the average salary of business students without an MIS concentration or a statistics minor with those who have (i) an MIS concentration but not a statistics minor, (ii) a statistics minor but not an MIS concentration, and (iii) an MIS concentration and a statistics minor. Then, conduct hypothesis tests to determine whether the average salary in the (i), (ii), and (iii) categories are greater than $70,000. Use a reasonable significance level for the tests.

CONCEPTUAL REVIEW

LO 9.1 Define the null hypothesis and the alternative hypothesis.

Every hypothesis test contains two competing hypotheses: the null hypothesis, denoted H_0, and the alternative hypothesis, denoted H_A. We can think of the null hypothesis as corresponding to a presumed default state of nature or status quo, whereas the alternative hypothesis contradicts the default state or status quo.

On the basis of sample information, we either reject H_0 or do not reject H_0. As a general guideline, whatever we wish to establish is placed in the alternative hypothesis. If we reject the null hypothesis, we are able to conclude that the alternative hypothesis is true.

Hypothesis tests can be one-tailed or two-tailed. A one-tailed test allows the rejection of the null hypothesis only on one side of the hypothesized value of the population parameter. In a two-tailed test, the null hypothesis can be rejected on both sides of the hypothesized value of the population parameter.

LO 9.2 Distinguish between Type I and Type II errors.

A Type I error is committed when we reject the null hypothesis when it is true. On the other hand, a Type II error is made when we do not reject the null hypothesis when it is false. We denote the probability of a Type I error by α and the probability of a Type II error by β. For a given sample size n, a decrease (increase) in α will increase (decrease) β. However, both α and β will decrease if the sample size n increases.

LO 9.3 Conduct a hypothesis test for the population mean when σ is known.

A four-step procedure is followed for every hypothesis test.

Step 1. Specify the null and the alternative hypothesis. We identify the relevant population parameter of interest, determine whether it is a one- or a two-tailed test and, include some form of the equality sign in the null hypothesis and place whatever we wish to establish in the alternative hypothesis.

Step 2. Specify the significance level. Before implementing a hypothesis test, we first specify α, which is the significance level or the allowed probability of making a Type I error.

Step 3. Calculate the value of the test statistic and the p-value. When testing the population mean μ when the population standard deviation σ is known, the value of the test statistic is calculated as $z = \frac{\bar{x} - \mu_0}{\sigma/\sqrt{n}}$. The p-value is the probability that this test statistic is as extreme as its value computed from the given sample. The p-value is calculated as

- $P(Z \geq z)$ for a right-tailed test,
- $P(Z \leq z)$ for a left-tailed test, or
- $2P(Z \geq z)$ if $z > 0$ or $2P(Z \leq z)$ if $z < 0$ for a two-tailed test.

Step 4. State the conclusion and interpret the results. The decision rule is to reject the null hypothesis if the p-value $< \alpha$ and not reject the null hypothesis if the p-value $\geq \alpha$. We always interpret the results in the context of the problem.

LO 9.4 Conduct a hypothesis test for the population mean when σ is unknown.

The four-step procedure for conducting a hypothesis test remains the same. The only change is the test statistic. When testing the population mean μ when the population standard deviation σ is unknown, the value of the test statistic is calculated as $t_{df} = \frac{\bar{x} - \mu_0}{s/\sqrt{n}}$, where s is the sample standard deviation, n is the sample size, and the degrees of freedom $df = n - 1$. The p-value is calculated as

- $P(T_{df} \geq t_{df})$ for a right-tailed test,
- $P(T_{df} \leq t_{df})$ for a left-tailed test, or
- $2P(T_{df} \geq t_{df})$ if $t_{df} > 0$ or $2P(T_{df} \leq t_{df})$ if $t_{df} < 0$ for a two-tailed test.

LO 9.5 Conduct a hypothesis test for the population proportion.

The four-step procedure for conducting a hypothesis test remains the same. The only change is the test statistic. When testing the population proportion p, the value of the test statistic is computed as $z = \frac{\bar{p} - p_0}{\sqrt{p_0(1 - p_0)/n}}$. The p-value is calculated as

- $P(Z \geq z)$ for a right-tailed test,
- $P(Z \leq z)$ for a left-tailed test, or
- $2P(Z \geq z)$ if $z > 0$ or $2P(Z \leq z)$ if $z < 0$ for a two-tailed test.

ADDITIONAL EXERCISES

72. A pharmaceutical company has developed a new drug for depression. There is a concern, however, that the drug also raises the blood pressure of its users. A researcher wants to conduct a test to validate this claim. Would the manager of the pharmaceutical company be more concerned about a Type I error or a Type II error? Explain.

73. A company has developed a new diet that it claims will lower one's weight by more than 10 pounds. Health officials decide to conduct a test to validate this claim.
    a. Would the manager of the company be more concerned about a Type I error or a Type II error? Explain.
    b. Would the consumers be more concerned about a Type I error or a Type II error? Explain.

74. An advertisement for a popular weight loss clinic suggests that participants in its new diet program lose, on average, more than 10 pounds. A consumer activist decides to test the authenticity of the claim. She follows the progress of 18 women who recently joined the weight reduction program. She calculates the mean weight loss of these participants as 10.8 pounds with a standard deviation of 2.4 pounds.
    a. Set up the competing hypotheses to test the advertisement's claim.
    b. Calculate the value of the test statistic and the p-value.
    c. At the 5% significance level, what does the consumer activist conclude?

75. A promising start-up wants to compete in the cell phone market. It understands that the lead product has a battery life of approximately 12 hours. The start-up claims that while its new cell phone is more expensive, its battery life is more than twice as long as that of the leading product. In order to test the claim, a researcher samples 45 units of the new cell phone and finds that the sample battery life averages 24.5 hours with a sample standard deviation of 1.8 hours.
    a. Set up the competing hypotheses to test the start-up's claim.
    b. Calculate the value of the test statistic and the p-value.
    c. Test the start-up's claim at $\alpha = 0.05$.

76. A city council is deciding whether or not to spend additional money to reduce the amount of traffic. The council decides that it will increase the transportation budget if the amount of waiting time for drivers exceeds 20 minutes. A sample of

32 main roads results in a mean waiting time of 22.08 minutes with a standard deviation of 5.42 minutes. Conduct a hypothesis test at the 1% level of significance to determine whether or not the city should increase its transportation budget.

77. FILE ***Rental.*** A real estate analyst examines the rental market in a college town. The accompanying data file shows the data that she has gathered on the monthly rent and the square footage for 40 rentals.
    a. The analyst believes that the average monthly rent is less than $1,400. At the 5% significance level, is her belief supported by the data?
    b. The analyst believes that the average square footage is more than 1,200 square feet. At the 5% significance level, is her belief supported by the data?

78. According to a poll, 33% of those surveyed said America was headed in the right direction. Suppose this poll was based on a sample of 1,000 people. Does the sample evidence suggest that the proportion of Americans who feel that America is headed in the right direction is below 35%? Use a 5% level of significance for the analysis. What if the sample size was 2,000?

79. A retailer is looking to evaluate its customer service. Management has determined that if the retailer wants to stay competitive, then it will have to have at least a 90% satisfaction rate among its customers. Management will take corrective actions if the satisfaction rate falls below 90%. A survey of 1,200 customers showed that 1,068 were satisfied with their customer service.
    a. State the hypotheses to test if the retailer needs to improve its services.
    b. What is the value of the test statistic?
    c. Find the p-value.
    d. Interpret the results at $\alpha = 0.05$.

80. One-fifth of Britains are not using the internet (bbc.com, September 9, 2019). A researcher believes that the proportion of Americans who do not use the internet is less than Britain's proportion. She surveys 200 Americans and finds that 30 of them do not use the internet. Test the researcher's claim at the 5% significance level.

81. A television network is deciding whether or not to give its newest television show a spot during prime viewing time at night. For this to happen, it will have to move one of its most viewed shows to another slot. The network conducts a survey asking its viewers which show they would rather watch. The network will keep its current lineup of shows unless the majority of the customers want to watch the new show. The network receives 827 responses, of which 428 indicate that they would like to see the new show in the lineup.
    a. Set up the hypotheses to test if the television network should give its newest television show a spot during prime viewing time at night.
    b. Calculate the value of the test statistic and the p-value.
    c. At $\alpha = 0.01$, what should the television network do?

82. A survey finds that 17% of Americans cannot part with their landlines. A researcher in the rural South collects data from 200 households and finds that 45 of them still have landlines.
    a. The researcher believes that the proportion of households with landlines in the rural South is not representative of the national proportion. Specify the competing hypotheses to test her claim.
    b. Calculate the value of the test statistic and the p-value.
    c. At the 5% significance level, do the sample data support the researcher's belief?

83. FILE ***Stock_Return.*** Using data from the past 25 years, an investor wants to test whether the average return on a stock is greater than 12%. Assume returns are normally distributed with a population standard deviation of 30%.
    a. State the null and the alternative hypotheses for the test.
    b. Calculate the value of the test statistic and the p-value.
    c. At $\alpha = 0.05$, what is the conclusion? Is the average stock return greater than 12%?

84. FILE ***Midwest_Drivers.*** On average, Americans drive 13,500 miles per year (carinsurance.com, November 26, 2019). An economist gathers data on the driving habits of 50 residents in the Midwest.
    a. The economist believes that the average number of miles driven annually by Midwesterners is different from the U.S. average. Specify the competing hypotheses to test the economist's claim.
    b. Calculate the value of the test statistic and the p-value.
    c. At the 10% significance level, do the data support the researcher's claim? Explain.

85. FILE ***Convenience_Stores.*** An entrepreneur examines monthly sales (in $1,000s) for 40 convenience stores in Rhode Island.
    a. State the null and the alternative hypotheses in order to test whether average sales differ from $130,000.
    b. Calculate the value of the test statistic and the p-value.
    c. At $\alpha = 0.05$, what is your conclusion to the test? Do average sales differ from $130,000?

86. FILE ***DJIA_Volume.*** A portfolio analyst wonders if the average trading volume on the Dow Jones Industrial Average (DJIA) has decreased since the beginning of the year. She gathers data on daily trading volumes for 30 days.

   a. The average trading volume in the beginning of the year was about 4,000 shares (in millions). Specify the competing hypotheses to test her claim.
   b. Calculate the value of the test statistic and the p-value.
   c. At the 5% significance level, does it appear that the trading volume has decreased since the beginning of the year?

87. FILE ***Study_Hard.*** A report suggests that business majors spend the least amount of time on course work than do all other college students. A provost of a university conducts a survey of 50 business and 50 nonbusiness students. Students are asked if they study hard, defined as spending at least 20 hours per week on course work. The response shows "yes" if they study hard or "no" otherwise; a portion is shown in the following table.

Business Majors	Nonbusiness Majors
Yes	No
No	Yes
⋮	⋮
Yes	Yes

   a. At the 5% level of significance, determine if the percentage of business majors who study hard is less than 20%.
   b. At the 5% level of significance, determine if the percentage of nonbusiness majors who study hard is more than 20%.

88. FILE ***MI_Life.*** The average life expectancy for residents of Hawaii is 81.48 years (travelandleisure.com, July 16, 2018). A sociologist collects data on the age at death for 50 recently deceased Michigan residents.

   a. The sociologist believes that the average life expectancy for Michigan residents is less than the average life expectancy for Hawaiian residents. Specify the competing hypotheses to test this belief.
   b. Calculate the value of the test statistic and the p-value.
   c. At the 1% significance level, do the data support the sociologist's belief?

89. According to a survey, half of U.S. households have no emergency savings (*The Wall Street Journal,* April 16, 2020). An analyst in the Midwest collects data on 200 households and finds that 84 of them have no emergency savings.

   a. The analyst believes that the proportion of Midwestern households with no emergency savins is not representative of the national proportion. Specify the competing hypotheses to test the analyst's claim.
   b. Calculate the value of the test statistic and the p-value.
   c. At the 1% significance level, do the sample data support the analyst's claim?

APPENDIX 9.1 The Critical Value Approach

We always use sample evidence and the chosen significance level α to conduct hypothesis tests. The p-value approach makes the comparison in terms of probabilities. As discussed in Section 9.2, the value of the test statistic is used to compute the p-value, which is then compared with α in order to arrive at a decision. Most statistical software packages report p-values, so the p-value approach to hypothesis testing tends to be favored by most researchers and practitioners. The critical value approach, on the other hand, makes the comparison directly in terms of the value of the test statistic. This approach is particularly useful when a computer is unavailable and all calculations must be done manually. Both approaches, however, always lead to the same conclusion.

In Section 9.2, we used the p-value approach to validate a sociologist's claim that the mean retirement age in the United States is greater than 67 at the 5% significance level. In a random sample of 25 retirees, the average retirement age was 71. It was also assumed that the retirement age is normally distributed with a population standard deviation of 9 years. With the critical value approach, we still specify the competing hypotheses and calculate the value of the test statistic. In the retirement age example, the competing hypotheses are H_0: $\mu \leq 67$ versus H_A: $\mu > 67$ and the value of the test statistic is $z = \frac{\bar{x} - \mu_0}{\sigma/\sqrt{n}} = \frac{71 - 67}{9/\sqrt{25}} = 2.2222$.

The critical value approach specifies a region of values, also called the rejection region, such that if the value of the test statistic falls into this region, then we reject the null hypothesis. The critical value is a point that separates the rejection region from the nonrejection region. Once again we need to make distinctions between the three types of competing hypotheses. For a right-tailed test, the critical value is z_α, where $P(Z \geq z_\alpha) = \alpha$. The resulting rejection region includes values greater than z_α.

With α known, we can easily find the corresponding z_α from the z table. In the retirement age example with $\alpha = 0.05$, we evaluate $P(Z \geq z_\alpha) = 0.05$ to derive the critical value as $z_\alpha = z_{0.05} = 1.645$. Figure A9.1 shows the critical value as well as the corresponding rejection region for the test.

FIGURE A9.1
The critical value for a right-tailed test with $\alpha = 0.05$

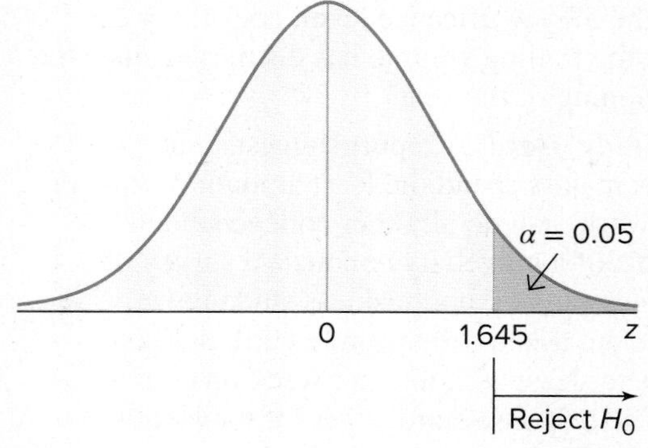

As shown in Figure A9.1, the decision rule is to reject H_0 if $z > 1.645$. Since the value of the test statistic, $z = 2.2222$, exceeds the critical value, $z_\alpha = 1.645$, we reject the null hypothesis and conclude that the mean age is greater than 67. Thus, we confirm the conclusion reached with the p-value approach.

We would like to stress that we always arrive at the same conclusion whether we use the p-value approach or the critical value approach. If z falls in the rejection region, then the p-value must be less than α. Similarly, if z does not fall in the rejection region, then the p-value must be greater than α. Figure A9.2 shows the equivalence of the two results in the retirement age example of a right-tailed test.

FIGURE A9.2
Equivalent conclusions resulting from the p-value and the critical value approaches

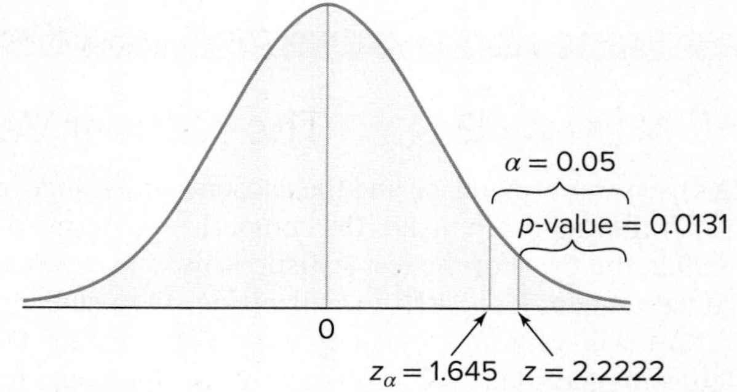

We reject the null hypothesis because the p-value $= 0.0131$ is less than $\alpha = 0.05$ or, equivalently, because $z = 2.2222$ is greater than $z_\alpha = 1.645$.

The retirement age example uses a right-tailed test to calculate the critical value as z_α. Given the symmetry of the z distribution around zero, the critical value for a left-tailed test is simply $-z_\alpha$. For a two-tailed test, we split the significance level in half to determine *two* critical values, $-z_{\alpha/2}$ and $z_{\alpha/2}$, where $P(Z \geq z_{\alpha/2}) = \alpha/2$.

For a given α, Figure A9.3 shows the three different scenarios of determining the critical value(s) depending on the specification of the competing hypotheses. For the illustration, we assume that the test statistic follows the z distribution.

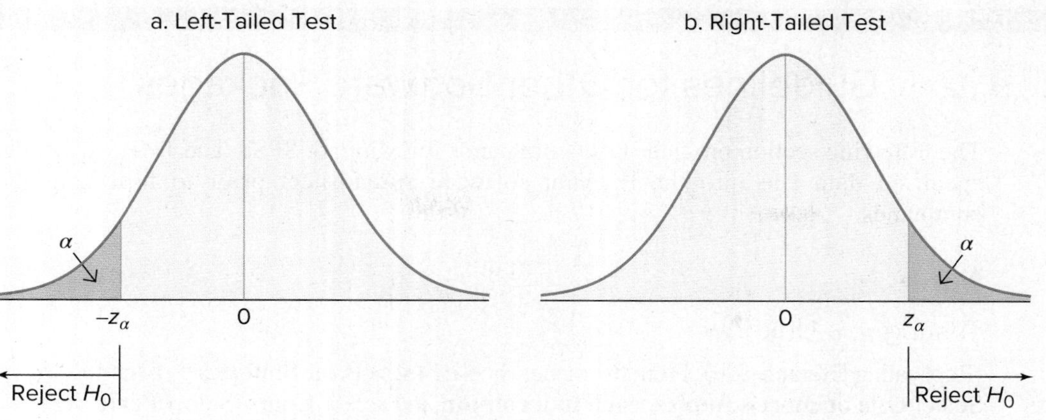

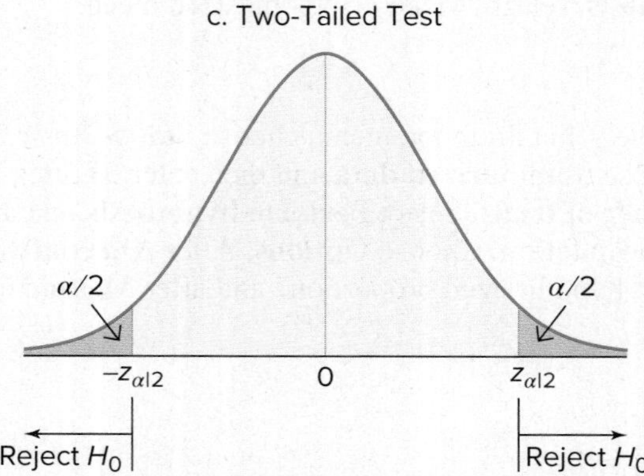

FIGURE A9.3 Critical values for one- and two-tailed tests

Figure A9.3a shows a negative critical value for a left-tailed test where we reject the null hypothesis if $z < -z_\alpha$. Similarly, Figure A9.3b shows a positive critical value for a right-tailed test where we reject the null hypothesis if $z > z_\alpha$. There are two critical values for a two-tailed test, where we reject the null hypothesis when $z < -z_{\alpha/2}$ or when $z > z_{\alpha/2}$ (see Figure A9.3c). We now summarize the general procedure for implementing the critical value approach.

THE FOUR-STEP PROCEDURE USING THE CRITICAL VALUE APPROACH

Step 1. Specify the null and the alternative hypotheses. This step is the same as in the *p*-value approach.

Step 2. Specify the significance level and find the critical value(s). We first specify α. The critical value(s) is a point that separates the rejection region from the nonrejection region. If the test statistic follows the *z* distribution, then, for a given α, we find the critical value(s) as

- z_α where $P(Z \geq z_\alpha) = \alpha$ for a right-tailed test,
- $-z_\alpha$ where $P(Z \geq z_\alpha) = \alpha$ for a left-tailed test, or
- $-z_{\alpha/2}$ and $z_{\alpha/2}$ where $P(Z \geq z_{\alpha/2}) = \alpha/2$ for a two-tailed test.

Z and z_α are replaced with T_{df} and t_{df} if the test statistic follows the t_{df} distribution with degrees of freedom, $df = n - 1$.

Step 3. Calculate the value of the test statistic. We calculate the value of the test statistic by converting the estimate of the relevant population parameter into its corresponding standardized value, either z or t_{df}.

Step 4. State the conclusion and interpret the results. The decision rule is to reject the null hypothesis if the test statistic falls in the rejection region. We interpret the results in the context of a problem.

APPENDIX 9.2 Guidelines for Other Software Packages

The following section provides brief commands for Minitab, SPSS, and JMP. Import the specified data file into the relevant software spreadsheet prior to following the commands.

Minitab

Testing μ, σ Unknown

(Replicating Example 9.10) From the menu, choose **Stat > Basic Statistics > 1-Sample t.** Select **One or more samples, each in a column** and select Hours. Select **Perform hypothesis test** and enter 14 after **Hypothesized mean.** Choose **Options.** After **Alternative hypothesis,** select "Mean $\neq$ hypothesized mean."

Testing p

(Replicating Example 9.11) From the menu, choose **Stat > Basic Statistics > 1-Proportion.** Choose **Summarized data** and then enter 67 after **Number of events** and 180 after **Number of trials.** Select **Perform hypothesis test** and enter 0.40 for **Hypothesized proportion.** Choose **Options.** After **Alternative hypothesis,** select "Proportion < hypothesized proportion" and after **Method** select "Normal approximation."

SPSS

Testing μ, σ Unknown

(Replicating Example 9.10). From the menu, choose **Analyze > Compare Means > One-Sample T-Test.** Under **Test Variable(s),** select Hours. After **Test Value,** enter 14.

JMP

Testing μ, σ Unknown

A. (Replicating Example 9.10). From the menu, choose **Analyze > Distribution.** Drag Hours to the **Y, Columns** box.

B. Click on the red triangle in the output window beside Hours. Choose **Test Mean.** After **Specify Hypothesized Mean,** enter 14.

10 Statistical Inference Concerning Two Populations

LEARNING OBJECTIVES

After reading this chapter you should be able to:

LO **10.1** **Make inferences about the difference between two population means based on independent sampling.**

LO **10.2** **Make inferences about the mean difference based on matched-pairs sampling.**

LO **10.3** **Make inferences about the difference between two population proportions based on independent sampling.**

In the preceding two chapters, we used estimation and hypothesis testing to analyze a single parameter, such as the population mean and the population proportion. In this chapter, we extend our discussion from the analysis of a single population to the comparison of two populations. In each of the statistical inferences concerning two populations, we first develop the procedure for estimation and then follow with hypothesis testing.

We first analyze differences between two population means. For instance, an economist may be interested in analyzing the salary difference between male and female employees. Similarly, a marketing researcher might want to compare the operating lives of two popular brands of batteries. In these examples, we use independent sampling for the analysis. We will also consider the mean difference of two populations based on matched-pairs sampling. An example would be a consumer group activist wanting to analyze the mean weight of customers before and after they enroll in a new diet program. Finally, we compare the difference between two population proportions. For instance, marketing executives and advertisers are often interested in the different preferences between males and females when determining where to target advertising dollars.

SMOCK JOHN/SIPA/Newscom

INTRODUCTORY CASE

Effectiveness of Mandatory Caloric Postings

In today's busy world, Americans eat and drink about one-third of their calories from foods prepared away from home. In general, these foods provide more calories, sodium, and saturated fat than meals consumed at home. The U.S. Food and Drug Administration believes that caloric labeling on menus can help the public make informed and healthful decisions about meals and snacks. Molly Hosler, a nutritionist in San Mateo, California, would like to study the effects of the caloric postings on consumer choices. She obtains transaction data for 40 customers at a popular cafe, and records their drink and food calories prior to the caloric postings and after the caloric postings. Table 10.1 shows a portion of the data.

TABLE 10.1 Caloric Intake Before and After Caloric Postings

FILE
Drink_Calories
Food_Calories

	Drink Calories		Food Calories	
Customer	Before	After	Before	After
1	141	142	395	378
2	137	140	404	392
⋮	⋮	⋮	⋮	⋮
40	147	141	406	400

Molly wants to use the sample information to

1. Determine whether the average calories of purchased drinks declined after caloric postings.
2. Determine whether the average calories of purchased food declined after caloric postings.
3. Assess the implications of caloric postings for cafes.

A synopsis of this case is provided at the end of Section 10.2.

10.1 INFERENCE CONCERNING THE DIFFERENCE BETWEEN TWO MEANS

LO 10.1

Make inferences about the difference between two population means based on independent sampling.

In this section, we consider statistical inference about the difference between two population means based on **independent random samples.** Independent random samples are samples that are completely unrelated to one another. Consider the example where we are interested in the difference between male and female salaries. For one sample, we collect data from the male population, while for the other sample we collect data from the female population. The two samples are considered to be independent because the selection of one is in no way influenced by the selection of the other. Similarly, in a comparison of battery lives between Brand A and Brand B, one sample comes from the Brand A population, while the other sample comes from the Brand B population. Again, both samples can be considered to be drawn independently.

> INDEPENDENT RANDOM SAMPLES
>
> Two (or more) random samples are considered independent if the process that generates one sample is completely separate from the process that generates the other sample. The samples are clearly delineated.

Confidence Interval for $\mu_1 - \mu_2$

As discussed in earlier chapters, we use sample statistics to estimate the population parameter of interest. For example, the sample mean $\overline{X}$ is the point estimator for the population mean μ. In a similar vein, the difference between the two sample means $\overline{X}_1 - \overline{X}_2$ is a point estimator for the difference between two population means $\mu_1 - \mu_2$, where μ_1 is the mean of the first population and μ_2 is the mean of the second population. The estimate is found by taking the difference of the sample means $\bar{x}_1$ and $\bar{x}_2$ computed from two independent random samples with n_1 and n_2 observations, respectively.

Let's first discuss the sampling distribution of $\overline{X}_1 - \overline{X}_2$. As in the case of a single population mean, this estimator is unbiased; that is, $E(\overline{X}_1 - \overline{X}_2) = \mu_1 - \mu_2$. Moreover, recall that the statistical inference regarding the population mean μ is based on the condition that the sample mean $\overline{X}$ is normally distributed. Similarly, for statistical inference regarding $\mu_1 - \mu_2$, it is imperative that the sampling distribution of $\overline{X}_1 - \overline{X}_2$ is normally distributed. Therefore, if we assume that the two sample means are derived from two independent and normally distributed populations, then $\overline{X}_1 - \overline{X}_2$ is also normally distributed. If the underlying populations cannot be assumed to be normally distributed, then by the central limit theorem, the sampling distribution of $\overline{X}_1 - \overline{X}_2$ is approximately normally distributed only if both sample sizes are sufficiently large—that is, $n_1 \geq 30$ and $n_2 \geq 30$.

As in the case of a single population mean, we consider two scenarios. If we know the variances of the two populations σ_1^2 and σ_2^2 (or the standard deviations σ_1 and σ_2), then we use the z distribution for the statistical inference. A more common case is to use the t_{df} distribution, where the sample variances s_1^2 and s_2^2 are used in place of the unknown population variances. When σ_1^2 and σ_2^2 are not known, we will examine two cases: (i) they can be assumed equal ($\sigma_1^2 = \sigma_2^2$) or (ii) they cannot be assumed equal ($\sigma_1^2 \neq \sigma_2^2$).

The confidence interval for the difference in means is based on the same procedure outlined in Chapter 8. In particular, the formula for the confidence interval will follow the standard format given by: Point Estimate $\pm$ Margin of Error.

We use sample data to calculate the point estimate for $\mu_1 - \mu_2$ as the difference between the two sample means $\bar{x}_1 - \bar{x}_2$. The margin of error equals $z_{\alpha/2}$ or $t_{\alpha/2,df}$ (which one depends on whether or not the population variances are known) multiplied by the standard error $se(\overline{X}_1 - \overline{X}_2)$.

CONFIDENCE INTERVAL FOR $\mu_1 - \mu_2$

A $100(1 - \alpha)\%$ confidence interval for the difference between two population means $\mu_1 - \mu_2$ is given by

1. $(\bar{x}_1 - \bar{x}_2) \pm z_{\alpha/2}\sqrt{\frac{\sigma_1^2}{n_1} + \frac{\sigma_2^2}{n_2}}$, if the population variances, σ_1^2 and σ_2^2, are known.
2. $(\bar{x}_1 - \bar{x}_2) \pm t_{\alpha/2,df}\sqrt{s_p^2\left(\frac{1}{n_1} + \frac{1}{n_2}\right)}$, if σ_1^2 and σ_2^2 are unknown but assumed equal. A pooled estimate of the common variance is $s_p^2 = \frac{(n_1 - 1)s_1^2 + (n_2 - 1)s_2^2}{n_1 + n_2 - 2}$, where s_1^2 and s_2^2 are the corresponding sample variances and the degrees of freedom $df = n_1 + n_2 - 2$.
3. $(\bar{x}_1 - \bar{x}_2) \pm t_{\alpha/2,df}\sqrt{\frac{s_1^2}{n_1} + \frac{s_2^2}{n_2}}$, if σ_1^2 and σ_2^2 are unknown and cannot be assumed equal. The degrees of freedom $df = \frac{(s_1^2/n_1 + s_2^2/n_2)^2}{(s_1^2/n_1)^2/(n_1 - 1) + (s_2^2/n_2)^2/(n_2 - 1)}$. Since the resultant value for df is rarely an integer, we generally round the value down. Software packages use various rounding rules when reporting the resultant value for df.

These formulas are valid only if $\bar{X}_1 - \bar{X}_2$ (approximately) follows a normal distribution.

Note that in the case when we construct a confidence interval for $\mu_1 - \mu_2$ where σ_1^2 and σ_2^2 are unknown but assumed equal, we calculate a pooled estimate of the common variance s_p^2. In other words, because the two populations are assumed to have the same population variance, the two sample variances s_1^2 and s_2^2 are simply two separate estimates of this population variance. We estimate the population variance by a *weighted* average of s_1^2 and s_2^2, where the weights applied are their respective degrees of freedom relative to the total number of degrees of freedom. In the case when σ_1^2 and σ_2^2 are unknown and cannot be assumed equal, we cannot calculate a pooled estimate of the population variance.

EXAMPLE 10.1

A consumer advocate analyzes the nicotine content in two brands of cigarettes. A sample of 20 cigarettes of Brand A resulted in an average nicotine content of 1.68 milligrams with a standard deviation of 0.22 milligram; 25 cigarettes of Brand B yielded an average nicotine content of 1.95 milligrams with a standard deviation of 0.24 milligram.

Brand A	Brand B
$\bar{x}_1 = 1.68$	$\bar{x}_2 = 1.95$
$s_1 = 0.22$	$s_2 = 0.24$
$n_1 = 20$	$n_2 = 25$

Construct the 95% confidence interval for the difference between the two population means. Nicotine content is assumed to be normally distributed. In addition, the population variances are unknown but assumed equal.

SOLUTION: We wish to construct a confidence interval for $\mu_1 - \mu_2$ where μ_1 is the mean nicotine level for Brand A and μ_2 is the mean nicotine level for Brand B. Since the population variances are unknown but assumed equal, we use the formula

$$(\bar{x}_1 - \bar{x}_2) \pm t_{\alpha/2,df}\sqrt{s_p^2\left(\frac{1}{n_1} + \frac{1}{n_2}\right)}.$$

We calculate the point estimate $\bar{x}_1 - \bar{x}_2 = 1.68 - 1.95 = -0.27$. In order to find $t_{\alpha/2,df}$, we determine $df = n_1 + n_2 - 2 = 20 + 25 - 2 = 43$. For the 95% confidence interval ($\alpha = 0.05$), we find $t_{0.025,43} = 2.017$.

We then calculate the pooled estimate of the population variance as

$$s_p^2 = \frac{(n_1 - 1)s_1^2 + (n_2 - 1)s_2^2}{n_1 + n_2 - 2} = \frac{(20 - 1)(0.22)^2 + (25 - 1)(0.24)^2}{20 + 25 - 2} = 0.0535.$$

Inserting the appropriate values into the formula, we have

$$-0.27 \pm 2.017\sqrt{0.0535\left(\frac{1}{20} + \frac{1}{25}\right)} = -0.27 \pm 0.14.$$

In other words, the 95% confidence interval for the difference between the two means ranges from −0.41 to −0.13. Shortly, we will use this interval to conduct a two-tailed hypothesis test.

Hypothesis Test for $\mu_1 - \mu_2$

As always, when specifying the competing hypotheses, it is important to (1) identify the relevant population parameter, (2) determine whether a one- or a two-tailed test is appropriate, and (3) include some form of the equality sign in the null hypothesis and use the alternative hypothesis to establish a claim. In order to conduct a hypothesis test concerning the parameter $\mu_1 - \mu_2$, the competing hypotheses will take one of the following general forms:

Two-Tailed Test	Right-Tailed Test	Left-Tailed Test
$H_0: \mu_1 - \mu_2 = d_0$	$H_0: \mu_1 - \mu_2 \leq d_0$	$H_0: \mu_1 - \mu_2 \geq d_0$
$H_A: \mu_1 - \mu_2 \neq d_0$	$H_A: \mu_1 - \mu_2 > d_0$	$H_A: \mu_1 - \mu_2 < d_0$

In most applications, the hypothesized difference d_0 between two population means μ_1 and μ_2 is zero. In this scenario, a two-tailed test determines whether the two means differ from one another, a right-tailed test determines whether μ_1 is greater than μ_2, and a left-tailed test determines whether μ_1 is less than μ_2.

We can also construct hypotheses where the hypothesized difference d_0 is a value other than zero. For example, if we wish to determine if the mean return of an emerging market fund (Population 1) is more than two percentage points higher than that of a developed market fund (Population 2), the resulting hypotheses are $H_0: \mu_1 - \mu_2 \leq 2$ versus $H_A: \mu_1 - \mu_2 > 2$.

EXAMPLE 10.2

Revisit Example 10.1.

a. Specify the competing hypotheses in order to determine whether the average nicotine levels differ between Brand A and Brand B.

b. Using the 95% confidence interval, what is the conclusion to the test?

SOLUTION:

a. We want to determine if the average nicotine levels differ between the two brands, or $\mu_1 \neq \mu_2$, so we formulate a two-tailed hypothesis test as

$$H_0: \mu_1 - \mu_2 = 0$$
$$H_A: \mu_1 - \mu_2 \neq 0$$

b. In Example 10.1, we calculated the 95% confidence interval for the difference between the two means as -0.27 ± 0.14 or, equivalently, the confidence interval ranges from −0.41 to −0.13. This interval does not contain zero, the value hypothesized under the null hypothesis. This information allows us to reject H_0; the sample data support the conclusion that average nicotine levels between the two brands differ at the 5% significance level.

While it is true that we can use confidence intervals to conduct two-tailed hypothesis tests, the four-step procedure outlined in Chapter 9 can be implemented to conduct one- or two-tailed hypothesis tests. (It is possible to adjust the confidence interval to accommodate a one-tailed test, but we do not discuss this modification.) The only real change in the process is the specification of the test statistic. We derive the value of the test statistic, z or t_{df}, by dividing $(\bar{x}_1 - \bar{x}_2) - d_0$ by the standard error of the estimator $se(\bar{X}_1 - \bar{X}_2)$.

TEST STATISTIC FOR TESTING $\mu_1 - \mu_2$

The value of the test statistic for a hypothesis test concerning the difference between two population means, $\mu_1 - \mu_2$, is computed using one of the following three formulas:

1. If σ_1^2 and σ_2^2 are known, then the value of the test statistic is computed as $z = \dfrac{(\bar{x}_1 - \bar{x}_2) - d_0}{\sqrt{\frac{\sigma_1^2}{n_1} + \frac{\sigma_2^2}{n_2}}}$.
2. If σ_1^2 and σ_2^2 are unknown but assumed equal, then the value of the test statistic is computed as $t_{df} = \dfrac{(\bar{x}_1 - \bar{x}_2) - d_0}{\sqrt{s_p^2\left(\frac{1}{n_1} + \frac{1}{n_2}\right)}}$, where $s_p^2 = \frac{(n_1 - 1)s_1^2 + (n_2 - 1)s_2^2}{n_1 + n_2 - 2}$ and $df = n_1 + n_2 - 2$.
3. If σ_1^2 and σ_2^2 are unknown and cannot be assumed equal, then the value of the test statistic is computed as $t_{df} = \dfrac{(\bar{x}_1 - \bar{x}_2) - d_0}{\sqrt{\frac{s_1^2}{n_1} + \frac{s_2^2}{n_2}}}$, where $df = \frac{(s_1^2/n_1 + s_2^2/n_2)^2}{(s_1^2/n_1)^2/(n_1 - 1) + (s_2^2/n_2)^2/(n_2 - 1)}$. For df, we generally round the value down; software packages use various rounding rules when reporting the resultant value for df.

These formulas are valid only if $\bar{X}_1 - \bar{X}_2$ (approximately) follows a normal distribution.

EXAMPLE 10.3

An economist claims that average weekly food expenditure for households in City 1 is more than the average weekly food expenditure for households in City 2. She surveys 35 households in City 1 and obtains an average weekly food expenditure of $164. A sample of 30 households in City 2 yields an average weekly food expenditure of $159. Prior studies suggest that the population standard deviation for City 1 is $12.50 and the population standard deviation for City 2 is $9.25.

City 1	City 2
$\bar{x}_1 = 164$	$\bar{x}_2 = 159$
$\sigma_1 = 12.50$	$\sigma_2 = 9.25$
$n_1 = 35$	$n_2 = 30$

a. Specify the competing hypotheses to test the economist's claim.

b. Calculate the value of the test statistic and the p-value.

c. At the 5% significance level, is the economist's claim supported by the data?

SOLUTION:

a. The relevant parameter of interest is $\mu_1 - \mu_2$, where μ_1 is the mean weekly food expenditure for City 1 and μ_2 is the mean weekly food expenditure for City 2. The economist wishes to determine if the mean weekly food expenditure in City 1 is more than that of City 2; that is, $\mu_1 > \mu_2$. This is an example of a right-tailed test where the appropriate hypotheses are

$$H_0: \mu_1 - \mu_2 \leq 0$$
$$H_A: \mu_1 - \mu_2 > 0$$

b. Since the population standard deviations are known, we compute the value of the test statistic as

$$z = \frac{(\bar{x}_1 - \bar{x}_2) - d_0}{\sqrt{\frac{\sigma_1^2}{n_1} + \frac{\sigma_2^2}{n_2}}} = \frac{(164 - 159) - 0}{\sqrt{\frac{(12.50)^2}{35} + \frac{(9.25)^2}{30}}} = \frac{5}{2.70} = 1.8485.$$

The p-value of the right-tailed test is computed as p-value $= P(Z \geq 1.8485) = 0.0323$. In order to find the p-value in Excel, we enter `=1-NORM.DIST(1.8485,0,1,TRUE)`; in R, we enter `pnorm(1.8485,0,1,lower.tail=FALSE)`.

c. We reject the null hypothesis because the p-value is less than the chosen $\alpha = 0.05$. Therefore, at the 5% significance level, the economist concludes that average weekly food expenditure in City 1 is more than that of City 2.

Using Excel and R for Testing Hypotheses about $\mu_1 - \mu_2$

Excel and R provide several options that simplify the steps when conducting a hypothesis test about $\mu_1 - \mu_2$. Consider the following example.

EXAMPLE 10.4

Table 10.2 shows a portion of the annual returns (in %) for 10 firms in the gold industry and 10 firms in the oil industry. Can we conclude at the 5% significance level that the average returns in the two industries differ? Here we assume that the sample data are drawn independently from normally distributed populations. The variance is a common measure of risk when analyzing financial returns and we cannot assume that the risk from investing in the gold industry is the same as the risk from investing in the oil industry.

FILE *Gold_Oil*

TABLE 10.2 Annual Returns (in percent)

Gold	Oil
6	−3
15	15
⋮	⋮
16	15

SOLUTION: We let μ_1 denote the mean return for the gold industry and μ_2 denote the mean return for the oil industry. Since we wish to test whether the mean returns differ, we set up the null and alternative hypotheses as

$$H_0: \mu_1 - \mu_2 = 0$$
$$H_A: \mu_1 - \mu_2 \neq 0$$

Given that we are testing the difference between two means when the population variances are unknown and not equal, we need to calculate $t_{df} = \frac{(\bar{x}_1 - \bar{x}_2) - d_0}{\sqrt{\frac{s_1^2}{n_1} + \frac{s_2^2}{n_2}}}$. Recall that the calculation for the degrees of freedom for the corresponding test statistic is rather involved. Fortunately, Excel and R provide the degrees of freedom, the value of the test statistic, and the p-value.

Using Excel

a. Open the ***Gold_Oil*** data file.

b. Choose **Data > Data Analysis > t-Test: Two-Sample Assuming Unequal Variances > OK**. (Note: Excel provides two other options when we want to test the difference between two population means from independent samples and we have access to the raw data. If the population variances are known, we use the option **z-Test: Two-Sample for Means.** If the population variances are unknown but assumed equal, we use the option **t-Test: Two-Sample Assuming Equal Variances**.)

c. See Figure 10.1. In the dialog box, choose *Variable 1 Range* and select the Gold observations. Then, choose *Variable 2 Range* and select the Oil observations. Enter a *Hypothesized Mean Difference* of 0 because $d_0 = 0$ and check the *Labels* box if you include Gold and Oil as headings. Click **OK**.

FIGURE 10.1 Excel's dialog box for *t*-test with unequal variances

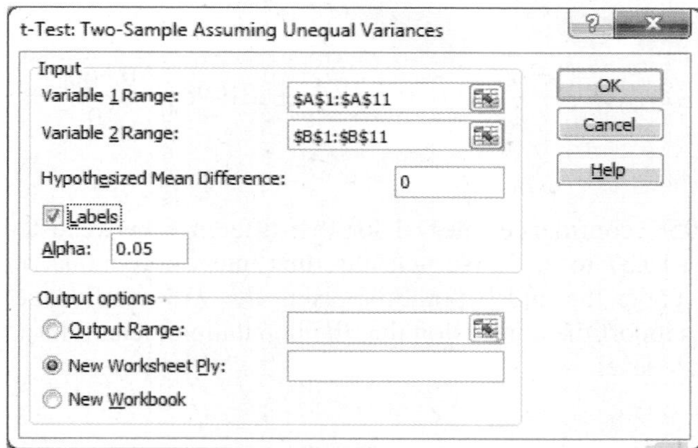

Table 10.3 shows the Excel output.

The value of the test statistic and the p-value for this two-tailed test are -0.3023 and 0.7661, respectively (see these values in boldface in Table 10.3). At the 5% significance level, we cannot reject H_0 since the p-value is greater than 0.05. While average returns in the oil industry seem to slightly outperform average returns in the gold industry ($\bar{x}_2 = 17.3 > 16.0 = \bar{x}_1$), the difference is not statistically significant.

TABLE 10.3 Excel's Output for t-Test concerning $\mu_1 - \mu_2$

	Gold	Oil
Mean	16	17.3
Variance	70.6667	114.2333
Observations	10	10
Hypothesized Mean Difference	0	
Df	17	
t Stat	**−0.3023**	
P(T ≤ t) one-tail	0.3830	
t Critical one-tail	1.7396	
P(T ≤ t) two-tail	**0.7661**	
t Critical two-tail	2.1098	

Given the information in Table 10.3, it is also possible to calculate the corresponding 95% confidence interval for $\mu_1 - \mu_2$. Recall that when we estimate the difference between two population means when the population variances are unknown and cannot be assumed equal, we use $t_{\alpha/2,df}$ in its construction. By default, Excel provides $t_{\alpha/2,df}$ for a 95% confidence interval - see Figure 10.1 where Alpha is set to 0.05. (We can easily adjust Alpha if we would like to construct a different confidence interval.) In the last row of Table 10.3, Excel reports $t_{\alpha/2,df} = t_{0.025,17} = 2.1098$. We then calculate:

$$(\bar{x}_1 - \bar{x}_2) \pm t_{\alpha/2,df}\sqrt{\frac{s_1^2}{n_1} + \frac{s_2^2}{n_2}} = (16.0 - 17.3) \pm 2.1098\sqrt{\frac{70.6667}{10} + \frac{114.2333}{10}}$$
$$= -1.3 \pm 9.07.$$

That is, the 95% confidence interval for the difference between the two means ranges from -10.37 to 7.77. We note that this interval contains zero, the value hypothesized under the null hypothesis. Using the 95% confidence interval, we again cannot support the conclusion that the population mean returns differ at the 5% significance level.

Using R

a. Import the ***Gold_Oil*** data file into a data frame (table) and label it myData.

b. We use R's **t.test** function to test $\mu_1 - \mu_2$. For options within the **t.test** function we use *alternative* to denote the specification of the alternative hypothesis (denoted as "two.sided" for a two-tailed test, "less" for a left-tailed test, and "greater" for a right-tailed test), *mu* to denote the value of the hypothesized difference, *paired* to indicate if we have a matched-pairs sample, *var.equal* to indicate if the variances are assumed equal, and *conf.level* to specify the confidence level. When testing $\mu_1 - \mu_2$ under the assumption that the variances are unknown and not equal, we enter

```
> t.test(myData$Gold, myData$Oil,alternative="two.sided",
  mu=0, paired=FALSE,var.equal=FALSE, conf.level=0.95)
```

Table 10.4 shows the R output. We have put the value of the test statistic, the p-value, and the 95% confidence level in boldface. The results are consistent with the Excel output; that is, since the p-value $= 0.7661 > 0.05 = \alpha$, we cannot reject the null hypothesis. Equivalently, the 95% confidence interval for $\mu_1 - \mu_2$ is $[-10.37, 7.77]$ which includes 0, the hypothesized value under the null hypothesis. At the 5% significance level, we cannot conclude that average returns between the gold industry and the oil industry differ.

TABLE 10.4 R's Output for t-Test concerning $\mu_1 - \mu_2$

```
Welch Two Sample t-test

data: myData$Gold and myData$Oil
t = -0.30233, df = 17.053 p-value = 0.7661
alternative hypothesis: true difference in means is not equal to 0
    95 percent confidence interval:
    -10.37005 7.77005
sample estimates:
mean of x mean of y
      16.0       17.3
```

A Note on the Assumption of Normality

In Example 10.4, we made an assumption that the populations were normally distributed. We could not invoke the central limit theorem, as we had small sample sizes. In Chapter 12, we will explore tests that check for normality. If we wish to draw inferences about $\mu_1 - \mu_2$ from nonnormal populations, we can use the nonparametric Wilcoxon rank-sum test for independent samples, discussed in Chapter 20.

EXERCISES 10.1

Mechanics

1. Consider the following data drawn independently from normally distributed populations:

$$\bar{x}_1 = 25.7 \quad \bar{x}_2 = 30.6$$
$$\sigma_1^2 = 98.2 \quad \sigma_2^2 = 87.4$$
$$n_1 = 20 \quad n_2 = 25$$

   a. Construct the 95% confidence interval for the difference between the population means.
   b. Specify the competing hypotheses in order to determine whether or not the population means differ.
   c. Using the confidence interval from part a, can you reject the null hypothesis? Explain.

2. Consider the following data drawn independently from normally distributed populations:

$$\bar{x}_1 = -10.5 \quad \bar{x}_2 = -16.8$$
$$s_1^2 = 7.9 \quad s_2^2 = 9.3$$
$$n_1 = 15 \quad n_2 = 20$$

   a. Construct the 95% confidence interval for the difference between the population means. Assume that the population variances are equal.
   b. Specify the competing hypotheses in order to determine whether or not the population means differ.
   c. Using the confidence interval from part a, can you reject the null hypothesis? Explain.

3. Consider the following competing hypotheses and accompanying sample data drawn independently from normally distributed populations.

$$H_0: \mu_1 - \mu_2 = 0$$
$$H_A: \mu_1 - \mu_2 \neq 0$$

$$\bar{x}_1 = 57 \quad \bar{x}_2 = 63$$
$$\sigma_1 = 11.5 \quad \sigma_2 = 15.2$$
$$n_1 = 20 \quad n_2 = 20$$

   Test whether the population means differ at the 5% significance level.

4. Consider the following competing hypotheses and accompanying sample data. The two populations are known to be normally distributed.

$$H_0: \mu_1 - \mu_2 \leq 0$$
$$H_A: \mu_1 - \mu_2 > 0$$

$\bar{x}_1 = 20.2$	$\bar{x}_2 = 17.5$
$s_1 = 2.5$	$s_2 = 4.4$
$n_1 = 10$	$n_2 = 12$

a. Implement the test at the 5% significance level under the assumption that the population variances are equal.
b. Repeat the analysis at the 10% significance level.

5. Consider the following competing hypotheses and accompanying sample data drawn independently from normally distributed populations.

$$H_0: \mu_1 - \mu_2 \geq 0$$
$$H_A: \mu_1 - \mu_2 < 0$$

$\bar{x}_1 = 249$	$\bar{x}_2 = 262$
$s_1 = 35$	$s_2 = 23$
$n_1 = 10$	$n_2 = 10$

a. Implement the test at the 5% significance level under the assumption that the population variances are equal.
b. Implement the test at the 5% significance level under the assumption that the population variances are not equal.

6. Consider the following competing hypotheses and accompanying sample data.

$$H_0: \mu_1 - \mu_2 = 5$$
$$H_A: \mu_1 - \mu_2 \neq 5$$

$\bar{x}_1 = 57$	$\bar{x}_2 = 43$
$s_1 = 21.5$	$s_2 = 15.2$
$n_1 = 22$	$n_2 = 18$

Assume that the populations are normally distributed with equal variances.

a. Calculate the value of the test statistic and the p-value.
b. At the 5% significance level, can you conclude that the difference between the two means differs from 5?

7. **FILE** ***Exercise_10.7.*** The accompanying file contains sample data drawn independently from normally distributed populations with equal population variances.
a. Construct the relevant hypotheses to test if the mean of the second population is greater than the mean of the first population.
b. Implement the test at the 1% significance level.
c. Implement the test at the 10% significance level.

8. **FILE** ***Exercise_10.8.*** The accompanying file contains sample data drawn independently from normally distributed populations with unequal population variances.
a. Construct the relevant hypothesis to test if the means of the two populations differ.
b. What is the value of the test statistic and the p-value?
c. At the 10% significance level, do the two population means differ?

Applications

9. You collect the following sample data concerning average life expectancies for female and male residents in Boston. You assume a population standard deviation of 8.2 years for females and 8.6 years for males.

Female	Male
$\bar{x}_1 = 81.1$	$\bar{x}_2 = 74.8$
$n_1 = 32$	$n_2 = 32$

a. Set up the hypotheses to test whether the average life expectancy of female Bostonians is higher than that of male Bostonians.
b. Calculate the value of the test statistic and the p-value.
c. At the 10% significance level, can you conclude that female Bostonians live longer than male Bostonians?

10. A report finds that graduates with a bachelor's degree who transferred from a community college earn less than those who start at a four-year school; this occurrence is referred to as the "community college penalty." Lucille Barnes wonders if a similar pattern applies to her university. In a sample of 100 graduates who transferred from a community college, she finds that their average salary was $52,000. In a sample of 100 graduates who did not transfer from a community college, she finds that their average salary was $54,700. Lucille believes that the population standard deviation is $4,400 for graduates who transferred from a community college and $1,500 for graduates who did not transfer from a community college.
a. Set up the hypotheses to test if the report's conclusion also applies to Lucille's university.
b. Calculate the value of the test statistic and the p-value.
c. At the 5% significance level, can we conclude that there is a "community college penalty" at Lucille's university?

11. The Chartered Financial Analyst (CFA) designation is fast becoming a requirement for serious investment professionals. It is an attractive alternative to getting an MBA for students wanting a career in investment. A student of finance is curious to know if a CFA designation is a more lucrative option than an MBA. He collects data on 38 recent CFAs with a mean salary of $138,000 and a standard deviation of $34,000. A sample of 80 MBAs results in a mean salary of $130,000 with a standard deviation of $46,000.

a. Specify the hypotheses to test whether a CFA designation is more lucrative than an MBA.
b. Calculate the value of the test statistic and the p-value. Do not assume that the population variances are equal.
c. At the 5% significance level, is a CFA designation more lucrative than an MBA?

12. An entrepreneur owns some land that he wishes to develop. He identifies two development options: build condominiums or build apartment buildings. Accordingly, he reviews public records and derives the following summary measures concerning annual profitability based on a random sample of 30 for each such local business venture. For the analysis, he uses a historical (population) standard deviation of $22,500 for condominiums and $20,000 for apartment buildings.

Condominiums	Apartment Buildings
$\bar{x}_1 = 244{,}200$	$\bar{x}_2 = 235{,}800$
$n_1 = 30$	$n_2 = 30$

a. Set up the hypotheses to test whether the mean profitability differs between condominiums and apartment buildings.
b. Calculate the value of the test statistic and the p-value.
c. At the 5% significance level, what is the conclusion to the test? What if the significance level is 10%?

13. David Anderson has been working as a lecturer at Michigan State University for the last three years. He teaches two large sections of introductory accounting every semester. While he uses the same lecture notes in both sections, his students in the first section outperform those in the second section. He believes that students in the first section not only tend to get higher scores, they also tend to have lower variability in scores. David decides to carry out a formal test to validate his hunch regarding the difference in average scores. In a random sample of 18 students in the first section, he computes a mean and a standard deviation of 77.4 and 10.8, respectively. In the second section, a random sample of 14 students results in a mean of 74.1 and a standard deviation of 12.2.
a. Construct the null and the alternative hypotheses to test David's hunch.
b. Compute the value of the test statistic. What assumption regarding the populations is necessary to implement this step?
c. Implement the test at $\alpha = 0.01$ and interpret your results.

14. A design engineer at Sperling Manufacturing, a supplier of high-quality ball bearings, claims a new machining process can result in a higher daily output rate. Accordingly, the production group is conducting an experiment to determine if this claim can be substantiated. The mean and the standard deviation of bearings in a sample of 8 days' output using the new process equal 2,613.63 and 90.78, respectively. A similar sample of 10 days' output using the old process yields a mean and a standard deviation of 2,485.10 and 148.22, respectively.
a. Set up the hypotheses to test whether the mean output rate of the new process exceeds that of the old process. Assume normally distributed populations and equal population variances for each process.
b. Compute the value of the test statistic and the p-value.
c. At the 5% significance level, what is the conclusion of the experiment?
d. At the 1% significance level, what is the conclusion of the experiment?

15. A promising start-up wants to compete in the cell phone market. The start-up believes that the battery life of its cell phone is more than two hours longer than the leading product. A recent sample of 120 units of the leading product provides a mean battery life of 5 hours and 40 minutes with a standard deviation of 30 minutes. A similar analysis of 100 units of the start-up's product results in a mean battery life of 8 hours and 5 minutes and a standard deviation of 55 minutes. It is not reasonable to assume that the population variances of the two products are equal.
a. Set up the hypotheses to test if the start-up's product has a battery life more than two hours longer than the leading product.
b. Implement the test at the 5% significance level.

16. A sales manager of a used car dealership believes that it takes an average of 30 days longer to sell a sports-utility vehicle (SUV) as compared to a small car. In the last two months, he sold 18 SUVs that took an average of 95 days to sell with a standard deviation of 32 days. He also sold 38 small cars with an average of 48 days to sell and a standard deviation of 24 days.
a. Construct the null and the alternative hypotheses to contradict the manager's claim.
b. Compute the value of the test statistic and the p-value. Assume that the populations are normally distributed and that the variability of selling time for the SUVs and the small cars is the same.
c. Implement the test at $\alpha = 0.10$ and interpret your results.

17. **FILE** ***Longevity.*** A consumer advocate researches the length of life between two brands of refrigerators, Brand A and Brand B. He collects data (measured in years) on the longevity of 40 refrigerators for Brand A and repeats the

sampling for Brand B. A portion of the data is shown in the accompanying table.

Brand A	Brand B
16	16
14	20
⋮	⋮
18	17

a. Specify the competing hypotheses to test whether the average length of life differs between the two brands.

b. Calculate the value of the test statistic and the p-value. Assume that $\sigma_A^2 = 4.4$ and $\sigma_B^2 = 5.2$.

c. At the 5% significance level, what is the conclusion?

18. FILE ***Searches.*** The "See Me" marketing agency wants to determine if time of day for a television advertisement influences website searches for a product. They have extracted the number of website searches occurring during a one-hour period after an advertisement was aired for a random sample of 30 day and 30 evening advertisements. A portion of the data is shown in the accompanying table.

Day	Evening
96670	118379
97855	111005
⋮	⋮
95103	114721

a. Set up the hypotheses to test whether the mean number of website searches differs between the day and evening advertisements.

b. Calculate the value of the test statistic and the p-value. Assume that the population variances are equal.

c. At the 5% significance level, what is the conclusion?

19. FILE ***Diets.*** According to a report, overweight people on low-carbohydrate diets lost more weight and got greater cardiovascular benefits than people on a conventional low-fat diet (healthline.com, March 24, 2020). A nutritionist wishes to verify these results and documents the weight loss (in pounds) of 30 dieters on the low carbohydrate diet and 30 dieters on the low-fat diet. A portion of the data is shown in the accompanying table.

Low_carb	Low_fat
9.5	6.5
8.1	5.8
...	...
9.0	3.9

a. Set up the hypotheses to test the claim that the mean weight loss for those on the low carbohydrate diet is greater than the mean weight loss for those on a conventional low-fat diet.

b. Calculate the value of the test statistic and the p-value. Assume that the population variances are equal.

c. At the 5% significance level, can the nutritionist conclude that people on the low carbohydrate diet lost more weight than people on a conventional low-fat diet?

20. FILE ***Tractor_Times.*** The production department at Greenside Corporation, a manufacturer of lawn equipment, has devised a new manual assembly method for its lawn tractors. Now it wishes to determine if it is reasonable to conclude that the mean assembly time of the new method is less than the old method. Accordingly, they have randomly sampled assembly times (in minutes) from 40 tractors using the old method and 32 tractors using the new method. A portion of the data is shown in the accompanying table.

Old	New
32	30
36	32
⋮	⋮

a. Set up the hypotheses to test the claim that the mean assembly time using the new method is less than the old method.

b. Calculate the value of the test statistic and the p-value. Assume that the population variances are not equal.

c. At the 5% significance level, what is the conclusion? What if the significance level is 10%?

21. FILE ***Nicknames.*** Baseball has always been a favorite pastime in America and is rife with statistics and theories. One study found that major league players who have nicknames live an average of 2½ years longer than those without them. You do not believe in this result and decide to collect data on the lifespan of 30 baseball players along with a nickname variable that equals 1 if the player had a nickname and 0 otherwise. A portion of the data is shown in the accompanying table.

Years	Nickname
74	1
62	1
⋮	⋮
64	0

a. Create two subsamples consisting of players with and without nicknames. Calculate the average longevity for each subsample.

b. Specify the hypotheses to contradict the claim made by the researchers.

c. Calculate the value of the test statistic and the p-value. Assume that the population variances are equal.

d. What is the conclusion of the test using a 5% level of significance?

22. FILE ***Salaries.*** A report suggests that graduating from college during bad economic times can impact the graduate's earning power for a long time. The admissions director at a regional state university wants to determine if the starting

salary of his college graduates has declined from 2018 to 2020. He expects the variance of the salaries to be different between these two years. A portion of the data is shown in the accompanying table.

Salary_2018	Salary_2020
35000	34000
56000	62000
⋮	⋮
47000	54000

At the 5% significance level, determine if the mean starting salary has decreased from 2018 to 2020.

23. **FILE** ***Spending.*** Researchers have found that men and women shop for different reasons. While women enjoy the shopping experience, men are on a mission to get the job done. Men do not shop as frequently, but when they do, they make big purchases like expensive electronics. The accompanying table shows a portion of the amount spent (in $) over the weekend by 40 men and 60 women at a local mall.

Men	Women
85	90
102	79
⋮	⋮

At the 1% significance level, determine if the mean amount spent by men is more than that by women. Assume that the population variances are equal.

10.2 INFERENCE CONCERNING MEAN DIFFERENCES

LO 10.2

Make inferences about the mean difference based on matched-pairs sampling.

One of the crucial assumptions in Section 10.1 concerning differences between two population means is that the samples are drawn independently. As mentioned in that section, two samples are independent if the selection of one is not influenced by the selection of the other. When we want to conduct tests on two population means based on samples that we believe are not independent, we need to employ a different methodology.

A common case of dependent sampling, commonly referred to as **matched-pairs sampling,** is when the samples are paired or matched in some way. Such samples are useful in evaluating strategies because the comparison is made between "apples" and "apples." For instance, an effective way to assess the benefits of a new medical treatment is by evaluating the same patients before and after the treatment. If, however, one group of people is given the treatment and another group is not, then it is not clear if the observed differences are due to the treatment or due to other important differences between the groups.

For matched-pairs sampling, the parameter of interest is referred to as the mean difference μ_D where $D = X_1 - X_2$, and the random variables X_1 and X_2 are matched in a pair. The statistical inference regarding μ_D is based on the estimator $\overline{D}$, representing the sample mean difference. It requires that $X_1 - X_2$ is normally distributed or that the sample size is sufficiently large ($n \geq 30$).

Recognizing a Matched-Pairs Experiment

It is important to be able to determine whether a particular experiment uses independent or matched-pairs sampling. In general, two types of matched-pairs sampling occur:

1. The first type of matched-pairs sample is characterized by a measurement, an intervention of some type, and then another measurement. We generally refer to these experiments as "before" and "after" studies. For example, an operation manager of a production facility wants to determine whether a new workstation layout improves productivity at her plant. She first measures output of employees before the layout change. Then she measures output of the same employees after the change. Another classic before-and-after example concerns weight loss of clients at a diet center. In these examples, the same individual gets sampled before and after the experiment.

2. The second type of matched-pairs sample is characterized by a pairing of observations, where it is not the same individual who gets sampled twice. Suppose an agronomist wishes to switch to an organic fertilizer but is unsure what the effects might be on his crop yield. It is important to the agronomist that the yields be similar. He matches 20 adjacent plots of land using the nonorganic fertilizer on one half of the plot and the organic fertilizer on the other. Similarly, two portfolio returns over a specific time period also represent a matched-pairs sample because they are both influenced by the state of the economy.

In order to recognize a matched-pairs experiment, we watch for a natural pairing between one observation in the first sample and one observation in the second sample. If a natural pairing exists, then the experiment involves matched samples.

Confidence Interval for μ_D

When constructing a confidence interval for the mean difference μ_D, we follow the same standard format given by: Point Estimate $\pm$ Margin of Error.

CONFIDENCE INTERVAL FOR μ_D

A $100(1 - \alpha)\%$ confidence interval for the mean difference μ_D is given by

$$\bar{d} \pm t_{\alpha/2,df} s_D / \sqrt{n}$$

where $\bar{d}$ and s_D are the mean and the standard deviation, respectively, of the n sample differences and $df = n - 1$. This formula is valid only if $\bar{D}$ (approximately) follows a normal distribution.

In the next example, the values for $\bar{d}$ and s_D are explicitly given; we will outline the calculations when we discuss hypothesis testing.

EXAMPLE 10.5

A manager is interested in improving productivity at a plant by changing the layout of the workstation. For each of 10 workers, she measures the time it takes to complete a task before the change and again after the change. She calculates the following summary statistics for the sample difference: $\bar{d} = 8.5$, $s_D = 11.38$ and $n = 10$. Construct the 95% confidence interval for the mean difference, assuming that the productivity variable, defined as before minus after, is normally distributed.

SOLUTION: In order to construct the 95% confidence interval for the mean difference, we use $\bar{d} \pm t_{\alpha/2,df} s_D / \sqrt{n}$. With $df = n - 1 = 10 - 1 = 9$ and $\alpha = 0.05$, we find $t_{\alpha/2,df} = t_{0.025,9} = 2.262$. Plugging the relevant values into the formula, we calculate $8.5 \pm 2.262(11.38/\sqrt{10}) = 8.5 \pm 8.14$. That is, the 95% confidence interval for the mean difference ranges from 0.36 to 16.64. This represents a fairly wide interval, caused by the high standard deviation s_D of the 10 sample differences.

Hypothesis Test for μ_D

In order to conduct a hypothesis test concerning the parameter μ_D, the competing hypotheses will take one of the following general forms:

Two-Tailed Test	Right-Tailed Test	Left-Tailed Test
$H_0: \mu_D = d_0$ $H_A: \mu_D \neq d_0$	$H_0: \mu_D \leq d_0$ $H_A: \mu_D > d_0$	$H_0: \mu_D \geq d_0$ $H_A: \mu_D < d_0$

In practice, the competing hypotheses tend to be based on $d_0 = 0$. For example, when testing if the mean difference differs from zero, we use a two-tailed test with the competing hypotheses defined as H_0: $\mu_D = 0$ versus H_A: $\mu_D \neq 0$. If, on the other hand, we wish to determine whether or not the mean difference differs by some amount, say by 5 units, we set $d_0 = 5$ and define the competing hypotheses as H_0: $\mu_D = 5$ versus H_A: $\mu_D \neq 5$. One-tailed tests are defined similarly.

EXAMPLE 10.6

Using the information from Example 10.5, can the manager conclude at the 5% significance level that there has been a change in productivity since the adoption of the new workstation?

SOLUTION: In order to determine whether or not there has been a change in the mean difference, we formulate the null and the alternative hypotheses as

$$H_0: \mu_D = 0$$

$$H_A: \mu_D \neq 0$$

In Example 10.5, we found that the 95% confidence interval for the mean difference ranges from 0.36 to 16.64. Although the interval is very wide, the entire range is above the hypothesized value of zero. Therefore, at the 5% significance level the sample data suggest that the mean difference differs from zero. In other words, there has been a change in productivity due to the different layout in the workstation.

We now examine the four-step procedure to conduct one- or two-tailed hypothesis tests concerning the mean difference. We again find the value of the t_{df} statistic by dividing the difference between the sample mean difference and the hypothesized mean difference by the standard error of the estimator $se(\overline{D})$.

TEST STATISTIC FOR TESTING μ_D

The value of the test statistic for a hypothesis test concerning the population mean difference μ_D is computed as

$$t_{df} = \frac{\bar{d} - d_0}{s_D / \sqrt{n}},$$

where $df = n - 1$, $\bar{d}$ and s_D are the mean and the standard deviation, respectively, of the n sample differences, and d_0 is the hypothesized mean difference. This formula is valid only if $\overline{D}$ (approximately) follows a normal distribution.

We should note that a hypothesis test for μ_D is equivalent to finding the differences between the paired items and then using the one-sample t-test discussed in Chapter 9.

EXAMPLE 10.7

FILE
Drink_Calories

Recall from the introductory case that chain restaurants are required to post caloric information on their menus. A nutritionist wants to examine whether average drink calories declined at a popular cafe after the caloric postings. The nutritionist obtains transaction data for 40 customers and records each customer's drink calories prior to the caloric postings and then after the caloric postings. A portion of the data is shown in Table 10.5. Can she conclude at the 5% significance level that the ordinance reduced average drink calories?

SOLUTION: We first note that this is a matched-pairs experiment; specifically, it conforms to a "before" and "after" type of study. Moreover, we want to find out whether average drink calories prior to the caloric postings are greater than average drink calories after the caloric postings. Thus, we want to test if the mean difference μ_D is greater than zero, where $D = X_1 - X_2$, X_1 denotes drink calories before the caloric postings, and X_2 denotes drink calories after the caloric postings for a randomly selected customer. We specify the competing hypotheses as

$$H_0: \mu_D \leq 0$$

$$H_A: \mu_D > 0$$

The normality condition for the test is satisfied since the sample size $n \geq 30$. The value of the test statistic is calculated as $t_{df} = \frac{\bar{d} - d_0}{s_D/\sqrt{n}}$ where d_0 equals 0. In order to determine $\bar{d}$ and s_D, we first calculate the difference d_i for each customer. For instance, customer 1 consumes 141 calories prior to the caloric postings and 142 calories after the caloric postings, for a difference of $d_1 = 141 - 142 = -1$. The differences for a portion of the other customers appear in the fourth column of Table 10.5.

TABLE 10.5 Data and Calculations for Example 10.7, $n = 40$

Customer	Before	After	d_i	$(d_i - \bar{d})^2$
1	141	142	−1	$(-1 - 2.1)^2 = 9.61$
2	137	140	−3	$(-3 - 2.1)^2 = 26.01$
⋮	⋮	⋮	⋮	⋮
40	147	141	6	$(6 - 2.1)^2 = 15.21$

We obtain the average of the differences as

$$\bar{d} = \frac{\Sigma d_i}{n} = \frac{84}{40} = 2.10.$$

Similarly, in the fifth column of Table 10.5, we square the differences between d_i and $\bar{d}$. Summing these squared differences yields the numerator in the formula for the sample variance s_D^2. The denominator is simply $n - 1$, so

$$s_D^2 = \frac{\Sigma(d_i - \bar{d})^2}{n - 1} = \frac{2{,}593.60}{40 - 1} = 66.5026.$$

As usual, the standard deviation is the positive square root of the sample variance—that is, $s_D = \sqrt{66.5026} = 8.1549$. We compute the value of the t_{df} test statistic with $df = n - 1 = 40 - 1 = 39$ as

$$t_{39} = \frac{\bar{d} - d_0}{s_D/\sqrt{n}} = \frac{2.10 - 0}{8.1549/\sqrt{40}} = 1.629.$$

Given a right-tailed hypothesis test with $df = 39$, we can use the t table to approximate the p-value $= P(T_{39} \geq 1.629)$, as $0.05 < p\text{-value} < 0.10$. Recall that in order to find the exact p-value in Excel, we enter `=T.DIST.RT(1.629, 39)` and in R, we enter `pt(1.629, 39, lower.tail=FALSE)`. Both software return a p-value of 0.056. Because the p-value > 0.05, we do not reject H_0. At the 5% significance level, we cannot conclude that the posting of caloric information decreases average drink calories.

Using Excel and R for Testing Hypotheses about μ_D

Excel and R provide several options that simplify the steps when conducting a hypothesis test about μ_D. Consider the following example.

EXAMPLE 10.8

The nutritionist from Example 10.7 also wants to use the data from the 40 customers in order to determine if the posting of caloric information has reduced average food calories. This test is also conducted at the 5% significance level.

SOLUTION: We set up the same competing hypotheses as in Example 10.7 since we want to know if average food calories were greater before the caloric postings as compared to after the caloric postings.

$$H_0: \mu_D \leq 0$$
$$H_A: \mu_D > 0$$

Using Excel

a. Open the ***Food_Calories*** data file.

b. Choose **Data > Data Analysis > *t*-Test: Paired Two Sample for Means > OK.**

c. See Figure 10.2. In the dialog box, choose *Variable 1 Range* and select the observations in the Before column. Choose *Variable 2 Range* and select the observations in the After column. Enter a *Hypothesized Mean Difference* of 0 since $d_0 = 0$ and check the *Labels* box if you include Before and After as headings. Click **OK.**

FIGURE 10.2 Excel's dialog box for *t*-test with paired sample

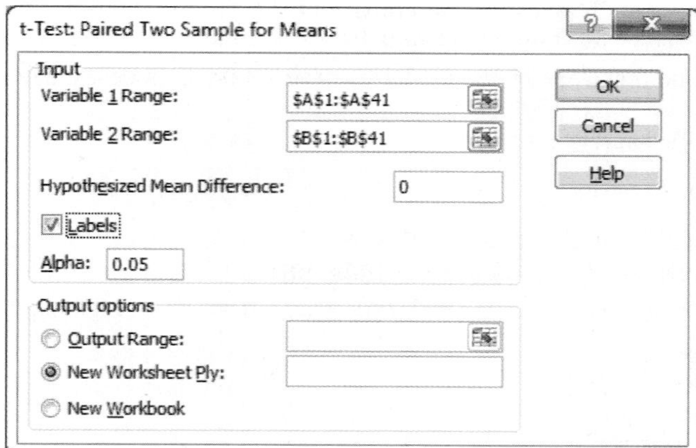

Table 10.6 shows the Excel output. The value of the test statistic and the p-value for this one-tailed test are 6.7795 and 2.15E-08, respectively (see these values in boldface in Table 10.6). We can reject H_0 because the p-value < 0.05. Thus, at the 5% significance level, we can conclude that average food calories have declined after the caloric postings.

TABLE 10.6 Excel's Output for *t*-Test concerning μ_D

	Before	After
Mean	400.275	391.475
Variance	49.9481	42.3583
Observations	40	40
Pearson Correlation	0.27080	
Hypothesized Mean Difference	0	
Df	39	
t Stat	**6.7795**	
P(T ≤ t) one-tail	**2.15E-08**	
t Critical one-tail	1.6849	
P(T ≤ t) two-tail	4.31E-08	
t Critical two-tail	2.0227	

Note: Although Excel calculates the *p*-value correctly, the expression it uses to denote the *p*-value is not always correct. In this example with a positive value for the test statistic, the expression should be "P(T ≥ t) one-tail" rather than "P(T ≤ t) one-tail."

Using R

a. Import the ***Food_Calories*** data file into a data frame (table) and label it myData.

b. We use the **t.test** function, discussed in Section 10.1, For options within the **t.test** function we use *alternative, mu,* and *paired.* We enter

```
> t.test(myData$Before,myData$After, alternative="greater",
  mu=0, paired=TRUE)
```

Table 10.7 shows the R output. We have put the value of the test statistic and the *p*-value in boldface. The results are consistent with the Excel output; that is, since the *p*-value < 0.05, we reject the null hypothesis. At the 5% significance level, we can conclude that average food calories have declined since the caloric postings.

TABLE 10.7 R's Output for *t*-Test concerning μ_D

```
Paired t-test

data: myData$Before and myData$After
t = 6.7795, df = 39, p-value = 2.154e-08
alternative hypothesis: true difference in means is greater
than 0
95 percent confidence interval:
 6.612988     Inf
sample estimates:
mean of the differences
                    8.8
```

One Last Note on the Matched-Pairs Experiment

Similar to our remarks in the last section, when making inferences concerning μ_D, we require that $\overline{D}$ (approximately) follows a normal distribution. If $\overline{D}$ is not normally distributed, we can use the nonparametric Wilcoxon signed-rank test for matched pairs, discussed in Chapter 20.

SYNOPSIS OF INTRODUCTORY CASE

Chris Hondros/Getty Images

In an effort to make it easier for consumers to select healthier options, many restaurants and cafes have started to post caloric information on their menus. A nutritionist studies the effects of the caloric postings at a popular cafe in San Mateo, California. She obtains transaction data for 40 customers and records each customer's drink and food calories prior to the caloric postings and then after the caloric postings. Two hypothesis tests are conducted. The first test examines whether average drink calories are less since the caloric postings. After conducting a test on the mean difference at the 5% significance level, the nutritionist infers that the caloric postings did not prompt customers to reduce their consumption of drink calories. The second test investigates whether average food calories are less since the caloric postings. At the 5% significance level, the sample data suggest that customers have reduced their consumption of food calories since the caloric postings. In sum, these results are consistent with research that has shown mixed results on whether mandatory caloric postings are prompting customers to select healthier foods.

EXERCISES 10.2

Mechanics

24. A sample of 20 paired observations generates the following data: $\bar{d} = 1.3$ and $s_D^2 = 2.6$. Assume that the differences are normally distributed.
    a. Construct the 90% confidence interval for the mean difference μ_D.
    b. Using the confidence interval, test whether the mean difference differs from zero. Explain.

25. **FILE** ***Exercise_10.25.*** The accompanying data file contains information on matched sample observations whose differences are normally distributed.
    a. Construct the 95% confidence interval for the mean difference μ_D.
    b. Specify the competing hypotheses in order to test whether the mean difference differs from zero.
    c. Using the confidence interval from part a, are you able to reject H_0? Explain.

26. Consider the following competing hypotheses and accompanying results from a matched-pairs sample:

$$H_0: \mu_D \geq 0; H_A: \mu_D < 0$$
$$\bar{d} = -2.8, s_D = 5.7, n = 12$$

    a. Calculate the value of the test statistic and the p-value, assuming that the sample difference is normally distributed.
    b. At the 5% significance level, what is the conclusion to the hypothesis test?

27. Consider the following competing hypotheses and accompanying results from a matched-pairs sample:

$$H_0: \mu_D \leq 2; H_A: \mu_D > 2$$
$$\bar{d} = 5.6, s_D = 6.2, n = 10$$

    a. Calculate the value of the test statistic and the p-value, assuming that the sample difference is normally distributed.
    b. Use the 1% significance level to make a conclusion.

28. A sample of 35 paired observations generates the following results: $\bar{d} = 1.2$ and $s_D = 3.8$.
    a. Specify the appropriate hypotheses to test if the mean difference is greater than zero.
    b. Calculate the value of the test statistic and the p-value.
    c. At the 5% significance level, can you conclude that the mean difference is greater than zero? Explain.

29. **FILE** ***Exercise_10.29.*** The accompanying data file shows matched-pairs observations for a before-and-after experiment. Assume that the sample differences are normally distributed.
    a. Construct the competing hypotheses to determine if the experiment increases the magnitude of the observations.
    b. Implement the test at the 5% significance level.
    c. Do the results change if we implement the test at the 1% significance level?

Applications

30. **FILE** ***Industrial.*** A manager of an industrial plant asserts that workers on average do not complete a job using Method A in the same amount of time as they would using Method B. Seven workers are randomly selected. Each worker's completion time (in minutes) is recorded by the use of Method A and Method B. A portion of the data is shown in the accompanying table.

Worker	Method_A	w
1	15	16
2	21	25
⋮	⋮	⋮
7	20	20

    a. Specify the null and alternative hypotheses to test the manager's assertion.
    b. Assuming that the completion time difference is normally distributed, calculate the value of the test statistic.
    c. Find the *p*-value.
    d. At the 10% significance level, is the manager's assertion supported by the data?

31. **FILE** ***Diet_Center.*** A diet center claims that it has the most effective weight loss program in the region. Its advertisements say, "Participants in our program lose more than 5 pounds within a month." Six clients of this program are weighed on the first day (Before) of the diet and then one month later (After). A portion of the data is shown in the accompanying table.

Client	Before	After
1	158	151
2	205	200
⋮	⋮	⋮
6	135	129

    a. Specify the null and alternative hypotheses that test the diet center's claim.
    b. Assuming that weight loss is normally distributed, calculate the value of the test statistic.
    c. Find the *p*-value.
    d. At the 5% significance level, do the data support the diet center's claim?

32. **FILE** ***Appraisers.*** A bank employs two appraisers. When approving borrowers for mortgages, it is imperative that the appraisers value the same types of properties consistently. To make sure that this is the case, the bank examines six properties (in $1,000s) that the appraisers had valued recently. A portion of the data is shown in the accompanying table.

Property	Appraiser_1	Appraiser_2
1	235	239
2	195	190
⋮	⋮	⋮
6	515	525

    a. Specify the competing hypotheses that determine whether there is any difference between the values estimated by Appraiser 1 and Appraiser 2.
    b. Assuming that the value difference is normally distributed, calculate the value of the test statistic.
    c. Find the *p*-value.
    d. At the 5% significance level, is there sufficient evidence to conclude that the appraisers are inconsistent in their estimates? Explain.

33. **FILE** ***Defects.*** The quality department at ElectroTech is examining which of two microscope brands (Brand A or Brand B) to purchase. Using each microscope, an inspector examines six circuit boards and records the number of defects (e.g., solder voids, misaligned components, etc.). The accompanying table shows a portion of the results.

Board	Brand_A	Brand_B
1	12	14
2	8	9
⋮	⋮	⋮
6	13	15

    a. Specify the null and alternative hypotheses to test for mean differences in the defects found between the microscope brands.
    b. Assuming that the difference in defects is normally distributed, calculate the value of the test statistic and the *p*-value.
    c. At the 5% significance level, is there a difference between the microscope brands?

34. **FILE** ***Speed.*** A computer technology firm wishes to check whether the speed of a new processor exceeds that of an existing processor when used in one of its popular laptop computer models. Accordingly, it measures the time required (in seconds) to complete seven common tasks on two otherwise identical computers, one with the new processor and one with the existing processor. A portion of the time required for both processors is shown in the accompanying table.

Task	New	Existing
1	1.47	1.68
2	2.59	2.99
⋮	⋮	⋮
7	5.75	6.19

    a. Specify the null and alternative hypotheses to test whether the time required for the new processor is less than the existing processor.

b. Assuming that the difference in time is normally distributed, calculate the value of the test statistic and the p-value.

c. At the 5% significance level, is the new processor faster than the old processor?

35. FILE ***SAT_Scores.*** A report criticizes SAT-test-preparation providers for promising big score gains without any hard data to back up such claims. Suppose eight college-bound students take a mock SAT, complete a three-month test-prep course, and then take the real SAT. A portion of the data is shown in the accompanying table.

Student	Mock	Real
1	1830	1840
2	1760	1800
⋮	⋮	⋮
8	1710	1780

a. Specify the competing hypotheses that determine whether completion of the test-prep course increases a student's score on the real SAT.

b. Calculate the value of the test statistic and the p-value. Assume that the SAT scores difference is normally distributed.

c. At the 5% significance level, do the sample data support the test-prep providers' claims?

36. FILE ***Premiums.*** The marketing department at Insure-Me, a large insurance company, wants to advertise that customers can save, on average, more than $100 on their annual automotive insurance policies (relative to their closest competitor) by switching their policies to Insure-Me. However, to avoid potential litigation for false advertising, they select a random sample of 50 policyholders and compare their premiums to those of their closest competitor. A portion of the data is shown in the accompanying table.

Policyholder	Competitor	Insure-Me
1	958	1086
2	1034	366
⋮	⋮	⋮
50	1161	964

a. Specify the competing hypotheses to determine whether the mean difference between the competitor's premium and *Insure-Me's* premium is over $100.

b. Calculate the value of the test statistic and the p-value.

c. What is the conclusion at the 5% significance level? What is the conclusion at the 10% significance level?

37. FILE ***Returns.*** The accompanying table shows a portion of the annual returns for Stock A and Stock B over the past nine years.

Year	Stock_A	Stock_B
1	−14.23	−21.89
2	−50.54	−30.40
⋮	⋮	⋮
9	84.99	14.39

a. Set up the hypotheses to test the claim that the mean difference between the returns differs from zero.

b. Calculate the value of the test statistic and the p-value.

c. At the 5% significance level, does the mean difference between the returns differ from zero?

38. FILE ***Labor_Costs.*** The labor quotation department at Excabar, a large manufacturing company, wants to verify the accuracy of their labor bidding process (estimated cost per unit versus actual cost per unit). They have randomly chosen 35 product quotations that subsequently were successful (meaning the company won the contract for the product). A portion of the data is shown in the accompanying table.

Product	Estimated	Actual
1	13.90	12.90
2	18.80	15.80
⋮	⋮	⋮
35	17.80	14.80

a. Specify the competing hypotheses to determine whether there is a difference between the estimated cost and the actual cost.

b. Calculate the value of the test statistic and the p-value.

c. At the 1% significance level, what is the conclusion?

39. FILE ***Smoking.*** It is fairly common for people to put on weight when they quit smoking. While a small weight gain is normal, excessive weight gain can create new health concerns that erode the benefits of not smoking. The accompanying table shows a portion of the weight data for 50 women before quitting and six months after quitting.

Woman	Before	After
1	140	155
2	144	142
⋮	⋮	⋮
50	135	147

a. Construct and interpret the 95% confidence interval for the mean gain in weight.

b. Use the confidence interval to determine if the mean gain in weight differs from 5 pounds.

40. FILE ***Shift.*** When faced with a power hitter, many baseball teams utilize a defensive shift. A shift usually involves putting three infielders on one side of second base against pull hitters. Many believe that a power hitter's batting average is lower when he faces a shift defense as compared to when he faces

a standard defense. The accompanying table shows a portion of the batting averages of 10 power hitters when they faced a shift defense versus when they faced a standard defense.

Player	Shift	Standard
1	0.239	0.270
2	0.189	0.230
⋮	⋮	⋮
10	0.211	0.205

a. Specify the competing hypotheses to determine whether the use of the defensive shift lowers a power hitter's batting average.

b. Calculate the value of the test statistic and the *p*-value. Assume that the batting average difference is normally distributed.

c. At the 5% significance level, is the defensive shift effective in lowering a power hitter's batting average?

LO 10.3

10.3 INFERENCE CONCERNING THE DIFFERENCE BETWEEN TWO PROPORTIONS

Make inferences about the difference between two population proportions based on independent sampling.

In the preceding two sections, we focused on the difference between two population means under independent sampling and matched-pairs sampling. Now we turn our attention to the difference between two population proportions under independent sampling. This technique has many practical applications.

Consider an investor who may want to determine if the bankruptcy rate is the same in the technology and construction industries. The resulting analysis will help determine the relative risk of investing in these two industries. Or perhaps a marketing executive maintains that the proportion of women who buy a firm's product is greater than the proportion of men who buy the product. If this claim is supported by the data, it provides information as to where the firm should advertise. In another case, a consumer advocacy group may state that the proportion of young adults who carry health insurance is less than the proportion of older adults. Health and government officials might be particularly interested in this type of information.

All of the above examples deal with comparing two population proportions. Our parameter of interest is $p_1 - p_2$, where p_1 and p_2 denote the proportions in the first and second populations, respectively. The estimator for the difference between two population proportions is $\overline{P}_1 - \overline{P}_2$.

Confidence Interval for $p_1 - p_2$

Since the population proportions p_1 and p_2 are unknown, we estimate them by $\overline{p}_1$ and $\overline{p}_2$, respectively. The first sample proportion is computed as $\overline{p}_1 = x_1/n_1$ where x_1 denotes the number of successes in n_1 observations drawn from population 1. Similarly, $\overline{p}_2 = x_2/n_2$ is the sample proportion derived from population 2 where x_2 is the number of successes in n_2. The difference $\overline{p}_1 - \overline{p}_2$ is a point estimate of $p_1 - p_2$.

Recall from Chapter 7 that the standard errors for the estimators $\overline{P}_1$ and $\overline{P}_2$ are $se(\overline{P}_1) = \sqrt{\frac{p_1(1-p_1)}{n_1}}$ and $se(\overline{P}_2) = \sqrt{\frac{p_2(1-p_2)}{n_2}}$, respectively. Therefore, for two independently drawn samples, the standard error, $se(\overline{P}_1 - \overline{P}_2) = \sqrt{\frac{p_1(1-p_1)}{n_1} + \frac{p_2(1-p_2)}{n_2}}$. Since p_1 and p_2 are unknown, we estimate the standard error by $\sqrt{\frac{\overline{p}_1(1-\overline{p}_1)}{n_1} + \frac{\overline{p}_2(1-\overline{p}_2)}{n_2}}$. Finally, when both n_1 and n_2 are sufficiently large, the sampling distribution of $\overline{P}_1 - \overline{P}_2$ can be approximated by the normal distribution.

We construct a confidence interval for the difference between two population proportions using the following formula.

CONFIDENCE INTERVAL FOR $p_1 - p_2$

A $100(1 - \alpha)\%$ confidence interval for the difference between two population proportions $p_1 - p_2$ is given by:

$$(\bar{p}_1 - \bar{p}_2) \pm z_{\alpha/2}\sqrt{\frac{\bar{p}_1(1-\bar{p}_1)}{n_1} + \frac{\bar{p}_2(1-\bar{p}_2)}{n_2}}.$$

As noted, the above formula is valid only when the two samples are sufficiently large; the general guideline is that n_1p_1, $n_1(1 - p_1)$, n_2p_2, and $n_2(1 - p_2)$ must all be greater than or equal to 5, where p_1 and p_2 are evaluated at $\bar{p}_1$ and $\bar{p}_2$, respectively.

EXAMPLE 10.9

Despite his inexperience, Candidate A appears to have gained support among the electorate. Three months ago, in a survey of 120 registered voters, 55 said that they would vote for Candidate A. Today, 41 registered voters in a sample of 80 said that they would vote for Candidate A. Construct the 95% confidence interval for the difference between the two population proportions.

SOLUTION: Let p_1 and p_2 represent the population proportion of the electorate who support the candidate today and three months ago, respectively. In order to calculate the 95% confidence interval for $p_1 - p_2$, we use the formula $(\bar{p}_1 - \bar{p}_2) \pm z_{\alpha/2}\sqrt{\frac{\bar{p}_1(1-\bar{p}_1)}{n_1} + \frac{\bar{p}_2(1-\bar{p}_2)}{n_2}}$. We compute the sample proportions as

$$\bar{p}_1 = x_1/n_1 = 41/80 = 0.5125 \quad \text{and} \quad \bar{p}_2 = x_2/n_2 = 55/120 = 0.4583.$$

Note that the normality condition is satisfied because $n_1\bar{p}_1$, $n_1(1 - \bar{p}_1)$, $n_2\bar{p}_2$, and $n_2(1 - \bar{p}_2)$ all exceed 5. For the 95% confidence interval, we use the z table to find $z_{\alpha/2} = z_{0.05/2} = z_{0.025} = 1.96$. Substituting the values into the formula, we find

$$(0.5125 - 0.4583) \pm 1.96\sqrt{\frac{0.5125(1-0.5125)}{80} + \frac{0.4583(1-0.4583)}{120}}$$
$$= 0.0542 \pm 0.1412 \text{ or } [-0.0870, 0.1954].$$

With 95% confidence, we can report that the percentage change of support for the candidate is between −8.70% and 19.54%.

Hypothesis Test for $p_1 - p_2$

The null and alternative hypotheses for testing the difference between two population proportions under independent sampling will take one of the following forms:

Two-Tailed Test	Right-Tailed Test	Left-Tailed Test
$H_0: p_1 - p_2 = d_0$	$H_0: p_1 - p_2 \leq d_0$	$H_0: p_1 - p_2 \geq d_0$
$H_A: p_1 - p_2 \neq d_0$	$H_A: p_1 - p_2 > d_0$	$H_A: p_1 - p_2 < d_0$

We use the symbol d_0 to denote a given hypothesized difference between the unknown population proportions p_1 and p_2. In most cases, d_0 is set to zero. For example, when testing if the population proportions differ—that is, if $p_1 \neq p_2$—we use a two-tailed test, with the competing hypotheses defined as H_0: $p_1 - p_2 = 0$ versus H_A: $p_1 - p_2 \neq 0$. If, on the other hand, we wish to determine whether or not the proportions differ by some amount, say 0.20, we set $d_0 = 0.20$ and define the competing hypotheses as H_0: $p_1 - p_2 = 0.20$ versus H_A: $p_1 - p_2 \neq 0.20$. One-tailed tests are defined similarly.

EXAMPLE 10.10

Let's revisit Example 10.9. Specify the competing hypotheses in order to determine whether the proportion of those who favor Candidate A has changed over the three-month period. Using the 95% confidence interval, what is the conclusion to the test? Explain.

SOLUTION: In essence, we would like to determine whether $p_1 \neq p_2$, where p_1 and p_2 represent the population proportion of the electorate who support the candidate today and three months ago, respectively. We formulate the competing hypotheses as

$$H_0: p_1 - p_2 = 0$$

$$H_A: p_1 - p_2 \neq 0$$

In Example 10.9, we constructed the 95% confidence interval for the difference between the population proportions as [−0.0870, 0.1954]. We note that the interval contains zero, the value hypothesized under the null hypothesis. Therefore, we are unable to reject the null hypothesis. In other words, from the given sample data, we cannot conclude at the 5% significance level that the support for Candidate A has changed.

We now introduce the standard four-step procedure for conducting one- or two-tailed hypothesis tests concerning the difference between two proportions $p_1 - p_2$. We transform its estimate $\bar{p}_1 - \bar{p}_2$ into a corresponding z statistic by subtracting the hypothesized difference d_0 from this estimate and dividing by the standard error of the estimator $se(\bar{P}_1 - \bar{P}_2)$. When we developed the confidence interval for $p_1 - p_2$, we assumed $se(\bar{P}_1 - \bar{P}_2) = \sqrt{\frac{\bar{p}_1(1-\bar{p}_1)}{n_1} + \frac{\bar{p}_2(1-\bar{p}_2)}{n_2}}$. However, if d_0 is zero—that is, H_0: $p_1 = p_2$—both $\bar{p}_1$ and $\bar{p}_2$ are essentially the estimates of the same unknown population proportion. For this reason, the standard error can be improved upon by computing the pooled estimate $\bar{p} = (x_1 + x_2)/(n_1 + n_2)$ for the unknown population proportion, which is now based on a larger sample.

TEST STATISTIC FOR TESTING $p_1 - p_2$

The value of the test statistic for a hypothesis test concerning the difference between two proportions $p_1 - p_2$ is computed using one of the following two formulas:

1. If the hypothesized difference d_0 is zero, then the value of the test statistic is

$$z = \frac{\bar{p}_1 - \bar{p}_2}{\sqrt{\bar{p}(1-\bar{p})\left(\frac{1}{n_1} + \frac{1}{n_2}\right)}},$$

where $\bar{p}_1 = \frac{x_1}{n_1}$, $\bar{p}_2 = \frac{x_2}{n_2}$, and $\bar{p} = \frac{x_1 + x_2}{n_1 + n_2}$.

2. If the hypothesized difference d_0 is not zero, then the value of the test statistic is

$$z = \frac{(\bar{p}_1 - \bar{p}_2) - d_0}{\sqrt{\frac{\bar{p}_1(1-\bar{p}_1)}{n_1} + \frac{\bar{p}_2(1-\bar{p}_2)}{n_2}}}.$$

As in the case of the confidence interval, the above formulas are valid only when the two samples are sufficiently large.

EXAMPLE 10.11

An analyst claims that the proportion of men who regularly make online purchases is greater than the proportion of women. Of the 6,000 men that the analyst surveyed, 5,400 of them said they regularly make online purchases, compared with 8,600 of the 10,000 women surveyed. Test the analyst's claim at the 5% significance level.

SOLUTION: Let p_1 and p_2 denote the population proportions of men and of women who make online purchases, respectively. We wish to test whether the proportion of men who make online purchases is greater than the proportion of women; that is, $p_1 - p_2 > 0$. Therefore, we construct the competing hypotheses as

$$H_0: p_1 - p_2 \leq 0$$

$$H_A: p_1 - p_2 > 0$$

Since the hypothesized difference is zero, or $d_0 = 0$, we compute the value of the test statistic as $z = \frac{\bar{p}_1 - \bar{p}_2}{\sqrt{\bar{p}(1-\bar{p})\left(\frac{1}{n_1} + \frac{1}{n_2}\right)}}$. We first compute the sample proportions $\bar{p}_1 = x_1/n_1 = 5{,}400/6{,}000 = 0.90$ and $\bar{p}_2 = x_2/n_2 = 8{,}600/10{,}000 = 0.86$. The normality condition is satisfied since $n_1\bar{p}_1$, $n_1(1-\bar{p}_1)$, $n_2\bar{p}_2$, and $n_2(1-\bar{p}_2)$ all exceed 5. Next we calculate $\bar{p} = \frac{x_1 + x_2}{n_1 + n_2} = \frac{5{,}400 + 8{,}600}{6{,}000 + 10{,}000} = 0.875$. Thus,

$$z = \frac{(0.90 - 0.86)}{\sqrt{0.875(1 - 0.875)\left(\dfrac{1}{6{,}000} + \dfrac{1}{10{,}000}\right)}} = 7.4066.$$

The p-value, computed as $P(Z \geq 7.4066)$, is approximately zero. Since the p-value $< \alpha = 0.05$, we reject H_0. At the 5% significance level, the analyst's claim is supported by the sample data; that is, the proportion of men who regularly make online purchases is greater than the proportion of women. The results appear consistent with the decision by so many retailers to redesign their websites to attract male customers.

EXAMPLE 10.12

While we expect relatively expensive wines to have more desirable characteristics than relatively inexpensive wines, people are often confused in their assessment of the quality of wine in a blind test (npr.com, May 24, 2016). In a recent experiment at a local winery, the same wine is served to two groups of people but with different price information. In the first group, 60 people are told that they are tasting a \$25 wine, of which 48 like the wine. In the second group, only 20 of 50 people like the wine when they are told that it is a \$10 wine. The experiment is conducted to determine if the proportion of people who like the wine in the first group is more than 20 percentage points higher than in the second group. Conduct this test at the 5% significance level.

SOLUTION: Let p_1 and p_2 denote the proportions of people who like the wine in groups 1 and 2, respectively. We want to test if the proportion of people who like the wine in the first group is more than 20 percentage points higher than in the second group. Thus, we construct the competing hypotheses as

$$H_0: p_1 - p_2 \leq 0.20$$
$$H_A: p_1 - p_2 > 0.20$$

We first compute the sample proportions as $\bar{p}_1 = x_1/n_1 = 48/60 = 0.80$ and $\bar{p}_2 = x_2/n_2 = 20/50 = 0.40$ and note that the normality condition is satisfied since $n_1\bar{p}_1$, $n_1(1-\bar{p}_1)$, $n_2\bar{p}_2$, and $n_2(1-\bar{p}_2)$ all exceed 5.

Since $d_0 = 0.20$, the value of the test statistic is computed as

$$z = \frac{(\bar{p}_1 - \bar{p}_2) - d_0}{\sqrt{\dfrac{\bar{p}_1(1-\bar{p}_1)}{n_1} + \dfrac{\bar{p}_2(1-\bar{p}_2)}{n_2}}} = \frac{(0.80 - 0.40) - 0.20}{\sqrt{\dfrac{0.80(1-0.80)}{60} + \dfrac{0.40(1-0.40)}{50}}} = 2.3146.$$

For this right-tailed test, we compute the p-value as $P(Z \geq 2.3146) = 0.0103$. Recall that in order to find the p-value in Excel, we enter `=1-NORM.DIST(2.3146,0,1,TRUE)` and in R, we enter `pnorm(2.3146, 0, 1,lower.tail=FALSE)`. Since the p-value $< \alpha = 0.05$, we reject the null hypothesis. At the 5% significance level, we conclude that the proportion of people who like the wine in the first group is more than 20 percentage points higher than in the second group. Overall, this result is consistent with scientific research, which has demonstrated the power of suggestion in wine tasting.

EXERCISES 10.3

Mechanics

41. Given $\bar{p}_1 = 0.85$, $n_1 = 400$, $\bar{p}_2 = 0.90$, $n_2 = 350$, construct the 90% confidence interval for the difference between the population proportions. Is there a difference between the population proportions at the 10% significance level? Explain.

42. Given $x_1 = 50$, $n_1 = 200$, $x_2 = 70$, $n_2 = 250$, construct the 95% confidence interval for the difference between the population proportions. Is there a difference between the population proportions at the 5% significance level? Explain.

43. Consider the following competing hypotheses and accompanying sample data.

$$H_0: p_1 - p_2 \geq 0$$
$$H_A: p_1 - p_2 < 0$$
$$x_1 = 250 \qquad x_2 = 275$$
$$n_1 = 400 \qquad n_2 = 400$$

   a. Calculate the value of the test statistic.
   b. Find the p-value.
   c. At the 5% significance level, what is the conclusion to the test? Is p_1 less than p_2?

44. Consider the following competing hypotheses and accompanying sample data.

$$H_0: p_1 - p_2 = 0$$
$$H_A: p_1 - p_2 \neq 0$$
$$x_1 = 100 \qquad x_2 = 172$$
$$n_1 = 250 \qquad n_2 = 400$$

   a. Calculate the value of the test statistic.
   b. Find the p-value.
   c. At the 5% significance level, what is the conclusion to the test? Do the population proportions differ?

45. Consider the following competing hypotheses and accompanying sample data.

$$H_0: p_1 - p_2 = 0$$
$$H_A: p_1 - p_2 \neq 0$$
$$x_1 = 300 \qquad x_2 = 325$$
$$n_1 = 600 \qquad n_2 = 500$$

   a. Calculate the value of the test statistic.
   b. Find the p-value.
   c. At the 5% significance level, what is the conclusion to the test? Do the population proportions differ?

46. Consider the following competing hypotheses and accompanying sample data.

$$H_0: p_1 - p_2 = 0.20$$
$$H_A: p_1 - p_2 \neq 0.20$$
$$x_1 = 150 \qquad x_2 = 130$$
$$n_1 = 250 \qquad n_2 = 400$$

   a. Calculate the value of the test statistic.
   b. Find the p-value.
   c. At the 5% significance level, what is the conclusion to the test? Can you conclude that the difference between the population proportions differs from 0.20?

Applications

47. A study claims that girls and boys do not do equally well on math tests taken from the 2nd to 11th grades. Suppose in a representative sample, 344 of 430 girls and 369 of 450 boys score at proficient or advanced levels on a standardized math test.
    a. Construct the 95% confidence interval for the difference between the population proportions of girls and boys who score at proficient or advanced levels.
    b. Develop the appropriate null and alternative hypotheses to test whether the proportion of girls who score at proficient or advanced levels differs from the proportion of boys.
    c. At the 5% significance level, what is the conclusion to the test? Do the results support the study's claim?
48. Reducing scrap of 4-foot planks of hardwood is an important factor in reducing cost at a wood-flooring manufacturing company. Accordingly, engineers at Lumberworks are investigating a potential new cutting method involving lateral sawing that may reduce the scrap rate. To examine its viability, samples of planks were examined under the old and new methods. Sixty-two of the 500 planks were scrapped under the old method, whereas 36 of the 400 planks were scrapped under the new method.
    a. Construct the 95% confidence interval for the difference between the population scrap rates between the old and new methods.
    b. Specify the null and alternative hypotheses to test for differences in the population scrap rates between the old and new cutting methods.
    c. Using the results from part (a), can we conclude at the 5% significance level that the scrap rate of the new method is different than the old method?
49. A recent report finds that 14.6% of newly married couples had a spouse of a different race or ethnicity. In a similar survey in 1980, only 6.8% of newlywed couples reported marrying outside their race or ethnicity. Suppose both of these surveys were conducted on 500 newly married couples.
    a. Specify the competing hypotheses to test the claim that there is an increase in the proportion of people who marry outside their race or ethnicity.
    b. Calculate the value of the test statistic and the p-value.
    c. At the 5% level of significance, what is the conclusion to the test?
50. A study suggests that boys are more likely than girls to grow out of childhood asthma when they hit their teenage years. The study followed 500 boys and 500 girls between the ages of 5 and 12, all of whom had mild to moderate asthma. By the age of 18, 27% of the boys and 14% of the girls had grown out of asthma.
    a. Develop the hypotheses to test whether the proportion of boys who grow out of asthma in their teenage years is more than that of girls.
    b. Test the assertion in part (a) at the 5% significance level.
    c. Suppose a medical researcher has asserted that the proportion of boys who grow out of asthma in their teenage years is more than 0.10 than that of girls. Test this assertion at the 5% significance level.
51. From an employment perspective, jobseekers are no longer calling up friends for help with job placement, as they can now get help online. In a recent survey of 150 jobseekers, 67 said they used LinkedIn to search for jobs. A similar survey of 140 jobseekers, conducted three years ago, had found that 58 jobseekers had used LinkedIn for their job search. Is there sufficient evidence to suggest that more people are now using LinkedIn to search for jobs as compared to three years ago? Use a 5% level of significance for the analysis.
52. The director of housekeeping at *Elegante,* a luxury resort hotel with two locations (*Seaside* and *Oceanfront*), wants to evaluate housekeeping performance at those two locations. Random samples of 100 rooms were inspected at each location for defects (e.g., missing towels, missing soap, dirty floors or showers, dusty tables) after being cleaned. It was found that 21 of the rooms at *Seaside* had some housekeeping defects, and 28 rooms at *Oceanfront* had some housekeeping defects.
    a. Develop the hypotheses to test whether the proportion of housekeeping defects differs between the two hotel locations.
    b. Calculate the value of the test statistic and the p-value.
    c. Do the results suggest that the proportion of housekeeping defects differs between the two hotel locations at the 5% significance level?
    d. Construct the 95% confidence interval for the difference between the population housekeeping defect rates at the two hotel locations. How can this confidence interval be used to reach the same conclusion as in part (c)?
53. In an effort to make children's toys safer and more tamper-proof, toy packaging has become cumbersome for parents to remove in many cases. Accordingly, the director of marketing at Toys4Tots, a large toy manufacturer, wants to evaluate the effectiveness of a new packaging design that engineers claim will reduce customer complaints by more than 10 percentage points. Customer satisfaction surveys were sent to 250 parents who registered toys packaged under the old design and 250 parents who registered toys packaged under the new design. Of these, 85 parents expressed dissatisfaction with packaging of the old design, and 40 parents expressed dissatisfaction with packaging of the new design.
    a. Specify the null and alternative hypotheses to test whether customer complaints have been reduced by more than 10 percentage points under the new packaging design.
    b. Calculate the value of the test statistic and the p-value.
    c. At the 5% significance level, do the results support the engineers' claim?
    d. At the 1% significance level, do the results support the engineers' claim?

54. According to a report, 32.2% of American adults are obese. Among ethnic groups in general, African American women are more overweight than Caucasian women, but African American men are less obese than Caucasian men. Sarah Weber, a recent college graduate, is curious to determine if the same pattern also exists in her hometown on the West Coast. She randomly selects 220 African American adults and 300 Caucasian adults for the analysis. The following table contains the sample information.

Race	Sex	Obese	Not Obese
African Americans	Males	36	94
	Females	35	55
Caucasians	Males	62	118
	Females	31	89

a. Test if the proportion of obese African American men is less than the proportion of obese Caucasian men at $\alpha = 0.05$.

b. Test if the proportion of obese African American women is more than the proportion of obese Caucasian women at $\alpha = 0.05$.

c. Test if the proportion of obese African American adults differs from the proportion of obese Caucasian adults at the 5% significance level.

55. A report finds that only 26% of psychology majors are satisfied with their career paths as compared to 50% of accounting majors. Suppose these results were obtained from a survey of 300 psychology majors and 350 accounting majors.

a. Develop the null and alternative hypotheses to test whether the proportion of accounting majors satisfied with their career paths is higher than that of psychology majors by more than 20 percentage points.

b. Calculate the value of the test statistic and the p-value.

c. At the 5% significance level, what is the conclusion?

56. Due to late delivery problems with an existing supplier, the director of procurement at ElectroTech began to place orders for electrical switches with a new supplier as part of a "dual-source" (two-supplier) strategy. Now she wants to revert to a "single-source" (i.e., one supplier) strategy to simplify purchasing activities. She wishes to conduct a test to infer whether the new supplier will continue to outperform the old supplier. Based on recent sample data, she found that 27 of 150 orders placed with the old supplier arrived late, whereas 6 of 75 orders placed with the new supplier arrived late.

a. Specify the null and alternative hypotheses to test for whether the proportion of late deliveries with the new supplier is less than that of the old supplier.

b. Calculate the value of the test statistic and the p-value.

c. At the 5% significance level, what is the conclusion?

57. A report suggests that business majors spend the least amount of time on course work than all other college students. A provost of a university decides to conduct a survey where students are asked if they study hard, defined as spending at least 20 hours per week on course work. Of 120 business majors included in the survey, 20 said that they studied hard, as compared to 48 out of 150 nonbusiness majors who said that they studied hard. At the 5% significance level, can we conclude that the proportion of business majors who study hard is less than that of nonmajors? Provide the details.

58. Many believe that it is not feasible for men and women to be just friends, while others argue that this belief may not be true anymore since gone are the days when men worked and women stayed at home and the only way they could get together was for romance. In a recent survey, 200 heterosexual college students were asked if it was feasible for male and female students to be just friends. Thirty-two percent of females and 57% of males reported that it was not feasible for men and women to be just friends. Suppose the study consisted of 100 female and 100 male students. At the 5% significance level, can we conclude that there is a greater than 10 percentage point difference between the proportion of male and female students with this view? Provide the details.

JGI/Blend Images LLC

10.4 | WRITING WITH DATA

Case Study

Online dating has made it as likely for would-be couples to meet via e-mail or other virtual matchmaking services as through friends and family. One study found that women put greater emphasis on the race and financial stability of a partner, while men mostly look for physical attractiveness. It is reported that 13% of women and 8% of men want their partner to be of the same ethnic background. Moreover, 36% of women and 13% of men would like to meet someone who makes as much money as they do.

Anka Wilder, working for a small matchmaking service in Cincinnati, Ohio, wants to know if a similar pattern also exists with her customers. She has access to the preferences of 160 women and 120 men customers. In this sample, she finds that 28 women and 12 men customers want their partner to be of the same ethnicity. Also, 50 women and 10 men want their partner to make as much money as they do.

Anka wants to use this sample information to determine whether the proportion of women who want their partner to be of the same ethnic background is greater than that of men. In addition she wants to determine whether the proportion of women who want their partner to make as much money as they do is more than 20 percentage points greater than that of men.

STOCK4B-RF/Getty Images

Sample Report—Online Dating Preferences

With the advent of the Internet, there has been a surge in online dating services that connect individuals with similar interests, religions, and cultural backgrounds for personal relationships. In 1992, when the Internet was still in its infancy, less than 1% of Americans met their partners through online dating services. Today, about 39% of heterosexual couples reported meeting online (stanford.edu, August 21, 2019). A recent survey suggested that a higher proportion of women than men would like to meet someone with a similar ethnic background. Also, the difference between the proportion of women and men who would like to meet someone who makes as much money as they do is greater than 20%.

A couple of hypothesis tests were performed to determine if similar gender differences existed for online dating customers in Cincinnati, Ohio. The sample consisted of responses from 160 women and 120 men. The summary of the test results is presented in Table 10.8.

TABLE 10.8 Test Statistics and *p*-values for Hypothesis Tests

Hypotheses	Test Statistic	*p*-value
$H_0: p_1 - p_2 \leq 0$ $H_A: p_1 - p_2 > 0$	$z = \dfrac{0.175 - 0.10}{\sqrt{0.1429(1 - 0.1429)\left(\frac{1}{160} + \frac{1}{120}\right)}} = 1.7748$	0.038
$H_0: p_1 - p_2 \leq 0.20$ $H_A: p_1 - p_2 > 0.20$	$z = \dfrac{0.3125 - 0.0833 - 0.20}{\sqrt{\frac{0.3125(1 - 0.3125)}{160} + \frac{0.0833(1 - 0.0833)}{120}}} = 0.6556$	0.256

First, it was tested if the proportion of women, denoted p_1, who want their partner to be of the same ethnicity is greater than that of men, denoted p_2. It was found that 28 out of 160 women valued this trait, yielding a sample proportion of $\bar{p}_1 = 28/160 = 0.175$; a similar proportion for men was calculated as $\bar{p}_2 = 12/120 = 0.10$. The first row of Table 10.8 shows the competing hypotheses, the value of the test statistic, and the *p*-value for this test. At the 5% significance level, the proportion of women who want the same ethnicity was greater than that of men. In the second test, p_1 and p_2 denoted the proportion of women and men, respectively, who would like their partner to make as much money as they do; here $\bar{p}_1 = 50/160 = 0.3125$ and $\bar{p}_2 = 10/120 = 0.0833$. The second row of Table 10.8 shows the competing hypotheses, the value of the test statistic, and the *p*-value for this test. At the 5% significance level, the proportion of women who want their partner to make as much income as they do is not more than 20 percentage points greater than that of men. Online dating is a relatively new market and any such information is important for individuals looking for relationships as well as for service providers.

Suggested Case Studies

Report 10.1 Repeat the analysis performed in this section, but collect your own survey data on dating preferences or any other issue of your choice.

Report 10.2 Recent data report that the average salary is $61,261 in Denver and $63,381 in Chicago. Suppose these data were based on 100 employees in each city where the population standard deviation is $16,000 in Denver and $14,500 in Chicago. The same report states that 20% of the population are in their twenties in Denver; the corresponding percentage in Chicago is 22%. In a report, use the sample information to determine whether the average starting salary in Chicago is greater than Denver's average starting salary. Also, determine whether the proportion of the population in their twenties differs in these two cities. Use a reasonable level of significance for the tests.

Report 10.3 Go to https://finance.yahoo.com/ to extract two years of monthly adjusted close price data for two of Fidelity's mutual funds For each fund, calculate monthly returns as the percentage change in adjusted close prices from the previous month, giving 23 months of return data. Use summary measures to compare the risk and reward for each fund. At the 5% significance level, determine whether the mean returns differ. (*Hint:* This is a matched-pairs sample.) Discuss any assumptions that you made for the analysis.

CONCEPTUAL REVIEW

LO 10.1 Make inferences about the difference between two population means based on independent sampling.

Independent samples are samples that are completely unrelated to one another. A $100(1 - \alpha)\%$ confidence interval for the difference between two population means $\mu_1 - \mu_2$, based on independent samples, is

- $(\bar{x}_1 - \bar{x}_2) \pm z_{\alpha/2}\sqrt{\frac{\sigma_1^2}{n_1} + \frac{\sigma_2^2}{n_2}}$, if σ_1^2 and σ_2^2 are known.
- $(\bar{x}_1 - \bar{x}_2) \pm t_{\alpha/2,df}\sqrt{s_p^2\left(\frac{1}{n_1} + \frac{1}{n_2}\right)}$, if σ_1^2 and σ_2^2 are unknown but assumed equal. The pooled sample variance is $s_p^2 = \frac{(n_1 - 1)s_1^2 + (n_2 - 1)s_2^2}{n_1 + n_2 - 2}$ and $df = n_1 + n_2 - 2$.
- $(\bar{x}_1 - \bar{x}_2) \pm t_{\alpha/2,df}\sqrt{\frac{s_1^2}{n_1} + \frac{s_2^2}{n_2}}$, if σ_1^2 and σ_2^2 are unknown and cannot be assumed equal. The degrees of freedom are calculated as $df = \frac{(s_1^2/n_1 + s_2^2/n_2)^2}{(s_1^2/n_1)^2/(n_1 - 1) + (s_2^2/n_2)^2/(n_2 - 1)}$.

When conducting hypothesis tests about the difference between two means $\mu_1 - \mu_2$, based on independent samples, the value of the test statistic is

- $z = \dfrac{(\bar{x}_1 - \bar{x}_2) - d_0}{\sqrt{\frac{\sigma_1^2}{n_1} + \frac{\sigma_2^2}{n_2}}}$, if σ_1^2 and σ_2^2 are known.
- $t_{df} = \dfrac{(\bar{x}_1 - \bar{x}_2) - d_0}{\sqrt{s_p^2\left(\frac{1}{n_1} + \frac{1}{n_2}\right)}}$, if σ_1^2 and σ_2^2 are unknown but assumed equal.
- $t_{df} = \dfrac{(\bar{x}_1 - \bar{x}_2) - d_0}{\sqrt{\frac{s_1^2}{n_1} + \frac{s_2^2}{n_2}}}$, if σ_1^2 and σ_2^2 are unknown and cannot be assumed equal.

Here, d_0 is the hypothesized difference between μ_1 and μ_2 and the degrees of freedom for the last two test statistics are the same as the ones defined for the corresponding confidence intervals. The formulas for estimation and testing are valid only if $\bar{X}_1 - \bar{X}_2$ (approximately) follows a normal distribution.

LO 10.2 **Make inferences about the mean difference based on matched-pairs sampling.**

A common case of dependent sampling, commonly referred to as matched-pairs sampling, is when the samples are paired or matched in some way.

For matched-pairs sampling, the population parameter of interest is referred to as the mean difference μ_D where $D = X_1 - X_2$, and the random variables X_1 and X_2 are matched in a pair. A $100(1 - \alpha)\%$ confidence interval for the mean difference μ_D, based on a matched-pairs sample, is given by $\bar{d} \pm t_{\alpha/2,df} s_D/\sqrt{n}$, where $\bar{d}$ and s_D are the mean and the standard deviation, respectively, of the n sample differences, and $df = n - 1$. When conducting a hypothesis test about μ_D the value of the test statistic is calculated as $t_{df} = \frac{\bar{d} - d_0}{s_D/\sqrt{n}}$, where d_0 is the hypothesized mean difference and $df = n - 1$.

LO 10.3 **Make inferences about the difference between two population proportions based on independent sampling.**

A $100(1 - \alpha)\%$ confidence interval for the difference between two population proportions $p_1 - p_2$ is given by $(\bar{p}_1 - \bar{p}_2) \pm z_{\alpha/2}\sqrt{\frac{\bar{p}_1(1-\bar{p}_1)}{n_1} + \frac{\bar{p}_2(1-\bar{p}_2)}{n_2}}$. When conducting hypothesis tests about the difference between two proportions $p_1 - p_2$, the value of the test statistic is calculated as

- $z = \dfrac{\bar{p}_1 - \bar{p}_2}{\sqrt{\bar{p}(1-\bar{p})\left(\frac{1}{n_1} + \frac{1}{n_2}\right)}}$, if the hypothesized difference d_0 between p_1 and p_2 is zero. The pooled sample proportion is $\bar{p} = \frac{x_1 + x_2}{n_1 + n_2}$.
- $z = \dfrac{(\bar{p}_1 - \bar{p}_2) - d_0}{\sqrt{\frac{\bar{p}_1(1-\bar{p}_1)}{n_1} + \frac{\bar{p}_2(1-\bar{p}_2)}{n_2}}}$, if the hypothesized difference d_0 between p_1 and p_2 is not zero.

ADDITIONAL EXERCISES

59. A study has found that, on average, 6- to 12-year-old children are spending less time on household chores today compared to 1981 levels. Suppose two samples representative of the study's results report the following summary statistics for the two periods:

1981	Today
$\bar{x}_1 = 30$ minutes	$\bar{x}_2 = 24$ minutes
$s_1 = 4.2$ minutes	$s_1 = 3.9$ minutes
$n_1 = 30$	$n_2 = 30$

a. Specify the competing hypotheses to test the study's claim that children today spend less time on household chores as compared to children in 1981.
b. Calculate the value of the test statistic assuming that the unknown population variances are equal.
c. Find the p-value.
d. At the 5% significance level, do the data support the study's claim? Explain.

60. Do men really spend more money on St. Patrick's Day as compared to women? A survey found that men spend an average of $43.87 while women spend an average of $29.54. Assume that these data were based on a sample of 100 men and 100 women and the population standard deviations of spending for men and women are $32 and $25, respectively.

a. Specify the competing hypotheses to determine whether men spend more money on St. Patrick's Day as compared to women.
b. Calculate the value of the test statistic.
c. Find the p-value.
d. At the 1% significance level, do men spend more money on St. Patrick's Day as compared to women? Explain.

61. **FILE** ***Mutual_Funds.*** The accompanying table shows a portion of the annual returns (in %) for Mutual Fund A and Mutual Fund B over the past nine years.

Year	Fund_A	Fund_B
1	−3.02	−20.30
2	−9.52	−17.95
⋮	⋮	⋮
9	20.05	31.91

a. Set up the hypotheses to test whether the mean returns of the two funds differ. (*Hint:* This is a matched-pairs comparison.)
b. Calculate the value of the test statistic and the p-value. Assume that the return difference is normally distributed.
c. At the 5% significance level, what is the conclusion?

62. **FILE** ***Cholesterol.*** Cholesterol levels vary by age, weight, and sex. A recent college graduate working at a local blood lab has access to the cholesterol data of 50 men and 50 women in the 20–40 age group. The accompanying table shows a portion of the data.

Men	Women
181	178
199	193
⋮	⋮
190	182

At the 1% significance level, determine if there are any differences in the mean cholesterol levels for men and women in the age group. It is fair to assume that the population variances for men and women are equal.

63. **FILE** ***Fertilizer.*** A farmer is concerned that a change in fertilizer to an organic variant might change his crop yield. He subdivides six lots and uses the old fertilizer on one half of each lot and the new fertilizer on the other half. The accompanying table shows a portion of the data.

Lot	Old	New
1	10	12
2	11	10
⋮	⋮	⋮
6	11	12

a. Specify the competing hypotheses that determine whether there is any difference between the average crop yields from the use of the different fertilizers.
b. Assuming that differences in crop yields are normally distributed, calculate the value of the test statistic.
c. Find the p-value.
d. Is there sufficient evidence to conclude that the crop yields are different? Should the farmer be concerned?

64. **FILE** ***Pregnancy.*** It is important for women to gain the right amount of weight during pregnancy by eating a healthy, balanced diet. It is recommended that a woman of average weight before pregnancy should gain 25 to 35 pounds during pregnancy (cdc.com, January 17, 2019). The accompanying table shows a portion of the weight data for 40 women before and after pregnancy.

Woman	Before	After
1	114	168
2	107	161
⋮	⋮	⋮
40	136	157

a. At the 5% level of significance, determine if the mean weight gain of women due to pregnancy is more than 30 pounds.
b. At the 5% level of significance, determine if the mean weight gain of women due to pregnancy is more than 35 pounds.

65. A study finds that 14% of females suffer from asthma as opposed to 6% of males. Suppose 250 females and 200 males responded to the study.
a. Develop the appropriate null and alternative hypotheses to test whether the proportion of females suffering from asthma is greater than the proportion of males.
b. Calculate the value of the test statistic and the p-value.
c. At the 5% significance level, what is the conclusion? Do the data suggest that females suffer more from asthma than males?

66. **FILE** ***Health_Info.*** A financial analyst is studying the annual returns (in %) for firms in the health and information technology (IT) industries. He randomly samples 20 firms in each industry. A portion of the data is shown in the accompanying table. At the 5% significance level, determine whether the average returns in each industry differ. Assume that the population variances are not equal.

Health	IT
10.29	4.77
32.17	1.14
⋮	⋮
13.21	22.61

67. Depression engulfs millions of Americans every day. A study finds that 10.9% of adults aged 18–24 identified with some level of depression versus 6.8% of adults aged 65 or older. Suppose 1,000 young adults (18–24 years old) and 1,000 older adults (65 years old and older) responded to the study.
    a. Develop the appropriate null and alternative hypotheses to test whether the proportion of young adults suffering from depression is greater than the proportion of older adults suffering from depression.
    b. Calculate the value of the test statistic and the p-value.
    c. At the 5% significance level, do the sample data suggest that young adults suffer more from depression than older adults?

68. A transportation analyst is interested in comparing the performance at two major international airports, namely Kennedy International (JFK) in New York and O'Hare International in Chicago. She finds that 70% of the flights were on time at JFK compared with 63% at O'Hare. Suppose these proportions were based on 200 flights at each of these two airports. The analyst believes that the proportion of on-time flights at JFK is more than five percentage points higher than that of O'Hare.
    a. Develop the competing hypotheses to test the transportation analyst's belief.
    b. Calculate the value of the test statistic and the p-value.
    c. At the 5% significance level, do the data support the transportation analyst's belief? Explain.

69. **FILE** ***Safety_Program.*** An engineer wants to determine the effectiveness of a safety program. He collects annual loss of hours due to accidents in 12 plants before and after the program was put into operation. The accompanying table shows a portion of the data.

Plant	Before	After
1	100	98
2	90	88
⋮	⋮	⋮
12	104	98

    a. Specify the competing hypotheses that determine whether the safety program was effective.
    b. Calculate the value of the test statistic and the p-value. Assume that the hours difference is normally distributed.
    c. At the 5% significance level, is there sufficient evidence to conclude that the safety program was effective? Explain.

APPENDIX 10.1 Guidelines for Other Software Packages

The following section provides brief commands for Minitab, SPSS, and JMP. Import the specified data file into the relevant software spreadsheet prior to following the commands.

Minitab

Testing $\mu_1 - \mu_2$

Gold_Oil

(Replicating Example 10.4) From the menu, choose **Stat > Basic Statistics > 2-Sample t.** Choose **Each sample is in its own column,** and after **Sample 1,** select Gold and after **Sample 2,** select Oil. Choose **Options.** After **Alternative hypothesis,** select "Difference ≠ hypothesized difference."

Testing μ_D

Food_Calories

(Replicating Example 10.8) From the menu, choose **Stat > Basic Statistics > Paired t. Each sample is in its own column,** and after **Sample 1,** select Before and after **Sample 2,** select After. Choose **Options.** After **Alternative hypothesis,** select "Difference > hypothesized difference."

Testing $p_1 - p_2$

(Replicating Example 10.11) From the menu, choose **Stat > Basic Statistics > 2 Proportions.** Choose **Summarized data.** Under **Sample 1,** enter 5,400 for **Number of**

events and 6,000 for **Number of trials.** Under **Sample 2,** enter 8,600 for **Number of events** and 10,000 for **Number of trials.** Choose **Options.** After **Alternative hypothesis,** select "Difference > hypothesized difference." After **Test method,** select "Use the pooled estimate for the proportion."

SPSS

Testing $\mu_1 - \mu_2$

A. (Replicating Example 10.4) Reconfigure data so that all observations are in one column, labeled Returns, and the associated industry is in the adjacent column, labeled Industry. From the menu, choose, **Data > Restructure > Restructure selected variables into cases**, and then follow the prompts.

B. From the menu, choose **Analyze > Compare Means > Independent-Samples T-Test.** Select Returns as **Test Variable(s)** and Industry as **Grouping Variable.** Select **Define Groups,** and enter 1 for **Group 1** and 2 for **Group 2.**

Testing μ_D

(Replicating Example 10.8) From the menu, choose **Analyze > Compare Means > Paired-Samples T-Test.** Select Before as **Variable1** and After as **Variable2.**

JMP

Testing $\mu_1 - \mu_2$

FILE *Gold_Oil*

A. (Replicating Example 10.4) From the menu, choose **Table > Stack** and stack the Gold and Oil variables.

B. From the menu, choose **Analyze > Fit Y by X.** Drag Data to the **Y, Response** box and drag Label to the **X, Factor** box.

C. Click on the red triangle next to the header that reads **Oneway Analysis of Data by Label** and select **t-test** (to use a pooled variance, select **Means/Anova/Pooled t**).

Testing μ_D

FILE *Food_Calories*

(Replicating Example 10.8) From the menu, choose **Analyze > Specialized Modeling > Matched Pairs.** Drag Before and After to the **Y, Paired Response** box.

11 Statistical Inference Concerning Variance

LEARNING OBJECTIVES

After reading this chapter you should be able to:

LO **11.1** **Discuss features of the χ^2 distribution.**

LO **11.2** **Make inferences about the population variance.**

LO **11.3** **Discuss features of the *F* distribution.**

LO **11.4** **Make inferences about the ratio of two population variances.**

So far, when conducting statistical inference concerning numerical variables, we have restricted our attention to the population mean. The mean is the primary measure of central location, but in many instances we are also interested in making inferences about measures of variability or dispersion. For instance, quality-control studies use the variance (or the standard deviation) to measure the variability of the weight, size, or volume of a product. Also, within the investment industry, the standard deviation tends to be the most common measure of risk. In this chapter, we study statistical inference with respect to the population variance as well as the ratio of two population variances.

In order to construct confidence intervals or conduct hypothesis tests regarding the population variance, we use a new distribution called the χ^2 (chi-square) distribution. We then turn our attention to analyzing the ratio of two population variances. In order to construct confidence intervals or conduct hypothesis tests concerning this ratio, we use another new distribution called the *F* distribution.

Hero Images/Getty Images

INTRODUCTORY CASE

Assessing the Risk of Mutual Fund Returns

In Chapter 3, investment counselor Dorothy Brennan examined annual return data for two mutual funds: Vanguard's Growth Index mutual fund (henceforth, Growth) and Vanguard's Value Index mutual fund (henceforth, Value). Table 11.1 shows relevant descriptive statistics for the two funds for the years 1984–2019. Dorothy measures the reward of investing by its average return and the risk of investing by its standard deviation. A client of Dorothy's has specific questions related to the risk of investing, measured by the standard deviation of returns. He would like to invest a portion of his money in the Growth fund so long as the risk does not exceed 20%. He also wonders if the risk of investing in the Value fund differs from 15%. Finally, he would like to know if the risk from investing in the Growth fund is greater than the risk from investing in the Value fund.

TABLE 11.1 Summary Statistics (in percent) for the Growth and the Value funds, $n = 36$

	Growth	Value
Mean	15.755	12.005
Standard Deviation	23.7993	17.9792

Growth_Value

Dorothy will use the above sample information to

1. Determine whether the standard deviation of the Growth fund exceeds 20%.
2. Determine whether the standard deviation of the Value fund differs from 15%.
3. Determine whether the risk from investing in the Growth fund is greater than the risk from investing in the Value fund.

A synopsis of this case is provided at the end of Section 11.2.

11.1 INFERENCE CONCERNING THE POPULATION VARIANCE

The population variance (or the population standard deviation) is used in quality-control studies to measure the variability of the weight, size, or volume of a product. Consider, for example, a bottler who wishes its production line to fill a certain amount of beverage in each bottle. It is important not only to get the desired average amount filled in the bottles, but also to keep the variability of the amount filled below some tolerance limit. Similarly, an investor may want to evaluate the risk of a particular investment, where the standard deviation typically corresponds to risk. Other examples for the relevance of making inference regarding the population variance include evaluating the variability of customer spending on an online purchase, the speeds on a highway, and the repair costs of a certain automobile.

Recall that we use the sample mean $\overline{X}$ as the estimator of the population mean μ. Similarly, we use the sample variance S^2 as an estimator of the population variance σ^2. Using a random sample of n observations drawn from the population, we compute $s^2 = \frac{\Sigma(x_i - \bar{x})^2}{n-1}$ as an estimate of σ^2. In order to examine the techniques for statistical inferences regarding σ^2, we first need to analyze the sampling distribution of S^2.

LO 11.1

Discuss features of the χ^2 distribution.

Sampling Distribution of S^2

Statistical inferences regarding σ^2 are based on the χ^2 or **chi-square distribution.** Like the t distribution, the χ^2 distribution is characterized by a family of distributions, where each distribution depends on its particular degrees of freedom df. It is common, therefore, to refer to it as the χ^2_{df} distribution.

In general, the χ^2_{df} distribution is the probability distribution of the sum of several independent, squared standard normal random variables. Here df is defined as the number of squared standard normal random variables included in the summation. Recall that the estimator S^2 of the population variance is based on the squared differences between the sample values and the sample mean. If S^2 is computed from a random sample of n observations drawn from an underlying normal population, then we can define the χ^2_{df} variable as $\frac{(n-1)S^2}{\sigma^2}$.

THE SAMPLING DISTRIBUTION OF $\frac{(n-1)S^2}{\sigma^2}$

If a sample of size n is taken from a normal population with a finite variance, then the statistic $\chi^2_{df} = \frac{(n-1)S^2}{\sigma^2}$ follows the χ^2_{df} distribution with $df = n - 1$.

In earlier chapters, we denoted the random variables by uppercase letters and particular values of the random variables by the corresponding lowercase letters. For instance, the statistics Z and T_{df} are random variables, and their values are given by z and t_{df}, respectively. It is cumbersome to continue with the distinction between the random variable and its value in this chapter. Here, we use the notation χ^2_{df} to represent a random variable as well as its value. Similarly, for the $F_{(df_1,df_2)}$ distribution introduced in Section 11.2, we will use $F_{(df_1,df_2)}$ to represent both a random variable and its value.

From Figure 11.1, we note that the χ^2_{df} distributions are positively skewed, where the extent of skewness depends on the degrees of freedom. As the df grow larger, the χ^2_{df} distribution tends to the normal distribution. For instance, as shown in Figure 11.1, the χ^2_{20} distribution resembles the shape of the normal distribution.

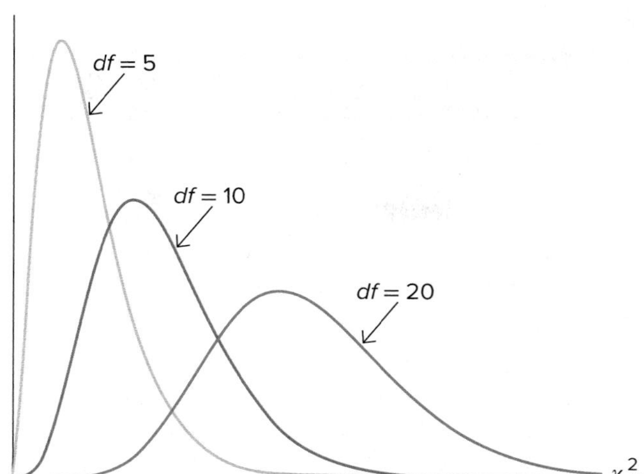

FIGURE 11.1 The χ^2_{df} distribution with various degrees of freedom

> **SUMMARY OF THE χ^2_{df} DISTRIBUTION**
>
> - The χ^2_{df} distribution is characterized by a family of distributions, where each distribution depends on its particular degrees of freedom *df*.
> - The values of the χ^2_{df} distribution range from zero to infinity.
> - The χ^2_{df} distribution is positively skewed, and the extent of skewness depends on the *df*. As the *df* grow larger, the χ^2_{df} distribution approaches the normal distribution.

Finding χ^2_{df} Values and Probabilities

For a χ^2_{df} distributed random variable, we use the notation $\chi^2_{\alpha,df}$ to represent a value such that the area in the upper (right) tail of the distribution is α. In other words, $P(\chi^2_{df} \geq \chi^2_{\alpha,df}) = \alpha$. Figure 11.2 illustrates the notation $\chi^2_{\alpha,df}$, which we use to locate χ^2_{df} values and probabilities from the χ^2 table.

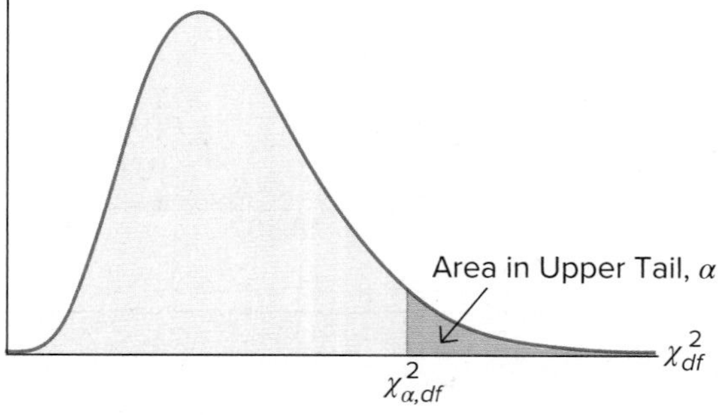

FIGURE 11.2 Graphical depiction of $P(\chi^2_{df} \geq \chi^2_{\alpha,df}) = \alpha$

A portion of the upper tail areas and the corresponding values for the χ^2_{df} distributions are given in Table 11.2. Table 3 of Appendix B provides a more complete table.

Suppose we want to find the value of $\chi^2_{\alpha,df}$ with $\alpha = 0.05$ and $df = 10$; that is, $\chi^2_{0.05,10}$. Using Table 11.2, we look at the first column labeled *df* and find the value 10. We then continue along this row until we reach the column 0.050. Here we see the value $\chi^2_{0.05,10} = 18.307$ such that $P(\chi^2_{10} \geq 18.307) = 0.05$.

We can use Excel's **CHISQ.INV** function to find a particular $\chi^2_{\alpha,df}$ value. We enter =CHISQ. INV(*cumulprob, df*), where *cumulprob* is the cumulative probability associated with the value $\chi^2_{\alpha,df}$, and *df* are the degrees of freedom. In order to find $\chi^2_{0.05,10}$, we enter `=CHISQ.INV(0.95, 10)`, and Excel returns 18.307. We can also use R's **qchisq** function to find a particular $\chi^2_{\alpha,df}$ value. We enter qchisq(*cumulprob, df, lower.tail=TRUE*), where *cumulprob* is the cumulative probability associated with the $\chi^2_{\alpha,df}$ value, and *df* are the degrees of freedom. In order to find $\chi^2_{0.05,10}$, we enter: `qchisq(0.95, 10, lower.tail=TRUE)` and R returns: 18.307; alternatively, we can enter: `qchisq(0.05, 10, lower.tail=FALSE)`.

TABLE 11.2 Portion of the χ^2 table

	Area in Upper Tail, α									
df	0.995	0.990	0.975	0.950	0.900	0.100	0.050	0.025	0.010	0.005
1	0.000	0.000	0.001	0.004	0.016	2.706	3.841	5.024	6.635	7.879
⋮	⋮	⋮	⋮	⋮	⋮	⋮	⋮	⋮	⋮	⋮
10	2.156	2.558	3.247	**3.940**	4.865	15.987	**18.307**	20.483	23.209	25.188
⋮	⋮	⋮	⋮	⋮	⋮	⋮	⋮	⋮	⋮	⋮
100	67.328	70.065	74.222	77.929	82.358	118.342	124.342	129.561	135.807	140.170

Sometimes we need to derive values in the lower (left) tail of the distribution. Unlike z and t_{df} distributions that are symmetric around a zero mean, the value on the lower tail of the χ^2_{df} distribution does not equal the negative of the value on the upper tail. As mentioned earlier, the χ^2_{df} distribution is not only positively skewed, its values range from 0 to infinity. However, given that the area under any probability distribution equals one, if the area to the left of a given value equals α, then the area to the right must equal $1 - \alpha$. In other words, the relevant value on the lower tail of the distribution is $\chi^2_{1-\alpha,df}$ where $P(\chi^2_{df} \geq \chi^2_{1-\alpha,df}) = 1 - \alpha$.

Suppose that we want to find the value such that the area to the left of the χ^2_{10} variable equals 0.05. Given that the area to the left of this value is 0.05, we know that the area to its right is $1 - 0.05 = 0.95$; thus, we need to find $\chi^2_{1-0.05,10} = \chi^2_{0.95,10}$. Again, we find $df = 10$ in the first column and follow this row until we intersect the column 0.95 and find the value 3.940. This is the value such that $P(\chi^2_{10} \geq 3.940) = 0.95$ or $P(\chi^2_{10} < 3.940) = 0.05$. In order to find $\chi^2_{0.95,10}$ in Excel, we enter `=CHISQ.INV(0.05, 10)`, and in R we enter `qchisq(0.05, 10, lower.tail=TRUE)`. Figure 11.3 graphically depicts the probability $\alpha = 0.05$ on both sides of the χ^2_{10} distribution and the corresponding χ^2_{10} values.

FIGURE 11.3 Graph of the probability $\alpha = 0.05$ on both sides of χ^2_{10}

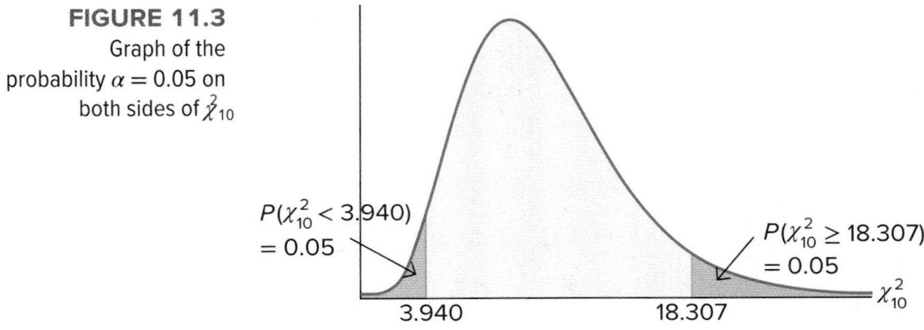

FINDING χ^2_{df} VALUES

- For a χ^2_{df} distributed random variable, $\chi^2_{\alpha,df}$ represents a value such that $P(\chi^2_{df} \geq \chi^2_{\alpha,df}) = \alpha$.
- Similarly, for a χ^2_{df} distributed random variable, $\chi^2_{1-\alpha,df}$ represents a value such that $P(\chi^2_{df} \geq \chi^2_{1-\alpha,df}) = 1 - \alpha$, or, equivalently, $P(\chi^2_{df} < \chi^2_{1-\alpha,df}) = \alpha$.

EXAMPLE 11.1

Find the value x for which:

a. $P(\chi^2_5 \geq x) = 0.025$

b. $P(\chi^2_8 < x) = 0.025$

SOLUTION

a. We find the value x such that the area in the upper tail of the distribution equals 0.025. Referencing Table 3 in Appendix B, we find $df = 5$ in the first column, follow this row until we intersect the column 0.025, and find the value 12.833; therefore, $x = 12.833$.

Using Excel, we enter `=CHISQ.INV(0.975, 5)`, and using R we enter `qchisq(0.975, 5, lower.tail=TRUE)`.

b. We find the value x such that the area in the lower tail of the distribution equals 0.025. We solve this problem as $P(\chi_8^2 \geq x) = 1 - 0.025 = 0.975$. Again referencing Table 3 in Appendix B, we find $df = 8$ in the first column, follow this row until we intersect the column 0.975, and find $x = 2.180$. This is equivalent to $P(\chi_8^2 < 2.180) = 0.025$.

Using Excel, we enter `=CHISQ.INV(0.025, 8)`, and using R we enter `qchisq(0.025, 8, lower.tail=TRUE)`.

We will now make inferences about the population variance and, subsequently, the population standard deviation, starting with confidence intervals.

LO 11.2

Make inferences about the population variance.

Confidence Interval for the Population Variance

Consider a χ_{df}^2 distributed random variable. We can use the notation that we just introduced to make the following probability statement concerning this random variable:

$$P(\chi_{1-\alpha/2,df}^2 \leq \chi_{df}^2 \leq \chi_{\alpha/2,df}^2) = 1 - \alpha.$$

This indicates that the probability that χ_{df}^2 falls between $\chi_{1-\alpha/2,df}^2$ and $\chi_{\alpha/2,df}^2$ is equal to $1 - \alpha$, where $1 - \alpha$ can be thought of as the familiar confidence coefficient. Substituting $\chi_{df}^2 = \frac{(n-1)S^2}{\sigma^2}$ into the probability statement yields

$$P\left(\chi_{1-\alpha/2,df}^2 \leq \frac{(n-1)S^2}{\sigma^2} \leq \chi_{\alpha/2,df}^2\right) = 1 - \alpha.$$

After manipulating this equation algebraically, we arrive at the formula for the confidence interval for σ^2.

CONFIDENCE INTERVAL FOR σ^2

A $100(1 - \alpha)\%$ confidence interval for the population variance σ^2 is computed as

$$\left[\frac{(n-1)s^2}{\chi_{\alpha/2,df}^2}, \frac{(n-1)s^2}{\chi_{1-\alpha/2,df}^2}\right],$$

where $df = n - 1$. This formula is valid only when the random sample is drawn from a normally distributed population.

Note that the confidence interval is not in the usual format of point estimate ± margin of error. Since the confidence intervals for the population mean and the population proportion are based on the z or the t_{df} distributions, the symmetry of these distributions around a zero mean leads to the same margin of error that is added to and subtracted from the point estimate. However, for a nonsymmetric χ_{df}^2 distribution, what is added to and subtracted from the point estimate of the population variance is not the same. Finally, since the standard deviation is just the positive square root of the variance, a $100(1 - \alpha)\%$ confidence interval for the population standard deviation is computed as

$$\left[\sqrt{\frac{(n-1)s^2}{\chi_{\alpha/2,df}^2}}, \sqrt{\frac{(n-1)s^2}{\chi_{1-\alpha/2,df}^2}}\right].$$

EXAMPLE 11.2

Compute the 95% confidence intervals for the population standard deviation for the Growth fund and the Value fund using the data from Table 11.1 in the introductory case. Assume that returns are normally distributed.

SOLUTION: For the years 1984–2019 ($n = 36$), the sample standard deviation for the Growth fund is $s = 23.7993$, while the sample standard deviation for the Value fund is $s = 17.9792$.

We first determine the 95% confidence interval for the population variance for the Growth fund. Given $n = 36$, $df = 36 - 1 = 35$. For the 95% confidence interval, $\alpha = 0.05$ and $\alpha/2 = 0.025$. Thus, we find $\chi^2_{\alpha/2,df} = \chi^2_{0.025,35} = 53.203$ and $\chi^2_{1-\alpha/2,df} = \chi^2_{0.975,35} = 20.569$. The 95% confidence interval for the population variance is

$$\left[\frac{(n-1)s^2}{\chi^2_{\alpha/2,df}}, \frac{(n-1)s^2}{\chi^2_{1-\alpha/2,df}}\right] = \left[\frac{(36-1)(23.7993)^2}{53.203}, \frac{(36-1)(23.7993)^2}{20.569}\right]$$
$$= [372.61, 963.79].$$

Taking the positive square root of the limits of this interval, we find the corresponding 95% confidence interval for the population standard deviation as [19.30, 31.04]. With 95% confidence, we report that the standard deviation of the return for the Growth fund is between 19.30% and 31.04%. Similarly, for the Value fund, we can show that the 95% confidence interval for the population standard deviation is between 14.58% and 23.45%.

Note: Answers may differ slightly due to rounding.

Hypothesis Test for the Population Variance

Let's now develop the four-step procedure for conducting a hypothesis test concerning the population variance. Following the methodology used in the last two chapters, the null and the alternative hypotheses will take one of the following forms:

Two-Tailed Test	Right-Tailed Test	Left-Tailed Test
$H_0: \sigma^2 = \sigma_0^2$	$H_0: \sigma^2 \leq \sigma_0^2$	$H_0: \sigma^2 \geq \sigma_0^2$
$H_A: \sigma^2 \neq \sigma_0^2$	$H_A: \sigma^2 > \sigma_0^2$	$H_A: \sigma^2 < \sigma_0^2$

Here, σ_0^2 is the hypothesized value of the population variance σ^2. As before, we can use confidence intervals to implement two-tailed hypothesis tests; however, for one-tailed tests concerning the population variance, we implement the four-step procedure.

TEST STATISTIC FOR σ^2

The value of the test statistic for the hypothesis test for the population variance σ^2 is computed as

$$\chi^2_{df} = \frac{(n-1)s^2}{\sigma_0^2},$$

where $df = n - 1$, s^2 is the sample variance, and σ_0^2 is the hypothesized value of the population variance. This formula is valid only if the underlying population is normally distributed.

EXAMPLE 11.3

Recall the introductory case. Dorothy Brennan's client asks if the standard deviation of returns for the Growth fund exceeds 20%. This is equivalent to testing if the variance exceeds $400(\%)^2$. Based on the sample information provided in Table 11.1, conduct this test at the 5% significance level. (Assume that returns are normally distributed.)

SOLUTION: In this example, the relevant parameter of interest is the population variance σ^2. Since we wish to determine whether the variance is greater than $400(\%)^2$, we specify the competing hypotheses as

$$H_0: \sigma^2 \leq 400$$
$$H_A: \sigma^2 > 400$$

The χ^2 test is valid because the underlying population is assumed to be normally distributed. Given that $n = 36$ and $s = 23.7993$, we compute the value of the test statistic as

$$\chi^2_{df} = \frac{(n-1)s^2}{\sigma_0^2} = \frac{(36-1)(23.7993)^2}{400} = 49.561.$$

Since this is a right-tailed test, we compute the p-value as $P(\chi^2_{35} \geq 49.561)$. Referencing the χ^2 table for $df = 35$, we see that 49.561 lies between the values 46.059 and 49.802, implying that the p-value is between 0.05 and 0.10. We use Excel or R (as explained in Example 11.4) to find the exact p-value as 0.052. Since the p-value is greater than 0.05, we do not reject H_0. At the 5% significance level, the variance of the Growth fund is not greater than $400(\%)^2$. Equivalently, the standard deviation does not exceed 20%, implying that the risk associated with this investment is not more than what the client wants to accept.

Note: Answers may differ slightly due to rounding.

Note on Calculating the p-Value for a Two-Tailed Test Concerning σ^2

Recall that the p-value is the probability of obtaining a value of the test statistic that is at least as extreme as the one that we actually observed, given that the null hypothesis is true as an equality. For a two-tailed test, we double the probability that is considered extreme. For example, for a two-tailed test for the population mean μ with a z statistic, the p-value is computed as $2P(Z \geq z)$ if $z > 0$ or $2P(Z \leq z)$ if $z < 0$. Note that $z > 0$ if $\bar{x} > \mu_0$ and $z < 0$ if $\bar{x} < \mu_0$. Similarly, for a two-tailed test for the population variance σ^2, the p-value is computed as two times the area in the right-tail of the distribution if $s^2 > \sigma_0^2$ or two times the area in the left-tail of the distribution if $s^2 < \sigma_0^2$.

Using Excel and R to Test σ^2

EXAMPLE 11.4

FILE
Growth_Value

Dorothy Brennan's client from the introductory case also wonders if the standard deviation of returns for the Value fund differs from 15%. This is equivalent to testing if the variance differs from $225(\%)^2$. Conduct this test at the 5% significance level. (Assume that returns are normally distributed.)

SOLUTION: This is an example of a two-tailed test for the population variance σ^2. We specify the competing hypotheses for the test as

$$H_0: \sigma^2 = 225$$
$$H_A: \sigma^2 \neq 225$$

Given $n = 36$ and $s = 17.9792$, it is easy to simply plug these values into the formula, $\chi^2_{df} = \frac{(n-1)s^2}{\sigma_0^2}$, and obtain the value of the test statistic. We include the steps for obtaining the value of the test statistic in Excel for continuity; in R, we use a function that computes the value. Both Excel and R are especially useful when you have access to the raw data.

Using Excel

a. Open the ***Growth_Value*** data file. Note that the observations for the variable Value are in cells C2 through C37.

b. We use Excel's **VAR.S** function to help in the calculation of the value of the test statistic $\chi^2_{df} = \frac{(n-1)s^2}{\sigma_0^2}$. We enter =(36 – 1)*VAR.S(C2:C37)/225 and Excel returns 50.284, so $\chi^2_{35} = 50.284$.

c. We use Excel's **CHISQ.DIST.RT** function to find the p-value. If we enter =CHISQ. DIST.RT(x, df), where x is the value to be evaluated and df are the degrees of freedom, then Excel returns the probability in the right-tail of the distribution or, equivalently, the p-value for a right-tailed test. Similarly, the p-value for a left-tailed test can be found as =1-CHISQ.DIST.RT(x, df). Since we have a two-tailed test and $s^2 > \sigma_0^2$ $(17.982^2 > 15^2)$, we compute the p-value as two times the area in the right-tail of the distribution. We enter `=2*CHISQ.DIST.RT(50.284, 35)`. Excel returns 0.091.

Using R

a. Import the ***Growth_Value*** data file into a data frame (table) and label it myData.

b. Install and load the *EnvStats* package. Enter:

```
>install.packages("EnvStats")
>library(EnvStats)
```

c. We use R's **varTest** function to obtain both the test statistic and the p-value. For options within this function, we use *alternative* to denote the specification of the alternative hypothesis (denoted as "two.sided" for a two-tailed test, "less" for a left-tailed test, and "greater" for a right-tailed test) and *sigma-squared* to denote the hypothesized value of the variance. Another feature of this function is that it automatically provides the 95% confidence interval for the mean by default; other levels can be found using the option *conf.level.* We enter

```
>varTest(myData$Value, alternative = "two.sided", sigma.squared = 225)
```

Figure 11.4 shows R's output. We have put the value of the test statistic and the p-value in boldface.

FIGURE 11.4 R's output using varTest function

```
      Chi-squared Test on Variance

data: myData$value
Chi-squared = 50.284, df = 35, p-value = 0.09097
alternative hypothesis: true variance is not equal to 225
95 percent confidence interval:
  212.6519 550.0308
sample estimates:
variance
323.2512
```

Note: If we do not have access to the raw data and only have summary statistics, then we could use R's **pchisq** function to find the p-value. For the p-value for the two-tailed test in this example, we enter `2*pchisq(50.284, 35, lower.tail=FALSE)`.

Summary

We do not reject the null hypothesis because the p-value $= 0.091$ is more than $\alpha = 0.05$. Therefore, at the 5% level, we cannot conclude that the risk, measured by the variance of the return, differs from $225(\%)^2$ or, equivalently, that the standard deviation differs from 15%.

EXERCISES 11.1

Concepts

1. Find the value x for which:
   a. $P(\chi^2_8 \geq x) = 0.025$
   b. $P(\chi^2_8 \geq x) = 0.05$
   c. $P(\chi^2_8 < x) = 0.025$
   d. $P(\chi^2_8 < x) = 0.05$

2. Find the value x for which:
   a. $P(\chi^2_{20} \geq x) = 0.005$
   b. $P(\chi^2_{20} \geq x) = 0.01$
   c. $P(\chi^2_{20} < x) = 0.005$
   d. $P(\chi^2_{20} < x) = 0.01$

3. In order to construct a confidence interval for the population variance, a random sample of n observations is drawn from a normal population. Use this information to find $\chi^2_{\alpha/2,df}$ and $\chi^2_{1-\alpha/2,df}$ under the following scenarios.
   a. A 95% confidence level with $n = 18$
   b. A 95% confidence level with $n = 30$
   c. A 99% confidence level with $n = 18$
   d. A 99% confidence level with $n = 30$

4. A random sample of 25 observations is used to estimate the population variance. The sample mean and the sample standard deviation are calculated as 52.5 and 3.8, respectively. Assume that the population is normally distributed.
   a. Construct the 90% interval estimate for the population variance.
   b. Construct the 99% interval estimate for the population variance.
   c. Use your answers to discuss the impact of the confidence level on the width of the interval.

5. The following values are drawn from a normal population.

20	29	32	27	34	25	30	31

   a. Calculate the point estimates for the population variance and the population standard deviation.
   b. Construct the 95% confidence interval for the population variance and the population standard deviation.

6. In order to conduct a hypothesis test for the population variance, you compute $s^2 = 75$ from a sample of 21 observations drawn from a normally distributed population. Conduct the following tests at $\alpha = 0.10$.
   a. $H_0: \sigma^2 \leq 50; H_A: \sigma^2 > 50$
   b. $H_0: \sigma^2 = 50; H_A: \sigma^2 \neq 50$

7. Consider the following hypotheses:

$$H_0: \sigma^2 = 200$$
$$H_A: \sigma^2 \neq 200$$

   Find the p-value based on the following sample information, where the sample is drawn from a normally distributed population.
   a. $s^2 = 300; n = 25$
   b. $s^2 = 100; n = 25$
   c. Which of the above sample information enables us to reject the null hypothesis at $\alpha = 0.05$?

8. You would like to test the claim that the variance of a normally distributed population is more than 2 squared units. You draw a random sample of 10 observations as 2, 4, 1, 3, 2, 5, 2, 6, 1, 4. At $\alpha = 0.10$, test the claim.

Applications

9. A research analyst is examining a stock for possible inclusion in his client's portfolio. Over a 10-year period, the sample mean and the sample standard deviation of annual returns on the stock were 20% and 15%, respectively. The client wants to know if the risk, as measured by the standard deviation, differs from 18%.
   a. Construct the 95% confidence intervals for the population variance and the population standard deviation.
   b. What assumption did you make in constructing the confidence intervals?
   c. Based on the results in part (a), does the risk differ from 18%?

10. A replacement part for a machine must be produced within close specifications in order for it to be acceptable to customers. A random sample of 20 parts drawn from a normally distributed population yields a sample variance of $s^2 = 0.03$.
   a. Construct the 95% confidence interval for the population variance.
   b. Production specifications call for the variance in the lengths of the parts to be exactly 0.05. Comment on whether or not the specifications are being violated.

11. The manager of a supermarket would like the variance of the waiting times of the customers not to exceed 3 minutes-squared. She would add a new cash register if the variance exceeds this threshold. She regularly checks the waiting times of the customers to ensure that the variance does not rise above the allowed level. In a recent random sample of 28 customer waiting times, she computes the sample variance as 4.2 minutes-squared. She believes that the waiting times are normally distributed.

a. State the null and the alternative hypotheses to test if the threshold has been crossed.
b. Conduct the test at $\alpha = 0.05$.
c. What should the manager do?

12. Metalworks, a supplier of machine parts, fabricates bearings in which the standard deviation of the bearing diameter must be within 0.002 inch maximum. Otherwise, problems with fit will occur. The engineering department is conducting an experiment to investigate adherence to this requirement. A sample of 25 bearings has revealed a sample standard deviation of 0.0025 inch.
   a. State the null and alternative hypotheses to test if the requirement has been violated.
   b. Compute the value of the test statistic. What assumption did you make regarding the bearing diameters?
   c. Conduct the test at $\alpha = 0.05$. What is your conclusion?
   d. Would your conclusion change at the 10% significance level?

13. Some transportation experts claim that it is the variability of speeds, rather than the level of speeds, that is a critical factor in determining the likelihood of an accident occurring. One of the experts claims that driving conditions are dangerous if the variance of speeds exceeds 80 $(\text{mph})^2$. On a heavily traveled highway, a random sample of 61 cars revealed a mean and a variance of speeds of 57.5 mph and 88.7 $(\text{mph})^2$, respectively.
   a. Set up the competing hypotheses to test if the variance of speeds exceeds 80 $(\text{mph})^2$.
   b. At the 5% significance level, can you conclude that driving conditions are dangerous on this highway? Explain.

14. A consumer advocacy group is concerned about the variability in the cost of prescription medication. The group surveys eight local pharmacies and obtains the following prices (in $) for a particular brand of medication:

25.50	32.00	33.50	28.75	29.50	35.00	27.00	29.00

   a. Calculate the point estimate for the population variance.
   b. The group assumes that the prices represent a random sample drawn from a normally distributed population. Construct the 90% interval estimate for the population variance.
   c. The group decides to begin a lobbying effort on its members' behalf if the variance in the price does not equal 4. What should the group do?

15. **FILE** ***Wage.*** An economist is interested in the variability of hourly wages at a production plant. She collects data on 50 hourly wage earners.
   a. Set up the competing hypotheses to test whether the variance of hourly wages exceeds 35 $(\$^2)$.
   b. Calculate the value of the test statistic.
   c. Find the p-value.
   d. At the 5% significance level, does the variance of hourly wages exceed 35 $(\$^2)$? Explain.

16. **FILE** ***Sewing.*** To maintain high consistency in its manual sewing operations, a custom manufacturer of high-quality fashion clothing has a goal in which all sewing employees should score within a standard deviation of 9 on a sewing dexterity test. To test adherence to this goal, a random sample of 30 employees was subjected to a needle-board dexterity test.
   a. State the hypotheses to test whether the standard deviation of the dexterity test scores exceeds 9.
   b. Calculate the value of the test statistic. Assume that dexterity scores are normally distributed.
   c. Find the p-value.
   d. Make a conclusion at each of the following significance levels: 1%, 5%, and 10%.

17. **FILE** ***MPG.*** The data accompanying this exercise show miles per gallon (mpg) for 25 cars.
   a. State the null and the alternative hypotheses in order to test whether the variance differs from 62 mpg^2.
   b. Assuming that mpg is normally distributed, calculate the value of the test statistic.
   c. Find the p-value.
   d. Make a conclusion at $\alpha = 0.01$.

18. **FILE** ***MV_Houses.*** A realtor in Mission Viejo, California, believes that the standard deviation of house prices is more than 100 units, where each unit equals $1,000. Assume house prices are normally distributed.
   a. State the null and the alternative hypotheses for the test.
   b. Calculate the value of the test statistic.
   c. Find the p-value.
   d. At $\alpha = 0.05$, what is the conclusion? Is the realtor's claim supported by the data?

19. **FILE** ***Profits.*** A restaurant owner is aware of the lack of consistency in profits. He would be very concerned if the standard deviation of the weekly profits is greater than $700. Refer to the weekly profits in the accompanying data file to inform the owner if there is a cause for concern. Assume that profits are normally distributed.
   a. State the appropriate hypotheses to validate the owner's concern.
   b. Calculate the value of the test statistic and the p-value.
   c. At the 5% significance level, should the owner be very concerned?

20. **FILE** ***Discovery.*** Fidelity's Growth Discovery Fund (FDSVX) is a highly rated growth fund that invests in companies that have above-average growth potential in domestic and foreign markets. An investor is concerned that foreign markets tend to be more volatile because of exchange rate, economic, and political risks. She has decided to purchase this fund only if the variance of its weekly returns is below 4. Refer to the 2019 weekly returns in the accompanying file to help the investor with the decision. Assume that weekly returns are normally distributed.
   a. State the appropriate hypotheses for the variance test.
   b. Calculate the value of the test statistic and the p-value.
   c. At the 10% significance level, should the investor invest in this fund?

21. **FILE** ***Shoppers.*** While the frequency of online shopping is lower for men as compared to women, men are the big spenders when it comes to making costly online purchase. A manager at the online retail store has complied the annual revenue from the store's 80 men and 80 women online shoppers. Assume that revenues are normally distributed. The accompanying table shows shows a portion of the data.

Men	Women
1676	2043
1493	2023
⋮	⋮
1685	2051

a. At the 5% level of significance, test if the standard deviation of the revenue for the store's online men shoppers differs from 100.

b. At the 5% level of significance, test if the standard deviation of the revenue for the store's online women shoppers differs from 100.

22. **FILE** ***Rentals.*** Real estate investment in college towns continues to promise good returns. With rents holding up, this is good news for investors but the same cannot be said for students. The investment company is concerned about the variability in rents and would invest only if the standard deviation is below $220. Consider monthly rents (in $) of two-bedroom apartments in two campus towns. Assume that monthly rents are normally distributed. A portion of the data is shown in the accompanying table.

Town 1	Town 2
1000	1500
1150	1150
⋮	⋮
1300	1350

a. At the 5% level of significance, test if the standard deviation of the rent in Town 1 is below 220. Should the investment company invest in this campus town? Explain

b. At the 5% level of significance, test if the standard deviation of the rent in Town 2 is below 220. Should the investment company invest in this campus town? Explain.

11.2 INFERENCE CONCERNING THE RATIO OF TWO POPULATION VARIANCES

In this section, we turn our attention to comparing two population variances, σ_1^2 and σ_2^2. It is common to compare products on the basis of the relative variability of their weight, size, or volume. For example, a bottler may want to compare two production facilities based on the relative variability of the amount of beverage filled at each facility. Similarly, an investor may want to compare the relative risk of two investment strategies, where variance is used as a measure of risk. Other examples for the relevance of comparing two population variances include comparing the relative variability of customer spending on online purchases, the speeds on highways, and the repair costs of different makes of automobiles.

We specify the parameter of interest as the ratio of the population variances σ_1^2/σ_2^2 rather than their difference $\sigma_1^2 - \sigma_2^2$. Note that the condition $\sigma_1^2 = \sigma_2^2$ is equivalent to $\sigma_1^2 - \sigma_2^2 = 0$ as well as $\sigma_1^2/\sigma_2^2 = 1$. We use the ratio of the sample variances S_1^2/S_2^2 as an estimator of σ_1^2/σ_2^2, where the sample variances are computed from independent random samples drawn from two normally distributed populations. In order to examine the methodologies for statistical inference, we first need to analyze the sampling distribution of S_1^2/S_2^2.

Sampling Distribution of S_1^2/S_2^2

LO 11.3

Discuss features of the *F* distribution.

We use the sampling distribution of S_1^2/S_2^2 to define a new distribution, called the ***F* distribution.**[1] Like the t_{df} and χ^2_{df} distributions, the F distribution is characterized by a family of distributions; however, each distribution depends on *two* degrees of freedom: the numerator degrees of freedom df_1 and the denominator degrees of freedom df_2. It is common to refer to it as the $F_{(df_1,df_2)}$ distribution. As mentioned earlier, we will use the notation $F_{(df_1,df_2)}$ to represent both a random variable and its value.

[1]The *F* distribution is named in honor of Sir Ronald Fisher, who discovered the distribution in 1922.

In general, the $F_{(df_1,df_2)}$ distribution is the probability distribution of the ratio of two independent chi-square variables, where each variable is divided by its own degrees of freedom; that is, $F_{(df_1,df_2)} = \frac{\chi^2_{df_1}/df_1}{\chi^2_{df_2}/df_2}$.

THE SAMPLING DISTRIBUTION OF S_1^2/S_2^2 WHEN $\sigma_1^2 = \sigma_2^2$

If independent samples of size n_1 and n_2 are drawn from normal populations with equal variances, then the statistic $F_{(df_1,df_2)} = S_1^2/S_2^2$ follows the $F_{(df_1,df_2)}$ distribution with $df_1 = n_1 - 1$ and $df_2 = n_2 - 1$.

Like the χ^2_{df} distribution, the $F_{(df_1,df_2)}$ distribution is positively skewed, with values ranging from zero to infinity, but becomes increasingly symmetric as df_1 and df_2 increase. Figure 11.4 shows the $F_{(df_1,df_2)}$ distribution with various degrees of freedom. Note that each $F_{(df_1,df_2)}$ distribution is positively skewed; however, as df_1 and df_2 grow larger, the $F_{(df_1,df_2)}$ distribution becomes less skewed and approaches the normal distribution. For instance, $F_{(20,20)}$ is relatively less skewed as compared to $F_{(2,8)}$ or $F_{(6,8)}$.

FIGURE 11.4 The $F_{(df_1,df_2)}$ distribution with various degrees of freedom

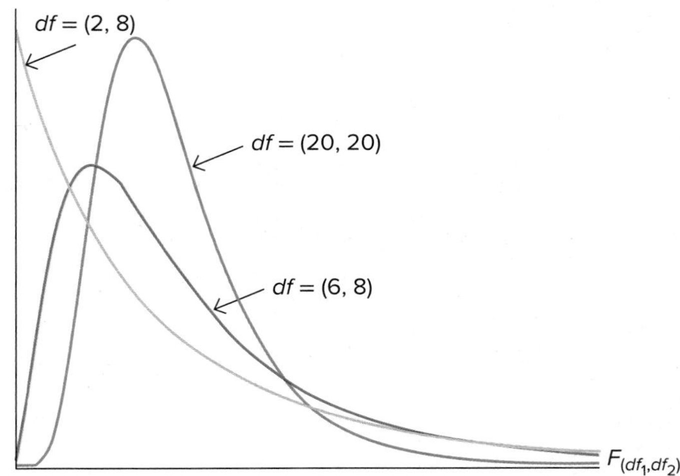

SUMMARY OF THE $F_{(df_1,df_2)}$ DISTRIBUTION

- The $F_{(df_1,df_2)}$ distribution is characterized by a family of distributions, where each distribution depends on two degrees of freedom, df_1 and df_2.
- The values of the $F_{(df_1,df_2)}$ distribution range from zero to infinity.
- The $F_{(df_1,df_2)}$ distribution is positively skewed, where the extent of skewness depends on df_1 and df_2. As df_1 and df_2 grow larger, the $F_{(df_1,df_2)}$ distribution approaches the normal distribution.

Finding $F_{(df_1,df_2)}$ Values and Probabilities

As with other distributions, we use the notation $F_{\alpha,(df_1,df_2)}$ to represent a value such that the area in the upper (right) tail of the distribution is α. In other words, $P(F_{(df_1,df_2)} \geq F_{\alpha,(df_1,df_2)}) = \alpha$. Figure 11.5 illustrates this notation.

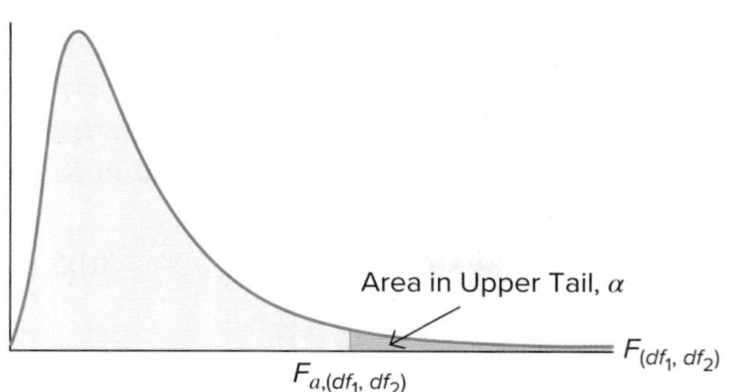

FIGURE 11.5 Graphical depiction of $P(F_{(df_1,df_2)} \geq F_{\alpha,(df_1,df_2)}) = \alpha$

A portion of the upper tail areas and the corresponding values for the $F_{(df_1,df_2)}$ distribution are given in Table 11.3. Table 4 of Appendix B provides a more complete table.

TABLE 11.3 Portion of the *F* Table

		df_1		
df_2	Area in Upper Tail, α	6	7	8
6	0.10	3.05	3.01	2.98
	0.05	4.28	4.21	**4.15**
	0.025	5.82	5.70	5.60
	0.01	8.47	8.26	8.10
7	0.10	2.83	2.78	2.75
	0.05	3.87	3.79	3.73
	0.025	5.12	4.99	4.90
	0.01	7.19	6.99	6.84
8	0.10	2.67	2.62	2.59
	0.05	**3.58**	3.50	3.44
	0.025	4.65	4.53	4.43
	0.01	6.37	6.18	6.03

Suppose we want to find $F_{\alpha,(df_1,df_2)}$ with $\alpha = 0.05$, $df_1 = 6$, and $df_2 = 8$; that is, $F_{0.05,(6,8)}$. With $df_1 = 6$ (read from the top row), $df_2 = 8$ (read from the first column), and then $\alpha = 0.05$ (read from the second column), we see that $F_{0.05,(6,8)} = 3.58$ such that $P(F_{(6,8)} \geq 3.58) = 0.05$.

We can use Excel's **F.INV** function to find a particular $F_{\alpha,(df_1,df_2)}$ value. We enter =F.INV(*cumulprob*, df_1, df_2), where *cumulprob* is the cumulative probability associated with the value $F_{\alpha,(df_1,df_2)}$, and df_1 and df_2 are the degrees of freedom in the numerator and the denominator, respectively. In order to find $F_{0.05,(6,8)}$, we enter `=F.INV(0.95, 6, 8)`, and Excel returns 3.58058. We use R's **qf** function to find a particular $F_{\alpha,(df_1,df_2)}$ value. We enter qf(*cumulprob*, df_1, df_2, *lower.tail=TRUE*), where *cumulprob* is the cumulative probability associated with the $F_{\alpha,(df_1,df_2)}$ value and df_1 and df_2 are the degrees of freedom in the numerator and the denominator, respectively. In order to find $F_{0.05,(6,8)}$, we enter `qf(0.95, 6, 8, lower.tail=TRUE)` and R returns: 3.58058; alternatively, we can enter `qf(0.05, 6, 8, lower.tail=FALSE)`.

Sometimes we need to derive values such that the area to the left of a given value is equal to α. Given that the area under any distribution equals one, the area to the right of the given value must equal $1 - \alpha$. As in the case of the χ^2_{df} distribution, we let $F_{1-\alpha,(df_1,df_2)}$ denote the value such that the area to its right equals $1 - \alpha$ and, thus, the area to its left equals α. It is convenient, however, to find $F_{1-\alpha,(df_1,df_2)}$ using a simple rule that $F_{1-\alpha,(df_1,df_2)} = \frac{1}{F_{\alpha,(df_2,df_1)}}$. Note that the rule reverses the order of the numerator and the denominator degrees of freedom.

Suppose we need to find $F_{1-\alpha,(df_1,df_2)}$ where $\alpha = 0.05$, $df_1 = 6$, and $df_2 = 8$. We find $F_{0.95,(6,8)} = \frac{1}{F_{0.05,(8,6)}} = \frac{1}{4.15} = 0.24$. In other words, the lower (left) tail area is $P(F_{(6,8)} < 0.24) = 0.05$. We do not need to make this adjustment when using Excel or R. In order to find to find $F_{0.95,(6,8)}$ in Excel, we enter `=F.INV(0.05, 6, 8)`, and in R we enter `qf(0.05, 6, 8, lower.tail=TRUE)`. Both Excel and R return 0.2411.

Figure 11.6 graphically depicts $P(F_{(6,8)} \geq 3.58) = 0.05$ and $P(F_{(6,8)} < 0.24) = 0.05$.

FIGURE 11.6 Graph of the probability $\alpha = 0.05$ on both sides of $F_{(6,8)}$

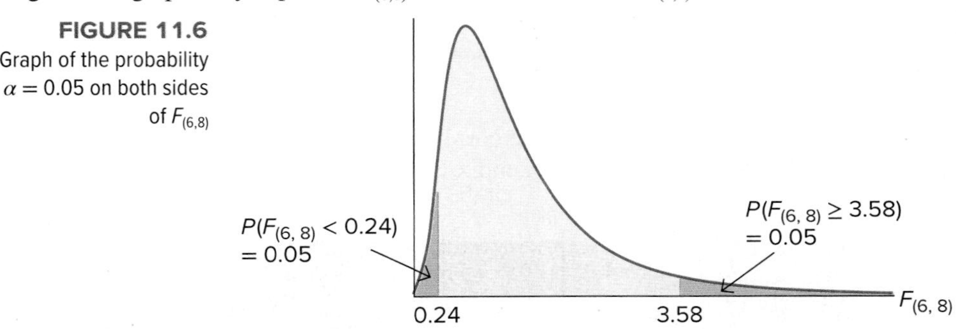

FINDING $F_{(df_1,df_2)}$ VALUES

- For a $F_{(df_1,df_2)}$ distributed random variable, $F_{\alpha,(df_1,df_2)}$ represents a value such that $P(F_{(df_1,df_2)} \geq F_{\alpha,(df_1,df_2)}) = \alpha$.
- Similarly, for a $F_{(df_1,df_2)}$ distributed random variable, $F_{1-\alpha,(df_1,df_2)}$ represents a value such that $P(F_{(df_1,df_2)} \geq F_{1-\alpha,(df_1,df_2)}) = 1 - \alpha$; equivalently, $P(F_{(df_1,df_2)} < F_{1-\alpha,(df_1,df_2)}) = \alpha$. When relying on the F table, it is convenient to reverse the order of degrees of freedom and find $F_{1-\alpha,(df_1,df_2)}$ as $\frac{1}{F_{\alpha,(df_2,df_1)}}$. We do not need to make this adjustment when using Excel or R.

EXAMPLE 11.5

Find the value x for which:

a. $P(F_{(7,10)} \geq x) = 0.025$

b. $P(F_{(7,10)} < x) = 0.05$

SOLUTION:

a. We find the value x such that the area in the upper tail of the distribution equals 0.025. Referencing Table 4 in Appendix B, we follow the column corresponding to $df_1 = 7$ until it intersects with the row corresponding to $df_2 = 10$ and $\alpha = 0.025$; we find the value 3.95. Therefore, $x = 3.95$ because $P(F_{(7,10)} \geq 3.95) = 0.025$. In order to find to find this value in Excel, we enter `=F.INV(0.975, 7, 10)`, and in R we enter `qf(0.975, 7, 10, lower.tail=TRUE)`.

b. We find the value x such that the area in the lower tail of the distribution equals 0.05, or, equivalently, the area in the upper tail of the distribution equals 0.95. We have $F_{0.95,(7,10)} = \frac{1}{F_{0.05,(10,7)}} = \frac{1}{3.64} = 0.27$. Therefore, $x = 0.27$ because $P(F_{(7,10)} < 0.27) = 0.05$. In order to find to find this value in Excel, we enter `=F.INV(0.05, 7, 10)`, and in R we enter `qf(0.05, 7, 10, lower.tail=TRUE)`.

LO 11.4

Make inferences about the ratio of two population variances.

We will now make statistical inferences about the ratio of two population variances, starting with confidence intervals.

Confidence Interval for the Ratio of Two Population Variances

The formula for a confidence interval for the ratio of the population variances σ_1^2/σ_2^2 is derived in a manner analogous to previous confidence intervals. Here, we simply show the end result.

CONFIDENCE INTERVAL FOR σ_1^2/σ_2^2

A 100(1 − α)% confidence interval for the ratio of the population variances σ_1^2/σ_2^2 is computed as

$$\left[\left(\frac{s_1^2}{s_2^2}\right)\frac{1}{F_{\alpha/2,(df_1,df_2)}}, \left(\frac{s_1^2}{s_2^2}\right)F_{\alpha/2,(df_2,df_1)}\right],$$

where for samples of size n_1 and n_2, $df_1 = n_1 - 1$ and $df_2 = n_2 - 1$. Note that the order of the degrees of freedom for the right part of the interval is reversed.

This formula is valid if the sample variances are computed from independently drawn samples from two normally distributed populations.

EXAMPLE 11.6

Students of two sections of a statistics course took a common final examination. A professor examines the variability in scores between the two sections. Random samples of $n_1 = 11$ and $n_2 = 16$ yield sample variances of $s_1^2 = 182.25$ and $s_2^2 = 457.96$. Construct the 95% confidence interval for the ratio of the population variances. Assume that the samples are independently drawn from two normally distributed populations.

SOLUTION: In order to construct the 95% confidence interval for the ratio of the population variances, we determine $\left[\left(\frac{s_1^2}{s_2^2}\right)\frac{1}{F_{\alpha/2,(df_1,df_2)}}, \left(\frac{s_1^2}{s_2^2}\right)F_{\alpha/2,(df_2,df_1)}\right]$. We find the degrees of freedom as $df_1 = n_1 - 1 = 11 - 1 = 10$ and $df_2 = n_2 - 1 = 16 - 1 = 15$. From the F table and given $\alpha = .05$, we find

$$F_{\alpha/2,(df_1,df_2)} = F_{0.025,(10,15)} = 3.06 \quad \text{and} \quad F_{\alpha/2,(df_2,df_1)} = F_{0.025,(15,10)} = 3.52.$$

The confidence interval is

$$\left[\left(\frac{182.25}{457.96}\right)\frac{1}{3.06}, \left(\frac{182.25}{457.96}\right)3.52\right] = [0.13, 1.40]$$

Therefore, the 95% confidence interval for the ratio of the population variances ranges from 0.13 to 1.40. In other words, the variance of scores in the first section is between 13% and 140% of the variance of scores in the second section.

As we have done in earlier chapters, we will be able to use this confidence interval to conduct a two-tailed hypothesis test.

Hypothesis Test for the Ratio of Two Population Variances

When comparing two population variances σ_1^2 and σ_2^2, the competing hypotheses will take one of the following forms:

Two-Tailed Test	Right-Tailed Test	Left-Tailed Test
$H_0: \sigma_1^2/\sigma_2^2 = 1$	$H_0: \sigma_1^2/\sigma_2^2 \leq 1$	$H_0: \sigma_1^2/\sigma_2^2 \geq 1$
$H_A: \sigma_1^2/\sigma_2^2 \neq 1$	$H_A: \sigma_1^2/\sigma_2^2 > 1$	$H_A: \sigma_1^2/\sigma_2^2 < 1$

A two-tailed test determines whether the two population variances differ. As noted earlier, the condition $\sigma_1^2 = \sigma_2^2$ is equivalent to $\sigma_1^2/\sigma_2^2 = 1$. A right-tailed test examines whether σ_1^2 is greater than σ_2^2, whereas a left-tailed test examines whether σ_1^2 is less than σ_2^2.

EXAMPLE 11.7

Let's revisit Example 11.6.

a. Specify the competing hypotheses in order to determine whether or not the variances in the two statistics sections differ.

b. Using the 95% confidence interval, what is the conclusion to the test?

SOLUTION:

a. Since we want to determine if the variances differ between the two sections, we formulate a two-tailed hypothesis test as

$$H_0: \sigma_1^2/\sigma_2^2 = 1$$
$$H_A: \sigma_1^2/\sigma_2^2 \neq 1$$

b. We calculated the 95% confidence interval for the ratio of the two variances that ranged from 0.13 to 1.40. We note that this interval contains the value 1; thus, we do not reject H_0. The sample data do not suggest that the variances between the two statistics sections differ at the 5% significance level.

Now we use the four-step procedure to implement one- or two-tailed hypothesis tests. We use the ratio of the values of the sample variances s_1^2/s_2^2 to conduct hypothesis tests regarding the ratio of the population variances σ_1^2/σ_2^2.

TEST STATISTIC FOR σ_1^2/σ_2^2

The value of the test statistic for the hypothesis test for the ratio of two population variances σ_1^2/σ_2^2 is computed as

$$F_{(df_1,df_2)} = s_1^2/s_2^2,$$

where for samples of size n_1 and n_2, $df_1 = n_1 - 1$ and $df_2 = n_2 - 1$. The $F_{(df_1,df_2)}$ test statistic is valid if the sample variances are computed from independently drawn samples from normally distributed populations.

Note that a left-tailed test can easily be converted into a right-tailed test by interchanging the variances of the two populations. For instance, we can convert $H_0: \sigma_1^2/\sigma_2^2 \geq 1$ versus $H_A: \sigma_1^2/\sigma_2^2 < 1$ into $H_0: \sigma_2^2/\sigma_1^2 \leq 1$ versus $H_A: \sigma_2^2/\sigma_1^2 > 1$.

PLACING THE LARGER SAMPLE VARIANCE IN THE NUMERATOR

It is preferable to place the larger sample variance in the numerator of the $F_{(df_1,df_2)}$ statistic. The resulting value allows us to focus only on the upper (right) tail of the distribution.

In other words, we define the hypotheses such that the resulting test statistic is computed as s_1^2/s_2^2 when $s_1^2 > s_2^2$ and as s_2^2/s_1^2 when $s_2^2 > s_1^2$; the degrees of freedom is adjusted accordingly. This saves us the additional work required to find the area in the lower (left) tail of the $F_{(df_1,df_2)}$ distribution.

Using Excel and R to Test σ_1^2/σ_2^2

EXAMPLE 11.8

Growth_Value

Let's again revisit the introductory case. Dorothy Brennan's client wonders if the Growth fund is riskier than the Value fund. For reference, we repeat the relevant information for the two funds.

$$\text{Growth fund: } s_1 = 23.7993, \quad n_1 = 36$$
$$\text{Value fund: } s_2 = 17.9792, \quad n_2 = 36$$

Assume that returns are normally distributed to implement the test at the 5% significance level.

SOLUTION: We define the population variance as the measure of risk, which is equivalent to defining risk in terms of the standard deviation. Let σ_1^2 and σ_2^2 denote the population variances of the Growth and the Value funds, respectively. Since we wish to determine whether the variance of the Growth fund is greater than that of the Value fund, we specify the competing hypotheses as

$$H_0: \sigma_1^2/\sigma_2^2 \leq 1$$
$$H_A: \sigma_1^2/\sigma_2^2 > 1$$

Note that this specification is appropriate since $s_1 > s_2$. If it were the case that $s_2 > s_1$, then would have specified the hypotheses in terms of σ_2^2/σ_1^2 instead of σ_1^2/σ_2^2.

As in Section 11.1, even though we could easily calculate $F_{(df_1, df_2)} = s_1^2/s_2^2$ given the summary statistics, we include the steps for obtaining this statistic in Excel for continuity; in R, we use a function that computes the value. Both Excel and R are especially useful when you have access to the raw data.

Using Excel

a. Open the ***Growth_Value*** data file. Note that the values for the variables Growth and Value are in cells B2 through C37.

b. We use Excel's **VAR.S** function to calculate the value of the test statistic $F_{(df_1, df_2)} = s_1^2/s_2^2$. We enter =VAR.S(B2:B37)/VAR.S(C2:C37) and Excel returns 1.7522; so, $F_{(35, 35)} = 1.7522$.

c. We use Excel's **F.DIST.RT** function to find the p-value. If we enter =F. DIST.RT(x, df_1, df_2), where x is the value to be evaluated, df_1 is degrees of freedom in the numerator, and df_2 is degrees of freedom in the denominator, then Excel returns the probability in the right-tail of the distribution, or equivalently, the p-value for a right-tailed test. Since we have a right-tailed test, we enter `=F.DIST.RT(1.7522, 35, 35)`. Excel returns 0.051.

Using R

a. Import the ***Growth_Value*** data file into a data frame (table) and label it myData.

b. We use R's **var.test** function to obtain both the test statistic and the p-value. For options within this function, we use *ratio* to denote the hypothesized value of the variance ratio and *alternative* to denote the specification of the alternative hypothesis (denoted as "two.sided" for a two-tailed test, "less" for a left-tailed test, and "greater" for a right-tailed test). Another feature of this function is that it automatically provides the 95% confidence interval for the mean by default; other levels can be found using the option *conf.level*. We enter

```
> var.test(myData$Growth, myData$Value, ratio=1,
  alternative = "greater")
```

Figure 11.7 shows R's output. We have put the value of the test statistic and the p-value in boldface. Because we conducted a right-tailed test, R reports a one-tailed confidence interval for the variance ratio, which we do not discuss in the text.

FIGURE 11.7 R's output using var.test function

```
      F test to compare two variances
data: myData$Growth and myData$Value
F = 1.7522, num df = 35, denom df = 35, p-value = 0.05084
alternative hypothesis: true ratio of variances is greater than 1
95 percent confidence interval:
 0.9971982      Inf
sample estimates:
ratio of variances
         1.752216
```

Note: If we do not have access to the raw data and only have summary statistics, then we could use R's ***pf*** function to find the p-value. For the p-value for the right-tailed test in this example, we enter `pf(1.7522, 35, 35, lower.tail=FALSE)`.

Summary

We do not reject the null hypothesis because the p-value $= 0.051$ is more than $\alpha = 0.05$. Therefore, at the at the 5% significance level, we cannot conclude that the Growth fund is riskier than the Value fund.

Note: As before, the p-value for a two-tailed can be found by multiplying the right-tailed probability by two.

SYNOPSIS OF INTRODUCTORY CASE

The annual return data for Vanguard's Growth Index mutual fund (Growth) and Vanguard's Value Index mutual fund (Value) were examined for the years 1984 through 2019. Over this time period, the average annual return for the Growth and the Value mutual funds were 15.76% and 12.01%, respectively. The averages imply that the Growth mutual fund offers a higher reward due to its higher average return. The average return gauges the reward of investing, but it says nothing about the risk of investing when both reward and risk are important. Can we conclude that an investment in one fund may be riskier than an investment in the other?

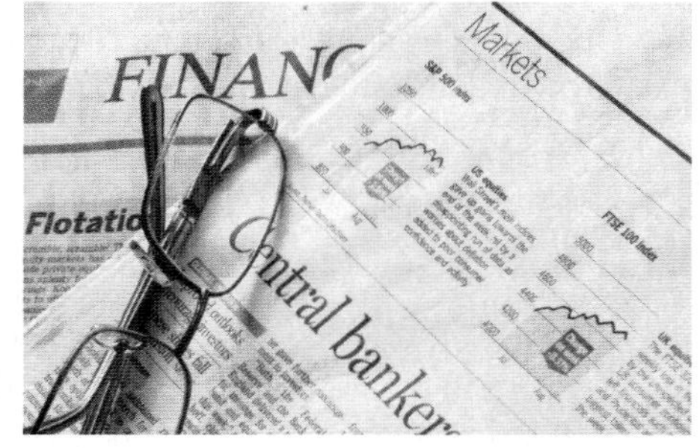

dani3315/Shutterstock

Variance and standard deviation tend to be the most common measures of risk with financial data, so a number of tests were conducted to assess the risk of investing in either of these mutual funds. Over this time period, the standard deviations of return for the Growth and the Value mutual funds were 23.80% and 17.98%, respectively. The first test examined if the standard deviation of the Growth fund was greater than 20%—a level of risk that a client did not want to exceed. At the 5% significance level, it was found that the standard deviation was not greater than 20%. The second test investigated if the standard deviation of the Value fund differed from 15%. At the 5% significance level, the results suggested that the standard deviation did not differ from 15%. Finally, it was found that the standard deviation of the Growth mutual fund is not greater than the standard deviation of the Value mutual fund at the 5% significance level.

A cursory glance of the standard deviation for the Growth and the Value mutual funds may lead an investor to incorrectly conclude that the Growth mutual fund has higher risk than the Value fund. Formal testing did not support that the Growth fund is riskier than the Value fund. Based on this analysis, and assuming similar performance into the future, it appears that the investor should not favor one mutual fund over the other. Since the two investment styles of growth and value investing often complement each other, it might be advisable for the investor to add diversity to his portfolio by using the funds together.

EXERCISES 11.2

Concepts

23. Find the value x for which:
    a. $P(F_{(4,8)} \geq x) = 0.025$
    b. $P(F_{(4,8)} \geq x) = 0.05$
    c. $P(F_{(4,8)} < x) = 0.025$
    d. $P(F_{(4,8)} < x) = 0.05$
24. Find the following probabilities.
    a. $P(F_{(10,8)} \geq 3.35)$
    b. $P(F_{(10,8)} < 0.42)$
    c. $P(F_{(10,8)} \geq 4.30)$
    d. $P(F_{(10,8)} < 0.26)$
25. Construct the 90% interval estimate for the ratio of the population variances using the following results from two independently drawn samples from normally distributed populations.

    Sample 1: $\bar{x}_1 = 157$, $s_1^2 = 23.2$, and $n_1 = 9$
    Sample 2: $\bar{x}_2 = 148$, $s_2^2 = 19.9$, and $n_2 = 8$
26. Consider the following measures based on independently drawn samples from normally distributed populations:

    Sample 1: $s_1^2 = 220$, and $n_1 = 20$
    Sample 2: $s_2^2 = 196$, and $n_2 = 15$

    a. Construct the 95% interval estimate for the ratio of the population variances.
    b. Using the confidence interval from part (a), test if the ratio of the population variances differs from 1 at the 5% significance level. Explain.
27. Consider the following competing hypotheses and relevant summary statistics:

$$H_0: \sigma_1^2/\sigma_2^2 = 1$$
$$H_A: \sigma_1^2/\sigma_2^2 \neq 1$$

    Sample 1: $\bar{x}_1 = 48.5$, $s_1^2 = 18.7$, and $n_1 = 10$
    Sample 2: $\bar{x}_2 = 50.2$, $s_2^2 = 12.9$, and $n_2 = 8$

    Assume that the two populations are normally distributed. Conduct this test at the 5% significance level.
28. Consider the following competing hypotheses and relevant summary statistics:

$$H_0: \sigma_1^2/\sigma_2^2 \leq 1$$
$$H_A: \sigma_1^2/\sigma_2^2 > 1$$

    Sample 1: $s_1^2 = 935$ and $n_1 = 14$
    Sample 2: $s_2^2 = 812$ and $n_2 = 11$

    Conduct this test at the 5% significance level. State your assumptions.
29. Consider the following competing hypotheses and relevant summary statistics:

$$H_0: \sigma_1^2/\sigma_2^2 \geq 1$$
$$H_A: \sigma_1^2/\sigma_2^2 < 1$$

    Sample 1: $s_1^2 = 1{,}315$ and $n_1 = 17$
    Sample 2: $s_2^2 = 1{,}523$ and $n_2 = 19$

    Conduct this hypothesis test at the 5% significance level. State your assumptions. (*Hint:* You may want to first convert the above left-tailed test into a right-tailed test by switching the two variances.)

Applications

30. A firm has just developed a new cost-reducing technology for producing a certain replacement part for automobiles. Since a replacement part must be produced within close specifications in order for it to be acceptable to customers, the new technology's specifications must not deviate drastically from the older version. Suppose the sample variance for 26 parts produced using the older version is $s_1^2 = 0.28$, while the sample variance for 26 parts produced using the new technology is $s_2^2 = 0.48$. Assume that the two samples are drawn independently from normally distributed populations.
    a. Develop the hypotheses to test whether the population variances differ.
    b. Calculate the value of the test statistic and the p-value.
    c. Can you conclude that the variances are different at the 5% significance level? Given that all other criteria are satisfied, should the company adopt the new technology?
31. Two basketball players on a school team are working hard on consistency of their performance. In particular, they are hoping to bring down the variance of their scores. The coach believes that the players are not equally consistent in their games. Over a 10-game period, the scores of these two players are shown in the accompanying table. Assume that the two samples are drawn independently from normally distributed populations.

Player 1	13	15	12	18	14	15	11	13	11	16
Player 2	11	21	18	9	20	11	13	11	19	8

    a. Develop the hypotheses to test whether the players differ in consistency.
    b. Test the coach's claim at $\alpha = 0.05$.
32. The quality manager at a battery manufacturing company wants to determine if lithium-ion batteries have less variability in discharge time than nickel-cadmium batteries. Using products with similar power draws, he has measured the time until discharge (in hours) for random samples of 16 lithium-ion batteries and 26 nickel-cadmium batteries. The sample variance of the discharge times is 0.44 hours^2 for the lithium-ion batteries and 0.89 hours^2 for the nickel-cadmium batteries.

a. State the hypotheses to test whether the variance in discharge time for the lithium-ion batteries is less than the variance for the nickel-cadmium batteries.
b. Compute the value of the test statistic. What assumption did you make?
c. Find the p-value.
d. Make a conclusion at the 5% significance level.
e. Would your conclusion change at the 10% significance level?

33. FILE ***Shoppers.*** The data accompanying this exercise include a store's annual revenue from 80 men and 80 women online shoppers.
   a. Specify the competing hypotheses in order to test whether the variance in revenues is greater for men than for women.
   b. Calculate the value of the test statistic. Assume that revenues are normally distributed.
   c. Find the p-value.
   d. At $\alpha = 0.01$, what is your conclusion?

34. FILE ***Fidelity.*** The following table shows the 2019 weekly returns (in percent) for Fidelity's 500 Index (Index) and Blue Chip (Bluechip) funds.

Week	Index	Bluechip
1	2.58	4.07
2	2.90	2.64
⋮	⋮	⋮
52	−0.56	−1.00

Test if the population variances differ at the 5% significance level. State your assumptions.

35. FILE ***Purchase_Amounts.*** A marketing analyst is studying the variability in customer purchase amounts between shopping mall stores and "big box" discount stores. She suspects the variability is different between those stores due to the nature of the customers involved. To investigate this issue in detail, she compiled two random samples, each consisting of 26 purchase amounts at shopping mall stores and discount stores.
   a. State the hypotheses to test whether the variance of the purchase amounts differs between the two types of stores.
   b. Construct the 95% confidence interval for the ratio of the population variances. Assume that purchase amounts are normally distributed.
   c. Use the confidence interval to test whether the variance of the purchase amounts differs between the two stores at the 5% significance level.
   d. Confirm your conclusion using the p-value approach.

36. FILE ***Coffee.*** A portion of the monthly stock prices for Starbucks Corp. and Dunkin' Brands Group, Inc. from 2017 to 2019 are reported in the following table.

Date	Starbucks	Dunkin'
Jan-17	51.77	48.37
Feb-17	53.31	51.30
⋮	⋮	⋮
Dec-19	87.51	75.09

   a. State the null and the alternative hypotheses in order to determine if the variance of price differs for the two firms. Assume that prices are normally distributed.
   b. Compute the value of the test statistic and the p-value.
   c. At $\alpha = 0.05$, what is your conclusion?

37. FILE ***Packaging.*** A variety of packaging solutions exist for products that must be kept within a specific temperature range. Cold chain distribution is particularly useful in the food and pharmaceutical industries. A packaging company is trying out a new packaging material that might reduce the variation of temperatures in the box. Inspectors randomly select 16 boxes of new and old packages, and report the temperatures in degrees Celsius 24 hours after they are sealed for shipment. A portion of the data is shown in the accompanying table. Assume that the two samples are drawn independently from normally distributed populations.

New Package	Old Package
3.98	5.79
4.99	6.42
⋮	⋮
4.95	5.95

   a. State the hypotheses to test whether the new packaging material reduces the variation of temperatures in the box.
   b. Compute the value of the test statistic and the p-value.
   c. Make a conclusion at the 5% significance level.

38. FILE ***Rentals.*** The data accompanying this exercise include monthly rents for a two-bedroom apartment in two campus towns. At the 5% significance level, test if the variance of rent in campus town 1 is less than the variance of rent in campus town 2. State your assumptions clearly.

11.3 WRITING WITH DATA

Case Study

Many environmental groups and politicians are suggesting a return to the federal 55-mile-per-hour speed limit on America's highways. They argue that a lower national speed limit will improve traffic safety, save fuel, and reduce greenhouse emissions. Elizabeth Connolly believes that more focus should be put on the variability of speed limits as opposed to average speed limits. She points to recent research that suggests that increases in speed variability decrease overall safety. Specifically, Elizabeth feels that traffic accidents are more likely to occur when the standard deviation of speeds exceeds 5 mph. She records the speeds of 40 cars from a highway with a speed limit of 55 mph (Highway 1) and the speeds of 40 cars from a highway with a speed limit of 65 mph (Highway 2). A portion of the data is shown in Table 11.4.

Dmitry Kalinovsky/Shutterstock

Elizabeth would like to use this sample information to determine whether the standard deviation on the 55-mph highway exceeds 5 mph. She would also like to determine whether the variability on the 55-mph highway is more than the variability on the 65-mph highway.

TABLE 11.4 Speeds of Cars from Highway 1 and Highway 2

FILE *Highway_Speeds*

Highway 1 (55-mph limit)	Highway 2 (65-mph limit)
60	70
55	65
⋮	⋮
52	65

Sample Report—Traffic Safety and the Variation in Speed

Increasing greenhouse emissions are prompting conservationists to lobby for a return to the federal 55-mile-per-hour (mph) speed limit on America's highways. In addition, advocates point to potential money and fuel savings, noting that fuel efficiency worsens at speeds above 60 mph. It is not clear, however, if the return to 55 mph will increase traffic safety. Many believe that traffic safety is based on the variability of the speed rather than the average speed that people are driving—the more variation in speed, the more dangerous the roads.

In this report, the variability of speeds on two highways is compared. The sample consists of the speeds of 40 cars recorded on a highway with a 55-mph speed limit (Highway 1) and the speeds of 40 cars recorded on a highway with a 65-mph speed limit (Highway 2). Table 11.5 shows the most relevant descriptive measures for the analysis.

TABLE 11.5 Summary Measures for Highway 1 and Highway 2

	Highway 1 (55-mph speed limit)	Highway 2 (65-mph speed limit)
Mean	56.60	66.00
Standard deviation	6.98	3.00
Number of cars	40	40

While it is true that cars travel at a slower speed, on average, on Highway 1 (56.60 mph < 66.00 mph), the variability of speeds is greater on Highway 1, as measured by the standard deviation (6.98 mph > 3.00 mph).

Two hypothesis tests are conducted. The first test examines whether or not the standard deviation on Highway 1 is greater than 5 mph at the 5% significance level or, alternatively, $\sigma^2 > 25$. The second test analyzes whether the standard deviation on Highway 1 is greater than the standard deviation on Highway 2 or, alternatively, $\sigma_1^2/\sigma_2^2 > 1$. The results of the tests are summarized in Table 11.6.

TABLE 11.6 Competing Hypotheses, Test Statistics, and *p*-values

Hypotheses	Test Statistic	*p*-value
$H_0: \sigma^2 \leq 25$ $H_A: \sigma^2 > 25$	$\chi^2_{39} = \frac{(n-1)s^2}{\sigma^2} = \frac{(40-1)(6.98)^2}{25} = 76.00$	≈ 0.00
$H_0: \sigma_1^2/\sigma_2^2 \leq 1$ $H_A: \sigma_1^2/\sigma_2^2 > 1$	$F_{39,39} = \frac{s_1^2}{s_2^2} = \frac{(6.98)^2}{(3.00)^2} = 5.41$	≈ 0.00

When testing whether or not the standard deviation is greater than 5 mph on Highway 1, a test statistic of 76.00 is obtained with a corresponding *p*-value that is approximately equal to zero. The null hypothesis regarding the population variance is rejected at any reasonable level of significance. In other words, the sample data suggest that the standard deviation is greater than 5 mph on Highway 1. The second hypothesis test reveals that the variance for Highway 1 is greater than the variance for Highway 2 given a test statistic of 5.41 and a corresponding *p*-value that is approximately equal to zero.

American drivers love to drive fast, which explains why safety advocates and conservationists are losing the long-running debate over lowering highway speed limits. While a 55-mph speed limit will save fuel and reduce greenhouse emissions, it is still an open question as to whether it will also enhance safety. If traffic safety is based on the variability of the speeds that people are driving rather than the average speed, then the data suggest that a return to a federal 55-mph speed limit may not necessarily enhance safety.

Suggested Case Studies

Report 11.1 FILE ***Gasoline.*** Due to environmental concerns and the never-ending volatility of gas prices, drivers are becoming more concerned with their cars' gasoline consumption. Cameron White, a research analyst at a nonprofit organization, shares these concerns and wonders whether his car's gas consumption is as efficient as it was when he first bought the new car five years ago. Despite his best intentions, he has been a bit lax in his upkeep of the car and feels that this may adversely influence its performance. At the time he purchased the car, he was told that his car would average 29 miles per gallon (mpg) on highways, with a standard deviation of 1 mpg. The accompanying data file shows his car' mpg from the last 20 fill-ups.

In a report, use the information to construct a confidence interval for the population standard deviation. Use a reasonable confidence level and discuss any assumptions that you make for the analysis. Then determine whether the variability has increased from the original standard deviation of 1 mpg. Use a reasonable significance level.

Report 11.2 FILE ***Math_Scores.*** For decades, people have believed that boys are innately more capable than girls in math. In other words, due to the intrinsic differences in brains, boys are better suited for doing math than girls. Recent research challenges this stereotype, arguing that gender differences in math performance have more to do with culture than innate aptitude. In the United States, for example, girls perform just as well on standardized math tests as boys. Others argue, however, that while the average may be the same, there is more variability in math ability for boys than girls, resulting in some boys with soaring math skills. A portion of representative data on math scores for boys and girls is shown in the accompanying data file.

In a report, use the information to construct and interpret a confidence interval for the ratio of the variance of math scores for boys and for girls. Use a reasonable confidence level and discuss the assumptions that you make for the analysis. Then determine if boys have more variability in math scores than girls. Use a reasonable significance level.

Report 11.3 Go to https://finance.yahoo.com/ to extract three-years of monthly adjusted stock price data for two large technology firms. For each firm, calculate monthly returns as the percentage change in adjusted close prices from the previous month, giving 35 months of return data. Use summary measures to compare the risk and reward for the two firms. For each firm, determine if the risk, measured by the standard deviation, is statistically different from 120 at the 5% significance level. Also, determine if the seemingly riskier. Use a reasonable significance level and discuss any assumptions that you make for the analysis.

CONCEPTUAL REVIEW

LO 11.1 Discuss features of the χ^2 distribution.

The χ^2 distribution is characterized by a family of distributions, where each distribution depends on its particular degrees of freedom *df*. It is common, therefore, to refer to it as the χ^2_{df} distribution. It is positively skewed with values ranging from zero to infinity. As the *df* grows larger, the χ^2_{df} distribution tends to the normal distribution.

LO 11.2 Make inferences about the population variance.

Statistical inferences regarding σ^2 are based on the χ^2_{df} distribution. The $100(1-\alpha)\%$ confidence interval for σ^2 is computed as $\left[\frac{(n-1)s^2}{\chi^2_{\alpha/2,df}}, \frac{(n-1)s^2}{\chi^2_{1-\alpha/2,df}}\right]$. The value of the test statistic for the hypothesis test for σ^2 is computed as $\chi^2_{df} = \frac{(n-1)s^2}{\sigma_0^2}$, where σ_0^2 is the hypothesized value of the population variance. These formulas are valid when σ^2 is computed using a random sample drawn from a normally distributed population.

LO 11.3 Discuss features of the F distribution.

The F distribution is also characterized by a family of distributions; however, each distribution depends on *two* degrees of freedom: the numerator degrees of freedom df_1 and the denominator degrees of freedom df_2. It is common to refer to it as the $F_{(df_1,df_2)}$ distribution. The $F_{(df_1,df_2)}$ distribution is positively skewed with values ranging from zero to infinity, but becomes increasingly symmetric as df_1 and df_2 increase.

LO 11.4 Make inferences about the ratio of two population variances.

Statistical inferences regarding σ_1^2/σ_2^2 are based on the $F_{(df_1,df_2)}$ distribution. The $100(1-\alpha)\%$ confidence interval for σ_1^2/σ_2^2 is computed as $\left[\left(\frac{s_1^2}{s_2^2}\right)\frac{1}{F_{\alpha/2,(df_1,df_2)}}, \left(\frac{s_1^2}{s_2^2}\right)F_{\alpha/2,(df_2,df_1)}\right]$. The value of the test statistic for the hypothesis test of σ_1^2/σ_2^2 is computed as $F_{(df_1,df_2)} = s_1^2/s_2^2$, with $df_1 = n_1 - 1$ and $df_2 = n_2 - 1$. These formulas are valid when s_1^2 and s_2^2 are computed using independently drawn samples from two normally distributed populations.

ADDITIONAL EXERCISES

39. A replacement part for a machine must be produced within close specifications in order for it to be acceptable to customers. A production process is considered to be working properly as long as the variance in the lengths of the parts does not exceed 0.05 squared-units. Suppose the sample variance computed from 30 parts turns out to be $s^2 = 0.07$. Use this sample evidence to test if the production specification is not being met at the 5% level of significance.

40. **FILE** ***Generic.*** A consumer advocacy group is concerned about the variability in the cost of a generic drug. There is cause for concern if the

variance of the cost exceeds 5. The group surveys 48 local pharmacies and obtains prices (in $) for a particular generic drug; refer to the data in the accompanying file. Test if there is a cause for concern for the consumer group at the 1% significance level.

41. **FILE** ***Checkout_Arrivals.*** For staffing purposes, a retail store manager would like to standardize the number of checkout lanes to keep open on a particular shift. She believes that if the standard deviation of the hourly customer arrival rates is 8 customers or less, then a fixed number of checkout lanes can be staffed without excessive customer waiting time or excessive clerk idle time. However, before determining how many checkout lanes (and thus clerks) to use, she must verify that the standard deviation of the arrival rates does not exceed 8. Accordingly, a sample of 25 hourly customer arrival rates was compiled for that shift over the past week.
    a. State the hypotheses to test whether the standard deviation of the customer arrival rates exceeds 8.
    b. Calculate the value of the test statistic. Assume that customer arrival rates are normally distributed.
    c. Find the p-value.
    d. At $\alpha = 0.05$, what is your conclusion? Would your conclusion change at the 1% significance level?

42. **FILE** ***Beverage.*** Fizzco, a beverage manufacturing company, is interested in determining whether the standard deviation of their dispensing process has changed from a required level of 5 milliliters. They have taken a random sample of 36 bottles and have measured the amount of beverage dispensed into each bottle (in milliliters); refer to the data in the accompanying file.
    a. Construct the 95% confidence interval for the population standard deviation. Assume the amount of beverage dispensed follows a normal distribution.
    b. At the 5% significance level, can we conclude that the standard deviation of the amount of beverage dispensed differs from the required level of 5 milliliters?

43. John Daum and Chris Yin are star swimmers at a local college. They are preparing to compete at the NCAA Division II national championship meet, where they both have a good shot at earning a medal in the men's 100-meter freestyle event. The coach feels that Chris is not as consistent as John, even though they clock about the same average time. In order to determine if the coach's concern is valid, you clock their time in the last 20 runs and compute a standard deviation of 0.85 seconds for John and 1.20 seconds for Chris. It is fair to assume that clock time is normally distributed for both John and Chris.
    a. Specify the hypotheses to test if the variance of time for John is smaller than that of Chris.
    b. Carry out the test at the 10% level of significance.
    c. Who has a better likelihood of breaking the record at the meet? Explain.

44. **FILE** ***Pizza.*** Roberto Esposito owns two pizza delivery restaurants, one on the east side of campus and the other on the west side. He tells one of his employees, who studies business, that he has noticed that the variation of pizza deliveries is lower on the east side of the campus than on the west side. She wonders whether the owner's hunch is real or due to chance. She decides to bring her knowledge of statistics to use by recording the number of pizza deliveries on weekdays. The accompanying table shows shows a portion of the data.

East	West
206	229
216	176
⋮	⋮
221	178

At the 5% level of significance, test the owner's hunch. Provide the details.

45. At BurgerJoint, consistency in product and service is the new motto. Accordingly, management has invested in an automated French-fry dispenser to replace the manual dispensing method. The goal is to standardize the number of fries provided. The accompanying table shows the number of fries dispensed in a large-sized container based on samples of 10 orders before and after the process change. Assume these samples were drawn randomly and independently from normally distributed populations.

Manual	27	39	29	31	30	37	41	29	38	31
Automated	30	35	37	38	34	35	35	32	35	32

    a. State the hypotheses to test whether the variance of the new automated dispensing method is lower than the previous manual method.
    b. Calculate the value of the test statistic and the p-value.
    c. What is the conclusion at the 1% significance level?

46. **FILE** ***Safety_Stock.*** An automotive parts distributor wants to standardize its safety stock level

for two parts, A and B. ("Safety stock" is the excess inventory carried above the expected demand level to provide protection against demand variability.) Consequently, the distributor has randomly sampled daily demand for each part over the past 30 days.

a. State the null and alternative hypotheses to test if the variances of the daily demand values for the two parts are different.
b. Calculate the value of the test statistic and the p-value. Assume demand is normally distributed.
c. Make a conclusion at the 5% significance level.

47. FILE ***Wait_Times.*** Barbara Dwyer, the manager at Lux Hotel, makes every effort to ensure that customers attempting to make phone reservations do not have to wait too long to speak with a reservation specialist. Since the hotel accepts phone reservations 24 hours a day, Barbara is especially interested in maintaining consistency in service. Barbara wants to determine if the variance of wait time in the early morning shift (12:00 am – 6:00 am) differs from that in the late morning shift (6:00 am – 12:00 pm). She uses independently drawn samples of wait time for phone reservations for both shifts for the analysis; a portion of the data is shown in the accompanying table. Assume that wait times are normally distributed.

Early	Late
67	98
48	100
⋮	⋮
69	106

a. Specify the hypotheses to test if the variance of wait time in the early morning shift differs from that in the late morning shift.
b. At the 1% significance level, what is your conclusion?

APPENDIX 11.1 Guidelines for Other Software Packages

The following section provides brief commands for Minitab and JMP; SPSS does not provide applications suitable to this chapter. Import the specified data file into the relevant software spreadsheet prior to following the commands.

Minitab

Confidence Interval for σ^2

Growth_Value

(Replicating Example 11.2) From the menu, choose **Stat > Basic Statistics > 1 Variance.** Choose **One or more samples, each in a column.** Select Growth and Value. Choose **Options.** Enter 95.0 for **Confidence Interval.**

Testing σ^2

(Replicating Example 11.4) From the menu, choose **Stat > Basic Statistics > 1 Variance.** Choose **One or more samples, each in a column**. Select Value. Select **Perform hypothesis test,** select **Hypothesized variance,** and enter the value 225. Choose **Options**. Select "Variance ≠ hypothesized variance."

Confidence Interval for σ_1^2/σ_2^2

(Replicating Example 11.6) From the menu, choose **Stat > Basic Statistics > 2 Variances.** Choose **Sample variances,** and under **Sample 1,** enter 36 for **Sample size** and 566.41 for **Variance.** Under **Sample 2,** enter 36 for **Sample size** and 323.25 for **Variance.** Choose **Options.** Enter 95.0 for **Confidence Interval.**

Testing σ_1^2/σ_2^2

(Replicating Example 11.8) From the menu, choose **Stat > Basic Statistics > 2 Variances.** Choose **Sample standard deviations,** and under **Sample 1,** enter 36 for **Sample size** and 23.7993 for **Standard deviation.** Under **Sample 2,** enter 36 for **Sample size** and 17.9792 for **Standard deviation.** Choose **Options.** Select "Ratio > hypothesized ratio."

JMP

Confidence Interval for σ^2

Growth_Value

A. (Replicating Example 11.2) From the menu, choose **Analyze > Distribution.** Drag Growth and Value to the **Y, Columns** box.

B. Click the red triangle in the output window next to Growth and Value, and hover over **Confidence Interval** and select 0.95. Note that JMP only provides confidence interval for σ.

Testing σ^2

A. (Replicating Example 11.4) From the menu, choose **Analyze > Distribution.** Drag Value to the **Y, Columns** box.

B. Click the red triangle in the output window next to Value, and select **Test Std Dev.** After **Specify Hypothesized Standard Deviation,** enter 15.

12 Chi-Square Tests

LEARNING OBJECTIVES

After reading this chapter you should be able to:

LO **12.1** **Conduct a goodness-of-fit test for a multinomial experiment.**

LO **12.2** **Conduct a test for independence.**

LO **12.3** **Conduct a goodness-of-fit test for normality.**

LO **12.4** **Conduct the Jarque-Bera test.**

In this chapter, we focus on the χ^2 (chi-square) distribution to develop statistical tests that compare observed data with what we would expect from a population with a specific distribution. A goodness-of-fit test is commonly used with a frequency distribution representing sample data of a categorical variable. For instance, we may want to substantiate a claim that market shares in the automotive industry have changed dramatically over the past 10 years. Whereas a goodness-of-fit test focuses on a single categorical variable, a test for independence is used to compare two categorical variables. For example, we may want to determine whether a person's sex influences his/her purchase of a product.

We extend the goodness-of-fit test to contest the assumption that sample data are drawn from a normal population. Since we use the normal distribution with a numerical variable, we first convert the raw data into a frequency distribution. Finally, we introduce the Jarque-Bera test, which allows us to test for normality using the data in their raw form.

Shutterstock

INTRODUCTORY CASE

Sportswear Brands

In the introductory case to Chapter 4, Janet Williams, a manager at 24/7 Fitness Center, wishes to develop a data-driven strategy for selecting which new open house attendees to contact. From 400 past open house attendees, she knows the enrollment outcome (Enroll or Not Enroll) of a follow-up phone call regarding a club membership. In addition, she has information on the age of attendees in years, where age is binned into groups Under 30, Between 30 and 50, and Over 50.

Janet uses the data to construct a contingency table, shown in Table 12.1, that is cross-classified by enrollment outcome and age group. A cursory look at the relevant empirical probabilities concerning age and enrollment seems to suggests that the probability of enrollment depends on the age of the attendees. Before she uses this information to identify individual open house attendees who are likely to purchase a gym membership, Janet wants to ensure that the results are backed by a thorough statistical analysis.

TABLE 12.1 Enrollment and Age Frequencies of Attendees

	Age Group		
Enrollment Outcome	**Under 30 (*U*)**	**Between 30 and 50 (*B*)**	**Over 50 (*O*)**
Enroll (*E*)	24	72	44
Not Enroll (*N*)	84	88	88

Janet wants to use the above sample information to

1. Determine whether the two variables (Age Group and Enrollment Outcome) are related at the 5% significance level.
2. Discuss how the findings from the test for independence can be used.

A synopsis of this case will be provided in Section 12.2.

12.1 GOODNESS-OF-FIT TEST FOR A MULTINOMIAL EXPERIMENT

LO 12.1

Conduct a goodness-of-fit test for a multinomial experiment.

In Chapter 10, we compared the difference between two population proportions. Here we extend the analysis to test if two or more population proportions differ from each other or any predetermined (hypothesized) set of values. There are many instances where we may want to make inferences of this type. For instance, in a heavily concentrated industry consisting of four firms, we may want to determine whether market shares differ between the firms. Or, in a political contest, we may want to contest the prediction that Candidates A, B, and C will receive 70%, 20%, and 10% of the vote, respectively. Before conducting a test of this type, we must first ensure that the random experiment satisfies the conditions of a **multinomial experiment,** which is simply a generalization of the Bernoulli process first introduced in Chapter 5.

Recall that a Bernoulli process, also referred to as a binomial experiment, is a series of n independent and identical trials of an experiment, where each trial has only two possible outcomes, conventionally labeled "success" and "failure." For the binomial experiment, we generally denote the probability of success as p and the probability of failure as $1 - p$. Alternatively, we could let p_1 and p_2 represent these probabilities, where $p_1 + p_2 = 1$. Now let us assume that the number of outcomes per trial is k where $k \geq 2$.

A MULTINOMIAL EXPERIMENT

A multinomial experiment consists of a series of n independent and identical trials, such that for each trial:

- There are k possible outcomes or categories.
- The probability p_i associated with the ith category remains the same.
- The sum of the probabilities is one; that is, $p_1 + p_2 + \cdots + p_k = 1$.

Note that when $k = 2$, the multinomial experiment specializes to a binomial experiment.

Numerous experiments fit the conditions of a multinomial experiment. For instance,

- As compared to the previous day, a stockbroker records whether the price of a stock rises, falls, or stays the same. This example has three possible categories ($k = 3$).
- A consumer rates service at a restaurant as excellent, good, fair, or poor ($k = 4$).
- The admissions office records which of the six business concentrations a student picks ($k = 6$).

When setting up the competing hypotheses for a multinomial experiment, we have essentially two choices. We can set all population proportions equal to the same specific value or, equivalently, equal to one another. For instance, if we want to judge on the basis of sample data whether the proportion of voters who favor four different candidates is not the same, the competing hypotheses would take the following form:

$$H_0\text{: } p_1 = p_2 = p_3 = p_4 = 0.25$$
$$H_A\text{: Not all population proportions are equal to 0.25.}$$

Note that the hypothesized value under the null hypothesis is 0.25 because the population proportions must sum to one. We can also set each population proportion equal to a different predetermined (hypothesized) value. Suppose we want to contest the prediction that 40% of the voters favor Candidate 1, 30% favor Candidate 2, 20% favor Candidate 3, and 10% favor Candidate 4. The competing hypotheses are formulated as

H_0: $p_1 = 0.40$, $p_2 = 0.30$, $p_3 = 0.20$, and $p_4 = 0.10$
H_A: Not all population proportions equal their hypothesized values.

When conducting a test, we take a random sample and determine whether the sample proportions are close enough to the hypothesized population proportions. For this reason, this type of test is called a **goodness-of-fit test.** Under the usual assumption that the null hypothesis is true, we derive the expected frequencies of the categories in a multinomial experiment and compare them with observed frequencies. The objective is to determine whether we can reject the null hypothesis in favor of the alternative hypothesis. To see how to conduct a goodness-of-fit test, consider the following example.

One year ago, the management at a restaurant chain surveyed its patrons to determine whether changes should be made to the menu. One question on the survey asked patrons to rate the quality of the restaurant's entrées. The percentages of the patrons responding Excellent, Good, Fair, or Poor are listed in the following table:

Excellent	Good	Fair	Poor
15%	30%	45%	10%

Based on responses to the overall survey, management decided to revamp the menu. Recently, the same question concerning the quality of entrées was asked of a random sample of 250 patrons. Their responses are shown below:

Excellent	Good	Fair	Poor
46	83	105	16

At the 5% significance level, we want to determine whether there has been any change in the population proportions calculated one year ago.

Since we want to determine whether the responses of the 250 patrons are inconsistent with the earlier proportions, we let the earlier population proportions denote the hypothesized proportions for the test. Thus, denote p_1, p_2, p_3, and p_4 as the population proportions of those who responded Excellent, Good, Fair, or Poor, respectively, and construct the following competing hypotheses.

H_0: $p_1 = 0.15$, $p_2 = 0.30$, $p_3 = 0.45$, and $p_4 = 0.10$
H_A: Not all population proportions equal their hypothesized values.

The first step in calculating the value of the test statistic is to calculate the expected frequency for each category. That is, we need to estimate the frequencies that we would expect to get if the null hypothesis is true. In general, in order to calculate the expected frequency e_i for category i, we multiply the sample size n by the respective hypothesized value of the population proportion p_i. For example, consider the category Excellent. If H_0 is true, then we expect that 15% ($p_1 = 0.15$) of 250 patrons will find the quality of entrées to be excellent. Therefore, the expected frequency of Excellent responses is 37.5 ($= 250 \times 0.15$), whereas the corresponding observed frequency is 46. Expected frequencies for other responses are found similarly.

When computing the value of the test statistic, we compare expected frequencies with observed frequencies. The test statistic follows the χ^2 (chi-square) distribution that was discussed in Chapter 11. Because the distribution is characterized by a family of distributions, where each distribution depends on its particular degrees of freedom, *df*, it is common to make reference to it using the notation χ^2_{df}.

TEST STATISTIC FOR GOODNESS-OF-FIT TEST

For a multinomial experiment with k categories, the value of the test statistic is calculated as

$$\chi^2_{df} = \Sigma \frac{(o_i - e_i)^2}{e_i},$$

where $df = k - 1$, o_i is the observed frequency of the ith category, $e_i = np_i$ is the expected frequency of the ith category, and n is the number of observations.

Note: The test is valid when the expected frequencies for each category are five or more.

Table 12.2 shows the expected frequency e_i for each category. The condition that each expected frequency e_i must equal five or more is satisfied here. As we will see shortly, sometimes it is necessary to combine observations from two or more categories to achieve this result.

TABLE 12.2 Calculation of Expected Frequency for Restaurant Example

	Hypothesized Proportion, p_i	Expected Frequency, $e_i = np_i$
Excellent	0.15	$250 \times 0.15 = 37.5$
Good	0.30	$250 \times 0.30 = 75.0$
Fair	0.45	$250 \times 0.45 = 112.5$
Poor	0.10	$250 \times 0.10 = 25.0$
		$\Sigma e_i = 250$

As a check on the calculations, the sum of the expected frequencies Σe_i must equal the sample size n, which in this example equals 250. Once the expected frequencies are estimated, we are ready to calculate the value of the test statistic.

The χ^2_{df} statistic measures how much the observed frequencies deviate from the expected frequencies. In particular, χ^2_{df} is computed as the sum of the standardized squared deviations. The smallest value that χ^2_{df} can assume is zero—this occurs when each observed frequency equals its expected frequency. Rejection of the null hypothesis occurs when χ^2_{df} is significantly greater than zero. As a result, these tests of hypotheses regarding multiple population proportions ($p_1, p_2, p_3, \ldots$) are always implemented as right-tailed tests. However, since the alternative hypothesis states that not all population proportions equal their hypothesized values, rejection of the null hypothesis does not indicate which proportions differ from these values.

In the Restaurant example, there are four categories ($k = 4$), so $df = k - 1 = 3$. The value of the test statistic is calculated as

$$\chi^2_{df} = \chi^2_3 = \Sigma \frac{(o_i - e_i)^2}{e_i}$$

$$= \frac{(46 - 37.5)^2}{37.5} + \frac{(83 - 75)^2}{75} + \frac{(105 - 112.5)^2}{112.5} + \frac{(16 - 25)^2}{25}$$

$$= 6.520.$$

Since a goodness-of-fit test is a right-tailed test, we calculate the p-value as $P(\chi^2_3 \geq 6.520)$. We show a portion of the χ^2 table from Appendix B in Table 12.3.

For $df = 3$, we see that 6.520 lies between the values 6.251 and 7.815, implying that the p-value is between 0.05 and 0.10. As explained in Chapter 11, we can use Excel's CHISQ.DIST.RT function or R's pchisq function to find the exact p-value. In Excel, we enter `=CHISQ.DIST.RT(6.520, 3)`, and in R, we enter `pchisq(6.520, 3, lower.tail=FALSE)`. Both software return a p-value of 0.089. Because the p-value is greater than 0.05, we do not reject H_0. We cannot conclude that the proportions differ from the ones from one year ago at the 5% significance level. Management may find this news disappointing if the

TABLE 12.3 Portion of the χ^2 table

	Area in Upper Tail, α									
df	0.995	0.990	0.975	0.950	0.900	0.100	0.050	0.025	0.010	0.005
1	0.000	0.000	0.001	0.004	0.016	2.706	3.841	5.024	6.635	7.879
2	0.010	0.020	0.051	0.103	0.211	4.605	5.991	7.378	9.210	10.597
3	0.072	0.115	0.216	0.352	0.584	6.251	7.815	9.348	11.345	12.838

goal of the menu change was to improve customer satisfaction. Responses to other questions on the survey may shed more light on whether the goals of the menu change met or fell short of expectations.

As mentioned earlier, the chi-square test is valid when the expected frequencies for each category are five or more. Sometimes it is necessary to combine two or more categories to achieve this result, as illustrated in Example 12.1.

EXAMPLE 12.1

Table 12.4 lists the market shares in 2019 for the five firms that manufacture a particular product. A marketing analyst wonders whether the market shares have changed since 2019. He surveys 200 customers. The last column of Table 12.4 shows the number of customers who recently purchased the product at each firm.

TABLE 12.4 Market Share of Five Firms

Firm	Market_Share	Recent_Customers
1	0.40	70
2	0.32	60
3	0.24	54
4	0.02	10
5	0.02	6

a. Specify the competing hypotheses to test whether the market shares have changed since 2019.

b. Calculate the value of the test statistic.

c. Use $a = 0.05$ to determine if the market shares have changed since 2019.

SOLUTION:

a. Let p_i denote the market share for the *i*th firm. In order to test whether the market shares have changed since 2019, we *initially* set up the competing hypotheses as

$$H_0: p_1 = 0.40, p_2 = 0.32, p_3 = 0.24, p_4 = 0.02, \text{ and } p_5 = 0.02$$
$$H_A: \text{Not all market shares equal their hypothesized values.}$$

b. The value of the test statistic is calculated as $\chi^2_{df} = \Sigma\frac{(o_i - e_i)^2}{e_i}$. The last column of Table 12.4 shows each firm's observed frequency o_i. Before applying the formula, we first calculate each firm's expected frequency e_i:

$$\begin{aligned} e_1 &= 200 \times 0.04 = 80 \\ e_2 &= 200 \times 0.32 = 64 \\ e_3 &= 200 \times 0.24 = 48 \\ \left.\begin{aligned} e_4 &= 200 \times 0.02 = 4 \\ e_5 &= 200 \times 0.02 = 4 \end{aligned}\right\} & 8 \end{aligned}$$

We note that the expected frequencies for firms 4 and 5 are less than five. For the test to be valid, the expected frequencies in each category must be five or more. In order to achieve this result, we combine the expected frequencies for firms 4 and 5 to obtain a combined frequency of eight ($e_4 + e_5 = 8$). We could have made other combinations, say e_4 with e_1 and e_5 with e_2, but we preferred to maintain a category for the less dominant firms. Table 12.15 shows the reconfigured market shares. For ease of exposition, we denote the combination of firms 4 and 5 as simply firm 4.

SHARE

TABLE 12.5 Reconfigured Market Shares

Firm	Market_Share	Recent_Customers
1	0.40	70
2	0.32	60
3	0.24	54
4	0.04	16

After making this combination, we now respecify the competing hypotheses as

H_0: $p_1 = 0.40, p_2 = 0.32, p_3 = 0.24$, and $p_4 = 0.04$
H_A: Not all market shares equal their hypothesized values.

With $df = k - 1 = 3$, we calculate the value of the test statistic as

$$\chi_3^2 = \Sigma\frac{(o_i - e_i)^2}{e_i} = \frac{(70-80)^2}{80} + \frac{(60-64)^2}{64} + \frac{(54-48)^2}{48} + \frac{(16-8)^2}{8}$$
$$= 10.250.$$

c. We calculate the p-value as $P(\chi_3^2 \geq 10.250)$. From Table 12.3, we see that 10.520 lies between the values 9.348 and 11.345, implying that the p-value is between 0.01 and 0.025. In order to find the exact p-value in Excel, we enter `=CHISQ.DIST.RT(10.250, 3)`; and in R, we enter `pchisq(10.250, 3, lower.tail=FALSE)`. Both software return a p-value of 0.017. Since the p-value is less than 0.05, we reject H_0. At the 5% significance level, we conclude that market shares have changed.

As mentioned earlier, one limitation of this type of chi-square test is that we cannot tell which proportions differ from their hypothesized values. However, given the divergence between the observed and expected frequencies for the less dominant firms, it appears that they may be making some headway in this industry. Further analysis is needed to determine if this is the case.

Using R to Conduct a Goodness-of-Fit Test

Unfortunately, the current version of Excel does not provide a simple function to implement a goodness-of-fit test. However, we can use R's **chisq.test** function and easily replicate the results from Example 12.1. We follow these steps.

a. Import the ***Share*** data file into a data frame (table) and label it myData.

b. We use R's **chisq.test** function to calculate the value of the test statistic and the p-value. Within the **chisq.test** function, we use the option p to indicate the location of the hypothesized proportions. Enter:

```
> chisq.test(myData$Recent_Customers, p = myData$Market_Share)
```

And R returns:

```
Chi-squared test for given probabilities
data:  myData$Recent_Customers
X-squared = 10.25, df = 3, p-value = 0.01656
```

Note that the test statistic and the p-value (in boldface) match those from Example 12.1.

EXERCISES 12.1

Mechanics

1. Consider a multinomial experiment with $n = 250$ and $k = 4$. The null hypothesis to be tested is H_0: $p_1 = p_2 = p_3 = p_4 = 0.25$. The observed frequencies resulting from the experiment are:

Category	1	2	3	4
Frequency	70	42	72	66

   a. Specify the alternative hypothesis.
   b. Calculate the value of the test statistic and the p-value.
   c. At the 5% significance level, what is the conclusion to the hypothesis test?

2. Consider a multinomial experiment with $n = 400$ and $k = 3$. The null hypothesis is H_0: $p_1 = 0.60$, $p_2 = 0.25$, and $p_3 = 0.15$. The observed frequencies resulting from the experiment are:

Category	1	2	3
Frequency	250	94	56

   a. Specify the alternative hypothesis.
   b. Calculate the value of the test statistic and the p-value.
   c. At the 5% significance level, what is the conclusion to the hypothesis test?

3. A multinomial experiment produced the following results:

Category	1	2	3	4	5
Frequency	57	63	70	55	55

   Can we conclude at the 1% significance level that not all population proportions are equal to 0.20?

4. A multinomial experiment produced the following results:

Category	1	2	3
Frequency	128	87	185

   At the 1% significance level, can we reject H_0: $p_1 = 0.30$, $p_2 = 0.20$, and $p_3 = 0.50$?

Applications

5. You suspect that an unscrupulous employee at a casino has tampered with a die; that is, he is using a loaded die. In order to test this claim, you roll the die 200 times and obtain the following frequencies:

Category	1	2	3	4	5	6
Frequency	40	35	33	30	33	29

   a. Specify the null and alternative hypotheses in order to test your claim.
   b. Calculate the value of the test statistic and the p-value.
   c. At the 10% significance level, can you conclude that the die is loaded?

6. A study found that fewer than half of employers who hired fresh college graduates last academic year plan to definitely do so again. Suppose the hiring intentions of the respondents were as follows:

Definitely Hire	Likely to Hire	Hire Uncertain	Will not Hire
37%	17%	28%	18%

   Six months later, a sample of 500 employers were asked their hiring intentions and gave the following responses:

Definitely Hire	Likely to Hire	Hire Uncertain	Will not Hire
170	100	120	110

   a. Specify the competing hypotheses to test whether the proportions from the initial study have changed.
   b. Calculate the value of the test statistic and the p-value.
   c. At the 5% significance level, what is the conclusion to the hypothesis test? Interpret your results.

7. A rent-to-own (RTO) agreement appeals to low-income and financially distressed consumers. It allows immediate access to merchandise, and by making all payments, the consumer acquires the merchandise. At the same time, goods can be returned at any point without penalty. Suppose a recent study documents that 65% of RTO contracts are returned, 30% are purchased, and the remaining 5% default. In order to test the validity of this study, an RTO researcher looks at the transaction data of 420 RTO contracts, of which 283 are returned, 109 are purchased, and the rest defaulted.
   a. Set up the competing hypothesis to test whether the return, purchase, and default probabilities of RTO contracts differ from 0.65, 0.30, and 0.05, respectively.
   b. Compute the value of the test statistic.
   c. Conduct the test at the 5% level of significance, and interpret the test results.

8. Despite Zimbabwe's shattered economy, with endemic poverty and widespread political strife and repression, thousands of people from overseas still head there every year. Main attractions include the magnificent Victoria Falls, the ruins of Great Zimbabwe, and herds of roaming wildlife. A tourism director claims that Zimbabwe visitors are equally represented by Europe, North America, and the rest of the world. Records show that of the 380 tourists who recently visited Zimbabwe, 148 were from Europe, 106 were from North America, and 126 were from the rest of the world.
   a. A recent visitor to Zimbabwe believes that the tourism director's claim is wrong. Set up the competing hypotheses to test the visitor's belief.
   b. Conduct the test at the 5% significance level. Do the sample data support the visitor's belief?
9. In 2003, the distribution of the world's people worth $1 million or more was as follows:

Region	Millionaires
Europe	35.7%
North America	31.4%
Asia Pacific	22.9%
Latin America	4.3%
Middle East	4.3%
Africa	1.4%

A recent sample of 500 global millionaires produces the following results:

Region	Number of Millionaires
Europe	153
North America	163
Asia Pacific	139
Latin America	20
Middle East	20
Africa	5

   a. Test whether the distribution of millionaires today is different from the distribution in 2003 at $\alpha = 0.05$.
   b. Would the conclusion change if we tested it at $\alpha = 0.10$?
10. A couple of years ago, a survey found that 38% of American drivers favored U.S. cars, while 33% preferred Asian brands, with the remaining 29% going for other foreign cars. A researcher wonders whether today's preferences for cars have changed. He surveys 200 Americans and finds that the number of respondents who prefer American, Asian, and other foreign cars are 66, 70, and 64, respectively. At the 5% significance level, can the researcher conclude that today's preferences have changed?
11. The quality department at an electronics company has noted that, historically, 92% of the units of a specific product pass a test operation, 6% fail the test but are able to be repaired, and 2% fail the test and need to be scrapped. Due to recent process improvements, the quality department would like to test if the rates have changed. A recent sample of 500 parts revealed that 475 parts passed the test, 18 parts failed the test but were repairable, and 7 parts failed the test and were scrapped.
   a. State the null and alternative hypotheses to test if the current proportions are different than the historical proportions.
   b. Calculate the value of the test statistic and the p-value.
   c. At the 5% significance level, what is your conclusion? Would your conclusion change at the 1% significance level?
12. An agricultural grain company processes and packages various grains purchased from farmers. A high-volume conveyor line contains four chutes at the end, each of which is designed to receive and dispense equal proportions of grain into bags. Each bag is then stamped with a date code and the number of the chute from which it came. If the chute output proportions are not relatively equal, then a bottleneck effect is created upstream and the conveyor cannot function at peak output. Recently, a series of repairs and modifications have led management to question whether the grains still are being equally distributed among the chutes. Packaging records from 800 bags yesterday indicate that 220 bags came from Chute 1, 188 bags from Chute 2, 218 bags from Chute 3, and 174 bags from Chute 4.
   a. State the null and alternative hypotheses to test if the proportion of bags filled by any of the chutes is different from 0.25.
   b. Calculate the value of the test statistic and the p-value.
   c. What is your conclusion at the 10% significance level? Would your conclusion change at the 5% significance level?

LO 12.2

12.2 CHI-SQUARE TEST FOR INDEPENDENCE

Conduct a test for independence.

In this section, we conduct a **test for independence**—also called a **chi-square test of a contingency table**—to assess the relationship between two categorical variables. Many examples of the use of this test arise, especially in marketing, biomedical research, and courts of law. For instance, a retailer may be trying to determine whether there is a relationship between the age of its clientele and where it chooses to advertise. Doctors might want to investigate whether or not the new vaccine is equally effective for people of all age groups. Or one party in a discrimination lawsuit may be trying to show that a person's sex and promotion are related. All of these examples lend themselves to applications of the hypothesis test discussed in this section.

Recall from Chapters 2 and 4 that a contingency table shows the frequencies for two categorical variables, x and y, where each cell represents a mutually exclusive combination of the pair of x and y values. In the introductory case study, we are presented with a contingency table cross-classified by the variables Age Group and Enrollment Outcome. Specifically, we want to determine whether the likelihood of gym enrollment depends on the age of open house attendees. We will conduct this test at the 5% significance level.

In general, the competing hypotheses for a statistical test for independence are formulated such that rejecting the null hypothesis leads to the conclusion that the two categorical variables are dependent. Formally,

H_0: The two categorical variables are independent.

H_A: The two categorical variables are dependent.

In the Gym example, the criteria upon which we classify the data are Age Group and Enrollment Outcome; thus, we write the competing hypotheses as

H_0: Age Group and Enrollment Outcome are independent.

H_A: Age Group and Enrollment Outcome are dependent.

Table 12.6 reproduces Table 12.1 of the introductory case. The variable Enrollment Outcome has two possible categories: (1) Enroll (E) and (2) Not Enroll (N). The variable Age Group has three possible categories: (1) Under 30 (U), (2) Between 30 and 50 (B), and (3) Over 50 (O). Each cell in this table represents an observed frequency o_{ij}, where the subscript ij refers to the ith row and the jth column. For example, o_{13} refers to the cell in the first row and the third column. Here, $o_{13} = 44$, or, equivalently, there are 44 open house attendees who are over 50 years of age and enrolled in the gym.

TABLE 12.6 Enrollment and Age Frequencies of Attendees

	Age Group		
Enrollment Outcome	Under 30 (*U*)	Between 30 and 50 (*B*)	Over 50 (*O*)
Enroll (*E*)	24	72	44
Not Enroll (*N*)	84	88	88

We will use the independence assumption postulated under the null hypothesis to derive an expected frequency for each cell from the sample data. In other words, we first find expected frequencies as if no relationship exists between age and enrollment. Then we compare these expected frequencies with the observed frequencies to compute the value of the test statistic.

Calculating Expected Frequencies

For ease of exposition, we let events E and N represent "Enroll" and "Not Enroll", respectively. Similarly, U, B and O represent "Under 30", "Between 30 and 50", and "Over 50", respectively. We then sum the frequencies for each column and row. For instance, the sum of the frequencies for Event E is 140; this is obtained by summing the values in row E: 24, 72, and 44. Totals for the other rows and columns are shown in Table 12.7.

TABLE 12.7 Row and Column Totals

	Age Group			
Enrollment Outcome	*U*	*B*	*O*	Row Total
E	e_{11}	e_{12}	e_{13}	140
N	e_{21}	e_{22}	e_{23}	260
Column Total	108	160	132	400

Our goal is to calculate the expected frequency e_{ij} for each cell, where the subscript ij refers to the ith row and the jth column. Thus, e_{13} refers to the cell in the first row and the third column, or the expected number of open house attendees who are over 50 years of age and enrolled in the gym.

Before we can arrive at the expected frequencies, we first calculate marginal row probabilities (the proportion of open house attendees who enrolled in the gym and those who did not enroll in the gym) and marginal column probabilities (the proportion of open house attendees who are under 30, between 30 and 50, and over 50 years of age). We calculate a marginal row (column) probability by dividing the row (column) sum by the total sample size:

Marginal Row Probabilities:

$$P(E) = \frac{140}{400} \text{ and } P(N) = \frac{260}{400}$$

Marginal Column Probabilities:

$$P(U) = \frac{108}{400}, \ P(B) = \frac{160}{400}, \text{ and } P(O) = \frac{132}{400}$$

We can now calculate each cell probability by applying the multiplication rule for independent events from Chapter 4. That is, if two events are independent, say events E and U (our assumption under the null hypothesis), then their joint probability is

$$P(E \cap U) = P(E)P(U) = \left(\frac{140}{400}\right)\left(\frac{108}{400}\right) = 0.0945.$$

Multiplying this joint probability by the sample size yields the expected frequency for e_{11}; that is, the expected number of customers who are under 30 years of age and enroll in the gym is

$$e_{11} = 400 \times 0.0945 = 37.80.$$

CALCULATING THE EXPECTED FREQUENCY FOR EACH CELL IN A CONTINGENCY TABLE

The expected frequency e_{ij} for each cell in a contingency table is calculated as

$$e_{ij} = \frac{(\text{Row } i \text{ total})(\text{Column } j \text{ total})}{\text{Sample Size}},$$

where the subscript ij refers to the ith row and the jth column of the contingency table.

Applying the formula, we calculate all expected frequencies as

$$e_{11} = \frac{(140)(108)}{400} = 37.80 \qquad e_{12} = \frac{(140)(160)}{400} = 56.00 \qquad e_{13} = \frac{(140)(132)}{400} = 46.20$$

$$e_{21} = \frac{(260)(108)}{400} = 70.20 \qquad e_{22} = \frac{(260)(160)}{400} = 104.00 \qquad e_{23} = \frac{(260)(132)}{400} = 85.80$$

Table 12.8 shows the expected frequency e_{ij} for each cell. In order to satisfy subsequent assumptions, each expected frequency e_{ij} *must equal five or more*. This condition is satisfied here. As we saw in Example 12.1, it may be necessary to combine two or more rows or columns to achieve this result in other applications.

TABLE 12.8 Expected Frequencies for Contingency Table

Enrollment Outcome	Age Group			Row Total
	U	*B*	*O*	
E	37.80	56.00	46.20	140
N	70.20	104.00	85.80	260
Column Total	108	160	132	400

When conducting a test for independence, we calculate the value of the chi-square test statistic χ^2_{df}. Analogous to the discussion in Section 12.1, χ^2_{df} measures how much the observed frequencies deviate from the expected frequencies. The smallest value that χ^2_{df} can assume is zero—this occurs when each observed frequency equals its expected frequency. Thus, a test for independence is also implemented as a *right-tailed test.*

TEST STATISTIC FOR A TEST FOR INDEPENDENCE

For a test for independence applied to a contingency table with *r* rows and *c* columns, the value of the test statistic is calculated as

$$\chi^2_{df} = \sum_i \sum_j \frac{(o_{ij} - e_{ij})^2}{e_{ij}},$$

where $df = (r-1)(c-1)$, and o_{ij} and e_{ij} are the observed frequency and the expected frequency, respectively, for each cell in a contingency table.

Note: This test is valid when the expected frequencies for each cell are five or more.

With two rows and three columns in the contingency table, degrees of freedom are calculated as $df = (r-1)(c-1) = (2-1)(3-1) = 2$. We apply the formula to compute the value of the test statistic as

$$\begin{aligned}\chi^2_2 &= \frac{(24-37.80)^2}{37.80} + \frac{(72-56.00)^2}{56.00} + \frac{(44-46.20)^2}{46.20} \\ &+ \frac{(84-70.20)^2}{70.20} + \frac{(88-104.00)^2}{104.00} + \frac{(88-85.80)^2}{85.80} \\ &= 14.945.\end{aligned}$$

For $df = 2$, we calculate the *p*-value as $P(\chi^2_2 \geq 14.945)$. Referring to Table 12.3, we see that 14.945 is greater than 10.597, implying that the *p*-value is less than 0.005. In order to find the *p*-value in Excel, we enter `=CHISQ.DIST.RT(14.945, 2)`, and in R, we enter `pchisq(14.945, 2, lower.tail=FALSE)`. Both software return a *p*-value of 0.001. Because the *p*-value is less than 0.05, we reject H_0. At the 5% significance level, we conclude that the two categorical variables are dependent; that is, there is a relationship between the age of an open house attendee and the enrollment outcome.

SYNOPSIS OF INTRODUCTORY CASE

Halfpoint/Shutterstock

Janet Williams, a manager at 24/7 Fitness Center, analyzes data from the gym's past open house. She wants to gain a better insight into which attendees are likely to purchase a gym membership after attending this event.

After careful analysis of the contingency table representing frequencies for age groups and enrollment outcome of attendees, several interesting observations are made. From a sample of 400 past attendees, 35% ended up enrolling in the gym. Further inspection revealed that 45% of the attendees in the 30 to 50 age group enrolled in the gym compared to only 22% for under 30 years old and 33% for over 50 years old. While these results seem to indicate that the probability of enrollment depends on the age of the attendees, Janet wants to ensure that the results are backed by a thorough statistical analysis.

A formal test for independence is conducted to determine if there is a relationship between the age of an attendee and his/her decision to enroll in the gym. At the 5% significance level, it is concluded that the variables, age group and enrollment outcome, are dependent; that is, there is a statistically significant relationship between the two. Janet uses this information to identify individual open house attendees who are likely to purchase a gym membership.

EXAMPLE 12.2

In general, Latinx and Caucasians use social media networks equally, but there are some differences in their preferences for specific social media sites (www.pewresearch.org, February 5, 2015). In particular, Instagram is more popular among Latinx while Pinterest is more popular among Caucasians. Kate Dawson, a junior in college, decides to test if similar differences exist among students on her campus. She collects data on 400 students cross-classified by Race (Latinx versus Caucasians) and Social Media Preference (Instagram versus Pinterest). The results are shown in Table 12.9. At the 10% significance level, determine whether the sample data support racial differences in social media preferences.

FILE *Social_Media*

TABLE 12.9 Social Media Preference by Race

	Social Media Preference		
Race	Instagram	Pinterest	Row Total
Latinx	50	60	110
Caucasians	120	170	290
Column Total	170	230	400

SOLUTION: In order to determine whether social media preference depends on race, we specify the competing hypotheses as

H_0: Race and Social Media Preference are independent.

H_A: Race and Social Media Preference are dependent.

The value of the test statistic is calculated as $\chi^2_{df} = \sum_i \sum_j \frac{(o_{ij} - e_{ij})^2}{e_{ij}}$. Table 12.9 provides each cell's observed frequency o_{ij}, so before applying the formula, we first calculate each cell's expected frequency e_{ij}:

$$e_{11} = \frac{(110)(170)}{400} = 46.75 \qquad e_{12} = \frac{(110)(230)}{400} = 63.25$$

$$e_{21} = \frac{(290)(170)}{400} = 123.25 \qquad e_{22} = \frac{(290)(230)}{400} = 166.75$$

With two rows and two columns in the contingency table, degrees of freedom are calculated as $df = (r - 1)(c - 1) = (2 - 1)(2 - 1) = 1$. The value of the test statistic is calculated as

$$\chi^2_1 = \frac{(50 - 46.75)^2}{46.75} + \frac{(60 - 63.25)^2}{63.25} + \frac{(120 - 123.25)^2}{123.25} + \frac{(170 - 166.75)^2}{166.75}$$
$$= 0.2259 + 0.1670 + 0.0857 + 0.0633 = 0.542.$$

In order to find the p-value in Excel, we enter =`CHISQ.DIST.RT(0.542, 1)`, and in R, we enter `pchisq(0.542, 1, lower.tail=FALSE)`. Both software return a p-value of 0.462. Because the p-value is greater than 0.10, we do not reject H_0. At the 10% significance level, the sample data do not support racial differences in social media preferences.

Using R to Conduct a Test for Independence

In addition to being used in a goodness-of-fitness test, R's **chisq.test** function can be used to implement a test for independence. To replicate the results from Example 12.2, we follow these steps.

a. Import the **Social_Media** data file into a data frame (table) and label it myData.

FILE
Social_Media

b. We use R's chisq.test function to calculate the value of the test statistic and the p-value. Within the chisq.test function, we indicate that the relevant data are in columns 2 and 3 of the data frame. In addition, we set correct=FALSE so that a continuity correction is not applied in the calculation of the test statistic. Enter:

```
> chisq.test(myData[, 2:3], correct = FALSE)
```

And R returns:

```
Pearson's Chi-squared test
data:  myData[, 2:3]
X-squared = 0.54198, df = 1, p-value = 0.4616
```

Note that the test statistic and the p-value (in boldface) match those from Example 12.2.

EXERCISES 12.2

Mechanics

13. Given the following contingency table, conduct a test for independence at the 5% significance level.

	Variable A	
Variable B	1	2
1	23	47
2	32	53

14. Given the following contingency table, conduct a test for independence at the 1% significance level.

	Variable A			
Variable B	1	2	3	4
1	120	112	100	110
2	127	115	120	124
3	118	115	110	124

Applications

15. According to an online survey, more than half of IT workers say they have fallen asleep at work. The same is also true for government workers. Assume that the following contingency table is representative of the survey results.

	Job Category	
Slept on the Job?	IT Professional	Government Professional
Yes	155	256
No	145	144

   a. Specify the competing hypotheses to determine whether sleeping on the job is associated with job category.
   b. Calculate the value of the test statistic.
   c. Find the *p*-value.
   d. At the 5% significance level, can you conclude that sleeping on the job depends on job category?

16. A market researcher for an automobile company suspects differences in preferred color between male and female buyers. Advertisements targeted to different groups should take such differences into account, if they exist. The researcher examines the most recent sales information of a particular car that comes in three colors.

	Sex of Automobile Buyer	
Color	Male	Female
Silver	470	280
Black	535	285
Red	495	350

   a. Specify the competing hypotheses to determine whether color preference depends on the automobile buyer's sex.
   b. Calculate the value of the test statistic and the *p*-value.
   c. Does your conclusion suggest that the company should target advertisements differently for males versus females? Explain.

17. The following sample data reflect shipments received by a large firm from three different vendors and the quality of those shipments.

Vendor	Defective	Acceptable
1	14	112
2	10	70
3	22	150

   a. Specify the competing hypotheses to determine whether quality is associated with the source of the shipments.
   b. Conduct the test at the 1% significance level.
   c. Should the firm be concerned about the source of the shipments? Explain.

18. A marketing agency would like to determine if there is a relationship between union membership and type of vehicle owned (domestic or foreign brand). The goal is to develop targeted advertising campaigns for particular vehicle brands likely to appeal to specific groups of customers. A survey of 500 potential customers revealed the following results.

	Union Member	Not Union Member
Domestic brand	133	147
Foreign brand	67	153

   a. Specify the competing hypotheses to determine whether vehicle brand (domestic, foreign) is associated with union membership.
   b. Conduct the test at the 10% significance level. What is your conclusion?
   c. Is the conclusion reached in part (b) sensitive to the choice of significance level?

19. The quality manager believes there may be a relationship between the experience level of an inspector and whether a product passes or fails inspection. Inspection records were reviewed for 630 units of a particular product, and the number of units which passed and failed inspection was determined based on three inspector experience levels. The results are shown in the following table.

	Experience Level		
Decision	Low (< 2 years)	Medium (2–8 years)	High (> 8 years)
Pass	152	287	103
Fail	16	46	26

   a. Specify the competing hypotheses to determine whether the inspector pass/fail decision depends on experience level.
   b. Calculate the value of the test statistic.
   c. Find the *p*-value.
   d. At the 5% significance level, what is your conclusion? Does your conclusion change at the 1% significance level?

20. Firms routinely conduct surveys to gauge their customer satisfaction levels. The marketing manager of a firm wants to know if the satisfaction level depends on the customer's age. Survey responses are tabulated in the following table.

Age	Very Happy	Somewhat Happy	Not Happy
20 up to 40	23	50	18
40 up to 60	51	38	16
60 and older	19	45	20

   a. Specify the competing hypotheses to test the claim that satisfaction level depends on the age of the customer.
   b. Calculate the value of the test statistic.

c. Find the p-value.
d. At the 1% level of significance, can we infer that satisfaction level of customers is dependent on age?

21. A study by the Massachusetts Community & Banking Council found that black people, and, to a lesser extent, Latinx, remain largely unable to borrow money at the same interest rate as whites (*The Boston Globe,* February 28, 2008). The following contingency table shows representative data for the city of Boston, cross-classified by race and type of interest rate received:

	Type of Interest Rate on Loan	
Race	**High Interest Rate**	**Low Interest Rate**
Black	553	480
Latinx	265	324
White	491	3,701

At the 5% significance level, do the data indicate that the interest rate received on a loan is dependent on race? Provide the details.

22. In a survey of 3,000 Facebook users, the designers looked at why Facebook users break up in a relationship.

Reasons for Breakup	Sex of Respondent	
	Percentage of Men	**Percentage of Women**
Nonapproval	3	4
Distance	21	16
Cheating	18	22
Lost Interest	28	26
Other	30	32

Suppose the survey consisted of 1,800 men and 1,200 women. Use the data to determine whether the reasons for breakup depend on one's sex at the 1% significance level. Provide the details.

23. FILE ***CarCrash.*** The California Highway Patrol (CHP) routinely compiles car crash data in California. The accompanying table shows shows a portion of the data for Santa Clara county. It shows information on the type of car crash (Head-On or Not Head-On) and light (Daylight or Not Daylight).

ID	Crash	Light
1	Not Head-On	Not Daylight
2	Not Head-On	Daylight
⋮	⋮	⋮
290	Not Head-On	Not Daylight

a. Use the data to construct a contingency table.
b. Specify the competing hypotheses to determine whether crash type is related to light.
c. Conduct the test at the 1% significance level and make a conclusion.

24. FILE ***Happiness.*** There have been numerous attempts that relate happiness with income. In a recent survey, 290 individuals were asked to evaluate their state of happiness (Happy or Not Happy) and income (Low, Medium, or High). The accompanying table shows shows a portion of the data.

Individual	Income	State
1	Low	Not Happy
2	Low	Happy
⋮	⋮	⋮
290	High	Happy

a. Use the data to construct a contingency table.
b. Specify the competing hypotheses to determine whether happiness is related to income.
c. Conduct the test at the 5% significance level and make a conclusion.

12.3 CHI-SQUARE TESTS FOR NORMALITY

The goodness-of-fit test for a multinomial experiment can also be used to test a hypothesis that a population has a particular probability distribution. For instance, we can use this test to determine whether the sample data fit the binomial or the Poisson distributions. However, due to its wide applicability, we focus on the normal distribution. We first describe the **goodness-of-fit test for normality.** We then introduce another chi-square test for normality referred to as the Jarque-Bera test.

The Goodness-of-Fit Test for Normality

LO 12.3

Conduct a goodness-of-fit test for normality.

Suppose an economist claims that annual household income in a small Midwestern city is not normally distributed. We will use the representative data (in \$1,000s) in Table 12.10 to test this claim at the 5% significance level.

FILE
Income

TABLE 12.10 Household Income (in \$1,000s)

Household Income
90
15
⋮
58

We first compute the sample mean and the sample standard deviation as

$$\bar{x} = 63.80 \quad \text{and} \quad s = 45.78.$$

For illustration, we use the above mean and standard deviation, rounded to two decimal places. We want to determine whether or not the observations represent a random sample from a population having a normal distribution and, therefore, specify the null and the alternative hypotheses accordingly.

H_0: Income (in \$1,000s) follows a normal distribution with mean \$63.80 and standard deviation \$45.78.

H_A: Income (in \$1,000s) does not follow a normal distribution with mean \$63.80 and standard deviation \$45.78.

The null hypothesis implies that the underlying distribution is normal and that the population mean and the population standard deviation equal their estimates, or, equivalently, $\mu = 63.80$ and $\sigma = 45.78$. As discussed in Section 12.1, the goodness-of-fit test for a multinomial experiment deals with a single population for a categorical variable. Because the normal distribution describes a numerical variable, we need to convert the variable into a categorical format in order to apply the goodness-of-fit test. After computing the sample mean and the sample standard deviation, we divide the observations of the variable into k non-overlapping intervals (categories); in other words, we construct a frequency distribution. The intervals are chosen somewhat arbitrarily. The first two columns of Table 12.12 show the frequency distribution for the raw data from Table 12.11, divided up into five non-overlapping intervals.

TABLE 12.12 Calculations for the Normality Test Example

Income (in \$1,000s)	Observed Frequency, o_i	p_i if H_0 is True	Expected Frequency, $e_i = n \times p_i$	Standardized Squared Deviation, $\frac{(o_i - e_i)^2}{e_i}$
Income < 20	6	0.1693	$50 \times 0.1693 = 8.4673$	$\frac{(6 - 8.467)^2}{8.467} = 0.7190.$
20 ≤ Income < 40	10	0.1322	$50 \times 0.1322 = 6.6114$	1.7368
40 ≤ Income < 60	13	0.1653	$50 \times 0.1653 = 8.2675$	2.7091
60 ≤ Income < 80	10	0.1714	$50 \times 0.1714 = 8.5678$	0.2394
Income ≥ 80	11	0.3617	$50 \times 0.3617 = 18.086$	2.7762
	$\Sigma o_i = 50$	$\Sigma p_i = 1$	$\Sigma e_i = 50$	$\Sigma \frac{(o_i - e_i)^2}{e_i} = 8.180$

Earlier, we were able to calculate expected frequencies by multiplying the sample size n by the hypothesized probabilities (proportions) p_i under the null hypothesis. Here, we first calculate the probabilities under the assumption that the null hypothesis is true and then use them to calculate expected frequencies. For example, under the null hypothesis that income is normally distributed with $\mu = 63.80$ and $\sigma = 45.78$, we find the probability that an individual's income is less than 20, or

$$P(X < 20) = P\left(\frac{X - \mu}{\sigma} < \frac{20 - 63.80}{45.78}\right) = P(Z < -0.9567) = 0.1693.$$

Recall that we obtain this probability in Excel by entering =`NORM.DIST(20, 63.80, 45.78, TRUE)`, and in R by entering `pnorm(20, 63.80, 45.78, lower.tail=TRUE)`. We proceed with the other intervals in a like manner.

$$P(20 \leq X < 40) = P(-0.9567 \leq Z < -0.5199) = 0.1322$$
$$P(40 \leq X < 60) = P(-0.5199 \leq Z < -0.0830) = 0.1653$$
$$P(60 \leq X < 80) = P(-0.0830 \leq Z < 0.3539) = 0.1714$$
$$P(X \geq 80) = P(Z \geq 0.3539) = 0.3617$$

The third column of Table 12.12 shows these probabilities. We are then able to compute the expected frequencies for each interval as $n \times p_i$. The fourth column of Table 12.12 shows the values for the expected frequencies. It is important to ensure that the expected frequency is five or more in each interval. In this example, this condition is satisfied; however in other applications, it may be necessary to combine adjacent intervals until this condition is achieved.

As in Section 12.1, the appropriate test statistic follows the χ^2_{df} distribution, and its value is calculated as $\chi^2_{df} = \Sigma \frac{(o_i - e_i)^2}{e_i}$. The only difference is that the degrees of freedom is equal to the number of intervals k minus one, minus the number of parameters estimated. Since we estimate two parameters—the population mean and the population standard deviation—from the sample data, the degrees of freedom for the chi-square test for normality is always $k - 1 - 2 = k - 3$. In this example we formed five intervals ($k = 5$); therefore, we calculate $df = 5 - 3 = 2$.

TEST STATISTIC FOR THE GOODNESS-OF-FIT TEST FOR NORMALITY

For a goodness-of-fit test for normality, the value of the test statistic is calculated as

$$\chi^2_{df} = \Sigma \frac{(o_i - e_i)^2}{e_i},$$

where $df = k - 3$, k is the number of intervals in the frequency distribution, o_i is the observed frequency of the ith interval, and e_i is the expected frequency of the ith interval.

Note: The test is valid when the expected frequencies for each interval are five or more.

As shown in the last column of Table 12.12, we sum the standardized squared deviations to find the value of the chi-square test statistic as $\chi^2_{df} = \chi^2_2 = 8.180$. Like before, the goodness-of-fit test for normality is a right-tailed test. In order to find the p-value in Excel, we enter =`CHISQ.DIST.RT(8.180, 2)`, and in R, we enter `pchisq(8.180, 2, lower.tail=FALSE)`. Both software return a p-value of 0.017. Because the p-value is less than 0.05, we reject H_0. At the 5% significance level, we conclude that income in this Midwestern city does not follow a normal distribution with a mean of $63,800 and a standard deviation of $45,780.

We would like to point out that R offers a number of options when testing for normality. For the goodness-of-fit test for normality, R internally finds the nonoverlapping intervals (categories). We do not pursue R in this section because of inconsistencies between the R and the manually computed results based on specific nonoverlapping intervals.

LO 12.4

Conduct the Jarque-Bera test.

The Jarque-Bera Test

A criticism of the goodness-of-fit test for normality is that we first have to convert raw data into a frequency distribution by grouping them into a set of arbitrary intervals or categories. The resulting value of the chi-square test statistic depends on how the data are grouped. An alternative to the goodness-of-fit test for normality is the **Jarque-Bera test.** In this test, it is not necessary to convert the numerical variable into a categorical form.

For the Jarque-Bera test, we first calculate the **skewness coefficient** S and the (excess) **kurtosis coefficient** K of the sample data. A skewness coefficient of zero indicates that the data are symmetric about the mean. The kurtosis coefficient measures whether a distribution is more or less peaked than a normal distribution. The skewness coefficient and the (excess) kurtosis coefficient for the normal distribution are both equal to zero.

When testing whether sample observations are derived from the normal distribution, the null hypothesis consists of the joint hypothesis that both the skewness coefficient and the (excess) kurtosis coefficient are zero. It can be shown that the Jarque-Bera test statistic follows the χ^2_{df} distribution with two degrees of freedom.

THE TEST STATISTIC FOR THE JARQUE-BERA TEST

When testing whether the sample observations are derived from a normal distribution using the Jarque-Bera (JB) test, the value of the test statistic is calculated as

$$JB = \chi^2_2 = (n/6)[S^2 + K^2/4],$$

where $df = 2$, n is the sample size, S is the skewness coefficient, and K is the (excess) kurtosis coefficient.

EXAMPLE 12.3

Income

At the 1% significance level, use the Jarque-Bera test to determine whether the observations in the ***Income*** data file are derived from a normal distribution.

SOLUTION: The competing hypotheses take the following form:

$$H_0: S = 0 \text{ and } K = 0$$
$$H_A: S \neq 0 \text{ or } K \neq 0$$

In order to compute the value of the test statistic, we first need to compute the skewness and (excess) kurtosis coefficients, S and K. We use Excel's SKEW and KURT functions to find that $S = 2.3190$ and $K = 6.7322$. The value of the test statistic is calculated as

$$JB = \chi^2_2 = (n/6)[S^2 + K^2/4] = (50/6)[2.3190^2 + 6.7322^2/4] = 139.237.$$

In order to find the p-value in Excel, we enter `=CHISQ.DIST.RT(139.237, 2)`, and in R, we enter `pchisq(139.237, 2, lower.tail=FALSE)`. Both software return a p-value of 0.000. Because the p-value is less than 0.01, we reject H_0. At the 1% significance level, we conclude that income in this Midwestern city does not follow a normal distribution.

In the preceding examples, the conclusion with the Jarque-Bera test and the goodness-of-fit test for normality is the same. This result is not surprising, as it is fairly well documented that income distribution, in general, is skewed to the right (not normally distributed), with a few households accounting for most of the total income. For this reason, we prefer to use the median rather than the mean to get a more accurate reflection of income.

Like in the case of goodness-of-fit test, we do not pursue R for the Jarque-Bera test because it calculates the test statistic using slightly different formulas for the skewness and (excess) kurtosis coefficients, as compared to the ones used by Excel.

EXERCISES 12.3

Mechanics

25. Consider the following sample data with mean and standard deviation of 20.5 and 5.4, respectively.

Class	Frequency
Less than 10	25
10 up to 20	95
20 up to 30	65
30 or more	15

a. Using the goodness-of-fit test for normality, specify the competing hypotheses in order to determine whether or not the data are normally distributed.

b. Calculate the value of the test statistic and the *p*-value.

c. What is the conclusion at the 5% significance level?

26. The following frequency distribution has a sample mean of −3.5 and a sample standard deviation of 9.7.

Class	Frequency
Less than −10	70
−10 up to 0	40
0 up to 10	80
10 or more	10

At the 1% significance level, use the goodness-of-fit test for normality to determine whether or not the data are normally distributed.

27. You are given the following summary statistics from a sample of 50 observations:

Mean	77.25
Standard Deviation	11.36
Skewness	1.12
Kurtosis	1.63

a. Using the Jarque-Bera test, specify the null and alternative hypotheses to determine whether or not the data are normally distributed.

b. Calculate the value of the test statistic and the *p*-value.

c. At the 5% significance level, what is the conclusion? Can you conclude that the data do not follow the normal distribution? Explain.

Applications

28. An economics professor states on her syllabus that final grades will be distributed using the normal distribution. The final averages of 300 students are calculated, and she groups the data into a frequency distribution as shown in the accompanying table. The mean and the standard deviation of the final are $\bar{x} = 72$ and $s = 10$.

Final Averages	Frequency
F: Less than 50	5
D: 50 up to 70	135
C: 70 up to 80	105
B: 80 up to 90	45
A: 90 or above	10

a. Using the goodness-of-fit test for normality, state the competing hypotheses in order to determine if the normal distribution is inappropriate for making grades.

b. Calculate the value of the test statistic and the *p*-value.

c. At the 5% significance level, what is the conclusion to the test?

29. Fifty cities provided information on vacancy rates (in percent) in local apartments in the following frequency distribution. The sample mean and the sample standard deviation are 9% and 3.6%, respectively.

Vacancy Rate	Frequency
Less than 6	10
6 up to 9	10
9 up to 12	20
12 or more	10

Apply the goodness-of-fit test for normality at the 5% significance level. Do the sample data suggest that vacancy rates do not follow the normal distribution?

30. The quality department at an electronics component manufacturer must ensure that their components will operate at pre-specified levels. The accompanying table shows a frequency distribution with measured resistance values (in ohms) for a sample of 520 resistors. The sample mean and the sample standard deviation are 4,790 ohms and 40 ohms, respectively.

Resistance	Frequency
Under 4,740	44
4,740 up to 4,780	145
4,780 up to 4,820	197
4,820 up to 4,860	107
4,860 or more	27

a. Using the goodness-of-fit test for normality, state the competing hypotheses to test if the sample data suggest that resistance does not follow the normal distribution.
b. At $\alpha = 0.05$, what is the conclusion to the test?
c. Would your conclusion change at the 10% significance level?

31. The following frequency distribution shows the distribution of monthly returns (in %) for a retail firm over the recent five year period ($n = 60$)

Monthly Return	Frequency
Less than −5	14
−5 up to 0	9
0 up to 5	18
5 up to 10	11
10 or more	8

Over this time period, the following summary statistics are provided:

Mean	Median	Standard Deviation	Skewness	Kurtosis
1.16%	1.79%	7.38%	−0.31	−0.65

a. Conduct a goodness-of-fit test for normality at the 5% significance level. Can you conclude that monthly returns do not follow the normal distribution?
b. Conduct the Jarque-Bera test at the 5% significance level. Can you conclude that monthly returns do not follow the normal distribution?

32. Total compensation (in $ millions) for 238 CEOs is reported in the following frequency distribution. Total compensation includes salary, bonuses, stock and incentives, the potential value of stock options, and gains from stock options exercised.

Total Compensation	Frequency
Less than 5	43
5 up to 10	65
10 up to 15	32
15 up to 20	38
20 or more	60

Other summary statistics for CEO compensation are as follows:

Mean	Median	Standard Deviation	Skewness	Kurtosis
19.03	11.02	27.61	5.26	35.53

a. Conduct a goodness-of-fit test for normality of CEO compensation at the 1% significance level. Does total compensation of CEOs not follow the normal distribution?
b. Conduct the Jarque-Bera test at the 1% significance level. Does total compensation of CEOs not follow the normal distribution?

33. **FILE** ***Shaft_Diameter.*** Fabco, a precision machining shop, uses statistical process control (SPC) techniques to ensure quality and consistency of their steel shafts. The control limits used in their SPC charts are based on the assumption that shaft diameters are normally distributed. To verify this assumption, a quality engineer has measured the diameters for a sample of 50 of its popular 1/2-inch shafts.
a. Using the Jarque-Bera test, state the competing hypotheses in order to determine whether or not the data follow the normal distribution.
b. Calculate the value of the Jarque-Bera test statistic and the p-value.
c. At $\alpha = 0.10$, can you conclude that the shaft diameters are not normally distributed?
d. Would your conclusion change at the 5% significance level?

34. **FILE** ***Improvement.*** The accompanying data file shows weekly stock prices for a home improvement firm.
a. Using the Jarque-Bera test, state the competing hypotheses in order to determine whether or not the firm's weekly stock prices follow the normal distribution.
b. Calculate the value of the Jarque-Bera test statistic and the p-value.
c. At $\alpha = 0.05$, can you conclude that stock prices are not normally distributed?

35. **FILE** ***MPG.*** The accompanying data file shows miles per gallon (MPG) for a sample of 25 cars.
a. Using the Jarque-Bera test, state the competing hypotheses in order to determine whether or not MPG follows the normal distribution.
b. Calculate the value of the Jarque-Bera test statistic and the p-value.
c. At $\alpha = 0.05$, can you conclude that MPG is not normally distributed?

12.4 WRITING WITH DATA

Case Study

Jirapong Manustrong/Shutterstock

The S&P 500 is a stock market index that measures the stock performance of 500 large companies listed on stock exchanges in the United States. Javier Gonzalez is in the process of writing a comprehensive analysis of the distribution of the S&P 500 index returns. Before he makes any inferences concerning the return data, he would first like to determine whether or not the returns follow a normal distribution. Table 12.13 shows a portion of the monthly returns of the S&P 500 index for the years 2012 through 2019. Javier wants to use the sample information to conduct the goodness-of-fit test for normality and the Jarque-Bera test to determine if the S&P 500 index monthly returns do not follow a normal distribution.

TABLE 12.13 Monthly Returns of the S&P 500 Index

Date	Return
Jan-12	4.36
Feb-12	4.06
⋮	⋮
Dec-19	2.86

FILE
SP500

Sample Report—Assessing Whether Data Follow the Normal Distribution

One of the key assumptions in modern portfolio theory is that stock returns follow a normal distribution. Arguably, while the distribution of monthly stock returns can be symmetric about its mean, the tails are fatter. In other words, the likelihood of extreme returns is more than what would be expected with normal distributions. Table 12.14 shows relevant summary statistics for monthly returns of the S&P 500 Index.

TABLE 12.14 Summary Measures for the S&P 500 Index Monthly Returns

Mean	Median	Standard Deviation	Skewness	Kurtosis
1.0376%	1.6250%	3.1736%	−0.6525	1.0434

The average monthly return for the S&P 500 index for the years 2012–2019 is 1.0376%, with a median of 1.6250%. A mean that is smaller than the median is indicative of a negatively skewed distribution. The skewness coefficient of −0.6525 supports this claim. Moreover, the (excess) kurtosis coefficient of 1.0434 suggests a distribution that is slightly more peaked than the normal distribution. A formal test will determine whether this seemingly non-normal behavior can be deemed real or due to chance.

The goodness-of-fit test for normality is first applied. The raw data are converted into a frequency distribution with five intervals ($k = 5$). Expected frequencies are calculated by multiplying the sample size $n = 96$ by the hypothesized proportions p_i, under the null hypothesis that the data follow the normal distribution with mean 1.0376% and standard deviation 3.1736%. Finally, the value of the chi-square test statistic is computed by summing the standardized squared deviations. All of these calculations are shown in Table 12.15.

The top half of Table 12.16 shows the competing hypotheses, the value of the test statistic, and the p-value that result from applying the goodness-of-fit test for normality. Given a p-value of 0.0198, we reject the null hypothesis that returns are normally distributed at the 5% significance level.

TABLE 12.15 Calculations for the Goodness-of-Fit Test for Normality

Return (in %)	Observed Frequency, o_i	p_i if Normally Distributed	Expected Frequency, $e_i = n \times p_i$	Standardized Squared Deviation, $\frac{(o_i - e_i)^2}{e_i}$
Return < −2	13	0.1692	16.2479	0.6492
$-2 \leq$ Return < 0	14	0.2026	19.4502	1.5272
$0 \leq$ Return < 2	32	0.2473	23.7403	2.8737
$2 \leq$ Return < 4	25	0.2056	19.7332	1.4057
Return ≥ 4	12	0.1753	16.8284	1.3854
	$\Sigma o_i = 96$	$\Sigma p_i = 1$	$\Sigma e_i = 96$	$\Sigma \frac{(o_i - e_i)^2}{e_i} = 7.8412$

TABLE 12.16 Test Statistics and *p*-values for Hypothesis Tests

Hypotheses	Test Statistic	*p*-value
Goodness-of-Fit Test: H_0: Returns are normally distributed. H_A: Returns are not normally distributed.	$\chi^2_2 = 7.8412$	$P(\chi^2_2 \geq 7.8412) = 0.0198$
Jarque-Bera Test: H_0: $S = 0$ and $K = 0$ H_0: $S = 0$ or $K = 0$	$\chi^2_2 = 11.1665$	$P(\chi^2_2 \geq 11.1665) = 0.0038$

The bottom half of Table 12.16 shows the results from conducting the Jarque-Bera (JB) test. The value for the JB test statistic is 11.1665 and its associated *p*-value is 0.0038; thus, at the 5% significance level, the null hypothesis that skewness and kurtosis are both zero is rejected. This result is consistent with the conclusion drawn from the goodness-of-fit test for normality. Therefore, at the 5% level of significance, we conclude that the S&P 500 index returns do not follow the normal distribution. It is noteworthy that the negative skewness exhibited by the stock returns is indicative of frequent small gains and a few extreme losses and it must be taken into account when making investment decisions.

Suggested Case Studies

Report 12.1 A 2018 survey conducted by Pew Research Center shows the percentage of Americans who view issues such as drug addiction and gun violence as 'very big' national problems. The following table lists some of the problems along with the percentage of Americans (Percentage) who treat them as 'very big'.

Problem	Percentage
Drug Addition	68%
Sexism	34%
Racism	46%
Gun Violence	53%
Climate Change	43%
Terrorism	53%
College Affordability	63%

Create your own survey with responses from at least 50 of your college students on the above national problems. In a report, interpret the proportions derived from your survey results. Further, determine whether your college proportions differ from national proportions. Use a reasonable significance level for the test.

Report 12.2 FILE ***Machine.*** Being able to predict machine failures before they happen can save millions of dollars. This allows manufacturers to perform preventive maintenance or repairs in advance to minimize machine downtime. A manager wants to explore the effect of percentage humidity (Low, Medium, or High) on machine failure (Yes or No). In a report, use the data in the accompanying table to construct a contingency table and interpret the results. Further, determine if machine failure is significantly related to humidity levels. Use a reasonable significance level for the test.

Report 12.3 FILE ***Returns.*** Investors are often curious about the distribution of their stock returns. A concern is that with fatter tails, the likelihood of extreme returns is more than what would be expected with the normal distribution. The accompanying data file shows 2012–2019 monthly stock returns for three major firms—Apple (AAPL), Proctor and Gamble (PG), and McDonald's (MCD). In a report, use summary statistics to compare stock returns for the firms. Further, for each firm, determine if stock returns follow a normal distribution at the 5% level of significance.

CONCEPTUAL REVIEW

LO 12.1 Conduct a goodness-of-fit test for a multinomial experiment.

A multinomial experiment consists of a series of n independent and identical trials such that on each trial there are k possible outcomes or categories; the probability p_i associated with the ith category remains the same; and the sum of the probabilities is one.

A goodness-of-fit test is conducted to determine if the population proportions differ from some predetermined (hypothesized) values. The value of the test statistic is calculated as $\chi^2_{df} = \Sigma \frac{(o_i - e_i)^2}{e_i}$, where $df = k - 1$, o_i is the observed frequency of the ith category, $e_i = np_i$ is the expected frequency of the ith category, and n is the number of observations. The test is valid when the expected frequencies for each category are five or more. This test is always implemented as a right-tailed test.

LO 12.2 Conduct a test for independence.

A test for independence, also called a chi-square test of a contingency table, analyzes the relationship between two categorical variables. In order to determine whether or not the two variables are related, we again compare observed frequencies with expected frequencies. The expected frequency for each cell in a contingency table, e_{ij}, is calculated as $e_{ij} = \frac{(\text{Row } i \text{ total})(\text{Column } j \text{ total})}{\text{Sample Size}}$, where the subscript ij refers to the ith row and the jth column of the contingency table.

The value of the chi-square test statistic is calculated as $\chi^2_{df} = \sum_i \sum_j \frac{(o_{ij} - e_{ij})^2}{e_{ij}}$, where o_{ij} is the observed frequency in the ith row and jth column of the contingency table. Degrees of freedom df is calculated as $(r - 1)(c - 1)$, where r and c refer to the number of rows and columns, respectively, in the contingency table. The test for independence is implemented as a right-tailed test and is valid when the expected frequencies for each cell are five or more.

LO 12.3 Conduct a goodness-of-fit test for normality.

The goodness-of-fit test for normality is conducted to contest that a given population follows the normal distribution. We first construct a frequency distribution of the sample observations with k intervals. We then calculate the probability of observing the ith interval p_i under the assumption of a normal distribution, and then use this probability to calculate the expected frequency as $e_i = n \times p_i$. The value of the test statistic is calculated as $\chi^2_{df} = \Sigma \frac{(o_i - e_i)^2}{e_i}$, with $df = k - 3$. The goodness-of-fit test for normality is implemented as a right-tailed test and is valid when the expected frequencies for each interval are five or more.

LO 12.4 Conduct the Jarque-Bera test.

An alternative to the goodness-of-fit test for normality is the Jarque-Bera test. We use the skewness coefficient S and the (excess) kurtosis coefficient K of the sample observations to conduct the test. The value of the Jarque-Bera JB test statistic is calculated as $JB = \chi^2_2 = (n/6)[S^2 + K^2/4]$, where n is the sample size. The Jarqe-Bera test is implemented as a right-tailed test.

ADDITIONAL EXERCISES

36. The following table lists the market shares of the four firms in a particular industry in 2019 and total sales (in $ billions) for each firm in 2020.

Firm	Market Share in 2019	Total Sales in 2020
1	0.40	200
2	0.30	180
3	0.20	100
4	0.10	70

a. Specify the competing hypotheses to test whether the market shares in 2019 are not valid in 2020.

b. Calculate the value of the test statistic and the *p*-value.

c. At the 1% significance level, do the sample data suggest that the market shares changed from 2019 to 2020?

37. A study suggests that airlines have increased restrictions on cheap fares by raising overnight requirements. This forces business travelers to pay more for their flights, since they tend to need the most flexibility and want to be home on weekends. A year ago, the overnight stay requirements were as follows:

One night	Two nights	Three nights	Saturday night
37%	17%	28%	18%

A recent sample of 644 flights found the following restrictions:

One night	Two nights	Three nights	Saturday night
117	137	298	92

a. Specify the competing hypotheses to test whether the proportions cited by the study have changed.

b. Calculate the value of the test statistic.

c. At the 5% significance level, what is the conclusion to the hypothesis test? Interpret your results.

38. In a survey by Facebook, young users were asked about their preference for delivering the news about breaking up a relationship. One of the shocking results was that only 47% of users preferred to break the news in person. A researcher decides to verify the survey results of Facebook by taking her own sample of 200 young Facebook users. The preference percentages from Facebook and the researcher's survey are presented in the following table.

Delivery Method	Facebook Results	Researcher's Results
In Person	47%	55%
Phone	30%	25%
E-mail	4%	6%
Facebook	5%	5%
Instant Message	14%	9%

At the 5% level of significance, test if the researcher's results are inconsistent with the survey results conducted by Facebook. Provide the details.

39. A local TV station claims that 60% of people support Candidate A, 30% support Candidate B, and 10% support Candidate C. A survey of 500 registered voters is taken. The accompanying table indicates how they are likely to vote.

Candidate A	Candidate B	Candidate C
350	125	25

a. Specify the competing hypotheses to test whether the TV station's claim can be rejected by the data.
b. Test the hypothesis at the 1% significance level.

40. Given a shaky economy and high heating costs, more and more households are struggling to pay utility bills. Particularly hard hit are households with homes heated with propane or heating oil. A representative sample of 500 households was taken to investigate if the type of heating influences whether or not a household is delinquent in paying its utility bill. The following table reports the results.

Delinquent in Payment?	Type of Heating			
	Natural Gas	Electricity	Heating Oil	Propane
Yes	50	20	15	10
No	240	130	20	15

At the 5% significance level, test whether the type of heating influences a household's delinquency in payment. Interpret your results.

41. An analyst is trying to determine whether the prices of certain stocks on the NASDAQ are independent of the industry to which they belong. She examines four industries and, within each industry, categorizes each stock according to its price (high-priced, average-priced, low-priced).

Stock Price	Industry			
	I	II	III	IV
High	16	8	10	14
Average	18	16	10	12
Low	7	8	4	9

a. Specify the competing hypotheses to determine whether stock price depends on the industry.
b. Calculate the value of the test statistic and the p-value.
c. At the 1% significance level, what can the analyst conclude?

42. Many parents have turned to St. John's wort, an herbal remedy, to treat their children with attention deficit hyperactivity disorder (ADHD). In a study, children with ADHD were randomly assigned to take either St. John's wort capsules or placebos. The contingency table below shows the results.

Treatment	Effect on ADHD	
	No Change in ADHD	Improvement in ADHD
St. John's wort	12	15
Placebo	14	13

At the 5% significance level, do the data indicate that St. John's wort affects children with ADHD?

43. A poll asked 3,228 Americans aged 16 to 21 whether they are likely to serve in the U.S. military. The following table, cross-classified by a person's sex and race, reports those who responded that are likely or very likely to serve in the active-duty military.

Sex	Race		
	Hispanic	Black	White
Male	1,098	678	549
Female	484	355	64

a. State the competing hypotheses to test whether a person's sex and race are dependent when making a choice to serve in the military.
b. Conduct the test at the 5% significance level.

44. FILE ***HomePrice.*** The accompanying data file shows various variables, including price and square footage, for 36 single-family homes sold in St. Louis.
a. Use the Jarque-Bera test to test if house prices are not normally distributed at $\alpha = 0.05$.
b. Use the Jarque-Bera test to test if square footage is not normally distributed at $\alpha = 0.05$.

45. The following frequency distribution shows the monthly stock returns (in percent) for a construction company in the last five years.

Monthly Returns	Observed Frequency
Less than −5	13
−5 up to 0	16
0 up to 5	20
5 or more	11

Over this time period, the following summary statistics are provided:

Mean	Median	Standard Deviation	Skewness	Kurtosis
0.31%	0.43%	6.49%	0.15	0.38

a. Conduct a goodness-of-fit test for normality at the 5% significance level. Can you conclude that monthly stock returns do not follow the normal distribution?
b. Conduct the Jarque-Bera test at the 5% significance level. Are your results consistent with your answer in part (a)?

46. Color coding is often used in manufacturing operations to display production status or to identify/prioritize materials. For example, suppose "green" status indicates that an assembly line

is operating normally, "yellow" indicates it is down waiting on personnel for set up or repair, "blue" indicates it is down waiting on materials to be delivered, and "red" indicates an emergency condition. Management has set realistic goals whereby the assembly line should be operating normally 80% of the time, waiting on personnel 9% of the time, waiting on materials 9% of the time, and in an emergency condition 2% of the time. Based on 250 recent status records, the status was green 185 times, yellow 24 times, blue 32 times, and red 9 times.

a. State the appropriate null and alternative hypotheses to test if the proportions of assembly line statuses differ from the goals set by management.
b. Calculate the value of the test statistic and the p-value.
c. Are management's goals being met at $\alpha = 0.05$? Will your conclusion change at $\alpha = 0.01$?

47. An automotive parts company has been besieged with poor publicity over the past few years due to several highly publicized product recalls that have tarnished its public image. This has prompted a series of quality improvement initiatives. Currently, the marketing manager would like to determine if these initiatives have been successful in changing public perception about the company. The accompanying table show the results of two surveys, each of 600 random adults. Survey 1 was conducted prior to the quality initiatives. Survey 2 was conducted after the quality initiatives were implemented and publicized.

	Public Perception		
	Negative	Neutral	Positive
Survey 1	324	180	96
Survey 2	246	146	208

a. State the appropriate null and alternative hypotheses to test if the public perception has changed since the quality initiatives have been implemented.
b. Make a conclusion at the 1% significance level.

48. The human resources department would like to consolidate the current set of retirement plan options offered to specific employee pay groups into a single plan for all pay groups (salaried, hourly, or piecework). A sample of 585 employees of various pay groups were asked which of three potential plans they preferred (A, B, or C). The results are shown in the accompanying table. The human resources department is hoping to conclude that the retirement plan preferred by the majority of employees is independent of pay group, in order to avoid the impression that the preferred plan may favor a particular group.

Preferred Plan	Employee Pay Group		
	Salaried	Hourly	Piecework
A	78	98	37
B	121	95	30
C	51	57	18

a. Specify the competing hypotheses to determine whether the preferred retirement plan depends on employee pay group.
b. Calculate the value of the test statistic and the p-value.
c. What is your conclusion at the 10% significance level? What about the 5% significance level?

49. The operations manager at ElectroTech, an electronics manufacturing company, believes that workers on particular shifts may be more likely to phone in "sick" than those on other shifts. To test this belief, she has compiled the following table containing frequencies based on work shift and days absent over the past year.

	First Shift	Second Shift	Third Shift
0–2 days absent	44	20	10
3–6 days absent	38	25	12
7–10 days absent	14	9	13
11 or more days absent	4	6	5

a. Specify the competing hypotheses to determine whether days absent depend on work shift.
b. Calculate the value of the test statistic and the p-value.
c. What is your conclusion at the 5% significance level? What about the 1% significance level?

50. FILE ***Reorder*** Reorder point decisions for a particular part at an automotive parts distributor are based on the assumption that weekly demand is normally distributed. (Note: "Reorder point" is the inventory level at which a replenishment order is placed; it should be high enough to cover demand during the order fulfillment period, but low enough to avoid excessive inventory holding costs.) To examine the validity of this assumption, the logistics department has compiled weekly demand values for the past year.

a. Using the Jarque-Bera test, state the competing hypotheses in order to determine whether or not weekly demand values follow the normal distribution.
b. Calculate the value of the Jarque-Bera test statistic and the p-value.
c. At $\alpha = 0.05$, can you conclude that the weekly demand values are not normally distributed? Is the conclusion sensitive to the choice of significance level?

51. A software company develops and markets a popular business simulation/modeling program. A random number generator contained in the program provides random values from various probability distributions. The software design group would like to validate that the program is properly generating random numbers. Accordingly, they generated 5,000 random numbers from a normal distribution and grouped the results into the accompanying frequency distribution. The sample mean and sample standard deviation are 100 and 10, respectively.

Value	Frequency
Under 70	12
70 up to 80	99
80 up to 90	658
90 up to 100	1734
100 up to 110	1681
110 up to 120	697
120 up to 130	112
130 or more	7

a. Using the goodness-of-fit test for normality, state the competing hypotheses to test if the random numbers generated do not follow the normal distribution.

b. Calculate the value of the test statistic and the p-value.

c. What is the conclusion to the test at the 1% significance level? Is your conclusion sensitive within the range of typical significance levels?

52. FILE ***Degrees.*** The accompanying table shows the proportions of college degrees awarded in 2010 by colleges and universities, categorized by a graduate's race and ethnicity. The race and ethnicity of 500 recent graduates are recorded and shown in the last column of the table.

Race/Ethnicity	2010 Proportions	Recent Numbers
White	0.73	350
Black	0.10	50
Hispanic	0.09	60
Asian	0.08	40

At the 5% significance level, test if the proportions have changed since 2010.

APPENDIX 12.1 Guidelines for Other Software Packages

The following section provides brief commands for Minitab, SPSS, and JMP. Import the specified data file into the relevant software spreadsheet prior to following the commands.

Minitab

Goodness-of-Fit Test

Share

(Replicating Example 12.1) From the menu, choose **Stat** > **Tables** > **Chi-Square Goodness-of-Fit Test (One Variable).** Choose **Observed counts** and then select Recent_Numbers. Under **Test,** select **Proportions specified by historical counts,** and then select Market_Share. Choose **Results** and select **Display test results.**

Test for Independence

Social_Media

(Replicating Example 12.2) From the menu, choose **Stat** > **Tables** > **Cross Tabulation and Chi-Square.** Select "Summarized data in a two-way table." Under **Columns containing the table,** select Instagram and Pinterest. Choose Chi-Square and select **Chi-square test.**

SPSS

Goodness-of-Fit Test

Share

A. (Replicating Example 12.1) From the menu, choose **Data** > **Weight Cases.** Select **Weight cases by,** and under **Frequency Variable,** select Recent_Numbers.

B. Select **Analyze > Nonparametric Tests > Legacy Dialogs > Chi-square.**

C. Under **Test Variable List,** select Firm. Under **Expected Values,** select **Values,** and **Add** 0.40, 0.32, 0.24, and 0.04.

Test for Independence

A. (Replicating Example 12.2) In order to conduct this test in SPSS, the data need to be reconfigured. Label Columns 1, 2, and 3 as Race, Media, Frequency respectively. In the first row, enter Latinx, Instagram, 50; in the second row, enter Latinx, Pinterest, 60; in the third row, enter Caucasians, Instagram, 120; and in the forth row enter Caucasians, PInterest,170.

B. From the menu, choose **Data > Weight Cases.** Select **Weight cases by,** and under **Frequency Variable,** select Frequency.

C. From the menu, select **Analyze > Descriptive Statistics > Crosstabs.** Under **Rows,** select Race, and under **Columns,** select Media. Choose **Statistics,** check **Chi-square.**

JMP

Goodness-of-Fit Test

A. (Replicating Example 12.1) Select Analyze > Distribution. Drag Firm to the **Y, Columns** box and drag Recent_Numbers to the **Freq** box. (Make sure that the Firm variable is recognized as a nominal variable.)

B. Click on the red arrow beside **Distributions** and select **Stack**. Click on the red arrow beside **Firm** and select **Test Probabilities**. Under **Hypoth Prob**, enter 0.40, 0.32, 0.24, and 0.04.

Test for Independence

A. (Replicating Example 12.2) In order to conduct this test in JMP, the data need to be reconfigured. Follow Step A under the SPSS instructions for Test for Independence.

B. From the menu, select **Analyze > Fit Y by X.** Drag Race to the **Y, Response** box, drag Media to the **X, Factor box**, and drag Frequency to the **Freq** box.

13 Analysis of Variance

LEARNING OBJECTIVES

After reading this chapter you should be able to:

LO **13.1** **Conduct and evaluate a one-way ANOVA test.**

LO **13.2** **Use Fisher's LSD method and Tukey's HSD method to determine which means differ.**

LO **13.3** **Conduct and evaluate a two-way ANOVA test with no interaction.**

LO **13.4** **Conduct and evaluate a two-way ANOVA test with interaction.**

In this chapter, we study analysis of variance, which is more commonly referred to as ANOVA. ANOVA is a statistical technique used to determine if differences exist between the means of three or more populations under independent sampling. We can think of the ANOVA test as a generalization of the two-sample *t* test with equal but unknown variances discussed in Chapter 10.

We begin with one-way ANOVA, where we examine how the mean may be influenced by one categorical variable or one factor. For instance, we may want to determine if the average miles per gallon of small hybrid cars vary by brand. Or we may wish to compare the effectiveness of different fertilizers on the average yield per acre.

We then move on to two-way ANOVA, where we examine how the mean may be influenced by two categorical variables or two factors. For instance, we may want to determine if the average miles per gallon of small hybrid cars vary by brand and octane rating of gasoline. Or we may wish to determine if the average yield per acre is influenced by the fertilizer and the acidity level of the soil. Tests based on two-way ANOVA can be conducted *with* or *without* the interaction of the categorical variables or factors.

INTRODUCTORY CASE

Store Layout

Despite the growth in online grocery outlets, most American consumers still prefer to do their grocery shopping in brick-and-mortar stores. These stores provide the shopping experience and allow consumers to inspect and pick out products. Driven by competition, grocery stores are always experimenting with layouts that appeal to their customers and increase sales.

Sean Cox is vice president of sales and marketing for a large grocery chain. He wants to know if mean sales differ depending on the store layout. Sean implements three different store layouts at 10 different stores for one month and measures total sales for each store at the end of the month. Table 13.1 shows a portion of the results as well as the relevant summary statistics.

FILE *Store_Layout*

TABLE 13.1 Monthly Sales (in $ millions)

Layout 1	Layout 2	Layout 3
1.3	2.0	2.3
1.8	2.2	2.3
⋮	⋮	⋮
2.0	1.8	2.2
$\bar{x}_1 = 1.92$ $s_1^2 = 0.0973$	$\bar{x}_2 = 2.08$ $s_2^2 = 0.1062$	$\bar{x}_3 = 2.42$ $s_3^2 = 0.0373$

Sean wants to use the above sample information to

1. Determine whether there are differences in mean monthly sales among these three store layouts at the 5% significance level.
2. Determine which means differ at the 5% significance level, if it is found that differences exist in the mean monthly sales among the layouts.

A synopsis of this case is provided in Section 13.2.

LO 13.1

13.1 ONE-WAY ANOVA TEST

Conduct and evaluate a one-way ANOVA test.

We use an **analysis of variance (ANOVA) test** to determine if differences exist between the means of three or more populations under independent sampling. The ANOVA test can be thought of as a generalization of the two-sample t test with equal but unknown variances discussed in Chapter 10. This test is based on the $F_{(df_1, df_2)}$ distribution that was introduced in Chapter 11. A **one-way ANOVA test** compares population means based on one categorical variable or factor. In general, it is used for testing c population means under the following assumptions:

1. The populations are normally distributed.
2. The population standard deviations are unknown but assumed equal.
3. The samples are selected independently.

In the store layout example from the introductory case, we want to determine whether some differences exist in the mean monthly sales of a grocery store depending on one of three possible store layouts. We thus delineate sales by store layout and formulate the following competing hypotheses:

$$H_0: \mu_1 = \mu_2 = \mu_3$$
$$H_A: \text{Not all population means are equal.}$$

Note that H_A does not require that all means must differ from one another. In principle, the sample data may support the rejection of H_0 in favor of H_A even if only two means differ.

When conducting the equality of means test, you might be tempted to set up a series of hypothesis tests, comparing μ_1 and μ_2, μ_1 and μ_3, and μ_2 and μ_3, and then use the two-sample t test with equal variances discussed in Section 10.1. However, such an approach is not only cumbersome, but also flawed. In this example, where we evaluate the equality of three means, we would have to compare three combinations of two means at a time. Also, by conducting numerous pairwise comparisons, we inflate the risk of the Type I error α; that is, we increase the risk of incorrectly rejecting the null hypothesis. In other words, if we conduct all three pairwise tests at the 5% level of significance, the resulting significance level for the overall test will be greater than 5%.

Fortunately, the ANOVA technique avoids this problem by providing one test that simultaneously evaluates the equality of several means. In the store layout example, if the three population means are equal, we would expect the resulting sample means, $\bar{x}_1$, $\bar{x}_2$, and $\bar{x}_3$, to be relatively close to one another. Figure 13.1a illustrates the distribution of the sample

FIGURE 13.1 The logic of ANOVA

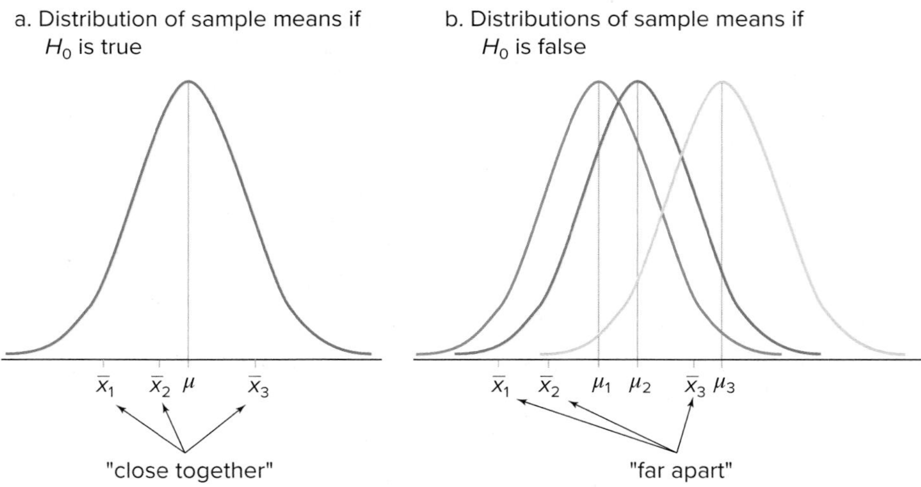

means if H_0 is true. Here, the relatively small variability in the sample means can be explained by chance. What if the population means differ? Figure 13.1b shows the distributions of the sample means if the sample data support H_A. In this scenario, the sample means are relatively far apart since each sample mean is calculated from a population with a different mean. The resulting variability in the sample means cannot be explained by chance alone.

The term *treatments* is often used to identify the c populations being examined. The practice of referring to different populations as different treatments is due to the fact that many ANOVA applications were originally developed in connection with agricultural experiments where different fertilizers were regarded as different treatments applied to soil.

In order to determine if significant differences exist between some of the population means, we develop two independent estimates of the common population variance σ^2. One estimate of σ^2 can be attributed to the variability *between* the sample means. It is referred to as **between-treatments variance.** The other estimate of σ^2 can be attributed to the variability of the observations *within* each sample; that is, the variability due to chance. It is referred to as **within-treatments variance.**

If the two independent estimates of σ^2 are relatively close together, then it is likely that the variability of the sample means can be explained by chance and the null hypothesis of equal population means is not rejected. However, if the between-treatments variance is significantly greater than the within-treatments variance, then the null hypothesis of equal population means is rejected. This is equivalent to concluding that the ratio of between-treatments variance to within-treatments variance is significantly greater than one. We will come back to this ratio shortly.

Between-Treatments Estimate of σ^2: *MSTR*

The between-treatments variance is based on a weighted sum of squared differences between the sample means and the overall mean of the data set, referred to as the **grand mean** and denoted as $\bar{\bar{x}}$. We compute the grand mean by summing all observations in the data set and dividing by the total number of observations.

Each squared difference of a sample mean from the grand mean $(\bar{x}_i - \bar{\bar{x}})^2$ is multiplied by the respective sample size, n_i, for each treatment. After summing the weighted squared differences, we arrive at a value called the **sum of squares due to treatments** or *SSTR*. When we divide *SSTR* by its degrees of freedom $c - 1$, we obtain the mean square for treatments; or equivalently, the between-treatments estimate of σ^2, which we denote by *MSTR*.

CALCULATIONS FOR *MSTR*

- The grand mean: $\bar{\bar{x}} = \frac{\sum_{i=1}^{c}\sum_{j=1}^{n_i} x_{ij}}{n_T}$,
- The sum of squares due to treatments: $SSTR = \sum_{i=1}^{c} n_i(\bar{x}_i - \bar{\bar{x}})^2$, and
- The between-treatments estimate of σ^2: $MSTR = \frac{SSTR}{c-1}$,

where c is the number of populations (treatments), $\bar{x}_i$ and n_i are the sample mean and the sample size of the ith sample, respectively, and n_T is the total sample size.

Referring back to the store layout example, we first find the sample mean $\bar{x}_i$ and the sample size n_i, for each layout. Table 13.1 shows that the sample means for Layout 1, Layout 2, and Layout 3 are $\bar{x}_1 = 1.92$, $\bar{x}_2 = 2.08$, and $\bar{x}_3 = 2.42$, respectively. There are

10 observations in each of the three samples, so $n_1 = n_2 = n_3 = 10$, which implies that the total sample size n_T is equal to 30. The calculations for $\bar{\bar{x}}$, *SSTR,* and *MSTR* for the public transportation example are as follows:

$$\bar{\bar{x}} = \frac{\sum_{i=1}^{c}\sum_{j=1}^{n_i} x_{ij}}{n_T} = \frac{1.3 + 1.8 + \cdots + 2.2}{30} = 2.14$$

$$SSTR = \sum_{i=1}^{c} n_i(\bar{x}_i - \bar{\bar{x}})^2 = 10(1.92 - 2.14)^2 + 10(2.08 - 2.14)^2 + 10(2.42 - 2.14)^2 = 1.304.$$

$$MSTR = \frac{SSTR}{c - 1} = \frac{1.304}{3 - 1} = 0.652$$

Within-Treatments Estimate of σ^2: *MSE*

We just calculated a value of *MSTR* equal to 0.652. Is this value of *MSTR* large enough to indicate that the population means differ? To answer this question, we compare *MSTR* to the variability that we expect due to chance. In other words, we compare this between-treatments variance to the within-treatments variance. In order to calculate the within-treatments variance, we first calculate the **error sum of squares,** denoted as *SSE. SSE* provides a measure of the degree of variability that exists even if all population means are the same. We calculate *SSE* as a weighted sum of the sample variances of each treatment. When we divide *SSE* by its degrees of freedom $n_T - c$, we arrive at the **mean square error** or, equivalently, the within-treatments estimate of σ^2, which we denote by *MSE.*

CALCULATIONS FOR *MSE*

- The error sum of squares: $SSE = \sum_{i=1}^{c} (n_i - 1)s_i^2$, and
- The within-treatments estimate of σ^2: $MSE = \frac{SSE}{n_T - c}$,

where c is the number of populations (treatments), s_i^2 and n_i are the sample variance and the sample size of the ith sample, respectively, and n_T is the total sample size.

Table 13.1 shows that the sample variances for Layout 1, Layout 2, and Layout 3 are $s_1^2 = 0.0973$, $s_2^2 = 0.1062$, and $s_3^2 = 0.0373$, respectively. The values of *SSE* and *MSE* for the store layout example are calculated as follows:

$$SSE = \sum_{i=1}^{c} (n_i - 1)s_i^2 = (10 - 1)0.0973 + (10 - 1)0.1062 + (10 - 1)0.0373 = 2.168$$

$$MSE = \frac{SSE}{n_T - c} = \frac{2.168}{30 - 3} = 0.0803$$

As mentioned earlier, if the ratio of the between-treatments variance to the within-treatments variance is significantly greater than one, then this finding provides evidence for rejecting the null hypothesis of equal population means. We use this ratio to develop the test statistic for a one-way ANOVA test.

TEST STATISTIC FOR A ONE-WAY ANOVA TEST

The value of the test statistic for testing whether differences exist between the population means is computed as

$$F_{(df_1,df_2)} = \frac{MSTR}{MSE},$$

where $df_1 = c - 1$, $df_2 = n_T - c$, and n_T is the total sample size; $MSTR$ is the between-treatments variance and MSE is the within-treatments variance.

The values for $MSTR$ and MSE are based on independent samples drawn from c normally distributed populations with a common variance. ANOVA tests are always implemented as right-tailed tests.

We are now in a position to conduct a four-step hypothesis test at the 5% significance level for the store layout example.

Step 1. Specify the null and the alternative hypotheses. For completeness, we repeat the competing hypotheses to determine whether mean sales differ between the three store layouts:

H_0: $\mu_1 = \mu_2 = \mu_3$

H_A: Not all population means are equal.

Step 2. Specify the significance level. We conduct the hypothesis test at the 5% significance level, so $\alpha = 0.05$.

Step 3. Calculate the value of the test statistic and the *p*-value. Given $MSTR = 0.652$, $MSE = 0.0803$, $df_1 = c - 1 = 3 - 1 = 2$ and $df_2 = n_T - c = 30 - 3 = 27$, we compute the value of the test statistic as

$$F_{(df_1,df_2)} = F_{(2,27)} = \frac{MSTR}{MSE} = \frac{0.652}{0.0803} = 8.1199.$$

Since the ANOVA test is a right-tailed test, we calculate the p-value as $P(F_{2,27} \geq 8.1199)$. We show a portion of the F table from Appendix B in Table 13.2.

TABLE 13.2 Portion of the *F* table

df_2	Area in Upper Tail	df_1: 1	2	3
27	0.10	2.90	2.51	2.30
	0.05	4.21	3.35	2.96
	0.025	5.63	4.24	3.65
	0.01	7.68	5.49	4.60

For $df_1 = 2$ and $df_2 = 27$, we see that 8.1199 is greater than 5.49, implying that the p-value is less than 0.01. As explained in Chapter 11, we can use Excel's F.DIST.RT function or R's pf function to find the exact p-value. In Excel, we enter `=F.DIST.RT(8.1199, 2,27)`, and in R, we enter `pf(8.1199, 2, 27, lower.tail=FALSE)`. Both software return a p-value of 0.002.

Step 4. State the conclusion and interpret the results. Since the p-value is less than 0.05, we reject H_0. Therefore, at the 5% significance level, we conclude that the mean monthly sales differ between the three store layouts.

It is important to note that if we reject the null hypothesis, we can only conclude that not all population means are equal. The one-way ANOVA test does not allow us to infer which individual means differ. Therefore, even though the sample mean is the highest for Layout 3, we cannot conclude that Layout 3 produces the highest sales. Further analysis of the difference between paired population means is addressed in Section 13.2.

The One-Way ANOVA Table

Most software packages summarize the ANOVA calculations in a table. The general format of the ANOVA table is presented in Table 13.3.

TABLE 13.3 General Format of a One-Way ANOVA Table

Source of Variation	SS	df	MS	F	p-value
Between Groups	$SSTR$	$c - 1$	$MSTR$	$F_{(df_1,df_2)} = \dfrac{MSTR}{MSE}$	$P\left(F_{(df_1,df_2)} \geq \dfrac{MSTR}{MSE}\right)$
Within Groups	SSE	$n_T - c$	MSE		
Total	SST	$n_T - 1$			

We should also note that **total sum of squares *SST*** is equal to the sum of the squared differences of each observation from the grand mean. This is equivalent to summing *SSTR* and *SSE;* that is, $SST = SSTR + SSE$.

> DECOMPOSING TOTAL VARIATION IN A ONE-WAY ANOVA TEST
>
> In a one-way ANOVA test, the total sum of squares, *SST,* of the variable is partitioned into two distinct components: the sum of squares due to treatments, *SSTR,* and the error sum of squares, *SSE.* That is, $SST = SSTR + SSE$.

FILE
Store_Layout

Using Excel and R to Construct a One-Way ANOVA Table

Fortunately, we can follow simple steps to construct a one-way ANOVA table in Excel and R.

EXAMPLE 13.1

Use Excel and R to obtain the ANOVA table for the store layout example.

SOLUTION:

Using Excel

a. Open the ***Store_Layout*** data file.

b. From the menu, choose **Data > Data Analysis > ANOVA: Single Factor.**

c. In the *ANOVA: Single Factor* dialog box, as shown in Figure 13.2, choose the box next to *Input range,* and then select cells A1 through C11. Check the box in front of *Labels in First Row.* Click **OK.**

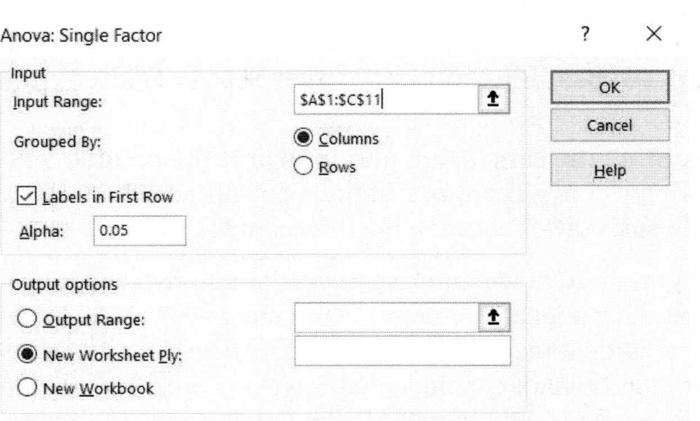

FIGURE 13.2 Excel's ANOVA: Single Factor dialog box

Table 13.4 shows Excel's results for the store layout example. The top portion of the table provides summary statistics for the three different layouts. The bottom portion of the table shows the ANOVA table. You should verify that all values in the ANOVA table match our manual calculations. We have highlighted the value of the test statistic, $F_{(2,27)} = 8.1199$, as well as its corresponding p-value of 0.002. As found earlier, we can conclude at the 5% significance level that mean monthly sales are not the same for the three store layouts. (Excel also provides a statistic called F-crit (not shown) which would be useful if we were using the critical-value approach to conduct a hypothesis test.)

TABLE 13.4 Excel-Produced ANOVA Table for Store Layout Example

SUMMARY					
Groups	**Count**	**Sum**	**Average**	**Variance**	
Layout 1	10	19.2	1.92	0.097333	
Layout 2	10	20.8	2.08	0.106222	
Layout 3	10	24.2	2.42	0.037333	
ANOVA					
Source of Variation	***SS***	***df***	***MS***	***F***	***p*-value**
Between Groups	1.304	2	0.652	**8.119926**	**0.001734**
Within Groups	2.168	27	0.080296		
Total	3.472	29			

Using R

a. Import the ***Store_Layout*** data file into a data frame (table) and label it myData.

b. We reconfigure the data frame using the **stack** function and label it Stacked. The reconfigured data frame will consist of two variables: sales and layout type. For clarity, we use the **colnames** function to label the columns in Stacked as Sales and Layout, respectively. Enter

```
> Stacked <- stack(myData)
> colnames(Stacked) <- c("Sales", "Layout")
```

(You can make sure that your data has been properly reconfigured by entering Stacked at the prompt sign.)

c. We then use the **aov** function, which creates an analysis of variance model object; we label this object as Store. Within the **aov** function, we first specify the numerical variable of interest as a function of the categorical variable(s) or treatment(s). In this example, we are interested in Sales as a function of Layout. We also need to specify the data frame. Enter

```
> Store <- aov(Sales ~ Layout, data = Stacked)
```

d. To obtain the ANOVA table, we use the **anova** function with the object created in Step c. Enter

```
> anova(Store)
```

Table 13.5 shows the R-produced ANOVA results. Note that these results match our calculations as well as the Excel-produced ANOVA table.

TABLE 13.5 R-Produced ANOVA Table for the Store Layout Example

```
Analysis of Variance Table
Response: Sales
            Df     Sum      Sq Mean      Sq F value     Pr(>F)
Layout       2     1.304    0.6520       8.1199         0.001734 **
Residuals   27     2.168    0.0803
---
Signif. codes: 0 '***' 0.001 '**' 0.01 '*' 0.05 '.' 0.1 ' ' 1
```

EXERCISES 13.1

Mechanics

1. **FILE** ***Exercise_13.1.*** A random sample of five observations from three normally distributed populations produced the following data:

Treatments		
A	B	C
22	20	19
25	25	22
27	21	24
24	26	21
22	23	19
$\bar{x}_A = 24$	$\bar{x}_B = 23$	$\bar{x}_C = 21$
$s_A^2 = 4.5$	$s_B^2 = 6.5$	$s_C^2 = 4.5$

   a. Calculate the grand mean.
   b. Calculate *SSTR* and *MSTR*.
   c. Calculate *SSE* and *MSE*.
   d. Specify the competing hypotheses in order to determine whether some differences exist between the population means.
   e. Calculate the value of the $F_{(df_1,df_2)}$ test statistic and the *p*-value.
   f. At the 5% significance level, what is the conclusion to the test?

2. **FILE** ***Exercise_13.2.*** Random sampling from four normally distributed populations produced the following data:

Treatments			
A	B	C	D
−11	−8	−8	−12
−13	−13	−13	−13
−10	−15	−8	−15
	−12	−13	
		−10	

   a. Calculate the grand mean.
   b. Calculate *SSTR* and *MSTR*.
   c. Calculate *SSE* and *MSE*.
   d. Specify the competing hypotheses in order to determine whether some differences exist between the population means.
   e. Calculate the value of the $F_{(df_1,df_2)}$ test statistic and the *p*-value.
   f. At the 10% significance level, what is the conclusion to the test?

3. Given the following information obtained from three normally distributed populations, construct an ANOVA table and perform an ANOVA test of mean differences at the 1% significance level.

   $SSTR = 220.7; SSE = 2252.2; c = 3; n_1 = n_2 = n_3 = 8$

4. Given the following information obtained from four normally distributed populations, construct an ANOVA table and perform an ANOVA test of mean differences at the 5% significance level.

   $SST = 70.47; SSTR = 11.34; c = 4; n_1 = n_2 = n_3 = n_4 = 15$

5. An analysis of variance experiment produced a portion of the accompanying ANOVA table. Assume normality in the underlying populations

Source of Variation	*SS*	*df*	*MS*	*F*	*p-value*
Between Groups	25.08	3	?	?	0.000
Within Groups	92.64	76	?		
Total	117.72	79			

   a. Specify the competing hypotheses in order to determine whether some differences exist between the population means.
   b. Fill in the missing statistics in the ANOVA table.
   c. At the 5% significance level, what is the conclusion to the test?

6. An analysis of variance experiment produced a portion of the following ANOVA table. Assume normality in the underlying populations.

Source of Variation	*SS*	*df*	*MS*	*F*	*p-value*
Between Groups	?	5	?	?	?
Within Groups	4321.11	54	?		
Total	4869.48	59			

   a. Specify the competing hypotheses in order to determine whether some differences exist between the population means.
   b. Fill in the missing statistics in the ANOVA table.
   c. At the 10% significance level, what is the conclusion to the test?

Applications

7. A report finds that Asian residents in Boston have the highest average life expectancy of any racial or ethnic group—a decade longer than black residents. The report included the following summary statistics.

Asian	Black	Latino	White
$\bar{x}_1 = 83.7$ years	$\bar{x}_2 = 73.5$ years	$\bar{x}_3 = 80.6$ years	$\bar{x}_4 = 79.0$ years
$s_1^2 = 26.3$	$s_2^2 = 27.5$	$s_3^2 = 28.2$	$s_4^2 = 24.8$
$n_1 = 20$	$n_2 = 20$	$n_3 = 20$	$n_4 = 20$

a. Specify the competing hypotheses to test whether there are some differences in average life expectancies between the four ethnic groups.

b. Construct an ANOVA table. Assume life expectancies are normally distributed.

c. At the 5% significance level, what is the conclusion to the test?

8. **FILE** ***Detergent.*** A well-known conglomerate claims that its detergent "whitens and brightens better than all the rest." In order to compare the cleansing action of the top three brands of detergents, 24 swatches of white cloth were soiled with red wine and grass stains and then washed in front-loading machines with the respective detergents. A portion of the whiteness readings are included in the accompanying table.

Detergent		
1	2	3
84	78	87
79	74	80
⋮	⋮	⋮
83	79	78

a. Specify the competing hypotheses to test whether there are some differences in the average whitening effectiveness of the three detergents.

b. At the 5% significance level, what is the conclusion to the test? Assume whiteness readings are normally distributed.

9. A survey finds that the cost of long-term care in the United States varies significantly, depending on where an individual lives. An economist collects data from the five states with the highest annual costs (Alaska, Massachusetts, New Jersey, Rhode Island, and Connecticut), in order to determine if his sample data are consistent with the survey's conclusions. The economist provides the following portion of the relevant ANOVA table:

Source of Variation	*SS*	*df*	*MS*	*F*	*p-value*
Between Groups	635.0542	4	?	?	?
Within Groups	253.2192	20	?		
Total	888.2734	24			

a. Specify the competing hypotheses to test whether some differences exist in the mean long-term care costs in these five states.

b. Complete the ANOVA table. Assume that long-term care costs are normally distributed.

c. At the 5% significance level, do mean costs differ?

10. **FILE** ***Sports.*** An online survey finds that household income of recreational athletes varies by sport. In order to verify this claim, an economist samples five sports enthusiasts participating in each of four different recreational sports and obtains each enthusiast's income (in $1,000s), as shown in the accompanying table.

Snorkeling	Sailing	Windsurfing	Bowling
90.9	87.6	75.9	79.3
86.0	95.0	75.6	75.8
93.6	94.6	83.1	79.6
98.8	87.2	74.4	78.5
98.4	82.5	80.5	73.2

a. Specify the competing hypotheses in order to test the survey's claim.

b. Do some average incomes differ depending on the recreational sport? Explain. Assume incomes are normally distributed.

11. The following output summarizes the results of an analysis of variance experiment in which the treatments were three different hybrid cars and the variable measured was the miles per gallon (mpg) obtained while driving the same route. Assume mpg is normally distributed.

Source of Variation	*SS*	*df*	*MS*	*F*	*p-value*
Between Groups	1034.51	2	517.26	19.86	4.49E-07
Within Groups	1302.41	50	26.05		
Total	2336.92	52			

At the 5% significance level, can we conclude that average mpg differs between the hybrids? Explain.

12. Do energy costs vary dramatically depending on where you live in the United States? Annual energy costs are collected from 25 households in four regions in the United States. A portion of the ANOVA table is shown.

Source of Variation	*SS*	*df*	*MS*	*F*	*p-value*
Between Groups	7531769	3	?	?	7.13E-24
Within Groups	3492385	96	?		
Total	11024154	99			

a. Complete the ANOVA table. Assume energy costs are normally distributed.
b. At the 1% significance level, can we conclude that average annual energy costs vary by region?

13. **FILE** ***Buggies.*** Wenton Powersports produces dune buggies. They have three assembly lines, "Razor," "Blazer," and "Tracer," named after the particular dune buggy models produced on those lines. Each assembly line was originally designed using the same target production rate. However, over the years, various changes have been made to the lines. Accordingly, management wishes to determine whether the assembly lines are still operating at the same average hourly production rate. The accompanying table shows a portion of the production data (in dune buggies/hour) for the last eight hours.

Razor	Blazer	Tracer
11	10	9
10	8	9
⋮	⋮	⋮
11	8	9

a. Specify the competing hypotheses to test whether there are some differences in the mean production rates across the three assembly lines.
b. At the 5% significance level, what is the conclusion to the test? What about the 10% significance level? Assume production rates are normally distributed.

14. **FILE** ***Fill_Volumes.*** In the carbonated beverage industry, dispensing pressure can be an important factor in achieving accurate fill volumes. Too little pressure can slow down the dispensing process. Too much pressure can create excess "fizz" and, thus, inaccurate fill volumes. Accordingly, a leading beverage manufacturer wants to conduct an experiment at three different pressure settings to determine if differences exist in the mean fill volumes. Forty bottles with a target fill volume of 12 ounces were filled at each pressure setting, and the resulting fill volumes (in ounces) were recorded. A portion of the data is shown in the accompanying table.

Low	Medium	High
12.00	12.00	11.56
11.97	11.87	11.55
⋮	⋮	⋮
12.00	12.14	11.80

a. Specify the competing hypotheses to test whether there are differences in the mean fill volumes across the three pressure settings.
b. At the 5% significance level, what is the conclusion to the test? What about the 1% significance level?

15. **FILE** ***Exam_Scores.*** A statistics instructor wonders whether significant differences exist in her students' final exam scores in her three different sections. She randomly selects the scores from 10 students in each section. A portion of the data is shown in the accompanying table. Assume exam scores are normally distributed.

Section 1	Section 2	Section 3
85	91	74
68	84	69
⋮	⋮	⋮
74	75	73

Do these data provide enough evidence at the 5% significance level to indicate that there are some differences in final exam scores among these three sections?

16. **FILE** ***Patronage.*** The accompanying table shows a portion of the number of customers that frequent a restaurant on weekend days over the past 52 weeks.

Fridays	Saturdays	Sundays
391	450	389
362	456	343
⋮	⋮	⋮
443	441	376

At the 5% significance level, can we conclude that the average number of customers that frequent the restaurant differs by weekend day?

17. **FILE** ***Revenues.*** The accompanying table shows a portion of quarterly revenues (in $ millions) for a large firm over the past 10 years. Assume revenues are normally distributed.

Quarter 1	Quarter 2	Quarter 3	Quarter 4
2637	2199	2170	2483
2614	2337	2260	2682
⋮	⋮	⋮	⋮
4799	4406	4733	5077

Use a one-way ANOVA test to determine if the data provide enough evidence at the 5% significance level to indicate that there are quarterly differences in the firm's revenue.

18. **FILE** ***Field_Score.*** A human resource specialist wants to determine whether the average job satisfaction score (on a scale of 0 to 100) differs depending on a person's field of employment. She collects scores from 30 employees in three different fields. A portion of the data is shown in the accompanying table.

Field 1	Field 2	Field 3
80	76	81
76	73	77
⋮	⋮	⋮
79	67	80

At the 10% significance level, can we conclude that the average job satisfaction differs by field?

13.2 MULTIPLE COMPARISON METHODS

LO 13.2

Use Fisher's LSD method and Tukey's HSD method to determine which means differ.

In Section 13.1, we used a one-way ANOVA test to determine whether differences exist between population means. Suppose that for a given sample we reject the null hypothesis of equal means. As noted earlier, while the ANOVA test determines that not all population means are equal, it does not indicate which ones differ. To find out which population means differ requires further analysis of the direction and the statistical significance of the difference between paired population means ($\mu_i - \mu_j$). By constructing confidence intervals for all pairwise differences for the population means, we can identify which means significantly differ from one another. The first method we discuss is often referred to as **Fisher's Least Significant Difference (LSD) method.**

We also introduce an improved method, developed by the renowned 20th-century statistician John Tukey (1915–2000). This is often referred to as **Tukey's Honestly Significant Difference (HSD) method.**

It is important to note that we can employ Fisher's or Tukey's methods only if the ANOVA test determines that not all population means are equal. There are no significant differences to find if the ANOVA test does not reject the null hypothesis of equal means.

Fisher's Least Significant Difference (LSD) Method

In Chapter 10, we stated that, when the population variances are unknown but assumed equal, the 100(1 − α)% confidence interval for the difference between two population means $\mu_i - \mu_j$ is

$$(\bar{x}_i - \bar{x}_j) \pm t_{\alpha/2, n_i+n_j-2}\sqrt{s_p^2\left(\frac{1}{n_i} + \frac{1}{n_j}\right)}.$$

Here, s_p^2 is a pooled estimate of the common population variance and is computed as

$$s_p^2 = \frac{(n_i - 1)s_i^2 + (n_j - 1)s_j^2}{n_i + n_j - 2}.$$

Fisher's innovation is to substitute the mean square error *MSE* from the one-way ANOVA test for s_p^2. This is a preferred approach because *MSE* uses all samples whereas s_p^2 uses only two of the samples for the pairwise comparison. Recall that when we conduct a one-way ANOVA test, we assume that we are sampling from populations that have the same population variance σ^2. We still apply the t_{df} distribution, but we use the degrees of freedom corresponding to *MSE*, or $df = n_T - c$.

FISHER'S CONFIDENCE INTERVAL FOR $\mu_i - \mu_j$

Fisher's 100(1 − α)% confidence interval for the difference between two population means $\mu_i - \mu_j$ is given by

$$(\bar{x}_i - \bar{x}_j) \pm t_{\alpha/2, n_T-c}\sqrt{MSE\left(\frac{1}{n_i} + \frac{1}{n_j}\right)},$$

where the mean square error *MSE* is estimated from the one-way ANOVA test.

EXAMPLE 13.2

Recall in Example 13.1 that we concluded that there are differences between mean monthly sales among the three store layouts. Use the information from Table 13.4 to calculate 95% confidence intervals for the difference between all possible pairings of the three population means. Comment on the direction and the significance of the differences at the 5% level.

SOLUTION: Table 13.4 shows that the sample means for Layout 1, Layout 2, and Layout 3 are $\bar{x}_1 = 1.92$, $\bar{x}_2 = 2.08$, and $\bar{x}_3 = 2.42$, respectively. There are 10 observations in each of the three samples, so $n_1 = n_2 = n_3 = 10$. Also, $MSE = 0.0803$, $n_T - c = 27$, and $t_{\alpha/2, n_T - c} = t_{0.025,27} = 2.052$. Table 13.6 shows the 95% confidence intervals.

Store_Layout

TABLE 13.6 Fisher's 95% Confidence Intervals for Store Layout Example

Population Mean Differences	Confidence Interval
$\mu_1 - \mu_2$	$(1.92 - 2.08) \pm 2.052\sqrt{0.0803\left(\frac{1}{10} + \frac{1}{10}\right)} = -0.16 \pm 0.26$ or $[-0.42, 0.10]$
$\mu_1 - \mu_3$	$(1.92 - 2.42) \pm 2.052\sqrt{0.0803\left(\frac{1}{10} + \frac{1}{10}\right)} = -0.50 \pm 0.26$ or $[-0.76, -0.24]$*
$\mu_2 - \mu_3$	$(2.08 - 2.42) \pm 2.052\sqrt{0.0803\left(\frac{1}{10} + \frac{1}{10}\right)} = -0.34 \pm 0.26$ or $[-0.60, -0.08]$*

The 95% confidence interval for $\mu_1 - \mu_2$ is given by -0.16 ± 0.26 which is $[-0.42, 0.10]$. Since this interval contains the value zero, we cannot reject the null hypothesis, given by H_0: $\mu_1 - \mu_2 = 0$, at the 5% significance level. In other words, we cannot conclude that mean monthly sales differ between Layout 1 and Layout 2. The interval for $\mu_1 - \mu_3$ is $[-0.76, -0.24]$ and the interval for $\mu_2 - \mu_3$ is $[-0.60, -0.08]$. Both intervals are below the value zero, implying that mean monthly sales differ between Layout 1 and Layout 3, as well as between Layout 2 and Layout 3. We mark each of these intervals with the asterisk * which indicates that the means significantly differ—this is a common marking in computer output.

In Example 13.2, we have three paired tests. As noted before, if we use the 5% significance level for each test, the probability that we would make a Type I error (incorrectly rejecting a null hypothesis of equal means) on *at least* one of these individual tests will be greater than 5%. The more means we compare, the more the Type I error becomes inflated. We will now discuss Tukey's method that avoids this problem.

Tukey's Honestly Significant Difference (HSD) Method

An improved multiple comparison technique is Tukey's honestly significant difference (HSD) method. The original Tukey's HSD method was introduced with **balanced** data, but it was subsequently modified for **unbalanced** data. If there are an equal number of observations in each sample—that is, when $n_1 = n_2 = \cdots = n_c$—then the data are balanced. In situations where different numbers of observations occur in each sample—that is, when $n_i \neq n_j$—the data are unbalanced. Tukey's method uses the **studentized range distribution,** which has broader, flatter, and thicker tails than the t_{df} distribution. In other words, for a given probability under the right tail of the distribution, the studentized range value will be larger than the corresponding t_{df} value. Therefore, Tukey's HSD method protects against an inflated risk of a Type I error.

TUKEY'S CONFIDENCE INTERVAL FOR $\mu_i - \mu_j$

Tukey's 100(1 − α)% confidence interval for the difference between two population means $\mu_i - \mu_j$ is given by

- $(\bar{x}_i - \bar{x}_j) \pm q_{\alpha,(c,n_T-c)}\sqrt{\frac{MSE}{n}}$ for balanced data ($n_i = n_j = n$), and
- $(\bar{x}_i - \bar{x}_j) \pm q_{\alpha,(c,n_T-c)}\sqrt{\frac{MSE}{2}\left(\frac{1}{n_i}+\frac{1}{n_j}\right)}$ for unbalanced data ($n_i \neq n_j$),

where $q_{\alpha,(c,n_T-c)}$ is the studentized range value.

Tukey's method ensures that the probability of a Type I error equals α, irrespective of the number of pairwise comparisons.

The studentized range value $q_{\alpha,(c,n_T-c)}$ varies with the significance level α, the number of populations c, and $n_T - c$. Table 13.7 shows a portion of the studentized range table; Table 5 in Appendix B provides a more comprehensive table. For example, with $\alpha = 0.05$, $c = 6$, and $n_T - c = 19$, we find $q_{0.05,(6,19)} = 4.47$. With $\alpha = 0.01$, $c = 3$, and $n_T - c = 20$, we find $q_{0.01,(3,20)} = 4.64$. These values are in boldface in Table 13.7.

TABLE 13.7 Portion of Values for $q_{\alpha,(c,n_T-c)}$ in Tukey's HSD Method

		c = number of means							
$n_T - c$	α	2	3	4	5	6	7	8	9
19	0.05	2.96	3.59	3.98	4.25	**4.47**	4.65	4.79	4.92
	0.01	4.05	4.67	5.05	5.33	5.55	5.73	5.89	6.02
20	0.05	2.95	3.58	3.96	4.23	4.45	4.62	4.77	4.90
	0.01	4.02	**4.64**	5.02	5.29	5.51	5.69	5.84	5.97

In instances where we do not see values for $n_T - c$ in Table 5 of Appendix B, we can either round down or interpolate between two values. For example, in the store layout example, $n_T - c = 27$, a value that does not appear in Table 5 of Appendix B. If we want the value for $q_{0.05,(3,27)}$, then we can take the average between $q_{0.05,(3,24)}$ and $q_{0.05,(3,30)}$ which is equal to $(3.53 + 3.49)/2 = 3.51$. We will use this value in Example 13.3.

EXAMPLE 13.3

Repeat Example 13.2 using Tukey's HSD method instead of Fisher's LSD method.

SOLUTION: We use Tukey's confidence interval for balanced data since each sample size is the same ($n_1 = n_2 = n_3 = 10$). Given $\alpha = 0.05$, $c = 3$, and $n_T - c = 30 - 3 = 27$, we refer to Table 5 in Appendix B to approximate $q_{\alpha,(c,n_T-c)} = q_{0.05,(3,27)} = 3.51$. We use $(\bar{x}_i - \bar{x}_j) \pm q_{\alpha,(c,n_T-c)}\sqrt{\frac{MSE}{n}}$ to compute 95% confidence intervals for all pairwise differences of the means. The results are shown in Table 13.8.

Store_Layout

TABLE 13.8 Tukey's 95% Confidence Intervals for Store Layout Example

Population Mean Differences	Confidence Interval
$\mu_1 - \mu_2$	$(1.92 - 2.08) \pm 3.51\sqrt{\frac{0.0803}{10}}$ or [−0.4745, 0.1545]
$\mu_1 - \mu_3$	$(1.92 - 2.42) \pm 3.51\sqrt{\frac{0.0803}{10}}$ or [−0.8145, −0.1855]*
$\mu_2 - \mu_3$	$(2.08 - 2.42) \pm 3.51\sqrt{\frac{0.0803}{10}}$ or [−0.6545, −0.0255]*

The asterisk * shows that the confidence interval does not include the value zero, thus indicating that the corresponding means are different at the 5% significance level. The results are consistent with those found in Example 13.2; that is, at the 5% significance level, we cannot conclude that mean monthly sales differ between Layout 1 and Layout 2. However, at the 5% significance level, mean monthly sales using Layout 3 differ from mean monthly sales using Layout 1 and Layout 2.

Using R to Construct Tukey Confidence Intervals for $\mu_1 - \mu_2$

Unfortunately, Excel does not generate Fisher's LSD or Tukey's HSD confidence intervals. R does generate both types of confidence intervals; however, it is more straightforward, and ultimately more useful, to obtain Tukey's HSD confidence intervals with R. To replicate the results from Example 13.3, we follow these steps.

a. Import the ***Store_Layout*** data file into a data frame (table) and label it myData.

b. In order to reconfigure the data frame, we use the **stack** function and label the reconfigured data frame as Stacked. We use the **colnames** function to label the columns in Stacked as Sales and Layout, respectively. We use the **aov** function to create an analysis of variance model object, which we label as Store, and specify Sales as a function of Layout. Enter

```
> Stacked <- stack(myData)
> colnames(Stacked) <- c("Sales", "Layout")
> Store <- aov(Sales ~ Layout, data=Stacked)
```

c. We use the **TukeyHSD** function to obtain Tukey's HSD confidence intervals. Within the function, we specify the object from Step b, and we use the option *conf.level* to specify the confidence level. Enter

```
> TukeyHSD(Store,  conf.level = 0.95)
```

Table 13.9 shows the R-produced Tukey's HSD confidence intervals for the store layout example.

TABLE 13.9 R-Produced Tukey Confidence Intervals for the store layout example

```
  Tukey multiple comparisons of means
    95% family-wise confidence level
Fit: aov(formula = Sales ~ Layout, data = Stacked)
$Layout
                   diff         lwr       upr       p adj
Layout 2-Layout 1  0.16  -0.15420454  0.4742045  0.4279695
Layout 3-Layout 1  0.50   0.18579546  0.8142045  0.0014376
Layout 3-Layout 2  0.34   0.02579546  0.6542045  0.0319536
```

Note that the only difference in the results for the confidence intervals reported in Tables 13.8 and 13.9 is the order when finding the differences; this results in inverse values for the lower and upper limits. R also reports the p-values for testing pairwise differences, which confirm the results found in Example 13.3. At the 5% significance level, the average sales do not differ between Layout 1 and Layout 2; however, at the 5% significance level, average sales using Layout 3 differ from average sales using Layout 1 and Layout 2.

SYNOPSIS OF INTRODUCTORY CASE

Driven by lower profit margins, grocery stores are under constant pressure to make their stores better than their competitors. One of the effective ways to do that is by changing the store's layout. Grocery stores rely on consumer psychology for getting customers to spend more money, often by buying items that they had not planned on buying.

Ariel Skelley/DigitalVision/Getty Images

Sean Cox, vice president of sales and marketing at a large grocery chain, wants to determine whether mean monthly sales differ depending on the store layout. He implements three different store layouts at 10 different stores for one month and measures total sales for each store at the end of the month. An ANOVA test produces an F-statistic of 8.1199 with a p-value of 0.002. At the 5% significance level, Sean is able to conclude that there are differences in mean monthly sales depending on the store layout.

Sean also constructs confidence intervals for all pairwise differences to identify pairings of layouts that have statistically different mean monthly sales. At the 5% significance level, mean monthly sales do not differ between Layout 1 and Layout 2. However, significant differences exist between Layout 1 and Layout 3 and between Layout 2 and Layout 3. Sean is able to conclude that mean monthly sales are highest when Layout 3 is used.

EXERCISES 13.2

Mechanics

19. The following statistics are computed by sampling from three normal populations whose variances are equal:

$\bar{x}_1 = 25.3, n_1 = 8; \bar{x}_2 = 31.5, n_2 = 10; \bar{x}_3 = 32.3, n_3 = 6;$
$MSE = 27.2$

a. Calculate 95% confidence intervals for $\mu_1 - \mu_2, \mu_1 - \mu_3$, and $\mu_2 - \mu_3$ to test for mean differences with Fisher's LSD approach.

b. Repeat the analysis with Tukey's HSD approach.

c. Which of these two approaches would you use to determine whether differences exist between the population means? Explain.

20. The following statistics are calculated by sampling from four normal populations whose variances are equal:

$\bar{x}_1 = 149, n_1 = 10; \bar{x}_2 = 154, n_2 = 10; \bar{x}_3 = 143, n_3 = 10;$
$\bar{x}_4 = 139, n_4 = 10; MSE = 51.3$

a. Use Fisher's LSD method to determine which population means differ at $\alpha = 0.01$.

b. Use Tukey's HSD method to determine which population means differ at $\alpha = 0.01$.

c. Do all population means differ? Explain.

21. A one-way analysis of variance experiment produced the following ANOVA table. Assume normality in the underlying populations.

SUMMARY					
Groups	Count		Average		
Column 1	6		0.57		
Column 2	6		1.38		
Column 3	6		2.33		
Source of Variation	SS	df	MS	F	p-value
Between Groups	9.12	2	4.56	12.84	0.0006
Within Groups	5.33	15	0.36		
Total	14.46	17			

a. Conduct an ANOVA test at the 5% significance level to determine if some population means differ.
b. Calculate 95% confidence interval estimates for $\mu_1 - \mu_2$, $\mu_1 - \mu_3$, and $\mu_2 - \mu_3$ with Tukey's HSD approach.
c. Given your response to part (b), which means significantly differ?

22. A one-way analysis of variance experiment produced the following ANOVA table. Assume normality in the underlying populations.

SUMMARY					
Groups	Count		Average		
Column 1	10		349		
Column 2	10		348		
Column 3	10		366		
Column 4	10		365		
Source of Variation	*SS*	*df*	*MS*	*F*	*p-value*
Between Groups	2997.11	3	999.04	15.54	1.2E-06
Within Groups	2314.71	36	64.30		
Total	5311.82	39			

a. Use Fisher's LSD method to determine which means differ at the 5% level of significance.
b. Use Tukey's HSD method to determine which means differ at the 5% level of significance.
c. Given your responses to parts (a) and (b), do the population means differ at the 5% significance level?

Applications

23. The following output summarizes the results for a one-way analysis of variance experiment in which the treatments were three different hybrid cars and the variable measured was the miles per gallon (mpg) obtained while driving the same route. Assume that mpg is normally distributed.

Hybrid 1: $\bar{x}_1 = 38, n_1 = 20$
Hybrid 2: $\bar{x}_2 = 48, n_2 = 15$
Hybrid 3: $\bar{x}_3 = 39, n_3 = 18$

Source of Variation	*SS*	*df*	*MS*	*F*	*p-value*
Between Groups	1034.51	2	517.26	19.86	4.49E-07
Within Groups	1302.41	50	26.05		
Total	2336.92	52			

a. At the 5% significance level, can we conclude that average mpg differs between the hybrids?
b. If significant differences exist, use Tukey's HSD method at the 5% significance level to determine which hybrids' means differ.

24. In an attempt to improve efficiency, a coffee chain has implemented "lean" Japanese techniques at many of its locations. By reducing the time employees spend on bending, reaching, and walking, they will have more time to interact with customers. Suppose the coffee chain adopts the lean technique at Store 1 but makes no changes at Stores 2 and 3. On a recent Monday morning between the hours of 7:00 AM and 8:00 AM, the following statistics were obtained relating to average time per order (in seconds):

Store 1: $\bar{x}_1 = 56, n_1 = 18$
Store 2: $\bar{x}_2 = 66, n_2 = 12$
Store 3: $\bar{x}_3 = 63, n_3 = 14$

The following ANOVA table was produced:

Source of Variation	*SS*	*df*	*MS*	*F*	*p-value*
Between Groups	811.70	2	405.85	52.11	5.5E-12
Within Groups	319.30	41	7.79		
Total	1131.00	43			

a. At the 5% significance level, can we conclude that average times per order vary by technique? Assume that time per order is normally distributed.
b. Compute 95% confidence interval estimates for all paired differences for the means using Fisher's LSD approach.
c. Repeat the analysis with Tukey's HSD approach.
d. Which of these two approaches is more reliable? Explain.

25. Do energy costs vary dramatically depending on where you live in the United States? Annual energy costs are collected from 25 households in four regions in the United States. Sample means for each region and a portion of the ANOVA table is shown in the accompanying table.

SUMMARY		
Groups	Count	Average
West	25	1491
Northeast	25	2391
Midwest	25	1768
South	25	1758

Source of Variation	SS	df	MS	F	p-value
Between Groups	7531769	3	?	?	7.13E-24
Within Groups	3492385	96	?		
Total	11024154	99			

a. Complete the ANOVA table.
b. At the 1% significance level, can we conclude that average annual energy costs vary by region?
c. If significant differences exist, use Tukey's HSD method at the 1% significance level to determine which regions' means differ.

26. Elastotech, a plastics company, is trying to determine whether four successive daily batches of their Lexan polycarbonate have the same mean hardness value. Four daily samples of polycarbonate were taken, and the resulting hardness values were measured (using the Rockwell *R* scale). The following output was obtained.

Day 1	Day 2	Day 3	Day 4
$\bar{x}_1 = 115.75$	$\bar{x}_2 = 108.00$	$\bar{x}_3 = 121.39$	$\bar{x}_4 = 119.53$
$n_1 = 20$	$n_2 = 16$	$n_3 = 18$	$n_4 = 17$

Source of Variation	SS	df	MS	F	p-value
Between Groups	1751.62	3	583.87	19.29	0.000
Within Groups	2028.26	67	30.27		
Total	3779.89	70			

a. At the 1% significance level, can we conclude that the mean hardness differs among the four daily batches? Assume that hardness is normally distributed.
b. If significant differences exist, use Tukey's HSD method at the 1% significance level to determine which batches have different mean hardness values.

27. Producers of a new grass seed claim that grass grown using its seed blend requires less maintenance as compared to other brands. For instance, grass grown using the new grass seed needs mowing only once a month. Suppose an independent tester wants to test whether the average height of grass after one month's growth is the same between the new grass seed and the other two top-selling brands. The independent tester measures 25 grass blades using each of the three seeds (glass blades are measured in inches), and constructs the following ANOVA table with supporting descriptive statistics.

SUMMARY		
Groups	Count	Average
New Grass Seed	25	4.83
Top Brand 1	25	6.50
Top Brand 2	25	6.99

Source of Variation	SS	df	MS	F	p-value
Between Groups	64.43	2	32.21	121.67	8.09E-24
Within Groups	19.06	72	0.26		
Total	83.49	74			

a. At the 5% significance level, can the independent tester conclude that the average heights of grass blades differ by brand? Assume that heights are normally distributed.
b. If significant differences exist, use Tukey's HSD method at the 5% significance level to determine which brands differ.

28. **FILE** ***Employee_Absences.*** A production manager is examining whether work shift is related to employee absenteeism. The number of days absent over the past year was tallied for random samples of 25 workers on each shift. A portion of the data is shown in the accompanying table.

First Shift	Second Shift	Third Shift
14	5	19
7	10	9
⋮	⋮	⋮
2	9	10

a. At the 5% significance level, can the production manager conclude that the mean days of absenteeism differ among the three shifts? Does the conclusion change at the 10% significance level? Assume that days are normally distributed.
b. If significant differences exist, use Fisher's LSD method at the 10% significance level to determine which shifts have different mean days of absenteeism.

29. **FILE** ***Patronage.*** The accompanying table shows a portion of the number of customers that ate at a restaurant on weekend days over the past 52 weeks.

Fridays	Saturdays	Sundays
391	450	389
362	456	343
⋮	⋮	⋮
443	441	376

a. Verify that the average number of customers that frequent the restaurant differs by weekend day at the 5% significance level.
b. Use Tukey's HSD method at the 5% significance level to determine which weekend days differ.

LO 13.3

13.3 TWO-WAY ANOVA TEST: NO INTERACTION

Conduct and evaluate a two-way ANOVA test with no interaction.

A one-way ANOVA test is used to compare population means based on one categorical variable or one factor. For instance, we can use a one-way ANOVA test to determine whether differences exist in average miles per gallon depending on the brand name of hybrid cars. A **two-way ANOVA test** extends the analysis by measuring the effects of two factors simultaneously. Suppose we want to determine if the brand of a hybrid car and the octane level of gasoline influence average miles per gallon. Whereas a one-way ANOVA test is able to assess either the brand effect or the octane-level effect in isolation, a two-way ANOVA test is able to assess the effect of one factor while controlling for the other factor. The additional factor explains some of the unexplained variation in miles per gallon, or equivalently, reduces the error sum of squares *SSE* for a more discriminating $F_{(df_1,df_2)}$ test statistic.

Another feature of a two-way ANOVA test is that it can be extended to capture the interaction between the factors. In the miles per gallon example, if we believe that some brands of a hybrid car react more positively to the octane levels than others, then we can include the interaction of these factors in examining miles per gallon. We use a test that determines whether the factors do indeed interact.

A two-way ANOVA test is used to simultaneously examine the effect of two factors on the population mean. This test can be conducted with or without the interaction of the factors.

In the following example, we initially conduct a one-way ANOVA test and quickly recognize its limitations. We then introduce a two-way ANOVA test without interaction. In Section 13.4, we discuss a two-way ANOVA test with interaction.

EXAMPLE 13.4

Julia Hayes is an undergraduate who is completely undecided as to what career she should pursue. To help in her decision process, she wants to determine whether or not there are significant differences in annual incomes depending on the field of employment. Initially, she confines her analysis to the following three fields: educational services, financial services, and medical services. As a preliminary experiment, she surveys four workers from each of these three fields and asks how much he/she earns annually. Table 13.10 shows the results (in \$1,000s) from the experiment.

TABLE 13.10 Data for Example 13.4

Educational Services	Financial Services	Medical Services
35	58	110
18	90	62
75	25	26
46	45	43

FILE
One_Factor

At the 5% significance level, conduct a one-way ANOVA test to determine if differences exist among mean incomes depending on the field of employment. Assume that incomes are normally distributed.

SOLUTION: Table 13.11 shows the relevant results from implementing a one-way ANOVA test.

TABLE 13.11 ANOVA Results for Example 13.4

ANOVA					
Source of Variation	*SS*	*df*	*MS*	*F*	*p-value*
Between Groups	579.5	2	289.75	0.330	0.727
Within Groups	7902.75	9	878.0833		
Total	8482.25	11			

In order to determine whether mean incomes differ by field of employment, we specify the following hypotheses:

$$H_0: \mu_{\text{Education}} = \mu_{\text{Financial}} = \mu_{\text{Medical}}$$
$$H_A: \text{Not all population means are equal.}$$

The value of the test statistic is $F_{(2,9)} = 0.330$ with a corresponding p-value of 0.727. Since the p-value is greater than 0.05, we do not reject H_0. At the 5% significance level, we cannot conclude that mean incomes differ by field.

Julia is surprised by these results, since she feels that those in the educational services industry probably earn less than those in the other two fields. Julia is advised that she must interpret these results with caution because many other factors influence annual income—one of which is an individual's education level. We can capture the true influence of field of employment on income only when education level is held fixed.

As mentioned earlier, a two-way ANOVA test helps us find a more discriminating $F_{(df_1,df_2)}$ test statistic, since the additional factor reduces the resulting *SSE*. An added requirement for a two-way ANOVA test is that all groups must have the same sample size.

To show how a two-way ANOVA test works, we redo the income example, but this time we allow the variation in income to be affected by field of employment (factor *A*) *and* education level (factor *B*). We match a worker from each field according to his or her highest degree. For example, we randomly select a worker from the educational services industry who does not have a high school degree. We then randomly select three more workers from this field whose highest education level is a high school degree, a bachelor's degree, or a master's degree, respectively. We repeat this process for the other two fields. The outcomes in this experiment are matched or blocked in the sense that one worker is randomly selected from each field of employment depending on his/her education level. In general, blocks are the levels at which we hold an extraneous factor fixed, so that we can measure its contribution to the total variation of the variable. This experimental design is called a **randomized block design.** The experiment in this example is designed to eliminate the variability in income attributable to differences in education level.

Table 13.12 shows the incomes (in $1,000s) for 12 workers according to their field of employment and highest education level. The observations can be found in the ***Two_Factor*** data file. Table 13.12 also shows the factor means.

FILE
Two_Factor

TABLE 13.12 Data for Two-Factor Income Example (No Interaction)

Education Level (Factor *B*)	Field of Employment (Factor *A*) Educational Services	Financial Services	Medical Services	Factor *B* Means
No High School	18	25	26	$\bar{x}_{No\ High\ School} = 23.00$
High School	35	45	43	$\bar{x}_{High\ School} = 41.00$
Bachelor's	46	58	62	$\bar{x}_{Bachelor's} = 53.3333$
Master's	75	90	110	$\bar{x}_{Master's} = 91.6667$
Factor *A* Means	$\bar{x}_{Education} = 43.50$	$\bar{x}_{Financial} = 54.50$	$\bar{x}_{Medical} = 60.25$	$\bar{\bar{x}} = 52.75$

The goal of the analysis is to answer the following two questions:

- At the 5% significance level, do average annual incomes differ by field of employment?
- At the 5% significance level, do average annual incomes differ by education level?

A one-way ANOVA test is based on one factor for which we used the notation "sum of squares due to treatments *SSTR*" to capture the variability *between* the levels of this factor. Since we are now examining two factors, we use the notation *SSA* to capture the variability *between* the levels of factor *A* and *SSB* to capture the variability *between* the levels of factor *B*.

DECOMPOSING TOTAL VARIATION IN A TWO-WAY ANOVA TEST WITHOUT INTERACTION

In a two-way ANOVA test without interaction, the total sum of squares, *SST*, of the variable is partitioned into three distinct components: the sum of squares for factor *A*, *SSA*; the sum of squares for factor *B*, *SSB*; and the error sum of squares, *SSE*. That is, $SST = SSA + SSB + SSE$.

The Sum of Squares for Factor *A*, *SSA*

We calculate the sum of squares for factor *A*, *SSA*, as we did before; that is, we first calculate the sum of the squared differences between the mean for each level of factor *A* (field of employment) and the grand mean. We then multiply this sum by the number of rows in the randomized block design *r*, or equivalently, the number of factor B categories. For the two-factor income example, *r* equals 4. We calculate *SSA* as

$$\begin{aligned} SSA &= r\sum_{i=1}^{c}(\bar{x}_i - \bar{\bar{x}})^2 \\ &= 4[(43.50 - 52.75)^2 + (54.50 - 52.75)^2 + (60.25 - 52.75)^2] \\ &= 579.50. \end{aligned}$$

Dividing *SSA* by its degrees of freedom, $c - 1$, (where *c* is the number of columns in the randomized block design, or equivalently, the number of factor A categories) yields the mean square for factor *A*, *MSA*. For the two-factor income example, *c* equals 3, so *MSA* is

$$MSA = \frac{SSA}{c-1} = \frac{579.50}{3-1} = 289.75.$$

The Sum of Squares for Factor *B*, *SSB*

In order to obtain the sum of squares for factor B (education level), SSB, we calculate the sum of the squared differences between the mean for each level of factor B and the grand mean. We multiply this sum by c; thus, for the two-factor income example, we calculate SSB as

$$\begin{aligned} SSB &= c\sum_{j=1}^{r}(\bar{x}_j - \bar{\bar{x}})^2 \\ &= 3[(23.00 - 52.75)^2 + (41.00 - 52.75)^2 + (55.3333 - 52.75)^2 \\ &\quad + (91.6667 - 52.75)^2] \\ &= 7{,}632.9167. \end{aligned}$$

Dividing SSB by its degrees of freedom, $r - 1$, yields the mean square for factor B, MSB, or

$$MSB = \frac{SSB}{r-1} = \frac{7{,}632.9167}{4-1} = 2{,}544.3056$$

The Error Sum of Squares, *SSE*

As mentioned earlier, in a two-way ANOVA test without interaction, $SST = SSA + SSB + SSE$. We can calculate SSE by rewriting this expression as $SSE = SST - (SSA + SSB)$. We calculate SST as the sum of squared differences between each observation and the grand mean, or equivalently, $SST = \sum_{i=1}^{c}\sum_{j=1}^{r}(x_{ij} - \bar{\bar{x}})^2$. For the two-factor income example, we calculate SST as

$$\begin{aligned} SST &= \sum_{i=1}^{c}\sum_{j=1}^{r}(x_{ij} - \bar{\bar{x}})^2 \\ &= (18 - 52.75)^2 + (35 - 52.75)^2 + \cdots + (110 - 52.75)^2 \\ &= 8{,}482.25. \end{aligned}$$

We then compute SSE as

$$SSE = SST - (SSA + SSB) = 8{,}482.25 - (579.50 + 7{,}632.9167) = 269.8333.$$

We can make some generalizations about the difference in the magnitudes of the SSE values for the one-way ANOVA versus the two-way ANOVA income examples. When we used one factor (field of employment) to explain annual incomes, the value of SSE was 7,902.75 (see Table 13.11). By ignoring the second factor (education level), we could not establish that annual incomes were different by field of employment. However, once we include this second factor, the value of SSE declines dramatically to 269.8333. We will show shortly that by accounting for the effect of education level on income, the $F_{(df_1, df_2)}$ test allows Julia to conclude that significant differences do exist among annual incomes by field of employment.

Dividing SSE by its degrees of freedom ($n_T - c - r + 1$) yields the mean square error, MSE, or

$$MSE = \frac{SSE}{n_T - c - r + 1} = \frac{269.8333}{12 - 3 - 4 + 1} = 44.9722.$$

The test statistics for conducting a two-way ANOVA test without interaction can be summarized as follows.

TEST STATISTICS FOR A TWO-WAY ANOVA TEST—NO INTERACTION

When testing for differences between the factor A means (the column means), the value of the test statistic is computed as

$$F_{(df_1,df_2)} = \frac{MSA}{MSE},$$

where $df_1 = c - 1$, $df_2 = n_T - c - r + 1$, MSA is the mean square for factor A, and MSE is the mean square error.

When testing for differences between the factor B means (the row means), the value of the test statistic is computed as

$$F_{(df_1,df_2)} = \frac{MSB}{MSE},$$

where $df_1 = r - 1$, $df_2 = n_T - c - r + 1$, MSB is the mean square for factor B, and MSE is the mean square error.

In these tests, c represents the number of columns, r the number of rows, and n_T the total sample size. An ANOVA test is always specified as a right-tailed test.

As we will show shortly, Excel and R easily provide these statistics. Table 13.13 shows the general format of an ANOVA table when conducting a two-way ANOVA test without interaction.

TABLE 13.13 General Format of ANOVA Table for Randomized Block Design

Source of Variation	SS	df	MS	F	p-value
Rows	SSB	$r - 1$	$MSB = \frac{SSB}{r-1}$	$F_{(df_1,df_2)} = \frac{MSB}{MSE}$	$P\left(F_{(df_1,df_2)} \geq \frac{MSB}{MSE}\right)$
Columns	SSA	$c - 1$	$MSA = \frac{SSA}{c-1}$	$F_{(df_1,df_2)} = \frac{MSA}{MSE}$	$P\left(F_{(df_1,df_2)} \geq \frac{MSA}{MSE}\right)$
Error	SSE	$n_T - c - r + 1$	$MSE = \frac{SSE}{n_T - c - r + 1}$		
Total	SST	$n_T - 1$			

Using Excel and R for a Two-Way ANOVA Test—No Interaction

We rarely use manual calculations to perform a two-way ANOVA test. Consider the following example where we complete the analysis of the two-factor income example.

EXAMPLE 13.5

FILE *Two_Factor*

Here, we first use Excel and R to obtain the ANOVA table for the two-factor income example. Then, we answer the two questions posed at the beginning of the analysis:

- At the 5% significance level, do average annual incomes differ by field of employment?
- At the 5% significance level, do average annual incomes differ by education level?

SOLUTION:

Using Excel

a. Open the ***Two_factor*** data file.

b. From the menu, choose **Data > Data Analysis > ANOVA: Two Factor Without Replication.**

c. In the *ANOVA: Two Factor Without Replication* dialog box, as shown in Figure 13.3, choose the box next to *Input range,* and then select all the data, including the labels. Check the *Labels* box. Click **OK.**

FIGURE 13.3 Excel's ANOVA: Two-Factor Without Replication dialog box.

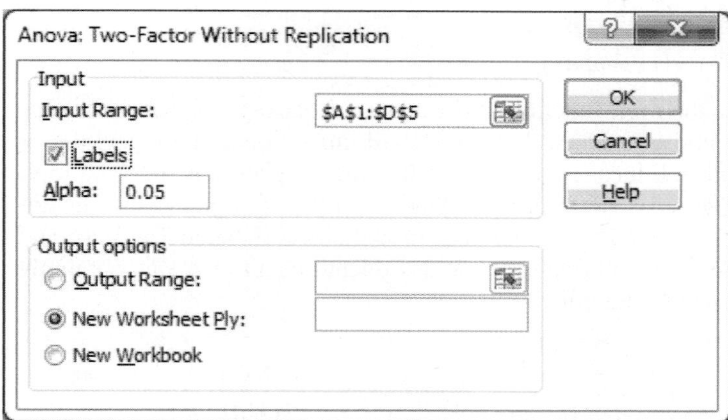

Table 13.14 shows a portion of the Excel-produced results. Note that the sum of squares and the mean sum of squares are identical to the ones calculated manually.

TABLE 13.14 Excel-Produced ANOVA Table for Two-Factor Income Example

Source of Variation	*SS*	*df*	*MS*	*F*	*p-value*
Rows	7632.9167	3	2544.3056	56.575	8.6E-05
Columns	579.50	2	289.75	6.443	0.032
Error	269.8333	6	44.9722		
Total	8482.25	11			

In order to determine whether annual incomes differ by field of employment, we specify the competing hypotheses as:

$$H_0: \mu_{\text{Education}} = \mu_{\text{Financial}} = \mu_{\text{Medical}}$$
$$H_A: \text{Not all population means are equal.}$$

When testing whether the factor A (column) means differ, the value of the test statistic is $F_{(df_1,df_2)} = \frac{MSA}{MSE} = \frac{289.75}{44.9722} = 6.443$ where $df_1 = c - 1 = 3 - 1 = 2$ and $df_2 = n_T - c - r + 1 = 12 - 3 - 4 + 1 = 6$; that is, $F_{(2,6)} = 6.443$ with an accompanying p-value of 0.032. Since the p-value is less than 0.05, we reject H_0. Therefore, contrary to the results derived earlier with a one-way ANOVA test, average annual salaries do differ by field of employment at the 5% significance level.

In order to determine whether annual incomes differ by education level, we specify the competing hypotheses as

$$H_0: \mu_{\text{No High School}} = \mu_{\text{High School}} = \mu_{\text{Bachelor's}} = \mu_{\text{Master's}}$$
$$H_A: \text{Not all population means are equal.}$$

When testing whether the factor B (row) means differ, the value of the test statistic is $F_{(df_1,df_2)} = \frac{MSB}{MSE} = \frac{2{,}544.3056}{44.9722} = 56.575$ where $df_1 = r - 1 = 4 - 1 = 3$

and $df_2 = n_T - c - r + 1 = 12 - 3 - 4 + 1 = 6$; that is, $F_{(3,6)} = 56.575$ with an accompanying p-value of 0 (approximately). Since the p-value is less than 0.05, we reject H_0. At the 5% significance level, average annual incomes differ by education level. Since education level exerts a significant influence on income, its influence must be incorporated in ANOVA testing.

Using R

a. Import the ***Two_Factor*** data file into a data frame (table) and label it myData

b. In order to reconfigure the data frame, we need to install and load the *reshape2* package. Enter:

```
> install.packages("reshape2")
> library(reshape2)
```

c. We use the **melt** function in the *reshape2* package and label the reconfigured data frame as Stacked. We use the **colnames** function to label the columns in Stacked as Education, Field, and Income, respectively. In order to view the reconfigured data frame, type Stacked at the prompt. We use the **aov** function to create an analysis of variance model object, labeled TwoWay, and specify Income as an additive function of Education and Field. To obtain the ANOVA table, we use the **anova** function. Enter:

```
> Stacked <- melt(myData)
> colnames(Stacked) <- c("Education", "Field", "Income")
> TwoWay <- aov(Income ~ Education + Field, data = Stacked)
> anova(TwoWay)
```

Table 13.15 shows the R-produced ANOVA table. The values are identical to the ones produced by Excel in Table 13.14. Thus, the conclusions to our questions are the same. At the 5% significance level, average annual incomes differ by field of employment as well as by education level.

TABLE 13.15 R-Produced ANOVA Table for Two-Factor Income Example

```
Analysis of Variance Table
Response: Income
           Df  Sum Sq  Mean Sq  F value    Pr(>F)
Education  3   7632.9  2544.31  56.5750  8.595e-05 ***
Field      2   579.5   289.75   6.4429     0.03207 *
Residuals  6   269.8   44.97
---
Signif. codes:  0 '***' 0.001 '**' 0.01 '*' 0.05
'.' 0.1 ' ' 1
```

We would like to point out that, analogous to the last section, we can apply the *MSE* estimate from the two-way ANOVA test to construct useful confidence intervals for the paired differences in population means using Fisher's LSD method. The only significant modification to these confidence intervals is with respect to degrees of freedom, which are now given by $df = n_T - c - r + 1$. Similarly, we can also use Tukey's HSD method to determine which column means or row means are significantly different from one another. The value for the margin of error in the confidence interval will depend on whether we are assessing differences between the column means or the row means. When constructing the confidence interval for the difference between two column means, we calculate the margin of error as $q_{\alpha,(c, n_T - c - r + 1)}\sqrt{\frac{MSE}{n}}$, where n is the number of observations in each column. When constructing the confidence interval for the difference between two row means, we calculate the margin of error as $q_{\alpha,(r, n_T - c - r + 1)}\sqrt{\frac{MSE}{n}}$, where n is the number of observations in each row.

EXERCISES 13.3

Mechanics

30. The following observations were obtained when conducting a two-way ANOVA experiment with no interaction. Assume normality in the underlying populations.

	Factor *A*			
Factor *B*	1	2	3	$\bar{x}_j$ for Factor *B*
1	4	8	12	8
2	2	10	3	5
3	0	6	0	2
4	2	4	0	2
$\bar{x}_i$ for Factor *A*	2	7	3.75	$\bar{\bar{x}} = 4.25$

a. Calculate *SST, SSA, SSB,* and *SSE.*
b. Calculate *MSA, MSB,* and *MSE.*
c. Construct an ANOVA table.
d. At the 5% significance level, can you conclude that the column means differ?
e. At the 5% significance level, can you conclude that the row means differ?

31. The following observations were obtained when conducting a two-way ANOVA experiment with no interaction. Assume normality in the underlying populations.

	Factor *A*				
Factor *B*	1	2	3	4	$\bar{x}_j$ for Factor *B*
1	2	3	2	4	2.75
2	6	5	7	6	6.00
3	8	10	9	10	9.25
$\bar{x}_i$ for Factor *A*	5.3333	6	6	6.6667	$\bar{\bar{x}} = 6$

a. Calculate *SST, SSA, SSB,* and *SSE.*
b. Calculate *MSA, MSB,* and *MSE.*
c. Construct an ANOVA table.
d. At the 5% significance level, do the levels of Factor *B* differ?
e. At the 5% significance level, do the levels of Factor *A* differ?

32. A two-way ANOVA experiment with no interaction is conducted. Factor *A* has four levels (columns) and Factor *B* has three levels (rows). Assume normality in the underlying populations. The results include the following sum of squares terms:

$$SST = 1,630.7 \quad SSB = 532.3 \quad SSE = 374.5$$

a. Construct an ANOVA table.
b. At the 1% significance level, can you conclude that the factor A means differ?
c. At the 1% significance level, can you conclude that the factor B means differ?

33. A two-way ANOVA experiment with no interaction is conducted. Factor *A* has three levels (columns) and Factor *B* has five levels (rows). Assume normality in the underlying populations. The results include the following sum of squares terms:

$$SST = 311.7 \quad SSA = 201.6 \quad SSE = 69.3$$

a. Construct an ANOVA table.
b. At the 5% significance level, can you conclude that the row means differ?
c. At the 5% significance level, can you conclude that the column means differ?

34. The following table summarizes a portion of the results for a two-way ANOVA experiment with no interaction. Assume normality in the underlying populations.

Source of Variation	*SS*	*df*	*MS*	*F*	*p-value*
Rows	1057	5	$MSB = ?$	$F_{\text{Factor B}} = ?$	0.006
Columns	7	2	$MSA = ?$	$F_{\text{Factor A}} = ?$	0.900
Error	330	10	$MSE = ?$		
Total	1394	17			

a. Find the missing values in the ANOVA table.
b. At the 5% significance level, can you conclude that the column means differ?
c. At the 5% significance level, can you conclude that the row means differ?

35. The following table summarizes a portion of the results for a two-way ANOVA experiment with no interaction. Assume normality in the underlying populations.

Source of Variation	*SS*	*df*	*MS*	*F*	*p-value*
Rows	25.17	2	$MSB = ?$	$F_{\text{Factor B}} = ?$	0.083
Columns	142.25	3	$MSA = ?$	$F_{\text{Factor A}} = ?$	0.004
Error	19.50	6	$MSE = ?$		
Total	186.92	11			

a. Find the missing values in the ANOVA table.
b. At the 5% significance level, can you conclude that the column means differ?
c. At the 5% significance level, can you conclude that the row means differ?

Applications

36. **FILE** ***Golf.*** During a typical Professional Golf Association (PGA) tournament, the competing golfers play four rounds of golf, where the hole locations are changed for each round. The accompanying table shows the scores for the top five finishers at a recent tournament. Assume that scores are normally distributed.

	Round 1	Round 2	Round 3	Round 4
Player 1	69	64	70	73
Player 2	69	70	69	70
Player 3	67	70	70	71
Player 4	67	65	70	76
Player 5	70	78	79	72
	Grand mean: $\bar{\bar{x}} = 70.45$			

The following statistics were computed:

$$SST = 272.95 \quad SSB = 93.2 \quad SSE = 127.6$$

a. Construct the ANOVA table.
b. At the 5% significance level, can you conclude that the average scores produced by the four different rounds differ?
c. At the 5% significance level, can you conclude that the average scores produced by the five different players differ?

37. The following output summarizes a portion of the results for a two-way ANOVA experiment with no interaction. Factor *A* (columns) consists of four different kinds of organic fertilizers, Factor *B* (rows) consists of three different kinds of soil acidity levels, and the variable measured is the height (in inches) of a plant at the end of four weeks. Assume that height is normally distributed.

Source of Variation	*SS*	*df*	*MS*	*F*	*p-value*
Rows	0.13	2	$MSB = ?$	$F_{Factor\ B} = ?$	0.818
Columns	44.25	3	$MSA = ?$	$F_{Factor\ A} = ?$	0.000
Error	1.88	6	$MSE = ?$		
Total	46.26	11			

a. Find the missing values in the ANOVA table.
b. At the 5% significance level, can you conclude that the average growth of the plant differs by organic fertilizer?
c. At the 5% significance level, can you conclude that the average growth of the plant differs by acidity level?

38. **FILE** ***Shift_Output.*** Metalworks, a supplier of fabricated industrial parts, wants to determine if the average output rate for a particular component is the same across the three work shifts. However, since any of four machines can be used, the machine effect must be controlled for within the sample. The accompanying table shows output rates (in units) for the previous day. Assume that output rates are normally distributed.

	Shift 1	Shift 2	Shift 3
Machine A	1392	1264	1334
Machine B	1228	1237	1107
Machine C	1173	1108	1186
Machine D	1331	1342	1387

a. At the 5% significance level, can you conclude that the average output rate differs across the work shifts?
b. At the 5% significance level, can you conclude that the average output rate differs across the machines?
c. If significant differences exist across the machines, use Tukey's HSD method at the 5% significance level to determine which machines have different average output rates.

39. **FILE** ***Restaurants.*** Given a recent outbreak of illness caused by *E. coli* bacteria, the mayor in a large city is concerned that some of his restaurant inspectors are not consistent with their evaluations of a restaurant's cleanliness. In order to investigate this possibility, the mayor has five restaurant inspectors grade (scale of 0 to 100) the cleanliness of three restaurants. The results are shown in the accompanying table. Assume that grades are normally distributed.

	Restaurant 1	Restaurant 2	Restaurant 3
Inspector 1	72	54	84
Inspector 2	68	55	85
Inspector 3	73	59	80
Inspector 4	69	60	82
Inspector 5	75	56	84

a. At the 5% significance level, can you conclude that the average grades differ by restaurant?
b. If the average grades differ by restaurant, use Tukey's HSD method at the 5% significance level to determine which averages differ.
c. At the 5% significance level, can you conclude that the average grades differ by inspector? Does the mayor have cause for concern?

40. **FILE** ***YumYum.*** The marketing manager at YumYum, a large deli chain, is testing the effectiveness of four potential advertising strategies. After a two-week trial period for each advertising strategy, sales were evaluated. However, since some store locations have higher customer traffic than other locations, the effect of location on sales must be controlled for within the sample. The accompanying table shows sales (in $1,000s) achieved over the 2-week trial period using each advertising strategy at three different store locations. Assume that sales are normally distributed.

	Newspaper only	Internet only	TV only	Internet & TV
City	511	644	585	712
Suburban	458	548	503	614
Rural	388	298	347	421

a. At the 5% significance level, can you conclude that the mean sales differ among the advertising strategies? What about the 10% significance level?
b. At the 5% significance level, can you conclude that the mean sales differ across the store locations?
c. If significant differences exist across advertising strategies, use Fisher's LSD method at the 10% significance level to find which strategies have different mean sales.

41. FILE ***Houses.*** First National Bank employs three real estate appraisers whose job is to establish a property's market value before the bank offers a mortgage to a prospective buyer. It is imperative that each appraiser values a property with no bias. Suppose First National Bank wishes to check the consistency of the recent values that its appraisers have established. The bank asked the three appraisers to value (in $1,000s) three different types of homes: a cape, a colonial, and a ranch. The accompanying table shows the results. Assume that values are normally distributed.

	Appraiser_1	Appraiser_2	Appraiser_3
Cape	425	415	430
Colonial	530	550	540
Ranch	390	400	380

a. At the 5% significance level, can you conclude that the average values differ by appraiser? Should the bank be concerned with appraiser inconsistencies?
b. At the 5% significance level, can you conclude that the average values differ by house type?
c. If average values differ by house type, use Tukey's HSD method at the 5% significance level to determine which averages differ.

13.4 TWO-WAY ANOVA TEST: WITH INTERACTION

LO 13.4

Conduct and evaluate a two-way ANOVA test with interaction.

We use a two-way ANOVA test with interaction to capture the possible relationship between factors A and B. Such a test allows the influence of factor A to change over levels of factor B and the influence of factor B to change over levels of factor A. In the two-factor income example from Section 13.3, field of employment may interact with education level. In other words, the influence of field of employment may vary between levels of education. Similarly, the influence of education level may not be the same for all fields of employment.

DECOMPOSING TOTAL VARIATION IN A TWO-WAY ANOVA TEST WITH INTERACTION

In a two-way ANOVA test with interaction, the total sum of squares, SST, of the variable is partitioned into four distinct components: the sum of squares for factor A, SSA; the sum of squares for factor B, SSB; the sum of squares for the interaction between the two factors, $SSAB$; and the error sum of squares, SSE. That is,

$$SST = SSA + SSB + SSAB + SSE.$$

While we still use a randomized block design, we need at least two observations for each combination of the ith level of factor A and the jth level of factor B. In other words, we need more than one observation per cell. In a two-way ANOVA test with interaction, we let w equal the number of observations for each combination of the ith level of factor A and the jth level of factor B.

To illustrate two-way ANOVA with interaction, we reanalyze the income example, using new data with three incomes for each combination; thus, $w = 3$. A portion of the data is shown in Table 13.16. It shows the values in the ***Interaction*** data file along with factor headings.

Interaction

TABLE 13.16 Data for the Two-Factor Income Example with Interaction

Education Level (Factor *B*)	Field of Employment (Factor *A*)		
	Educational Services	Financial Services	Medical Services
No High School	20	27	26
	25	25	24
	22	25	25
⋮	⋮	⋮	⋮
Master's	79	90	90
	78	92	100
	74	95	105

We are specifically interested in whether field of employment and education level interact with respect to average annual income. In order to find the relevant sum of squares for the test, we first compute the cell means and the factor means. For example, the cell mean for workers in the field of educational services with no high school education is computed as $(20 + 25 + 22)/3 = 22.3333$. Table 13.17 shows the cell means $\bar{x}_{ij}$, factor means $\bar{x}_i$ and $\bar{x}_j$, and the grand mean $\bar{\bar{x}}$ for the data.

TABLE 13.17 Cell and Factor Means for the Two-Factor Income Example with Interaction

Education Level (Factor *B*)	Field of Employment (Factor *A*)			Factor *B* Means
	Educational Services	Financial Services	Medical Services	
No High School	22.3333	25.6667	25.00	24.3333
High School	33.00	46.00	43.3333	40.7778
Bachelor's	47.6667	54.6667	59.3333	53.8889
Master's	77.00	92.3333	98.3333	89.2222
Factor *A* Means	45.00	54.6667	56.50	$\bar{\bar{x}} = 52.0556$

The Total Sum of Squares, *SST*

SST is computed as $SST = \sum_{i=1}^{c}\sum_{j=1}^{r}\sum_{k=1}^{w}(x_{ijk} - \bar{\bar{x}})^2$. Using all observations from the ***Interaction*** data file and the grand mean from Table 13.17, we calculate

$$SST = (20 - 52.0556)^2 + (25 - 52.0556)^2 + \cdots + (105 - 52.0556)^2$$
$$= 22{,}007.8889$$

The Sum of Squares for Factor *A*, *SSA*, and the Sum of Squares for Factor *B*, *SSB*

The calculations for *SSA* and *SSB* are analogous to the two-way ANOVA discussion in Section 13.3 with one minor modification. For two-way ANOVA without interaction, *SSA* and *SSB* were calculated as $r\sum_{i=1}^{c}(\bar{x}_i - \bar{\bar{x}})^2$ and $c\sum_{j=1}^{r}(\bar{x}_j - \bar{\bar{x}})^2$, respectively. Now each formula is multiplied by the number of observations per cell w. So, $SSA = wr\sum_{i=1}^{c}(\bar{x}_i - \bar{\bar{x}})^2$ and $SSB = wc\sum_{j=1}^{r}(\bar{x}_j - \bar{\bar{x}})^2$. Given the means in Table 13.17 with $w = 3$, $c = 3$, and $r = 4$, we calculate

$$SSA = (3 \times 4)[(45.00 - 52.0556)^2 + (54.6667 - 52.0556)^2 + (56.50 - 52.0556)^2]$$
$$= 916.2222,$$

and

$$SSB = (3 \times 3)[(24.3333 - 52.0556)^2 + (40.7778 - 52.0556)^2 + (53.8889 - 52.0556)^2 + (89.2222 - 52.0556)^2] = 20{,}523.8889.$$

We divide by the respective degrees of freedom to obtain the mean square for factor *A*, *MSA*, and the mean square for factor *B*, *MSB*, as

$$MSA = \frac{SSA}{c-1} = \frac{916.2222}{3-1} = 458.1111 \quad \text{and}$$

$$MSB = \frac{SSA}{r-1} = \frac{20,523.8889}{4-1} = 6{,}841.2963.$$

The Sum of Squares for the Interaction of Factor *A* and Factor *B*, *SSAB*

When two factors interact, the effect of one factor on the mean depends upon the specific value or level present for the other factor. Interaction exists between these factors when two mathematical expressions, denoted Expression 1 and Expression 2, are significantly different from one another.

Expression 1 is defined as the difference of a cell mean from the grand mean, or equivalently, $(\bar{x}_{ij} - \bar{\bar{x}})$. Using the means in Table 13.17 with $i = 1$ and $j = 1$, one such difference would be $(\bar{x}_{11} - \bar{\bar{x}}) = (22.3333 - 52.0556)$.

Expression 2 is defined as the *combined* differences of the corresponding factor *A* mean from the grand mean and the corresponding factor *B* mean from the grand mean, or equivalently, $(\bar{x}_i - \bar{\bar{x}}) + (\bar{x}_j - \bar{\bar{x}})$. Using the means in Table 13.17 with $i = 1$ and $j = 1$, one such calculation would be $(45.00 - 52.0556) + (24.3333 - 52.0556)$.

If the difference between Expression 1 and Expression 2 is nonzero, then there is evidence of interaction. If we let *I* denote interaction, then we can measure *I* as

$$I = (\bar{x}_{ij} - \bar{\bar{x}}) - [(\bar{x}_i - \bar{\bar{x}}) + (\bar{x}_j - \bar{\bar{x}})].$$

This expression can be simplified to

$$I = \bar{x}_{ij} - \bar{x}_i - \bar{x}_j + \bar{\bar{x}}.$$

The sum of squares for the interaction between factor *A* and factor *B*, *SSAB*, is then based on a weighted sum of the squared interactions (I^2) where the weight equals the number of observations per cell *w*:

$$SSAB = w \sum_{i=1}^{c} \sum_{j=1}^{r} (\bar{x}_{ij} - \bar{x}_i - \bar{x}_j + \bar{\bar{x}})^2.$$

Using the means in Table 13.17, we calculate

$$SSAB = 3[(22.3333 - 45.00 - 24.3333 + 52.0556)^2 + (33.00 - 45.00 - 40.7778 + 52.0556)^2 + \cdots + (98.3333 - 56.50 - 89.2222 + 52.0666)^2] = 318.4444.$$

We obtain the mean square for interaction, *MSAB*, by dividing *SSAB* by its degrees of freedom $(c - 1)(r - 1)$, or

$$MSAB = \frac{SSAB}{(c-1)(r-1)} = \frac{318.4444}{(3-1)(4-1)} = 53.0741.$$

The Error Sum of Squares, *SSE*

We solve for *SSE* by rearranging $SST = SSA + SSB + SSAB + SSE$; that is,

$$SSE = SST - (SSA + SSB + SSAB) = 22{,}007.8889 - (916.2222 + 20{,}523.8889 + 318.4444) = 249.3334.$$

Finally, we divide *SSE* by its degrees of freedom $rc(w - 1)$ and obtain the mean square error, *MSE,* as

$$MSE = \frac{SSE}{rc(w-1)} = \frac{249.3333}{(4 \times 3)(3-1)} = 10.3889.$$

We now summarize the test statistics when conducting a two-way ANOVA test with interaction. The first two statistics are used to examine the main effects—potential differences in factor *A* means (column means) or potential differences in factor *B* means (row means). The third test statistic is used to test whether there is interaction between factor *A* and factor *B*.

TEST STATISTICS FOR A TWO-WAY ANOVA TEST—WITH INTERACTION

When testing for differences between the factor *A* means (the column means), the value of the test statistic is computed as

$$F_{(df_1, df_2)} = \frac{MSA}{MSE},$$

where $df_1 = c - 1$, $df_2 = rc(w - 1)$, *MSA* is the mean square for factor *A,* and *MSE* is the mean square error.

When testing for differences between the factor *B* means (the row means), the value of the test statistic is computed as

$$F_{(df_1, df_2)} = \frac{MSB}{MSE},$$

where $df_1 = r - 1$, $df_2 = rc(w - 1)$, *MSB* is the mean square for factor *B,* and *MSE* is the mean square error.

When testing for interaction between factor *A* and factor *B,* the value of the test statistic is computed as

$$F_{(df_1, df_2)} = \frac{MSAB}{MSE},$$

where $df_1 = (c - 1)(r - 1)$, $df_2 = rc(w - 1)$, *MSAB* is the mean square for interaction, and *MSE* is the mean square error.

In these tests, *c* represents the number of columns, *r* the number of rows, *w* the number of observations for each combination of the *i*th row and *j*th column, and n_T the total sample size. An ANOVA test is always specified as a right-tailed test.

Using Excel and R for a Two-Way ANOVA Test—With Interaction

Fortunately, Excel and R easily calculate all of the statistics that we have just discussed. Consider the following example where we complete the analysis of the two-factor income with interaction example.

EXAMPLE 13.6

FILE *Interaction*

Here, we first use Excel and R to obtain the ANOVA table for the two-factor income with interaction example. Then, we determine whether the field of employment and education level interact with respect to average income at the 5% significance level.

SOLUTION:

Using Excel

a. Open the ***Interaction*** data file.

b. From the menu, choose **Data** > **Data Analysis** > **ANOVA: Two Factor With Replication.**

c. In the *ANOVA: Two Factor With Replication* dialog box, as shown in Figure 13.4, choose the box next to *Input range,* and then select all the data, including the labels. Enter 3 for *Rows Per Sample.* Click **OK.**

FIGURE 13.4 Excel's ANOVA: Two-Factor With Replication dialog box

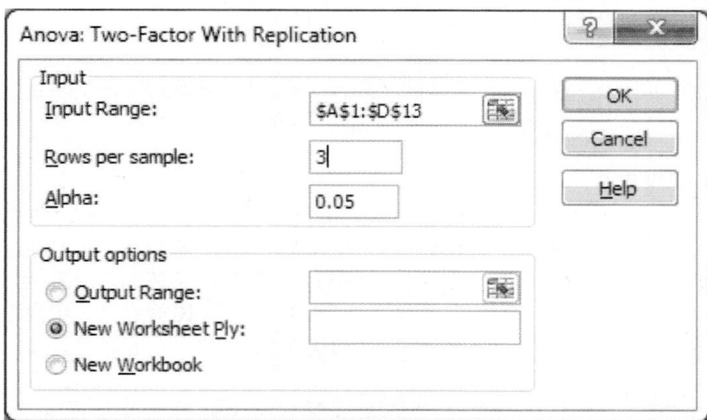

Table 13.18 shows a portion of the Excel-produced results. Note that the values that we calculated manually match those in Table 13.18.

TABLE 13.18 Excel-Produced ANOVA Table for Two-Factor Income with Interaction Example

Source of Variation	*SS*	*df*	*MS*	*F*	*p-value*
Sample (Rows)	20523.8889	3	6841.2963	658.521	3.58E-23
Columns	916.2222	2	458.1111	44.096	9.18E-09
Interaction	318.4444	6	53.0741	5.109	0.002
Within (Error)	249.3333	24	10.3889		
Total	22007.8889	35			

Using R

a. Import the ***Interaction*** data file into a data frame (table) and label it myData. If you view myData, you will notice that there are missing observations in the first column. Each level of education is not repeated three times. In order to correct this issue, we replace the first column using the **rep** function to replicate each entry three times and the **c** function to combine the resulting columns into one larger column. Enter

```
> myData[, 1] <- c(rep("No High School", 3), rep("High School", 3),
  rep("Bachelor's", 3), rep("Master's", 3))
```

If you view myData now, you should see no missing observations.

b. Then, as we did in Section 13.3, we install and load the *reshape2* package if we have not done so already. We use the **melt** function and label the reconfigured data frame as Stacked. We use the **colnames** function to label the columns in Stacked as Education, Field, and Income, respectively. We use the **aov** function to create an analysis of variance model object, which is labeled Interact, and specify Income as a multiplicative function of Education and Field. (Recall when we estimated a two-way ANOVA with no interaction, we used an additive function.) To obtain the ANOVA table, we use the **anova** function. Enter

```
> install.packages("reshape2")
> library(reshape2)
> Stacked <- melt(myData)
> colnames(Stacked) <- c("Education", "Field", "Income")
> Interact <- aov(Income ~ Education*Field, data=Stacked)
> anova(Interact)
```

Table 13.19 shows the R-produced ANOVA table. The values are identical to the ones produced by Excel in Table 13.18.

TABLE 13.19 R-Produced ANOVA Table for the Two-Factor Income with Interaction Example

```
Analysis of Variance Table
Response: Income
                  Df    Sum Sq   Mean Sq   F value        Pr(>F)
Field              2     916.2     458.1   44.0963    9.183e-09 ***
Education          3   20523.9    6841.3  658.5205    < 2.2e-16 ***
Education Field:   6     318.4      53.1    5.1087     0.001659 **
Residuals         24     249.3      10.4
---
Signif. codes:    0    '***'  0.001  '**'  0.01  '*'  0.05 '.'  0.1 ' '  1
```

Summary

In order to determine whether interaction exists between field of employment and education level, we specify the competing hypotheses as

H_0: There is no interaction between factors A and B.
H_A: There is interaction between factors A and B.

The value of the test statistic is $F_{(df_1,df_2)} = \frac{MSAB}{MSE} = \frac{53.0741}{10.3889} = 5.109$ where $df_1 = (r-1)(c-1) = (4-1)(3-1) = 6$ and $df_2 = rc(w-1) = (4 \times 3)(3-1) = 24$, or $F_{(6,24)} = 5.109$ with a corresponding p-value of 0.002. At the 5% significance level, we reject H_0 and conclude that there is an interaction between the field of employment and education level. This result implies that the average income with an advanced degree is higher in some fields than in others. Analogously, the average income in a particular field depends on the education level.

Note that due to the interaction, the differences between education levels are not the same for all fields of employment. Such an outcome serves to complicate the interpretation of the main effects, because differences in one factor are not consistent across the other factor. This is why we should perform the interaction test before making any conclusions using the other two $F_{(df_1,df_2)}$ statistics. If the interaction effect is not significant, then we can proceed by focusing on the main effects: testing whether or not the row means or the column means differ. If the interaction effect is significant, as it is here, one option is to use another technique called regression analysis. Regression analysis is discussed in the next four chapters.

EXERCISES 13.4

Mechanics

42. A two-way ANOVA experiment with interaction was conducted. Factor *A* had four levels (columns), factor *B* had three levels (rows), and five observations were obtained for each combination. Assume normality in the underlying populations. The results include the following sum of squares terms:

$SST = 2500 \quad SSA = 1200 \quad SSB = 1000 \quad SSE = 280$

   a. Construct an ANOVA table.
   b. At the 5% significance level, can you conclude that there is interaction between factor *A* and factor *B*?
   c. At the 5% significance level, can you conclude that the factor *A* means differ?
   d. At the 5% significance level, can you conclude that the factor *B* means differ?

43. A two-way ANOVA experiment with interaction was conducted. Factor *A* had three levels (columns), factor *B* had five levels (rows), and six observations were obtained for each combination. Assume normality in the underlying populations. The results include the following sum of squares terms:

$SST = 1558 \quad SSA = 1008 \quad SSB = 400 \quad SSAB = 30$

   a. Construct an ANOVA table.
   b. At the 1% significance level, can you conclude that there is interaction between factor *A* and factor *B*?
   c. At the 1% significance level, can you conclude that the factor *A* means differ?
   d. At the 1% significance level, can you conclude that the factor *B* means differ?

44. A researcher conducts a two-way ANOVA test with interaction and provides the following ANOVA table. Assume normality in the underlying populations.

Source of Variation	*SS*	*df*	*MS*	*F*	*p-value*
Sample	30.827	1	30.827	11.690	0.003
Columns	169.861	2	84.930	32.208	1.13E-06
Interaction	4.241	2	2.120	0.804	0.463
Within	47.465	18	2.637		
Total	252.393	23			

   a. At the 1% significance level, can you conclude that there is interaction between the two factors?
   b. Are you able to conduct tests based on the main effects? If yes, conduct these tests at the 1% significance level. If no, explain.

45. A researcher conducts a two-way ANOVA test with interaction and provides the following ANOVA table. Assume normality in the underlying populations.

Source of Variation	*SS*	*df*	*MS*	*F*	*p-value*
Sample	752.78	2	*MSB* = ?	$F_{Factor\ B}$ = ?	0.012
Columns	12012.50	1	*MSA* = ?	$F_{Factor\ A}$ = ?	5.62E-09
Interaction	58.33	2	*MSAB* = ?	$F_{Interaction}$ = ?	0.612
Within	683.33	12	*MSE* = ?		
Total	13506.94	17			

   a. Find the missing values in the ANOVA table.
   b. At the 5% significance level, can you conclude that there is an interaction effect?
   c. At the 5% significance level, can you conclude that the column means differ?
   d. At the 5% significance level, can you conclude that the row (sample) means differ?

Applications

46. The engineering department at a steel mill is studying the tensile strength of a particular grade of steel when fabricated at various pressures (Factor *A*) and temperatures (Factor *B*). The accompanying ANOVA table shows a portion of the results from conducting a two-way ANOVA test with interaction. Assume that tensile strength is normally distributed.

Source of Variation	*SS*	*df*	*MS*	*F*	*p-value*
Sample (*B*, temperature)	150.22	1	150.22		
Columns (*A*, pressure)			62.06		
Interaction	24.11	2	12.06		
Within			26.11		
Total	611.78	17			

   a. How many levels did pressure have?
   b. How many observations were run for each combination of pressure-temperature settings?
   c. At the 5% significance level, can you conclude that there is interaction between pressure and temperature?
   d. At the 5% significance level, can you conclude that the main effect of pressure is significant?
   e. At the 5% significance level, can you conclude that the main effect of temperature is significant?

47. The effects of detergent brand name (factor *A*) and the temperature of the water (factor *B*) on the brightness of washed fabrics are being studied. Four brand names and two temperature levels are used; six observations for each combination are examined. The following ANOVA table is produced. Assume that brightness readings are normally distributed.

Source of Variation	*SS*	*df*	*MS*	*F*	*p-value*
Sample	75	1	75	63.38	8.92E-10
Columns	130.25	3	43.42	36.69	1.45E-11
Interaction	8.67	3	2.89	2.44	0.078
Within	47.33	40	1.18		
Total	261.25	47			

a. Can you conclude that there is interaction between the detergent brand name and the temperature of the water at the 5% significance level?

b. Are you able to conduct tests based on the main effects? If yes, conduct these tests at the 5% significance level. If no, explain.

48. **FILE** ***Buy4Less.*** The marketing group at Buy4Less, a local retail chain, is examining the effect of advertising at various times of day and on various local television channels. Based on 12-week cycles (4 time periods × 3 local channels), three observations (cycles) of weekly sales data (in $1,000s) have been obtained for each time period-channel combination. The results are shown in the accompanying data file. Assume sales are normally distributed.

a. At the 5% significance level, can you conclude that there is interaction between the time of day and the local channel used for advertising?

b. Are you able to conduct tests based on the main effects? If yes, conduct them at the 5% significance level. If no, explain why.

49. **FILE** ***Brand_Garage.*** A consumer advocate examines whether the longevity of car batteries (measured in years) is affected by the brand name (factor A) and whether or not the car is kept in a garage (factor *B*). Interaction is suspected. The results are shown in the accompanying data file. Assume longevity is normally distributed.

a. At the 5% significance level, is there interaction between the brand name and whether a car is garaged?

b. At the 5% significance level, can you conclude that the average battery lives differ by brand name?

c. At the 5% significance level, can you conclude that the average battery lives differ depending on whether a car is garaged?

50. **FILE** ***Job_Satisfaction.*** A human resource specialist wants to determine whether the average job satisfaction score (on a scale of 0 to 100) is the same for three different industries and three types of work experience. A randomized block experiment with interaction is performed. The results are shown in the accompanying data file. Assume that scores are normally distributed.

a. At the 5% significance level, is there interaction between industry and work experience?

b. At the 5% significance level, can you conclude that job satisfaction differs by industry?

c. At the 5% significance level, can you conclude that job satisfaction differs by work experience?

51. **FILE** ***Salaries.*** It is generally believed that a practical major such as business or engineering can really pay off for college graduates. Other studies have shown that it is not just the major but also how students perform, as measured by their GPA, that influences their salaries. Henry Chen, an employee of PayScale.com, wants to measure the effect of major and GPA on starting salaries of graduates of the University of California at Irvine. He samples starting salaries of five graduates for a given GPA range from the schools of business, engineering, and social sciences. The sample data are shown in the accompanying data file. Assume that salaries are normally distributed.

a. At the 5% significance level, is there interaction between major and GPA?

b. At the 5% significance level, can you conclude that starting salary differs between majors?

c. At the 5% significance level, can you conclude that starting salary depends on GPA?

Comstock/Stockbyte/Getty Images

13.5 WRITING WITH DATA

Case study

A study finds that the average U.S. driver languished in rush-hour traffic for 36.1 hours. This congestion also wasted approximately 2.81 billion gallons in fuel, or roughly three weeks' worth of gas per traveler. John Farnham, a research analyst at an environmental firm, is stunned by some of the report's conclusions. John is asked to conduct an independent study in order to see if differences exist in congestion depending on the city where the commuter drives. He selects 25 commuters from each of the five cities that suffered from the worst congestion, and asks each commuter to approximate the time spent in traffic (in hours) over the last calendar year. John assumes that the underlying populations are normally distributed. Table 13.20 shows a portion of his sample results.

TABLE 13.20 Annual Hours of Delay per Commuter in Five Cities

FILE *Congestion*

Los Angeles	Washington, DC	Atlanta	Houston	San Francisco
71	64	60	58	57
60	64	58	56	56
⋮	⋮	⋮	⋮	⋮
68	57	57	59	56

John wants to use the sample information to

- Determine whether significant differences exist in congestion, depending on the city where the commuter drives.
- Use Tukey's method to establish where commuters experience the least and the worst delays.

Sample Report—Evaluating Traffic Congestion by City

Does traffic congestion vary by city? A study is conducted to determine if traffic congestion, measured by annual hours of delay per commuter, differs in the worst-congested cities: Los Angeles, Washington, D.C., Atlanta, Houston, and San Francisco. Twenty-five commuters in each of these cities were asked how many hours they wasted in traffic over the past calendar year. Table 13.21 reports the summary statistics. The sample data indicate that Los Angeles residents waste the most time sitting in traffic, with an average of 69.2 hours per year. Washington, DC, residents rank a close second, spending an average of 62 hours per year in traffic. Residents in Atlanta, Houston, and San Francisco spend on average, 57.0, 56.5, and 55.6 hours per year in traffic, respectively.

TABLE 13.21 Summary Statistics for Traffic Congestion

Los Angeles	Washington, DC	Atlanta	Houston	San Francisco
$\bar{x}_1 = 69.24$	$\bar{x}_2 = 61.96$	$\bar{x}_3 = 57.00$	$\bar{x}_4 = 56.52$	$\bar{x}_5 = 55.56$
$s_1 = 4.60$	$s_2 = 4.74$	$s_3 = 4.81$	$s_4 = 5.37$	$s_5 = 3.66$

A one-way ANOVA test was conducted to determine if significant differences exist in the average number of hours spent in traffic in these five worst-congested cities. The value of the test statistic is $F_{(4,120)} = 37.251$ with a p-value of approximately zero. Therefore, at the 5% level of significance, traffic congestion does vary by city.

In order to determine which cities had significantly different average delays per commuter, Tukey's HSD method was used. The 95% confidence interval for the difference between two population means $\mu_i - \mu_j$ was computed as $(\bar{x}_i - \bar{x}_j) \pm q_{\alpha,(c,n_T-c)}\sqrt{\frac{MSE}{n}}$. Referencing the studentized range table and the ANOVA test output, the margin of error for the confidence interval was calculated as 3.66. The 95% confidence intervals for the difference between all pairings of cities showed that travelers in Los Angeles suffered the most hours of congestion, followed by travelers in Washington, DC. Congestion was not significantly different in the cities of Atlanta, Houston, and San Francisco.

Suggested Case Studies

Report 13.1 FILE ***Industry_Returns.*** The accompanying data file contains annual stock returns (in %) for 10 firms in the energy industry, 13 firms in the retail industry, and 16 firms in the utilities industry. In a report, use the sample information to determine whether significant differences exist in the annual returns for the three industries. Then, construct 95% confidence intervals for the difference between annual returns for each pairing using Tukey's HSD method. Evaluate which means (if any) significantly differ from one another. Use a reasonable level of significance for the tests and state your assumptions clearly.

Report 13.2 FILE ***Grocery_Prices.*** The accompanying data file contains prices (in $) of 11 products at three different grocery stores in the Boston area. Assume that prices are normally distributed. In a report, use the sample information to determine whether differences exist in the average prices across (a) stores and (b) products. In addition, determine which stores' prices differ using Tukey's HSD method, if it is found that differences exist in the average prices among three stores. Use a reasonable level of significance for the tests.

Report 13.3 FILE ***Review_SAT.*** A manager of an SAT review program wonders whether the program's instructor and the time that has elapsed since the student completed the program affect a student's performance on the SAT. Four time intervals and three instructors are examined. Ten student scores for each combination are sampled. The results are shown in the accompanying data file. Assume that SAT scores are normally distributed. In a report, use the sample information to determine if there is any interaction between instructor and elapsed time. In addition, establish whether average SAT scores differ across (a) instructors and (b) elapsed time. Use a reasonable level of significance for the tests and state your assumptions clearly.

CONCEPTUAL REVIEW

LO 13.1 Conduct and evaluate a one-way ANOVA test.

A one-way analysis of variance (ANOVA) test is used to determine if differences exist between three or more population means. This test examines the amount of variability *between* the samples relative to the amount of variability *within* the samples.

The value of the test statistic for testing for differences between the c population means is calculated as $F_{(df_1,df_2)} = \frac{MSTR}{MSE}$, where $MSTR$ is the mean square for treatments, MSE is the mean square error, $df_1 = c - 1$, $df_2 = n_T - c$, and n_T is the total sample size. The values for $MSTR$ and MSE are based on independent samples drawn from c normally distributed populations with a common variance. An ANOVA test is always specified as a right-tailed test.

LO 13.2 Use Fisher's LSD method and Tukey's HSD method to determine which means differ.

Fisher's $100(1 - \alpha)\%$ confidence intervals for mean differences $\mu_i - \mu_j$ is computed as $(\bar{x}_i - \bar{x}_j) \pm t_{\alpha/2, n_T-c}\sqrt{MSE\left(\frac{1}{n_i} + \frac{1}{n_j}\right)}$ where MSE is estimated from the ANOVA test. If the computed interval does not include the value zero, then we reject the null hypothesis H_0: $\mu_i - \mu_j = 0$.

When pairwise comparisons are made with Fisher's LSD method, we inflate the risk of the Type I error α. Tukey's HSD method uses the studentized range distribution, which has broader, flatter, and thicker tails than the t_{df} distribution, and therefore protects against an inflated risk of a Type I error. Tukey's $100(1 - \alpha)\%$ confidence interval for $\mu_i - \mu_j$ is computed as $(\bar{x}_i - \bar{x}_j) \pm q_{\alpha,(c,n_T-c)}\sqrt{\frac{MSE}{n}}$ for balanced data ($n_i = n_j = n$) and $(\bar{x}_i - \bar{x}_j) \pm q_{\alpha,(c,n_T-c)}\sqrt{\frac{MSE}{2}\left(\frac{1}{n_i} + \frac{1}{n_j}\right)}$ for unbalanced data ($n_i \neq n_j$), where $q_{\alpha,(c,n_T-c)}$ is the studentized range value.

LO 13.3 Conduct and evaluate a two-way ANOVA test with no interaction.

Whereas a one-way ANOVA test is used to compare population means based on one factor, a two-way ANOVA test extends the analysis to measure the effects of two factors. The additional factor explains some of the unexplained variation, or equivalently, reduces the error sum of squares SSE for a more discriminating $F_{(df_1,df_2)}$ statistic. A two-way ANOVA test can be conducted with or without interaction between the factors.

In a two-way ANOVA test without interaction, we find the value of two $F_{(df_1,df_2)}$ test statistics. The first test statistic $F_{(df_1,df_2)} = \frac{MSB}{MSE}$, where $df_1 = r - 1$ and $df_2 = n_T - c - r + 1$, is used to test for differences between the factor B means (the row means). The second test statistic $F_{(df_1,df_2)} = \frac{MSA}{MSE}$, where $df_1 = c - 1$ and $df_2 = n_T - c - r + 1$, is used to test for differences between the factor A means (the column means).

LO 13.4 Conduct and evaluate a two-way ANOVA test with interaction.

In a two-way ANOVA test with interaction, we find the values of three $F_{(df_1,df_2)}$ test statistics. Two test statistics are used to examine the main effects—differences in the means of factor B ($F_{(df_1,df_2)} = \frac{MSB}{MSE}$, where $df_1 = r - 1$ and $df_2 = rc(w - 1)$) and differences in the means of factor A ($F_{(df_1,df_2)} = \frac{MSA}{MSE}$, where $df_1 = c - 1$ and $df_2 = rc(w - 1)$). The third test statistic ($F_{(df_1,df_2)} = \frac{MSAB}{MSE}$, where $df_1 = (r - 1)(c - 1)$ and $df_2 = rc(w - 1)$) is used to test for interaction between factor A and factor B.

We perform the tests for the differences in factor means only if the interaction effect is found to be insignificant.

ADDITIONAL EXERCISES

52. FILE ***Transportation.*** A government agency wants to determine whether the average salaries of four kinds of transportation operators differ. A random sample of 30 employees in each of the four categories yields the salary data (in $1,000s) given in the accompanying data file.
    a. Specify the competing hypotheses in order to determine whether the average salaries of the transportation operators differ.
    b. At the 5% significance level, what is the conclusion to the test?

53. FILE ***Foodco.*** The Marketing Manager at Foodco, a large grocery store, wants to determine if store display location influences sales of a particular grocery item. He instructs employees to rotate the display location of that item every week and then tallies the weekly sales at each location over a 24-week period (8 weeks per location). The sample information is in the accompanying data file.
    a. Specify the competing hypotheses to test whether there are some differences in the mean weekly sales across the three store display locations.
    b. At the 5% significance level, what is the conclusion to the test? Assume sales are normally distributed.

54. FILE ***Generic.*** A consumer advocate in California is concerned with the price of a common generic drug. Specifically, he feels that one region of the state has significantly different prices for the drug than two other regions. He divides the state into three regions and collects the generic drug's price (in $) from 10 pharmacies in each region. The sample information is in the accompanying data file.
    a. At the 5% significance level, do differences exist between the mean drug prices in the three regions? Assume that prices are normally distributed.
    b. If significant differences exist, use Tukey's HSD method to determine which regions' means differ at the 5% significance level.

55. FILE ***Concrete_Mixing.*** Compressive strength of concrete is affected by several factors, including composition (sand, cement, etc.), mixer type (batch vs. continuous), and curing procedure. Accordingly, a concrete company is conducting an experiment to determine how mixing technique affects the resulting compressive strength. Four potential mixing techniques have been identified. Subsequently, samples of 20 specimens have been subjected to each mixing technique, and the resulting compressive strengths (in pounds per square inch, psi) were measured. The sample information is in the accompanying data file.

a. Specify the competing hypotheses to test whether there are some differences in the mean compressive strengths across the four mixing techniques.

b. At the 5% significance level, what is the conclusion to the test? What about the 1% significance level? Assume that compressive strengths are normally distributed.

56. **FILE** ***Plywood.*** An engineer wants to determine whether the average strength of plywood boards (in pounds per square inch, psi) differs depending on the type of glue used. For three types of glue, she measures the strength of 20 plywood boards. The sample information is in the accompanying data file. At the 5% significance level, can she conclude that the average strength of the plywood boards differs by the type of glue used? Assume that the strength of plywood boards is normally distributed.

57. **FILE** ***Route.*** An employee of a small software company in Minneapolis bikes to work during the summer months. He can travel to work using one of three routes and wonders whether the average commute times (in minutes) differ between the three routes. He uses each route for one week and records the commute times. The sample information is in the accompanying data file.

a. Determine at the 1% significance level whether the average commute times differ between the three routes. Assume that commute times are normally distributed.

b. If differences exist, use Tukey's HSD method at the 1% significance level to determine which routes' average times differ.

58. **FILE** ***PEratios.*** An economist wants to determine whether average price/earnings (P/E) ratios differ for firms in three industries. He records the P/E ratios for five firms in each industry. The sample information is in the accompanying data file.

a. At the 5% significance level, determine whether average P/E ratios differ in the three industries. Assume that P/E ratios are normally distributed.

b. If differences exist, use Tukey's HSD method at the 5% significance level to determine which industries' mean P/E ratios differ.

59. Do hourly wages differ for hotel maids depending on where they work? Hourly wages (in $) are collected from 25 hotel maids in Las Vegas, Phoenix, and Orlando. The following summary statistics and ANOVA table are produced.

SUMMARY					
Groups	Count	Average			
Las Vegas	25	13.91			
Phoenix	25	8.82			
Orlando	25	8.83			
Source of Variation	*SS*	*df*	*MS*	*F*	*p*-value
Between Groups	430.87	2	215.44	202.90	2.58E-30
Within Groups	76.44	72	1.06		
Total	507.31	74			

a. At the 5% significance level, do mean hourly rates for hotel maids differ between the three cities? Assume that hourly wages are normally distributed.

b. If differences exist, use Tukey's HSD method to determine which cities' mean hourly rates differ at the 5% significance level.

60. The marketing department for an upscale retail catalog company wants to determine if there are differences in the mean customer purchase amounts across the available purchase sources (Internet, phone, or mail-in). Accordingly, samples were taken for 20 random orders for each purchase source. The following output was compiled. Assume purchase amounts are normally distributed.

Internet	Phone	Mail-in
$\bar{x}_1 = 214.05$	$\bar{x}_2 = 212.45$	$\bar{x}_3 = 182.40$

Source of Variation	SS	df	MS	F	p-value
Between Groups	12715.23	2	6357.62	0.433	0.651
Within Groups	836704.70	57	14679.03		
Total	849419.93	59			

a. At the 5% significance level, can we conclude that the mean purchase amount is different across the three purchase sources?

b. If significant differences exist, use Fisher's LSD method at the 5% significance level to determine which purchase sources have different mean purchase amounts.

61. An accounting professor wants to know if students perform the same on the departmental final exam irrespective of the accounting section they attend. She randomly selects the exam scores of 20 students from three sections. A portion of the

output from conducting a one-way ANOVA test is shown in the accompanying table. Assume that exam scores are normally distributed.

Source of Variation	SS	df	MS	F	p-value
Between Groups	57.39	2	$MSTR = ?$	$F_{2,57} = ?$	0.346
Within Groups	$SSE = ?$	57	$MSE = ?$		
Total	1570.19	59			

a. Find the missing values in the ANOVA table.
b. At the 5% significance level, can you conclude that average grades differ in the accounting sections?

62. **FILE** ***Website.*** A data analyst for an online store wonders whether average customer visits to the store's website vary by day of the week. He collects daily unique visits to the website for a 12-week period. The sample information is in the accompanying data file. At the 5% significance level, what conclusion can the data analyst make? Discuss any assumptions that you make for the analysis.

63. **FILE** ***Battery_Times.*** Electrobat, a battery manufacturer, is investigating how storage temperature affects the performance of one of its popular deep-cell battery models used in recreational vehicles. Samples of 30 fully charged batteries were subjected to a light load under each of four different storage temperature levels. The hours until deep discharge (meaning $\leq 20\%$ of charge remaining) were measured. The sample information is in the accompanying data file.
   a. At the 5% significance level, can you conclude that mean discharge times differ across the four storage temperature levels? What about the 1% significance level?
   b. If significant differences exist, use Tukey's HSD method at the 5% significance level to determine which temperature levels have different mean discharge times.

64. The accompanying table shows a portion of the results from conducting a two-way ANOVA test with no interaction in which five different production methods (factor *A*, columns) were evaluated in terms of labor cost per unit. Operator experience was used as a blocking factor (factor *B*, rows) and was considered at four levels. Assume that cost is normally distributed.

Source of Variation	SS	df	MS	F	p-value
Rows (Experience level)	$SSB = ?$	3	$MSB = ?$	$F_B = ?$	$p\text{-}val_B = ?$
Columns (Prod. method)	$SSA = ?$	$df_A = ?$	$MSA = 0.720$	$F_A = ?$	$p\text{-}val_A = ?$
Error	3.072	12	$MSE = ?$		
Total	10.998	19			

   a. Find the missing values in the ANOVA table.
   b. At the 5% significance level, can you conclude that labor cost per unit differs by production method? What about the 10% significance level?
   c. At the 5% significance level, can you conclude that labor cost per unit differs by operator experience level?

65. The following output summarizes a portion of the results for a two-way ANOVA test without interaction where factor *A* (column) represents three income categories (low, medium, high), factor *B* (rows) consists of three different kinds of political parties (Democrat, Republican, Independent), and the variable measured was the amount (in $) contributed to the political party during the most recent presidential election. Assume that contributions are normally distributed.

Source of Variation	SS	df	MS	F	p-value
Rows	25416.67	2	$MSB = ?$	$F_{\text{Factor B}} = ?$	0.099
Columns	42916.67	2	$MSA = ?$	$F_{\text{Factor A}} = ?$	0.046
Error	11666.67	4	$MSE = ?$	$MSE = ?$	
Total	80000	8			

   a. Find the missing values in the ANOVA table.
   b. At the 5% significance level, can you conclude that average contributions differ by political party?
   c. At the 5% significance level, can you conclude that average contributions differ by income level?

66. **FILE** ***Headlight_Design.*** An automotive parts manufacturer is testing three potential halogen headlight designs, one of which ultimately will be promoted as providing best-in-class nighttime vision. The distance at which a traffic sign can be read in otherwise total darkness is the variable of interest. Since older drivers often have lower visual acuity, driver age must be controlled in this experiment. The following results (in feet) were obtained from sampling 12 drivers (four age groups for each headlight design).

	Design 1	Design 2	Design 3
Below 30	293	268	270
30–45	254	243	254
46–59	224	249	231
60–up	238	214	205

a. At the 5% significance level, can you conclude that the mean nighttime viewing distance is different among the headlight designs? Assume that distance is normally distributed. Practically speaking, what does your conclusion imply?

b. At the 5% significance level, was including the blocking variable *Driver Age* beneficial to this experiment? Explain.

67. FILE ***Gymnastics.*** At a gymnastics meet, three judges evaluate the balance beam performances of five gymnasts. The judges use a scale of 1 to 10, where 10 is a perfect score. The accompanying data file contains the scores of the most recent gymnastic meet. Assume that scores are normally distributed.

a. At the 1% significance level, can you conclude that average scores differ by judge? Can you conclude that the judges seem inconsistent with their scoring?

b. At the 1% significance level, can you conclude that average scores differ by gymnast?

c. If average scores differ by gymnast, use Tukey's HSD method at the 1% significance level to determine which gymnasts' performances differ.

68. FILE ***Fuel_Hybrid.*** An environmentalist wants to examine whether average fuel consumption (measured in miles per gallon) is affected by fuel type (factor *A*) and type of hybrid (factor *B*). The accompanying data file shows the results from her analysis.

a. Perform a two-way ANOVA test with interaction. Assume that fuel consumption is normally distributed. At the 5% significance level, is there interaction between fuel type and hybrid type?

b. At the 5% significance level, can you conclude that average fuel consumption differs by fuel type?

c. At the 5% significance level, can you conclude that average fuel consumption differs by type of hybrid?

69. A management consultant wants to determine whether the age and sex of a restaurant's wait staff influence the size of the tip the customer leaves. Three age brackets (factor *A* in columns: young, middle-age, older) and sex (factor *B* in rows: male, female) are used to construct a two-way ANOVA experiment with interaction. For each combination, the percentage of the total bill left as a tip for 10 wait staff is examined. The consultant assumes that the percentages are normally distributed and produces the following ANOVA table.

Source of Variation	SS	df	MS	F	p-value
Sample	0.04278	1	0.04278	16.595	0.000
Columns	0.01793	2	0.00897	3.479	0.038
Interaction	0.00561	2	0.00281	1.089	0.344
Within	0.1392	54	0.00258		
Total	0.20552	59			

a. Can you conclude that there is interaction between age and sex at the 1% significance level?

b. Are you able to conduct tests based on the main effects? If yes, conduct these tests at the 1% significance level. If no, explain.

70. FILE ***Training_Experience.*** A production manager is investigating whether the operator training method (factor *A*) will affect the resulting output for a particular product. Three training methods were studied: a full-day workshop (most intensive), in-line training, and as-needed training (least intensive). Since the value of training likely depends on the operator experience level, experience level (factor *B*) was also studied. Five operators for each training method-experience level category were randomly chosen. The accompanying data file shows the total output rates (in units produced) for the previous week. Assume that output rates are normally distributed.

a. At the 5% significance level, can you conclude that there is interaction between the training method and operator experience level? Explain why this is reasonable from a practical standpoint.

b. Are you able to conduct tests based on the main effects? If yes, conduct them at the 5% significance level. If no, explain why. Explain why your conclusion is reasonable from a practical standpoint.

71. FILE ***BestCuts.*** The cutting department at BestCuts, a furniture manufacturer, is examining the effect of depth of cut and feed rate on the surface roughness of table legs used in a popular dining room table model. The accompanying data file shows the surface roughness results for six

replicates involving three different depth-of-cut settings and two different feed rate settings. Assume that surface roughness is normally distributed.

a. At the 5% significance level, can you conclude that there is interaction between depth of cut and feed rate?

b. Are you able to conduct tests based on the main effects? If yes, conduct them at the 5% significance level. If no, explain why.

c. Explain why your conclusion in part (b) is reasonable from a practical standpoint.

APPENDIX 13.1 Guidelines for Other Software Packages

The following section provides brief commands for Minitab, SPSS, and JMP. Import the specified data file into the relevant software spreadsheet prior to following the commands.

Minitab

One-Way ANOVA; Fisher and Tukey Confidence Intervals

(Replicating Examples 13.1, 13.2, and 13.3) From the menu, choose **Stat > ANOVA > One-Way.** Select "**Response data are in a separate column for each factor level.**" Under **Responses,** select Layout 1, Layout 2, and Layout 3. Choose **Comparisons.** Enter the value 5 after **Error rate for comparisons.** After **Comparisons procedures assuming equal variances,** select **Tukey** and **Fisher.**

Two-Way ANOVA (No Interaction)

A. (Replicating Example 13.5) Stack all income observations into Column 1 and label Income. In Column 2 (label Education), denote all income observations associated with no high school education with N, all income observations associated with a high school education with H, all income observations associated with a bachelor's degree with B, and all income observations associated with a master's degree with M. In Column 3 (label Field), denote all income observations associated with Education with E, all income observations associated with Financial with F, and all income observations associated with Medical with Med.

B. From the menu, choose **Stat > ANOVA > Balanced ANOVA.** For **Response,** select Income, and for **Model,** select Education and Field.

Two-Way ANOVA (with Interaction)

A. (Replicating Example 13.6) In order to reconfigure the data, follow the Minitab instructions for Two-Way ANOVA (No Interaction), step A.

B. From the menu, choose **Stat > ANOVA > General Linear Model > Fit General Linear Model.**

C. For **Response,** select Income, and for **Factors,** select Education and Field.

D. Choose **Model,** and under **Factors and covariates,** select Education and Field, then **Add.**

SPSS

One-Way ANOVA; Fisher and Tukey Confidence Intervals

A. (Replicating Examples 13.1, 13.2, and 13.3) Stack all observations in one column and label Sales. In adjacent column (label Layout), denote all Layout 1 sales with value 1, all Layout 2 sales with value 2, and all Layout 3 sales with value 3.

B. From the menu, choose **Analyze > Compare Means > One-Way ANOVA.**

C. Under **Dependent, List,** select Sales, and under **Factor,** select Layout. Choose **Post Hoc,** and select **LSD** and **Tukey.**

Two_Factor

Two-Way ANOVA (No Interaction)

A. (Solving Example 13.5) In order to reconfigure the data, follow the Minitab instructions for Two-Way ANOVA (No Interaction), step A.

B. From the menu, select **Analyze > General Linear Model > Univariate.** Under **Dependent Variable,** select Income, and under **Fixed Factor(s),** select Education and Field. Choose **Model.** Under **Specify Model,** select **Build terms**. Under **Model,** select Education and Field. Under **Type,** select **All 2-way.** Deselect **Include Intercept in Model.**

Interaction

Two-Way ANOVA (with Interaction)

A. (Replicating Example 13.6) In order to arrange the data, follow the Minitab instructions for Two-Way ANOVA (No Interaction), step A.

B. From the menu, select **Analyze > General Linear Model > Univariate.** Under **Dependent Variable,** select Income, and under **Fixed Factor(s),** select Education and Field. Choose **Model.** Under **Specify Model,** select **Full factorial.** Deselect **Include Intercept in Model.**

JMP

Store_Layout

One-Way ANOVA; Fisher and Tukey Confidence Intervals

A. (Replicating Examples 13.1, 13.2, and 13.3) From the menu, choose **Table > Stack** and stack the Layout 1, Layout 2, and Layout 3 variables.

B. From the menu, select **Analyze > Fit Y by X.** Drag Data to the **Y, Factor** box and drag Label to the **X, Factor** box.

C. Click on the red triangle next to **Oneway Analysis of Data by Label** and select **Means/Anova.**

D. For Fisher confidence intervals, click on the red triangle next to **Oneway Analysis of Data by Label** and select **Compare Means > Each Pair, Student's t.**

E. For Tukey confidence intervals, click on the red triangle next to **Oneway Analysis of Data by Label** and select **Compare Means > All Pairs, Tukey HSD.**

Two_Factor

Two-Way ANOVA (No Interaction)

A. (Replicating Example 13.5) In order to reconfigure the data, follow the Minitab instructions for Two-Way ANOVA (No Interaction), step A.

B. From the menu, select **Analyze > Fit Model.** Drag Income to the **Y** box. Simultaneously select Education and Field and then select **Macros > Full Factorial**. Double-click on Education*Field in order to deselect this variable.

Interaction

Two-Way ANOVA (with Interaction)

A. (Replicating Example 13.6) In order to reconfigure the data, follow the Minitab instructions for Two-Way ANOVA (No Interaction), step A.

B. From the menu, select **Analyze > Fit Model.** Drag Income to the **Y** box. Simultaneously select Education and Field and then select **Macros > Full Factorial**.

14 Regression Analysis

LEARNING OBJECTIVES

After reading this chapter you should be able to:

LO **14.1** **Conduct a hypothesis test for the population correlation coefficient.**

LO **14.2** **Estimate and interpret a simple linear regression model.**

LO **14.3** **Estimate and interpret a multiple linear regression model.**

LO **14.4** **Interpret goodness-of-fit measures.**

As researchers or analysts, we often need to examine the relationship between two or more variables. We begin this chapter with a review of the correlation coefficient, first discussed in Chapter 3, and then conduct a hypothesis test to determine if two variables are correlated.

Next, we introduce regression analysis, which is one of the most widely used statistical techniques in business, engineering, and the social sciences. It is commonly used to predict and/or describe changes in a variable of interest, called the response variable, on the basis of several input variables, called the explanatory variables. For example, if a firm increases advertising expenditures by $100,000, then we may want to know the likely impact on sales. Or, we may want to predict the price of a house based on its size and location. Regression analysis can be applied in both of these scenarios.

We first explore the procedure for estimating a linear relationship between two variables, referred to as the simple linear regression model. We then extend the simple linear regression model to the case involving several variables, referred to as the multiple linear regression model. Finally, since we often must choose between various regression models, we examine a number of goodness-of-fit measures in order to assess how well an estimated model fits the data.

Blend Images - JGI/Jamie Grill/Getty Images

INTRODUCTORY CASE

Consumer Debt Payments

A study finds that American consumers are making average monthly debt payments of $983. However, it turns out that the actual amount a consumer pays depends a great deal on where the consumer lives. For instance, residents of Washington, D.C. pay the most, while Pittsburgh residents pay the least. Madelyn Davis, an economist at a large bank, believes that income differences between cities are the primary reason for the disparate debt payments. For example, the Washington, D.C. area's high incomes have likely contributed to its placement on the list. She is unsure about the likely effect of the unemployment rate on consumer debt payments. On the one hand, higher unemployment rates may reduce consumer debt payments, as consumers forgo making major purchases such as large appliances and cars. On the other hand, higher unemployment rates may raise consumer debt payments as consumers struggle to pay their bills.

In order to analyze the relationship between consumer debt payments, income, and the unemployment rate, Madelyn gathers data on average consumer debt (Debt in $), the annual median household income (Income in $1,000s), and the monthly unemployment rate (Unemployment in %) from 26 metropolitan areas in the United States. Table 14.1 shows a portion of the data.

FILE _Payments

TABLE 14.1 Average Consumer Debt, Median Income, and the Unemployment Rate

Metropolitan Area	Debt	Income	Unemployment
Washington, D.C.	1285	103.50	6.3
Seattle	1135	81.70	8.5
⋮	⋮	⋮	⋮
Pittsburgh	763	63.00	8.3

Madelyn would like to use the sample information in Table 14.1 to

1. Determine if debt payments and income are correlated.
2. Use regression analysis to make predictions for debt payments for given values of income and the unemployment rate.
3. Use various goodness-of-fit measures to determine the regression model that best fits the data.

A synopsis of this case is provided at the end of Section 14.3.

14.1 HYPOTHESIS TEST FOR THE CORRELATION COEFFICIENT

LO 14.1

Conduct a hypothesis test for the population correlation coefficient.

Recall from Chapter 2 that a scatterplot graphically shows the relationship between two variables. Using the ***Debt_Payments*** data file from the introductory case, Figure 14.1 shows a scatterplot of debt payments against income. We may infer that the two variables have a positive relationship; as one increases, the other one tends to increase.

FIGURE 14.1 Scatterplot of debt payments against income

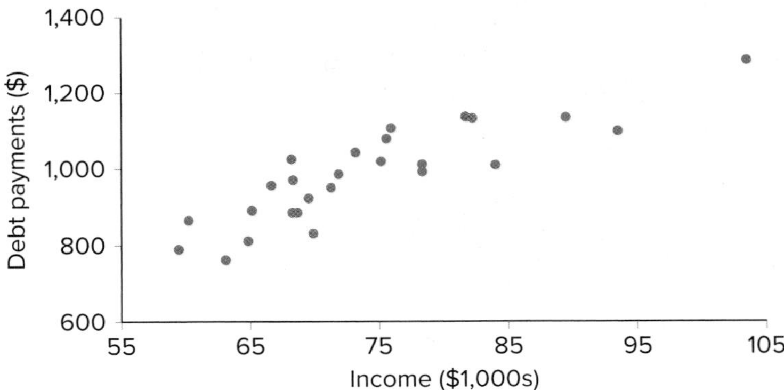

In Chapter 3 we examined the covariance and the correlation coefficient which are measures that quantify the linear relationship between two variables. The sample covariance s_{xy} measures the direction of the linear relationship between two variables x and y. A positive value of s_{xy} implies that x and y have a positive linear relationship, whereas a negative value of s_{xy} implies that x and y have a negative linear relationship.

Further interpretation of the covariance is difficult because it is sensitive to the units of measurement. For instance, the covariance between two variables might be 100 and the covariance between two other variables might be 1,000, yet all we can conclude is that both sets of variables are positively related. In other words, we cannot comment on the strength of the linear relationships.

An easier measure to interpret is the **sample correlation coefficient** r_{xy}, which describes both the direction and the strength of the linear relationship between x and y.

THE SAMPLE CORRELATION COEFFICIENT

The sample correlation coefficient gauges the direction and the strength of the linear relationship between two variables x and y. We calculate the sample correlation coefficient r_{xy} as

$$r_{xy} = \frac{s_{xy}}{s_x s_y},$$

where s_{xy} is the sample covariance, s_x and s_y are the sample standard deviations of x and y, respectively, and $-1 \leq r_{xy} \leq 1$.

In short, the sample correlation coefficient r_{xy} is unit-free and its value falls between -1 and 1. If r_{xy} equals 1, then a perfect positive linear relationship exists between x and y. Similarly, a perfect negative linear relationship exists if r_{xy} equals -1. If r_{xy} equals zero, then no linear relationship exists between x and y. Other values for r_{xy} must be interpreted with reference to −1, 0, and 1. As the absolute value of r_{xy} approaches 1, the stronger the linear relationship. For instance, $r_{xy} = -0.80$ indicates a strong negative linear relationship, whereas $r_{xy} = 0.12$ indicates a weak positive linear relationship. However, we should comment on the direction of the relationship only if the correlation coefficient is found to be statistically significant—a topic which we address next.

Testing the Correlation Coefficient ρ_{xy}

We conduct a hypothesis test to determine whether the apparent relationship between the two variables, implied by the sample correlation coefficient, is real or due to chance. Let ρ_{xy} denote the population correlation coefficient. When testing whether the population correlation coefficient differs from zero, is greater than zero, or is less than zero, the competing hypotheses will take one of the following forms:

Two-Tailed Test	Right-Tailed Test	Left-Tailed Test
$H_0: \rho_{xy} = 0$	$H_0: \rho_{xy} \leq 0$	$H_0: \rho_{xy} \geq 0$
$H_A: \rho_{xy} \neq 0$	$H_A: \rho_{xy} > 0$	$H_A: \rho_{xy} < 0$

As in all hypothesis tests, the next step is to specify and calculate the value of the test statistic.

TEST STATISTIC FOR ρ_{XY}

The value of the test statistic for the hypothesis test concerning the population correlation coefficient ρ_{xy} is calculated as

$$t_{df} = \frac{r_{xy}}{s_r},$$

where $df = n - 2$ and s_r is the standard error of the sample correlation coefficient, r_{xy}, and is calculated as $\sqrt{(1 - r_{xy}^2)/(n - 2)}$.

Or, equivalently,

$$t_{df} = \frac{r_{xy}\sqrt{n-2}}{\sqrt{1 - r_{xy}^2}}.$$

Using Excel and R to Conduct a Hypothesis Test for ρ_{xy}

Here, we rely on Excel and R to help us conduct a hypothesis test concerning the population correlation coefficient. Consider the following example.

EXAMPLE 14.1

Use the ***Debt_Payments*** data file from the introductory case to solve the following problems.

Debt_Payments

a. Calculate and interpret the correlation coefficient between Debt and Income.

b. At the 5% significance level, determine whether the correlation coefficient is significant.

SOLUTION:

Using Excel

a. Open the ***Debt_Payments*** data file. Note that the observations for Debt are in cells B2 through B27, and the observations for Income are in cells C2 through C27. We use Excel's **CORREL** function to calculate the correlation coefficient. So, we enter `=CORREL(B2:B27, C2:C27)`, and Excel returns 0.8675. The correlation coefficient of 0.8675 indicates that Debt and Income have a positive linear relationship.

b. When testing whether the correlation coefficient between Income (x) and Debt (y) is significant, we set up the following competing hypotheses:

$$H_0: \rho_{xy} = 0$$
$$H_A: \rho_{xy} \neq 0$$

In order to find the value of the test statistic, $t_{df} = \frac{r_{xy}\sqrt{n-2}}{\sqrt{1-r_{xy}^2}}$ with $df = n - 2 = 24$, we enter `=(CORREL(B2:B27, C2:C27)*sqrt(26-2))/(sqrt(1-CORREL(B2:B27, C2:C27)^2))`. Excel returns 8.544, so $t_{24} = 8.544$. For this two-tailed test with $t_{df} > 0$, we find the p-value by entering `=2*T.DIST.RT(8.544,24)`, and Excel returns 9.66E-09. Since the p-value is approximately equal to zero, we reject H_0. At the 5% significance level, we conclude that the population correlation coefficient between Debt and Income differs from zero.

Using R

a. Import the ***Debt_Payments*** data file into a data frame (table) and label it myData.

b. It is possible to use R's **cor** function, first introduced in Chapter 3, to find the correlation coefficient. However, the **cor.test** function generates the correlation coefficient as well as the value of the test statistic and the p-value. Within the function, we first specify the x and y variables. We then use the option *alternative* to denote the specification of the alternative hypothesis (specified as "two.sided" for a two-tailed test, "less" for a left-tailed test, and "greater" for a right-tailed test). Enter:

```
> cor.test(myData$Income, myData$Debt, alternative="two.sided")
```

Table 14.2 shows the R output. We have put the sample correlation coefficient, the value of the test statistic, and the p-value in boldface. The results are identical to the Excel output. That is, the correlation between Debt and Income, found at the bottom of Table 14.2, is 0.8675. Also, since the p-value is approximately 0, we reject the null hypothesis. At the 5% significance level, we conclude that the population correlation coefficient between Debt and Income differs from zero.

TABLE 14.2 R's Output for Hypothesis Test Concerning the Correlation Coefficient

```
          Pearson's product-moment correlation
data: myData[, "Income"] and myData[, "Debt"]
t = 8.544, df = 24, p-value = 9.66e-09
alternative hypothesis: true correlation is not equal to 0
95 percent confidence interval:
0.7231671 0.9392464
sample estimates:
    cor
0.8675115
```

Correlation analysis has a number of limitations. Recall that the correlation coefficient measures the strength of the linear relationship between two variables. There are many instances where we may want to know how three or more variables are related, such as the relationship between salary, education, and work experience. Or, we may have reason to believe that the relationship between two variables is nonlinear. In these instances, correlation analysis is not appropriate, but regression analysis is. Much of the remainder of this text is devoted to regression analysis, which also allows us to make predictions regarding a variable of interest.

EXERCISES 14.1

Mechanics

1. The covariance between two random variables x and y is 100. The sample standard deviation for x is 10 and the sample standard deviation for y is 12.5. Calculate and interpret the correlation coefficient.
2. The covariance between two random variables x and y is −250. The sample standard deviation for x is 40 and the sample standard deviation for y is 50. Calculate and interpret the correlation coefficient.
3. Consider the following competing hypotheses:

$$H_0: \rho_{xy} = 0$$
$$H_A: \rho_{xy} \neq 0$$

The sample consists of 25 observations and the sample correlation coefficient is 0.15.

   a. Calculate the value of the test statistic and the p-value.
   b. At the 5% significance level, what is the conclusion to the test? Explain.

4. Consider the following competing hypotheses:

$$H_0: \rho_{xy} \geq 0$$
$$H_A: \rho_{xy} < 0$$

The sample consists of 30 observations and the sample correlation coefficient is −0.60.

   a. Calculate the value of the test statistic and the p-value.
   b. At the 5% significance level, what is the conclusion to the test? Explain.

5. A sample of 10 observations provides the following statistics:

$$s_x = 13, \quad s_y = 18, \quad \text{and} \quad s_{xy} = 117.22$$

   a. Calculate and interpret the sample correlation coefficient r_{xy}.
   b. Specify the competing hypotheses to determine whether the population correlation coefficient is positive.
   c. Calculate the value of the test statistic and the p-value.
   d. At the 5% significance level, what is the conclusion to the test? Explain.

6. A sample of 25 observations provides the following statistics:

$$s_x = 2, \quad s_y = 5, \quad \text{and} \quad s_{xy} = -1.75$$

   a. Calculate and interpret the sample correlation coefficient r_{xy}.
   b. Specify the competing hypotheses in order to determine whether the population correlation coefficient differs from zero.
   c. At the 5% significance level, what is the conclusion to the test? Explain.

Applications

7. **FILE** ***Rain.*** A sociologist studies the relationship between weather and crime in a city. Specifically, she believes that dreary weather is a key factor in reducing fatal and nondeadly shootings. She collects data on the number of rainy days and the number of shootings that occurred over the past five months. A portion of the data is shown in the accompanying table.

Month	Rainy	Shootings
1	7	31
2	15	46
⋮	⋮	⋮
5	22	15

   a. Calculate the sample correlation coefficient between the number of rainy days and crime.
   b. Specify the competing hypotheses in order to determine whether the population correlation coefficient between the number of rainy days and crime is negative.
   c. Calculate the value of the test statistic and the p-value.
   d. At the 5% significance level, what is the conclusion to the test? Does it appear that dreary weather and crime are negatively correlated?

8. **FILE** ***Stock_Returns.*** Diversification is considered important in finance because it allows investors to reduce risk by investing in a variety of assets. It is especially effective when the correlation between the assets is low. Consider the accompanying table, which shows a portion of monthly data on closing stock prices of four firms over the past year.

Month	Firm 1	Firm 2	Firm 3	Firm 4
Jan	27.61	49.52	15.13	15.64
Feb	28.22	54.88	16.61	15.72
⋮	⋮	⋮	⋮	⋮
Dec	27.91	55.58	13.34	18.29

a. Calculate the sample correlation coefficients between all pairs of stock prices.
b. Suppose an investor already has a stake in Firm 1 and would like to add another asset to her portfolio. Which of the remaining three assets will give her the maximum benefit of diversification? (*Hint:* Find the asset with the lowest correlation with Firm 1.)
c. Suppose an investor does not own any of these four stocks. Pick two stocks so that she gets the maximum benefit of diversification.

9. FILE ***Taxes.*** A realtor studies the relationship between the size of a house (in square feet) and the property taxes (in $) owed by the owner. The accompanying table shows a portion of the data for 20 homes in a suburb 60 miles outside of New York City.

Taxes	Size
21928	2449
17339	2479
⋮	⋮
29235	2864

a. Calculate and interpret r_{xy}.
b. Specify the competing hypotheses in order to determine whether the population correlation coefficient between the size of a house and property taxes differs from zero.
c. Calculate the value of the test statistic and the p-value.
d. At the 5% significance level, what is the conclusion to the test?

10. FILE ***Happiness_Age.*** Many attempts have been made to relate happiness with various factors. One such study relates happiness with age and finds that holding everything else constant, people are least happy when they are in their mid-40s. The accompanying table shows a portion of data on a respondent's age and his/her perception of well-being on a scale from 0 to 100.

Respondent	Happiness	Age
1	62	49
2	66	51
⋮	⋮	⋮
24	72	69

a. Calculate and interpret the sample correlation coefficient between age and happiness.
b. Is the correlation coefficient statistically significant at the 1% level?
c. Construct a scatterplot to point out a flaw with this correlation analysis.

11. FILE ***Points.*** A sports analyst for the National Basketball Association wonders whether there is a relationship between a basketball player's average points per game (PPG) and his average minutes per game (MPG). The accompanying table lists a portion of the data that he collected for ten players.

Player	PPG	MPG
1	30.2	38.6
2	28.4	37.7
⋮	⋮	⋮
10	22.6	37.2

a. Calculate and interpret the sample correlation coefficient between PPG and MPG.
b. Specify the competing hypotheses in order to determine whether the population correlation coefficient between PPG and MPG is positive.
c. Calculate the value of the test statistic and the p-value.
d. At the 5% significance level, what is the conclusion to the test? Is this result surprising? Explain.

LO 14.2

14.2 THE LINEAR REGRESSION MODEL

Estimate and interpret a simple linear regression model.

Regression analysis is one of the most widely used statistical methodologies in business, engineering, and the social sciences. It presumes that one variable, called the **response variable,** is influenced by other variables, called the **explanatory variables.** Consequently, we use information on the explanatory variables to predict and/or describe changes in the response variable. Alternative names for the explanatory variables are predictor variables or input variables, while the response variable is often referred to as the target variable.

Correlation and regression analyses are related in a sense that they both measure some form of association between variables. As discussed in Section 14.1, the correlation coefficient measures the strength of the linear relationship between two variables, whereas regression extends the analysis to capture the relationship between the response variable and multiple explanatory variables. A regression model also allows us to make predictions regarding the response variable based on the known values of the explanatory variables.

Regression models are known to perform well for making predictions. Oftentimes, however, they fail to establish a cause-and-effect relationship between the variables because of the largely non-experimental nature of business applications. A regression model may appear to search for causality when it basically detects correlation. Causality can only be established through randomized experiments and/or advanced statistical models, which are outside the scope of this text.

In the introductory case, Madelyn is interested in examining how median income and the unemployment rate might influence debt payments in a metropolitan area. In another scenario, we may want to predict a firm's sales based on its advertising; estimate an individual's salary based on education and years of experience; predict the selling price of a house on the basis of its size and location; or describe auto sales with respect to consumer income, interest rates, and price discounts. In all of these examples, we can use regression analysis to describe the relationship between the variables of interest.

No matter the response variable that we choose to examine, we cannot expect to predict its exact value. If the value of the response variable is uniquely determined by the values of the explanatory variables, we say that the relationship between the variables is **deterministic.** This is often the case in the physical sciences. For example, momentum p is the product of the mass m and velocity v of an object; that is, $p = mv$. In most fields of research, however, we tend to find that the relationship between the explanatory variables and the response variable is **stochastic,** due to the omission of relevant variables (sometimes not measurable) that influence the response variable. For instance, debt payments are likely to be influenced by costs associated with the household size—a variable that is not included in the introductory case. Similarly, when trying to predict an individual's salary, the individual's natural ability is often omitted since it is extremely difficult, if not impossible, to quantify.

DETERMINISTIC VERSUS STOCHASTIC RELATIONSHIPS

The relationship between the response variable and the explanatory variables is deterministic if the value of the response variable is uniquely determined by the explanatory variables; otherwise, the relationship is stochastic.

Our objective is to develop a mathematical model that captures the relationship between the response variable y and the k explanatory variables $x_1, x_2, \ldots, x_k$. The model must also account for the stochastic nature of the relationship. In order to develop a linear regression model, we start with a deterministic component that approximates the relationship we want to model, and then add a random term to it, making the relationship stochastic.

The Simple Linear Regression Model

We first focus on the **simple linear regression model,** which uses one explanatory variable, denoted x_1, to explain the variation in the response variable, denoted y. For ease of exposition when discussing the simple linear regression model, we often drop the subscript on the explanatory variable and refer to it solely as x. We then extend the simple linear regression model to the **multiple linear regression model,** where more than one explanatory variable is presumed to have a linear relationship with the response variable.

A fundamental assumption underlying the simple linear regression model is that the expected value of y lies on a straight line, denoted by $\beta_0 + \beta_1 x$, where β_0 and β_1 (the Greek letters read as betas) are the unknown intercept and slope parameters, respectively. (You have actually seen this relationship before, but you just used different notation. Recall the equation for a line: $y = \text{m}x + \text{b}$, where b and m are the intercept and the slope, respectively, of the line.)

The expression $\beta_0 + \beta_1 x$ is the deterministic component of the simple linear regression model, which can be thought of as the expected value of y for a given value of x. In other words, conditional on x, $E(y) = \beta_0 + \beta_1 x$. The slope parameter β_1 determines whether the linear relationship between x and $E(y)$ is positive ($\beta_1 > 0$) or negative ($\beta_1 < 0$); $\beta_1 = 0$ indicates that there is no linear relationship. Figure 14.2 shows the expected value of y for various values of the intercept β_0 and the slope β_1 parameters.

FIGURE 14.2 Various examples of a simple linear regression model

Positive linear relationship

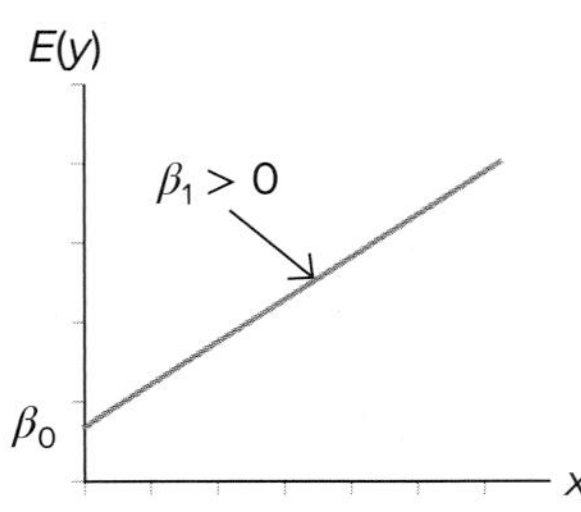

Negative linear relationship

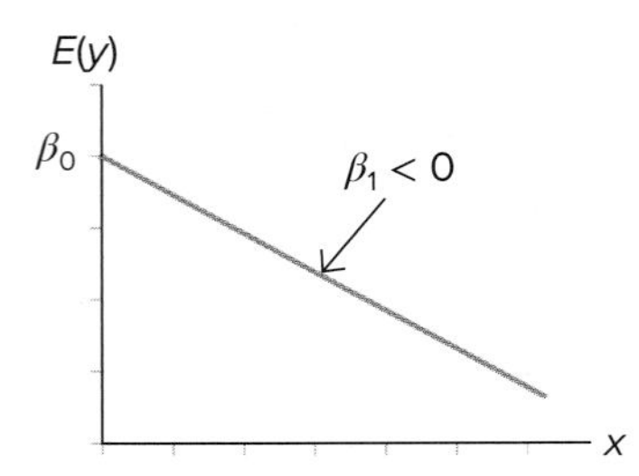

No linear relationship

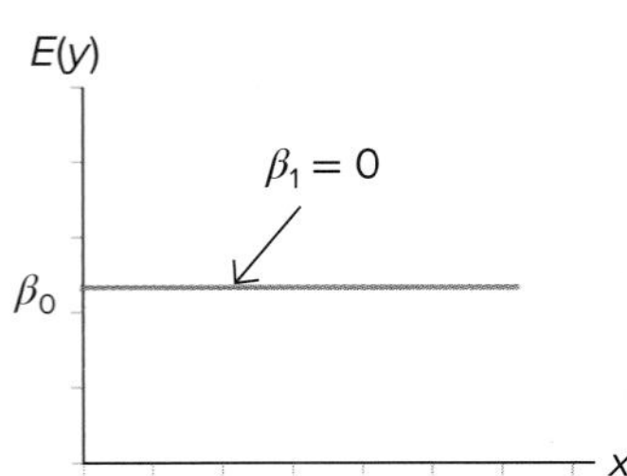

As noted earlier, the observed value y may differ from the expected value $E(y)$. Therefore, we add a random error term ε (the Greek letter read as epsilon) to develop a simple linear regression model.

> THE SIMPLE LINEAR REGRESSION MODEL
>
> The simple linear regression model is defined as
>
> $$y = \beta_0 + \beta_1 x + \varepsilon,$$
>
> where y and x are the response variable and the explanatory variable, respectively, and ε is the random error term. The coefficients β_0 and β_1 are the unknown parameters to be estimated.

The population parameters β_0 and β_1 used in the simple linear regression model are unknown, and, therefore, must be estimated. As always, we use sample data to estimate the population parameters of interest. Here sample data consist of n pairs of observations on y and x.

Let b_0 and b_1 represent the estimates of β_0 and β_1, respectively. We form the sample regression equation as $\hat{y} = b_0 + b_1 x$, where $\hat{y}$ (read as y-hat) is the predicted value of the response variable given a specified value of the explanatory variable x. For a given value of x, the observed and the predicted values of the response variable are likely to be different since many factors besides x influence y. We refer to the difference between the observed and the predicted values of y, that is $y - \hat{y}$, as the **residual** e.

> THE SAMPLE REGRESSION EQUATION FOR THE SIMPLE LINEAR REGRESSION MODEL
>
> The sample regression equation for the simple linear regression model is denoted as
>
> $$\hat{y} = b_0 + b_1 x,$$
>
> where b_0 and b_1 are the estimates of β_0 and β_1, respectively.
>
> The difference between the observed and the predicted values of y represents the residual e—that is, $e = y - \hat{y}$.

Before estimating a simple linear regression model, it is useful to visualize the relationship between y and x by constructing a scatterplot. Here, we explicitly place y on the vertical axis and x on the horizontal axis. In Figure 14.3, we use the data from the introductory case to show a scatterplot of Debt against Income. We then superimpose a linear trendline through the points on the scatterplot.

The superimposed line in Figure 14.3 is the sample regression equation, $\hat{y} = b_0 + b_1 x$, where y and x represent Debt and Income, respectively. The upward slope of the line suggests that as income increases, the predicted debt payments also increase. Also, the vertical distance between any data point on the scatterplot (y) and the corresponding point on the line ($\hat{y}$) represents the residual, $e = y - \hat{y}$.

FIGURE 13.3 Scatterplot with a superimposed trendline

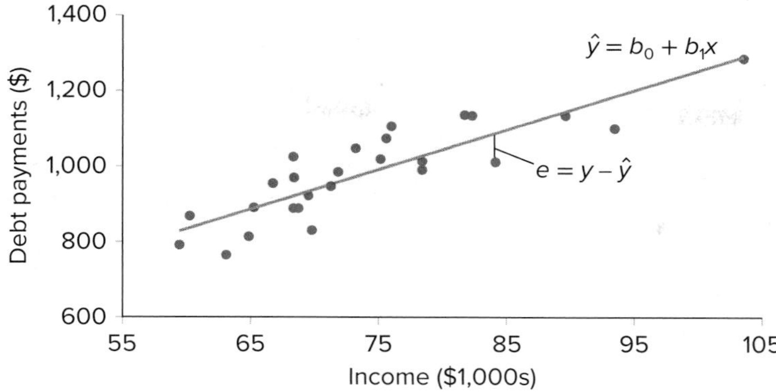

A common approach to fitting a line to the scatterplot is the **method of least squares,** also referred to as **ordinary least squares (OLS).** In other words, we use OLS to estimate the parameters β_0 and β_1. OLS estimators have many desirable properties if certain assumptions hold. (These assumptions are discussed in Chapter 15.) The OLS method chooses the line whereby the **error sum of squares, *SSE*,** is minimized, where $SSE = \Sigma(y_i - \hat{y}_i)^2 = \Sigma e_i^2$. *SSE* is the sum of the squared difference between the observed value y and its predicted value $\hat{y}$ or, equivalently, the sum of the squared distances from the regression equation. Thus, using this distance measure, we say that the OLS method produces the straight line that is "closest" to the data. In the context of Figure 14.3, the superimposed line has been estimated by OLS.

Using calculus, equations have been developed for b_0 and b_1 that satisfy the OLS criterion. These equations, or formulas, are as follows.

CALCULATING THE REGRESSION COEFFICIENTS b_1 AND b_0

The slope b_1 and the intercept b_0 of the sample regression equation are calculated as

$$b_1 = \frac{\Sigma(x_i - \bar{x})(y_i - \bar{y})}{\Sigma(x_i - \bar{x})^2} \quad \text{and}$$

$$b_0 = \bar{y} - b_1\bar{x}.$$

Fortunately, virtually every statistical software package produces values for b_1 and b_0. So we can focus on interpreting these regression coefficients rather than performing the grueling calculations. The slope estimate b_1 represents the change in $\hat{y}$ when x increases by one unit. As we will see in the following example, it is not always possible to provide an economic interpretation of the intercept estimate b_0; mathematically, however, it represents the predicted value of $\hat{y}$ when x has a value of zero.

EXAMPLE 14.2

Use the ***Debt_Payments*** data file from the introductory case to estimate Debt as a function of Income in a simple linear regression model.

Debt_Payments

a. What is the sample regression equation?

b. Interpret b_1.

c. Interpret b_0.

d. Predict debt payments if income is $80,000.

SOLUTION: Table 14.3 shows the Excel-produced output from estimating the model: Debt $= \beta_0 + \beta_1$ Income $+ \varepsilon$, or simply, $y = \beta_0 + \beta_1 x + \varepsilon$, where y and x represent Debt and Income, respectively. We provide Excel and R instructions for obtaining regression output at the end of this section.

TABLE 14.3 Excel-Produced Regression Results for Example 14.2

Regression Statistics						
Multiple R		0.8675				
R Square		0.7526				
Adjusted R Square		0.7423				
Standard Error		63.2606				
Observations		26				
ANOVA						
	df	*SS*	*MS*	*F*	*Significance F*	
Regression	1	292136.91	292136.91	72.9996	9.66E-09	
Residual	24	96045.55	4001.90			
Total	25	388182.46				
	Coefficients	*Standard Error*	*t Stat*	*p-Value*	*Lower 95%*	*Upper 95%*
Intercept	**210.2977**	91.3387	2.3024	0.0303	−21.78	398.81
Income	**10.4411**	1.2220	8.5440	9.66E-09	7.92	12.96

a. As Table 14.3 shows, Excel produces quite a bit of information. In order to formulate the sample regression equation, we need estimates for β_0 and β_1, which are found at the bottom of the table (see values in boldface). We address the remaining information in the next section of this chapter, as well as in Chapter 15. We find that $b_0 = 210.2977$ and $b_1 = 10.4411$. Thus, the sample regression equation is $\hat{y} = 210.2977 + 10.4411x$; that is, $\widehat{\text{Debt}} = 210.2977 + 10.4411\text{Income}$.

b. The estimated slope coefficient of 10.4411 suggests a positive relationship between Debt and Income. If median household income increases by one unit, or by \$1,000 (since Income is measured in \$1,000s), then we predict consumer debt payments to increase by b_1—that is, by \$10.44.

c. The estimated intercept coefficient of 210.2977 suggests that if Income equals zero, then predicted debt payments are \$210.30. In this particular application, we may be tempted to make this conclusion because a household with no income still needs to make debt payments for any credit card use, automobile loans, and so on. However, we should be careful about predicting y when we use a value for x that is not included in the sample range of x. In the ***Debt_Payments*** data set, the lowest and highest values for Income are 59.40 and 103.50, respectively; plus, the scatterplot suggests that a line fits the data well within this range of the explanatory variable. Unless we assume that Debt and Income will maintain the same linear relationship for observations of Income less than 59.40 and more than 103.50, we should refrain from making predictions based on observations of the explanatory variable outside the sample range.

d. Recall that Income is measured in \$1,000s. So if we are predicting debt payments for an income of \$80,000, then we input the value of 80 for Income in the sample regression equation. Thus, we find

$$\widehat{\text{Debt}} = 210.2977 + 10.4411 \times 80 = 1{,}045.59.$$

That is, debt payments are predicted to be \$1,045.59.

The Multiple Linear Regression Model

LO 14.3

Estimate and interpret the multiple linear regression model

The simple linear regression model allows us to analyze the linear relationship between one explanatory variable and the response variable. However, by restricting the number of explanatory variables to one, we sometimes reduce the potential usefulness of the model. In Chapter 15, we will discuss how the OLS estimates can be quite misleading when important explanatory variables are excluded. A multiple linear regression model allows us to examine how the response variable is influenced by two or more explanatory variables. The choices of the explanatory variables are based on economic theory, intuition, and/or prior research. The multiple linear regression model is a straight-forward extension of the simple linear regression model.

THE MULTIPLE LINEAR REGRESSION MODEL

The multiple linear regression model is defined as

$$y = \beta_0 + \beta_1 x_1 + \beta_2 x_2 + \cdots + \beta_k x_k + \varepsilon,$$

where y is the response variable, $x_1, x_2, \ldots, x_k$ are the k explanatory variables, and ε is the random error term. The coefficients $\beta_0, \beta_1, \ldots, \beta_k$ are the unknown parameters to be estimated.

As in the case of the simple linear regression model, we apply the OLS method that minimizes *SSE*, where $SSE = \Sigma(y_i - \hat{y}_i)^2 = \Sigma e_i^2$.

THE SAMPLE REGRESSION EQUATION FOR THE MULTIPLE LINEAR REGRESSION MODEL

The sample regression equation for the multiple linear regression model is denoted as

$$\hat{y} = b_0 + b_1 x_1 + b_2 x_2 + \cdots + b_k x_k,$$

where $b_0, b_1, \cdots, b_k$ are the estimates of $\beta_0, \beta_1, \cdots, \beta_k$.

The difference between the observed and the predicted values of y represents the residual e—that is, $e = y - \hat{y}$.

For each explanatory variable x_j ($j = 1, \ldots, k$), the corresponding slope coefficient b_j is the estimate of β_j. We slightly modify the interpretation of the slope coefficients in the context of a multiple linear regression model. Here b_j measures the change in the predicted value of the response variable $\hat{y}$ given a unit increase in the associated explanatory variable x_j, *holding all other explanatory variables constant.* In other words, it represents the partial influence of x_j on $\hat{y}$.

EXAMPLE 14.3

FILE
Debt_Payments

Use the ***Debt_Payments*** data file from the introductory case to estimate Debt as a function of Income and Unemployment in a multiple linear regression model.

a. What is the sample regression equation?

b. Interpret the regression coefficients.

c. Predict debt payments if income is \$80,000 and the unemployment rate is 7.5%.

SOLUTION:

a. Table 14.4 shows the Excel-produced output from estimating the model: Debt $= \beta_0 + \beta_1$Income $+ \beta_2$Unemployment $+ \varepsilon$. We provide Excel and R instructions for obtaining this output shortly.

TABLE 14.4 Excel-Produced Regression Output for Example 14.3

Regression Statistics						
Multiple R	0.8676					
R Square	0.7527					
Adjusted R Square	0.7312					
Standard Error	64.6098					
Observations	26					
ANOVA						
	df	***SS***	***MS***	***F***	***Significance F***	
Regression	2	292170.77	146085.39	34.9954	1.05E-07	
Residual	23	96011.69	4174.42			
Total	25	388182.46				
	Coefficients	***Standard Error***	***t Stat***	***p-Value***	***Lower 95%***	***Upper 95%***
Intercept	**198.9956**	156.3619	1.2727	0.2159	−124.46	522.45
Income	**10.5122**	1.4765	7.1120	2.98E-07	7.46	13.57
Unemployment	**0.6186**	6.8679	0.0901	0.9290	−13.59	14.83

Using the boldface estimates from Table 14.4, $b_0 = 198.9956$, $b_1 = 10.5122$, and $b_2 = 0.6186$, we derive the sample regression equation as

$$\widehat{\text{Debt}} = 198.9956 + 10.5122\text{Income} + 0.6186\text{Unemployment}.$$

b. The regression coefficient of Income is 10.5122. Since Income is measured in \$1,000s, the model suggests that if income increases by \$1,000, then debt payments are predicted to increase by \$10.51, holding the unemployment rate constant. Similarly, the regression coefficient of Unemployment is 0.6186, implying that a 1 percentage point increase in the unemployment rate leads to a predicted increase in debt payments of \$0.62, holding income constant. It seems that the predicted impact of Unemployment, with Income held constant, is rather small. In fact, the influence of the unemployment rate is not even statistically significant at any reasonable level; we will discuss such tests of significance in the next chapter.

c. If income is \$80,000 and the unemployment rate is 7.5%, we find

$$\widehat{\text{Debt}} = 198.9956 + 10.5122 \times 80 + 0.6186 \times 7.5 = 1{,}044.61.$$

That is, debt payments are predicted to be \$1,044.61.

Using Excel and R to Estimate a Linear Regression Model

Debt_Payments

We replicate Table 14.4 from Example 14.3.

Using Excel

A. Open the ***Debt_Payments*** data file.

B. Choose **Data** > **Data Analysis** > **Regression** from the menu.

C. See Figure 14.4. In the *Regression* dialog box, click on the box next to *Input Y Range,* and then select the Debt observations, including its heading. For *Input X Range, simultaneously* select the Income and the Unemployment observations, including their headings. Check *Labels.* Click **OK.** Your results should be identical to Table 14.4.

FIGURE 14.4 Excel's Regression dialog box

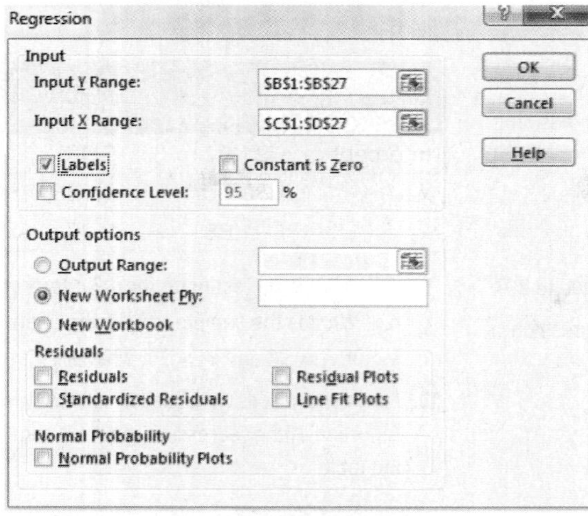

Using R

A. Import the ***Debt_Payments*** data file into a data frame and label it myData.

B. By default, R will report the regression output using scientific notation. We opt to turn this option off using the following command:

```
> options(scipen=999)
```

In order to turn scientific notation back on, we would enter options(scipen=0) at the prompt.

C. We use the **lm** function to create a linear model. In R terminology, this is referred to as an object. We label this object as Multiple. Within the lm function, we specify Debt as a function of Income and Unemployment, using the '+' sign to add explanatory variables. If we only enter the lm function, then we will not see the output. We use the **summary** function preceded by a semi-colon, to view the regression output. Enter:

```
> Multiple <- lm(Debt ~ Income + Unemployment, data = myData);
  summary(Multiple)
```

D. We use the **predict** function accompanied with the **data.frame** function to predict Debt if Income equals 80 and Unemployment equals 7.5. Enter:

```
> predict(Multiple, data.frame(Income=80,Unemployment=7.5))
```

And R returns: 1044.608

Table 14.5 shows the R regression output. We have put the intercept and the slope coefficients in boldface. As expected, these values are identical to the ones obtained using Excel.

TABLE 14.5 R-Produced Regression Output for Example 14.3

```
Call:
lm(formula = Debt ~ Income + Unemployment, data = Debt_Payments)
Residuals:
     Min          1Q          Median         3Q           Max
-110.456     -38.454        -5.836       51.156       102.121
Coefficients:
                  Estimate Std.   Error        t value       Pr(>|t|)
(Intercept)        198.9956     156.3619       1.273          0.216
Income              10.5122       1.4765       7.120       2.98e-07 ***
Unemployment         0.6186       6.8679       0.090          0.929
---
Signif. codes: 0 '***' 0.001 '**' 0.01 '*' 0.05 '.' 0.1 ' ' 1
Residual standard error: 64.61 on 23 degrees of freedom
Multiple R-squared: 0.7527, Adjusted R-squared: 0.7312
F-statistic: 35 on 2 and 23 DF, p-value: 1.054e-07
```

EXERCISES 14.2

Mechanics

12. In a simple linear regression, the following sample regression equation is obtained:

$$\hat{y} = 15 + 2.5x.$$

a. Predict y if x equals 10.
b. What happens to this prediction if x doubles in value to 20?

13. In a simple linear regression, the following sample regression equation is obtained:

$$\hat{y} = 436 - 17x.$$

a. Interpret the slope coefficient.
b. Predict y if x equals –15.

14. In a multiple regression, the following sample regression equation is obtained:

$$\hat{y} = -8 + 2.6x_1 - 47.2x_2.$$

a. Predict y if x_1 equals 40 and x_2 equals –10.
b. Interpret the slope coefficient of x_2.

15. In a multiple regression, the following sample regression equation is obtained:

$$\hat{y} = 152 + 12.9x_1 - 2.7x_2.$$

a. Predict y if x_1 equals 20 and x_2 equals 35.
b. Interpret the slope coefficient of x_1.

16. Thirty observations were used to estimate $y = \beta_0 + \beta_1 x + \varepsilon$. A portion of the results is shown in the accompanying table.

	Coefficients	Standard Error	t Stat	p-value
Intercept	41.82	8.58	4.87	3.93E-05
x	0.49	0.10	4.81	4.65E-05

a. What is the estimate for β_1? Interpret this value.
b. What is the sample regression equation?
c. If $x = 30$, what is $\hat{y}$?

17. Twenty-four observations were used to estimate $y = \beta_0 + \beta_1 x + \varepsilon$. A portion of the regression results is shown in the accompanying table.

	Coefficients	Standard Error	t Stat	p-value
Intercept	2.25	2.36	0.95	0.3515
x	−0.16	0.30	−0.53	0.6017

a. What is the estimate for β_1? Interpret this value.
b. What is the sample regression equation?
c. What is the predicted value for y if $x = 2$? If $x = -2$?

18. Thirty observations were used to estimate $y = \beta_0 + \beta_1 x_1 + \beta_2 x_2 + \varepsilon$. A portion of the regression results is shown in the accompanying table.

	Coefficients	Standard Error	t Stat	p-value
Intercept	21.97	2.98	7.37	6.31E-08
x_1	30.00	2.23	13.44	1.75E-13
x_2	−1.88	0.27	−6.96	1.75E-07

a. What is the estimate for β_1? Interpret this value.
b. What is the sample regression equation?
c. If $x_1 = 30$ and $x_2 = 20$, what is $\hat{y}$?

19. Forty observations were used to estimate $y = \beta_0 + \beta_1 x_1 + \beta_2 x_2 + \varepsilon$. A portion of the regression results is shown in the accompanying table.

	Coefficients	Standard Error	t Stat	p-value
Intercept	13.83	2.42	5.71	1.56E-06
x_1	−2.53	0.15	−16.87	5.84E-19
x_2	0.29	0.06	4.83	2.38E-05

a. What is the estimate for β_1? Interpret this value.
b. What is the sample regression equation?
c. What is the predicted value for y if $x_1 = -9$ and $x_2 = 25$?

Applications

20. If a firm spends more on advertising, is it likely to increase sales? Data on annual sales (in \$100,000s) and advertising expenditures (in \$10,000s) were collected for 20 firms in order to estimate the model Sales $= \beta_0 + \beta_1$Advertising $+ \varepsilon$. A portion of the regression results is shown in the accompanying table.

	Coefficients	Standard Error	t Stat	p-value
Intercept	−7.42	1.46	−5.09	7.66E-05
Advertising	0.42	0.05	8.70	7.26E-08

a. Is the sign on the slope as expected? Explain.
b. What is the sample regression equation?
c. Predict the sales for a firm that spends \$500,000 annually on advertising.

21. The owner of several used-car dealerships believes that the selling price of a used car can best be predicted using the car's age. He uses data on the recent selling price (in \$) and age of 20 used sedans to estimate Price $= \beta_0 + \beta_1$Age $+ \varepsilon$. A portion of the regression results is shown in the accompanying table.

	Coefficients	Standard Error	t Stat	p-value
Intercept	21187.94	733.42	28.89	1.56E-16
Age	−1208.25	128.95	−9.37	2.41E-08

a. What is the estimate for β_1? Interpret this value.
b. What is the sample regression equation?
c. Predict the selling price of a 5-year-old sedan.

22. On the first day of class, an economics professor administers a test to gauge the math preparedness of her students. She believes that the performance on this math test and the number of hours studied per week on the course are the primary factors that predict a student's score on the final exam. Using data from her class of 60 students, she estimates Final $= \beta_0 + \beta_1$Math $+ \beta_2$Hours $+ \varepsilon$. A portion of the regression results is shown in the following table.

	Coefficients	*Standard Error*	*t Stat*	*p-value*
Intercept	40.55	3.37	12.03	2.83E-17
Math	0.25	0.04	6.06	1.14E-07
Hours	4.85	0.57	8.53	9.06E-12

a. What is the slope coefficient of Hours?
b. What is the sample regression equation?
c. What is the predicted final exam score for a student who has a math score of 70 and studies 4 hours per week?

23. Using data from 50 workers, a researcher estimates Wage $= \beta_0 + \beta_1$Education $+ \beta_2$Experience $+ \beta_3$Age $+ \varepsilon$, where Wage is the hourly wage rate and Education, Experience, and Age are the years of higher education, the years of experience, and the age of the worker, respectively. A portion of the regression results is shown in the following table.

	Coefficients	*Standard Error*	*t Stat*	*p-value*
Intercept	7.87	4.09	1.93	0.0603
Education	1.44	0.34	4.24	0.0001
Experience	0.45	0.14	3.16	0.0028
Age	−0.01	0.08	−0.14	0.8920

a. Interpret the estimates for β_1 and β_2.
b. What is the sample regression equation?
c. Predict the hourly wage rate for a 30-year-old worker with 4 years of higher education and 3 years of experience.

24. A sociologist believes that the crime rate in an area is significantly influenced by the area's poverty rate and median income. Specifically, she hypothesizes that crime will increase with poverty and decrease with income. She collects data on the crime rate (crimes per 100,000 residents), the poverty rate (in %), and the median income (in $1,000s) from 41 New England cities. A portion of the regression results is shown in the following table.

	Coefficients	*Standard Error*	*t Stat*	*p-value*
Intercept	−301.62	549.71	−0.55	0.5864
Poverty	53.16	14.22	3.74	0.0006
Income	4.95	8.26	0.60	0.5526

a. Are the signs as expected on the slope coefficients?
b. Interpret the slope coefficient for Poverty.
c. Predict the crime rate in an area with a poverty rate of 20% and a median income of $50,000.

25. Osteoporosis is a degenerative disease that primarily affects women over the age of 60. A research analyst wants to forecast sales of StrongBones, a prescription drug for treating this debilitating disease. She uses the model Sales $= \beta_0 + \beta_1$Population $+ \beta_2$Income $+ \varepsilon$, where Sales refers to the sales of StrongBones (in $ millions), Population is the number of women over the age of 60 (in millions), and Income is the average income of women over the age of 60 (in $1,000s). She collects data on 38 cities across the United States and obtains the following regression results:

	Coefficients	*Standard Error*	*t Stat*	*p-value*
Intercept	10.35	4.02	2.57	0.0199
Population	8.47	2.71	3.12	0.0062
Income	7.62	6.63	1.15	0.2661

a. What is the sample regression equation?
b. Interpret the slope coefficients.
c. Predict sales if a city has 1.5 million women over the age of 60 and their average income is $44,000.

26. **FILE** ***GPA.*** The director of graduate admissions at a large university is analyzing the relationship between scores on the math portion of the Graduate Record Examination (GRE) and subsequent performance in graduate school, as measured by a student's grade point average (GPA). She uses a sample of 24 students who graduated within the past five years. A portion of the data is as follows:

GPA	GRE
3.0	700
3.5	720
⋮	⋮
3.5	780

a. Find the sample regression equation for the model: GPA $= \beta_0 + \beta_1$GRE $+ \varepsilon$.
b. What is a student's predicted GPA if he/she scored 710 on the math portion of the GRE?

27. **FILE** ***Education.*** A social scientist would like to analyze the relationship between educational attainment (in years of higher education) and annual salary (in $1,000s). He collects data on 20 individuals. A portion of the data is as follows:

Salary	Education
40	3
53	4
⋮	⋮
38	0

a. Find the sample regression equation for the model: Salary $= \beta_0 + \beta_1$Education $+ \varepsilon$.
b. Interpret the coefficient for Education.
c. What is the predicted salary for an individual who completed 7 years of higher education?

28. FILE ***Consumption.*** The consumption function, first developed by John Maynard Keynes, captures one of the key relationships in economics. It expresses consumption as a function of disposable income, where disposable income is income after taxes. The accompanying table shows a portion of quarterly data for average U.S. annual consumption (in $) and disposable income (in $) for the years 2000–2016.

Date	Consumption	Income
Q1, 2000	28634	31192
Q2, 2000	28837	31438
⋮	⋮	⋮
Q4, 2016	35987	39254

a. Find the sample regression equation for the model, Consumption $= \beta_0 + \beta_1$Income $+ \varepsilon$.
b. In this model, the slope coefficient is called the marginal propensity to consume. Interpret its meaning.
c. What is predicted consumption if disposable income is $35,000?

29. FILE ***Pitchers.*** A sports analyst for Major League Baseball wonders whether there is a relationship between a pitcher's salary (in $ millions) and his earned run average (ERA). The accompanying table lists a portion of the data that she collected for 10 pitchers.

Pitcher	Salary	ERA
1	17.0	2.53
2	4.0	2.54
⋮	⋮	⋮
10	0.5	3.09

a. Estimate the model: Salary $= \beta_0 + \beta_1$ERA $+ \varepsilon$ and interpret the coefficient of ERA.
b. Use the estimated model to predict the salary for each player, given his ERA. For example, use the sample regression equation to predict the salary for Pitcher 1 with ERA $= 2.53$.
c. Derive the corresponding residuals and explain why the residuals might be so high.

30. FILE ***Happiness_Age.*** Refer to the accompanying data file on happiness and age to answer the following questions.
a. Estimate Happiness as a function of Age in a simple linear regression model. What is the sample regression equation?
b. Use the sample regression equation to predict Happiness when Age equals 25, 50, and 75.
c. Construct a scatterplot of Happiness against Age. Discuss why your predictions might not be accurate.

31. FILE ***Taxes.*** The accompanying table shows a portion of data that refers to the property taxes owed by a homeowner (in $) and the size of the home (in square feet) in an affluent suburb 30 miles outside New York City.

Taxes	Size
21928	2449
17339	2479
⋮	⋮
29235	2864

a. Estimate the sample regression equation that enables us to predict property taxes on the basis of the size of the home.
b. Interpret the slope coefficient.
c. Predict the property taxes for a 1,500-square-foot home.

32. FILE ***Test_Scores.*** The accompanying table shows a portion of the scores that 32 students obtained on the final and the midterm in a course in statistics.

Final	Midterm
86	78
94	97
⋮	⋮
91	47

a. Estimate the sample regression equation that enables us to predict a student's final score on the basis of his/her midterm score.
b. Predict the final score of a student who received an 80 on the midterm.

33. FILE ***Fertilizer.*** A horticulturist is studying the relationship between tomato plant height and fertilizer amount. Thirty tomato plants grown in similar conditions were subjected to various amounts of fertilizer (in ounces) over a four-month period, and then their heights (in inches) were measured. A portion of the data is shown in the accompanying table.

Height	Fertilizer
20.4	1.9
49.2	5.0
⋮	⋮
46.4	3.1

a. Estimate the model: Height $= \beta_0 + \beta_1$Fertilizer $+ \varepsilon$.
b. Interpret the coefficient of Fertilizer. Does the y-intercept make practical sense?
c. Use the estimated model to predict, after four months, the height of a tomato plant which received 3.0 ounces of fertilizer.

34. FILE ***Dexterity.*** Finger dexterity, the ability to make precisely coordinated finger movements to grasp or assemble very small objects, is important in jewelry making. Thus, the manufacturing manager at Gemco, a manufacturer of high-quality watches, wants to develop a regression model to predict the productivity (in watches per shift) of new employees based on dexterity. He has subjected a sample of 20 current employees to the O'Connor dexterity test in which the time required to place 3 pins in each of 100 small holes using tweezers is measured in seconds. A portion of the data is shown in the accompanying table.

Watches	Time
23	513
19	608
⋮	⋮
20	437

a. Estimate the model: Watches $= \beta_0 + \beta_1$Time $+ \varepsilon$.
b. Interpret the coefficient of Time.
c. Explain why the *y*-intercept makes no practical sense in this particular problem.
d. Suppose a new employee takes 550 seconds on the dexterity test. How many watches per shift is she expected to produce?

35. FILE ***Homes.*** A realtor in a suburb outside of Chicago is analyzing the relationship between the sale price of a home (Price in $), its square footage (Sqft), the number of bedrooms (Beds), and the number of bathrooms (Baths). She collects data on 36 recent sales. A portion of the data is shown in the accompanying table.

Price	Sqft	Beds	Baths
840000	2768	4	3.5
822000	2500	4	2.5
⋮	⋮	⋮	⋮
307500	850	1	1

a. Estimate the model Price $= \beta_0 + \beta_1$Sqft $+ \beta_2$Beds $+ \beta_3$Baths $+ \varepsilon$.
b. Interpret the slope coefficients.
c. Predict the price of a 2,500-square-foot home with three bedrooms and two bathrooms.

36. FILE ***Engine_Overhaul.*** The maintenance manager at a trucking company wants to build a regression model to forecast the time (in years) until the first engine overhaul based on four explanatory variables: (1) annual miles driven (in 1,000s of miles), (2) average load weight (in tons), (3) average driving speed (in mph), and (4) oil change interval (in 1,000s of miles). Based on driver logs and onboard computers, data have been obtained for a sample of 25 trucks. A portion of the data is shown in the accompanying table.

Time	Miles	Weight	Speed	Oil
7.9	42.8	19	46	15
0.9	98.5	25	46	29
⋮	⋮	⋮	⋮	⋮
6.1	61.2	24	58	19

a. For each explanatory variable, discuss whether it is likely to have a positive or negative influence on the time until the first engine overhaul.
b. Estimate the regression model (use all four explanatory variables).
c. Based on part (a), are the signs of the regression coefficients as expected?
d. Predict the time before the first engine overhaul for a particular truck driven 60,000 miles per year with an average load of 22 tons, an average driving speed of 57 mph, and 18,000 miles between oil changes.

37. FILE ***MCAS.*** Education reform is one of the most hotly debated subjects on both state and national policy makers' list of socioeconomic topics. Consider a linear regression model that relates school expenditures and family background to student performance in Massachusetts using 224 school districts. The response variable is the mean score on the MCAS (Massachusetts Comprehensive Assessment System) exam given to 10th graders. Four explanatory variables are used: (1) STR is the student-to-teacher ratio in %, (2) TSAL is the average teacher's salary in $1,000s, (3) INC is the median household income in $1,000s, and (4) SGL is the percentage of single-parent households. A portion of the data is shown in the accompanying table.

Score	STR	TSAL	INC	SGL
227.00	19.00	44.01	48.89	4.70
230.67	17.90	40.17	43.91	4.60
⋮	⋮	⋮	⋮	⋮
230.67	19.20	44.79	47.64	5.10

a. For each explanatory variable, discuss whether it is likely to have a positive or negative influence on Score.
b. Find the sample regression equation. Are the signs of the slope coefficients as expected?
c. What is the predicted score if STR = 18, TSAL = 50, INC = 60, and SGL = 5?
d. What is the predicted score if everything else is the same as in part (c) except INC = 80?

38. FILE ***Electricity_Cost.*** The facility manager at a pharmaceutical company wants to build a regression model to forecast monthly electricity cost. Three main variables are thought to dictate electricity cost (in $): (1) average outdoor temperature (Temp in °F), (2) working days per month, and (3) tons of product produced. A portion of the past year's monthly data is shown in the accompanying table.

Cost	Temp	Days	Tons
24100	26	24	80
23700	32	21	73
⋮	⋮	⋮	⋮
26000	39	22	69

a. For each explanatory variable, discuss whether it is likely to have a positive or negative influence on monthly electricity cost.

b. Estimate the regression model. What is the sample regression equation?

c. Are the signs of the regression coefficients as expected? If not, speculate as to why this could be the case.

d. What is the predicted electricity cost in a month during which the average outdoor temperature is 65°, there are 23 working days, and 76 tons are produced?

39. FILE ***Quarterbacks.*** American football is the highest paying sport on a per-game basis. The quarterback, considered the most important player on the team, is appropriately compensated. A sports statistician wants to estimate a multiple linear regression model that links the quarterback's salary (in $ millions) with his pass completion percentage (PC), total touchdowns scored (TD), and his age. He collects data for 32 quarterbacks during a recent season. A portion of the data is shown in the accompanying table.

Quarterback	Salary	PC	TD	Age
1	25.5566	65.2	28	27
2	22.0441	60.5	27	26
⋮	⋮	⋮	⋮	⋮
32	0.6260	63.1	26	29

a. Estimate the model defined as Salary $= \beta_0 + \beta_1$PC $+ \beta_2$TD $+ \beta_3$Age $+ \varepsilon$.

b. Are you surprised by the estimated coefficients?

c. Quarterback 8 earned 12.9895 million dollars. According to the model, what is his predicted salary if PC = 70.6, TD = 34, and Age = 30?

d. Quarterback 16 earned 8.0073 million dollars. According to the model, what is his predicted salary if PC = 65.7, TD = 28, and Age = 32?

e. Compute and interpret the residual salary for Quarterback 8 and Quarterback 16.

40. FILE ***Rentals.*** The accompanying table shows a portion of data consisting of the rent, the number of bedrooms, the number of bathrooms, and the square footage for 40 apartments in a college town.

Rent	Bed	Bath	Sqft
645	1	1	500
675	1	1	648
⋮	⋮	⋮	⋮
2400	3	2.5	2700

a. Determine the sample regression equation that enables us to predict the rent of an apartment on the basis of the number of bedrooms, the number of bathrooms, and the square footage.

b. Interpret the slope coefficient of Bath.

c. Predict the rent for a 1,500-square-foot apartment with 2 bedrooms and 1 bathroom.

41. FILE ***Car_Prices.*** The accompanying table shows a portion of data consisting of the selling price, the age, and the mileage for 20 used sedans.

Selling Price	Age	Mileage
13590	6	61485
13775	6	54344
⋮	⋮	⋮
11988	8	42408

a. Estimate the sample regression equation that enables us to predict the price of a sedan on the basis of its age and mileage.

b. Interpret the slope coefficient of Age.

c. Predict the selling price of a five-year-old sedan with 65,000 miles.

LO 14.4

14.3 GOODNESS-OF-FIT MEASURES

Interpret goodness-of-fit measures.

So far we have focused on the estimation and the interpretation of the linear regression models. By simply observing the sample regression equation, we cannot assess how well the explanatory variables explain the variation in the response variable. We rely on several objective "goodness-of-fit" measures that summarize how well the sample regression equation fits the data. If each predicted value $\hat{y}$ is equal to its observed value y, then we have a perfect fit. Since that almost never happens, we evaluate the models on a relative basis.

In the introductory case study, we were interested in analyzing consumer debt payments. In the last section, we estimated the following two linear regression models:

$$\text{Model 1: Debt} = \beta_0 + \beta_1\text{Income} + \varepsilon$$
$$\text{Model 2: Debt} = \beta_0 + \beta_1\text{Income} + \beta_2\text{Unemployment} + \varepsilon$$

For ease of exposition, we use the same notation to refer to the coefficients in Models 1 and 2. We note, however, that these coefficients and their estimates have a different meaning depending on which model we are referencing.

If you had to choose one of these models to predict debt payments, which model would you choose? It may be that by using more explanatory variables, you can better describe the response variable. However, for a given sample, *more* is not always better. In order to select the preferred model, we need to examine goodness-of-fit measures. We will study three goodness-of-fit measures: the standard error of the estimate, the coefficient of determination, and the adjusted coefficient of determination.

The Standard Error of the Estimate

We first describe goodness-of-fit measures in the context of a simple linear regression model, or Model 1. Figure 14.5 reproduces the scatterplot of debt payments against income, as well as the superimposed sample regression line. Recall that the residual e represents the difference between an observed value and the predicted value of the response variable—that is, $e = y - \hat{y}$. If all the observation points had fallen on the line, then each residual would be zero; in other words, there would be no dispersion between the observed and the predicted values. Since in practice we rarely, if ever, obtain this result, we evaluate models on the basis of the relative magnitude of the residuals. The sample regression equation provides a good fit when the dispersion of the residuals is relatively small.

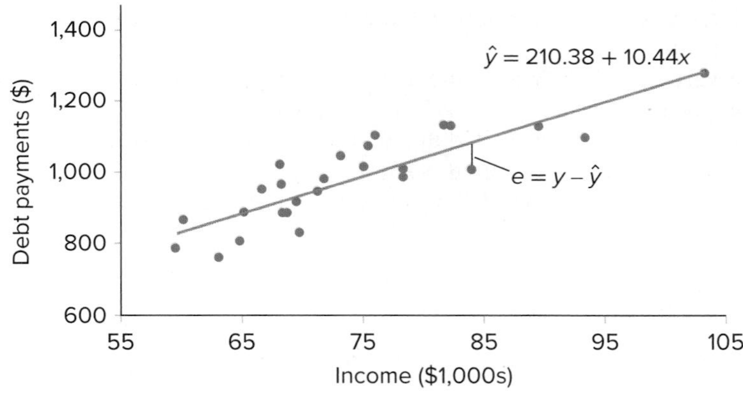

FIGURE 14.5
Scatterplot of debt payments y against income x

A numerical measure that gauges dispersion from the sample regression equation is the sample variance of the residual, denoted s_e^2. This measure is defined as the average squared difference between y_i and $\hat{y}_i$. The numerator of the formula is the error sum of squares, $SSE = \Sigma(y_i - \hat{y}_i)^2 = \Sigma e_i^2$. Dividing SSE by its respective degrees of freedom $n - k - 1$ yields s_e^2. Recall that k denotes the number of explanatory variables in the linear regression model; thus, for a simple linear regression model, k equals one. Instead of s_e^2, we generally report the standard deviation of the residual, denoted s_e, more commonly referred to as the **standard error of the estimate.** As usual, s_e is the positive square root of s_e^2. The less the dispersion, the smaller the s_e, which typically implies that the model provides a good fit for the sample data.

THE STANDARD ERROR OF THE ESTIMATE

The standard error of the estimate s_e is calculated as

$$s_e = \sqrt{\frac{SSE}{n-k-1}},$$

where *SSE* is the error sum of squares. Theoretically, s_e can assume any value between zero and infinity, $0 \leq s_e < \infty$. When comparing models with the same response variable, the model with the smaller s_e is preferred.

For a given sample size *n*, increasing the number *k* of the explanatory variables reduces both the numerator (*SSE*) and the denominator ($n - k - 1$) in the formula for s_e. The net effect, shown by the value of s_e, allows us to determine if the added explanatory variables improve the fit of the model.

Virtually all statistical software packages report s_e. Excel reports s_e in the *Regression Statistics* portion of the regression output and refers to it as Standard Error. R reports s_e in the bottom portion of the regression output and refers to it as Residual standard error.

The Coefficient of Determination, R^2

Like the standard error of the estimate, the **coefficient of determination,** commonly referred to as R^2, evaluates how well the sample regression equation fits the data. In particular, R^2 quantifies the sample variation in the response variable *y* that is explained by the sample regression equation. It is computed as the ratio of the explained variation of the response variable to its total variation. For example, if $R^2 = 0.72$, we say that 72% of the sample variation in the response variable is explained by the sample regression equation. Other factors, which have not been included in the model, account for the remaining 28% of the sample variation.

We use analysis of variance (ANOVA) in the context of the linear regression model, to derive R^2. We denote the total variation in *y* as $\Sigma(y_i - \bar{y})^2$, which is the numerator in the formula for the variance of *y*. This value, called the total sum of squares *SST*, can be broken down into two components: explained variation and unexplained variation. Figure 14.6 illustrates the decomposition of the total variation in *y* into its two components for a simple linear regression model.

FIGURE 14.6 Total, explained, and unexplained differences

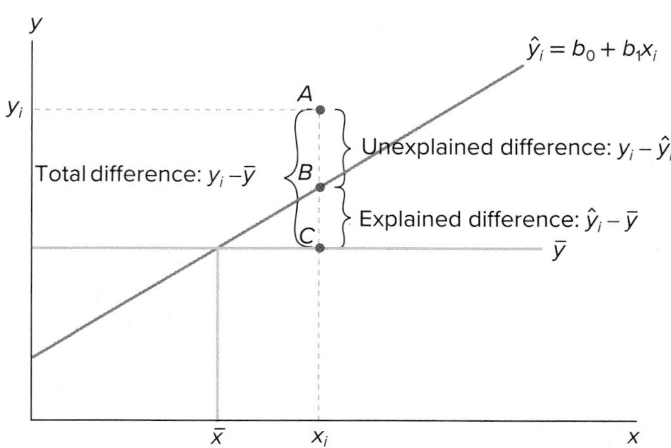

For ease of exposition, we show a scatterplot with all the points removed except one (point A). Point A refers to the observation (x_i, y_i). The blue line represents the estimated regression equation based on the entire sample data; the horizontal and vertical green lines represent the sample means $\bar{y}$ and $\bar{x}$, respectively. The vertical distance between the data point A and $\bar{y}$ (point C) is the difference $y_i - \bar{y}$ (distance AC). For each data point, we square these differences and then find their sum—this amounts to $SST = \Sigma(y_i - \bar{y})^2$. Recall that SST is a measure of the total variation in y.

Now, we focus on the distance between the predicted value $\hat{y}_i$ (point B) and $\bar{y}$; that is, the explained difference (distance BC). It is called "explained" because the difference between $\hat{y}_i$ and $\bar{y}$ can be explained by the difference between x_i and $\bar{x}$. Squaring all such differences and summing them yields the regression sum of squares, SSR, where $SSR = \Sigma(\hat{y}_i - \bar{y})^2$. SSR is a measure of the explained variation in y.

The distance between the particular observation and its predicted value (distance AB) is the unexplained difference. This is the portion that remains unexplained; it is due to random error or chance. Squaring all such differences and summing them yields the familiar error sum of squares, $SSE = \Sigma\,(y_i - \hat{y}_i)^2$. SSE is a measure of the unexplained variation in y.

Thus, the total variation in y can be decomposed into explained and unexplained variation as follows:

$$SST = SSR + SSE.$$

We derive the formula for R^2 by dividing both sides by SST and rearranging:

$$R^2 = \frac{SSR}{SST} = 1 - \frac{SSE}{SST}.$$

The value of R^2 falls between zero and one, $0 \leq R^2 \leq 1$. The closer R^2 is to one, the stronger the fit; the closer it is to zero, the weaker the fit.

THE COEFFICIENT OF DETERMINATION, R^2

The coefficient of determination, R^2, is the proportion of the sample variation in the response variable that is explained by the sample regression equation. We compute R^2 as

$$R^2 = \frac{SSR}{SST}, \text{ or equivalently, } R^2 = 1 - \frac{SSE}{SST},$$

where $SSR = \Sigma(\hat{y} - \bar{y})^2$, $SSE = \Sigma(y_i - \hat{y}_i)^2$, and $SST = \Sigma(y_i - \bar{y})^2$. R^2 can also be computed as $R^2 = r^2_{y\hat{y}}$, where $r_{y\hat{y}}$ is the sample correlation coefficient between y and $\hat{y}$.

The value of R^2 falls between zero and one; the closer the value is to one, the better the fit.

Most statistical packages, including Excel and R, report the coefficient of determination. Excel reports R^2 in the *Regression Statistics* portion of the regression output and refers to it as R Square. R reports R^2 in the bottom portion of the regression output and refers to it as Multiple R-squared.

Our objective in adding another explanatory variable to a linear regression model is to increase the model's usefulness. It turns out that we cannot use R^2 for model comparison when the competing models do not include the same number of explanatory variables. This occurs because R^2 never decreases as we add more explanatory variables to the model. A popular model selection method in such situations is to choose the model that has the highest adjusted R^2 value, a topic that we discuss next.

The Adjusted R^2

Because R^2 never decreases as we add more explanatory variables to the linear regression model, it is possible to increase its value unintentionally by including a group of explanatory variables that may have no economic or intuitive foundation in the linear regression model. This is true especially when the number of explanatory variables k is large relative to the sample size n. In order to avoid the possibility of R^2 creating a false impression, virtually all software packages, including Excel and R, include **adjusted R^2**. Unlike R^2, adjusted R^2 explicitly accounts for the number of explanatory variables k. It is common to use adjusted R^2 for model selection because it imposes a penalty for any additional explanatory variable that is included in the analysis.

ADJUSTED R^2

The adjusted coefficient of determination is calculated as

$$\text{Adjusted } R^2 = 1 - (1 - R^2)\left(\frac{n-1}{n-k-1}\right).$$

Adjusted R^2 is used to compare competing linear regression models with different numbers of explanatory variables; the higher the adjusted R^2, the better the model.

If SSE is substantially greater than zero and k is large compared to n, then adjusted R^2 will differ substantially from R^2. Adjusted R^2 may be negative if the correlation between the response variable and the explanatory variables is sufficiently low.

We would also like to point out that both the standard error of the estimate and the adjusted R^2 are useful for comparing the linear regression models with different numbers of explanatory variables. Adjusted R^2, however, is the more commonly used criterion for model selection.

EXAMPLE 14.4

Recall the two models that we estimated in Section 14.2:
Model 1: Debt $= \beta_0 + \beta_1$Income $+ \varepsilon$
Model 2: Debt $= \beta_0 + \beta_1$Income $+ \beta_2$Unemployment $+ \varepsilon$

Table 14.6 reports the goodness-of-fit measures for both of these models.

TABLE 14.6 Goodness-of-Fit Measures for Model 1 and Model 2

	Model 1	Model 2
Standard Error	63.2606	64.6098
R Square	0.7526	0.7527
Adjusted R Square	0.7423	0.7312

a. Which of the two models is the preferred model? Justify your response with two goodness-of-fit measures.

b. Interpret the coefficient of determination for the preferred model.

c. What percentage of the sample variation in consumer debt payments is unexplained by the preferred model?

SOLUTION:

a. Model 1 has the lower standard error of the estimate as compared to Model 2 (63.2606<64.6098). Model 1 also has the higher adjusted R^2 (0.7423>0.7312). Thus, Model 1 is the preferred model. Note that we cannot use the coefficient of determination R^2 to compare the two models because the models have different numbers of explanatory variables.

b. The coefficient of determination R^2 for Model 1 is 0.7526 which means that 75.26% of the sample variation in Debt is explained by changes in Income.

c. If 75.26% of the sample variation in Debt is explained by changes in Income, then 24.74% (1 − 0.7526) is unexplained by the regression equation.

SYNOPSIS OF INTRODUCTORY CASE

Andy Dean Photography/Alamy Stock Photo

A study shows substantial variation in consumer debt payments depending on where the consumer resides. A possible explanation is that a linear relationship exists between consumer debt payments and an area's median household income. In order to substantiate this claim, relevant data on 26 metropolitan areas are collected. The correlation coefficient between debt payments and income is computed as 0.87, suggesting a strong positive linear relationship between the two variables. A simple test confirms that the correlation coefficient is statistically significant at the 5% level.

Two regression models are also estimated for the analysis. A simple linear regression model (Model 1), using consumer debt payments as the response variable and median household income as the explanatory variable, is estimated as $\widehat{Debt} = 210.30 + 10.44 Income$. For every $1,000 increase in median household income, consumer debt payments are predicted to increase by $10.44. In an attempt to improve upon the prediction, a multiple regression model (Model 2) is proposed, where median household income and the unemployment rate are used as explanatory variables. The sample regression line for Model 2 is $\widehat{Debt} = 199.00 + 10.51 Income + 0.62 Unemployment$. Given its slope coefficient of only 0.62, the economic impact of the unemployment rate on consumer debt payments, with median household income held fixed, seems extremely weak. Goodness-of-fit measures confirm that Model 1 provides a better fit than Model 2 because it has a lower standard error of the estimate and a higher adjusted R^2. The preferred model explains 75.26% of the sample variation in Debt by changes in Income. For an area's median household income of $80,000, consumer debt payments are predicted to be about $1,046.

A Cautionary Note Concerning Goodness-of-fit Measures

Unfortunately, all of these goodness-of-fit measures do not help us gauge how well an estimated model will predict in an unseen sample. It is possible for a model to perform really well with the data set used for estimation, but then perform miserably once a new data set is used. We often call modelling of this sort overfitting. Overfitting occurs when an estimated model begins to describe the quirks of the data rather than the real relationships between variables. By making the model conform too closely to the given data, the model's predictive power is compromised. A useful method to assess the predictive power of a model is to test it on a data set not used in estimation. Cross-validation is a technique that evaluates predictive models by partitioning the original sample into a training set to build (train) the model and a validation set to evaluate (validate) it. The cross-validation method is beyond the scope of this text.

EXERCISES 14.3

Mechanics

42. In a simple linear regression based on 25 observations, it is found that $SSE = 1{,}250$ and $SST = 1{,}500$.
    a. Calculate s_e^2 and s_e.
    b. Calculate R^2.
43. In a simple linear regression based on 30 observations, it is found that $SSE = 2{,}540$ and $SST = 13{,}870$.
    a. Calculate s_e^2 and s_e.
    b. Calculate R^2.
44. In a multiple regression with two explanatory variables, and 50 observations, it is found that $SSE = 35$ and $SST = 90$.
    a. Calculate the standard error of the estimate s_e.
    b. Calculate the coefficient of determination R^2.
45. In a multiple regression with four explanatory variables and 100 observations, it is found that $SSR = 4.75$ and $SST = 7.62$.
    a. Calculate the standard error of the estimate s_e.
    b. Calculate the coefficient of determination R^2.
    c. Calculate adjusted R^2.
46. The accompanying table lists goodness-of-fit measures that were obtained when estimating the following two simple linear regression models:

    Model 1: $y = \beta_0 + \beta_1 x_1 + \varepsilon$
    Model 2: $y = \beta_0 + \beta_1 x_2 + \varepsilon$

	Model 1	Model 2
R^2	0.459	0.496
Adjusted R^2	0.445	0.483
s_e	104.914	101.274

Which model provides a better fit for *y*? Justify your response with two goodness-of-fit measures.

47. The accompanying table lists goodness-of-fit measures that were obtained when estimating the following linear regression models:

    Model 1: $y = \beta_0 + \beta_1 x_1 + \varepsilon$
    Model 2: $y = \beta_0 + \beta_1 x_1 + \beta_2 x_2 + \varepsilon$

	Model 1	Model 2
R^2	0.751	0.752
Adjusted R^2	0.748	0.747
s_e	13.652	13.694

Which model provides a better fit for *y*? Justify your response with two goodness-of-fit measures.

48. The accompanying table lists goodness-of-fit measures that were obtained when estimating the following linear regression models:

    Model 1: $y = \beta_0 + \beta_1 x_1 + \varepsilon$
    Model 2: $y = \beta_0 + \beta_1 x_1 + \beta_2 x_2 + \beta_3 x_3 + \varepsilon$

	Model 1	Model 2
R^2	0.804	0.828
Adjusted R^2	0.801	0.819
s_e	17.746	16.924

Which model provides a better fit for *y*? Justify your response with two goodness-of-fit measures.

49. The accompanying table lists goodness-of-fit measures that were obtained when estimating the following linear regression models:

    Model 1: $y = \beta_0 + \beta_1 x_1 + \beta_2 x_2 + \varepsilon$
    Model 2: $y = \beta_0 + \beta_1 x_3 + \beta_2 x_4 + \varepsilon$

	Model 1	Model 2
R^2	0.640	0.610
Adjusted R^2	0.627	0.597
s_e	34.706	36.103

Which model provides a better fit for *y*? Justify your response with two goodness-of-fit measures.

Applications

50. An analyst estimates the sales of a firm as a function of its advertising expenditures using the model: Sales = $\beta_0 + \beta_1$Advertising $+ \varepsilon$. Using 20 observations, he finds that $SSR = 199.93$ and $SST = 240.92$.
    a. What proportion of the sample variation in sales is explained by advertising expenditures?
    b. What proportion of the sample variation in sales is unexplained by advertising expenditures?
51. **FILE** ***Test_Scores.*** The accompanying data file shows the midterm and final scores for 32 students in a statistics course.
    a. Estimate a student's final score as a function of his/her midterm score. What is the sample regression equation?
    b. Find the standard error of the estimate.
    c. Find and interpret the coefficient of determination.
52. The director of college admissions at a local university is trying to determine whether a student's high school GPA or SAT score is a better predictor of the student's subsequent college GPA. She formulates two models:

    Model 1. College GPA = $\beta_0 + \beta_1$High School GPA $+ \varepsilon$
    Model 2. College GPA = $\beta_0 + \beta_1$SAT Score $+ \varepsilon$

    She estimates these models and obtains the following goodness-of-fit measures.

	Model 1	Model 2
R^2	0.5595	0.5322
Adjusted R^2	0.5573	0.5298
s_e	40.3684	41.6007

Which model provides a better fit for *y*? Justify your response with two goodness-of-fit measures.

53. **FILE** ***Taxes.*** The accompanying data file shows the square footage and associated property taxes for 20 homes in an affluent suburb 30 miles outside New York City.
   a. Estimate a home's property taxes as a linear function of its square footage. What is the sample regression equation?
   b. What proportion of the sample variation in property taxes is explained by the home's size?
   c. What proportion of the sample variation in property taxes is unexplained by the home's size?

54. **FILE** ***Car_Prices.*** The accompanying data file shows the selling price of a used sedan, its age, and its mileage. Estimate two models:

   Model 1: $\text{Price} = \beta_0 + \beta_1\text{Age} + \varepsilon$
   Model 2: $\text{Price} = \beta_0 + \beta_1\text{Age} + \beta_2\text{Mileage} + \varepsilon$

   Which model provides a better fit for *y*? Justify your response with two goodness-of-fit measures.

55. For a sample of 41 New England cities, a sociologist studies the crime rate in each city as a function of its poverty rate and its median income. He finds that $SSE = 4{,}182{,}663$ and $SST = 7{,}732{,}451$.
   a. Calculate the standard error of the estimate.
   b. What proportion of the sample variation in crime rate is explained by the variability in the explanatory variables? What proportion is unexplained?

56. A financial analyst uses the following model to estimate a firm's stock return: $\text{Return} = \beta_0 + \beta_1\text{P/E} + \beta_2\text{P/S} + \varepsilon$, where P/E is a firm's price-to-earnings ratio and P/S is a firm's price-to-sales ratio. For a sample of 30 firms, she finds that $SSE = 4{,}402.786$ and $SST = 5{,}321.532$.
   a. Calculate the standard error of the estimate.
   b. Calculate and interpret the coefficient of determination.
   c. Calculate the adjusted R^2.

57. **FILE** ***Football.*** Is it defense or offense that wins football games? Consider the following portion of data, which includes a team's winning record (Win in %), the average number of yards gained, and the average number of yards allowed during a recent NFL season.

Team	Win	Gained	Allowed
1	62.50	344.40	346.40
2	56.30	340.40	348.90
⋮	⋮	⋮	⋮
32	25.00	312.50	319.70

   a. Compare two simple linear regression models, where Model 1 predicts the winning percentage based on yards gained and Model 2 uses yards allowed.
   b. Estimate a multiple linear regression model, Model 3, that applies both yards gained and yards allowed to forecast the winning percentage. Is this model an improvement over the other two models? Explain.

58. **FILE** ***Executive_Compensation.*** Executive compensation has risen dramatically beyond the rising levels of an average worker's wage over the years. Consider the following portion of data which links total compensation (in $ millions) for 455 CEOs with three measures: industry-adjusted return on assets (ROA), industry-adjusted stock return (Return) and the firm's size (Assets in $ millions).

Compensation	ROA	Return	Assets
16.58	2.53	−0.15	20917.5
26.92	1.27	0.57	32659.5
⋮	⋮	⋮	⋮
2.3	0.45	0.75	44875.0

   a. Estimate three simple linear regression models that use Compensation as the response variable with ROA, Return, or Assets as the explanatory variable. Which model do you select? Explain.
   b. Estimate multiple linear regression models that use various combinations of two, or all three, explanatory variables. Which model do you select? Explain.

14.4 WRITING WITH DATA

Case Study

Kick Images/Getty Images

Matthew Farnham is an investment consultant who always recommends a well-diversified portfolio of mutual funds to his clients. He knows that a key concept in benefiting from diversification is correlation. If all of an investor's assets move in lockstep, or are highly correlated, then the investor is either all right or all wrong. In order to reduce risk, it is considered good practice to invest in assets with relatively low correlation with each other.

Matthew is approached by a client who has already invested in Vanguard's 500 Index Fund—a fund that mimics the Standard & Poor's 500 Index.

She seeks advice for choosing her next investment from one of the following Vanguard funds:

- Inflation-Protected Securities Index
- Intermediate-Term Bond Index
- Real Estate Index
- Small Cap Index

Matthew collects five years of monthly return data for each mutual fund for the analysis. A portion of the data is shown in Table 14.7. He is tasked with using correlations to make a recommendation for a mutual fund.

Vanguard

TABLE 14.7 Monthly Return Data for Five Mutual Funds, January 2015–December 2019

	500 Index	Inflation-Protected Securities	Intermediate-Term Bond	Real Estate	Small Cap
January 2015	−0.0249	0.0450	0.0386	0.0959	0.0017
February 2015	0.0573	−0.0140	−0.0147	−0.0359	0.0574
⋮	⋮	⋮	⋮	⋮	⋮
December 2019	0.0253	−0.0075	−0.0020	−0.0023	0.0203

Sample Report–Making Investment Decisions by Diversifying

In attempting to create a well-diversified portfolio, an analysis of the correlation between the assets' returns is crucial. The correlation coefficient measures the direction and the strength of the linear relationship between the assets' returns. This statistic can aid in the hunt for assets to consider when forming a portfolio. An investor has already chosen Vanguard's 500 Index mutual fund as part of her portfolio. When choosing to add to her portfolio, she considers four mutual funds from the Vanguard family.

Five years of monthly return data for each of these prospective funds, as well as the 500 Index, are collected. The first row of Table 14.8 shows the sample correlation coefficients between the 500 Index and each mutual fund.

TABLE 14.8 Analysis of Correlations between the 500 Index and Each Mutual Fund

	Inflation-Protected Securities	Intermediate-Term Bond	Real Estate	Small Cap
Correlation Coefficient	0.0881	−0.1839	0.4827*	0.8808*
Test Statistic	0.673	−1.425	4.200	14.149
p-value	0.503	0.160	0.000	0.000

Note: * represents significance at the 5% level.

The correlation coefficient always assumes a value between −1 and 1; an absolute value close to 1 implies that the two assets move in sync. In this sample, the highest sample correlation coefficient is between the 500 Index and the Small Cap Index, with a value of 0.8808. Next on the list is the correlation coefficient 0.4827 between the 500 Index and the Real Estate Index. Investors often choose to invest across a range of asset classes that earn respectable returns but are relatively uncorrelated. This way, if one asset in a portfolio suffers, the rest may be unaffected. Given that the Inflation-Protected Securities Index and the Intermediate-Term Bond Index have correlation coefficients close to zero, these may prove to be desirable additions to the investor's portfolio.

A hypothesis test is conducted to determine whether the fund returns are correlated at the 5% significance level. The null hypothesis is that the returns are uncorrelated and the alternative hypothesis suggests either a positive or a negative correlation. Rows 2 and 3 of Table 14.8 show the value of the test statistics and the corresponding *p*-values. For instance, given a *p*-value of 0.503, the correlation coefficient between the 500 Index and the Inflation-Protected Securities Index is not different from zero at the 5% significance level. This same conclusion holds for the correlation coefficient between the 500 Index and the Intermediate-Term Bond Index. On the other hand, given *p*-values of 0.000 for both of the test statistics associated with the correlation coefficient between the 500 Index and the Real Estate Index and the 500 Index and the Small Cap Index, we can conclude that the returns of these funds are correlated with the returns of the 500 Index fund.

It is well documented that combining assets that have a low correlation with each other reduce the overall risk of the portfolio. Assuming that the correlation between assets is likely to remain stable in the future, then it might make sense for the investor to add either the Inflation-Protected Securities Index or the Intermediate Bond Index to her portfolio. Compared to the other two funds, these funds would offer the maximum benefit from diversification in the sense of reducing investment risk.

Suggested Case Studies

Here are some suggestions for analysis.

Report 14.1 Perform a similar analysis to the one conducted in this section, but choose similar mutual funds from a different investment firm, such as Fidelity or T. Rowe Price. Go to https://finance.yahoo.com/ to extract monthly prices for each mutual fund. Calculate the monthly return as $(P_t - P_{t-1})/P_{t-1}$, were P_t is the adjusted close price at time t and P_{t-1} is the adjusted close price at time $t-1$.

Report 14.2 FILE ***House_Price.*** Choose a college town. Find the model that best predicts the sale price of a house. Use goodness-of-fit measures to find the appropriate explanatory variables.

Report 14.3 FILE ***College_Admissions.*** Choose a college of interest and use the sample of enrolled students to best predict a student's college grade point average. Use goodness-of-fit measures to find the appropriate explanatory variables. In order to estimate these models, you have to first filter the data to include only the enrolled students.

CONCEPTUAL REVIEW

LO 14.1 Conduct a hypothesis test for the population correlation coefficient.

When conducting tests concerning the population correlation coefficient ρ_{xy}, the value of the test statistic is calculated as $t_{df} = \dfrac{r_{xy}\sqrt{n-2}}{\sqrt{1-r_{xy}^2}}$, where r_{xy} is the sample correlation coefficient and $df = n - 2$.

LO 14.2 Estimate and interpret the simple linear regression model.

Regression analysis presumes that one variable, called the response variable, is influenced by other variables, called the explanatory variables. The simple linear regression model uses only one explanatory variable to predict and/or describe changes in the response variable. The model is specifed as $y = \beta_0 + \beta_1 x + \varepsilon$, where y and x are the response variable and the explanatory variable, respectively, and ε is the random error term. The coefficients β_0 and β_1 are the unknown parameters to be estimated.

We apply the ordinary least squares (OLS) method to find a sample regression equation $\hat{y} = b_0 + b_1x$, where $\hat{y}$ is the predicted value of the response variable and b_0 and b_1 are the estimates of β_0 and β_1, respectively. The estimated slope coefficient b_1 represents the change in $\hat{y}$ when x changes by one unit. The units of b_1 are the same as those of y.

LO 14.3 Estimate and interpret the multiple linear regression model.

The multiple linear regression model allows more than one explanatory variable to be linearly related with the response variable y. It is specifed as $y = \beta_0 + \beta_1x_1 + \beta_2x_2 + \cdots + \beta_kx_k + \varepsilon$, where y is the response variable, $x_1, x_2, \ldots, x_k$ are the k explanatory variables, and ε is the random error term. The coefficients $\beta_0, \beta_1, \ldots, \beta_k$ are the unknown parameters to be estimated. We again use the OLS method to arrive at the following sample regression equation: $\hat{y} = b_0 + b_1x_1 + b_2x_2 + \cdots + b_kx_k$, where $b_0, b_1, \ldots, b_k$ are the estimates of $\beta_0, \beta_1, \ldots, \beta_k$, respectively.

For each explanatory variable x_j ($j = 1, \ldots, k$), the corresponding slope coefficient b_j is the estimated regression coefficient. It measures the change in the predicted value of the response variable $\hat{y}$, given a unit increase in the associated explanatory variable x_j, *holding all other explanatory variables constant.* In other words, it represents the partial influence of x_j on $\hat{y}$.

LO 14.4 Interpret goodness-of-fit measures.

The standard error of the estimate s_e is the standard deviation of the residual and is calculated as $s_e = \sqrt{\frac{SSE}{n-k-1}}$, where SSE is the error sum of squares. The standard error of the estimate is a useful goodness-of-fit measure when comparing models; the model with the smaller s_e is preferred.

The coefficient of determination R^2 is the proportion of the sample variation in the response variable that is explained by the sample regression equation. It falls between 0 and 1; the closer the value is to 1, the better the model fits the sample data.

Adjusted R^2 adjusts R^2 by accounting for the number of explanatory variables k used in the regression. In comparing competing models with different numbers of explanatory variables, the preferred model will have the highest adjusted R^2.

R^2 cannot be used to compare the linear regression models with different numbers of explanatory variables. Both the standard error of the estimate and the adjusted R^2 are appropriate for making such comparisons.

ADDITIONAL EXERCISES

59. FILE ***Energy_Health.*** The following table shows a portion of the monthly returns data (in percent) from 2010–2016 for two of Vanguard's mutual funds: the Energy Fund and the Healthcare Fund.

Date	Energy	Healthcare
Jan-10	−4.86	−0.13
Feb-10	1.50	0.58
⋮	⋮	⋮
Dec-16	−0.30	−5.26

a. Calculate and interpret the sample correlation coefficient r_{xy}.

b. Specify the competing hypotheses in order to determine whether the population correlation coefficient is different from zero.

c. At the 5% significance level, what is the conclusion to the test? Are the returns on the mutual funds correlated?

60. FILE ***Yields.*** While the Federal Reserve controls short-term interest rates, long-term interest rates essentially depend on supply and demand dynamics, as well as longer-term interest rate expectations. The accompanying table shows a portion of data for the annualized rates for the 10-year Treasury yield (in %) and the

3-month Treasury yield (in %) over a ten-year period.

Year	Ten_Year	Three_Month
1	5.02	3.47
2	4.61	1.63
⋮	⋮	⋮
10	3.21	0.14

a. Construct and interpret a scatterplot of the 10-year treasury yield against the 3-month yield.
b. Calculate and interpret the sample correlation coefficient. Use $\alpha = 0.05$ to test if the population correlation coefficient is different from zero.
c. Estimate and interpret a regression model using the 10-year yield as the response variable and the 3-month yield as the explanatory variable.

61. FILE ***Home_Ownership.*** In order to determine if the homeownership rate in the United States is linked with income, state-level data on the homeownership rate (Ownership in %) and median household income (Income in $) were collected. A portion of the data is shown in the accompanying table.

State	Ownership	Income
Alabama	74.1	39980
Alaska	66.8	61604
⋮	⋮	⋮
Wyoming	73.8	52470

a. Estimate and interpret the model: Ownership $= \beta_0 + \beta_1$Income $+ \varepsilon$.
b. What is the standard error of the estimate?
c. Interpret the coefficient of determination.

62. FILE ***Return.*** A research analyst is trying to determine whether a firm's price-earnings (PE) and price-sales (PS) ratios can explain the firm's stock performance over the past year. A PE ratio is calculated as a firm's share price compared to the income or profit earned by the firm per share. Generally, a high PE ratio suggests that investors are expecting higher earnings growth in the future compared to companies with a lower PE ratio. The PS ratio is calculated by dividing a firm's share price by the firm's revenue per share for the trailing 12 months. In short, investors can use the PS ratio to determine how much they are paying for a dollar of the firm's sales rather than a dollar of its earnings (PE ratio). In general, the lower the PS ratio, the more attractive the investment. The accompanying table shows a portion of the year-to-date returns (Return in %) and the PE and PS ratios for 30 firms.

Firm	Return	PE	PS
1	4.4	14.37	2.41
2	−4.5	11.01	0.78
⋮	⋮	⋮	⋮
30	16.3	13.94	1.94

a. Estimate: Return $= \beta_0 + \beta_1$PE $+ \beta_2$PS $+ \varepsilon$. Are the signs on the coefficients as expected? Explain.
b. Interpret the slope coefficient of the PS ratio.
c. What is the predicted return for a firm with a PE ratio of 10 and a PS ratio of 2?
d. What is the standard error of the estimate?
e. Interpret R^2.

63. FILE ***SAT.*** There has been a lot of discussion regarding the relationship between Scholastic Aptitude Test (SAT) scores and test-takers' family income. It is generally believed that the wealthier a student's family, the higher the SAT score. Another commonly used predictor for SAT scores is the student's grade point average (GPA). Consider the following portion of data collected on 24 students.

Student	SAT	Income	GPA
1	1651	47000	2.79
2	1581	34000	2.97
⋮	⋮	⋮	⋮
24	1940	113000	3.96

a. Estimate three models:
   (i) SAT $= \beta_0 + \beta_1$Income $+ \varepsilon$,
   (ii) SAT $= \beta_0 + \beta_1$GPA $+ \varepsilon$, and
   (iii) SAT $= \beta_0 + \beta_1$Income $+ \beta_2$GPA $+ \varepsilon$.
b. Use goodness-of-fit measures to select the best-fitting model.
c. Use the preferred model to predict SAT given the mean value of the explanatory variable(s).

64. FILE ***Startups.*** Many of today's leading companies, including Google, Microsoft, and Facebook, are based on technologies developed within universities. Lisa Fisher is a business school professor who would like to analyze university factors that enhance innovation. She collects data on 143 universities for a regression where the response variable is the number of startups (Startups), which is used as a measure for innovation. The explanatory variables include the university's research expenditure (Research in $ millions), the number of patents issued (Patents), and the age of its technology transfer office

(Duration in years). A portion of the data is shown in the accompanying table.

University	Startups	Research	Patents	Duration
1	1	145.52	8	23
2	1	237.52	16	23
⋮	⋮	⋮	⋮	⋮
143	1	154.38	3	9

a. Estimate: Startups $= \beta_0 + \beta_1$Research $+ \beta_2$Patents $+ \beta_3$Duration $+ \varepsilon$.
b. Predict the number of startups for a university that spent $120 million on research, that was issued 8 patents, and has had a technology transfer office for 20 years.
c. How much more research expenditure is needed for the university to have an additional predicted startup, with everything else being the same?

65. FILE ***Wage.*** A researcher interviews 50 employees of a large manufacturer and collects data on each worker's hourly wage (Wage in $), years of higher education (Educ), years of experience (Exper), and age (Age). A portion of the data is shown in the accompanying table.

Wage	Educ	Exper	Age
37.85	11	2	40
21.72	4	1	39
⋮	⋮	⋮	⋮
24.18	8	11	64

a. Estimate: Wage $= \beta_0 + \beta_1$Educ $+ \beta_2$Exper $+ \beta_3$Age $+ \varepsilon$.
b. Are the signs as expected?
c. Interpret the coefficient of Educ.
d. Interpret the coefficient of determination.
e. Predict the hourly wage of a 40-year-old employee who has 5 years of higher education and 8 years of experience.

APPENDIX 14.1 Guidelines for Other Software Packages

The following section provides brief commands for Minitab, SPSS, and JMP. Import the specified data file into the relevant software spreadsheet prior to following the commands.

Minitab

Correlation Analysis

Debt_Payments

(Replicating Example 14.1) From the menu, choose **Stat > Basic Statistics > Correlation.** Select Debt and Income for **Variables.** Under **Results,** select **Pairwise correlation table.**

Estimating a Regression Model

(Replicating Example 14.3) From the menu, choose **Stat > Regression > Regression > Fit Regression Model.** Select Debt for **Responses,** and select Income and Unemployment for **Continuous predictors.**

SPSS

Correlation Analysis

Debt_Payments

(Replicating Example 14.1) From the menu, choose **Analyze > Correlate > Bivariate.** Select Debt and Income as **Variables.**

Estimating a Regression Model

(Replicating Example 14.3) From the menu, choose **Analyze > Regression > Linear.** Select Debt as **Dependent,** and Income and Unemployment as **Independent(s).**

JMP

Correlation Analysis

A. (Replicating Example 14.1) From the menu, choose **Analyze > Multivariate Methods > Multivariate.** Drag Debt and Income to the **Y, Columns** box.

B. Click on the red triangle next to **Multivariate** and select **Pairwise Correlations.**

Estimating a Regression Model

(Replicating Example 14.3) From the menu, choose **Analyze > Fit Model.** Drag Debt to the **Y** box, and drag Income and Unemployment to the box under **Construct Model Effects.**

15 Inference with Regression Models

LEARNING OBJECTIVES

After reading this chapter you should be able to:

LO **15.1** **Conduct tests of significance.**

LO **15.2** **Conduct a general test of linear restrictions.**

LO **15.3** **Calculate and interpret confidence intervals and prediction intervals.**

LO **15.4** **Address common violations of the OLS assumptions.**

In Chapter 14, we employed regression analysis to capture a relationship between a response variable and one or more explanatory variables. We also studied goodness-of-fit measures that assess how well the sample regression equation fits the data. While the estimated regression models and goodness-of-fit measures are useful, it is not clear if the relationships inferred from the estimated coefficients are real or due to chance.

In this chapter, we focus on statistical inference with regression models. In particular, we develop hypothesis tests that enable us to determine the joint and individual significance of the explanatory variables. We also develop interval estimates for a prediction from the sample regression equation.

Finally, we examine the importance of the assumptions on the statistical properties of the ordinary least squares (OLS) estimator, as well as the validity of the testing procedures. We address common violations to the model assumptions, the consequences when these assumptions are violated, and offer some remedial measures.

Rob Tringali/MLB/Getty Images

INTRODUCTORY CASE

Analyzing the Winning Percentage in Baseball

On a recent radio talk show, two sports analysts quarreled over which statistic was a better predictor of a Major League Baseball team's winning percentage (Win). One argued that the team's batting average (BA) was a better predictor of a team's success since the team with the higher batting average has won approximately 75% of the World Series contests. The other insisted that a team's pitching is clearly the main factor in determining wins—the lower a team's earned run average (ERA), the higher the team's winning percentage. In order to determine if these claims are backed by the data, relevant information is collected for the 14 American League (AL) and 16 National League (NL) teams during a recent season. A portion of the data is shown in Table 15.1.

TABLE 15.1 Winning Percentage, Batting Average, and Earned Run Average in Baseball

FILE *Baseball*

Team	League	Win	BA	ERA
1	AL	0.407	0.259	4.59
2	AL	0.549	0.268	4.20
⋮	⋮	⋮	⋮	⋮
30	NL	0.426	0.250	4.13

Use the sample information to

1. Conduct joint and individual tests of significance on the preferred model.
2. Evaluate the expected winning percentage for a team with a batting average of 0.25 and an earned run average of 4.

A synopsis of this case is provided at the end of Section 15.3.

LO 15.1

15.1 TESTS OF SIGNIFICANCE

Conduct tests of significance.

In this section, we continue our assessment of the linear regression model by turning our attention to hypothesis tests about the unknown parameters (coefficients) $\beta_0, \beta_1, \ldots, \beta_k$. In particular, we test for joint and individual significance to determine whether there is evidence of a linear relationship between the response variable and the explanatory variables. We note that for the tests to be valid, certain conditions about the model must be met. We discuss the underlying assumptions of the linear regression model in Section 15.4.

Test of Joint Significance

Consider the following linear regression model, which links the response variable y with k explanatory variables $x_1, x_2, \ldots, x_k$:

$$y = \beta_0 + \beta_1 x_1 + \beta_2 x_2 + \ldots + \beta_k x_k + \varepsilon.$$

If all of the slope coefficients equal zero, then all of the explanatory variables drop out of the model; this implies that none of the explanatory variables has a linear relationship with the response variable. Conversely, if at least one of the slope coefficients does not equal zero, then at least one explanatory variable has a linear relationship with the response variable.

When we assess a linear regression model, a test of joint significance is often regarded as a test of the overall usefulness of a regression. This test determines whether the explanatory variables $x_1, x_2, \ldots, x_k$ have a joint statistical influence on y. If we reject the null hypothesis that all slope coefficients equal zero, then we are able to conclude that at least one explanatory variable influences the response variable. The competing hypotheses for a test of joint significance take the following form:

$$H_0: \beta_1 = \beta_2 = \ldots = \beta_k = 0$$
$$H_A: \text{At least one } \beta_i \neq 0$$

To conduct the test of joint significance, we employ a right-tailed F test. (Recall that the $F_{(df_1, df_2)}$ distribution was used for hypothesis testing in Chapters 11 and 13.) The test statistic measures how well the regression equation explains the variability in the response variable. It is defined as the ratio of the mean square regression (MSR) to the mean square error (MSE) where $MSR = SSR/k$ and $MSE = SSE/(n - k - 1)$. Recall from Chapter 14 that SSR is the regression sum of squares and SSE is the error sum of squares.

A TEST OF JOINT SIGNIFICANCE

For the linear regression model, $y = \beta_0 + \beta_1 x_1 + \beta_2 x_2 + \ldots + \beta_k x_k + \varepsilon$, the following competing hypotheses are used for a test of joint significance:

$$H_0: \beta_1 = \beta_2 = \ldots = \beta_k = 0$$
$$H_A: \text{At least one } \beta_i \neq 0$$

The value of the test statistic is calculated as:

$$F_{(df_1, df_2)} = \frac{SSR/k}{SSE/(n-k-1)} = \frac{MSR}{MSE}$$

where $df_1 = k$, $df_2 = n - k - 1$, SSR is the regression sum of squares, SSE is the error sum of squares, MSR is the mean square regression, and MSE is the mean square error.

- If the null hypothesis is not rejected, then the explanatory variables are not jointly significant; the model is not useful.
- If the null hypothesis is rejected, then the explanatory variables are jointly significant; the model is useful.

Most statistical computer packages, including Excel and R, produce an ANOVA table that decomposes the total variability of the response variable y into two components: (1) the variability explained by the regression and (2) the variability that is unexplained. In addition, the value for the $F_{(df_1,df_2)}$ test statistic and its p-value are also provided. Table 15.2 shows the general format of an ANOVA table. Excel explicitly provides an ANOVA table with its regression output, with the p-value reported under the heading *Significance F.* R provides the value for the $F_{(df_1,df_2)}$ test statistic and its p-value with its regression output, which is sufficient to conduct a test of joint significance. (If we use R's **anova** function, R generates an ANOVA table that is even more detailed than the one provided by Excel; R's ANOVA table breaks down the contribution of each explanatory variable in explaining the total variability in the response variable.)

TABLE 15.2 General Format of an ANOVA Table for Regression

ANOVA	*df*	*SS*	*MS*	*F*	Significance *F*
Regression	k	SSR	$MSR = \frac{SSR}{k}$	$F_{(df_1,df_2)} = \frac{MSR}{MSE}$	$P\left(F_{(df_1,df_2)} \geq \frac{MSR}{MSE}\right)$
Residual	$n - k - 1$	SSE	$MSE = \frac{SSE}{n-k-1}$		
Total	$n - 1$	SST			

Before we conduct a test of joint significance, let's recall the baseball example from the introductory case. The objective is to predict a team's winning percentage (Win) on the basis of its batting average (BA), its earned run average (ERA), or by both BA and ERA. For those readers who do not follow baseball, BA is a ratio of hits divided by times at bat, and ERA is the average number of earned runs given up by a pitcher per nine innings pitched. A priori, we expect that a higher BA positively influences a team's winning percentage, while a higher ERA negatively affects a team's winning percentage. We estimate three models:

Model 1: $\text{Win} = \beta_0 + \beta_1\text{BA} + \varepsilon$

Model 2: $\text{Win} = \beta_0 + \beta_1\text{ERA} + \varepsilon$

Model 3: $\text{Win} = \beta_0 + \beta_1\text{BA} + \beta_2\text{ERA} + \varepsilon.$

Table 15.3 shows the relevant goodness-of-fit measures for the three models; we advise you to replicate these results using the ***Baseball*** data file.

TABLE 15.3 Goodness-of-Fit Measures for the Models

	Model 1	Model 2	Model 3
Standard Error	0.0614	0.0505	0.0375
R Square	0.2112	0.4656	0.7156
Adjusted *R* Square	0.1830	0.4465	0.6945

We choose Model 3 to predict the winning percentage because it has the lowest standard error of the estimate and the highest adjusted R^2. Remember, we cannot compare these models on the basis of R^2, because Models 1 and 2 use only one explanatory variable, whereas Model 3 uses two.

EXAMPLE 15.1

Table 15.4 shows the ANOVA portion of the regression results from estimating Model 3: $\text{Win} = \beta_0 + \beta_1\text{BA} + \beta_2\text{ERA} + \varepsilon$. Conduct a test to determine if BA and ERA are jointly significant in explaining winning percentage at $\alpha = 0.05$.

Baseball

TABLE 15.4 Portion of Regression Results for Model 3: Win = $\beta_0 + \beta_1$BA + β_2ERA + ε

ANOVA	*df*	*SS*	*MS*	*F*	*Significance F*
Regression	2	0.09578	0.04789	33.966	4.25E-08
Residual	27	0.038068	0.00141		
Total	29	0.133848			

SOLUTION: When testing whether the explanatory variables are jointly significant in explaining winning percentage, we set up the following competing hypotheses:

$$H_0: \beta_1 = \beta_2 = 0$$
$$H_A: \text{At least one } \beta_j \neq 0.$$

Given $n = 30$ and $k = 2$, we find that $df_1 = k = 2$ and $df_2 = n - k - 1 = 27$. Although shown in Table 15.4, we can verify that

$$F_{(2,27)} = \frac{0.09578/2}{0.038068/(30 - 2 - 1)} = \frac{0.04789}{0.00141} = 33.966$$

Also reported in Table 15.4 is the p-value, $P(F_{(2,27)} \geq 33.966)$. We can verify this value in Excel by entering `=F.DIST.RT(33.966, 2, 27)`; in R, we enter `pf(33.966, 2, 27, lower.tail=FALSE)`. Both software return a p-value of 4.25E-08. Because the p-value is approximately zero ($= 4.25 \times 10^{-8}$), we reject H_0. At the 5% significance level, batting average and earned run average are jointly significant in explaining winning percentage.

Test of Individual Significance

In addition to testing all slope coefficients jointly, we often want to conduct tests on a single coefficient. Again consider the following linear regression model, which links the response variable y with k explanatory variables $x_1, x_2, \ldots, x_k$:

$$y = \beta_0 + \beta_1 x_1 + \beta_2 x_2 + \ldots + \beta_k x_k + \varepsilon.$$

If, for example, the slope coefficient β_1 equals zero, then the explanatory variable x_1 basically drops out of the equation, implying that x_1 does not influence y. In other words, if β_1 equals zero, then there is no linear relationship between x_1 and y. Conversely, if β_1 does not equal zero, then x_1 influences y.

In general, when we want to test whether the population coefficient β_j is different from, greater than, or less than β_{j0}, where β_{j0} is the hypothesized value of β_j, then the competing hypotheses take one of the following forms:

Two-Tailed Test	Right-Tailed Test	Left-Tailed Test
$H_0: \beta_j = \beta_{j0}$	$H_0: \beta_j \leq \beta_{j0}$	$H_0: \beta_j \geq \beta_{j0}$
$H_A: \beta_j \neq \beta_{j0}$	$H_A: \beta_j > \beta_{j0}$	$H_A: \beta_j < \beta_{j0}$

When testing whether x_j significantly influences y, we set $\beta_{j0} = 0$ and specify a two-tailed test as $H_0: \beta_j = 0$ and $H_A: \beta_j \neq 0$. We could easily specify one-tailed competing hypotheses for a positive linear relationship ($H_0: \beta_j \leq 0$ and $H_A: \beta_j > 0$) or a negative linear relationship ($H_0: \beta_j \geq 0$ and $H_A: \beta_j < 0$).

Although tests of significance are commonly based on $\beta_{j0} = 0$, in some situations we might wish to determine whether the slope coefficient differs from a nonzero value. For instance, if we are analyzing the relationship between students' exam scores on the basis of hours studied, we may want to determine if an extra hour of review before the exam will increase a student's score by more than five points. Here, we formulate the hypotheses as H_0: $\beta_j \leq 5$ and H_A: $\beta_j > 5$. Finally, although in most applications we are interested in conducting hypothesis tests on the slope coefficient(s), there are instances where we may also be interested in testing the intercept, β_0. The testing framework for the intercept remains the same; that is, if we want to test whether the intercept differs from zero, we specify the competing hypotheses as H_0: $\beta_0 = 0$ and H_A: $\beta_0 \neq 0$.

As in all hypothesis tests, the next step is to define the appropriate test statistic.

TEST OF INDIVIDUAL SIGNIFICANCE

For the linear regression model, $y = \beta_0 + \beta_1 x_1 + \beta_2 x_2 + \ldots + \beta_k x_k + \varepsilon$, the following competing hypotheses are used to conduct a test of individual significance:

$$H_0: \beta_j = \beta_{j0}$$
$$H_A: \beta_j \neq \beta_{j0}$$

The value of the test statistic is calculated as

$$t_{df} = \frac{b_j - \beta_{j0}}{se(b_j)},$$

where $df = n - k - 1$, b_j is the estimate for β_j, $se(b_j)$ is the standard error of the estimator b_j, and β_{j0} is the hypothesized value of β_j. If $\beta_{j0} = 0$, the value of the test statistic reduces to $t_{df} = \frac{b_j}{se(b_j)}$.

Suppose the competing hypotheses are H_0: $\beta_j = 0$ versus H_A: $\beta_j \neq 0$.

- If the null hypothesis is not rejected, then x_j is not significant.
- If the null hypothesis is rejected, then x_j is significant.

We would like to note that while the test of joint significance is important for a multiple linear regression model, it is redundant for a simple linear regression model. In fact, for a simple linear regression model, the p-value of the F-test is identical to that of the t-test on the single slope coefficient. We advise you to verify this fact.

EXAMPLE 15.2

Let's again revisit Model 3: Win $= \beta_0 + \beta_1$BA $+ \beta_2$ERA $+ \varepsilon$. Table 15.5 shows a portion of the regression results from estimating this model. Conduct a hypothesis test to determine whether BA influences Win at the 5% significance level.

Baseball

TABLE 15.5 Portion of Regression Results for Model 3: Win $= \beta_0 + \beta_1$BA $+ \beta_2$ERA $+ \varepsilon$

	Coefficients	Standard Error	t Stat	p-value	Lower 95%	Upper 95%
Intercept	0.1269	0.1822	0.696	0.492	−0.2470	0.5008
BA	3.2754	0.6723	4.872	4.3E-05	1.8960	4.6549
ERA	−0.1153	0.0167	−6.920	1.95E-07	−0.1494	−0.0811

SOLUTION: We set up the following competing hypotheses in order to determine whether BA influences Win:

$$H_0: \beta_1 = 0$$
$$H_A: \beta_1 \neq 0$$

From Table 15.5, we find that $b_1 = 3.2754$ and $se(b_1) = 0.6723$. In addition, given $n = 30$ and $k = 2$, we find $df = n - k - 1 = 30 - 2 - 1 = 27$. The value of the test statistic is found as $t_{27} = \frac{b_1 - \beta_{10}}{se(b_1)} = \frac{3.2754 - 0}{0.6723} = 4.872$. Note that this calculation is not necessary since virtually all statistical computer packages automatically provide the value of the test statistic and its associated p-value.

It is important to note that the computer-generated results are valid only in a standard case where a two-tailed test is implemented to determine whether a regression coefficient differs from zero. Here, we can use the computer-generated results because this example represents a standard case. Shortly, we will see an application with a nonstandard case.

As usual, the decision rule is to reject H_0 if the p-value $< \alpha$. Since the p-value is approximately zero ($= 4.3 \times 10^{-5}$), we reject H_0. At the 5% significance level, batting average is significant in explaining winning percentage.

Using a Confidence Interval to Determine Individual Significance

In earlier chapters, we constructed a confidence interval to conduct a two-tailed hypothesis test. When assessing whether the regression coefficient differs from zero, we can apply the same methodology.

CONFIDENCE INTERVAL FOR β_j

A $100(1 - \alpha)\%$ confidence interval for the regression coefficient β_j is computed as

$$b_j \pm t_{\alpha/2,df} se(b_j) \quad \text{or} \quad [b_j - t_{\alpha/2,df} se(b_j),\ b_j + t_{\alpha/2,df} se(b_j)],$$

where $se(b_j)$ is the standard error of b_j and $df = n - k - 1$.

Excel automatically provides a 95% confidence interval for the regression coefficients; it will provide other levels if prompted. In R, we can easily obtain confidence intervals for the regression coefficients using the **confint** function. As explained in Chapter 14, if we have estimated Model 3 by constructing an object labeled Multiple, then at the prompt sign we would enter confint(Multiple, level = 0.95); R would return 95% confidence intervals for all regression coefficients.

For a two-tailed test, if the confidence interval for the slope coefficient contains the value zero, then the explanatory variable associated with the regression coefficient is not significant. Conversely, if the confidence interval does not contain the value zero, then the explanatory variable associated with the regression coefficient is statistically significant. The next example is based on the confidence interval approach.

EXAMPLE 15.3

Let's again revisit Model 3, Win $= \beta_0 + \beta_1$BA $+ \beta_2$ERA $+ \varepsilon$, and the regression results in Table 15.5.

a. Specify the competing hypotheses in order to determine if ERA is significant in explaining Win.

b. Construct the 95% confidence interval for β_2. Use the confidence interval to determine if ERA is significant in explaining Win.

SOLUTION:

a. For testing whether ERA is statistically significant, we set up the following competing hypotheses:

$$H_0: \beta_2 = 0$$
$$H_A: \beta_2 \neq 0$$

b. For the 95% confidence interval, $\alpha = 0.05$ and $\alpha/2 = 0.025$. With $n = 30$ and $k = 2$, we use $df = 30 - 2 - 1 = 27$ to find $t_{\alpha/2,df} = t_{0.025,27} = 2.052$. Recall that in order to get this value, we enter `=T.INV(0.975, 27)` in Excel and `qt(0.975, 27, lower.tail=TRUE)` in R. Given $b_2 = -0.1153$ and $se(b_2) = 0.0167$ (from Table 15.5), the 95% confidence interval for the population coefficient β_2 is

$$b_2 \pm t_{\alpha/2,df}se(b_2) = -0.1153 \pm 2.052 \times 0.0167 = -0.1153 \pm 0.0343.$$

Thus, the lower and upper limits of the confidence interval are −0.1496 and −0.0810, respectively. Note that Table 15.5 also provides these values. (Slight differences are due to rounding.) Since the 95% confidence interval does not contain the value zero, we can conclude that ERA is significant in explaining Win at $\alpha = 0.05$.

Confidence intervals provide a useful alternative to conducting a two-tailed test for individual significance. In this text, we do not discuss the modification to confidence intervals to accommodate a one-tailed test. We generally rely on the standard four-step testing procedure for all tests of significance.

As noted above, the computer-generated results for a four-step procedure are valid only in a standard case where a two-tailed test is implemented to determine whether a regression coefficient differs from zero. In Example 15.2 we could use the computer-generated value of the test statistic as well as the corresponding p-value because it represented a standard case. For a one-tailed test with $\beta_{j0} = 0$, the value of the test statistic is valid, but the p-value is not; in most cases, the computer-generated p-value must be divided in half. For a one- or two- tailed test to determine if the regression coefficient differs from a nonzero value, both the computer-generated value of the test statistic and the p-value become invalid. These facts are summarized below.

COMPUTER-GENERATED TEST STATISTIC AND THE p-VALUE

Virtually all statistical packages report a value of the test statistic and its associated p-value for a two-tailed test that assesses whether the regression coefficient differs from zero.

- If we specify a one-tailed test, then we need to divide the computer-generated p-value in half.
- If we test whether the coefficient differs from a nonzero value, then we cannot use the value of the computer-generated test statistic and its p-value.

We would also like to point out that for a one-tailed test with $\beta_{j0} = 0$, there are rare instances when the computer-generated p-value is invalid. This occurs when the sign of b_j (and the value of the accompanying test statistic) is not inconsistent with the null hypothesis. For example, for a right-tailed test, H_0: $\beta_j \leq 0$ and H_A: $\beta_j > 0$, the null hypothesis cannot be rejected if the estimate b_j (and the value of the accompanying test statistic t_{df}) is negative. Similarly, no further testing is necessary if $b_j > 0$ (and thus $t_{df} > 0$) for a left-tailed test. In these rare instances, the reported p-value is invalid.

A Test for a Nonzero Slope Coefficient

In Examples 15.2 and 15.3, the null hypothesis included a zero value for the slope coefficient—that is, $\beta_{j0} = 0$. We now motivate a test where the hypothesized value is not zero by using a renowned financial application referred to as the capital asset pricing model (CAPM).

Let R represent the return on a stock or portfolio of interest. Given the market return R_M and the risk-free return R_f, the CAPM expresses the risk-adjusted return of an asset, $R - R_f$, as a function of the risk-adjusted market return, $R_M - R_f$. It is common to use the return of the S&P 500 index for R_M and the return on a Treasury bill for R_f. For empirical estimation, we express the CAPM as

$$R - R_f = \alpha + \beta(R_M - R_f) + \varepsilon.$$

We can rewrite the model as $y = \alpha + \beta x + \varepsilon$, where $y = R - R_f$ and $x = R_M - R_f$. Note that this is essentially a simple linear regression model that uses α and β, in place of the usual β_0 and β_1, to represent the intercept and the slope coefficients, respectively. The slope coefficient β, called the stock's beta, measures how sensitive the stock's return is to changes in the level of the overall market. When β equals 1, any change in the market return leads to an identical change in the given stock return. A stock for which $\beta > 1$ is considered more "aggressive" or riskier than the market, whereas one for which $\beta < 1$ is considered "conservative" or less risky. We also give importance to the intercept coefficient α, called the stock's alpha. The CAPM theory predicts α to be zero, and thus a nonzero estimate indicates abnormal returns. Abnormal returns are positive when $\alpha > 0$ and negative when $\alpha < 0$.

EXAMPLE 15.4

FILE
J&J

Johnson & Johnson (J&J) was founded more than 120 years ago on the premise that doctors and nurses should use sterile products to treat people's wounds. Since that time, J&J products have become staples in most people's homes. Consider the CAPM where the J&J risk-adjusted stock return $R - R_f$ is used as the response variable and the risk-adjusted market return $R_M - R_f$ is used as the explanatory variable. A portion of 60 months of data is shown in Table 15.6.

TABLE 15.6 Risk-Adjusted Stock Return of J&J and Market Return

Month	Year	$R - R_f$	$R_M - R_f$
Jan	2012	−0.0129	0.0403
Feb	2012	0.0216	0.0304
⋮	⋮	⋮	⋮
Dec	2016	−0.0221	0.0128

a. J&J stock is often considered less risky because the company sells several consumer staples that people will buy whether the economy is good or bad. At the 5% significance level, is the beta coefficient less than one?

b. At the 5% significance level, are there abnormal returns? In other words, is the alpha coefficient significantly different from zero?

SOLUTION: Using the CAPM notation, we estimate the model, $R - R_f = \alpha + \beta(R_M - R_f) + \varepsilon$; the relevant portion of the regression output is presented in Table 15.7.

TABLE 15.7 Portion of CAPM Regression Results for J&J

	Coefficients	Standard Error	*t* Stat	*p*-value
Intercept	0.0048	0.0042	1.127	0.2645
$R_M - R_f$	0.7503	0.1391	5.395	1.32E-06

a. The estimate for the beta coefficient is 0.7503 and its standard error is 0.1391. In order to determine whether the beta coefficient is significantly less than one, we formulate the hypotheses as

$$H_0: \beta \geq 1$$
$$H_A: \beta < 1$$

Given 60 data points, $df = n - k - 1 = 60 - 1 - 1 = 58$. We cannot use the test statistic value or the p-value reported in Table 15.7 because the hypothesized value of β is not zero. Using unrounded calculations, we find the value of the test statistic as $t_{58} = \frac{b_j - \beta_{j0}}{se(b_j)} = \frac{0.7503 - 1}{0.1391} = -1.796$. We can use the t table to approximate the p-value, $P(T_{58} \leq -1.796)$, as a value that is between 0.025 and 0.05. In order to find the exact p-value in Excel, we enter `=1-T.DIST.RT(−1.796, 58)` and in R, we enter `pt(−1.796, 58, lower.tail=TRUE)`. Both software return a p-value of 0.039. Because the p-value $< \alpha = 0.05$, we reject H_0 and conclude that β is significantly less than one; that is, the return on J&J stock is less risky than the return on the market.

b. Abnormal returns exist when α is significantly different from zero. Thus, the competing hypotheses are H_0: $\alpha = 0$ versus H_A: $\alpha \neq 0$. Because it is a standard case, where the hypothesized value of the coefficient is zero, we can use the reported test statistic value of 1.127 with an associated p-value of 0.2645. We cannot reject H_0 at any reasonable level of significance. Therefore, we cannot conclude that there are abnormal returns for J&J stock.

Reporting Regression Results

Regression results are often reported in a "user-friendly" table. Table 15.8 reports the regression results for the three models that explain a baseball team's winning percentage. The explanatory variables are batting average in Model 1, earned run average in Model 2, and both batting average and earned run average in Model 3. If we were supplied with only this table, we would be able to compare these models, construct the sample regression equation of the chosen model, and perform a respectable assessment of the model with the statistics provided. Many tables contain a Notes section at the bottom explaining some of the notation. We choose to put the p-values in parentheses next to all estimated coefficients; however, some analysts place the standard errors of the coefficients or the values of the test statistics in parentheses. Whichever format is chosen, it must be made clear to the reader in the Notes section.

TABLE 15.8 Estimates of Regression Models for Explaining Winning Percentage

Variable	Model 1	Model 2	Model 3
Intercept	−0.2731 (0.342)	0.9504* (0.000)	0.1269 (0.492)
Batting Average	3.0054* (0.011)	NA	3.2754* (0.000)
Earned Run Average	NA	−0.1105* (0.000)	−0.1153* (0.000)
s_e	0.0614	0.0505	0.0375
R^2	0.2112	0.4656	0.7156
Adjusted R^2	0.1830	0.4465	0.6945
F-test (p-value)			33.966* (0.000)

Notes: Parameter estimates are in the top half of the table with the p-values in parentheses; * represents significance at the 5% level. NA denotes not applicable. The lower part of the table contains goodness-of-fit measures.

EXERCISES 15.1

Mechanics

1. In a simple linear regression based on 30 observations, it is found that $b_1 = 3.25$ and $se(b_1) = 1.36$. Consider the hypotheses:

$$H_0: \beta_1 = 0 \text{ and } H_A: \beta_1 \neq 0.$$

   a. Calculate the value of the test statistic.
   b. Find the p-value.
   c. At the 5% significance level, what is the conclusion? Is the explanatory variable statistically significant?

2. In a simple linear regression based on 25 observations, it is found that $b_1 = 0.5$ and $se(b_1) = 0.3$. Consider the hypotheses:

$$H_0: \beta_1 \leq 0 \text{ and } H_A: \beta_1 > 0.$$

   a. Calculate the value of the test statistic and the p-value.
   b. At the 5% significance level, what is the conclusion to the test?

3. In a simple linear regression based on 30 observations, it is found that $b_1 = 7.2$ and $se(b_1) = 1.8$. Consider the hypotheses:

$$H_0: \beta_1 \geq 10 \text{ and } H_A: \beta_1 < 10.$$

   a. Calculate the value of the test statistic and the p-value.
   b. At the 5% significance level, what is the conclusion to the test?

4. Consider the following regression results based on 20 observations.

	Coefficients	*Standard Error*	*t Stat*	*p-value*
Intercept	34.2123	4.5665	7.420	0.000
x_1	0.1223	0.1794	0.682	0.504

   a. Specify the hypotheses to determine if the intercept differs from zero. Perform this test at the 5% significance level.
   b. Construct the 95% confidence interval for the slope coefficient. At the 5% significance level, does the slope differ from zero? Explain.

5. Consider the following regression results based on 40 observations.

	Coefficients	Standard Error	*t* Stat	*p*-value
Intercept	43.1802	12.6963	3.401	0.002
x_1	0.9178	0.9350	0.982	0.333

   a. Specify the hypotheses to determine if the slope differs from minus one.
   b. Calculate the value of the test statistic and the p-value.
   c. At the 5% significance level, does the slope differ from minus one? Explain.

6. When estimating a multiple linear regression model based on 30 observations, the following results were obtained.

	Coefficients	Standard Error	*t* Stat	*p*-value
Intercept	152.27	119.70	1.272	0.214
x_1	12.91	2.68	4.817	5.06E-05
x_2	2.74	2.15	1.274	0.213

   a. Specify the hypotheses to determine whether x_1 is linearly related to y. At the 5% significance level, are x_1 and y linearly related?
   b. What is the 95% confidence interval for β_2? Using this confidence interval, is x_2 significant in explaining y? Explain.
   c. At the 5% significance level, can you conclude that β_1 is less than 20? Show the relevant steps of the hypothesis test.

7. The following ANOVA table was obtained when estimating a multiple linear regression model.

ANOVA	*df*	*SS*	*MS*	*F*	*Significance F*
Regression	2	22016.75	11008.375		0.0228
Residual	17	39286.93	2310.996		
Total	19	61303.68			

   a. How many explanatory variables were specified in the model? How many observations were used?
   b. Specify the hypotheses to determine whether the explanatory variables are jointly significant.
   c. Compute the value of the test statistic.
   d. At the 5% significance level, what is the conclusion to the test? Explain.

Applications

8. A marketing manager analyzes the relationship between the annual sales of a firm (in \$100,000s) and its advertising expenditures (in \$10,000s). He collects data from 20 firms and estimates Sales $= \beta_0 + \beta_1$Advertising $+ \varepsilon$. A portion of the regression results is shown in the accompanying table.

	Coefficients	Standard Error	*t* Stat	*p*-value
Intercept	−7.42	1.46	−5.082	7.66E-05
Advertising	0.42	0.15		0.0118

   a. Specify the competing hypotheses in order to determine whether advertising expenditures and sales have a positive linear relationship.
   b. Calculate the value of the test statistic.
   c. At the 1% significance level, do advertising expenditures and sales have a positive linear relationship? Explain.

9. In order to examine the relationship between the selling price of a used car and its age, an analyst uses data from 20 recent transactions and estimates Price = $\beta_0 + \beta_1$Age + ε. A portion of the regression results is shown in the accompanying table.

	Coefficients	Standard Error	t Stat	p-value
Intercept	21187.94	733.42	28.889	1.56E-16
Age	−1208.25	128.95		2.41E-08

a. Specify the competing hypotheses in order to determine whether the selling price of a used car and its age are linearly related.
b. Calculate the value of the test statistic.
c. At the 5% significance level, is the age of a used car significant in explaining its selling price? Explain.
d. Conduct a hypothesis test at the 5% significance level in order to determine if β_1 differs from −1000. Show all of the relevant steps.

10. **FILE** ***Dash.*** A study on the evolution of mankind shows that, with a few exceptions, world-record holders in the 100-meter dash have progressively gotten bigger over time. The accompanying data file lists record holders, along with their record-holding times (in seconds) and heights (in inches):

a. Estimate the model: Time = $\beta_0 + \beta_1$Height + ε. Specify the sample regression equation.
b. Specify the hypotheses to determine whether Height and Time have a negative linear relationship.
c. At the 5% significance level, do Height and Time have a negative linear relationship? Explain.

11. An economist examines the relationship between changes in short-term interest rates and long-term interest rates. He believes that changes in short-term rates are significant in explaining long-term interest rates. Using five years of monthly data (n = 60), he estimates the model Dlong = $\beta_0 + \beta_1$Dshort + ε, where Dlong is the change in the long-term interest rate (10-year Treasury bill) and Dshort is the change in the short-term interest rate (3-month Treasury bill). A portion of the regression results is shown in the accompanying table.

	Coefficients	Standard Error	t Stat	p-value
Intercept	−0.0038	0.0088	−0.427	0.671
Dshort	0.0473	0.0168	2.813	0.007

Use a 5% significance level to determine whether there is a linear relationship between Dshort and Dlong.

12. For a sample of 20 New England cities, a sociologist studies the crime rate in each city (crimes per 100,000 residents) as a function of its poverty rate (in %) and its median income (in $1,000s). A portion of the regression results is shown in the accompanying table.

ANOVA	df	SS	MS	F	Significance F
Regression	2	188246.8	94123.40	35.20	9.04E-07
Residual	17	45457.32	2673.96		
Total	19	233704.1			

	Coefficients	Standard Error	t Stat	p-value
Intercept	−301.7927	549.7135	−0.549	0.590
Poverty	53.1597	14.2198	3.738	0.002
Income	4.9472	8.2566	0.599	0.557

a. Specify the sample regression equation.
b. At the 5% significance level, are the poverty rate and income jointly significant in explaining the crime rate?
c. At the 5% significance level, show whether the poverty rate and the crime rate are linearly related.
d. Construct the 95% confidence interval for the slope coefficient of income. Using the confidence interval, determine whether income influences the crime rate at the 5% significance level.

13. Akiko Hamaguchi is a manager at a small sushi restaurant in Phoenix, Arizona. Akiko is concerned that the weak economic environment has hampered foot traffic in her area, thus causing a dramatic decline in sales. In order to offset the decline in sales, she has pursued a strong advertising campaign. She believes advertising expenditures have a positive influence on sales. To support her claim, Akiko estimates the following linear regression model: Sales = $\beta_0 + \beta_1$Unemployment + β_2Advertising + ε. A portion of the regression results is shown in the accompanying table.

ANOVA	df	SS	MS	F	Significance F
Regression	2	72.6374	36.3187	8.760	0.003
Residual	14	58.0438	4.1460		
Total	16	130.681			

	Coefficients	Standard Error	t Stat	p-value
Intercept	17.5060	3.9817	4.397	0.007
Unemployment	−0.6879	0.2997	−2.296	0.038
Advertising	0.0266	0.0068	3.932	0.002

a. At the 5% significance level, test whether the explanatory variables jointly influence sales.
b. At the 1% significance level, test whether the unemployment rate is negatively related with sales.
c. At the 1% significance level, test whether advertising expenditures are positively related with sales.

14. **FILE** ***Returns.*** The accompanying data file contains the annual stock return (in %), the price-to-earnings ratio (PE), and the price-to-sales ratio (PS) for 30 firms.

a. Estimate the model: Return $= \beta_0 + \beta_1$PE $+ \beta_2$PS $+ \varepsilon$. Specify the sample regression equation.
b. At the 10% significant level, are PE and PS jointly significant? Show the relevant steps of the test.
c. Are both explanatory variables individually significant at the 10% significance level? Show the relevant steps of the test.

15. FILE ***Test_Scores.*** The accompanying data file shows midterm and final grades for 32 students. Estimate a student's final grade as a linear function of a student's midterm grade. At the 1% significance level, is a student's midterm grade significant in explaining a student's final grade? Show the relevant steps of the test.

16. FILE ***Taxes.*** The accompanying data file shows the square footage and associated property taxes for 20 homes in an affluent suburb 30 miles outside of New York City. Estimate a home's property taxes as a linear function of its square footage. At the 5% significance level, is square footage significant in explaining property taxes? Show the relevant steps of the test.

17. FILE ***Fertilizer.*** A horticulturist is studying the relationship between tomato plant height and fertilizer amount. Thirty tomato plants grown in similar conditions were subjected to various amounts of fertilizer (in ounces) over a four-month period, and then their heights (in inches) were measured.
a. Estimate the regression model: Height $= \beta_0 + \beta_1$Fertilizer $+ \varepsilon$.
b. At the 5% significance level, determine if an ounce of fertilizer increases height by more than 3 inches. Show the relevant steps of the test.

18. FILE ***Dexterity.*** Finger dexterity, the ability to make precisely coordinated finger movements to grasp or assemble very small objects, is important in jewelry making. Thus, the manufacturing manager at Gemco, a manufacturer of high-quality watches, wants to develop a regression model to predict the productivity, measured by watches per shift, of new employees based on the time required (in seconds) to place 3 pins in each of 100 small holes using tweezers. He has subjected a sample of 20 current employees to the O'Connor dexterity test in which the time required to place the pins and the number of watches produced per shift are measured.
a. Estimate the regression model: Watches $= \beta_0 + \beta_1$Time $+ \varepsilon$.
b. The manager claims that for every extra second taken on placing the pins, the number of watches produced decreases by more than 0.02. Test this claim at the 5% significance level. Show the relevant steps of the test.

19. FILE ***Engine_Overhaul.*** The maintenance manager at a trucking company wants to build a regression model to forecast the time until the first engine overhaul (Time in years) based on four explanatory variables: (1) annual miles driven (Miles in 1,000s), (2) average load weight (Load in tons), (3) average driving speed (Speed in mph), and (4) oil change interval (Oil in 1,000s miles). Based on driver logs and onboard computers, data have been obtained for a sample of 25 trucks.
a. Estimate the time until the first engine overhaul as a function of all four explanatory variables.
b. At the 10% significance level, are the explanatory variables jointly significant? Show the relevant steps of the test.
c. Are the explanatory variables individually significant at the 10% significance level? Show the relevant steps of the test.

20. FILE ***Electricity_Cost.*** The facility manager at a pharmaceutical company wants to build a regression model to forecast monthly electricity cost. Three main variables are thought to dictate electricity cost: (1) average outdoor temperature (Temp in °F), (2) working days per month (Days), and (3) tons of product produced (Tons).
a. Estimate the regression model.
b. At the 10% significance level, are the explanatory variables jointly significant? Show the relevant steps of the test.
c. Are the explanatory variables individually significant at the 10% significance level? Show the relevant steps of the test.

21. FILE ***Caterpillar.*** Caterpillar, Inc. manufactures and sells heavy construction equipment worldwide. The performance of Caterpillar's stock is likely to be strongly influenced by the economy. For instance, during the subprime mortgage crisis, the value of Caterpillar's stock plunged dramatically. Monthly data for Caterpillar's risk-adjusted return (Cat_Adj) and the risk-adjusted market return (Market_Adj) are collected for a five-year period ($n = 60$).
a. Estimate the CAPM: Cat_Adj $= \beta_0 + \beta_1$(Market_Adj) $+ \varepsilon$. Show the regression results in a well-formatted table.
b. At the 5% significance level, determine if investment in Caterpillar is riskier than the market (beta significantly greater than 1).
c. At the 5% significance level, is there evidence of abnormal returns?

22. FILE ***Houses.*** A realtor examines the factors that influence the price of a house in a suburb outside of Boston, Massachusetts. He collects data on 36 recent house sales (Price) and notes each house's square footage (Sqft) as well as its number of bedrooms (Beds) and number of bathrooms (Baths).
a. Estimate: Price $= \beta_0 + \beta_1$Sqft $+ \beta_2$Beds $+ \beta_3$Baths $+ \varepsilon$. Show the regression results in a well-formatted table.
b. At the 5% significance level, are the explanatory variables jointly significant in explaining Price?
c. At the 5% significance level, are all explanatory variables individually significant in explaining Price?

23. FILE ***Final_Test.*** On the first day of class, an economics professor administers a test to gauge the math preparedness of her students. She believes that the performance on this math test and the number of hours studied per week on the

course are the primary factors that predict a student's score on the final exam. She collects data from 60 students.

a. Estimate the sample regression equation that enables us to predict a student's final exam score on the basis of his/her math score and the number of hours studied per week.

b. At the 5% significance level, are a student's math score and the number of hours studied per week jointly significant in explaining a student's final exam score?

c. At the 5% significance level, is each explanatory variable individually significant in explaining a student's final exam score?

15.2 A GENERAL TEST OF LINEAR RESTRICTIONS

LO 15.2

Conduct a general test of linear restrictions.

The significance tests discussed in the preceding section can also be referred to as tests of linear restrictions. For example, the two-tailed t-test is a test of one linear restriction that determines whether or not a slope coefficient differs from zero. Similarly, the F test is a test of k linear restrictions that determines whether or not at least one of the slope coefficients is nonzero. In this section, we introduce a general **test of linear restrictions;** the resulting F test is often referred to as the **partial F test.** We can apply this test to any subset of the regression coefficients.

Consider a multiple regression model with three explanatory variables:

$$y = \beta_0 + \beta_1 x_1 + \beta_2 x_2 + \beta_3 x_3 + \varepsilon.$$

As mentioned earlier, we use a t-test for a test of one restriction, $\beta_j = 0$, and an F test for a test of three restrictions, $\beta_1 = \beta_2 = \beta_3 = 0$. What if we wanted to test if x_2 and x_3 are jointly significant? This is an example of a test of two restrictions, $\beta_2 = \beta_3 = 0$. Similarly, we may wish to test if the influence of x_3 is identical to that of x_2. This would be a test of one restriction, $\beta_2 = \beta_3$. When conducting a partial F test, the null hypothesis implies that the restrictions are valid. In these two examples, the null hypothesis would be specified as H_0: $\beta_2 = \beta_3 = 0$ and H_0: $\beta_2 = \beta_3$, respectively. As usual, the alternative hypothesis implies that the null hypothesis is not true. We conclude that the restrictions implied by the null hypothesis are not valid if we reject the null hypothesis.

In order to conduct the partial F test, we estimate the model with and without the restrictions. The **restricted model** is a reduced model where we do not estimate the coefficients that are restricted to a specific value under the null hypothesis. The **unrestricted model** is a complete model that imposes no restrictions on the coefficients; therefore, all coefficients are estimated. If the restrictions are valid—that is, the null hypothesis is true—then the error sum of squares of the restricted model SSE_R will not be significantly larger than the error sum of squares of the unrestricted model SSE_U. With the partial F test, we basically analyze the ratio of (SSE_R – SSE_U) to SSE_U. If this ratio, suitably adjusted for the degrees of freedom, is significantly large, then we reject the null hypothesis and conclude that the restrictions implied by the null hypothesis are not valid.

TEST STATISTIC FOR THE TEST OF LINEAR RESTRICTIONS

When testing linear restrictions, the value of the test statistic is calculated as

$$F_{(df_1, df_2)} = \frac{(SSE_R - SSE_U)/df_1}{SSE_U/df_2},$$

where df_1 is equal to the number of linear restrictions, $df_2 = n - k - 1$ where k is the number of explanatory variables in the unrestricted model; SSE_R and SSE_U are the error sum of squares for the restricted and the unrestricted models, respectively.

- If the null hypothesis is not rejected, the linear restrictions are not invalid.
- If the null hypothesis is rejected, the linear restrictions are invalid.

We will consider two examples of the partial F test.

EXAMPLE 15.5

A manager at a car wash company in Missouri wants to measure the effectiveness of price discounts and various types of advertisement expenditures on sales. For the analysis, he uses varying price discounts (Discount) and advertisement expenditures on radio (Radio) and newspapers (Newspaper) in 40 counties in Missouri. A portion of the monthly data on sales (in \$1,000s), price discounts (in percent), and advertisement expenditures (in \$1,000s) on radio and newspapers are shown in Table 15.9. At the 5% level, determine if the advertisement expenditures on radio and newspapers have a statistically significant influence on sales.

Car_Wash

TABLE 15.9 Sales, Price Discounts, and Advertising Expenditures, $n = 40$

County	Sales	Discount	Radio	Newspaper
1	62.72	40	2.27	3.00
2	49.65	20	3.78	1.78
⋮	⋮	⋮	⋮	⋮
40	49.95	40	3.57	1.57

SOLUTION: Consider the unrestricted model (U) that does not impose restrictions on the coefficients and is specified as

$$\text{(U)} \qquad \text{Sales} = \beta_0 + \beta_1 \text{Discount} + \beta_2 \text{Radio} + \beta_3 \text{Newspaper} + \varepsilon.$$

A test that determines whether advertisement expenditures on radio and newspapers have a significant influence on sales is equivalent to a test that determines whether the Radio and Newspaper variables are jointly significant. We formulate the competing hypotheses as

H_0: $\beta_2 = \beta_3 = 0$
H_A: At least one of the coefficients is nonzero.

In order to implement the partial F test, we then create the restricted (R) model. Note that we do not estimate the coefficients that are restricted to zero under the null hypothesis. Therefore, we exclude Radio and Newspaper and specify the model as

$$\text{(R)} \qquad \text{Sales} = \beta_0 + \beta_1 \text{Discount} + \varepsilon.$$

For ease of exposition, we use the same notation to refer to the coefficients in models U and R. We note, however, that these coefficients and their estimates have a different meaning depending on which model we are referencing. Table 15.10 shows the relevant portion of the regression results.

TABLE 15.10 Relevant Regression Output for Example 15.5

Variable	Restricted	Unrestricted
Intercept	43.4541* (0.000)	6.7025 (0.356)
Discount	0.4016* (0.000)	0.3417* (0.000)
Radio	NA	6.0624* (0.001)
Newspaper	NA	9.3968* (0.000)
SSE	2,182.5649	1,208.1348

Notes: Parameter estimates are in the main body of the table with the p-values in parentheses; * represents significance at the 5% level. NA denotes not applicable. The last row presents the error sum of squares.

We use $df_1 = 2$, since we are testing for two restrictions, $\beta_2 = 0$ and $\beta_3 = 0$, and $df_2 = n - k - 1 = 40 - 3 - 1 = 36$. Taking the appropriate *SSE* values from Table 15.10, we calculate the value of the test statistic as

$$F_{(2,36)} = \frac{(SSE_R - SSE_U)/df_1}{SSE_U/df_2} = \frac{(2{,}182.5649 - 1{,}208.1348)/2}{1{,}208.1348/36} = 14.518.$$

We can use the *F* table to approximate the *p*-value, $P(F_{(2,36)} \geq 14.518)$, as a value that is less than 0.01. In order to find the exact *p*-value in Excel,we enter `=F.DIST.RT(14.518, 2, 36)`, and in R, we enter `pf(14.518, 2, 36, lower.tail=FALSE)`. Both software return a *p*-value of 2.38E-0.5. Because the *p*-value is approximately zero ($= 2.38 \times 10^{-5}$), we reject H_0. At the 5% level, we conclude that the advertisement expenditures on radio and newspapers have a significant influence on sales.

EXAMPLE 15.6

Car_Wash

In Example 15.5, we showed that the advertisement expenditures on radio and newspapers have a statistically significant influence on sales. The manager believes that the influence of the advertisement expenditure on radio differs from the influence of the advertisement expenditure on newspapers. Conduct the appropriate partial *F* test at the 5% level to verify the manager's belief.

SOLUTION: We again specify the unrestricted model (U) as

(U) $\quad \text{Sales} = \beta_0 + \beta_1 \text{Discount} + \beta_2 \text{Radio} + \beta_3 \text{Newspaper} + \varepsilon.$

Because β_2 and β_3 capture the influence of the advertisement expenditures on radio and newspapers, respectively, we formulate the competing hypotheses as

$$H_0: \beta_2 = \beta_3$$
$$H_A: \beta_2 \neq \beta_3$$

In order to implement the partial *F* test, we then create the restricted (R) model. Note that under the restriction that $\beta_2 = \beta_3$, so the unrestricted model simplifies to

$\quad \text{Sales} = \beta_0 + \beta_1 \text{Discount} + \beta_2 \text{Radio} + \beta_2 \text{Newspaper} + \varepsilon$; that is,

(R) $\quad \text{Sales} = \beta_0 + \beta_1 \text{Discount} + \beta_2 (\text{Radio} + \text{Newspaper}) + \varepsilon.$

Thus, the restricted model uses only two explanatory variables, where the new second explanatory variable is defined as the sum of Radio and Newspaper. For this regression, we have to first create a new explanatory variable by adding up the Radio and Newspaper observations. Further, given the restriction, $\beta_2 = \beta_3$, the estimated coefficient for this new explanatory variable applies to both Radio and Newspaper. Note that the restricted model imposes one restriction, as there is one fewer coefficient to estimate. Table 15.11 presents the relevant portion of the regression results.

TABLE 15.11 Relevant Regression Output for Example 15.6

Variable	Restricted	Unrestricted
Intercept	7.9524 (0.274)	6.7025 (0.356)
Discount	0.3517* (0.000)	0.3417* (0.000)
Radio	NA	6.0624* (0.001)
Newspaper	NA	9.3968* (0.000)
Radio + Newspaper	7.1831* (0.000)	NA
SSE	1,263.6243	1,208.1348

Notes: Parameter estimates are in the main body of the table with the *p*-values in parentheses; * represents significance at the 5% level. NA denotes not applicable. The last row presents the error sum of squares.

We use $df_1 = 1$ since we are testing for only one restriction, and $df_2 = n - k - 1 = 40 - 3 - 1 = 36$. Using the appropriate SSE values from Table 15.11, we calculate the value of the test statistic as

$$F_{(1,36)} = \frac{(SSE_R - SSE_U)/df_1}{SSE_U/df_2} = \frac{(1{,}263.6243 - 1{,}208.1348)/1}{1{,}208.1348/36} = 1.653.$$

We can use the F table to approximate the p-value, $P(F_{(1,36)} \geq 1.653)$, as a value that is greater than 0.10. In order to find the exact p-value in Excel,we enter `=F.DIST.RT(1.653, 1, 36)`, and in R, we enter `pf(1.653, 1, 36, lower.tail=FALSE)`. Both software return a p-value of 0.207. Because the p-value $> \alpha = 0.05$, we do not reject H_0. At the 5% significance level, we cannot conclude that the influence of the advertisement expenditures on radio is different from the influence of the advertisement expenditures on newspapers.

Using R to Conduct Partial F Tests

FILE
Car_Wash

R offers an easy way to conduct a partial F test. We replicate the findings from Example 15.5 and Example 15.6 using R.

A. Import the **Car_Wash** data file into a data frame and label it myData.

B. We use the **lm** function to create the objects for the unrestricted model and the restricted model (Restricted_1) in Example 15.5, as well as the restricted model (Restricted_2) in Example 15.6. When creating the 'Radio + Newspaper' variable in Restricted_2, we use the I function which isolates or insulates the expression inside the parentheses. Enter:

```
> Unrestricted < - lm(Sales ~ Discount + Radio + Newspaper, data=myData)
> Restricted_1 < - lm(Sales ~ Discount, data=myData)
> Restricted_2 < - lm(Sales ~ Discount + I(Radio + Newspaper),
  data=myData)
```

C. Use the **anova** function to obtain the F-statistic and the accompanying p-value for each example. Enter:

```
> anova(Unrestricted, Restricted_1)
> anova(Unrestricted, Restricted_2)
```

EXERCISES 15.2

Mechanics

24. Consider the multiple linear regression model, $y = \beta_0 + \beta_1 x_1 + \beta_2 x_2 + \beta_3 x_3 + \varepsilon$. You wish to test whether the slope coefficients β_1 and β_3 are jointly significant. Define the restricted and unrestricted models needed to conduct the test.

25. Consider the multiple linear regression model, $y = \beta_0 + \beta_1 x_1 + \beta_2 x_2 + \beta_3 x_3 + \varepsilon$. You wish to test whether the slope coefficients β_1 and β_3 are statistically different from each other. Define the restricted and unrestricted models needed to conduct the test.

26. Consider the multiple linear regression model, $y = \beta_0 + \beta_1 x_1 + \beta_2 x_2 + \varepsilon$. Define the restricted and unrestricted models if the hypotheses are

$$H_0\colon \beta_1 + \beta_2 = 1 \quad \text{and} \quad H_A\colon \beta_1 + \beta_2 \neq 1.$$

27. Consider a portion of simple linear regression results,

$$\hat{y} = 105.40 + 39.17x_1; \quad SSE = 407{,}308; \quad n = 30$$

In an attempt to improve the results, two explanatory variables are added. The relevant regression results are the following:

$$\hat{y} = 4.87 + 19.47x_1 - 26.31x_2 + 7.31x_3; \quad SSE = 344{,}784; \quad n = 30$$

a. Formulate the hypotheses to determine whether x_2 and x_3 are jointly significant in explaining y.

b. Calculate the value of the test statistic and the p-value.

c. At the 5% significance level, what is the conclusion to the test?

Applications

28. A real estate analyst estimates the following regression, relating a house price to its square footage (Sqft):

$$\widehat{\text{Price}} = 48.39 + 52.74\text{Sqft}; \quad SSE = 56{,}944; \quad n = 50$$

In an attempt to improve the results, he adds two more explanatory variables: the number of bedrooms (Beds) and the number of bathrooms (Baths). The estimated regression equation is

$$\widehat{\text{Price}} = 28.11 + 40.17\text{Sqft} + 10.08\text{Beds} + 16.14\text{Baths};$$
$$SSE = 48{,}074; \quad n = 50$$

a. Formulate the hypotheses to determine whether Beds and Baths are jointly significant in explaining Price.
b. Calculate the value of the test statistic and the p-value.
c. At the 5% significance level, what is the conclusion to the test?

29. A financial analyst believes that the best way to predict a firm's returns is by using the firm's price-to-earnings ratio (P/E) and its price-to-sales ratio (P/S) as explanatory variables. He estimates the following regression, using 30 large firms:

$$\widehat{\text{Return}} = -33.40 + 3.97\text{P/E} - 3.37\text{P/S};$$
$$SSE = 5{,}021.63; \quad n = 30$$

A colleague suggests that he can improve on his prediction if he also includes the P/E-to-growth ratio (PEG) and the dividend yield (DIV). He re-estimates the model by including these explanatory variables and obtains

$$\widehat{\text{Return}} = -31.84 + 4.26\text{P/E} - 2.16\text{P/S} - 11.49\text{PEG} + 3.82\text{DIV}; \quad SSE = 4{,}149.21; \quad n = 30$$

At the 5% significance level, is the colleague's claim substantiated by the data? Explain.

30. Lisa Fisher is a business school professor who would like to analyze university factors that enhance innovation. She collects data on 143 universities for a regression where the response variable is the number of startups (Startups), which is used as a measure for innovation. Lisa believes that the amount of money that a university directs toward research (Research) is the most important factor influencing Startups. She estimates Startups as a function of Research and obtains

$$\widehat{\text{Startups}} = 0.21 + 0.01\text{Research};$$
$$SSE = 1{,}434.78; \quad n = 143$$

Two other explanatory variables are also likely to influence Startups: the number of patents issued (Patents), and the age of its technology transfer office in years (Duration). Lisa then includes these additional variables in the model and obtains

$$\widehat{\text{Startups}} = 0.42 + 0.01\text{Research} + 0.05\text{Patents} - 0.02\text{Duration}; \quad SSE = 1{,}368.14; \quad n = 143$$

At the 5% significance level, should Lisa include Patents and Duration in the model predicting Startups?

31. **FILE** ***Wage.*** A researcher interviews 50 employees of a large manufacturer and collects data on each worker's hourly wage (Wage in $), years of higher education (EDUC), experience (EXPER), and age (AGE).

a. Estimate:
$\text{Wage} = \beta_0 + \beta_1\text{EDUC} + \beta_2\text{EXPER} + \beta_3\text{AGE} + \varepsilon.$
b. The researcher wonders if the influence of experience is different from that of age, or if $\beta_2 \neq \beta_3$. Specify the competing hypotheses for this test.
c. What is the restricted model given that the null hypothesis is true? Estimate this model.
d. At the 5% significance level, can you conclude that the influence of experience is different from that of age?

32. **FILE** ***Mobile_Phones.*** The manager of a local Costo store is in the process of making hiring decisions for selling mobile phone contracts. She believes that the sale of mobile phone contracts depends crucially on the number of hours clocked by male and female employees. She collects the weekly data on last year's sales of mobile phone contracts (Sale) along with work hours of male (Hours_Males) and female (Hours_Females) employees.

a. Report the sample regression equation of the appropriate model.
b. At the 5% significance level, are the explanatory variables jointly significant? Are they individually significant?
c. The manager would like to determine whether there is a difference in productivity of male and female employees. In other words, for the same work hours, whether the number of sales of mobile contracts varies between male and female employees. Conduct the appropriate test at the 5% level of significance. Provide the details.

33. **FILE** ***Football.*** A multiple regression model is used to predict an NFL team's winning record (Win in %). For the explanatory variables, the average rushing yards (Rush) and the average passing yards (Pass) are used to capture offense, and the average yards allowed are used to capture defense (Allowed).

a. Estimate the model: $\text{Win} = \beta_0 + \beta_1\text{Rush} + \beta_2\text{Pass} + \beta_3\text{Allowed} + \varepsilon.$
b. Conduct a test at the 10% significance level to determine whether the impact of Rush is different from that of Pass in explaining Win, or $\beta_1 \neq \beta_2$.

34. **FILE** ***Union_Pay.*** An automotive workers union, in conjunction with top management, is negotiating a new hourly pay policy for union workers based on three variables: (1) job class, (2) years with the company, and (3) years as a union member at any company. The goal is to develop an equitable model that can objectively specify hourly pay, thereby reducing pay disparity grievances. Fifty union workers have been sampled and will be used as the basis for the pay model.

a. Report the sample regression equation of the appropriate model.
b. At the 5% significance level, are the explanatory variables jointly significant? Are they individually significant?
c. Predict hourly pay for a worker in Job Class 48 with 18 years experience at the company and 14 years with the union.
d. A manager wonders if the years with the company and the years as a union member matter in negotiating hourly pay. At the 5% significance level, can you conclude that the influence of these two explanatory variables is jointly significant? Provide the details.

15.3 INTERVAL ESTIMATES FOR THE RESPONSE VARIABLE

LO 15.3

Calculate and interpret confidence intervals and prediction intervals.

In the introductory case, we analyzed the winning percentage of a baseball team on the basis of its batting average (BA) and earned run average (ERA). The preferred model was estimated as $\widehat{\text{Win}} = 0.1269 + 3.2754\text{BA} - 0.1153\text{ERA}$. Suppose we want to predict a team's winning percentage given its batting average of 0.25 and earned run average of 4. Using unrounded coefficient estimates with BA = 0.25 and ERA = 4, we can easily derive the predicted winning percentage as

$$\widehat{\text{Win}} = 0.1269 + 3.2754 \times 0.25 - 0.1153 \times 4 = 0.4847.$$

Predictions, such as the one above, are certainly useful, but we need to be aware that such predictions are subject to sampling variations. In other words, the prediction will change if we use a different sample to estimate the regression model. Recall from Chapter 8 that the point estimate along with the margin of error is used to construct the relevant interval estimate. In the baseball example, 0.4847 represents the point estimate.

In this section, we will make a distinction between the interval estimate for the mean (expected value) of the response variable y and the interval estimate for the individual value of y. It is common to refer to the former as the **confidence interval** and the latter as the **prediction interval.** For given values of the explanatory variables, we can think of the confidence interval as the range that contains the mean of y and the prediction interval as the range that contains the individual value of y. We use the same point estimate for constructing both interval estimates. In the context of the baseball example, 0.4847 is the point estimate for the mean winning percentage as well as the individual winning percentage given the team's batting average of 0.25 and earned run average of 4. Due to the added uncertainty in predicting the individual value of y, the prediction interval is always wider than the corresponding confidence interval.

CONFIDENCE INTERVAL AND PREDICTION INTERVAL

We construct two types of interval estimates regarding the response variable y for given values of the explanatory variables.

- The confidence interval is for the mean (expected value) of y.
- The prediction interval is wider than the confidence interval.

We will now describe the general procedure for constructing the confidence interval and the prediction interval. Consider a multiple regression model $y = \beta_0 + \beta_1 x_1 + \beta_2 x_2 + \cdots + \beta_k x_k + \varepsilon$ with k explanatory variables, $x_1, x_2, \ldots, x_k$. In the context of the baseball example, $k = 2$ and x_1 and x_2 represent the team's batting average and earned run average, respectively. Moreover, let

$$y^0 = \beta_0 + \beta_1 x_1^0 + \beta_2 x_2^0 + \cdots + \beta_k x_k^0 + \varepsilon^0,$$

where $x_1^0, x_2^0, \ldots, x_k^0$ denote specific values for $x_1, x_2, \ldots, x_k$ at which y^0 is evaluated and ε^0 is the (unobserved) random error term. In the baseball example, we used $x_1^0 = 0.25$ and $x_2^0 = 4$. We can evaluate the expected value of the response variable at $x_1^0, x_2^0, \ldots, x_k^0$ as

$$E(y^0) = \beta_0 + \beta_1 x_1^0 + \beta_2 x_2^0 + \cdots + \beta_k x_k^0.$$

The expected value equation assumes that the expected value of the random error term is zero; that is, $E(\varepsilon^0) = 0$. Note that the prediction interval is wider than the confidence interval because it also incorporates the additional uncertainty due to ε^0. We first derive the confidence interval for $E(y^0)$, followed by the prediction interval for y^0.

The predicted value, $\hat{y}^0 = b_0 + b_1 x_1^0 + b_2 x_2^0 + \cdots + b_k x_k^0$, is the point estimate for $E(y^0)$. In the baseball example, 0.4847 is the point estimate of $E(y^0)$ when $x_1^0 = 0.25$ and $x_2^0 = 4$.

We form the $100(1-\alpha)\%$ confidence interval for $E(y^0)$ as $\hat{y}^0 + t_{\alpha/2,df}\, se(\hat{y}^0)$, where $se(\hat{y}^0)$ is the estimated standard error of $\hat{y}^0$. While there is a simple formula to compute the standard error $se(\hat{y}^0)$ for a simple linear regression model, it is very cumbersome to do so for a multiple linear regression model. Next we describe a relatively easy way to construct a confidence interval that works for both simple and multiple linear regression models.

CONFIDENCE INTERVAL FOR THE EXPECTED VALUE OF y

For specific values of $x_1, x_2, \ldots, x_k$, denoted by $x_1^0, x_2^0, \ldots, x_k^0$, the $100(1-\alpha)\%$ confidence interval for the expected value of y is computed as

$$\hat{y}^0 + t_{\alpha/2,df}\, se(\hat{y}^0),$$

where $df = n - k - 1$ and $se(\hat{y}^0)$ is the standard error of $\hat{y}^0$.

To derive $\hat{y}^0$ together with $se(\hat{y}^0)$, we first estimate a modified regression model where y is the response variable and the explanatory variables are defined as $x_1^* = x_1 - x_1^0, x_2^* = x_2 - x_2^0, \ldots, x_k^* = x_k - x_k^0$. The resulting estimate of the intercept and its standard error equal $\hat{y}^0$ and $se(\hat{y}^0)$, respectively.

EXAMPLE 15.7

Using the regression model Win $= \beta_0 + \beta_1$BA $+ \beta_2$ERA $+ \varepsilon$, construct the 95% confidence interval for the expected winning percentage if BA is 0.25 and ERA is 4.

SOLUTION: Let y, x_1, and x_2 denote Win, BA, and ERA, respectively. In order to construct a confidence interval for $E(y^0)$, we follow the above-mentioned procedure to derive $\hat{y}^0$ as well as $se(\hat{y}^0)$. First, given $x_1^0 = 0.25$ and $x_2^0 = 4$, we define two modified explanatory variables as $x_1^* = x_1 - 0.25$ and $x_2^* = x_2 - 4$. Table 15.12 shows a portion of the computed observations.

TABLE 15.12 Computing the Values of Modified Explanatory Variables (Example 15.7)

y	x_1	x_2	$x_1^* = x_1 - 0.25$	$x_2^* = x_2 - 4$
0.407	0.259	4.59	0.259 − 0.25 = 0.009	4.59 − 4 = 0.59
0.549	0.268	4.20	0.268 − 0.25 = 0.018	4.20 − 4 = 0.20
⋮	⋮	⋮	⋮	⋮
0.426	0.250	4.13	0.250 − 0.25 = 0.000	4.13 − 4 = 0.13

The regression output for a multiple regression model that uses y as the response variable and x_1^* and x_2^* as the explanatory variables is presented in Table 15.13.

TABLE 15.13 Regression Results with Modified Explanatory Variables (Example 15.7)

Regression Statistics					
Multiple R	0.8459				
R Square	0.7156				
Adjusted R Square	0.6945				
Standard Error	**0.0375**				
Observations	30				
ANOVA					
	df	*SS*	*MS*	*F*	*Significance F*
Regression	2	0.0958	0.0479	33.966	4.25E-08
Residual	27	0.0381	0.0014		
Total	29	0.1338			

	Coefficients	Standard Error	t Stat	p-value	Lower 95%	Upper 95%
Intercept	**0.4847**	**0.0085**	57.258	0.000	**0.4673**	**0.5021**
x_1^*	3.2754	0.6723	4.872	0.000	1.8960	4.6549
x_2^*	−0.1153	0.0167	−6.920	0.000	−0.1494	−0.0811

We note that the modified regression output is identical to the original regression output (see Table 15.8), except for the estimates of the intercept term. Here the intercept estimate is 0.4847 and its standard error is 0.0085 (see values in boldface in Table 15.13). Therefore, we use $\hat{y}^0 = 0.4847$ and $se(\hat{y}^0) = 0.0085$ in constructing the confidence interval. Note that the computer-generated calculation for $\hat{y}^0$ is the same as our earlier estimate, $\hat{y}^0 = 0.4847$.

For the 95% confidence level and $df = n - k - 1 = 30 - 2 - 1 = 27$, we find $t_{\alpha/2,df} = t_{0.025,27} = 2.052$. The 95% confidence interval for $E(y^0)$, using unrounded coefficient estimates, is

$$\hat{y}^0 \pm t_{\alpha/2,df} se(\hat{y}^0) = 0.4847 \pm 2.052 \times 0.0085 = 0.4847 \pm 0.0174.$$

Or, with 95% confidence,

$$0.4673 \leq E(y^0) \leq 0.5021.$$

Using this 95% confidence interval, we can state that the mean winning percentage of a team with a batting average of 0.25 and earned run average of 4 falls between 0.4673 and 0.5021. Note that the lower and upper confidence limits for the 95% confidence interval for $E(y^0)$ are identical to the lower and upper confidence limits for the 95% confidence interval for the intercept (see values in boldface in Table 15.13).

As mentioned earlier, the prediction interval pertains to the individual value of the response variable defined for specific explanatory variables as $y^0 = \beta_0 + \beta_1 x_1^0 + \beta_2 x_2^0 + \cdots + \beta_k x_k^0 + \varepsilon^0$. The prediction interval is wider than the confidence interval because it incorporates the variability of the random error term ε^0. The higher variability makes it more difficult to predict accurately, thus necessitating a wider interval.

PREDICTION INTERVAL FOR AN INDIVIDUAL VALUE OF y

For specific values of $x_1, x_2, \ldots, x_k$, denoted by $x_1^0, x_2^0, \ldots, x_k^0$, the $100(1 - \alpha)\%$ prediction interval for an individual value of y is computed as

$$\hat{y}^0 \pm t_{\alpha/2,df}\sqrt{(se(\hat{y}^0))^2 + s_e^2},$$

where $df = n - k - 1$, $se(\hat{y}^0)$ is the standard error of $\hat{y}^0$, and s_e is the standard error of the estimate that captures the variability of the random error term ε^0.

EXAMPLE 15.8

a. Using the information in Table 15.13, construct the 95% prediction interval for Win if BA is 0.25 and ERA is 4.

b. Comment on any differences between this prediction interval and the confidence interval constructed in Example 15.7.

SOLUTION:

a. As in the calculation for the confidence interval, we find $\hat{y}^0 = 0.4847$, $se(\hat{y}^0) = 0.0085$, and $t_{\alpha/2,df} = t_{0.025,27} = 2.052$. The only thing missing from the prediction interval formula is the standard error of the estimate s_e. From

Table 15.13, we extract the value, $s_e = 0.0375$ (see value in boldface). The 95% prediction interval, using unrounded coefficient estimates, is

$$\hat{y}^0 \pm t_{\alpha/2,df}\sqrt{(se(\hat{y}^0))^2 + s_e^2} = 0.4847 \pm 2.052\sqrt{0.0085^2 + 0.0375^2}$$
$$= 0.4847 \pm 0.0790.$$

Or, with 95% confidence,

$$0.4057 \leq y^0 \leq 0.5637.$$

b. Using this 95% prediction interval, we can state that the winning percentage of a team with a batting average of 0.25 and earned run average of 4 falls between 0.4057 and 0.5637. In the previous example, the corresponding 95% confidence interval was between 0.4673 and 0.5021. As expected, the prediction interval is wider because it also accounts for the variability caused by the random error term. The higher variability, captured by the standard error of the estimate s_e, makes it more difficult to predict accurately, thus necessitating a wider interval.

Using R to Find Interval Estimates for the Response Variable

Baseball

R offers an easy way to find the confidence and prediction intervals for the response variable. We replicate the findings from Example 15.7 and Example 15.8 using R.

A. Import the ***Baseball*** data file into a data frame and label it myData.

B. Use the **lm** function to create the object (the regression model) which is labeled Baseball. Enter:

```
> Baseball <- lm(Win ~ BA + ERA, data=myData)
```

C. Use the **predict** function accompanied with the **data.frame** function to construct confidence intervals for Win with BA=0.25 and ERA=4. Use the option *level* set equal to 0.95 for 95% confidence and prediction intervals. For the confidence interval, use the option *interval* set equal to "confidence" and for the prediction interval, use the option *interval* set equal to "prediction". Enter:

```
> predict(Baseball, data.frame(BA=0.25, ERA=4), level=0.95,
  interval="confidence")
> predict(Baseball, data.frame(BA=0.25, ERA=4), level=0.95,
  interval="prediction")
```

SYNOPSIS OF INTRODUCTORY CASE

Two sports analysts have conflicting views over how best to predict a Major League Baseball (MLB) team's winning percentage. One argues that the team's batting average is a better predictor of a team's success, since the team with the higher batting average has won approximately 75% of the World Series contests. The other analyst insists that a team's pitching is clearly the main factor in determining wins. Three regression models are used to analyze a baseball team's winning percentage (Win). The explanatory variables are batting average (BA) in Model 1, earned run average (ERA) in Model 2, and both BA and ERA in Model 3.

Mark Cunningham/MLB Photos/Getty Images

After estimating the models using data from 30 MLB teams, it appears that neither analyst is totally right nor totally wrong. This is because Model 3, which includes both BA and

ERA, provides the best overall fit. Model 3 has the lowest standard error and the highest adjusted R^2 value. Its sample regression equation is $\widehat{\text{Win}} = 0.13 + 3.28\text{BA} - 0.12\text{ERA}$. Further testing of this preferred model reveals that the two explanatory variables are jointly as well as individually significant in explaining the winning percentage at the 5% significance level.

Lastly, for a team with a batting average of 0.25 and an earned run average of 4, the model predicts a winning percentage of 0.4847. With 95% confidence, the expected winning percentage will lie between 0.4673 and 0.5021.

EXERCISES 15.3

MECHANICS

35. In a simple linear regression based on 30 observations, the following information is provided: $\hat{y} = -6.92 + 1.35x$ and $s_e = 2.78$. Also, $se(\hat{y}^0)$ evaluated at $x = 30$ is 1.02.
    a. Construct the 95% confidence interval for $E(y)$ if $x = 30$.
    b. Construct the 95% prediction interval for y if $x = 30$.
    c. Which interval is narrower? Explain.

36. In a simple linear regression based on eight observations, the following sample regression is obtained: $\hat{y} = 9.15 + 1.46x$ with $s_e = 2.67$. Also, when x equals 15, $se(\hat{y}^0) = 1.06$.
    a. Construct the 95% confidence interval for $E(y)$ if $x = 15$.
    b. Construct the 95% prediction interval for y if $x = 15$.
    c. Which interval is wider? Explain.

37. In a multiple linear regression with 40 observations, the following sample regression equation is obtained: $\hat{y} = 12.8 + 2.6x_1 - 1.2x_2$ with $s_e = 5.84$. Also, when x_1 equals 15 and x_2 equals 6, $se(\hat{y}^0) = 2.20$.
    a. Construct the 95% confidence interval for $E(y)$ if x_1 equals 15 and x_2 equals 6.
    b. Construct the 95% prediction interval for y if x_1 equals 15 and x_2 equals 6.
    c. Which interval is wider? Explain.

38. In a multiple linear regression based on eight observations, the following sample regression is obtained: $\hat{y} = 22.81 + 0.85x_1 - 0.71x_2$ with $s_e = 4.69$. Also, when x_1 equals 50 and x_2 equals 20, $se(\hat{y})^0 = 2.18$.
    a. Construct the 95% confidence interval for $E(y)$ if $x_1 = 50$ and $x_2 = 20$.
    b. Construct the 95% prediction interval for y if $x_1 = 50$ and $x_2 = 20$.
    c. Which interval is narrower? Explain.

Applications

39. FILE ***Education.*** Estimate: Salary $= \beta_0 + \beta_1$Education $+ \varepsilon$, where Salary is measured in \$1,000s and Education refers to years of higher education.
    a. Construct the 90% confidence interval for the expected salary for an individual who completed 6 years of higher education.
    b. Construct the 90% prediction interval for salary for an individual who completed 6 years of higher education.
    c. Comment on the difference in the widths of these intervals.

40. FILE ***Fertilizer.*** Estimate: Height $= \beta_0 + \beta_1$Fertilizer $+ \varepsilon$, where Height is a tomato plant's height (in inches) and Fertilizer is the fertilizer amount (in ounces).
    a. Calculate and interpret the 90% confidence interval for the mean height of a tomato plant that receives 3.0 ounces of fertilizer.
    b. Calculate and interpret the 90% prediction interval for a tomato plant that receives 3.0 ounces of fertilizer.

41. FILE ***GPA.*** Estimate: GPA $= \beta_0 + \beta_1$GRE $+ \varepsilon$, where GRE is a student's score on the math portion of the Graduate Record Examination (GRE) and GPA is the student's grade point average in graduate school.
    a. Construct the 90% confidence interval for the expected GPA for an individual who scored 710 on the math portion of the GRE.
    b. Construct the 90% prediction interval for GPA for an individual who scored 710 on the math portion of the GRE.

42. FILE ***Debt_Payments.*** Estimate: Debt $= \beta_0 + \beta_1$Income $+ \varepsilon$, where Debt (in \$) is the average debt payments for a household in a particular city and Income (in \$1,000s) is the city's median income.
    a. Construct the 95% confidence interval for expected debt payments if income is \$80,000.
    b. Construct the 95% prediction interval for debt payments if income is \$80,000.

43. FILE ***Houses.*** Estimate: Price $= \beta_0 + \beta_1$Sqft $+ \beta_2$Beds $+ \beta_2$Baths $+ \varepsilon$, where Price, Sqft, Beds, and Baths refer to home price, square footage, number of bedrooms, and number of bathrooms, respectively. Construct the 95% confidence interval for the expected price of a 2,500-square-foot home with three bedrooms and two bathrooms. Construct the corresponding prediction interval for an individual home. Interpret both intervals.

44. FILE ***Engine_Overhaul.*** The maintenance manager at a trucking company wants to build a regression model to

forecast the time until the first engine overhaul (Time in years) based on four explanatory variables: (1) annual miles driven (Miles in 1,000s), (2) average load weight (Load in tons), (3) average driving speed (Speed in mph), and (4) oil change interval (Oil in 1,000s miles). Based on driver logs and onboard computers, data have been obtained for a sample of 25 trucks.

a. Estimate the regression model to predict the time before the first engine overhaul for a truck driven 60,000 miles per year with an average load of 22 tons, an average driving speed of 57 mph, and 18,000 miles between oil changes. (Note that both annual miles driven and oil change interval are measured in 1,000s.)
b. Use the prediction in part a to calculate and interpret the 90% confidence interval for the mean time before the first engine overhaul.
c. Use the prediction in part a to calculate and interpret the corresponding 90% prediction interval for the time before the first engine overhaul.

15.4 MODEL ASSUMPTIONS AND COMMON VIOLATIONS

LO 15.4

Address common violations of the OLS assumptions.

So far we have focused on the estimation and the assessment of linear regression models. It is important to understand that the statistical properties of the ordinary least squares (OLS) estimator, as well as the validity of the testing procedures, depend on the assumptions of the classical linear regression model. In this section, we discuss these assumptions. We also address common violations to the assumptions, discuss the consequences when the assumptions are violated, and, where possible, offer some remedies.

Under the assumptions of the classical linear regression model, the OLS estimators have desirable properties. In particular, the OLS estimators of the regression coefficients β_j are unbiased; that is, $E(b_j) = \beta_j$. Moreover, among all linear unbiased estimators, they have minimum variations between samples. These desirable properties of the OLS estimators become compromised as one or more model assumptions are violated. Aside from coefficient estimates, the validity of the significance tests is also impacted by the assumptions. For certain violations, the estimated standard errors of the OLS estimators are inappropriate; in these cases it is not possible to make meaningful inferences from the t and the F test results.

Residual Plots

The assumptions of the classical linear regression model are, for the most part, based on the error term ε. Since the residuals, or the observed error term, $e = y - \hat{y}$, contain useful information regarding ε, it is common to use the residuals to investigate the assumptions. In this section, we will rely on **residual plots** to detect some of the common violations to the assumptions. These graphical plots are easy to use and provide informal analysis of the estimated regression models. Formal tests are beyond the scope of this text.

RESIDUAL PLOTS

For the regression model, $y = \beta_0 + \beta_1 x_1 + \beta_2 x_2 + \cdots + \beta_k x_k + \varepsilon$, the residuals are computed as $e = y - \hat{y}$, where $\hat{y} = b_0 + b_1 x_1 + b_2 x_2 + \cdots + b_k x_k$. These residuals can be plotted sequentially or against an explanatory variable x_j or against predicted values $\hat{y}$ to look for model inadequacies.

Residual plots can also be used to detect outliers. Recall that outliers are observations that stand out from the rest of the data. For an outlier observation, the resulting residual will appear distinct in a plot; it will stand out from the rest. While outliers can greatly impact the estimates, it is not always clear what to do with them. As mentioned in Chapter 3, outliers may indicate bad data due to incorrectly recorded (or included) observations in the data set. In such cases, the relevant observation should be corrected or simply deleted. Alternatively, outliers may just be due to random variations, in which case the relevant observations should remain. In any event, residual plots help us identify potential outliers so that we can take corrective actions, if needed.

It is common to plot the residuals e on the vertical axis and the explanatory variable x_j, or the predicted values $\hat{y}$ on the horizontal axis. In Figure 15.1, we present a hypothetical residual plot when none of the assumptions has been violated. Note that all the points are randomly dispersed around the zero value of the residuals. Also, there is no evidence of outliers since no residual stands out from the rest. Any discernible pattern of the residuals indicates that one or more assumptions have been violated.

Next we discuss the OLS assumptions, describe common violations, and offer remedies. At the end of this section, we outline how to obtain residual plots in Excel and R.

FIGURE 15.1 Residual plot of a correctly specified model

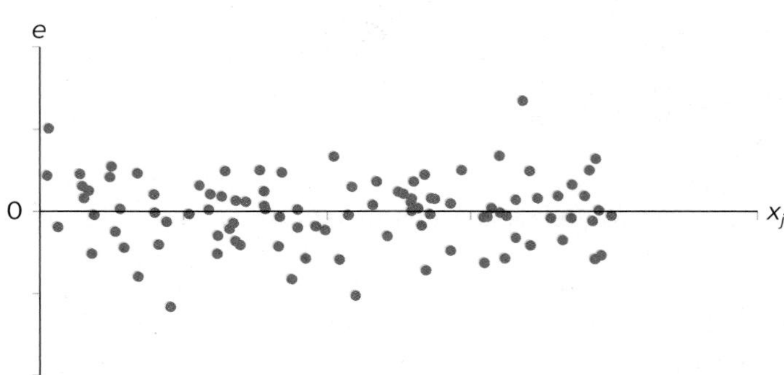

Assumption 1. The regression model given by $y = \beta_0 + \beta_1 x_1 + \beta_2 x_2 + \ldots + \beta_k x_k + \varepsilon$ is linear in the parameters and is correctly specified.

Note that Assumption 1 requires linearity in the parameters ($\beta_0, \beta_1, \ldots, \beta_k$), but not the variables ($y, x_1, x_2, \ldots, x_k$). Assumption 1 also requires that we correctly specify the model. The model should make economic and intuitive sense, include all relevant explanatory variables, and incorporate any nonlinearities between the response and explanatory variables.

Detecting Nonlinearities

We can use residual plots to identify nonlinear patterns. Linearity is justified if the residuals are randomly dispersed across the observations of an explanatory variable. A discernible trend in the residuals is indicative of a nonlinear pattern.

EXAMPLE 15.9

A sociologist wishes to study the relationship between age and happiness. He interviews 24 individuals and collects data on each person's age and happiness, where happiness is measured on a scale from 0 to 100. A portion of the data is shown in Table 15.14. Use a residual plot to determine whether the regression model, Happiness $= \beta_0 + \beta_1$Age $+ \varepsilon$, is correctly specified.

FILE *Happiness_Age*

TABLE 15.14 Happiness and Age

Happiness	Age
62	46
66	51
⋮	⋮
72	69

SOLUTION: We start the analysis with a scatterplot of Happiness against Age. Figure 15.2 shows the scatterplot and the superimposed trend line, which is based on the sample regression equation, $\widehat{Happiness} = 56.18 + 0.28Age$. It is clear from Figure 15.2 that the model does not appropriately capture the relationship between Happiness and Age. In other words, it is misleading to conclude that a person's happiness increases by 0.28 units every year.

FIGURE 15.2 Scatterplot and the superimposed trendline

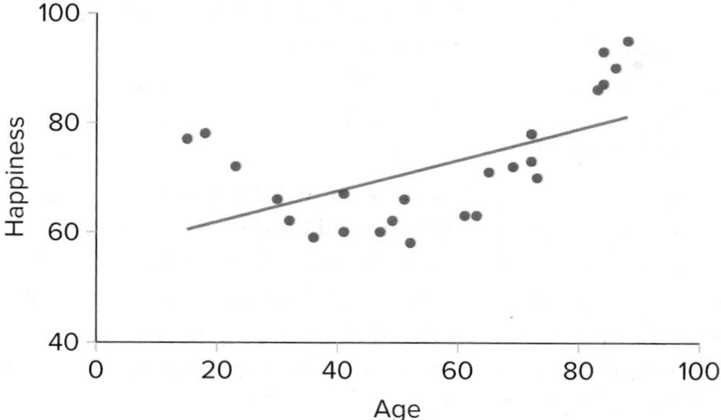

Figure 15.3 shows a residual plot against Age. It highlights the nonlinear, U-shaped relationship between Happiness and Age. The residuals decrease until the age of 50 and steadily increase thereafter. The model is inappropriate as it underestimates at lower and higher age levels and overestimates in the middle.

FIGURE 15.3 Residual plot against Age

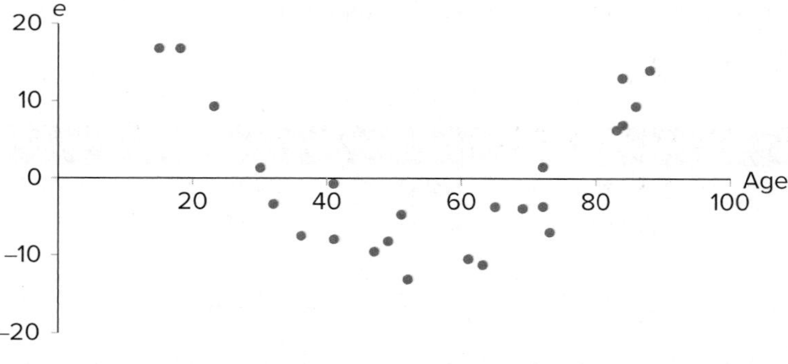

Remedy

If the residual plot exhibits strong nonlinear patterns, then we should accommodate nonlinearity by making simple transformations of the response variable and/or the explanatory variable. In Chapter 16, we will discuss how we can easily capture certain nonlinear patterns within a linear regression model framework.

> **Assumption 2.** There is no exact linear relationship among the explanatory variables; or, in statistical terminology, there is no perfect multicollinearity.

Perfect multicollinearity exists when two or more explanatory variables have an exact linear relationship. Consider the model $y = \beta_0 + \beta_1 x_1 + \beta_2 x_2 + \varepsilon$, where y is bonus, x_1 is the number of cars sold, and x_2 is the number of cars remaining in the lot. If all car salesmen started with the same inventory, we have a case of *perfect* multicollinearity

(x_2 = Constant − x_1). Perfect multicollinearity is easy to detect because the model cannot be estimated. However, if x_2 represents the proportion of positive reviews from customers, we have *some* **multicollinearity** because the number of cars sold and the proportion of positive reviews are likely to be correlated. In most applications, some degree of correlation exists between the explanatory variables.

The problem with (non-perfect) multicollinearity is similar to that of small samples. Multicollinearity does not violate any of the assumptions; however, its presence results in imprecise estimates of the slope coefficients. In other words, multicollinearity makes it difficult to disentangle the separate influences of the explanatory variables on the response variable. If multicollinearity is severe, we may find insignificance of important explanatory variables; some coefficient estimates may even have wrong signs.

Detecting Multicollinearity

The detection methods for multicollinearity are mostly informal. The presence of a high R^2 coupled with individually insignificant explanatory variables can indicate multicollinearity. Sometimes researchers examine the correlations between the explanatory variables to detect severe multicollinearity. One such guideline suggests that multicollinearity is severe if the sample correlation coefficient between any two explanatory variables is more than 0.80 or less than −0.80. Seemingly wrong signs of the estimated regression coefficients may also indicate multicollinearity.

EXAMPLE 15.10

Examine the multicollinearity issue in a linear regression model that uses median home values (in $) as the response variable and median household incomes (in $), per capita incomes (in $), and the proportion of owner-occupied homes (in %) as the explanatory variables. A portion of the data for all states in the United States is shown in Table 15.15.

Home_Values

TABLE 15.15 Home Values and Other Factors

State	Home Value	HH Income	Per Cap Inc	Pct Owner Occ
Alabama	117600	42081	22984	71.1
Alaska	229100	66521	30726	64.7
⋮	⋮	⋮	⋮	⋮
Wyoming	174000	53802	27860	70.2

SOLUTION: We estimate three models to examine the multicollinearity issue; Table 15.16 presents the regression results.

TABLE 15.16 Summary of Model Estimates (Example 15.10)

Variable	Model 1	Model 2	Model 3
Intercept	417,892.04* (0.001)	348,187.14* (0.002)	285,604.08 (0.083)
HH income	9.04* (0.000)	7.74* (0.000)	NA
Per Cap Inc	−3.27 (0.309)	NA	13.21* (0.000)
Pct Owner Occ	−8,744.30* (0.000)	−8,027.90* (0.000)	−6,454.08* (0.001)
Adjusted R^2	0.8071	0.8069	0.6621

Notes: The table contains parameter estimates with *p*-values in parentheses; * represents significance at the 5% level. NA denotes not applicable. Adjusted R^2, reported in the last row, is used for model selection.

Model 1 uses all three explanatory variables to explain home values. Surprisingly, the per capita income variable has a negative estimated coefficient of −3.27 and, with a p-value of 0.31, is not even statistically significant at the 5% level. Multicollinearity might be the reason for this surprising result since household income and per capita income are likely to be correlated. We compute the sample correlation coefficient between these two variables as 0.8582, which suggests that multicollinearity is severe.

We estimate two more models where one of these collinear variables is removed; Model 2 removes per capita income and Model 3 removes household income. Note that per capita income in Model 3 now exerts a positive and significant influence on home values. Between these two models, Model 2 is preferred to Model 3 because of its higher adjusted R^2 (0.8069 > 0.6621). The choice between Model 1 and Model 2 is unclear. In general, Model 1, with the highest adjusted R^2 value of 0.8071, is preferred if the sole purpose of the analysis is to make predictions. However, if the coefficient estimates need to be evaluated, then Model 2 may be the preferred choice.

Remedy

Inexperienced researchers tend to include too many explanatory variables in their quest not to omit anything important and in doing so may include redundant variables that essentially measure the same thing. When confronted with multicollinearity, a good remedy is to drop one of the collinear variables. The difficult part is to decide which of the collinear variables is redundant and, therefore, can safely be removed. Another option is to obtain more data, since the sample correlation may get weaker as we include more observations. Sometimes it helps to express the explanatory variables differently so that they are not collinear. At times, the best approach may be to *do nothing* when there is a justification to include all explanatory variables. This is especially so if the estimated model yields a high R^2, which implies that the estimated model is good for prediction.

Assumption 3. Conditional on $x_1, x_2, \ldots, x_k$, the variance of the error term ε is the same for all observations (constant variability); or in statistical terminology, there is no heteroskedasticity.

The assumption of constant variability of observations often breaks down in studies with cross-sectional data. Consider the model $y = \beta_0 + \beta_1 x + \varepsilon$, where y is a household's consumption expenditure and x is its disposable income. It may be unreasonable to assume that the variability of consumption is the same across a cross-section of household incomes. For example, we would expect higher-income households to have a higher variability in consumption as compared to lower-income households. Similarly, home prices tend to vary more as homes get larger, and sales tend to vary more as firm size increases.

In the presence of **changing variability,** the OLS estimators are still unbiased. However, the estimated standard errors of the OLS estimators are inappropriate. Consequently, we cannot put much faith in the standard t or F tests since they are based on these estimated standard errors.

Detecting Changing Variability

We can use residual plots to gauge changing variability. The residuals are generally plotted against each explanatory variable x_j; for a multiple regression model, we can also plot them against the predicted value $\hat{y}$. There is no violation if the residuals are randomly dispersed across the values of x_j. On the other hand, there is a violation if the variability increases or decreases over the values of x_j.

Stores

EXAMPLE 15.11

Consider a simple regression model that relates monthly sales (Sales in \$1,000s) from a chain of convenience stores with the square footage (Sqft) of the store. A portion of the data used for the analysis is shown in Table 15.17. Estimate the model and use a residual plot to determine if the observations have a changing variability.

TABLE 15.17 Sales and Square Footage of Convenience Stores

Sales	Sqft
140	1810
160	2500
⋮	⋮
110	1470

SOLUTION: The sample regression is given by

$$\begin{array}{ccc} \widehat{\text{Sales}} = & 22.0795 + & 0.0591\text{Sqft}, \\ (se) & (10.4764) & (0.0057) \end{array}$$

where we have put the standard errors of the coefficients in parentheses. We will reference these values when we incorporate R instructions at the end of this section.

A residual plot of the estimated model is shown in Figure 15.4. Note that the residuals seem to fan out across the horizontal axis. Therefore, we conclude that changing variability is a likely problem in this application relating sales to square footage. This result is not surprising, since you would expect sales to vary more as square footage increases. For instance, a small convenience store is likely to include only bare essentials for which there is a fairly stable demand. A larger store, on the other hand, may include specialty items, resulting in more fluctuation in sales.

FIGURE 15.4 Residual plot against square footage

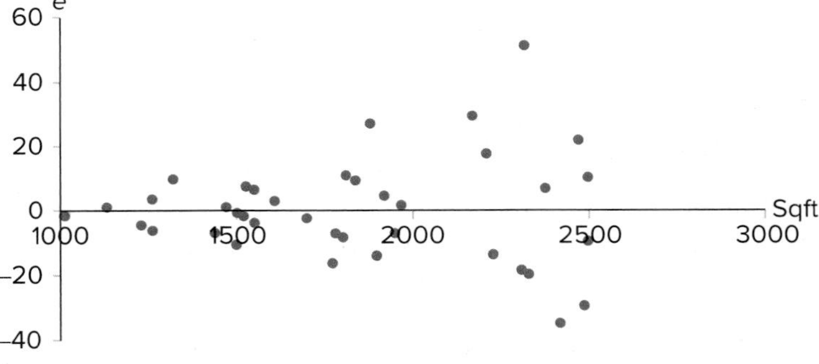

Remedy

As mentioned earlier, in the presence of changing variability, the OLS estimators are unbiased but their estimated standard errors are inappropriate. Therefore, OLS still provides reasonable coefficient estimates, but the t and the F tests are no longer valid. This has prompted some researchers to use the OLS estimates along with a correction for the standard errors, often referred to as White's robust standard errors. Unfortunately, the current version of Excel does not include a correction for the standard errors. However, it is available on many statistical computer packages, including R. At the end of this section, we use R to make the necessary correction in Example 15.11. With robust standard errors, we can then perform legitimate t-tests.

Assumption 4. Conditional on $x_1, x_2, \ldots, x_k$, the error term ε is uncorrelated across observations; or in statistical terminology, there is no serial correlation.

When obtaining the OLS estimators, we assume that the observations are uncorrelated. This assumption often breaks down in studies with time series data. Variables such as GDP, employment, and asset returns exhibit business cycles. As a consequence, successive observations are likely to be correlated.

In the presence of **correlated observations,** the OLS estimators are unbiased, but their estimated standard errors are inappropriate. Generally, these standard errors are distorted downward, making the model look better than it really is with a spuriously high R^2. Furthermore, the t and F tests may suggest that the explanatory variables are individually and jointly significant when this is not true.

Detecting Correlated Observations

We can plot the residuals sequentially over time to look for correlated observations. If there is no violation, then the residuals should show no pattern around the horizontal axis. A violation is indicated when a positive residual in one period is followed by positive residuals in the next few periods, followed by negative residuals for a few periods, then positive residuals, and so on. Although not as common, a violation is also indicated when a positive residual is followed by a negative residual, then a positive residual, and so on.

EXAMPLE 15.12

Consider $y = \beta_0 + \beta_1 x_1 + \beta_2 x_2 + \varepsilon$ where y represents sales (in \$1,000s) at a sushi restaurant and x_1 and x_2 represent advertising costs (in \$) and the unemployment rate (in %), respectively. Data for these variables are collected for 17 consecutive months, a portion of which is shown in Table 15.18. Inspect the behavior of the residuals in order to comment on serial correlation.

FILE *Sushi*

TABLE 15.18 Sales, Advertising Costs, and Unemployment Data

Month	Sales	AdCost	Unemp
1	27.0	550	4.6
2	24.2	425	4.3
⋮	⋮	⋮	⋮
17	27.4	550	9.1

SOLUTION: The model is estimated as

$$\begin{array}{llll} & \hat{y} = 17.5060 & + \; 0.0266x_1 & - \; 0.6879x_2, \\ (se) & (3.9817) & (0.0068) & (0.2997) \end{array}$$

where we have put the standard errors of the coefficients in parentheses. We will reference these values when we incorporate R instructions at the end of this section.

In order to detect serial correlation, we plot the residuals sequentially against time t, where t is given by 1, 2, . . . , 17 for the 17 months of time series data. Figure 15.5 shows a wavelike movement in the residuals over time, first clustering below the horizontal axis, then above the horizontal axis, and so on. Given this pattern around the horizontal axis, we conclude that the observations are correlated.

FIGURE 15.5 Scatterplot of residuals against time t

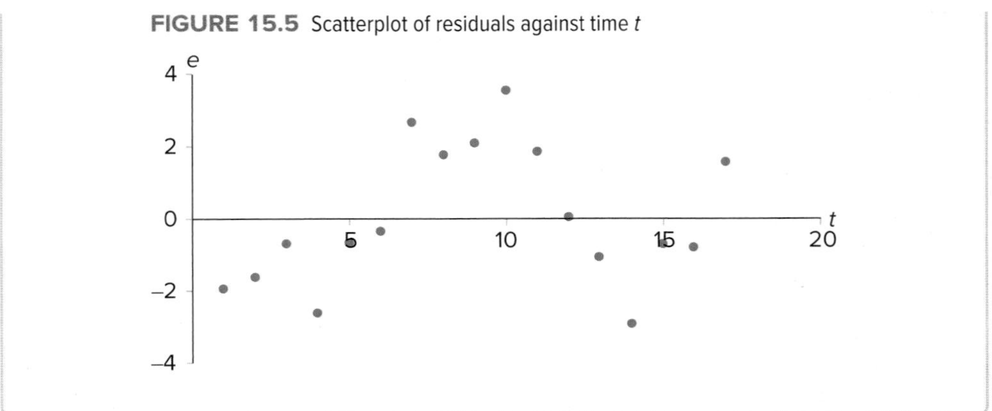

Remedy

As mentioned earlier, in the presence of correlated observations, the OLS estimators are unbiased but their standard errors are inappropriate and generally distorted downward, making the model look better than it really is. Therefore, OLS still provides reasonable coefficient estimates, but the t and the F tests are no longer valid. This has prompted some researchers to use the OLS estimates along with a correction for the standard errors, often referred to as Newey-West robust standard errors. As in the case of changing variability, the current version of Excel does not include this correction. However, it is available on many statistical computer packages, including R. At the end of this section, we use R to make the necessary correction in Example 15.12. With robust standard errors, we can then perform legitimate t-tests.

Assumption 5. The error term ε is not correlated with any of the explanatory variables $x_1, x_2, \ldots, x_k$; or in statistical terminology, there is no endogeneity.

Another crucial assumption in a linear regression model is that the error term is not correlated with the explanatory variables; that is, the explanatory variables are exogenous. In general, this assumption breaks down when important explanatory variables are excluded. If one or more of the relevant explanatory variables are excluded, then the resulting OLS estimators are biased. The extent of the bias depends on the degree of the correlation between the included and the excluded explanatory variables.

Suppose we want to estimate $y = \beta_0 + \beta_1 x + \varepsilon$, where y is salary and x is years of education. This model excludes innate ability, which is an important ingredient for salary. Since ability is omitted, it gets incorporated in the error term and the resulting error term is likely to be correlated with years of education. Now consider someone who is highly educated and also commands a high salary. The model will associate high salary with education, when, in fact, it may be the person's unobserved high level of innate ability that has raised both education and salary. In sum, the violation of assumption 5 leads to unreliable coefficient estimates and, therefore, the linear regression models are unable to establish causality.

Remedy

It is important that we include all relevant explanatory variables in the regression model. An important first step before running a regression model is to compile a comprehensive list of potential explanatory variables. We can then build down to perhaps a smaller list of explanatory variables using the adjusted R^2 criterion. Sometimes, due to data limitations, we are unable to include all relevant variables. For example, innate ability may be an important explanatory variable for a model that explains salary, but we are unable to include it since innate ability is not observable. Specialized models that can be used to establish causality are outside the scope of this text.

Assumption 6. Conditional on $x_1, x_2, \ldots, x_k$, the error term ε is normally distributed.

Given Assumptions 1 through 5, the OLS estimators are unbiased and, among all linear unbiased estimators, they have minimum variations between samples. Assumption 6 allows us to construct interval estimates and conduct tests of significance. If ε is not normally distributed, then the interval estimates and the hypothesis tests are valid only for large samples.

Summary of Regression Modeling

Regression models are an integral part of business statistics. It takes practice to become an effective user of the regression methodology. We should think of regression modeling as an iterative process. We start with a clear understanding of what the regression model is supposed to do. We define the relevant response variable and compile a comprehensive list of potential explanatory variables. The emphasis should be to pick a model that makes economic and intuitive sense and avoid explanatory variables that more or less measure the same thing, thus causing multicollinearity. We then apply this model to data and refine and improve its fit. Specifically, from the comprehensive list, we build down to perhaps a smaller list of explanatory variables using significance tests and goodness-of-fit measures such as the standard error of the estimate and the adjusted R^2. It is important that we explore residual plots to look for signs of changing variability and correlated observations in cross-sectional and time series studies, respectively. If we identify any of these two violations, we can still trust the point estimates of the regression coefficients. However, we cannot place much faith in the standard t or F tests of significance unless we employ the necessary correction.

Using Excel and R for Residual Plots, and R for Robust Standard Errors

Using Excel to Replicate Figure 15.4

Stores

A. Open the ***Stores*** data file.

B. From the menu, choose **Data > Data Analysis > Regression**.

C. For *Input Y Range,* select the Sales observations, and for *Input X Range,* select the Sqft observations.
Select *Residual Plots.* Click **OK.** You should see a graph very similar to Figure 15.4. Formatting (regarding colors, axes, etc.) can be done by selecting **Format** from the menu.

Using R to Replicate Figure 15.4 and Obtain White's Robust Standard Errors

A. Import the ***Stores*** data file into a data frame (table) and label it myData.

B. Install and load the *lmtest* and *sandwich* packages. We use these packages to calculate robust standard errors. Enter:

```
> install.packages("lmtest"); library(lmtest)
> install.packages("sandwich"); library(sandwich)
```

C. Use the **lm** function to estimate the linear regression model. Enter:

```
> Model <- lm(Sales ~ Sqft, data=myData)
```

D. Use the **resid** function to obtain the residuals. Enter:

```
> Residuals <- resid(Model)
```

E. Use the **plot** function to create a scatterplot of the residuals against the explanatory variable, Sqft. We use the *xlab* and *ylab* options to add labels to the x- and y-axes. Enter:

```
> plot(Residuals ~ myData$Sqft, xlab="Sqft", ylab="e")
```

The scatterplot that R returns should look very similar to Figure 15.4.

F. Given the residual plot from Figure 15.4, changing variability is an issue in the model of Sales as a function of Sqft. We use the **coeftest** function to calculate robust standard errors for the OLS estimators. By using the option *type* = "HC1", we are asking R to apply a widely used formula for calculating robust standard errors (other designations within *type* are available in R). Enter:

```
> coeftest(Model, vcov = vcovHC(Model, type = "HC1"))
```

R returns:

	Estimate	Std. Error	t value	Pr(>|t|)
(Intercept)	22.0795111	9.5630163	2.3088	0.02649*
Sqft	0.0591479	0.0064415	9.1823	3.46e-11***

The corrected standard errors for the intercept and Sqft are 9.5630 and 0.0064, respectively. Recall from Example 15.11 that the OLS-generated standard errors for the intercept and Sqft were 10.4764 and 0.0057, respectively. With the corrected standard errors, we can now perform valid t tests of significance.

Sushi

Using Excel to Replicate Figure 15.5

A. Open the ***Sushi*** data file.

B. From the menu, choose **Data > Data Analysis > Regression.**

For *Input Y Range,* select the Sales data, and for *Input X Range,* simultaneously select the AdCost and Unemp observations. Select *Residuals.* Click **OK.**

C. Given the regression output, select the residuals and choose **Insert > Scatter;** choose the option on the top left. (If you are having trouble finding this option after selecting **Insert,** look for the graph with data points above **Charts.**) You should see a graph very similar to Figure 15.5. Formatting (regarding colors, axes, etc.) can be done by selecting **Format** from the menu.

Using R to Replicate Figure 15.5 and Obtain Newey-West Robust Standard Errors

A. Import the ***Sushi*** data file and follow steps A through D from the instructions for Replicating Figure 15.4. Enter:

```
> install.packages("lmtest"); library(lmtest)
> install.packages("sandwich"); library(sandwich)
> Model <- lm(Sales ~ AdCost + Unemp, data=myData)
> Residuals <- resid(Model)
```

B. Use the **plot** function to plot Residuals against time and then use the **abline** function to insert a line at the x-axis. Enter:

```
> plot(Residuals ~ myData$Month, xlab="t", ylab="e"); abline(h=0)
```

The scatterplot that R returns should look very similar to Figure 15.5.

C. Given the scatterplot, correlated observations are an issue in the multiple linear regression model of Sales as a function of AdCost and Unemp. We use the **coeftest** function to find Newey-West standard errors (other options are available in R). Enter:

```
> coeftest(Model, vcov = NeweyWest(Model))
```

R returns:

	Estimate	Std. Error	t value	Pr(>|t|)
(Intercept)	17.5059699	4.7733757	3.6674	0.002536**
AdCost	0.0265511	0.0069616	3.8140	0.001898**
Unemp	−0.6878632	0.3546461	−1.9396	0.072852

The corrected standard errors for the intercept, AdCost, and Unemp are 4.7734, 0.0070, and 0.3546, respectively. Recall from Example 15.12 that the OLS-generated standard errors for the intercept, AdCost, and Unemp were 3.9817, 0.0068, and 0.2997, respectively. The corrected standard errors are all higher than the OLS estimates, which is typically what we expect when observations are correlated. With the corrected standard errors, we can now perform valid t tests of significance.

EXERCISES 15.4

Mechanics

45. Using 20 observations, the multiple regression model $y = \beta_0 + \beta_1 x_1 + \beta_2 x_2 + \varepsilon$ was estimated. A portion of the regression results is as follows:

	df	*SS*	*MS*	*F*	*Significance F*	
Regression	2	2.12E+12	1.06E+12	56.556	3.07E-08	
Residual	17	3.19E+11	1.88E+10			
Total	19	2.44E+12				
	Coefficients	*Standard Error*	*t Stat*	*p-value*	*Lower 95%*	*Upper 95%*
Intercept	−987557	131583	−7.505	0.000	−1265173	−709941
x_1	29233	32653	0.895	0.383	−39660	98125
x_2	30283	32645	0.928	0.367	−38592	99158

a. At the 5% significance level, are the explanatory variables jointly significant?
b. At the 5% significance level, is each explanatory variable individually significant?
c. What is the likely problem with this model?

46. A simple linear regression, $y = \beta_0 + \beta_1 x + \varepsilon$, is estimated with cross-sectional data. The resulting residuals e along with the values of the explanatory variable x are shown in the accompanying table.

x	1	2	5	7	10	14	15	20	24	30
e	−2	1	−3	2	4	−5	−6	8	11	−10

a. Graph the residuals e against the values of the explanatory variable x and look for any discernible pattern.
b. Which assumption is being violated? Discuss its consequences and suggest a possible remedy.

47. A simple linear regression, $y = \beta_0 + \beta_1 x + \varepsilon$, is estimated with time series data. The resulting residuals e and the time variable t are shown in the accompanying table.

t	1	2	3	4	5	6	7	8	9	10
e	−5	−4	−2	3	6	8	4	−5	−3	−2

a. Graph the residuals against time and look for any discernible pattern.
b. Which assumption is being violated? Discuss its consequences and suggest a possible remedy.

Applications

48. **FILE** ***Television.*** Numerous studies have shown that watching too much television hurts school grades. Others have argued that television is not necessarily a bad thing for children. Like books and stories, television not only entertains, it also exposes a child to new information about the world. While watching too much television is harmful, a little bit may actually help. Researcher Matt Castle gathers information on the grade point average (GPA) of 28 middle-school children and the number of hours of television they watched per week. Estimate the model $\text{GPA} = \beta_0 + \beta_1\text{Hours} + \varepsilon$ and plot the residuals against the explanatory variable. Does the model appear correctly specified? Explain.

49. **FILE** ***Delivery.*** Quick2U, a delivery company, would like to standardize its delivery charge model for shipments (Charge in \$) such that customers will better understand their delivery costs. Three explanatory variables are used: (1) distance (in miles), (2) shipment weight (in lbs), and (3) number of boxes. A sample of 30 recent deliveries is collected.
a. Estimate the model $\text{Charge} = \beta_0 + \beta_1\text{Distance} + \beta_2\text{Weight} + \beta_3\text{Boxes} + \varepsilon$ and examine the joint and individual significance of the explanatory variables at the 1% level.
b. Is there any evidence of multicollinearity?
c. Graph the residuals against the predicted values and determine if there is any evidence of changing variability.

50. Consider the results of a survey where students were asked about their GPA and also to break down their typical 24-hour day into study, leisure (including work), and sleep. Consider the model $\text{GPA} = \beta_0 + \beta_1\text{Study} + \beta_2\text{Leisure} + \beta_3\text{Sleep} + \varepsilon$.
a. What is wrong with this model?
b. Suggest a simple way to reformulate the model.

51. **FILE** ***Rental.*** Consider the monthly rent (Rent in \$) of an apartment as a function of the number of bedrooms (Beds), the number of bathrooms (Baths), and square footage (Sqft).
a. Estimate: $\text{Rent} = \beta_0 + \beta_1\text{Beds} + \beta_2\text{Baths} + \beta_3\text{Sqft} + \varepsilon$.
b. Which of the explanatory variables might cause changing variability? Explain.
c. Use residual plots to verify your economic intuition.

52. **FILE** ***Work_Experience.*** Consider the data on salary (in \$) and work experience (in years) of 100 employees in a marketing firm. Estimate the model: $\text{Salary} = \beta_0 + \beta_1\text{Experience} + \varepsilon$.
a. Explain why you would be concerned about changing variability in this application.
b. Use a residual plot to confirm your economic intuition.

53. **FILE** ***Healthy_Living.*** Healthy living has always been an important goal for any society. Consider a regression model that conjectures that fruits and vegetables and regular exercising have a positive effect on health and smoking has a negative effect on health. The sample consists of the percentage of these variables observed in various states in the United States.

a. Estimate the model Healthy $= \beta_0 + \beta_1$FV $+ \beta_2$Exercise $+ \beta_3$Smoke $+ \varepsilon$.

b. Analyze the data to determine if multicollinearity and changing variability are present.

54. **FILE** ***J&J.*** Estimate the capital asset pricing model (CAPM) for Johnson & Johnson where the risk-adjusted stock return (JJ_Adj) is the response variable and the risk-adjusted market return (Market_Adj) is the explanatory variable. Since serial correlation may occur with time series data, it is prudent to inspect the behavior of the residuals. Construct a scatterplot of the residuals against time to comment on correlated observations.

55. **FILE** ***Consumption.*** The consumption function is one of the key relationships in economics, where consumption y depends on disposable income x. The accompanying data file shows quarterly data for these seasonally adjusted variables, measured in billions of dollars.

a. Estimate $y = \beta_0 + \beta_1 x + \varepsilon$. Plot the residuals against time to determine if there is a possibility of correlated observations.

b. Discuss the consequences of correlated observations and suggest a possible remedy.

56. **FILE** ***Mowers.*** The marketing manager at Turfco, a lawn mower company, believes that monthly sales across all outlets (stores, online, etc.) are influenced by three key variables: (1) outdoor temperature (in °F), (2) advertising expenditures (in $1,000s), and (3) promotional discounts (in %). The accompanying data file shows monthly sales data over the past two years.

a. Estimate the model Sales $= \beta_0 + \beta_1$Temperature $+ \beta_2$Advertising $+ \beta_3$Discount $+ \varepsilon$, and test for the joint and individual significance of the explanatory variables at the 5% level.

b. Examine the data for evidence of multicollinearity. Provide two reasons why it might be best to do nothing about multicollinearity in this application.

c. Examine the residual plots for evidence of changing variability.

15.5 WRITING WITH BIG DATA

Case Study

FILE
House_Price

Develop a predictive model for the price of a house in the college town of Ames, Iowa. Before evaluating various models, you first have to filter out the ***House_Price*** data to get the appropriate subset of observations for selected variables. After you have obtained the preferred model, summarize your findings as well as predict the price of a house in Ames, Iowa, given typical values of the explanatory variables.

Sample Report—Investing In College Town Real Estate

Dmytro Zinkevych/Shutterstock

Investing in college town real estate can be a smart move. First, students offer a steady stream of rental demand as many cash-strapped public universities are unable to house their students beyond freshman year. Second, this demand is projected to grow. The National Center for Education Statistics predicts that college enrollment in the U.S. will reach 19.8 million students by 2025, an increase of 14% from its 2014 enrollment of 17.3 million.

A regression analysis is conducted to determine the factors that influence the sale price of a single-family house in Ames, Iowa—home to Iowa State University. For a sample of 209 single-family houses, the following data are collected: the house's sale price (Price in $), the number of bedrooms (Beds), the number of bathrooms (Baths), the square footage (Sqft), and the lot size

(LSize in square feet). Table 15.19 shows the mean values of the relevant variables for newer houses (those built in 2000 or after), old houses (those built prior to 2000), and for all houses in the sample. Median values are shown in parentheses.

TABLE 15.19 The Mean (Median) of Variables for New, Old, and All Houses

Variables	New Houses	Old Houses	All Houses
Price	326,134 (292,000)	209,552 (190,500)	230,191 (215,000)
Beds	3.68 (4.00)	3.22 (3.00)	3.30 (3.00)
Baths	3.06 (3.00)	2.20 (2.00)	2.36 (2.00)
Sqft	1,867 (1,691)	1,596 (1,444)	1,644 (1,515)
LSize	18,137 (10,361)	19,464 (10,123)	19,229 (10,171)
Number of Observations	37	172	209

The average sale price for the newer houses is substantially more than that for the older houses. For all houses, given that the mean is higher than the median, the house price distribution is positively skewed, indicating that a few expensive houses have pulled up the mean above the median. The square footage and the lot size are also positively skewed. Finally, relatively newer houses have more bedrooms, bathrooms, and square footage but a smaller lot size. This is consistent with a 2017 article in *Building* magazine that found that newer houses have become 24% bigger over the past 15 years, while lot sizes have shrunk 16%.

In order to analyze the factors that may influence the price of a house, the following linear regression model is considered:

$$\text{Price} = \beta_0 + \beta_1\,\text{Beds} + \beta_2\,\text{Baths} + \beta_3\,\text{Sqft} + \beta_4\,\text{Lsize} + \varepsilon$$

It is expected that Beds, Bath, Sqft, and Lsize will have a positive relationship with Price; that is, a house with more bedrooms and bathrooms is expected to obtain a higher price than one with fewer bedrooms and bathrooms. Similarly, a bigger house, or one on a bigger lot, is expected to obtain a higher price. Column 2 of Table 15.20 shows the regression results from estimating this complete model.

TABLE 15.20 Estimates of Alternative Regression Models to Predict House Price, $n = 209$

Variables	Complete Model	Restricted Model
Intercept	−14,209.45 (0.455)	−6,873.47 (0.634)
Beds	4,029.47 (0.552)	NA
Baths	43,792.52* (0.000)	45,141.73* (0.000)
Sqft	73.26* (0.000)	75.04* (0.000)
Lsize	0.40* (0.001)	0.39* (0.001)
s_e	68,867.60	68,759.21
R^2	0.6220	0.6214
Adjusted R^2	0.6146	0.6158
F-stat (p-value)	83.93* (0.000)	112.14* (0.000)

Notes: Parameter estimates are in the top half of the table with the p-values in parentheses; * represents significance at the 5% level. NA denotes not applicable. The lower part of the table contains goodness-of-fit measures.

With the exception of Beds, all explanatory are correctly signed and statistically significant. Perhaps the lack of significance of Beds is due to multicollinearity because the number of bedrooms is likely to be correlated with the number of bathrooms as well as square footage. An alternative explanation might be that additional bedrooms add value only in houses with large square footage. For comparison, a restricted model is estimated that omits Beds from the list of explanatory variables; see Column 3 of Table 15.20 for the results.

The following observations are made:

- The restricted model is preferred because it has the lower standard error of the estimate s_e and the higher adjusted R^2.
- Holding other factors constant, an additional bathroom adds about $45,142 in value. Similarly, a 100-square-foot increase in a house adds $7,504 in value and a 1,000-square-foot increase in the lot size adds $390 in value.
- The coefficient of determination reveals that 62.14% of the variability in sale price is explained by the explanatory variables, implying that approximately 37.86% is unexplained. This is not surprising because other factors, such as the condition of the house or its proximity to nearby amenities, are likely to influence the sales price.
- Suppose a 1,600-square-foot house with two bathrooms sits on a 15,000-square-foot lot. Given the preferred model, its predicted sale price is $209,320.

Suggested Case Studies

Report 15.1 FILE ***House_Price.*** Perform a similar analysis to the one conducted in this section, but choose another college town.

Report 15.2 FILE ***College_Admissions.*** Choose a college of interest and use the sample of enrolled students to best predict a student's college grade point average. Use tests of significance along with goodness-of-fit measures to find the best predictive model. Use the preferred model to construct and interpret relevant confidence and prediction intervals based on select values of the explanatory variables. In order to estimate these models, you have to first filter the data to include only the enrolled students.

Report 15.3 FILE ***TechSales_Reps.*** Develop a regression model for predicting the salary of a sales representative in the software product group. Explore models that include personality type variables along with other relevant explanatory variables. Use the preferred model to test if personality type variables are jointly significant. Consider grouping sentinels with analysts and explorers with diplomats for improved predictability.

CONCEPTUAL REVIEW

LO 15.1 Conduct tests of significance.

A test of joint significance determines whether the explanatory variables $x_1, x_2, \ldots, x_k$ in a multiple regression model have a joint statistically significant influence on y. The value of the test statistic is calculated as $F_{(df_1, df_2)} = \frac{MSR}{MSE}$, where $df_1 = k$, $df_2 = n - k - 1$, MSR is the mean square regression, and MSE is the mean square error. If the null hypothesis is rejected, then the explanatory variables are jointly significant.

A test of individual significance determines whether the explanatory variable x_j has an individual statistical influence on y. The value of the test statistic is calculated as $t_{df} = \frac{b_j - \beta_{j0}}{se(b_j)}$, where $df = n - k - 1$, $se(b_j)$ is the standard error of the OLS estimator b_j, and β_{j0} is the hypothesized value of β_j. If $\beta_{j0} = 0$, the value of the test statistic reduces to $t_{df} = \frac{b_j}{se(b_j)}$. If the null hypothesis is rejected, then the explanatory variable x_j is significant.

The $100(1 - \alpha)\%$ confidence interval for the regression coefficient β_j is given by $b_j \pm t_{\alpha/2, df}\, se(b_j)$, where $df = n - k - 1$.

LO 15.2 **Conduct a general test of linear restrictions.**

When testing linear restrictions, the value of the test statistic is calculated as $F_{(df_1,df_2)} = \frac{(SSE_R - SSE_U)/df_1}{SSE_U/df_2}$, where df_1 is equal to the number of linear restrictions, $df_2 = n - k - 1$ (k is the number of explanatory variables in the unrestricted model), and SSE_R and SSE_U are the error sum of squares of the restricted and unrestricted models, respectively. If the null hypothesis is rejected, then the linear restrictions are not valid.

LO 15.3 **Calculate and interpret confidence intervals and prediction intervals.**

For specific values of $x_1, x_2, \ldots, x_k$, denoted by $x_1^0, x_2^0, \ldots, x_k^0$, the $100(1 - \alpha)\%$ confidence interval for the expected value of y is given by $\hat{y}^0 \pm t_{\alpha/2,df} se(\hat{y}^0)$, where $df = n - k - 1$ and $se(\hat{y}^0)$ is the standard error of $\hat{y}^0$. To derive $\hat{y}^0$ together with $se(\hat{y}^0)$, we first estimate a modified regression model where y is the response variable and the explanatory variables are defined as $x_1^* = x_1 - x_1^0, x_2^* = x_2 - x_2^0, \ldots, x_k^* = x_k - x_k^0$. The resulting estimate of the intercept and its standard error equal $\hat{y}^0$ and $se(\hat{y}^0)$, respectively.

For specific values of $x_1, x_2, \ldots, x_k$, denoted by $x_1^0, x_2^0, \ldots, x_k^0$, the $100(1 - \alpha)\%$ prediction interval for an individual value of y is given by $\hat{y} \pm t_{\alpha/2,df} \sqrt{(se(\hat{y}^0))^2 + s_e^2}$, where $df = n - k - 1$, $se(\hat{y}^0)$ is the standard error of $\hat{y}^0$, and s_e is the standard error of the estimate derived from the modified regression model used for the confidence interval.

LO 15.4 **Address common violations of the OLS assumptions.**

Under the assumptions of the classical linear regression model, OLS provides the best estimates.

The assumptions are as follows:

Assumption 1. The regression model given by $y = \beta_0 + \beta_1 x_1 + \beta_2 x_2 + \ldots + \beta_k x_k + \varepsilon$ is linear in the parameters and is correctly specified.

Assumption 2. There is no exact linear relationship among the explanatory variables; or, in statistical terminology, there is no perfect multicollinearity.

Assumption 3. Conditional on $x_1, x_2, \ldots, x_k$, the variance of the error term ε is the same for all observations (constant variability); or in statistical terminology, there is no heteroskedasticity.

Assumption 4. Conditional on $x_1, x_2, \ldots, x_k$, the error term ε is uncorrelated across observations; or in statistical terminology, there is no serial correlation.

Assumption 5. The error term ε is not correlated with any of the explanatory variables $x_1, x_2, \ldots, x_k$; or in statistical terminology, there is no endogeneity.

Assumption 6. Conditional on $x_1, x_2, \ldots, x_k$, the error term ε is normally distributed.

However, the desirable properties of the OLS estimators become compromised as one or more model assumptions are violated. In addition, for certain violations, the estimated standard errors of the OLS estimators are inappropriate; in these cases it is not possible to make meaningful inferences from the t and F test results.

ADDITIONAL EXERCISES

57. **FILE** ***Apple.*** The accompanying data file has the monthly returns (in %) for Apple over a five-year period. Estimate the capital asset pricing model (CAPM) for Apple where the risk-adjusted stock return (Apple_Adj) is the response variable and the risk-adjusted market return (Market_Adj) is the explanatory variable.
    a. At the 5% significance level, is Apple's return riskier than that of the market?
    b. At the 5% significance level, do abnormal returns exist?
    c. Use a residual plot to analyze the potential problem of correlated observations.

58. **FILE** ***Quotations.*** The labor estimation group at Sturdy Electronics, a contract electronics manufacturer of printed circuit boards, wants to simplify the process it uses to quote production costs to potential customers. They have identified the primary drivers for production time (and thus production cost) as being the number of electronic parts that can be machine-installed and the number of parts that must be manually installed. Accordingly, they develop a multiple regression model to predict production time, measured as minutes per board, using a random sample of 25 recent product quotations.
   a. Predict production time for a circuit board with 475 machine-installed components and 16 manually installed components.
   b. What proportion of the sample variability in production time is explained by the two explanatory variables?
   c. At the 5% significance level, are the explanatory variables jointly significant? Are they individually significant?

59. **FILE** ***Happiness_Age.*** A sociologist wishes to study the relationship between happiness and age. He interviews 24 individuals and collects data on each person's age and happiness, where happiness is measured on a scale from 0 to 100. Estimate: Happiness $= \beta_0 + \beta_1$Age $+ \varepsilon$. At the 1% significance level, is Age significant in explaining Happiness?

60. **FILE** ***Home_Ownership.*** In order to determine if home ownership (Ownership, in %) is linked with income (Income in \$), an analyst uses state-level data and estimates the model: Ownership $= \beta_0 + \beta_1$Income $+ \varepsilon$.
   a. At the 5% significance level, is Income linearly related to Ownership?
   b. Construct the 95% confidence interval for the expected value of Ownership if Income is \$50,000.
   c. Compare the above confidence interval with the 95% prediction interval for Ownership if Income is \$50,000.

61. **FILE** ***SAT.*** A researcher studies the relationship between SAT scores, the test-taker's family income (Income), and his/her grade point average (GPA). Data are collected from 24 students. She estimates the following model: SAT $= \beta_0 + \beta_1$Income $+ \beta_2$GPA $+ \varepsilon$.
   a. At the 5% significance level, are Income and GPA jointly significant?
   b. At the 5% significance level, are Income and GPA individually significant?
   c. With 95% confidence, construct the prediction interval for the individual SAT score if Income is \$80,000 and GPA is 3.5.

62. **FILE** ***Turnover_Expense.*** George believes that the returns of mutual funds are influenced by annual turnover rates and annual expense ratios. In order to substantiate his claim, he collects data on 20 mutual funds and estimates the following model:

$$\text{Return} = \beta_0 + \beta_1 \text{Turnover} + \beta_2 \text{Expense} + \varepsilon.$$

   a. Conduct appropriate tests to verify George's theory at the 5% significance level.
   b. Discuss the potential problems of multicollinearity and changing variability.

63. **FILE** ***Crime.*** A government researcher examines the factors that influence a city's crime rate. For 41 cities, she collects the crime rate (crimes per 100,000 residents), the poverty rate (in %), the median income (in \$1,000s), the percent of residents younger than 18, and the percent of residents older than 65.
   a. Estimate: Crime $= \beta_0 + \beta_1$Poverty $+ \beta_2$Income $+ \beta_3$Under 18 $+ \beta_4$Over 65 $+ \varepsilon$. Discuss the individual and joint significance of the explanatory variables at the 5% significance level.
   b. At the 5% level, conduct a partial F test to determine if the influence of Under 18 is different from that of Over 65.
   c. Which explanatory variables are likely to be collinear? Find their sample correlation coefficients to confirm.

64. **FILE** ***Quarterbacks.*** American football is the highest paying sport on a per-game basis. The quarterback, considered the most important player on the team, is appropriately compensated. A sports statistician wants to estimate a multiple linear regression model that links the quarterback's salary (in \$ millions) with his pass completion percentage (PC), total touchdowns scored (TD), and his age. He collects data for 32 quarterbacks during a recent season.
   a. Estimate: Salary $= \beta_0 + \beta_1$PC $+ \beta_2$TD $+ \beta_3$Age $+ \varepsilon$. Show the regression results in a well-formatted table.
   b. Determine whether the explanatory variables are jointly significant at the 5% significance level.
   c. Establish whether the explanatory variables are individually significant at the 5% significance level.
   d. Determine whether PC and Age are jointly significant at the 5% significance level.
   e. Construct the 95% confidence interval for the expected salary of a quarterback using average values of PC, TD, and Age.

65. **FILE** ***Smoking.*** A nutritionist wants to understand the influence of income and healthy food on the incidence of smoking. He collects data on the percentage of smokers in each state in the U.S. and

the corresponding median income (in \$) and the percentage of the population that regularly eats fruits and vegetables.

a. Estimate: Smoke $= \beta_0 + \beta_1$FV $+ \beta_2$Income $+ \varepsilon$.

b. At the 5% level of significance, are the explanatory variables jointly and individually significant? Explain.

c. Use the sample correlation coefficients to evaluate the potential problem of multicollinearity.

66. FILE ***PerCapita.*** Consider a regression model for per capita income, y. The explanatory variables consist of the percentage of the population in the U.S. that is (a) without a high school diploma, x_1, (b) foreign born, x_2, and (c) non-English speaking, x_3.

a. Estimate the model, $y = \beta_0 + \beta_1 x_1 + \beta_2 x_2 + \beta_3 x_3 + \varepsilon$, and test for the joint and individual significance of the explanatory variables at the 5% level.

b. What proportion of the sample variability in per capita income is explained by the explanatory variables?

c. Do you suspect multicollinearity in the model? Use sample data to confirm.

67. FILE ***MCAS.*** A researcher examines the factors that influence student performance. She gathers data on 224 school districts in Massachusetts. The response variable is the students' mean score on a standardized test (Score). She uses four explanatory variables in her analysis: the student-to-teacher ratio (STR in %), the average teacher's salary (TSAL in \$1,000s), the median household income (INC in \$1,000s), and the percentage of single family households (SGL).

a. Estimate: Score $= \beta_0 + \beta_1$STR $+ \beta_2$TSAL $+ \beta_3$INC $+ \beta_4$SGL $+ \varepsilon$. Show the regression results in a well-formatted table.

b. Suppose you want to test if school input factors, STR and TSAL, are significant in explaining Score. Specify the competing hypotheses. Estimate the restricted model. At the 5% significance level, can you conclude that STR and TSAL are jointly significant?

c. Suppose you want to test if socioeconomic factors, INC and SGL, are significant in explaining Score. Specify the competing hypotheses. Estimate the restricted model. At the 5% significance level, can you conclude that INC and SGL are jointly significant?

68. FILE ***Starts.*** An analyst for a mortgage company wants to better understand the quantitative relationship between housing starts (in 1,000s), the mortgage rate (in %), and the unemployment rate (in %). She gathers seasonally adjusted monthly data on these variables for a five-year period, and estimates a multiple regression model for housing starts as a function of the mortgage rate and the unemployment rate.

a. At the 5% significance level, are the explanatory variables jointly and individually significant?

b. Examine the potential problems of multicollinearity and correlated observations in this time series data application.

APPENDIX 15.1 Guidelines for Other Software Packages

The following section provides brief commands for Minitab, SPSS, and JMP. Import the specified data file into the relevant software spreadsheet prior to following the commands.

Minitab

Confidence and Prediction Intervals for *y*

FILE *Baseball*

A. (Replicating Examples 15.7 and 15.8) From the menu, choose **Stat > Regression > Regression > Fit Regression Model.** Select Win as Response and select BA and ERA as **Continuous Predictors.**

B. From the menu, choose **Stat > Regression > Regression > Predict.** Enter 0.25 for BA and 4 for ERA.

Residual Plots—Changing Variability

Stores

(Replicating Figure 15.4) From the menu, choose **Stat > Regression > Regression > Fit Regression Model.** Select Sales as **Response** and select Sqft as **Continuous Predictors.** Choose **Graphs.** Under **Residuals Plots,** select **Individual plots,** and under **Residuals versus the variables,** select Sqft.

Residual Plots—Correlated Observations

(Replicating Figure 15.5) From the menu, choose **Stat > Regression > Regression > Fit Regression Model.** Select Sales as **Response** and select AdCost and Unemp as **Continuous Predictors.** Choose **Graphs.** Under **Residuals Plots,** select **Individual plots,** and then select **Residuals versus order.**

SPSS

Residual Plots—Changing Variability

A. (Replicating Figure 15.4) From the menu, choose **Analyze > Regression > Linear.** Select Sales as **Dependent** and select Sqft as **Independent(s).** Choose **Save,** and under **Residuals,** select **Unstandardized.**

B. From the menu, choose **Graphs > Legacy Dialogs > Scatter/Dot > Simple Scatter.** Select Unstandardized Residual as **Y Axis** and select Sqft as **X Axis.**

Residual Plots—Correlated Observations

A. (Replicating Figure 15.5)
From the menu, choose **Analyze > Regression > Linear.** Select Sales as **Dependent** and select AdCost and Unemp as **Independent(s).** Choose **Save,** and under **Residuals,** select **Unstandardized.**

B. From the menu, choose **Graphs > Legacy Dialogs > Scatter/Dot > Simple Scatter.** Select Unstandardized Residual as **Y Axis** and select Month as **X Axis.**

JMP

Confidence and Prediction Intervals for *y*

A. (Replicating Examples 15.7 and 15.8) In the ***Baseball*** spreadsheet, add the observations 0.25 for BA and 4 for ERA in the 31st row.

B. From the menu, choose **Analyze > Fit Model.** Drag Win to the **Y** box, and drag BA and ERA to the box under **Construct Model Effects.**

C. Click on the red triangle next to **Response Win,** and select **Save Columns > Mean Confidence Interval;** then click on the red triangle next to **Response Win,** and select **Save Columns > Indiv Confidence Interval.**

Residual Plots—Changing Variability

A. (Replicating Figure 15.4) From the menu, choose **Analyze > Fit Y by X.** Drag Sales to the **Y, Response** box and drag Sqft to the **X, Factor** box.

B. Click on the red triangle next to **Bivariate Fit Sales by Sqft,** and select **Fit Line.**

C. Click on the red triangle next to **Linear Fit,** and select **Plot Residuals.**

Residual Plots—Correlated Observations

A. (Replicating Figure 15.5) From the menu, choose **Analyze > Fit Model.** Drag Sales to the **Y** box, and drag AdCost and Unemp to the box under **Construct Model Effects.**

B. Click on the red triangle next to **Response Sales,** select **Row Diagnostics > Plot Residual by Row.**

16 Regression Models for Nonlinear Relationships

LEARNING OBJECTIVES

After reading this chapter you should be able to:

LO **16.1** **Use and evaluate polynomial regression models.**

LO **16.2** **Use and evaluate log-transformed models.**

LO **16.3** **Describe the method used to compare linear models with log-transformed models.**

In Chapters 14 and 15, we discussed linear regression models where the partial effect of an explanatory variable on the response variable is constant. For example, when evaluating salaries, a linear regression model assumes that each year the salary changes by the same amount, regardless of age.

There are numerous applications where the relationship between the explanatory variable and the response variable cannot be represented by a straight line and, therefore, must be captured by an appropriate curve. Continuing with the salary example, it is common to find an inverted U-shaped relationship between salary and age, where the salary increases with age up to a point and then it decreases. There are also examples where each year the salary increase is more than the increase in the previous year.

In this chapter, we will discuss common nonlinear specifications by making simple transformations of the variables. These transformations include squares and natural logarithms, which capture interesting nonlinear relationships while still allowing easy estimation within the framework of a linear regression model.

Finally, we will discuss goodness-of-fit measures, including R^2 and adjusted R^2, that allow us to choose between linear and nonlinear specifications.

Yellow Dog Productions/Getty Images

INTRODUCTORY CASE

Rental Market in College Towns

Real estate investment in college towns often promises good returns (*The College Investor*, August 22, 2017). First, students offer a steady stream of rental demand as cash-strapped public universities are unable to house their students beyond freshman year. Second, this demand is projected to grow as more children of baby boomers head to college. Marcela Treisman works for an investment firm in Michigan. Her assignment is to analyze the rental market in campus towns around the country.

Marcela wants to understand the type of off-campus homes that promise good rental income. She gathers data on monthly rent (Rent, in $) in a Midwestern campus town, along with three characteristics of the home: number of bedrooms (Beds), number of bathrooms (Baths), and square footage (Sqft). A portion of the data is shown in Table 16.1.

TABLE 16.1 Rental Homes in a Midwestern Campus Town

Rent	Beds	Baths	Sqft
645	1	1	500
675	1	1	648
⋮	⋮	⋮	⋮
2400	3	2.5	2700

College_Town

Marcela would like to use the sample information to

1. Evaluate various regression models that quantify the relationship between rent and home characteristics.
2. Use model selection criteria to select the most appropriate model.
3. Make predictions for rental income for specific values of home characteristics.

A synopsis of this case is provided at the end of Section 16.2.

LO 16.1

16.1 POLYNOMIAL REGRESSION MODELS

Use and evaluate polynomial regression models.

Linear regression models are often justified on the basis of their computational simplicity. An implication of a simple linear regression model, $y = \beta_0 + \beta_1 x + \varepsilon$, is that if x goes up by one unit, the expected value of y changes by β_1, irrespective of the value of x. However, in many applications, the relationship cannot be represented by a straight line and, therefore, must be captured by an appropriate curve. We note that the linearity assumption discussed in Chapter 15 places the restriction of linearity on the parameters and not on the variables. Consequently, we can capture many interesting nonlinear relationships, within the framework of a linear regression model, by making simple transformations of the response and/or the explanatory variables.

The Quadratic Regression Model

If you ever studied microeconomics, you may have learned that a firm's (or industry's) average cost curve tends to be U-shaped. Due to economies of scale, the average cost y of a firm initially decreases as output x increases. However, as x increases beyond a certain point, its impact on y turns positive. Other applications show the influence of the explanatory variable initially positive but then turning negative, leading to an inverted U shape. The **quadratic regression model** appropriately captures these shapes where the influence of x on y, changes in magnitude as well as sign.

A quadratic regression model with one explanatory variable is specified as $y = \beta_0 + \beta_1 x + \beta_2 x^2 + \varepsilon$; we can easily extend it to include multiple explanatory variables. The expression $\beta_0 + \beta_1 x + \beta_2 x^2$ is the deterministic component of a quadratic regression model. In other words, conditional on x, $E(y) = \beta_0 + \beta_1 x + \beta_2 x^2$. This model can easily be estimated by running a regression of y on x and x^2.

Figure 16.1 shows two scatterplots of sample data with superimposed trendlines for the quadratic regression model. Although the linear trendline is not included in either panel, it is clear that the quadratic regression model provides a better fit.

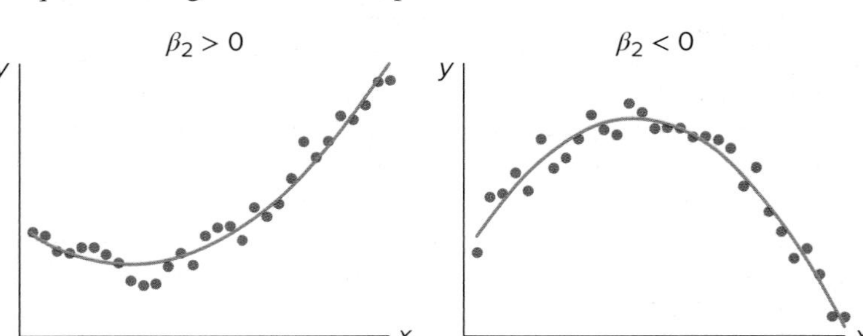

FIGURE 16.1 Scatterplots of y against x with superimposed quadratic trendlines

It is important to be able to determine whether a quadratic regression model provides a better fit than the linear regression model. Recall from Chapters 14 and 15 that we cannot compare these models on the basis of their respective R^2 values because the quadratic regression model uses one more parameter than the linear regression model. For comparison purposes, we will use adjusted R^2, which imposes a penalty for the additional parameter.

In order to estimate the quadratic regression model $y = \beta_0 + \beta_1 x + \beta_2 x^2 + \varepsilon$, we have to first create a variable x^2 that contains the squared values of x. The quadratic model is estimated in the usual way as $\hat{y} = b_0 + b_1 x + b_2 x^2$, where b_1 and b_2 are the estimates of β_1 and β_2, respectively. It is advisable to use unrounded coefficient estimates for making predictions.

Interpretation of coefficients in the quadratic regression model: It does not make sense to think of b_1 in the estimated quadratic regression equation as being the effect of changing x by one unit, holding the square of x constant. In nonlinear models, the sample regression equation is best interpreted by calculating, and even graphing, the predicted effect on the response variable over a range of values for the explanatory variable. We will elaborate on this point in Examples 16.2 and 16.3.

Evaluating the marginal effect of *x* on *y* in the quadratic regression model: It is important to evaluate the estimated marginal (partial) effect of the explanatory variable x

on the predicted value of the response variable; that is, we want to evaluate the change in $\hat{y}$ due to a one-unit increase in x. In the estimated linear regression equation $\hat{y} = b_0 + b_1x$, the partial (marginal) effect is constant, estimated by the slope coefficient b_1. In a quadratic regression model, it can be shown that the partial effect of x on $\hat{y}$ can be approximated by $b_1 + 2b_2x$. This partial effect, unlike in the case of a linear regression model, depends on the value at which x is evaluated. In addition, $\hat{y}$ reaches a maximum ($b_2 < 0$) or minimum ($b_2 > 0$) when the partial effect equals zero. The value of x when this happens is obtained from solving the equation $b_1 + 2b_2x = 0$, as $x = \frac{-b_1}{2b_2}$. (Note that the optimum is obtained where the first derivative, $b_1 + 2b_2x$, equals zero and the second derivative, $2b_2$, is negative for a maximum and positive for a minimum.)

THE QUADRATIC REGRESSION MODEL

In a quadratic regression model $y = \beta_0 + \beta_1x + \beta_2x^2 + \varepsilon$, the coefficient β_2 determines whether the relationship between x and y is U-shaped ($\beta_2 > 0$) or inverted U-shaped ($\beta_2 < 0$).

- Predictions with a quadratic model are made by $\hat{y} = b_0 + b_1x + b_2x^2$, where b_0, b_1, and b_2 are the coefficient estimates.
- It is common to use adjusted R^2 to choose between linear and quadratic regression models.
- $\hat{y}$ reaches a maximum or a minimum where $x = \frac{-b_1}{2b_2}$.
- It is advisable to use unrounded coefficient estimates for making predictions.

EXAMPLE 16.1

Table 16.2 shows a portion of the average cost (AC, in \$) and annual output (in millions of units) for 20 manufacturing firms. We also include a column of Output^2, which we created for estimating the quadratic regression model.

TABLE 16.2 Average Cost and Output Data for 20 Manufacturing Firms

AC	Output	Output^2
9.61	4	16
9.55	5	25
⋮	⋮	⋮
9.62	11	121

Average_Cost

a. Use the scatterplot of average cost against output to suggest an appropriate regression model.

b. Estimate the linear and the quadratic regression models. Determine which model fits the data best.

c. Use the best-fitting model to predict the average cost for a firm that produces 7 million units.

SOLUTION:

a. It is always informative to begin with a scatterplot of the response variable against the explanatory variable. Make sure that the response variable is on the vertical axis. Figure 16.2 shows average cost against output. We also superimpose linear and quadratic trendlines on the scatterplot. (In Excel, right-click on the scatterpoints, add Trendline, and choose Linear and Polynomial with Order 2.). At lower and higher levels of output, average costs are highest, implying that the relationship between average cost and output in this industry is U-shaped. It appears that average cost would best be estimated using a quadratic regression model.

FIGURE 16.2 Scatterplot of average cost versus output

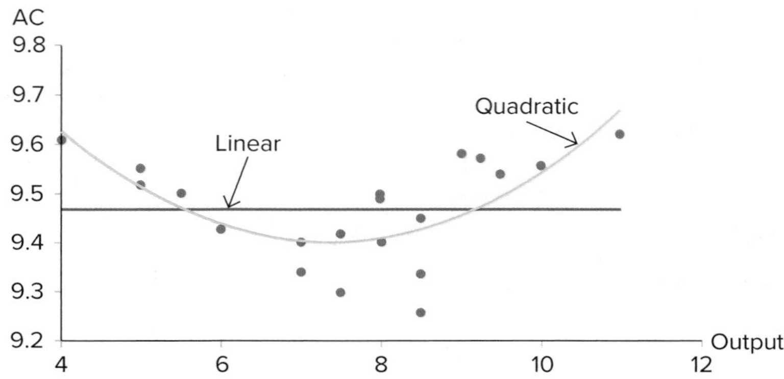

b. The second column of Table 16.3 shows the regression results for the linear regression model: $AC = \beta_0 + \beta_1 Output + \varepsilon$. The linear regression model provides a poor fit, which is not surprising given the scatterplot in Figure 16.2. Not only is Output statistically insignificant, the adjusted R^2 is negative. In order to estimate a quadratic regression model, we have to first create the squared Output variable. A portion of the observations for this variable, computed by squaring Output, is shown in Table 16.2. The third column of Table 16.3 shows the regression results for the quadratic regression model: $AC = \beta_0 + \beta_1 Output + \beta_2 Output^2 + \varepsilon$. In the quadratic regression model, Output is now significant. In addition, the slope coefficient of $Output^2$ is positive and significant, indicating a U-shaped relationship between average cost and output.

TABLE 16.3 Estimates of the Linear and the Quadratic Regression Models for Example 16.1

Variable	Linear Regression Model	Quadratic Regression Model
Intercept	9.4461* (0.000)	10.5225* (0.000)
Output	0.0029 (0.841)	−0.3073* (0.001)
$Output^2$	NA	0.0210* (0.001)
Adjusted R^2	−0.0531	0.4540

Notes: Parameter estimates are in the main body of the table with the p-values in parentheses; NA denotes not applicable; * represents significance at the 5% level. The last row presents adjusted R^2 for model comparison.

Given the adjusted R^2 of 0.4540, the quadratic regression model is clearly better than the linear regression model in explaining average cost.

c. Using unrounded coefficient estimates of the quadratic regression model, the predicted average cost for a firm that produces 7 million units is

$$\widehat{AC} = 10.5225 - 0.3073 \times 7 + 0.0210 \times 7^2 = \$9.40.$$

EXAMPLE 16.2

Use the results from estimating the quadratic regression model in Example 16.1 to answer the following questions.

a. What is the change in average cost going from an output level of 4 million units to 5 million units?

b. What is the change in average cost going from an output level of 8 million units to 9 million units? Compare this result to the result found in part a.

c. What is the output level that minimizes average cost?

SOLUTION:

We will again use unrounded estimates for the analysis.

a. The predicted average cost for a firm that produces 4 million units is:

$$\widehat{AC} = 10.5225 - 0.3073 \times 4 + 0.0210 \times 4^2 = \$9.63.$$

The predicted average cost for a firm that produces 5 million units is:

$$\widehat{AC} = 10.5225 - 0.3073 \times 5 + 0.0210 \times 5^2 = \$9.51.$$

An increase in output from 4 to 5 million units (a one-unit increase in x) results in a \$0.12 decrease (\$9.63 – \$9.51) in predicted average cost.

b. The predicted average cost for a firm that produces 8 million units is:

$$\widehat{AC} = 10.5225 - 0.3073 \times 8 + 0.0210 \times 8^2 = \$9.41.$$

The predicted average cost for a firm that produces 9 million units is:

$$\widehat{AC} = 10.5225 - 0.3073 \times 9 + 0.0210 \times 9^2 = \$9.46.$$

An increase in output from 8 to 9 million units (a one-unit increase in x) results in a \$0.05 increase in predicted average cost. Comparing this result to the one found in part a, we note that a one-unit change in x depends on the value at which x is evaluated. A one-unit increase in output from 4 to 5 million units results in a \$0.12 decrease in predicted average cost, while a one-unit increase in output from 8 to 9 million units results in a \$0.05 increase in predicted average cost. Depending on the value at which x is evaluated, a one-unit change in x may have a positive or negative influence on y, and the magnitude of this effect is not constant.

c. Given $b_1 = -0.3073$ and $b_2 = 0.0210$, the output level that minimizes average cost is $x = \frac{-b_1}{2b_2} = \frac{-(-0.3073)}{2 \times 0.0210} = 7.30$ million units. This result is consistent with the lowest point on the superimposed quadratic trendline in Figure 16.2.

Let's now turn to an example with an inverted U-shaped relationship.

EXAMPLE 16.3

It is widely believed that wages of workers decline as they get older. A young worker can expect wages to rise with age only up to a certain point, beyond which wages begin to fall. Ioannes Papadopoulos works in the human resources department of a large manufacturing firm and is examining the relationship between wages (in \$), education (in years of school), and age. Specifically, he wants to verify the quadratic effect of age on wages. He gathers data on 80 workers in his firm with information on their hourly wage, education, and age. A portion of the data is shown in Table 16.4.

TABLE 16.4 Hourly Wage, Education, and Age; $n = 80$

Wage	Education	Age
17.54	12	76
20.93	10	61
⋮	⋮	⋮
23.66	12	49

Wages

a. Estimate a linear regression model for Wage using Education and Age as explanatory variables and then extend it to allow for a possible quadratic effect of Age. Choose between the two models using the appropriate scatterplot and goodness-of-fit measure.

b. Use the preferred model to predict hourly wages for someone with 16 years of education and Age equal to 30, 50, and 70.

c. According to the preferred model, at what Age is Wage maximized?

SOLUTION:

a. Figure 16.3 shows a scatterplot of Wage against Age with superimposed linear and quadratic trendlines. It seems that the quadratic regression model provides a better fit for the data as compared to the linear regression model.

FIGURE 16.3 Scatterplot of Wage versus Age

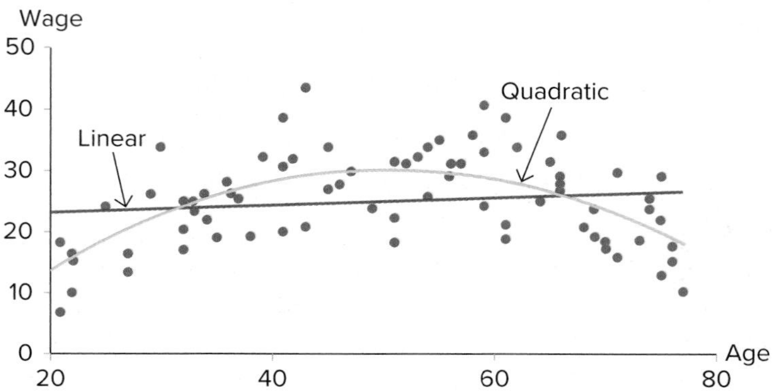

We estimate two regression models.

Linear Model: $\text{Wage} = \beta_0 + \beta_1\text{Education} + \beta_2\text{Age} + \varepsilon$

Quadratic Model: $\text{Wage} = \beta_0 + \beta_1\text{Education} + \beta_2\text{Age} + \beta_3\text{Age}^2 + \varepsilon$

For ease of exposition, we use the same notation for the coefficients in the linear and the quadratic models even though they have a different meaning depending on the model we reference. Note that in order to estimate the quadratic regression model, we first create observations for the variable Age^2. Table 16.5 shows the relevant regression results for the linear and the quadratic regression models.

TABLE 16.5 Estimates of the Linear and the Quadratic Regression Models for Example 16.3

Variable	Linear Model	Quadratic Model
Intercept	2.6381 (0.268)	−22.7219* (0.000)
Education	1.4410* (0.000)	1.2540* (0.000)
Age	0.0472 (0.127)	1.3500* (0.000)
Age^2	NA	−0.0133* (0.000)
Adjusted R^2	0.6088	0.8257

Notes: Parameter estimates are in the main body of the table with the *p*-values in parentheses; NA denotes not applicable; * represents significance at the 5% level. The last row presents adjusted R^2 for model comparison.

In the linear regression model, Age has an estimated coefficient of only 0.0472, which is not statistically significant (p-value = 0.127) even at the 10% significance level. However, results change dramatically when Age^2 is included along with Age. In the quadratic regression model, both of these variables, with p-values of approximately zero, are statistically significant at any reasonable level. Also, the adjusted R^2 is higher for the quadratic regression model ($0.8257 > 0.6088$), making it a better choice for prediction. This conclusion is consistent with our visual impression from the scatterplot in Figure 16.3, which suggested a weak linear but strong quadratic relationship between Wage and Age.

b. From Table 16.5, the estimated regression equation for the quadratic regression model is

$$\widehat{Wage} = -22.7219 + 1.2540\text{Education} + 1.3500\text{Age} - 0.0133\text{Age}^2.$$

Therefore, using unrounded coefficient estimates, the predicted hourly wage for a 30-year-old person with 16 years of education is

$$\widehat{Wage} = -22.7219 + 1.2540 \times 16 + 1.3500 \times 30 - 0.0133 \times 30^2 = \$25.85.$$

Similarly, the predicted hourly wage for a 50- and a 70-year-old person is \$31.54 and \$26.56, respectively. Note that the hourly wage increases as a person ages from 30 to 50, but then decreases as a person ages from 50 to 70.

c. In part b, we predicted the hourly wage for a 30-, 50-, and 70-year-old person with 16 years of education. Therefore, of the three ages considered, a 50-year-old person earns the highest wage. In Figure 16.4, we plot the predicted wage with 16 years of education and vary age from 20 to 80 with increments of 1.

FIGURE 16.4 Predicted wages with 16 years of education and varying age

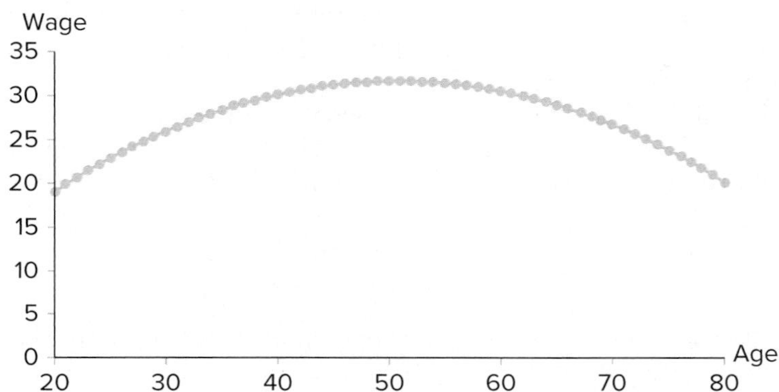

In order to determine the optimal age at which wage is maximized, we also solve for $x = \frac{-b_2}{2b_3} = \frac{-(1.3500)}{2(-0.0133)} = 50.67$. The optimal age at which the wage is maximized is 50.67 years, with a wage of \$31.54. It is worth noting that at a different education level, predicted wages will not be the same, yet the highest wage will still be achieved at the same 50.67 years of age. Students are encouraged to plot a similar graph with 12 years of education and varying age levels.

Using R to Estimate a Quadratic Regression Model

We replicate the results for Example 16.3.

A. Import the ***Wages*** data file into a data frame (table) and label it myData.

B. We use the **lm** function to estimate and the **summary** function to view the regression output for the linear and the quadratic regression models. When specifying the Age^2 variable in the quadratic regression model, we use the **I** function which isolates or insulates the expression inside the parentheses. Enter:

```
> Linear_Model <- lm(Wage ~ Education + Age, data = myData);
  summary(Linear_Model)
> Quadratic_Model <- lm(Wage ~ Education + Age + I(Age^2), data = myData);
  summary(Quadratic_Model)
```

C. We use the **predict** function accompanied with the **data.frame** function to predict wages for someone with 16 years of education and age equal to 30. Enter:

```
> predict(Quadratic_Model, data.frame(Education=16, Age=30))
```

And R returns: 25.85187

Predictions at ages 50 and 70 are found similarly.

D. We use the **coef** function to extract the estimated coefficients of the quadratic model. Using the 3rd and 4th coefficient values for Age and Age-squared, respectively, we determine the age at which the wages are maximized. Enter:

```
> Coeff <- coef(Quadratic_Model)
> -Coeff[3]/(2*Coeff[4])
```

And R returns: 50.66904

The Cubic Regression Model

The quadratic regression model allows one sign change of the slope capturing the influence of x on y. It is a special case of a **polynomial regression model**. Polynomial regression models describe various numbers of sign changes. Sometimes a quadratic regression model with one sign change of the slope is referred to as a polynomial regression model of order 2. In fact, a linear regression model is a polynomial regression model of order 1 with no sign change of the slope.

The linear and the quadratic regression models are the most common polynomial regression models. Sometimes, researchers use a polynomial regression model of order 3, also called the **cubic regression model**. The cubic regression model allows two sign changes of the slope.

THE CUBIC REGRESSION MODEL

A cubic regression model, $y = \beta_0 + \beta_1 x + \beta_2 x^2 + \beta_3 x^3 + \varepsilon$, allows two sign changes of the slope capturing the influence of x on y.

- Predictions with a cubic model are made by $\hat{y} = b_0 + b_1 x + b_2 x^2 + b_3 x^3$, where b_0, b_1, b_2, and b_3 are the coefficient estimates.
- It is common to use adjusted R^2 to choose between linear, quadratic, and cubic regression models.
- It is advisable to use unrounded coefficient estimates for making predictions.

The expression $\beta_0 + \beta_1 x + \beta_2 x^2 + \beta_3 x^3$ is the deterministic component of a cubic regression model; equivalently, conditional on x, $E(y) = \beta_0 + \beta_1 x + \beta_2 x^2 + \beta_3 x^3$. The shape of a cubic relationship depends on the coefficients. Figure 16.5 shows a scatterplot of sample data with the superimposed trendline for a cubic regression model when $\beta_1 > 0$, $\beta_2 < 0$, and $\beta_3 > 0$. Although the superimposed linear and quadratic trend lines are not shown, it is clear that the cubic regression model provides the best fit.

FIGURE 16.5 Scatterplot of y against x with trendline generated from estimating the cubic regression model

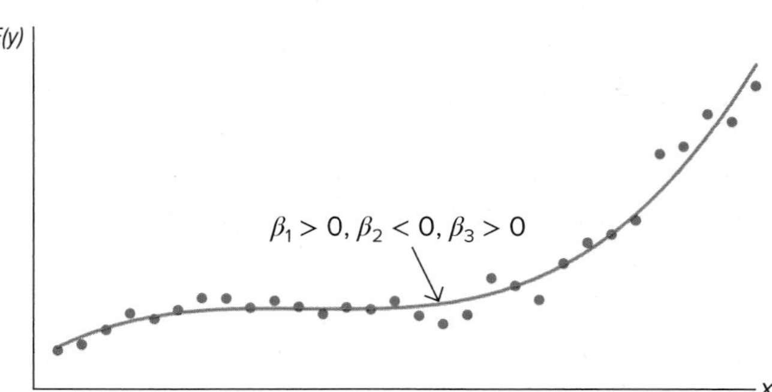

We often apply the cubic regression model when estimating the total cost curve of a firm. The total cost curve shows the relationship between a firm's total cost and its output in the short run. Consider an example of assembling a car in a factory. Initially, as more workers are hired, the total cost curve flattens. At some point, however, adding more workers will result in inefficiency as workers get in each other's way or wait for access to a machine. As a result, an extra unit of output costs more due to inputs being used less and less effectively. We can think of Figure 16.5 as a firm's typical total cost curve where x and y represent a firm's output and total cost, respectively.

A cubic regression model can easily be estimated within the framework of a linear regression model where we use y as the response variable and x, x^2, and x^3 as the explanatory variables. As before, we can compare polynomial models of various orders on the basis of adjusted R^2.

EXAMPLE 16.4

Table 16.6 shows a portion of data on the total cost (TC, in \$1,000s) and output for producing a particular product. We also include a portion of the squared output and cubed output variables; these variables will be used in the estimation process.

a. Use a cubic regression model to estimate total cost.

b. Predict the total cost if a firm produces 11 units of the product.

TABLE 16.6 Total Cost and Output, $n = 40$

Total_Cost

TC	Output	Output^2	Output^3
37.49	9	81	729
37.06	7	49	343
⋮	⋮	⋮	⋮
33.92	4	16	64

SOLUTION:

a. In order to estimate a cubic regression model, we first create observations for the squared output and the cubed output variables (see Table 16.6). We then estimate $\text{TC} = \beta_0 + \beta_1\text{Output} + \beta_2\text{Output}^2 + \beta_3\text{Output}^3 + \varepsilon$. Table 16.7 shows the relevant regression results. All variables are significant at the 5% level. In addition, the adjusted R^2 (not shown) is 0.8551, which is higher than the adjusted R^2 of 0.6452 and 0.8289 for the linear and the quadratic regression models, respectively. Students are encouraged to verify these results.

TABLE 16.7 Estimates of the Cubic Regression Model for Example 16.4

Variable	Cubic Regression Model
Intercept	17.1836* (0.000)
Output	6.4570* (0.000)
Output^2	−0.7321* (0.000)
Output^3	0.0291* (0.009)

Notes: p-values are in parentheses; * represents significance at the 5% level.

b. We use unrounded coefficient estimates to predict the total cost of production for a firm that produces 11 units of the product as $\widehat{\text{TC}} = 17.1836 + 6.4570 \times 11 - 0.7321 \times 11^2 + 0.0291 \times 11^3 = 38.34$, or \$38,340.

R instructions for estimating a cubic regression model are similar to those discussed earlier for the quadratic regression model.

EXERCISES 16.1

Mechanics

1. Consider the following two estimated models:

$$\hat{y} = 25 + 1.2x$$
$$\hat{y} = 30 + 1.4x - 0.12x^2$$

For each of the estimated models, predict y when x equals 5 and 10.

2. Consider the following three models:

$$\hat{y} = 80 + 1.2x$$
$$\hat{y} = 200 + 2.1x - 0.6x^2$$
$$\hat{y} = 100 + 16x - 2.2x^2 + 0.08x^3$$

For each of the estimated models, predict y when x equals 10 and 15.

3. Consider the estimated quadratic model $\hat{y} = 20 + 1.9x - 0.05x^2$.
   a. Predict y when x equals 10, 20, and 30.
   b. Find the value of x at which the predicted y is optimized. At this x value, is the predicted y maximized or minimized.

4. Consider the following sample regressions for the linear and quadratic models along with their respective R^2 and adjusted R^2.

	Linear	Quadratic
Intercept	13.3087	1.7656
x	0.3392	4.0966
x^2	NA	−0.2528
R^2	0.1317	0.5844
Adjusted R^2	0.0232	0.4657

   a. Use the appropriate goodness-of-fit measure to justify which model fits the data best.
   b. Given the best-fitting model, predict y for $x = 4$, 8, and 12.

5. Consider the following sample regressions for the linear, the quadratic, and the cubic models along with their respective R^2 and adjusted R^2.

	Linear	Quadratic	Cubic
Intercept	9.66	10.00	10.06
x	2.66	2.75	1.83
x^2	NA	−0.31	−0.33
x^3	NA	NA	0.26
R^2	0.810	0.836	0.896
Adjusted R^2	0.809	0.833	0.895

   a. Predict y for $x = 1$ and 2 with each of the estimated models.
   b. Select the most appropriate model. Explain.

6. Consider the following sample regressions for the linear, the quadratic, and the cubic models along with their respective R^2 and adjusted R^2.

	Linear	Quadratic	Cubic
Intercept	19.80	20.08	20.07
x	1.35	1.50	1.58
x^2	NA	−0.31	−0.27
x^3	NA	NA	−0.03
R^2	0.640	0.697	0.698
Adjusted R^2	0.636	0.691	0.689

   a. Predict y for $x = 2$ and 3 with each of the estimated models.
   b. Select the most appropriate model. Explain.

Applications

7. **FILE** ***Television.*** Studies have shown that watching too much television hurts school grades. Others argue that like books, television not only entertains, it also exposes a child to new information about the world. While watching too much television is harmful, a little bit may actually help. Researcher Matt Castle gathers information on the grade point average (GPA) of 28 middle school children and the number of hours of television they watched per week. A portion of the data is shown in the accompanying table.

GPA	Hours
3.24	19
3.10	21
⋮	⋮
3.31	4

   a. Estimate a quadratic regression model where the GPA of middle school children is regressed on hours and hours-squared.
   b. Is the quadratic term in this model justified? Explain.
   c. Find the optimal number of weekly hours of TV for middle school children.

8. **FILE** ***Crew_Size.*** The project manager at a construction company is evaluating how crew size affects the productivity of framing jobs. He has experimented with varying crew size (Crew, the number of workers) over the past 27 weeks and has recorded productivity (Jobs, jobs/week). A portion of the data is shown in the accompanying table.

Crew	Jobs
2	10
3	12
⋮	⋮
10	12

a. Create a scatterplot of the data. Based on the scatterplot alone, what crew size seems optimal?

b. Estimate the linear and the quadratic regression models. Evaluate the two models in terms of variable significance and adjusted R^2. Which model provides the best fit?

c. Use the best-fitting model to predict how many jobs a crew of 5 could be expected to complete in a week.

d. Estimate the cubic regression model. Does it improve the fit as compared to the quadratic regression model?

9. **FILE** ***Bids.*** Consider a sample comprised of firms that were targets of tender offers. Conduct an analysis where the response variable represents the number of bids (Bids) received prior to the takeover of the firm. The explanatory variables include the bid premium (Premium) and firm size (Size in $ billions). It is generally believed that a high initial bid premium, defined as the percentage excess of the firm's stock price, would deter subsequent bids. Moreover, while tender offers for large firms are likely to receive more media coverage and thereby attract the attention of opportunistic bidders, it also is a wealth constraint to potential bidders. A portion of the data is shown in the accompanying table.

Bids	Premium	Size
3	1.1905	0.7668
1	1.0360	0.1625
⋮	⋮	⋮
2	1.0329	3.4751

a. Estimate the model, Bids $= \beta_0 + \beta_1$Premium $+ \beta_2$Size $+ \beta_2$Size$^2 + \varepsilon$.

b. Justify the inclusion of the quadratic term in the model.

c. What firm size is likely to get the highest number of bids?

10. **FILE** ***Inspection.*** A lead inspector at ElectroTech, an electronics assembly shop, wants to convince management that it takes longer, on a per-component basis, to inspect large devices with many components than it does to inspect small devices because it is difficult to keep track of which components have already been inspected. To prove her point, she has collected data on the inspection time (Time in seconds) and the number of components per device (Components) from the last 25 devices. A portion of the data is shown in the accompanying table.

Time	Components
84	32
49	13
⋮	⋮
70	23

a. Estimate the linear, quadratic, and cubic regression models. Use the appropriate goodness-of-fit measure to identify the best fitting model.

b. Use the best model to predict the time required to inspect a device with 35 components.

11. **FILE** ***Debt_Payments.*** You collect data on 26 metropolitan areas to analyze average monthly debt payments (Debt in $) in terms of income (Inc in $1,000s) and the unemployment rate (Unemp in %). A portion of the data is shown in the accompanying table.

Metropolitan Area	Debt	Inc	Unemp
Washington, D.C.	1285	103.50	6.3
Seattle	1135	81.70	8.5
⋮	⋮	⋮	⋮
Pittsburgh	763	63.00	8.3

a. Estimate the model Debt $= \beta_0 + \beta_1$Inc $+ \beta_2$Unemp $+ \varepsilon$. Is unemployment significant at the 5% level?

b. You are told that the unemployment rate might have a quadratic influence on monthly debt payments. Estimate Debt $= \beta_0 + \beta_1$Inc $+ \beta_2$Unemp $+ \beta_3$Unemp$^2 + \varepsilon$ to determine if Unemp and Unemp^2 are jointly significant at the 5% level.

16.2 REGRESSION MODELS WITH LOGARITHMS

LO 16.2

Use and evaluate log-transformed models.

In the preceding section, we squared, and in some instances, cubed the explanatory variable in order to capture nonlinearities between the response variable and the explanatory variable. Another commonly used transformation is based on the natural logarithm. You may recall from your math courses that the natural logarithmic function is the inverse of the exponential function. It is useful to briefly review exponential and logarithmic functions before using them in regression models.

The exponential function is defined as

$$y = \exp(x) = e^x,$$

where $e \approx 2.718$ is a constant and x is the function argument. We can easily compute, for example, $e^2 = 7.3891$, or $e^5 = 148.4132$.

The inverse of the exponential function is the natural logarithm (or simply, log); that is, the logarithm with the base $e \approx 2.718$. In other words,

$$\text{if } y = e^x, \quad \text{then} \quad \ln(y) = x,$$

where $\ln(y)$ is the natural log of y. For example, if $y = e^2 = 7.3891$, then $\ln(y) = \ln(7.3891) = 2$. Similarly, if $y = e^5 = 148.4132$, then $\ln(y) = \ln(148.4132) = 5$. Since $\exp(\ln(x)) = x$, the exponential function is sometimes referred to as the anti-log function. Finally, the log of a negative or zero value is not defined. Therefore, we can log-transform only those variables that have positive values.

As mentioned earlier, in many applications, linearity is not justifiable. For instance, consider an estimated linear regression of annual food expenditure y on annual income x: $\hat{y} = 9{,}000 + 0.20x$. An estimated slope coefficient value of $b_1 = 0.20$ implies that a \$1,000 increase in annual income would lead to a \$200 increase in annual food expenditure, irrespective of whether the income increase is from \$20,000 to \$21,000 or from \$520,000 to \$521,000. Since we would expect the impact to be smaller at high income levels, it may be more meaningful to analyze what happens to food expenditure as income increases by a certain percentage rather than by a certain dollar amount.

Logarithms convert changes in variables into percentage changes, which is useful since many relationships are naturally expressed in terms of percentages. For instance, it is common to log-transform variables such as incomes, house prices, and sales. On the other hand, variables such as age, number of bedrooms, and scores are generally expressed in their original form. We rely both on economic intuition as well as statistical measures to find the appropriate form for the variables.

THE LOGARITHIMC TRANSFORMATION

The natural logarithm converts changes in a variable into percentage changes.

We first illustrate log models with only one explanatory variable, which we later extend to a multiple regression model.

A Log-Log Model

In a **log-log model,** both the response variable and the explanatory variable are transformed into natural logs. It is also referred to as the **power regression model.** We can write this model as

$$\ln(y) = \beta_0 + \beta_1 \ln(x) + \varepsilon,$$

where $\ln(y)$ is the log-transformed response variable and $\ln(x)$ is the log-transformed explanatory variable. With these transformations, the relationship between y and x is captured by a curve whose shape depends on the sign and magnitude of the slope coefficient β_1. Figure 16.6 shows two scatterplots of sample data with superimposed trendlines for the log-log regression model. Although the linear trendline is not included in either panel, it is clear that the log-log regression model provides a better fit.

For $0 < \beta_1 < 1$, the log-log model implies a positive relationship between x and $E(y)$; as x increases, $E(y)$ increases at a slower rate. This may be appropriate in the earlier example, where we expect food expenditure to react positively to changes in income, with the impact diminishing at higher income levels. If $\beta_1 < 0$, it suggests a negative relationship between x and $E(y)$; as x increases, $E(y)$ decreases at a slower rate. Finally, $\beta_1 > 1$

implies a positive and increasing relationship between x and y; this case is not shown in Figure 16.6. For any application, the estimated value of β_1 is determined by the data.

FIGURE 16.6 Scatterplots of y against x with superimposed log-log (power) trendlines

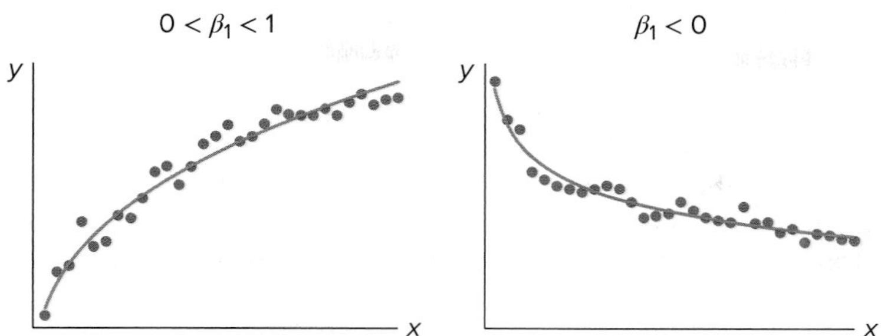

Note that while the log-log regression model is nonlinear in the variables, it is still linear in the coefficients, thus satisfying the requirement of the linear regression model. The only requirement is that we have to first transform both variables into natural logs before running the regression. We should also point out that in a log-log regression model, the slope coefficient β_1 measures the approximate percentage change in y for a small percentage change in x. In other words, β_1 is a measure of elasticity. In a log-log model, if y represents the quantity demanded of a particular good and x is its unit price, then β_1 measures the price elasticity of demand, a parameter of considerable economic interest. Suppose $\beta_1 = -1.2$; then a 1% increase in the price of this good is expected to lead to about a 1.2% decrease in its quantity demanded.

Finally, even though the response variable is transformed into logs, we still make predictions in regular units. Given $\widehat{\ln(y)} = b_0 + b_1 \ln(x)$, you may be tempted to use the anti-log function, to make predictions in regular units as $\hat{y} = \exp(\widehat{\ln(y)}) = \exp(b_0 + b_1\ln(x))$, where b_0 and b_1 are the coefficient estimates. However, this transformation is known to systematically underestimate the expected value of y. One relatively simple correction is to make predictions as $\hat{y} = \exp(b_0 + b_1 \ln(x) + s_e^2/2)$, where s_e is the standard error of the estimate from the log-log model. This correction is easy to implement since virtually all statistical packages report s_e.

THE LOG-LOG REGRESSION MODEL

A log-log model is specified as $\ln(y) = \beta_0 + \beta_1 \ln(x) + \varepsilon$, and β_1 measures the approximate percentage change in $E(y)$ when x increases by 1%.

- Predictions with a log-log model are made by $\hat{y} = \exp(b_0 + b_1\ln(x) + s_e^2/2)$, where b_0 and b_1 are the coefficient estimates and s_e is the standard error of the estimate.
- It is advisable to use unrounded coefficient estimates for making predictions.

EXAMPLE 16.5

Refer back to the food expenditure example where y represents expenditure on food and x represents income. Let the sample regression be $\widehat{\ln(y)} = 3.64 + 0.50\ln(x)$ with the standard error of the estimate $s_e = 0.18$.

a. Interpret the slope coefficient, $b_1 = 0.50$.

b. What is the predicted food expenditure for an individual whose income is \$20,000?

SOLUTION:

a. In the log-log model, a slope coefficient of $b_1 = 0.50$ implies that a 1% increase in income will lead to about a 0.5% increase in predicted food expenditure.

b. For income $x = 20{,}000$, we predict food expenditure as $\hat{y} = \exp(3.64 + 0.50 \times \ln(20{,}000) + 0.18^2/2) = \$5{,}474.98$.

The Logarithmic Model

A log-log specification transforms both the response variable and the explanatory variable into logs. It is also common to employ a **semi-log** model, in which only one of the variables is transformed into logs. We will discuss two types of semi-log models in the context of the simple linear regression model. A semi-log model that transforms only the explanatory variable is also referred to as the **logarithmic model,** and a semi-log model that transforms only the response variable is also referred to as the **exponential model.** We can have many variants of semi-log models when we extend the analysis to include multiple explanatory variables.

The logarithmic model is defined as

$$y = \beta_0 + \beta_1 \ln(x) + \varepsilon.$$

Like the log-log model, this model implies that an increase in x will lead to an increase ($\beta_1 > 0$) or decrease ($\beta_1 < 0$) in $E(y)$ at a decreasing rate. These models are especially attractive when only the explanatory variable is better captured in percentages. Figure 16.7 shows two scatterplots of sample data with superimposed trendlines for the logarithmic regression model. Although the linear trendline is not included in either panel, it is clear that the logarithmic regression model provides a better fit. Since the log-log and the logarithmic model can allow similar shapes, the choice between the two models can be tricky. We will use goodness-of-fit measures to compare these models later in this section.

FIGURE 16.7 Scatterplots of y against x with superimposed logarithmic trendlines

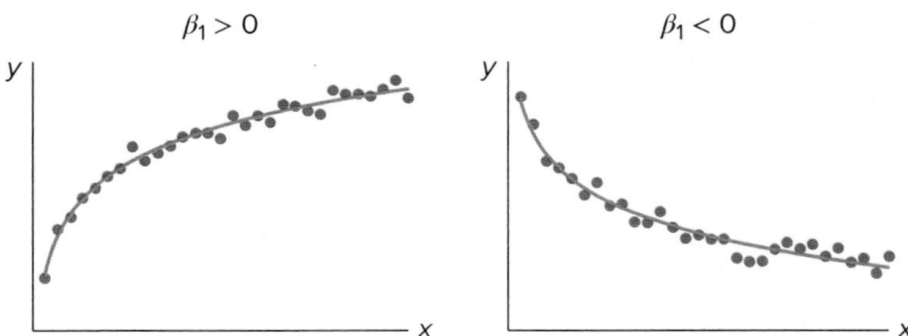

In the logarithmic model, the response variable is specified in regular units, but the explanatory variable is transformed into logs. Therefore, $\beta_1/100 = \beta_1 \times 0.01$ measures the approximate unit change in $E(y)$ when x increases by 1%. For example, if $\beta_1 = 5{,}000$, then a 1% increase in x leads to a 50 unit ($= 5{,}000 \times 0.01$) increase in $E(y)$. Since the response variable is already specified in regular units, no further transformation is necessary when making predictions.

> **THE LOGARITHMIC MODEL**
>
> A logarithmic model is specified as $y = \beta_0 + \beta_1 \ln(x) + \varepsilon$, and $\beta_1/100 = \beta_1 \times 0.01$ measures the approximate change in $E(y)$ when x increases by 1%.
>
> - Predictions with a logarithmic model are made by $\hat{y} = b_0 + b_1 \ln(x)$, where b_0 and b_1 are the coefficient estimates.
> - It is advisable to use unrounded coefficient estimates for making predictions.

EXAMPLE 16.6

Continuing with the earlier example of food expenditure, let the estimated regression be $\hat{y} = 12 + 566\ln(x)$.

a. Interpret the slope coefficient, $b_1 = 566$.

b. What is the predicted food expenditure for an individual whose income is \$20,000?

SOLUTION:

a. In the logarithmic model, a slope coefficient of $b_1 = 566$ implies that a 1% increase in income will lead to approximately a \$5.66 (= 566 × 0.01) increase in predicted food expenditure.

b. For income $x = 20{,}000$, we predict food expenditure as $\hat{y} = 12 + 566 \times \ln(20{,}000) = 5{,}617.37$.

The Exponential Model

Unlike the logarithmic model, in which we were interested in finding the unit change in $E(y)$ for a 1% increase in x, the exponential model allows us to estimate the percent change in $E(y)$ when x increases by one unit. The exponential model is defined as

$$\ln(y) = \beta_0 + \beta_1 x + \varepsilon.$$

Figure 16.8 shows two scatterplots of sample data with superimposed trendlines for the exponential regression model. Although the linear trendline is not included in either panel, it is clear that the exponential regression model provides a better fit.

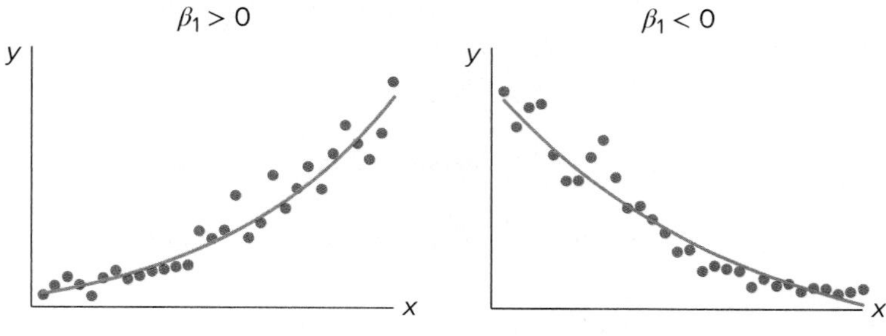

FIGURE 16.8 Scatterplots of y against x with superimposed exponential trendlines

For an exponential model, $\beta_1 \times 100$ measures the approximate percentage change in $E(y)$ when x increases by one unit. For example, a value of $\beta_1 = 0.05$ implies that a one-unit increase in x leads to a 5% (= 0.05 × 100) increase in $E(y)$. As in the case of a log-log model, we make a correction for making predictions, since the response variable is measured in logs.

THE EXPONENTIAL MODEL

An exponential model is specified as $\ln(y) = \beta_0 + \beta_1 x + \varepsilon$, and $\beta_1 \times 100$ measures the approximate percentage change in $E(y)$ when x increases by one unit.

- Predictions with an exponential model are made by $\hat{y} = \exp(b_0 + b_1 x + s_e^2/2)$, where b_0 and b_1 are the coefficient estimates and s_e is the standard error of the estimate.
- It is advisable to use unrounded coefficient estimates for making predictions.

EXAMPLE 16.7

Continuing again with the example of food expenditure, let the estimated regression be $\widehat{\ln(y)} = 7.60 + 0.00005x$ with the standard error of the estimate, $s_e = 0.20$.

a. Interpret the slope coefficient, $b_1 = 0.00005$.

b. What is the predicted food expenditure for an individual whose income is \$20,000?

SOLUTION:

a. In the exponential model, a slope coefficient of $b_1 = 0.00005$ implies that a \$1,000 increase in income will lead to approximately a 5% (= 1,000 × 0.00005 × 100) increase in predicted food expenditure.

b. For income $x = 20{,}000$, we predict food expenditure as $\hat{y} = \exp(7.60 + 0.00005 \times 20{,}000 + 0.20^2/2) = 5{,}541.39$.

As mentioned earlier, while log-transformed models are easily estimated within the framework of a linear regression model, care must be exercised in making predictions and interpreting the estimated slope coefficient. In addition, when interpreting the slope coefficient, keep in mind that logs essentially convert changes in variables into percentage changes. Table 16.8 summarizes the results.

TABLE 16.8 Summary of the Linear, Log-Log, Logarithmic, and Exponential Models

Model	Predicted Value	Estimated Slope Coefficient
$y = \beta_0 + \beta_1 x + \varepsilon$	$\hat{y} = b_0 + b_1 x$	b_1 measures the change in $\hat{y}$ when x increases by one unit.
$\ln(y) = \beta_0 + \beta_1 \ln(x) + \varepsilon$	$\hat{y} = \exp(b_0 + b_1 \ln(x) + s_e^2/2)$	b_1 measures the approximate percentage change in $\hat{y}$ when x increases by 1%.
$y = \beta_0 + \beta_1 \ln(x) + \varepsilon$	$\hat{y} = b_0 + b_1 \ln(x)$	$b_1 \times 0.01$ measures the approximate change in $\hat{y}$ when x increases by 1%.
$\ln(y) = \beta_0 + \beta_1 x + \varepsilon$	$\hat{y} = \exp(b_0 + b_1 x + s_e^2/2)$	$b_1 \times 100$ measures the approximate percentage change in $\hat{y}$ when x increases by one unit.

Note: It is advisable to use unrounded coefficient estimates for making predictions.

College_Town

EXAMPLE 16.8

The objective outlined in the introductory case was to evaluate the influence of the number of bedrooms (Beds), the number of bathrooms (Baths), and the square footage (Sqft) on monthly rent (Rent). Use the ***College_Town*** data file to answer the following:

a. Plot rent against each of the three explanatory variables and evaluate whether the relationship is best captured by a line or a curve. Identify variables that may require a log-transformation.

b. Estimate the linear and the relevant log-transformed models to predict rent for a 1,600-square-foot home with three bedrooms and two bathrooms.

SOLUTION: Given the nature of Beds and Baths, we will specify these variables only in regular units. We will, however, consider log-transformations for Rent and Sqft, since their changes are often expressed in percentages.

a. In Figure 16.9, we plot Rent against (a) Beds and (b) Baths and superimpose linear and exponential curves (recall that an exponential model log-transforms only the response variable).

FIGURE 16.9 Comparing Rent against (a) Beds and (b) Baths

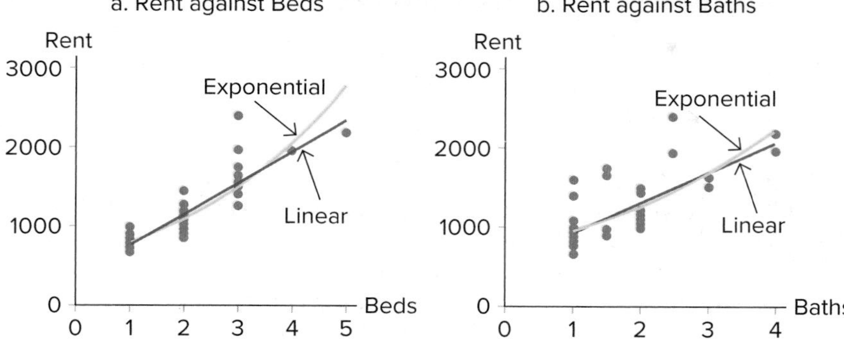

It is hard to tell from Figure 16.9 whether the relationship between Rent and Beds or Rent and Baths is better captured by a line or a curve. We will use goodness-of-fit measures for the selection.

We now plot Rent against Sqft in Figure 16.10.

FIGURE 16.10 Comparing Rent against Sqft

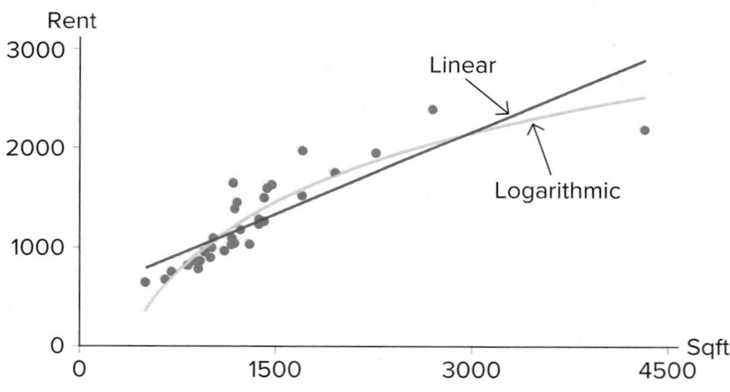

Here it appears that the relationship between Rent and Sqft is better captured by a curve than a line. Figure 16.10 shows that a logarithmic model that log-transforms Sqft fits the data better than the linear model, suggesting that as square footage increases, rent increases at a decreasing rate. In other words, the increase in Rent is higher when Sqft increases from 1,000 to 2,000 than from 2,000 to 3,000.

Two other models worth considering are the exponential model, where only Rent is log-transformed, and a log-log model, where both Rent and Sqft are log-transformed. In order to avoid a "cluttered" figure, these curves are not superimposed on the scatterplot in Figure 16.10; however, we will formally evaluate all models.

b. While the preceding visual tools are instructive, we evaluate four models and use goodness-of-fit measures to select the most appropriate model for prediction.

$$\text{Model 1: Rent} = \beta_0 + \beta_1 \text{Beds} + \beta_2 \text{Baths} + \beta_3 \text{Sqft} + \varepsilon$$
$$\text{Model 2: Rent} = \beta_0 + \beta_1 \text{Beds} + \beta_2 \text{Baths} + \beta_3 \ln(\text{Sqft}) + \varepsilon$$
$$\text{Model 3: } \ln(\text{Rent}) = \beta_0 + \beta_1 \text{Beds} + \beta_2 \text{Baths} + \beta_3 \text{Sqft} + \varepsilon$$
$$\text{Model 4: } \ln(\text{Rent}) = \beta_0 + \beta_1 \text{Beds} + \beta_2 \text{Baths} + \beta_3 \ln(\text{Sqft}) + \varepsilon$$

In order to estimate these models, we first log-transform Rent and Sqft; see the last two columns of Table 16.9.

TABLE 16.9 Transforming Rent and Sqft into Logs

Rent	Beds	Baths	Sqft	ln(Rent)	ln(Sqft)
645	1	1	500	6.4693	6.2146
675	1	1	648	6.5147	6.4739
⋮	⋮	⋮	⋮	⋮	⋮
2400	3	2.5	2700	7.7832	7.9010

In Models 1 and 2, we use Rent as the response variable with Beds and Baths, along with Sqft in Model 1 and ln(Sqft) in Model 2, as the explanatory variables. Similarly, in Models 3 and 4, we use ln(Rent) as the response variable with Beds and Baths, along with Sqft in Model 3 and ln(Sqft) in Model 4, as the explanatory variables. Model estimates are summarized in Table 16.10.

TABLE 16.10 Regression Results for Example 16.8

	Response Variable: Rent		Response Variable: ln(Rent)	
	Model 1	Model 2	Model 3	Model 4
Intercept	300.4116* (0.001)	−3,909.7415* (0.001)	6.3294* (0.000)	3.3808* (0.000)
Beds	225.8100* (0.001)	131.7781* (0.040)	0.2262* (0.000)	0.1246* (0.009)
Baths	89.2661 (0.119)	36.4255 (0.494)	0.0831 (0.060)	0.0254 (0.514)
Sqft	0.2096* (0.028)	NA	0.0001 (0.362)	NA
ln(Sqft)	NA	675.2648* (0.000)	NA	0.4742* (0.001)
s_e	193.1591	172.2711	0.1479	0.1262
R^2	0.8092	0.8482	0.8095	0.8613

Notes: Parameter estimates are followed with the *p*-values in parentheses; NA denotes not applicable; * represents significance at the 5% level.

For the most part, the number of bedrooms and the square footage of the house are statistically significant at the 5% level, while the number of bathrooms is insignificant. We use the model results to predict rent for a 1,600-square-foot home with three bedrooms and two bathrooms. In order to make a prediction with Models 3 and 4, which are both based on ln(Rent), we will add the correction term $s_e^2/2$.

$$\text{Model 1: } \widehat{\text{Rent}} = 300.4116 + 225.8100 \times 3 + 89.2661 \times 2 + 0.2096 \times 1{,}600 = \$1{,}492$$

$$\text{Model 2: } \widehat{\text{Rent}} = -3{,}909.7415 + 131.7781 \times 3 + 36.4255 \times 2 + 675.2648 \times \ln(1{,}600) = \$1{,}540$$

$$\text{Model 3: } \widehat{\text{Rent}} = \exp(6.3294 + 0.2262 \times 3 + 0.0831 \times 2 + 0.0001 \times 1{,}600 + (0.1479)^2/2) = \$1{,}463$$

$$\text{Model 4: } \widehat{\text{Rent}} = \exp(3.3808 + 0.1246 \times 3 + 0.0254 \times 2 + 0.4742 \times \ln(1{,}600) + 0.1262^2/2) = \$1{,}498$$

The predicted rent ranges from \$1,463 in Model 3 to \$1,540 in Model 2. We would like to know which model provides the best prediction, which we discuss shortly.

Using R to Estimate Log-Transformed Models

We replicate the results for Example 16.8.

A. Import the ***College_Town*** data file into a data frame (table) and label it myData.

B. We use the **lm** function to estimate and the **summary** function to view the regression output for linear and log-transformed models. We also use the **log** function to log-transform the variables Rent and Sqft. Enter:

```
> Model1 <- lm(Rent ~ Beds + Baths + Sqft, data = myData); summary(Model1)
> Model2 <- lm(Rent ~ Beds + Baths + log(Sqft), data = myData);
  summary(Model2)
> Model3 <- lm(log(Rent) ~ Beds + Baths + Sqft, data = myData);
  summary(Model3)
> Model4 <- lm(log(Rent) ~Beds + Baths + log(Sqft), data = myData);
  summary(Model4)
```

C. For Models 1 and 2, we use the **predict** function accompanied with the **data.frame** function to predict rent for a house with 3 bedrooms, 2 bathrooms, and 1600 square footage. Enter:

```
> predict(Model1, data.frame(Beds=3, Baths=2, Sqft=1600))
> predict(Model2, data.frame(Beds=3, Baths=2, Sqft=1600))
```

And R returns 1492 for Model 1 and 1540 for Model 2.

D. For Models 3 and 4, we compute the predicted rent as: $\widehat{\text{Rent}} = \exp(\ln(\widehat{\text{Rent}}) + s_e^2/2)$. We again use the **predict** function to compute $\ln(\widehat{\text{Rent}})$ and extract *se*, which R refers to as sigma, from the estimated model. We label $\ln(\widehat{\text{Rent}})$ as pred3 and pred4 and *se* as se3 and se4 for Models 3 and 4, respectively. Enter:

```
> pred3 <- predict(Model3, data.frame(Beds=3, Baths=2, Sqft=1600))
> se3 <- sigma(Model3)
> exp(pred3+se3^2/2)
> pred4 <- predict(Model4, data.frame(Beds=3, Baths=2, Sqft=1600))
> se4 <- sigma(Model4)
> exp(pred4 + se4^2/2)
```

And R returns 1463 for Model 3 and 1498 for Model 4.

Comparing Linear and Log-Transformed Models

LO 16.3

Describe the method used to compare linear models with log-transformed models.

As seen in Example 16.8, it is often not clear which regression model is best suited for an application. While we can use economic intuition and scatterplots for direction, we also justify our selection on the basis of goodness-of-fit measures. In Chapter 14, we introduced R^2 to compare models based on the same number of explanatory variables; we compared adjusted R^2 if the number of explanatory variables was different. Such comparisons are valid only when the response variable of the competing models is the same. Since R^2 measures the percentage of sample variations of the response variable explained by the model, we cannot compare the percentage of explained variations of y with that of $\ln(y)$. Comparing models based on the computer-generated R^2, that does not differentiate between y and $\ln(y)$, is like comparing apples with oranges.

For a valid comparison, we need to compute the percentage of explained variations of y even though the estimated model uses $\ln(y)$ as the response variable. To do this, we need to calculate R^2 from scratch for the model that uses $\ln(y)$ as the response variable. In Chapter 14, we calculated $R^2 = SSR/SST = 1 - SSE/SST$. Here, we will use an alternative and easy way to calculate R^2 which entails squaring the sample correlation coefficient of y and $\hat{y}$.

> **AN ALTERNATIVE WAY TO CALCULATE R^2**
>
> The coefficient of determination, R^2, can be calculated as $R^2 = (r_{y\hat{y}})^2$ where $r_{y\hat{y}}$ is the sample correlation coefficient between y and $\hat{y}$.

Example 16.9 elaborates on the method with Excel and R.

Using Excel and R to Compare Linear and Log-Transformed Models

EXAMPLE 16.9

Revisit the four regression models in Example 16.8 and determine which model is best suited for making predictions.

SOLUTION: From Table 16.10, Model 4 has the highest computer-generated R^2 value of 0.8613. However, this does not mean that Model 4 is necessarily the best because R^2 is based on Rent for Models 1 and 2 and on ln(Rent) for Models 3 and 4. Therefore, while we can infer that Model 2 is superior to Model 1 (0.8482 > 0.8092) and Model 4 is superior to Model 3 (0.8613 > 0.8095), we cannot directly compare Models 2 and 4 based on the computer-generated R^2. For a valid comparison, we compute R^2 for Model 4 from scratch; that is, R^2 is based on Rent, even though it uses ln(Rent) for estimation.

For Model 4, we first compute $\widehat{\text{Rent}} = \exp(b_0 + b_1\text{Beds} + b_2\text{Baths} + b_3\ln(\text{Sqft}) + s_e^2/2)$ for the given sample values of the explanatory variables. The next step is to find its sample correlation coefficient with Rent and square it.

College_Town

Excel and R are quite useful in performing the calculations for generating a value of R^2 for Model 4 based on Rent rather than ln(Rent).

Using Excel

a. Open the ***College_Town*** data file. Convert the Rent and Sqft variables into their respective logarithms by using Excel's **ln** function.

b. Estimate Model 4 by choosing **Data > Data Analysis > Regression** from the menu. For *Input Y Range*, select the ln(Rent) observations, and for *Input X Range*, simultaneously select the Beds, Baths, and ln(Sqft) observations. If you check the *Residuals* box, then Excel provides the predicted values for ln(Rent), or $\widehat{\ln(\text{Rent})}$. So check this box, and then click **OK.**

c. For convenience, paste the values for $\widehat{\ln(\text{Rent})}$ next to the observed values for Rent on the spreadsheet; the first two columns of Table 16.11 show a portion of the results. Next, we want to calculate: $\widehat{\text{Rent}} = \exp(b_0 + b_1\text{Beds} + b_2\text{Baths} + b_3\ln(\text{Sqft}) + s_e^2/2)$. Given the Excel-produced predicted values for ln(Rent), this equation simplifies to $\widehat{\text{Rent}} = \exp(\widehat{\ln(\text{Rent})} + s_e^2/2)$. Substituting the value for the standard error of the estimate from Model 4 into this equation yields: $\widehat{\text{Rent}} = \exp(\widehat{\ln(\text{Rent})} + 0.1262^2/2)$. In the calculations, we use the unrounded value for s_e from the regression output. The third column of Table 16.11 shows a portion of the results.

TABLE 16.11 Excel-Produced Predicted Values for Model 4

Rent	$\widehat{\ln(\text{Rent})}$	$\widehat{\text{Rent}} = \exp(\widehat{\ln(\text{Rent})} + 0.1262^2/2)$
645	6.4778	655.7335
675	6.6007	741.5211
⋮	⋮	⋮
2400	7.5648	1944.5761

d. Finally, use Excel's **CORREL** function to calculate the correlation between Rent and $\widehat{\text{Rent}}$ (columns 1 and 3 in Table 16.11) as $r_{y\hat{y}} = 0.8691$. Then, square the sample correlation coefficient to find the coefficient of determination, $R^2 = (0.8691)^2 = 0.7554$.

Using R

a. Import the ***College_Town*** data file into a data frame (table) and label it myData.

b. As shown earlier, we can easily estimate Model 4. Enter:

```
> Model4 <- lm(log(Rent) ~ Beds + Baths + log(Sqft), data = myData)
```

c. We use the estimated Model 4 to generate $\widehat{\ln(\text{Rent})}$, labeled as plogRent4, and to extract *se*, labeled as se4. Enter:

```
> plogRent4 <- predict(Model4)
> se4 <- sigma(Model4)
```

d. Next, we compute the predicted values for Rent: $\widehat{\text{Rent}} = \exp(\widehat{\ln(\text{Rent})} + s_e^2/2)$. Enter:

```
> pRent4 <- exp(plogRent4 + se4^2/2)
```

e. Finally, we use the **cor** function to calculate the correlation between Rent and $\widehat{\text{Rent}}$. We square this value to find the coefficient of determination, R^2. Enter:

```
> cor(myData$Rent, pRent4)^2
```

And R returns: 0.7554188, which is the same as obtained with Excel.

Summary The above $R^2 = 0.7554$, based on Rent and not ln(Rent), can now be compared with the computer-generated $R^2 = 0.8482$ for Model 2. We conclude that Model 2 is better suited for making predictions because $0.8482 > 0.7554$.

A Cautionary Note Concerning Goodness-of-fit Measures

As mentioned in Chapter 14, the goodness-of-fit measures described in this chapter do not help us gauge how well an estimated model will predict in an unseen sample. It is possible for a model to perform really well with the data set used for estimation, but then perform miserably once a new data set is used. Cross-validation is a useful technique that evaluates predictive models by partitioning the original sample into a training set to build (train) the model and a validation set to evaluate (validate) it. The cross-validation method is beyond the scope of this text.

SYNOPSIS OF INTRODUCTORY CASE

Cultura Creative/Alamy Stock Photo

The recession-resistance of campus towns has prompted many analysts to call investment in off-campus student housing a smart choice. First, there is a stable source of demand in college towns, as cash-strapped public universities are unable to house all students. Second, this demand may actually improve due to a projected increase in college enrollment. This report focuses on rental opportunities in a Midwestern campus town.

Four regression models analyze the monthly rent (Rent) on the basis of the number of bedrooms (Beds), the number of bathrooms (Baths), and the square footage (Sqft) of off-campus houses. Nonlinearities between the variables are captured by transforming Rent and/or Sqft into natural logs. The coefficient of determination R^2, computed in the original units, is used to select the best model. The selected model is estimated as $\widehat{\text{Rent}} = -3909.74 + 131.78\text{Beds} + 36.43\ \text{Baths} + 675.26\ \ln(\text{Sqft})$. The bedroom coefficient implies that for every additional bedroom, the monthly rent is predicted to go up by about \$132, holding other factors constant. Similarly, for every 1% increase in square footage, the monthly rent is predicted to increase by about \$6.75 (675 × 0.01).

The estimated regression model can also be used to make predictions for rent. For example, a 1,000-square-foot house with two bedrooms and one bathroom is predicted to rent for \$1,055. Similarly, a 1,600-square-foot house with three bedrooms and two bathrooms is predicted to rent for \$1,540. These results are useful to any investor interested in off-campus housing in this Midwestern campus town.

EXERCISES 16.2

Mechanics

12. Consider the following four estimated models:

$\hat{y} = 500 - 4.2x$

$\hat{y} = 1370 - 280\ln(x)$

$\widehat{\ln(y)} = 8.4 - 0.04x;\ s_e = 0.13$

$\widehat{\ln(y)} = 8 - 0.8\ln(x);\ s_e = 0.11$

a. Interpret the slope coefficient in each of these estimated models.

b. For each model, what is the predicted change in y when x increases from 100 to 101?

13. Consider the following estimated models:

$\hat{y} = 10 + 4.4x$

$\hat{y} = 2 + 23\ln(x)$

$\widehat{\ln(y)} = 3.0 + 0.1x;\ s_e = 0.07$

$\widehat{\ln(y)} = 2.6 + 0.6\ln(x);\ s_e = 0.05$

a. Interpret the slope coefficient in each of these estimated models.

b. For each model, what is the predicted change in y when x increases from 10 to 10.5?

14. Consider the sample regressions for the linear, the logarithmic, the exponential, and the log-log models. For each of the estimated models, predict y when x equals 100.

	Response Variable: y		Response Variable: $\ln(y)$	
	Model 1	Model 2	Model 3	Model 4
Intercept	240.42	−69.75	1.58	0.77
x	4.68	NA	0.05	NA
$\ln(x)$	NA	162.51	NA	1.25
s_e	83.19	90.71	0.12	0.09

15. Consider the sample regressions for the linear, the logarithmic, the exponential, and the log-log models. For each of the estimated models, predict y when x equals 50.

	Response Variable: y		Response Variable: $\ln(y)$	
	Model 1	Model 2	Model 3	Model 4
Intercept	18.52	−6.74	1.48	1.02
x	1.68	NA	0.06	NA
$\ln(x)$	NA	29.96	NA	0.96
s_e	23.92	19.71	0.12	0.10

16. Consider the following sample regressions for the linear and the logarithmic models.

	Linear	Logarithmic
Intercept	6.7904	−5.6712
x	1.0607	NA
$\ln(x)$	NA	10.5447*
s_e	2.4935	1.5231
R^2	0.8233	0.9341
Adjusted R^2	0.8013	0.9259

a. Justify which model fits the data best.

b. Use the selected model to predict y for $x = 10$.

17. Consider the following sample regressions for the log-log and the exponential models.

	Log-Log	Exponential
Intercept	1.8826	2.0219
x	NA	0.0513
$\ln(x)$	0.3663	NA
s_e	0.3508	0.2922
R^2	0.5187	0.6660
Adjusted R^2	0.4585	0.6242

a. Justify which model fits the data best.

b. Use the selected model to predict y for $x = 20$.

Applications

18. An economist is interested in examining how an individual's cigarette consumption (C) may be influenced by the price for a pack of cigarettes (P) and the individual's annual income (I). Using data from 50 individuals, she estimates a log-log model and obtains the following regression results.

$$\widehat{\ln(C)} = 3.90 - 1.25\ln(P) + 0.18\ln(I)$$
$$p\text{-values} = (0.000)\quad(0.005)\quad(0.400)$$

a. Interpret the value of the elasticity of demand for cigarettes with respect to price.

b. At the 5% significance level, is the price elasticity of demand statistically significant?

c. Interpret the value of the income elasticity of demand for cigarettes.

d. At the 5% significance level, is the income elasticity of demand statistically significant? Is this result surprising? Explain.

19. **FILE** ***BMI.*** According to the *World Health Organization*, obesity has reached epidemic proportions globally. While obesity has generally been linked with chronic disease and disability, researchers argue that it may also affect wages. Body Mass Index (BMI) is a widely used weight measure that also adjusts for height. A person is considered normal weight if BMI is between 18.5 to 25, overweight if BMI is between 25 to 30, and obese if BMI is over 30. The accompanying table shows a portion of data on the salary (in $1,000s) of 30 college-educated men with their respective BMIs.

Salary	BMI
34	33
43	26
⋮	⋮
45	21

a. Estimate a linear model with salary as the response variable and BMI as the explanatory variable. What is the estimated salary of a college-educated man with a BMI of 25? With a BMI of 30?

b. Estimate an exponential model using log of salary as the response variable and BMI as the explanatory variable. What is the estimated salary of a college-educated man with a BMI of 25? With a BMI of 30?

c. Which of the above two models is more appropriate for this application? Use R^2 for comparison.

20. **FILE** ***Dexterity.*** A manufacturing manager uses a dexterity test on 20 current employees in order to predict watch production based on time to completion (in seconds). A portion of the data is shown below.

Watches	Time
23	513
19	608
⋮	⋮
20	437

a. Estimate the linear model: Watches $= \beta_0 + \beta_1\text{Time} + \varepsilon$. Interpret the slope coefficient. If the time required to complete the dexterity test is 550 seconds, what is the predicted watch production?

b. Estimate the logarithmic model: Watches $= \beta_0 + \beta_1 \ln(\text{Time}) + \varepsilon$. Interpret the slope coefficient. If the time required to complete the dexterity test is 550 seconds, what is the predicted watch production?

c. Which model provides a better fit? Explain.

21. **FILE** ***Wine_Pricing.*** Professor Orley Ashenfelter of Princeton University is a pioneer in the field of wine economics. He claims that, contrary to old orthodoxy, the quality of wine can be explained mostly in terms of weather conditions. Wine romantics accuse him of undermining the whole wine-tasting culture. In an interesting co-authored paper that appeared in Chance magazine in 1995, he ran a multiple regression model where quality, measured by the average vintage price relative to 1961, is used as the response variable y. The explanatory variables were the average temperature x_1 (in degrees Celsius), the amount of winter rain x_2 (in millimeters), the amount of harvest rain x_3 (in millimeters), and the years since vintage x_4. A portion of the data is shown in the accompanying table.

y	x_1	x_2	x_3	x_4
0.3684	17.1167	600	160	31
0.6348	16.7333	690	80	30
⋮	⋮	⋮	⋮	⋮
0.1359	16.0000	578	74	3

a. Estimate the linear model: $y = \beta_0 + \beta_1 x_1 + \beta_2 x_2 + \beta_3 x_3 + \beta_4 x_4 + \varepsilon$. What is the predicted price if $x_1 = 16$, $x_2 = 600$, $x_3 = 120$, and $x_4 = 20$?

b. Estimate the exponential model: $\ln(y) = \beta_0 + \beta_1 x_1 + \beta_2 x_2 + \beta_3 x_3 + \beta_4 x_4 + \varepsilon$. What is the predicted price if $x_1 = 16$, $x_2 = 600$, $x_3 = 120$, and $x_4 = 20$?

c. Use R^2 to select the appropriate model for prediction.

22. **FILE** ***Electricity_Cost.*** The facility manager at a pharmaceutical company wants to build a regression model to forecast monthly electricity cost (Cost in \$). Three main variables are thought to influence electricity cost: (1) average outdoor temperature (Temp in °F), (2) working days per month (Days), and (3) tons of product produced (Tons). A portion of the past year's monthly data is shown in the accompanying table.

Cost	Temp	Days	Tons
24100	26	24	80
23700	32	21	73
⋮	⋮	⋮	⋮
26000	39	22	69

a. Estimate the linear model: $\text{Cost} = \beta_0 + \beta_1\text{Temp} + \beta_2\text{Days} + \beta_3\text{Tons} + \varepsilon$. What is the predicted electricity cost in a month during which the average outdoor temperature is 65°, there are 23 working days, and 76 tons are produced?

b. Estimate the exponential model: $\ln(\text{Cost}) = \beta_0 + \beta_1\text{Temp} + \beta_2\text{Days} + \beta_3\text{Tons} + \varepsilon$. What is the predicted electricity cost in a month during which the average outdoor temperature is 65°, there are 23 working days, and 76 tons are produced?

c. Based on R^2, which model provides the better fit?

23. **FILE** ***Rental.*** Chad Dobson has heard about the positive outlook for rental properties. He has access to monthly rents (in \$) for 27 houses, along with three characteristics of the home: number of bedrooms (Beds), number of bathrooms (Baths), and square footage (Sqft). A portion of the data is shown in the accompanying table.

Rent	Beds	Baths	Sqft
2950	4	4	1453
2400	4	2	1476
⋮	⋮	⋮	⋮
744	2	1	930

a. Estimate a linear model that uses Rent as the response variable. Estimate an exponential model that uses log of Rent as the response variable.

b. Compute the predicted rent for a 1,500-square-foot house with three bedrooms and two bathrooms for the linear and the exponential models (ignore the significance tests).

c. Use R^2 to select the appropriate model for prediction.

24. **FILE** ***Life_Expectancy.*** Life expectancy at birth is the average number of years that a person is expected to live. There is a huge variation in life expectancies between countries, with the highest being in Japan and the lowest in some African countries. An important factor for such variability is the availability of suitable health care. One measure of a person's access to health care is the people-to-physician ratio. We expect life expectancy to be lower for countries where this ratio is high. The accompanying table lists a portion of life expectancy of males and females in 40 countries and their corresponding people-to-physician ratio.

Country	Male	Female	Ratio
Argentina	67	74	370
Bangladesh	54	53	6166
⋮	⋮	⋮	⋮
Zaire	52	56	23193

a. Construct a scatterplot of female life expectancy against the people-to-physician ratio. Superimpose a linear trend and a logarithmic trend to determine the appropriate model.

b. Estimate a simple linear regression model with life expectancy of females as the response variable and the people-to-physician ratio as the explanatory variable. What happens to life expectancy of females as the people-to-physician ratio decreases from 1,000 to 500?

c. Estimate a logarithmic regression model with the natural log of the people-to-physician ratio as the explanatory variable. What happens to the life expectancy of females as the people-to-physician ratio decreases from 1,000 to 500?

d. Use R^2 to determine which of the preceding two models is more appropriate.

25. **FILE** ***Life_Expectancy.*** Use the data in Exercise 24 to answer the same four questions regarding life expectancy of males. Who is more likely to benefit from adding more physicians to the population? Explain.

26. **FILE** ***Production_Function.*** Economists often examine the relationship between the inputs of a production function and the resulting output. A common way of modeling this relationship is referred to as the Cobb–Douglas production function. This function can be expressed as $\ln(Q) = \beta_0 + \beta_1\ln(L) + \beta_2\ln(K) + \varepsilon$, where Q stands for output, L for labor, and K for capital. The accompanying table lists a portion of data with values representing indices.

State	Output	Labor	Capital
AL	3.1973	2.7682	3.1315
AR	7.7006	4.9278	4.7961
⋮	⋮	⋮	⋮
WY	1.2993	1.6525	1.5206

Estimate $\ln(Q) = \beta_0 + \beta_1 \ln(L) + \beta_2 \ln(K) + \varepsilon$.

a. What is the predicted change in output if labor increases by 1%, holding capital constant?

b. Holding capital constant, can we conclude at the 5% level that a 1% increase in labor will increase the output by more than 0.5%?

16.3 WRITING WITH DATA

Case Study

Photodisc/Getty Images

Numerous attempts have been made to understand happiness. Because there is no unique way to quantify it, researchers often rely on surveys to capture a subjective assessment of well-being. One study finds that holding everything else constant, people seem to be least happy when they are in their 40s (*Psychology Today*, April 27, 2018). Another study suggests that money does buy happiness, but its effect diminishes as incomes rise above $75,000 a year (*Money Magazine*, February 14, 2018).

Nick Fisher is a young business school graduate who is fascinated by these reports. He decides to collect his own data to better comprehend and also verify the results of these studies. He surveys working adults in his hometown and inputs information on the respondent's self-assessed happiness on a scale of 0 to 100, along with age and family income. A portion of the data is shown in Table 16.12.

FILE
Happiness

TABLE 16.12 Happiness, Age, and Income Data, $n = 100$.

Respondent	Happiness	Age	Income
1	69	49	52000
2	83	47	123000
⋮	⋮	⋮	⋮
100	79	31	105000

Nick would like to use the sample information to explore linear and nonlinear specifications for happiness and interpret the results for the best fitting model.

Sample Report—Understanding Happiness

In a survey of 100 working adults, respondents were asked to report their age and family income, as well as rate their happiness on a scale of 0 to 100. This report summarizes the analysis of several regression models that examine the influence of age and income on the perceived happiness of respondents. The models used various transformations to capture interesting nonlinearities suggested by recent research reports. For example, one such report shows that people get happier as they get older, despite the fact that old age is associated with a loss of hearing, vision, and muscle tone. In addition, while people start out feeling pretty good about themselves in their 20s, their self-assessed happiness deteriorates until around age 50 and then improves steadily thereafter. In order to quantify this possible quadratic effect, both age and age-squared variables are used for the regression. Also, the log transformation of income is considered to capture the possible diminishing effect on happiness of incomes above $75,000. The results of the various regression models are summarized in Table 16.13.

TABLE 16.13 Regression Results.

	Model 1	Model 2	Model 3	Model 4
Intercept	49.1938* (0.00)	118.5285* (0.00)	−81.0939* (0.00)	−13.3021 (0.39)
Age	0.2212* (0.00)	−2.4859* (0.00)	0.2309* (0.00)	−2.4296* (0.00)
Age-squared	NA	0.0245* (0.00)	NA	0.0241* (0.00)
Income	0.0001* (0.00)	0.0001* (0.00)	NA	NA
ln(Income)	NA	NA	12.6761* (0.00)	12.7210* (0.00)
Adjusted R^2	0.4863	0.6638	0.5191	0.6907

Notes: Parameter estimates are in the top portion of the table with the *p*-values in parentheses; NA denotes not applicable; * represents significance at the 5% level. The last row presents the adjusted R^2 values for model comparison.

Model 4 was selected as the most appropriate model because it has the highest adjusted R^2 value of 0.6907. The estimated parameters of this model were used to make predictions. For instance, with family income equal to $80,000, the predicted happiness for a 30-, 50-, and 70-year-old is 79.09, 69.00, and 78.17, respectively. Note that these results are consistent with those suggesting that happiness first decreases and then increases with age. Specifically, using the estimated coefficients for Age, a person is least happy at 50.48 years of age. These results are shown graphically in Figure16.11, panel a, where Happiness is plotted against Age, holding Income fixed at $80,000.

The regression results were also used to analyze the income effect. For instance, for a 60-year-old, the predicted happiness with family income of $50,000, $75,000, and $100,000 is 65.20, 70.36, and 74.02, respectively. Note that there is a greater increase in Happiness when income increases from $50,000 to $75,000 than when it increases from $75,000 to $100,000. These results are shown in Figure 16.11, panel b, where predicted Happiness is plotted against Income, holding Age fixed at 60 years. Overall, the results support recent research findings.

FIGURE 16.11 Predicted Happiness using Model 4 regression results

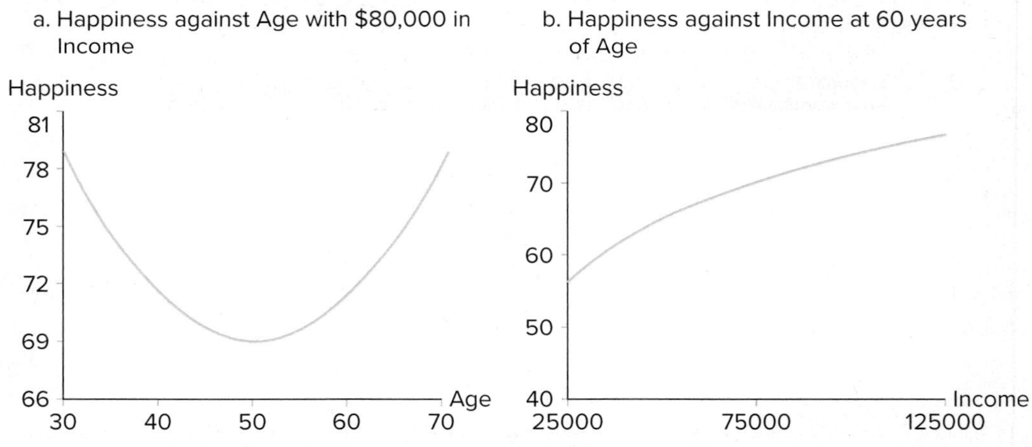

Suggested Case Studies

Report 16.1 FILE ***TechSales_Reps.*** Develop a regression model for predicting the salary of a sales representative in the software product group, using appropriate explanatory variables. Explore linear and nonlinear model specifications and use goodness-of-fit measures to find the best fitting model. Interpret your results with reference to graphs and tables.

Report 16.2. FILE ***House_Price.*** Choose two comparable college towns. Develop a regression model for predicting the sale price of a house for each college town, using appropriate explanatory variables. Explore linear and nonlinear model specifications and use goodness-of-fit measures to find the best fitting model. Interpret your results with reference to graphs and tables.

Report 16.3. FILE ***College_Admissions.*** Choose any college of interest and use the sample of enrolled students to predict a student's college grade point average. Explore linear and nonlinear model specifications and use goodness-of-fit measures to find the best fitting model. Interpret your results with reference to graphs and tables.

CONCEPTUAL REVIEW

LO 16.1 Use and evaluate polynomial regression models.

A quadratic regression model is specified as $y = \beta_0 + \beta_1 x + \beta_2 x^2 + \varepsilon$. Predictions with this model are made by $\hat{y} = b_0 + b_1 x + b_2 x^2$, where b_0 and b_1 are the coefficient estimates. It is advisable to use unrounded estimates for making predictions. In a quadratic regression model, $\hat{y}$ reaches a maximum (if $b_2 < 0$) or minimum (if $b_2 > 0$) at $x = \frac{-b_1}{2b_2}$.

A cubic regression model is specified as $y = \beta_0 + \beta_1 x + \beta_2 x^2 + \beta_3 x^3 + \varepsilon$. Predictions with this model are made by $\hat{y} = b_0 + b_1 x + b_2 x^2 + b_3 x^3$, where b_0, b_1, and b_2 are the coefficient estimates. It is advisable to use unrounded estimates for making predictions.

It is common to use adjusted R^2 to compare linear, quadratic, and cubic regression models.

LO 16.2 Use and evaluate log-transformed models.

A log-log regression model, also referred to as the power regression model, is specified as $\ln(y) = \beta_0 + \beta_1 \ln(x) + \varepsilon$. Predictions with this model are made by $\hat{y} = \exp(b_0 + b_1 \ln(x) + s_e^2/2)$, where b_0 and b_1 are the coefficient estimates and s_e is the standard error of the estimate. It is advisable to use unrounded estimates for making predictions.

A logarithmic regression model is specified as $y = \beta_0 + \beta_1 \ln(x) + \varepsilon$. Predictions with this model are made by $\hat{y} = b_0 + b_1 \ln(x)$, where b_0 and b_1 are the coefficient estimates. It is advisable to use unrounded estimates for making predictions.

An exponential regression model is specified as $\ln(y) = \beta_0 + \beta_1 x + \varepsilon$. Predictions with this model are made by $\hat{y} = \exp(b_0 + b_1 x + s_e^2/2)$, where b_0 and b_1 are the coefficient estimates and s_e is the standard error of the estimate. It is advisable to use unrounded estimates for making predictions.

LO 16.3 Describe the method used to compare linear models with log-transformed models.

We use the coefficient of determination R^2 to compare models that employ the same number of explanatory variables. Such comparisons are valid only when the response variable of the competing models is the same. In other words, we cannot compare the percentage of explained variations of y with that of $\ln(y)$. For a valid comparison, for any model that uses $\ln(y)$ as the response variable, we compute R^2 as $R^2 = (r_{y\hat{y}})^2$, where $r_{y\hat{y}}$ is the sample correlation coefficient between y and $\hat{y}$.

ADDITIONAL EXERCISES

27. FILE ***Fertilizer2.*** A horticulturist is studying the relationship between tomato plant height and fertilizer amount. Thirty tomato plants grown in similar conditions were subjected to various amounts of fertilizer (in ounces) over a four-month period, and then their heights (in inches) were

measured. A portion of the results is shown in the accompanying table.

Height	Fertilizer
20.4	1.9
29.1	5.0
⋮	⋮
36.4	3.1

a. Estimate the linear regression model: Height = $\beta_0 + \beta_1$Fertilizer + ε.
b. Estimate the quadratic regression model: Height = $\beta_0 + \beta_1$Fertilizer + β_2Fertilizer^2 + ε. Find the fertilizer amount at which the height reaches a minimum or maximum.
c. Use the best-fitting model to predict, after a four-month period, the height of a tomato plant that received 3.0 ounces of fertilizer.

28. **FILE** ***Sales_Reps.*** Brendan Connolly manages the human resource division of a high-tech company. He has access to the salary information of 300 sales agents along with each agent's age and net promoter score (NPS) which indicates customer satisfaction. A portion of the data is shown in the accompanying table.

Salary	Age	NPS
97000	44	9
50000	34	4
⋮	⋮	⋮
88000	36	10

a. Estimate a model using the natural log of salary as the response variable and Age, Age^2, and NPS as the explanatory variables.
b. Determine the optimal level of age at which the natural log of salary is maximized.
c. At the optimal age, predict the salary of an agent with NPS = 8.

29. **FILE** ***Homes.*** A realtor examines the factors that influence the price of a house. He collects data on the prices (in $) for 36 single-family homes in a suburb outside of Chicago. For explanatory variables, he uses the house's square footage (Sqft), as well as its number of bedrooms (Beds) and bathrooms (Baths). A portion of the data is shown in the accompanying table.

Price	Sqft	Beds	Baths
840000	2768	4	3.5
822000	2500	4	2.5
⋮	⋮	⋮	⋮
307500	850	1	1

a. Estimate the linear model: Price = $\beta_0 + \beta_1$Sqft + β_2Beds + β_3Baths + ε. Estimate the exponential model: ln(Price) = $\beta_0 + \beta_1$Sqft + β_2Beds + β_3Baths + ε.
b. Interpret the slope coefficients of the estimated models.
c. Use the coefficient of determination to choose the preferred model.

30. **FILE** ***Circuit_Boards.*** The operators manager at an electronics company believes that the time required for workers to build a circuit board is not necessarily proportional to the number of parts on the board. He wants to develop a regression model to predict time (in minutes) based on part quantity. He has collected data for the last 25 boards. A portion of this data is shown in the accompanying table.

Time	Parts
30.8	62
9.8	32
⋮	⋮
29.8	60

a. Estimate the linear regression model to predict time as a function of the number of parts. Then estimate the quadratic regression model to predict time as a function of Parts and Parts squared.
b. Evaluate the two models in terms of variable significance ($\alpha = 0.05$) and adjusted R^2.
c. Use the best-fitting model to predict how long it would take to build a circuit board consisting of 48 parts.

31. **FILE** ***Smoking.*** A nutritionist wants to understand the influence of income and healthy food on the incidence of smoking. He collects data on the percentage of smokers in each state in the United States, the percentage of the state's population that regularly eats fruits and vegetables and the state's median income (in $). A portion of the data is shown in the accompanying table.

State	Smoke	Fruits_ Vegetables	Income
AK	14.6	23.3	61604
AL	16.4	20.3	39980
⋮	⋮	⋮	⋮
WY	15.2	23.3	52470

a. Estimate: Smoke = $\beta_0 + \beta_1$Fruits_Vegetables + β_2Income + ε.
b. Compare this model with a model that log-transforms the income variable.

32. FILE ***Savings_Rate.*** The accompanying table shows a portion of monthly data on the personal savings rate (Savings in %) and personal disposable income (Income in $ billions) in the United States.

Savings	Income
2.2	10198.2
2.3	10252.9
⋮	⋮
5.5	11511.9

a. Estimate the linear model, Savings $= \beta_0 + \beta_1$Income $+ \varepsilon$, and a log-log model, ln(Savings) $= \beta_0 + \beta_1$ ln(Income) $+ \varepsilon$.
b. Which is the preferred model? Explain.

33. FILE ***Inventory_Cost.*** The inventory manager at a warehouse distributor wants to predict inventory cost (Cost in $) based on order quantity (Quantity in units). She thinks it may be a nonlinear relationship since its two primary components move in opposite directions: (1) order processing cost (costs of procurement personnel, shipping, transportation), which *decreases* as order quantity increases (due to fewer orders needed), and (2) holding cost (costs of capital, facility, warehouse personnel, equipment), which *increases* as order quantity increases (due to more inventory held). She has collected monthly inventory costs and order quantities for the past 36 months. A portion of the data is shown in the accompanying table.

Cost	Quantity
54.4	844
52.1	503
⋮	⋮
55.5	870

a. Create a scatterplot of inventory cost as a function of quantity. Superimpose a linear trendline and quadratic trendline.
b. Estimate the linear regression model to predict inventory cost as a function of order quantity. Then estimate the quadratic regression model to predict inventory cost as a function of order quantity and order quantity squared.
c. Evaluate the two models in terms of significance tests ($\alpha = 0.05$) and adjusted R^2.
d. Use the best-fitting model to predict monthly inventory cost for an order quantity of 800 units.

34. FILE ***Learning_Curve.*** Learning curves are used in production operations to estimate the time required to complete a repetitive task as an operator gains experience. Suppose a production manager has compiled 30 time values (in minutes) for a particular operator as she progressed down the learning curve during the first 100 units. A portion of this data is shown in the accompanying table.

Time	Unit
18.30	3
17.50	5
⋮	⋮
5.60	100

a. Create a scatterplot of time per unit against units built. Superimpose a linear trendline and a logarithmic trendline to determine visually the best-fitting model.
b. Estimate a simple linear regression model and a logarithmic regression model for explaining time per unit using unit number as the explanatory variable.
c. Based on R^2, use the best-fitting model to predict the time that was required for the operator to build Unit 50.

APPENDIX 16.1 Guidelines for Other Software Packages

The following section provides brief commands for Minitab, SPSS, and JMP. Import the specified data file into the relevant software spreadsheet prior to following the commands.

Minitab

Estimating Polynomial Regression Models

FILE *Wages*

A. (Replicating Example 16.3) To create the variable Age^2, from the menu, select **Calc > Calculator.** After **Store result in variable,** enter AgeSqu. After **Expression,** select Age, select *, and select Age.

B. Estimate the regression model using the standard commands.

Estimating Logarithmic Regression Models

A. (Replicating Example 16.8, Model 4) To create the variable ln(Rent), from the menu, select **Calc > Calculator.** After **Store result in variable,** enter ln(Rent). Under **Functions,** select **Natural log,** then select Rent. Repeat these steps to create the variable ln(Sqft).

B. Estimate the regression model using the standard commands.

Calculating a Comparable R^2

A. (Replicating Example 16.9) Create the variables ln(Rent) and ln(Sqft).

B. From the menu, choose **Stat > Regression > Regression > Fit Regression Model.** After **Responses,** select ln(Rent), and after **Continuous predictors,** select Bed, Bath, and ln(Sqft). Choose **Storage,** and then select **Fits.**

C. From the menu, select **Calc > Calculator.** After **Store result in variable,** enter yhat. After **Expression,** enter Exp(FITS1+0.1262*0.1262/2). (Recall that 0.1262 is the standard error of the estimate.)

D. From the menu, select **Stat > Basic Statistics > Correlation.** Under **Variables,** select Rent and yhat. Square the correlation coefficient to obtain R^2.

SPSS

Estimating Polynomial Regression Models

A. (Replicating Example 16.3) To create the variable Age^2, from the menu, select **Transform > Compute Variables.** Under **Target Variable,** enter AgeSqu. In the **Numeric Expression** dialog box, select Age, select *, and select Age.

B. Estimate the regression model using the standard commands.

Estimating Logarithmic Regression Models

A. (Replicating Example 16.8, Model 4) To create the variable ln(Rent), from the menu, select **Transform > Compute Variables.** Under **Target Variable,** enter lnRent. Under **Function group,** select **Arithmetic,** and under **Functions and Special Variables,** double-click on **Ln.** Under **Numeric Expression,** select Rent. Repeat these steps to calculate ln(Sqft).

B. Estimate the regression model using the standard commands.

Calculating a Comparable R^2

A. (Replicating Example 16.9) Create the variables lnRent and lnSqft.

B. From the menu, select **Analyze > Regression > Linear.**

C. Under **Dependent,** select lnRent, and under **Independent(s),** select Bed, Bath, and lnSqft. Choose **Save** and select **Predicted Values – Unstandardized.**

D. From the menu, select **Transform > Compute Variables.** Under **Target Variable,** enter yhat. Under **Numeric Expression,** input EXP(PRE_1+0.1262 ** 2/2). (Recall that 0.1262 is the standard error.)

E. From the menu, select **Analyze > Correlate > Bivariate.** Under **Variables,** select Rent and yhat. Square the correlation coefficient to obtain R^2.

JMP

Estimating Polynomial Regression Models

A. (Replicating Example 16.3) To create the variable Age^2, right-click on a new column and select **New Column,** and label it AgeSqu. Right-click on AgeSqu, and select **Formula.** Under **Table Columns,** select Age, select ×, and select Age.

B. Estimate the regression model using the standard commands.

Estimating Logarithmic Regression Models

FILE
College_Town

A. (Replicating Example 16.8, Model 4) To create the variable ln(Rent), right-click on a new column and select **New Column,** and label it ln(Rent). Right-click on ln(Rent), and select **Formula.** Under **Functions (grouped)**, select **Transcendental > Log,** and then select Rent in the bracket. Repeat these steps to create the variable ln(Sqft).

B. Estimate the regression model using the standard commands.

Calculating a Comparable R^2

College_Town

A. (Replicating Example 16.9) Create the variables ln(Rent) and ln(Sqft).

B. From the menu, choose **Analyze > Fit Model.** Drag ln(Rent) to the **Y** box, and drag Bed, Bath, and ln(Sqft) to the box under **Construct Model Effects.**

C. In the red triangle next to **Response ln(Rent)**, select **Save Columns > Predicted Values.** A new column named Predicted ln(Rent) should appear in the JMP spreadsheet.

D. In the JMP spreadsheet, right-click on a new column, select **New Column,** and enter yhat as the column name. Right-click on yhat, input **Formula > Transcendental > Exp.** In the bracket, input Predicted ln(Rent) + 0.1262 × 0.1262/2. (Recall that 0.1262 is the standard error.)

E. From the menu, select **Analyze > Multivariate Methods > Multivariate.** Drag Rent and yhat to the **Y, Columns** box. Square the correlation coefficient to obtain R^2.

17 Regression Models with Dummy Variables

LEARNING OBJECTIVES

After reading this chapter you should be able to:

LO **17.1** **Use a dummy variable to represent a categorical explanatory variable.**

LO **17.2** **Use and interpret the interaction between a dummy variable and a numerical variable.**

LO **17.3** **Estimate and interpret the linear probability model and the logistic regression model.**

Up until now, we have used regression models in applications where the response and the explanatory variables are numerical. There are other important applications of regression models that use categorical variables either as response and/or explanatory variables. For instance, if we want to examine whether women get paid as much as men for the same work, then we can use a categorical explanatory variable. Or, if we want to estimate the probability that a family buys a house, then we can use a categorical response variable.

Categorical variables require special attention in regression analysis because, unlike numerical variables, they cannot be used just as they are because regression models work only with numbers. In this chapter, we first convert categorical variables into dummy variables, that take on values 1 or 0, to describe two categories of the variable. Then, we show how a dummy variable is used in a regression model as an explanatory variable. We extend the analysis to explore the interaction between a dummy explanatory variable and a numerical explanatory variable.

Finally, we show how a dummy variable is used in a regression model as a response variable. We estimate and interpret two models in this scenario: the linear probability model and the logistic regression model.

Asia Images Group/Getty Images

INTRODUCTORY CASE

Is There Evidence of Wage Discrimination?

Several years ago, three female professors at Seton Hall University filed a lawsuit alleging that the University paid better salaries to younger instructors and male professors. Even though this particular case was eventually dismissed, other universities took notice.

Hannah Benson, a human resource specialist at a community college, was asked by the college's president to test for differences in salaries due to the professor's sex or age. For 42 professors, Hannah gathered information on annual salary (in $1,000s), years of experience, sex (Male or Female), and age (Younger or Older) where Younger and Older refer to age less than 60 years and 60 years or more, respectively. A portion of the data is shown in Table 17.1.

TABLE 17.1 Salary and Other Information on 42 Professors

FILE *Professor*

Salary	Experience	Sex	Age
67.50	14	Male	Younger
53.51	6	Male	Younger
⋮	⋮	⋮	⋮
73.06	35	Female	Older

Hannah would like to use the sample information in Table 17.1 to

1. Determine whether salary differs by a fixed amount between male and female professors.
2. Determine whether there is evidence of age discrimination in salaries.
3. Determine whether the salary difference between male and female professors increases with experience.

A synopsis of this case is provided in Section 17.2.

17.1 DUMMY VARIABLES

In Chapters 14 through 16, the explanatory variables and the response variable used in the regression applications have, for the most part, been numerical. For example, in Chapter 14, we used income and unemployment to explain variations in consumer debt. In empirical work, however, it is common to include some variables that are categorical. Although such variables can be described by several categories, they are commonly described by only two categories. Examples include a person's sex (male or female), homeownership (own or do not own), and loan default (yes or no).

In the first two sections of this chapter we focus on categorical explanatory variables. In the last section, we discuss how to estimate and interpret a regression model that uses a categorical response variable.

Given the professor salary data in the introductory case, we can estimate the model as $\hat{y} = 48.83 + 1.15x$ where y represents salary (in \$1,000s) and x is the usual numerical variable, representing experience (in years). The sample regression equation implies that the predicted salary increases by about \$1,150 (= 1.15 × 1,000) for every year of experience. Arguably, in addition to experience, variations in salary are also associated with a person's sex (male or female) and age (less than 60 years or at least 60 years).

A Categorical Explanatory Variable with Two Categories

LO 17.1

Use a dummy variable to represent a categorical explanatory variable.

A categorical variable requires special attention in regression analysis because, unlike a numerical variable, the observations of a categorical variable cannot be used in their original form—that is, in a non-numerical format. We convert a categorical variable into a **dummy variable,** also referred to as an **indicator variable.** A dummy variable d is defined as a variable that assumes a value of 1 for one of the categories and 0 for the other. For example, when categorizing a person's sex, we can define d as 1 for male and 0 for female. Alternatively, we can define d as 1 for female and 0 for male, with no change in inference.

Sometimes we define a dummy variable by converting a numerical variable into categories. In the introductory case, the age variable (less than 60 years or at least 60 years) was defined from a numerical variable. Similarly, in studying teen behavior, we may have access to numerical information on age, but we can generate a dummy variable that equals 1 for ages between 13 and 19 and 0 otherwise.

A DUMMY VARIABLE

A dummy variable d is defined as a variable that takes on values of 1 or 0. It is commonly used to describe a categorical variable with two categories.

For the sake of simplicity, we will first consider a model containing one numerical explanatory variable and one dummy variable. As we will see shortly, the model can easily be extended to include additional variables.

Consider the following model:

$$y = \beta_0 + \beta_1 x + \beta_2 d + \varepsilon,$$

where x is a numerical variable and d is a dummy variable with values of 1 or 0. We can use sample data to estimate the model as

$$\hat{y} = b_0 + b_1 x + b_2 d.$$

For a given x and $d = 1$, we can compute the predicted value as

$$\hat{y} = b_0 + b_1 x + b_2 = (b_0 + b_2) + b_1 x.$$

Similarly, for $d = 0$,

$$\hat{y} = b_0 + b_1 x.$$

Observe that the two regression lines, $\hat{y} = (b_0 + b_2) + b_1x$ and $\hat{y} = b_0 + b_1x$, have the same slope b_1. Thus, the sample regression equation $\hat{y} = b_0 + b_1x + b_2d$ accommodates two parallel lines; that is, the dummy variable d affects the intercept but not the slope. The difference between the intercepts is b_2 when d changes from 0 to 1. Figure 17.1 shows the two regression lines, one for each category, when $b_2 > 0$.

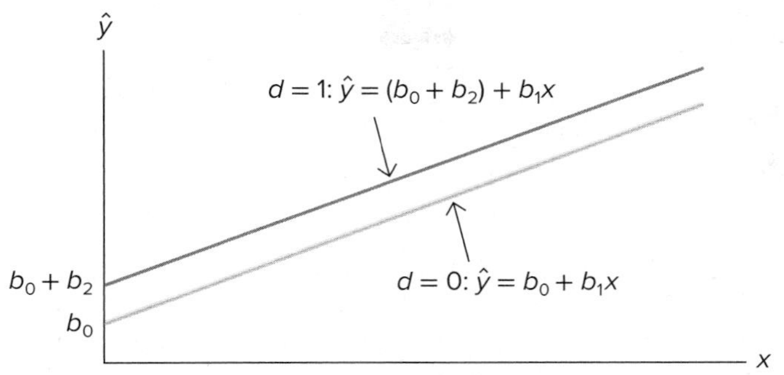

FIGURE 17.1 Using d for an intercept shift

EXAMPLE 17.1

Professor

The objective outlined in the introductory case is to determine if there are differences in salaries due to a professor's sex or age at a community college. Use the ***Professor*** data file to solve the following problems.

a. Estimate $y = \beta_0 + \beta_1x + \beta_2d_1 + \beta_3d_2 + \varepsilon$, where y is the annual salary (in \$1,000s) of a professor, x is the number of years of experience. For this regression, we have to first create a Male dummy variable d_1 that equals 1 if the professor is male and 0 otherwise, and an Older dummy variable d_2 that equals 1 if the professor is at least 60 years of age and 0 otherwise.

b. Compute the predicted salary of a 50-year-old male professor with 10 years of experience. Compute the predicted salary of a 50-year-old female professor with 10 years of experience. Discuss the impact of one's sex on predicted salary.

c. Compute the predicted salary of a 65-year-old female professor with 10 years of experience. Discuss the impact of age on predicted salary.

SOLUTION:

a. Table 17.2 shows a portion of the regression results; shortly, we will use Excel and R to convert a categorical variable into a dummy variable.

TABLE 17.2 Regression Results for Example 17.1

	Coefficients	*Standard Error*	*t Stat*	*p-Value*
Intercept	40.6060	3.6919	10.999	0.000
Experience (x)	1.1279	0.1790	6.300	0.000
Male (d_1)	13.9240	2.8667	4.857	0.000
Older (d_2)	4.3428	4.6436	0.935	0.356

The estimated model is $\hat{y} = 40.6060 + 1.1279x + 13.9240d_1 + 4.3428d_2$.

b. The predicted salary of a 50-year-old male professor ($d_1 = 1$ and $d_2 = 0$) with 10 years of experience ($x = 10$) is

$\hat{y} = 40.6060 + 1.1279 \times 10 + 13.9240 \times 1 + 4.3428 \times 0 = 65.8095$, or about \$65,810.

The corresponding salary of a 50-year-old female professor ($d_1 = 0$ and $d_2 = 0$) is

$\hat{y} = 40.6060 + 1.1279 \times 10 + 13.9240 \times 0 + 4.3428 \times 0 = 51.8855$, or about \$51,886.

The predicted difference in salary between a male and a female professor with 10 years of experience is \$13,924 (65,810 – 51,886). This difference can also be inferred from the estimated coefficient 13.924 of the male dummy variable d_1. Note that the salary difference does not change with experience. For instance, the predicted salary of a 50-year-old male with 20 years of experience is \$77,089. The corresponding salary of a 50-year-old female is \$63,165, for the same difference of \$13,924.

c. For a 65-year-old female professor ($d_1 = 0$ and $d_2 = 1$) with 10 years of experience ($x = 10$), the predicted salary is

$$\hat{y} = 40.6060 + 1.1279 \times 10 + 13.9240 \times 0 + 4.3428 \times 1 = 56.2283,$$
or about \$56,228.

Prior to any statistical testing, it appears that an older female professor earns, on average, about \$4,343 more than a younger female professor with the same experience. Again, this difference can be inferred from the estimated coefficient of 4.343 of the Older dummy variable d_2.

Using Excel and R to Make Dummy Variables

The following Excel and R instructions can be used to convert categorical variables into dummy variables.

Using Excel

A. Open the ***Professor*** data file.

B. We use the **IF** function to create a dummy variable for the Sex and Age variables. Enter the column heading Male in cell E1. In cell E2, enter the formula =IF(C2="Male", 1, 0). Fill the range E3:E43 with the formula in E2. Similarly, enter the column heading Older in cell F1. In cell F2, enter the formula =IF(D2="Older", 1, 0). Fill the range F3:F43 with the formula in F2.

Using R

A. Import the ***Professor*** data file into a data frame (table) and label it myData.

B. We use the **ifelse** function to create a dummy variable for the Sex and Age variables. Enter:

```
> myData$Male <- ifelse(myData$Sex == "Male", 1, 0)
> myData$Older <- ifelse(myData$Age == "Older", 1, 0)
```

Summary

We verify that the first two observations are 1 and 1 for male and 0 and 0 for Old. Regression models that use the male and old dummy variables can now be estimated easily.

Assessing Dummy Variable Models

Dummy variables are treated just like other explanatory variables; that is, all statistical tests and goodness-of-fit measures, discussed in earlier chapters remain valid. In particular, we can examine whether a particular dummy variable is statistically significant by using the standard t-test.

TESTING THE SIGNIFICANCE OF A DUMMY VARIABLE

In a model, $y = \beta_0 + \beta_1 x + \beta_2 d_1 + \beta_3 d_2 + \varepsilon$, we can perform the t-test to determine the significance of each dummy variable.

EXAMPLE 17.2

Refer to the regression results in Table 17.2.

a. Determine whether a male professor's salary differs from a female professor's salary at the 5% significance level.

b. Determine whether an older professor's salary differs from a younger professor's salary at the 5% significance level.

SOLUTION:

a. In order to test for a salary difference between male and female professors, we set up the competing hypotheses as H_0: $\beta_2 = 0$ against H_A: $\beta_2 \neq 0$. Given a value of the t_{df} test statistic of 4.857 with a p-value ≈ 0, we reject the null hypothesis and conclude that the Male dummy variable is statistically significant at the 5% level. We conclude that male and female professors do not make the same salary, holding other variables constant.

b. Here the competing hypotheses take the form H_0: $\beta_3 = 0$ against H_A: $\beta_3 \neq 0$. Given a value of the t_{df} test statistic of 0.935 with a p-value $= 0.356$, we cannot reject the null hypothesis. At the 5% significance level, we cannot conclude that an older professor's salary differs from a younger professor's salary.

We now turn our attention to selecting the preferred model for the analysis. Regression results are summarized in Table 17.3.

TABLE 17.3 Summary of Model Estimates

Variable	Model 1	Model 2	Model 3
Intercept	48.8274* (0.000)	39.4333* (0.000)	40.6060* (0.000)
Experience (x)	1.1455* (0.000)	1.2396* (0.000)	1.1279* (0.000)
Male (d_1)	NA	13.8857* (0.000)	13.9240* (0.000)
Older (d_2)	NA	NA	4.3428 (0.356)
Adjusted R^2	0.5358	0.7031	0.7022

Notes: The table contains parameter estimates with p-values in parentheses; NA denotes not applicable; * represents significance at the 5% level; adjusted R^2, reported in the last row, is used for model selection.

Model 1 uses only the numerical Experience variable. In addition to Experience, Model 2 includes the Male dummy variable, and Model 3 includes the Male and Older dummy variables. This raises an important question: which of the above three models should we use for making predictions? As discussed in Chapter 14, we usually rely on adjusted R^2 to compare models with different numbers of explanatory variables. Based on the adjusted R^2 values of the models, reported in the last row of Table 17.3, we select Model 2 as the preferred model because it has the highest adjusted R^2 value of 0.7031. This is consistent with the test results that showed that the Male dummy variable is significant, but the Older dummy variable is not significant, at the 5% level.

A Categorical Explanatory Variable with Multiple Categories

So far we have used dummy variables to describe explanatory variables with two categories. Sometimes, a categorical explanatory variable may be defined by more than two categories. In such cases, we use multiple dummy variables to capture all categories.

For example, the mode of transportation used to commute to work may be described by three categories: Public Transportation, Driving Alone, and Car Pooling. We can then define two dummy variables d_1 and d_2, where d_1 equals 1 for Public Transportation, 0 otherwise, and d_2 equals 1 for Driving Alone, 0 otherwise. For this three-category case, we need to define only two dummy variables; Car Pooling is indicated when $d_1 = d_2 = 0$.

Consider the following regression model:

$$y = \beta_0 + \beta_1 x + \beta_2 d_1 + \beta_3 d_2 + \varepsilon,$$

where y represents commuting expenditure, x represents distance to work, and d_1 and d_2 represent the Public Transportation and Driving Alone dummy variables, respectively. We can use sample data to estimate the model as

$$\hat{y} = b_0 + b_1 x + b_2 d_1 + b_3 d_2.$$

For $d_1 = 1$, $d_2 = 0$ (Public Transportation), $\hat{y} = b_0 + b_1 x + b_2 = (b_0 + b_2) + b_1 x$.

For $d_1 = 0$, $d_2 = 1$ (Driving Alone), $\hat{y} = b_0 + b_1 x + b_3 = (b_0 + b_3) + b_1 x$.

For $d_1 = d_2 = 0$ (Car Pooling), $\hat{y} = b_0 + b_1 x$.

Here Car Pooling is used as the reference category with the intercept b_0. The intercept changes to $(b_0 + b_2)$ for Public Transportation and $(b_0 + b_3)$ for Driving Alone. Therefore, we account for all three categories with just two dummy variables.

Given the intercept term, we exclude one of the dummy variables from the regression, where the excluded variable represents the reference category against which the others are assessed. If we include as many dummy variables as there are categories, then their sum will equal one. For instance, if we add a third dummy variable d_3 that equals 1 to denote Car Pooling, then for all observations, $d_1 + d_2 + d_3 = 1$. This creates the problem called perfect multicollinearity, a topic discussed in Chapter 15; recall that such a model cannot be estimated. This situation is sometimes referred to as the **dummy variable trap.**

AVOIDING THE DUMMY VARIABLE TRAP

Assuming that the linear regression model includes an intercept, the number of dummy variables representing a categorical variable should be *one less than the number of categories* of the variable.

EXAMPLE 17.3

A human resources manager at a software development firm would like to analyze the net promoter score (NPS) of sales representatives at the company. The NPS is a key indicator of customer satisfaction and loyalty, measuring how likely a customer would recommend a product or company to others on a scale of 0 (unlikely) to 10 (very likely). The manager believes that NPS is linked with the sales representative's personality type (Analyst, Diplomat, Explorer, and Sentinel) and the number of professional certifications (Certificates) he/she has earned. The manager collects data on NPS, personality types, and certificates for 120 sales representatives. A portion of the data is shown in Table 17.4.

NPS

TABLE 17.4 NPS, Certificates, and Personality Types; $n = 120$

NPS	Certificates	Analyst	Diplomat	Explorer	Sentinel
8	1	0	0	1	0
7	5	0	1	0	0
⋮	⋮	⋮	⋮	⋮	⋮
5	0	0	1	0	0

a. Estimate a linear regression model using NPS as the response variable and certificates along with three dummy variables representing Analyst, Diplomat, and Explorer as the explanatory variables. Note that Sentinel is used as the reference category.

b. Find the predicted NPS for a diplomat and a sentinel with three certificates.

c. Test if NPS differs between diplomats and sentinels at the 5% significance level.

SOLUTION:

a. We report a portion of the regression results of the estimated model in Table 17.5.

TABLE 17.5 Regression Results for Example 17.3

	Coefficients	Standard Error	*t* Stat	*p*-Value
Intercept	3.0998	0.461	6.721	0.000
Certificates	0.6123	0.103	5.971	0.000
Analyst	−0.1485	0.582	−0.255	0.799
Diplomat	2.5029	0.488	5.124	0.000
Explorer	1.9483	0.459	4.245	0.000

In addition to certificates, we find that personality types are linked with NPS. Among the four personality types, diplomats and explorers have the highest NPS values.

b. To predict NPS for a diplomat with three certificates, we set Certificates = 3, Analyst = 0, Diplomat = 1 and Explorer = 0 and calculate $\widehat{\text{NPS}} = 3.0998 + 0.6123 \times 3 + 2.5029 \times 1 = 7.44$. The corresponding NPS for a sentinel is $\widehat{\text{NPS}} = 3.0998 + 0.6123 \times 3 = 4.94$. The difference of 2.50 (7.44 − 4.94) can also be deduced from the estimated coefficient of 2.5029 for a diplomat.

c. With Sentinel as the reference category, the *p*-value for the Diplomat variable is approximately zero. Therefore, at the 5% significance level, we conclude that NPS differs between diplomats and sentinels.

EXAMPLE 17.4

Use the ***NPS*** data file to determine if NPS differs between diplomats and explorers. Conduct the test at the 5% significance level.

NPS

SOLUTION: We note that the regression results reported in Table 17.5 cannot be used to determine if NPS differs between diplomats and explorers. To conduct the relevant test, we must use either Diplomat or Explorer as the reference category against which the other is assessed. Table 17.6 shows a portion of the regression results using Explorer as the reference category.

TABLE 17.6 Regression Results for Example 17.4

	Coefficients	Standard Error	*t* Stat	*p*-Value
Intercept	5.0481	0.348	14.511	0.000
Certificates	0.6123	0.103	5.971	0.000
Analyst	−2.0968	0.501	−4.183	0.000
Diplomat	0.5546	0.388	1.428	0.156
Sentinel	−1.9483	0.459	−4.245	0.000

For a diplomat with three certificates, we set Certificates = 3, Analyst = 0, Diplomat = 1, Sentinel = 0 and calculate $\widehat{NPS} = 5.0481 + 0.6123 \times 3 + 0.5546 \times 1 = 7.44$, which is the same as the value obtained in Example 17.3. In fact, we can show that all predicted NPS values are identical to the corresponding values derived in Example 17.3. This shows that the choice of the reference category does not matter for making predictions.

With Explorer as the reference category, the p-value of 0.156 for the Diplomat variable is more than $\alpha = 0.05$. Therefore, we cannot conclude that NPS differs between diplomats and explorers at the 5% significance level.

EXERCISES 17.1

Mechanics

1. Consider a linear regression model where y represents the response variable, x is a numerical explanatory variable, and d is a dummy variable. The model is estimated as $\hat{y} = 14.8 + 4.4x - 3.8d$.
   a. Interpret the dummy variable coefficient.
   b. Compute $\hat{y}$ for $x = 3$ and $d = 1$.
   c. Compute $\hat{y}$ for $x = 3$ and $d = 0$.
2. Consider a linear regression model where y represents the response variable and d_1 and d_2 are dummy variables. The model is estimated as $\hat{y} = 160 + 15d_1 + 32d_2$.
   a. Compute $\hat{y}$ for $d_1 = 1$ and $d_2 = 1$.
   b. Compute $\hat{y}$ for $d_1 = 0$ and $d_2 = 0$.
3. Using 50 observations, the following regression output is obtained from estimating $y = \beta_0 + \beta_1 x + \beta_2 d_1 + \beta_3 d_2 + \varepsilon$.

	Coefficients	*Standard Error*	*t Stat*	*p-Value*
Intercept	−0.61	0.23	−2.75	0.007
x	3.12	1.04	3.01	0.003
d_1	−13.22	15.65	−0.85	0.401
d_2	5.35	1.25	4.27	0.000

   a. Compute $\hat{y}$ for $x = 250$, $d_1 = 1$, and $d_2 = 0$; compute $\hat{y}$ for $x = 250$, $d_1 = 0$, and $d_2 = 1$.
   b. Interpret d_1 and d_2. Are both dummy variables individually significant at the 5% level? Explain.

Applications

4. An executive researcher wants to better understand the factors that explain differences in salaries for marketing majors. He decides to estimate two models: $y = \beta_0 + \beta_1 d_1 + \varepsilon$ (Model 1) and $y = \beta_0 + \beta_1 d_1 + \beta_2 d_2 + \varepsilon$ (Model 2). Here y represents salary, d_1 is a dummy variable that equals 1 for male employees, and d_2 is a dummy variable that equals 1 for employees with an MBA.
   a. What is the reference group in Model 1?
   b. What is the reference group in Model 2?
   c. In the above models, would it matter if d_1 equaled 1 for female employees?
5. House price y is estimated as a function of the square footage of a house x and a dummy variable d that equals 1 if the house has ocean views. The estimated house price, measured in $1,000s, is given by $\hat{y} = 118.90 + 0.12x + 52.60d$.
   a. Compute the predicted price of a house with ocean views and square footage of 2,000 and 3,000, respectively.
   b. Compute the predicted price of a house without ocean views and square footage of 2,000 and 3,000, respectively.
   c. Discuss the impact of ocean views on the house price.
6. **FILE** ***Urban.*** A sociologist is studying the relationship between consumption expenditures of families in the United States (Consumption in $), family income (Income in $), and whether or not the family lives in an urban or rural community (Urban = 1 if urban, 0 otherwise). She collects data on 50 families, a portion of which is shown in the accompanying table.

Consumption	Income	Urban
62336	87534	0
60076	94796	1
⋮	⋮	⋮
59055	100908	1

   a. Estimate Consumption $= \beta_0 + \beta_1$Income $+ \beta_2$Urban $+ \varepsilon$. Use the estimated model to predict the consumption expenditure of urban families with an income of $80,000. What is the corresponding consumption expenditure of rural families?
   b. Estimate Consumption $= \beta_0 + \beta_1$Income $+ \beta_2$Rural $+ \varepsilon$ where the dummy variable Rural equals 1 if rural, 0 otherwise. Use the estimated model to predict the consumption expenditure of urban families with an income of $80,000. What is the corresponding consumption expenditure of rural families?
   c. Interpret the results of the preceding two models.
7. **FILE** ***IPO.*** One of the theories regarding initial public offering (IPO) pricing is that the initial return (Initial) on an IPO depends on the price revision (Revision). Another factor that may influence the initial return is whether or not the firm is high-tech. The following table shows a portion of the data on 264 IPO firms.

Initial	Revision	HighTech
33.93	7.14	No
18.68	−26.39	No
⋮	⋮	⋮
0.08	−29.41	Yes

a. Estimate $y = \beta_0 + \beta_1 x + \beta_2 d + \varepsilon$, where the dummy variable d equals 1 for firms that are high-tech and 0 otherwise. Use the estimated model to predict the initial return of a high-tech firm with a 10% price revision. Find the corresponding predicted return of a firm that is not high-tech.

b. Estimate $y = \beta_0 + \beta_1 x + \beta_2 d + \varepsilon$, where the dummy variable d equals 1 for firms that are not high-tech and 0 otherwise. Use the estimated model to predict the initial return of a high-tech firm with a 10% price revision. Find the corresponding predicted return of a firm that is not high-tech.

8. **FILE** ***BMI.*** According to the World Health Organization, obesity has reached epidemic proportions globally. While obesity has generally been linked with chronic disease and disability, researchers argue that it may also affect salaries. In other words, the body mass index (BMI) of an employee is a predictor for salary. The accompanying table shows a portion of salary data (in $1,000s) for 30 college-educated men with their respective BMI and a dummy variable that equals 1 for a white man and 0 otherwise.

Salary	BMI	White
34	33	1
43	26	1
⋮	⋮	⋮
45	21	1

a. Estimate a model for Salary using BMI and White as the explanatory variables. Determine if BMI influences Salary at the 5% level of significance.

b. What is the estimated salary of a white college-educated man with a BMI of 30? Compute the corresponding salary of a nonwhite man.

9. **FILE** ***Wage.*** A researcher wonders whether males get paid more, on average, than females at a large firm. She interviews 50 employees and collects data on each employee's hourly wage (Wage in $), years of higher education (EDUC), years of experience (EXPER), age (Age), and a Male dummy variable that equals 1 if male, 0 otherwise. A portion of the data is shown in the accompanying table.

Wage	EDUC	EXPER	Age	Male
37.85	11	2	40	1
21.72	4	1	39	0
⋮	⋮	⋮	⋮	⋮
24.18	8	11	64	0

a. Estimate: $\text{Wage} = \beta_0 + \beta_1\text{EDUC} + \beta_2\text{EXPER} + \beta_3\text{Age} + \beta_4\text{Male} + \varepsilon$.

b. Predict the hourly wage of a 40-year-old male employee with 10 years of higher education and 5 years experience. Predict the hourly wage of a 40-year-old female employee with the same qualifications.

c. Interpret the estimated coefficient for Male. Is the Male variable significant at the 5% level? Do the data suggest that sex discrimination exists at this firm?

10. **FILE** ***Nicknames.*** In the United States, baseball has always been a favorite pastime and is rife with statistics and theories. Researchers have shown that major league players who have nicknames live longer than those without them. The following table shows a portion of data on the lifespan (Years) of a player and a Nickname variable (Yes if the player had a nickname, No otherwise).

Years	Nickname
74	Yes
62	Yes
⋮	⋮
64	No

a. Create two subsamples, with one consisting of players with a nickname and the other one without a nickname. Calculate the average longevity for each subsample.

b. Estimate a linear regression model of Years on a dummy variable d with value 1 if the player had a nickname, 0 otherwise. Compute the predicted longevity of players with and without a nickname.

11. **FILE** ***SAT.*** The SAT has gone through many revisions over the years. People argue that female students generally do worse on math tests but better on writing tests. Consider the following portion of data on 20 students who took the SAT test last year. Information includes each student's score on the writing and math sections of the exam, the student's GPA, and a Female dummy variable that equals 1 if the student is female, 0 otherwise.

Writing	Math	GPA	Female
620	600	3.44	0
570	550	3.04	0
⋮	⋮	⋮	⋮
540	520	2.84	0

a. Estimate a linear regression model with Writing as the response variable and GPA and Female as the explanatory variables.

b. Compute the predicted writing score for a male student with a GPA of 3.5. Repeat the computation for a female student.

c. At the 5% significance level, determine if there is a difference in writing scores between males and females.

12. **FILE** ***SAT.*** Refer to the previous exercise for a description of the data. Estimate a linear regression model with Math as the response variable and GPA and Female as the explanatory variables.
   a. Compute the predicted math score for a male student with a GPA of 3.5. Repeat the computation for a female student.
   b. At the 5% significance level, determine if there is a difference in math scores between males and females.

13. **FILE** ***Ice_Cream.*** A manager at an ice cream store is trying to determine how many customers to expect on any given day. Overall business has been relatively steady over the past several years, but the customer count seems to have ups and downs. He collects data over 30 days and records the number of customers, the high temperature (in degrees Fahrenheit), and whether the day fell on a weekend (Weekend equals 1 if weekend, 0 otherwise). A portion of the data is shown in the accompanying table.

Customers	Temperature	Weekend
376	75	0
433	78	0
⋮	⋮	⋮
401	68	0

   a. Estimate: Customers $= \beta_0 + \beta_1$Temperature $+$ β_2Weekend $+ \varepsilon$.
   b. How many customers should the manager expect on a Sunday with a forecasted high temperature of 80°?
   c. Interpret the estimated coefficient for Weekend. Is it significant at the 5% level? How might this affect the store's staffing needs?

14. In an attempt to "time the market," a financial analyst studies the quarterly returns of a stock. He uses the model $y = \beta_0 + \beta_1 d_1 + \beta_2 d_2 + \beta_3 d_3 + \varepsilon$ where y is the quarterly return of a stock, d_1 is a dummy variable that equals 1 if quarter 1 and 0 otherwise, d_2 is a dummy variable that equals 1 if quarter 2 and 0 otherwise, and d_3 is a dummy variable that equals 1 if quarter 3 and 0 otherwise. The following table shows a portion of the regression results.

	Coefficients	*Standard Error*	*t Stat*	*p-Value*
Intercept	10.62	5.81	1.83	0.08
d_1	−7.26	8.21	−0.88	0.38
d_2	−1.87	8.21	−0.23	0.82
d_3	−9.31	8.21	−1.13	0.27

   a. Given that there are four quarters in a year, why doesn't the analyst include a fourth dummy variable in his model?
   b. At the 5% significance level, are the dummy variables individually significant? Explain.
   c. Explain how you would reformulate the model to determine if the quarterly return is higher in quarter 2 than in quarter 3, still accounting for all quarters.

15. **FILE** ***Industry.*** The issues regarding executive compensation have received extensive media attention. Consider a regression model that links CEO compensation (in \$ millions) with the total assets of the firm (in \$ billions) and the firm's industry. Dummy variables are used to represent four industries: Manufacturing Technology d_1, Manufacturing Other d_2, Financial Services d_3, and Nonfinancial Services d_4. A portion of the data for 455 CEOs is shown in the accompanying table.

Compensation	Assets	d_1	d_2	d_3	d_4
16.58	20.92	1	0	0	0
26.92	32.66	1	0	0	0
⋮	⋮	⋮	⋮	⋮	⋮
2.30	44.88	0	0	1	0

   a. Estimate the model: $y = \beta_0 + \beta_1 x + \beta_2 d_1 + \beta_3 d_2 + \beta_4 d_3 + \varepsilon$, where y and x denote compensation and assets, respectively. Here the reference category is the nonfinancial services industry.
   b. Use a 5% level of significance to determine which industries, relative to the nonfinancial services industry, have different executive compensation.
   c. Reformulate the model to determine, at the 5% significance level, if compensation is higher in Manufacturing Other than in Manufacturing Technology. Your model must account for total assets and all industry types.

16. **FILE** ***QuickFix.*** The general manager of QuickFix, a chain of quick-service, no-appointment auto repair shops, wants to develop a model to forecast monthly vehicles served at any particular shop based on four factors: garage bays (Garage), population within 5-mile radius (Population in 1,000s), interstate highway access (Access equals 1 if convenient, 0 otherwise), and time of year (Winter equals 1 if winter, 0 otherwise). He believes that, all else equal, shops near an interstate will service more vehicles and that more vehicles will be serviced in the winter due to battery and tire issues. A sample of 19 locations has been obtained. A portion of the data is shown in the accompanying table.

Vehicles	Garage	Population	Access	Winter
200	3	15	0	0
351	3	22	0	1
⋮	⋮	⋮	⋮	⋮
464	6	74	1	1

   a. Estimate the regression equation relating vehicles serviced to the four explanatory variables.
   b. Interpret each of the slope coefficients.
   c. At the 5% significance level, are the explanatory variables jointly significant? Are they individually significant? What about at the 10% significance level?
   d. What proportion of the variability in vehicles served is explained by the four explanatory variables?
   e. Predict vehicles serviced in a non-winter month for a particular location with 5 garage bays, a population of 40,000, and convenient interstate access.

17. FILE ***Retail.*** A government researcher is analyzing the relationship between retail sales (in $ millions) and the gross national product (GNP in $ billions). He also wonders whether there are significant differences in retail sales related to the quarters of the year. He collects 10 years of quarterly data. A portion is shown in the accompanying table.

Year	Quarter	Sales	GNP
1	1	696048	9740.5
1	2	753211	9983.5
⋮	⋮	⋮	⋮
10	4	985649	14442.8

a. Estimate $y = \beta_0 + \beta_1 x + \beta_2 d_1 + \beta_3 d_2 + \beta_4 d_3 + \varepsilon$ where y is retail sales, x is GNP, d_1 is a dummy variable that equals 1 if quarter 1 and 0 otherwise, d_2 is a dummy variable that equals 1 if quarter 2 and 0 otherwise, and d_3 is a dummy variable that equals 1 if quarter 3 and 0 otherwise. Here the reference category is quarter 4.

b. Predict retail sales in quarters 2 and 4 if GNP equals $13,000 billion.

c. Which of the quarterly sales are significantly different from those of the 4th quarter at the 5% level?

d. Reformulate the model to determine, at the 5% significance level, if sales differ between quarter 2 and quarter 3. Your model must account for all quarters.

17.2 INTERACTIONS WITH DUMMY VARIABLES

LO 17.2

Use and interpret the interaction between a dummy variable and a numerical variable.

So far we have used a dummy variable d to allow for a shift in the intercept. In other words, d allows the predicted y to differ between the two categories by a fixed amount across the values of x. We can also create an interaction variable, which allows the predicted y to differ between the two categories by a varying amount across the values of x. The interaction variable is a product term xd that captures the interaction between a numerical variable x and a dummy variable d. Together, the variables d and xd allow the intercept as well as the slope of the estimated linear regression line to vary between the two categories of a categorical variable.

Consider the following regression model:

$$y = \beta_0 + \beta_1 x + \beta_2 d + \beta_3 xd + \varepsilon.$$

We can use sample data to estimate the model as

$$\hat{y} = b_0 + b_1 x + b_2 d + b_3 xd.$$

For a given x and $d = 1$, we can compute the predicted value as

$$\hat{y} = b_0 + b_1 x + b_2 + b_3 x = (b_0 + b_2) + (b_1 + b_3)x.$$

Similarly, for $d = 0$,

$$\hat{y} = b_0 + b_1 x.$$

The dummy variable d along with the interaction variable xd affects the intercept as well as the slope of the estimated regression line. Note that the estimated intercept b_0 and slope b_1 when $d = 0$ shift to $(b_0 + b_2)$ and $(b_1 + b_3)$, respectively, when $d = 1$. Figure 17.2 shows a shift in the intercept and the slope of the estimated regression line when $d = 0$ changes to $d = 1$, given $b_2 > 0$ and $b_3 > 0$.

FIGURE 17.2 Using d and xd for intercept and slope shifts

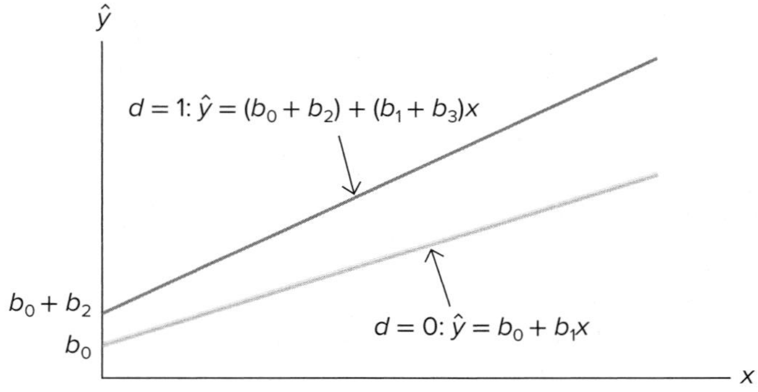

Prior to estimation, we use sample data to generate two variables, d and xd, which we use along with other explanatory variables in the regression. Tests of significance are performed as before.

SIGNIFICANCE TESTS WITH DUMMY VARIABLES

In a model $y = \beta_0 + \beta_1 x + \beta_2 d + \beta_3 xd + \varepsilon$, we can perform a t test for the individual significance of the dummy variable d and the interaction variable xd. Similarly, we can perform the partial F test for the joint significance of d and xd.

EXAMPLE 17.5

FILE *Professor*

In Section 17.1, we estimated a regression model to test for differences in salaries depending on a professor's sex and age. We found that the number of years of experience x and the Male dummy variable d_1 were significant in explaining salary differences; however, the Older dummy variable d_2 was insignificant. In an attempt to refine the model explaining salary, we drop d_2 and estimate three models using the ***Professor*** data file, where y represents annual salary (in $1,000s).

$$\text{Model 1: } y = \beta_0 + \beta_1 x + \beta_2 d_1 + \varepsilon$$
$$\text{Model 2: } y = \beta_0 + \beta_1 x + \beta_2 xd_1 + \varepsilon$$
$$\text{Model 3: } y = \beta_0 + \beta_1 x + \beta_2 d_1 + \beta_3 xd_1 + \varepsilon$$

a. Estimate and interpret each of the three models.

b. Select the most appropriate model.

c. Use the selected model to predict salaries for males and females over various years of experience.

SOLUTION:

a. In order to estimate the three models, we first generate data on d_1 and xd_1; shortly, we will use R to generate relevant variables and estimate this model. Table 17.7 shows a portion of the data.

TABLE 17.7 Generating xd_1 from the Data in Table 17.1

y	x	d_1	xd_1
67.50	14	1	$14 \times 1 = 14$
53.51	6	1	$6 \times 1 = 6$
⋮	⋮	⋮	⋮
73.06	35	0	$35 \times 0 = 0$

Table 17.8 summarizes the regression results for the three models.

TABLE 17.8 Summary of Model Estimates

	Model 1	Model 2	Model 3
Intercept	39.4333* (0.000)	47.0725* (0.000)	49.4188* (0.000)
Experience (x)	1.2396* (0.000)	0.8466* (0.000)	0.7581* (0.000)
Male (d_1)	13.8857* (0.000)	NA	−4.0013 (0.422)
Experience × Male (xd_1)	NA	0.7716* (0.000)	0.9303* (0.000)
Adjusted R^2	0.7031	0.7923	0.7905

Notes: The top portion of the table contains parameter estimates with p-values in parentheses; NA denotes not applicable; * represents significance at the 5% level; Adjusted R^2, reported in the last row, is used for model selection.

Model 1 uses the Male dummy variable d_1 to allow salaries between males and females to differ by a fixed amount, irrespective of experience. It is estimated as $\hat{y} = 39.4333 + 1.2396x + 13.8857d_1$. Since d_1 is associated with a p-value ≈ 0, we conclude at the 5% level that d_1 has a statistically significant influence on salary. The estimated model implies that, on average, males earn about \$13,886 (13.8857 × 1,000) more than females at all levels of experience.

Model 2 uses an interaction variable xd_1 to allow the difference in salaries between males and females to vary with experience. It is estimated as $\hat{y} = 47.0725 + 0.8466x + 0.7716xd_1$. Since xd_1 is associated with a p-value ≈ 0, we conclude that it is statistically significant at the 5% level. With every extra year of experience, the estimated difference in salaries between males and females increases by about \$772 (0.7716 × 1,000).

Model 3 uses d_1 along with xd_1 to allow a fixed as well as a varying difference in salaries between males and females. The estimated regression equation is $\hat{y} = 49.4188 + 0.7581x - 4.0013d_1 + 0.9303xd_1$. Interestingly, with a p-value of 0.422, the variable d_1 is no longer statistically significant at the 5% level. However, the variable xd_1 is significant, suggesting that with every extra year of experience, the estimated difference in salaries between males and females increases by about \$930 (0.9303 × 1,000).

b. While Model 1 shows that the dummy variable d_1 is significant and Model 2 shows that the interaction variable xd_1 is significant, Model 3 provides somewhat conflicting results. This raises an important question: which model should we trust? It is not uncommon to contend with such scenarios in business applications. As discussed earlier, we usually rely on adjusted R^2 to compare models that have a different number of explanatory variables. Based on the adjusted R^2 values of the models, reported in the last row of Table 17.8, we select Model 2 as the preferred model because it has the highest value of 0.7923.

c. In order to interpret the results further, we use Model 2 to predict salaries with varying levels of experience for both males and females. For example, with 10 years of experience, the predicted salary for males ($d_1 = 1$) is

$$\hat{y} = 47.0725 + 0.8466 \times 10 + 0.7716 \times 10 \times 1 = 63.255, \text{ or } \$63{,}255.$$

The corresponding predicted salary for females ($d_1 = 0$) is

$$\hat{y} = 47.0725 + 0.8466 \times 10 + 0.7716 \times 10 \times 0 = 55.539, \text{ or } \$55{,}539.$$

Therefore, with 10 years of experience, the salary difference between males and females is about \$7,716. Predicted salaries (in \$) for both males and females, and their salary difference, at other levels of experience are presented in Table 17.9.

TABLE 17.9 Predicted Salaries at Various Levels of Experience

Experience	Males	Females	Difference
1	\$48,691	\$47,919	\$772
2	\$50,309	\$48,766	\$1,543
3	\$51,927	\$49,612	\$2,315
4	\$53,546	\$50,459	\$3,087
5	\$55,164	\$51,306	\$3,858
10	\$63,255	\$55,539	\$7,716
15	\$71,346	\$59,772	\$11,574
20	\$79,438	\$64,005	\$15,433
25	\$87,529	\$68,239	\$19,290
30	\$95,620	\$72,472	\$23,148

Note that as experience increases, the salary difference between males and females becomes wider. For instance, the difference is $3,858 with 5 years of experience. However, the difference increases to $19,290 with 25 years of experience. This is consistent with the inclusion of the interaction variable in Model 2. The shift in the slope, implied by the predicted salaries in Table 17.9, is shown in Figure 17.3.

FIGURE 17.3 Predicted salaries of male and female professors

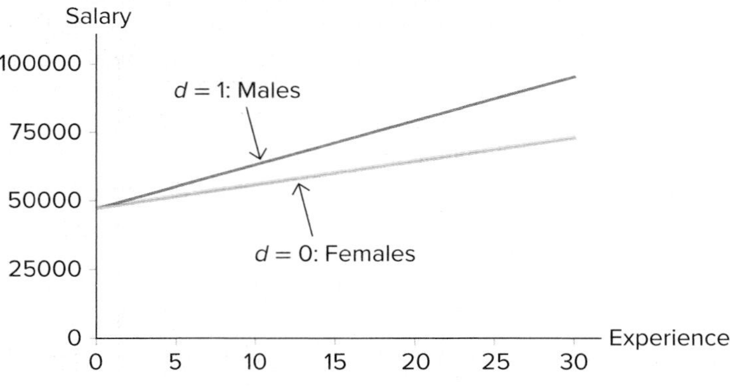

Using R to Estimate a Regression Model with a Dummy Variable and an Interaction Variable

The following instructions allow us to replicate the results for Example 17.5.

Professor

A. Import the ***Professor*** data into a data frame (table) in R and label it myData.

B. We use the **ifelse** function to create a dummy variable for the sex variable. Enter:

```
> myData$Male <- ifelse(myData$Sex == "Male", 1, 0)
```

C. We use the **lm** and **summary** functions to estimate and view three regression models, where Models 2 and 3 use the interaction variable created by multiplying Experience with Male. Enter:

```
> Model1 <- lm(Salary ~ Experience + Male, data = myData);
  summary(Model1)
> Model2 <- lm(Salary ~ Experience + I(Experience*Male),
  data = myData); summary(Model2)
> Model3 <- lm(Salary ~ Experience + Male + I(Experience*Male),
  data = myData); summary(Model3)
```

D. We use the **predict** function for Model 2 to predict the salary of a male and a female professor with 10 years of experience. Enter:

```
> predict(Model2, data.frame(Experience=c(10, 10), Male=c(1, 0)))
```

R returns: 63.25517 and 55.53896.

Predictions with other values for Experience can be found similarly.

SYNOPSIS OF INTRODUCTORY CASE

Hero Images/Getty Images

A lawsuit brought against Seton Hall University by three female professors alleged that the university engaged in both age and sex discrimination with respect to salaries (www.nj.com, November 23, 2010). Despite the fact that the case was eventually dismissed, the President of a community college wonders if the same can be said about its practices. For 42 professors, information is collected on annual salary, experience, whether a professor is male or female, and whether or not the professor is at least 60 years of age. A regression of annual salary against experience, a Male dummy variable, and an Older dummy variable reveal that the professor's sex is significant in explaining variations in salary, but the professor's age is not significant.

In an attempt to refine the model describing annual salary, various models are estimated that remove the Older dummy variable but use the Male dummy variable to allow both fixed and changing effects on salary. The sample regression line that best fits the data does not include the Male dummy variable for a fixed effect. However, the interaction variable, defined as the product of Male and Experience, is significant at any reasonable level, implying that males make about \$772 more than females for every year of experience. While the estimated difference in salaries between males and females is only \$772 with 1 year of experience, the difference increases to \$19,290 with 25 years of experience. In sum, the findings suggest that salaries do indeed differ by one's sex, and this difference increases with every extra year of experience.

EXERCISES 17.2

Mechanics

18. Consider a linear regression model where y represents the response variable and x and d are the explanatory variables; d is a dummy variable assuming values 1 or 0. A model with the dummy variable d and the interaction variable xd is estimated as $\hat{y} = 5.2 + 0.9x + 1.4d + 0.2xd$.
   a. Compute $\hat{y}$ for $x = 10$ and $d = 1$.
   b. Compute $\hat{y}$ for $x = 10$ and $d = 0$.

19. Using 20 observations, the following regression output is obtained from estimating $y = \beta_0 + \beta_1 x + \beta_2 d + \beta_3 xd + \varepsilon$.

	Coefficients	Standard Error	*t* Stat	*p*-Value
Intercept	13.56	3.31	4.09	0.001
x	4.62	0.56	8.31	0.000
d	−5.15	4.97	−1.04	0.316
xd	2.09	0.79	2.64	0.018

   a. Compute $\hat{y}$ for $x = 10$ and $d = 1$; compute $\hat{y}$ for $x = 10$ and $d = 0$.
   b. Are the dummy variable d and the interaction variable xd individually significant at the 5% level? Explain.

Applications

20. The annual salary of an employee y (in \$1,000s) is estimated as a function of years of experience x; a dummy variable d that equals 1 for college graduates and 0 for those graduating from high school but not college; and the interaction variable xd. The estimated salary is given by $\hat{y} = 30.3 + 1.2x + 15.5d + 2.0xd$.
   a. What is the predicted salary of a college graduate who has 5 years of experience? What is the predicted salary of a college graduate who has 15 years of experience?
   b. What is the predicted salary of a non-college graduate who has 5 years of experience? What is the predicted salary of a non-college graduate who has 15 years of experience?
   c. Discuss the impact of a college degree on salary.

21. House price y is estimated as a function of the square footage of a house x; a dummy variable d that equals 1 if the house has ocean views and 0 otherwise; and the interaction variable xd. The estimated house price, measured in \$1,000s, is given by $\hat{y} = 80 + 0.12x + 40d + 0.01xd$.
   a. Compute the predicted price of a house with ocean views and square footage of 2,000 and 3,000, respectively.
   b. Compute the predicted price of a house without ocean views and square footage of 2,000 and 3,000, respectively.
   c. Discuss the impact of ocean views on the house price.

22. **FILE** ***Urban.*** The accompanying data file shows consumption expenditures of families in the United States (Consumption in \$), family income (Income in \$), and whether or not the family lives in an urban or rural community (Urban = 1 if urban, 0 otherwise).

a. Estimate: Consumption $= \beta_0 + \beta_1$Income $+ \varepsilon$. Compute the predicted consumption expenditures of a family with income of $75,000.
b. Include the dummy variable Urban to predict consumption for a family with income of $75,000 in urban and rural communities.
c. Include the dummy variable Urban and an interaction variable (Income × Urban) to predict consumption for a family with income of $75,000 in urban and rural communities.
d. Which of the preceding models is most suitable for the data? Explain.

23. **FILE** ***BMI.*** The accompanying data file shows salary data (in $1,000s) for 30 college-educated men with their respective body mass index (BMI) and a dummy variable that represents 1 for a white man and 0 otherwise.
a. Estimate a model for Salary with BMI and White as the explanatory variables.
b. Reestimate the model with BMI, White, and a product of BMI and White as the explanatory variables.
c. Which of the models is most suitable? Explain. Use this model to estimate the salary for a white college-educated man with a BMI of 30. Compute the corresponding salary for a nonwhite man.

24. **FILE** ***Pick_Errors.*** The accompanying data file shows an employee's annual pick errors (Errors), experience (Exper in years), and whether or not the employee attended training (Train equals 1 if the employee attended training, 0 otherwise).
a. Estimate two models:
Errors $= \beta_0 + \beta_1$ Exper $+ \beta_2$ Train $+ \varepsilon$, and
Errors $= \beta_0 + \beta_1$ Exper $+ \beta_2$ Train $+ \beta_3$ Exper × Train $+ \varepsilon$.
b. Which model provides a better fit in terms of adjusted R^2 and the significance of the explanatory variables at the 10% level?
c. Use the chosen model to predict the number of pick errors for an employee with 10 years of experience who attended the training program, and for an employee with 20 years of experience who did not attend the training program.
d. Give a practical interpretation for the positive interaction coefficient.

25. **FILE** ***IPO.*** The accompanying data file shows information on 264 initial public offering (IPO) firms. The data include the initial return (Initial), price revision (Revision), and whether or not the firm is high-tech.
a. Estimate a model with the initial return as the response variable and the price revision and the high-tech dummy variable as the explanatory variables.
b. Reestimate the model with price revision along with the dummy variable and the product of the dummy variable and the price revision.
c. Which of these models is the preferred model? Explain. Use this model to estimate the initial return for a high-tech firm with a 15% price revision. Compute the corresponding initial return for a firm that is not high-tech.

26. **FILE** ***Savings.*** The accompanying data file shows monthly data on the personal savings rate (Savings in %) and personal disposable income (Income in $ billions) in the U.S. from January 2007 to November 2010.
a. Estimate and interpret a log-log model, ln (Savings) $= \beta_0 + \beta_1$ln (Income) $+ \varepsilon$. What is the predicted percentage change in savings when personal disposable income increases by 1%?
b. Suppose we want to test whether or not there has been a structural shift due to the financial crisis that erupted in the fall of 2008. Consider a dummy variable d that assumes a value 0 before August 2008 and a value of 1 starting August 2008 onwards. Estimate: ln (Savings) $= \beta_0 + \beta_1$ln (Income) $+ \beta_2 d + \beta_3$ln (Income) $\times d + \varepsilon$. What is the predicted percentage change in savings when personal disposable income increases by 1% prior to August 2008? What is the corresponding predicted percentage change starting in August 2008 onward?
c. At the 5% significance level, conduct the partial F test to determine whether or not β_2 and β_3 are jointly significant. Has there been a structural shift?

27. **FILE** ***BP_Race.*** Important risk factors for high blood pressure reported by the *National Institute of Health* include weight and ethnicity. High blood pressure is common in adults who are overweight and are African American. According to the American Heart Association, the systolic pressure (top number) should be below 120. In a recent study, a public policy researcher in Atlanta surveyed 150 adult men about 5′10″ in height and in the 55–60 age group. Data were collected on their systolic pressure, weight (in pounds), and race (African and Non-African); a portion of the data is shown in the accompanying data.

Systolic	Weight	Race
196	254	African
151	148	Non-African
⋮	⋮	⋮
170	228	Non-African

a. Use Race to create a dummy variable, labelled African, with values 1 for African and 0 otherwise. Estimate a regression model (Model 1) for Systolic with Weight and African as explanatory variables to predict the systolic pressure of African and non-African adult men with a weight of 180 pounds.
b. Extend the model in part a to include the interaction between Weight and African (Model 2) and use it to predict the systolic pressure of African and non-African adult men with a weight of 180 pounds.
c. Which of the two models is preferred for making predictions? Explain.

17.3 THE LINEAR PROBABILITY MODEL AND THE LOGISTIC REGRESSION MODEL

LO 17.3

Estimate and interpret the linear probability model and the logistic regression model.

So far we have considered regression models where dummy (binary) variables are used as explanatory variables. In this section, we analyze **binary choice (classification) models** where the response variable is a binary variable. The consumer choice literature is replete with applications such as whether or not to buy a house, join a health club, or go to graduate school. At the firm level, managers make decisions such as whether or not to run a marketing campaign, restructure debt, or approve a loan. In all such applications, the response variable is binary, where one of the choices can be designated as 1 (success) and the other as 0 (failure). Usually, this choice can be related to a host of factors—the explanatory variables. For instance, whether or not a family buys a house depends on explanatory variables such as household income, mortgage rates, and so on.

The Linear Probability Model

Consider a linear regression model $y = \beta_0 + \beta_1 x_1 + \beta_2 x_2 + \ldots + \beta_k x_k + \varepsilon$, where y is a binary variable; with an expected value, conditional on the explanatory variables, equal to $\beta_1 x_1 + \beta_2 x_2 + \ldots + \beta_k x_k$. Because y is a discrete random variable with only two possible outcomes, its conditional expected value also equals $0 \times P(y = 0) + 1 \times P(y = 1) = P(y = 1)$, or simply p. In other words, the probability of success p is a linear function of the explanatory variables; that is $p = \beta_1 x_1 + \beta_2 x_2 + \ldots + \beta_k x_k$. The linear regression model applied to a binary response variable is called the **linear probability model (LPM).**

THE LINEAR PROBABILITY MODEL

The linear probability model is specified as $y = \beta_0 + \beta_1 x_1 + \beta_2 x_2 + \ldots + \beta_k x_k + \varepsilon$, where y assumes a 1 or 0 value.

- Predictions with this model are made by $\hat{p} = \hat{y} = b_0 + b_1 x_1 + b_2 x_2 + \ldots + b_k x_k$, where $\hat{p}$ is the predicted probability of success and $b_0, b_1, b_2, \ldots, b_k$ are the coefficient estimates.
- It is advisable to use unrounded coefficient estimates for making predictions.

EXAMPLE 17.6

Mortgage

The Great Recession has forced financial institutions to be extra stringent in granting mortgage loans. Thirty recent mortgage applications are obtained to analyze the mortgage approval rate. The response variable y equals 1 if the mortgage loan is approved, 0 otherwise. It is believed that approval depends on the percentage of the down payment x_1 and the percentage of the income-to-loan ratio x_2. Table 17.10 shows a portion of the data.

TABLE 17.10 Mortgage Application Data

y	x_1	x_2
1	16.35	49.94
1	34.43	56.16
⋮	⋮	⋮
0	17.85	26.86

a. Estimate and interpret the linear probability model $y = \beta_0 + \beta_1 x_1 + \beta_2 x_2 + \varepsilon$.

b. Predict the loan approval probability for an applicant with a 20% down payment and a 30% income-to-loan ratio. What if the down payment was 30%?

SOLUTION:

a. Table 17.11 shows a portion of the regression results. The estimated regression equation is $\hat{p} = \hat{y} = -0.8682 + 0.0188x_1 + 0.0258x_2$. With p-values of 0.012 and 0.000, respectively, both explanatory variables exert a positive and statistically significant influence on loan approval, at a 5% level. Also, holding the income-to-loan ratio constant, $b_1 = 0.0188$ implies that a 1-percentage-point increase in down payment increases the approval probability by 0.0188, or by 1.88 percentage points. Similarly, holding down payment constant, a 1-percentage-point increase in the income-to-loan ratio increases the approval probability by 0.0258, or by 2.58 percentage points.

TABLE 17.11 The Linear Probability Model Results for Example 17.6

	Coefficients	Standard Error	*t* Stat	*p*-Value
Intercept	−0.8682	0.2811	−3.089	0.005
Down Payment (x_1)	0.0188	0.0070	2.695	0.012
Income-to-loan Ratio (x_2)	0.0258	0.0063	4.107	0.000

b. Using unrounded coefficient estimates, the predicted loan approval probability for an applicant with a 20% down payment and a 30% income-to-loan ratio is $\hat{p} = -0.8682 + 0.0188 \times 20 + 0.0258 \times 30 = 0.2836$. Similarly, the predicted loan approval probability with a down payment of 30% is $\hat{p} = -0.8682 + 0.0188 \times 30 + 0.0258 \times 30 = 0.4720$. In other words, as down payment increases by 10 percentage points, the predicted probability of loan approval increases by 0.188 (= 0.4720 − 0.2836), which is essentially the estimated slope, 0.0188, multiplied by 10. The estimated slope coefficient for the percentage of income-to-loan variable can be interpreted similarly.

Although it is easy to estimate and interpret the linear probability model, it has some shortcomings. The major shortcoming is that it can produce predicted probabilities that are greater than 1 or less than 0. For instance, for a down payment of 60%, with the same income-to-loan ratio of 30%, we get a predicted loan approval probability of $\hat{p} = -0.8682 + 0.0188 \times 60 + 0.0258 \times 30 = 1.04$, a probability greater than 1. Similarly, for a down payment of 4%, the model predicts a negative probability, $\hat{p} = -0.8682 + 0.0188 \times 4 + 0.0258 \times 30 = -0.02$. Furthermore, the linearity of the relationship may also be questionable. For instance, we would expect a big increase in the probability of loan approval if the applicant makes a down payment of 30% instead of 20%. This increase in probability is likely to be much smaller if the same 10-percentage-point increase in down payment is from 60% to 70%. The linear probability model cannot differentiate between these two scenarios. For these reasons, we introduce the logistic regression model, which is a more appropriate probability model for binary response variables.

The Logistic Regression Model

As mentioned above, the major shortcoming of the LPM is that for certain values of the explanatory variables, the predicted probability can be outside the [0,1] interval. For meaningful analysis, we would like a nonlinear specification that constrains the predicted probability between 0 and 1.

The probability of success, p, for the **logistic regression model** is specified as

$$p = \frac{\exp(\beta_0 + \beta_1 x_1 + \beta_2 x_2 + \ldots + \beta_k x_k)}{1 + \exp(\beta_0 + \beta_1 x_1 + \beta_2 x_2 + \ldots + \beta_k x_k)}$$

where $\exp(\beta_0 + \beta_1 x_1 + \beta_2 x_2 + \ldots + \beta_k x_k) = e^{\beta_0 + \beta_1 x_1 + \beta_2 x_2 + \ldots + \beta_k x_k}$ and $e \approx 2.718$. The logistic specification ensures that the predicted probability is between 0 and 1 for all values of the explanatory variables.

The logistic regression model cannot be estimated with standard ordinary least squares (OLS) procedures. Instead, we rely on the method of **maximum likelihood estimation (MLE).** While the MLE of the logistic regression model is not supported by Excel, it can easily be estimated with most statistical packages, including R. Given the relevance of the logistic regression model in business applications, it is important to be able to interpret and make predictions with the estimated model.

THE LOGISTIC REGRESSION MODEL

The probability of success, p, for the logistic regression model is specified as $p = \frac{\exp(\beta_0 + \beta_1 x_1 + \beta_2 x_2 + \ldots + \beta_k x_k)}{1 + \exp(\beta_0 + \beta_1 x_1 + \beta_2 x_2 + \ldots + \beta_k x_k)}$.

- Predictions with this model are made by $\hat{p} = \hat{y} = \frac{\exp(b_0 + b_1 x_1 + b_2 x_2 + \ldots + b_k x_k)}{1 + \exp(b_0 + b_1 x_1 + b_2 x_2 + \ldots + b_k x_k)}$, where $\hat{p}$ is the predicted probability of success and $b_0, b_1, b_2, \ldots, b_k$ are the coefficient estimates.
- It is advisable to use unrounded coefficient estimates for making predictions.

For illustration, let the binary response variable y be influenced by a single explanatory variable x. Figure 17.4 highlights the relationship between the predicted probability $\hat{p}$ and x for the linear probability model and the logistic regression model, given $b_1 > 0$. Note that in the linear probability model, the probability falls below 0 for small values of x and exceeds 1 for large values of x. The probabilities implied by the logistic regression model, however, are always constrained in the [0,1] interval. (For ease of exposition, we use the same notation to refer to the coefficients in the linear probability model and the logistic regression model. We note, however, that these coefficients and their estimates have a different meaning depending on which model we are referencing.)

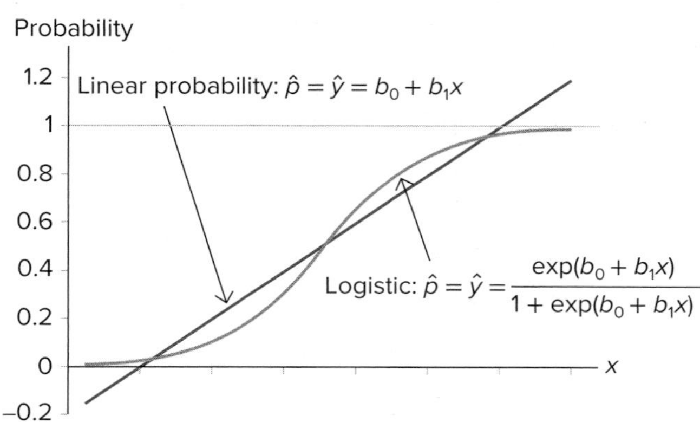

Figure 17.4 Predicted probabilities for the linear probability model and the logistic regression model, with $b_1 > 0$

It is important to be able to interpret the regression coefficients of the logistic regression model. In a linear probability model, the interpretation of a regression coefficient is straightforward. For instance, if the estimated linear probability model is $\hat{p} = -0.20 + 0.03x$, it implies that for every 1-unit increase in x, the predicted probability $\hat{p}$ increases by 0.03. We note that $\hat{p}$ increases by 0.03, whether x increases from 10 to 11 or from 20 to 21.

Now consider the estimated logistic regression model, $\hat{p} = \frac{\exp(-2.10 + 0.18x)}{1 + \exp(-2.10 + 0.18x)}$. Because the regression coefficient $b_1 = 0.18$ is positive, we can infer that x exerts a positive influence on $\hat{p}$. However, the exact impact based on the estimated regression coefficient is not obvious. A useful method to interpret the estimated coefficient is to highlight the changing impact of x on $\hat{p}$. For instance, given $x = 10$, we compute the predicted probability as $\hat{p} = \frac{\exp(-2.10 + 0.18 \times 10)}{1 + \exp(-2.10 + 0.18 \times 10)} = 0.4256$. Similarly, for $x = 11$, the predicted probability is $\hat{p} = 0.4700$.

Therefore, as x increases by one unit from 10 to 11, the predicted probability increases by 0.0444(= 0.4700 − 0.4256). However, the increase in $\hat{p}$ will not be the same if x increases from 20 to 21. We can show that $\hat{p}$ increases from 0.8176 when $x = 20$ to 0.8429 when $x = 21$, for a smaller increase of 0.0253. Note that when x is relatively large, its reduced influence on the predicted probability is consistent with the depiction of the logistic probabilities in Figure 17.4.

EXAMPLE 17.7

FILE *Mortgage*

Let's revisit Example 17.6.

a. Estimate and interpret the logistic regression model for the loan approval outcome y based on the applicant's percentage of down payment x_1 and the income-to-loan ratio x_2.

b. For an applicant with a 30% income-to-loan ratio, predict loan approval probabilities with down payments of 20% and 30%.

c. Compare the predicted probabilities based on the estimated logistic regression model with those from the estimated linear probability model in Example 17.6.

SOLUTION:

a. We use R to produce the logistic regression results shown in Table 17.12. (Instructions for estimating the logistic regression model with R are provided shortly.)

TABLE 17.12 Logistic Regression Results for Example 17.7

	Estimate	Std. Error	*z* value	*P* (>|z|)
(Intercept)	−9.3671	3.1958	−2.931	0.003
Down Payment (x_1)	0.1349	0.0640	2.107	0.035
Income-to-loan Ratio (x_2)	0.1782	0.0646	2.758	0.006

As in the case of the linear probability model, both explanatory variables exert a positive and statistically significant influence on loan approval at a 5% level, given positive estimated coefficients and p-values of 0.035 and 0.006, respectively. (In maximum likelihood estimation, the significance tests are valid only with large samples. Consequently, we conduct the z-test, in place of the usual t-test, to evaluate the statistical significance of a coefficient. The last column includes the p-values for a two-tailed test.)

b. The estimated probability equation is computed as

$$\hat{p} = \frac{\exp(-9.3671 + 0.1349x_1 + 0.1782x_2)}{1 + \exp(-9.3671 + 0.1349x_1 + 0.1782x_2)}.$$

The predicted loan approval probability with $x_1 = 20$ and $x_2 = 30$ is

$$\hat{p} = \frac{\exp(-9.3671 + 0.1349 \times 20 + 0.1782 \times 30)}{1 + \exp(-9.3671 + 0.1349 \times 20 + 0.1782 \times 30)} = 0.2103.$$

Similarly, the predicted loan approval probability with $x_1 = 30$ and $x_2 = 30$ is 0.5065. Note that, given the income-to-loan ratio of 30%, the predicted probability increases by 0.2962 (= 0.5065 − 0.2103) when the down payment increases from 20% to 30%. For the same income-to-loan ratio of 30%, it can be shown that the increase in the predicted probability is only 0.0449 (= 0.9833 − 0.9384) when the down payment increases from 50% to 60%.

c. Table 17.13 provides predicted probabilities for the linear probability and the logistic regression models for selected values of x_1 given $x_2 = 30$.

TABLE 17.13 Predicted Probabilities for the Linear Probability and the Logistic Regression Models

x_1	x_2	Linear Probability	Logistic
5	30	−0.0002	0.0340
20	30	0.2818	0.2103
30	30	0.4698	0.5065
50	30	0.8458	0.9384
60	30	1.0338	0.9833

As discussed earlier, with the linear probability model, the predicted probabilities can be negative or greater than one. The probabilities based on the logistic regression model stay between zero and one for all possible values of the explanatory variables. Therefore, whenever possible, it is preferable to use the logistic regression model over the linear probability model in binary choice models.

Sometimes, analysts prefer to interpret the estimated logistic model in terms of the **odds ratio**. The odds ratio is defined as the ratio of the probability of success $P(y = 1)$ to the probability of failure $P(y = 0)$, which is predicted as $\hat{p}/1 - \hat{p}$. The odds ratio metric is especially popular in sports and gambling. In this text, we focus on the probability of success and not on the odds ratio.

Using R to Estimate a Logistic Regression Model

We replicate the results for Example 17.7.

Mortgage

A. Import the ***Mortgage*** data file into a data frame (table) and label it myData.

B. We use the **glm** function to construct a logistic regression model object, which is a generalized version of the **lm** function; we label this object as Logistic_Model. Within the function, we specify the response and the explanatory variables, the binomial *family* option to denote a logistic model (default for binomial), and the data frame. Like the linear regression model, we use the **summary** function to view the output. Enter:

```
> Logistic_Model <- glm(y ~ x1 + x2, family = binomial, data = myData);
summary(Logistic_Model)
```

Note that the results are the same as those reported in Table 17.12.

C. We use the **predict** function to find predicted loan probabilities when $x_1 = 20$ and $x_2 = 30$, and when $x_1 = 30$ and $x_2 = 30$. Within the function we specify type ="response", to compute predicted probabilities. Enter:

```
> predict(Logistic_Model, data.frame(x1=c(20, 30), x2=c(30, 30)),
type = "response")
```

R returns: 0.2104205 and 0.5066462.

Note that in Example 17.7, we predicted the probabilities as 0.2103 and 0.5065; the differences are due to rounding. Other probabilities can be found similarly.

Accuracy of Binary Choice Models

There is no universal goodness-of-fit measure for binary choice models. Unlike in the case of the linear regression models, we cannot assess the performance of binary choice models based on the standard error of the estimate s_e, the coefficient of determination R^2, or adjusted R^2. These residuals-based measures are meaningless because the response variable can only take values 0 and 1, which then corresponds to two values for the residuals: $-\hat{y}$ for $y = 0$ and $1 - \hat{y}$ for $y = 1$.

It is common to assess the performance of the linear probability model and the logistic regression model on the basis of the accuracy rates defined as the percentage of correctly predicted outcomes. Using a default cutoff of 0.5, we first convert predictions of $\hat{y}$ into binary predictions that equal one if $\hat{y} \geq 0.5$ and zero if $\hat{y} < 0.5$. We then compare binary values of the response variable with binary predictions. The accuracy rate is calculated as the number of correct predictions divided by the total number of observations.

THE ACCURACY RATE OF A BINARY CHOICE MODEL

Using the default cutoff of 0.5, the binary predicted values are calculated as 1 for $\hat{y} \geq 0.5$ and 0 for $\hat{y} < 0.5$. These values are then compared with the binary y values to compute the accuracy rate as:

$$\frac{\text{number of correct predictions}}{\text{total number of observations}} \times 100$$

It is important to note that while the accuracy rate is a useful performance measure, it can sometimes be misleading. In applications with many ones and a few zeros, or many zeros and a few ones, the percentage of correctly predicted outcomes can be high even when the model predicts the less likely outcome poorly. For example, in the case of fraud detection, we are interested primarily in identifying the fraudulent cases where the number of fraudulent cases often account for a very small percentage (less than 1%) of the total number of cases. A fraud detection model that predicts all the nonfraudulent cases correctly but misses most of the fraudulent cases is not very useful despite having an extremely high accuracy rate (> 99%). Further details on cutoff values and other performance measures is beyond the scope of this text.

EXAMPLE 17.8

Mortgage

Continuing with the mortgage approval example, compare the accuracy rates of the estimated linear probability model (LPM) with the estimated logistic regression model.

SOLUTION: In order to compute the accuracy rates, we first find the predicted approval probabilities given the sample values of the explanatory variables. For the first sample observation, we find the predicted probability as:

$$\hat{y} = -0.8682 + 0.0188 \times 16.35 + 0.0258 \times 49.94 = 0.7276 \text{ (LPM), and}$$

$$\hat{y} = \frac{\exp(-9.3671 + 0.1349 \times 16.35 + 0.1782 \times 49.94)}{1 + \exp(-9.3671 + 0.1349 \times 16.35 + 0.1782 \times 49.94)} = 0.8504 \text{ (Logistic).}$$

Because the predicted values for both models are greater than 0.5, their corresponding binary predicted values are one. Predictions for other sample observations, and their binary conversions, are computed similarly; see Table 17.14 for a portion of these predictions.

TABLE 17.14 Computing the Accuracy Rates of Binary Choice Models

			Prediction		Binary Prediction	
y	x_1	x_2	LPM	Logistic	LPM	Logistic
1	16.35	49.94	0.7276	0.8504	1	1
1	34.43	56.16	1.2280	0.9950	1	1
⋮	⋮	⋮	⋮	⋮	⋮	⋮
0	17.85	26.86	0.1604	0.1022	0	0

We find that out of 30 observations, the binary predicted values match the values of y in 25 cases for the linear probability model and in 26 cases for the logistic regression model. Therefore, the accuracy rate is 83.33% for the linear probability model and 86.67% for the logistic regression model. We infer that the logistic regression model provides better predictions than the linear probability model.

Using R to Find the Accuracy Rate

We replicate the results for Example 17.8.

FILE
Mortgage

A. Import the ***Mortgage*** data file into a data frame (table) and label it myData.

B. We use the **lm** and **glm** functions to estimate the linear probability model and the logistic regression model, respectively. Enter:

```
> Linear_Model <- lm(y~x1+x2, data = myData)
> Logistic_Model <- glm(y ~ x1 + x2, family = binomial, data = myData)
```

C. We use the **predict** function to compute predicted probabilities for the sample data. Enter:

```
> PredLin <- predict(Linear_Model)
> PredLg <- predict(Logistic_Model, type = "response")
```

D. We use the **round** function to construct binary predictions. If a predicted probability is 0.50 or more, then its corresponding binary value is 1, and 0 otherwise. Enter:

```
> BinaryLin <- round(PredLin)
> BinaryLg <- round(PredLg)
```

E. We want to compute the percentage of the observations in the sample for which the actual outcome equals the predicted outcome. We use the double equal sign (==) to compare the two; if the two values are the same, the operator returns 1, and 0 otherwise. We use the **mean** function to compute the proportion of correctly classified observations, which we multiply by 100 to get a percentage. Enter:

```
> 100*mean(myData$y == BinaryLin)
> 100*mean(myData$y == BinaryLg)
```

R returns: 83.33333 for the linear probability model and 86.66667 for the logistic regression model.

EXERCISES 17.3

Mechanics

28. Consider a binary response variable y and an explanatory variable x that varies between 0 and 4. The linear model is estimated as $\hat{y} = -1.11 + 0.54x$.
    a. Compute the estimated probability for $x = 2$ and $x = 3$.
    b. For what values of x is the estimated probability negative or greater than one?

29. Consider a binary response variable y and an explanatory variable x. The following table contains the parameter estimates of the linear probability model (LPM) and the logistic regression model, with the associated p-values shown in parentheses.

Variable	LPM	Logistic
Constant	−0.72 (0.04)	−6.20 (0.04)
x	0.05 (0.06)	0.26 (0.02)

    a. Test for the significance of the intercept and the slope coefficients at the 5% level in both models.
    b. What is the predicted probability implied by the linear probability model for $x = 20$ and $x = 30$?
    c. What is the predicted probability implied by the logistic regression model for $x = 20$ and $x = 30$?

30. Consider a binary response variable y and two explanatory variables x_1 and x_2. The following table contains the parameter estimates of the linear probability model (LPM) and the logistic regression model, with the associated p-values shown in parentheses.

Variable	LPM	L ogistic
Constant	−0.40 (0.03)	−2.20 (0.01)
x_1	0.32 (0.04)	0.98 (0.06)
x_2	−0.04 (0.01)	−0.20 (0.01)

a. Comment on the significance of the variables at the 5% level.
b. What is the predicted probability implied by the linear probability model for $x_1 = 4$ with x_2 equal to 10 and 20?
c. What is the predicted probability implied by the logistic regression model for $x_1 = 4$ with x_2 equal to 10 and 20?

31. Using 30 observations, the following output was obtained when estimating the logistic regression model.

Predictor	Coef	SE	Z	P
Constant	−0.188	0.083	2.27	0.024
x	3.852	1.771	2.18	0.030

a. What is the predicted probability when $x = 0.40$?
b. Is x significant at the 5% level?

32. Using 40 observations, the following output was obtained when estimating the logistic regression model.

Predictor	Coef	SE	Z	P
Constant	1.609	1.405	1.145	0.252
x_1	−0.194	0.143	−1.357	0.177
x_2	0.202	0.215	0.940	0.348
x_3	0.223	0.086	2.593	0.010

a. What is the predicted probability when $x_1 = 15$, $x_2 = 10$, and $x_3 = -2$?
b. At the 5% significance level, which of the explanatory variables are significant?

33. FILE ***Exercise_17.33.*** The accompanying data file contains 20 observations on the binary response variable y along with the explanatory variables x_1 and x_2.
a. Estimate the linear probability model to compute $\hat{y}$ for $x_1 = 12$ and $x_2 = 8$.
b. Estimate the logistic regression model to compute $\hat{y}$ for $x_1 = 12$ and $x_2 = 8$.

34. FILE ***Exercise_17.34.*** The accompanying data file contains 20 observations on the binary response variable y along with the explanatory variables x_1 and x_2.
a. Estimate and interpret the linear probability model and the logistic regression model.
b. Compute the accuracy rates of both models.
c. Use the preferred model to compute $\hat{y}$ for $x_1 = 60$ and $x_2 = 18$.

Applications

35. FILE ***Purchase.*** Annabel, a retail analyst, has been following Under Armour, Inc., the pioneer in the compression-gear market. Compression garments are meant to keep moisture away from a wearer's body during athletic activities in warm and cool weather. Annabel believes that the Under Armour brand attracts a younger customer compared to other brands. In order to test her belief, she collects data on the age of the customers and whether or not they purchased Under Armour (1 for Under Armour, 0 otherwise). A portion of the data is shown in the accompanying table.

Purchase	Age
1	30
0	19
⋮	⋮
1	24

a. Estimate a linear probability model using Under Armour as the response variable and Age as the explanatory variable.
b. Compute the predicted probability of an Under Armour purchase for a 20-year-old customer and a 30-year-old customer.
c. Test Annabel's belief that the Under Armour brand attracts a younger customer, at the 5% level.

36. FILE ***Purchase.*** Refer to the previous exercise for a description of the data set. Estimate the logistic regression model where the Under Armour purchase depends on age.
a. Compute the predicted probability of an Under Armour purchase for a 20-year-old customer and a 30-year-old customer.
b. Test Annabel's belief that the Under Armour brand attracts a younger customer, at the 5% level.

37. FILE ***Insurance.*** According to the 2017 Census, just over 90% of Americans have health insurance. However, a higher percentage of Americans on the lower end of the economic spectrum are still without coverage. The accompanying table contains a portion of data showing insurance coverage (Insurance equals1 for coverage, 0 otherwise), the percentage of the premium paid by the employer (Premium in %), and the individual's income (Income in $1,000s) for 30 working adults in Georgia.

Insurance	Premium	Income
1	0	88
0	0	60
⋮	⋮	⋮
0	60	60

a. Analyze a linear probability model for insurance coverage with Premium and Income used as the explanatory variables.

b. Consider an individual with an income of $60,000. What is the probability that she has insurance coverage if her employer contributes 50% of the premium? What if her employer contributes 75% of the premium?

38. FILE ***Insurance.*** Refer to the previous exercise for a description of the data set. Estimate the logistic regression model where insurance coverage depends on Premium and Income. Consider an individual with an income of $60,000. What is the probability that she has insurance coverage if her employer contributes 50% of the premium? What if her employer contributes 75% of the premium?

39. FILE ***Admit.*** Unlike small selective colleges that pay close attention to personal statements, teacher recommendations, etc., large, public state university systems primarily rely on a student's grade point average (GPA) and scores on the SAT or ACT for the college admission decisions. Data were collected for 120 applicants on college admission (Admit equals 1 if admitted, 0 otherwise) along with the student's GPA and SAT scores. A portion of the data is shown in the accompanying table.

Admit	GPA	SAT
1	3.10	1550
0	2.70	1360
⋮	⋮	⋮
1	4.40	1320

a. Estimate the linear probability model and the logistic regression model.

b. Compute the accuracy rates of both models.

c. Use the preferred model to predict the probability of admission for a college student with GPA = 3.0 and SAT = 1400. What if GPA = 4.0?

40. FILE ***Divorce.*** Divorce has become an increasingly prevalent part of American society. According to a 2019 Gallup poll, 77% of U.S. adults say divorce is morally acceptable, which is a 17-point increase since 2001 (*Gallup*, May 29, 2019). In general, the acceptability is higher for younger adults who are not very religious. A sociologist conducts a survey in a small Midwestern town where 200 American adults are asked about their opinion on divorce (Acceptable equals 1 if morally acceptable, 0 otherwise), religiosity (Religious equals 1 if very religious, 0 otherwise), and their age. A portion of the data is shown in the accompanying table.

Acceptable	Religious	Age
1	0	78
1	0	20
⋮	⋮	⋮
1	0	22

a. Estimate the linear probability model and the logistic regression model.

b. Compute the accuracy rates of both models.

c. Use the preferred model to predict the probability that a 40-year old, very religious adult will find divorce morally acceptable. What if the adult is not very religious?

17.4 WRITING WITH DATA

Case Study

Create a sample report to analyze admission and enrollment decisions at a school of arts & letters in a selective four-year college in North America. For explanatory variables, include the applicant's sex, ethnicity, grade point average, and SAT scores. Make predictions for the admission probability and the enrollment probability using typical values of the explanatory variables. Before running the models, you have to first filter out the ***College_Admission*** data to get the appropriate subset of observations for selected variables.

Sample Report—College Admission and Enrollment

College admission can be stressful for both students and parents as there is no magic formula when it comes to admission decisions. Two important factors considered for admission are the student's high school record and performance on standardized tests.

Just as prospective students are anxious about receiving an acceptance letter, most colleges are concerned about meeting their enrollment targets. The number of acceptances a college sends out depends on its enrollment target and admissions yield, defined as the

Rawpixel.com/Shutterstock

percentage of students who enroll at the school after being admitted. It is difficult to predict admissions yield as it depends on the college's acceptance rate as well as the number of colleges to which students apply. As the number of applications for admission and the number of acceptances increase, the yield decreases.

In this report, we analyze factors that affect the probability of college admission and enrollment at a school of arts & letters in a selective four-year college in North America. Explanatory variables include the applicant's high school GPA, SAT score,[1] and the Male, White, and Asian dummy variables capturing the applicant's sex and ethnicity. In Table 17.15, we present the representative applicant profile.

TABLE 17.15 Applicant Profile for the School of Arts & Letters

Variable	Applied	Admitted	Enrolled
Male Applicant (%)	30.76	27.37	26.68
White Applicant (%)	55.59	61.13	69.83
Asian Applicant (%)	12.42	11.73	8.73
Other Applicant (%)	31.99	27.14	21.45
High School GPA (Average)	3.50	3.86	3.74
SAT Score (Average)	1,146	1,269	1,229
Number of Applicants	6,964	1,739	401

Of the 6,964 students who applied to the school of arts & letters, 30.76% were males; in addition, the percentages of white and Asian applicants were 55.59% and 12.42%, respectively, with about 32.00% from other ethnicities. The average applicant had a GPA of 3.50 and an SAT score of 1146. Table 17.15 also shows that 1,739 (or 24.97%) applicants were granted admission, of which 401 (23.06%) decided to enroll. As expected, the average GPA and SAT scores of admitted applicants are higher than those who applied and those who enrolled, but to a lesser extent.

Two logistic regression models are estimated using the same explanatory variables, one for predicting the admission probability and the other for predicting the enrollment probability. The entire pool of 6,964 applicants is used for the first regression, whereas 1,739 admitted applicants are used for the second regression. The results are presented in Table 17.16.

With accuracy rates of 81% and 77%, respectively, both models do a good job with predicting probabilities. It seems that the sex of the applicant plays no role in the admission or enrollment decisions. Interestingly, both white and Asian applicants have a lower probability of admission than those from other ethnicities. A higher admission rate for underrepresented applicants is consistent with the admission practices at colleges that believe that diversity

[1]The higher of SAT and ACT scores is included in the data where for comparison, ACT scores on reading and math are first converted into SAT scores.

TABLE 17.16 Logistic Regressions for College Admission and Enrollment

Variable	Admission	Enrollment
Constant	−17.5732* (−37.41)	7.2965* (8.48)
Male Dummy Variable	0.0459 (0.61)	−0.1433 (−1.05)
White Dummy Variable	−0.3498* (−4.43)	0.7653* (5.15)
Asian Dummy Variable	−0.4140* (−3.57)	−0.0074 (−0.03)
High School GPA	2.7629* (25.74)	−1.4265* (−7.17)
SAT Score	0.0056* (20.93)	−0.0028* (−5.99)
Accuracy (%)	81	77
Number of Observations	6,974	1,739

Notes: Parameter estimates are in the top half of the table with the *z*-statistics given in parentheses; * represents significance at the 5% level. Accuracy (%) measures the percentage of correctly classified observations.

enriches the educational experience for all. As expected, quality applicants, in terms of both GPA and SAT, are pursued for admission.

On the enrollment side, admitted applicants who are white are more likely to enroll than all other admitted applicants. Consider the case of a representative male applicant with an SAT score of 1300. For a white male, the predicted probabilities of admission and enrollment are 47% and 24%, respectively. The corresponding probabilities are 45% and 13%, respectively, for Asians, and 55% and 13%, respectively, for all other ethnicities.

The lower admission yield for underrepresented applicants is noteworthy. Perhaps the college should explore the reasons for the low yield and find ways to raise it. Finally, admitted applicants with high GPA and high SAT scores are less likely to enroll at this college. This is not surprising because academically strong applicants will have many offers, which lowers the probability that an applicant will accept the admission offer of a particular college.

Suggested Case Studies

Many different regression models can be estimated and assessed with the data that accompany this text. Here are some suggestions.

Report 17.1 FILE ***College_Admissions.*** Choose a college of interest and use the sample of enrolled students to best predict a student's college grade point average. Explore interactions with the appropriate dummy variables. In order to estimate these models, you have to first filter the data to include only the enrolled students.

Report 17.2 FILE ***House_Price.*** Choose two comparable college towns. Develop a predictive model for the sale price of a house for each college town. Explore linear and nonlinear model specifications with appropriate dummy variables to find a good fit. Interpret your results with reference to graphs and tables.

Report 17.3 FILE ***College_Admissions.*** Perform a similar analysis to the one conducted in this section, but choose a different college.

Report 17.4 FILE ***TechSales_Reps.*** The net promoter score (NPS) is a key indicator of customer satisfaction and loyalty. Use data on employees in the software product group with a college degree to develop the logistic regression model for predicting if an employee will score an NPS of 9 or more. In order to estimate this model, you have to first construct the (dummy) response variable, representing NPS ≥ 9. Also, subset the data to include only the employees who work in the software product group with a college degree.

CONCEPTUAL REVIEW

LO 17.1 Use dummy variables to represent categorical explanatory variables.

A dummy variable d is defined as a variable that takes on values of 1 or 0. Dummy variables are used to represent categories of a categorical variable. In a regression model that includes an intercept, the number of dummy variables needed should be one less than the number of categories of the categorical explanatory variable.

A regression model with a numerical variable x and a dummy variable d is specified as $y = \beta_0 + \beta_1 x + \beta_2 d + \varepsilon$. The dummy variable d allows the predicted y to differ between the two categories of a categorical variable by a fixed amount across the values of x. We estimate this model to make predictions as $\hat{y} = (b_0 + b_2) + b_1 x$ for $d = 1$ and as $\hat{y} = b_0 + b_1 x$ for $d = 0$.

LO 17.2 Use and interpret the interaction between a dummy variable and a numerical variable.

A regression model with a dummy variable d, a numerical variable x, and an interaction variable xd is specified by $y = \beta_0 + \beta_1 x + \beta_2 d + \beta_3 xd + \varepsilon$. We estimate this model to make predictions as $\hat{y} = (b_0 + b_2) + (b_1 + b_3)x$ for $d = 1$, and as $\hat{y} = b_0 + b_1 x$ for $d = 0$. The interaction variable xd allows the predicted y to differ between the two categories of a categorical variable by a varying amount across the values of x. In addition to performing a t test to determine the individual significance of d or xd, we can also implement the partial F test to determine their joint significance.

LO 17.3 Estimate and interpret the linear probability model and the logistic regression model.

Models that use a dummy (binary) variable as the response variable are called binary choice (classification) models.

A linear probability model (LPM) is specified as $y = \beta_0 + \beta_1 x_1 + \beta_2 x_2 + \cdots + \beta_k x_k + \varepsilon$. Predictions with this model are made by $\hat{p} = \hat{y} = b_0 + b_1 x + b_2 x_2 + \ldots + b_k x_k$, where $\hat{p}$ is the predicted probability of success and $b_0, b_1, b_2 \ldots, b_k$ are the coefficient estimates. It is advisable to use unrounded coefficient estimates for making predictions. The major shortcoming of the LPM is that it can produce predicted probabilities that are greater than one or less than zero.

A logistic regression model is a nonlinear specification that constrains the predicted probability within the [0, 1] interval. Predictions with this model are made by $\hat{p} = \frac{\exp(b_0 + b_1 x_1 + b_2 x_2 + \ldots + b_k x_k)}{1 + \exp(b_0 + b_1 x_1 + b_2 x_2 + \ldots + b_k x_k)}$, where $\hat{p}$ is the predicted probability of success and $b_0, b_1, b_2, \ldots b_k$ are the coefficient estimates. It is advisable to use unrounded coefficient estimates for making predictions.

ADDITIONAL EXERCISES

41. **FILE** ***Return.*** A financial analyst would like to determine whether the return on a mutual fund varies depending on the quarter; that is, if there is a seasonal component describing return. He collects 10 years of quarterly return data. A portion is shown in the accompanying table.

Observation	Quarter	Return
1	1	4.85
2	2	−3.96
⋮	⋮	⋮
40	4	4.06

a. Estimate $y = \beta_0 + \beta_1 d_1 + \beta_2 d_2 + \beta_3 d_3 + \varepsilon$, where y is the mutual fund's quarterly return, d_1 is a dummy variable that equals 1 if quarter 1 and 0 otherwise, d_2 is a dummy variable that equals 1 if quarter 2 and 0 otherwise, and d_3 is a dummy variable that equals 1 if quarter 3 and 0 otherwise.
b. Interpret the slope coefficients of the dummy variables.
c. Predict the mutual fund's return in quarters 2 and 4.

42. **FILE** ***Hiring.*** Researchers have documented race-based hiring in the Boston and Chicago labor markets. They sent out identical resumes to employers, half with African American sounding names and the other half with Caucasian sounding names and found a 53% difference in call-back rates between the two groups of people. A research fellow decides to repeat the same experiment in the Los Angeles labor market. She repeatedly sends out resumes for sales positions that are identical except for the difference in the names and ages of the applicants. She also records the call-back rate for each candidate. The accompanying table shows a portion of data on call-back rate (in %), age, and a Caucasian dummy that equals 1 for a Caucasian-sounding name, 0 otherwise.

CallBack	Age	Caucasian
12	60	1
9	56	0
⋮	⋮	⋮
15	38	0

a. Estimate a linear regression model with call-back as the response variable, and age and the Caucasian dummy variable as the explanatory variables.
b. Compute the call-back rate for a 30-year-old applicant with a Caucasian-sounding name. What is the corresponding call-back rate for a a 30-year-old applicant with a non-Caucasian-sounding name?
c. Conduct a test for race discrimination at the 5% significance level.

43. An analyst studies quarterly data on the relationship between retail sales (y, in $ millions), gross national product (x, in $ billions), and a quarterly dummy d that equals 1 if the sales are for the 4th quarter, 0 otherwise. He estimates the model $y = \beta_0 + \beta_1 x + \beta_2 d + \beta_3 xd + \varepsilon$. Relevant regression results are shown in the accompanying table.

	Coefficients	Standard Error	*t* Stat	*p*-Value
Intercept	186553.3	56421.1	3.31	0.002
x	55.0	4.6	12.08	0.000
d	112605.8	117053.0	0.96	0.342
xd	−4.7	9.3	−0.50	0.618

a. Interpret the dummy variable, d. Is it significant at the 5% level?
b. Interpret the interaction variable. Is it significant at the 5% level?

44. **FILE** ***Study.*** A researcher in the education department wants to determine if the number of hours that business students study per week at a state university varies by term. He conducts a survey where business students are asked how much they study per week in each of the three terms. He defines a Fall dummy variable that equals 1 if the survey was conducted in the fall term and 0 otherwise. The Winter and Spring dummy variables are defined similarly. The accompanying table shows a portion of the data for 120 students.

Hours	Fall	Winter	Spring
15	0	0	1
16	0	1	0
⋮	⋮	⋮	⋮
14	0	0	1

a. Estimate the appropriate model to determine, at the 5% significance level, if students study more in Fall and Winter as compared to Spring.
b. Find the predicted number of hours that students study per week in the fall, winter, and spring terms.

45. **FILE** ***Longevity.*** According to the Center for Disease Control and Prevention, life expectancy at age 65 in America is about 18.7 years. Medical researchers have argued that while excessive drinking is detrimental to health, drinking a little alcohol every day, especially wine, may be associated with an increase in life expectancy. Others have also linked longevity with income and a person's sex. The accompanying table shows a portion of data relating to the length of life after 65, average income (in $1,000s) at a retirement age of 65, a Female dummy variable, that equals 1 if the individual is female, 0 otherwise, and the average number of alcoholic drinks consumed per day.

Life	Income	Female	Drinks
19.00	64	0	1
19.30	43	1	3
⋮	⋮	⋮	⋮
20.24	36	1	0

a. Use the data to model life expectancy at 65 on the basis of Income, Female, and Drinks.

b. Conduct a one-tailed test at $\alpha = 0.01$ to determine if females live longer than males.

c. Predict the life expectancy at 65 of a male with an income of $40,000 and an alcoholic consumption of two drinks per day; repeat the prediction for a female.

46. **FILE** ***Shifts.*** The manager of a diner wants to reevaluate his staffing needs depending on variations in customer traffic during the day. He collects data on the number of customers served, along with the shift variable representing the morning, afternoon, evening, and night shifts. The accompanying table shows a portion of the data.

Customers	Shift
99	Night
148	Afternoon
⋮	⋮
111	Afternoon

a. Estimate a regression model using the number of customers as the response variable and the shift dummy variables as the explanatory variables; use Night as the reference category.

b. What is the predicted number of customers served during the morning, afternoon, evening, and night shifts?

47. **FILE** ***Overweight.*** According to the U.S. Department of Health and Human Services, African American women have the highest rates of being overweight compared to other groups in the United States. Individuals are considered overweight if their body mass index (BMI) is 25 or greater. Data are collected from 120 individuals. The following table shows a portion of data on each individual's BMI, a Female dummy variable that equals 1 if the individual is female, 0 otherwise, and a Black dummy variable that equals 1 if the individual is African American, 0 otherwise.

BMI	Female	Black
28.70	0	1
28.31	0	0
⋮	⋮	⋮
24.90	0	1

a. Estimate the model, $\text{BMI} = \beta_0 + \beta_1\text{Female} + \beta_2\text{Black} + \beta_3(\text{Female} \times \text{Black}) + \varepsilon$, to predict the BMI for white males, white females, black males, and black females.

b. Is the difference between white females and white males statistically significant at the 5% level?

c. Is the difference between white males and black males statistically significant at the 5% level?

48. **FILE** ***Compensation.*** To encourage performance, loyalty, and continuing education, the human resources department at a large company wants to develop a regression-based compensation model (Comp in $ per year) for mid-level managers based on three variables: (1) business unit-profitability (Profit in $1,000s per year), (2) years with the company (Years), and (3) whether or not the manager has a graduate degree (Grad equals 1 if graduate degree, 0 otherwise). The accompanying table shows a portion of data collected for 36 managers.

Comp	Profit	Years	Grad
118100	4500	37	1
90800	5400	5	1
⋮	⋮	⋮	⋮
85000	4200	29	0

a. Estimate the following model for compensation:
$$\text{Comp} = \beta_0 + \beta_1\text{Profit} + \beta_2\text{Years} + \beta_3\text{Grad} + \beta_4\text{Profit} \times \text{Grad} + \beta_5\text{Years} \times \text{Grad} + \varepsilon.$$

b. At the 5% significance level, is the overall regression model significant?

c. Which explanatory variables and interaction terms are significant at $\alpha = 0.05$?

d. Use the estimated model in part a to determine compensation for a manager having 15 years with the company, a graduate degree, and a business-unit profit of $4,800(000).

49. **FILE** ***Parole.*** Parole boards use risk assessment tools when trying to determine an individual's likelihood of returning to crime. Most of these models are based on a range of character traits and biographical facts about an individual. A sociologist collects data on 20 individuals who were released on parole two years ago. She notes if the parolee committed another crime over the last two years (Crime equals 1 if crime committed, 0 otherwise), the parolee's age at the time of release, and the parolee's sex. The accompanying table shows a portion of the data.

Crime	Age	Sex
1	25	Male
0	42	Male
⋮	⋮	⋮
0	30	Male

a. Estimate the linear probability model where crime depends on age and the parolee's sex.
b. Are the results consistent with the claims of other studies with respect to age and the parolee's sex?
c. Predict the probability of a 25-year-old male parolee committing another crime; repeat the prediction for a 25-year-old female parolee.

50. **FILE** ***Parole.*** Refer to the previous exercise for a description of the data set.
a. Estimate the logistic regression model where crime depends on age and the parolee's sex.
b. Are the results consistent with the claims of other studies with respect to age and the parolee's sex?
c. Predict the probability of a 25-year-old male parolee committing another crime; repeat the prediction for a 25-year-old female parolee.

51. **FILE** ***Assembly.*** Because assembly line work can be tedious and repetitive, it is not suited for everybody. Consequently, a production manager is developing a binary choice regression model to predict whether a newly hired worker will stay in the job for at least one year (Stay equals 1 if a new hire stays for at least one year, 0 otherwise). Three explanatory variables will be used: (1) Age; (2) a Female dummy variable that equals 1 if the new hire is female, 0 otherwise; and (3) an Assembly dummy variable that equals 1 if the new hire has worked on an assembly line before, 0 otherwise. The accompanying table shows a portion of data for 32 assembly line workers.

Stay	Age	Female	Assembly
0	35	1	0
0	26	1	0
⋮	⋮	⋮	⋮
1	38	0	1

a. Estimate and interpret the linear probability model and the logistic regression model where being on the job one year later depends on Age, Female, and Assembly.
b. Compute the accuracy rates of both models.
c. Use the preferred model to predict the probability that a 45-year-old female who has not worked on an assembly line before will still be on the job one year later. What if she has worked on an assembly line before?

52. **FILE** ***CFA.*** The Chartered Financial Analyst (CFA) designation is the de facto professional certification for the financial industry. Employers encourage their prospective employees to complete the CFA exam. Daniella Campos, an HR manager at SolidRock Investment, is reviewing 10 job applications. Given the low pass rate for the CFA Level 1 exam, Daniella wants to know whether or not the 10 prospective employees will be able to pass it. Historically, the pass rate is higher for those with work experience and a good college GPA. With this insight, she compiles the information on 263 current employees who took the CFA Level I exam last year, including the employee's success on the exam (1 for pass, 0 for fail), the employee's college GPA, and years of work experience. A portion of the data is shown in the accompanying table.

Pass	GPA	Experience
1	3.75	18
0	2.62	17
⋮	⋮	⋮
0	2.54	4

a. Estimate the linear probability model to predict the probability of passing the CFA Level I exam for a candidate with a college GPA of 3.80 and five years of experience.
b. Estimate the logistic regression model to predict the probability of passing the CFA Level I exam for a candidate with a college GPA of 3.80 and five years of experience.

53. **FILE** ***STEM.*** Several studies have reported lower participation in the science, technology, engineering, and mathematics (STEM) careers by female and minority students. A high school counselor surveys 240 college-bound students, collecting information on whether the student has

applied to a STEM field (1 if STEM, 0 otherwise), whether or not the student is female (1 if female, 0 otherwise), white (1 if white, 0 otherwise), and Asian (1 if Asian, 0 otherwise). Also included in the survey is the information on the student's high school GPA and SAT scores. A portion of the data is shown in the accompanying table.

STEM	GPA	SAT	White	Female	Asian
0	3.70	1420	0	0	1
0	4.40	1240	0	1	1
⋮	⋮	⋮	⋮	⋮	⋮
0	3.80	1390	0	1	0

a. Estimate and interpret the logistic regression model using STEM as the response variable, and GPA, SAT, White, Female, and Asian as the explanatory variables.
b. Find the predicted probability that a white male student will apply to a STEM field with GPA = 3.4 and SAT = 1400. Find the corresponding probabilities for an Asian male and a male who is neither white nor Asian.
c. Find the predicted probability that a white female student will apply to a STEM field with GPA = 3.4 and SAT = 1400. Find the corresponding probabilities for an Asian female and a female who is neither white nor Asian.

54. FILE ***Spam.*** Peter Derby works as a cyber security analyst at a private equity firm. He has been asked to implement a spam detection system on the company's e-mail server. He analyzes a sample of 500 spam and legitimate e-mails with the following relevant variables: spam (1 if spam, 0 otherwise), the number of recipients, the number of hyperlinks, and the number of characters in the message. A portion of the data is shown in the accompanying table.

Spam	Recipients	Hyperlinks	Characters
0	19	1	47
0	15	1	58
⋮	⋮	⋮	⋮
1	13	2	32

a. Estimate a logistic regression model for Spam using Recipients, Hyperlinks, and Characters as explanatory variables. Use the estimated model to predict the probability of spam if the number of recipients, hyperlinks, and characters are 20, 5, and 60, respectively.
b. Calculate the accuracy rate of the estimated model.

APPENDIX 17.1 Guidelines for Other Software Packages

The following section provides brief commands for Minitab, SPSS, and JMP. Import the specified data file into the relevant software spreadsheet prior to following the commands.

Minitab

Estimating a Logit Model

FILE *Mortgage*

(Replicating Example 17.7) From the menu, choose **Stat > Regression > Binary Logistic Regression > Fit Binary Logistic Model.** Select **Response in binary response/frequency format,** and after **Response,** select y. After **Continuous predictors,** select x1 and x2. Choose **Results,** and after **Display of results,** select **Expanded tables.**

SPSS

Estimating a Logit Model

FILE *Mortgage*

(Replicating Example 17.7) From the menu, select **Analyze > Regression > Binary Logistic.** Under **Dependent,** select y, and under **Covariates,** select x1 and x2.

JMP

Estimating a Logit Model

Mortgage

A. (Replicating Example 17.7) Right-click on y, select **Column Info,** and under **Modeling Type,** select **Nominal.**

B. From the menu, choose **Analyze > Fit Model.** Drag y to **Y** box and drag x_1 and x_2 to the box under **Construct Model Effect.** (Note: By default, JMP fits the 0 response. Thus, the results have opposite signs from those in the text.)

18 Forecasting with Time Series Data

LEARNING OBJECTIVES

After reading this chapter, you should be able to:

LO **18.1** **Describe the time series forecasting process.**

LO **18.2** **Use smoothing techniques to make forecasts.**

LO **18.3** **Use linear regression models to make forecasts.**

LO **18.4** **Use nonlinear regression models to make forecasts.**

LO **18.5** **Use lagged variable models to make forecasts.**

Observations of any variable recorded over time in sequential order are considered a time series. Forecasting with time series is an important aspect of analytics, providing guidance for decisions in all areas of business. In fact, the success of any business depends on the ability to accurately forecast vital variables. Sound forecasts not only improve the quality of business plans, but also help identify and evaluate potential risks. Examples include forecasting sales, product defects, the inflation rate, cyber attacks, or cash flows.

In this chapter, we focus on the trend, the seasonal, and the random components of a time series. Several models are introduced that capture one or more of these components. In particular, we use simple smoothing techniques for making forecasts when short-term fluctuations in the data represent random departures from the overall pattern with no discernible trend or seasonal fluctuations. Forecasting models based on linear and nonlinear regression models are introduced when trend and seasonal fluctuations are present in the time series. Finally, we introduce regression models that use lagged variables for making forecasts.

icon Stocker/Shutterstock

INTRODUCTORY CASE

Apple Revenue Forecast

On August 2, 2018, Apple Inc. reported its fourth consecutive quarter of record revenue and became the first publicly traded American company to surpass $1 trillion in market value. Its explosive growth has played a big role in the technology industry's ascent to the forefront of the global market economy (*The Wall Street Journal*, Aug. 2, 2018). Although the company designs, develops, and sells consumer electronics, computer software, and online services, the iPhones segment continues to be the company's core source of revenue.

Cadence Johnson, a research analyst at a small investment firm, is evaluating Apple's performance by analyzing the firm's revenue. She is aware that Apple could be seeing some resistance to its newly revamped and high-priced line of iPhones, stoking fears among investors that demand for iPhones is waning. Cadence hopes that Apple's past performance will aid in predicting its future performance. She collects quarterly data on Apple's revenue for the fiscal years 2010 through 2018, with the fiscal year concluding at the end of September. A portion of the data is shown in Table 18.1.

TABLE 18.1 Quarterly Revenue for Apple Inc. (in $ millions)

Year	Quarter	Revenue
2010	1	15,683
2010	2	13,499
⋮	⋮	⋮
2018	4	62,900

FILE *Revenue_Apple*

Cadence would like to use the information in Table 18.1 to

1. Explore models that capture the trend and seasonal components of Apple's revenue.
2. Forecast Apple's revenue for fiscal year 2019.

A synopsis of this case is provided at the end of Section 18.4.

18.1 THE FORECASTING PROCESS FOR TIME SERIES

In this chapter, we focus our attention on time series data. Observations of any variable recorded over time in sequential order are considered a time series. The time period can be expressed in terms of a year, a quarter, a month, a week, a day, an hour, or even a second. Examples of time series include the *hourly* volume of stocks traded on the New York Stock Exchange (NYSE) on five consecutive trading days; the *daily* number of loan applications over the months of June and July; the *monthly* sales for a retailer over a five-year period; and the *annual* growth rate of a country over the past 30 years.

Let $y_1, y_2, \ldots, y_T$ represent a sample of T observations of a variable y with y_t denoting the value of y at time t. With time series data, it is customary to use the notation T, instead of n, to represent the number of sample observations and to use a subscript t to identify time. For instance, if the number of daily loan applications over five days are 100, 94, 98, 110, 102, then $y_1 = 100, y_2 = 94, \ldots, y_5 = 102$.

LO **18.1**

Describe the time series forecasting process.

Time series consist of the trend, the seasonal, the cyclical, and the random components. The **trend** component represents long-term upward or downward movements of the series. For example, product sales or a firm's stock price may go up (or go down) over a certain time period. The **seasonal** component typically represents repetitions over a one-year period. For example, every year, sales of retail goods increase during the holiday season, and the number of vacation packages sold goes up during the summer. The **cyclical** component represents wavelike fluctuations or business cycles, often caused by expansion and contraction of the economy. The main distinction between seasonal and cyclical patterns is that seasonal patterns tend to repeat within periods of one year or less, whereas cyclical patterns last for one to several years—plus, the duration of a cycle differs from one cycle to the next. In addition, the magnitude of the up-and-down swings of the time series are more predictable with seasonal patterns as opposed to cyclical patterns. The **random** component is difficult to identify as it captures the unexplained movements of the time series. For example, there may be an increase or decrease in customers at a retail store for no apparent reason. In this text, we will focus on the trend, the seasonal, and the random components of a time series when making forecasts.

> TIME SERIES
>
> A time series is a set of sequential observations of a variable over time. It is generally characterized by the trend, the seasonal, the cyclical, and the random components.

FILE
Revenue_Apple

In the introductory case, we considered Apple's quarterly revenue from 2010 through 2018, with the fiscal year concluding at the end of September. Figure 18.1 is a scatterplot of the series, with the dots connected, where we have relabeled the nine years of quarterly observations from 1 to 36.

FIGURE 18.1 Scatterplot of Apple's quarterly revenue (in $ millions)

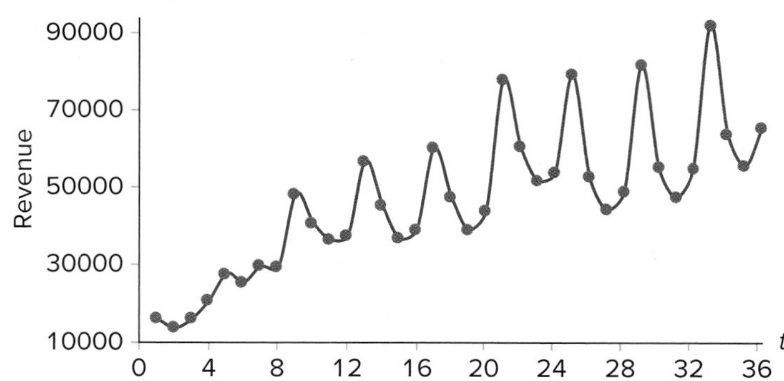

The graph highlights some important characteristics of Apple's revenue. First, there is a persistent upward movement with the series plateauing near the end of the observation period. Second, a seasonal pattern repeats itself year after year. For instance, revenue is consistently higher in the first quarter as compared to the other quarters. Note that given Apple's fiscal calendar, the first quarter, ending in December, encompasses the holiday period with usual strong sales.

Forecasting Methods

Forecasting methods are broadly classified as qualitative or quantitative. **Qualitative forecasting** methods are based on the judgment of the forecaster, who uses prior experience and expertise to make forecasts. On the other hand, **quantitative forecasting** methods use a formal model along with historical data for the variable of interest.

Qualitative forecasting is especially attractive when historical data are not available. For instance, a manager may use qualitative forecasts when she attempts to project sales for a new product. Similarly, we rely on qualitative forecasts when future results are suspected to depart markedly from results in prior periods, and, therefore, cannot be based on historical data. For example, major changes in market conditions or government policies will render the analysis from historical data misleading.

Although attractive in certain scenarios, qualitative forecasts are often criticized on the grounds that they are prone to some well-documented biases such as optimism and overconfidence. Decisions based on the judgment of an overly optimistic manager may prove costly to the business. Furthermore, qualitative forecasting is difficult to document, and its quality is totally dependent on the judgment and skill of the forecaster. Two people with access to similar information may offer different qualitative forecasts.

Formal quantitative models have been used extensively to forecast variables, such as product sales, product defects, house prices, inflation, stock prices, and cash flows.

FORECASTING METHODS

Forecasting methods are broadly classified as qualitative or quantitative. Qualitative methods are based on the judgment of the forecaster, whereas quantitative methods use a formal model to project historical data.

In this chapter, we focus on quantitative models to project historical data, where each model is specially designed to capture one or more components of a time series.

Model Selection Criteria

Numerous models can be used to make a forecast, with each model well-suited to capture a particular feature of the time series. It would be easy to choose the right model if we knew for certain which feature describes the given series. Unfortunately, such certainty rarely exists in the business world. Because we do not know which of the competing models is likely to provide the best forecast, it is common to consider several models. Model selection is one of the most important steps in forecasting. Therefore, it is important to understand model selection criteria before we even introduce any of the formal models.

Two types of model selection criteria are used to compare the performance of competing models. These are broadly defined as in-sample criteria and out-of-sample criteria. These criteria give rise to two important questions: How well does a model explain the given sample data? And how well does a model make out-of-sample forecasts? Ideally, the chosen model is best in terms of its in-sample predictability *and* its out-of-sample forecasting ability. In this chapter we will focus on in-sample criteria.

Model selection, using in-sample criteria, is based on the residuals $e_t = y_t - \hat{y}_t$, where y_t denotes the value of the series at time t and $\hat{y}_t$ denotes its forecast. Because there is no 'primary' model selection criterion, multiple performance measures are used for model selection. Commonly used performance measures for the comparison of competing forecasting models are the familiar mean square error (*MSE*), the mean absolute deviation (*MAD*), and the mean absolute percentage error (*MAPE*). Ideally, the preferred model will have the lowest *MSE, MAD,* and *MAPE* values. The formulas for *MSE, MAD,* and *MAPE* are shown in the following definition box.

PERFORMANCE MEASURES

Performance measures are based on the residuals $e_t = y_t - \hat{y}_t$, where y_t denotes the value of the series at time t and $\hat{y}_t$ denotes its forecast. Because there is no 'primary' performance measure, multiple measures are used for model selection. The mean square error (*MSE*), the mean absolute deviation (*MAD*), and the mean absolute percentage error (*MAPE*) are calculated as

$$MSE = \frac{1}{n}\sum e_t^2,$$

$$MAD = \frac{1}{n}\sum |e_t|, \text{ and}$$

$$MAPE = \frac{1}{n}\left(\sum \left|\frac{e_t}{y_t}\right|\right) \times 100,$$

where n is the number of observations used in the computation. Ideally, the preferred model will have the lowest values for *MSE*, *MAD*, and *MAPE*.

For any given model, there is no universal "good" value for the above performance measures; therefore, these are best used as model selection criteria. *MSE* heavily penalizes models with large residuals and, therefore, is preferred if relatively large residuals are particularly undesirable. Another popular measure is the root mean square error (*RMSE*), which is simply the square root of *MSE*. A large *RMSE* relative to *MAD* is indicative of relatively large errors in the forecast. The main attraction of using *MAPE* is that it shows the error as a percentage of the actual value, giving a sense of the magnitude of the errors.

We cannot use *MSE, MAD,* and *MAPE* to compare regression-based forecasting models that do not employ the same number of explanatory variables. For comparing regression-based forecasting models with different number of explanatory variables, we use adjusted R^2, which imposes a penalty for over-parameterization.

18.2 SIMPLE SMOOTHING TECHNIQUES

As mentioned earlier, a time series is a sequence of observations that are ordered in time. Inherently, any data collected over time is likely to exhibit some form of random variation. For instance, the checkout time at a campus bookstore or the weekly sales at a convenience store encounter random variations for no apparent reason. In this section we focus on applications where the time series is described primarily by random variations around an unknown level. In other words, there are no variations due to trend and/or seasonality.

A simple plot of the time series provides insights into its components. A jagged appearance, caused by abrupt changes in the series, indicates random variations.

Smoothing techniques are employed to reduce the effect of the random fluctuations. These techniques can also be used to provide forecasts if short-term fluctuations represent random departures from the structure, with no discernible patterns. These techniques are especially attractive when forecasts of multiple variables need to be updated frequently. For example, consider a manager of a convenience store who has to update the inventories of numerous items on a weekly basis. It is not practical in such situations to develop complex forecasting models for each item. We discuss two distinct smoothing techniques: the moving average technique and the simple exponential smoothing technique.

The Moving Average Technique

LO 18.2

Use smoothing techniques to make forecasts.

Due to its simplicity, the **moving average technique** ranks among the most popular techniques for smoothing a time series. The method is based on computing the average from a fixed number m of the most recent observations. For instance, a 3-period moving average is formed by averaging the three most recent observations. The term "moving" is used because as a new observation becomes available, the average is updated by including the newest observation and dropping the oldest observation.

CALCULATING A MOVING AVERAGE

An m-period moving average is computed as

$$\text{Moving Average} = \frac{\text{Sum of the } m \text{ most recent observations}}{m}.$$

EXAMPLE 18.1

In preparation for staffing during the upcoming summer months, an online retailer reviews the number of customer service calls received over the past three weeks (21 days). Table 18.2 shows a portion of the time series.

a. Construct a 3-period moving average series for the data.

b. Plot the time series and its corresponding 3-period moving average against days. Comment on any differences.

c. Using the 3-period moving average series, forecast the number of customer service calls for the 22nd day.

d. Calculate *MSE, MAD,* and *MAPE.*

TABLE 18.2 Daily Customer Service Calls

FILE
Service_Calls

Day	Calls
1	309
2	292
3	284
4	294
5	292
⋮	⋮
19	326
20	327
21	309

SOLUTION:

a. We would like to point out that the calculations are based on unrounded values even though we show rounded values in the text. For notational simplicity, let Calls be denoted by y_t and the corresponding moving average be denoted by $\bar{y}_t$. We form a 3-period moving average series by averaging all sets of three consecutive values of the original series. The first value of a 3-period moving average is calculated as

$$\bar{y}_2 = \frac{y_1 + y_2 + y_3}{3} = \frac{309 + 292 + 284}{3} = 295.$$

We designate this value $\bar{y}_2$ because it represents the average in days 1 through 3. The next moving average, representing the average in days 2 through 4, is

$$\bar{y}_3 = \frac{y_2 + y_3 + y_4}{3} = \frac{292 + 284 + 294}{3} = 290.$$

Other values of $\bar{y}_t$ are calculated similarly and are presented in column 3 of Table 18.3. Note that we lose one observation at the beginning and one observation at the end of the 3-period moving average series $\bar{y}_t$. (If it were a 5-period moving average, we would lose two observations at the beginning and two at the end.)

TABLE 18.3 3-Period Moving Averages, Forecasts, and Residuals

Day (1)	y (2)	$\bar{y}$ (3)	$\hat{y}$ (4)	$e = y - \hat{y}$ (5)
1	309	—	—	—
2	292	295	—	—
3	284	290	—	—
4	294	290	295	−1
5	292	290.33	290	2
⋮	⋮	⋮	⋮	⋮
19	326	320.67	304	22
20	327	320.67	309	18
21	309	—	320.67	−11.67

b. In Figure 18.2, we plot the time series and its corresponding 3-period moving average against days. Note that the original time series has a jagged appearance, suggesting the presence of an important random component of the series. The series of moving averages, on the other hand, presents a much smoother picture.

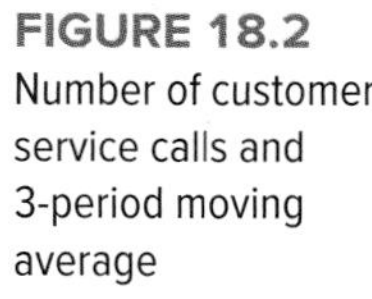

FIGURE 18.2 Number of customer service calls and 3-period moving average

c. As mentioned earlier, if the series exhibits primarily random variations, we can use moving averages to generate forecasts. Because $\bar{y}_2$ represents the average for days 1 through 3, it is the most updated estimate of the series prior to period 4. Therefore, we use $\hat{y}_4 = \bar{y}_2$ where $\hat{y}_4$ is the in-sample forecast for period 4. Similarly, $\hat{y}_5 = \bar{y}_3$ is the forecast for period 5, where $\bar{y}_3$ is the average for days 2 through 4, and so on. These forecasts, derived as $\hat{y}_t = \frac{y_{t-3} + y_{t-2} + y_{t-1}}{3}$, are shown in column 4 of Table 18.3. Following this simple process, we compute the out-of-sample forecast for day 22 as

$$\hat{y}_{22} = \bar{y}_{20} = \frac{y_{19} + y_{20} + y_{21}}{3} = \frac{326 + 327 + 309}{3} = 320.67.$$

Therefore, the forecast for the number of customer service calls for the 22nd day is 321 calls. One potential weakness when using the moving average technique is that all future forecasts take on the same value as the first out-of-sample forecast; that is, the forecast for the 23rd day is also 321 calls.

d. To calculate *MSE, MAD,* and *MAPE,* we first compute the residuals, $e_t = y_t - \hat{y}_t$, as shown in column 5 of Table 18.3.

$$MSE = \frac{1}{n}\sum e_t^2 = \frac{(-1)^2 + (2)^2 + \cdots + (-11.67)^2}{18} = 208.90,$$

$$MAD = \frac{1}{n}\sum |e_t| = \frac{|-1| + |2| + \cdots + |-11.67|}{18} = 11.85, \text{ and}$$

$$MAPE = \frac{1}{n}\left(\sum \left|\frac{e_t}{y_t}\right|\right) \times 100 = \frac{1}{18}\left(\left|\frac{-1}{294}\right| + \left|\frac{2}{292}\right| + \cdots + \left|\frac{-11.67}{309}\right|\right) \times 100 = 3.92.$$

These performance measures will prove useful when comparing alternative models.

The Simple Exponential Smoothing Technique

Although the moving average approach is popular, it has some shortcomings. First, the choice of the order *m* is arbitrary, although we can use trial and error to choose the value of *m* that results in the smallest values for *MSE, MAD,* and *MAPE.* Second, it may not be appropriate to give equal weight to all recent *m* observations. Whereas the moving average technique weighs all recent observations equally, the method called **simple exponential smoothing** assigns exponentially decreasing weights as the observations get older. As in the case of moving averages, exponential smoothing is a procedure for continually revising a forecast in light of more recent observations.

Let L_t denote the estimated level of the series at time *t,* where L_t is defined as

$$L_t = \alpha y_t + \alpha(1 - \alpha)y_{t-1} + \alpha(1 - \alpha)^2 y_{t-2} + \alpha(1 - \alpha)^3 y_{t-3} + \cdots, \text{ where } 0 < \alpha < 1.$$

That is, L_t is simply a weighted average of exponentially declining weights, with α dictating the speed of decline. For example, with $\alpha = 0.8$,

$$L_t = 0.8y_t + 0.16y_{t-1} + 0.032y_{t-2} + 0.0064y_{t-3} + \cdots.$$

Similarly, with $\alpha = 0.2$,

$$L_t = 0.2y_t + 0.16y_{t-1} + 0.128y_{t-2} + 0.1024y_{t-3} + \cdots.$$

Note that the speed of decline is higher when $\alpha = 0.8$ as compared to when $\alpha = 0.2$. Using algebra, it can be shown that the initial equation simplifies to

$$L_t = \alpha y_t + (1 - \alpha)L_{t-1}.$$

We use this representation to define the formula for exponential smoothing. Because L_t represents the most updated level at time *t,* we can use it to make a one-period-ahead forecast as $\hat{y}_{t+1} = L_t$. This equation shows that the forecast $\hat{y}_{t+1} = L_t$ depends on the current value, y_t, and its earlier forecast, $\hat{y}_t = L_{t-1}$. In other words, we continually revise the forecast in the light of more recent observations.

CALCULATING A SIMPLE EXPONENTIALLY SMOOTHED SERIES

The simple exponential smoothing technique continually updates the level of the series as

$$L_t = \alpha y_t + (1 - \alpha)L_{t-1},$$

where α represents the speed of decline. Forecasts are made as $\hat{y}_{t+1} = L_t$.

In order to implement this method, we need to determine α and the initial value of the series, L_1. Typically, the initial value is set equal to the first observation of the time series, that is, $L_1 = y_1$; the choice of the initial value is less important if the number of observations is large. The optimal value for α is determined by a trial-and-error method. We evaluate various values of α and choose the one that results in the smallest *MSE, MAD, MAPE,* or some other selection criteria.

EXAMPLE 18.2

Revisit the ***Service_Calls*** data from Example 18.1.

a. Construct the simple exponentially smoothed series with $\alpha = 0.20$ and $L_1 = y_1$.

b. Plot the time series and its corresponding exponentially smoothed series against days. Comment on any differences.

c. Using the exponentially smoothed series, forecast the number of customer service calls for the 22nd day.

d. Calculate *MSE, MAD,* and *MAPE.* Compare these values with those obtained using the 3-period moving average technique in Example 18.1.

SOLUTION: Again, the calculations are based on unrounded values even though we show rounded values in the text.

a. In Column 3 of Table 18.4, we present sequential estimates of L_t with the initial value $L_1 = y_1 = 309$. We use $L_t = \alpha y_t + (1 - \alpha)L_{t-1}$ to continuously update the level with $\alpha = 0.2$. For instance, for periods 2 and 3 we calculate

$$L_2 = 0.20 \times 292 + 0.80 \times 309 = 305.60, \text{ and}$$
$$L_3 = 0.20 \times 284 + 0.80 \times 305.60 = 301.28.$$

All other estimates of L_t are found in a like manner.

b. In Figure 18.3, we plot the original time series and its corresponding exponentially smoothed series against days. As mentioned earlier, while the original time series has the jagged appearance, the exponentially smoothed series removes most of the sharp points and, like the moving average series, presents a much smoother picture.

TABLE 18.4 Exponentially Smoothed Series with $\alpha = 0.20$, Forecasts, and Residuals

Day (1)	y (2)	L_t (3)	$\hat{y}$ (4)	$e = y - \hat{y}$ (5)
1	309	309.00	—	—
2	292	305.60	309.00	−17.00
3	284	301.28	305.60	−21.60
⋮	⋮	⋮	⋮	⋮
20	327	310.95	306.93	20.07
21	309	310.56	310.95	−1.95

FIGURE 18.3 Number of customer service calls and exponentially smoothed series

c. Forecasts, given by $\hat{y}_{t+1} = L_t$, are presented in column 4 of Table 18.4. For instance, for period 2, $\hat{y}_2 = L_1 = 309$. Similarly, $L_2 = 305.60$ is the forecast for $\hat{y}_3$. Therefore, the forecast for the 22nd day is computed as $\hat{y}_{22} = L_{21} = 0.20 \times 309 + 0.80 \times 310.95 = 310.56$, or 311 customer service calls. As with the moving average technique, any further out-of-sample forecasts also assume this same value; that is, the forecast for the 23rd day is also 311 customer service calls.

d. To calculate *MSE, MAD,* and *MAPE,* we first compute the residuals, $e_t = y_t - \hat{y}_t$, as shown in column 5 of Table 18.4.

$$MSE = \frac{1}{n}\sum e_t^2 = \frac{(-17.00)^2 + (-21.60)^2 + \cdots + (-1.95)^2}{20} = 217.16,$$

$$MAD = \frac{1}{n}\sum |e_t| = \frac{|-17.00| + |-21.60| + \cdots + |-1.95|}{20} = 12.91, \text{ and}$$

$$MAPE = \frac{1}{n}\left(\sum\left|\frac{e_t}{y_t}\right|\right) \times 100 = \frac{1}{20}\left(\left|\frac{-17.00}{292}\right| + \left|\frac{-21.60}{284}\right| + \cdots + \left|\frac{-1.95}{309}\right|\right) \times 100 = 4.32.$$

There is nothing special about $\alpha = 0.2$; we used this value primarily to illustrate the exponential smoothing technique. As we noted earlier, it is common to evaluate various values of α and choose the one that produces the smallest *MSE, MAD,* or *MAPE* values. In order to illustrate how α is chosen, we generate *MSE, MAD,* and *MAPE* with α values ranging from 0.1 to 0.9 with increments of 0.1. The results are summarized in Table 18.5.

Here, the choice of α depends on whether we employ *MSE, MAD,* or *MAPE* for model comparison. In this example, it may be appropriate to select $\alpha = 0.5$ because it leads to the smallest value for two out of three performance measures (*MAD* and *MAPE*). This model (with $\alpha = 0.5$) also outperforms the moving average model as measured by lower *MSE, MAD,* and *MAPE* values.

TABLE 18.5 Various Values of α and the Resulting *MSE, MAD,* and *MAPE*

α	0.1	0.2	0.3	0.4	0.5	0.6	0.7	0.8	0.9
MSE	257.20	217.16	192.44	180.42	175.40	173.61	172.82	171.79	169.97
MAD	13.60	12.91	12.18	11.42	11.10	11.11	11.25	11.41	11.43
MAPE	4.57	4.32	4.07	3.81	3.70	3.70	3.75	3.81	3.82

Using R for Exponential Smoothing

In Excel's Analysis Toolpak, there are functions that find the moving average of a time series as well as its exponentially smoothed series; however, Excel provides no simple functions that generate the performance measures. For this reason, we do not pursue smoothing techniques in Excel. We can find performance measures in R using a single function, but we need to make some modifications to the data frame. With moving averages, these modifications can be confusing depending on the value of m. Fortunately, the modifications are simple for exponential smoothing. Here, we replicate the exponential smoothing results in Example 18.2.

A. Import the ***Service_Calls*** data file into a data frame (table) and label it myData.

B. Load and install the *forecast* package. Enter:

```
> install.packages("forecast"); library(forecast)
```

C. We use the ***ses*** function in the *forecast* package to generate an exponentially smoothed series, which we label ExpSm. Within the function, we set *initial* to "simple" and *alpha* equal to 0.2. If we retype ExpSm, then we see that R reports the forecasts for time period 22 and beyond. (As expected, all of these values equal 310.5577.) Enter:

```
> ExpSm <-ses(myData$Calls, initial="simple", alpha=0.2); ExpSm
```

D. We use the **fitted** function to find the predicted calls in the sample and use the **accuracy** function to view the resulting performance measures. As we did in Example 18.2, we want to base the performance measures on observations 2 through 21, so we make that modification for each variable. Enter:

```
> accuracy(fitted(ExpSm)[(2:21)], myData$Calls[(2:21)])
```

Note that R denotes *MAD* as *MAE* and *MSE* is found by squaring the reported *RMSE*. These values are identical to those reported in Table 18.5 when $\alpha = 0.2$.

EXERCISES 18.2

Mechanics

1. **FILE** ***Exercise_18.1.*** The accompanying data file contains 10 observations for t and y_t.
   a. Construct the 3-period moving average and plot it along with the actual series. Comment on smoothing.
   b. Use the 3-period moving average to make in-sample forecasts and compute the resulting *MSE* and *MAD*.
   c. Make a forecast for period 11.

2. **FILE** ***Exercise_18.2.*** The accompanying data file contains 20 observations for t and y_t.
   a. Plot the series and discuss the presence of random variations.
   b. Use the exponential smoothing method to make in-sample forecasts with $\alpha = 0.2$. Compute the resulting *MSE* and *MAD*.
   c. Repeat the process with $\alpha = 0.4$.
   d. Use the preferred value of α to make a forecast for period 21.

Applications

3. **FILE** ***Convenience_Store.*** The owner of a convenience store near Salt Lake City in Utah has been tabulating weekly sales at the store, excluding gas. The accompanying table shows a portion of the sales for 30 weeks.

Week	Sales
1	5387
2	5522
⋮	⋮
30	5206

   a. Use the 3-period moving average to forecast sales for the 31st week.
   b. Use simple exponential smoothing with $\alpha = 0.3$ to forecast sales for the 31st week.
   c. Which is the preferred technique for making the forecast based on *MSE, MAD,* and *MAPE*?

4. **FILE** ***Spotify.*** Spotify is a music streaming platform that gives access to songs from artists all over the world. On February 28, 2018, Spotify filed for an initial public offering (IPO) on the New York Stock Exchange. The accompanying table shows a portion of the adjusted monthly stock price of Spotify from April 1, 2018, to February 1, 2019.

Date	Stock Price
Apr-18	161.67
May-18	157.71
⋮	⋮
Feb-19	134.71

   a. Use the 3-period moving average to forecast Spotify's stock price for March 2019.
   b. Use simple exponential smoothing with $\alpha = 0.2$ to forecast Spotify's stock price for March 2019.
   c. Which is the preferred technique for making the forecast based on *MSE, MAD,* and *MAPE?*

5. **FILE** ***FoodTruck.*** Food trucks have become a common sight on American campuses. They serve scores of hungry students strolling through campus and looking for trendy food served

fast. The owner of a food truck collects data on the number of students he serves on weekdays on a small campus in California. A portion of the data is shown in the accompanying table.

Weekday	Students
1	84
2	66
⋮	⋮
40	166

a. Use the 3-period moving average to make a forecast for Weekday 41.

b. Use the 5-period moving average to make a forecast for Weekday 41.

c. Which is the preferred technique for making the forecast based on *MSE, MAD,* and *MAPE*?

6. **FILE** ***Exchange_Rate.*** Consider the exchange rate of the $ (USD) with € (Euro) and $ (USD) with £ (Pound). The accompanying table shows a portion of the exchange rates from January 2017 to January 2019.

Date	Euro	Pound
Jan-17	1.0635	1.2367
Feb-17	1.0650	1.2495
⋮	⋮	⋮
Jan-19	1.1414	1.2845

a. Find the 3-period and the 5-period moving averages for Euro. Based on *MSE, MAD,* and *MAPE,* use the preferred model to forecast Euro for February 2019.

b. Find the simple exponential smoothing series for Pound with possible α values of 0.2, 0.4, 0.6. Based on *MSE, MAD,* and *MAPE,* use the preferred model to forecast Pound for February 2019.

7. **FILE** ***Downtown_Cafe.*** The manager of a trendy downtown café in Columbus, Ohio, collects weekly data on the number of customers it serves. A portion of the data is shown in the accompanying table.

Week	Customers
1	944
2	997
⋮	⋮
52	1365

a. Use the simple exponential smoothing technique with $\alpha = 0.2$ to make a forecast for Week 53.

b. Use the simple exponential smoothing technique with $\alpha = 0.4$ to make a forecast for Week 53.

c. Which is the preferred technique for making the forecast based on *MSE, MAD,* and *MAPE*?

8. **FILE** ***Gas_Prices.*** It is difficult to predict gas prices given a multitude of factors affecting them. Consider 22 weeks of the average weekly regular gasoline price ($ per gallon) in New England and the West Coast.

Date	New England	West Coast
9/3/2018	2.855	3.329
9/10/2018	2.864	3.336
⋮	⋮	⋮
1/28/2019	2.346	2.928

c. Find the 3-period and the 5-period moving averages for gas prices in New England. Based on *MSE, MAD,* and *MAPE,* use the preferred model to forecast gas prices for the first week of February 2019.

d. Find the simple exponential smoothing series with possible α values of 0.2, 0.4, 0.6 for gas prices on the West Coast. Based on *MSE, MAD,* and *MAPE,* use the preferred model to forecast gas prices for the first week of February 2019.

18.3 LINEAR REGRESSION MODELS FOR TREND AND SEASONALITY

The smoothing techniques discussed in Section 18.2 are used when the time series represent random fluctuations with no discernible trend or seasonal fluctuations. When trend and seasonal variations are present, we need to use special models for the analysis. In this section, we first focus on trend analysis, which extracts long-term upward or downward movements of the series. We then incorporate seasonal dummy variables that extract the repetitive movement of the series within a one-year period.

The Linear Trend Model

LO 18.3

Use linear regression models to make forecasts.

We estimate a **linear trend model** using the regression techniques described in earlier chapters. Let y_t be the value of the response variable at time t. Here we use t as the explanatory variable corresponding to consecutive time periods, such as 1, 2, 3, and so on.

THE LINEAR TREND MODEL

The linear trend model is used for a time series that is expected to grow by a fixed amount each time period. It is specified as

$$y_t = \beta_0 + \beta_1 t + \varepsilon_t,$$

where y_t is the value of the time series at time t.

- Forecasts with a linear trend model are made by $\hat{y}_t = b_0 + b_1 t$, where b_0 and b_1 are the coefficient estimates.
- It is advisable to use unrounded coefficient estimates for making forecasts.

Example 18.3 provides an application of the linear trend model for making forecasts.

EXAMPLE 18.3

A local organic food store carries several food products for health-conscious consumers. The store has witnessed a steady growth in the sale of chef-designed meals, which are especially popular with college-educated millennials. For planning purposes, the manager of the store would like to extract useful information from the weekly sales of chef-designed meals for the past year, a portion of which is shown in Table 18.6.

FILE
Organic

TABLE 18.6 Weekly Sales (in $) at Organic Food Store

Week	Sales
1	1925
2	2978
⋮	⋮
52	6281

a. Visually inspect the time series to confirm the existence of a trend.

b. Estimate and interpret the linear trend model for the sale of chef-designed meals.

c. Forecast the sale of chef-designed meals for the next four weeks.

SOLUTION:

a. As a first step, it is advisable to visually inspect the time series. Figure 18.4 is a scatterplot of the weekly sales of chef-designed meals for the past year with a superimposed linear trend line. We see an upward movement of the series over this time period.

FIGURE 18.4
Scatterplot of weekly sales of chef-designed meals

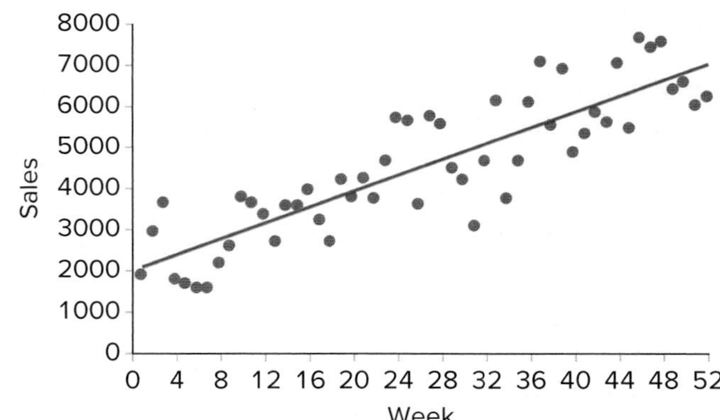

b. The linear trend model is specified as Sales $= \beta_0 + \beta_1$Week $+ \varepsilon$. The estimated linear trend equation is $\widehat{\text{Sales}} = 1998.2285 + 96.8383$ Week, implying that every week, sales increase by about \$96.84. The estimated $R^2 = 0.7538$ suggests that about 75.38% of the sample variations in sales are explained by the sample trend line.

c. We use Week = 53 to forecast sales for the next week as $\widehat{\text{Sales}} = 1998.2285 + 96.8383 \times 53 = \$7{,}130.66$. Similarly, we use Week = 54, 55, and 56 to forecast sales for the subsequent three weeks as \$7,227.49, \$7,324.33, \$7,421.17, respectively.

Trend forecasting models, like the model used in Example 18.3, extract long-term upward or downward movements of a time series. These models are appropriate when the time series does not exhibit seasonal variations or has been stripped of its seasonal variation; that is, it has been deseasonalized. We now move our attention to making forecasts that extract both trend and seasonal variations.

The Linear Trend Model with Seasonality

With seasonal data, we estimate a linear trend model that also includes dummy variables to capture the seasonal variations. Recall that a dummy variable is commonly used to describe a categorical variable with two categories. Here, we use dummy variables to describe seasons. For quarterly data, we usually to define only three dummy variables, using the fourth quarter as reference.

LINEAR TREND MODEL WITH SEASONAL DUMMY VARIABLES

With quarterly data, a linear trend model with seasonal dummy variables can be specified as

$$y = \beta_0 + \beta_1 d_1 + \beta_2 d_2 + \beta_3 d_3 + \beta_4 t + \varepsilon,$$

where d_1, d_2, and d_3 are the dummy variables representing the first three quarters.

- Forecasts are made as

  Quarter 1 ($d_1 = 1, d_2 = 0, d_3 = 0$): $\hat{y} = (b_0 + b_1) + b_4 t$,
  Quarter 2 ($d_1 = 0, d_2 = 1, d_3 = 0$): $\hat{y} = (b_0 + b_2) + b_4 t$,
  Quarter 3 ($d_1 = 0, d_2 = 0, d_3 = 1$): $\hat{y} = (b_0 + b_3) + b_4 t$,
  Quarter 4 ($d_1 = 0, d_2 = 0, d_3 = 0$): $\hat{y} = b_0 + b_4 t$,

where $b_0, b_1, \ldots b_4$ are the coefficient estimates.

- It is advisable to use unrounded coefficient estimates for making forecasts.

Note that the above forecasting equations can easily be modified if a different quarter is used as reference. Also, the model for the quarterly data can be modified to make forecasts with monthly or other forms of seasonal data. Example 18.4 provides an application with quarterly data.

EXAMPLE 18.4

With Amazon.com at the lead, e-commerce retail sales have increased substantially over the last decade. Consider quarterly data on e-commerce retail sales in the U.S. from the first quarter of 2010 to the first quarter of 2019, a portion of which is shown in Table 18.7.

TABLE 18.7 Quarterly e-Commerce Retail Sales (in $ millions)

Year	Quarter	Sales
2010	1	37059
2010	2	38467
⋮	⋮	⋮
2019	1	127265

a. Visually inspect the data to confirm the existence of trend and seasonality.

b. Estimate and interpret the linear trend model with seasonal dummy variables for e-commerce retail sales.

c. Forecast e-commerce retail sales for the last three quarters of 2019.

SOLUTION: Given quarterly data, we have to first construct relevant variables for the linear trend models with seasonal dummy variables. Table 18.8 presents a portion of the constructed data for seasonal dummy variables d_1, d_2, and d_3 representing the first three quarters (using the fourth quarter as reference), and the trend variable t representing the 37 quarters of data. (Shortly, we will provide R instructions for replicating the results.)

TABLE 18.8 Constructing Variables for Example 18.4

Year	Quarter	Sales	d_1	d_2	d_3	t
2010	1	37059	1	0	0	1
2010	2	38467	0	1	0	2
2010	3	40075	0	0	1	3
2010	4	54320	0	0	0	4
⋮	⋮	⋮	⋮	⋮	⋮	⋮
2018	4	158548	0	0	0	36
2019	1	127265	1	0	0	37

a. Figure 18.5 is a scatterplot of quarterly sales, with the dots connected, and the quarterly data relabeled from 1 to 37. The graph highlights some important characteristics of e-commerce retail sales. First, there is a persistent upward movement in sales. Second, a seasonal pattern repeats itself year after year. For instance, sales are consistently higher in the fourth quarter as compared to the other quarters. The graph makes a strong case for a model that captures both trend and seasonality.

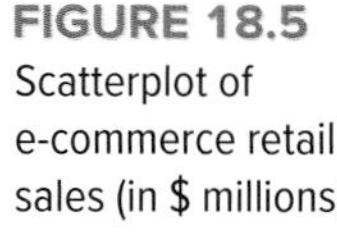
FIGURE 18.5 Scatterplot of e-commerce retail sales (in $ millions)

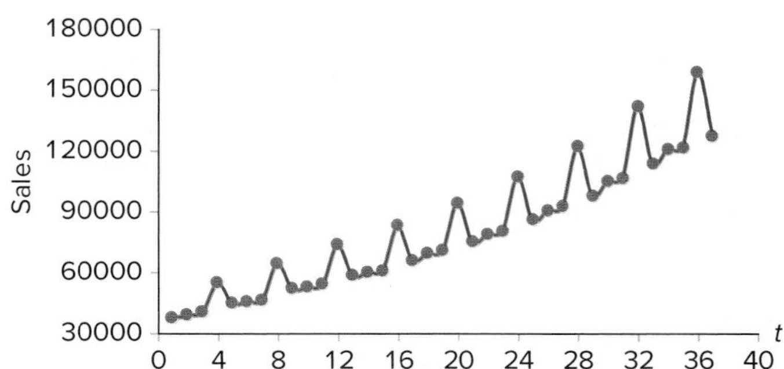

b. The estimated linear trend model with seasonal dummy variables is: $\widehat{\text{Sales}} = 46{,}682.6508 - 21{,}611.6437d_1 - 21{,}295.7984d_2 - 22{,}594.1214d_3 + 2{,}649.8786t$.

The coefficients for the seasonal dummy variables indicate that, relative to the 4th quarter, e-commerce sales are about $22,000 lower in the other three quarters. The estimated coefficient for the trend variable suggests that the predicted quarterly sales increase by about $2,650 million every quarter, in addition to the seasonal variations.

c. For the 2nd quarter of 2019, we use $d_1 = 0$, $d_2 = 1$, $d_3 = 0$, and $t = 38$ to forecast $\widehat{Sales} = 46{,}682.6508 - 21{,}295.7984 + 2{,}649.8786 \times 38 =$ \$126,082 million. Similarly, we use $d_1 = 0$, $d_2 = 0$, $d_3 = 1$, and $t = 39$ for the 3rd quarter and $d_1 = 0$, $d_2 = 0$, $d_3 = 0$, $t = 40$ for the 4th quarter to forecast sales as \$127,434 and \$152,678 million, respectively.

Estimating a Linear Trend Model with Seasonality with R

ECommerce

In order to replicate the results in Example 18.4, we follow these steps.

A. Import the ***ECommerce*** data file into a data frame (table) and label it myData.

B. Install and load the *forecast* package. Enter:

```
> install.packages("forecast")
> library(forecast)
```

C. We use the **ts** function to create a time series object and call it newData. Within the **ts** function, we specify the *start* and *end* periods as well as *frequency,* denoting the number of seasons in a year. Enter:

```
> newData <- ts(myData$Sales, start = c(2010,1), end = c(2019,1), frequency=4)
```

D. We use the **tslm** function to estimate the model and the **summary** function to view the regression output. Enter:

```
> TSReg <- tslm(newData ~ trend + season)
> summary(TSReg)
```

Note: By default, R uses the first quarter as the reference season, which explains why the intercept and the coefficient estimates for the dummy variables differ from those reported in Example 18.4. The forecasts, however, are not influenced by the choice of the reference dummy variable.

E. Use the **forecast** function where h denotes the number of forecasts. Enter:

```
> forecast(TSReg, h=3)
```

The forecasts are identical to those reported in Example 18.4.

A Note on Causal Models for Forecasting

So far, we have discussed noncausal, or purely time series, models that capture trend and seasonality for making forecasts. These models do not offer any explanation of the mechanism generating the target variable and simply provide a method for projecting historical data. Causal models, on the other hand, are standard regression models that exploit the relationship between the response and the explanatory variables for making forecasts. For example, we can use causal models to forecast product sales using explanatory variables such as the firm's advertising budget and its pricing strategy. The regression framework also allows us the flexibility to combine causal with time series effects. In other words, the list of explanatory variables may include k causal variables $x_1, x_2, \ldots, x_k$ along with the trend variable t and seasonal dummy variables $d_1, d_2, \ldots, d_{p-1}$ for p seasons.

For example, consider quarterly data for developing a forecasting model for product sales y. Let the explanatory variables include the firm's advertising budget x, the trend variable t, and seasonal dummy variables, d_1, d_2, d_3, representing the first three quarters. We can easily estimate the regression model to make forecasts as:

$$\hat{y} = b_0 + b_1 d_1 + b_2 d_2 + b_3 d_3 + b_4 t + b_5 x.$$

Note that in addition to the known future values of t, d_1, d_2, and d_3, this approach will work only if we also know, or can predict, the future value of the variable x. In other words, we cannot forecast product sales if the advertising budget in the future is not known.

EXERCISES 18.3

Mechanics

9. A linear trend model estimated from 30 days of data is given by $\hat{y}_t = 80.20 + 0.62t$. Use the estimated model to forecast y for the next two days.

10. Consider the following linear trend models estimated from 10 years of quarterly data with and without seasonal dummy variables d_1, d_2, and d_3. Here, $d_1 = 1$ for quarter 1, 0 otherwise; other dummy variables are defined similarly.

    Model 1: $\hat{y}_t = 48.00 + 0.44t$

    Model 2: $\hat{y}_t = 48.00 + 0.46t - 0.38d_1 - 0.42d_2 - 0.12d_3$

    a. Use each model to make a forecast for y for the first and the fourth quarter of the 11th year.
    b. Which is the preferred model for forecasting if, relative to Model 1, Model 2 has higher R^2 but lower adjusted R^2?

Applications

11. **FILE** ***Inquiries.*** Morgan Bank has been encouraging its customers to use its new mobile banking app. While this may be good for business, the bank has to deal with a number of inquiries it receives about the new app. The accompanying table contains a portion of weekly inquiries the bank has received over the past 30 weeks.

Week	Inquiries
1	286
2	331
⋮	⋮
30	219

Estimate the linear trend model to forecast the number of inquiries over the next two weeks.

12. **FILE** ***Apple_Price.*** Apple Inc. has performed extremely well in the last decade. After its stock price dropped to below 90 in May 2016, it made a tremendous comeback to reach about 146 by May 2017 (SeekingAlpha.com, May 1, 2017). An investor seeking to gain from the positive momentum of Apple's stock price analyzes 53 weeks of stock price data from 5/30/16 to 5/26/17. A portion of the data is shown in the accompanying table.

Date	Price
5/30/2016	97.92
6/6/2016	98.83
⋮	⋮
5/26/2017	153.57

a. Estimate and interpret the linear trend model (no seasonality).
b. Make a forecast for the next week (54th week).

13. **FILE** ***Tax_Revenue.*** In Colorado, sales of medical marijuana began in November 2012; however, the Department of Revenue did not report tax collection data until February of 2014. The accompanying table shows a portion of the monthly revenue from medical and retail marijuana tax and fee collections as posted in the Colorado state accounting system.

Date	Revenue
Feb-14	3,519,756
Mar-14	4,092,575
⋮	⋮
Oct-18	22,589,679

Use the linear trend model (no seasonality) to forecast the tax revenue for November and December of 2018.

14. **FILE** ***Revenue_Lowes.*** Lowe's Companies, Inc., is a home improvement company offering a range of products for maintenance, repair, remodeling, and decorating. The accompanying table contains a portion of quarterly data on Lowe's revenue (in $ millions) with its fiscal year concluding at the end of January.

Year	Quarter	Revenue
2010	1	12,388
2010	2	14,361
⋮	⋮	⋮
2018	3	17,415

a. Estimate and interpret the linear trend model with seasonal dummy variables.
b. Use the estimated model to forecast Lowe's revenue for the fourth quarter of 2018.

15. **FILE** ***Vacation.*** Vacation destinations often run on a seasonal basis, depending on the primary activities in that location. Amanda Wang is the owner of a travel agency in Cincinnati, Ohio. She has built a database of the number of vacation packages (Vacation) that she has sold over the last twelve years. The accompanying table contains a portion of quarterly data on the number of vacation packages sold.

Year	Quarter	Vacation
2008	1	500
2008	2	147
⋮	⋮	⋮
2019	4	923

a. Estimate the linear regression models using seasonal dummy variables with and without the trend term. Which is the preferred model?
b. Use the preferred model to forecast the quarterly number of vacation packages sold in the first two quarters of 2020.

18.4 NONLINEAR REGRESSION MODELS FOR TREND AND SEASONALITY

LO 18.4

Use nonlinear regression models to make forecasts.

Although the linear relationship assumed in Section 18.3 can be adequate, there are many cases in which a nonlinear functional form is more suitable. In this section, we discuss the exponential, the quadratic, and the cubic trend models with and without seasonal dummy variables.

The Exponential Trend Model

A linear trend model uses a straight line to capture the trend, thus implying that each period, the predicted value of the series changes by a fixed amount, given by the estimated coefficient b_1. The **exponential trend model** is attractive when the expected increase in the series gets larger over time. It is not uncommon for some variables to exhibit exponential growth over time. For example, in recent years, technology firms such as Amazon, Netflix, Spotify, Airbnb, and Paypal have exhibited exponential growth for which the linear trend model would clearly be inadequate.

Figure 18.6 presents a scatterplot of a time series with superimposed linear and exponential trend lines. While both trend lines capture positive growth, the exponential trend line (green) correctly allows the values to grow by an increasing amount over time. Here, the linear trend line (blue) would under-forecast future values.

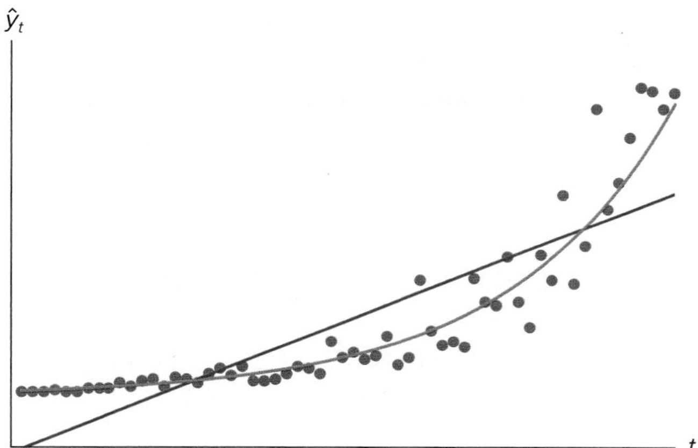

FIGURE 18.6 Scatterplot with superimposed linear and exponential trend lines

Recall from Chapter 16 that we specify an exponential model as $\ln(y_t) = \beta_0 + \beta_1 t + \varepsilon_t$. In order to estimate this model, we first generate the series in natural logs, $\ln(y_t)$, and then run a regression of $\ln(y_t)$ on t. Because the response variable is measured in logs, we make forecasts in regular units as $\hat{y}_t = \exp(b_0 + b_1 t + s_e^2/2)$, where s_e is the standard error of the estimate. Again, recall that the correction term $s_e^2/2$ is included because, without it, the forecasts are known to be systematically underestimated. This correction is easy to implement since virtually all statistical packages report s_e.

> **THE EXPONENTIAL TREND MODEL**
>
> The exponential trend model is specified as
>
> $$\ln(y_t) = \beta_0 + \beta_1 t + \varepsilon_t,$$
>
> where $\ln(y_t)$ is the natural log of y_t.
>
> - Forecasts are made as $\hat{y}_t = \exp(b_0 + b_1 t + s_e^2/2)$, where b_0 and b_1 are the coefficient estimates and s_e is the standard error of the estimate.
> - It is advisable to use unrounded coefficient estimates for making forecasts.

Example 18.5 provides an application of the linear and the exponential trend models for making forecasts.

EXAMPLE 18.5

According to data compiled by the World Bank, the world population has increased from 3.03 billion in 1960 to 7.53 billion in 2017. This rapid increase concerns environmentalists, who believe that our natural resources may not be able to support the ever-increasing population. Additionally, most of the rapid population growth has been in 34 low-income countries, many of which are located in Africa. Consider the population data, in millions, for low-income countries from 1960 to 2017, a portion of which is shown in Table 18.9.

FILE
Population_LowInc

TABLE 18.9 Population in Low-Income Countries

Year	Population
1960	166.5028
1961	170.2108
⋮	⋮
2017	732.4486

a. Estimate and interpret the linear and the exponential trend models.

b. Use *MSE, MAD,* and *MAPE* to select the appropriate model.

c. Forecast the population in low-income countries for 2018.

SOLUTION: As a first step, it is advisable to inspect the data visually. Figure 18.7 is a scatterplot of the population in low-income countries from 1960 through 2017. We relabel the 58 years of annual observations from 1 to 58 and superimpose the linear and exponential trends to the data.

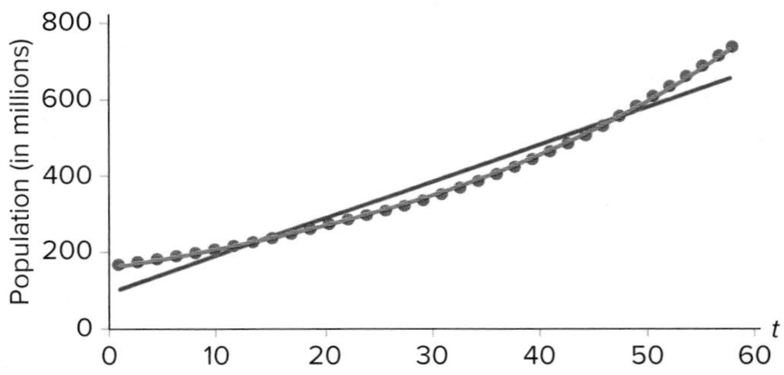

FIGURE 18.7 Population in low-income countries with superimposed trends

The scatterplot makes a strong case for the exponential trend model.

a. We estimate the linear and the exponential trend models, where the linear model is used for comparison with the visually preferred exponential model. To estimate the exponential trend model, we first transform the population series to natural logs. Table 18.10 shows a portion of the log-transformed population along with the explanatory variable *t*, relabeled from 1 to 58.

TABLE 18.10 Constructing Variables for Example 18.5

Year	Population	*t*	ln(Population)
1960	166.5028	1	5.1150
1961	170.2108	2	5.1370
⋮	⋮	⋮	⋮
2017	732.4486	58	6.5964

The estimated trend models, where *y* denotes population, are:

Linear: $\hat{y}_t = 92.9213 + 9.6799t$

Exponential: $\hat{y}_t = \exp(5.0614 + 0.0264t + \frac{0.0104^2}{2})$

(Shortly, we will provide R instructions for replicating the results.)

The slope coefficient of the linear trend model implies that the population grows by approximately 9.6799 million each year. The slope coefficient of the exponential trend model implies that the population grows by approximately 2.64% (= 0.0264 × 100) each year. The exact growth rate for the estimated exponential model can be calculated as 2.68% (= (exp(0.0264) – 1) × 100).

b. In Table 18.11, we present a portion of the series y_t along with $\hat{y}_t$ for both models using unrounded values of the coefficient estimates. As discussed in Section 18.2, we use the residuals, $e_t = y_t - \hat{y}_t$. to compute *MSE, MAD,* and *MAPE.* The *MSE, MAD,* and *MAPE* values for the linear and the exponential models are shown in the last three rows of Table 18.11.

TABLE 18.11 Analysis of Linear and Exponential Trend Models for Example 18.5

t	*y*	$\hat{y}$ (Linear)	$\hat{y}$ (Exponential)
1	166.5028	102.6011	162.0398
2	170.2108	112.2810	166.3719
⋮	⋮	⋮	⋮
58	732.4486	654.3529	729.0290
	MSE	1,176.74	12.28
	MAD	29.58	2.87
	MAPE	9.36	0.82

Consistent with the scatterplot, the exponential trend is clearly better suited to describe the population in low-income countries because it has lower *MSE, MAD,* and *MAPE* values than the linear trend model.

c. For 2018 ($t = 59$), we use unrounded values of the coefficient estimates to forecast the population as $\hat{y}_{59} = \exp(5.0614 + 0.0264 \times 59 + \frac{0.0104^2}{2}) = 748.52$ million.

Using R to Forecast with an Exponential Trend Model

We replicate the results for Example 18.5.

A. Import the ***Population_LowInc*** data file into a data frame (table) and label it myData.

B. We load the *forecast* package, assuming that it is already installed on your computer. Enter:

```
> library(forecast)
```

C. We use the **ts** function to create a time series object named newData and then estimate and view the linear and the exponential trend models. Enter:

```
> newData <- ts(myData$Population, start = c(1960), end = c(2017),
  frequency=1)
> Linear_Model <- tslm(newData ~ trend); summary(Linear_Model)
> Exponential_Model <- tslm(log(newData) ~ trend); summary(Exponential_Model)
```

D. We use the **fitted** function to find the predicted population in the sample and use the **accuracy** function to view the resulting performance measures. In order to find the predicted population for the exponential model, we also need to extract *se,* which R refers to as sigma. Enter:

```
> accuracy(fitted(Linear_Model), myData$Population)
> se <- sigma(Exponential_Model)
> accuracy(exp(fitted(Exponential_Model) + se^2/2), myData$Population)
```

Note that R denotes *MAD* as *MAE* and *MSE* is found by squaring the reported *RMSE*. These values are identical to those reported in Table 18.11.

E. We use the **forecast** function where *h* denotes the number of forecasts. We label ln(Population) as flg and use the unadjusted forecast in the object flg, which R refers to as mean, along with *se* to forecast for the next year. Enter:

```
> flg <- forecast(Exponential_Model, h=1)
> exp(flg$mean + se^2/2)
```

R returns: 748.5195.

The Polynomial Trend Model

In Chapter 16, we introduced the quadratic regression model, $yt = \beta_0 + \beta_1 x + \beta_2 x^2 + \varepsilon_t$. This particular polynomial model is appropriate when the relationship between the response variable and the explanatory variable is best captured by a U-shape or an inverted U-shape. Sometimes a time series reverses direction, due to any number of circumstances. **The quadratic trend** model allows for curvature and one change in the direction of a time series and is specified as

$$y_t = \beta_0 + \beta_1 t + \beta_2 t^2 + \varepsilon_t.$$

The coefficient β_2 determines whether the trend is U-shaped or inverted U-shaped. Figure 18.8 presents a scatterplot of a time series with superimposed linear (blue) and quadratic (green) trend lines. Here, the linear trend line would under-forecast future values when $\beta_2 > 0$ and over-forecast future values when $\beta_2 < 0$.

FIGURE 18.8 Scatterplots with superimposed linear and quadratic trend lines

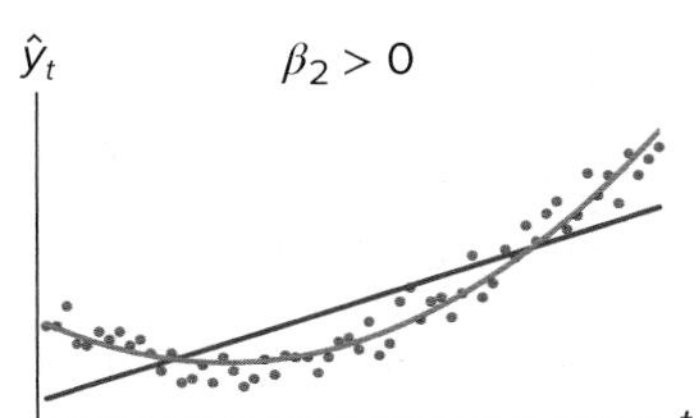

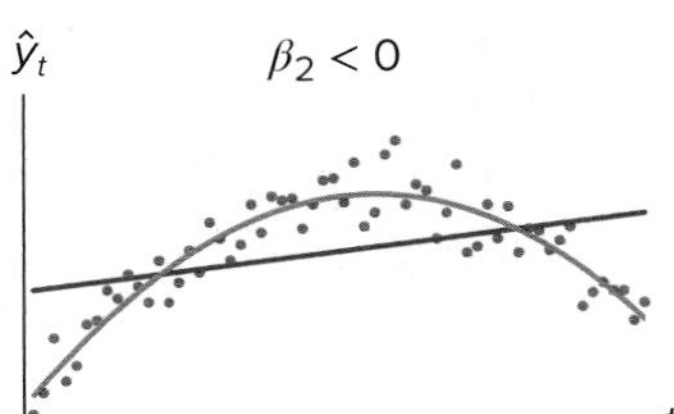

In order to estimate the quadratic trend model, we generate t^2, which is simply the square of *t*. Then, we run a multiple regression model that uses *y* as the response variable and both *t* and t^2 as the explanatory variables. The estimated model is used to make forecasts as

$$\hat{y}_t = b_0 + b_1 t + b_2 t^2.$$

Higher-order polynomial functions can be estimated similarly. For instance, the **cubic trend model** is specified as

$$y_t = \beta_0 + \beta_1 t + \beta_2 t^2 + \beta_3 t^3 + \varepsilon_t.$$

The cubic trend model allows for two changes in the direction of a series. In the cubic trend model, we basically generate two additional variables, t^2 and t^3, for the regression. A multiple regression model is run that uses *y* as the response variable and *t*, t^2, and t^3 as the explanatory variables. The estimated model is used to make forecasts as $\hat{y}_t = b_0 + b_1 t + b_2 t^2 + b_3 t^3$.

Note: We cannot use *MSE, MAD,* and *MAPE* to compare polynomial trend models because these values decrease as the order of the polynomial increases. The problem is similar to that of the coefficient of determination R^2 discussed in earlier chapters where R^2 increases as the number of explanatory variables increases. When comparing polynomial trend models, we use adjusted R^2, which imposes a penalty for over-parameterization.

THE POLYNOMIAL TREND MODEL

The polynomial trend model of order q is estimated as

$$y_t = \beta_0 + \beta_1 t + \beta_2 t^2 + \beta_3 t^3 + \cdots + \beta_q t^q + \varepsilon_t.$$

This model specializes to a linear trend model, quadratic trend model, and cubic trend model for $q = 1, 2,$ and 3, respectively.

- Forecasts are made as $\hat{y}_t = b_0 + b_1 t + b_2 t^2 + b_3 t^3 + \cdots + b_q t^q$, where $b_0, b_1, \ldots, b_q$ are the coefficient estimates.
- Adjusted R^2 is used to compare polynomial trend models with different orders.
- It is advisable to use unrounded coefficient estimates for making forecasts.

Nonlinear Trend Models with Seasonality

In Section 18.3, we incorporated seasonality in linear trend models; here we do the same for nonlinear models. The following two definition boxes summarize the exponential and the quadratic trend models with quarterly seasonal dummy variables. These models can be easily modified for monthly or other forms of seasonal data.

EXPONENTIAL TREND MODEL WITH SEASONAL DUMMY VARIABLES

With quarterly data, an exponential trend model with seasonal dummy variables is specified as

$$\ln(y) = \beta_0 + \beta_1 d_1 + \beta_2 d_2 + \beta_3 d_3 + \beta_4 t + \varepsilon.$$

- Forecasts are made as

  Quarter 1 ($d_1 = 1, d_2 = 0, d_3 = 0$): $\hat{y}_t = \exp((b_0 + b_1) + b_4 t + s_e^2/2)$,
  Quarter 2 ($d_1 = 0, d_2 = 1, d_3 = 0$): $\hat{y}_t = \exp((b_0 + b_2) + b_4 t + s_e^2/2)$,
  Quarter 3 ($d_1 = 0, d_2 = 0, d_3 = 1$): $\hat{y}_t = \exp((b_0 + b_3) + b_4 t + s_e^2/2)$,
  Quarter 4 ($d_1 = 0, d_2 = 0, d_3 = 0$): $\hat{y}_t = \exp(b_0 + b_4 t + s_e^2/2)$,

  where $b_0, b_1, \ldots b_4$ are the coefficient estimates and s_e is the standard error of the estimate.
- It is advisable to use unrounded coefficient estimates for making forecasts.

Note that for the exponential model, we compute $\hat{y}_t$ in regular units and not in natural logs. The resulting $\hat{y}_t$ also enables us to compare the linear and the exponential models in terms of their *MSE, MAD,* and *MAPE.*

QUADRATIC TREND MODEL WITH SEASONAL DUMMY VARIABLES

With quarterly data, a quadratic trend model with seasonal dummy variables is specified as

$$y = \beta_0 + \beta_1 d_1 + \beta_2 d_2 + \beta_3 d_3 + \beta_4 t + \beta_5 t^2 + \varepsilon.$$

- Forecasts are made as

  Quarter 1 ($d_1 = 1, d_2 = 0, d_3 = 0$): $\hat{y} = (b_0 + b_1) + b_4 t + b_5 t^2$,
  Quarter 2 ($d_1 = 0, d_2 = 1, d_3 = 0$): $\hat{y} = (b_0 + b_2) + b_4 t + b_5 t^2$,
  Quarter 3 ($d_1 = 0, d_2 = 0, d_3 = 1$): $\hat{y} = (b_0 + b_3) + b_4 t + b_5 t^2$,
  Quarter 4 ($d_1 = 0, d_2 = 0, d_3 = 0$): $\hat{y} = b_0 + b_4 t + b_5 t^2$,

  where $b_0, b_1, \ldots b_4$ are the coefficient estimates.
- It is advisable to use unrounded coefficient estimates for making forecasts.

We use adjusted R^2 to compare the linear and the quadratic models because of the added t^2 variable in the quadratic model. Example 18.6 provides an application of the quadratic trend model with seasonal dummy variables.

EXAMPLE 18.6

FILE
Revenue_Apple

The objective outlined in the introductory case is to forecast Apple's quarterly revenue, in $ millions, from 2010 to 2018. Use the ***Revenue_Apple*** data file to

a. Estimate the linear and the quadratic trend models with seasonal dummy variables for Apple's revenue.

b. Determine the preferred model and use it to forecast Apple's revenue for fiscal year 2019.

SOLUTION: In Section 18.1, we used Figure 18.1 to highlight important characteristics of Apple's revenue. First, there is a persistent upward movement with the series plateauing near the end of the observation period, which is suggestive of a quadratic trend model. Second, a seasonal pattern repeats itself year after year. For instance, revenue is consistently higher in the first quarter (September–December), as compared to the other quarters.

a. Given quarterly data, we first construct relevant variables for the linear and the quadratic trend models with seasonal dummy variables. (Shortly, we will provide R instructions for replicating the results.) Table 18.12 presents a portion of the data for the revenue variable y; three seasonal dummy variables d_1, d_2, and d_3 representing the first three quarters (using the fourth quarter as reference); and the trend variable t and its square t^2.

TABLE 18.12 Constructing Variables for Example 18.6

Year	Quarter	y	d_1	d_2	d_3	t	t^2
2010	1	15,683	1	0	0	1	1
2010	2	13,499	0	1	0	2	4
2010	3	15,700	0	0	1	3	9
2010	4	20,343	0	0	0	4	16
⋮	⋮	⋮	⋮	⋮	⋮	⋮	⋮
2018	3	53,265	0	0	1	35	1225
2018	4	62,900	0	0	0	36	1296

The estimated trend models are:

Linear: $$y_t = 13{,}969.3750 + 19{,}757.1382d_1 + 4{,}047.0181d_2 - 2{,}522.9910d_3 + 1{,}401.5646t;\ \text{Adjusted } R^2 = 0.8324$$

Quadratic: $$\hat{y}_t = 4{,}668.5985 + 19{,}757.1382d_1 + 3{,}967.2971d_2 - 2{,}602.7119d_3 + 2{,}876.4020t - 39.8605t^2;\ \text{Adjusted } R^2 = 0.8824$$

The coefficients for the seasonal dummy variables indicate that the revenue is about $19,757 million, or $19.76 billion, higher in the first quarter as compared to the fourth quarter. The results also suggest that compared to the fourth quarter, the revenue is somewhat higher in the second quarter and lower in the third quarter. The positive coefficient for the trend variable t in the linear model indicates an upward movement of the revenue. The positive coefficient for t along with a negative coefficient for t^2 in the quadratic model captures the inverted U-shape of the series. Recall from Chapter 16 that we can determine that the revenue reaches its maximum at $t = 36.08\left(= \frac{2{,}876.4020}{2 \times 39.8605}\right)$, which suggests that Apple's revenues reached their maximum in the fourth quarter of 2018.

b. The quadratic trend model with seasonal dummy variables is preferred for making forecasts because of a higher adjusted R^2 value (0.8824 > 0.8324). Therefore, the revenue forecasts for fiscal year 2019 are:

$$\hat{y}_{2019:01}\ (d_1 = 1, d_2 = 0, d_3 = 0, t = 37, t^2 = 1{,}369) = \$76{,}283.63 \text{ million}$$
$$\hat{y}_{2019:02}\ (d_1 = 0, d_2 = 1, d_3 = 0, t = 38, t^2 = 1{,}444) = \$60{,}380.65 \text{ million}$$
$$\hat{y}_{2019:03}\ (d_1 = 0, d_2 = 0, d_3 = 1, t = 39, t^2 = 1{,}521) = \$53{,}617.79 \text{ million}$$
$$\hat{y}_{2019:04}\ (d_1 = 0, d_2 = 0, d_3 = 0, t = 40, t^2 = 1{,}600) = \$55{,}947.93 \text{ million}$$

The quarterly forecasts result in a sum of $246,230 million in revenue, or $246.23 billion, for fiscal year 2019.

Using R to Forecast a Quadratic Trend Model with Seasons

We replicate the results for Example 18.6.

A. Import the ***Revenue_Apple*** data file into a data frame (table) and label it myData.

B. We load the *forecast* package, assuming that it is already installed on your computer. Enter:

```
> library(forecast)
```

C. We use the **ts** function to create a time series object named newData and then estimate and view the linear and the quadratic trend models. Enter:

```
> newData <- ts(myData$Revenue, start = c(2010,1), end = c(2018,4),
  frequency=4)
> Linear_Model <- tslm(newData ~ trend + season); summary(Linear_Model)
> Quadratic_Model <- tslm(newData ~ trend + I(trend^2) + season);
  summary(Quadratic_Model)
```

Recall that, by default, R uses the first quarter as the reference season, which explains why the intercept and the coefficient estimates for the dummy variables differ from those reported in Example 18.6. The forecasts, however, are not influenced by the choice of the reference dummy variable.

D. Finally, we use the **forecast** function for the preferred quadratic model where h denotes the number of forecasts. Enter:

```
> forecast(Quadratic_Model, h=4)
```

The forecasts are identical to those reported in Example 18.6.

SYNOPSIS OF INTRODUCTORY CASE

Pavel L Photo and Video/Shutterstock

Apple Inc. is an American multinational technology company headquartered in Cupertino, California. It designs, manufactures, and markets mobile communication and media devices, personal computers, and portable digital music players. It also sells a range of related software, streaming services, accessories, networking solutions, and third-party digital content and applications.

For several years, Apple's smartphone segment has been the company's core source of revenue, resulting in record revenue. A scatterplot of Apple's quarterly revenue for the fiscal years 2010 through 2018 highlights some important characteristics. First, there is a persistent upward movement with the revenue plateauing near the end of the observation period. Second, a seasonal pattern repeats itself. For each year, the revenue is the highest in the first quarter (October–December) followed by the second (January–March), fourth (July–September), and third (April–June) quarters.

The coefficients of the estimated quadratic trend model with seasonal dummy variables suggest that the revenue is about \$20 billion higher in the first quarter as compared to the fourth quarter. This is not surprising because given Apple's fiscal calendar, the first quarter encompasses the holiday period with usual strong sales. The positive coefficient for the trend variable t along with a negative coefficient for t^2 captures the plateauing of the series. In fact, given the coefficients, holding seasonality constant, the revenue reaches its maximum in the fourth quarter of 2018. This finding is consistent with the concern that while Apple is clearly doing well for now, its future growth may be murky partly because, in terms of the smartphone market, it only sells on the somewhat saturated mid-to-high-end range market. The quarterly revenue forecasts for 2019 are \$76.28, \$60.38, \$53.62, and \$55.95 billion, respectively, resulting in a whopping \$246.23 billion in revenue for fiscal year 2019.

EXERCISES 18.4

Mechanics

16. Consider the following estimated trend models. Use them to make a forecast for y at $t = 21$.
    a. Linear Trend: $\hat{y} = 13.54 + 1.08t$
    b. Quadratic Trend: $\hat{y} = 18.28 + 0.92t - 0.01t^2$
    c. Exponential Trend: $\widehat{\ln(y)} = 1.8 + 0.09t$; $s_e = 0.01$

17. Consider the following trend models estimated from 30 observations.

    Linear Model: $\hat{y} = 24 + 0.12t$

    Quadratic Model 2: $\hat{y} = 30 + 0.20t - 0.01t^2$

    a. Use each model to make a forecast for y at $t = 31$ and $t = 32$.
    b. Which is the preferred model for forecasting if, relative to the linear model, the quadratic model has higher R^2 but lower adjusted R^2?

Applications

18. **FILE** ***Whites.*** In 2016, demographers reported that deaths outnumbered births among white Americans in more than half the states in the U.S. (*The New York Times,* June 20, 2018). Consider the white American population, in millions, from 2005 through 2017; a portion of the data is shown in accompanying table.

Year	Whites
2005	215.33
2006	221.33
⋮	⋮
2017	235.51

    a. Use the scatterplot to explore linear and quadratic trends; the cubic trend is not considered. Which trend model do you think describes the time series better?
    b. Validate your intuition by comparing the appropriate goodness-of-fit measure for the two models. Use the preferred model to forecast the white population in 2018 and 2019.

19. **FILE** ***TrueCar.*** Investors are always reviewing past pricing history and using it to influence their future investment decisions. On May 16, 2014, online car buying system TrueCar launched its initial public offering (IPO), raising \$70 million in the stock offering. An investor, looking for a promising return, analyzes the monthly stock price data of TrueCar from June 2014 to May 2017. A portion of the data is shown in the accompanying table.

Date	Price
Jun-14	14.78
Jul-14	13.57
⋮	⋮
May-17	17.51

    a. Estimate the linear, the quadratic, and the cubic trend models.
    b. Determine the preferred model and use it to make a forecast for June 2017.

20. **FILE** ***Miles_Traveled.*** The number of cars sold in the United States in 2016 reached a record high for the seventh year in a row (CNNMoney, January 4, 2017). Consider monthly total miles traveled (in billions) in the United States from January 2010 to December 2016. A portion of the data is shown in the accompanying table.

Date	Miles
Jan-10	2953.305
Feb-10	2946.689
⋮	⋮
Dec-16	3169.501

    a. Estimate the quadratic and the cubic trend models.
    b. Determine the preferred model and use it to make a forecast for Miles in January 2017.

21. **FILE** ***Café_Sales.*** With a new chef and a creative menu, Café Venetian has witnessed a huge surge in sales. The accompanying table shows a portion of daily sales (in \$) at Café Venetian in the first 100 days after the changes.

Day	Sales
1	263
2	215
⋮	⋮
100	2020

Estimate the exponential trend model to forecast sales for the 101st day.

22. FILE ***Expenses.*** The controller of a small construction company is attempting to forecast expenses for the next year. He collects quarterly data on expenses (in $1,000s) over the past five years, a portion of which is shown in the accompanying table.

Year	Quarter	Expenses
2008	1	96.50
2008	2	54.00
⋮	⋮	⋮
2017	4	22335.30

Estimate the exponential trend model with seasonal dummy variables to forecast expenses for the first two quarters of 2018.

23. FILE ***Treasury_Securities.*** Treasury securities are bonds issued by the U.S. government. Consider a portion of quarterly data on treasury securities, measured in millions of U.S. dollars.

Year	Quarter	Securities
2010	1	927527
2010	2	1038881
⋮	⋮	⋮
2018	3	2284572

Estimate the exponential trend model with seasonal dummy variables to make a forecast for the fourth quarter of 2018.

24. FILE ***Housing_Starts.*** Housing starts are the number of new residential construction projects that have begun during any given month. It is considered to be a leading indicator of economic strength. The accompanying table contains a portion of monthly data on housing starts (in 1,000s) in the U.S. from Jan-11 to Nov-18.

Date	HStarts
Jan-11	40.2
Feb-11	35.4
⋮	⋮
Nov-18	95.9

Estimate the exponential seasonal trend model to forecast housing starts for December 2018.

25. FILE ***Weekly_Earnings.*** Data on weekly earnings are collected as part of the Current Population Survey, a nationwide sample survey of households in which respondents are asked how much each worker usually earns. The accompanying table contains a portion of quarterly data on weekly earnings (Earnings, adjusted for inflation) in the U.S. from 2010–2017.

Year	Quarter	Earnings
2010	1	347
2010	2	340
⋮	⋮	⋮
2017	4	347

a. Estimate the linear and the quadratic trend models with seasonal dummy variables. Which is the preferred model?
b. Use the preferred model to forecast earnings for the first two quarters of 2018.

18.5 CAUSAL FORECASTING METHODS

The models we have discussed so far are sometimes referred to as noncausal, or purely time series, models. These models do not offer any explanation of the mechanism generating the variable of interest and simply provide a method for projecting historical data. Although this approach can be effective, it provides no guidance on the likely effects of changes in policy (explanatory) variables.

Causal forecasting models are based on a regression framework, where the explanatory variables are associated with the outcome of the response variable. For instance, consider the following simple linear regression model:

$$y_t = \beta_0 + \beta_1 x_t + \varepsilon_t.$$

Here y is the response variable and x is the explanatory variable. Let the sample observations be denoted by $y_1, y_2, \ldots, y_T$ and $x_1, x_2, \ldots, x_T$, respectively. The model can easily be estimated to make a one-step-ahead forecast as

$$\hat{y}_{T+1} = b_0 + b_1 x_{T+1}.$$

Multi-step-ahead forecasts can be made similarly. Note that this approach works only if we know, or can predict, the future value of the explanatory variable x_{T+1}. For instance, let sales y be related to expenditure on advertisement x. We can forecast sales $\hat{y}_{T+1}$ only if we know the advertisement budget, x_{T+1}, for the next period.

LO 18.5

Use lagged variable models to make forecasts

Lagged Regression Models

For forecasting, sometimes we use a causal approach with lagged values of x and y as explanatory variables. For instance, consider the model

$$y_t = \beta_0 + \beta_1 x_{t-1} + \varepsilon_t,$$

where β_1 represents the slope of the lagged explanatory variable x. Note that if we have T sample observations, the estimable sample will consist of $T - 1$ observations, where $y_2, y_3, \ldots, y_T$ are matched with $x_1, x_2, \ldots, x_{T-1}$. Here a one-step-ahead forecast is easily made as

$$\hat{y}_{T+1} = b_0 + b_1 x_T.$$

This forecast does not require the future value of the explanatory variable because x_T is its last known sample value. We can generalize this model to include more lags. For example, we can specify a two-period lagged regression model as $y_t = \beta_0 + \beta_1 x_{t-1} + \beta_2 x_{t-2} + \varepsilon_t$. A one-step-ahead forecast is now made as $\hat{y}_{T+1} = b_0 + b_1 x_T + b_2 x_{T-1}$.

Another popular specification for causal forecasting uses lagged values of the response variable as an explanatory variable. For instance, consider the model

$$y_t = \beta_0 + \beta_1 y_{t-1} + \varepsilon_t,$$

where the parameter β_1 represents the slope of the lagged response variable y. This regression is also referred to as an **autoregressive model** of order one, or simply an AR(1). Higher-order autoregressive models can be constructed similarly.

Autoregressive models exploit time dependence in the given time series where future behavior can be predicted based on past behavior. A one-period-ahead forecast is made as

$$\hat{y}_{T+1} = b_0 + b_1 y_T.$$

Finally, we can also use lagged values of both x and y as the explanatory variables. For instance, consider

$$\hat{y}_t = \beta_0 + \beta_1 x_{t-1} + \beta_2 y_{t-1} + \varepsilon_t.$$

Here, a one-period-ahead forecast is made as

$$\hat{y}_{T+1} = b_0 + b_1 x_T + b_2 y_T.$$

In Example 18.7, we discuss forecasting models based on lagged variables.

EXAMPLE 18.7

Table 18.13 shows a portion of data on total dwellings and residential buildings started in the U.S. (Buildings, in 1,000s), and real gross domestic product (GDP, in $ billions). Estimate the following three models and use the most suitable model to make a forecast for buildings in 2020.

Model 1: $\text{Buildings}_t = \beta_0 + \beta_1 \text{GDP}_{t-1} + \varepsilon_t$.
Model 2: $\text{Buildings}_t = \beta_0 + \beta_1 \text{Buildings}_{t-1} + \varepsilon_t$.
Model 3: $\text{Buildings}_t = \beta_0 + \beta_1 \text{GDP}_{t-1} + \beta_2 \text{Buildings}_{t-1} + \varepsilon_t$.

TABLE 18.13 Buildings and GDP Data

Buildings

Year	Buildings	GDP
1990	99.38	9365.49
1991	84.50	9355.36
1992	99.97	9684.89
⋮	⋮	⋮
2019	107.49	19073.06

SOLUTION: In order to estimate these models, we first have to create lagged variables. This can easily be done in Excel; shortly, we will provide instructions for R. We create a new variable called LagGDP by copying the GDP observations from 1990 to 2018 and pasting it from 1991 to 2019. Note that the lagged GDP information for 1990 is not available. We repeat the process for the new lagged variable called LagBldg. Table 18.14 shows a portion of the data.

TABLE 18.14 Generating Lagged Values

Year	Buildings	GDP	LagGDP	LagBldg
1990	99.38	9365.49	-	-
1991	84.50	9355.36	9365.49	99.38
1992	99.97	9684.89	9355.36	84.50
⋮	⋮	⋮	⋮	⋮
2019	107.49	19073.06	18638.16	104.17

When estimating the three regression models in Excel, we make sure that the cell ranges for the response and explanatory variable(s) correspond to the years 1991-2019. Table 18.15 summarizes the regression results of the three models.

TABLE 18.15 Regression Models with Lagged Variables

Parameters	Model 1	Model 2	Model 3
Constant	160.2109* (0.000)	10.9114 (0.254)	27.6681 (0.157)
LagGDP	−0.0037 (0.101)	NA	−0.0010 (0.320)
LagBldg	NA	0.9019* (0.000)	0.8799* (0.000)
Adjusted R^2	0.0630	0.8087	0.8089

Notes: The top portion of the table contains parameter estimates with *p*-values in parentheses; NA denotes not applicable; the symbol * denotes significance at the 5% level.

As discussed earlier, it is preferable to compare competing regression models in terms of adjusted R^2 because it appropriately penalizes for overfitting. We choose Model 3 because it has the highest adjusted R^2 of 0.8089. To make a forecast for 2020, we use the 2019 values for GDP and Buildings, which represent their lagged values for 2020.

$$\widehat{\text{Building}}_{2020} = 27.6681 - 0.0010 \times 19073.06 + 0.8799 \times 107.49 = 102.59.$$

Therefore, we forecast that about 102,590 new dwellings and residential buildings will start in the U.S. in 2020.

Using R to Estimate Lagged Regression Models

Buildings

We replicate the results for Example 18.7.

A. Import the ***Buildings*** data file into a data frame (table) and label it myData.

B. We create a new variable for Buildings, labeled y, using observations 2 to 30 which correspond to the years 1991 to 2019. We also create the corresponding lagged variables for GDP and Buildings, labelled lagx and lagy, respectively, using observations 1 to 29. Enter:

```
> y <- myData$Buildings[c(2:30)]
> lagx <- myData$GDP[c(1:29)]
> lagy <- myData$Buildings[c(1:29)]
```

C. We use the **lm** and **summary** functions to estimate and view the regression output for Model 1, Model 2, and Model 3. Enter:

```
> Model1 <- lm(y ~ lagx); summary(Model1)
> Model2 <- lm(y ~ lagy); summary(Model2)
> Model3 <- lm(y ~ lagx + lagy); summary(Model3)
```

D. Finally, we use the **forecast** function for the preferred Model 3, using 2019 GDP and Buildings observations as lagged values for the 2020 forecast. Enter:

```
> predict(Model3, data.frame(lagx=19073.06, lagy=107.49))
And R returns: 102.5867.
```

EXERCISES 18.4

Mechanics

26. **FILE** ***Exercise_18.26.*** The accompanying file contains data for y and x. Estimate $y_t = \beta_0 + \beta_1 x_{t-1} + \beta_2 x_{t-2} + \varepsilon_t$ and use it to make a one-step-ahead forecast ($t = 13$) for y.

27. **FILE** ***Exercise_18.27.*** The accompanying file contains data for y.
    a. Estimate an autoregressive model of order 1, $y_t = \beta_0 + \beta_1 y_{t-1} + \varepsilon_t$, to make a one-step-ahead forecast ($t = 25$) for y.
    b. Estimate an autoregressive model of order 2, $y_t = \beta_0 + \beta_1 y_{t-1} + \beta_2 y_{t-2} + \varepsilon_t$, to make a one-step-ahead forecast ($t = 25$) for y.

28. **FILE** ***Exercise_18.28.*** The accompanying file contains data for y and x.
    a. Estimate $y_t = \beta_0 + \beta_1 x_{t-1} + \varepsilon_t$ to make a one-step-ahead forecast for period 13.
    b. Estimate $y_t = \beta_0 + \beta_1 y_{t-1} + \varepsilon_t$ to make a one-step-ahead forecast for period 13.

29. **FILE** ***Exercise_18.29.*** The accompanying file contains data for y and x.
    a. Estimate $y_t = \beta_0 + \beta_1 x_{t-1} + \varepsilon_t$.
    b. Estimate $y_t = \beta_0 + \beta_1 y_{t-1} + \varepsilon_t$.
    c. Estimate $y_t = \beta_0 + \beta_1 x_{t-1} + \beta_2 y_{t-1} + \varepsilon_t$.
    d. Use the most suitable model to make a one-step-ahead forecast ($t = 13$) for y.

Applications

30. Hiroshi Sato, an owner of a sushi restaurant in San Francisco, has been following an aggressive marketing campaign to thwart the effect of rising unemployment rates on business. He used monthly data on sales ($1,000s), advertising costs ($), and the unemployment rate (%) from January 2018 to May 2019 to estimate the following sample regression equation:

$$\widehat{Sales}_t = 17.51 + 0.03AdCost_{t-1} - 0.69Unemp_{t-1}.$$

    a. Hiroshi had budgeted $620 toward advertising costs in May 2019. Make a forecast for Sales for June 2019 if the unemployment rate in May 2019 was 9.1%.
    b. What will be the forecast if he raises his advertisement budget to $700?
    c. Reevaluate the above forecasts if the unemployment rate was 9.5% in May 2019.

31. **FILE** ***Profits.*** The owner of a popular restaurant wants to forecast weekly profits during the peak tourist season. The

accompanying table shows a portion of its profits y (in $1,000s) and its marketing expenditure x for 12 weeks.

Week	y	x
1	26.92	9321.40
2	25.89	9135.34
⋮	⋮	⋮
12	27.07	9496.28

Estimate three models: (a) $y_t = \beta_0 + \beta_1 x_{t-1} + \varepsilon_t$, (b) $y_t = \beta_0 + \beta_1 y_{t-1} + \varepsilon_t$, and (c) $y_t = \beta_0 + \beta_1 x_{t-1} + \beta_2 y_{t-1} + \varepsilon_t$. Use the most suitable model to forecast the restaurant's profit for Week 13.

32. **FILE** ***Phillips_Curve.*** The Phillips curve captures the inverse relation between the rate of unemployment and the rate of inflation; the lower the unemployment in an economy, the higher is the inflation rate. Consider the following portion of monthly data on the seasonally adjusted consumer price index (CPI) and the unemployment rates in the United States from January 2018 to December 2019.

Date	Unemployment	CPI
Jan-18	4.1	248.816
Feb-18	4.1	249.475
⋮	⋮	⋮
Dec-19	3.5	258.444

a. Estimate two models. Model 1 uses CPI as the response variable and lagged unemployment rate as the explanatory variable. Model 2 extends the model by including lagged CPI as another explanatory variable.

b. Determine the preferred model and use it to forecast CPI for January 2020.

18.6 WRITING WITH DATA

Case Study

feverpitched/123RF

Leading economic indicators, such as the stock market or the housing market, often change prior to large economic adjustments. For example, a rise in stock prices often means that investors are more confident of future growth in the economy. Or, a fall in building permits is likely a signal that the housing market is weakening – which is often a sign that other sectors of the economy are on the downturn.

Consider what happened prior to the 2008 recession. As early as October 2006, building permits for new homes were down 28% from October 2005. Analysts use economic indicators to predict future trends and gauge where the economy is heading. The information provided by economic indicators helps firms implement or alter business strategies.

Pooja Nanda is an analyst for a large investment firm in Chicago. She covers the construction industry and has been given the challenging task of forecasting housing starts for June 2019. She has access to seasonally adjusted monthly housing starts in the United States from January 2016 to May 2019. A portion of the data is shown in Table 18.16.

TABLE 18.16 Monthly Housing Starts (in 1,000s)

Starts

Date	Housing Starts
Jan-16	1114
Feb-16	1208
⋮	⋮
May-19	1269

Pooja would like to use the sample information to identify the best-fitting model to forecast housing starts for June 2019.

Sample Report—Forecasting Monthly Housing Starts

Leading economic indicators are often used to gauge where the economy is heading. The housing market is one of the most important indicators because it is a significant component of the economy. When this sector weakens, just about everyone and everything feels it – from homeowners and construction workers to government municipalities that rely on property taxes to operate. Given the importance of the housing market, this report will employ simple time series models to project historical data on housing starts.

A scatterplot of housing starts from January 2016 to May 2019 is shown in Figure 18.9. A casual observation of the scatterplot suggests quite a bit of random variation and possibly a slight upward trend. There is no concern for seasonality as the housing starts data represent seasonally adjusted annual rates.

FIGURE 18.9 Scatterplot of housing starts (in 1,000s)

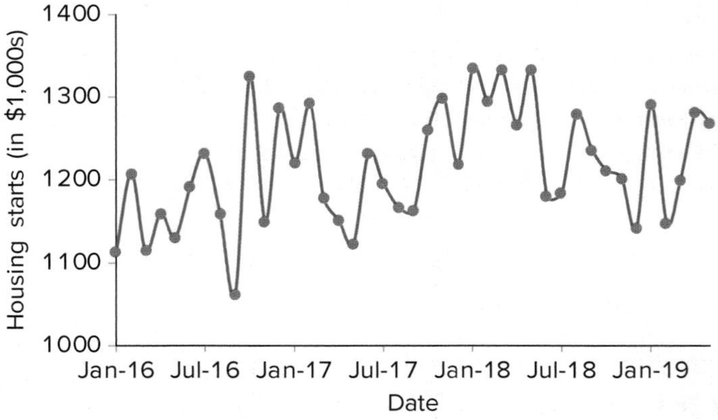

Given the findings from Figure 18.9, three models are estimated.

1. The three-period moving average model.
2. The simple exponential smoothing model with various values for the speed of decline α.
3. The simple linear trend model, $y_t = \beta_0 + \beta_{1t} + \varepsilon_t$, where y_t represents housing starts.

Three performance measures are used for model selection: mean square error (*MSE*), mean absolute deviation (*MAD*), and the mean absolute percentage error (*MAPE*). Ideally, the preferred model will have the lowest values for *MSE, MAD,* and *MAPE.* Table 18.17 shows the values of these three performance measures for the models.

TABLE 18.17 Performance Measures of Competing Models

	3-period Moving Average Model	Exponential Smoothing Model ($\alpha = 0.2$)*	Linear Regression Model
MSE	5,069.50	4,798.44	4,091.72
MAD	60.55	57.13	54.24
MAPE	4.96	4.65	4.46

*For the exponential smoothing model, $\alpha = 0.20$ provides the lowest values for *MSE, MAD,* and *MAPE.*

The linear trend model provides the best sample fit, as it has the lowest values for *MSE, MAD,* and *MAPE.* Therefore, the estimated linear trend model is used to derive the forecast for June 2019 as

$$\hat{y}_{42} = 1{,}170.2524 + 2.1413 \times 42 = 1{,}260.19.$$

Housing starts plays a key role in determining the health of the economy and is, therefore, always under scrutiny. The U.S. housing market seems to be on solid ground even though there has been a slowdown from its peak in early 2018.

Suggested Case Studies

Report 18.1 FILE ***Fried_Dough.*** Fried dough is a popular North American food associated with outdoor food stands at carnivals, amusement parks, fairs, festivals, and so on. Usually dusted with powdered sugar and drenched in oil, it is not particularly healthy, but it sure is tasty! Jose Sanchez owns a small stall at Boston Commons in Boston, Massachusetts, where he sells fried dough and soft drinks. Although business is good, he is apprehensive about the variation in sales for no apparent reason. The accompanying data file contains information on the number of plates of fried dough and soft drinks that he sold over the last 30 days. In a report, use the sample information to explore forecasting models, including moving averages and the simple exponential method, to smooth the time series for fried dough and soft drinks. Use the preferred method to forecast sales of fried dough and soft drinks for the next few days.

Report 18.2 FILE ***India_China.*** According to United Nations estimates, more than half of the world population live in just seven countries, with China, closely followed by India, leading the pack. The other five countries on the list include the United States, Indonesia, Brazil, Pakistan, and Nigeria. It is believed that India will overtake China to become the world's most populous nation much sooner than previously thought (*CNN*, June 2019). The accompanying data file, compiled by the World Bank, contains the population data, in millions, for India and China from 1960 to 2017. In a report, use the sample information to explore linear and nonlinear trend regression models to capture the population trend for both China and India. Use the preferred model to forecast the population of China and India from 2018–2020.

Report 18.3 FILE ***Revenue_Amazon.*** Amazon.com, Inc., was a money-losing company when it went public on May 15, 1997, with an IPO valued at a modest $438 million. Amazon has since had an epic 20-year run as a public company, worth about $460 billion in 2017. Many analysts attribute the success of the company to its dynamic leader, Jeff Bezos, who, according to the Bloomberg Billionaires Index, is the richest man in modern history (CNBC, July 2018). An important question for investors and other stakeholders is if Amazon's growth is sustainable. The accompanying data file contains quarterly data on Amazon's revenue for the fiscal years 2010 through 2018, with the fiscal year concluding at the end of December. In a report, use the sample information to explore linear and nonlinear regression models with trend and seasonality to capture Amazon's revenue. Use the preferred model to forecast Amazon's revenue for fiscal year 2019.

CONCEPTUAL REVIEW

LO 18.1 Describe the time series forecasting process.

Observations of any variable recorded over time in sequential order are considered a time series. The purpose of any forecasting model is to forecast the time series at time t, or $\hat{y}_t$. Forecasting methods are broadly classified as qualitative or quantitative. While qualitative forecasts are based on prior experience and the expertise of the forecaster, quantitative forecasts use a formal model, along with historical data, for making forecasts.

We use performance measures to compare competing models. Because there is no 'primary' performance measure, multiple measures are used for model selection. These measures are based on the residuals, $e_t = y_t - \hat{y}_t$, and include: $MSE = \frac{1}{n}\sum e_t^2$, $MAD = \frac{1}{n}\sum |e_t|$, and $MAPE = \frac{1}{n}\left(\sum\left|\frac{e_t}{y_t}\right|\right) \times 100$, where n is the number of observations used in the computation. We choose the model with the lowest *MSE, MAD,* and *MAPE* values. For comparing regression-based forecasting models with different number of explanatory variables, we use adjusted R^2, which imposes a penalty for over-parameterization.

LO 18.2 Use smoothing techniques to make forecasts.

Smoothing techniques are employed to provide forecasts if short-term fluctuations represent random departures from the structure with no discernible systematic patterns.

A moving average is the average from a fixed number of the m most recent observations. We use moving averages to make forecasts as $\hat{y}_t = \frac{y_{t-m} + y_{t-m+1} + \cdots + y_{t-1}}{m}$.

Exponential smoothing is a weighted average approach where the weights decline exponentially as they become more distant. The exponential smoothing method continually updates the level of the series as $A_t = \alpha y_t + (1 - \alpha)A_{t-1}$, where α represents the speed of decline. Forecasts are made as $\hat{y}_{t+1} = A_t$.

LO 18.3 Use linear regression models to make forecasts.

The linear trend model is specified as $y_t = \beta_0 + \beta_1 t + \varepsilon_t$. The model is estimated to make forecasts as $\hat{y}_t = b_0 + b_1 t$, where b_0 and b_1 are the coefficient estimates.

With seasonal data, we extend the linear trend model to include seasonal dummy variables. For example, with quarterly data, the model can be estimated as $\hat{y} = b_0 + b_1 d_1 + b_2 d_2 + b_3 d_3 + b_4 t$ where the dummy variables, d_1, d_2, and d_3 represent the first three quarters and b_1, b_2, b_3, and b_4 are the coefficient estimates. Forecasts are made as $\hat{y} = (b_0 + b_1) + b_4 t$ (Quarter 1), $\hat{y} = (b_0 + b_2) + b_4 t$ (Quarter 2), $\hat{y} = (b_0 + b_3) + b_4 t$ (Quarter 3), and $\hat{y} = b_0 + b_4 t$ (Quarter 4).

LO 18.4 Use nonlinear regression models to make forecasts.

The exponential trend model is specified as $\ln(y_t) = \beta_0 + \beta_1 t + \varepsilon$, where $\ln(y_t)$ is the natural log of y_t. The model is estimated to make forecasts as $\hat{y} = \exp(b_0 + b_1 t + s_e^2/2)$ where b_0 and b_1 are the coefficient estimates and s_e is the standard error of the estimate. We use *MSE, MAD,* and *MAPE* to compare linear and exponential trend models.

The polynomial trend model of order q is specified as $y = \beta_0 + \beta_1 t + \beta_2 t^2 + \beta_3 t^3 + \cdots + \beta_q t^q + \varepsilon$. It specializes to a linear trend model, a quadratic trend model, and a cubic trend model for $q = 1$, 2, and 3, respectively. The model is estimated to make forecasts as $\hat{y} = b_0 + b_1 t + b_2 t^2 + b_3 t^3 + b_q t^q$ where $b_0, b_1, \cdots, b_q$ are the coefficient estimates. We use adjusted R^2 to compare polynomial trend models of different orders.

With seasonal data, we can easily extend the exponential and the polynomial trend models to include seasonal dummy variables. Forecasts are made similarly.

LO 18.5 Use lagged variable models to make forecasts.

It is common to use lagged values of x and y for making forecasts. A model that uses a lagged explanatory variable is specified as

$y_t = \beta_0 + \beta_1 x_{t-1} + \varepsilon_t$ and a forecast is made as $\hat{y}_{T+1} = b_0 + b_1 x_T$. Another common model uses a lagged response variable as an explanatory variable and is specified as $y_t = \beta_0 + \beta_1 y_{t-1} + \varepsilon_t$; a forecast is made as $\hat{y}_{T+1} = b_0 + b_1 y_T$. Finally, a model may include lagged values of both x and y as explanatory variables. Here, the specification is $y_t = \beta_0 + \beta_1 x_{t-1} + \beta_2 y_{t-1} + \varepsilon_t$ and a forecast is made as $\hat{y}_{T+1} = b_0 + b_1 x_T + b_2 y_T$.

ADDITIONAL EXERCISES

33. FILE ***Yields.*** The U.S. housing market remains fragile despite historically low mortgage rates. Since the rate on 30-year mortgages is tied to the 10-year yield on Treasury bonds, it is important to be able to predict this yield accurately. The accompanying table shows a portion of the 10-year yield on Treasury bonds (in %) for 21 trading days.

Day	Yield
1	2.63
2	2.59
⋮	⋮
21	2.80

a. Use a 3-period moving average to make a forecast for the 22nd trading day.
b. Use the exponential smoothing method to make a forecast for 22nd trading day. Use $\alpha = 0.5$.

34. FILE ***Fried_Dough.*** Jose Sanchez owns a stall where he sells fried dough and soft drinks. He asks a friend to help him make a forecast for fried dough as well as soft drinks. The accompanying table shows a portion of data on the number of plates of fried dough and soft drinks that he sold over the last 20 days. Construct the exponentially smoothed series for fried dough and soft drinks using $\alpha = 0.30$ and make the resulting forecasts for day 21.

Day	Fried Dough	Soft Drinks
1	70	150
2	69	145
⋮	⋮	⋮
20	61	153

35. FILE ***UsedCars*** Used car dealerships generally have sales quotas that they strive to hit each month, quarter, and calendar year. Consequently, buying a used car toward the end of those periods presents a great opportunity to get a good deal on the car. A local dealership has compiled monthly sales data for used cars (Cars) from 2014-2019, a portion of which is shown in the accompanying table.

Date	Cars
Jan-2014	138
Feb-2014	179
⋮	⋮
Dec-2019	195

a. Estimate the linear regression models using seasonal dummy variables with and without the trend term. Which is the preferred model?
b. Use the preferred model to forecast sales for used cars in the first two months of 2020.

36. FILE ***Consumer_Sentiment.*** The accompanying table lists a portion of the University of Michigan's Consumer Sentiment index. This index is normalized to have a value of 100 in 1966 and is used to record changes in consumer morale.

Date	Sentiment
Jan-10	74.4
Feb-10	73.6
⋮	⋮
Nov-18	97.5

a. Estimate and interpret the linear trend model with seasonal dummy variables.
b. Use the estimated model to make a consumer sentiment index forecast for December 2018.

37. FILE ***Case_Shiller.*** The S&P's Case-Shiller home price index measures repeat-sales house price indices for the United States. The index, normalized to have a value of 100 in January 2000, captures price movements of the same homes relative to January 2000. The accompanying table shows a portion of the seasonally adjusted monthly series from January 2016 to November 2018.

Date	Price
Jan-16	177.412
Feb-16	177.828
⋮	⋮
Nov-18	206.263

a. Estimate the linear and the exponential trend models and calculate their *MSE, MAD,* and *MAPE.*
b. Use the preferred model to forecast the Case-Shiller index for December 2018.

38. FILE ***Population_Japan.*** For several years, Japan's declining population has led experts and lawmakers to consider its economic and social repercussions (*NPR,* December 21, 2018). The accompanying table shows a portion of Japan's population data, in millions, from 1960 to 2017.

Year	Population
1960	92.50
1961	94.94
⋮	⋮
2017	126.79

a. Estimate linear and quadratic trend models. Which is the preferred model for forecasting?
b. Use the preferred model to forecast the population in Japan for 2018 and 2019.

39. **FILE** ***House_Price.*** The West Census region for the U.S. includes Montana, Wyoming, Colorado, New Mexico, Idaho, Utah, Arizona, Nevada, California, Oregon, and Washington. The accompanying table shows a portion of the median house prices in the West Census region from 2010:01 through 2018:03.

Year	Quarter	Price
2010	1	263600
2010	2	264100
⋮	⋮	⋮
2018	3	404300

a. Estimate linear and quadratic trend models with seasonal dummy variables. Which is the preferred model?
b. Use the preferred model to forecast the median house price in the West Census region for the fourth quarter of 2018.

40. **FILE** ***Vehicle_Miles.*** The United States economy picked up speed in 2012 as businesses substantially built up their inventories and consumers increased their spending. This also led to an increase in domestic travel. The accompanying table shows a portion of the vehicle miles traveled in the U.S. (in millions) from January 2012 through September 2018.

Date	Miles
Jan-12	227527
Feb-12	218196
⋮	⋮
Sep-18	260555

a. Estimate the linear and the exponential trend models with seasonal dummy variables for vehicle miles and calculate their *MSE, MAD,* and *MAPE.*
b. Use the preferred model to forecast vehicle miles for the last three months of 2018.

41. **FILE** ***Consumption.*** The consumption function is one of the key relationships in economics, where consumption (y) depends on disposable income (x). The accompanying table shows a portion of quarterly data on personal consumption expenditure and disposable income for five years. Both variables are measured in billions of dollars and are seasonally adjusted.

Year	Quarter	y	x
1	1	9148.2	9705.2
1	2	9266.6	9863.8
⋮	⋮	⋮	⋮
5	4	10525.2	11514.7

a. Plot the consumption series. Estimate the appropriate polynomial trend model to forecast consumption expenditure for the 1st quarter of year 6.
b. Estimate $y_t = \beta_0 + \beta_1 x_{t-1} + \varepsilon_t$ to forecast consumption expenditure for the 1st quarter of year 6.
c. Which of these two models is more appropriate for making forecasts? Explain.

APPENDIX 18.1 Guidelines for Other Software Packages

The following section provides brief commands for Minitab, SPSS, and JMP. Import the specified data file into the relevant software spreadsheet prior to following the commands.

Minitab

A Linear Trend Model with Seasonality

Ecommerce

A. (Replicating Example 18.4) In order to create the trend variable, from the menu choose **Calc > Make Patterned Data > Simple Set of Numbers.** After **From first value,** enter 1, and after **To last value,** enter 37. In order to create seasonal dummy variables, from the menu choose **Calc > Make Indicator Variables.** After **Indicator variables for,** enter Quarter.

B. Estimate the regression model using the standard commands.

A Lagged Regression Model

FILE *Buildings*

A. (Replicating Example 18.7 – Model 3) In order to create GDP_{t-1}, choose **Calc > Calculator.** After **Store result in variable,** enter lagGDP, and after **Expression,** enter lag(GDP,1). Repeat these steps to create $Buildings_{t-1}$.

B. Estimate the regression model using the standard commands.

SPSS

A Linear Trend Model with Seasonality

Ecommerce

A. (Replicating Example 18.4) In order to create a trend variable, choose **Transform> Compute Variable.** Under **Target Variable** enter trend. After **Numeric Expression,** enter $CASENUM. In order to create seasonal dummy variables, from the menu choose **Transform > Create Dummy Variables.** Under **Create Dummy Variables for,** select Quarter. Select **Create main-effect dummies** and under **Root Names,** enter Quarter.

B. Estimate the regression model using the standard commands.

A Lagged Regression Model

Buildings

A. (Replicating Example 18.7 – Model 3) In order to create GDP_{t-1}, choose **Transform> Compute Variable.** Under **Target Variable** enter lagGDP. After **Numeric Expression,** enter lag(GDP,1). Repeat these steps to create $Buildings_{t-1}$.

B. Estimate the regression model using the standard commands.

JMP

A Linear Trend Model with Seasonality

Ecommerce

A. (Replicating Example 18.4) In order to create the trend variable, right-click on a new column in the spreadsheet and label it trend. Right-click on trend and select **Formula > Row > Sequence.** Enter 1 for **start,** 37 for **end,** and 1 for **incr.** In order to create a dummy variable for quarter 1, right-click on a new column in the spreadsheet and label it Q1. Right-click on Q1 and select **Formula > Comparison> a==b.** Enter Quarter for **a** and 1 for **b.** Repeat these steps to create the other seasonal dummy variables.

B. Estimate the regression model using the standard commands.

A Lagged Regression Model

Buildings

A. (Replicating Example 18.7 - Model 3) In order to create GDP_{t-1}, right-click on a new column in the spreadsheet and label it lagGDP. Right-click on lagGDP and select **Formula > Row > Lag.** Enter GDP for **x** and 1 for **n.** Repeat these steps to create $Buildings_{t-1}$.

B. Estimate the regression model using the standard commands.

19 Returns, Index Numbers, and Inflation

LEARNING OBJECTIVES

After reading this chapter you should be able to:

LO **19.1** Define and compute investment returns.

LO **19.2** Convert nominal returns into real returns and vice versa.

LO **19.3** Calculate and interpret a simple price index.

LO **19.4** Calculate and interpret an unweighted aggregate price index.

LO **19.5** Calculate and interpret the Laspeyres and the Paasche price indices.

LO **19.6** Use price indices to deflate an economic time series and derive the inflation rate.

In Chapter 18, we discussed deseasonalized time series. Policy makers often analyze time series in this deseasonalized format, as they are not particularly interested in its seasonal variations. Other transformations of time series also facilitate interpretation and statistical analysis. For example, financial analysts are interested in the analysis of investment returns. The underlying information on asset prices and income distributions can easily be transformed into investment returns.

Similarly, economists are often interested in measuring the magnitude of economic changes over time. Again, it is easy to create index numbers that transform the original values into percentage changes. We can do the transformation both for a single item or a group of items.

Finally, many time series are reported both in nominal as well as real terms. While the nominal values represent dollar amounts, the corresponding real values incorporate inflation to represent the purchasing power of money.

In this chapter, we will compute and interpret all such transformed time series.

imageBROKER/Alamy Stock Photo

INTRODUCTORY CASE

Analyzing Beer and Wine Price Changes

Jehanne-Marie Roche is the owner of a convenience store in Iowa City, which is the home of the University of Iowa. Although Jehanne-Marie sells selected grocery and household items, the major source of revenue is from the sale of liquor. Recently, the store has experienced a significant decline in consumer demand for liquor due to the opening of a supermarket in the neighborhood and further exacerbated by the COVID-19 pandemic in 2020.

Jehanne-Marie has been forced to offer numerous price discounts to sell beer and wine at the store. She asks her nephew to help her understand the price movement of liquor at her store during the 2018–2020 time period. She gives him the average price and quantity information for red wine, white wine, and beer, listed in Table 19.1.

TABLE 19.1 Average Price and Quantity of Wine and Beer

Year		Red Wine	White Wine	6-pack of Beer
2018	Price	\$12.30	\$11.90	\$8.10
	Quantity	1,560	1,410	2,240
2019	Price	\$12.10	\$11.05	\$8.25
	Quantity	1,490	1,390	2,310
2020	Price	\$9.95	\$10.60	\$7.95
	Quantity	1,280	1,010	2,190

Jehanne-Marie wants to use the above information to

1. Determine the percentage price change of red wine, white wine, and beer from 2018 to 2020.
2. Derive and interpret the aggregate price index of liquor.

A synopsis of this case is provided at the end of Section 19.2.

19.1 INVESTMENT RETURN

LO 19.1

Define and compute investment returns.

In earlier chapters, the focus of many examples was on the analysis of **investment returns.** Here we describe a simple method to compute them. The time period used for computing an investment return may be a day, a week, a month, a year, or multiple years, and the investment may be in assets such as stocks, bonds, currencies, Treasury bills, or real estate. The investment may be in an individual asset or a portfolio of assets (for example, a mutual fund).

An investment return consists of two components. The income component is the direct cash payments from the underlying asset, such as dividends, interest, or rental income. The price change component is the capital gain or loss resulting from an increase or decrease in the value of the asset.

Consider a share of a company's stock that an investor purchased a year ago for $25. If the price of this share jumps to $28 in a year, then $3 ($28 – $25) is the annual capital gain from this stock. In percentage terms, it is computed as $(3/25) \times 100 = 12\%$ and is referred to as the **capital gains yield.** If the company has also paid a dividend of $1 per share during the year, the income component, in percentage terms, is $(1/25) \times 100 = 4\%$ and is referred to as the **income yield.** Therefore, the total annual return from investing in this company is 16% (12% + 4%).

CALCULATING AN INVESTMENT RETURN

An investment return R_t at time t is calculated as

$$R_t = \frac{P_t - P_{t-1} + I_t}{P_{t-1}},$$

where P_t and P_{t-1} are the price of the asset at times t (current) and $t - 1$ (prior), respectively, and I_t is the income distributed during the investment period. The ratios $\frac{P_t - P_{t-1}}{P_{t-1}}$ and $\frac{I_t}{P_{t-1}}$ are the capital gains yield and the income yield, respectively.

The process for computing an investment return is the same for all assets. The income component is dividends for stocks, interest for bonds, and rental income for a real estate investment. For some assets, like Treasury bills, there is no income component and the investment return consists entirely of a capital gain or loss.

EXAMPLE 19.1

Helen Watson purchased a corporate bond for $950 a year ago. She received a coupon payment (interest) of $60 during the year. The bond is currently selling for $975. Compute Helen's (a) capital gains yield, (b) income yield, and (c) investment return.

SOLUTION:

a. We calculate the capital gains yield as $\frac{P_t - P_{t-1}}{P_{t-1}} = \frac{975 - 950}{950} = 0.0263$ or 2.63%.

b. Given the interest payment of $60, we calculate the income yield as $\frac{I_t}{P_{t-1}} = \frac{60}{950} = 0.0632$ or 6.32%.

c. The investment return is the sum of the capital gains yield and the income yield, that is, $0.0263 + 0.0632 = 0.0895$ or 8.95%. We can also compute it directly as $R_t = \frac{P_t - P_{t-1} + I_t}{P_{t-1}} = \frac{975 - 950 + 60}{950} = \frac{85}{950} = 0.0895$ or 8.95%.

EXAMPLE 19.2

Last year, Jim Hamilton bought a stock for $35 and recently received a dividend of $1.25. The stock is now selling for $31. Find Jim's (a) capital gains yield, (b) income yield, and (c) investment return.

SOLUTION:

a. The capital gains yield is $\frac{P_t - P_{t-1}}{P_{t-1}} = \frac{31 - 35}{35} = -0.1143$ or -11.43%.

b. The income yield is $\frac{I_t}{P_{t-1}} = \frac{1.25}{35} = 0.0357$ or 3.57%.

c. The investment return is $-0.1143 + 0.0357 = -0.0786$ or -7.86%. Equivalently, we can compute the investment return as

$$R_t = \frac{P_t - P_{t-1} + I_t}{P_{t-1}} = \frac{31 - 35 + 1.25}{35} = \frac{-2.75}{35} = -0.0786 \text{ or } -7.86\%.$$

Note that the investment return is unaffected by the decision to sell or hold assets. A common misconception is that if you do not sell an asset, there is no capital gain or loss involved, as a given price increase or decrease leads only to paper gain or loss. This misconception often leads an investor to hold a "loser" asset longer than necessary because of the reluctance to admit a bad investment decision. It is important to note that the nonrecognition of the loss is relevant for tax purposes because only realized income must be reported in tax returns. However, whether or not you have liquidated an asset is irrelevant when measuring its return.

The Adjusted Closing Price

Historical returns are often used by investors, analysts, and other researchers to assess past performance of a stock. In Example 19.2, we saw that the dividend payments also influence stock returns. Therefore, we need the dividend data along with the price data to compute historical returns. Similarly, we need information on stock splits and reverse stock splits in computing returns. Tabulating corporate decisions such as the announcement of dividends, stock splits, and reverse stock splits can be very cumbersome. For these reasons, most data sources for stock price information, such as *http://finance.yahoo.com,* also include data on the **adjusted closing price.** Here, price data are adjusted using appropriate dividend distributions and split multipliers.

Given that the adjustment has been made for all dividend distributions and applicable splits, we can compute the total investment return solely on the basis of the price appreciation or depreciation of the adjusted closing prices.

USING ADJUSTED CLOSING PRICES TO CALCULATE AN INVESTMENT RETURN

Let P_t^* and P_{t-1}^* represent the adjusted closing price of a stock at times t (current) and $t - 1$ (prior), respectively. The investment return R_t at the end of time t is calculated as

$$R_t = \frac{P_t^* - P_{t-1}^*}{P_{t-1}^*}.$$

EXAMPLE 19.3

Consider the adjusted closing stock prices of Tesla in Table 19.2. Find the monthly returns for April and May of 2020.

TABLE 19.2 Monthly Stock Prices for Tesla

Date	Adjusted Closing Price
April 1, 2020	781.88
May 1, 2020	835.00
June 1, 2020	972.84

SOLUTION: We compute the monthly return for April 2020 as $R_t = \frac{835.00 - 781.88}{781.88} = 0.0679$, or 6.79%. Similarly, the monthly return for May 2020 is $R_t = \frac{972.84 - 835.00}{835.00} = 0.1651$, or 16.51%. The surge in the stock price can be attributed to the volume production of its new commercial semi-truck.

LO 19.2

Convert nominal returns into real returns and vice versa.

Nominal versus Real Rates of Return

So far we have focused on **nominal return,** which makes no allowance for inflation. Financial rates, such as interest rates, discount rates, and rates of return, are generally reported in nominal terms. However, the nominal return does not represent a true picture because it does not capture the erosion of the purchasing power of money due to inflation.

Consider an investment of $100 that becomes $105 after one year. While the nominal return on this investment is 5%, the purchasing power of the money is likely to have increased by less than 5%. Once the effects of inflation have been factored in, investors can determine the real, or true, return on their investment. The **real return** is the return adjusted for inflation.

The relationship between the nominal return and the real return was developed by Irving Fisher (1867–1947), a prominent economist. The **Fisher equation** is a theoretical relationship between the nominal return, the real return, and the expected inflation rate.

THE FISHER EQUATION

Let R be the nominal rate of return, r the real rate of return, and i the expected inflation rate. The Fisher equation is defined as

$$1 + r = \frac{1 + R}{1 + i}.$$

When the expected inflation rate is relatively low, a reasonable approximation to the Fisher equation is $r = R - i$; we will not be using this approximation in this chapter.

EXAMPLE 19.4

The quoted rate of return on a one-year U.S. Treasury bill in January 2020 is 1.56%. Compute and interpret the real rate of return that investors can earn if the inflation rate is expected to be 2.1%.

SOLUTION: Using the Fisher equation, $1 + r = \frac{1+R}{1+i} = \frac{1.0156}{1.0210} = 0.9947$; we derive the real rate of return as $r = 0.9947 - 1 = -0.0053$, or -0.53%. The negative real rate of return implies that investors are cautious and are willing to accept a small drop in their purchasing power during this period.

EXAMPLE 19.5

A bond produces a real rate of return of 5.30% for a time period when the inflation rate is expected to be 3%. What is the nominal rate of return on the bond?

SOLUTION: The Fisher equation can be rewritten as $1 + R = (1 + r)(1 + i)$. Therefore, given the real rate of return of 5.30% and the inflation rate of 3%, we can easily compute, $1 + R = (1.053)(1.03) = 1.0846$ giving us the nominal return of $R = 1.0846 - 1 = 0.0846$, or 8.46%.

EXERCISES 19.1

1. You borrowed $2,000 to take a vacation in the Caribbean islands. At the end of the year, you had to pay back $2,200. What is the annual interest that you paid on your loan?
2. You bought a corporate bond last year for $980. You received a coupon payment (interest) of $60, and the bond is currently selling for $990. What is the (a) income yield, (b) capital gains yield, and (c) Investion return?
3. The year-end price and dividend information on a stock is given in the following table.

Year	Price	Dividend
1	23.50	NA
2	24.80	0.18
3	22.90	0.12

Note: NA denotes not applicable.

   a. What is the nominal return of the stock in years 2 and 3?
   b. What is the corresponding real return if the inflation rates for years 2 and 3 were 2.8% and 1.6%, respectively?
4. The price of a stock has gone up from $24 to $35 in one year. It also paid a year-end dividend of $1.20. What is the stock's (a) income yield, (b) capital gains yield, and (c) total return?
5. A portfolio manager invested $1,500,000 in bonds. In one year, the market value of the bonds dropped to $1,485,000. The interest payments during the year totaled $105,000.
   a. What was the manager's total rate of return for the year?
   b. What was the manager's real rate of return if the inflation rate during the year was 2.3%?
6. Bill Anderson purchased 1,000 shares of a company's stock for $17,100 at the beginning of 2019. At the end of the year, he sold all of his shares at $30.48 a share. He also earned a dividend of $0.52 per share during the year.
   a. What is Bill's total return on the investment?
   b. What is the dollar gain from the investment?
7. You would like to invest $20,000 for a year in a risk-free investment. A conventional certificate of deposit (CD) offers a 4.6% annual rate of return. You are also considering an "Inflation-Plus" CD which offers a real rate of return of 2.2% regardless of the inflation rate.
   a. What is the implied (expected) inflation rate?
   b. You decide to invest $10,000 in the conventional CD and $10,000 in the "Inflation-Plus" CD. What is your expected dollar value at the end of the year?
   c. Which of the two CDs is a better investment if the actual inflation rate for the year turns out to be 2.2%?
8. Consider the following adjusted closing stock prices of a company. Find the monthly returns for January and February of 2020.

Date	Adjusted Closing Price
January 1, 2020	36.82
February 1, 2020	36.20
March 1, 2020	36.07

9. Consider the following adjusted closing stock prices for two software development firms. Compute and compare the monthly returns for both firms from January 2020 to May 2020.

Date	Firm 1	Firm 2
1/1/2020	12.36	36.61
2/1/2020	12.53	36.84
3/1/2020	11.64	35.36
4/1/2020	11.47	34.64
5/1/2020	11.12	33.93
6/1/2020	11.35	34.45

19.2 INDEX NUMBERS

An **index number** is an easy-to-interpret numerical value that reflects a percentage change in price or quantity from a base value. In this chapter, we focus on price indices. The base value for a price index is set equal to 100 for the selected base period, and values in other periods are adjusted in proportion to the base. Thus, if the price index for a given year is 125, it implies that the price has increased by 25% from the base year. Similarly, a price index of 90 implies that the price has decreased by 10% from the base year. Index numbers enable policy makers and analysts to focus on the movements in variables rather than on their raw absolute values.

LO 19.3

Calculate and interpret a simple price index.

A Simple Price Index

Consider the price of a hot dog that increases from \$3.25 in 2015 to \$4.75 in 2020. We can easily determine that the price of a hot dog has increased by $\frac{4.75-3.25}{3.25} = 0.46$, or 46%. Alternatively, if we use 2015 as the base year with an index value of 100, then the corresponding index value for 2020 is 146, indicating a 46% increase in price. This is an example of a **simple price index.**

A SIMPLE PRICE INDEX

A simple price index for any item is the ratio of the price in period t, p_t, and the price in the base period, p_0, expressed as a percentage. It is calculated as $\frac{p_t}{p_0} \times 100$.

EXAMPLE 19.6

Consider the data presented in the introductory case of this chapter in Table 19.1. Use the base year of 2018 to compute and interpret the 2019 and 2020 simple price indices for:

a. Red wine

b. White wine

c. A 6-pack of beer

SOLUTION: Because 2018 is the base year, we set the corresponding index value equal to 100. The index values for other years are computed as follows.

a. For red wine, the simple price index for 2019 is

$$\frac{\text{Price in 2019}}{\text{Price in 2018}} \times 100 = \frac{12.10}{12.30} \times 100 = 98.37.$$

Similarly, for 2020, it is

$$\frac{\text{Price in 2020}}{\text{Price in 2018}} \times 100 = \frac{9.95}{12.30} \times 100 = 80.89.$$

Therefore, the average price of red wine in 2019 and 2020 was 98.37% and 80.89%, respectively, of what it was in 2018. In other words, as compared to 2018, the price of red wine dropped by 1.63% in 2019 and by 19.11% in 2020.

b. For white wine, the simple price index for 2019 is $(11.05/11.90) \times 100 = 92.86$ and $(10.60/11.90) \times 100 = 89.08$ for 2020. Therefore, relative to 2018, the average price of white wine dropped by 7.14% in 2019 and by 10.92% in 2020.

c. The simple price index for a six-pack of beer for 2019 is $(8.25/8.10) \times 100 = 101.85$ and $(7.95/8.10) \times 100 = 98.15$ for 2020. Interestingly, while the prices of both red and white wines experienced substantial declines, the price of beer stayed fairly stable. Relative to the base year of 2018, there was a 1.85% increase in the price of beer in 2019 and a 1.85% decline in 2020.

EXAMPLE 19.7

Table 19.3 shows the average price and corresponding price index for a product from 2010 to 2018, using 2010 as the base year. Interpret the price indices for 2011 and 2018.

TABLE 19.3 Price and Corresponding Price Index Base Year 2010

Year	2010	2011	2012	2013	2014	2015	2016	2017	2018
Price	1.51	1.46	1.36	1.59	1.88	2.30	2.59	2.80	3.27
Price index (Base = 2010)	100	96.69	90.07	105.30	124.50	152.32	171.52	185.43	216.56

SOLUTION: Since 2010 is treated as the base year, the index number for 2010 is 100. The index number for 2011 is calculated as $(1.46/1.51) \times 100 = 96.69$. Thus, the price in 2011 was 96.69% of what it was in 2010, or 3.31% lower. Given a price index of 216.56 in 2018, the price in 2018 was 116.56% higher relative to 2010.

In Figure 19.1, we plot the price and price indices for the product from 2010 to 2018. Note that although the units of the product's price and index number graphs are different, the basic shape of the two graphs is similar. This shows that the main purpose of index numbers is to provide an easy interpretation of the changes of the series over time.

FIGURE 19.1 Price and the corresponding index numbers for 2010–2018

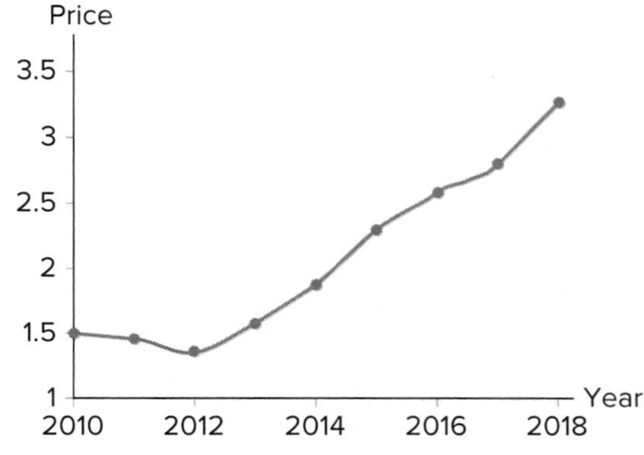

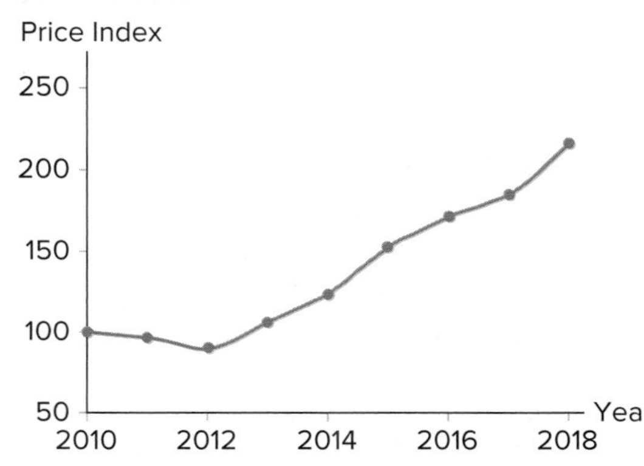

It is important to note that index numbers provide direct comparisons only with respect to the base year. Similar direct comparisons cannot be made between non–base years. For instance, based on the index numbers for 2015 and 2018 in Table 19.3, we cannot say that prices rose by 64.24% (216.56% − 152.32%) from 2015 to 2018. The actual percentage change from 2015 to 2018 is $\frac{216.56 - 152.32}{152.32} \times 100 = 42.17$, indicating that prices rose by 42.17% from 2015 to 2018.

Alternatively, we can use index numbers directly to compare prices between 2015 and 2018 by making 2015 the base year. It may be more meaningful to compare 2018 values with those in 2015 rather than the values in 2010. In fact, federal agencies routinely update the base year used in their calculations of statistical indices.

It is fairly simple to revise the base period of an index. We basically transform the index of the newly chosen base period as 100 and values in other periods are adjusted by the same proportion.

REVISING THE BASE PERIOD

A simple index can easily be updated with a revised base period as

$$\text{Updated Index} = \frac{\text{Old Index Value}}{\text{Old Index Value of New Base}} \times 100.$$

EXAMPLE 19.8

Update the index numbers in Table 19.3 with a base year revised from 2010 to 2015.

SOLUTION: With a revised base of 2015, the index number for 2015 is updated from 152.32 to 100. Other indices are adjusted according to the revision rule. For instance, the index number for 2016 is updated as (171.52/152.32) × 100 = 112.61. Table 19.4 contains index numbers that have been similarly updated.

TABLE 19.4 Price Index Using Base Years of 2010 and 2015

Year	2010	2011	2012	2013	2014	2015	2016	2017	2018
Price	1.51	1.46	1.36	1.59	1.88	2.30	2.59	2.80	3.27
Price Index (Base = 2010)	100	96.69	90.07	105.30	124.50	152.32	171.52	185.43	216.56
Price Index (Base = 2015)	65.65	63.48	59.13	69.13	81.74	100.00	112.61	121.74	142.17

With the revised base of 2015, we can directly see that the product's price in 2018 was 142.17% of what it was in 2015, or 42.17% higher.

LO 19.4

Calculate and interpret an unweighted aggregate price index.

An Unweighted Aggregate Price Index

An **aggregate price index** is used to represent relative price movements for a group of items. Examples include the closely watched consumer price index (CPI) and the producer price index (PPI). An aggregate price index can be weighted or unweighted. An **unweighted aggregate price index** is based entirely on aggregate prices with no emphasis placed on quantity. In other words, it does not incorporate the information that consumers may not be consuming equal quantities over the years of the items comprising the index. Weighted methods, on the other hand, use quantity as weights in the calculations.

AN UNWEIGHTED AGGREGATE PRICE INDEX

Let p_{it} represent the price of item i in period t, and let p_{i0} be the corresponding price in the base period ($t = 0$). The unweighted aggregate price index in period t is computed as

$$\frac{\Sigma p_{it}}{\Sigma p_{i0}} \times 100.$$

EXAMPLE 19.9

A real estate firm based in Florida collects data on the average selling price of condominiums, single-family homes, and multifamily homes that it sold over the last three years. Table 19.5 shows the results. Compute and interpret the unweighted price index for the properties, using 2018 as the base year.

TABLE 19.5 Average Price (in $1,000s) of Properties Sold in Florida

Year	Condominiums	Single Family	Multi-family
2018	290	410	490
2019	305	420	500
2020	260	430	460

SOLUTION: To find the unweighted aggregate price index, we first aggregate prices for each year by adding up the prices of condominiums, single-family homes, and multifamily homes. For 2018, the aggregate price is computed as $\Sigma p_{i0} = 290 + 410 + 490 = 1{,}190$. Similarly, the aggregate prices are $\Sigma p_{it} = 305 + 420 + 500 = 1{,}225$ for 2019 and $\Sigma p_{it} = 260 + 430 + 460 = 1{,}150$ for 2020. Using 2018 as the base year, the unweighted aggregate price indices are computed as

$$\text{Price Index for 2019} = \frac{1{,}225}{1{,}190} \times 100 = 102.94 \text{ and}$$

$$\text{Price Index for 2020} = \frac{1{,}150}{1{,}190} \times 100 = 96.64.$$

Thus, according to the unweighted aggregate price index, property values in 2019 were 102.94% of what they were in 2018, or equivalently, 2.94% higher. Similarly, relative to 2018, property values in 2020 were 3.36% lower.

Although the unweighted aggregate price index captured the overall price decline in 2020, relative to 2018, the price drop of 3.36% in Florida seemed more than what has been reported in the popular press. A possible explanation is that the unweighted index unfairly treats all property prices equally. The price decline in 2020, relative to 2018, would be smaller if we considered the fact that most properties sold in Florida consisted of single-family homes and the price decline was mostly confined to condominiums and multi-family homes.

A Weighted Aggregate Price Index

LO 19.5

Calculate and interpret the Laspeyres and the Paasche weighted price indices.

A **weighted aggregate price index** does not treat prices of different items equally. A higher weight is given to the items that are sold in higher quantities. However, there is no unique way to determine the weights, as they depend on the period in which the quantities are evaluated. One option is to evaluate the changing quantities over the years to derive the weighted average. However, in many applications, the quantity information is not readily available and we have to rely on its evaluation in a single time period. Two popular choices for weights are based on the quantities evaluated in the base period and in the current period. A **Laspeyres price index** uses the quantities evaluated in the base period to compute a weighted aggregate price index.

THE LASPEYRES PRICE INDEX

Let p_{it} and q_{it} represent the price and quantity of item i in period t, and let p_{i0} and q_{i0} be the corresponding values in the base period ($t = 0$). Using only the base period quantities q_{i0}, the Laspeyres price index for period t is computed as

$$\frac{\Sigma p_{it}q_{i0}}{\Sigma p_{i0}q_{i0}} \times 100.$$

EXAMPLE 19.10

Table 19.6 shows the number of condominiums, single-family homes, and multi-family homes sold in Florida. Use these quantities, along with the price information in Table 19.5, to compute and interpret the Laspeyres price index for real estate, using 2018 as the base year.

TABLE 19.6 Number of Properties Sold in Florida

Year	Condominiums	Single Family	Multi-family
2018	34	92	16
2019	35	96	18
2020	22	32	10

SOLUTION: The data show that the coronavirus resulted in a marked decline in the sale of all properties in 2020. Interestingly, while property values of condominiums and multi-family homes went down, there was a slight increase in the value of single-family homes in 2020. Perhaps the drop in inventory pushed up prices of single-family homes in Florida.

Recall that the Laspeyres price index evaluates the quantities in the base period, so, we will use the number of properties sold in 2018 in the calculation. Refer to Table 19.7 for the calculation of the Laspeyres price index.

TABLE 19.7 Calculation of the Laspeyres Price Index

Year	Weighted Price = $\Sigma p_{it}q_{i0}$	The Laspeyres Price Index
2018	290 × 34 + 410 × 92 + 490 × 16 = 55420	100
2019	305 × 34 + 420 × 92 + 500 × 16 = 57010	(57010/55420) × 100 = 102.87
2020	260 × 34 + 430 × 92 + 460 × 16 = 55760	(55760/55420) × 100 = 100.61

Based on the Laspeyres price index, aggregate property values in 2019 were 102.87% of what they were in 2018, or equivalently, 2.87% higher. Similarly, property values in 2020 were 0.61% higher than in 2018.

Recall that the unweighted price index showed a 3.36% decrease in property values in 2020 relative to 2018. However, based on the Laspeyres price index, property values increased slightly over this period. As noted earlier, this discrepancy is because most properties sold in Florida consisted of single-family homes, which did not experience a price decline. Unlike the unweighted price index that treats all property prices equally, the relative weight of properties is appropriately captured by the Laspeyres price index.

As mentioned earlier, the choice of weights for a weighted aggregate price index depends on the quantity evaluated in a given period. Whereas a Laspeyres price index uses the base period quantities as weights, a **Paasche price index** uses the current period quantities in deriving the weights. Since the choice of weights for the two methods are different, the Laspeyres and Paasche price indices differ for the period under evaluation.

THE PAASCHE PRICE INDEX

Let p_{it} and q_{it} represent the price and quantity of item i in period t, and let p_{i0} and q_{i0} be the corresponding values in the base period ($t = 0$). Using only the current period quantities q_{in}, where n represents the current period, the Paasche price index for period t is computed as

$$\frac{\Sigma p_{it} q_{in}}{\Sigma p_{i0} q_{in}} \times 100.$$

EXAMPLE 19.11

Consider Tables 19.5 and 19.6, representing the price and quantity data for properties sold in Florida. Use this information to compute the Paasche price index for real estate, using 2018 as the base year.

SOLUTION: Because the Paasche price index uses the quantities evaluated in the current period, we use only the numbers of properties sold in 2020 in the calculations. Refer to Table 19.8 for the calculation of the Paasche price index.

TABLE 19.8 Calculation of the Paasche Price Index

Year	Weighted Price = $\Sigma p_{it} q_{in}$	The Paasche Price Index
2018	290 × 22 + 410 × 32 + 490 × 10 = 24400	100
2019	305 × 22 + 420 × 32 + 500 × 10 = 25150	(25150/24400) × 100 = 103.07
2020	260 × 22 + 430 × 32 + 460 × 10 = 24080	(24080/24400) × 100 = 98.69

The Paasche price index is calculated as 103.07 for 2019 and 98.69 for 2020. Therefore, according to the Paasche price index, relative to 2018, property values increased by 3.07% in 2019 and decreased by 1.31% in 2020.

As noted earlier, according to the unweighted price index that treats all property prices equally, the price change in 2020, relative to 2018, was −3.36%. In contrast, the Laspeyres and the Paasche price indices appropriately capture the relative weight of properties in the base period and in the current period, respectively. The corresponding price change was 0.61% with the Laspeyres price index and −1.31% with the Paasche price index.

In general, the Laspeyres and Paasche price indices provide similar results if the periods being compared are not too far apart. The two price indices tend to differ when the length of time between the periods increases, since the relative quantities of items (weights) adjust to the changes in consumer demand over time. The Paasche price index is attractive because it incorporates current expenditure patterns. However, it requires that the weights be updated each year and the index numbers be recomputed for all of the previous years. The additional cost required to process current expenditure data, needed to revise the weights, can be substantial. Therefore, the Laspeyres price index is a more widely used weighted aggregate price index.

EXAMPLE 19.12

Let us revisit the introductory case with the data presented in Table 19.1.

a. Using 2018 as the base year, compute and interpret the Laspeyres price index for liquor.

b. Using 2018 as the base year, compute and interpret the Paasche price index for liquor.

SOLUTION: With 2018 used as the base year, its value for both indices is set equal to 100.

a. For the Laspeyres price index, the prices are weighted by the quantities evaluated in the base period of 2018. Therefore, the weighted price for each year is calculated as follows.

For 2018: $12.30 \times 1{,}560 + 11.90 \times 1{,}410 + 8.10 \times 2{,}240 = 54{,}111.$

For 2019: $12.10 \times 1{,}560 + 11.05 \times 1{,}410 + 8.25 \times 2{,}240 = 52{,}936.5$

For 2020: $9.95 \times 1{,}560 + 10.60 \times 1{,}410 + 7.95 \times 2{,}240 = 48{,}276.$

The corresponding price index for each year is calculated as follows.

For 2018: 100

For 2019: $(52{,}936.5/54{,}111) \times 100 = 97.83$

For 2020: $(48{,}276/54{,}111) \times 100 = 89.22$

Therefore, based on the Laspeyres price index, liquor prices were 97.83% in 2019 and 89.22% in 2020 of what they were in 2018. In other words, relative to 2018, overall liquor prices dropped by 2.17% in 2019 and by 10.78% in 2020.

b. For the Paasche price index, the prices are weighted by the quantities evaluated in the current period, which in our example is 2020. Therefore, the weighted price for each year is calculated as follows.

For 2018: $12.30 \times 1{,}280 + 11.90 \times 1{,}010 + 8.10 \times 2{,}190 = 45{,}502$

For 2019: $12.10 \times 1{,}280 + 11.05 \times 1{,}010 + 8.25 \times 2{,}190 = 44{,}716$

For 2020: $9.95 \times 1{,}280 + 10.60 \times 1{,}010 + 7.95 \times 2{,}190 = 40{,}852.5$

The corresponding price index for each year is calculated as follows.

For 2018: 100

For 2019: $(44{,}716/45{,}502) \times 100 = 98.27$

For 2020: $(40{,}852.5/45{,}502) \times 100 = 89.78$

Therefore, based on the Paasche price index, liquor prices were 98.27% in 2019 and 89.78% in 2020 of what they were in 2018. In other words, relative to 2018, overall liquor prices dropped by 1.73% in 2019 and by 10.22% in 2020.

SYNOPSIS OF INTRODUCTORY CASE

Koy Hipster/Shutterstock

Small businesses often have to fight an uphill battle to compete with big stores even though they are appealing to customers who value personalized attention. Jehanne-Marie, the owner of a small convenience store in Iowa City, has not been spared the effects of stiff competition from a new supermarket. The situation was further exacerbated by the COVID-19 pandemic in 2020. She has been forced to offer numerous price discounts to counter the plummeting demand for liquor. Interestingly, the cutbacks by consumers have not been uniform across red wine, white wine, and beer. While the price of red wine has dropped by 19.11% from 2018 to 2020, the corresponding drop in price has been 10.92% for white wine and only 1.85% for beer.

In order to capture the overall price movement of liquor, two weighted aggregate price indices are also computed. These indices devote a higher weight to the price of items that are sold in higher quantities. The weights are defined by the base period quantities for the Laspeyres index and the current period quantities for the Paasche index. Both indices suggest that, relative to 2018, Jehanne-Marie has experienced an overall price decline of about 2% in 2019 and a much larger price decline of about 10.50% in 2020.

Jehanne-Marie is advised to focus more on beer sales, rather than wine. A comprehensive analysis that includes other grocery items like bread, cheese, and soda would better describe the full impact of the competition from the new supermarket and the 2020 pandemic.

EXERCISES 19.2

Mechanics

10. FILE *Exercise_19.10.* The accompanying table shows a portion of the simple price index, using 2012 as the base year.

Year	2012	2013	...	2020
Price Index	100	107.2	...	114.7

a. Update the index numbers using a revised base year of 2016.
b. Determine the percentage change in price from 2012 to 2020.
c. Determine the percentage change in price from 2016 to 2020.

11. FILE *Exercise_19.11.* The accompanying table shows a portion of the price data from 2012 to 2020.

Year	2012	2013	...	2020
Price	62	60	...	70

a. Compute the simple price index using 2012 as the base year.
b. Determine the percentage change in prices from 2012 to 2016.

12. Consider the following price and quantity data for three products from 2018 to 2020.

Year		Product 1	Product 2	Product 3
2018	Price	$14.30	$13.90	$18.10
	Quantity	992	1,110	800
2019	Price	$14.90	$13.70	$18.50
	Quantity	980	1,220	790
2020	Price	$15.50	$13.80	$17.90
	Quantity	140	1,290	810

a. Compute the simple price index for each product, using 2018 as the base year.
b. Compare the relative price movements of the three products.

13. Use the price and quantity information in the previous exercise to compute the following aggregate price indices, given a base year of 2018.
a. The unweighted aggregate price index
b. The Laspeyres price index
c. The Paasche price index

Applications

14. FILE *Gasoline* The accompanying table shows a portion of the average monthly prices, for regular gasoline in 2019. ($ per gallan)

Month	Jan	Feb	...	Dec
Price	2.34	2.39	...	2.65

a. Construct a simple price index with January 2019 as the base.
b. Determine the percentage change in the average gasoline price from January to June.

15. FILE *Tech.* The accompanying table shows a portion of the monthly adjusted closing price per share of a technology firm.

Month	Jan	Feb	...	Dec
Price	16.6	15.8	...	30.3

a. Construct a simple price index with January as the base.
b. What is the percentage price change in July relative to January?
c. What is the percentage price change in December relative to January?

16. FILE *Returns.* According to dollar cost averaging, a fixed amount of money is invested periodically in a portfolio. Consequently, more units of a financial asset are purchased when prices are low and fewer units are purchased when prices are high. Robert Dudek follows dollar cost averaging by making a monthly investment of $500 toward retirement. His monthly investment is divided equally among equity and bond funds. The following table shows a portion of the monthly adjusted closing price of the funds.

Month	Equity	Bond
January	14.77	4.47
February	12.93	4.49
⋮	⋮	⋮
December	20.99	4.82

a. Compute and interpret the Laspeyres price index.
b. Compute and interpret the Paasche price index.

17. A private college in Wisconsin offers an MBA program for executives. The following table shows the tuition for the program from 2014 to 2019.

Year	2014	2015	2016	2017	2018	2019
Tuition (in $)	36,850	39,844	42,634	44,556	46,784	48,650

a. Use 2014 as the base year to form a simple price index for tuition.
b. Use 2017 as the base year to form a simple price index for tuition.
c. Compare the percentage tuition increase from 2014 through 2017 and 2017 through 2019.

18. JJ Diner is a small mom and pop restaurant in a small town. They offer three choices for breakfast: omelets, pancakes, or cereal. The average prices (in $) for these options for 2017, 2018, and 2019 are shown in the accompanying table.

Year	Omelet	Pancakes	Cereal
2017	4.75	3.50	3.50
2018	5.25	4.25	4.00
2019	5.00	4.50	4.25

a. Compute and interpret the simple price index for each breakfast, using 2017 as the base year.
b. Compute and interpret the unweighted aggregate price index for breakfast, using 2017 as the base year.

19. The following table shows the number (in 1,000s) of breakfasts sold at JJ Diner. Use this information, along with the price data provided in the previous exercise, to solve the following problems. Assume that the base year is 2017.

Year	Omelet	Pancakes	Cereal
2017	9.26	7.98	2.44
2018	11.82	9.20	2.62
2019	10.48	8.50	2.12

a. Compute and interpret the Laspeyres price index.
b. Compute and interpret the Paasche price index.

20. A software company offers several pricing options for its software as a service (SaaS) product. SaaS is a software licensing and delivery model in which software is licensed on a subscription basis and is centrally hosted. The pricing options include limited, medium, and unlimited access for users. The accompanying table shows the pricing options for 2018, 2019, and 2020.

Year	Limited	Medium	Unlimited
2018	290	480	1200
2019	340	520	1260
2020	380	540	1240

a. Construct and interpret the simple price index for each usage type, using 2018 as the base year.
b. Construct and interpret the unweighted aggregate price for usage, using 2018 as the base year.

21. The accompanying table shows the number of SaaS subscriptions for each type of usage for 2018, 2019, and 2020 described in the previous exercise. Use this information, along with the price data provided in the previous exercise, to solve the following problems. Assume that the base year is 2018.

Year	Limited	Medium	Unlimited
2018	120	80	80
2019	110	76	130
2020	100	60	150

a. Compute and interpret the Laspeyres price index.
b. Compute and interpret the Paasche price index.

19.3 USING PRICE INDICES TO DEFLATE A TIME SERIES

LO 19.6

Use price indices to deflate an economic time series and derive the inflation rate.

Most business and economic time series are generally reported in nominal terms, implying that they are measured in dollar amounts. The dollar differences, however, ignore price appreciation that is due to inflation which erodes the value of money. For instance, we cannot directly compare the starting salary of a recent college graduate with that of a college graduate five years ago. Due to price increases, the purchasing power of recent graduates may be lower even if they make more money than their predecessors. Similarly, a hardware store may have doubled its revenue over 20 years, but the true increase in value may be smaller once it has been adjusted for inflation.

An important function of price indices, introduced in the previous section, is to serve as deflators. A **deflated time series** is obtained by adjusting the given time series for price changes. We use the price index to remove the effect of inflation so that we can evaluate business and economic time series in a more meaningful way.

NOMINAL VERSUS REAL VALUES

A time series that has been deflated is said to be represented in real terms. The unadjusted time series is said to be represented in nominal terms. We use a price index to convert the nominal value of a time series into its real value as

$$\text{Real Value} = \frac{\text{Nominal Value}}{\text{Price Index}} \times 100.$$

Consider the following example. Lisa Redford has worked in a small marketing firm in Florida for the last three years. During this time, her salary has decreased from $80,000 in 2018 to $72,000 in 2020, mostly because of the pandemic. Along with her salary drop of 10%, there has been a slight increase in property values in Florida during the same time period. In Example 19.10, we used the base year of 2018 to derive the Laspeyres price index of 100.61 in 2020, implying that property values are 0.61% higher in 2020 than in 2018. It is more meaningful to compare Lisa's salary of $80,000 in 2018 (the base year) with the price-adjusted (real) salary of ($72,000/100.61) × 100 = $71,563 in 2020. Using the Laspeyres price index of property values for adjustment, the effect of the salary cut (nominal) for Lisa is slightly magnified.

We note that it is not reasonable to adjust Lisa's salary solely on the basis of the price index of property values in Florida. Because her expenditure is not limited to mortgage payments, a more comprehensive price index is needed to make the price adjustment to the salary. In fact, when we say that a series has been deflated, we imply that the series has been adjusted on the basis of the price of a comprehensive basket of goods and services.

The two price indices most commonly used to deflate economic time series are the **Consumer Price Index, CPI,** and the **Producer Price Index, PPI.** While both the CPI and PPI measure the percentage price change over time for a fixed basket of goods and services, they differ in the composition of the basket and in the types of prices used in the analysis.

The CPI is perhaps the best-known weighted aggregate price index. The U.S. Bureau of Labor Statistics (BLS) computes a monthly CPI based on the prices paid by urban consumers for a representative basket of goods and services. Currently, the base period for the CPI is 1982–1984; that is, all price changes are measured from a base that represents the average index level of the period encompassing 1982, 1983, and 1984. The prices of several hundred consumption items are included in the index. In addition, randomly selected consumers help determine the expenditure for the representative basket of goods and services. The corresponding quantities of items in the base year are then used for computing the weights for the index.

The PPI is a weighted aggregate price index of prices measured at the wholesale, or producer, level. Prior to 1978, the PPI was called the Wholesale Price Index, WPI. The BLS computes a monthly PPI based on the selling prices received by domestic producers for their entire marketed output. Currently, the base period for the PPI is 1982. The target set includes purchases of goods and services by consumers—directly from the producer or indirectly from a retailer—and by other producers as inputs to their production, or as capital investment.

Note that the CPI is based on out-of-pocket expenditures of an urban consumer and the PPI is based on the portion that is actually received by the producer. Therefore, although sales and excise taxes are included in the CPI, they are not included in the PPI because they do not represent revenue to the producer. The differences between the PPI and CPI are consistent with the way these indices are used for deflation. It is common to use the CPI to adjust wages for changes in the cost of living. The PPI, on the other hand, is useful to deflate revenue in order to obtain real growth in output.

Table 19.9 shows a portion of CPI and PPI values from 1990 to 2019. These values capture price appreciation over the years. For example, CPI shows that relative to the base period of 1982–1984, prices in 1990 were 30.70% higher. The corresponding price appreciation according to PPI, relative to the base period of 1982, was 19.20%.

TABLE 19.9 CPI and PPI from 1990–2019

Year	CPI	PPI
1990	130.70	114.50
1991	136.20	115.90
⋮	⋮	⋮
2019	255.66	196.80

It is important to note that the direction and magnitude of a price change often differs between CPI and PPI. In Figure 19.2, we use the ***CPI_PPI*** data to plot the annual CPI and PPI. We see that the prices that consumers paid far exceeded those received by producers, with the difference peaking in 2019.

FILE
CPI_PPI

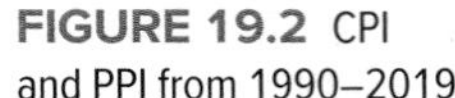

FIGURE 19.2 CPI and PPI from 1990–2019

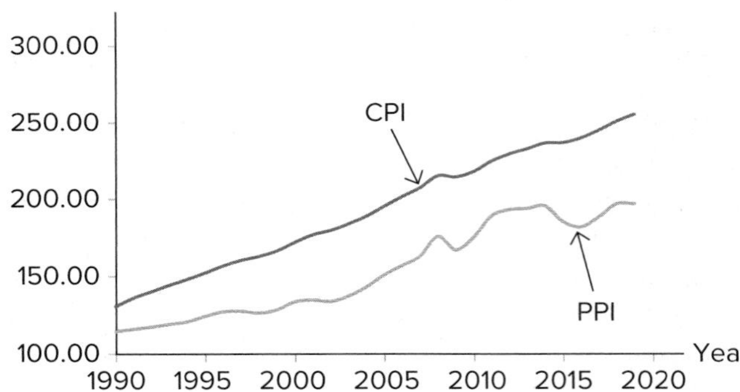

EXAMPLE 19.13

Tom Denio has been a project manager in a small construction firm in Atlanta since 2000. He started with a salary of \$52,000, which grew to \$90,000 in 2019. The revenue of the construction firm also grew over the years, increasing from \$13 million in 2000 to \$20 million in 2019. According to the Bureau of Labor Statistics, the values of the consumer price index with a base period of 1982–1984 for 2000 and 2019 are 172.20 and 255.66, respectively. The corresponding values of the producer price index with a base period of 1982 are 133.50 and 196.80, respectively.

a. Compute and analyze the nominal and real increase in Tom's salary.

b. Compute and analyze the nominal and real revenue growth of the construction firm.

SOLUTION:

a. Tom's nominal salary grew by $\frac{90,000 - 52,000}{52,000} = 0.7308$, or by 73.08%, from 2000 to 2019. This nominal salary makes no cost of living adjustment. We use the CPI to compute his real salary as $(52,000/172.20) \times 100 = \$30,197$ in 2000 and $(90,000/255.66) \times 100 = \$35,203$ in 2019. These are Tom's real salaries based on 1982–1984 prices. Thus, while Tom's salary increased by 73.08% in dollar amounts, his purchasing power increased by only $\frac{35,203 - 30,197}{30,197} = 0.1658$, or by 16.58%.

b. The nominal revenue of the construction firm grew by $\frac{20 - 13}{13} = 0.5385$, or by 53.85% from 2000 to 2019. We use the producer price index to compute the revenue growth in real terms. The real revenue is $(13/133.50) \times 100 = \$9.7378$ million in 2000 and $(20/196.80) \times 100 = \$10.1626$ million in 2019. Therefore, the real growth in revenue for the construction firm has been $\frac{10.1626 - 9.7378}{9.7378} =$ 0.0436, or 4.36%.

Inflation Rate

The **inflation rate** is the percentage rate of change of a price index over time. We generally use the CPI to compute the inflation rate in the United States. Also, although it is common to quote the inflation rate in annual terms, the CPI can be used to calculate the inflation rate for any time period.

CALCULATING THE INFLATION RATE

The reported inflation rate i_t for a given period is generally based on the consumer price index, CPI. It is computed as $i_t = \frac{CPI_t - CPI_{t-1}}{CPI_{t-1}}$.

EXAMPLE 19.14

The consumer price indices for the years 2017, 2018, and 2019 are reported as 245.12, 251.11, and 255.66, respectively. Use this information to compute the annual inflation rate for 2018 and 2019.

SOLUTION: The inflation rates for 2018 and 2019 are computed as

$$i_{2018} = \frac{CPI_{2018} - CPI_{2017}}{CPI_{2017}} = \frac{251.11 - 245.12}{245.12} = 0.0244, \text{ or } 2.44\%.$$

$$i_{2019} = \frac{CPI_{2019} - CPI_{2018}}{CPI_{2018}} = \frac{255.66 - 251.11}{251.11} = 0.0181, \text{ or } 1.81\%.$$

Therefore, the inflation rate decreased from 2.44% in 2018 to 1.81% in 2019.

EXERCISES 19.3

Mechanics

22. The nominal values for four years are given by 32, 37, 39, and 42. Convert these values to real terms if the price index values for the corresponding years are given by 100, 102, 103, and 108.
23. An item increases in value from 240 to 280 in one year. What is the percentage change in the value of this item? Compute the percentage change in real terms if overall prices have increased by 5% for the same period.
24. Let revenues increase by 10% from $100,000 to $110,000. Calculate the percentage change in real terms if the relevant price index increases by 4% from 100 to 104.
25. The following table represents the nominal values of an item and the corresponding price index for two years.

Year	Nominal Value	Price Index
1	38	112
2	40	120

  a. Compute the inflation rate for year 2.
  b. Compute the annual percentage change of the item in real terms.

26. The following table represents the nominal values of an item and the corresponding price index for three years.

Year	Nominal Value	Price Index
1	38	100
2	40	103
3	42	112

  a. Compare the percentage change in the nominal values with the corresponding percentage change in real values from year 1 to year 2.
  b. Compare the percentage change in the nominal values with the corresponding real values from year 2 to year 3.
  c. Use the price data to compute the inflation rate for year 2 to year 3.

Applications

27. Amy Lin's condominium that she bought in 2016 for $240,000 has gone up in value to $250,000 in 2019.
  a. What is the percentage price change of Amy's condominium from 2016 to 2019?
  b. What is the corresponding percentage price change in real terms if the CPI in 2016 and 2019 are 240.01 and 255.66, respectively?
28. The revenue of a software development firm grew from $10 million in 2000 to $22 million in 2019.
  a. What is the percentage price change of revenue from 2000 to 2019?
  b. What is the corresponding percentage price change in real terms if the PPI in 2000 and 2019 are 133.5 and 196.8, respectively?
29. FILE ***Sales.*** Economists often look at retail sales data to gauge the state of the economy. The accompanying table shows a portion of seasonally adjusted monthly nominal retail sales for 2019, measured in $ millions. Also included in the table is the corresponding producer price index (PPI).

Month	Sales	PPI
Jan	443420	194.3
Feb	442467	195.4
⋮	⋮	⋮
Dec	460512	196.4

a. How many times were nominal sales below that of the previous month?
b. Use the PPI to compute sales in real terms. How many times were real sales below that of the previous month?
c. Compute the total percentage increase in nominal as well as real retail sales in 2019 (January to December).

30. FILE ***Income.*** Personal income is the income that people receive for labor, land, and capital along with the net current transfer payments that they receive from business and government. The accompanying table shows a portion of personal income (Income, measured in $ billions), along with the corresponding consumer price index (CPI) for 2010 – 2019 in the U.S.

Year	Income	CPI
2010	10185.836	218.06
2011	10641.109	224.94
⋮	⋮	⋮
2019	14562.662	255.66

a. Use the CPI to compute real personal income. Which year(s) did real personal income decline from the previous year?
b. Compute the total percentage increase in personal income from 2010 to 2019.
c. Compute the total percentage increase in real personal income from 2010 to 2019.

31. FILE ***Houses.*** The accompanying table shows a portion of the median sales price of new houses sold in the United States, along with the corresponding consumer price index (CPI).

Year	Price	CPI
2010	221800	218.06
2011	227200	224.94
⋮	⋮	⋮
2019	321500	255.66

a. Use the CPI to compute the real sales price of new houses. Which year(s) did the real sales price decline from the previous year?
b. Compute the percentage increase in the sales price of new houses from 2010 to 2019.
c. Compute the percentage increase in the real sales price of new houses from 2010 to 2019.

32. The accompanying table shows the consumer price index for China, India, and the U.S. for 2018 and 2019, each using the base period of 2015. Compute the inflation rate for each country in 2019.

Year	China	India	U.S.
2018	105.775	112.783	105.945
2019	108.841	121.422	107.865

19.4 WRITING WITH DATA

Bettmann/Getty Images

Case Study

Valerie Barnes is a graduate student in the department of political science at Michigan State University. She has been asked to write a brief report on the changes in the economic climate during the presidency of Ronald Reagan from 1981–1989. Valerie collects information on various economic indicators at the beginning and the end of President Reagan's term, as shown in Table 19.10. She would like to use the information to evaluate nominal and real price changes during Reagan's presidency.

TABLE 19.10 Select Economic Indicators during the Reagan Presidency

Economic Indicators	1981	1989
Federal Debt ($ billions)	$994.8	$2,868.0
Median Household Income	$19,074	$28,906
Cost of a New Home	$83,000	$148,800
Dow Jones Industrial Average High	1,024	2,791
Cost of a Gallon of Regular Gasoline	$1.38	$1.12
Consumer Price Index (1982–1984 = 100)	90.9	124

Sample Report—Economic Indicators during Reagan's Presidency

Ronald Wilson Reagan became the 40th President of the United States in 1981 after serving eight years as governor of California. He took office at a time when the United States was experiencing economic stagnation and inflation. As president, Reagan advocated reduced business regulation and extensive tax cuts to boost economic growth. Arguably, the Reagan era signifies a period of significant growth as the economy recovered from the recession.

Crucial economic indicators were analyzed during Reagan's presidency. The consumer price index (CPI) values of 90.9 in 1981 and 124 in 1989 indicate that prices were 9.1% lower in 1981 and 24% higher in 1989 than during the base years of 1982–1984. The percentage price increase during Reagan's term is calculated as 36.41% (=(124−90.9)/90.9), resulting in an annualized inflation rate of $(1 + 0.3641)^{1/8} - 1 = 3.96\%$. The CPI is also used to deflate crucial economic indicators. For instance, while the median household income increased from $19,074 to $28,906, or by 51.55%, the corresponding deflated incomes increased from $20,984 to $23,311, or by 11.09%. Other similarly deflated economic indicators are presented in Table 19.11.

TABLE 19.11 Deflated Economic Indicators

Economic Indicators	1981	1989
Federal Debt ($ billions)	$1,094.4	$2,312.9
Median Household Income	$20,984	$23,311
Cost of a New Home	$91,309	$120,000
Dow Jones Industrial Average High	1,127	2,251
Cost of a Gallon of Regular Gasoline	$1.52	$0.90

The significant increase in the federal debt during the Reagan era is noteworthy. When Reagan took office, he used deficit spending through tax cuts to stimulate the economy. However, the debt continued to grow throughout the boom years. The resulting deflated federal debt rose sharply from $1,094.4 billion in 1981 to $2,312.9 billion in 1989, or by 111%. The deflated cost of a new home grew from $91,309 to $120,000, or by 31.42%. Therefore, despite the 11.09% growth in real income, a higher percentage increase in home values made owning a new home more difficult. Interestingly, the deflated Dow Jones Industrial Average High grew by a whopping 99.73% from 1,127 in 1981 to 2,251 in 1989. Finally, there was a steep decline of 40.79% in the deflated price of gasoline, from $1.52 per gallon to $0.90 per gallon. Perhaps the price decline was the consequence of the falling demand as consumers reacted to the energy crisis of the 1970s.

President Reagan's policies reflected his personal belief in individual freedom. According to Reagan supporters, his policies resulted in the largest peacetime economic boom in American history. His critics, on the other hand, argue that the Reagan era is associated with a widening of inequality, where the rich got richer with little economic gains for most Americans.

Suggested Case Studies

Report 19.1 Amazon, Google, and Facebook are some of the most well-known internet companies in the world. Go to https://finance.yahoo.com/ to extract the 2020 monthly adjusted stock price data for these companies. In a report, compute monthly returns for the companies for February through December and use them to compare their stock performance.

Report 19.2 FILE ***Beef.*** Jeff Watson is the manager of a popular hamburger restaurant. He is responsible for managing the operations as well as food and labor costs. He constantly monitors market conditions and, in his annual reports, analyzes the changing retail cost of the ingredients used in cooking. In his current report, he decides to analyze meat prices. He collects data on monthly average retail prices of three varieties of ground beef. This information is important, as the restaurant purchases about 1,400 pounds of ground beef, 800 pounds of ground chuck, and 500 pounds of lean ground beef each month. In a report, compute and interpret simple indices for each variety of beef as well as the weighted aggregate price index, using January as the base period.

Report 19.3 FILE ***CPI_PPI.*** Go to https://fred.stlouisfed.org/ to access nominal annual data for at least two economic series from 2010 to 2019. In a report, use the accompanying ***CPI_PPI*** data to compute and interpret the percentage changes in the series, in nominal and real terms, over the 10-year period.

CONCEPTUAL REVIEW

LO 19.1 Define and compute investment returns.

The investment return R_t is calculated as $R_t = \frac{P_t - P_{t-1} + I_t}{P_{t-1}}$, where $\frac{P_t - P_{t-1}}{P_{t-1}}$ and $\frac{I_t}{P_{t-1}}$ are the capital gains yield and the income yield, respectively.

The adjusted closing price makes appropriate adjustments for dividend distributions, stock splits, and reverse stock splits. Let P_t^* and P_{t-1}^* represent the adjusted closing price of a stock at times t (current) and $t - 1$ (prior), respectively. Using adjusted closing prices, the investment return R_t at the end of time t is calculated as $R_t = \frac{P_t^* - P_{t-1}}{P_{t-1}^*}$.

LO 19.2 Convert nominal returns into real returns and vice versa.

Unlike the nominal return, the real return is the return on an investment, adjusted for inflation. The Fisher equation, $1 + r = \frac{1+R}{1+i}$, represents the relationship between the nominal return R, the real return r, and the expected inflation rate i.

LO 19.3 Calculate and interpret a simple price index.

An index number reflects a percentage change in price or quantity from a base value. A simple price index is a ratio of the price in period t, p_t, and the price in the base period, p_0, expressed as a percentage. It is calculated as $\frac{p_t}{p_0} \times 100$.

It is common to update the base period over time. We update a simple index, with a revised base period, as Updated Index $= \frac{\text{Old Index Value}}{\text{Old Index Value of New Base}} \times 100$.

LO 19.4 Calculate and interpret an unweighted aggregate price index.

Let p_{it} represent the price of item i in period t, and let p_{i0} be the corresponding price in the base period ($t = 0$). An unweighted aggregate price index in period t is calculated as $\frac{\Sigma p_{it}}{\Sigma p_{i0}} \times 100$.

LO 19.5 Calculate and interpret the Laspeyres and the Paasche price indices.

Let p_{it} and q_{it} represent the price and quantity of item i in period t, and let p_{i0} and q_{i0} be the corresponding values in the base period ($t = 0$).

Using only the base period quantities q_{i0}, the Laspeyres price index for period t is calculated as $\frac{\Sigma p_{it} q_{i0}}{\Sigma p_{i0} q_{i0}} \times 100$.

Using only the current period quantities q_{in}, where n represents the current period, the Paasche price index for period t is calculated as $\frac{\Sigma p_{it} q_{in}}{\Sigma p_{i0} q_{in}} \times 100$.

LO 19.6 **Use price indices to deflate an economic time series and derive the inflation rate.**

A **deflated time series** is obtained by adjusting it for changes in prices, or inflation. A time series that has been deflated is said to be represented in real terms. The unadjusted time series is said to be represented in nominal terms.

We use a price index to convert the nominal value of a time series into its real value as Real Value $= \frac{\text{Nominal Value}}{\text{Price Index}} \times 100$.

Two price indices commonly used to deflate economic time series are the Consumer Price Index (CPI) and the Producer Price Index (PPI). It is common to use the CPI to adjust wages for changes in the cost of living. On the other hand, the PPI is useful to deflate revenue in order to obtain real growth in output.

The reported inflation rate i_t for a given period is generally based on the CPI and is computed as $i_t = \frac{CPI_t - CPI_{t-1}}{CPI_{t-1}}$.

ADDITIONAL EXERCISES

33. Kim Baek invested $20,000 for a year in corporate bonds. Each bond sold for $1,000 and earned a coupon payment of $80 during the year. The price of the bond at the end of the year dropped to $980.
   a. Calculate Kim's investment return.
   b. Calculate Kim's total dollar gain or loss on her investment.

34. The following table shows the monthly adjusted closing price per share of a manufacturing firm from October 2019 to March 2020.

Date	Adjusted Closing Price	Date	Adjusted Closing Price
October 2019	78.89	January 2020	77.00
November 2019	78.54	February 2020	74.83
December 2019	84.16	March 2020	79.56

   a. Form a simple price index with October 2019 as the base period.
   b. Update the simple price index, using January 2020 as the base period.
   c. What is the percentage price change from October 2019 to December 2019?
   d. What is the percentage price change from January 2020 to March 2020?

35. **FILE** ***Price***. The accompanying table shows a portion of price data from 2012 to 2020.

Year	2012	2013	⋯	2020
Price	3.20	3.46	⋯	4.70

   a. Compute the simple price index using 2012 as the base year.
   b. Update the index numbers with a base year revised from 2012 to 2015.

36. Consider the following price data from 2018 to 2020.

Year	Product 1	Product 2	Product 3
2018	38	94	45
2019	40	92	48
2020	42	98	56

   a. Compute and interpret the simple price index for each product, using 2018 as the base year.
   b. Compute and interpret the unweighted aggregate price index, using 2018 as the base year.

37. Let the quantities corresponding to the prices in the previous exercise be given by the following table.

Year	Product 1	Product 2	Product 3
2018	90	32	48
2019	82	34	46
2020	76	30	36

   a. Compute the Laspeyres price index, using 2018 as the base year.
   b. Compute the Paasche price index, using 2018 as the base year.

38. Consider the following table, representing the net revenue and net income of a startup over two years. Both variables are measured in millions of dollars.

Year	Net Revenue	Net Income
1	146.6	21.2
2	159.2	13.6

a. Compute and interpret the simple price index for net revenue, using Year 1 as the base year.
b. Compute and interpret the simple price index for net income, using Year 1 as the base year.

39. Lindsay Kelly bought 100 shares of a finance firm, 300 shares of a manufacturing firm, and 500 shares of a technology firm in Year 1. The adjusted closing prices of these stocks over the next three years are shown in the accompanying table.

Year	Finance	Manufacturing	Technology
1	195.62	24.11	13.36
2	432.66	26.14	16.54
3	505.00	28.83	19.83

a. Compute and interpret the unweighted aggregate price index for Lindsay's portfolio, using Year 1 as the base year.
b. Compute and interpret the corresponding weighted price index using the Laspeyres approach.

40. In January 2020, you bought 100 shares of Tesla stock for $65,057. In May 2020, the value of your investment increased to $83,500.
a. Find the nominal percentage price increase of your investment.
b. Find the percentage price increase in real terms if the consumer price index (CPI) in January and May of 2020 was 257.97 and 256.39, respectively.

41. The consumer price index (CPI), with a base of 1982-84, increased from 218.06 in 2010 to 255.66 in 2019. The corresponding increase in the producer price index (PPI) was from 175.40 in 2010 to 196.80 in 2019.
a. Use the appropriate price index to compute John's percentage change in real income if his (nominal) income increased from $52,000 in 2010 to $68,000 in 2019.
b. Use the appropriate index to compute the percentage change in real revenue of John's company if the nominal increase was from $10.4 million in 2010 to $12 million in 2019.

20 Nonparametric Tests

LEARNING OBJECTIVES

After reading this chapter you should be able to:

LO **20.1** **Make inferences about a population median.**

LO **20.2** **Make inferences about the population median difference based on matched-pairs sampling.**

LO **20.3** **Make inferences about the difference between two population medians based on independent sampling.**

LO **20.4** **Make inferences about the difference between three or more population medians.**

LO **20.5** **Conduct a hypothesis test for the population Spearman rank correlation coefficient.**

LO **20.6** **Make inferences about the difference between two populations of ordinal data based on matched-pairs sampling.**

LO **20.7** **Determine whether the elements of a sequence appear in a random order.**

The hypothesis tests presented in earlier chapters make certain assumptions about the underlying population. We refer to these tests as parametric tests. A t- or an F-test, for example, requires that the observations come from a normal distribution. These tests are quite "robust," in the sense that they are still useful when the assumptions are not exactly fulfilled, especially when the sample size is large.

In situations when the underlying population is markedly nonnormal and the sample size is not large, we apply distribution-free alternative techniques called nonparametric tests. Nonparametric tests are also useful for examining variables that are measured on a weaker scale, such as the ordinal scale. In this chapter, we explore a variety of nonparametric tests.

Getty Images

INTRODUCTORY CASE

Analyzing Mutual Fund Returns

Dorothy Brennan is a financial advisor at a large investment firm. One of her clients has narrowed his investment options to two mutual funds: a Growth Index mutual fund and a Value Index mutual fund. He has some final questions for Dorothy with respect to each fund's historical returns. Dorothy explains that her analysis will use techniques that do not rely on stringent assumptions concerning the distribution of the underlying population. This is because the distribution of returns often diverges from the normal distribution, and in this particular case, the sample size is small. Table 20.1 shows a portion of the annual return data for each fund and some relevant descriptive statistics over the past ten years.

TABLE 20.1 Annual Returns and Descriptive Statistics (in percent) for Growth and Value

FILE *Mutual_Funds*

Year	Growth	Value
1	12.56	0.09
2	−38.32	−35.97
⋮	⋮	⋮
10	5.99	16.75
	$\bar{x} = 10.088$ median = 13.015 $s = 20.448$	$\bar{x} = 7.560$ median = 13.655 $s = 18.459$

Dorothy will use the sample information to

1. Determine whether the median return for each fund is greater than 5%.
2. Determine whether the median difference between the two funds' returns differs from zero.
3. Determine whether the funds' returns are correlated.

A synopsis of this case is provided at the end of Section 20.4.

20.1 TESTING A POPULATION MEDIAN

The parametric tests presented in earlier chapters make certain assumptions about the underlying population. These conventional tests can be misleading if the underlying assumptions are not met. Nonparametric tests, also referred to as distribution-free tests, use fewer and weaker assumptions than those associated with parametric tests and are especially useful when the sample size is small. For instance, these tests do not assume that the sample observations originate from a normal distribution or that the sample size is sufficiently large for the central limit theorem to apply.

Nonparametric tests have disadvantages, too. If the parametric assumptions are valid yet we choose to use a nonparametric test, the nonparametric test is less powerful (more prone to Type II error) than its parametric counterpart. The reason for less power is that a nonparametric test uses the data less efficiently. As we will see shortly, nonparametric tests often focus on the rank of the observations rather than the magnitude of the observations, thus possibly ignoring useful information.

Table 20.2 summarizes some of the parametric tests that we examined in earlier chapters. The first column shows the parametric test of interest, the second column states the underlying assumptions of the test, and the third column lists where the test was covered in the text. Each one of these parametric tests has a nonparametric counterpart. At the end of Section 20.4, we will present a table that lists the corresponding nonparametric test for each parametric test.

TABLE 20.2 Summary of Select Parametric Tests

Parametric Test	Population Characteristics and Other Description	Reference Section
t-test concerning the population mean	Sampling from a normal population or large sample; σ unknown	9.3
t-test to determine whether the population mean difference differs based on matched-pairs sampling	Sampling from a normal population or large sample	10.2
t-test to determine whether two population means differ based on independent sampling	Sampling from normal populations or large samples; σ_1 and σ_2 unknown	10.1
F-test to determine whether three or more population means differ	Sampling from normal populations or large samples; $\sigma_1, \sigma_2, \sigma_3, \ldots$ unknown but assumed equal	13.1
t-test to determine whether two variables are correlated	Sampling from a normal population or large sample	14.1

The Wilcoxon Signed-Rank Test for a Population Median

LO 20.1

Make inferences about a population median.

In Chapter 9, we used a t-test to determine whether the population mean μ differs from some assumed value when the population standard deviation σ was unknown. However, as shown in Table 20.2, a t-test requires that we sample from a normal distribution or use a large sample size. In a small sample, if we cannot assume that the variable is normally distributed and/or we want to test whether the population *median* differs from some hypothesized value, we can apply the **Wilcoxon signed-rank test.** The Wilcoxon signed-rank test makes no assumptions concerning the distribution of the population except that it is continuous and symmetric.

Let's revisit the introductory case. In order to analyze a mutual fund's return, Dorothy chooses nonparametric methods because the distribution of returns often has "fatter tails" as compared to the normal distribution; that is, the likelihood of extreme returns (area under the tail) is higher for a fatter-tailed distribution than for a normal distribution. Figure 20.1 shows a normal distribution versus a distribution with fatter tails; note that both distributions are continuous and symmetric. If Dorothy were to rely on tests that incorrectly assume that returns are normally distributed, then there is a chance that she may make erroneous conclusions. She chooses to use the Wilcoxon signed-rank test for the population median.

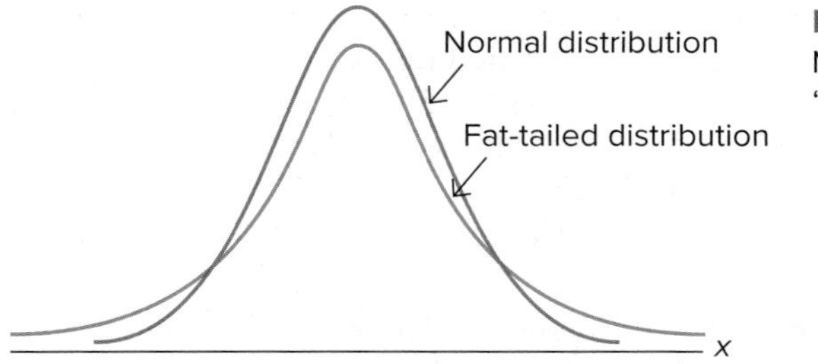

FIGURE 20.1 Normal distribution versus "fat-tailed" distribution

Following the methodology outlined in earlier chapters, when conducting a hypothesis test for the population median m, we want to test whether m differs from, is greater than, or is less than m_0, where m_0 is the value of the population median postulated in the null hypothesis. The null and alternative hypotheses will assume one of the following forms:

Two-Tailed Test	Right-Tailed Test	Left-Tailed Test
H_0: $m = m_0$	H_0: $m \leq m_0$	H_0: $m \geq m_0$
H_A: $m \neq m_0$	H_A: $m > m_0$	H_A: $m < m_0$

Given the ***Mutual_Funds*** data file from the introductory case, we would like to determine whether the median return for each fund is greater than 5%. We start with Growth and formulate the competing hypotheses for a one-tailed test as

$$H_0: m \leq 5$$
$$H_A: m > 5$$

To arrive at the sample value for the Wilcoxon signed-rank test statistic T, several calculations are necessary. It is important to point out this test statistic T is not related to the t_{df} distribution discussed in earlier chapters.

A. The first column of Table 20.3 shows the observations for Growth. We first calculate the difference d_i between each observation x_i and the hypothesized median, $m_0 = 5$; that is, we find $d_i = x_i - 5$. The second column of Table 20.3 shows the results.

TABLE 20.3 Calculations for the Wilcoxon Signed-Rank Test Statistic

Return, x (1)	$d = x - m_0$ (2)	$\|d\|$ (3)	Rank (4)	Ranks of Negative Differences (5)	Ranks of Positive Differences (6)
12.56	12.56 − 5 = 7.56	7.56	4		4
−38.32	−43.32	43.32	10	10	
36.29	31.29	31.29	9		9
16.96	11.96	11.96	7		7
1.71	−3.29	3.29	3	3	
16.89	11.89	11.89	6		6
32.16	27.16	27.16	8		8
13.47	8.47	8.47	5		5
3.17	−1.83	1.83	2	2	
5.99	0.99	0.99	1		1
				$T^- = 15$	$T^+ = 40$

B. We then take the absolute value of each difference, $|d_i|$; see the third column of Table 20.3. Any differences of zero are discarded from the sample. In this example, there are no zero differences. We calculate $|d_i|$ because if the median is equal to 5 (the null hypothesis is true), then positive or negative differences of a given magnitude are equally likely.

C. Next we rank the absolute value of each difference, assigning 1 to the smallest $|d|$ and n to the largest $|d|$. Note that n would be smaller than the original sample size if there were some zero-difference observations, which would have been discarded. Here, n equals the original sample size of 10. Any ties in the ranks of differences are assigned the average of the tied ranks. For instance, if two observations have the rank of 5 (occupying the 5th and 6th positions), each is assigned the rank of $(5 + 6)/2 = 5.5$. Or, if three observations have a ranking of 1, each is assigned a rank of $(1 + 2 + 3)/3 = 2$. For the Growth observations, there are no ties. The rankings for the differences are shown in the fourth column of Table 20.3.

D. We then sum the ranks of the negative differences (denoted T^-) and sum the ranks of the positive differences (denoted T^+). In this example we find three negative differences, whose rank sum is $T^- = 15$, and seven positive differences, whose rank sum is $T^+ = 40$. These calculations are shown in the fifth and sixth columns of Table 20.3.

The sum of T^- and T^+ should equal $n(n + 1)/2$, which is the formula for the sum of consecutive integers from 1 to n. In our example, $T^- + T^+ = 15 + 40 = 55$. Also, $n(n + 1)/2 = 10(10 + 1)/2 = 55$, which is equivalent to the sum of the integers from 1 to 10. If the null hypothesis were true, then both T^- and T^+ would equal about half of the total sum of ranks, or about $55/2 = 27.5$. For testing, we could analyze either T^- or T^+. In what follows, we will base the test on T^+. Although we do not use the value of T^- for the test, its calculation can help us avoid errors.

THE TEST STATISTIC T FOR THE WILCOXON SIGNED-RANK TEST

The test statistic T for the Wilcoxon signed-rank test is defined as $T = T^+$, where T^+ denotes the sum of the ranks of the positive differences from the hypothesized median m_0.

There are two scenarios when conducting the Wilcoxon signed-rank test:

1. If $n \leq 10$, then we use special tables to find the p-value. Alternatively, we rely on statistical packages, including R, to compute the value of the test statistic T and the resulting p-value.
2. If $n \geq 10$, the sampling distribution of T can be approximated by the normal distribution with mean $\mu_T = \frac{n(n+1)}{4}$ and standard deviation $\sigma_T = \sqrt{\frac{n(n+1)(2n+1)}{24}}$, and hence the value of the resulting test statistic is computed as $z = \frac{T - \mu_T}{\sigma_T}$.

For ease of exposition, we do not make a distinction between the random variable and the particular outcomes of the random variable. For example, we use the test statistic T to represent a random variable as well as its sample value. We adopt this same practice for the test statistics W, H, r_S, and R that we introduce in later sections.

EXAMPLE 20.1

Use the ***Mutual_Funds*** data file from the introductory case to determine whether the median return for Growth is greater than 5% with $\alpha = 0.05$.

FILE *Mutual_Funds*

SOLUTION: As shown earlier, the competing hypotheses for the test are

$$H_0: m \leq 5$$
$$H_A: m > 5$$

In this example, since the sample size equals exactly ten, we can implement the Wilcoxon test with or without the normal distribution approximation. Here, we implement the test without the normal approximation using R. (R instructions will be provided at the end of this section.) Table 20.4 reports a portion of the R output for a right-tailed test. We have put the value of the test statistic and the p-value in boldface. Even though R labels the value of the test statistic as V, it is identical to the one that we calculated manually—that is, $V = T = 40$. So, from Table 20.4 we see that the p-value = 0.1162. Since the p-value is greater than $\alpha = 0.05$, we do not reject H_0. At the 5% significance level, we cannot conclude that the median return for Growth is greater than 5%.

TABLE 20.4 R's Output for Example 20.1

```
            Wilcoxon signed rank test
V = 40, p-value = 0.1162
alternative hypothesis: true location is greater
than 5
```

Using a Normal Distribution Approximation for *T*

As mentioned earlier, the sampling distribution of T can be approximated by the normal distribution if n has at least 10 observations.[1] We can then easily implement a z test with this approximation.

EXAMPLE 20.2

Redo the test specified in Example 20.1 using the normal distribution approximation.

SOLUTION: Again we use the competing hypotheses, H_0: $m \leq 5$ versus H_A: $m > 5$, and the value of the test statistic, $T = 40$. Since there are 10 observations, we calculate the mean and the standard deviation of the sampling distribution of T as

$$\mu_T = \frac{n(n+1)}{4} = \frac{10(10+1)}{4} = 27.50 \text{ and}$$

$$\sigma_T = \sqrt{\frac{n(n+1)(2n+1)}{24}} = \sqrt{\frac{10(10+1)(2 \times 10+1)}{24}} = 9.8107.$$

[1]Since the normality assumption for parametric tests becomes less stringent in large samples, the main appeal of rank-based tests tends to be with relatively small samples. Note, however, the Wilcoxon test requires the sample size to be at least 10, as compared to 30 required for the parametric t-test.

The corresponding value of the test statistic Z is

$$z = \frac{T - \mu_T}{\sigma_T} = \frac{40 - 27.50}{9.8107} = 1.2741.$$

Therefore, with the normal distribution approximation, we can use Excel's NORM.DIST function or R's pnorm function to find the corresponding p-value as $P(Z \geq 1.2741) = 0.1013$. Since the p-value is greater than $\alpha = 0.05$, we do not reject H_0. This conclusion is consistent with the one made in Example 20.1; that is, at the 5% significance level, we cannot conclude that the median return is greater than 5%.

Using R to Test a Population Median

We can use a single function in R, the **wilcox.test** function, which greatly facilitates conducting a Wilcoxon signed-rank test.

EXAMPLE 20.3

Use the ***Mutual_Funds*** data file from the introductory case to determine whether the median return for Value is greater than 5% with $\alpha = 0.05$.

Mutual_Funds

SOLUTION: The competing hypotheses for the test are

$$H_0: m \leq 5$$
$$H_A: m > 5$$

a. Import the ***Mutual_Funds*** data file into a data frame (table) and label it myData.

b. We use R's **wilcox.test** function to find the value of the test statistic and the p-value. For options within the **wilcox.test** function, we use *mu* to specify the value of the hypothesized median and *alternative* to specify the alternative hypothesis (denoted as "two.sided" for a two-tailed test, "less" for a left-tailed test, and "greater" for a right-tailed test). Enter:

```
> wilcox.test(myData$Value, mu=5, alternative="greater")
```

Table 20.5 shows a portion of the R output.

TABLE 20.5 R's Output for Example 20.3

```
        Wilcoxon signed rank test
data: myData$Value
V = 39, p-value = 0.1377
alternative hypothesis: true location is greater
than 5
```

The value of the test statistic is $V = T = 39$ with a corresponding p-value of 0.1377 (see values in boldface). Since the p-value > 0.05, we do not reject the null hypothesis. At the 5% significance level, we cannot conclude that the median return for Value is greater than 5%.

We should note that, by default, R generates an exact p-value if the sample size is less than 50 and there are no ties. Otherwise, a normal approximation is used.

EXERCISES 20.1

*For exercises marked with an asterisk, it is advised that you use a statistical software package that accommodates the Wilcoxon signed-rank test.

Mechanics

1. Consider the following sample data:

25	18	21	27	30

   a. Specify the competing hypotheses to determine whether the median differs from 20.
   b. Calculate the value of the test statistic T.
   c. The p-value corresponding to the test statistic in part b is equal to 0.188. At the 5% significance level, does the median differ from 20? Explain.

2. Consider the following sample data:

150	145	138	155	141	152

   a. Specify the competing hypotheses to determine whether the median is greater than 140.
   b. Calculate the value of the test statistic T.
   c. The p-value corresponding to the test statistic in part b is equal to 0.047. At the 5% significance level, is the median greater than 140? Explain.

3. Consider the following sample data.

8	5	11	7	6	5

   a. Specify the competing hypotheses to determine whether the median is less than 10.
   b. Calculate the value of the test statistic T.
   c. The p-value corresponding to the test statistic in part b is approximately equal to 0.029. At the 5% significance level, what is the conclusion to the hypothesis test? Explain.

4. Consider the following competing hypotheses and sample data.

$$H_0: m \leq 150$$
$$H_A: m > 150$$
$$n = 30 \quad T^- = 200 \quad T^+ = 265$$

   a. Assuming that the sampling distribution of T is normally distributed, calculate the value of the test statistic.
   b. Calculate the p-value.
   c. At the 5% significance level, is the median greater than 150? Explain.

5. Consider the following sample data.

105	90	110	80	85	85	103	70	115	75

   Assume the normal approximation for T.
   a. Specify the competing hypotheses to determine whether the median differs from 100.
   b. Calculate the value of the test statistic and the p-value.
   c. At the 10% significance level, is the median different from 100? Explain.

Applications

6. A random sample of eight drugstores shows the following prices (in $) for a popular pain reliever:

5.00	4.25	3.75	5.50	5.75	6.25	5.25	4.25

   a. Specify the competing hypotheses to determine whether the median price is less than $6.00.
   b. Calculate the value of the test statistic.
   c. The p-value corresponding to the test statistic in part b is approximately equal to 0.012. At the 5% significance level, what is the conclusion to the hypothesis test? Explain.

7. FILE ***Balanced.*** The accompanying data file shows the annual returns (in %) for a mutual fund over a 10-year period.
   a. Specify the competing hypotheses to determine whether the median return is greater than 5%.
   b. Calculate the value of the test statistic, using a normal distribution approximation for T.
   c. At the 10% significance level, what is the conclusion to the hypothesis test?

8. FILE ***City_Rent.*** The accompanying data file lists the average rent per square foot (in $) for 10 cities.
   a. Specify the competing hypotheses to determine whether the median rent is greater than $25 per square foot.
   b. Calculate the value of the test statistic, using a normal distribution approximation for T.
   c. At the 1% significance level, can you conclude that the median rent exceeds $25 per square foot?

9.* FILE ***Wage.*** An economist wants to test whether the median hourly wage is less than $22.
   a. Specify the competing hypotheses for the test.
   b. At the 5% significance level, can you conclude that the median hourly wage is less than $22? Explain.

10.* FILE ***Houses.*** A realtor believes that the median price of a house is more than $500,000. The accompanying data is in $1,000s.
   a. Specify the competing hypotheses for the test.
   b. At the 5% significance level, is the realtor's claim supported by the data? Explain.

11.* FILE ***Convenience.*** An entrepreneur examines monthly sales (in $1,000s) for 40 convenience stores in Rhode Island.
   a. Specify the competing hypotheses to determine whether median sales differ from $130,000.
   b. At the 5% significance level, do median sales differ from $130,000? Explain.

20.2 TESTING TWO POPULATION MEDIANS

In Chapter 10, we presented t-tests to determine whether significant differences existed between population means from matched-pairs and independent samples. When using a t-test, we assume that we are sampling from normal populations. The **Wilcoxon signed-rank test** serves as the nonparametric counterpart to the matched-pairs t-test. The **Wilcoxon rank-sum test,** also referred to as the **Mann-Whitney test,** is used for independent samples. We again note that if the normality assumption is not unreasonable, then these tests are less powerful than the parametric t-tests. We begin this section by examining the Wilcoxon signed-rank test for a matched-pairs experiment, followed by the Wilcoxon rank-sum test for independent samples.

The Wilcoxon Signed-Rank Test for a Matched-Pairs Sample

LO 20.2

Make inferences about the population median difference based on matched-pairs sampling.

In this application of matched-pairs sampling, the parameter of interest is referred to as the median difference m_D, where $D = X - Y$, and the random variables X and Y are matched in a pair; refer to Chapter 10 for details on matched-pairs sampling. When we wish to test whether m_D differs from, is greater than, or is less than 0, we set up the competing hypotheses as follows.

Two-Tailed Test	Right-Tailed Test	Left-Tailed Test
H_0: $m_D = 0$	H_0: $m_D \leq 0$	H_0: $m_D \geq 0$
H_A: $m_D \neq 0$	H_A: $m_D > 0$	H_A: $m_D < 0$

The Wilcoxon signed-rank test for a matched-pairs sample is nearly identical to its use for a single sample. The only added step is that we first find the difference between each pairing. We illustrate the Wilcoxon signed-rank test for a matched-pairs sample using the Growth and Value observations from the introductory case.

Note that these samples are matched, in that each return observation is blocked by year. We apply the Wilcoxon signed-rank test to determine whether significant differences exist between the median difference of the returns and formulate the two-tailed test as

$$H_0: m_D = 0$$
$$H_A: m_D \neq 0$$

Table 20.6 summarizes the method for calculating the value of the test statistic T; that is, we first calculate differences between the returns (column 4), find absolute

TABLE 20.6 Calculations for Wilcoxon Signed-Rank Test

Year (1)	Growth x (2)	Value y (3)	$d = x - y$ (4)	$\|d\|$ (5)	Rank (6)	Ranks of Negative Differences (7)	Ranks of Positive Differences (8)
1	12.56	0.09	12.47	12.47	9		9
2	−38.32	−35.97	−2.35	2.35	5	5	
3	36.29	19.58	16.71	16.71	10		10
4	16.96	14.28	2.68	2.68	6		6
5	1.71	1.00	0.71	0.71	3		3
6	16.89	15.00	1.89	1.89	4		4
7	32.16	32.85	−0.69	0.69	2	2	
8	13.47	13.05	0.42	0.42	1		1
9	3.17	−1.03	4.20	4.2	7		7
10	5.99	16.75	−10.76	10.76	8	8	
						$T^- = 15$	$T^+ = 40$

differences (column 5), and determine rankings (column 6). Then we compute the sum of the ranks of negative differences (column 7, $T^- = 15$) and the sum of the ranks of positive differences (column 8, $T^+ = 40$). The value of the test statistic T is $T = T^+ = 40$.

As mentioned earlier, we generally rely on statistical packages to compute the value of the test statistic T and the resulting p-value. In Example 20.4, we show how to use R to implement the Wilcoxon signed-rank test for a matched-pairs sample.

Using R to Test for Median Differences from a Matched-Pairs Sample

EXAMPLE 20.4

FILE *Mutual_Funds*

Use the ***Mutual_Funds*** data file from the introductory case to determine whether the median difference between Growth and Value differs from zero at the 5% significance level.

SOLUTION: As discussed earlier, the competing hypotheses for the test are H_0: $m_D = 0$ versus H_A: $m_D \neq 0$.

a. Import the ***Mutual_Funds*** data file into a data frame (table) and label it myData.

b. As discussed in Section 20.1, we again use R's **wilcox.test** function to test m_D. For options within the **wilcox.test** function, we use *alternative* and *paired.* Enter:

```
> wilcox.test(myData$Growth, myData$Value,
alternative="two.sided", paired=TRUE)
```

Table 20.7 reports the R output when testing whether the median return difference between Growth and Value differs from zero. We have put the value of the test statistic and the p-value in boldface.

TABLE 20.7 R's Output for Example 20.4

```
        Wilcoxon signed rank test
V = 40, p-value = 0.2324
alternative hypothesis: true location shift is
not equal to 0
```

The value of the test statistic is identical to the one that we calculated manually—that is, $V = T = 40$. Since the p-value is equal to 0.2324, which is greater than $\alpha = 0.05$, we do not reject H_0. At the 5% significance level, we cannot conclude that the median difference between the funds' returns differs from zero.

The Wilcoxon Rank-Sum Test for Independent Samples

LO 20.3

Make inferences about the difference between two population medians based on independent sampling.

Next we discuss whether significant differences exist between two population medians when the underlying populations are nonnormal and the samples are independent. In this situation, we use the Wilcoxon rank-sum test. The parameter of interest is the difference between two population medians $m_1 - m_2$. When we wish to test whether $m_1 - m_2$ differs from, is greater than, or is less than 0, we set up the competing hypotheses as follows.

Two-Tailed Test	Right-Tailed Test	Left-Tailed Test
H_0: $m_1 - m_2 = 0$	H_0: $m_1 - m_2 \leq 0$	H_0: $m_1 - m_2 \geq 0$
H_A: $m_1 - m_2 \neq 0$	H_A: $m_1 - m_2 > 0$	H_A: $m_1 - m_2 < 0$

We illustrate the Wilcoxon rank-sum test with the following example.

An undergraduate at a local university cannot decide whether she should pursue business or journalism. She wonders whether her choice will influence her salary upon graduation. She gathers salary data (in \$1,000s) on 10 recent graduates who majored in business and 10 recent graduates who majored in journalism. A portion of the data is shown in Table 20.8.

TABLE 20.8 Business and Journalism Salaries (in \$1,000s)

FILE *Salaries*

Business	Journalism
66	61
60	52
⋮	⋮
69	46

In order to determine whether salaries differ across majors, we apply the Wilcoxon rank-sum test. Let m_1 and m_2 denote the population median salary for business and journalism majors, respectively. We formulate the two-tailed test as

$$H_0\colon m_1 - m_2 = 0$$
$$H_A\colon m_1 - m_2 \neq 0$$

To arrive at the value of the test statistic W for the Wilcoxon rank-sum test, several steps are necessary.

A. We first pool the n_1 observations data from sample 1 (Business) with the n_2 observations from sample 2 (Journalism), and then arrange **all** the data in ascending order of magnitude. That is, we treat the independent samples as if they are one large sample of size $n_1 + n_2 = n$. See column 1 of Table 20.9.

B. We rank the observations from smallest to largest, assigning the numbers 1 to n. Since we have a multiple tie at ranks 4, 5, and 6, we assign to each of the tied observations the mean of the ranks which they jointly occupy, or $(4 + 5 + 6)/3 = 5$. See columns 2 and 3 of Table 20.9. We note that the journalism salaries occupy the lower ranks, whereas the business salaries occupy the higher ranks.

C. We sum the ranks of the business salaries (denoted W_1) and then sum the ranks of the journalism salaries (denoted W_2). Here we find that $W_1 = 149$ and $W_2 = 61$; see columns 4 and 5 of Table 20.9. To check that we have performed the calculations properly, we confirm that the sum of the rank sums, $W_1 + W_2$, equals $\frac{(n_1 + n_2)(n_1 + n_2 + 1)}{2}$, which is equivalent to the sum of the integers from 1 to $n_1 + n_2$. We first find that $W_1 + W_2 = 149 + 61 = 210$. Since $n_1 = 10$ and $n_2 = 10$, we then find that $\frac{(n_1 + n_2)(n_1 + n_2 + 1)}{2} = \frac{(10 + 10)(10 + 10 + 1)}{2} = 210$.

TABLE 20.9 Calculations for Wilcoxon Rank-Sum Test

Salary (1)	Sample of Origin (2)	Rank (3)	Business Ranks (4)	Journalism Ranks (5)
46	Journalism	1		1
47	Journalism	2		2
50	Journalism	3		3
52	Journalism	5		5
52	Journalism	5		5
52	Journalism	5		5
54	Journalism	7		7
55	Journalism	8		8
58	Business	9	9	
59	Business	10	10	
60	Business	11	11	
61	Journalism	12		12
62	Journalism	13		13
64	Business	14	14	
65	Business	15	15	
66	Business	16	16	
67	Business	17	17	
68	Business	18	18	
69	Business	19	19	
70	Business	20	20	
			$W_1 = 149$	$W_2 = 6$

If the median salary of business majors is equal to the median salary of journalism majors, then we would expect each major to produce about as many low ranks as high ranks, so that both W_1 and W_2 are about equal to half of the total sum of ranks of 210, or about 105. However, if the median salaries are significantly different, then most of the higher ranks will be occupied by one major and most of the lower ranks will be occupied by the other major. For testing, we could analyze either W_1 or W_2. In what follows, we will base the Wilcoxon rank-sum test on W_1.

THE TEST STATISTIC *W* FOR THE WILCOXON RANK-SUM TEST

The test statistic W for the Wilcoxon rank-sum test is defined as $W = W_1$, where W_1 denotes the sum of the ranks of the values in sample 1.

There are two scenarios when conducting the Wilcoxon rank-sum test:

1. If $n_1 \leq 10$ and $n_2 \leq 10$, then we use special tables to find the p-value. Alternatively, we rely on statistical packages, including R, to compute the value of the test statistic W and the resulting p-value.
2. If $n_1 \geq 10$ and $n_2 \geq 10$, then the sampling distribution of W can be approximated by the normal distribution with mean $\mu_W = \frac{n_1(n_1 + n_2 + 1)}{2}$ and standard deviation $\sigma_W = \sqrt{\frac{n_1 n_2(n_1 + n_2 + 1)}{12}}$, and hence the value of the resulting test statistic is computed as $z = \frac{W - \mu_W}{\sigma_W}$.

Using R to Test for Median Differences from Independent Samples

In Example 20.5, we use R to implement the Wilcoxon rank-sum test for independent samples.

EXAMPLE 20.5

Use the ***Salaries*** data file to determine whether the median business salary differs from the median journalism salary at the 5% significance level.

Salaries

SOLUTION: As discussed earlier, the competing hypotheses for the test are H_0: $m_1 - m_2 = 0$ versus H_A: $m_1 - m_2 \neq 0$.

a. Import the ***Salaries*** data file into a data frame (table) and label it myData.

b. We again use R's **wilcox.test** function with options *alternative* and *paired.* Enter:

```
> wilcox.test(myData$Business, myData$Journalism,
  alternative="two.sided", paired=FALSE)
```

Table 20.10 reports the R output when testing whether the median salaries differ. We have put the value of the test statistic and the p-value in boldface.

TABLE 20.10 R's Output for Example 20.5

```
Wilcoxon rank-sum test with continuity correction
W = 94, p-value = 0.0009904
alternative hypothesis: true location shift is not equal to 0
```

It is important to point out that the value of the test statistic $W = 94$ reported by R is not the same as the value $W = W_1 = 149$ that we computed manually in Table 20.9. The value of W in Table 20.9 is often referred to as the unadjusted sum of ranks because it does not adjust for the sample size from which W is derived. To compute adjusted sum of ranks, we first compute $n_1(n_1 + 1)/2$ where n_1 is the number of observations in the first sample. We then subtract this value from W. In this example, since $n_1 = 10$, we find $10(10 + 1)/2 = 55$. So, the adjusted sum of ranks is equal to $149 - 55 = 94$. To avoid confusion, we refer to the adjusted sum of ranks derived by R as W^*. The p-values based on W or W^* are the same. The p-value for the two-tailed test reported by R is approximately equal to 0. Therefore, at $\alpha = 0.05$, we reject H_0. At the 5% significance level, we can conclude that the median business salary differs from the median journalism salary.

Using a Normal Distribution Approximation for *W*

When n_1 and n_2 both have at least 10 observations, we can use the normal distribution approximation to implement a z test.

EXAMPLE 20.6

Assuming that the distribution of W is approximately normal, let's again determine whether the median business salary differs from the median journalism salary at the 5% significance level.

SOLUTION: We specify the same competing hypotheses, H_0: $m_1 - m_2 = 0$ versus H_A: $m_1 - m_2 \neq 0$, and compute the value of the test statistic as $W = W_1 = 149$. Note that we use the manually derived value of W, and not the one reported by R. We now compute the mean and the standard deviation as

$$\mu_W = \frac{n_1(n_1 + n_2 + 1)}{2} = \frac{10(10 + 10 + 1)}{2} = 105, \text{ and}$$

$$\sigma_W = \sqrt{\frac{n_1 n_2(n_1 + n_2 + 1)}{12}} = \sqrt{\frac{(10 \times 10)(10 + 10 + 1)}{12}} = 13.2288.$$

The value of the test statistic Z is calculated as

$$z = \frac{W - \mu_W}{\sigma_W} = \frac{149 - 105}{13.2288} = 3.3261.$$

We can use Excel's NORM.DIST function or R's pnorm function to, find the p-value as $2 \times P(Z \geq 3.3261) = 0.0004$. Since the p-value is less than the significance level of $\alpha = 0.05$, we reject H_0 and conclude, as before, that the median business salary differs from the median journalism salary.

EXERCISES 20.2

*For exercises marked with an asterisk, it is advised that you use a statistical software package that accommodates the Wilcoxon signed-rank test or the Wilcoxon rank-sum test.

Mechanics

12. A matched-pairs sample of 20 observations produced a test statistic of $T = 165$.
    a. Specify the competing hypotheses in order to determine whether the median difference is greater than zero.
    b. Determine the value of the test statistic using a normal approximation for T.
    c. Calculate the p-value.
    d. At the 5% significance level, what is the conclusion to the hypothesis test? Explain.

13. Consider the following competing hypotheses and accompanying sample data drawn from a matched-pairs sample.

    H_0: $m_D = 0$
    H_A: $m_D \neq 0$ $\quad n = 50 \quad T^- = 400 \; T^+ = 875$

    a. Determine the value of the test statistic using a normal approximation for T.
    b. Calculate the p-value.
    c. At the 5% significance level, what is the conclusion? Explain.

14.* FILE ***Exercise_20.14.*** The accompanying data file contains information on a matched-pairs sample.
    a. Specify the competing hypotheses that determine whether the median difference between Population 1 and Population 2 is less than zero.
    b. At the 5% significance level, what is the conclusion to the hypothesis test? Explain.

15. FILE ***Exercise_20.15.*** The accompanying data file contains information on a matched-pairs sample.
    a. Specify the competing hypotheses that determine whether the median difference differs from zero.
    b. Assuming a normal approximation for T, determine the value of the test statistic.
    c. Calculate the p-value.
    d. At the 1% significance level, what is the conclusion?

16. FILE ***Exercise_20.16.*** Random samples were drawn from two independent populations. The accompanying data file shows the results.
    a. Specify the competing hypotheses to determine whether the median of Population 1 is less than the median of Population 2.
    b. Find the unadjusted sum of ranks, W.
    c. The p-value for the test is found to be equal to 0.034. At the 5% significance level, what is the conclusion to the hypothesis test? Explain.

17. FILE ***Exercise_20.17.*** Random samples were drawn from two independent populations. The accompanying data file shows the results.
    a. Specify the competing hypotheses to determine whether the median of Population 1 is greater than the median of Population 2.
    b. Find the unadjusted sum of ranks, W.
    c. The p-value for the test is found to be equal to 0.180. At the 5% significance level, what is the conclusion to the hypothesis test? Explain.

18. The following data are provided for two samples drawn from independent populations: $W = 700$, $n_1 = 25$, and

$n_2 = 20$. Suppose the distribution of W is approximately normal.

a. Calculate the mean and the standard deviation of the distribution of W.
b. Specify the competing hypotheses to determine whether the median of Population 1 is greater than the median of Population 2.
c. Calculate the value of the test statistic Z.
d. At the 5% significance level, what is the conclusion to the hypothesis test?

19. The following data are provided for two samples drawn from independent populations: $W = 545$, $n_1 = 25$, and $n_2 = 25$. Suppose the distribution of W is approximately normal.
    a. Calculate the mean and the standard deviation of the distribution of W.
    b. Specify the competing hypotheses to determine whether the median of Population 1 differs from the median of Population 2.
    c. Calculate the value of the test statistic, Z.
    d. At the 10% significance level, what is the conclusion to the hypothesis test?

Applications

20.* FILE ***Mock_SAT.*** Suppose eight college-bound students take a mock SAT, complete a three-month test-prep course, and then take the real SAT.
    a. Specify the competing hypotheses to determine whether the median score on the real SAT is greater than the median score on the mock SAT.
    b. At the 5% significance level, is there sufficient evidence to conclude that the median score on the real SAT is greater than the median score on the mock SAT? Explain.

21. FILE ***Diet.*** A diet center claims that it has the most effective weight loss program in the region. Its advertisement says, "Participants in our program really lose weight." Five clients of this program are weighed on the first day of the diet and then three months later.
    a. Specify the null and alternative hypotheses to test whether the median difference for weight loss supports the diet center's claim.
    b. Find the value of the test statistic, T.
    c. The p-value for the test is found to be equal to 0.139. At the 5% significance level, do the data support the diet center's claim? Explain.

22. FILE ***Appraisals.*** A bank employs two appraisers. When approving borrowers for mortgages, it is imperative that the appraisers provide consistent appraisals to the same types of properties. To make sure that this is the case, the bank asks the appraisers to value 10 different properties (in $).
    a. Specify the competing hypotheses to determine whether the median difference between the appraisals differs from zero.
    b. Calculate the value of the test statistic, T. Assume the normal approximation for T.
    c. Calculate the p-value.
    d. At the 5% significance level, is there sufficient evidence to conclude that the appraisers are not consistent in their appraisals? Explain.

23.* FILE ***Statistics.*** A professor teaches two sections of an introductory statistics course. He gives each section the same final and wonders if any significant differences exist between the medians of these sections. The accompanying data file shows seven scores from Section A and six scores from Section B.
    a. Set up the hypotheses to test the claim that the median test score in Section A differs from the median test score in Section B.
    b. At the 5% significance level, do the median test scores differ? Explain.

24.* FILE ***Income.*** A study suggests that married men have a higher median income than unmarried men. The accompanying data file shows the incomes (in $1,000s) of six married men and seven unmarried men.
    a. Set up the hypotheses to test the claim that the median income of married men is greater than the median income of unmarried men.
    b. At the 5% significance level, is the claim supported by the data? Explain.

25.* FILE ***Spending.*** Researchers at the Wharton School of Business have found that men and women shop for different reasons. While women enjoy the shopping experience, men are on a mission to get the job done. Men do not shop as frequently, but when they do, they make big purchases like expensive electronics. The accompanying data file shows the amount spent (in $) over the weekend by 40 men and 60 women at a local mall.
    a. Specify the competing hypotheses to determine whether the median amount spent by men is more than the amount spent by women.
    b. At the 5% significance level, is there sufficient evidence to conclude that the median amount spent by men is greater than the median amount spent by women? Explain.

26. FILE ***South_Koreans.*** According to a study, South Koreans spend more hours per year on the job than people in any other developed country. The accompanying data file reports the number of hours worked in the last year by 10 workers in South Korea and by 10 workers in the United States.
    a. Set up the hypotheses to test the claim that the median annual hours worked in South Korea is greater than the median annual hours worked in the United States.
    b. Calculate the unadjusted sum of ranks, W.
    c. Assume the normal approximation for W. With $\alpha = 0.05$, is the claim supported by the data? Explain.

20.3 TESTING THREE OR MORE POPULATION MEDIANS

In Chapter 13, we applied the one-way ANOVA F-test to compare three or more population means. In order to implement this test, we assumed that for each population the variable of interest was normally distributed with the same variance. The **Kruskal-Wallis test** is a nonparametric alternative to the one-way ANOVA test that can be used when the assumptions of normality and/or equal population variances cannot be validated. It is based on ranks and is used for testing the equality of three or more population medians. Since the Kruskal-Wallis test is essentially an extension of the Wilcoxon rank-sum test, we discuss its application through an example.

The Kruskal-Wallis Test for Population Medians

LO 20.4

Make inferences about the difference between three or more population medians.

A marketing manager for a large grocery chain wants to know if sales differ depending on the store layout. She collects monthly sales (in $1,000s) from a representative sample of stores that use one of four possible layouts. Table 20.11 shows the results. She decides not to pursue the one-way ANOVA test because of the small sample size and the possibility that the population variances may not be equal. Instead she chooses to apply the Kruskal-Wallis test.

TABLE 20.11 Monthly Sales (in $1,000s) by Store Layout

FILE
Layout

Layout_1	Layout_2	Layout_3	Layout_4
1246	1267	1581	1623
1148	1228	1649	1550
1300	1450	981	1936
1404	1351	1877	1800
1396	1280	1629	1750
1450		1800	
		1423	

Let m_1, m_2, m_3, and m_4 denote the median monthly sales for Layout 1, Layout 2, Layout 3, and Layout 4, respectively. We formulate the competing hypotheses as

$$H_0: m_1 = m_2 = m_3 = m_4$$
$$H_A: \text{Not all population medians are equal.}$$

As in the Wilcoxon rank-sum test, we follow several steps to arrive at the value for the Kruskal-Wallis test statistic H.

A. First, we pool the k independent samples (here, $k = 4$) and then rank the observations from 1 to n. Since the total number of observations is 23, we rank the scores from 1 to 23. As before, if there are any ties, then we assign to each of the tied observations the mean of the ranks which they jointly occupy. In this sample, two stores have sales of 1450, and each is assigned the rank of 12.5, since the observations jointly occupy the 12th and 13th ranks. Also, two stores have sales of 1800, and each is assigned the rank of 20.5. Table 20.12 shows the rank for each sale.

B. We then calculate a ranked sum, denoted R_i, for each of the k samples. For instance, the ranked sum for Layout 1 is calculated as $4 + 2 + 7 + 10 + 9 + 12.5 = 44.5$. These sums are shown in the second-to-last row of Table 20.12.

TABLE 20.12 Calculations for the Kruskal-Wallis Test

Layout_1	Rank	Layout_2	Rank	Layout_3	Rank	Layout_4	Rank
1246	4	1267	5	1581	15	1623	16
1148	2	1228	3	1649	18	1550	14
1300	7	1450	12.5	981	1	1936	23
1404	10	1351	8	1877	22	1800	20.5
1396	9	1280	6	1629	17	1750	19
1450	12.5			1800	20.5		
				1423	11		
$R_1 = 44.5$		$R_2 = 34.5$		$R_3 = 104.5$		$R_4 = 92.5$	
$\frac{R_1^2}{n_1} = 330.0417$		$\frac{R_2^2}{n_2} = 238.05$		$\frac{R_3^2}{n_3} = 1560.0357$		$\frac{R_4^2}{n_4} = 1711.25$	

If median sales across different layouts are the same, we expect the ranked sums to be relatively close to one another. However, if some sums deviate substantially from others, then this is evidence that not all population medians are the same. We determine whether the variability of some ranked sums differs significantly from others by first calculating the value of the test statistic H.

THE TEST STATISTIC H FOR THE KRUSKAL-WALLIS TEST

The test statistic H for the Kruskal-Wallis test is defined as

$$H = \left(\frac{12}{n(n+1)} \times \sum_{i=1}^{k} \frac{R_i^2}{n_i}\right) - 3(n+1),$$

where R_i and n_i are the rank sum and the size of the ith sample, respectively, $n = \sum_{i=1}^{k} n_i$, and k is the number of populations (independent samples). If $n_i \geq 5$ for $i = 1, 2, \ldots, k$, then H can be approximated by the χ^2 distribution with $k - 1$ degrees of freedom.

For small sample values ($n_i < 5$), the test may be based on special tables; however, we will not pursue that case. The Kruskal-Wallis test is always a right-tailed test.

EXAMPLE 20.7

Use the data in Table 20.12 to determine whether some median sales differ by layout at the 5% significance level.

SOLUTION: As discussed earlier, the appropriate hypotheses for the test are

$$H_0: m_1 = m_2 = m_3 = m_4$$
$$H_A: \text{Not all population medians are equal.}$$

We compute the value of the test statistic H as

$$\begin{aligned} H &= \left(\frac{12}{n(n+1)} \times \sum_{i=1}^{k} \frac{R_i^2}{n_i}\right) - 3(n+1) \\ &= \left(\frac{12}{23(23+1)} \times (330.0417 + 238.05 + 1560.0357 + 1711.25)\right) - 3(23+1) \\ &= 11.465 \end{aligned}$$

With $k = 4$, degrees of freedom equal $df = k - 1 = 3$. We find the p-value as $P(\chi^2_3 \geq 11.465)$. Referencing the χ^2 table for $df = 3$, we see that 11.465 lies between the values 11.345 and 12.838, implying that the p-value is between 0.005 and 0.01. Using Excel's CHISQ.DIST.RT function or R's pchisq function, we find the exact p-value as 0.009. Since the p-value is less than 0.05, we reject H_0. At the 5% significance level, not all median sales across different layouts are the same.

It is important to note that if we reject the null hypothesis, we can only conclude that not all population medians are equal. The Kruskal-Wallis test does not allow us to infer which medians differ.

Using R to Conduct a Kruskal-Wallis Test

We generally rely on computer software to perform the calculations involved in a Kruskal-Wallis test. Next, we redo Example 20.7 using R.

FILE
Layout

A. Import the ***Layout*** data file into a data frame (table) and label it myData.

B. We reconfigure the data frame using the **stack** function and label it Stacked. The reconfigured data frame will consist of two variables: Sales and Layout. For clarity, we use the **colnames** function to label the columns in Stacked as Sales and Layout, respectively. Enter:

```
> Stacked <- stack(myData)
> colnames(Stacked) <- c("Sales", "Layout")
```

C. We then apply the **kruskal.test** function by referencing the Sales and Layout variables from the Stacked data frame. Make sure that you first input the numerical variable (Sales), followed by the categorical variable (Layout). Enter

```
> kruskal.test(Stacked$Sales, Stacked$Layout)
```

Table 20.13 reports the R output when testing whether the median sales differ between the four layouts. We have put the value of the test statistic and the p-value in boldface.

TABLE 20.13 R's Output for the Kruskal-Wallis Test

```
Kruskal-Wallis rank sum test
data: Stacked$Sales and Stacked$Layout
Kruskal-Wallis chi-squared = 11.476, df = 3, p-value = 0.009411
```

The value of the test statistic computed by R is $H = 11.476$. Note that this is slightly different from the value of 11.465 that we calculated in Example 20.7. This difference occurs because R adjusts for ties differently. If there are no ties, then the H value calculated manually or with R is the same.

EXERCISES 20.3

*For exercises marked with an asterisk, it is advised that you use a statistical software package that accommodates the Kruskal-Wallis test.

Mechanics

27. Consider the following sample information: $k = 3$ and $H = 4.5$.
    a. Specify the competing hypotheses to test whether some differences exist between the medians.
    b. At the 10% significance level, do some medians differ? Explain.

28. Consider the following sample information: $k = 5$ and $H = 12.4$.
    a. Specify the competing hypotheses to test whether some differences exist between the medians.
    b. At the 5% significance level, do some medians differ? Explain.

29. FILE ***Exercise_20.29.*** Random samples were drawn from three independent populations. The accompanying data file shows the results.

a. Specify the competing hypotheses to test whether some differences exist between the medians.
b. Calculate the value of the test statistic H.
c. At the 10% significance level, do some medians differ? Explain.

30.* FILE ***Exercise_20.30.*** Random samples were drawn from four independent populations. The accompanying data file shows the results.

a. Specify the competing hypotheses to test whether some differences exist between the medians.
b. At the 5% significance level, do some medians differ? Explain.

Applications

31. FILE ***Unemployment.*** A research analyst wants to test whether the median unemployment rate differs from one region of the country to another. She collects the unemployment rate (in percent) of similar-sized cities in three regions of the United States. The accompanying data file shows the results.

a. Specify the competing hypotheses to test whether some differences exist in the median unemployment rates between the three regions.
b. Calculate the value of the test statistic H.
c. At the 10% significance level, do some unemployment rates differ by region? Explain.

32. FILE ***Bulb.*** A quality-control manager wants to test whether there is any difference in the median length of life of light bulbs between three different brands. Random samples were drawn from each brand, where the duration of each light bulb (in hours) was measured. The results are shown in the accompanying table.

a. Specify the competing hypotheses to test whether some differences exist in the median length of life of light bulbs between the three brands.
b. Calculate the value of the test statistic H.
c. At the 10% significance level, do some differences exist between the median length of life of light bulbs by brand? Explain.

33. FILE ***Industry_Returns.*** A research analyst examines annual returns (in percent) for Industry A, Industry B, and Industry C. The accompanying data file shows the results.

a. Specify the competing hypotheses to test whether some differences exist in the median returns by industry.
b. Calculate the value of the test statistic H.
c. At the 10% significance level, do some differences exist between the median returns by industry. Explain.

34. FILE ***Detergents.*** In order to compare the cleansing action of the top three detergents, 15 swatches of white cloth were soiled with red wine and grass stains and then washed in front-loading machines with the respective detergents. The accompanying data file shows the whiteness readings for each detergent.

a. Specify the competing hypotheses to test whether some differences exist in the median cleansing action of the three detergents.
b. Calculate the value of the test statistic H.
c. At the 1% significance level, do some differences exist between the median cleansing action by detergent? Explain.

35.* FILE ***Exam_Scores.*** A statistics instructor wonders whether significant differences exist in her students' median exam scores in her three different sections. She randomly selects scores from 10 different students in each section. The accompanying data file shows the results. Do these data provide enough evidence at the 5% significance level to indicate that there are some differences in median scores in the three sections?

36.* FILE ***Job_Satisfaction.*** A human resource specialist wants to determine whether the median job satisfaction score (on a scale of 0 to 100) differs depending on a person's field of employment. She collects scores from 30 employees in three different fields. The accompanying data file shows the results. At the 10% significance level, can the specialist conclude that there are some differences in job satisfaction depending on field of employment?

20.4 THE SPEARMAN RANK CORRELATION TEST

Recall from earlier chapters that the correlation coefficient, also referred to as the Pearson correlation coefficient, measures the direction and strength of the linear relationship between two random variables. The value of the correlation coefficient falls between −1 and +1; as its absolute value approaches one, the linear relationship becomes stronger. The **Spearman rank correlation coefficient** also measures the correlation between two random variables. Like the Pearson correlation coefficient, its value falls between −1 and +1, and it is interpreted in a similar way. As we will see shortly, the Spearman rank correlation coefficient is based on the ranked observations for each variable rather than the raw data.

Using the ***Mutual_Funds*** data file from the introductory case, Figure 20.2 shows a scatterplot of Value against Growth. Each point in the scatterplot represents a pairing of each fund's return for a given year. It appears that the two funds are positively related.

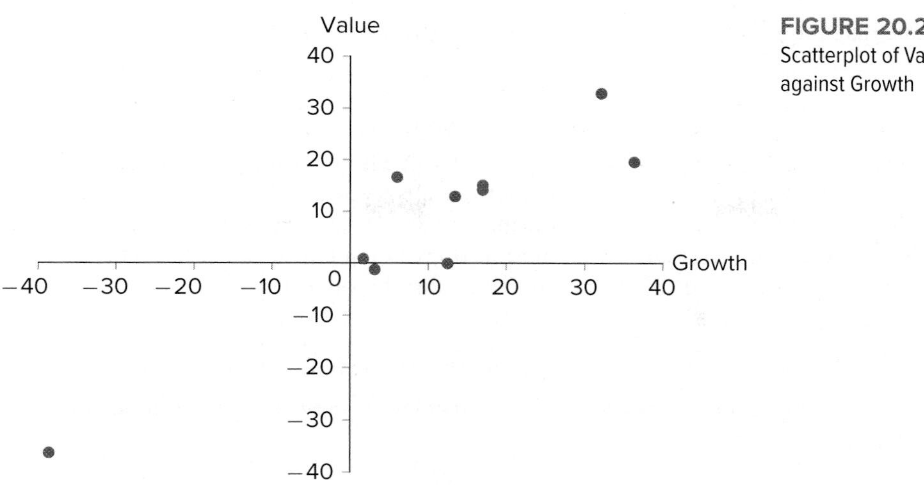

FIGURE 20.2
Scatterplot of Value against Growth

In order to calculate the sample Spearman rank correlation coefficient r_S between Value and Growth, we follow these steps.

A. We rank the observations for Growth from smallest to largest. In the case of ties, we assign to each tied observation the average of the ranks that they jointly occupy. We perform the same procedure for Value. Columns 2 and 3 of Table 20.14 show the original observations for the variables, and columns 4 and 5 show the ranked values.

TABLE 20.14 Calculations for the Spearman Rank Correlation Coefficient

Year (1)	Growth x (2)	Value y (3)	Rank for Growth (4)	Rank for Value (5)	Difference d (6)	Difference Squared d^2 (7)
1	12.56	0.09	5	3	2	4
2	−38.32	−35.97	1	1	0	0
3	36.29	19.58	10	9	1	1
4	16.96	14.28	8	6	2	4
5	1.71	1.00	2	4	−2	4
6	16.89	15.00	7	7	0	0
7	32.16	32.85	9	10	−1	1
8	13.47	13.05	6	5	1	1
9	3.17	−1.03	3	2	1	1
10	5.99	16.75	4	8	−4	16
					$\Sigma d_i = 0$	$\Sigma d_i^2 = 32$

B. We calculate the difference d_i between the ranks of each pair of observations. See column 6 of Table 20.14. As a check, when we sum the differences, Σd_i, we should obtain zero.

C. We then sum the squared differences. The resulting value is shown in the last cell of column 7 in Table 20.14—that is, $\Sigma d_i^2 = 32$.

The sample Spearman rank correlation coefficient between two variables x and y is calculated as

$$r_S = 1 - \frac{6\,\Sigma d_i^2}{n(n^2 - 1)}$$

We calculate the sample Spearman correlation coefficient r_S between Growth and Value as

$$r_S = 1 - \frac{6\,\Sigma d_i^2}{n(n^2-1)} = 1 - \frac{6 \times 32}{10 \times (10^2 - 1)} = 0.8061.$$

A value of $r_S = 0.8061$ implies that Growth and Value have a strong positive relationship.

Suppose we want to determine whether the observed relationship between two variables is real or due to chance. The Spearman rank correlation test offers a nonparametric alternative when the normality assumption does not seem reasonable. The following definition box summarizes the Spearman rank correlation test.

LO 20.5

Conduct a hypothesis test for the population Spearman rank correlation coefficient.

THE SPEARMAN RANK CORRELATION TEST

The sample Spearman rank correlation coefficient r_S between two variables x and y is defined as

$$r_S = 1 - \frac{6\Sigma d_i^2}{n(n^2-1)},$$

where d_i is the difference between the ranks of observations x_i and y_i.

There are two scenarios when conducting the Spearman rank correlation test:

1. If $n \leq 10$, then we use special tables to find the p-value. Alternatively, we rely on statistical packages, including R, to compute the value of the test statistic r_S and the resulting p-value.
2. If $n \geq 10$, then the sampling distribution of r_S can be approximated by the normal distribution with zero mean and standard deviation of $\sqrt{\frac{1}{n-1}}$, and the value of the resulting test statistic is computed as $z = r_S \times \sqrt{n-1}$.

EXAMPLE 20.8

At the 5% significance level, determine whether the Spearman rank correlation coefficient between Growth and Value differs from zero. Assume that the sampling distribution of r_S is normally distributed.

SOLUTION: We let ρ_s denote the population Spearman rank correlation coefficient and formulate the competing hypotheses as

$$H_0: \rho_s = 0$$
$$H_A: \rho_s \neq 0$$

We found that $r_s = 0.8061$. Under normality, the value of the corresponding test statistic Z is calculated as $z = 0.8061 \times \sqrt{10-1} = 2.4183$. We can use Excel's NORM.DIST function or R's pnorm function to find the p-value of $2 \times (Z \geq 2.4183) = 0.0156$. Since the p-value is less than $\alpha = 0.05$, we reject H_0 and conclude that the Spearman rank correlation coefficient between Growth and Value differs from zero.

Using R to Conduct the Spearman Rank Correlation Test

Here, we redo Example 20.8 using R.

A. Import the ***Mutual_Funds*** data file into a data frame (table) and label it myData.

B. As discussed in Chapter 14, we again use the **cor.test** function—the only difference is that we include the option *method* in order to designate the correlation coefficient that is to be used. Enter:

```
> cor.test(myData$Growth, myData$Value,
  alternative = "two.sided", method = "spearman")
```

Table 20.15 shows a portion of the R output when conducting the Spearman rank correlation test. Note that the sum of the squared rank differences (see S = 32) and the Spearman rank correlation coefficient (see the value of 0.8060606 under rho) match the values that we calculated manually. Note that the p-value differs from the one in Example 20.8 because the test implemented in R does not assume normality.

TABLE 20.15 R's Output for Example 20.8

```
                Spearman's rank correlation rho
S = 32, p-value = 0.008236
alternative hypothesis: true rho is not equal to 0
sample estimates:
      rho
0.8060606
```

Summary of Parametric and Nonparametric Tests

Table 20.16 summarizes the select parametric tests referenced in Section 20.1 and their nonparametric counterparts. Nonparametric tests use fewer and weaker assumptions than those associated with parametric tests and are especially attractive when the underlying population is markedly nonnormal. However, a nonparametric test ignores useful information since it focuses on the rank rather than the magnitude of the sample observations. Therefore, in situations when the parametric assumptions are valid, the nonparametric test is less powerful than its parametric counterpart. In general, when the assumptions for a parametric test are met, it is preferable to use a parametric test rather than a nonparametric test. Since the normality assumption for parametric tests is less stringent in large samples, the main appeal of nonparametric tests tends to be with relatively small samples.

TABLE 20.16 Parametric Test versus Nonparametric Alternative

Parametric Test	Nonparametric Alternative
t-test concerning the population mean	Wilcoxon signed-rank test concerning the population median
t-test to determine whether the population mean difference differs from zero based on matched-pairs sampling	Wilcoxon signed-rank test to determine whether the population median difference differs from zero based on matched-pairs sampling
t-test to determine whether two population means differ based on independent sampling	Wilcoxon rank-sum test to determine whether two population medians differ based on independent sampling
F-test to determine whether three or more population means differ	Kruskal-Wallis test to determine whether three or more population medians differ
t-test to determine whether two variables are correlated	Spearman rank correlation test to determine whether two variables are correlated

SYNOPSIS OF INTRODUCTORY CASE

An analysis of annual return data over the past ten years for a Growth Index mutual fund and a Value Index mutual fund provides important information for an investor trying to determine his next investment steps. Given that return data often have "fatter tails" than the normal distribution, the analysis focuses on nonparametric techniques. These techniques do not rely on the normality assumption concerning the underlying population.

When applying the Wilcoxon signed-rank test at the 5% significance level, it is found that the median return for the Growth fund is not greater than 5%. The same conclusion is also found for the Value fund. The Wilcoxon signed-rank test is

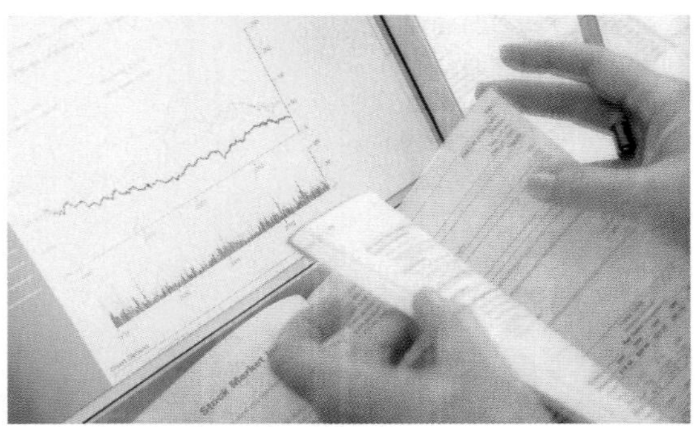

Ken Reid/Photographer's Choice/Getty Images

also used to determine whether the median difference between the returns differs from zero. At the 5% significance level, it is found that the median difference does not differ from zero. Finally, the sample Spearman rank correlation coefficient is calculated as 0.8061, implying a strong positive relationship between the returns of the two funds. A test conducted at the 5% significance level finds that the population Spearman rank correlation coefficient is different from zero. Interestingly, even though the approaches of growth and value investing use different fundamentals, the performance of the returns of these two funds is highly correlated over this ten-year period.

EXERCISES 20.4

Mechanics

*For exercises marked with an asterisk, it is advised that you use a statistical software package that accommodates the Spearman rank correlation test.

37. FILE ***Exercise_20.37.*** The accompanying data file shows six observations for two variables, x and y.
    a. Specify the competing hypotheses to determine whether the Spearman rank correlation coefficient differs from zero.
    b. Calculate and interpret r_S.
    c. The p-value associated with the test statistic in part b is 0.017. At the 5% significance level, what is the conclusion to the hypothesis test?

38. FILE ***Exercise_20.38.*** The accompanying data file shows six observations for two variables, x and y.
    a. Specify the competing hypotheses to determine whether the Spearman rank correlation coefficient is less than zero.
    b. Calculate and interpret r_S.
    c. The p-value associated with the test statistic in part b is 0.029. At the 5% significance level, what is the conclusion to the hypothesis test?

39. Consider the following competing hypotheses and accompanying sample data.

$$H_0: \rho_s = 0 \qquad r_s = 0.85 \text{ and } n = 65$$
$$H_A: \rho_s \neq 0$$

    a. What is the value of the test statistic and its associated p-value? Assume the normal approximation for r_S.
    b. At the 10% significance level, what is the conclusion?

40. Consider the following competing hypotheses and accompanying sample data.

$$H_0: \rho_s \leq 0 \qquad r_s = 0.64 \text{ and } n = 50$$
$$H_A: \rho_s > 0$$

    a. What is the value of the test statistic and its associated p-value? Assume the normal approximation for r_S.
    b. At the 1% significance level, what is the conclusion?

Applications

41. FILE ***Judge_Ranking.*** The accompanying data file shows the ranks given by two judges to the performance of six finalists in a men's figure skating competition.
    a. Specify the competing hypotheses to determine whether the Spearman rank correlation coefficient is different from zero.
    b. Calculate and interpret the Spearman rank correlation coefficient r_S.
    c. The p-value for the test is found to be equal to 0.033. At the 5% significance level, does the Spearman rank correlation coefficient differ from zero? Explain.

42. FILE ***WB_Ranking.*** The accompanying data file shows the ranking of the richest countries, as measured by per capita GNP. In addition, it gives each country's rank with respect to infant mortality. A higher rank indicates a lower mortality rate.
    a. Specify the competing hypotheses to determine whether the Spearman rank correlation coefficient is different from zero.
    b. Calculate and interpret the Spearman rank correlation coefficient r_S.
    c. At the 5% significance level, are GNP and the infant mortality rate correlated? Assume the normal distribution approximation.

43. FILE ***Assets.*** You are interested in whether the returns on Asset A (in %) are negatively correlated with the returns on Asset B (in %). You collect six years of annual return data on the two assets.
    a. Specify the competing hypotheses to determine whether the Spearman rank correlation coefficient is less than zero.
    b. Calculate and interpret the Spearman rank correlation coefficient r_S.
    c. The p-value for the test is found to be equal to 0.051. At the 1% significance level, are the returns negatively correlated? Explain.

44.* FILE ***Price_Days.*** The accompanying data file shows the price of a house (Price in $1,000s) and the number of days it takes to sell the house (Days) for a sample of eight recent transactions.

a. Specify the competing hypotheses to determine whether the Spearman rank correlation coefficient differs from zero.
b. At the 5% significance level, can you conclude that the price of a home and the number of days it takes to sell the home are correlated? Explain.

45.* FILE ***GRE_GPA.*** The director of graduate admissions at a local university is analyzing the relationship between scores on the Graduate Record Examination (GRE) and subsequent performance in graduate school, as measured by a student's grade point average (GPA). She uses a sample of seven students who graduated within the past five years.

a. Specify the competing hypotheses to determine whether the Spearman rank correlation coefficient is greater than zero.
b. At the 5% significance level, are GRE and GPA positively correlated?

46. A social scientist analyzes the relationship between educational attainment and salary. For 65 individuals, he collects data on each individual's educational attainment (in years) and his/her salary (in $1,000s). He then calculates a Spearman rank correlation coefficient of 0.85.

a. Specify the competing hypotheses to determine whether the Spearman rank correlation coefficient differs from zero.
b. Assume that the distribution of r_s is approximately normal. Calculate the value of the test statistic and the *p*-value of the test.
c. At the 5% significance level, are educational attainment and salary correlated?

47. An engineer examines the relationship between the weight of a car and its average miles per gallon (MPG). For a sample of 100 cars, he calculates a Spearman rank correlation coefficient of −0.60.

a. Specify the competing hypotheses to determine whether the Spearman rank correlation coefficient is less than zero.
b. Assume that the distribution of r_s is approximately normal. Calculate the value of the test statistic and the *p*-value.
c. At the 5% significance level, does a negative relationship exist between a car's weight and its average MPG?

48.* FILE ***Happiness.*** Many attempts have been made to relate happiness with various factors. One such study relates happiness with age and finds that, holding everything else constant, people are least happy when they are in their mid-40s. The accompanying data file shows a respondent's age and his/her perception of well-being on a scale from 0 to 100. Using the Spearman rank correlation coefficient, determine whether age and happiness are positively correlated at the 5% significance level.

49.* FILE ***Gambling.*** The accompanying data file shows the number of cases of crime related to gambling and offenses against the family and children for the 50 states in the United States. Using the Spearman rank correlation coefficient, determine whether gambling and family abuse are correlated at the 5% significance level.

20.5 THE SIGN TEST

In some applications, a matched-pairs sample originates from a categorical variable of ordinal observations rather than from a numerical variable (interval- or ratio-scaled observations). Let's review the definition of an ordinal-scaled variable first introduced in Chapter 1. With ordinal-scaled observations, we are able to categorize and rank the observations with respect to some characteristic or trait. The weakness with an ordinal variable is that we cannot interpret the difference between the ranked observations because the actual numbers used are arbitrary. For example, suppose you are asked to classify the service at a particular hotel as excellent, good, fair, or poor. A standard way to record the ratings is

Category	Rating
Excellent	4
Good	3
Fair	2
Poor	1

Here the value attached to excellent (4) is higher than the value attached to good (3), indicating that the response of excellent is preferred to good. However, another representation of the ratings might be

Category	Rating
Excellent	100
Good	80
Fair	70
Poor	40

LO 20.6

Make inferences about the difference between two populations of ordinal data based on matched-pairs sampling.

Excellent still receives a higher value than good, but now the difference between the two categories is 20 (100–80), as compared to a difference of 1 (4–3) when we use the first classification. In other words, differences between categories are meaningless with ordinal-scaled observations.

If we have a matched-pairs sample of ordinal-scaled observations, we can use the **sign test** to determine whether there are significant differences between the populations. When applying the sign test, we are only interested in whether the difference between two observations in a pair is different from, greater than, or less than zero. The difference between each pairing is replaced by a plus sign (+) if the difference is positive (that is, the first observation is greater than the second observation) or by a minus sign (−) if the difference between the pair is negative. If the difference between the pair is zero, we discard that particular outcome from the sample.

If significant differences do not exist between the two populations, then we expect just as many plus signs as minus signs. Equivalently, we expect plus signs 50% of the time and minus signs 50% of the time. Suppose we let p denote the population proportion of plus signs. (We could just as easily allow p to represent the population proportion of minus signs without loss of generality.) The competing hypotheses for the sign test take one of the following forms.

Two-Tailed Test	Right-Tailed Test	Left-Tailed Test
$H_0: p = 0.50$	$H_0: p \leq 0.50$	$H_0: p \geq 0.50$
$H_A: p \neq 0.50$	$H_A: p > 0.50$	$H_A: p < 0.50$

A two-tailed test allows us to determine whether the proportion of plus signs differs from the proportion of minus signs. A right-tailed test allows us to determine whether the proportion of plus signs is greater than the proportion of minus signs. A left-tailed test is interpreted in a similar manner.

Let $\overline{P} = X/n$ be the estimator of the population proportion of plus signs. The mean and standard error of $\overline{P}$ are $E(\overline{P}) = p$ and $se(\overline{P}) = \sqrt{p(1-p)/n}$, respectively (as discussed in Section 7.3). As long as the number of matched pairs is 10 or more, $n \geq 10$, then we can use the normal approximation to conduct the sign test. When $n < 10$, we rely on the binomial distribution to conduct the sign test; we will not consider such cases.

THE TEST STATISTIC FOR THE SIGN TEST

Assuming a probability of success $p = 0.50$ and $se(\overline{P}) = 0.5/\sqrt{n}$, the value of the test statistic for the sign test is computed as $z = \frac{\overline{p} - 0.5}{0.5/\sqrt{n}}$, where $\overline{p} = x/n$ is the sample proportion of plus signs. The test is valid when $n \geq 10$.

Note that this sign test is a special case of the test of the population proportion discussed in Chapter 9.

EXAMPLE 20.9

A large pizza chain claims that its reformulated recipe for pizza is a vast improvement over the old recipe. Suppose 20 customers are asked to sample the old recipe and then sample the new recipe. Each person is asked to rate the pizzas on a 5-point scale, where 1 = inedible and 5 = very tasty. The ratings are shown in Table 20.17. Do these data provide sufficient evidence to conclude that the new recipe is preferred to the old recipe? Use $\alpha = 0.05$.

TABLE 20.17 Calculations for Sign Test in Example 20.9

Customer	Old Recipe	New Recipe	Sign	Customer	Old Recipe	New Recipe	Sign
1	3	4	−	11	3	4	−
2	3	2	+	12	4	5	−
3	2	5	−	13	1	2	−
4	4	4	0	14	3	3	0
5	2	5	−	15	5	3	+
6	1	3	−	16	3	4	−
7	3	2	+	17	1	5	−
8	1	2	−	18	4	2	+
9	2	4	−	19	3	4	−
10	4	5	−	20	2	5	−

SOLUTION: If customers feel that there is no difference between the old recipe and the new recipe, then we expect 50% of the customers to prefer the old recipe and 50% to prefer the new recipe. Let p denote the population proportion of consumers who prefer the old recipe. We want to specify the competing hypotheses such that rejection of the null hypothesis provides evidence that customers prefer the new recipe (implying that p is significantly less than 0.50). We set up the competing hypotheses as

$$H_0: p \geq 0.50$$
$$H_A: p < 0.50$$

Table 20.17 shows the signs for each customer. For example, customer 1 ranks the old recipe with the value 3 and the new recipe with the value 4, which yields a minus sign when the difference between the old recipe and the new recipe is calculated: $3 - 4 = -1$. This difference indicates that this customer prefers the new recipe. We find 4 positive signs, 14 negative signs, and 2 ties (signs of zero). We then let n denote the number of matched-paired observations such that the sign between the rankings is nonzero; thus, n equals 18. We denote $\overline{p}$ as the sample proportion of plus signs, or the sample proportions of customers who prefer the old recipe. Given that there are four plus signs, the sample proportion is calculated as $\overline{p} = 4/18 = 0.2222$. We calculate the value of the test statistic as

$$z = \frac{\overline{p} - 0.5}{0.5/\sqrt{n}} = \frac{0.2222 - 0.5}{0.5/\sqrt{18}} = -2.3570.$$

We can use Excel's NORM.DIST function or R's pnorm function to find the corresponding p-value as $P(Z \leq -2.3570) = 0.0092$. Since the p-value is less than the significance level of $\alpha = 0.05$, we reject H_0 and conclude that customers prefer the reformulated version as compared to the old recipe at the 5% significance level.

Note that we could define p as the population proportion of customers who prefer the new recipe and conduct an equivalent right-tailed hypothesis test.

We can also use R's prop.test function to conduct the sign test. It produces a χ^2 test statistic rather than a Z test statistic. The p-values generated from each test statistic turn out to be identical, however, because of the underlying properties of the two distributions. Thus, the conclusion to the hypothesis test is the same. For the sake of consistency and to avoid any potential confusion, we do not elaborate on R's prop.test function here.

Finally, the sign test can be used for a numerical variable (interval- or ratio-scaled observations). However, because the sign test ignores the magnitude in the difference between two observations, it is advisable to use the Wilcoxon signed-rank test if interval- or ratio-scaled observations are available.

EXERCISES 20.5

Mechanics

50. Consider the following competing hypotheses and sample data.

$$H_0: p = 0.50 \qquad n = 40 \quad \bar{p} = 0.30$$
$$H_A: p \neq 0.50$$

a. Calculate the value of the test statistic for the sign test.
b. Calculate the p-value.
c. At the 5% significance level, what is the conclusion? Explain.

51. Consider the following competing hypotheses and sample data.

$$H_0: p \leq 0.50 \qquad n = 25 \quad \bar{p} = 0.64$$
$$H_A: p > 0.50$$

a. Calculate the value of the test statistic for the sign test.
b. Calculate the p-value.
c. At the 1% significance level, what is the conclusion? Explain.

52. Consider the following sign data, produced from a matched-pairs sample of ordinal-scaled observations.

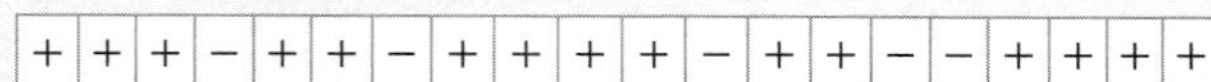

+	+	+	−	+	+	−	+	+	+	+	−	+	+	−	−	+	+	+	+

a. Specify the competing hypotheses to determine whether the proportion of negative signs differs from the proportion of positive signs.
b. Calculate the value of the test statistic.
c. Calculate the p-value.
d. At the 5% significance level, what is the conclusion? Explain.

53. Consider the following sign data, produced from a matched-pairs sample of ordinal-scaled observations.

+	−	−	+	−	−	+	−	+	−	+	−	−	−	+	−

a. Specify the competing hypotheses to determine whether the proportion of negative signs is significantly greater than the proportion of positive signs.
b. Calculate the value of the test statistic.
c. Calculate the p-value.
d. At the 1% significance level, what is the conclusion? Explain.

Applications

54. Last year, 100 registered voters were asked to rate the effectiveness of the president of the United States. This year, these same people were again asked to make the same assessment. Seventy percent of the second ratings were lower than the first ratings and 30% were higher.

a. Using the sign test, specify the competing hypotheses to determine whether the president's rating has significantly declined.
b. Calculate the value of the test statistic.
c. Calculate the p-value.
d. At the 5% significance level, do the data suggest that the president's rating has significantly declined?

55. **FILE** ***Water.*** Concerned with the increase of plastic water bottles in landfills, a leading environmentalist wants to determine whether there is any difference in taste between the local tap water and the leading bottled water. She randomly selects 14 consumers and conducts a blind taste test. She asks the consumers to rank the taste on a scale of 1 to 5 (where a score of 5 indicates excellent taste). The accompanying data file shows the results.

a. Using the sign test, specify the competing hypotheses to determine whether there are significant differences in preferences between tap water and bottled water.
b. Calculate the value of the test statistic.
c. Calculate the p-value.
d. At the 5% significance level, what is the conclusion? Do the results indicate that significant differences exist in preferences?

56. A new diet and exercise program claims that it significantly lowers a participant's cholesterol level. In order to test this claim, a sample of 60 participants is taken. Their cholesterol levels are measured before and after the three-month program. Forty of the participants recorded lower cholesterol levels at the end of the program, 18 participants recorded higher cholesterol levels, and 2 participants recorded no change.

a. Using the sign test, specify the competing hypotheses to test the program's claim.
b. Calculate the value of the test statistic.
c. Calculate the p-value.
d. At the 5% significance level, do the data support the program's claim? Explain.

57. **FILE** ***PhD_Rating.*** For scholarship purposes, two graduate faculty members rate 12 applicants to the PhD program on a scale of 1 to 10 (with 10 indicating an excellent candidate). These ratings are shown in the accompanying data file.
a. Using the sign test, specify the competing hypotheses to determine whether the ratings differ between the two faculty members.
b. Calculate the value of the test statistic.
c. Calculate the p-value.
d. At the 10% significance level, do the data suggest that faculty ratings differ? Explain.

20.6 TESTS BASED ON RUNS

LO 20.7

Determine whether the elements of a sequence appear in a random order.

In many applications, we wish to determine whether some observations occur in a truly random fashion or whether some form of a nonrandom pattern exists. In other words, we want to test if the elements of the sequence are mutually independent. We use the **Wald-Wolfowitz runs test,** or simply the **runs test,** to examine whether the elements in a sequence appear in a random order. It can be applied to either categorical or numerical variables so long as we can separate the sample observations into two categories.

Suppose we observe a machine filling 16-ounce cereal boxes. Since a machine is unlikely to dispense exactly 16 ounces in each box, we expect the weight of each box to deviate from 16 ounces. We might conjecture that a machine is operating properly if the deviations from 16 ounces occur in a random order. Let's sample 30 cereal boxes and denote those boxes that are overfilled with the letter O and those that are underfilled with the letter U. The following sequence of O's and U's is produced:

Sequence: OOOOUUUOOOOUOOOUUUUOOOOUUOOOOO

One possible way to test whether or not a machine is operating properly is to determine if the elements of a particular sequence of O's and U's occur randomly. If we observe a long series of consecutive O's (or U's), then the machine is likely overfilling (or underfilling) the cereal boxes. Adjustment of the machine is necessary if this is the case. Given the observed sequence, can we conclude that the machine needs adjustment in the sense that the series of O's and U's do not occur randomly?

In general, when applying the runs test, we specify the competing hypotheses as

H_0: The elements occur randomly.
H_A: The elements do not occur randomly.

In this particular application, the null hypothesis implies that the machine properly fills the boxes, and the alternative hypothesis implies that it does not. Before deriving the test statistic, it is first necessary to introduce some terminology. We define a **run** as an uninterrupted sequence of one letter, symbol, or attribute, such as O or U. We rewrite the observed sequence but now include single horizontal lines below the letter O. The five single lines indicate that we observe five runs of O, or $R_O = 5$. Similarly, the double horizontal lines below the letter U show that we have four runs of U, or $R_U = 4$. Thus, the total number of runs R is equal to 9: $R = R_O + R_U = 5 + 4 = 9$. Also, note that we have a total of 30 observations, of which 20 are Os and 10 are Us, or $n = n_O + n_U = 20 + 10 = 30$.

Sequence: $\underline{\text{OOOO}}\ \underline{\underline{\text{UUU}}}\ \underline{\text{OOOO}}\ \underline{\underline{\text{U}}}\ \underline{\text{OOO}}\ \underline{\underline{\text{UUUU}}}\ \underline{\text{OOOO}}\ \underline{\underline{\text{UU}}}\ \underline{\text{OOOOO}}$

We then ask: "Are 9 runs consisting of 30 observations too few or too many compared with the number of runs expected in a strictly random sequence of 30 observations?"

In general, the runs test is a two-tailed test; that is, too many runs are deemed just as unlikely as too few runs. For example, consider the following two sequences:

Sequence A: OOOOOOOOOOOO UUUUUU OOOOOOOOOOOO
Sequence B: O U O U O U O U O U O U O U O U O U O U O U O U O U O U O U

If the null hypothesis of randomness is true, Sequence A seems unlikely in the sense that there appear to be too few runs given a sample of 30 observations. Sequence B also seems unlikely since O and U alternate systematically, or equivalently, there appear to be too many runs. It is more readily apparent in the machine-filling application that a sequence that produces too few runs indicates a machine that is not operating properly; that is, the machine has a pattern of consistently overfilling and/or underfilling the cereal boxes. However, a machine that exhibits a perfect regularity of overfilling, underfilling, overfilling, underfilling, etc. (too many runs) may be just as problematic. If there are too many runs, then this may indicate some sort of repeated alternating pattern.

Let n_1 and n_2 denote the numbers of O's and U's in an n-element sequence. In general, the sampling distribution of R (the distribution for the runs test) is quite complex. However, if $n_1 \geq 10$ and $n_2 \geq 10$, then the distribution of R is approximately normal.

THE TEST STATISTIC R FOR THE WALD-WOLFOWITZ RUNS TEST

The value of the test statistic for the Wald-Wolfowitz runs test is computed as $z = \frac{R - \mu_R}{\sigma_R}$, where R represents the number of runs with mean $\mu_R = \frac{2n_1n_2}{n} + 1$ and standard deviation $\sigma_R = \sqrt{\frac{2n_1n_2(2n_1n_2 - n)}{n^2(n-1)}}$; n_1 and n_2 are the number of elements in a sequence possessing and not possessing a certain attribute; and $n = n_1 + n_2$. The test is valid when $n_1 \geq 10$ and $n_2 \geq 10$.

For the machine example, we found that $R = 9$; in addition, we have $n_1 = n_O = 20$ and $n_2 = n_U = 10$. We calculate the mean and the standard deviation of the distribution of R as

$$\mu_R = \frac{2n_1n_2}{n} + 1 = \frac{2(20)(10)}{30} + 1 = 14.3333 \text{ and}$$

$$\sigma_R = \sqrt{\frac{2n_1n_2(2n_1n_2 - n)}{n^2(n-1)}} = \sqrt{\frac{(2 \times 20 \times 10)(2 \times 20 \times 10 - 30)}{30^2(30-1)}} = \sqrt{\frac{148{,}000}{26{,}100}} = 2.3813.$$

Thus, the expected number of runs in a sample with 30 observations is 14.3333 and the standard deviation is 2.3813. We calculate the value of the test statistic as $z = \frac{R - \mu_R}{\sigma_R} = \frac{9 - 14.3333}{2.3813} = -2.2397$. We can use Excel's NORM.DIST function or R's pnorm function to find the p-value for a two-tailed test as $2 \times P(Z \leq -2.2397) = 0.0251$. Since the p-value is less than $\alpha = 0.05$, we reject H_0 and conclude that the machine does not properly fill the boxes. At the 5% significance level, adjustment of the machine is necessary.

The Method of Runs Above and Below the Median

As mentioned earlier, the runs test can also be applied to a numerical variable. For example, any sample with meaningful numerical observations can be treated similarly by using letters, say A and B, to denote observations falling above and below the median. The resulting A's and B's can be tested for nonrandomness by applying the **method of runs above and below the median.** This test is especially useful in detecting a trend or a cyclical pattern in economic data. A finding of too few runs is suggestive of a trend; that is, we first observe mostly A's and later mostly B's (or vice versa). In computing the value of the test statistic, we omit observations that are equal to the median. A systematic alternation of A's and B's—that is, too many runs—implies a cyclical pattern. Consider the following example.

EXAMPLE 20.10

Table 20.18 shows a portion of the growth rate in the gross domestic product (GDP) for the United States from 1990–2018. Use the method of runs above and below the median with a significance level of 10% to test the null hypothesis of randomness against the alternative that a trend or cyclical pattern exists.

TABLE 20.18 GDP Growth Rates (in percent)

FILE
US_GDP

Year	GDP
1990	1.89
1991	−0.11
⋮	⋮
2018	2.93

SOLUTION: Since we are testing the null hypothesis of randomness against the alternative that there is a trend or a cyclical pattern, we formulate the competing hypotheses as

H_0: The GDP growth rate is random.

H_A: The GDP growth rate is not random.

We first calculate the median GDP growth rate as 2.68%. Letting A denote an observation that falls above the median and B denote an observation that falls below the median, we rewrite the observations using the following sequence of A's and B's:

Sequence: BB AAAAAAAA BB AAAA BBBBBBBB A BB A

We see that the number of runs below the median R_B is 4 and the number of runs above the median R_A is also 4, so the total number of runs R is 8. Also, because one observation was discarded because it was equal to the median, the total number of observations is $n = 28$, where the number of observations above the median and the number of observations below the median are $n_A = 14$ and $n_B = 14$, respectively. Using this information, we compute the mean and the standard deviation of the distribution of R as

$$\mu_R = \frac{2n_An_B}{n} + 1 = \frac{2(14)(14)}{28} + 1 = 15 \text{ and}$$

$$\sigma_R = \sqrt{\frac{2n_An_B(2n_An_B - n)}{n^2(n-1)}} = \sqrt{\frac{(2 \times 14 \times 14)(2 \times 14 \times 14 - 28)}{28^2(28-1)}} = 2.5963.$$

Thus, the value of the test statistic is $z = \frac{R - \mu_R}{\sigma_R} = \frac{8 - 15}{2.5963} = -2.6962$. We can use Excel's NORM.DIST function or R's pnorm function to find the p-value for this two-tailed test as $2 \times P(Z \leq -2.6962) = 0.0070$. Since the p-value is less than $\alpha =$ 0.10, we reject H_0 and conclude that the observations are not random. In fact, since the observed number of runs ($R = 8$) is significantly less than the expected number of runs ($\mu_R = 15$), there is evidence of a trend. The test results, however, do not enable us to determine whether there is an upward or downward trend in the data.

Using R to Conduct the Runs Test

A. Import the ***US_GDP*** data file into a data frame (table) and label it myData. In order to implement the runs test, we then install and load the *randtests* package. Enter:

```
> install.packages("randtests")
> library(randtests)
```

B. We use R's **runs.test** function to find the value of the test statistic and the p-value. Enter

```
> runs.test(myData$GDP)
```

Table 20.19 shows the R output. We have put the value of the test statistic and the p-value in boldface; these values match those that we calculated by hand in Example 20.10.

TABLE 20.19 R's Output for the Runs Test

```
                    Runs Test
data:  myData$GDP
statistic = −2.6962, runs = 8, n1 = 14, n2 = 14, n = 28,
p-value = 0.007015
alternative hypothesis: nonrandomness
```

EXERCISES 20.6

*For exercises marked with an asterisk, it is advised that you use a statistical software package that accommodates the runs test.

Mechanics

58. Consider the following information: $n_1 = 24$, $n_2 = 28$, and $R = 18$, where R is the number of runs, n_1 and n_2 are the number of elements in a sequence possessing and not possessing a certain attribute, and $n_1 + n_2 = n$.
    a. Specify the competing hypotheses to test for nonrandomness.
    b. Calculate the value of the test statistic.
    c. Calculate the p-value.
    d. At the 5% significance level, are the observations nonrandom?

59. Consider the following information: $n_1 = 10$, $n_2 = 13$, and $R = 8$, where R is the number of runs, n_1 and n_2 are the number of elements in a sequence possessing and not possessing a certain attribute, and $n_1 + n_2 = n$.
    a. Specify the competing hypotheses to test for nonrandomness.
    b. Calculate the value of the test statistic.
    c. Calculate the p-value.
    d. At the 5% significance level, are the observations nonrandom?

60. Let A and B be two possible outcomes of a single experiment. The sequence of the outcomes is as follows:

    BBAABAABBABABBBABBAAABABBABBABA

    At the 5% significance level, conduct a hypothesis test to determine if the outcomes are nonrandom.

61. Let D denote a desirable outcome and U denote an undesirable outcome. The sequence of the outcomes is as follows:

    DDDUUDUUUUUDDDUUDUUUDDDUUUUDDD

    At the 1% significance level, conduct a hypothesis test to determine if the outcomes are nonrandom.

Applications

62. Given the digits zero through nine, a computer program is supposed to generate even and odd numbers randomly. The computer produced the following sequence of numbers:

    5 3 4 6 8 0 2 9 7 7 1 6 8 3 1 5 2 4 3 3 9 2

    a. Specify the competing hypotheses to test for nonrandomness.
    b. What is the value of the test statistic?
    c. At the 1% significance level, is the program operating improperly? Explain.

63. A gambler suspects that a coin may be weighted more heavily toward the outcome of tails (T) over heads (H). He flips the coin 25 times and notes the following sequence:

    T T H T T T H H T H T T H T T T H H T H T H T T H

    a. Specify the competing hypotheses to test the gambler's belief on nonrandomness.
    b. What is the value of the test statistic?
    c. Calculate the p-value.
    d. At the 5% significance level, is the gambler's belief supported by the data?

64.* FILE ***India_GDP.*** The accompanying data file shows the growth rate in the gross domestic product (GDP) for India from 1990 through 2018. Use the method of runs above and below the median with a significance level of 5% to test the null hypothesis of randomness against the alternative that there is a trend or a cyclical pattern.

65.* FILE ***Absenteeism.*** The superintendent of a large suburban high school must decide whether to close the school for at least two days due to the spread of flu. If she can confirm a trend in absenteeism, then she will close the high school. The accompanying data file shows the number of students absent from the high school on 25 consecutive school days. Use the method of runs above and below the median and $\alpha = 0.05$ to test the null hypothesis of randomness against the alternative hypothesis of nonrandomness.

66.* FILE *BioTech.* A financial analyst follows the daily stock price of a biotechnology firm over the past year. She wants to test the random walk hypothesis that suggests that stock prices move randomly over time with no discernible pattern.

a. Use the method of runs above and below the median to test the null hypothesis of randomness against the alternative hypothesis of nonrandomness.

b. Can the research analyst conclude that the movement of the stock price is inconsistent with the random walk hypothesis?

20.7 WRITING WITH DATA

Case Study

Lisovskaya Natalia/Shutterstock

Meg Suzuki manages a trendy sushi restaurant in Chicago, Illinois. She is planning an aggressive advertising campaign to offset the loss of business due to competition from other restaurants. She knows advertising costs increase overall costs, but she hopes this effort will positively affect sales, as it has done in the past under her tenure. She collects monthly data on sales (in $1,000s) and advertising costs (in $) over the past two years and produces the following regression equation:

$$\text{Estimated Sale} = 17.77 + 0.03\text{Advertising Costs}$$
$$t\text{-statistics} = (17.77)\ (21.07)$$

At the 5% significance level, Meg initially concludes that advertising is significant in explaining sales. However, to estimate this regression model, she had to make certain assumptions that might not be valid. Specifically, with a time series analysis, the assumption maintaining the independence of the error terms often breaks down. In other words, the regression model often suffers from correlated observations. Table 20.20 shows a portion of the residuals from the regression. Meg would like to use the runs test to determine whether the positive and negative residuals occur randomly at the 5% significance level.

FILE *Residuals*

TABLE 20.20 Residuals

Observation	Residual
1	−0.31
2	−0.80
⋮	⋮
24	0.12

Sample Report—Testing the Independence of Residuals

One of the underlying assumptions of a linear regression model is that the error term is uncorrelated across observations. In a regression model relating sales to advertising costs, there is reason to believe that correlated observations may be a problem because the data are time series. Figure 20.3 is a scatterplot of the residuals against time. If the residuals show no pattern around the horizontal axis, then the observations are not likely correlated. Given the wavelike movement in the residuals over time (clustering below the horizontal axis, then above the horizontal axis, and so on), the observations are likely correlated.

FIGURE 20.3 Scatterplot of Residuals against Time

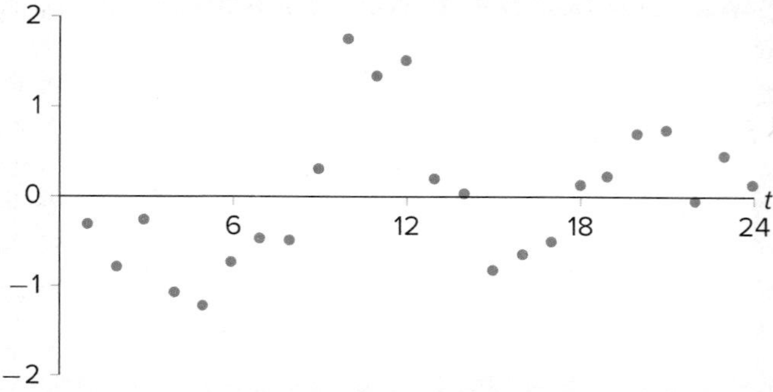

The graphical analysis is supplemented with a runs test to determine if the residuals fail to follow a random pattern. A residual is given a + symbol if the residual is positive and a – symbol if the residual is negative. There are 12 positive residuals and 12 negative residuals, or $n_+ = 12$ and $n_- = 12$, respectively. A run is then defined as an uninterrupted sequence of a + or a − sign. The sample data exhibit three positive runs, $R_+ = 3$, and three negative runs, $R_- = 3$, for a total number of runs equal to six, $R = 6$.

Are six runs consisting of 24 observations too few or too many compared with the number of runs expected in a strictly random sequence of 24 observations? To answer this question, the mean and the standard deviation for the distribution of R are calculated. The mean number of runs in a sample of 24 observations is 13 with a standard deviation of 2.3956. Table 20.21 provides summary data to conduct the runs test.

TABLE 20.21 Runs Test, $n = 24$

- Mean number of runs, $\mu_R = 13$, versus actual number of runs, $R = 6$.
- Standard deviation of the sampling distribution of R: $\sigma_R = 2.3956$
- z-statistic = −2.92; the p-value (two-tailed) = 0.0035

The sample value of the test statistic is $z = -2.92$ with an associated p-value of 0.0035. The null hypothesis of the randomness of the residuals is rejected at the 5% level; the pattern of the residuals is nonrandom. Corrective measures should be taken before statistical inference is conducted on the regression model.

Suggested Case Studies

Report 20.1 FILE ***California.*** The accompanying data file shows the sale prices (in $1,000s) for 20 homes in Southern California and 20 homes in the Inland Empire. Use the sample information to calculate and interpret relevant summary measures for home prices in these two regions of California. Use the appropriate test to determine whether the median home price in Southern California is greater than the median home price in the Inland Empire. Justify the choice of the test used for the analysis.

Report 20.2 FILE ***Compensation.*** There has been a lot of discussion lately surrounding the levels and structure of executive compensation. It is well documented that, in general, compensation received by senior executives has risen steeply in recent years. The accompanying data file shows total compensation (in $ millions) for the top 10 CEOs in four industry classifications: Manufacturing (technology); Manufacturing (other); Services (financial); Services (other). Use the sample information to calculate and interpret relevant summary measures for executive compensation in these four industries. Use the appropriate test to determine whether some median compensations vary across classifications. Justify the choice of the test used for the analysis.

Report 20.3 Go to https://finance.yahoo.com/ and extract two years of monthly adjusted closing price data for two mutual funds. For each fund, calculate monthly returns as the percentage change in adjusted closing prices from the previous month, giving 23 months of return data. Use the sample information to calculate and interpret relevant summary measures for the returns for the two mutual funds. Use the appropriate test to determine whether the median difference between the returns differs. Justify the choice of the test used for the analysis.

Report 20.4 FILE ***Consumption.*** The consumption function, developed by John Maynard Keynes, captures one of the key relationships in economics. It expresses consumption as a function of disposable income, where disposable income is defined as income after taxes. The accompanying data file shows quarterly observations for U.S. per-capita consumption (in $) and U.S. per-capita disposable income (in $) for the years 2000 through 2016. Estimate the consumption function and compute the residuals. Then perform an analysis similar to the one conducted in this section in order to determine if the regression model suffers from correlated observations.

CONCEPTUAL REVIEW

LO 20.1 Make inferences about a population median.

We use the Wilcoxon signed-rank test to test the population median. The value of the test statistic T for the Wilcoxon signed-rank test is $T = T^+$, where T^+ denotes the sum of the ranks of the positive differences from the hypothesized median m_0.

- If the sample size $n \leq 10$, then we use special tables to find the p-value. Alternatively, we rely on statistical packages, including R, to compute the value of the test statistic T and the resulting p-value.
- If the sample size $n \geq 10$, then the sampling distribution of T can also be approximated by the normal distribution. With the normal approximation, the value of the test statistic is calculated as $z = \frac{T - \mu_T}{\sigma_T}$, where $\mu_T = \frac{n(n+1)}{4}$ and $\sigma_T = \sqrt{\frac{n(n+1)(2n+1)}{24}}$.

LO 20.2 Make inferences about the population median difference based on matched-pairs sampling.

We use the Wilcoxon signed-rank test to determine whether the population median difference differs from zero based on matched-pairs sampling. The measurement of interest is the difference between paired observations, or $d_i = x_i - y_i$. We conduct the test by following steps analogous to those applied for a one-sample Wilcoxon signed-rank test.

LO 20.3 Make inferences about the difference between two population medians based on independent sampling.

We use the Wilcoxon rank-sum test to determine whether two populations have different medians based on independent sampling. We pool the data and calculate the rank sum of sample 1, W_1, and the rank sum of sample 2, W_2. The test statistic W for the Wilcoxon rank-sum test is defined as $W = W_1$.

- If either sample is less than or equal to 10, then we use special tables to find the p-value. Alternatively, we rely on statistical packages, including R, to compute the value of the test statistic W and the resulting p-value.
- If both sample sizes are greater than or equal to 10, then the sampling distribution of W can be approximated by the normal distribution. The value of the test statistic is calculated as $z = \frac{W - \mu_W}{\sigma_W}$, where $\mu_W = \frac{n_1(n_1 + n_2 + 1)}{2}$ and $\sigma_W = \sqrt{\frac{n_1 n_2(n_1 + n_2 + 1)}{12}}$.

LO 20.4 **Make inferences about the difference between three or more population medians.**

We use the Kruskal-Wallis test to test the differences between the medians of k populations. The value of the test statistic is $H = \left(\frac{12}{n(n+1)} \times \sum_{i=1}^{k} \frac{R_i^2}{n_i}\right) - 3(n+1)$, where R_i and n_i are the rank sum and the size of the ith sample, $n = \sum_{i=1}^{k} n_i$, and k is the number of populations (independent samples). So long as $n_i \geq 5$, the test statistic H follows the χ^2 distribution with $k - 1$ degrees of freedom.

LO 20.5 **Conduct a hypothesis test for the population Spearman rank correlation coefficient.**

The Spearman rank correlation coefficient r_S measures the sample correlation between two random variables. It is computed as $r_S = 1 - \frac{6\Sigma d_i^2}{n(n^2 - 1)}$, where d_i is the difference between the ranks assigned to the variables.

- If $n \leq 10$, then we use special tables to find the p-value. Alternatively, we rely on statistical packages, including R, to compute the value of the test statistics r_S and the resulting p-value.
- If the sample size $n \geq 10$, then it is reasonable to assume that the distribution of r_S is approximately normal. The resulting value of the test statistic is calculated as $z = r_S\sqrt{n - 1}$.

LO 20.6 **Make inferences about the difference between two populations of ordinal data based on matched-pairs sampling.**

We use the sign test to determine whether significant differences exist between two matched-pairs populations of ordinal-scaled observations. The value of the test statistic is computed as $z = \frac{\overline{p} - 0.5}{0.5/\sqrt{n}}$, where $\overline{p}$ is the sample proportion of plus signs. The test is valid when $n \geq 10$.

LO 20.7 **Determine whether the elements of a sequence appear in a random order.**

We use the Wald-Wolfowitz runs test to examine whether or not the attributes in a sequence appear in a random order. The sampling distribution of R, representing the number of runs, can be approximated by the normal distribution if $n_1 \geq 10$ and $n_2 \geq 10$. The value of the test statistic is computed as $z = \frac{R - \mu_R}{\sigma_R}$ where $\mu_R = \frac{2n_1n_2}{n} + 1$ and $\sigma_R = \sqrt{\frac{2n_1n_2(2n_1n_2 - n)}{n^2(n-1)}}$. We can use the runs test for a numerical variable to investigate whether the observations randomly fall above and below the sample's median. This test is also used to detect a trend or a cyclical pattern in economic data.

ADDITIONAL EXERCISES

*For exercises marked with an asterisk, it is advised to use a statistical software package that accommodates the relevant nonparametric test.

67. FILE ***PharmFirm.*** The accompanying data file shows the closing stock price (in $) for a phamaceutical firm over the past five days.
    a. Specify the competing hypotheses to determine whether the median stock price is greater than $61.25.
    b. Calculate the value of the Wilcoxon signed-rank test statistic T.
    c. The p-value for the test is found to be equal to 0.156. At the 5% significance level, is the median stock price greater than $61.25? Explain.

68. FILE ***Comparison.*** The accompanying data file shows the returns for Stock 1 and Stock 2 over the past 11 years.
    a. Specify the competing hypotheses to determine whether the median difference between the returns differs from zero.
    b. Calculate the value of the Wilcoxon signed-rank test statistic T. Assume normality of T.
    c. At the 5% significance level, does the median difference between the returns differ from zero? Explain.

69. FILE ***Fertilizer.*** A farmer is concerned that a change in fertilizer to an organic variant might change his crop yield. He subdivides six lots and uses the old fertilizer on one half of each lot and the new fertilizer on the other half. The accompanying data file shows the results.
    a. Specify the competing hypotheses to determine whether the median difference between the crop yields differs from zero.
    b. Calculate the value of the Wilcoxon signed-rank test statistic T.
    c. The p-value for the test is found to be equal to 0.915. At the 5% significance level, is there sufficient evidence to conclude that the median difference between the crop yields differs from zero? Should the farmer be concerned? Explain.

70.* FILE ***Refrigerator.*** A consumer advocate researches the length of life between two brands of refrigerators, Brand A and Brand B. He collects data on the longevity of 40 refrigerators for Brand A and repeats the sampling for Brand B. The accompanying data file shows the results.
    a. Specify the competing hypotheses to test whether the median length of life differs between the two brands.
    b. With $\alpha = 0.05$, does median longevity differ between the two brands? Explain.

71.* FILE ***Test_Centers.*** A psychiatrist believes that the location of a test center may influence a test taker's performance. To test his claim, he collects SAT scores from four different locations. The accompanying data file shows the results.
    a. Specify the competing hypotheses to test whether some median test scores differ by location.
    b. At the 5% significance level, do the data support the psychiatrist's belief? Explain.

72. FILE ***PE_Ratio.*** An economist wants to determine whether the Price/Earnings (P/E) ratio is the same for firms in three industries. Five firms were randomly selected from each industry. The accompanying data file shows the results.
    a. Specify the competing hypotheses to test whether some median P/E ratios differ by industry.
    b. Calculate the value of the test statistic H.
    c. At the 5% significance level, do some P/E ratios differ by industry? Explain.

73. A research analyst believes that a positive relationship exists between a firm's advertising expenditures and its sales. For 65 firms, she collects data on each firm's yearly advertising expenditures and subsequent sales. She calculates the Spearman rank correlation coefficient as $r_S = 0.45$.
    a. Specify the competing hypotheses to determine whether the Spearman rank correlation coefficient is greater than zero.
    b. Assume that the sampling distribution of r_S is approximately normal. Calculate the value of the test statistic and the p-value.
    c. At the 5% significance level, are advertising and sales positively correlated? Explain.

74. FILE ***Mutual_Funds2.*** The accompanying data file shows the annual returns (in %) for two mutual funds over the past 10 years.
    a. Specify the competing hypotheses to determine whether the Spearman rank correlation coefficient differs from zero.
    b. Calculate and interpret the Spearman correlation coefficient.

c. At the 5% significance level, are the returns correlated? Explain. Assume the sampling distribution of r_S is approximately normal.

75. FILE ***Inspectors.*** In order to ensure the public's health and safety, state health inspectors are required to rate the cleanliness and quality of all restaurants in the state. Restaurants that consistently score below a certain level often lose their licenses to operate. From a sample of 10 restaurants, two health inspectors give the ratings where a score of 10 denotes excellence in cleanliness and quality. The accompanying data file shows the results.
    a. Using the sign test, specify the competing hypotheses to determine whether the ratings differ between the two health inspectors.
    b. Calculate the value of the test statistic.
    c. Calculate the p-value.
    d. At the 5% significance level, do the data suggest that the ratings differ?

76.* FILE ***China_GDP.*** The accompanying data file shows the gross domestic product (GDP) for China from 1990 through 2018. Use the method of runs above and below the median with a significance level of 5% to test the null hypothesis of randomness against the alternative that there is a trend or cyclical pattern.

77.* FILE ***DJIA.*** The accompanying data file shows the daily Dow Jones Industrial Average (DJIA) for the 251 trading days in 2019. At the 5% significance level, use the method of runs above and below the median to test the random walk hypothesis that suggests that prices move randomly over time with no discernible pattern. Can you conclude that the movement of the DJIA is inconsistent with the random walk hypothesis?

78.* FILE The accompanying data file shows the U.S. inflation rate as measured by the consumer price index from 1990 through 2019. Use the method of runs above and below the median with a significance level of 5% to test the null hypothesis of randomness against the alternative hypothesis of nonrandomness.

APPENDIX 20.1 Guidelines for Other Software Packages

The following section provides brief commands for Minitab, SPSS, and JMP. Import the specified data file into the relevant software spreadsheet prior to following the commands.

Minitab

The Wilcoxon Signed-Rank Test

FILE *Mutual_Funds*

(Replicating Example 20.3) From the menu, choose **Stat > Nonparametrics > 1-Sample Wilcoxon.** Select Value for **Variables**. Select **Test median** and enter the value 5. After **Alternative,** select "greater than."

The Wilcoxon Rank-Sum Test

FILE *Salaries*

(Replicating Example 20.5) From the menu, choose **Stat > Nonparametrics > Mann-Whitney.** Select Business for the **First Sample,** and then select Journalism for the **Second Sample.** After **Alternative,** select "not equal."

The Kruskal-Wallis Test

FILE *Layout*

A. (Replicating Example 20.7) From the menu, choose **Data > Stack > Columns.** Under **Stack the following columns,** select Layout_1, Layout_2, Layout_3, and Layout_4. Label the first column of the new worksheet Layout and the second column Sales.

B. From the menu, choose **Stat, > Nonparametrics > Kruskal-Wallis.** Select Sales for **Response** and Layout for **Factor**.

The Spearman Rank Correlation Test

FILE *Mutual_Funds*

(Replicating Example 20.8) From the menu, choose **Stat > Basic Statistics > Correlation.** Under **Variables,** select Growth and Value. Select **Options** and next to **Method,** select Spearman correlation.

The Runs Test

(Replicating Example 20.10) From the menu, choose **Stat > Nonparametrics > Runs Test.** Select GDP for **Variables**. Select **Above and below,** and enter the value 2.68.

US_GDP

SPSS

The Wilcoxon Signed-Rank Test

(Replicating Example 20.3) From the menu, select **Analyze > Nonparametric Tests > One-Sample.** Select the **Settings** tab. Select **Customize tests** and then **Compare median to hypothesized (Wilcoxon signed-rank test).** Enter 5 for **Hypothesized median.**

Mutual_Funds

The Wilcoxon Rank-Sum Test

A. (Replicating Example 20.5) Reconfigure data so that all salary observations are in one column and the associated major is in the adjacent column. From the menu, choose, **Data > Restructure > Restructure selected variables into cases,** and then follow the prompts.

Salaries

B. From the menu, select **Analyze > Nonparametric Test > Legacy Dialogs > 2 Independent Samples.** Under **Test Variable,** select the salary observations and under **Grouping Variable,** select Index1 (the major). Define Group 1 and Group 2 as 1 and 2, respectively.

The Kruskal-Wallis Test

A. (Replicating Example 20.7) Reconfigure data so that all sales observations are in one column and the associated layout is in the adjacent column. From the menu, choose, **Data > Restructure > Restructure selected variables into cases,** and then follow the prompts.

Layout

B. From the menu, select **Analyze > Nonparametric Test > Legacy Dialogs > K Independent Samples.** Under **Test Variable,** select the sales observations and under **Grouping Variable,** select Index1 (layout labels). Define the Minimum and Maximum values for the Grouping Variable as 1 and 4, respectively.

The Spearman Rank Correlation Test

(Replicating Example 20.8) From the menu, choose **Analyze > Correlate > Bivariate.** Under **Variables,** select Growth and Value. Under **Correlation Coefficients,** select Spearman.

Mutual_Funds

The Runs Test

(Replicating Example 20.10) From the menu, select **Analyze > Nonparametric Tests > Legacy Dialogs > Runs.** Select GDP for **Test Variable List**. Under Cut Point, select Median.

US_GDP

JMP

The Wilcoxon Signed-Rank Test

A. (Replicating Example 20.3) From the menu, select **Analyze > Distribution.** Drag Value to **Y, Columns.**

Mutual_Funds

B. Click on the red triangle next to **Value,** and select **Test Mean.** After **Specify Hypothesized Mean,** enter 5, and check the box before **Wilcoxon Signed Rank.**

The Wilcoxon Rank-Sum Test

Salaries

A. (Replicating Example 20.5) From the menu, select **Tables > Stack.** Next to **Stack Columns,** select Business and Journalism.

B. From the menu, select **Analyze > Fit Y by X.** Drag Data to **Y, Response** and drag Label to **X, Factor**.

C. Click on the red triangle next to **Oneway Analysis of Data By Label** and select **Nonparametric > Wilcoxon Test.**

The Kruskal-Wallis Test

Layout

A. (Replicating Example 20.7) From the menu, select **Tables > Stack.** Next to **Stack Columns,** select Layout_1, Layout_2, Layout_3, and Layout_4.

B. From the menu, select **Analyze > Fit Y by X.** Drag Data to **Y, Response** and drag Label to **X, Factor.**

C. Click on the red triangle next to **Oneway Analysis of Data By Label** and select **Nonparametric > Wilcoxon Test.**

The Spearman Rank Correlation Test

Mutual_Funds

A. (Replicating Example 20.8) From the menu, choose **Analyze > Multivariate Methods > Multivariate.** Drag Growth and Value to **Y, Columns.**

B. Click the red triangle beside **Multivariate.** Select **Nonparametric Correlations > Spearman's ρ.**

Getting Started with R

What is R?

R is a powerful computer language that merges the convenience of statistical packages with the power of coding. It is open source as well as cross-platform compatible. This means that there is zero cost to download R, and it can be run on Windows, macOS, or Linux. In this appendix, we will introduce you to some fundamental features of R and provide instructions on how to obtain solutions for many of the exercises in the text.

What is RStudio?

RStudio is a program that makes R easier to use. On its own, R acts like a programming language and, as such, comes with a minimal user interface. As standalone software, R shows a single prompt for you to enter commands; this is called the Console. While everything we will ever need from R can be done by combining Console commands with other programs, things can quickly get messy. To make coding in R easier, we use an integrated development environment (IDE). IDEs are programs that combine in one place many common features needed in programming and give them a graphical user interface.[1] In this text, we use an open source version of an IDE called RStudio, which is very popular among students, professionals, and researchers who use R.

Installation

Installation of both R and RStudio is straightforward and requires no special modifications to your system. However, it should be noted that RStudio does not come with R; *therefore, both pieces of software need to be installed separately.* Also, these instructions were written in the summer of 2020. Given the constant innovation in technology, you may need to refer to the internet if some of the steps provided below do not work.

Installing R

A. Navigate to https://cran.r-project.org/.

B. In the Download and Install R box, select the link that corresponds with your operating system (Linux, Mac, or Windows). After installation, the instructions provided in the text will work regardless of your operating system.

C. Select the link *install R for the first time.*

D. Download the latest version of R, then select *Open and Run.*

E. Select *Yes* when asked about verifying the software publisher, and then select the language that you prefer. We select *English.*

F. Follow the instructions in the R Setup window.

Installing RStudio

A. Navigate to https://www.rstudio.com/products/rstudio/.

B. Select *RStudio Desktop,* then select *Download RStudio Desktop.*

[1]More formally, this is called a "graphical user interface," or a GUI. In practice, this means that charts, graphs, and buttons can be seen and used.

C. Scroll down to the *Installers for Supported Platforms* section, select the link that corresponds to your operating system, and then select *Open* or *Run*.

D. Select *Yes* when asked about verifying the software publisher.

E. Follow the instructions in the RStudio Setup window.

The Interface

Installation should now be complete. You can close all windows and then double-click on the RStudio icon.

The RStudio interface consists of several panes. By default, three panes are visible. We will refer to these by the names of the default tab shown in each: Console, Environment, and Help. We will also briefly discuss the Source pane, which is hidden until you open it. Figure A.1 shows what you should see when you open RStudio for the first time.

FIGURE A.1 The Console, Environment, and Help Panes

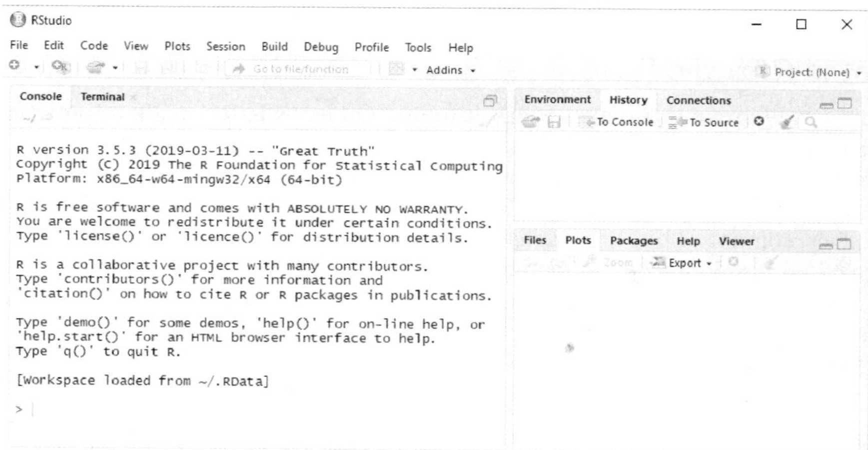

- **Console pane:** The Console pane is the primary way that you interact with R. It is here that you input commands (at the > prompt) and then view most of your output.
- **Environment pane:** Two relevant tabs in the Environment pane are: the Environment tab and the History tab. A common feature between them is the broom icon, which clears the content of each tab. The Environment tab shows the data, objects, and variables in the current R session. The History tab provides a list of all console commands issued in the session.
- **Help pane (or Files pane):** The Help pane has five tabs. We discuss two of these here: Help and Plots.
  - The Help tab is where you can view R documentation (help files). For example, to learn about the **print** function, select the Help tab and then enter print next to the magnifying glass icon. (You can also view R documentation by entering a question mark followed immediately by the topic of interest in the Console pane; so, for this example, you would enter `?print` after the prompt.)
  - The Plots tab is where you can see all graphs and charts. Any graph or chart can be cleared with the broom icon.
- **The Source pane:** The Source pane is hidden by default in R. This is where you can write your own scripts. As you will see, most of what we do in this text can be accomplished by importing a data set and then using a single command in the Console pane. Nonetheless, here is an example of how you would write a simple script:

  A. From the menu, select **File > New File > R Script**

B. In the new window, enter the following:

```
print("This is my first script.")
print("This is easy!")
```

Save the script with **File > Save As.** Name your script `Script1`. Figure A.2 shows what you should see in the Source pane.

Important: Due to different fonts and type settings, copying and pasting formulas and functions from this text directly into R may cause errors. When such errors occur, you may need to replace special characters such as quotation marks and parentheses or delete extra spaces in the functions.

FIGURE A.2 The Source Pane After Writing First Script

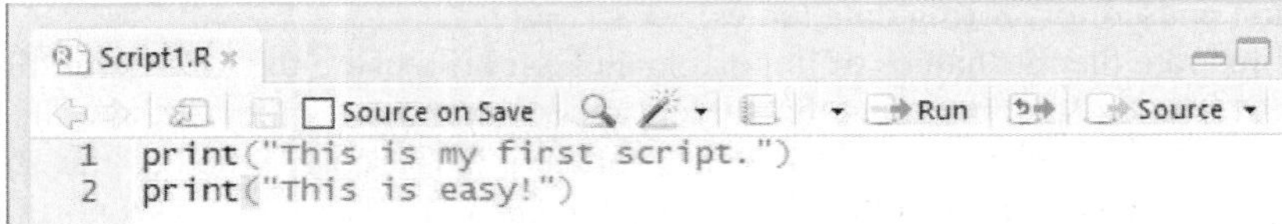

C. Again refer to Figure A.2. Click the Source button from the menu on the Source pane; this tells R to read and execute the script. Figure A.3 shows what you should see in the Console pane after executing your first script.

FIGURE A.3 The Console Pane After Executing First Script

```
Console ~/
> source('~/Script1.R')
[1] "This is my first script."
[1] "This is easy!"
>
```

R executes complete statements in the order that they appear. Unique to RStudio, there is also a way to run specific sections of scripts. This is done by highlighting the desired section of the script in RStudio and selecting the Run button from the menu on the Source pane.

Entering Data and Using Functions

Throughout this text, our goal is to provide the simplest way to obtain the relevant output. Seasoned users of R might argue that there are "better" approaches than the ones we suggest, but we feel that they may distract from learning the important concepts.

Like Excel and other statistical packages, R has many built-in formulas or functions. In the text, we denote all function names in **boldface.** Within each function, R also provides various options, such as labeling the axes of a graph, inserting colors in a chart, and so on. We will not use every option within a function; rather, we use those that we feel are most useful and least cumbersome. We denote all option names in *italics.*

Most of the time we will be importing data files, as we explain in the next section. However, suppose we want to use R to perform a simple calculation. Suppose we want to calculate the mean given the following data: −4, 0, 6, 1, −3, −4. In order to input these values into R, we use the **c** function, which combines the values to form a list; or, perhaps more mathematically precise, the **c** function combines the values to form a vector. We label this data as Example_1 and use the expression "<-" which is equivalent to the equal sign. We enter:

```
Example_1 <- c(-4, 0, 6, 1, -3, -4)
```

You should see Example_1 listed in the Environment pane. You can view the data in the Console pane by entering Example_1 after the prompt. Additionally, you can use the **View** function and the data will appear in the Source pane. (Note that R is case sensitive.) We enter:

```
View(Example_1)
```

Another common function is the **mean** function which we discuss in more detail in Chapter 3. In order to calculate the mean of the data, we enter:

```
> mean(Example_1)
```

And R returns: −0.6666667.

Importing Data and Using Functions

All the data for *Business Statistics—Communicating with Numbers* have been stored in Excel spreadsheets. We will assume that you have stored all the relevant spreadsheets in a Data folder. When we import a spreadsheet into R, it is referred to as a data frame. A data frame is a table, or two-dimensional array-like structure, in which each column contains measurements on one variable and each row contains one observation, record, or case. A data frame is used for storing data tables.

We illustrate the mechanics of importing an Excel file using the ***Admission*** data from Chapter 2. The data set contains the student record number (Student), the college decision on acceptance (Admit or Deny), the student's SAT score, whether the student is female (Yes or No), and the student's high school GPA. Table A.1 shows a portion of the ***Admission*** data.

Admission

TABLE A.1 Portion of the Admission Data

Student	Decision	SAT	Female	HSGPA
1	Deny	873	No	2.57
2	Deny	861	Yes	2.65
⋮	⋮	⋮	⋮	⋮
1230	Admit	1410	No	4.28

In order to import this data file into R, we select **File > Import Dataset > From Excel,** as shown in Figure A.4.[2] (The first time you import data, R might prompt you to add updates. Simply follow the steps to add the relevant updates.)

FIGURE A.4 Importing the Admission Data into R

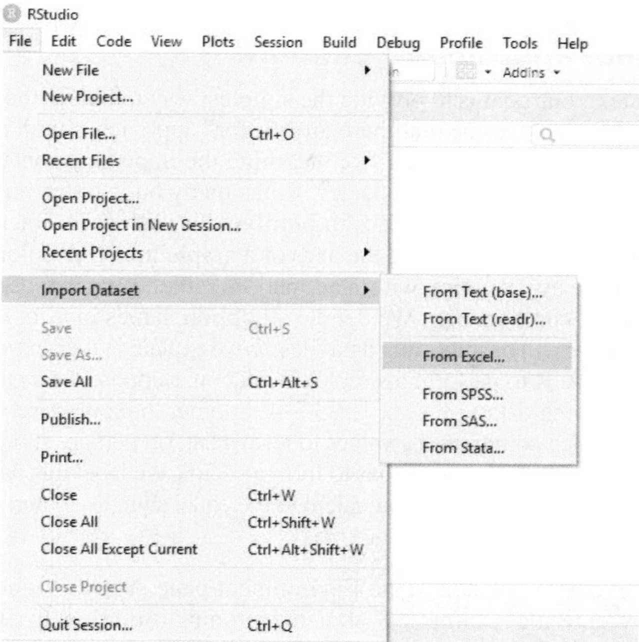

[2]Note that you can also import a comma- or tab-delimited text file by selecting **File > Import Dataset > From Text (base)** or **File > Import Dataset > From Text (readr)**, respectively.

See Figure A.5. We select the Browse button on the top right and then navigate to the ***Admission*** data in the Data folder. Once we select the ***Admission*** data, we should see the data in the *Data Preview* dialog box. In the R instructions in this text, we label all data files as myData for simplicity and consistency. Because of this, in the *Import Options* dialog box, replace Admission with myData. Once you select the Import button (see the bottom of Figure A.5), you have successfully imported the data. You can verify this in a number of ways. For instance, you should now see myData in the Environment pane under Data, or you can enter `View(myData)` in the Console pane and a portion of the data will appear in the Source pane.

FIGURE A.5 Viewing the Admission Data Prior to Importing

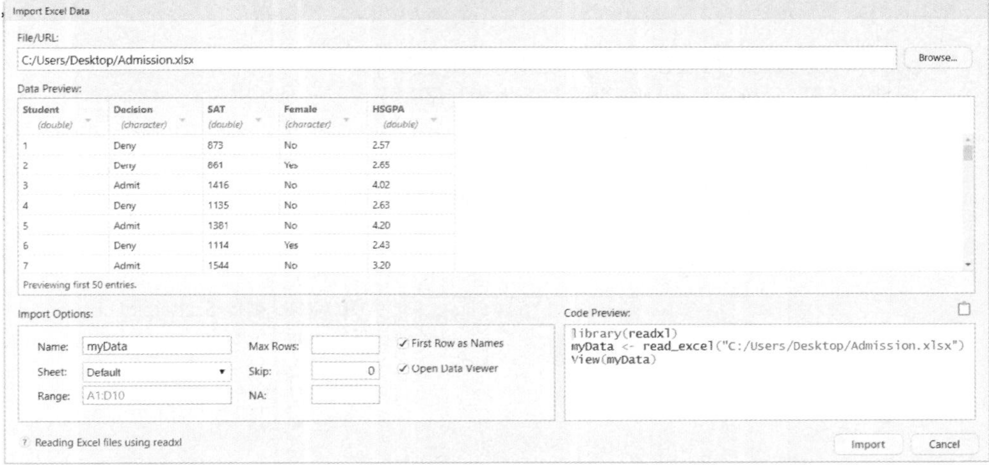

Note: For an Excel file with multiple worksheets, select the appropriate worksheet from the *Sheet* drop-down option.

Suppose we want to calculate the mean SAT score in myData. We use the mean function, and within the function, we specify the data frame and select the variable of interest by attaching the expression $Variable to the name of the data frame. Here, we enter:

```
> mean(myData$SAT)
```

And R returns: 1197.348.

If the variable name in the data frame is more than one word or numeric (such as year), then it is necessary to enclose the variable name with single quotation marks. For instance, if the variable name was SAT score instead of SAT, then we would have entered mean(myData$'SAT score').

Another function that we discuss in Chapter 3 is the **summary** function. This function provides various summary measures for all variables in a data frame. We could enter `summary(myData)` and R would return summary measures for all the variables in the myData data frame, including the categorical variables. Suppose we would like summary measures only on SAT and HSGPA. In this case, we attach square brackets to the name of the data frame, and within the brackets we indicate the columns that should be included in the calculations using the **c** function. In order to obtain summary measures for SAT (third variable) and HSGPA (fifth variable), we enter:

```
> summary(myData[,c(3,5)])
```

Notice in the above command that we enter a comma directly after the left square bracket. This implies that we are including all 1,230 observations (all 1,230 rows) in the calculations. If for some reason we only wanted to include the first 100 observations in the calculations, we would have entered `summary(myData[1:100,c(3,5)])`.

Finally, suppose we want to delete the myData data frame. We use the **rm** function and enter:

```
> rm(myData)
```

You will find that myData no longer appears under Data in the Environment pane.

A Note on Line Breaks

The commands that we have outlined here have been relatively short. There are some instances, however, when the commands get long and become difficult to read. To mitigate this, we can break up a command into parts. R will prompt you to finish the command with plus + symbols in lines following the first line. For example, in Chapter 3 we discuss a scatterplot. Suppose we want to construct a scatterplot of SAT against HSGPA for the first 20 observations using R's **plot** function. In addition to constructing the scatterplot, we use the *ylab* and *xlab* options to add titles on the *y*-axis and the *x*-axis. Two entries for constructing a scatterplot are shown below. Entry 1 uses a single line in R (even though two lines are shown on the page). Entry 2 uses three lines. Both entries result in the same scatterplot, as shown in Figure A.6.

Entry 1:

```
> plot(myData$SAT[1:20] ~ myData$HSGPA[1:20],
  ylab="SAT Score", xlab="High School GPA")
```

Entry 2:

```
> plot(myData$SAT[1:20] ~ myData$HSGPA[1:20],
  + ylab="SAT Score",
  + xlab="High School GPA")
```

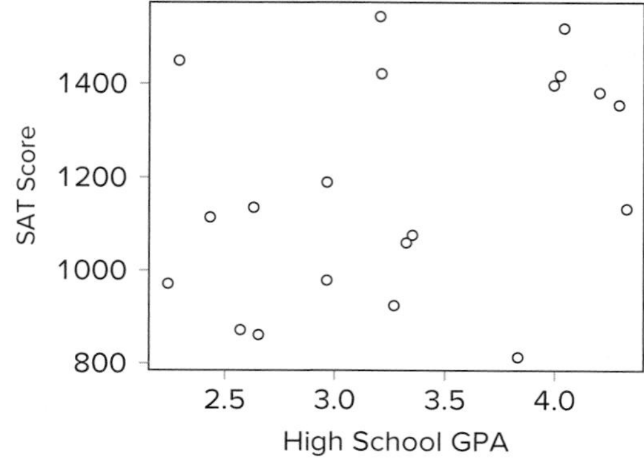

FIGURE A.6 Scatterplot of SAT against HSGPA

Packages

Part of what makes R so powerful is its large collection of packages, or collections of objects not included in the base version. Packages greatly expand what can be done with R by adding custom functions and data structures.

To use a package, you must install it and then load it. We use the *forecast* package to demonstrate how this is done. We enter:

```
> install.packages("forecast")
> library(forecast)
```

The **install.packages** function connects to the official R servers (CRAN), downloads the specified package(s) and those it depends on, and installs it. This must be done with each package only once on each computer used. The **library** function loads the installed package.

Sometimes, R may prompt you to install additional packages. If this is the case, follow the steps outlined here to download and install these additional packages.

Note that each package only needs to be loaded once per R session. Once the package is downloaded and loaded, documentation for commands it contains can be viewed in R using the help feature discussed earlier. Documentation files for an entire package can be viewed online. All information associated with available packages can be found at https://cran.r-project.org/web/packages/.

APPENDIX B

Tables

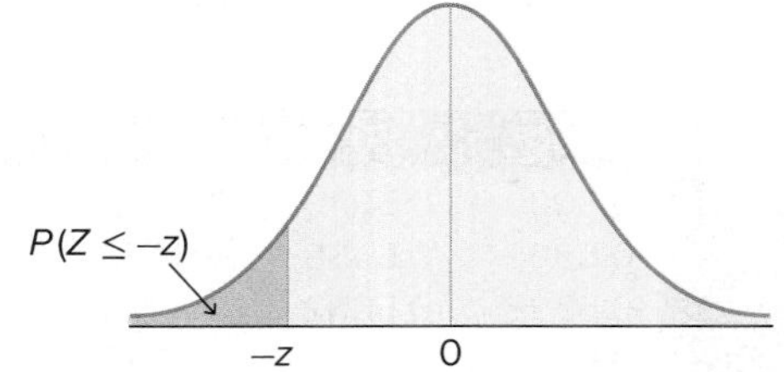

TABLE 1 Standard Normal Curve Areas

Entries in this table provide cumulative probabilities, that is, the area under the curve to the left of $-z$. For example, $P(Z \leq -1.52) = 0.0643$.

z	0.00	0.01	0.02	0.03	0.04	0.05	0.06	0.07	0.08	0.09
−3.9	0.0000	0.0000	0.0000	0.0000	0.0000	0.0000	0.0000	0.0000	0.0000	0.0000
−3.8	0.0001	0.0001	0.0001	0.0001	0.0001	0.0001	0.0001	0.0001	0.0001	0.0001
−3.7	0.0001	0.0001	0.0001	0.0001	0.0001	0.0001	0.0001	0.0001	0.0001	0.0001
−3.6	0.0002	0.0002	0.0001	0.0001	0.0001	0.0001	0.0001	0.0001	0.0001	0.0001
−3.5	0.0002	0.0002	0.0002	0.0002	0.0002	0.0002	0.0002	0.0002	0.0002	0.0002
−3.4	0.0003	0.0003	0.0003	0.0003	0.0003	0.0003	0.0003	0.0003	0.0003	0.0002
−3.3	0.0005	0.0005	0.0005	0.0004	0.0004	0.0004	0.0004	0.0004	0.0004	0.0003
−3.2	0.0007	0.0007	0.0006	0.0006	0.0006	0.0006	0.0006	0.0005	0.0005	0.0005
−3.1	0.0010	0.0009	0.0009	0.0009	0.0008	0.0008	0.0008	0.0008	0.0007	0.0007
−3.0	0.0013	0.0013	0.0013	0.0012	0.0012	0.0011	0.0011	0.0011	0.0010	0.0010
−2.9	0.0019	0.0018	0.0018	0.0017	0.0016	0.0016	0.0015	0.0015	0.0014	0.0014
−2.8	0.0026	0.0025	0.0024	0.0023	0.0023	0.0022	0.0021	0.0021	0.0020	0.0019
−2.7	0.0035	0.0034	0.0033	0.0032	0.0031	0.0030	0.0029	0.0028	0.0027	0.0026
−2.6	0.0047	0.0045	0.0044	0.0043	0.0041	0.0040	0.0039	0.0038	0.0037	0.0036
−2.5	0.0062	0.0060	0.0059	0.0057	0.0055	0.0054	0.0052	0.0051	0.0049	0.0048
−2.4	0.0082	0.0080	0.0078	0.0075	0.0073	0.0071	0.0069	0.0068	0.0066	0.0064
−2.3	0.0107	0.0104	0.0102	0.0099	0.0096	0.0094	0.0091	0.0089	0.0087	0.0084
−2.2	0.0139	0.0136	0.0132	0.0129	0.0125	0.0122	0.0119	0.0116	0.0113	0.0110
−2.1	0.0179	0.0174	0.0170	0.0166	0.0162	0.0158	0.0154	0.0150	0.0146	0.0143
−2.0	0.0228	0.0222	0.0217	0.0212	0.0207	0.0202	0.0197	0.0192	0.0188	0.0183
−1.9	0.0287	0.0281	0.0274	0.0268	0.0262	0.0256	0.0250	0.0244	0.0239	0.0233
−1.8	0.0359	0.0351	0.0344	0.0336	0.0329	0.0322	0.0314	0.0307	0.0301	0.0294
−1.7	0.0446	0.0436	0.0427	0.0418	0.0409	0.0401	0.0392	0.0384	0.0375	0.0367
−1.6	0.0548	0.0537	0.0526	0.0516	0.0505	0.0495	0.0485	0.0475	0.0465	0.0455
−1.5	0.0668	0.0655	0.0643	0.0630	0.0618	0.0606	0.0594	0.0582	0.0571	0.0559
−1.4	0.0808	0.0793	0.0778	0.0764	0.0749	0.0735	0.0721	0.0708	0.0694	0.0681
−1.3	0.0968	0.0951	0.0934	0.0918	0.0901	0.0885	0.0869	0.0853	0.0838	0.0823
−1.2	0.1151	0.1131	0.1112	0.1093	0.1075	0.1056	0.1038	0.1020	0.1003	0.0985
−1.1	0.1357	0.1335	0.1314	0.1292	0.1271	0.1251	0.1230	0.1210	0.1190	0.1170
−1.0	0.1587	0.1562	0.1539	0.1515	0.1492	0.1469	0.1446	0.1423	0.1401	0.1379
−0.9	0.1841	0.1814	0.1788	0.1762	0.1736	0.1711	0.1685	0.1660	0.1635	0.1611
−0.8	0.2119	0.2090	0.2061	0.2033	0.2005	0.1977	0.1949	0.1922	0.1894	0.1867
−0.7	0.2420	0.2389	0.2358	0.2327	0.2296	0.2266	0.2236	0.2206	0.2177	0.2148
−0.6	0.2743	0.2709	0.2676	0.2643	0.2611	0.2578	0.2546	0.2514	0.2483	0.2451
−0.5	0.3085	0.3050	0.3015	0.2981	0.2946	0.2912	0.2877	0.2843	0.2810	0.2776
−0.4	0.3446	0.3409	0.3372	0.3336	0.3300	0.3264	0.3228	0.3192	0.3156	0.3121
−0.3	0.3821	0.3783	0.3745	0.3707	0.3669	0.3632	0.3594	0.3557	0.3520	0.3483
−0.2	0.4207	0.4168	0.4129	0.4090	0.4052	0.4013	0.3974	0.3936	0.3897	0.3859
−0.1	0.4602	0.4562	0.4522	0.4483	0.4443	0.4404	0.4364	0.4325	0.4286	0.4247
−0.0	0.5000	0.4960	0.4920	0.4880	0.4840	0.4801	0.4761	0.4721	0.4681	0.4641

Source: Probabilities calculated with Excel.

TABLE 1 *(Continued)*

Entries in this table provide cumulative probabilities, that is, the area under the curve to the left of z. For example, $P(Z \leq 1.52) = 0.9357$.

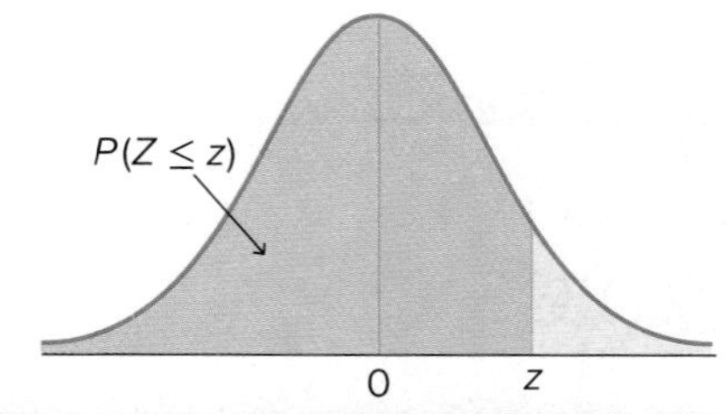

z	0.00	0.01	0.02	0.03	0.04	0.05	0.06	0.07	0.08	0.09
0.0	0.5000	0.5040	0.5080	0.5120	0.5160	0.5199	0.5239	0.5279	0.5319	0.5359
0.1	0.5398	0.5438	0.5478	0.5517	0.5557	0.5596	0.5636	0.5675	0.5714	0.5753
0.2	0.5793	0.5832	0.5871	0.5910	0.5948	0.5987	0.6026	0.6064	0.6103	0.6141
0.3	0.6179	0.6217	0.6255	0.6293	0.6331	0.6368	0.6406	0.6443	0.6480	0.6517
0.4	0.6554	0.6591	0.6628	0.6664	0.6700	0.6736	0.6772	0.6808	0.6844	0.6879
0.5	0.6915	0.6950	0.6985	0.7019	0.7054	0.7088	0.7123	0.7157	0.7190	0.7224
0.6	0.7257	0.7291	0.7324	0.7357	0.7389	0.7422	0.7454	0.7486	0.7517	0.7549
0.7	0.7580	0.7611	0.7642	0.7673	0.7704	0.7734	0.7764	0.7794	0.7823	0.7852
0.8	0.7881	0.7910	0.7939	0.7967	0.7995	0.8023	0.8051	0.8078	0.8106	0.8133
0.9	0.8159	0.8186	0.8212	0.8238	0.8264	0.8289	0.8315	0.8340	0.8365	0.8389
1.0	0.8413	0.8438	0.8461	0.8485	0.8508	0.8531	0.8554	0.8577	0.8599	0.8621
1.1	0.8643	0.8665	0.8686	0.8708	0.8729	0.8749	0.8770	0.8790	0.8810	0.8830
1.2	0.8849	0.8869	0.8888	0.8907	0.8925	0.8944	0.8962	0.8980	0.8997	0.9015
1.3	0.9032	0.9049	0.9066	0.9082	0.9099	0.9115	0.9131	0.9147	0.9162	0.9177
1.4	0.9192	0.9207	0.9222	0.9236	0.9251	0.9265	0.9279	0.9292	0.9306	0.9319
1.5	0.9332	0.9345	0.9357	0.9370	0.9382	0.9394	0.9406	0.9418	0.9429	0.9441
1.6	0.9452	0.9463	0.9474	0.9484	0.9495	0.9505	0.9515	0.9525	0.9535	0.9545
1.7	0.9554	0.9564	0.9573	0.9582	0.9591	0.9599	0.9608	0.9616	0.9625	0.9633
1.8	0.9641	0.9649	0.9656	0.9664	0.9671	0.9678	0.9686	0.9693	0.9699	0.9706
1.9	0.9713	0.9719	0.9726	0.9732	0.9738	0.9744	0.9750	0.9756	0.9761	0.9767
2.0	0.9772	0.9778	0.9783	0.9788	0.9793	0.9798	0.9803	0.9808	0.9812	0.9817
2.1	0.9821	0.9826	0.9830	0.9834	0.9838	0.9842	0.9846	0.9850	0.9854	0.9857
2.2	0.9861	0.9864	0.9868	0.9871	0.9875	0.9878	0.9881	0.9884	0.9887	0.9890
2.3	0.9893	0.9896	0.9898	0.9901	0.9904	0.9906	0.9909	0.9911	0.9913	0.9916
2.4	0.9918	0.9920	0.9922	0.9925	0.9927	0.9929	0.9931	0.9932	0.9934	0.9936
2.5	0.9938	0.9940	0.9941	0.9943	0.9945	0.9946	0.9948	0.9949	0.9951	0.9952
2.6	0.9953	0.9955	0.9956	0.9957	0.9959	0.9960	0.9961	0.9962	0.9963	0.9964
2.7	0.9965	0.9966	0.9967	0.9968	0.9969	0.9970	0.9971	0.9972	0.9973	0.9974
2.8	0.9974	0.9975	0.9976	0.9977	0.9977	0.9978	0.9979	0.9979	0.9980	0.9981
2.9	0.9981	0.9982	0.9982	0.9983	0.9984	0.9984	0.9985	0.9985	0.9986	0.9986
3.0	0.9987	0.9987	0.9987	0.9988	0.9988	0.9989	0.9989	0.9989	0.9990	0.9990
3.1	0.9990	0.9991	0.9991	0.9991	0.9992	0.9992	0.9992	0.9992	0.9993	0.9993
3.2	0.9993	0.9993	0.9994	0.9994	0.9994	0.9994	0.9994	0.9995	0.9995	0.9995
3.3	0.9995	0.9995	0.9995	0.9996	0.9996	0.9996	0.9996	0.9996	0.9996	0.9997
3.4	0.9997	0.9997	0.9997	0.9997	0.9997	0.9997	0.9997	0.9997	0.9997	0.9998
3.5	0.9998	0.9998	0.9998	0.9998	0.9998	0.9998	0.9998	0.9998	0.9998	0.9998
3.6	0.9998	0.9998	0.9999	0.9999	0.9999	0.9999	0.9999	0.9999	0.9999	0.9999
3.7	0.9999	0.9999	0.9999	0.9999	0.9999	0.9999	0.9999	0.9999	0.9999	0.9999
3.8	0.9999	0.9999	0.9999	0.9999	0.9999	0.9999	0.9999	0.9999	0.9999	0.9999
3.9	1.0000	1.0000	1.0000	1.0000	1.0000	1.0000	1.0000	1.0000	1.0000	1.0000

Source: Probabilities calculated with Excel.

TABLE 2 Student's *t* Distribution

Entries in this table provide the values of $t_{\alpha,df}$ that correspond to a given upper-tail area α and a specified number of degrees of freedom df. For example, for $\alpha = 0.05$ and $df = 10$, $P(T_{10} \geq 1.812) = 0.05$.

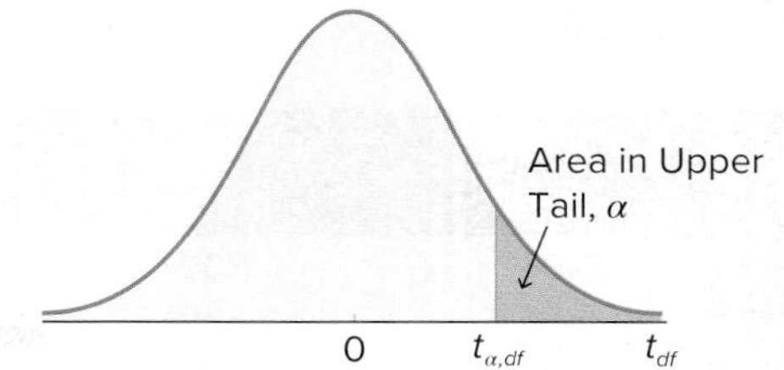

	α					
df	**0.20**	**0.10**	**0.05**	**0.025**	**0.01**	**0.005**
1	1.376	3.078	6.314	12.706	31.821	63.657
2	1.061	1.886	2.920	4.303	6.965	9.925
3	0.978	1.638	2.353	3.182	4.541	5.841
4	0.941	1.533	2.132	2.776	3.747	4.604
5	0.920	1.476	2.015	2.571	3.365	4.032
6	0.906	1.440	1.943	2.447	3.143	3.707
7	0.896	1.415	1.895	2.365	2.998	3.499
8	0.889	1.397	1.860	2.306	2.896	3.355
9	0.883	1.383	1.833	2.262	2.821	3.250
10	0.879	1.372	1.812	2.228	2.764	3.169
11	0.876	1.363	1.796	2.201	2.718	3.106
12	0.873	1.356	1.782	2.179	2.681	3.055
13	0.870	1.350	1.771	2.160	2.650	3.012
14	0.868	1.345	1.761	2.145	2.624	2.977
15	0.866	1.341	1.753	2.131	2.602	2.947
16	0.865	1.337	1.746	2.120	2.583	2.921
17	0.863	1.333	1.740	2.110	2.567	2.898
18	0.862	1.330	1.734	2.101	2.552	2.878
19	0.861	1.328	1.729	2.093	2.539	2.861
20	0.860	1.325	1.725	2.086	2.528	2.845
21	0.859	1.323	1.721	2.080	2.518	2.831
22	0.858	1.321	1.717	2.074	2.508	2.819
23	0.858	1.319	1.714	2.069	2.500	2.807
24	0.857	1.318	1.711	2.064	2.492	2.797
25	0.856	1.316	1.708	2.060	2.485	2.787
26	0.856	1.315	1.706	2.056	2.479	2.779
27	0.855	1.314	1.703	2.052	2.473	2.771
28	0.855	1.313	1.701	2.048	2.467	2.763
29	0.854	1.311	1.699	2.045	2.462	2.756
30	0.854	1.310	1.697	2.042	2.457	2.750

TABLE 2 *(Continued)*

	α					
df	**0.20**	**0.10**	**0.05**	**0.025**	**0.01**	**0.005**
31	0.853	1.309	1.696	2.040	2.453	2.744
32	0.853	1.309	1.694	2.037	2.449	2.738
33	0.853	1.308	1.692	2.035	2.445	2.733
34	0.852	1.307	1.691	2.032	2.441	2.728
35	0.852	1.306	1.690	2.030	2.438	2.724
36	0.852	1.306	1.688	2.028	2.434	2.719
37	0.851	1.305	1.687	2.026	2.431	2.715
38	0.851	1.304	1.686	2.024	2.429	2.712
39	0.851	1.304	1.685	2.023	2.426	2.708
40	0.851	1.303	1.684	2.021	2.423	2.704
41	0.850	1.303	1.683	2.020	2.421	2.701
42	0.850	1.302	1.682	2.018	2.418	2.698
43	0.850	1.302	1.681	2.017	2.416	2.695
44	0.850	1.301	1.680	2.015	2.414	2.692
45	0.850	1.301	1.679	2.014	2.412	2.690
46	0.850	1.300	1.679	2.013	2.410	2.687
47	0.849	1.300	1.678	2.012	2.408	2.685
48	0.849	1.299	1.677	2.011	2.407	2.682
49	0.849	1.299	1.677	2.010	2.405	2.680
50	0.849	1.299	1.676	2.009	2.403	2.678
51	0.849	1.298	1.675	2.008	2.402	2.676
52	0.849	1.298	1.675	2.007	2.400	2.674
53	0.848	1.298	1.674	2.006	2.399	2.672
54	0.848	1.297	1.674	2.005	2.397	2.670
55	0.848	1.297	1.673	2.004	2.396	2.668
56	0.848	1.297	1.673	2.003	2.395	2.667
57	0.848	1.297	1.672	2.002	2.394	2.665
58	0.848	1.296	1.672	2.002	2.392	2.663
59	0.848	1.296	1.671	2.001	2.391	2.662
60	0.848	1.296	1.671	2.000	2.390	2.660
80	0.846	1.292	1.664	1.990	2.374	2.639
100	0.845	1.290	1.660	1.984	2.364	2.626
150	0.844	1.287	1.655	1.976	2.351	2.609
200	0.843	1.286	1.653	1.972	2.345	2.601
500	0.842	1.283	1.648	1.965	2.334	2.586
1000	0.842	1.282	1.646	1.962	2.330	2.581
∞	0.842	1.282	1.645	1.960	2.326	2.576

Source: *t* values calculated with Excel.

TABLE 3 χ^2 (Chi-Square) Distribution

Entries in this table provide the values of $\chi^2_{\alpha,df}$ that correspond to a given upper-tail area α and a specified number of degrees of freedom df. For example, for $\alpha = 0.05$ and $df = 10$, $P(\chi^2_{10} \geq 18.307) = 0.05$.

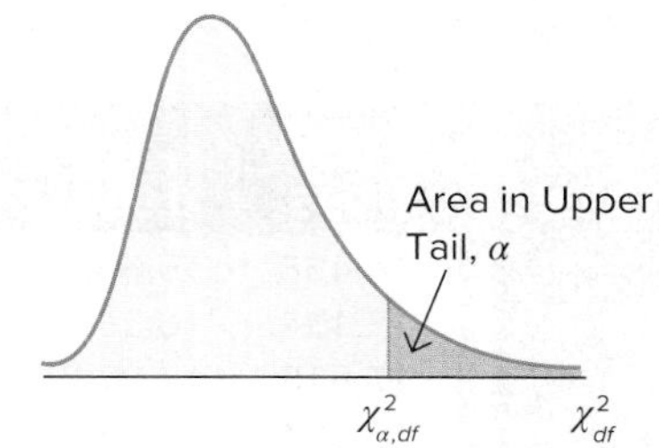

df	α = 0.995	0.990	0.975	0.950	0.900	0.100	0.050	0.025	0.010	0.005
1	0.000	0.000	0.001	0.004	0.016	2.706	3.841	5.024	6.635	7.879
2	0.010	0.020	0.051	0.103	0.211	4.605	5.991	7.378	9.210	10.597
3	0.072	0.115	0.216	0.352	0.584	6.251	7.815	9.348	11.345	12.838
4	0.207	0.297	0.484	0.711	1.064	7.779	9.488	11.143	13.277	14.860
5	0.412	0.554	0.831	1.145	1.610	9.236	11.070	12.833	15.086	16.750
6	0.676	0.872	1.237	1.635	2.204	10.645	12.592	14.449	16.812	18.548
7	0.989	1.239	1.690	2.167	2.833	12.017	14.067	16.013	18.475	20.278
8	1.344	1.646	2.180	2.733	3.490	13.362	15.507	17.535	20.090	21.955
9	1.735	2.088	2.700	3.325	4.168	14.684	16.919	19.023	21.666	23.589
10	2.156	2.558	3.247	3.940	4.865	15.987	18.307	20.483	23.209	25.188
11	2.603	3.053	3.816	4.575	5.578	17.275	19.675	21.920	24.725	26.757
12	3.074	3.571	4.404	5.226	6.304	18.549	21.026	23.337	26.217	28.300
13	3.565	4.107	5.009	5.892	7.042	19.812	22.362	24.736	27.688	29.819
14	4.075	4.660	5.629	6.571	7.790	21.064	23.685	26.119	29.141	31.319
15	4.601	5.229	6.262	7.261	8.547	22.307	24.996	27.488	30.578	32.801
16	5.142	5.812	6.908	7.962	9.312	23.542	26.296	28.845	32.000	34.267
17	5.697	6.408	7.564	8.672	10.085	24.769	27.587	30.191	33.409	35.718
18	6.265	7.015	8.231	9.390	10.865	25.989	28.869	31.526	34.805	37.156
19	6.844	7.633	8.907	10.117	11.651	27.204	30.144	32.852	36.191	38.582
20	7.434	8.260	9.591	10.851	12.443	28.412	31.410	34.170	37.566	39.997
21	8.034	8.897	10.283	11.591	13.240	29.615	32.671	35.479	38.932	41.401
22	8.643	9.542	10.982	12.338	14.041	30.813	33.924	36.781	40.289	42.796
23	9.260	10.196	11.689	13.091	14.848	32.007	35.172	38.076	41.638	44.181
24	9.886	10.856	12.401	13.848	15.659	33.196	36.415	39.364	42.980	45.559
25	10.520	11.524	13.120	14.611	16.473	34.382	37.652	40.646	44.314	46.928
26	11.160	12.198	13.844	15.379	17.292	35.563	38.885	41.923	45.642	48.290
27	11.808	12.879	14.573	16.151	18.114	36.741	40.113	43.195	46.963	49.645
28	12.461	13.565	15.308	16.928	18.939	37.916	41.337	44.461	48.278	50.993
29	13.121	14.256	16.047	17.708	19.768	39.087	42.557	45.722	49.588	52.336
30	13.787	14.953	16.791	18.493	20.599	40.256	43.773	46.979	50.892	53.672

TABLE 3 *(Continued)*

	α									
df	0.995	0.990	0.975	0.950	0.900	0.100	0.050	0.025	0.010	0.005
31	14.458	15.655	17.539	19.281	21.434	41.422	44.985	48.232	52.191	55.003
32	15.134	16.362	18.291	20.072	22.271	42.585	46.194	49.480	53.486	56.328
33	15.815	17.074	19.047	20.867	23.110	43.745	47.400	50.725	54.776	57.648
34	16.501	17.789	19.806	21.664	23.952	44.903	48.602	51.966	56.061	58.964
35	17.192	18.509	20.569	22.465	24.797	46.059	49.802	53.203	57.342	60.275
36	17.887	19.233	21.336	23.269	25.643	47.212	50.998	54.437	58.619	61.581
37	18.586	19.960	22.106	24.075	26.492	48.363	52.192	55.668	59.893	62.883
38	19.289	20.691	22.878	24.884	27.343	49.513	53.384	56.896	61.162	64.181
39	19.996	21.426	23.654	25.695	28.196	50.660	54.572	58.120	62.428	65.476
40	20.707	22.164	24.433	26.509	29.051	51.805	55.758	59.342	63.691	66.766
41	21.421	22.906	25.215	27.326	29.907	52.949	56.942	60.561	64.950	68.053
42	22.138	23.650	25.999	28.144	30.765	54.090	58.124	61.777	66.206	69.336
43	22.859	24.398	26.785	28.965	31.625	55.230	59.304	62.990	67.459	70.616
44	23.584	25.148	27.575	29.787	32.487	56.369	60.481	64.201	68.710	71.893
45	24.311	25.901	28.366	30.612	33.350	57.505	61.656	65.410	69.957	73.166
46	25.041	26.657	29.160	31.439	34.215	58.641	62.830	66.617	71.201	74.437
47	25.775	27.416	29.956	32.268	35.081	59.774	64.001	67.821	72.443	75.704
48	26.511	28.177	30.755	33.098	35.949	60.907	65.171	69.023	73.683	76.969
49	27.249	28.941	31.555	33.930	36.818	62.038	66.339	70.222	74.919	78.231
50	27.991	29.707	32.357	34.764	37.689	63.167	67.505	71.420	76.154	79.490
55	31.735	33.570	36.398	38.958	42.060	68.796	73.311	77.380	82.292	85.749
60	35.534	37.485	40.482	43.188	46.459	74.397	79.082	83.298	88.379	91.952
65	39.383	41.444	44.603	47.450	50.883	79.973	84.821	89.177	94.422	98.105
70	43.275	45.442	48.758	51.739	55.329	85.527	90.531	95.023	100.425	104.215
75	47.206	49.475	52.942	56.054	59.795	91.061	96.217	100.839	106.393	110.286
80	51.172	53.540	57.153	60.391	64.278	96.578	101.879	106.629	112.329	116.321
85	55.170	57.634	61.389	64.749	68.777	102.079	107.522	112.393	118.236	122.325
90	59.196	61.754	65.647	69.126	73.291	107.565	113.145	118.136	124.116	128.299
95	63.250	65.898	69.925	73.520	77.818	113.038	118.752	123.858	129.973	134.247
100	67.328	70.065	74.222	77.929	82.358	118.498	124.342	129.561	135.807	140.169

Source: χ^2 values calculated with Excel.

TABLE 4 *F* Distribution

Entries in this table provide the values of $F_{\alpha,(df_1,df_2)}$ that correspond to a given upper-tail area α and a specified number of degrees of freedom in the numerator df_1 and degrees of freedom in the denominator df_2. For example, for $\alpha = 0.05$, $df_1 = 8$, and $df_2 = 6$, $P(F_{(8,6)} \geq 4.15) = 0.05$.

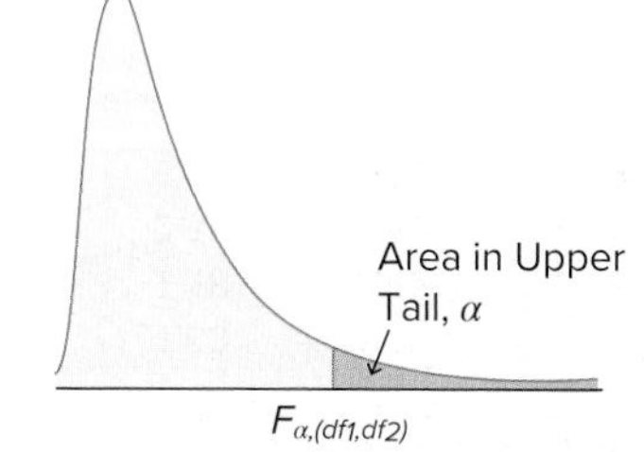

df_2	α	df_1 1	2	3	4	5	6	7	8	9	10	15	25	50	100	500
1	0.10	39.86	49.50	53.59	55.83	57.24	58.2	58.91	59.44	59.86	60.19	61.22	62.05	62.69	63.01	63.26
	0.05	161.45	199.50	215.71	224.58	230.16	233.99	236.77	238.88	240.54	241.88	245.95	249.26	251.77	253.04	254.06
	0.025	647.79	799.50	864.16	899.58	921.85	937.11	948.22	956.66	963.28	968.63	984.87	998.08	1008.12	1013.17	1017.24
	0.01	4052.18	4999.50	5403.35	5624.58	5763.65	5858.99	5928.36	5981.07	6022.47	6055.85	6157.28	6239.83	6302.52	6334.11	6359.50
2	0.10	8.53	9.00	9.16	9.24	9.29	9.33	9.35	9.37	9.38	9.39	9.42	9.45	9.47	9.48	9.49
	0.05	18.51	19.00	19.16	19.25	19.30	19.33	19.35	19.37	19.38	19.40	19.43	19.46	19.48	19.49	19.49
	0.025	38.51	39.00	39.17	39.25	39.30	39.33	39.36	39.37	39.39	39.40	39.43	39.46	39.48	39.49	39.50
	0.01	98.50	99.00	99.17	99.25	99.30	99.33	99.36	99.37	99.39	99.40	99.43	99.46	99.48	99.49	99.50
3	0.10	5.54	5.46	5.39	5.34	5.31	5.28	5.27	5.25	5.24	5.23	5.20	5.17	5.15	5.14	5.14
	0.05	10.13	9.55	9.28	9.12	9.01	8.94	8.89	8.85	8.81	8.79	8.70	8.63	8.58	8.55	8.53
	0.025	17.44	16.04	15.44	15.10	14.88	14.73	14.62	14.54	14.47	14.42	14.25	14.12	14.01	13.96	13.91
	0.01	34.12	30.82	29.46	28.71	28.24	27.91	27.67	27.49	27.35	27.23	26.87	26.58	26.35	26.24	26.15
4	0.10	4.54	4.32	4.19	4.11	4.05	4.01	3.98	3.95	3.94	3.92	3.87	3.83	3.80	3.78	3.76
	0.05	7.71	6.94	6.59	6.39	6.26	6.16	6.09	6.04	6.00	5.96	5.86	5.77	5.70	5.66	5.64
	0.025	12.22	10.65	9.98	9.60	9.36	9.20	9.07	8.98	8.90	8.84	8.66	8.50	8.38	8.32	8.27
	0.01	21.20	18.00	16.69	15.98	15.52	15.21	14.98	14.80	14.66	14.55	14.20	13.91	13.69	13.58	13.49
5	0.10	4.06	3.78	3.62	3.52	3.45	3.40	3.37	3.34	3.32	3.30	3.24	3.19	3.15	3.13	3.11
	0.05	6.61	5.79	5.41	5.19	5.05	4.95	4.88	4.82	4.77	4.74	4.62	4.52	4.44	4.41	4.37
	0.025	10.01	8.43	7.76	7.39	7.15	6.98	6.85	6.76	6.68	6.62	6.43	6.27	6.14	6.08	6.03
	0.01	16.26	13.27	12.06	11.39	10.97	10.67	10.46	10.29	10.16	10.05	9.72	9.45	9.24	9.13	9.04
6	0.10	3.78	3.46	3.29	3.18	3.11	3.05	3.01	2.98	2.96	2.94	2.87	2.81	2.77	2.75	2.73
	0.05	5.99	5.14	4.76	4.53	4.39	4.28	4.21	4.15	4.10	4.06	3.94	3.83	3.75	3.71	3.68
	0.025	8.81	7.26	6.60	6.23	5.99	5.82	5.70	5.60	5.52	5.46	5.27	5.11	4.98	4.92	4.86
	0.01	13.75	10.92	9.78	9.15	8.75	8.47	8.26	8.10	7.98	7.87	7.56	7.30	7.09	6.99	6.90
7	0.10	3.59	3.26	3.07	2.96	2.88	2.83	2.78	2.75	2.72	2.70	2.63	2.57	2.52	2.50	2.48
	0.05	5.59	4.74	4.35	4.12	3.97	3.87	3.79	3.73	3.68	3.64	3.51	3.40	3.32	3.27	3.24
	0.025	8.07	6.54	5.89	5.52	5.29	5.12	4.99	4.90	4.82	4.76	4.57	4.40	4.28	4.21	4.16
	0.01	12.25	9.55	8.45	7.85	7.46	7.19	6.99	6.84	6.72	6.62	6.31	6.06	5.86	5.75	5.67

TABLE 4 (*Continued*)

df_2	α	df_1 1	2	3	4	5	6	7	8	9	10	15	25	50	100	500
8	0.10	3.46	3.11	2.92	2.81	2.73	2.67	2.62	2.59	2.56	2.54	2.46	2.40	2.35	2.32	2.30
	0.05	5.32	4.46	4.07	3.84	3.69	3.58	3.50	3.44	3.39	3.35	3.22	3.11	3.02	2.97	2.94
	0.025	7.57	6.06	5.42	5.05	4.82	4.65	4.53	4.43	4.36	4.30	4.10	3.94	3.81	3.74	3.68
	0.01	11.26	8.65	7.59	7.01	6.63	6.37	6.18	6.03	5.91	5.81	5.52	5.26	5.07	4.96	4.88
9	0.10	3.36	3.01	2.81	2.69	2.61	2.55	2.51	2.47	2.44	2.42	2.34	2.27	2.22	2.19	2.17
	0.05	5.12	4.26	3.86	3.63	3.48	3.37	3.29	3.23	3.18	3.14	3.01	2.89	2.80	2.76	2.72
	0.025	7.21	5.71	5.08	4.72	4.48	4.32	4.20	4.10	4.03	3.96	3.77	3.60	3.47	3.40	3.35
	0.01	10.56	8.02	6.99	6.42	6.06	5.80	5.61	5.47	5.35	5.26	4.96	4.71	4.52	4.41	4.33
10	0.10	3.29	2.92	2.73	2.61	2.52	2.46	2.41	2.38	2.35	2.32	2.24	2.17	2.12	2.09	2.06
	0.05	4.96	4.10	3.71	3.48	3.33	3.22	3.14	3.07	3.02	2.98	2.85	2.73	2.64	2.59	2.55
	0.025	6.94	5.46	4.83	4.47	4.24	4.07	3.95	3.85	3.78	3.72	3.52	3.35	3.22	3.15	3.09
	0.01	10.04	7.56	6.55	5.99	5.64	5.39	5.20	5.06	4.94	4.85	4.56	4.31	4.12	4.01	3.93
11	0.10	3.23	2.86	2.66	2.54	2.45	2.39	2.34	2.30	2.27	2.25	2.17	2.10	2.04	2.01	1.98
	0.05	4.84	3.98	3.59	3.36	3.20	3.09	3.01	2.95	2.90	2.85	2.72	2.60	2.51	2.46	2.42
	0.025	6.72	5.26	4.63	4.28	4.04	3.88	3.76	3.66	3.59	3.53	3.33	3.16	3.03	2.96	2.90
	0.01	9.65	7.21	6.22	5.67	5.32	5.07	4.89	4.74	4.63	4.54	4.25	4.01	3.81	3.71	3.62
12	0.10	3.18	2.81	2.61	2.48	2.39	2.33	2.28	2.24	2.21	2.19	2.10	2.03	1.97	1.94	1.91
	0.05	4.75	3.89	3.49	3.26	3.11	3.00	2.91	2.85	2.80	2.75	2.62	2.50	2.40	2.35	2.31
	0.025	6.55	5.10	4.47	4.12	3.89	3.73	3.61	3.51	3.44	3.37	3.18	3.01	2.87	2.80	2.74
	0.01	9.33	6.93	5.95	5.41	5.06	4.82	4.64	4.50	4.39	4.30	4.01	3.76	3.57	3.47	3.38
13	0.10	3.14	2.76	2.56	2.43	2.35	2.28	2.23	2.20	2.16	2.14	2.05	1.98	1.92	1.88	1.85
	0.05	4.67	3.81	3.41	3.18	3.03	2.92	2.83	2.77	2.71	2.67	2.53	2.41	2.31	2.26	2.22
	0.025	6.41	4.97	4.35	4.00	3.77	3.60	3.48	3.39	3.31	3.25	3.05	2.88	2.74	2.67	2.61
	0.01	9.07	6.70	5.74	5.21	4.86	4.62	4.44	4.30	4.19	4.10	3.82	3.57	3.38	3.27	3.19
14	0.10	3.10	2.73	2.52	2.39	2.31	2.24	2.19	2.15	2.12	2.10	2.01	1.93	1.87	1.83	1.80
	0.05	4.60	3.74	3.34	3.11	2.96	2.85	2.76	2.70	2.65	2.60	2.46	2.34	2.24	2.19	2.14
	0.025	6.30	4.86	4.24	3.89	3.66	3.50	3.38	3.29	3.21	3.15	2.95	2.78	2.64	2.56	2.50
	0.01	8.86	6.51	5.56	5.04	4.69	4.46	4.28	4.14	4.03	3.94	3.66	3.41	3.22	3.11	3.03
15	0.10	3.07	2.70	2.49	2.36	2.27	2.21	2.16	2.12	2.09	2.06	1.97	1.89	1.83	1.79	1.76
	0.05	4.54	3.68	3.29	3.06	2.90	2.79	2.71	2.64	2.59	2.54	2.40	2.28	2.18	2.12	2.08
	0.025	6.20	4.77	4.15	3.80	3.58	3.41	3.29	3.20	3.12	3.06	2.86	2.69	2.55	2.47	2.41
	0.01	8.68	6.36	5.42	4.89	4.56	4.32	4.14	4.00	3.89	3.80	3.52	3.28	3.08	2.98	2.89
16	0.10	3.05	2.67	2.46	2.33	2.24	2.18	2.13	2.09	2.06	2.03	1.94	1.86	1.79	1.76	1.73
	0.05	4.49	3.63	3.24	3.01	2.85	2.74	2.66	2.59	2.54	2.49	2.35	2.23	2.12	2.07	2.02
	0.025	6.12	4.69	4.08	3.73	3.50	3.34	3.22	3.12	3.05	2.99	2.79	2.61	2.47	2.40	2.33
	0.01	8.53	6.23	5.29	4.77	4.44	4.20	4.03	3.89	3.78	3.69	3.41	3.16	2.97	2.86	2.78

df_2	α	df_1 = 1	2	3	4	5	6	7	8	9	10	15	25	50	100	500
17	0.10	3.03	2.64	2.44	2.31	2.22	2.15	2.10	2.06	2.03	2.00	1.91	1.83	1.76	1.73	1.69
	0.05	4.45	3.59	3.20	2.96	2.81	2.70	2.61	2.55	2.49	2.45	2.31	2.18	2.08	2.02	1.97
	0.025	6.04	4.62	4.01	3.66	3.44	3.28	3.16	3.06	2.98	2.92	2.72	2.55	2.41	2.33	2.26
	0.01	8.40	6.11	5.18	4.67	4.34	4.10	3.93	3.79	3.68	3.59	3.31	3.07	2.87	2.76	2.68
18	0.10	3.01	2.62	2.42	2.29	2.20	2.13	2.08	2.04	2.00	1.98	1.89	1.80	1.74	1.70	1.67
	0.05	4.41	3.55	3.16	2.93	2.77	2.66	2.58	2.51	2.46	2.41	2.27	2.14	2.04	1.98	1.93
	0.025	5.98	4.56	3.95	3.61	3.38	3.22	3.10	3.01	2.93	2.87	2.67	2.49	2.35	2.27	2.20
	0.01	8.29	6.01	5.09	4.58	4.25	4.01	3.84	3.71	3.60	3.51	3.23	2.98	2.78	2.68	2.59
19	0.10	2.99	2.61	2.40	2.27	2.18	2.11	2.06	2.02	1.98	1.96	1.86	1.78	1.71	1.67	1.64
	0.05	4.38	3.52	3.13	2.90	2.74	2.63	2.54	2.48	2.42	2.38	2.23	2.11	2.00	1.94	1.89
	0.025	5.92	4.51	3.90	3.56	3.33	3.17	3.05	2.96	2.88	2.82	2.62	2.44	2.30	2.22	2.15
	0.01	8.18	5.93	5.01	4.50	4.17	3.94	3.77	3.63	3.52	3.43	3.15	2.91	2.71	2.60	2.51
20	0.10	2.97	2.59	2.38	2.25	2.16	2.09	2.04	2.00	1.96	1.94	1.84	1.76	1.69	1.65	1.62
	0.05	4.35	3.49	3.10	2.87	2.71	2.60	2.51	2.45	2.39	2.35	2.20	2.07	1.97	1.91	1.86
	0.025	5.87	4.46	3.86	3.51	3.29	3.13	3.01	2.91	2.84	2.77	2.57	2.40	2.25	2.17	2.10
	0.01	8.10	5.85	4.94	4.43	4.10	3.87	3.70	3.56	3.46	3.37	3.09	2.84	2.64	2.54	2.44
21	0.10	2.96	2.57	2.36	2.23	2.14	2.08	2.02	1.98	1.95	1.92	1.83	1.74	1.67	1.63	1.60
	0.05	4.32	3.47	3.07	2.84	2.68	2.57	2.49	2.42	2.37	2.32	2.18	2.05	1.94	1.88	1.83
	0.025	5.83	4.42	3.82	3.48	3.25	3.09	2.97	2.87	2.80	2.73	2.53	2.36	2.21	2.13	2.06
	0.01	8.02	5.78	4.87	4.37	4.04	3.81	3.64	3.51	3.40	3.31	3.03	2.79	2.58	2.48	2.38
22	0.10	2.95	2.56	2.35	2.22	2.13	2.06	2.01	1.97	1.93	1.90	1.81	1.73	1.65	1.61	1.58
	0.05	4.30	3.44	3.05	2.82	2.66	2.55	2.46	2.40	2.34	2.30	2.15	2.02	1.91	1.85	1.80
	0.025	5.79	4.38	3.78	3.44	3.22	3.05	2.93	2.84	2.76	2.70	2.50	2.32	2.17	2.09	2.02
	0.01	7.95	5.72	4.82	4.31	3.99	3.76	3.59	3.45	3.35	3.26	2.98	2.73	2.53	2.42	2.33
23	0.10	2.94	2.55	2.34	2.21	2.11	2.05	1.99	1.95	1.92	1.89	1.80	1.71	1.64	1.59	1.56
	0.05	4.28	3.42	3.03	2.80	2.64	2.53	2.44	2.37	2.32	2.27	2.13	2.00	1.88	1.82	1.77
	0.025	5.75	4.35	3.75	3.41	3.18	3.02	2.90	2.81	2.73	2.67	2.47	2.29	2.14	2.06	1.99
	0.01	7.88	5.66	4.76	4.26	3.94	3.71	3.54	3.41	3.30	3.21	2.93	2.69	2.48	2.37	2.28
24	0.10	2.93	2.54	2.33	2.19	2.10	2.04	1.98	1.94	1.91	1.88	1.78	1.70	1.62	1.58	1.54
	0.05	4.26	3.40	3.01	2.78	2.62	2.51	2.42	2.36	2.30	2.25	2.11	1.97	1.86	1.80	1.75
	0.025	5.72	4.32	3.72	3.38	3.15	2.99	2.87	2.78	2.70	2.64	2.44	2.26	2.11	2.02	1.95
	0.01	7.82	5.61	4.72	4.22	3.90	3.67	3.50	3.36	3.26	3.17	2.89	2.64	2.44	2.33	2.24

TABLE 4 *(Continued)*

		df_1														
df_2	α	1	2	3	4	5	6	7	8	9	10	15	25	50	100	500
25	0.10	2.92	2.53	2.32	2.18	2.09	2.02	1.97	1.93	1.89	1.87	1.77	1.68	1.61	1.56	1.53
	0.05	4.24	3.39	2.99	2.76	2.60	2.49	2.40	2.34	2.28	2.24	2.09	1.96	1.84	1.78	1.73
	0.025	5.69	4.29	3.69	3.35	3.13	2.97	2.85	2.75	2.68	2.61	2.41	2.23	2.08	2.00	1.92
	0.01	7.77	5.57	4.68	4.18	3.85	3.63	3.46	3.32	3.22	3.13	2.85	2.60	2.40	2.29	2.19
26	0.10	2.91	2.52	2.31	2.17	2.08	2.01	1.96	1.92	1.88	1.86	1.76	1.67	1.59	1.55	1.51
	0.05	4.23	3.37	2.98	2.74	2.59	2.47	2.39	2.32	2.27	2.22	2.07	1.94	1.82	1.76	1.71
	0.025	5.66	4.27	3.67	3.33	3.10	2.94	2.82	2.73	2.65	2.59	2.39	2.21	2.05	1.97	1.90
	0.01	7.72	5.53	4.64	4.14	3.82	3.59	3.42	3.29	3.18	3.09	2.81	2.57	2.36	2.25	2.16
27	0.10	2.90	2.51	2.30	2.17	2.07	2.00	1.95	1.91	1.87	1.85	1.75	1.66	1.58	1.54	1.50
	0.05	4.21	3.35	2.96	2.73	2.57	2.46	2.37	2.31	2.25	2.20	2.06	1.92	1.81	1.74	1.69
	0.025	5.63	4.24	3.65	3.31	3.08	2.92	2.80	2.71	2.63	2.57	2.36	2.18	2.03	1.94	1.87
	0.01	7.68	5.49	4.60	4.11	3.78	3.56	3.39	3.26	3.15	3.06	2.78	2.54	2.33	2.22	2.12
28	0.10	2.89	2.50	2.29	2.16	2.06	2.00	1.94	1.90	1.87	1.84	1.74	1.65	1.57	1.53	1.49
	0.05	4.20	3.34	2.95	2.71	2.56	2.45	2.36	2.29	2.24	2.19	2.04	1.91	1.79	1.73	1.67
	0.025	5.61	4.22	3.63	3.29	3.06	2.90	2.78	2.69	2.61	2.55	2.34	2.16	2.01	1.92	1.85
	0.01	7.64	5.45	4.57	4.07	3.75	3.53	3.36	3.23	3.12	3.03	2.75	2.51	2.30	2.19	2.09
29	0.10	2.89	2.50	2.28	2.15	2.06	1.99	1.93	1.89	1.86	1.83	1.73	1.64	1.56	1.52	1.48
	0.05	4.18	3.33	2.93	2.70	2.55	2.43	2.35	2.28	2.22	2.18	2.03	1.89	1.77	1.71	1.65
	0.025	5.59	4.20	3.61	3.27	3.04	2.88	2.76	2.67	2.59	2.53	2.32	2.14	1.99	1.90	1.83
	0.01	7.60	5.42	4.54	4.04	3.73	3.50	3.33	3.20	3.09	3.00	2.73	2.48	2.27	2.16	2.06
30	0.10	2.88	2.49	2.28	2.14	2.05	1.98	1.93	1.88	1.85	1.82	1.72	1.63	1.55	1.51	1.47
	0.05	4.17	3.32	2.92	2.69	2.53	2.42	2.33	2.27	2.21	2.16	2.01	1.88	1.76	1.70	1.64
	0.025	5.57	4.18	3.59	3.25	3.03	2.87	2.75	2.65	2.57	2.51	2.31	2.12	1.97	1.88	1.81
	0.01	7.56	5.39	4.51	4.02	3.70	3.47	3.30	3.17	3.07	2.98	2.70	2.45	2.25	2.13	2.03
50	0.10	2.81	2.41	2.20	2.06	1.97	1.90	1.84	1.80	1.76	1.73	1.63	1.53	1.44	1.39	1.34
	0.05	4.03	3.18	2.79	2.56	2.40	2.29	2.20	2.13	2.07	2.03	1.87	1.73	1.60	1.52	1.46
	0.025	5.34	3.97	3.39	3.05	2.83	2.67	2.55	2.46	2.38	2.32	2.11	1.92	1.75	1.66	1.57
	0.01	7.17	5.06	4.20	3.72	3.41	3.19	3.02	2.89	2.78	2.70	2.42	2.17	1.95	1.82	1.71
100	0.10	2.76	2.36	2.14	2.00	1.91	1.83	1.78	1.73	1.69	1.66	1.56	1.45	1.35	1.29	1.23
	0.05	3.94	3.09	2.70	2.46	2.31	2.19	2.10	2.03	1.97	1.93	1.77	1.62	1.48	1.39	1.31
	0.025	5.18	3.83	3.25	2.92	2.70	2.54	2.42	2.32	2.24	2.18	1.97	1.77	1.59	1.48	1.38
	0.01	6.90	4.82	3.98	3.51	3.21	2.99	2.82	2.69	2.59	2.50	2.22	1.97	1.74	1.60	1.47
500	0.10	2.72	2.31	2.09	1.96	1.86	1.79	1.73	1.68	1.64	1.61	1.50	1.39	1.28	1.21	1.12
	0.05	3.86	3.01	2.62	2.39	2.23	2.12	2.03	1.96	1.90	1.85	1.69	1.53	1.38	1.28	1.16
	0.025	5.05	3.72	3.14	2.81	2.59	2.43	2.31	2.22	2.14	2.07	1.86	1.65	1.46	1.34	1.19
	0.01	6.69	4.65	3.82	3.36	3.05	2.84	2.68	2.55	2.44	2.36	2.07	1.81	1.57	1.41	1.23

Source: *F*-values calculated with Excel.

TABLE 5 Studentized Range Values $q_{\alpha,(c,n_T-c)}$ for Tukey's HSD Method

$n_T - c$	α	The number of means, c										
		2	3	4	5	6	7	8	9	10	11	12
4	0.05	3.93	5.04	5.76	6.29	6.71	7.05	7.35	7.60	7.83	8.03	8.21
	0.01	6.51	8.12	9.17	9.96	10.58	11.10	11.54	11.92	12.26	12.57	12.84
5	0.05	3.64	4.60	5.22	5.67	6.03	6.33	6.58	6.80	6.99	7.17	7.32
	0.01	5.70	6.98	7.80	8.42	8.91	9.32	9.67	9.97	10.24	10.48	10.70
6	0.05	3.46	4.34	4.90	5.30	5.63	5.90	6.12	6.32	6.49	6.65	6.79
	0.01	5.24	6.33	7.03	7.56	7.97	8.32	8.61	8.87	9.10	9.30	9.48
7	0.05	3.34	4.16	4.68	5.06	5.36	5.61	5.82	6.00	6.16	6.30	6.43
	0.01	4.95	5.92	6.54	7.01	7.37	7.68	7.94	8.17	8.37	8.55	8.71
8	0.05	3.26	4.04	4.53	4.89	5.17	5.40	5.60	5.77	5.92	6.05	6.18
	0.01	4.75	5.64	6.20	6.62	6.96	7.24	7.47	7.68	7.86	8.03	8.18
9	0.05	3.20	3.95	4.41	4.76	5.02	5.24	5.43	5.59	5.74	5.87	5.98
	0.01	4.60	5.43	5.96	6.35	6.66	6.91	7.13	7.33	7.49	7.65	7.78
10	0.05	3.15	3.88	4.33	4.65	4.91	5.12	5.30	5.46	5.60	5.72	5.83
	0.01	4.48	5.27	5.77	6.14	6.43	6.67	6.87	7.05	7.21	7.36	7.49
11	0.05	3.11	3.82	4.26	4.57	4.82	5.03	5.20	5.35	5.49	5.61	5.71
	0.01	4.39	5.15	5.62	5.97	6.25	6.48	6.67	6.84	6.99	7.13	7.25
12	0.05	3.08	3.77	4.20	4.51	4.75	4.95	5.12	5.27	5.39	5.51	5.61
	0.01	4.32	5.05	5.50	5.84	6.10	6.32	6.51	6.67	6.81	6.94	7.06
13	0.05	3.06	3.73	4.15	4.45	4.69	4.88	5.05	5.19	5.32	5.43	5.53
	0.01	4.26	4.96	5.40	5.73	5.98	6.19	6.37	6.53	6.67	6.79	6.90
14	0.05	3.03	3.70	4.11	4.41	4.64	4.83	4.99	5.13	5.25	5.36	5.46
	0.01	4.21	4.89	5.32	5.63	5.88	6.08	6.26	6.41	6.54	6.66	6.77
15	0.05	3.01	3.67	4.08	4.37	4.59	4.78	4.94	5.08	5.20	5.31	5.40
	0.01	4.17	4.84	5.25	5.56	5.80	5.99	6.16	6.31	6.44	6.55	6.66
16	0.05	3.00	3.65	4.05	4.33	4.56	4.74	4.90	5.03	5.15	5.26	5.35
	0.01	4.13	4.79	5.19	5.49	5.72	5.92	6.08	6.22	6.35	6.46	6.56
17	0.05	2.98	3.63	4.02	4.30	4.52	4.70	4.86	4.99	5.11	5.21	5.31
	0.01	4.10	4.74	5.14	5.43	5.66	5.85	6.01	6.15	6.27	6.38	6.48
18	0.05	2.97	3.61	4.00	4.28	4.49	4.67	4.82	4.96	5.07	5.17	5.27
	0.01	4.07	4.70	5.09	5.38	5.60	5.79	5.94	6.08	6.20	6.31	6.41
19	0.05	2.96	3.59	3.98	4.25	4.47	4.65	4.79	4.92	5.04	5.14	5.23
	0.01	4.05	4.67	5.05	5.33	5.55	5.73	5.89	6.02	6.14	6.25	6.34

TABLE 5 *(Continued)*

		The number of means, c										
$n_T - c$	α	2	3	4	5	6	7	8	9	10	11	12
20	0.05	2.95	3.58	3.96	4.23	4.45	4.62	4.77	4.90	5.01	5.11	5.20
	0.01	4.02	4.64	5.02	5.29	5.51	5.69	5.84	5.97	6.09	6.19	6.28
24	0.05	2.92	3.53	3.90	4.17	4.37	4.54	4.68	4.81	4.92	5.01	5.10
	0.01	3.96	4.55	4.91	5.17	5.37	5.54	5.69	5.81	5.92	6.02	6.11
30	0.05	2.89	3.49	3.85	4.10	4.30	4.46	4.60	4.72	4.82	4.92	5.00
	0.01	3.89	4.45	4.80	5.05	5.24	5.40	5.54	5.65	5.76	5.85	5.93
40	0.05	2.86	3.44	3.79	4.04	4.23	4.39	4.52	4.63	4.73	4.82	4.90
	0.01	3.82	4.37	4.70	4.93	5.11	5.26	5.39	5.50	5.60	5.69	5.76
60	0.05	2.83	3.40	3.74	3.98	4.16	4.31	4.44	4.55	4.65	4.73	4.81
	0.01	3.76	4.28	4.59	4.82	4.99	5.13	5.25	5.36	5.45	5.53	5.60
120	0.05	2.80	3.36	3.68	3.92	4.10	4.24	4.36	4.47	4.56	4.64	4.71
	0.01	3.70	4.20	4.50	4.71	4.87	5.01	5.12	5.21	5.30	5.37	5.44
∞	0.05	2.77	3.31	3.63	3.86	4.03	4.17	4.29	4.39	4.47	4.55	4.62
	0.01	3.64	4.12	4.40	4.60	4.76	4.88	4.99	5.08	5.16	5.23	5.29

Source: E. S. Pearson and H. O. Hartley, *Biometrika Tables for Statisticians*, vol. 1 (Cambridge: Cambridge University Press, 1966).

Answers to Selected Even-Numbered Exercises

Chapter 1

1.2 35 is the estimated population average; impossible to reach all video game players.

1.4 a. The population is all recent college graduates with an engineering degree.
b. No, the average salary is computed from a sample.

1.6 Cross-sectional data that will vary due to sampling

1.8 Unstructured; does not conform to a well-defines row-column format.

1.10 Structured; time series; vary due to sampling

1.18 a. Nominal
b. Interval
c. Ratio

1.26 a. 1
b. 9
c. 5 for Exercise, 2 for Marriage, and 3 for Income
d. 281 married; 134 not married
e. 69 exercise; 74 don't exercise

1.28 a. missing values in Travel Plan
b. 300 observations removed
c. 2 observations in the subset

1.30 a. Observations 25 missing in Yards, 28 in Attempts, and 29 in Interceptions
b. 3 observations removed
c. 5 observations removed

1.32 a. Population: all US citizens born in 2019
b. Averages computed from samples

1.36 a. Year measured on the interval scale
b. Quarter measured on the nominal scale
c. Vacation measured on the ratio scale

1.38 a. 616 males and 614 females
b. 49.35% males and 57.33% females
c. 2
d. 6
e. Males: highest 1600, lowest 1055; Females: highest 1599, lowest 1062

1.40 a. All variables other than Name have missing values; 9 missing values in the data set
b. 367 complete observations
c. 61 observations remain

Chapter 2

2.2 a. 0.302
b. Large-sized shirts had the highest frequency; small-sized shirts had the lowest frequency.

2.4 a. 19.3%
b. South has the highest relative frequency.

2.6 a. A rating of 5 has the highest frequency.
b. The higher ratings have the higher frequencies.

2.8 a. Not Religious is the most common response.
b. 35% responded "Not Religious" which is consistent with the earlier study.

2.10 No, by using a relatively high value as an upper limit on the vertical axis ($500), the rise in stock price appears dampened.

2.12 a. 378.
b. 46
c. 80
d. 14

2.14 a. 202; 60
b. 0.7030; 0.5588
c. Beer is the popular drink at this bar; both men and women are more likely to choose beer over the other two options.

2.18 a. 120; 68
b. 0.1667; 0.3200
c. The majority of both business and nonbusiness students do not study hard, but nonbusiness students are more likely to study hard.

2.20 a. 0.317
b. 104
c. 0.867; 0.133

2.26 a. 0.40
b. 200

2.28 a. 47
b. 0.31; 0.13
c. Approximately 0.70 of the observations are less than 15.

2.30 a. 125; 0.71
b. The distribution is symmetric.
c. 0.80

2.34 a. $2.30 < x \leq 2.60$; 6
b. No, the distribution is not symmetric. It is positively skewed.

2.36 a. $800 < x \leq 900$ (171 students); 157 students; 0.114.
b. The distribution is relatively symmetric.
c. 0.50

2.38 Negative relationship

2.40 No relationship; so investing in both would diversify risk.

2.42 a. Negative relationship
b. Negative relationship
c. 7
d. Negative relationship between age and price is consistent for cars of both mileage categories.

2.44 Both countries have a clear and consistent upward trend, but China's begins to stall slightly around 2000. India has slightly higher population growth over the past 40 years.

2.46 a. Observations ranged from a low of −87 to a high of −50.
b. The distribution is not symmetric; it is positively skewed. Most of the numbers are in the lower stems of −8 and −7.

2.48 Temperatures ranged from a low of 73 to a high of 107. The distribution is not symmetric; it has negative skew. Temperatures in 90s were the most frequent.

2.52 a. 220; 0.10
b. The majority of respondents, 55%, felt that parents do too much for their adult children; only 10% of respondents felt that parents do too little for their adult children.

2.54 a. 109 M red t-shirts were sold; 183 XL white t-shirts were sold
b. White S and White XS are the two most popular color/size combinations; Black S and Gray XS are the two least popular color/size combinations.

2.56 a. 0.851; 0.075
b. Approximately symmetric
c. 0.50

2.58 a. Positive relationship between health and exercise.
b. Negative relationship

2.60 a. Negative relationship
b. Negative relationship between birth rate and life expectancy; in general, developed countries have lower birth rates and higher life expectancies compared to developing countries.

2.62 Starbucks saw positive growth rates in revenues in every year. McDonald's experienced five years of positive growth rates and five years of negative growth rates.

2.64 a. PEG ratios ranged from 0.8 to 3.7. The 1.0 to 1.9 range had the highest frequency.
b. Distribution is positively skewed; there are a few firms with relatively high PEG ratios.

Chapter 3

3.2 Mean = −2.67: Median = −3.5; Mode = −4

3.4 Mean = 18.33; Median = 20; the distribution is bimodal: 15 and 20 are the two modes.

3.6 Mean = 2.31; Median = 2.18

3.8 Mean = 1,306.94; Median = 1,287.50

3.10 a. Mean Food = 4,416.44; Mean Travel = 2,405.27.
b. Mean food spending for homeowners = 4,048.90; Mean food spending for non-homeowners = 4,566.70; Non-homeowners spend more on food.
c. Mean travel spending for homeowners = 1,960.35; Mean travel spending for non-homeowners = 2,569.05; Non-homeowners spend more on travel.

3.14 Average weight = 7.72

3.16 25th percentile: 64; 50th percentile: 112; 75th percentile: 149.25

3.20 a. Q1: 200; Q3: 550.
b. IQR = 350; Limit: 1.5 × IQR = 1.5 × 350 = 525; at least one outlier on the right side of the distribution.
c. The distribution is not symmetric; positively skewed

3.22 a. Q1: 40; Q2: 46; Q3: 51
b. IQR = 11; 1.5 × IQR = 16.5; no outliers

3.24 a. There are no outliers; positively skewed.
b. There are two outliers; positively skewed.

3.26 G_g = 0.0313, or 3.13%.

3.28 G_R = −0.006, or −0.6%.

3.30 G_R = 0.0647, or 6.47%.

3.32 a. Year 1 – Year 2: 0.0667; Year 2 – Year 3: 0.0781; Year 3 – Year 4: 0.1014
b. G_g = 0.082, or 8.2%.

3.34 a. 12.98%
b. 12.84%
c. $1,621,26

3.36 a. 3.56%
b. 3.00%
c. $23,185.48

3.40 a. 18
b. 4.8
c. 36.80
d. 6.07

3.42 a. 22
b. 7.33
c. 81.2; 9.01

3.44 a. Firm A: s^2 = 162.65, s = 12.75; Firm B: s^2 = 173.51, s = 13.17.
b. Firm B (13.17 > 12.75)
c. Firm B (0.24 > 0.22)

3.46 a. CV_A = 0.13
b. CV_B = 0.14
c. Corporation B (0.14 > 0.13)

3.48 a. Investment B provides a higher return. Investment A provides less risk.
b. $Sharpe_A$ = 1.72; $Sharpe_B$ = 1.36. Investment A provides a higher reward per unit of risk.

3.50 a. Investment 2.
b. Investment 1
c. $Sharpe_1$ = 0.34; $Sharpe_2$ = 0.42; Investment 2

3.54 a. At least 75%
b. At least 89%

3.56 a. At least 75%
b. At least 89%

3.58 a. 16%
b. 80

3.60 a. 97.5%
b. 2.5%

3.64 a. At least 75%
b. At least 89%

3.66 a. 68%
b. 95%; 2.5%
c. 16%

3.68 a. At least 75%
b. 95%

3.70 a. No outliers
b. No outliers

3.72 a. −12.3.
b. −0.96; strong, negative linear relationship

3.74 a. 631.39
b. 0.45; moderate, positive linear relationship

3.76 a. 66.79
b. 0.90; strong positive linear relationship
3.78 a. 0.82; strong, positive linear relationship
b. 0.61; moderate, positive linear relationship
c. −0.46; moderate, negative linear relationship
3.80 a. Firm A: $\bar{x} = 75.39$; $s^2 = 52.02$; $s = 7.21$;
Firm B: $\bar{x} = 106.07$; $s^2 = 319.21$; $s = 17.87$
b. Firm B
c. Firm B
3.82 1,820
3.84 a. G_g(Firm 1) = −0.050, or −5%; G_g(Firm 2) = −0.012, or −1.2%
b. Firm 2
3.86 0.5518; moderate, positive linear relationship.
3.90 a. 2.3122; 2.18
b. Q1 = 2.01; Q3 = 2.55
c. $s^2 = 0.1482$; $s = 0.3849$
d. Boxplot shows outlier in upper part of the distribution.
e. No outliers using *z*-scores. Because distribution is positively skewed, use boxplot to identify outliers.
3.92 a. 3.15; 1282.72
b. Mean College GPA for white students = 3.26; mean College GPA for nonwhite students = 2.99
c. Mean SAT for white students = 1280.09; mean SAT for nonwhite students = 1286.67

Chapter 4

4.6 a. A union
b. An intersection
4.8 a. Not exhaustive; may not get any offer
b. Not mutually exclusive; may get both offers
4.16 $P(A) = 0.40$, $P(B) = 0.50$, and $P(A^c \cap B^c) = 0.24$
a. $P(A^c|B^c) = 0.48$
b. $P(A^c \cup B^c) = 0.86$.
c. $P((A \cup B)^c) = 0.76$
4.18 Let event *O* correspond to "students who ever go to their professor during office hours", and events *MI* and *MA* to "minor clarification" and "major clarification", respectively. $P(O) = 0.2$, $P(MI|O) = 0.3$, $P(MA|O) = 0.7$
a. $P(MI \cap O) = 0.06$
b. $P(MA \cap O) = 0.14$
4.20 Let event *A* correspond to "Firm raising an alarm", and event *F* to "Fraudulent Transaction". We have $P(A) = 0.05$, $P(A|F) = 0.80$, and $P(F) = 0.01$

$$P(F|A^c) = \frac{0.002}{1 - 0.05} = 0.0021$$

4.24 a. $P(A) = 0.70$, $P(A^c) = 0.30$, $P(B) = 0.50$
b. $(A \cap B) \neq 0$; not mutually exclusive
c. Mike's preference is described by $A \cap B$
4.28 For $i = 1,2$, let event A_i be "the *i*-th selected member is in favor of the bonus".
a. $P(A_1 \cap A_2) = 0.4286$
b. $P(A_1^c \cap A_2^c) = 0.0952$
4.32 Let event *H* correspond to "Woman faces sexual harassment", and event *T* to "Woman uses public transportation". We have $P(H) = 0.6667$, $P(H|T) = 0.82$, and $P(T) = 0.28$.
a. $P(H \cap T) = 0.2296$
b. $P(T|H) = 0.3444$
4.36 b. $P(N|B) = 0.8333$
c. $P(Y) = 0.2519$
d. $P(B|Y) = 0.2941$ and $P(B^c|Y) = 0.7059$
4.38 Let even *L* correspond to "Low", *M* to "Medium", *H* to "High", *N* to "No", and *Y* to "Yes".
b. $P(Y) = 0.5828$
c. $P(Y|L) = 0.50$; $P(Y|M) = 0.60$; $P(Y|H) = 0.63$
d. Yes, because $P(Y|L)$, $P(Y|M)$, and $P(Y|H)$ are not equal.
4.46 Let event *D* be "Experience a decline", and event *N* be "Ratio is negative". We have $P(D) = 0.20$, $P(N|D) = 0.70$, and $P(N|D^c) = 0.15$. $P(D|N) = 0.54$
4.48 Let event *O* correspond to "obese" woman, *W* to "white", *B* to "black", *H* to "Hispanic", and *A* to "Asian". We have $P(O|W) = 0.33$, $P(O|B) = 0.496$, $P(O|H) = 0.43$, $P(O|A) = 0.089$, $P(W) = 0.48$, $P(B) = 0.19$, $P(H) = 0.26$, and $P(A) = 0.07$.
a. $P(O) = 0.3707$
b. $P(W|O) = 0.4273$
c. $P(B|O) = 0.2542$
d. $P(A|O) = 0.0168$
4.50 Let *F* = "Player is fully fit to play", *S* = "Player is somewhat fit to play", *N* = "Player is not able to play", and *W* = "The Lakers win the game".
a. $P(W) = 0.62$
b. $P(F|W) = 0.52$
4.56 a. 336
b. 0.0030
c. 56
d. 0.0179
4.60 Let event *C* correspond to "Churn", *F* to "Female", and *M* to "Male". We are given that $P(C|F) = 0.12$, $P(C|M) = 0.09$, $P(F) = 0.62$; $P(M) = 1 - 0.62 = 0.38$. We find $P(M \cap C) = 0.0342$
4.62 a. 0.209
b. 0.0245
c. 0.498
d. 0.1388
e. 0.3791
f. No, the probability of the intersection is not zero
g. No, $0.0290 \neq 0.209 \times 0.0765$
4.64 Let event *S* correspond to "Biggest smilers", *F* to "Biggest frowners", and *D* to "Divorced". We have $P(D|S) = 0.11$ and $P(D|F) = 0.31$.
a. $P(S) = 0.1818$
b. $P(F \cap D) = 0.0775$
4.66 For $i = 1,2$, let event D_i be "the *i*-th selected mango is damaged".
a. $P(D_1^c) = 0.85$
b. $P(D_1^c \cap D_2^c) = 0.7158$
c. $P(D_1 \cap D_2) = 0.0158$
4.68 Let event *O* correspond to "Optimism about the global economy", *U* to "Respondents from the U.S.", and *A* to "Respondents from Asia". We have $P(O) = 0.18$, $P(O|U) = 0.22$, and $P(O|A) = 0.09$.
a. $P(O^c|A) = 0.91$
b. $P(O \cap U) = 0.0616$
c. $P(A|O) = 0.11$

4.72 a. $P(G) = 0.3245$
b. $P(S) = 0.1815$
c. $P(S|G) = 0.1470$
d. $P(G|S) = 0.2628$
e. Not independent; resources should be available at all times.

4.74 Let A correspond to "US economy performs well" and B to "Asian countries perform well". We have $P(A) = 0.40$, $P(B|A) = 0.80$, and $P(B|A^c) = 0.30$.
a. $P(A \cap B) = 0.32$
b. $P(B) = 0.50$
c. $P(A|B) = 0.64$

4.76 Let event M correspond to "Men", W to "Women", and H to "Healthy weight". We have $P(H|W) = 0.365$, $P(H|M) = 0.266$, and $P(W) = 0.5052$.
a. $P(H) = 0.3160$
b. $P(W|H) = 0.5835$
c. $P(M|H) = 0.4165$

4.80 Let event A correspond to "Asians", B to "black", W to "white", H to "Hispanic", and T to "Both parents at home". It is known that $P(T|A) = 0.85$, $P(T|W) = 0.78$, $P(T|H) = 0.70$, $P(T|B) = 0.38$. Also, $P(A) = 0.10$, $P(W) = 0.56$, $P(H) = 0.20$, and $P(B) = 0.14$.
a. $P(T) = 0.7150$
b. $P(A|T) = 0.1189$
c. $P(B|T) = 0.0744$

4.82 a. 35
b. 840
c. 20

Chapter 5

5.4 a. $P(X \leq 0) = 0.50$
b. $P(X = 50) = 0.25$
c. Yes

5.10 a. $P(X = 2) = 0.20$
b. $P(2 \leq X \leq 3) = 0.25$

5.14 $\mu = 10.75$; $\sigma^2 = 28.19$; $\sigma = 5.31$

5.22 Let X be the amount spent on warranty; $E(X) = \$30$
Let Y be the revenue earned by store; $E(Y) = \$3{,}600$

5.30 a. $w_X = 0.40$; $w_Y = 0.60$
b. $E(R_p) = 10.40$
c. $SD(R_P) = 14.60$

5.34 a. $P(X = 0) = 0.1160$
b. $P(X = 1) = 0.3124$
c. $P(X \leq 1) = 0.4284$

5.36 a. $P(3 < X < 5) = 0.1569$
b. $P(3 < X \leq 5) = 0.2160$
c. $P(3 \leq X \leq 5) = 0.4828$

5.40 a. $P(X = 5) = 0.4437$
b. $P(X \leq 2) = 0.0270$
c. $P(X \geq 4) = 0.835$
d. $E(X) = 4.25$
e. $\sigma^2 = 0.6375$; $\sigma = 0.7984$

5.42 a. $P(X < 2) = 0.7213$
b. $P(X < 2) = 0.4580$

5.46 a. $P(X > 2) = 0.3125$
b. $P(X > 2) = 0.5276$
c. $P(X > 2) = 0.1362$

5.50 a. $P(X = 10) = 0.1171$
b. $P(X \leq 10) = 0.8725$
c. $P(X \geq 15) = 0.0016$

5.52 a. $P(X = 1) = 0.3347$
b. $P(X = 2) = 0.2510$
c. $P(X \geq 2) = 0.4422$

5.56 a. $P(X < 14) = 0.0661$
b. $P(X \geq 20) = 0.5297$
c. $P(X = 25) = 0.0446$
d. $P(18 \leq X \leq 23) = 0.4905$

5.60 a. $\mu = 360/60 = 6$; $P(X = 2) = 0.0446$
b. $P(X \geq 2) = 0.9826$
c. $\mu = 60$; $P(X = 40) = 0.001$

5.64 a. $P(X \leq 4) = 0.8153$
b. $P(X \geq 3) = 0.5768$

5.66 a. $\mu = 304$; $P(X > 320) = 0.1717$
b. $\mu = 2128$; $P(X > 2200) = 0.0586$

5.68 a. $P(X = 0) = 0.5783$
b. $P(X = 1) = 0.3652$
c. $P(X \leq 1) = 0.9435$

5.72 $P(X \geq 8) = 0.0777$
$E(X) = 5$; $SD(X) = 1.7408$

5.74 a. $P(X = 0) = 0.5020$
b. $P(X \geq 1) = 0.4980$

5.78 $P(X = 2) = 0.0316$

5.80 a. $P(X = 2) = 0.0495$
b. $P(X = 5) = 0.0000002$
c. $P(X = 1) = 0.0256$
d. 0.00000000512

5.84 a. $P(X = 3) = 0.45$
b. $P(X \geq 2) = 0.90$
c. $E(X) = 2.6$; $\sigma^2 = 0.94$; $\sigma = 0.97$

5.86 a. $P(X = 1) = 0.13$; $P(X = 3) = 0.02$; $E(X) = 2.79$; $\sigma = 1.3137$
b. $E(P) = 41.85$; $E(120P) = 5022$

5.90 a. $P(X = 2) = 0.3747$
b. $P(X = 4) = 0.0677$
c. $E(X) = 51$; $\sigma^2 = 24.99$; $\sigma = 4.999$

5.92 a. $P(X = 10) = 0.0272$
b. $P(10 \leq X \leq 20) = 0.0451$
c. $P(X \leq 8) = 0.8996$

5.96 a. $P(X = 3) = 0.0129$
b. $P(X \leq 2) = 0.9871$
c. 0.0258.

5.98 a. $P(X = 5) = 0.2748$
b. $P(X > 5) = 0.3626$

Chapter 6

6.2 a. $P(X < 0) = 0.30$
b. $P(2.5 \leq X \leq 4) = 0.16$
c. $P(0 \leq X \leq 4) = 0.70$

6.4 a. $f(x) = 0.0333$
b. $\mu = 20$; $\sigma = 8.66$
c. $P(X > 10) = 0.8325$

6.8 Let X represent the price of electricity.
a. $E(X) = 16$.
b. $f(x) = 0.125$; $P(X < 15.5) = 0.4375$
c. $f(x) = 0.125$; $P(X > 14) = 0.75$

6.12 Let X represent the date when the peach tree will bloom; $f(x) = 0.0833$
a. $P(X > 25) = 0.4167$
b. $P(X \leq 20) = 0.1667$

6.14 a. $P(Z > 1.32) = 0.0934$
b. $P(Z \leq -1.32) = 0.0934$
c. $P(1.32 \leq Z \leq 2.37) = 0.0845$
d. $P(-1.32 \leq Z \leq 2.37) = 0.8977$

6.20 a. $P(X \leq 0) = 0.0062$
b. $P(X > 2) = 0.9772$
c. $P(4 \leq X \leq 10) = 0.4332$
d. $P(6 \leq X \leq 14) = 0.6827$

6.26 a. $P(X > -12) = 0.3694$
b. $P(0 \leq X \leq 5) = 0.0347$
c. $P(Z \leq z) = 0.25; x = -21.07$
d. $P(Z > z) = 0.25; x = -8.93$

6.30 Let X equal points scored in a game.
a. $P(60 < X < 100) = 0.9545$
b. $P(X > 100) = 0.0228$; 1.87 games

6.34 a. $P(X \geq 40) = 0.0382$
b. $P(30 \leq X \leq 35) = 0.4953$
c. $P(X \leq x) = 0.99;\ x = 41.94$

6.44 a. $P(50 \leq X \leq 80) = 0.5328$
b. $P(20 \leq X \leq 40) = 0.1359$
c. $P(X \geq x) = 0.15;\ x = 80.73$
d. $P(X < x) = 0.10; x = 34.37$

6.54 a. μ(Posson) = 4; μ(Exponential) = 2.5
b. $P(X \leq 2.5) = 0.6321$
c. $P(1 \leq X \leq 2) = 0.2210$

6.58 a. $P(X \leq 1) = 0.3935$
b. $P(2 < X < 4) = 0.2325$
c. $P(X > 10) = 0.0067$

6.60 a. $\mu_Y = 54.60; \sigma_Y^2 = 19{,}045.51$
b. $\mu_Y = 403.42; \sigma_Y^2 = 1{,}039{,}849.49$
c. $\mu_Y = 665.14; \sigma_Y^2 = 8{,}443{,}697.13$

6.62 a. $\mu_X = 2.5859; \sigma_X^2 = 0.1064$
b. $\mu_X = 2.9690; \sigma_X^2 = 0.0535$
c. $\mu_X = 2.8646; \sigma_X^2 = 0.2624$

6.64 a. μ(Poisson) = 10; μ(Exponential) = 6
b. $P(X > 15) = 0.0821$
c. $P(15 \leq X \leq 20) = 0.0464$

6.72 a. $P(X < 1) = 1 - e^{-2(1)} = 0.8647$
b. $P(X > 5) = 0.0001$

6.74 Let X represent the delivery time.
a. $\mu = 3; \sigma^2 = 1.3333$
b. $f(x) = 0.25$; $P(X > 4) = 0.25$
c. $P(X < 2.5) = 0.375$

6.76 Let X represent diastolic (a) and systolic readings (b).
a. $P(80 \leq X \leq 90) = 0.3245$
b. $P((120 \leq X \leq 139) = 0.4106$

6.84 a. $P(X \leq 10) = 0.1151$
b. 1,000(271.225) = 271,225.

6.86 a. $P(50{,}000 \leq X \leq 65{,}000) = 0.8536$
b. $P(X > 70{,}000) = 0.0004$
c. 62401.84
d. 53859.94

6.90 a. $\mu = 0.365$
b. $\lambda = 2.7397$
c. $P(X \leq 1) = 0.9354$

6.96 Let Y denote income; $\mu_X = 11.1$ and $\sigma_X = 0.4$
a. $P(Y < 50000) = 0.2418$
b. $P(Y > 60000) = 0.5967$
c. $P(Y > y) = 0.99$; $y = 167{,}801.86$ (unrounded)
d. $P(Y < y) = 0.10$; $y = 39{,}631.49$ (unrounded)

Chapter 7

7.2 Nonresponse bias if some people are less likely to stop at the booth. Selection bias since the booth is only open on the weekend.

7.4 a. Nonresponse bias if the people who respond are systematically different from those who do not respond.
b. Selection bias if those who frequent the store in the morning are likely to prefer an earlier opening time.
c. Selection bias if not everyone reads a newspaper. Nonresponse bias if the people who respond are systematically different from those who do not respond.

7.8 a. $E(\overline{X}) = E(X) = 80$; $se(\overline{X}) = \dfrac{14}{\sqrt{100}} = 1.4$
b. $P(77 \leq \overline{X} \leq 85) = 0.9838$
c. $P(\overline{X} > 84) = 0.0021$

7.12 a. $P(\overline{X} \geq 18) = 0.0142$
b. $P(\overline{X} \geq 17.5) = 0.0022$
c. Janice's findings are more likely.

7.14 a. $E(\overline{X}) = 22$ and $se(\overline{X}) = 1.25$. The sample mean has a normal distribution because the population is normally distributed.
b. $P(\overline{X} > 25) = 0.0082$
c. $P(18 \leq \overline{X} \leq 24) = 0.9445$

7.20 a. $P(X < 90) = 0.2660$
b. $P(\overline{X} < 90) = 0.1056$
c. $(P(X < 90))^4 = (0.2660)^4 = 0.0050$.

7.24 a. $P(\overline{P} < 0.30) = 0.9014$
b. $P(\overline{P} > 0.75) = 0.3736$

7.26 a. $E(\overline{P}) = p = 0.20$ and $se(\overline{P}) = 0.0283$; the normal approximation criteria are met because $np = 200(0.20) = 40 > 5$ and $n(1 - p) = 200(1 - 0.20) = 160 > 5$.
b. $P(\overline{P} > 0.25) = 0.0385$

7.34 $n = 120$, $N = 1{,}000$; apply the finite population correction; $E(\overline{P}) = 0.6667$ and $se(\overline{P}) = 0.0404$; $P(\overline{P} > 0.625) = 0.8491$.

7.36 a. No, not necessary because n is less than 5 percent of N.
b. $E(\overline{X}) = 10.32$ *and* $se(\overline{X}) = 2.8232$
c. The normal approximation is not justified because we do not know if the population has a normal distribution and $n < 30$.

7.40 a. Centerline: $\mu = 20$; UCL = 26; LCL = 14
c. The last two points are outside the upper control limit. There is also an upward trend, suggesting the process is becoming increasingly out of control.

7.42 a. Centerline: $p = 0.34$; UCL = 0.404; LCL = 0.276
c. Although there are no points outside the control limits, the positive trend suggests that the process may become out of control if the upward trend continues.

7.44 a. Centerline: $\mu = 5.125$; UCL = 5.25; LCL = 5
b. Although there are no points outside the control limits, the positive trend suggests that the process may become out of control if the upward trend continues.

7.46 a. Centerline: $\mu = 94$; UCL = 97.43; LCL = 90.57
b. Kalwant's average speed is out of control; the coach's concern is justified.

7.48 a. Centerline: $p = 0.04$; UCL = 0.066; LCL = 0.014
b. Yes, because all sample proportions are within the control limits and there is no apparent trend.

7.50 a. Centerline: $p = 0.15$; UCL = 0.27; LCL = 0.03
b. 3 out of 6 months were out of the control limits, which is a good justification for why the corporation chose to direct customers away from Country X call centers.

7.54 a. $E(\overline{X}) = 68$ and $se(\overline{X}) = 0.8333$
b. By the Central Limit Theorem, $\overline{X}$ is approximately normally distributed because $n = 36$.
c. $P(\overline{X} \leq 66) = 0.0082$

7.56 a. $P(X < 79) = 0.3085$
b. $P(\overline{X} < 79) = 0.0569$
c. $P(\overline{X} < 79) = 0.0031$

7.58 a. $P(X > 500) = 0.2791$
b. $P(\overline{X} > 500) = 0.1208$
c. $(P(X > 500))^4 = (0.2791)^4 = 0.0061$.

7.60 a. $P(\overline{P} > 0.80) = 0.1913$
b. $P(\overline{P} < 0.70) = 0.0208$

7.62 a. Centerline: $\mu = 5$; UCL = 5.32; LCL = 4.68
b. The last two points are outside the upper control limit, and there is a positive trend, suggesting that the process is out of control.

Chapter 8

8.2 a. For 89%, $z_{0.055} = 1.598$
b. For 92%, $z_{0.04} = 1.751$
c. For 96%, $z_{0.02} = 2.054$

8.6 a. $\bar{x} = 78.1$
b. $1.645\frac{4.5}{\sqrt{50}} = 1.05$.
c. 78.1 ± 1.05 or [77.05, 79.15]

8.10 a. $2.576\frac{500}{\sqrt{100}} = 128.79$
b. $7{,}790 \pm 128.79$ or [7,661.21, 7,918.79]

8.14 For 90% confidence interval: [18.81, 21.61]; for 99% confidence interval: [18.02, 22.40]. The 99% confidence interval is wider.

8.22 a. $2.11\frac{9.2}{\sqrt{18}} = 4.58$.
b. 12.5 ± 4.58 or [7.92, 17.08]

8.24 a. $2.724\frac{10}{\sqrt{36}} = 4.54$.
b. 100 ± 4.54 or [95.46, 104.54]

8.26 a. $17.25 \pm 3.499\frac{5.95}{\sqrt{8}}$ or [9.89, 24.61].
b. The population is normally distributed.

8.28 a. $2.447\frac{2.33}{\sqrt{7}} = 2.15$.
b. Increase the sample size.
c. 6.6 ± 2.15 or [4.45, 8.75]

8.30 a. Firm A: $18 \pm 4.604\frac{20.70}{\sqrt{5}}$ or [−24.62, 60.62];
Firm B: $14.8 \pm 4.604\frac{6.50}{\sqrt{5}}$ or [1.42, 28.18].
b. Annual return for each firm has a normal distribution, since the sample size is less than 30.
c. Firm A; it has higher sample standard deviation.

8.34 $1{,}080 \pm 2.032\frac{260}{\sqrt{35}}$ or [990.69, 1169.31]; the manager is wrong because 1200 is not within the 95% confidence interval.

8.36 a. Microeconomics: [68.74, 74.91]; Macroeconomics: [66.16, 74.64]
b. The widths are different because the sample standard deviations are different.

8.40 a. $0.6 \pm 1.960\sqrt{\frac{0.6(1-0.6)}{50}}$ or [0.464, 0.736]
b. $0.6 \pm 1.960\sqrt{\frac{0.6(1-0.6)}{200}}$ or [0.532, 0.668]; with larger n, the interval is narrower.

8.42 a. $\overline{p} = \frac{40}{100} = 0.40$
b. $0.40 \pm 1.645\sqrt{\frac{0.40(1-0.40)}{100}}$ or [0.319, 0.481]
c. Yes, because 0.5 does not fall within the interval.
d. No, because 0.5 falls within the interval.

8.44 $0.05 \pm 1.960\sqrt{\frac{0.05(1-0.05)}{400}}$ or [0.029, 0.071].

8.46 a. $0.37 \pm 1.645\sqrt{\frac{0.37(1-0.37)}{5{,}324}}$ or [0.359, 0.381]
b. $0.37 \pm 2.576\sqrt{\frac{0.37(1-0.37)}{5{,}324}}$ or [0.353, 0.387]
c. The margin of error in part b is greater because it uses a higher confidence level.

8.48 a. $0.44 \pm 1.645\sqrt{\frac{0.44(1-0.44)}{1000}}$ or [0.414, 0.466].
b. $1.645\sqrt{\frac{0.44(1-0.44)}{1000}} = 0.026$.
c. $2.576\sqrt{\frac{0.44(1-0.44)}{1000}} = 0.040$.

8.50 a. $0.275 \pm 1.645\sqrt{\frac{0.275(1-0.275)}{400}}$ or [0.238, 0.312]
b. No, because 0.30 falls in the interval.

8.52 a. $1.960\sqrt{\frac{0.55(1-0.55)}{600}} = 0.040$
b. 0.55 ± 0.040 or [0.510, 0.590]
c. Increase the sample size

8.56 $n = 62$

8.58 $n = 24$; $n = 68$

8.60 With $E = 0.08, n = 139$; with $E = 0.12$, $n = 62$.

8.62 $n = 182$

8.64 a. $n = 102$
b. $n = 40$
c. With higher standard deviation, Fund A requires a larger sample size to achieve the same margin of error.

8.66 a. With $E = 5, n = 50$
b. With $E = 3$, $n = 139$

8.68 $n = 1{,}680$.

8.72 10 ± 10.73 or $[-0.73, 20.73]$

8.74 a. $16 \pm 1.971 \frac{12}{\sqrt{225}}$ or $[14.42, 17.58]$
b. Yes, because the interval does not include 14.

8.76 $27{,}500 \pm 2{,}429.77$ or $[25{,}070.41, 29{,}929.59]$

8.82 a. $[77.14, 79.72]$
b. It differs because 81.3 is not contained in the interval.

8.84 a. Monday: 7.89; Tuesday: 4.41
b. Monday: $[214.48, 230.25]$; Tuesday: $[185.65, 194.48]$
c. For both Monday and Tuesday, the population mean differs from 200 because 200 does not belong to either of the two confidence intervals.

8.86 a. 0.032
b. 0.20 ± 0.032 or $[0.168, 0.232]$.

8.90 a. 0.2 ± 0.111 or $[0.089, 0.311]$
b. 0.4 ± 0.136 or $[0.264, 0.536]$

8.92 $n = 260$

Chapter 9

9.4 a. Incorrect; we never accept the null hypothesis.
b. Correct
c. Incorrect; we establish a claim only if the null hypothesis is rejected.
d. Correct

9.10 a. Type I error; the new software is purchased even though it does not reduce assembly costs.
b. Type II error; the new software is not purchased even though it reduces assembly costs.

9.12 a. Type I error; the restaurant is incorrectly implicated for using higher fat content.
b. Type II error; the restaurant escapes being implicated for using higher fat content.

9.14 a. $z = -2$
b. p-value $= 0.0456$
c. Reject H_0; at the 10% significance level, we conclude that the population mean differs from 100.

9.16 a. $H_0: \mu \leq 45$; $H_A: \mu > 45$
b. $z = 1.50$
c. p-value $= 0.0668$
d. Do not reject H_0; at the 5% significance level, we cannot conclude that the population mean is greater than 45.

9.18 $z = 1.4142$; p-value $= 0.0787$. Do not reject H_0; at the 5% significance level, we cannot conclude that the population mean is greater than -5.

9.20 $z = -3.57$; p-value $= 0.0004$. Reject H_0; at the 1% significance level, we conclude that the population mean differs from -100.

9.24 a. $H_0: \mu \leq 90$; $H_A: \mu > 90$
b. $z = 1.5811$; p-value $= 0.0569$
c. Do not reject H_0; the manager's claim is not supported at the 1% significance level.

9.28 a. $H_0: \mu = 30$; $H_A: \mu \neq 30$
b. $z = 2.40$; p-value $= 0.0164$
c. Reject H_0; at the 5% significance level, we conclude that the average weekly price differs from \$30.

9.36 $H_0: \mu = 16$; $H_A: \mu \neq 16$; $t_{31} = -7.54$; p-value $= 0$ (approximately). Reject H_0; at the 1% significance level, we conclude that the population mean differs from 16.

9.42 a. $H_0: \mu \leq 5$; $H_A: \mu > 5$
b. $t_{19} = 3.049$; p-value $= 0.003$; population normally distributed
c. Reject H_0; at the 10% significance level, we can conclude that the average waiting time is more than 5 minutes.

9.44 a. $H_0: \mu = 12$; $H_A: \mu \neq 12$
b. No, since $n > 30$
c. $t_{47} = -1.732$; p-value $= 0.09$
d. Do not reject H_0; at the 5% significance level, we cannot conclude that the bottling process has fallen out of adjustment.

9.46 $H_0: \mu \leq 6.6$; $H_A: \mu > 6.6$; $t_{35} = 2.7$; p-value $= 0.005$; reject H_0. At the 5% significance level, we conclude that the mean increase in home prices in the West is greater than the increase in the Midwest.

9.50 a. $H_0: \mu = 95$; $H_A: \mu \neq 95$
b. $t_{24} = 0.71$; p-value $= 0.484$
c. Do not reject H_0; at the 5% significance level, we cannot conclude that the average MPG differs from 95.

9.56 a. $z = -0.2955$; p-value $= 0.7676$
b. $z = 2.0477$; p-value $= 0.0406$
c. $z = 1.0847$; p-value $= 0.2781$
d. $z = 1.7257$; p-value $= 0.0844$

9.64 a. $H_0: p \leq 0.20$; $H_A: p > 0.20$
b. $z = 2.1764$; p-value $= 0.0148$
c. Reject H_0; at the 5% significance level, the economist's concern is supported.

9.66 $H_0: p \leq 0.75$; $H_A: p > 0.75$; $z = 1.0135$; p-value $= 0.1554$. Do not reject H_0; at the 5% significance level, we cannot conclude that more than 75% of the websites are prone to fraud.

9.78 $H_0: p \geq 0.35$; $H_A: p < 0.35$
Case 1: $z = -1.3260$; p-value $= 0.0924$. Do not reject H_0; at the 5% significance level, we cannot conclude that the percentage of Americans who feel that the country is headed in the right direction is below 35%.
Case 2: $z = -1.8752$; p-value $= 0.0304$. Reject H_0; at the 5% significance level, we conclude that the percentage of Americans who feel that the country is headed in the right direction is below 35%.

9.82 a. $H_0: p = 0.17$; $H_A: p \neq 0.17$
b. $z = 2.07$; p-value $= 0.0384$
c. Reject H_0; at the 5% significance level, we conclude that the proportion of households in the rural South is not representative of the national proportion.

9.84. a. H_0: $\mu = 13{,}500$; H_A: $\mu \neq 13{,}500$
b. $t_{49} = 2.593$; p-value $= 0.012$
c. Reject H_0; at the 10% significance level, we conclude that the average number of miles driven by Midwesterners differs from the U.S. average.

Chapter 10

10.4 a. $t_{20} = 1.719$; p-value $= 0.051$. Do not reject H_0; at the 5% significance level, we cannot conclude that μ_1 is greater than μ_2.
b. At the 10% significance level, we conclude that μ_1 is greater than μ_2.

10.8 a. H_0: $\mu_1 - \mu_2 = 0$; H_A: $\mu_1 - \mu_2 \neq 0$
b. $t_8 = -1.667$; p-value $= 0.134$
c. Do not reject H_0; at the 10% significance level, we cannot conclude that the population means differ.

10.10 a. H_0: $\mu_1 - \mu_2 \geq 0$; H_A: $\mu_1 - \mu_2 < 0$
b. $z = -5.81$; p-value $= 0$ (approximately)
c. Reject H_0; at the 5% significance level, we conclude that there is a "community college penalty" at Lucille's university.

10.14 a. H_0: $\mu_1 - \mu_2 \leq 0$; H_A: $\mu_1 - \mu_2 > 0$ (Population 1 = New Process and Population 2 = Old Process)
b. $t_{16} = 2.145$; p-value $= 0.024$
c. Reject H_0; at the 5% significance level, we conclude that the mean output rate of the new process exceeds that of the old process.
d. Do not reject H_0; at the 1% significance level, we cannot conclude that the mean output rate of the new process exceeds that of the old process.

10.20 a. H_0: $\mu_1 - \mu_2 \geq 0$; H_A: $\mu_1 - \mu_2 < 0$ (Population 1 = New Method and Population 2 = Old Method)
b. $t_{66} = -1.436$; p-value $= 0.078$
c. We conclude that the mean assembly time using the new method is less than the old method only at the 10% significance level.

10.28 a. H_0: $\mu_D \leq 0$; H_A: $\mu_D > 0$
b. $t_{34} = 1.868$; p-value $= 0.035$
c. Reject H_0; at the 5% significance level, we conclude that there is a positive mean difference.

10.30 a. H_0: $\mu_D = 0$; H_A: $\mu_D \neq 0$ (Mean difference between Method A and Method B)
b. $t_6 = -2.10$
c. p-value $= 0.08$
d. Reject H_0; at the 10% significance level, the manager's assertion is supported by the data.

10.34 a. H_0: $\mu_D \geq 0$; H_A: $\mu_D < 0$ (Mean time difference between New Processor and Existing Processor)
b. $t_6 = -3.682$; p-value $= 0.005$
c. Reject H_0; at the 5% significance level, we conclude that the mean difference between the new and the existing processing time is less than zero. Yes, there is evidence the new processor is faster than the old processor.

10.42 $(0.25 - 0.28) \pm 1.96$

$$\sqrt{\frac{0.25(1-0.25)}{200} + \frac{0.28(1-0.28)}{250}}, \text{ or } [-0.112, 0.052]$$

At the 5% significance level, we cannot conclude that the population proportions differ.

10.44 a. $z = -0.7543$
b. p-value $= 0.451$
c. Do not reject H_0; at the 5% significance level, we cannot conclude that the population proportions differ.

10.50 a. H_0: $p_1 - p_2 \leq 0$; H_A: $p_1 - p_2 > 0$ (Population 1 = Boys and Population 2 = Girls)
b. $z = 5.09$; p-value $= 0$ (approximately)
Reject H_0; at the 5% significance level, we conclude that the proportion of boys growing out of asthma is more than that of girls.
c. H_0: $p_1 - p_2 \leq 0.10$; H_A: $p_1 - p_2 > 0.10$; $z = 1.19$; p-value $= 0.117$
Do not reject H_0; at the 5% significance level, we cannot conclude that the proportion of boys who grow out of asthma exceeds that of girls by more than 0.10.

10.54 a. H_0: $p_1 - p_2 \geq 0$; H_A: $p_1 - p_2 < 0$ (Population 1 = African American Men and Population 2 = Caucasian Men)
$z = -1.2613$; p-value $= 0.1036$; do not reject H_0. At the 5% significance level, we cannot conclude that the proportion of obese African American men is less than their Caucasian counterparts.
b. H_0: $p_1 - p_2 \leq 0$; H_A: $p_1 - p_2 > 0$ (Population 1 = African American Women and Population 2 = Caucasian Women)
$z = 2.0175$; p-value $= 0.0218$; reject H_0.
At the 5% significance level, we conclude that the proportion of obese African American women is greater than their Caucasian counterparts.
c. H_0: $p_1 - p_2 = 0$; H_A: $p_1 - p_2 \neq 0$ (Population 1 = African American Adults and Population 2 = Caucasian Adults)
$z = 0.3079$; p-value $= 0.7581$; do not reject H_0.
At the 5% significance level, we cannot conclude that the proportion of obese African American adults differs from their Caucasian counterparts.

10.58 H_0: $p_1 - p_2 \leq 0.10$; H_A: $p_1 - p_2 > 0.10$ (Population 1 = Male Students and Population 2 = Female Students)
$z = 2.2052$; p-value $= 0.0137$; reject H_0.
At the 5% significance level, we conclude that there is a greater than 10 percentage point difference between the proportion of male and female students who think it is not feasible for men and women to be just friends.

10.60 a. H_0: $\mu_1 - \mu_2 \leq 0$; H_A: $\mu_1 - \mu_2 > 0$ (Population 1 = Men and Population 2 = Women)
b. $z = 3.53$
c. p-value $= 0.0002$
d. Reject H_0; at the 1% significance level, we conclude that men spend more money than women on St. Patrick's Day.

10.62 H_0: $\mu_1 - \mu_2 = 0$; H_A: $\mu_1 - \mu_2 \neq 0$ (Population 1 = Men and Population 2 = Women)
$t_{28} = 3.285$; p-value $= 0.002$
At the 1% significance level, we conclude that the mean cholesterol levels for men and women are different.

10.64 a. H_0: $\mu_D \leq 30$; H_A: $\mu_D > 30$ (Mean difference between after and before pregnancy weight)

$t_{39} = 3.932$; p-value = 0 (approximately); reject H_0. At the 5% significance level, we conclude that the mean weight gain of women due to pregnancy is more than 30 pounds.

b. H_0: $\mu_D \leq 35$; H_A: $\mu_D > 35$ (Mean difference between after and before pregnancy weight)

$t_{39} = 0.655$; p-value = 0.258; do not reject H_0. At the 5% significance level, we cannot conclude that the mean weight gain of women due to pregnancy is more than 35 pounds.

10.68 a. H_0: $p_1 - p_2 \leq 0.05$; H_A: $p_1 - p_2 > 0.05$ (Population 1 = JFK and Population 2 = O'Hare)

b. $z = 0.4249$; p-value = 0.3355

c. Do not reject H_0; at the 5% significance level, we cannot conclude that the proportion of on-time flights at JFK is more than 5 percentage points higher than that of O'Hare.

Chapter 11

11.8 $H_0{:}\sigma^2 \leq 2; H_A{:}\sigma^2 > 2$; $\chi^2_9 = 13$; p-value = 0.163; do not reject H_0; at the 10% significance level, we cannot conclude that the variance is more than 2.

11.10 a. [0.02, 0.06]

b. We cannot conclude with 95% confidence that the specification is violated.

11.12 a. $H_0{:}\sigma^2 = 0.002^2; H_A{:}\sigma^2 \neq 0.002^2$

b. $\chi^2_{24} = 37.50$; assume the bearing diameters are normally distributed.

c. p-value = 0.078; do not reject H_0; at the 5% significance level, we cannot conclude that the standard deviation differs from 0.002 inches.

d. reject H_0; at the 10% significance level, we conclude that the standard deviation differs from 0.002 inches.

11.20 a. $H_0{:}\sigma^2 \geq 4; H_A{:}\sigma^2 < 4$

b. $\chi^2_{51} = 36.096$; p-value = 0.057

c. Reject H_0; the investor should invest in this fund.

11.22 a. $H_0{:}\sigma^2 \geq 48400; H_A{:}\sigma^2 < 48400; \chi^2_{49} = 32.902$; p-value = 0.038; reject H_0; at the 5% significance level, we conclude that the standard deviation for Town 1 is less than 220.

b. $H_0{:}\sigma^2 \geq 48400; H_A{:}\sigma^2 < 48400$; $\chi^2_{49} = 36.347$; p-value = 0.090; do not reject H_0; at the 5% significance level, we cannot conclude that the standard deviation for Town 2 is less than 220.

11.30 a. $H_0{:}\sigma^2_2/\sigma^2_1 = 1, H_A{:}\sigma^2_2/\sigma^2_1 \neq 1$

b. $F_{(25,25)} = 1.714$; p-value = 0.185

c. Do not reject H_0; the company should adopt the new cost-cutting technology.

11.32 a. $H_0{:}\sigma^2_2/\sigma^2_1 \leq 1, H_A{:}\sigma^2_2/\sigma^2_1 > 1$ (Lithium-ion is population 1)

b. $F_{(25,15)} = 2.023$; assume normally distributed populations

c. p-value = 0.058

d. Do not reject H_0; at the 5% significance level, we cannot conclude that the variance in discharge time for the lithium-ion battery is less than the nickel-cadmium battery.

e. Yes; at the 10% significance level, we conclude that the variance in discharge time for the lithium-ion battery is less than the nickel-cadmium battery.

11.34 $H_0{:}\sigma^2_2/\sigma^2_1 = 1, H_A{:}\sigma^2_2/\sigma^2_1 \neq 1$ (Index is population 1); $F_{(51,51)} = 1.563$; p-value = 0.1138. Do not reject H_0; at the 5% level, we cannot conclude that the population variances differ; assume normally distributed populations

11.38 $H_0{:}\sigma^2_2/\sigma^2_1 \leq 1, H_A{:}\sigma^2_2/\sigma^2_1 > 1$; $F_{(49,49)} = 1.1047$; p-value = 0.3644; do not reject H_0; at the 5% significance level, we cannot conclude that the variance of rents in Town 1 is less than that of Town 2.

11.40 a. $H_0{:}\sigma^2 \leq 5; H_A{:}\sigma^2 > 5$; $\chi^2_{47} = 70.60$; p-value = 0.015; do not reject H_0; at the 1% significance level, we cannot conclude that the variance exceeds 5; no cause for concern for the advocacy group.

b. Assume that the generic drug prices are normally distributed.

11.42 a. [4.89, 7.86]

b. We cannot conclude with 95% confidence that the standard deviation differs from the required level of 5 milliliters.

11.46 a. $H_0{:}\sigma^2_1/\sigma^2_2 = 1, H_A{:}\sigma^2_1/\sigma^2_2 \neq 1$ (Part A is population 1)

b. $F_{(29,29)} = 1.105$; p-value = 0.789

c. Do not reject H_0; at the 5% significance level, we cannot conclude that the variances differ; carrying the same safety stock level for each part is reasonable.

Chapter 12

12.8 a. $H_0{:}p_1 = p_2 = p_3 = 1/3$; H_A: Not all proportions equal 1/3

b. $\chi^2_2 = 6.968$; p-value = 0.031; reject H_0; at the 5% significance level the visitor's claim is supported.

12.10 $H_0{:}p_1 = 0.38, p_2 = 0.33, p_3 = 0.29$; H_A: At least one population proportion differs from its hypothesized value; $\chi^2_2 = 2.179$; p-value = 0.336. do not reject H_0; at the 5% significance level, the researcher cannot conclude that car preferences have changed.

12.12 a. $H_0{:}p_1 = p_2 = p_3 = p_4 = 0.25; H_A$: Not all proportions equal 0.25

b. $\chi^2_3 = 7.720$. p-value = 0.052

c. At 10% significance level, we conclude that the proportion of bags filled by at least one chute differs from 0.25. At the 5% significance level we cannot conclude that the proportion of bags filled by at least one chute differs from 0.25.

12.14 H_0: The two categories are independent; H_A: The two categories are dependent; $\chi^2_6 = 1.249$; p-value = 0.974; do not reject H_0; at the 1% significance level, we cannot conclude that the two categories are dependent.

12.16 a. H_0: Color preference is independent of sex; H_A: Color preference is dependent on sex

b. $\chi^2_2 = 7.996$; p-value = 0.018

c. Do not reject H_0; at the 1% significance level, we cannot conclude that color preference is dependent on sex; no need to target advertisements differently to males versus females.

12.20 a. H_0: Satisfaction level and age are independent; H_A: Satisfaction level and age are dependent

b. $\chi^2_{df} = \chi^2_4 = 18.358$

c. p-value = 0.001

d. Reject H_0; at the 1% significance level, we conclude that the satisfaction level among the firm's customers is dependent on age.

12.26 H_0: the variable is normally distributed with mean −3.5 and standard deviation 9.7; H_A: the variable is not not normally distributed with mean −3.5 and standard deviation 9.7; $\chi^2_1 = 39.568$; p-value = 0 (approximately); reject H_0; at the 1% significance level, we conclude that the variable is not normally distributed.

12.28 a. H_0: The final grades are normally distributed with mean 72 and standard deviation 10; H_A: The final grades are not normally distributed with mean 72 and standard deviation 10.

b. $\chi^2_2 = 2.988$. The p-value = 0.224

c. Do not reject H_0; at the 5% significance level, we cannot conclude that the normal distribution is inappropriate for making grades.

12.30 a. H_0: Resistance is normally distributed with mean 4790 and standard deviation 40; H_A: Resistance is not normally distributed with mean 4790 and standard deviation 40.

b. $\chi^2_2 = 5.593$; p-value = 0.061; do not reject H_0; at the 5% significance level, we cannot conclude the resistance is not normally distributed.

c. At a 10% significance level, we conclude the resistance is not normally distributed.

12.32 a. H_0: CEO compensation is normally distributed with mean \$19.03 million and standard deviation \$27.61 million; H_A: CEO compensation is not normally distributed with mean \$19.03 million and standard deviation \$27.61 million; $\chi^2_2 =$ 232.493; p-value = 0 (approximately); reject H_0; at the 1% significance level, we conclude that CEO compensation is not normally distributed.

b. H_0: $S = 0$ and $K = 0$; H_A: $S \neq 0$ or $K \neq 0$; $\chi^2_2 = 13616.092$.; p-value = 0 (approximately); at the 1% significance level, we conclude that CEO compensation is not normally distributed.

12.34 a. H_0: $S = 0$ and $K = 0$; H_A: $S \neq 0$ or $K \neq 0$

b. $\chi^2_2 = 1.040$; p-value = 0.595

c. Do not reject H_0; at the 5% significance level, we cannot conclude that the stock prices are not normally distributed.

12.36 a. H_0:$p_1 = 0.40$, $p_2 = 0.30$, $p_3 = 0.20$, $p_4 = 0.10$; H_A: At least one population proportion differs from its hypothesized value.

b. $\chi^2_3 = 8.182$.

c. p-value = 0.042; do not reject H_0; at the 1% significance level, we cannot conclude that the market shares have changed.

12.40 H_0: Delinquency is independent of the type of heating; H_A: delinquency is dependent on the type of heating; $\chi^2_3 = 23.82$; p-value = 0 (approximately); reject H_0; at the 5% significance level, we conclude that delinquency is dependent on the type of heating.

12.46 a. H_0:$p_1 = 0.54$, $p_2 = 0.30$, $p_3 = 0.16$; H_A: At least one population proportion differs from its hypothesized value.

b. $\chi^2_2 = 155.867$; p-value = 0 (approximately); reject H_0; at the 1% significance level, we conclude that the proportions have changed.

12.50 a. H_0: $S = 0$ and $K = 0$; H_A: $S \neq 0$ or $K \neq 0$

b. $\chi^2_2 = 1.861$; p-value = 0.394

c. Do not reject H_0; at the 5% significance level, we cannot conclude that weekly demand values are not normally distributed; the conclusion is not sensitive to the choice of the significance level.

Chapter 13

13.6 a. H_0: $\mu_1 = \mu_2 = \mu_3 = \mu_4 = \mu_5 = \mu_6$
H_A: Not all population means are equal.

c. $F_{(5,54)} = 1.371$; p-value = 0.250; do not reject H_0. At the 5% significance level, we cannot conclude that not all population means are equal.

13.8. a. H_0: $\mu_1 = \mu_2 = \mu_3$
H_A: Not all population means are equal.

b. $F_{(2,21)} = 2.804$; p-value = 0.083; do not reject H_0. At the 5% significance level, we cannot conclude that there are differences in the effectiveness of the three detergents.

13.14 a. H_0: $\mu_{Low} = \mu_{Medium} = \mu_{High}$
H_A: Not all population means are equal.

b. $F_{(2,117)} = 10.591$; p-value = 0 (approximately). At the 1% and 5% significance levels, we conclude that the mean fill volumes are not equal.

13.18 H_0: $\mu_1 = \mu_2 = \mu_3$
H_A: Not all population means are equal.
$F_{(2,87)} = 11.4794$; p-value = 0 (approximately); reject H_0. At the 10% significance level, we conclude that the average job satisfaction differs by field.

13.24 b. $\mu_1 - \mu_2$: [−12.10, −7.90]*
$\mu_1 - \mu_3$: [−9.01, −4.99]*
$\mu_2 - \mu_3$: [0.78, 5.22]*

c. $\mu_1 - \mu_2$: [−12.53, −7.47]*
$\mu_1 - \mu_3$: [−9.42, −4.58]*
$\mu_2 - \mu_3$: [0.33, 5.67]*

d. Tukey's HSD approach is more reliable because it protects against an inflated risk of Type I error.

13.26 a. H_0: $\mu_{Day1} = \mu_{Day2} = \mu_{Day3} = \mu_{Day4}$
H_A: Not all population means are equal.
Reject H_0; at the 1% significance level, we conclude that the mean hardness is not the same.

b. $\mu_1 - \mu_2$: [1.76, 13.74]*
$\mu_1 - \mu_3$: [−11.44, 0.16]
$\mu_1 - \mu_4$: [−9.67, 2.11]
$\mu_2 - \mu_3$: [−19.53, −7.25]*
$\mu_2 - \mu_4$: [−17.75, −5.31]*
$\mu_3 - \mu_4$: [−4.18, 7.90]
At the 1% significance level, we conclude that the mean hardness of the Day 2 batch differs from those of the Day 1, 3, and 4 batches.

13.28 a. H_0: $\mu_{First} = \mu_{Second} = \mu_{Third}$
H_A: Not all population means are equal.

$F_{(2,72)} = 2.759$; p-value = 0.07; do not reject H_0. We conclude only at the 10% significance level (not at 5%) that the mean absenteeism differs across the three work shifts.

b. $\mu_1 - \mu_2$: [−5.81, 0.13]

$\mu_1 - \mu_3$: [−7.05, −1.11]*

$\mu_2 - \mu_3$: [−4.21, 1.73]

At the 10% significance level, we conclude that the mean absenteeism differs between the first and third shift workers.

13.30 a. $SST = 176.25$; $SSA = 51.5$; $SSB = 74.25$; $SSE = 50.5$

b. $MSA = 25.75$; $MSB = 24.75$; $MSE = 8.4167$

d. p-value = 0.1214; do not reject H_0. At the 5% significance level, we cannot conclude that the Factor A means differ.

e. p-value = 0.1209; do not reject H_0. At the 5% significance level, we cannot conclude that the Factor B means differ.

13.34 b. p-value = 0.900; do not reject H_0. At the 5% significance level, we cannot conclude that the column means differ.

c. p-value = 0.006; reject H_0. At the 5% significance level, we conclude that the row means differ.

13.36 b. p-value = 0.233; do not reject H_0. At the 5% significance level, we cannot conclude that average scores differ between rounds.

c. p-value = 0.132; do not reject H_0. At the 5% significance level, we cannot conclude that the average scores differ across players.

13.42 b. p-value = 0.751; do not reject H_0. At the 5% significance level, we cannot conclude that there is interaction between factors A and B.

c. p-value = 0 (approximately); reject H_0. At the 5% significance level, the means differ for factor A.

d. p-value = 0 (approximately); reject H_0. At the 5% significance level, the means differ for factor B.

13.44 a. p-value = 0.463; do not reject H_0. At the 1% significance level, we cannot conclude that there is interaction between the two factors.

b. Yes. At the 1% significance level, the column means as well as the row means differ.

13.48 a. p-value = 0.296; do not reject H_0. At the 5% significance level, we cannot conclude that there is interaction between the two factors.

b. Yes. At the 5% significance level, we conclude that differences in the mean weekly sales depend on the time of day used for advertising. At the 5% significance level, we cannot conclude that differences in the mean weekly sales depend on the local channel used for advertising.

13.52 a. H_0: $\mu_1 = \mu_2 = \mu_3 = \mu_4$

H_A: Not all population means are equal.

b. p-value = 0 (approximately); reject H_0. At the 5% significance level, we conclude that the average salaries of the four different transportation operators differ.

13.56 H_0: $\mu_1 = \mu_2 = \mu_3$

H_A: Not all population means are equal.

p-value = 0.020; reject H_0. At the 5% significance level, we conclude that the average strength of the plywood boards differs by the type of glue used.

13.58 a. H_0: $\mu_A = \mu_B = \mu_C$

H_A: Not all population means are equal.

p-value = 0.003; reject H_0. At the 5% significance level, we conclude that the mean P/E ratios of these three industries differ.

b. $\mu_A - \mu_B$: [−8.93, 3.58]

$\mu_A - \mu_C$: [−16.10, −3.58]*

$\mu_B - \mu_C$: [−13.42, −0.91]*

At the 5% significance level, the mean P/E ratio differs between A and C, and between B and C.

13.60 a. H_0: $\mu_{Internet} = \mu_{Phone} = \mu_{Mail\text{-}in}$

H_A: Not all population means are equal.

p-value = 0.651; do not reject H_0. At the 5% significance level, we cannot conclude that the mean purchase amounts differ across the three purchase sources.

b. Fisher's LSD method is not necessary since we did not find differences in means.

13.62 H_0: $\mu_1 = \mu_2 = \mu_3 = \mu_4 = \mu_5 = \mu_6 = \mu_7$

H_A: Not all population means are equal.

p-value = 0 (approximately); reject H_0. At the 5% significance level, we conclude that the mean visits to the website differ by day of the week.

13.68 a. p-value = 0.221; do not reject H_0. At the 5% significance level, we cannot conclude that there is interaction between fuel type and hybrid type.

b. p-value = 0.010; reject H_0. At the 5% significance level, we conclude that average fuel consumption differs by fuel type.

c. p-value = 0.160; do not reject H_0. At the 5% significance level, we cannot conclude that average fuel consumption differs by type of hybrid.

13.70 a. p-value = 0.001; reject H_0. At the 5% significance level, we conclude that there is interaction between the training method and operator experience level.

b. Given significant interaction, we cannot use results to conduct tests on the main effects.

Chapter 14

14.6 a. $r_{xy} = -0.175$; negative linear relationship

b. H_0: $r_{xy} = 0$; H_A: $r_{xy} \neq 0$

c. $t_{23} = -0.852$; p-value = 0.402; do not reject H_0. At the 5% significance level, we cannot conclude that the population correlation coefficient differs from zero.

14.8 a. $r_{1,2} = 0.5662$; $r_{1,3} = 0.6264$; $r_{1,4} = 0.8231$; $r_{2,3} = 0.0445$; $r_{2,4} = 0.6278$; $r_{3,4} = 0.4594$

b. Firm 2

c. Firm 2 and Firm 3

14.12 a. $\hat{y} = 40$

b. $\hat{y}$ increases by 25

14.14 a. $\hat{y} = 568$

b. If x_2 increases by 1 unit, $\hat{y}$ decreases by 47.2 units, holding x_1 constant.

14.18 a. $b_1 = 30$; if x_1 increases by 1 unit, $\hat{y}$ increases by 30 units, holding x_2 as constant.

b. $\hat{y} = 21.97 + 30x_1 - 1.88x_2$

c. $\hat{y} = 884.37$

14.24 a. The positive sign for the Poverty coefficient is as expected; the slope coefficient for Income is not as expected.
b. As Poverty increases by 1%, Crime is predicted to rise by 53.16, holding Income constant.
c. $\widehat{Crime} = 1009.08$

14.26 a. $\widehat{GPA} = 0.4256 + 0.0041GRE$
b. $\widehat{GPA} = 3.35$

14.28 a. $\widehat{Consumption} = 2{,}365.67 + 0.8465Income$
b. As disposable income increases by $1, consumption is predicted to increase by $0.85
c. $\widehat{Consumption} = 31.992.75$

14.32 a. $\widehat{Final} = 27.5818 + 0.6774Midterm$
b. $\widehat{Final} = 81.77$

14.40 a. $\widehat{Rent} = 300.4116 + 225.81Bed + 89.2661Bath + 0.2096Sqft$
b. For every additional bathroom, the predicted rent increases by $89.27, holding number of bedrooms and square feet constant.
c. $\widehat{Rent} = 1{,}155.70$

14.42 a. $s_e^2 = 54.3478; s_e = 7.3721$
b. $R^2 = 0.1667$

14.44 a. $s_e = 0.8629$
b. $R^2 = 0.6111$

14.46 Model 2, since it has a smaller s_e and a higher R^2. We need not use adjusted R^2 since both models have the same number of explanatory variables.

14.48 Model 2, since it has a smaller s_e and a higher adjusted R^2.

14.50 a. 82.99% of the sample variability in sales is explained.
b. 17.01% of the sample variability in sales is not explained.

14.54 Model 2, since it has a smaller s_e (1475 versus 1509) and a higher adjusted R^2 (0.8283 versus 0.8204).

14.56 a. $s_e = 12.7697$
b. $R^2 = 0.1726$
c. Adjusted $R^2 = 0.1113$

14.64 a. $\widehat{Startups} = 0.4190 + 0.0087Research + 0.0517Patents - 0.0194Duration$
b. $\widehat{Startups} = 1.48$
c. $114.94 million

Chapter 15

15.8 a. $H_0: \beta_1 \leq 0; H_A: \beta_1 > 0$
b. $t_{18} = 2.80$; p-value $= 0.0118/2 = 0.0059$
c. Reject H_0; at the 1% significance level, we conclude that advertising expenditures and sales have a positive linear relationship.

15.10 a. $\widehat{Time} = 13.8359 - 0.05463Height$
b. $H_0: \beta_1 = 0; H_A: \beta_1 \neq 0$
c. p-value $= 0.022/2 = 0.011$; reject H_0. At the 5% significance level, Height and Time have a negative linear relationship.

15.14 a. $\widehat{Return} = -33.9966 + 3.9674P/E - 3.36809P/S$
b. $H_0: \beta_1 = \beta_2 = 0; H_A$: At least one $\beta_j \neq 0$
$F_{(2,27)} = 9.104$; p-value $= 0.001$; reject H_0. At the 10% significance level, the two explanatory variables are jointly significant.
c. At the 10% significance level, P/E is not significant but P/S is not significant.

15.16 $\widehat{Taxes} = 6{,}499.4126 + 6.8063Size$
$H_0: \beta_1 = 0$ and $H_A: \beta_1 \neq 0$
p-value $= 0$ (approximately); reject H_0. At the 5% significance level, home size is significant.

15.20 a. $\widehat{Cost} = 14{,}039.1873 + 92.7827Temp + 446.1406Days - 27.0033Tons$
b. $H_0: \beta_1 = \beta_2 = \beta_3 = 0; H_A$: At least one $\beta_j \neq 0$ p-value $= 0.026$; reject H_0. At the 10% significance level, the explanatory variables are jointly significant.
c. At the 10% significance level, the average temperature is significant, the number of work days is not significant, and the tons produced is not significant.

15.24 Restricted Model: $y = \beta_0 + \beta_2 x_2 + \varepsilon$
Unrestricted Model: $y = \beta_0 + \beta_1 x_1 + \beta_2 x_2 + \beta_3 x_3 + \varepsilon$

15.26 Restricted Model: $(y - x_2) = \beta_0 + \beta_1(x_1 - x_2) + \varepsilon$
Unrestricted Model: $y = \beta_0 + \beta_1 x_1 + \beta_2 x_2 + \varepsilon$

15.30 $H_0: \beta_2 = \beta_3 = 0; H_A$: At least one of the coefficients is nonzero.
$F_{(2,139)} = 3.385$; p-value $= 0.037$; reject H_0. At the 5% level, Patents and Duration are jointly significant. Lisa should add both variables for predicting Startups.

15.32 a. $\widehat{Sale} = 23.3045 + 0.5184MaleHours + 0.6779FemaleHours$
b. At the 5% significance level, both explanatory variables are jointly significant.
At the 5% significance level, both explanatory variables are individually significant.
c. $H_0: \beta_1 = \beta_2; H_A: \beta_1 \neq \beta_2$
$F_{(1,49)} = 2.260$; p-value $= 0.139$; do not reject H_0. At the 5% significance level, we cannot conclude that there is a difference in productivity between male and female employees.

15.36 a. $28.46 \leq E(y^0) \leq 33.64$
b. $24.02 \leq y^0 \leq 38.08$
c. The prediction interval because it incorporates the non-zero error term.

15.38 a. $45.51 \leq E(y^0) \leq 56.71$
b. $37.81 \leq y^0 \leq 64.41$
c. The confidence interval because the prediction interval incorporates the non-zero error term.

15.40 a. $31.60 \leq E(y^0) \leq 36.93$
b. $19.49 \leq y^0 \leq 49.03$

15.44 a. $\hat{y}^0 = 6.1871$
b. $5.83 \leq E(y^0) \leq 6.55$
c. $4.75 \leq y^0 \leq 7.63$

15.46 b. Since the residuals fan out when plotted against x, it suggests a problem of changing variability (heteroskedasticity). This means that the estimators are not efficient and the significance tests are not valid. A common solution is to use robust standard errors for conducting significance tests.

15.48 The scatterplot shows that a simple linear regression model is not appropriate as GPA is positively related to Hours at lower levels but negatively related at higher levels of Hours.

15.50 a. Perfect multicollinearity, since Study + Sleep + Leisure = 24; the proposed model cannot be estimated.

b. Drop the Sleep variable.

15.52 a. Experienced (older) employees are likely to have more variability in salaries because not all employees reach the same level of success over time.

b. The residuals fan out when plotted against experience, confirming the changing variability (heteroskedasticity) problem.

15.54 There does not appear to be an issue with correlated observations, as the residuals do not show any pattern around the horizontal axis.

15.58 a. $\widehat{Time} = 14.13$ minutes

b. 85.30%

c. At the 5% significance level, the explanatory variables are jointly significant.

In addition, at the 5% significance level, the explanatory variables are individually significant.

15.60 a. At the 5% significance level, we cannot conclude that Ownership is linearly related to Income.

b. $67.58 \leq E(y^0) \leq 70.82$

c. $57.49 \leq y^0 \leq 80.91$; the prediction interval is wider since it accounts for the non-zero random error term.

15.62 a. At the 5% significance level, the explanatory variables are not jointly or individually significant. George's theory is not valid.

b. Multicollinearity is not likely a problem since the sample correlation coefficient between Turnover and Expense is only −0.247. There does not seem to be a problem of changing variability since the residuals appear randomly dispersed around zero when plotted against Turnover and Expense.

Chapter 16

16.4 a. The quadratic model with a higher adjusted R^2 is preferred.

b. For $x = 4$, $\hat{y} = 3.82$; for $x = 6$, $\hat{y} = 2.75$; for $x = 12$, $\hat{y} = 11.83$

16.6 a. Linear Model: for $x = 2$, $\hat{y} = 22.50$; for $x = 3$, $\hat{y} = 23.85$

Quadratic Model: for $x = 2$, $\hat{y} = 21.84$; for $x = 3$, $\hat{y} = 21.79$

Cubic Model: for $x = 2$, $\hat{y} = 21.91$; for $x = 3$, $\hat{y} = 21.57$

16.8 a. From the scatter plot, crew sie of 6 or 7 seem optimal.

b. Linear Model: $\widehat{Jobs} = 13.0741 + 0.1111$ Crew

Quadratic Model: $\widehat{Jobs} = 2.1111 + 4.5960$ Crew -0.3737 Crew^2

The quadratic model with a higher adjusted R^2 is preferred.

c. $\widehat{Jobs} = 15.75$

d. $\widehat{Jobs} = 0.6852 + 5.5407$ Crew Size -0.5505 Crew $\text{Size}^2 + 0.0098$ Crew Size^3; the quadratic model is still preferred.

16.12 a. Model 1: As x increases by one unit, $\hat{y}$ decreases by 4.2 units.

Model 2: As x increases by one percent, $\hat{y}$ decreases by about 2.8 units.

Model 3: As x increases by one unit, $\hat{y}$ decreases by about 4%

Model 4: As x increases by one percent, $\hat{y}$ decreases by about 0.8%

b. Model 1: $\hat{y}$ decreases by 4.2 (= 75.8 − 80)

Model 1: $\hat{y}$ decreases by 2.78 (= 77.77 − 80.55)

Model 3: $\hat{y}$ decreases by 3.22 (= 78.92 − 82.14)

Model 4: $\hat{y}$ decreases by 0.59 (= 74.74 − 75.33)

16.14 Model 1: $\hat{y} = 708.42$

Model 2: $\hat{y} = 678.64$

Model 3: $\hat{y} = 725.75$

Model 4: $\hat{y} = 685.75$

16.16 a. The logarithmic model is preferred because it has a lower standard error of the estimate and a higher R^2.

b. $\hat{y} = 18.61$

16.20 a. $\widehat{Watches} = 35.909 - 0.0261$ Time; as the time increases by 1 second, the number of predicted watches decrease by 0.0261; $\widehat{Watches} = 21.57$

b. $\widehat{Watches} = 123.1125 - 16.2124\ln(\text{Time})$; as the time increases by 1% the number of predicted watches decrease by about 0.1621; $\widehat{Watches} = 20.81$

c. The logarithmic model with a higher R^2 is preferred.

16.22 a. $\widehat{Cost} = \$28{,}279$

b. $\widehat{Cost} = \$28{,}238$

c. The linear model with a higher R2 is preferred; 0.6659 > 0.6544

16.28 a. $\widehat{Salary} = \exp(9.8895 + 0.0780\text{NPS} + 0.0360\text{Age} -0.0004\text{Age}^2 + \frac{0.2245^2}{2}$

b. Optimal age = 47.82

c. $\widehat{Salary} = \$89{,}243$

16.30 a. Linear Model: $\widehat{Time} = -14.4886 + 0.7502$ Parts;

Quadratic Model: $\widehat{Time} = -6.7165 + 0.4476$ Parts + 0.0025 Parts^2

b. The quadratic model with a higher adjusted R^2 is preferred.

c. $\widehat{Time} = 20.59$ minutes.

16.32 a. Linear Model: $\widehat{Savings} = -40.8632 + 0.0041$ Income

Log-log Model: $\ln(\widehat{Savings}) = -112.0910 + 12.2033\ln(\text{Income})$

b. The linear model with a higher R^2 is preferred; 0.7001 > 0.6497

Chapter 17

17.2 a. $\hat{y} = 207$

b. $\hat{y} = 160$

17.6 a. For Urban, $\widehat{Consumption} = 55{,}103.68$; for rural, $\widehat{Consumption} = 48{,}559.26$

b. For urban, $\widehat{Consumption} = 55{,}103.68$; for rural, $\widehat{Consumption} = 48{,}559.26$

c. Same results

17.8 a. BMI is significant at the 5% level

b. $\widehat{\text{Salary}} = 38.01$

c. $\widehat{\text{Salary}} = 33.52$

17.16 a. $\widehat{\text{Vehicles}} = 135.3913 + 23.5056\text{ Garage} + 0.5955\text{ Population} + 84.5998\text{ Access} + 77.4646\text{ Winter}$

c. The explanatory variables are jointly significant at the 5% and 10% levels; Garage is significant only at the 10% level; Population is not significant at the 5% or 10% levels; Access is significant at the 5% and 10% levels; Winter is significant at the 5% and 10% levels

d. 87.39%

e. 361.34

17.20 a. For 5 years, $\widehat{\text{Salary}} = \$61{,}800$; for 15 years $\widehat{\text{Salary}} = \$93{,}800$

b. For 5 years, $\widehat{\text{Salary}} = \$36{,}300$; for 15 years, $\widehat{\text{Salary}} = \$48{,}300$

c. Positive impact

17.24 a. $\widehat{\text{Errors}} = 37.9305 - 1.2814\text{Exper} - 7.4241\text{Train}$; $\widehat{\text{Errors}} = 42.7765 - 1.6991\text{Exper} - 23.1111\text{Train} + 0.9785(\text{Exper} \times \text{Train})$

b. Second model

c. For 10 years, $\widehat{\text{Errors}} = 12.46$; for 20 years, $\widehat{\text{Errors}} = 8.79$

d. Less experienced employees benefit more from training (reduced errors)

17.32 a. $\hat{y} = 0.57$

b. Only x_3 is significant at the 5% level

17.40 a. LPM: $\widehat{\text{Acceptable}} = 0.9900 - 0.0037\text{Age} - 0.2019\text{Religious}$

Logistic: $\widehat{\text{Acceptable}} = \dfrac{\exp(2.5028 - 0.0209\text{Age} - 1.0396\text{Religious})}{1 + \exp(2.5028 - 0.0209\text{Age} - 1.0396\text{Religious})}$

b. 74% for LPM and 74.5 for logistic

c. For religious, $\widehat{\text{Acceptable}} = 0.6516$; for non-religious, $\widehat{\text{Acceptable}} = 0.8410$

17.44 a. $\widehat{\text{Hours}} = 13.7647 + 4.5144\text{Fall} + 1.6074\text{Winter}$

At the 5% significance level, students study more in fall and winter than in spring.

b. For fall, $\widehat{\text{Hours}} = 18.28$; for winter, $\widehat{\text{Hours}} = 15.37$; for spring, $\widehat{\text{Hours}} = 13.76$

17.46 a. $\widehat{\text{Customers}} = 103.9643 - 1.9208\text{Morning} + 18.2710\text{Afternoon} - 39.6830\text{Evening}$

b. For morning, $\widehat{\text{Customers}} = 102.04$; for afternoon, $\widehat{\text{Customers}} = 122.24$, for evening, $\widehat{\text{Customers}} = 64.28$, for night, $\widehat{\text{Customers}} = 103.96$

17.48 a. $\widehat{\text{Comp}} = 2677.1892 + 10.3154\text{Profit} + 1227.6866\text{Years} + 36655.1363\text{Grad} - 0.5227(\text{Profit} \times \text{Grad}) - 193.1612(\text{Years} \times \text{Grad})$

b. At the 5% level, the explanatory variables are jointly significant

c. At the 5% significance level, profit is significant, years is significant, grad is significant, but both interaction variables are not significant.

d. $\widehat{\text{Comp}} = \$101{,}855$

17.50 a. $\text{Crime} = \dfrac{\exp(9.0293 - 0.3454x_1 + 1.2729x_2)}{1 + \exp(9.0293 - 0.3454x_1 + 1.2729x_2)}$

b. Age is significant at the 10% level, but Gender is not significant at any reasonable level.

c. For male, $\widehat{\text{Crime}} = 0.84$; for female, $\widehat{\text{Crime}} = 0.60$

17.52 a. $\widehat{\text{Pass}} = 0.4343$

b. $\widehat{\text{Pass}} = 0.4282$

17.54 a. $\widehat{\text{STEM}} = 0.51$

b. 79.4%

Chapter 18

18.4 a. $MSE = 649.9512$; $MAD = 20.3975$; $MAPE = 14.4617\%$; $\hat{y}_{12} = 127.8867$

b. $MSE = 551.5359$; $MAD = 19.9401$; $MAPE = 14.0331\%$; $\hat{y}_{12} = 146.0634$

c. Choose exponential smoothing

18.6 a. 3-period moving average: $MSE = 0.0009$; $MAD = 0.0244$; $MAPE = 2.0832$

5-period moving average: $MSE = 0.0016$; $MAD = 0.0344$; $MAPE = 2.9274$

Use 3-period moving average; $\hat{y}_{26} = 1.1386$

b. $\alpha = 0.2$: $MSE = 0.0018$; $MAD = 0.0384$; $MAPE = 2.8923$

$\alpha = 0.4$: $MSE = 0.0010$; $MAD = 0.0276$; $MAPE = 2.0791$

$\alpha = 0.6$: $MSE = 0.0007$; $MAD = 0.0213$; $MAPE = 1.6115$

Use $\alpha = 0.6$; $\hat{y}_{26} = 1.2819$

18.12 a. $\hat{y}_t = 90.4938 + 1.1124t$; positive trend

b. $\hat{y}_{54} = 150.56$

18.14 a. $\hat{y}_t = 9324.1892 + 1655.6701d_1 + 4094.4722d_2 + 1124.83d_3 + 189.4201t$; positive trend; lowest revenue in the 4th quarter

b. $\hat{y}_{2018:04} = 16143.31$

18.18 a. Quadratic trend seems appropriate

b. Linear: $\hat{y}_t = 219.31 + 1.437802t$; adjusted $R^2 = 0.8349$

Quadratic: $\hat{y}_t = 213.7527 + 3.6607t - 0.1588t^2$; adjusted $R^2 = 0.9550$

Choose quadratic because it has higher adjusted R^2; $\hat{y}_{2018} = 233.88$; $\hat{y}_{2019} = 232.94$

18.20 a. Quadratic: $\hat{y}_t = 2975.811 - 2.3423t + 0.0552t^2$; adjusted $R^2 = 0.9741$

Cubic: $\hat{y}_t = 2953.7899 + 0.6775t - 0.0331t^2 + 0.0007t^3$; adjusted $R^2 = 0.9886$

b. Choose cubic because it has higher adjusted R^2; $\hat{y}_{\text{Jan-17}} = 3197.89$

18.22 $\hat{y}_t = \exp(4.0278 + 0.4087d_1 + 0.2025d_2 - 0.3273d_3 + 0.1552t + \dfrac{(0.4481)^2}{2})$

$\hat{y}_{2018:1} = 54080.47$; $\hat{y}_{2018:2}$ 51387.09

18.24 $\hat{y}_t = \exp(3.8397 - 0.0350d_1 - 0.0287d_2 + 10.1563d_3 + 0.2533d_4 + 0.2679d_5 + 0.2909d_6 + 0.2839$

$d_7 + 0.2100d_8 + 0.2335d_9 + 0.2114d_{10} + 0.0988$

$d_{11} + 0.0082t + \left(\frac{(0.1041)^2}{2}\right)$; $\hat{y}_{2018:12} = 102.59$

18.32 a. Model 1: $\hat{y}_t = 303.161 - 13.079x_{t-1}$; adjusted $R^2 = 0.7347$

Model 2: $\hat{y}_t = -4.389 + 0.120x_{t-1} + 1.017y_{t-1}$; adjusted $R^2 = 0.9867$

b. Model 2 because it has higher adjusted R^2; $\hat{y}_{25} = 258.92$

18.34 a. Fried Dough: $\hat{y}_{21} = 63.03$; Soft Drinks: $\hat{y}_{21} = 151.73$

18.38 a. Linear: $\hat{y}_t = 99.9518 + 0.6071t$; adjusted $R^2 = 0.8536$

Quadratic: $\hat{y}_t = 90.2568 + 1.5766t - 0.01643t^2$; adjusted $R^2 = 0.9966$

Quadratic because it has higher adjusted R^2

b. $\hat{y}_{2018} = 126.07$; $\hat{y}_{2019} = 125.69$

18.40 a. Linear: $MSE = 8889968$; $MAD = 2383$; $MAPE = 0.9461$

Exponential: $MSE = 7909245$; $MAD = 2288$; $MAPE = 0.9037$

b. Choose exponential; $\hat{y}_{2018:10} = 281708$; $\hat{y}_{2018:11} = 261166$; $\hat{y}_{2018:12} = 267964$

Chapter 19

19.2 a. 6.12%

b. 1.02%

c. 7.14%.

19.4 a. 5.00%

b. 45.83%

c. 50.83%

19.8 January: −1.68%; February: −0.36%

19.10 a. In 2012, we update the price index as $\frac{100}{109.4} \times 100 = 91.41$; others are updated similarly.

b. Prices increased by 14.7% from 2012 to 2020.

c. Prices increased by 4.84% from 2016 to 2020.

19.14 a. Relative to January, the price peaked in May with an increase of 26.07%. The smallest price increase of 2.14% was in February.

b. Relative to January, the price was 19.66% higher in June.

19.16

Price Index	Jan	Feb	...	Nov	Dec
Laspeyres	100	93.99	...	123.99	124.97
Paasche	100	94.88	...	121.86	122.62

a. The Laspeyres price index suggests that the prices in December were 24.97% higher than what they were in January.

b. The Paasche price index suggests that the prices in December were 22.62% higher than what they were in January.

19.20

Year	Limited	Medium	Unlimited	Aggregate Price Index
2018	100.00	100.00	100.00	100.00
2019	117.24	108.33	105.00	107.61
2020	131.03	112.50	103.33	109.64

a. Relative to 2018, price appreciation was the most for limited usage, followed by medium and unlimited usage.

b. Relative to 2018, the prices of the three usage types increased by 7.61% and 9.64% in 2019 and 2020, respectively.

19.22

Nominal Value	Real Value
32	32.00
37	36.27
39	37.86
42	38.89

19.24 5.77% increase

19.26 a. Nominal values increased by 5.26% compared to 2.20% increase in real values.

b. Nominal values increased by 5.00% compared to 3.44% decrease in real values.

c. The inflation rate is 3.00% for 2010 and 8.74% in 2011.

19.28 a. 120% increase

b. 49.24% increase

19.30 a. Real income declined from the previous year in 2013.

b. 48.25%

c. 26.45%

19.40 a. 28.35%

b. 29.14%

Chapter 20

20.2. a. $H_0{:}m \leq 140$; $H_A{:}m > 140$

b. $T = T^+ = 19$

c. At the 5% significance level, we conclude that the median is greater than 140.

20.6. a. $H_0{:}m \geq 6$; $H_A{:}m < 6$

b. $T = T^+ = 1.5$

c. At the 5% significance level, we conclude that the median price is less than $6.

20.8. a. $H_0{:}m \leq 25$; $H_A{:}m > 25$

b. $z = \frac{35 - 27.50}{9.8107} = 0.76$

c. p-value $= 0.2236$.

d. At the 1% significance level, we cannot conclude that the median rent exceeds $25 per square foot.

20.10 a. $H_0{:}m \leq 500$; $H_A{:}m > 500$

b. Using R, p-value $= 0.3131$. At the 5% significance level, the realtor's claim is not supported by the data.

20.12 a. $H_0{:}m_D \leq 0$; $H_A{:}m_D > 0$

b. $z = \frac{165 - 105}{26.7862} = 2.24$.

c. p-value $= 0.0125$.

d. At the 5% significance level, the population median difference is greater than 0.

20.14 a. $H_0{:}m_D \geq 0$; $H_A{:}m_D < 0$

b. Using R, p-value $= 0.045$. At the 5% significance level, the population median difference is less than 0.

20.18 a. $\mu_W = 575$; $\sigma_W = 43.7798$

b. $H_0{:}m_1 - m_2 \leq 0$; $H_A{:}m_1 - m_2 > 0$

c. $z = \dfrac{700 - 575}{43.7798} = 2.86.$

d. At the 5% significance level, the median of Population 1 is greater than the median of Population 2.

20.20 a. $H_0{:}m_D \leq 0$; $H_A{:}m_D > 0$

b. Using R, p-value $= 0.069 > \alpha = 0.05$. At the 5% significance level, we cannot conclude the median score on the real SAT is greater than the median score on the mock SAT.

20.22 a. $H_0{:}m_D = 0$; $H_A{:}m_D \neq 0$

b. $z = \dfrac{14 - 27.50}{9.8107} = -1.38.$

c. p-value $= 0.1676$.

d. At the 5% significance level, we cannot conclude that the median difference between the two appraisal values differs from zero.

20.24 a. $H_0{:}m_1 - m_2 \leq 0$; $H_A{:}m_1 - m_2 > 0$

b. Using R, p-value $= 0.008 < \alpha = 0.05$. At the 5% significance level, the median income of married men is higher than that of unmarried men.

20.26 a. $H_0{:}m_1 - m_2 \leq 0$; $H_A{:}m_1 - m_2 > 0$

b. $W = W_1 = 138$

c. $z = \dfrac{138 - 105}{13.2288} = 2.49$; p-value $= 0.0064$.

The data support that South Koreans spend more hours per year on the job than American workers at the 5% significance level.

20.30 a. $H_0{:}m_1 = m_2 = m_3 = m_4$; H_A:Not all population medians are equal.

b. Using R, p-value $= 0.015$. At the 5% significance level, some medians differ.

20.32 a. $H_0{:}m_1 = m_2 = m_3$; H_A:Not all population medians are equal.

b. $H = 9.105$.

c. At the 10% significance level, some median lengths differ between the three brands.

20.34 a. $H_0{:}m_1 = m_2 = m_3$; H_A:Not all population medians are equal.

b. $H = 1.505$.

c. At the 1% significance level, we cannot conclude that some medians differ.

20.36 $H_0{:}m_1 = m_2 = m_3$; H_A:Not all population medians are equal.

Using R, p-value = 6.649e-05. At the 10% significance level, some differences exist in the median job satisfaction scores between the fields of employment.

20.38 a. $H_0{:}\rho_S \geq 0$; $H_A{:}\rho_S < 0$;

b. $r_S = -0.829$; relatively strong, negative relationship

c. At the 5% significance level, the Spearman correlation coefficient is less than 0.

20.42 a. $H_0{:}\rho_S = 0$; $H_A{:}\rho_S \neq 0$;

b. $r_S = 0.212$; weak negative relationship

c. At the 5% significance level, we cannot conclude that GNP and infant mortality are correlated.

20.44 a. $H_0{:}\rho_S = 0$; $H_A{:}\rho_S \neq 0$

b. Using R, p-value $= 0.2166$. At the 5% significance level, we cannot conclude that the price of a home and the number of days it takes to sell the home are correlated.

20.48 $H_0{:}\rho_S \leq 0$; $H_A{:}\rho_S > 0$; using R, p-value $= 0.0029$. At the 5% significance level, we can conclude that age and happiness are positively correlated.

20.50 a. $z = -2.53$

b. p-value $= 0.0114$.

c. At the 5% significance level, we conclude that the population proportions differ.

20.52 a. $H_0{:}p = 0.50$; $H_A{:}p \neq 0.50$ (p represents the proportion of plus signs)

b. $z = 2.24$.

c. p-value $= 0.0250$.

d. At the 5% significance level, the proportion of positive signs is different from that of negative signs.

20.54 a. $H_0{:}p \geq 0.50$; $H_A{:}p < 0.50$ (p represents the proportion of ratings that have improved)

b. $z = -4.00$

c. p-value ≈ 0.

d. At the 5% significance level, the rating is significantly lower this year as compared to last year.

20.62 a. H_0:Even and odd numbers occur randomly; H_A:Even and odd numbers do not occur randomly

b. $z = -1.72$.

c. At the 1% significance level, we cannot conclude that the computer program is operating improperly.

20.64 H_0:GDP growth rate in India is random; H_A:GDP growth rate in India is not random

Using R, p-value $= 0.05413$. We cannot conclude that India GDP growth rate is non-random at the 5% significance level.

20.68 a. $H_0{:}m_D = 0$; $H_A{:}m_D \neq 0$

b. $z = -0.89$

c. At the 5% significance level, we cannot conclude that the median difference between the stock returns differs from zero.

20.72 a. $H_0{:}m_1 = m_2 = m_3$; H_A:Not all population medians are equal.

b. $H = 7.98$.

c. At the 5% significance level, some median P/E ratios differ by industry.

A

Acceptance sampling A statistical quality control technique in which a portion of the completed products is inspected.

Accuracy Rate For the linear probability and the logistic regression models, the accuracy rate is defined as the percentage of correctly predicted outcomes.

Addition rule The probability that A or B occurs, or that at least one of these events occurs, is $P(A \cup B) = P(A) + P(B) - P(A \cap B)$.

Adjusted closing price Stock price adjusted using appropriate dividend and split multipliers.

Adjusted R^2 A modification of the coefficient of determination that imposes a penalty for using additional explanatory variables in the linear regression model.

Aggregate price index A representation of relative price movements for a group of items.

Alpha In the capital asset pricing model (CAPM), it measures whether abnormal returns exist.

Alternative hypothesis (H_A) In a hypothesis test, the alternative hypothesis contradicts the default state or status quo specified in the null hypothesis.

Analysis of variance (ANOVA) A statistical technique used to determine if differences exist between three or more population means.

Annualized return A measure equivalent to the geometric mean return.

Arithmetic mean The average value of a variable; the most commonly used measure of central location, also referred to as the mean or the average.

Assignable variation In a production process, the variation that is caused by specific events or factors that can usually be identified and eliminated.

Autoregressive model A regression model where lagged values of the response variable are used as explanatory variables.

Average See *Arithmetic mean.*

Average growth rate For growth rates $g_1, g_2 \ldots, g_n$, the average growth rate G_g is computed as $G_g = \sqrt[n]{(1+g_1)(1+g_2)\cdots(1+g_n)} - 1$, where n is the number of multi-period growth rates.

B

Balanced data A completely randomized ANOVA design with an equal number of observations in each sample.

Bar chart A graph that depicts the frequency or relative frequency of each category of a categorical variable as a series of horizontal or vertical bars, the lengths of which are proportional to the values that are to be depicted.

Bayes' theorem The rule for updating probabilities is $P(B|A) = \dfrac{P(A|B)P(B)}{P(A|B)P(B) + P(A|B^c)P(B^c)}$, where $P(B)$ is the prior probability and $P(B|A)$ is the posterior probability.

Bell curve See *Normal curve.*

Bell-shaped distribution See *Normal distribution.*

Bernoulli process A series of n independent and identical trials of an experiment such that each trial has only two possible outcomes, and each time the trial is repeated, the probabilities of success and failure remain the same.

Beta In the capital asset pricing model (CAPM), it measures the sensitivity of the stock's return to changes in the level of the overall market.

Between-treatments variance In ANOVA, a measure of the variability between sample means.

Bias The tendency of a sample statistic to systematically overestimate or underestimate a population parameter.

Big data A massive volume of both structured and unstructured data that are often difficult to manage, process, and analyze using traditional data processing tools.

Binary choice models Regression models that use a dummy (binary) variable as the response variable.

Binomial distribution A description of the probabilities associated with the possible values of a binomial random variable.

Binomial random variable The number of successes achieved in the n trials of a Bernoulli process.

Boxplot A graphical display of the minimum value, quartiles, and the maximum value of a variable.

C

***c* chart** A control chart that monitors the count of defects per item in statistical quality control.

Capital asset pricing model (CAPM) A regression model used in finance to examine an investment return.

Capital gains yield The gain or loss resulting from the increase or decrease in the value of an asset.

Categorical variable A variable that uses labels or names to identify the distinguishing characteristics of observations.

Causal (forecasting) model Quantitative forecast based on a regression framework, where the variable of interest is related to an explanatory variable(s).

Centerline In a control chart, the centerline represents a variable's expected value when the production process is in control.

Central limit theorem (CLT) The CLT states that the sum or mean of a large number of independent observations from the same underlying distribution has an approximate normal distribution.

Chance variation In a production process, the variation that is caused by a number of randomly occurring events that are part of the production process.

Changing variability In regression analysis, a violation of the assumption that the variance of the error term is the same for all observations. It is also referred to as heteroskedasticity.

Chebyshev's theorem For any variable, the proportion of observations that lie within k standard deviations from the mean will be at least $1 - 1/k^2$, where k is any number greater than 1.

Chi-square test of a contingency table See *Test for independence.*

Chi-square (X^2) distribution A family of distributions where each distribution depends on its particular degrees of freedom *df*. It is positively skewed, with values ranging from zero to infinity, but becomes increasingly symmetric as *df* increase.

Classical probability A probability often used in games of chance. It is based on the assumption that all outcomes are equally likely.

Cluster sampling A population is first divided up into mutually exclusive and collectively exhaustive groups of observations, called clusters. A cluster sample includes observations from randomly selected clusters.

Coefficient of determination (R^2) The proportion of the sample variation in the response variable that is explained by the sample regression equation.

Coefficient of variation (CV) The ratio of the standard deviation of a variable to its mean; a relative measure of dispersion.

Combination formula The number of ways to choose x objects from a total of n objects, where the order in which the x objects is listed *does not matter*, is ${}_nC_x = \binom{n}{x} = \frac{n!}{(n-x)!x!}$.

Complement The complement of event A, denoted A^c, is the event consisting of all outcomes in the sample space that are not in A.

Complement rule The probability of the complement of an event is $P(A^c) = 1 - P(A)$.

Conditional probability The probability of an event given that another event has already occurred.

Confidence coefficient The probability that the estimation procedure will generate an interval that contains the population parameter of interest.

Confidence interval A range of values that, with a certain level of confidence, contains the population parameter of interest.

Consistency An estimator is consistent if it approaches the unknown population parameter being estimated as the sample size grows larger.

Consumer price index (CPI) A monthly weighted aggregate price index, computed by the U.S. Bureau of Labor Statistics, based on the prices paid by urban consumers for a representative basket of goods and services.

Contingency table A table that shows frequencies for two categorical variables, x and y, where each cell represents a mutually exclusive combination of the pair of x and y observations.

Continuous (random) variable A variable that assumes uncountable values in an interval.

Continuous uniform distribution A distribution describing a continuous random variable that has an equally likely chance of assuming a value within a specified range.

Control chart A plot of statistics of a production process over time.

Correlated observations In regression analysis, a violation of the assumption that the observations are uncorrelated. It is also referred to as serial correlation.

Correlation coefficient A measure that describes the direction and strength of the linear relationship between two variables.

Covariance A measure that describes the direction of the linear relationship between two variables.

Critical value In a hypothesis test, the critical value is a point that separates the rejection region from the nonrejection region.

Cross-sectional data Observations of a characteristic of many subjects at the same point in time or approximately the same point in time.

Cubic regression model In regression analysis, a model that allows two sign changes of the slope capturing the influence of the explanatory variable on the response variable.

Cubic trend model In time series analysis, a model that allows for two changes in the direction of the series.

Cumulative distribution function A probability that the value of a random variable X is less than or equal to a particular value x, $P(X \leq x)$.

Cumulative frequency distribution A distribution for a numerical variable recording the number of observations that falls below the upper limit of each interval.

Cumulative relative frequency distribution A distribution for a numerical variable recording the fraction (proportion) of observations that falls below the upper limit of each interval.

Cyclical component Wave-like fluctuations or business cycles of a time series, often caused by expansion and contraction of the economy.

D

Deflated time series An economic time series that has been adjusted for changes in prices, or inflation.

Degrees of freedom The number of independent pieces of information that goes into the calculation of a given statistic. Many probability distributions are identified by the degrees of freedom.

Dependent events The occurrence of one event is related to the probability of the occurrence of the other event.

Descriptive statistics The summary of a data set in the form of tables, graphs, or numerical measures.

Detection approach A statistical quality control technique that determines at which point the production process does not conform to specifications.

Deterministic relationship A relationship in which the value of the response variable is uniquely determined by the values of the explanatory variables.

Discrete choice models See *Binary choice models.*

Discrete uniform distribution A symmetric distribution where the random variable assumes a finite number of values and each value is equally likely.

Discrete (random) variable A variable that assumes a countable number of values.

Dummy variable A variable that takes on values of 0 or 1.

Dummy variable trap A regression model where the number of dummy variables equals the number of categories of a categorical variable; the resulting model cannot be estimated.

E

Efficiency An unbiased estimator is efficient if its standard error is lower than that of other unbiased estimators.

Empirical probability A probability based on observing the relative frequency with which an event occurs.

Empirical rule Given a sample mean $\bar{x}$, a sample standard deviation s, and a relatively symmetric and bell-shaped distribution, approximately 68% of all observations fall in the interval $\bar{x} \pm s$; approximately 95% of all observations fall in the interval $\bar{x} \pm 2s$; and almost all observations fall in the interval $\bar{x} \pm 3s$.

Endogeneity See *Excluded variables.*

Error sum of squares (SSE) In ANOVA, a measure of the degree of variability that exists even if all population means are the same. In regression analysis, it measures the unexplained variation in the response variable.

Estimate A particular value of an estimator.

Estimator A statistic used to estimate a population parameter.

Event A subset of a sample space.

Excluded variables In regression analysis, a situation where important explanatory variables are excluded from the regression. It often leads to the violation of the assumption that the error term is uncorrelated with the (included) explanatory variables.

Exhaustive events When all possible outcomes of an experiment are included in the events.

Expected return of a portfolio A weighted average of the expected returns of the assets comprising the portfolio.

Expected value A weighted average of all possible values of a random variable.

Experiment A process that leads to one of several possible outcomes.

Explanatory variables In regression analysis, the variables that influence the response variable. They are also called the independent variables, predictor variables, control variables, or regressors.

Exponential distribution A continuous, nonsymmetric probability distribution used to describe the time that has elapsed *between* occurrences of an event.

Exponential regression model A regression model in which only the response variable is transformed into natural logs.

Exponential smoothing In time series analysis, a smoothing technique based on a weighted average where the weights decline exponentially as they become more distant.

Exponential trend model A regression model used for a time series that is expected to grow by an increasing amount each period.

F

***F* distribution** A family of distributions where each distribution depends on two degrees of freedom: the numerator degrees of freedom df_1 and the denominator degrees of freedom df_2. It is positively skewed, with values ranging from zero to infinity, but becomes increasingly symmetric as df_1 and df_2 increase.

Factorial formula The number of ways to assign every member of a group of size n to n slots is $n! = n \times (n-1) \times (n-2) \times (n-3) \times \ldots \times 1$.

Finite population correction factor A correction factor that accounts for the added precision gained by sampling a larger percentage of the population. It is implemented when the sample constitutes at least 5% of the population.

Fisher equation A theoretical relationship between the nominal return, the real return, and the expected inflation rate.

Fisher's least significant difference (LSD) method In ANOVA, a test that determines which means significantly differ by computing all pairwise differences of the means.

Frequency distribution A table that groups the observations of a variable into categories or intervals and records the number of observations that fall into each category or interval.

G

Geometric mean The geometric mean is a multiplicative average of a variable.

Geometric mean return For multiperiod returns R_1, R_2 . . ., R_n, the geometric mean return G_R is computed as $G_R = \sqrt[n]{(1+R_1)(1+R_2)\cdots(1+R_n)} - 1$, where n is the number of multiperiod returns.

Goodness-of-fit test A chi-square test used to determine if the sample proportions resulting from a multinomial experiment differ from the hypothesized population proportions specified in the null hypothesis.

Goodness-of-fit test for normality A chi-square test used to determine if sample data are drawn from a normally distributed population.

Grand mean In ANOVA, the sum of all observations in a data set divided by the total number of observations.

H

Heteroskedasticity See *Changing variability.*

Histogram A graphical depiction of a frequency or a relative frequency distribution for a numerical variable; series of rectangles where the width and height of each rectangle represent the interval width and frequency (or relative frequency) of the respective interval.

Hypergeometric distribution A description of the probabilities associated with the possible values of a hypergeometric random variable.

Hypergeometric random variable The number of successes achieved in the n trials of a two-outcome experiment, where the trials are not assumed to be independent.

Hypothesis test A statistical procedure to resolve conflicts between two competing claims (hypotheses) on a particular population parameter of interest.

I

Imputation strategy When missing values exist, this strategy recommends replacing them with some reasonable imputed values.

Income yield The direct cash payments from an underlying asset, such as dividends, interest, or rental income.

Independent events The occurrence of one event does not affect the probability of the occurrence of the other event.

Independent random samples Two (or more) random samples are independent if the process that generates one sample is completely separate from the process that generates the other sample.

Index number A numerical value that reflects a percentage change in price or quantity from a base value.

Indicator variable See *dummy variable.*

Inferential statistics The practice of extracting useful information from a sample to draw conclusions about a population.

Inflation rate The percentage rate of change of a price index over time.

Interaction variable In a regression model, a product of two explanatory variables.

Interquartile range (IQR) The difference between the third and first quartiles.

Intersection The intersection of two events A and B, denoted $A \cap B$, is the event consisting of all outcomes in A and B.

Interval scale Observations of a variable can be categorized and ranked, and differences between observations are meaningful.

Interval estimate See *Confidence interval.*

Inverse transformation A standard normal variable Z can be transformed to the normally distributed random variable X with mean μ and standard deviation σ as $X = \mu + Z\sigma$.

Investment return The net gain or loss in value of an investment over a time period.

J

Jarque–Bera test A test that uses the skewness and kurtosis coefficients to determine if sample observations are drawn from a normally distributed population.

Joint probabilities The values in the interior of a joint probability table, representing the probabilities of the intersection of two events.

Joint probability table A contingency table whose frequencies have been converted to relative frequencies.

K

Kruskal–Wallis test A nonparametric test to determine whether differences exist between several population medians.

Kurtosis coefficient A measure of whether data is more or less peaked than a normal distribution.

L

Laspeyres price index A weighted aggregate price index based on quantities evaluated in the base period.

Law of large numbers In probability theory, if an experiment is repeated a large number of times, its empirical probability approaches its classical probability.

Left-tailed test In hypothesis testing, when the null hypothesis is rejected on the left side of the hypothesized value of the population parameter.

Line Chart A graph that connects the consecutive observations of a numerical variable with a line.

Linear probability model (LPM) A linear regression model applied to a binary response variable.

Linear trend model A regression model used for a time series that is expected to grow by a fixed amount each time period.

Logarithmic regression model A regression model in which only the explanatory variable is transformed into natural logs.

Logit model A nonlinear regression model that ensures that the predicted probability of the binary response variable falls between zero and one.

Log-log regression model A regression model in which both the response variable and the explanatory variable(s) are transformed into natural logs.

Lognormal distribution A continuous nonsymmetric probability distribution used to describe random variables that are known to be positively skewed.

Lower control limit In a control chart, the lower control limit indicates excessive deviation below the expected value of the variable of interest.

M

Mann–Whitney test See *Wilcoxon rank-sum test.*

Margin of error A value that accounts for the standard error of the estimator and the desired confidence level of the interval.

Marginal probabilities The values in the margins of a joint probability table that represent unconditional probabilities.

Matched-pairs sample When a sample is matched or paired in some way.

Maximum likelihood estimation (MLE) An estimation technique used to estimate models such as the logit models.

Mean See *Arithmetic mean.*

Mean absolute deviation (MAD) The average of the absolute differences between the observations and the mean.

Mean square error (MSE) The average of the error (residual) sum of squares, where the residual is the difference between the observed and the predicted values of a variable.

Mean square regression The average of the sum of squares due to regression.

Mean-variance analysis The idea that the performance of an asset is measured by its rate of return, and this rate of return is evaluated in terms of its reward (mean) and risk (variance).

Median The middle value of the ordered observations of a variable.

Method of least squares See *Ordinary least squares (OLS).*

Method of runs above and below the median A nonparametric test to determine randomness for a numerical variable.

Mode The most frequently occurring observation of a variable.

Moving average (MA) method In time series analysis, a smoothing technique based on computing the average from a fixed number m of the most recent observations.

Multicollinearity In regression analysis, a situation where two or more explanatory variables are correlated.

Multinomial experiment A series of n independent and identical trials, such that on each trial there are k possible outcomes, called categories; the probability p_i associated with the ith category remains the same; and the sum of the probabilities is one.

Multiple linear regression model In regression analysis, more than one explanatory variable is used to explain the variability in the response variable.

Multiplication rule The probability that A and B both occur is $P(A \cap B) = P(A|B)P(B)$.

Mutually exclusive events Events that do not share any common outcome of an experiment.

N

Negatively skewed (left-skewed) distribution A distribution in which extreme values are concentrated in the left tail of the distribution.

Nominal scale Observations of a variable differ merely by name or label.

Nominal return Investment return that has not been adjusted for a change in purchasing power due to inflation.

Nominal terms A representation of a time series that is not adjusted for inflation.

Noncausal (forecasting) model Quantitative forecast that does not present any explanation of the mechanism generating the variable of interest and simply provides a method for projecting historical data.

Nonparametric tests Statistical tests that rely on fewer assumptions concerning the distribution of the underlying population. These tests are often used when the underlying distribution is not normal and the sample size is small.

Nonresponse bias A systematic difference in preferences between respondents and nonrespondents of a survey or a poll.

Normal curve A graph depicting the normal probability density function; also referred to as the bell curve.

Normal (probability) distribution The most extensively used probability distribution in statistical work and the cornerstone of statistical inference. It is symmetric and bell-shaped and is completely described by the mean and the variance.

Null hypothesis (H_0) In a hypothesis test, the null hypothesis corresponds to a presumed default state of nature or status quo.

Numerical variable A variable that assumes meaningful numerical values for observations.

O

Ogive For a numerical variable, a graph of the cumulative frequency or cumulative relative frequency distribution in which lines connect a series of neighboring points, where each point represents the upper limit of each interval and its corresponding cumulative frequency or cumulative relative frequency.

Omission strategy When missing values exist, this strategy recommends excluding these observations from subsequent analysis.

One-tailed hypothesis test A test in which the null hypothesis is rejected only on one side of the hypothesized value of the population parameter.

One-way ANOVA A statistical technique that analyzes the effect of one categorical variable (factor) on the mean.

Ordinal scale Observations of a variable can be categorized and ranked.

Ordinary least squares (OLS) A regression technique for fitting a straight line whereby the error (residual) sum of squares is minimized.

Outliers Extreme small or large observations.

P

$\bar{p}$ chart A control chart that monitors the proportion of defectives (or some other characteristic) of a production process.

***p*-value** In a hypothesis test, the probability of observing a sample result that is at least as extreme as the one derived from the given sample, under the assumption that the null hypothesis is true.

Paasche price index A weighted aggregate price index based on quantities evaluated in the current period.

Parameter See *Population parameter.*

Partial *F* test See *test of linear restrictions.*

Percentile The pth percentile divides a data set into two parts: approximately p percent of the observations have values less than the pth percentile and approximately $(100 - p)$ percent of the observations have values greater than the pth percentile.

Permutation formula The number of ways to choose x objects from a total of n objects, where the order in which the x objects is listed *does matter,* is ${}_nP_x = \frac{n!}{(n-x)!}$.

Pie chart A segmented circle portraying the categories and relative sizes for a categorical variable.

Point estimate The value of the point estimator derived from a given sample.

Point estimator A function of the random sample used to make inferences about the value of an unknown population parameter.

Poisson distribution A description of the probabilities associated with the possible values of a Poisson random variable.

Poisson process An experiment in which the number of successes within a specified time or space interval equals any integer between zero and infinity; the number of successes counted in nonoverlapping intervals is independent from one another; and the probability that success occurs in any interval is the same for all intervals of equal size and is proportional to the size of the interval.

Poisson random variable The number of successes over a given interval of time or space in a Poisson process.

Polygon For a numerical variable, a graph of a frequency or relative frequency distribution in which lines connect a series of neighboring points, where each point represents the midpoint of a particular interval and its associated frequency or relative frequency.

Polynomial regression model In regression analysis, a model that allows sign changes of the slope capturing the influence of an explanatory variable on the response variable.

Population All members of a specified group.

Population parameter A characteristic of a population.

Portfolio A collection of assets.

Positively skewed (right-skewed) distribution A distribution in which extreme values are concentrated in the right tail of the distribution.

Posterior probability The updated probability, conditional on the arrival of new information.

Prediction interval In regression analysis, an interval that pertains to the individual value of the response variable defined for specific values of the explanatory variables.

Prior probability The unconditional probability before the arrival of new information.

Probability A numerical value between 0 and 1 that measures the likelihood that an event occurs.

Probability density function The probability density function provides the probability that a continuous random variable falls within a particular range of values.

Probability distribution Every random variable is associated with a probability distribution that describes the variable completely. It is used to compute probabilities associated with the variable.

Probability mass function The probability mass function provides the probability that a discrete random variable takes on a particular value.

Probability tree A graphical representation of the various possible sequences of an experiment.

Producer price index (PPI) A monthly weighted aggregate price index, computed by the U.S. Bureau of Labor Statistics, based on prices measured at the wholesale or producer level.

Q

Quadratic regression model In regression analysis, a model that allows one sign change of the slope capturing the influence of the explanatory variable on the response variable.

Quadratic trend model In time series analysis, a model that captures either a U-shaped trend or an inverted U-shaped trend.

Qualitative forecasts Forecasts based on the judgment of the forecaster using prior experience and expertise.

Quantitative forecasts Forecasts based on a formal model using historical data for the variable of interest.

Quartiles Any of the three values that divide the ordered observations of a variable into four equal parts, where the first, second, and third quartiles refer to the 25th, 50th, and 75th percentiles, respectively.

R

***R* chart** A control chart that monitors the variability of a production process.

Random error In regression analysis, random error is due to the omission of factors that influence the response variable.

Random variable A function that assigns numerical values to the outcomes of an experiment.

Randomized block design In ANOVA, allowing the variation in the means to be explained by two factors.

Range The difference between the maximum and the minimum values of a variable.

Ratio scale Observations of a variable can be categorized and ranked, differences between observations are meaningful, and a true zero point (origin) exists.

Real return Investment return that is adjusted for the change in purchasing power due to inflation.

Real terms A representation of a time series that is adjusted for inflation.

Regression analysis A statistical method for analyzing the relationship between variables.

Rejection region In a hypothesis test, a range of values such that if the value of the test statistic falls into this range, then the decision is to reject the null hypothesis.

Relative frequency distribution A frequency distribution that shows the fraction (proportion) of observations in each category or interval for the variable.

Residual (*e*) In regression analysis, the difference between the observed value and the predicted value of the response variable, that is, $e = y - \hat{y}$.

Residual plots In regression analysis, the residuals are plotted sequentially or against an explanatory variable to identify model inadequacies. The model is adequate if the residuals are randomly dispersed around the zero value.

Response variable In regression analysis, the variable that is influenced by the explanatory variable(s). It is also called the dependent variable, the explained variable, the predicted variable, or the regressand.

Restricted model A regression model that imposes restrictions on the coefficients.

Right-tailed test In hypothesis testing, when the null hypothesis is rejected on the right side of the hypothesized value of the population parameter.

Risk-averse consumer Someone who takes risk only if it entails a suitable compensation and may decline a risky prospect even if it offers a positive expected gain.

Risk-loving consumer Someone who may accept a risky prospect even if the expected gain is negative.

Risk-neutral consumer Someone who is indifferent to risk and makes his/her decisions solely on the basis of the expected gain.

Run In the Wald–Wolfowitz runs test, a run is an uninterrupted sequence of one letter, symbol, or attribute.

Runs test See the *Wald–Wolfowitz runs test.*

S

***s* chart** A control chart that monitors the variability of a production process.

Sample A subset of a population of interest.

Sample correlation coefficient A sample measure that describes both the direction and strength of the linear relationship between two variables.

Sample covariance A sample measure that describes the direction of the linear relationship between two variables.

Sample space A record of all possible outcomes of an experiment.

Sample statistic A random variable used to estimate the unknown population parameter of interest.

Sampling distribution The probability distribution of an estimator.

Scatterplot For two numerical variables, a graph where each point in the graph represents a pair of observations of the two variables.

Scatterplot with a categorical variable A modification of a basic scatterplot that incorporates a categorical variable.

Seasonal component Repetitions of a time series over a one-year period.

Seasonal dummy variables Dummy variables used to capture the seasonal component from a time series.

Seasonally adjusted series A time series that is free of seasonal variations.

Selection bias A systematic underrepresentation of certain groups from consideration for a sample.

Serial correlation See *Correlated observations.*

Sharpe ratio A ratio calculated by dividing the difference of the mean return from the risk-free rate by the asset's standard deviation.

Sign test A nonparametric test to determine whether significant differences exist between two populations using matched-pairs sampling with ordinal data.

Significance level The allowed probability of making a Type I error.

Simple linear regression model In regression analysis, one explanatory variable is used to explain the variability in the response variable.

Simple price index For any item, the ratio of the price in a given time period to the price in the base period, expressed as a percentage.

Simple random sample A sample of n observations that has the same probability of being selected from the population as any other sample of n observations.

Skewness When the distribution is not symmetric.

Skewness coefficient A measure that determines if the observations of a variable are symmetric about the mean. A symmetric distribution has a skewness coefficient of zero.

Smoothing techniques In time series analysis, methods to provide forecasts if short-term fluctuations represent random departures from the structure with no discernible systematic patterns.

Social-desirability bias A systematic difference between a group's "socially acceptable" responses to a survey or poll and this group's ultimate choice.

Spearman rank correlation coefficient Measures the correlation between two variables based on rank orderings.

Stacked column chart Graph of a contingency table; depicts more than one categorical variable and allows for the comparison of composition within each category.

Standard deviation The positive square root of the variance; a common measure of dispersion.

Standard error The standard deviation of an estimator.

Standard error of the estimate The standard deviation of the residual; used as a goodness-of-fit measure for regression analysis.

Standard normal distribution A special case of the normal distribution with a mean equal to zero and a standard deviation (or variance) equal to one.

Standard normal table See *z table.*

Standard transformation A normally distributed random variable X with mean μ and standard deviation σ can be transformed into the standard normal random variable Z as $Z = (X - \mu)/\sigma$.

Standardize A technique used to convert a value into its corresponding z-score.

Statistic See *Sample statistic.*

Statistical quality control Statistical techniques used to develop and maintain a firm's ability to produce high-quality goods and services.

Stem-and-leaf diagram A visual method of displaying a numerical variable where each observation is separated into two parts: a stem, which consists of the leftmost digits, and a leaf, which consists of the last digit.

Stochastic relationship A relationship in which the value of the response variable is not uniquely determined by the values of the explanatory variables.

Stratified random sampling A population is first divided up into mutually exclusive and collectively exhaustive groups, called strata. A stratified sample includes randomly selected observations from each stratum. The number of observations per stratum is proportional to the stratum's size in the population. The data for each stratum are eventually pooled.

Structured data Data that conform to a predefined row-column format.

Student's *t* distribution See *t distribution.*

Studentized range distribution A distribution used in Tukey's HSD method that has broader, flatter, and thicker tails than the t distribution.

Subjective probability A probability value based on personal and subjective judgment.

Subsetting The process of extracting a portion of a data set.

Sum of squares due to regression (SSR) In regression analysis, it measures the explained variation in the response variable.

Sum of squares due to treatments (SSTR) In ANOVA, a weighted sum of squared differences between the sample means and the overall mean of the data.

Symmetry When one side of a distribution is a mirror image of the other side.

T

***t* distribution** A family of distributions that are similar to the z distribution except that they have broader tails. They are identified by their degrees of freedom *df.*

Test for independence A goodness-of-fit test analyzing the relationship between two categorical variables. Also called a chi-square test of a contingency table.

Test of individual significance In regression analysis, a test that determines whether an explanatory variable has an individual statistical influence on the response variable.

Test of joint significance In regression analysis, a test to determine whether the explanatory variables have a joint statistical influence on the response variable.

Test of linear restrictions In regression analysis, a test to determine if the restrictions specified in the null hypothesis are invalid.

Test statistic A sample-based measure used in hypothesis testing.

Time series A set of sequential observations of a variable over time.

Total probability rule A rule that expresses the unconditional probability of an event, $P(A)$, in terms of probabilities conditional on various mutually exclusive and exhaustive events. The total probability rule conditional on two events B and B^c is $P(A) = P(A \cap B) + P(A \cap B^c) = P(A|B)P(B) + P(A|B^c)P(B^c)$.

Total sum of squares (SST) In regression analysis, it measures the total variation in the response variable.

Trend A long-term upward or downward movement of a time series.

Tukey's honestly significant difference (HSD) method In ANOVA, a method that determines which means significantly differ by comparing all pairwise differences of the means.

Two-tailed hypothesis test A test in which the null hypothesis can be rejected on either side of the hypothesized value of the population parameter.

Two-way ANOVA test A statistical technique that analyzes the effect of two categorical variables on the mean. A two-way ANOVA test can be conducted with or without interaction between the categorical variables.

Type I error In a hypothesis test, this error occurs when the decision is to reject the null hypothesis when the null hypothesis is true.

Type II error In a hypothesis test, this error occurs when the decision is to not reject the null hypothesis when the null hypothesis is false.

U

Unbalanced data A completely randomized ANOVA design where the number of observations are not the same for each sample.

Unbiased An estimator is unbiased if its expected value equals the unknown population parameter being estimated.

Unconditional probability The probability of an event without any restriction.

Union The union of two events A and B, denoted $A \cup B$, is the event consisting of all outcomes in A or B.

Unrestricted model A regression model that imposes no restrictions on the coefficients.

Unstructured data Data that do not conform to a predefined row-column format.

Unweighted aggregate price index An aggregate price index based entirely on aggregate prices with no emphasis placed on quantity.

Upper control limit In a control chart, the upper control limit indicates excessive deviation above the expected value of the variable of interest.

V

Value One of the V's describing big data; information derived from big data should have value.

Variable A general characteristic being observed on a set of people, objects, or events, where each observation varies in kind or degree.

Variance The average of the squared differences from the mean; a common measure of dispersion.

Variety One of the V's describing big data; data come in all types, forms, and granularity.

Velocity One of the V's describing big data; data from a variety of sources get generated at a rapid speed.

Veracity One of the V's describing big data; refers to the credibility and quality of data.

Volume One of the V's describing big data; an immense amount of data is compiled from a single source or a wide range of sources.

W

Wald–Wolfowitz runs test A nonparametric test to determine whether the elements in a sequence appear in a random order.

Weighted aggregate price index An aggregate price index that gives higher weight to the items sold in higher quantities.

Weighted mean When some observations contribute more than others in the calculation of an average.

Wilcoxon rank-sum test A nonparametric test to determine whether two population medians differ under independent sampling. Also known as the Mann–Whitney test.

Wilcoxon signed-rank test A nonparametric test to determine whether a sample could have been drawn from a population having a hypothesized value as its median; this test can also be used to determine whether the median difference differs from zero under matched-pairs sampling.

Within-treatments variance In ANOVA, a measure of the variability within each sample.

X

$\bar{x}$ chart A control chart that monitors the central tendency of a production process.

Z

***z*-score** The relative position of an observation within a distribution; it is also used to detect outliers.

***z* table** A table providing cumulative probabilities for positive or negative values of the standard normal random variable Z.

D

E

F

G

H

I

J

K

L

M

N

O

P

Q

R

S

O

P

Q

R

S

T

U

V

W

X

Y

Z